Wolfgang J. Koschnick Standard-Wörterbuch für Werbung
Standard Dictionary of Advertising

Wolfgang J. Koschnick

Standard Dictionary of Advertising Mass Media and Marketing

German–English

Walter de Gruyter · Berlin · New York 1987

Wolfgang J. Koschnick

Standard Wörterbuch für Werbung Massenmedien und Marketing

Deutsch–Englisch

Walter de Gruyter · Berlin · New York 1987

Library of Congress Cataloging in Publication Data

Koschnick, Wolfgang J., 1942–
Standard-Wörterbuch für Werbung, Massenmedien und Marketing.
Deutsch-Englisch / Wolfgang J. Koschnick.
p. cm. Title on added t.p.: Standard dictionary of advertising, mass media and marketing, German-English.
ISBN 0-89925-293-1 (U.S.) : $66.00 (est.) (DM 120.00 W. Ger. : est.)
1. Advertising--Dictionaries. 2. Mass media--Dictionaries. 3. Marketing--Dictionaries. 4. English language--Dictionaries--German. I. Title.
II. Title: Standard dictionary of advertising, mass media, and marketing. German-English.
HF5803.K67 1987   87-19928
659.1'03'21--dc 19

CIP-Kurztitelaufnahme der Deutschen Bibliothek

Koschnik, Wolfgang J.:
Standard dictionary of advertising, mass media and marketing / Wolfgang J. Koschnick. – Berlin ; New York : de Gruyter
Parallelsacht.: Standard-Wörterbuch für Werbung, Massenmedien und Marketing
NE: HST
German-English. – 1987.
ISBN 3-11-008985-8

© Copyright 1987 by Walter de Gruyter · Berlin · New York.
All rights reserved, including those of translation into foreign languages. No part of this book may be reproduced in any form – by photoprint, microfilm or any other means nor transmitted nor translated into a machine language without written permission from the publisher. – Data Processing: Mohndruck Graphische Betriebe GmbH, Gütersloh. – Printing: Gerike GmbH, Berlin. – Binding: Lüderitz & Bauer Buchgewerbe GmbH, Berlin. – Cover Design: Rudolf Huebler, Berlin. – Printed in Germany.

Preface

It is four years ago now that the first, English-German volume of this dictionary of marketing, advertising, and mass media was published. This German-English volume has turned out to be even more comprehensive than the first. It lists almost 25,000 technical terms along with the pertinent explanations in English, wherever this appeared to be useful and advisable.
Both volumes thus add up to form a two-volume encyclopedia in two languages which, I hope, leaves few questions unanswered.
While working on the first English-German volume was characterized by fascination about the lucidity and terseness of the modern American language, compiling this volume was rather characterized by a considerable amount of resignation about how little resistance the German language offers toward its gradual and persistent Americanization.

Allensbach on Lake Constance　　　　　　　　　　　　　　Wolfgang J. Koschnick
July 1987

Vorwort

Vier Jahre ist es nun her, seit der erste, englisch-deutsche Band dieses Wörterbuchs für Marketing, Werbung und Massenmedien erschien. Der deutsch-englische Band ist noch etwas umfangreicher als der erste geworden. Er verzeichnet fast 25000 Fachtermini mit den zugehörigen Übersetzungen und mit englischsprachigen Erläuterungen, wo immer das geraten erscheint.
Beide Bände fügen sich so zu einem fast enzyklopädischen Kompendium in zwei Sprachen zusammen, das – wie ich hoffe – wenige Fragen offen läßt. Überwog noch bei der Arbeit an dem englisch-deutschen Band die Faszination über den Einfallsreichtum und den Wortschatz der amerikanischen Werbesprache, so stand bei diesem Band ein wenig Resignation darüber im Vordergrund, wie willenlos sich die deutsche Werbe- und Marketingsprache vom amerikanischen Englisch überwältigen läßt, ohne wenigstens ein Rückzugsgefecht zu versuchen.

Allensbach am Bodensee   Wolfgang J. Koschnick
im Juli 1987

Abbreviations — Abkürzungen

abbr	abbreviation	Abkürzung
adj	adjective	Adjektiv
adv	adverb	Adverb
advtsg	advertising	Werbung
advtsg res	advertising resarch	Werbeforschung
Am	American English	amerikanisches Englisch
attr	attribute	Attribut
brit	British English	britisches Englisch
cf.	confer	vergleiche
colloq	colloquial speech	umgangssprachlich
derog	derogatory	derogatorisch
econ	economics	Volkswirtschaft/Betriebswirtschaft
e. g.	for example	z. B., zum Beispiel
electr.	electronics	Elektronik
etc.	etcetera	usw.
f	feminine	feminin, weiblich
fig	figuratively	figürlich, bildlich
interj	interjection	Interjektion, Ausruf
i. e.	that is	d. h., das heißt
lat	Latin	lateinisch
m	masculine	männlich, maskulin
market res	market research	Marktforschung
marketing res	marketing research	Marketingforschung
media res	media research	Mediaforschung
n	neuter	neutrum, sächlich
obsol	obsolete	obsolet, veraltet
panel res	panel research	Panelforschung
outdoor advtsg	outdoor advertising	Außenwerbung
phot	photography	Photographie
pl	plural	Plural
POP advtsg	POP advertising	POP-Werbung
psy	psychology	Psychologie
readership res	readership research	Leserschaftsforschung
res	research	Forschung
sg	singular	Singular
soc res	social research	Sozialforschung
stat	statistics	Statistik
stoch.	stochastics	Stochastik
survey res	survey research	Umfrageforschung
TM	trademark	Warenzeichen
transit advtsg	transit advertising	Verkehrsmittelwerbung
typ	typography	Typographie
vgl.	confer	vergleiche
v/i	intransitive verb	intransitives Verb
v/t	transitive verb	transitives Verb
→	see, see also	siehe, siehe auch

A

A-Leser *m*
→ Abonnements-Leser, A + E-Leser
A + E-Leser *m*
→ AE
A-Rolle *f*
→ A-Wicklung
A-Stück *n*
→ A + E-Leser
A-Wicklung *f* **(A-Rolle** *f*) *(film)* A roll, A winding
vgl. B-Wicklung
ab I *prep* **1.** *(econ)* less, minus: ab Skonto — less cash discount **2.** (Preis) from...upward(s) **3.** *(econ)* ab Lager — ex warehouse; ab Werk — ex factory, ex works **II** *adv* **4.** (zeitlich) from...on, beginning, as of, effective **5.** *(Regieanweisung/Bühnenanweisung)* exit!; mehrere Personen: exeunt **III** *interj* **6.** cue! roll! go ahead! run! (Film/Band)
A/B-Kopierverfahren *n* **(A-B-Kopier-Schnittechnik** *f*) *(film)* A and B printing, A & B winding
Emulsion location on either side of 16mm single-perforation film base. "A wind." (emulsion toward reel hub) is generally for contact printing; "B wind" (base toward reel hub) is for camera raw stock, projection printing and optical work.
abändern *v/t* to alter, to change, to modify, to revise
Abänderung *f* alteration, modification, change, revision
Abbau *m* **1.** dismantling, dismantlement **2.** *(econ)* (Kosten) reduction, retrenchment **3.** *(film/TV)* (Dekoration) strike
abbauen *v/t* **1.** to dismantle, to disassemble, to pull down **2.** *(econ)* (Kosten) to reduce, to cut, to cut down, to retrench **3.** *(econ)* (Auftragsbestand, Arbeitsüberhang) to work off **4.** *(film/TV)* (Dekoration) to strike (a set), to pull down (a set), *Am* to kill (a set)
abbestellen *v/t* **1.** (Waren) to cancel an order for, to countermand **2.** (Abonnement) to cancel (a subscription), to discontinue the subscription of), *colloq* to stop the paper **3.** (beim Kabelfernsehen) to disconnect
Abbestellquote *f*
→ Abbestellungsrate
Abbestellung *f* **1.** cancellation, *Am* auch cancelation, countermand **2.** (Abonnement/Zeitung) cancellation, discontinuance **3.** (beim Kabelfernsehen) disconnect
Abbestellungsfrist *f* cancellation date
Abbestellungsrate *f* **(Abbestellquote** *f*) **1.** rate of cancellations, cancellation rate, percentage of cancellations **2.** (beim Kabelfernsehen) disconnect rate
The percentage of cable subscribers discontinuing service over a year.
abbilden *v/t* **1.** to reproduce, to copy **2.** (darstellen) to portray, to illustrate, to picture, to depict **3.** (nachbilden) to model, to represent **4.** (zeichnen) to draw **5.** (graphisch darstellen) to plot
Abbildung *f* **1.** reproduction, copy **2.** (Darstellung) portrayal, portraiture, illustration, picture, depiction **3.** (Nachbildung) representation, model **4.** (Zeichnung) drawing **5.** (graphische Darstellung) diagram
Abbildungsebene *f (phot)* image plane
Abbildungsfehler *m (phot)* defect of an image, image defect
→ Aberration, Astigmatismus, Bildfeldwölbung, Koma, Verzeichnung
Abbildungsgüte *f* **(Abbildungsqualität** *f*) **1.** *(phot)* picture quality, quality of a picture **2.** *(TV)* definition of an image
→ Auflösungsvermögen
Abbildungslinse *f (phot)* objective lens, image lens
Abbildungsmaßstab *m (phot/print/TV)* scale of a picture (an image), image scale, scale of reproduction, reproduction scale
Abbildungsrechte *n/pl* copyright, reproduction right(s) *(pl)*
Abbildungsverzeichnis *n* list of illustrations

Abbildungsvorlage f
→ Vorlage
abbinden v/t *(print)* (Kolumnenschnur) to untie (the page cord)
Abblende f
→ Abblenden (Abblendung)
abblenden I v/t **1.** to fade down, to fade out **2.** (Licht) to dim, to dim out, to turn down, to fade to black, to go to black, to brown out, *brit* to dip (the light)
   To fade out the image completely.
3. (Ton) to fade out, to fade down, to fade, *brit* to dip (the sound) II v/i **4.** to fade, to fade down, to fade out **5.** (Licht) to dim, to dim down, to dim out, *brit* to dip **6.** (Ton) to fade, to fade down, to fade out, to dip **7.** (Objektiv) to iris out, to focus out, to circle out **8.** (Blende) to stop down: auf Blende 16 abblenden - to stop down to 16 **9.** (abrupt abblenden) to pop off
Abblenden n **(Abblendung** f) **1.** fade, fade-down, fade-out, fading, dimming **2.** (Licht) dim, dimming, dimming-out, dimming-down, fade, fade to black, fade-down, fade-out, brownout **3.** (Ton) fade, fade-down, fade-out, sound fade **4.** (Blende) stop **5.** (abruptes Abblenden) pop-off
Abblendregler m *(TV)* fade-out, fader, TV fader
Abblendschalter m **(Abblendvorrichtung** f) dimmer, dim switch, *brit* dipper, dip switch
abbrechen v/t *(print)* (Wort, Zeile) to break, to divide; nicht abbrechen (Satzanweisung): run on
Abbreviatur f
→ Abkürzung
ABC-Analyse f *(econ)* ABC analysis, ABC inventory management, ABC inventory-control system
   The practice of dividing inventories into three categories (A,B,C) based on relative high or low usage and/or high or low costs. This arrangement makes analysis of most economical order quantity (EOQ) (optimale Bestellmenge) more efficient by providing for selective inventory control.
Abdeckband n
→ Abdeckstreifen
Abdeckblech n cover plate, cover sheet, guard cover
abdecken v/t **1.** *(phot/print)* (Teil einer Vorlage) to mask, to mask out, to opaque, to cover, to block out, to spot **2.** *(phot/print)* (abdecken oder wegschneiden) to crop **3.** *(phot/print)* (mit Tinte) to ink out **4.** *(phot)* (Objektiv/Linse) to cap, to cover, to stop out, to occult **5.** (Licht) to screen off, to stop out **6.** (Marketing/Medien) to cover
→ Haushaltsabdeckung, Reichweite
Abdecker m opaquer, spotter
Abdeckfarbe f
→ Abdecklack
Abdeckfolie f **1.** *(phot)* (für Diapositive) metal foil mask **2.** (beim Kopieren) transparent ruby mask **3.** → Abdeckstreifen
Abdecklack m **(Abdeckfarbe** f**)** opaque, opaque lacquer, opaque color, *brit* colour, opaque ink, acid resist, resist
Abdeckmaske f *(phot/print)* frisket, mask
   A mask placed over areas of a photograph or illustration not to be disturbed during airbrushing or placed over dead areas of a plate during proofing.
Abdeckpapier n masking paper, goldenrod paper, opaque paper
Abdeckrahmen m **(Maskierrahmen** m**)** masking frame, frisket
Abdeckstreifen m **(Abdeckband** n**, Kreppband** n**)** masking tape
   An adhesive opaque black or red cellulose tape, used for masking of artwork or photographic negatives. It can be removed without damaging the surface texture or image.
Abdeckung f **(Abdecken** n**) 1.** *(phot/print)* (Teile einer Vorlage) masking, masking out, opaquing, covering, blocking-out, spotting **2.** *(phot/print)* (Abdecken oder Wegschneiden) cropping **3.** *(phot)* (Objektiv/Linse) cap, cover, **4.** (Licht) screening-off **5.** → Haushaltsabdeckung, Reichweite
abdrehen v/t *(film)* (Aufnahmen) to finish (shooting)
Abdruck m *(print)* **1.** (Produkt) print, copy **2.** (erster Abdruck) first proof **3.** (Abdruck vor der Schrift) proof before letters **4.** (Abdruck mit angelegter Schrift) lettered proof **5.** (Abdruck mit ausgeführter Schrift) print state **6.** (Vorgang) printing, copying, proofing
abdruckbar adj printable; nicht abdruckbar: unprintable

Abdruckbewilligung f
→ Abdruckgenehmigung
abdrucken v/t to print, to print off, to work off, to reproduce; (wieder abdrucken) to reprint
Abdruckerlaubnis f
→ Abdruckgenehmigung
Abdruckgebühr f
→ Nachdruckgebühr (Nachdrucklizenzgebühr)
Abdruckgenehmigung f **(Abdruckerlaubnis** f, **Abdruckrecht** n) right of reproduction, permission to reprint, permission grant, copyright permission
Abdruckhöhe f (einer Anzeige) advertisement heigth, depth of space
Abdruckrecht n
→ Abdruckgenehmigung, Nachdruckrecht
Abdruckstempel m (print) impression stamp
abdunkeln v/t 1. (Licht) to dim, to darken, to turn down, to dim down 2. (vollständig abdunkeln) to black out, to fade to black 3. (TV) to blank, to gate 4. (Farbe) to deepen, to darken
Abdunkelung f **(Abdunkeln** n)
1. (Licht) dimming, darkening, dimming-out, dimming-down, brownout 2. (vollständig) blackout, fade to black 3. (TV) blanking
Abendausgabe f (einer Zeitung) evening edition
Abendblatt n **(Abendzeitung** f) evening paper, evening newspaper
abendfüllender Film m full-length film, feature film, A picture
Abendnachrichten f/pl (radio/TV) evening news pl (construed as sg)
Abendpresse f evening newspapers pl, evening papers pl, evening press (the evening press)
Abendprogramm n (radio/TV) evening program, brit programme, evening radio program, evening TV program, (abendliche Sendezeit) (die Sendezeit von 19:00 Uhr bis Sendeschluß) brit evening time, (im Radio) night time
Abendsendung f (radio/TV) evening broadcast, evening show
Abendvorstellung f (Kino) evening performance
Abendzeitung f
→ Abendblatt
Abenteuerfilm m adventure film

Abenteuerzeitschrift f adventure magazine
Aberration f (phot) aberration
→ chromatische Aberration, sphärische Aberration
abfahren (Regieanweisung) interj
→ ab 5., 6.
Abfall m
→ Schnittabfall
abfallen v/i to slip
abfallender Rand m
→ Anschnitt
abfallendes Bild n
→ Anschnitt
Abfangen n **(von Kunden)** **(Abfangwerbung** f) touting, pulling-in (of customers)
abfärben
→ abliegen
abfasen v/t (print) to bevel
Abfasen n (print) beveling
Abfindung f severance pay
Abflußquote f **(Abflußrate** f)
1. (marketing) customer decay rate, decay rate
 The proportion of customers lost in a year as a result of brand switching. The rate indicates the amount of weakening of the effects of prior marketing efforts.
2. (radio/TV) audience loss, audience loss rate
Abfrage f **(Abfrageverfahren** n) (survey res) pre-coded question, prechoice question, pre-quoted question, vertical question order
→ Werbeträgerabfrage
abgedeckte Anzeige f
→ maskierte Anzeige
abgeleitete Nachfrage f **(abgeleiteter Bedarf** m) secondary demand, derived demand
abgepackte Waren f/pl **(Produkte** n/pl)
→ Fertigwaren
abgequetscht adj (print) battered: abgequetschte Type — battered type
abgesetzt adj/adv (print) 1. (gesetzt) in type 2. (einen Absatz bildend) set off
Abgießen n **(Abgießung** f) (print) stereotyping
Abgleich m **(Abgleichung** f, **Abgleichen** n) 1. balance, balancing, adjustment 2. (radio) tracking 3. (film)
→ Weißabgleich, Schwarzabgleich

Abgrenzung 4

4. (Direktmarketing) → Adressenabgleich
5. *(print)* → Ausrichtung, Ausgleich
Abgrenzung *f* regionaler Teilmärkte zoning
Abguß *m (print)* plate, stereotyped plate
abhängige Variable *f* (**abhängige Veränderliche** *f*) *(res)* dependent variable
   Dependent variables are the behaviors, attitudes, or knowledge whose variance the researcher is attempting to explain. Independent variables are those variables used to explain the variance in the dependent variable. Whether variables such as occupation or income are dependent or independent variables depends on the purposes of the researcher and the model used.
   vgl. unabhängige Variable
Abhängigkeit *f* dependence
Abhängigkeitsanalyse *f*
   → Dependenzanalyse
Abholabonnement *n* (Zeitschrift) call-at-office subscription
Abholabonnent *m* (Zeitschrift) call-at-office subscriber
Abholdienst *m* collection service, pickup service
Abhörbericht *m (radio)* listening report, monitoring report
Abhörbox *f (radio)* sound booth, control cubicle, listening cubicle, monitoring cubicle
Abhördienst *m (radio)* monitoring service, listening service
abhören *v/t* **1.** to monitor, to listen **2.** *(radio/TV/film)* (Aufnahme abspielen) to play back
Abhörer *m* monitor
Abhörkabine *f* (**Abhörbox** *f,* **Abhörraum** *m*) *(radio/TV/film)* sound booth, control room, control cubicle, monitoring cubicle
Abhörkontrolle *f* monitoring
Abhörlautsprecher *m* monitoring loudspeaker, monitor, control loudspeaker
Abhörmikrophon *n* (**Abhörmikrofon** *n*) miniphone
Abhörverstärker *m* monitoring amplifier
abklammern *(phot/print) v/t* to crop
   To mark a photograph or the like to indicate a portion or portions to be deleted in final processing.
Abklammern *n (phot/print)* cropping

Abklatsch *m*
   → Stereo
abklatschen
   → abdrucken, stereotypieren
abklopfen *v/t (print)* (Bürstenabzug) to strike off, (Druckform) to plane down
abkupfern *v/t*
   → kupfern
abkürzen *v/t* to abbreviate, to shorten
Abkürzung *f* abbreviation
Ablage *f* (**Satzablage** *f*) *(print)* dump, dead bank
Ablagetisch *m (print)* delivery table
Ablaufdiagramm *n*
   → Flußdiagramm
Ablaufordnungsfrage *f (survey res)*
   → Filterfrage, Gabelungsfrage
abläuten *v/i (film/TV)* to give the red light
ablegen (des Satzes) *v/t (print)* **1.** to distribute, *colloq* to diss, to dump, to kill (the type) **2.** (Satzanweisung) kill
Ablegen *n* (**des Satzes**) *(print)* distribution (of type)
Ableger *m (print)* distributor, *colloq* diss hand
Ablegesatz *m (print)* dead matter, dead copy, (Ablegeklischee) dead plate
Ablegewalze *f (print)* distributing cylinder
Ablegung *f (print)*
   → Ablegen
Ableiter *m (print)* (Auswurfgreifer) delivery gripper
ablichten *v/t* to photocopy, to copy, to photostat, to make a photocopy of
Ablichtung *f*
   → Photokopie
abliegen (abfärben) *v/i (print)* to set off
   → abschmieren
Abliegen *n* (**Abfärben** *n*) *(print)* offsetting
   → Abschmieren
Abnahme *f* (**Annahme** *f*)
1. acceptance **2.** (Manuskriptannahme) acceptance of a manuscript, *(radio/TV)* continuity acceptance, continuity clearance
3. (von Entwürfen in einer Agentur) review
4. → Abnahmeprüfung, Qualitätskontrolle
Abnahmekopie *f (phot/print)* final proof, final copy, final print, fine cut,

(film) answer print (AP), optical answer print (APO), *(radio/TV)* transmission copy, transmission print, transmission tape
Abnahmeprüfung *f* inspection, quality control, acceptance test
Abnehmer *m* 1. *(econ)* buyer, purchaser, customer, client 2. *(print)* fly, flier(flyer)
Abnehmerbefragung *f*
→ Käuferbefragung
Abnehmerbindung(en) *f(pl)*
→ Absatzbindung(en)
Abnehmerfinanzierung *f*
→ Absatzfinanzierung
Abnehmerverhalten *n*
→ Käuferverhalten, Konsumverhalten
Abnutzung *f* **(Abnutzungseffekt** *m* **(in der Werbung)** advertising wearout, wearout effect, advertising decay, wearout
  The point at which an advertisement loses its effectiveness due to excessive exposure and consequent disregard.
Abo *n colloq* Abonnement
Abonnement *n* subscription
  The contractual agreement by an individual or firm to purchase one or more copies of a periodical publication for a given period which conforms to established rules.
Abonnementsauflage *f* paid subscription, subscription sales *pl*, subscription circulation
  The aggregate of those copies of a periodical publication that are paid for in advance by subscribers and mailed or otherwise distributed regularly.
Abonnementsbedingungen *f/pl* terms *pl* of subscription
Abonnementsbestellschein *m* subscription order form, subscription form
Abonnementsdauer *f* length of a subscription
Abonnementsermäßigung *f* reduced subscription rate, reduced subscription
Abonnementserneuerung *f*
1. (Vorgang) renewal of a subscription, subscription renewal
2. (Mitteilung) renewal notice, renewal
Abonnementsfernsehen *n* subscription television (STV, S.T.V.)
  Transmission for a monthly fee of television signals to home receivers attached to a cable network. It is pay TV,

(→) Münzfernsehen, on a monthly fee basis.
Abonnements-Leser *m* **(A-Leser** *m***)** (Zeitung/Zeitschrift) paid subscriber
  Purchaser of publication on a term contract, whose subscription qualifies as paid circulation (→ Verkaufsauflage).
Abonnementspreis *m* **(Abonnementstarif** *m***)** subscription rate, subscription price
Abonnementsrückgang *m* decline of subscriptions, decrease of subscriptions
Abonnementswerber *m* **(Abo-Werber** *m***)** 1. subscription agent, subscription canvasser, canvasser, magazine subscription canvasser, subscription salesman
  One who, as a regular or temporary or part-time vocation, solicits subscriptions for a paper or periodical. He may receive his compensation on either salary or commission basis, or both.
2. subscription agency, book agent
  An individual, firm or corporation obtaining subscriptions for two or more publications.
Abonnementszeitschrift *f* **(Abo-Zeitschrift** *f***)** subscription magazine, subscription journal
  A periodical publication that is preponderantly or exclusively distributed by means of subscriptions.
Abonnementszeitung *f* **(Abo-Zeitung** *f* **)** subscription newspaper, subscription paper
Abonnent(in) *m(f)* subscriber
Abonnentenexemplare *n/pl* **(A-Exemplare** *n/pl*, **A-Stücke** *n/pl* **)**
→ A + E-Exemplare
Abonnentenkartei *f* **(Abonnentenliste** *f* **)** list of subscribers, mailing list
Abonnentenwerber *m*
→ Abonnementswerber
Abonnentenwerbung *f*
→ Abonnementswerbung
Abonnentenzahl *f* number of subscribers
abonnieren *v/t* to subscribe to, to be a subscriber of, to have subscribed to, *colloq* to take in (a magazine)
abonnierte Auflage *f* **(abonnierte Stücke** *n/pl* **)**
→ Abonnementsauflage
abpacken *v/t* to package, to pack, to pack up
Abpacken *n*
→ Verpacken

abpausen v/t to trace, to copy, to trace out, to trace over
Abpausen n tracing, copying
abpressen v/t (print) to back (a book)
Abpressen n backing (of a book)
Abpreßfalz m (print) joint
Abpreßmaschine f (print) **1.** backing machine, machine backer, backing press **2.** pressing machine, press
abquetschen v/t (print) to batter
Abrechnungsverfahren n (**Abrechnungssystem** n) advertising agency remuneration, agency remuneration system
Abreibbuchstabe m rub-on letter, rub-off letter
Abreißband n (print) breaking band
Abreißblock m (**Abreißkalender** m) tear-off pad, tear-off block, tear-off calendar block
Abreißgutschein m (**Abreißkupon** m, **abtrennbarer Gutschein** m) tear-off coupon, (TM) Ad-A Card
Abreißkarte f (**abtrennbare Rückantwortkarte** f) tear-out card, tear-off card
Abreißschiene f (print) cutting ruler
Abriebfestigkeit f resistance to abrasion
abrücken (print)
→ absetzen
Abruffernsehen n
→ Münzfernsehen
Absage f (radio/TV) **1.** (am Ende einer Sendung) closing announcement, billboard, credits pl, credit title, (kurze Absage) tag, trailer, tag line, back cue
In broadcasting, an addition to a commercial or a program, such as a voice-over message following a transcribed message, or an announcement or musical bit that serves as a finale.
2. (bei Sendeschluß) sign-off
absagen v/t (radio/TV) to close a program, brit programme, to make the closing announcement, to sign off
Absahnplan m (**Absahnstrategie** f, **Marktabschöpfungspolitik** f) (marketing) cream plan, creaming, creaming strategy, milking strategy, skimming policy, skimming strategy, profit-taking strategy
The introduction of a new product at a high price, with subsequent reductions as sales develop.
Absatz m (econ) **1.** sales pl **2.** (Tätigkeit) selling **3.** (print) paragraph, colloq graf, (Satzanweisung) break, run out; kein Absatz (Satzanweisung) run on, set continuous)
Absatz-
→ Distribution-, Marketing-, Vertrieb-
Absatz m **ohne Einzug** (print) block paragraph, book style
Absatz m **über ausgewählte Absatzmittler**
→ selektiver Vertrieb
Absatzaktivität(en) f(pl) (econ) sales activity (activities pl)
Absatzanalyse f (econ) **1.** sales analysis **2.** distribution analysis
→ Vertriebsanalyse
3. marketing analysis
Absatzaußenorganisation f
→ Verkaufsaußenorganisation
Absatzbarometer n (econ) sales barometer
A means of comparing the level of sales performance against preset standards.
Absatzbeobachtung f (econ) **1.** sales observation **2.** distribution observation
→ Vertriebsbeobachtung
3. marketing observation
Absatzberater m
→ Marketingberater
Absatzbereich m
→ Absatzgebiet
Absatzbezirk m (econ) sales district
→ Absatzgebiet
Absatzbudget n (econ) sales budget
A tabulation of anticipated accounting figures covering sales revenue and direct selling costs shown in predetermined divisions of time, products, territory or market segment. Used as a means of control by comparing actual with budgeted performance and taking remedial action, where possible, to restore any shortfalls.
Absatzchance(n) f(pl) (econ) sales prospects pl, prospective sales pl
Absatzdaten n/pl (econ) **1.** sales data pl **2.** distribution data pl
Absatzdestinatar m
→ Zielperson
Absatzelastizität f (econ) sales elasticity
→ Elastizität, Nachfrageelastizität
Absatzentwicklung f (econ) development of sales, sales development

Absatzerfolg m **(Absatzwirkung** f)
(econ) sales effectiveness
Absatzertrag m
→ realisierter Ertrag
Absatzerwartung(en) f(pl) (econ) sales
expectation(s) (pl)
Absatzfinanzierung f (econ) financing
of sales, sales financing
Absatzflaute f (econ) period of slack
sales, sales stagnation
Absatzförderung f (econ) sales
promotion, promotion, merchandising
 Any non-face-to-face activity concerned
 with the promotion of sales, but often
 taken also to include advertising.
→ Verkaufsförderung, Merchandising
Absatzförderungsinstrument n (econ)
instrument of sales promotion
Absatzförderungsmaterial n
(Absatzförderungsmittel n) (econ)
1. promotional material, promotion
matter, promotool 2. (zusammen-
hängendes Paket von Materialien)
promotional kit, promotional package
Absatzförderungsnachlaß m (econ)
promotion allowance, merchandising
allowance
Absatzform(en) f(pl) distribution
organization, brit organisation
Absatzforschung f **(Absatzlehre** f)
(econ) sales research
Absatzfunktion(en) f(pl)
→ Handelsfunktionen
Absatzgarantie f (econ) sales
guarantee
Absatzgebiet n **(Absatzbereich** m)
(econ) sales area, sales territory, area
of distribution, distribution area,
trading area, trading zone
 A district whose size is usually
 determined by the boundaries within
 which it is economical in terms of
 volume and cost for a marketing unit or
 group to sell and/or deliver a good or
 service.
Absatzgemeinkosten pl (econ) 1. sales
overhead cost 2. distribution overhead
cost
Absatzgenossenschaft f (econ)
cooperative marketing association
Absatzgeschwindigkeit f (econ) sales
turnover
Absatzhelfer m **(Absatzhilfsbetriebe**
m/pl)
→ Handelsvertreter, Handelsmakler,
Kommissionär, Auktionär, Makler,
Marketingberater, Marktforschungsinstitut, Werbemittler, Werbeagentur

Absatzhonorar n royalty on sales,
author's royalty
Absatzindex m
→ Absatzkennzahl
Absatzinnenorganisation f
→ Verkaufsinnenorganisation
Absatzinstrument f **(Absatz-
instrumentarium** n)
→ absatzpolitische Instrumente
Absatzkanal m (econ) 1. sales
channel, channel of sales 2. channel
of distribution, distribution channel,
trade channel
 The structure of intra-company
 organization units and extra-company
 agents and dealers, wholesale and retail,
 through which a commodity, product, or
 service is marketed, including both a
 firm's internal marketing organization
 units and the outside business units it
 uses in its marketing work and both the
 channel structure of the individual firm
 and the entire complex available to all
 firms.
→ Vertriebskanal
3. marketing channel
Absatzkartell n
→ Vetriebskartell
Absatzkennzahl f **(Absatzkennziffer**
f) (econ) 1. sales index, sales index
number 2. marketing index,
marketing index number
3. → Vertriebskennzahl (Vertriebs-
kennziffer)
Absatzkette f (econ) chain of
distribution, trade chain
Absatzkontingent n
→ Absatzquote
Absatzkontrolle f (econ) sales control,
control of sales, sales audit
 The use of a system or procedures to
 enable the supervisory personnel in a
 business company to monitor the
 performance of the selling operation,
 particularly in relation to the field force,
 using predetermined aims or goals.
Absatzkonzept n **(Absatzkonzeption**
f)
→ Marketingkonzept
Absatzkooperation f
→ Marketingkooperation
Absatzkredit m (econ) sales credit,
sales loan
Absatzlage f
→ Marktlage
Absatzlehre f
→ Absatzforschung
Absatzleistung f
→ Marktleistung

Absatzlenkung

Absatzlenkung f *(econ)* sales control, distribution control, controlled distribution
→ Absatzkontrolle
Absatzmarketing n *(econ)* sales marketing, business marketing
vgl. Beschaffungsmarketing
Absatzmarkt m *(econ)* sales market
vgl. Beschaffungsmarkt
Absatzmarktforschung f sales market research
vgl. Beschaffungsmarktforschung
Absatzmaximierung f *(econ)* maximization of sales, sales maximization, *brit* maximisation
Absatzmenge f **(Absatzvolumen** n**)** *(econ)* sales volume, total number of sales, sales *pl*, quantity sold
  Sales achievement expressed in quantitative, physical or volume terms.
Absatzmethode f *(econ)* sales method
→ Absatzpolitik, Absatzweg(e)
Absatzminimierung f *(econ)* minimization of sales, sales minimization, *brit* minimisation
Absatzmittler m
→ Marketingmittler
Absatzorgan n
→ Marketingorgan, Vertriebsorgan
Absatzorganisation f
→ Marketingorganisation, Vertriebsorganisation
Absatzpflege f
→ Marketing
Absatzplan m *(econ)* sales plan
→ Marketingplan
Absatzplanung f *(econ)* sales planning
  That part of the marketing planning work which is concerned with making sales forecasts, devising programs for reaching the sales target, and deriving a sales budget.
→ Marketingplanung
Absatzpolitik f **(absatzpolitische Instrumente** n/pl**)** *(econ)* sales policy
  The company policies enjoined upon the sales force in order to promote uniform achievement of marketing objectives.
→ Marketingpolitik, Marktpolitik, Marketing-Mix
absatzpolitisches Ziel n **(absatzpolitische Ziele** n/pl**)** *(econ)* objective(s) *(pl)* of sales policy
→ Absatzziel(e)
Absatzpotential n **(unternehmensspezifisches Absatzpotential** n**)** *(econ)* sales potential
  The maximum possible sales achievement of an individual company ignoring all constraints on feasibility or desirability.
vgl. Marktpotential
Absatzprognose f *(econ)* sales forecast, sales prognosis
  An estimate of sales, in monetary or physical units for a specified future period under a proposed marketing plan or program and under an assumed set of economic and other forces outside the unit for which the forecast is made. The forecast may be for a specified item of merchandise or for an entire line.
Absatzquote f *(econ)* sales quota, sales proportion, sales ratio
→ Verkaufsquote
Absatzradius m
→ Einzugsgebiet
Absatzregelung(en) f(pl) *(econ)*
1. sales regulations *pl*, trade regulations *pl* 2. marketing regulations *pl*
3. → Absatzkontrolle
Absatzregion f
→ Absatzgebiet
Absatzrevision f *(econ)* sales audit, auditing of sales
Absatzrisiko n
→ Marktrisiko
Absatzrückgang m *(econ)* decline of sales, decrease of sales
Absatzschwankung(en) f(pl) *(econ)* sales fluctuation, fluctuation of sales
Absatzsegment n *(econ)* segment of sales
→ Marktsegment
Absatzsegmentierung f
→ Marktsegmentierung
Absatzsegmentrechnung f
→ Deckungsbeitragsrechnung, Marktsegmentrechnung
Absatzsoll n **(Absatzsollziffer** f**)**
→ Verkaufsquote
Absatzstatistik f *(econ)* sales statistics *pl (construed as sg)*
Absatzsteigerung f *(econ)* increase in sales, sales increase, (planmäßig) sales drive
Absatzstockung f *(econ)* slump in sales, slowdown of sales, stagnation of sales
Absatzstrategie f *(econ)* sales strategy
  A plan of the sales activities undertaken to achieve set objectives including

territory targets, methods of selling, rates of calling and budgets.
→ Marketingstrategie, Vertriebsstrategie
Absatzstruktur f
→ Marktstruktur
Absatzsystem n
→ Vertriebssystem
Absatztaktik f *(econ)* sales tactics pl *(construed as sg)*
→ Marketingtaktik, Vertriebstaktik
Absatztechnik f
→ Absatzmethode
Absatztheorie f
→ Marketingtheorie
Absatzverbund m
→ Absatzkooperation, Marketingkooperation
Absatzvolumen n
→ Absatzmenge
Absatzweg(e) m(pl) *(econ)* 1. sales channel, channel of sales 2. channel of distribution, distribution channel, trade channel
  The means by which goods and services are transferred from the original manufacturer or supplier to users or consumers implying change of ownership or possession.
→ Vertriebsweg(e)
3. marketing channel
Absatzwegeeffizienz f *(econ)* channel efficiency
Absatzwege-Manager m
→ Markt-Manager
Absatzwegepolitik f *(econ)* channel policy, sales channel policy, distribution channel policy, trade channel policy, marketing channel policy
Absatzwegkapitän m *(econ)* channel captain
  The firm acting in leadership of a trade channel which has become a single, integrated system. This is not yet common in the marketplace. The position is earned by leadership ability and market power, rather than by appointment by anyone.
channel leader
  A channel member which because of its position or economic power can stipulate marketing policies to other channel members, in effect exercising control over some or all of their decisions and activities.
Absatzwerbung f **(Verkaufswerbung** f) sales advertising, short-circuit

approach (of advertising), direct-action advertising
Absatzwirtschaft f *(econ)* marketing industry
absatzwirtschaftlicher Indikator m *(econ)* marketing indicator
absatzwirtschaftliche Kennzahl f
→ Absatzkennzahl, Absatzkennziffer
Absatzzahl f **(Absatzziffer** f) *(econ)* sales figure
Absatzzeichen n *(print)* paragraph mark, break mark, *colloq* graf mark
Absatzzentrum n *(econ)* distribution center, *brit* centre
Absatzziel n *(econ)* sales objective, sales target
  The volume of sales set for an individual salesman taking into consideration his record and capabilities, territorial conditions, competition and potential, as well as the company's overall sales forecast.
→ Marketingziel
abschalten v/t *(radio/TV)* to switch off, to turn off
Abschattung f *(radio/TV)* fading
→ Schwund
Abschätzung f **des Satzumfangs**
→ Satzumfangsberechnung
abschirmen v/t to shield, to screen
abschlagen *(print)* v/t 1. (Matrize) to stereotype, to dab 2. (Format) to strip, to untie, to unlock
Abschluß-Auftrag m **(beim Mediaeinkauf)** *(advtsg)* rate holder
  A minimum size advertisement placed in a publication during a contract period to hold a time or quantity discount rate.
Abschlußjahr n **(Geschäftsjahr** n) *(econ/advtsg)* contract year
Abschlußtermin m **(Abschlußstichtag** m) *(econ)* (für Abonnements, Anzeigen etc.) closing date
Abschlußzwang m
→ Kontrahierungszwang
abschmieren v/i *(print)* to set off, to slur
Abschmutzbogen m **(Schmutzbogen** m) *(print)* set-off sheet
Abschneidelinie f **(Abschneidemarkierung** f, **Abschneidestrich** m) crop mark (beim Bild)
  A marking placed at the edges of an original or on a guide sheet to indicate the area desired in reproduction, with the negative or the plate trimmed (cropped) at the markings.
abschneiden v/t 1. (Bild) to crop

Abschneidestufe

To trim or cut away a part of a print or a photograph to eliminate some undesirable portion or to improve the composition. **2.** to trim, to cut off (Anzeige, Seite, Buchblock **3.** (anschneiden) to bleed
Abschneidestufe f *(TV)* clipping circuit, clipper
Abschneideverfahren n **(Auswahl** f **nach dem Konzentrationsprinzip)** *(stat)* cut-off sampling
Abschnitt m
→ Absatz
Abschnittsschlußverkauf m **(Abschnittsverkauf** m) *(retailing)* seasonal closing-out sale, seasonal sale
Abschnittzeichen n *(print)* section mark
abschöpfen v/t *(econ)* to cream, to cream off, to skim, to skim off, to milk
Abschöpfung f **(Abschöpfungsstrategie** f, **Skimming-Strategie** f **)** *(econ)* creaming, creaming strategy, skimming, skimming strategy skimming policy, milking, milking strategy, profit taking, profit-taking strategy
vgl. Durchdringung (Marktdurchdringung, Penetrations-Strategie)
Abschöpfungspreis m *(econ)* skimming price, skim-the-cream price
  The setting of price high initially with the objective of getting the best out of the market rather than the most. The intent is to appeal to those persons in the market who are interested in new things and are little, if at all, conscious of price.
Abschöpfungspreispolitik f *(econ)* skimming pricing
abschrägen v/t *(print)* to bevel
Abschrägen n **(Abschrägung** f **)** *(print)* beveling, *brit auch* bevelling
Abschräghobel m **(Abschrägmaschine** f **)** *(print)* beveling machine, beveling plane, beveler *brit auch* bevelling machine
  A machine for cutting a narrow rabbet or bevel around the edges of square and rectangular printing plates, so as to provide a channel or flange for nailing plates on wooden blocks.
abschreiben v/t
→ ablichten, kopieren, plagiieren
Abschrift f
→ Kopie

abschwächen I v/t **1.** (Text) to soften, to mitigate, to modify, to extenuate (verwässern) to water down, to extenuate **2.** (Farbe) to tone down, to subdue, (verdünnen) to dilute **3.** *(phot)* (Negativ, Bild) to reduce **4.** (Ton) to tone down, to reduce, to attenuate, to thin down **II** v/reflex (sich abschwächen) (Bild, Ton) to become blurred, to grow blurred
Abschwächer m **1.** *(print/phot)* reducer **2.** *(radio)* attenuater, fader
Abschwächung f **1.** (Text) softening down, mitigation, extenuation, modification, (Verwässerung) watering down **2.** *(phot)* (Negativ, Bild) reduction **3.** (Ton) toning down, attenuation, reduction
absenden (abschicken) v/t to dispatch, *auch* despatch, to send off, to send away, (mit der Post) to mail, *brit* to post
Absender m sender
Absenderangabe f **(Absenderadresse** f **)** sender's address
Absendetag m **(Absendetermin** m**)** day of dispatch, date of dispatch
Absendung f **(Absenden** f **)** dispatch, dispatching, mailing, mail-out
absetzbar *adj* **1.** (saleable, *auch* salable, marketable; (leicht oder schwer absetzbar) easy to sell, difficult to sell **2.** (steuerlich) deductible, subject to tax exemption **3.** *(radio/TV)* preemptible
absetzen v/t **1.** *(print)* to set, to set (a manuscript) up in type, to put (a manuscript) in type, to typeset
→ setzen
2. *(print)* (abdrücken) to set apart **3.** *(print)* → Abliegen **4.** *(radio/TV)* (Programm, Sendung vom Spielplan absetzen) to preempt, to remove (a broadcast, a commercial) from the program, *brit* programme, to take (a broadcast, a commercial) out of the program **5.** *(econ)* (Ware, Leistungen) to sell, to market
Absetzen n
→ Absatz, Absetzung
Absetzlinie f **(Trennungslinie** f **)** *(print)* break-off rule, dividing rule
Absetzung f **(Absetzen** n) **1.** *(print)* setting, typesetting, composition **2.** *(radio/TV)* (einer Sendung vom Spielplan) cancellation, *Am auch*

cancelation, removal (from the program), preemption
absolute Abweichung f (**absoluter Wert** m **der Abweichung**) *(stat)* absolute deviation
The value taken without regard to sign of the difference between a value x and a value a from which it is regarded as deviating.
absolute Häufigkeit f (**Zahl** f **der Fälle**) *(stat)* absolute frequency
The actual frequency of a variate, as distinct from the relative frequency, namely the ratio of the frequency to the total frequency of all variate values.
absolute Wahrnehmungsschwelle f (**Reizschwelle** f) *(psy)* absolute threshold, absolute threshold of perception, just noticeable difference (JND), absolute limen
The minimum level at which an individual can detect a specific stimulus. The level tends to increase with constant stimulation, so that a degree of accommodation occurs which requires that the stimulus be ever stronger if it is to be detected.
absolute Zahl f absolute number
absolutes Maß n *(stat)* absolute measure
absoluter Fehler m *(stat)* absolute error
The absolute deviation of an observation from its "true" value.
Absolutskala f
→ Verhältnisskala (Ratioskala)
absorbieren v/t to absorb
absorbierende Markoff-Kette f (**Markov-Kette** f) *(stoch)* absorbing Markov chain
absorbierender Bereich m *(stoch)* absorbing region
absorbierender Rand m *(stoch)* absorbing barrier
absorbierender Zustand m *(stoch)* absorbing state, (absorbierender Zustand einer homogenen Markov-Kette) absorbing state of a homogeneous Markov chain
Absorption f *(phot/stoch)* absorption
Absorptionsmittel n *(phot)* absorbent, absorber, absorbing agent, dope
Abspann m (**Abspanntitel** m, **Nachspann** m) *(film/TV)* end titles *pl*, credits *pl*, credit title, screen credits *pl*, end credits *pl*, close, closing, (bei Patronatssendungen) sponsor identification, I.D. (ID)

Abspenstigmachen n (**von Kunden**)
→ Abwerbung
Abspieldauer f
→ Spieldauer
abspielen v/t (Band) to play, to play back
Abspielerchassis n tape deck
Abspielgerät n recorder, playback machine, (Ton) replay machine, (MAZ) reproducer
→ Plattenspieler, Tonbandgerät, Recorder, Videorecorder
Abspielgeschwindigkeit f speed of replay, replay speed, speed of playback, playback speed
Abspielkopf m playback head
Abspielnadel f reproducing stylus, stylus
Abspielung f (**Abspielen** n) playback, replay, reproduction
Abstand m
→ Distanz
Abstaubpinsel m *(phot)* lens brush
Absteigerung f
→ Auktion auf Abstrich (Abstrichverfahren)
abstellen v/t *(print)* (Walzen) to throw off
Absteller m (**Druckabsteller** m) *(print)* throwoff
Absterbetafel f *(stat)* life table, mortality table
Abstimmanzeiger m *(radio)* tuning indicator, tuning eye, magic eye
Abstimmbereich m *(radio)* tuning range
abstimmen v/t 1. (Farbe) to harmonize, to match, to tune, to adjust 2. (Sender, Empfänger) to tune, to tune in, to tune to, (modulieren) to modulate
Abstimmknopf m *(radio/TV)* 1. tuning knob 2. station selector
Abstimmkreis m *(radio/TV)* tuning circuit
Abstimmschärfe f *(radio/TV)* selectivity, tuning sharpness, tuning resonance
Abstimmskala f *(radio/TV)* tuning dial, tuning scale, dial
Abstimmton m *(radio/TV)* tuning note, tuning tone, line-up tone
Abstimmung f (**Abstimmen** n) 1. (Farben) harmonization, adjustment, tuning 2. (Sender, Empfänger) tuning, tuning-in,

Abstimmvariometer

(Modulation) modulation, syntonization, *brit auch* syntony
Abstimmvariometer *m* tuner, tuning variometer
Abstimmvorrichtung *f* tuning device, tuner, tuning control
abstoßen *v/t* **1.** *(print)* (Rand an einer Stereoplatte) to knock off, to edge off **2.** *(binding)* to round **3.** → verramschen
abstreichen *v/t (print)* (Walze) to scrape down
abstreifen *v/t (print)* to squeegee
Abstreifer *m (print)* squeegee
Abstrich *m* **1.** *(typ)* downstroke, downward stroke **2.** *(print)* stem **3.** → Auktion auf Abstrich (Abstrichverfahren)
abstufen *v/t* **1.** (Farben) to shade, to grade, to gradate, to tone **2.** *(econ)* (Preise) → staffeln
Abstufung *f* **1.** (Farben) shading, gradation, grading, toning **2.** (Preise) *(econ)* → Staffelung
Abszisse *f* (x-Achse *f*) abscissa
Abtastband *n (TV)* scanning belt
Abtastblende *f (phot)* scanning diaphragm, scanning aperture
Abtastbreite *f* (Kamera) track width
Abtastdose *f* (beim Plattenspieler) pickup, pick-up cartridge, pick-up box
abtasten *v/t* to scan
Abtasten *n* (**Abtastung** *f*) scanning
   The electronic process of breaking down the optical television image into horizontal lines.
Abtaster *m* scanner, scanning device
Abtastfeld *n (TV)* scanning field, scanning frame
Abtastfläche *f* scan area
Abtastfrequenz *f* (**Abtastrate** *f*) scanning frequency
Abtastkopf *m* (beim Plattenspieler) pick-up head, pickup
Abtastgerät *n*
→ Abtaster
Abtastgeschwindigkeit *f* scanning speed
Abtastnadel *f*
→ Abspielnadel
Abtastpunkt *m* (**Abtastfleck** *m*) *(TV)* scanning spot
Abtastrate *f*
→ Abtastfrequenz
Abtastraum *m* scanner area, scanning room, telecine area
Abtaströhre *f* scanning bulb

Abtastscheibe *f* (**Nipkowsche Scheibe** *f*) scanning disc, scanner
Abtastsignal *n* scanning signal
Abtastspalt *m* scanning gap, gap
Abtastspannung *f* scanning voltage
Abtaststelle *f*
→ Abtastpunkt
Abtaststrahl *m* scanning beam, scanning ray, scan
   The horizontal electron beam sweep across the television camera target or picture tube in 1/15 millisecond.
Abtastung *f*
→ Abtasten
Abtastvorrichtung *f*
→ Abtaster
Abtastwinkel *m* scanning angle
Abtastzeile *f* (**Bildzeile** *f*, **Rasterlinie** *f*) scanning line, scanline
   Single horizontal path traced across television picture tube by the electron beam.
Abtastzeit *f* scanning time
Abteilplakat *n (transit advstg)* car card, inside car card, inside transit poster, inside bus card, bulkhead card, square-end card, interior car card
Abteilungsorganisation *f* (einer Werbeagentur) departmental system, departmental organization structure, concentric system
Abteilungszeichen *n (print)* division mark, hyphen
abtrennbar *adj* tear-out, tear-off
abtrennbare Rückantwortkarte *f* tear-out card, tear-off card, *colloq* bingo card
Abverkaufsgeschwindigkeit *f (econ)* number of sales at the point of sale, sales rate at the point of purchase
Abwehrpreis *m (econ)* keep-out price, preemptive price, stay-out price
   A price set so low that the market is made unattractive to potential entrants, who might become formidable competitors.
Abwehrvergleich *m etwa* corrective counteradvertisement, corrective comparison advertisement
Abwehrzeichen *n*
→ Defensivzeichen
Abweichung *f (stat)* deviation
Abweichung *f* (**vom Mittelwert**) *(stat)* deviation from the mean
→ durchschnittliche Abweichung, mittlere quadratische Abweichung, Standardabweichung

Abweichungsanalyse *f*
→ Soll-Ist-Vergleich
abwerben *v/t* **1.** (abspenstigmachen) to lure (customers) away, to entice (customers) away **2.** to lure someone away from his job
Abwerbung *f* **1.** luring away of customers, enticing customers away **2.** luring someone away from his job
abwickeln *v/t* **1.** (Aufträge) to handle **2.** (Kabel) to unwind, unreel, to unroll, to uncoil
Abwickelspule *f* **(Abwickeltrommel** *f*) *(phot/film/TV)* feed reel, spool, feed spool, supply spool, supply reel, (beim Projektor) upper spool
Abwicklung *f* **(Abwickeln** *n*)
1. (Aufträge) handling
2. *(phot/film/TV)* unwinding, unreeling, unrolling, uncoiling
Abwicklungsgebühr *f*
→ Bearbeitungsgebühr
Abwicklungsprovision *f (econ)* handling commission
Abzeichen *n* badge
Abziehapparat *m* **(Abziehpresse** *f*) *(print)* **1.** galley press, proof press, proofing press **2.** mimeograph, photostat
Abziehbild *n* **(Abziehplakat** *n*) transfer picture, transfer, decalcomania, decal
   A transparent and adhesive film carrying printed material, such as an advertising message, which can be transferred to any smooth surface.
abziehen *v/t* **1.** *(print)* (Abzug, Bogen) to pull, to print, to strike off; einen Korrekturbogen abziehen: to pull a proof, to proof **2.** (vervielfältigen) to mimeograph, to photostat **3.** *(phot)* to print **4.** (Abziehbild, Lithographie) to transfer
Abziehen *n* **1.** *(print)* proofing, proving, printing, striking-off
2. (Vervielfältigung) mimeograph, photostat **3.** *(phot)* printing
4. (Abziehbild, Lithographie) transfer
Abzieher *m (print)* proofer, prover
Abziehlack *m (print)* stripping varnish
Abziehpapier *n (print)* proof paper, proofing paper
Abziehplakat *n*
→ Abziehbild
Abziehpresse *f*
→ Abziehapparat

Abzug *m* **1.** *(econ)* → Nachlaß, Preisnachlaß, Rabatt **2.** *(print)* (Korrekturabzug) proof, pull, (Fahnenabzug) galley proof, galley, (Bürstenabzug) brush proof, (Handabzug) hand proof, hand pull, (Maschinenabzug) machine proof, machine pull, press proof, (Revisionsabzug vor dem Matern) foundry proof, (erster Korrekturabzug) first proof, (letzter) final proof **3.** *(phot)* print, copy, (photographischer Abzug) photoprint **4.** *(print)* (Abklatsch) impression **5.** *(print)* (Abzug auf Kunstdruckpapier) art pull **6.** *(print)* (Abzug ohne Zurichtung) flat proof, flat pull, flat impression, stone proof **7.** *(print)* (Barytabzug) repro proof, reproduction proof, cameraready proof
Abzugbogen *m (print)* proof sheet, proof
Abzugpapier *n* **1.** *(print)* proof paper, proofing paper
2. → Kopierpapier (Umdruckpapier)
abzugsfähig *adj* (Werbungskosten) deductible
Abzugsfähigkeit *f* deductibility
Accelerator *m*
→ Terminer
Account *m*
→ Etat, Werbeetat, Kundenetat, Klient
Account Executive *m*
→ Kontakter, Kundenbetreuer
Account-Management *n* account management
→ Key-Account-Management, Special-Account-Management
Account Supervisor *m*
→ Etatdirektor, Kontaktgruppenleiter
Acetat *n*
→ Azetat
Achromat *m* **(achromatische Linse** *f*) *(phot)* achromat, achromatic lens
   A photographic lens corrected for chromatic aberration, → chromatische Aberration, or one bringing visual and actinic rays to the same focus.
Achsel *f* **(Achselfläche** *f*) *(typ)* shoulder (of a type)
   The portions of a unit of type which extend above and below the type character, and which do not print.
Achsensprung *m* **(Achssprung** *m*) *(film/TV)* reverse shot (RevS), reverse-

Achtelgeviert

angle shot, reverse angle, reverse action
  Shooting or printing normal film action backwards frame-by-frame to create a special visual effect.
Achtelgeviert *n (print)* em space
Achtelseite *f* (Anzeige) one eighth of a page
Achtermikrophon *n* (**-mikrofon** *n*) bidirectional microphone, figure-of-eight microphone
Achtpunktschrift *f (typ)* eight-point type, brevier
Acquisition *f*
  → Akquisition
Ad-hoc-Gruppe *f (res)* ad-hoc group
Ad-hoc-Studie *f* (**Ad-hoc-Untersuchung** *f*) *(res)* ad-hoc study, ad-hoc investigation
Adaptation *f* (**Adaptierung** *f*) **1.** *(psy)* adaptation **2.** (Filmbearbeitung) adaptation, film adaptation, screen adaptation, cinematization, filmization
Adaptations-Niveau-Theorie *f (psy)* adaptation-level theory, theory of adaptation level (H. Helson)
adaptieren *v/t* to adapt
Adäquanz *f* adequacy
adäquate Stichprobe *f*
  → zulängliche Stichprobe
ADC *abbr* Art Directors Club für Deutschland e.V.
Additionstheorem *n* (**Additionsregel** *f*) *(prob)* addition theorem, addition rule
additive Belichtung *f* (**additives Belichtungssystem** *n*) *(phot)* additive exposure
  A proposed system of exposure nomenclature offered by the American Standards Association (ASA) which would replace conventional f-stops and shutter speeds with a set of Aperture Values (AV) and Time Values (TV). Scene brightness would be indicated by a sequence of Brightness Values (BV) and film speed by a set of Speed Values (SV) which would replace the conventional ASA exposure index numbers. The equation for the system is AV + TV = EV (Exposure Value) = BV + SV.
additive Farbmischung *f* additive color mixing, *brit* colour mixing
  vgl. subtraktive Farbmischung
additiver Prozeß *m*
  → Random-Walk-Prozeß
additives Modell *n (stat)* additive model
additives Belichtungssystem *n (phot)* additive exposure system
Additivität *f (stat)* additivity, additive property, additive effect
Additivsynthese *f (phot)* additive synthesis
  Those three-color processes wherein colored lights are blended together to form the sensation of white.
Adequacy-Importance-Modell *n* adequacy-importance model
adjustieren
  → justieren
ADM *m abbr* Arbeitskreis Deutscher Marktforschungsinstitute
AD-ME-SIM *abbr* Advertising Media Simulation
Admira-System *n*
  → Schneeballverfahren
Adopter *m* adopter
  An individual who adopts an innovation.
Adoption *f* adoption
Adoptionsmodell *n* adoption model
Adoptionsprozeß *m* adoption process
  The mental activity which occurs from the time an individual first becomes aware of an innovation until he accepts it, usually buying it.
Adoptions-Prozeß-Modell *n* adoption process model
adra *m abbr* Adreßbuchausschuß der Deutschen Wirtschaft
Adressat *m*
  → Empfänger
Adressatenzahl *f obsol*
  → Zielgruppe
Adreßbuch *n* directory, city directory, (Branchenverzeichnis) trade directory, classified directory, commercial directory
Adreßbuchanzeige *f* (**Adreßbuchinserat** *n*) directory advertisement, directory ad
Adreßbuchausschuß *m* **der Deutschen Wirtschaft (adra)** *etwa* Directory Advertising Committee of German Industry
Adreßbuchwerbung *f* directory advertising
  Advertising in printed directories, such as telephone, industrial, trade and city directories.
Adresse *f* (**Anschrift** *f*) address
Adressenänderung *f* change of address
Adressenaufkleber *m* address label
Adressenauswahl *f* selection of addresses

Adressenbereinigung f (**Adressenkontrolle** f) mailing list control
Adressenbüro n
→ Adressenverlag
Adressenhandel m
→ Adressenvermittlung
Adressenkartei f
→ Bezieherkartei, Kundenkartei, Abonnentenkartei
Adressenliste f list of addresses, mailing list, list
   In direct mail advertising, the completed assembly of the names and addresses of the persons to whom the advertiser wishes to send his message.
Adressenmittler m (**Adressenvermittler** m) list broker, list supplier, list house, mailing house
   A commission agent who rents direct mail lists to advertisers.
Adressenpflege f
→ Adressenbereinigung
Adressenquelle f address source
Adressenverlag m (**Adressenbüro** n, **Adressenverleger** m) list broker, list supplier, list house, mailing house
   An independent businessman who arranges the rental to one advertiser of the lists compiled by another advertiser. He is paid a fee or a commission for his services.
Adressenvermietung f list broking
Adressenvermittler m
→ Adressenmittler
Adressenvermittlung f list broking, supply of lists
Adressenverzeichnis n
→ Adreßbuch
adressieren v/t to address (a letter), (maschinell) to addressograph
Adressiergerät n (**Adressiermaschine** f) addressing machine, adressograph, addresser, mailer
ADV m obsol abbr Allgemeiner Direktwerbe- und Direktmarketing-Verband e.V.
→ DDV
AdZ f abbr Arbeitsgemeinschaft der Zeitungen
AE abbr Annoncen-Expedition
A + E-Auflage f (**A + E-Exemplar** n/pl) abbr Abbonements- und Einzelverkaufsauflage f (Zeitungen/Zeitschrift) primary circulation, net paid circulation, net paid, total net paid (einschließlich der Sammelbezieher) total net paid including bulk, (ohne Sammelbezieher) total net paid excluding bulk
   The number of copies of a publication sold per issue through subscription, newsstand sales, etc.
A + E-Exemplar n (Zeitung/Zeitschrift) original purchase unit
A + E-Leser m (Zeitung/Zeitschrift) paid reader, buyer-reader
AE-Provision f (**Annoncen-Expeditions-Provision** f) agency commission, advertising agency commission, media commission
→ Agenturkommission
Affekt m affect
Affekthandlung f (**affektives Verhalten** n) affect-related behavior, brit behaviour
Affektionswert m obsol
→ Zusatznutzen
affektiv-kognitive Konsistenz f (psy) affective-cognitive consistency (Leon Festinger)
Affektkauf m
→ Impulskauf
Affiche m obsol
→ Bogenanschlag, Anschlag, Plakat, Poster
Affidavit n (**Affidavitanzeige** f, **Affidavitwerbung** f) obsol
→ Testimonial
Affinität f
→ Ähnlichkeit, Zielgruppenaffinität
affordable-Methode f (der Werbebudgetierung)
→ finanzmittelbezogene Budgetierung
After-sales-Service m
→ Nachkaufwerbung
AGB f/pl abbr Allgemeine Geschäftsbedingungen
AGB-Gesetz n abbr Gesetz über Allgemeine Geschäftsbedingungen
AGD f abbr Allianz deutscher Grafik-Designer
Agent m agent
   A business unit which negotiates purchases or sells or both but does not take title to the goods in which it deals. The agent usually performs fewer marketing functions than does the merchant. He commonly receives his remuneration in the form of a commission or fee. He usually does not represent both buyer and seller in the same transaction.
Agentenprovision f agent's commission

Agentur f agency
Agenturbeilage f (**Agentur-Supplement** n) syndicated supplement
A supplement supplied to several newspapers or periodicals for simultaneous publication.
Agenturbeleg m (**-exemplar** n) agency copy, advertising agency copy
Agentur-Briefing n agency briefing
→ Briefing
Agentureinkommen n (**Netto-Umsatz** m **einer Werbeagentur**) gross income
Agenturgebühr f agency fee, advertising agency fee, fee
A specified amount charged by an agency for service rendered an advertiser which is not covered by the usual agency commission.
Agenturgeschäft n agency business
Agenturgruppe f
→ Agenturkette
Agenturhonorar n agency fee
Agenturkette f (**Agenturnetz** n) agency chain, agency network
A group of independent and non-competing agencies that collaborate in specified areas.
Agenturleistungen f/pl agency services pl
Agenturnachlaß m (**Agentur-Bonus** m) agency discount
A reduction from a stated advertising rate, generally the cardrate, which an advertising agency receives from advertising media on billings to advertisers.
Agentur-Netto n net cost, net plus, net
The cost of a service provided by an advertising agency aside from the agency commission or an advertising rate after deduction of all applicable discounts, including the agency commission.
Agenturnetz n
→ Agenturkette
Agenturpersonal n (**Agenturmitarbeiter** m/pl) agency personnel, advertising agency personnel
Agenturpräsentation f agency presentation, (Wettbewerbspräsentation) agency pitch, pitch
An accumulation of facts, figures and ideas, both graphic and written, used in presenting and selling an advertising campaign to a client.
Agenturprovision f agency commission, media commission, commission, 15 and 2 (15 & 2)
The percentage of advertising costs earned by an advertising agency for its services to advertisers. It is usually 15 percent of gross media expenditures (time, talent, facilities, space, etc.) and 17.65 percent of net advertising production expenses for artwork, photography, typesetting, engravings etc.
Agenturstück n
→ Agenturbeleg
Agenturumsatz m agency billings pl, billings pl
→ Honorarumsatz
Agenturvergütung f agency remuneration, advertising agency remuneration
Agenturvertrag m agency agreement
Agenturvertreter m agency representative, representative of an agency
Agglomeration f (**im Einzelhandel**) retail agglomeration
aggressive Werbung f (**aggressive Verkaufswerbung** f) aggressive advertising, hard-selling advertising, hardselling advertisement, combative advertising
AGLA f abbr Arbeitsgemeinschaft Leseranalyse e.V.
AG.MA f abbr Arbeitsgemeinschaft Media-Analyse e.V.
Agostini-Ansatz m (media res) Agostini approach, Agostini method
Agrarmarketing n agricultural marketing
AgV f abbr Arbeitsgemeinschaft der Verbraucher
AGZV f abbr Arbeitsgemeinschaft Zeitschriftenverlage des Börsenvereins des Deutschen Buchhandels
Ahle f (print) bodkin
Ähnlichkeit f (stat) similarity
Ähnlichkeitskoeffizient m (stat) coefficient of similarity
Ähnlichkeitsmaß n (stat) similarity measure
→ Proximitätsmaß; vgl. Distanzmaß, Korrelationsmaß
AID-Verfahren n
→ Baumanalyse
AIDA-Formel f (**AIDA-Modell** n) AIDA, AIDA-model
An explanation of how prospects buy as a result of advertising exposure. It is thought that they go through a series of mental states: Attention, or focusing on the salesman and permitting him to begin his presentation; Interest, or

wishing to hear more; Desire, or a strong urge to acquire the salesman's offering; and Action, or placing the order.
Aided Recall *m* **(Aided-Recall-Verfahren** *n***)**
→ gestützte Erinnerung
AIR *m abbr* Arbeitskreis Incentive-Reiseveranstalter
AIW *m abbr* Arbeitskreis Fachagenturen und Berater für Industrie-Werbung
Ajzen-Fishbein-Modell *n* Ajzen Fishbein model
Akkolade *f (print)* brace, accolade, curly bracket
Akkomodation *f* accomodation
Akkumulation *f*
→ Kumulation
Akkuranz *f* **(Treffgenauigkeit** *f,* **Genauigkeit** *f* **)** (stat) accuracy
 The closeness of an estimate or a computation to the true or the exact value.
vgl. Wiederholungsgenauigkeit
Akquieszenz *f* **(Ja-Sage-Tendenz** *f* **)** *(survey res)* acquiescence
akquirieren *v/t* to acquire, to make acquisitions
Akquisiteur *m*
→ Abonnentenwerber (Abo-Werber), Anzeigenakquisiteur, Kundenwerber
Akquisition *f*
→ Abonnentenwerbung, Anzeigenakquisition, Kundenwerbung, persönlicher Verkauf
Akquisitionsanalyse *f* acquisition analysis
Akquisitionspolitik *f*
→ persönlicher Verkauf
akquisitorische Distribution *f etwa* acquisitory distribution
akquisitorisches Potential *n* (Erich Gutenberg) **(Marktpotential** *n***)** (Herbert Gross) *etwa* acquisitory potential, market potential, company goodwill
Akronym *n* acronym
Aktinität *f (phot)* actinity
Aktion *f* action, campaign
Aktionsfeld *n* **der Preispolitik** (Heribert Meffert) action parameters *pl* of price policy, action parameters *pl* of pricing
vgl. Datenfeld, Erwartungsfeld
Aktionsfilm *m* action movie
Aktionsforschung *f* **(Handlungsforschung** *f* **)** action research

Aktionsparameter *m* parameter of action
Aktionswerbung *f* **(Rücklaufwerbung** *f* **)** 1. direct-action advertising
 Advertising the goal of which it is to get the audience to act right away. This may be mail-order asking for money for the product, or advertising for leads in which prospects are encouraged to write for information. Some type of affirmative action is called for.
 2. direct-response advertising
 Essentially the same as direct mail advertising except that the message may be delivered by any medium such as television or radio as well as the postal system.
Aktivation *f* **(Aktivierung** *f* **)** activation
Aktivationsforschung *f* **(Aktivierungsforschung** *f,* **Kaufentschlußforschung** *f* **)** activation research, sales activation research
 A research technique to check the effect of advertising on sales. The effect of advertising is traced back from an actual purchase a respondent has made. He is asked to describe the effect advertising had on his buying decision and prove his statement about the influence of advertising (where did he see the ad?). Effects of particular ads are compared and the campaign is revised accordingly. The technique was developed by Gallup & Robertson.
Aktivationsinterview *n* activation interview
Aktivationsumfrage *f* **(Aktivationsbefragung** *f,* **Kaufentschlußumfrage** *f* **)** activation survey
Aktivator *m* *(print)* activator
aktiver Bekanntheitsgrad *m* **(ungestützte Erinnerung** *f* **)**
1. unaided recall, pure recall, spontaneous recall
 Recall that respondents have of a product (brand), a brand name, an advertisement or a medium without being exposed to any recall aids, (→) Gedächtnisstütze.
 top-of-mind awareness
 The first brand, advertisement or advertising campaign that comes to a respondent's mind in an interview.
 2. share of mind
→ Erinnerung; *vgl.* passiver Bekanntheitsgrad
Aktüberblendzeichen *n* *(film/TV)* changeover cues *pl,* cue mark, cue dots *pl*

aktuelle Illustrierte

A projectionist's changeover warning, usually several frames of a tiny white circle in advance of a film's beginning or end.
aktuelle Illustrierte f
→ Illustrierte
aktuelles Heft n (Zeitschrift) current issue
akustische Werbung f (Tonwerbung f) auditory advertising
Akzelerator m
→ Terminer
Akzeptanz f acceptance
Akzeptanzregion f
→ Annahmebereich
akzessorische Werbung f
→ flankierende Werbung
akzidentelle Werbung f (Extensivwerbung f)
→ flankierende Werbung
Akzidenzen f/pl (**Akzidenzdruck** m, **Akzidenzsatz** m) job printing, job, jobbing, job work, jobbing work, job composition
vgl. Werksatz
Akzidenzabteilung f (print) jobbing department
Akzidenzarbeit f
→ Akzidenzen
Akzidenzbuchbinderei f job bindery
Akzidenzdruck m
→ Akzidenzen
Akzidenzdrucker m job printer, jobbing printer
A printer who does small commercial printing, such as letterheads, business cards and envelopes.
Akzidenzdruckerei f job printer, jobbing printer, jobbing office
Akzidenzdrucksache(n) f(pl) job printing
Akzidenzeinband m job binding, extra binding
Akzidenzsetzer m (print) job compositor, (für Werbung) advertographer
A typesetter who sets commercial printing.
Akzidenzschrift f
A small assortment of type in any one size and style used for job composition.
Akzidenzsetzer m (print) job compositor
Akzidenzsetzerei f (print) jobbing case room, jobbing office

Akzidenzsetzgerät n (**Akzidenzsetzmaschine** f) (print) job press, jobber
A press used for job composition.
Akzidenzsetzkasten m (print) job case
aleatorische Werbung f aleatory advertising
Alfapapier n (**Espartopapier** n, **Halfapapier** n) alfalfa paper, esparto paper
Alinea n (**Alineazeichen** n) (typ) paragraph mark, new paragraph, colloq graf
alineieren v/t
→ absetzen 2.
Alkoholwerbung f advertising for alcoholic beverages, liquor advertising
Allbereichsverstärker m (radio) wideband amplifier
alle Rechte vorbehalten all rights reserved
allegatorische Werbung f (zitierende Werbung f) etwa advertising (oder advertisement) using quotes from research studies, scientific publications or test results, advertising using endorsements and testimonials
Alleinauslieferer m exclusive distributor
Alleinauslieferung f (**Exklusivvertrieb** f) exclusive distribution, exclusive outlet selling, exclusive agency method of distribution
The practice of confining the carrying of a particular service or brand in an area to just one retailer or one wholesaler, usually with some type of contractual agreement. The seller who wishes to use such an arrangement generally anticipates maximum promotional cooperation from his dealers.
alleinstehende Anzeige f island advertisement, island ad, solus advertisement
A newspaper or magazine advertisement entirely surrounded by reading matter or margin.
alleinstehende halbseitige Anzeige f island half-page advertisement, island half page, half-page island advertisement
alleinstehende Warenauslage f (POP advtsg) island display, merchandise island, island

A store display fixture centered in an open space and, therefore, accessible on all sides.
alleinstehender Werbespot *m (radio/ TV)* island commercial, isolated commercial,
The preferred location of a television commercial where program content separates it from the other commercials.
(alleinstehender 30-Sekundenspot) isolated 30
A 30-second commercial surrounded by program matter and thus enjoying an island position.
Alleinstellung *f* 1. (Position) island position, solus position
A preferred position of an advertisement in a newspaper or a magazine being completely surrounded by either editorial matter or margin.
2. (Vorgang) island positioning, solus positioning, *(radio/TV)* isolation
The preferred position of a television or radio commercial with program content directly before and after it.
3. → Alleinstellungswerbung
Alleinstellungswerbung *f* (**Alleinstellung** *f*) *etwa* advertising using untrue and misleading superlatives, advertising using superiority claims
Alleinverkauf *m* exclusive sale, exclusive selling, exclusive dealing
A practice under which a dealer agrees to refrain from handling competing products in return for being supplied with the manufacturer's goods. This usually is the result of an agreement between a manufacturer (or other supplier) with a particular wholesaler or retailer not to sell to other wholesalers or retailers in the same market.
Alleinvertreter *m* (**Exklusivvertreter** *m*) exclusive representive, exclusive agent
Alleinvertretung *f* exclusive representation
Alleinvertrieb *m* (**Exklusivvertrieb** *m*) exclusive distribution
→ Alleinauslieferung
Alleinvertriebsklausel *f* (**Alleinvertriebsvertrag** *m*)
→ Ausschließlichkeitsklausel (Ausschließlichkeitsvertrag)
Alleinwerbung *f*
→ Einzelwerbung
Allensbacher Werbeträger-Analyse (AWA) *f* Allensbach Advertising Media Analysis, Allensbach Market-Media Analysis

alles in Versalien *(print)* all capital letters, all caps (Satzanweisung)
allgemeine Anschlagstelle *f*
→ Allgemeinstelle
allgemeine Betriebsunkosten *pl (econ)* overhead cost, overhead
Those expenses of a general nature which apply to a business as a whole.
allgemeine Geschäftsbedingungen (AGB) *f/pl etwa* general business conditions *pl*, general business terms *pl*
allgemeine Zeitschrift *f*
→ Publikumszeitschrift
Allgemeiner Direktwerbe- und Direktmarketing-Verband (ADV) e.V. *m etwa* General Association of Direct Advertisers and Direct Marketers (in West Germany)
→ Deutscher Direktmarketing-Verband e.V. (DDV)
Allgemeines Einzelhandelspanel *n*
→ Einzelhandelspanel
Allgemeinstelle *f* (**allgemeine Anschlagstelle** *f*) *etwa* poster panel, general poster panel, billboard, billboard hoarding
Allgemeinstreuung *f* (**Allgemeinumwerbung** *f*) *etwa* scatter planning, shotgun approach (in media planning), advertising addressed to the general public
→ ungezielte Streuung
Allianz *f* deutscher Grafik-Designer AGD e.V. Association of German Graphic Artists
Alligatorklammer *f* (**Alligatorklemme** *f*) alligator clip
Alliteration *f* (**Stabreim** *m*) alliteration
All-Media-Analyse *f (media res)* all-media analysis
Allokation *f*
→ optimale Allokation
Allokation *f* (**der Marketingmittel, der Werbemittel**) allocation of marketing expenditure, of advertising expenditure
→ Budgetierung, Werbebudgetierung
Allonge *f* 1. *(print)* flyleaf 2. *(TV)* identification leader, protection leader
Allstromgerät *n* (**Allstromempfänger** *m*) all-mains receiver, all-mains set, AC/DC receiver, AC/DC set

All-you-can-afford-Methode f (der Werbebudgetierung)
→ finanzmittelbezogene Budgetierung
Allzweckstichprobe f *(stat)* general-purpose sample
Alpha-Fehler m (**α-Fehler** m)
→ Fehler 1. Art
alphamerisch *adj* alphamerical
→ alphanumerisch
alphanumeric(al) *adj* alphanumerisch
alt *adj (print)* dead
→ Altzeug
alter Satz m (**Ablegesatz** m) *(print)* dead matter
    Composed type that is no longer needed.
altes Klischee n (**Ablegeklischee** n) *(print)* dead plate
    A plate that is no longer needed.
Altarfalz m (**Altarfalzanzeige** f)
Dutch door, Dutch door advertisement, Dutch door ad, Dutch door spread
    A special magazine advertising space that consists of two-part, full-page gatefolds folding to a common center (hence the reference to altar in the German word), or stacked or single half-page gatefolds.
älteres Heft n (**ältere Ausgabe** f **einer Zeitschrift**) back issue, back copy, back number, backlog issue, backlog copy, backlog number
Alternativfrage f *(survey res)* dichotomous question, quantal question, yes-no question, bipolar scale question, bipolar question
    Bipolar questions are those expressed in terms of either end of a dimension, such as "favor/oppose" or "satisfied/dissatisfied." Unipolar questions are asked only in terms of one end of a dimension with a neutral or "not-X" point — for example, "Do you favor X or not?" A bipolar question assumes that the attitude runs from positive to negative values, with a neutral point in the middle; unipolar questions assume that the attitude runs from positive to neutral or from negative to neutral but that a positive view is not necessarily the opposite of a negative view.
Alternativhypothese f (H_1, H_A) alternative hypothesis
    In the theory of testing hypotheses, (→) Hypothesenprüfung, any hypothesis alternative to the one under test, i.e. the null hypothesis.
vgl. Nullhypothese

Alternativdaten n/pl (**Alternativinformationen** f/pl) alternative data pl, quantal data pl
Alternativprognose f alternative forecast, alternative prognosis
Altries n
→ Ries
Altzeug n *(print)* dead metal, bearers pl
    In hot-metal composition, any metal left or inserted in blank areas of an engraving or type form to evenly distribute the pressure of molding.
AM *abbr* Amplitudenmodulation
am Fuß einer Seite bottom of a page
Amateurfunk m
→ CB-Funk
Ambivalenz f ambivalence, *(selten)* ambivalency
Ambivalenzkonflikt m
→ Appetenzkonflikt
ambulanter Handel m *(retailing)* nonstationary trade, itinerant trade
→ Hausierhandel, mobiler Straßenhandel, zentrumorientierter Straßenhandel; *vgl.* stationärer Handel
ambulanter Zeitungsverkauf m
→ Straßenverkauf
ambulanter Zeitungsverkäufer m newsboy, street vendor, newsvendor
amerikanisches System n (**amerikanisches Abrechnungsverfahren** n) service fee system, fee basis (of advertising agency remuneration)
    The system of advertising agency remuneration whereby a fee is paid by an advertiser to the agency, either in the form of a retainer for general services or in the form of a special compensation for particular jobs beyond the agency's usual services.
AMF m *abbr* Arbeitskreis Media-Informationen Fachzeitschriften
Ammoniak-Entwicklung f *(phot)* ammonia process
Ammoniaklösung f *(phot)* ammonia solution, dilute ammonia
Amoroso-Robinson-Gleichung f (**Amoroso-Robinson-Relation** f) *(econ)* Amoroso-Robinson equation
Ampex n (**Ampex-Verfahren** n)
→ Magnetaufzeichnung (MAZ)
Amplitude f amplitude
Amplitudenmodulation (AM) f amplitude modulation (AM), medium wave

The original audio transmission technique, utilizing frequencies from 550 to 1,600 kilohertz. It is subject to atmospheric and local signal interference.
AMT *f abbr* Arbeitsgemeinschaft mittlerer Tageszeitungen e.v.
amtliche Anzeige *f* **(amtliche Bekanntmachung** *f***)** public service advertisement, public service ad
Amtsblatt *n* **(amtliche Zeitung** *f*, **Amtszeitung** *f***)** gazette
Anaglyphe *f (phot)* anaglyph
An illustration giving a stereoscopic or relief effect when viewed through proper color filters or spectacles, such as an anaglyphoscope.
Anaglyphenbrille *f* **(3-D-Brille** *f***)** anaglyphoscope
Anaglyptik *f* **(Anaglyphendruck** *m***)** anaglyptic(al) print, anaglyptical printing, anaglyptics *pl (construed as sg)*
analog *adj* analogous
Analog-Marketing *n* **(Analog-Werbung** *f***)**
→ Einweg-Kommunikation; *vgl.* Digital-Marketing (Digital-Werbung)
Analog-Methode *f* **(Analogiemethode** *f* **der Standortwahl)** *(econ/retailing)* analogue method of store site determination, analogue method of determining retail locations, *Am auch* analog method
analoge Farben *f/pl (phot/print)* analogous colors *pl, brit* colours *pl*
Analogiemethode *f* (Heribert Meffert)
→ warenspezifische Analogiemethode
Analyse *f* **(Auswertung** *f***)** analysis
→ Datenanalyse
Analyse *f* **der relevanten Vergleichsmarken** *(market res)* brand-set analysis, evoked set analysis
Analyse *f* **des Leserkreises**
→ Leserschaftsanalyse
analytische Befragung *f* **(analytische Umfrage** *f* **)** analytic(al) survey
A design for statistical observations to provide a basis for dealing with the factors causal to a situation. This type of study, dealing with a process, produces information which can only be regarded as a sample from that process, which could continue indefinitely without its conditions changing. A complete set of such observations is called an infinite population.
vgl. enumerative Befragung (Zählbefragung)

analytische Statistik *f*
→ Inferenzstatistik
analytisches Konstrukt *n*
→ hypothetisches Konstrukt
Anamorphot *m (phot)* anamorphic lens, "A" lens, shrink lens
A camera lens used to compress and a projector lens to expand the image, adapting the standard width camera film to widescreen projection formats.
anamorphotisches Bild *n (phot)* anamorphic picture, anamorphotic picture
anastatischer Druck *m* **1.** (Verfahren) anastatic printing **2.** (Produkt) anastatic print
Anastigmat *m* **(anastigmatisches Objektiv** *n***)** *(phot)* anastigmatic lens, anastigmat
A photographic lens corrected for astigmatism.
Anbieter *m (econ)* supplier
Anbietergemeinschaft *f* **(Anbieterkoalition** *f***)**
→ Selling Center
Anbieter-Nachfrager-Interaktionen *f/pl (econ)* interactions *pl* between suppliers and demanders
Anbieterverhalten *n (econ)* supplier behavior, *brit* behaviour, behavior of suppliers
anbringen *v/t* (ein Plakat an der Anschlagfläche) to post (a poster), to poster, to put up, (ein Schild) to attach (a sign), to fix (a sign)
ändern *v/t* (Teile eines Textes) to alter, to modify, to make changes, to change
Änderung *f* (im Text) alteration, modification, change
Änderungsblatt *n*
→ Korrekturblatt
Andienungssystem *n*
→ Bedienungsformen
Andruck *m (print)* final proof, final pull, preprint
The complete and proofread version of any copy, such as an advertisement, as it will be published.
andrucken *(print)* **1.** *v/t* to pull a proof, to pull a final proof, to make a preprint **2.** *v/i* to start printing
Andruckkufe *f* **(Andruckschiene** *f***)** *(film)* pressure pad, skid
Andruckmagnet *m* pressure solenoid
Andruckmaschine *f* **(Andruckpresse** *f***)**
→ Abziehapparat 1.

Andruckpapier *n*
→ Abziehpapier
Andruckplatte *f (film)* pressure plate
Andruckrolle *f* pressure roller, pinch roller, capstan idler, lay-on roller
aneinanderreihen *v/t (print)* (Typen) to stick
Anerkennungsschreiben *n*
→ Dankschreiben
Anfang *m*
→ Einleitung
Anfangsauflage *f*
→ Erstauflage
Anfangsaufmerksamkeit *f* initial attention
Anfangsbuchstabe *m*
→ Initial
Anfangsmoment *n* (gewöhnliches Moment *n*) *(stat)* initial moment
→ Moment
Anfangstotale *f (film)* establishing shot
  The initial master scene identifying the location of a scene and/or the relationship of on-camera talent.
Anfangszeile *f (print)* opening line, first line
Anfrage *f* inquiry, enquiry, query
  Any request from a prospective buyer or customer made in response to an advertisement.
Anfragenkontrolltest *m* (**Anfragetest** *m*) response control test, inquiry test, enquiry test
  A test of advertising or advertising medium effectiveness based on responses such as inquiries or coupon returns and comparing the number of inquiries received through different advertisements and/or different media.
Anführungszeichen *n/pl (print)* quotation marks *pl*, inverted commas *pl*
Angebot *n* 1. *(econ)* supply (Angebot und Nachfrage: supply and demand)
2. *(econ)* (Gebot bei Ausschreibungen) bid, tender
  A stated offer to purchase a product or a service at a specified price, usually under circumstances where the seller has not specified a price, or where there exists the potential for the seller of finding other competitive buyers for an item or service in scarce supply.
3. offer, proposition, proposal
→ verstecktes Angebot
Angebot machen *v/i* (bei Ausschreibungen) to bid, to tender

Angebotselastizität *f (econ)* elasticity of supply, supply elasticity
vgl. Nachfrage-Elastizität
Angebotsform(en) *f(pl)*
→ Marktformen des Angebots
Angebotsfunktion *f* (**Angebotskurve** *f*) *(econ)* supply function, supply curve
Angebotsmacht *f (econ)* etwa economic strength of a supplier
vgl. Nachfragemacht
Angebotsmappe *f* advertising portfolio, sales portfolio, sales kit
Angebotslage *f (econ)* supply situation
Angebotsmonopol *n (econ)* supplier monopoly, supply-side monopoly
Angebots-Nachfrage-Funktion *f*
→ Nachfragefunktion
Angebotsmuster *n*
→ Muster
Angebotspreis *m* advertised, quoted price
  The price for a product or a service as stated in an advertisement.
Angebotsstatistik *f (econ)* supply statistics *pl (construed as sg)*
Angebotsstruktur *f (econ)* structure of supply, supply structure
angehängt *adj/adv (print)* run-on, run-in, set continuous
angehren
→ gehren
angeklebtes Werbemittel *n* (**Ankleber** *m*, **Aufkleber** *m*) tip-on
  A coupon, a reply card, or a sample glued to an advertisement by one edge.
Angel *f (film/radio/TV)* (im Studio) boom arm, batten
  A pipe suspended above the studio and used for hanging lights or scenery.
angemessener Preis *m (econ)* adequate price, fair price
angeschnitten *adj (print)* bled, bled-off, bleed, trimmed
angeschnittene Anzeige *f* bleed advertisement, bleed ad, bled-off ad(vertisement)
  An advertisement which is not confined to the editorial margins of the publication, but printed to the very edge of the page. Sold at a premium rate.
angeschnittene Seite *f* bleed page, bleed, bled-off page
  A page (usually a full-page advertisement) of a publication with an illustration area that is printed to the very edges of the page, or is trimmed so that the illustration runs to the very edges.

(im Bundsteg angeschnittene Doppelseite) bleed in the gutter page, gutter bleed, bridge
A page (usually a double-page spread) of a publication with an illustration area that bleeds or prints to the gutter (Bundsteg), i.e. running uninterrupted across the gutter of the spread.
angeschnittener Druck *m* **(Druck** *m* **angeschnittener Seiten)** bleed printing, bleeding
angeschnittenes Klischee *n* **(Klischee** *n* **für eine angeschnittene Seite)** bleed plate, bleed
angeschnittenes Plakat *n* **(Plakat** *n* **ohne weißen Rand)** bleed face, bleed poster, bleed
An outdoor painted bulletin or poster which has no frame molding or (white) margin, with the design area extending to the very edges.
angestrahlte Werbefläche *f* illuminated outdoor poster, glow panel, glow bulletin board, glow bulletin
angewandte Kunst *f* applied art
angewandte Psychologie *f* applied psychology
angewandte Soziologie *f* applied sociology
Angst *f* **(Angstappell** *m***)** anxiety, anxiety creating advertising
vgl. furchterzeugende Werbung
anhängen *v/t (print)* to run on, (Satzanweisung) run, set continuous
Anhänger *m* **(Anhängeetikett** *n,* **Anhängezettel** *m***)** *(promotion)* tag, label, (Flaschenanhänger) bottle hanger, (Deckenanhänger) dangler, mobile, (Packungsanhänger) package outsert, outsert
anheften *v/t* (Bekanntmachung an einem Brett) to attach a notice on a bulletin board, (Preisschild an eine Ware) to attach a price tag to a product
Anilindruck *m* **1.** (Produkt) aniline print, flexographic print
An insolubilized image of glue or cold enamel that has been stained with an aniline dye either during or after development, the dyed print promoting greater visibility.
2. (Vorgang/Verfahren) aniline printing, flexography, flexographic printing

Animatic *n* **(Animatic-Verfahren** *n***)** animatic, animated storyboard, limited animation technique
An animatic is a draft television commercial produced by a mechanical animation technique from semi-finished artwork. Animatics are generally used for test purposes only.
Animatic-Test *m* animatic test
Animation *f*
→ Trickfilm, Zeichentrickfilm
Animator *m*
→ Trickfilmzeichner
animieren *v/t (film)* to animate
ankeilen
→ Form schließen
Ankerreiz *m (psy)* anchor stimulus, anchorage, anchoring point
ankleben *v/t* (Plakat) to post (a poster), to poster, to stick (a bill), to put up (a poster), (ankleistern) to paste (a poster) on, (an einer Ecke) to tip on
Ankleben *n* **(Plakatkleben** *n***)** billsticking, billposting, posting
Ankleber *m* **(Plakatkleber** *m***)** billsticker, billposter
Anlage *f (print)* **(Bogenanlegen** *n***)** feeding
Anlageblatt *n (print)* rider
An emendation to a manuscript which is indicated on a separate piece of paper.
Anlagegüter *n/pl*
→ Investitionsgüter
Anlagegüterwerbung *f*
→ Investmentwerbung
Anlaßfenster *n (POP advtsg)* theme display window, special occasion window
The use of window display to create a certain theme appropriate to the merchandise shown in the display. The theme may be related to a holiday, such as Christmas, or Easter. Or it may revolve around some local, national, or international event that is likely to be of interest to segments of the store's target market.
Anlegeapparat *m (print)* feeder, margin stop
Anlegekante *f* **(Anlegesteg** *m***)** *(print)* gripper margin, feed edge, lay margin
Anlegemarke *f (print)* gauge pin, centering arrow, lay gauge, lay mark
anlegen 1. *(print) v/t* (Bogen) to feed, to mark something sheetwise, (Formatstege) to dress **2.** *(radio/TV)* to dub, to put in sync, to sync up

Anlegen

Anlegen *n* 1. *(print)* (Bogen) feeding, (Formatstege) dressing 2. *(radio/TV)* putting in sync, dubbing
Anleger *m (print)* feeder, gripper
Anlegespan *m (print)* scale board
Anlegesteg *m*
→ Anlegekante
Anlegetisch *m (print)* feed table, horse
Anlegevorrichtung *f*
→ Anlegeapparat
anlehnende Werbung *f*
1. → Nachahmung
2. → Vorspannen
Anlocken *n* **(Anlocken** *n* **von Kunden)** bait advertising, bait-and-switch advertising, bait-and-switch selling, bait-and-switch tactics *pl (construed as sg)*, switch selling
 Advertising exceptional prices or some other alluring or irresistible terms for a product in order to attract prospects to a store, where they find it difficult or impossible to buy the product as advertised.
→ Anreißen (anreißerische Werbung), Zusendung (→) unbestellter Ware, Lockvogelangebot, marktschreierische Werbung
Anlöseschablone *f*
→ Siebdruckschablone
Anmeldekartell *n*
→ Erlaubniskartell
anmoderierter Werbespot *m* **(Programm-Spot** *m*) *(radio/TV)* lead-in commercial, cast commercial, cast-delivered commercial, integrated commercial
 A broadcast commercial that is presented as part of the program entertainment, so that either no perceptible interruption of the action takes place or, if it does, the commercial is acted out by members of the program to which it belongs or introduced by members or one member of the cast of the program preceding.
→ programmunterbrechender Werbespot
Anmutung *f (psy)* etwa first stage of emotional perception, first impression
Anmutungsqualität *f (psy)* etwa valence
Annahmeschluß *m* **(Anzeigen)** forms close date, forms close, closing date, cancellation date
 The final date on which advertising mustbe delivered to a medium if it is to appear in a specific issue or program.

firm order date
 The date after which an order for advertising space or time cannot be cancelled.
→ Anzeigenschluß
Annahmestelle *f*
→ Anzeigenannahme
Annonce *f obsol*
→ Anzeige
Annoncenakquisiteur *m*
→ Anzeigenakquisiteur
Annoncenblatt *n*
→ Anzeigenblatt
Annoncen-Expedition (AE) *f* space broker, advertisement broker, advertising agency
→ Anzeigenmittler, Werbungsmittler
Annoncenwesen *n*
→ Anzeigenwerbung
anonyme Anzeige *f* blind advertisement, blind ad
→ Chiffre-Anzeige
anonyme Ware *f* **(anonymer Artikel** *m*) *(econ)* unbranded product, unbranded goods *pl*, no-name product, no-name goods *pl*
→ weiße Ware, Schüttware; *vgl.* Gattungsmarke, Herstellermarke, Handelsmarke
anonyme Werbung *f*
→ Kennzifferwerbung
anonymer Test *m* **(anonymer Produkttest** *m*)
→ Blindtest
Anordnungsverfahren *n*
→ Rangordnungsstatistik
anpappen *v/t*
→ ankleben, einhängen
Anpassung *f* 1. → Adaptation 2. *(stat)* goodness of fit
 The goodness of agreement between an observed set of values and a second set which are derived wholly or partly on a hypothetical basis. The term is used especially in relation to the fitting of theoretical distributions to observation and the fitting of regression lines. The excellence of the fit is often measured by some criterion depending on the squares of differences between observed and theoretical value, and if the criterion has a minimum value the corresponding fit is said to be "best".
Anpassungstest *m* **(Gütetest** *m*) *(stat)* goodness-of-fit test
 A chi-square test, (→) Chi-Quadrat-Test, used for testing whether a particular theoretical model or set of a priori probabilities fits a set of data. For

example, the frequency with which each wrong alternative is selected on a multiple-choice question, (→) Auswahlfrage, may be used to test the hypothesis that all choices are equally likely to be selected. Similarly, a grouped frequency distribution may be used to test the hypothesis that the data came from a normal distribution, by comparing obtained frequencies within expected frequencies derived from a table of the normal distribution, (→) Normalverteilung.
→ Anpassung 2.
anpreisen v/t **1.** (Waren, Leistungen) to praise, to recommend, to boost, to promote, to glamorize **2.** (marktschreierisch anpreisen) to ballyhoo, to bally, to puff
Anpreiser m barker, booster
Anpreisung f (**Anpreisen** n) **1.** praise, recommendation, boost **2.** (marktschreierische Anpreisung) ballyhoo, bally, puff, puffery, puffing, puffing advertising, puffing publicity, claptrap, borax
Anreibemaschine f (print) **1.** (in der Buchbinderei) roughening machine **2.** (Farbanreibemaschine) ink mill
anreiben v/t (print) **1.** to roughen, to paste on **2.** (Farben) to grind, to mill (inks)
Anreiben n (**Anreibung** f) (print) **1.** roughening **2.** inking, grinding inks, milling inks
Anreißen n (**anreißerische Werbung** f) touting, borax advertising
Anreißer m touter, puller-in
Anreiz m **1.** (psy) stimulus (pl stimuli) **2.** (Anreizprämie) incentive, incentive bonus
Anreiz-Beitrags-Theorie f (psy) etwa stimulus-contribution theory
Anreiz-Marketing n stimulational marketing (Philip Kotler)
 The task of converting no demand to positive demand.
 vgl. Entwicklungsmarketing, Konversionsmarketing, Erhaltungsmarketing, Kontra-Marketing, Reduktions-Marketing, Revitalisierungs-Marketing, Synchro-Marketing
Anreizprämie f incentive, incentive bonus, sales incentive
 In general, a reward offered to inspire a desired performance. More specifically, in sales mangement a monetary or other reward in excess of salary or commission provided to a salesperson in return for achieving a stated sales goal.
Ansage f (radio/TV) **1.** announcement, opening announcement **2.** (Werbeansage) spot announcement, advertising announcement
 An advertising message, usually one minute or less in duration when broadcast between programs, but generally between 30 seconds to two minutes when within a program. **3.** (Ansage oder Absage des Werbungtreibenden) billboard, credits pl, credit title, sponsor identification (S.I.), identification spot, identification commercial, ID commercial, ID
 The brief sponsor identification near the beginning or the end of a sponsored radio or television broadcast.
ansagen (radio/TV) **1.** v/t (Sendung/Person) to announce, to introduce, to present **2.** v/i to be an announcer
Ansager m (**Ansagerin** f) (radio/TV) announcer, presenter
 A person employed by a broadcasting station or network to introduce programs and to deliver information and make announcements.
Ansaugplatte f (**Vakuumplatte** f) (print/phot) vacuum holder, vacuum copyboard
 A perforated or channeled metal plate on which films and negative papers are held in position in the focal plane of darkroom cameras by withdrawing the air between the film and support, the material then being securely held by the pressure of the atmosphere.
anschaffen
→ beschaffen, einkaufen, kaufen
Anschaffung f
→ Beschaffung, Einkauf, Kauf
Anschauungsmaterial n visual aids pl, illustrative material
Anschlag m **1.** → Bogenanschlag, Plakatanschlag **2.** (typ) character or space
 An individual letter, figure, or other unit of type or space.
Anschlagauftrag m (**Anschlaganweisung** f) (outdoor advtsg) billposting order, posting order, space order, space buy
Anschlagbeginn m (outdoor advtsg) posting date
Anschlagbogen m (outdoor advtsg) poster sheet
Anschlagbrett n (**Anschlagfläche** f, **Anschlagtafel** f) (outdoor advtsg)

Anschlagdauer 26

billboard, board, call board, *brit* notice-board, show board
Anschlagdauer *f* posting period
   The number of days an advertiser's message appears for display on a poster panel of outdoor or transit advertising.
anschlagen *v/t* (ein Plakat) to post, to billpost, to poster, to put up a poster
Anschläger *m*
→ Plakatanschläger
Anschlagfläche *f* **(Anschlagtafel** *f* **)** *(outdoor advtsg)* billboard, poster panel, panel, advertising panel, display surface, bulletin board
   A standardized outdoor structure upon which an advertising poster is pasted.
(gemalte) painted bulletin board, painted display, painted wall
Anschlagflächenkapazität *f (outdoor advtsg)* plant capacity
   The number of message structures under the control of an individual poster plant.
Anschlagflächenpächter *m* **(Anschlagpächter** *m*, **Plakatpächter** *m*) poster advertising operator, billposter, billposting agency, poster contractor, poster plant, outdoor advertising contractor, plant operator
   The organization or the person owning the plant which builds and services poster panels and hangs poster sheets on them.
Anschlagkontakt *m*
→ Plakatkontakt
Anschlagkontrolle *f* **(Plakatkontrolle** *f*) site inspection, riding the showing, riding the boards (die Anschlagkontrolle durchführen, die Anschlagstellen inspizieren: to ride the showing, to ride the boards)
   The process of surveying outdoor advertising showings from the street to see them from the perspective of passers-by.
Anschlagkontrolleur *m (outdoor advtsg)* site inspector
Anschlagkosten *pl* **(Anschlagpreis** *m*) space charge, space rate
   The charge for space bought in posters, bulletin boards, signs, car cards, etc. in outdoor and transit advertising.
Anschlagort *m* **(Anschlagstellenstandort** *m*) *(outdoor advtsg)* space position, poster site, site location, board location
   The space position of an outdoor poster panel is the measure of efficiency with which it dominates the effective traffic circulation to which it is exposed.

Anschlagpächter *m*
→ Anschlagflächenpächter
Anschlagplakat *n*
→ Anschlag, Plakat
Anschlagrichtung *f* **(Sichtrichtung** *f* **eines Anschlags)** *(outdoor advtsg)* facing
   The surface of the standard outdoor advertising structure upon or against which the advertising message is exhibited.
Anschlagsäule *f* **(Litfaßsäule** *f*) *(outdoor advtsg)* poster pillar, advertising pylon, pylon
Anschlagstelle *f* **(Plakatstelle** *f*) *(outdoor advtsg)* poster site, site
Anschlagstellenkarte *f* **(Anschlagstellenverzeichnis** *n* *(outdoor advtsg)* spotted map, spotting map
   A map of a locale, such as a city, town, district, or market, marked to show the locations of outdoor advertisements in a campaign or the poster sites operated by a plant.
Anschlagtafel *f* **(Plakattafel** *f*) *(outdoor advtsg)* billboard, poster panel, show board, advertisement board
Anschlagunternehmen *n* **(Plakatanschlagunternehmen** *n*) *(outdoor advtsg)* billposter, billposting agency, billposting company, plant operator, poster plant
   The local organization that builds and maintains standard outdoor advertising facilities.
Anschlagwand *f* **(Anschlagzaun** *m*) *(outdoor advtsg)* billboard hoarding, billboard, *brit* hoarding, poster hoarding
Anschlagwerbetest *m* **(Plakattest** *m*) *(outdoor advtsg)* billboard test, poster test
Anschlagwerbeunternehmen *n* **(Plakatwerbeunternehmen** *n*) *(outdoor advtsg)* billposter, billposting agency, billposting company, plant operator, poster advertising agency, poster advertising company, poster contractor, poster plant, poster advertising plant
Anschlagwerbung *f* **(Plakatwerbung** *f* **)** poster advertising, billboard advertising
vgl. Außenwerbung, Verkehrsmittelwerbung
Anschlagzählung *f (typ)* (bei der Satzumfangskalkulation) character count

Anschlagzaun m *(outdoor advtsg)* billboard, *brit* hoarding
Anschlagzettel m *(outdoor advtsg)* placard, card, bill
Anschleichen n
→ anlehnende Werbung
anschließen *(typ)*
→ anhängen
Anschlußanzeige f **(Fortsetzungsanzeige** f) follow-on advertisement, follow-on ad, follow-up advertisement, follow-up ad
Anschlußauftrag m **(Anschlußbestellung** f) *(econ/advtsg)* follow-on order
Anschlußfehler m
→ Kamerafehler (Regiefehler)
Anschlußkauf m
→ Wiederholungskauf
Anschlußrabatt m *(econ)* continuing discount
Anschlußwerbung f follow-up advertising
Anschmiermaschine f *(bookbinding)* glueing machine, gluing machine
anschneiden (beschneiden) v/t (Satzspiegel) to bleed, to cut, to bleed off, to trim, to cut, (Bild) to crop
  To remove portions of an illustration by trimming the edges, either to eliminate undesirable content or to change illustration proportions.
Anschneiden n **(Beschneiden** n) bleeding, bleeding-off, cutting, trimming; (Bild) cropping
→ Beschnitt
Anschnitt m **(Beschnitt** m) bleed, cut, trim, bleeding
  Printing to the very edge of the page, leaving no margin.
(Anschnitt im Bund) bleed in the gutter
→ Bunddurchdruck
Anschnittdrucken n bleed printing
Anschreiben n
→ Brief, Intervieweranweisung
Anschrift f
→ Adresse
Anschwärzung f **(Anschwärzen** n, **anschwärzende Werbung** f) denigration, denigratory advertising, *brit* knocking copy
  Advertising that unfairly attacks or discredits competing products.
Ansetzblatt n *(print)* fly leaf
Ansetzfalz m *(print)* hinge, guard
Ansichtsexemplar n **(Ansichtsheft** n, **Ansichtsnummer** f) (Zeitung/ Zeitschrift) complimentary copy, courtesy copy, specimen copy
  A free copy of a magazine or paper given as a courtesy.
Ansichtsmuster n
→ Muster
Ansoffsche Strategien-Matrix f **(Matrix** f **der Marketingstrategien)** Ansoff's matrix of marketing strategies, fourfold table of marketing strategies
Ansprechbarkeit f responsiveness
Ansprechgruppe f
→ Zielgruppe
Anspruchsanpassung f adaptation of aspiration
Anspruchsniveau n (Kurt Lewin) *(psy)* level of aspiration
Anstalt f 1. (Anstalt des öffentlichen Rechts) public service institution, public utility
→ öffentlich-rechtlicher Rundfunk
2. → lithographische Anstalt
Anstaltshaushalt m *(res)* institutional household
vgl. privater Haushalt
ansteckende Verteilung f **(Ansteckungsverteilung** f) *(stat)* contagious distribution
  A compound probability distribution, usually derived from probability distributions dependent on parameters by regarding those parameters as themselves having probability distributions.
Ansteckmikrophon n **(Ansteckmikrofon** n) lapel microphone, lapel mike
Ansteckplakette f **(Ansteckknopf** m, **Ansteckmadel** f) badge, pin
Ansteckung f
→ soziale Ansteckung
Ansteckungsfehler m **(Ansteckungs-Bias** m) *(res)* contagious bias
Anstiegzeit f *(radio/TV)* build-up time, (Impuls) rise time, (Verstärker) attack time
anstößige Werbung f offensive advertising, indecent advertising
→ unzüchtige Werbung
anstrahlen v/t (Plakatwand, Gebäude) to illuminate, (mit Scheinwerfern) to floodlight, to spotlight
Anstrahlen n **(Anstrahlung** f) illumination
Ansturm m **(Kundenansturm** m) rush, great rush, run

Antecedensbedingung

Antecedensbedingung f (Antecedens n) antecedent condition, antecedent
Antenne f antenna, *brit* aerial
Antext m *(radio/TV)* lead-in, introduction, intro, cue
   An introductory monologue at the beginning of a radio or television show.
Antikdruckpapier n (**Romandruckpapier** n) antique wove paper, antique wove, antique finish, antique paper, antique
   A rough-textured printing paper, available in various grades and weights, both in book paper and cover stock. It is suitable for printing type and line engravings.
Antimarketing n counter marketing
Antiqua f (**Antiquaschrift** f) *(typ)* Roman type, roman type, Roman type face, roman type face, roman
   A race of type distinguished by variation in the weight of strokes and the inclusion of serifs.
Antireflexbelag m (**Antireflexschicht** f) *(phot)* coating, blooming
Anti-Verbrauchswerbung f (**Anti-Werbung** f, **Anti-Konsumwerbung** f) counter advertising, counter publicity
   The advertising done by consumerist groups allegedly operating in the public interest to persuade consumers against the use of products these groups deem harmful.
antizyklische Werbung f anticyclical advertising
   Advertising aimed at countering business cycles, by advertising heavily in recessions and moderately in periods of boom.
vgl. prozyklische Werbung (zyklische Werbung)
Antrieb m (**Antriebskräfte** f/pl, **Trieb** m) *(psy)* drive, drive stimulus
Antriebsniveau n (**Triebniveau** n) *(psy)* drive level
Antritt m *(print)* (an der Presse) footstep
Antwort f 1. (allg.) answer, reply
2. (Gutscheinwerbung, Befragungen) response, reply
Antwortausfall m
→ Ausfälle (Non-Response)
Antwortfehler m (bei Befragungen) response error, response bias, answer error, answer bias
Antwortgutschein m (**Rückantwortkupon** m) *(direct-response advtsg)* reply coupon

Antwortkarte f (**Rückantwortkarte** f) *(direct-response advtsg)* reply card, business reply card, return card, (in Kennzifferanzeigen) reader service card, *colloq* bingo card
   A self-addressed postcard attached to or printed into an advertisement to encourage prospective customers' inquiries or orders.
→ Werbeantwort
Antwortkategorie f *(survey res)* (bei Befragungen) response category
Antwortquote f (**Antwortrate** f, **Rücklaufquote** f) 1. *(survey res)* response rate
   The percentage of persons in a sample who answer interview questions.
2. *(direct-response advtsg)* rate of returns, return rate
   The percentage of inquiries or other types of reaction to direct-response advertisements in relation to the total amount of possible returns.
→ Rücklaufquote
Antwortschein m
→ Antwortgutschein
Antwortschema n (**Antwortmuster** n, **Reaktionsmuster** n) response pattern
Antwortschreiben n
→ Antwortkarte
Antwortstabilität f
→ Konsistenz
Antwortstil m (**Reaktionsstil** m) *(survey res)* response style
Antworttendenz f (**Reaktionseinstellung** f, **Response Set** m) *(survey res)* response set
   The tendency of some respondents to answer all of a series of questions in the same way, regardless of the differences in content of the individual questions. For example, a respondent who answered the first of a series of questions "Yes" or "Agree" might answer all remaining questions the same way, particularly if the items were ambiguous or not salient.
Antwortverweigerer m *(survey res)* non-respondent
Antwortverweigerung f (**Non-Response** m, **Ausfälle** m/pl) *(survey res)* non-response, (Verweigerungsrate) non-response rate
   The failure to obtain data from respondents who where designated part of the sample under investigation.
Antwortvorgabe f *(survey res)* (im Fragebogen) response alternative,

pre-quoted response, pre-choice question
→ Vorgabefrage
Anwender m user
Anwendungsberatung f consultancy, consulting
→ Gebrauchsanleitung
anwerben v/t (Personal) to recruit
Anwerber m recruiter
Anwerbung f (Anwerben n) (von Personal) recruitment, recruiting
Anzahl f number
Anzapfen n
→ Bettelei
Anzeige f 1. (Annonce, Inserat) advertisement, ad, *Am seltener* advertizement, *brit auch* advert 2. (Ankündigung) announcement 3. *(tech)* indication, reading
Anzeige f **im Kasten** box ad(vertisement), boxed ad(vertisement)
Anzeige f **im redaktionellen Teil**
→ redaktioneller Hinweis, textanschließende Anzeige
anzeigen v/t to advertise, to announce, *(tech)* to indicate
Anzeigenabteilung f (**Anzeigenakquisition** f) advertising sales department, advertisement sales department
Anzeigenabzug m advertisement proof, ad proof, (für Archivzwecke) file proof, (Agenturbeleg) agency copy, advertising agency copy
Anzeigenagentur f
→ Annoncen-Expedition
Anzeigenakquisiteur m space salesman, space representative, space rep, advertisement canvasser, advertising canvasser, ad canvasser, newspaper representative, publisher's representative
  A representative or a salesman for a publication who sells advertising space.
Anzeigenakquisition f space selling, advertising space selling, advertisement canvassing, advertising canvassing ad canvassing, advertisement sales *pl*
  The sale of advertising space for a publication.
Anzeigenanalyse f advertisement analysis, advertising analysis
Anzeigenannahme f (**-abteilung** f) (bei einer Zeitung/Zeitschrift) advertisement office

Anzeigenannahmeschluß m (**-termin** m)
→ Anzeigenschluß
Anzeigenanteil m (einer Publikation) advertising share, advertising content advertising ratio, ratio of advertising, advertising to editorial ratio
  That portion of a publication or those pages devoted to advertising, as distinguished from the editorial content. It is usually expressed in terms of page units, linage or percent of the publication's contents.
Anzeigenarchiv n advertisement file, advertising file
Anzeigenart f (**Anzeigenkategorie** f) advertisement category
Anzeigenaufkommen n advertising, amount of advertising, amount of advertisements, advertising weight, advertising support, advertising volume
→ Anzeigenvolumen
Anzeigenaufmachung f (**Anzeigengestaltung** f) advertisement format, advertisement makeup
Anzeigenauftrag m space order, space buy, insertion order, advertisement order
  An advertiser's positive order for media space, including the written authorization for a publication to print an advertisement of specified size in a particular issue at a stated rate.
Anzeigenausschnitt m
→ Anzeigenbeleg
Anzeigenbeachtung f advertisement noting, ad noting, eyes open in front of advertisement (E.O.F.A.), (Anzeigenbeachtung pro Seite) ad-page audience
vgl. Anzeigenkontakt
Anzeigenbedingungen f/pl
→ Allgemeine Geschäftsbedingungen
Anzeigenbeihefter m (**Anzeigenbeilage** f, **Anzeigenbeipack** m)
→ Beihefter, Beilage, Beipack
Anzeigenbeleg m (für den Werbungtreibenden) advertiser's copy, (für die Agentur) agency copy, advertising agency copy, (einzelne Seite) tearsheet, *auch* tear sheet
Anzeigenbelegung f (**Anzeigeneinkauf** m, **Media-Einkauf** m) space buying, advertising media buying
  Buying space for advertising in print media.

Anzeigenberechnung *f*
→ Satzumfangsberechnung
Anzeigenbewertung *f* **(Anzeigenevaluierung** *f*) advertisement
→ Werbemittelbewertung
evaluation, ad evaluation
Anzeigenblatt *n* **(Offertenblatt** *n*)
giveaway paper, non-paid publication, free paper, free publication, freebee, shopper, *brit auch* advertiser
  A paper or other publication distributed free of charge to its readers or subscribers.
Anzeigenbüro *n*
→ Anzeigenabteilung
Anzeigenchiffre *f*
→ Chiffre
Anzeigenchiffrierung *f* keying of an advertisement
→ Verschlüsselung
Anzeigen-Copy-Test *m*
→ Copy-Test
Anzeigendirektor *m*
→ Anzeigenleiter
Anzeigendisposition *f* space schedule, space scheduling
  The scheduling of the media to be used, the dates on which advertising is to appear, including the size of advertisements and cost of space.
Anzeigeneinkauf *m*
→ Anzeigenverkauf
Anzeigeneinnahmen *f/pl* advertising revenue, advertising receipts *pl*
Anzeigenerfolgskontrolle *f*
advertisement effectiveness control, ad effectiveness control
Anzeigenerinnerung *f* advertisement recall, ad recall
→ Erinnerung, Werbemittelerinnerung
Anzeigenerinnerungstest *m* (*res*)
advertisement recall test, ad recall test
→ Erinnerung, Werbemittelerinnerung
Anzeigenerlös *m* (*meist pl*
Anzeigenerlöse) advertisement revenue, advertisement payout, advertisement payback
  The profit return on an investment of advertisement expenditure.
Anzeigenetat *m* advertising budget, ad budget
Anzeigenexpedition *f*
→ Annoncenexpedition
Anzeigenfachmann *m* adman, *auch* ad man, advertising man

Anzeigenfestpreis *m*
→ Festpreis
Anzeigenfließsatz *m*
→ Fließsatz
Anzeigenformat *n* size of an advertisement, form of an advertisement, space size, space form
Anzeigenfriedhof *m* clutter, clutter of advertisements
Anzeigengemeinschaft *f*
→ Gemeinschaftsanzeige
Anzeigengeschäft *n* advertising business, advertising sales *pl*, advertising
Anzeigengestaltung *f* **1.** (Art und Weise, in der eine Anzeige gestaltet ist) design of an advertisement, makeup of an advertisement, advertisement makeup, advertisement format **2.** (Vorgang der Gestaltung) design of advertisements, designing of ads, creating advertisemt copy and artwork
Anzeigengröße *f* space size, size of an advertisement, advertisement size, (nach Zeilen) advertisement lineage, lineage of an ad
Anzeigengrundpreis *m* (**Listenpreis** *m*) base rate (of an advertisement) basic rate, card rate, flat rate, full rate-card cost, one-time rate, open rate
  A fixed charge for advertising space in a publication regardless of the amount of space used or the frequency of insertions.
Anzeigenhauptteil *m* (**-haupttext** *m*) body copy, body text, body
  The main copy section of the reading matter in an advertisement, as distinguished from the headline, the name plate and base line.
Anzeigenhöhe *f* depth of space, depth of column, depth of an advertisement, advertisement depth, advertisement height
Anzeigeninhalt *m* content of an advertisement
Anzeigenkampagne *f* advertisement campaign, advertising campaign
Anzeigenkategorie *f* type of advertisement, advertisement category
Anzeigenkauf *m* space buying
Anzeigenkäufer *m* space buyer
  An employee of an advertiser or advertising agency who buys advertising space in periodical publications.

Anzeigenklischee n *(print)*
advertising block, advertising plate
Anzeigenkodierung f
→ Anzeigenchiffrierung
Anzeigenkollektiv n **(Kollektivanzeige** f **)** composite page
Anzeigenkompaß m
→ Starch-Verfahren
Anzeigenkontakt m advertisement exposure, ad exposure, advertising exposure
Audience contact with a specific advertisement. Depth of exposure is an indication of audience consciousness of an advertising message.
Anzeigenkontaktchance f
→ Kontaktchance
Anzeigenkoppelung f
→ Koppelgeschäft
Anzeigenkunde m space buyer, advertising space buyer, advertising customer, advertiser
An advertiser or advertising agency who buys periodical space.
Anzeigenleiter m **(Anzeigendirektor** m**)** advertising manager, head of advertising sales department, advertisement manager
Anzeigenleserschaft f **(Anzeigenleser** m/pl**)** *(media res)* ad audience
Anzeigenmalstaffel f
→ Malstaffel
Anzeigen-Marketing n space marketing, advertisement marketing
Anzeigenmarkt m advertising market
Anzeigenmater f *(print)* ad mat, advertisement matrix
Anzeigenmittler m space broker, space buyer, advertisement space broker
→ Werbemittler
Anzeigennachlaß m **(Anzeigenpreisnachlaß** m**)** advertising discount, discount on advertising
Anzeigen-Nach-Test m
→ Anzeigen-Posttest
Anzeigenpächter m
→ Anzeigenmittler
Anzeigenplacierung f **(Anzeigenplazierung** f**)** placement of an ad(vertisement), positioning of an ad(vertisement), advertising position
The placement of an advertisement in a publication in terms of page number, page size or place on a page.
Anzeigenplanung f advertising planning
→ Mediaplanung

Anzeigenposition f
→ Anzeigenplazierung
Anzeigen-Posttest m advertising post test
Anzeigenpreis m **(Anzeigentarif** m**)** ad rate, adrate, advertisement rate, space rate, space charge, advertising rate
The charge made for the placement of an advertisement in a publication.
Anzeigenpreis m **minus Provision (abzüglich Provision)** gross less
The actual rate that has to be paid for an advertisement after the agency commission, the cash discount and any other discounts were deducted.
Anzeigenpreisliste f **(Preisliste** f**)** ad(vertisement) rate card, rate card, space rates pl
A card issued by a publication giving the space rates, mechanical requirements, closing dates, etc.
Anzeigen-Pretest m advertising pretest
Anzeigenprovision f **(AE-Provision** f**)** agency commission, commission, advertising agency commission
Anzeigenpyramide f advertising pyramid, pyramid makeup
A newspaper page makeup in which advertisements are positioned from top to bottom, in diminishing sizes, so that they form steps from the top to the bottom to the outside.
Anzeigenrabatt m **(Anzeigenpreisnachlaß** m**)** advertising discount
Anzeigenraum m **(Anzeigenfläche** f**)** advertising space
→ Anzeigengröße
Anzeigenreichweite f *(media res)* advertising coverage, advertising reach, advertising audience
→ Reichweite
Anzeigenrubrik f
→ Rubrikanzeige
Anzeigensatz m *(typ)* 1. (Produkt) type set for an ad(vertisement)
2. (Vorgang) advertisement composition, ad composition, advertising typography
Anzeigensatzspiegel m *(typ)* advertisement type area, advertising type area, adpage plan
Anzeigenschluß m **(Anzeigenschlußtermin** m**)** closing date, closing day, closing time, ad closing, copy date, deadline

Anzeigenseite

The hour or day after which advertising will not be accepted for appearance in a specific edition of a publication. (Annahmeschluß für Druckunterlagen) forms close date, forms close
The day when all copy and plates must arrive at the publication if an advertisement is to appear in a particular issue.
Anzeigenseite f advertising page, adpage, *auch* ad page, advertisement page
Anzeigenseitenbeachtung f
→ Anzeigenseitenkontakt, Seitenkontakt
Anzeigenseitenkontakt m *(media res)* advertising page exposure(apx), adpage exposure (Alfred Politz Research)
A term used to describe the estimate of how frequently readers look at an average advertising page in a magazine issue. Specifically, ad-page exposure occurs whenever a reader opens a page containing an ad.
Anzeigenseitenspiegel m *(print)* advertising page plan, adpage plan
Anzeigenseiten-Tausenderpreis m cost per page per thousand circulation
The cost per thousand copies, (→) Tausenderpreis, of an issue for the placement of a full-page black-and-white advertisement in a periodical.
Anzeigenserie f series of ads, series of advertisements
Anzeigensetzer m *(typ)* advertising typographer, advertisement typographer, advertographer
Anzeigensetzerei f *(typ)* advertising typography, (in einer Setzerei) ad side, ad alley
Anzeigensonderform f
→ Flexformanzeige
Anzeigenspalte f ad column, advertising column
Anzeigenspiegel m advertisement type area, advertisement page plan
Anzeigen-Split m alternate-bundles run, A-B split (a/b split), split-run advertising, split-run circulation, split run
The insertion of an advertisement in only a part of the total copies of a publication distributed, or the insertion of two or more different forms of an advertiser's message in different copies or issues, to test the effectiveness of one advertisement against another or to appeal to regional or other specified markets.
Anzeigen-Splitting n split-run advertising
→ Anzeigen-Split
Anzeigenstatistik f advertising statistics *pl (construed as sg)*
Anzeigensteuer f
→ Werbesteuer
Anzeigenstrecke f advertising clutter, clutter
Anzeigentarif m
→ Anzeigenpreis, Tarifpreis
Anzeigenteil m advertising section, advertisement section, advertising content, adpages *pl*, advertising pages *pl*, advertising columns *pl*, ad columns *pl*
That portion of a publication devoted to advertising.
Anzeigen-Terminplan m advertising schedule, media schedule
Anzeigentest m advertisement test, advertising test, (Starch-Test) reading/noting study
Anzeigentext m advertisement copy, advertising copy, copy, advertising lineage, (der reine Textteil) body copy
Anzeigentexter m copywriter, advertising copywriter
Anzeigentextteil m advertising matter, advertising copy
Anzeigen-Text-Verhältnis n advertising-to-editorial ratio, editorial-to-advertising ratio
Anzeigenträger m
→ Werbeträger
Anzeigentyp m
→ Anzeigenkategorie
Anzeigenumbruch m advertisement makeup, advertisement format
Anzeigenumfang m
→ Anzeigengröße
Anzeigenumsatz m advertising turnover, advertising sales *pl*
Anzeigenverbund m regional facilities *pl*
Anzeigenverkauf m advertisement sales *pl*, advertising sales *pl*, space sales *pl*
Anzeigenverkaufsleiter m advertisement manager
Anzeigenvermittler m
→ Anzeigenmittler
Anzeigenvertrag m **(Werbevertrag** m**)** advertising contract, space contract
→ Mediavertrag

Anzeigenvertreter *m* space representative, advertisement representative, space rep, advertisement canvasser, advertising canvasser, ad canvasser, newspaper representative, publisher's representative
  An independent organization or individual that sells advertising space for a publication or group of them.
Anzeigenvolumen *n* advertising volume, total advertising, advertising sales *pl*, advertising weight, advertising support, support
  The total number of advertising messages published in print media used in or planned for a campaign.
Anzeigenvorlage *f* copy, advertisement copy, advertising copy
Anzeigenvorspann *m*
→ Vorspann
Anzeigen-Vor-Test *m*
→ Anzeigen-Pretest
Anzeigenwerbeleiter *m*
→ Anzeigenleiter
Anzeigenwerbung *f* press advertising, print advertising, newspaper and magazine advertising, publication advertising
Anzeigenwiedererkennung *f* **(Werbemittel-Wiedererkennung** *f*) *(media res)* advertisement recognition, ad recognition
  The remembrance of respondents' prior exposure to an advertisement provoked by repeated exposure during an investigation.
Anzeigenwiedererkennungstest *m* **(Werbemittel-Wiedererkennungstest** *m*) *(media res)* advertisement recognition test, ad recognition test
  An aided-recall technique for determining whether respondents in a survey had previously been exposed to an advertisement. The respondents are shown the advertisement and asked whether they had seen it before.
→ Wiedererkennungstest
Anzeigenwirkung *f* **(Werbewirkung** *f* **einer Anzeige)** advertisement effect, effect of an advertisement, advertising effect
Anzeiger *m*
→ Amtsblatt, Anzeigenblatt
Anziehungskraft *f* attraction, attractive power, drawing power, pull, pulling power, appeal, (Anziehungskraft der Werbung) advertising appeal

AOL *f abbr* Arbeitsgemeinschaft organisationsgebundene Landpresse
Apartverkauf *m*
→ Einzelverkauf
aperiodisch *adj* aperiodic, nonperiodical
Apertur *f (phot)* aperture
→ Blende
Aperturkorrektur *f* **(Kantenkorrektur** *f*) *(phot)* aperture correction
Aplanat *m* **(aplanatisches Objektiv** *n*) *(phot)* aplanatic lense, aplanat
  A lens corrected for spherical aberration.
A-posteriori-Analyse *f (res)* a posteriori analysis
A-posteriori-Wahrscheinlichkeit *f (res)* a posteriori probability
Apotheke *f Am* pharmacy, *brit* chemist's shop
apothekenpflichtes Heilmittel *n etwa* patent medicine, proprietary pharmaceutical, OTC medicine, over-the-counter medicine
  A drug or a product containing a drug sold over the counter at retail by pharmacists without a doctor's prescription.
Apothekenverwerbung *f* advertising of pharmacies
apparative Verfahren *f/pl (res)* apparative techniques *pl*
Appeal *m* appeal
Appell *m* appeal
Apperzeption *f* **(Apperzeptionswirkung** *f*) apperception
Appetenz *f* **(Appetenzverhalten** *n*) *(psy)* approach, approach behavior, *brit* behaviour
Appetenzkonflikt *m* **(Konflikt** *m* **zwischen Annährungstendenzen)** approach-approach conflict
Appetite Appeal *m (advtsg)* appetite appeal
A-priori-Analyse *f (res)* a priori analysis
A-priori-Wahrscheinlichkeit *f (res)* a priori probability
Aquarell *n* **(Aquarellzeichnung** *f*) wash drawing
  A drawing similar to water color, executed with a brush in varying shades of gray and black; reproduced by halftone engraving.
Aquarelldruck *m* watercolor print, *brit* water-colour print

aquarellierte Strichzeichnung *f* line and wash drawing
An artist's rendering employing a combination of line and wash techniques.
Aquarellkarton *m*
→ Malkarton
Äquivokation *f* equivocation
The rate of loss of selective information at the receiver's end of a channel, due to the noise (measured in bits per second or per signs as stated).
Arbeitsgemeinschaft *f* **Anzeigenblätter der Zeitungen (AdZ)** Association of Giveaway Papers Published by Newspapers
Arbeitsgemeinschaft *f* **Leseranalyse (AGLA) e.V.** Working Group Readership Analysis
Arbeitsgemeinschaft *f* **Media-Analyse e.V. (AG.MA)** Working Group Media Analysis
Arbeitsgemeinschaft *f* **der öffentlich-rechtlichen Rundfunkanstalten der Bundesrepublik Deutschland (ARD)** Association of Public-Service Broadcast Organizations of the Federal Republic of Germany
Arbeitsgemeinschaft *f* **der Verbraucher (AGV)** Association of Consumer Associations
Arbeitsgemeinschaft *f* **Incentive-Reiseveranstalter e.V. (AIR)** Association of Incentive Travel Agencies
Arbeitsgemeinschaft *f* **organisationsgebundene Landpresse (AOL)** Working Group of Organizational Farm Publications
Arbeitsgemeinschaft *f* **Rundfunkwerbung (ARW)** Association of Regional Broadcast Advertising Media
Arbeitshypothese (H_a, H_A, H_1) *f* working hypothesis
vgl. Nullhypothese
Arbeitskopie *f* **(Rushprint** *m*) *(film/phot)* work print, rush print, rush, daily rush, daily, *meist pl* dailies, cutting-copy print
A processed, but unedited motion picture or television commercial print as it comes directly from the laboratory.
Arbeitskreis *m* **der Deutschen Werbefachschulen (ASW)** Working Group of the German Advertising Colleges
Arbeitskreis *m* **Deutscher Markforschungsinstitute (ADM)** Association of German (Full-Service) Market Research Institutes
Arbeitskreis *m* **Fachagenturen und Berater für Industrie-Werbung (AIW)** Association of Specialized Industrial Advertising and Consultancy Agencies
Arbeitskreis *m* **Industrie-Zielgruppen (AIZ)** Working Group Industrial Target Groups
Arbeitskreis *m* **Media-Information Fachzeitschriften (AMF)** Working Group Media Information on Professional and Special Magazines
Arbeitskreis *m* **Werbefernsehen der deutschen Wirtschaft (AKW)** Working Group Television Advertising of German Industry
Arbeitskreis *m* **Werbemittel e.V. (AKW)** Working Group Specialty Advertising
Arbeitsmarktforschung *f* labor market research, *brit* labour market research
Arbeitsprojektor *m* **(Overhead-Projektor** *m*) overhead projector, overhead
Arbeitstitel *m* working title, preliminary title, *(typ)* slug
The catchline by which any copy is designated.
Arbeitstransparent *n* **(Overhead-Transparent** *n*) overhead transparency
Archiv *n* archives *pl*, records *pl*, library
→ Bildarchiv, Filmarchiv, Zeitungsarchiv, Redaktionsarchiv
Archivaufnahme *f* **(Archivbild** *n*) *(film/TV)* stock shot, library film, library shot, *(phot)* library picture, library still
A film or single shot of people, events, or objects that has been filed for later use in motion pictures, commercials or television shows.
Archivexemplar *n* record copy, file copy, file proof
Proof of an advertisement or a publication for record purposes rather than for corrections.
Archivfilm *m* stock footage, library film, file copy
ARD *f abbr* Arbeitsgemeinschaft der öffentlich-rechtlichen Rundfunkanstalten der Bundesrepublik Deutschland

Area-Methode f **(Area-Sampling** n)
→ Flächenauswahl(verfahren)
Argument n argument, point
Argumentation f **(Argumentations-weise** f) argumentation
argumentative Werbung f argumentative copy, argumentative advertising, reason-why copy, reason-why advertising, long-circuit appeal
 An advertising message offering objectively stated arguments in support of its object's benefits.
arithmetische Abweichung f
→ mittlere Abweichung
arithmetische Verteilung f *(stat)* arithmetic distribution
arithmetisches Mittel n *(stat)* arithmetic mean, mean
 The arithmetic mean of a set of values, $x_1, x_2, ... x_n$ is their sum divided by their number, namely for a continuous distribution with the distribution function F(x) the arithmetic mean is the integral

$$\frac{1}{n} \sum_{j=1}^{n} x_j.$$

Art-Buyer m art buyer
 An employee in an advertising agency or commercial studio who keeps a file of artists and photographers and is responsible for the purchase of art material and photography for advertising reproduction. No original German term exists.
Art-Buying n art buying
Art-Direktor m **(Art-Director** m) art director (A.D., AD), art editor
 An employee in an advertising agency who designs the graphic form of the finished advertisement, supervises the final artwork and selects the artists to execute the finished art. No original German term exists.
Art Directors Club m **für Deutschland e.V. (ADC)** Art Directors' Club of Germany
Artikel m **(Produkt** n, **Ware** f) *(econ)* article, product, commodity
Artikel m/pl **des täglichen Bedarfs** *(econ)* convenience goods pl
 The type of item which the consumer usually desires to purchase with a minimum of effort at the most convenient and accessible place.
Artikelausgleich m
→ kalkulatorischer Ausgleich

Artikelnumerierung f **(Artikelcodierung** f)
→ Strichkodierung
Artikelspanne f **(Stückspanne** f) *(econ)* unit margin, profit margin per unit
Art-Work n
→ Gebrauchsgraphik
ARW f *abbr* Arbeitsgemeinschaft Rundfunkwerbung
Arzneimittel n drug, medicine, (verschreibungspflichtig) ethical drug, ethical medicine, (nicht verschreibungspflichtig) over-the-counter drug, OTC drug, over-the-counter medicine, OTC medicine
Arzneimittelwerbung f pharmaceutical advertising, ethical advertising
Ärzte m/pl **in der Werbung (Werbung** f **mit Ärzten)** white coat advertising
AS-Signal n
→ Austastsignal, Synchronsignal
ASA-Empfindlichkeitssystem n *(phot)* ASA-rating system, ASA rating
Asphaltkopierverfahren n **(Asphaltverfahren** n) *(phot)* asphalt process, bitumen process
Asphaltlack m *(print)* asphalt varnish
Asphaltpresse f
→ Boulevardpresse
ASSESSOR-Modellkomplex m ASSESSOR model
Assimilation f assimilation
Assimilations-Kontrast-Theorie f *(psy)* assimilation-contrast theory
Assimilationsprozeß m assimilation, assimilation process, process of assimilation
Assoziation f *(psy/stat)* association
 1. In *psychology*, the spontaneous linking of two ideas or words in the mind of an individual. 2. In *statistics*, the degree of dependence, or independence between two or more variates whether they be measured quantitatively or qualitatively. More narrowly, the relationship between variates which are simply dichotomised, namely in a 2 × 2 table, (→) Vierfeldertafel, as distinct from contingency, (→) Kontingenz, which measures relationships in an m × n table of attributes, and correlation, (→) Korrelation, which measures relationships in a classification according to specified ranges of variate-values.
Assoziationsforschung f *(psy)* association research

Assoziationskoeffizient m *(stat)* coefficient of association
A measure of association for categorical data classified on two dichotomous dimensions and arranged in a fourfold table, (→) Vierfeldertafel, The coefficient is:

$$Q = \frac{ad - bc}{ad + bc}$$

where a, b, c, and d are the cell frequencies. It ranges from − 1 to + 1, with 0 being no association and + 1 being perfect positive and - 1 perfect negative association.
→ Yule-Koeffizient
Assoziationsmaß n *(stat)* measure of association
Assoziationsmatrix f *(stat)* matrix of association
→ Vierfeldertafel
Assoziationspsychologie f psychology of association, associationist psychology
Assoziationsreihentest m *(psy)* serial association test
Assoziationstabelle f
→ Vierfeldertafel
Assoziationstest m *(psy)* association test
A procedure for determining a subject's associations to various stimuli, usually verbal. The task may be simply to name a visually presented stimulus, which may be a word, letter, number, color, etc. In free association for words, the stimulus may be any word, and the response can be whatever other word first comes to mind. In controlled association, the response word must be one that stands in some specified relation to the stimulus word, such as a superordinate, coordinate, or subordinate, a rhyme, a synonym, or antonym, etc. Associative reaction time (i.e., the interval between the presentation of the stimulus and the subject's response) is often obtained.
Assoziationswerbung f associative advertising
Ästhetik f aesthetics *pl (construed as sg)*, esthetics *pl (construed as sg)*
ästhetischer Test m
→ Geschmackstest
astigmatisch (stabsichtig, zerrsichtig) *adj (phot)* astigmatic(al)
Astigmatismus m **(Stabsichtigkeit** f, **Zerrsichtigkeit** f) *(phot)* astigmatism
The inability of a photographic lens to sharply focus vertical and horizontal lines, especially near the margin of the field or image.
Asymmetrie f dissymmetry, asymmetry
asymmetrische Anordnung f **(asymmetrisches Anzeigenlayout** n**)** informal balance, occult balance, asymmetrical balance
A method of layout in which the advertisement is pleasing to the eye, yet the elements comprising the advertisement are not evenly spaced or weighted.
asynchron *adj/attr* out of sync, asynchronous, non-synchronous
Atelier n studio
Atelierarbeiter m
→ Bühnenarbeiter
Atelieraufnahme f studio shot, studio photo, studio photograph
Atelierdrehtag m *(film)* day in the studio, day on the stage
Atelierfundus m
→ Requisiteur, Requisiten
Ateliergelände n **(Aufnahmegelände** n**)** lot, studio area
Atelierkamera f **(Studiokamera** f **)** stand camera, studio camera
Atelierleiter m **(Studioleiter** m, **Leiter** m **der graphischen Abteilung)** studio manager
Atelierleitung f **(Studioleitung** f **)** studio management
Ateliersekretärin f **(Studiosekretärin** f **)** *(film/TV)* script girl, continuity girl
Atemfrequenzmessung f *(res)* measurement of breathing frequency, meaurement of respiratory rate, respiratory rate measurement
Atlasformat n *(print)* atlas format, large square folio
Atlaspapier n satin paper, glazed paper
Atmen n **des Bildes** *(phot)* breathing (of a picture)
Atmosphäre f **(Atmo** f **)** *(film/TV)* wild track effects *pl*, atmosphere
The recording of non-synchronized sound, i.e. a sound track recorded separately from visual images it will accompany.
At Random
→ Zufallsauswahl
Attitüde f
→ Einstellung
Attitüdenkonzeption f des Image
→ Einstellung, Image

Attitüdenmessung f
→ Einstellungsmessung
Attitüdenwandel m
→ Einstellungsänderungen
Attraktion f attraction
attraktiv adj attractive
Attraktivität f attractiveness, pulling power, drawing power
Attrappe f **(Schaupackung** f**)** dummy, dummy package, display package, (im Originalformat) mockup, auch mock-up
    An empty package or package reproduction used for display or in a package test. In direct advertising, a model indicating the size, shape, and layout of the finished printed product.
Attrappenforschung f dummy research
    Package research using dummies.
Attribution f **(Attribuierung** f**)** attribution
Attributionsforschung f **(Attribuierungsforschung** f**)** attribution research
Attributionstheorie f **(Attribuierungstheorie** f**)** theory of attribution, attribution theory
Ätzdruck m
→ Heliogravure, Photogravüre
ätzen v/t (print) to etch, to bite, to engrave
Ätzer m (print) etcher, aqua fortis
Ätzflüssigkeit f (print) etchant, etching ink, aqua fortis, nitric acid, mordant
    A greasy ink of resinous constituency, used as an acid resist in conjunction with etching powders applied to the inked print or plate. In etching, an acid or other corrosive liquid capable of eating into and dissolving a metal surface.
Ätzgrund m (print) etching varnish, etching ground, resist
Ätzlösung f **(Ätzbad** n**)** (print) etching bath, (Behälter) etching tub
    The solution or mordant used for etching. A stonewear or acid proofed tray or trough, mechanically oscillated to cause an acid solution to flow back and forth over a metal plate during etching.
Ätzlauge f (print) etching lye
Ätzmaschine f (print) etching machine
    A mechanically operated apparatus for accelerating the process of etching by agitation of the mordant and discharge of the solution against the surface of a metal plate.
Ätznadel f (print) etching needle, etching pointer, etching point
    A sharp-pointed steel instrument for drawing lines into an acid-resisting surface.
Ätzrückstand m (auf dem Klischee) (print) hickey
    Any speck on the printing area of an engraving that remains after the etch.
Ätzstaub m **(Drachenblut** n**)** (print) etching powder, dragon's blood
    A finely ground mixture of resins used for dusting relief plates during etching to protect the top and sides of lines and dots.
Ätzstaubverfahren n **(Ätzstaubbehandlung** f, **Drachenblutverfahren** n**)** (print) dragon's blood process
    A method of relief etching in which the sides of lines and dots are protected against undercutting by dusting the plate on all four sides with dragon's blood or etching powder, then heating the dusted plate to melt the powder and cause it to form an acid-resisting coating on the top and sides of the relief formations.
Ätztiefe f (print) etching depth, etched depth, depth, printing depth
Ätztinte f **(Ätzfarbe** f**)** (print) etching ink
Ätzung f **(Ätzen** n**)** (print) etching, engraving
Ätzverfahren n (print) etching process, engraving process
Ätzwasser n
→ Ätzflüssigkeit
Ätzzeichnung f (print) etched copperplate
Audilog n (TV res) Audilog, audilog
    A log of programs watched by television viewers in a Nielsen television panel survey, as prepared by an (→) Audimeter. Not used in Germany.
Audimeter n (TV res) Audimeter, audimeter
    A patented A.C. Nielsen Company device which monitors TV set usage and station selection in a sample of households. Cooperators return audimeter records to Nielsen by mail where their findings are matched against station lineups to produce "Nielsen Ratings" for network programs. Since audimeter records are complete and continuous, they permit the tabulation of household audience accumulation and duplication patterns as well as minute-by-minute viewing levels. The system is not used in Germany.

Audio-Mixer m
→ Tonmischpult
Audiovision f (**Kassettenfernsehen** n)
audiovision
Audiovisionsmedium n
→ audiovisuelles Kommunikationsmittel
audiovisuell adj audiovisual
audiovisuelle Kommunikation f (**AV-Kommunikation** f) audiovisual communication
audiovisuelles Kommunikationsmittel n (**AV-Medium** n) audiovisual medium, audiovisual communication medium
audiovisuelle Werbung f (**AV-Werbung** f) audiovisual advertising
Audit m
→ Revision
Aufbauskizze f
→ Layout
Aufbauten m/pl (film/TV/studio) set, built set
aufbereiten v/t to process
Aufbereitung f
→ Datenaufbereitung
Aufbereitungsfehler m (stat) processing error, data processing error
Aufbewahrung f (von **Druckunterlagen**) storage
aufbinden
→ binden
aufblasen (vergrößern)
→ vergrößern
Aufblasen n
→ Vergrößern
Aufblende f
→ Aufblenden (Aufblendung)
aufblenden I. v/t 1. to fade up, to fade in 2. (Licht) to turn up, to fade up 3. (Ton) to fade up, to fade in II. v/i 4. to fade, to fade up, to fade in 5. (Licht/Ton) to fade up, to fade in 6. (Objektiv) to iris in, to focus in, to circle in 7. (abrupt aufblenden) to pop in, to pop on
Aufblenden n (**Aufblendung** f) 1. (Licht, Ton) fading-up, fade-up, fading-in, fade-in 2. (Objektiv) iris-in, focus-in, circle-in 3. (abrupt) pop-in, pop-on
aufdringliche Werbung f borax advertising, borax, tum-tum
Aufdruck m
→ Eindruck, Firmeneindruck

aufdrucken
→ eindrucken
aufeinanderfolgende Werbesendungen f/pl back-to-back commercials pl, wall-to-wall commercials pl, adjacent commercials pl, adjacencies pl
  Two commercials shown directly one after the other.
Aufeinanderüberblendung f (film/TV) match dissolve
  A type of dissolve, (→) Überblendung, in which the principal figures or objects in the close of the preceding scene appear in the same positions in the new one.
auffällige Muße f
→ demonstrative Muße
auffälliger Konsum m
→ demonstrativer Konsum
Aufforderungscharakter m (**Aufforderungsgrad** m) (psy) valence
Aufforderungsgradient m (psy) gradient of valence
aufgezeichnete Kommunikation f recorded communication
aufgezeichnete Sendung f (**Sendeaufzeichnung** f) (radio/TV) recorded broadcast, transcribed programm, brit programme, colloq canned copy, canned broadcast
Aufgliederung f (stat) breakdown, classification
Aufhängedekoration f (POP advtsg) mobile, dangler, banner, overwire hanger
→ Deckenaufhänger
Aufhängekreuz n (POP advtsg) peel
Aufhänger m 1. (im Text) peg, news peg, lead-in, catchline, attention getter 2. → Aufhängedekoration, Deckenaufhänger 3. → Aufhängung
Aufhängung f suspension
Aufhellblende f 1. (phot) silver foil reflector, silvered reflector 2. → Aufheller
Aufhellen n (**Nachbelichtung** f) (phot) filling-in, balancing
Aufheller m (**Aufhell-Licht** n) (phot/film/TV) fill-in light, fill light, balancing light, klieg light, kleig light
  Lights that are used in addition to the main lights in portraiture or other photography by artificial light to fill in the dark shadow portions of subjects.
Aufhellschirm m (phot) reflector screen, reflector

Aufhellung f (Nachbeleuchtung f)
(film/TV) filler lighting, balancing,
klieg lighting, kleig lighting
aufkaufen
→ einkaufen, kaufen
Aufkaufhandel m (**Aufkaufgroßhandel** m)
aufkeilen v/t *(print)* to unlock
aufklappbar adj fold-out
aufklappen v/t to fold out, to flap up,
to unfold
aufklärende Werbung f (**Aufklärungswerbung** f)
→ informative Werbung
Aufklärungsvergleich m
→ vergleichende Werbung
aufklebbar adj adhesive
Aufklebeadresse f adhesive label,
adhesive address label, (gummiert)
gummed address label, gummed label,
(Cheshire) Cheshire address label
Aufklebeetikett n adhesive label, selfadhesive label, sticker, (gummiert)
gummed label
Aufklebekarton m adhesive
cardboard, stick-on cardboard
Aufkleber m adhesive label, selfadhesive label, sticker, (Aufklebestreifen) paster, snipe, overlay, tip-on
Aufklebezettel m
→ Aufklebeetikett, Aufkleber
aufklotzen v/t *(print)* to block, to
mount
aufkreisen v/t *(phot/film/TV)*
(Objektiv) to iris out
   An optical effect in which the picture
   grows progressively smaller in a circle
   until it shrinks to a dot and disappears.
Aufladung f
→ statische Aufladung
Auflage f (Zeitung/Zeitschrift)
circulation
   The (average) number of copies of a
   single edition or issue of a newspaper,
   magazine or other periodical publication
   sold or distributed free over a period of
   time.
→ Druckauflage, Abonnementsauflage, Einzelverkaufsauflage,
verkaufte Auflage (Verkaufsauflage),
tatsächlich verbreitete Auflage,
unentgeltlich vertriebene Auflage,
Remittenden, Deckungsauflage,
Kalkulationsauflage, garantierte
Auflage, kontrollierte Auflage, Bindeauflage, beglaubigte Auflage,
berechnete Auflage, gedruckte
Auflage

Auflagemaß n *(phot)* back focal
distance
Auflagenanalyse n (Zeitung/
Zeitschrift) circulation analysis,
circulation breakdown
Auflagenbeglaubigung f (**Auflagenbetätigung** f) (Zeitung/Zeitschrift)
certification of circulation, circulation
certification
→ beglaubigte Auflage
Auflagebestand m
→ Lagerbestand
Auflagendruck m
→ Druckauflage
Auflagengarantie f (Zeitung/
Zeitschrift) circulation rate base, rate
base
→ garantierte Auflage
Auflagenhöhe f (**Auflagenzahl** f)
(Zeitung/Zeitschrift) circulation,
circulation figure
Auflagenkontrolle f (**Auflagenprüfung**
f) (Zeitung/Zeitschrift) circulation
audit, auditing (of circulation)
   A formal unbiased check of circulation
   figures particularly of advertising media
   by an independent non-profit
   organization such as the German Audit
   Bureau of Circulations (→) Informationsgemeinschaft zur Feststellung der
   Verbreitung von Werbeträgern e.V. (IVW).
Auflagenmeldung f (des Verlages)
(Zeitung/Zeitschrift) publisher's
statement of circulation, publisher's
statement
   The statement of circulation issued by a
   publisher.
Auflagenprüfung f
→ Auflagenkontrolle
Auflagenprüfungsbericht m (Zeitung/
Zeitschrift) audit of circulation report,
audit report
   The report of annual official findings of
   an audit bureau of circulations as a
   result of its examination of a medium's
   records.
Auflagenrest m
→ Restauflage
Auflagenspaltung f (**Auflagensplit** m)
→ Anzeigen-Splitting
auflagenschwach adj low-circulation
auflagenstark adj high-circulation
Auflagenstruktur f (Zeitung/
Zeitschrift) structure of circulation,
circulation breakdown
Auflagenüberschuß m bonus
circulation
vgl. Drucküberschuß

Auflagenüberwachungsstelle f Audit Bureau of Circulations (ABC, A.B.C.)
→ Informationsgemeinschaft zur Feststellung der Verbreitung von Werbeträgern e.V. (IVW)
Auflagenverteilung f
→ Auflagenstruktur
Auflagenwachstum n **(Auflagenzuwachs** m) (Zeitung/Zeitschrift) circulation growth
Auflagenzahl f **(Auflagenziffer** f) (Zeitung/Zeitschrift) circulation figure
Auflagenzuschuß m
→ Zuschußexemplare
Auflegemaske f *(print)* overlay, tissue overlay
  A cover of tissue or layout paper placed over art work so that corrections can be made on the overlay rather than the original.
auflegen v/t **1.** (Waren) → auslegen **2.** *(print)* to publish, to print, to issue (neu auflegen: to reissue, to reprint)
Aufleger m *(print)* feeder, layer-on
Auflicht n *(phot)* reflected light
auflösen v/t *(phot)* to resolve, to dissolve
Auflösung f *(chem)* dissolution, solution, *(opt)* resolution, dissolution, definition
  The quality of picture detail, in printing, reproduction, and television.
Auflösungsgrenze f *(opt)* limit of resolution
Auflösungskeil m *(TV)* resolution wedge
Auflösungstestbild n
→ Testbild
Auflösungsvermögen n *(phot)* resolving power, resolution,
  The ability of a lens and the sensitized surface of a photographic material to sharply transmit and record very fine detail or lines.
(chem) dissolving power, solvent power
  A particularly small grain of photographic emulsion.
aufmachen v/t (Artikel, Text) (mit) to lead in (with), to open (with)
Aufmacher m (Zeitung/Zeitschrift) lead-in, lead, lead story, front-page story, hook, approach
Aufmachung f (einer Ware) makeup, *auch* make-up, styling, design, getup, *brit* get-up, appearance, styling
Aufmachungsmuster n
→ Attrappe

Aufmerksamkeit f attention
Aufmerksamkeitsauslöser m **(aufmerksamkeitsauslösendes Werbeelement** n) attention getter, attention-getting element, attention incentive, teaser, hook, eye catcher
  Any element in an advertisement designed to stimulate attention.
Aufmerksamkeitsfaktor m attention factor
Aufmerksamkeitshascherei f
→ Effekthascherei
Aufmerksamkeitsintensität f **(Aufmerksamkeitsgrad** m) attentiveness
aufmerksamkeitsstark adj attention-getting, eye catching
Aufmerksamkeitswert m attention value
Aufmerksamkeitswirkung f **(eines Werbemittels)** stopping power (of an advertisement)
Aufnahme f **1.** *(econ)* (günstige Aufnahme eines neuen Produkts etc.) acceptance, market acceptance **2.** (Ton-, Bildaufnahme) record, recording **3.** *(phot)* shot, snapshot, picture **4.** (Einbeziehung) inclusion, incorporation
Aufnahme f **in Teilbildern** *(print/ phot)* exposure in sections, composite photo, composite photograph, composite shot, double print, double printing
Aufnahmebereitschaft f
→ Aufnahme 1.
Aufnahmebericht m *(film)* camera sheet, dope sheet, report sheet
Aufnahmebogen m **(Aufnahmeplan** m) *(radio/TV/film)* cue sheet, *brit* dubbing chart
Aufnahmebrett n **(Aufnahmerahmen** m) copyboard
Aufnahmeeinheit f recording unit
Aufnahmefähigkeit f
→ Aufnahme 1.
Aufnahmefilm m camera film
Aufnahmefilter m *(phot)* color filter, *brit* colour filter, light filter
  A sheet of colored gelatin, glass or plastic used on lenses to absorb certain colors for better rendition of others while photographing subjects or originals.
Aufnahmeformat n
→ Filmformat
Aufnahmegelände n
→ Ateliergelände

Aufnahmegerät n (Ton) recorder, recording equipment, *(film/TV)* camera equipment
Aufnahmegeschwindigkeit f (Kamera) camera speed, running speed of film, (Ton) recording speed
Aufnahmekamera f cinecamera, film camera, movie camera, motion-picture camera
→ Filmkamera
Aufnahmekanal m recording channel
Aufnahmekette f recording chain
Aufnahmekopf m recording head
Aufnahmeleiter m *(film/TV)* floor manager, studio manager (S.M., SM), stage manager (S.M., SM),
   The director's representative in charge of movie or television studio floor activity.
Aufnahmeleitung f studio management, stage management
Aufnahmelicht n (**Aufnahmewarnlicht** n) *(film/TV)* camera cue, cue light, tally light, warning light
Aufnahmemaschine f
→ Aufnahmegerät
Aufnahmematerial n *(film)* camera stock, raw stock, stock footage, stock music, stock shots pl, (Ton) recording material, stock music
Aufnahmeobjektiv n *(phot)* camera lens, objective, shooting lens, taking lens, photographic lens
Aufnahmeort m
→ Aufnahmegelände
Aufnahmeplan m *(film/TV)* shooting schedule, film schedule
   A schedule of shots for a motion picture or television show, giving the actual chronological sequence of shots as they are to be taken rather than as they are to be assembled for the completed film.
Aufnahmeprobe f (für Werbung) session
Aufnahmeraum m *(radio/film/TV)* recording room, recording hall, recording theater, *brit* theatre
Aufnahmeröhre f *(film/TV)* camera tube, pickup tube
Aufnahmestab m *(radio/film/TV)* production team
Aufnahmestandort m (**Übertragungsstandort** m) *(radio/TV)* pickup point, pickup
   The point of origin of a broadcast.
Aufnahmestudio n *(radio/TV)* recording studio
Aufnahmesystem n *(radio/TV)* recording system

Aufnahmetaste f recording key
Aufnahmeteam n *(radio/film/TV)* production team
Aufnahmetechnik f *(phot)* shooting technique, photographic technique, radio recording technique
Aufnahmetonband n master tape, original
Aufnahmewagen m
→ Übertragungswagen
Aufnahme-Wiedergabegerät n recording-reproducing unit, record-replay equipment
Aufnahmewinkel m *(film/TV/phot)* camera angle, view angle, shooting angle, taking angle, (Objektiv) lens angle
   The point of view from which an object is photographed.
aufnehmen v/t **1.** *(phot)* to photograph, to shoot, to take a photograph of **2.** *(film)* to shoot, to take **3.** *(radio)* to record, to transcribe **4.** *(TV)* to record, to telerecord, to shoot **5.** *(econ)* (der Markt) to absorb, to take up, (neue Produkte), to accept **6.** (Anzeigen) to accept (advertisements), to admit (advertising), to carry (advertisements or advertising)
Aufprojektion f (**Aufpro** f) *(film)* front projection
   A scenic background effect achieved by low-intensity projection of location slides or films directly on performers and on a huge Scotchlite screen behind them.
aufquellen *(v/i)* (Kopierwerk) to soak
Aufquellen n (Kopierwerk) soaking
aufrastern
→ rastern
Aufrasterung f
→ Raster
Aufreißer m
→ Anreißer
Aufriß m (**Aufrißbild** n **Aufrißzeichnung** f) ghosted view, x-ray illustration, phantom section
   A drawing or rendering showing the exterior of an object as if it were transparent, so as to reveal its interior detailing.
aufrollen v/t (Spule) to reel, to wind up to roll up
Aufschlag m
→ Preisaufschlag
aufschlagbar
→ aufklappbar, ausschlagbar
aufschlagen v/t (Zeitung) to open

aufschließen v/t (print) (Druckform) to unlock, to untie
Aufschlüsselungsmethode f (data analysis) break-down method
Aufschrift f
→ Etikett
auf Sendung attr (radio/TV) on the air
Aufsichtaufnahme f (film) crane shot
Aufsichtfaltung f
→ Kreuzbruchfalz
Aufsichtvorlage f (print) opaque copy
aufspulen v/t
→ aufrollen
Aufstechbogen m (**Abschmutzbogen** m, **Ölbogen** m) (print) tympan sheet, tympan, waste sheet
Aufstecker m (POP advtsg) header, topper, crowner, (Flaschenaufstecker) bottle topper
Aufsteigerung f
→ Auktion auf Aufstrich (Aufstrichverfahren)
Aufsteller m (**Aufstellplakat** n) (Kleinplakat) showcard, tent card, A board, A frame, (Tresenaufsteller) counter card, display card
 A small, folded display card, so as to be legible from two directions.
Aufstellerfüße m/pl crow's feet
Aufstellpackung f display package, display carton, display outer
 A merchandise package or carton designed to fold out into a POP display without removing the merchandise.
Aufstellplakat n
→ Aufsteller
aufstoßen (print) v/t
→ geradestoßen
Aufstrich m 1. (typ) upstroke, upward stroke 2. → Auktion auf Aufstrich (Aufstrichverfahren)
aufsummierte Abweichung f (stat) accumulated deviation
Aufteilung f (**eines Werbebudgets**) allocation of advertising expenditure
Auftrag m (econ) order, commission, firm order, (Liefervertrag) contract
→ Anzeigenauftrag, Media-Vertrag, Druckauftrag
auftragen v/t (print) (Farbe) to distribute, (Farbe auf die Form auftragen) to roll the form(e), (Farbe durch Walzen auftragen) to roll on the ink
Auftraggeber m (econ) client, customer

Auftraggebereffekt m (survey res) sponsorship bias
Auftragsausführung f (econ) execution of an order
Auftragsbearbeitung f (**Auftragsabwicklung** f) (econ) order processing
Auftragsbestand m (econ) order books pl, stock of orders
Auftragsbestätigung f (econ) confirmation of an order, order confirmation, (radio/TV) confirmation of broadcast order (C.B.O., CBO)
Auftragsdeckungsbeitrag m
→ Deckungsbeitrag
Auftragsdienst m telephone answering service
Auftragsfilm m commissioned film, commissioned movie
Auftragsforschung f commissioned research
Auftragsformular n order form
Auftragsproduktion f commissioned production
Auftragsrückstand m (econ) back orders pl, backlog of orders
Auftragsstatistik f (econ) order statistics pl (construed as sg)
Auftragstasche f (print) job bag, docket
Aufwärmzeit f (TV) warming-up time
Aufwendungen f/pl expenses pl
Aufwickelgeschwindigkeit f (film) take-up speed
Aufwickelkassette f (film) take-up magazine
aufwickeln (film) v/t to spool (up), to reel (up), to wind (up), to coil (up), to take up
Aufwickelspule f (film) film reel, take-up reel, film spool, take-up spool
Aufwickelsystem n (film) take-up system
Aufwickelteller m (film) take-up plate
Auf-Wunsch-Kommunikation f (**On Demand Communication** f)
→ Kommunikation auf Wunsch
aufzeichnen v/t 1. (aufschreiben) to note down, to write down, (protokollieren) to record 2. (skizzieren) to outline, to sketch 3. (zeichnen) to draw 4. (Tonband, Video) to record, to tape
Aufzeichnung f recording, record
→ Fernsehaufzeichnung, Filmaufzeichnung, Bandaufzeichnung, Magnetbandaufzeichnung

Aufzeichnungsanlage f (**Aufzeichnungsgerät** n) recording device, recording equipment, recording system
Aufzeichnungsgeschwindigkeit f recording speed
Aufzeichnungskette f recording chain
Aufzeichnungskopf m recording head
Aufzeichnungspegelanzeiger m recording level indicator, indicator of recording level
Aufzeichnungsprotokoll n continuity log
Aufzeichnungsstrom m recording current
Aufzeichnungsverluste m/pl recording loss
Aufzeichnungswagen m
→ Übertragungswagen
aufziehen v/t 1. *(print)* (aufmontieren) to mount
→ aufkleben, aufmontieren
2. *(print)* (Buchrücken) to stick
Aufziehen n
→ Aufkleben, Aufmontieren, Aufklotzen
Aufziehkarton m *(phot/print)* mounting board, mount
Aufziehleinwand f *(print)* mount
Aufzug m *(phot)* winding knob
Aufzugshebel m *(phot)* (an der Kamera) winding lever
Augenanpassung f
→ Akkommodation
Augenbewegung f (**Blickverlauf** m) *(res)* eye movement, eye flow, eye direction, gaze motion, eye gaze
  The exact course a reader's or viewer's eyes take over a page or other object he reads or watches.
→ Blickaufzeichnung
Augenblinzeln n
→ Blinzeln, Blinzeltest
Augenempfindlichkeit f sensitivity of the eye
Augenempfindlichkeitskurve f relative sensitivity (of the eye) curve
Augenhöhe f (**Augenperspektive** f) *(phot)* eye level, eye line
Augenkamera f (**Blickbewegungskamera** f) *(res)* eye-movement camera, eye camera
  A camera-like device used in media and advertising research for recording eye movements.
Augenfälligkeit f (**optisch ansprechender Charakter** m) eye appeal

Augenlicht n (**Augenlichtlampe** f) *(phot/film/TV)* (Beleuchtung) catch light, eye light
  A low-level illumination, usually from a camera-mounted lamp, producing a specular reflection from a performer's eyes and teeth.
Augenmuschel f (**Augenmuschelkissen** n) (an der Kamera) eye guard
Augenzeugenbericht m eye-witness report, eye-witness account, *(radio/TV)* running commentary
Auktion f (**Versteigerung** f) *(econ)* auction, auction sale, sale by auction, commercial auction
  An agent business unit which effects the sale of goods through an auctioneer, who, under specific rules, solicits bids or offers from buyers and has power to accept the highest bids of responsible bidders and, thereby, consummates the sale. The auctioneer usually but not always is a paid employee of an auction company which is in the business of conducting auctions.
Auktion f **auf Abstrich** (**Absteigerung** f, **Abstrich** m) *(econ)* Dutch auction
  A type of auction in which the auctioneer offers the items at a high price and lowers the price gradually until a bidder responds.
Auktion f **auf Aufstrich** (**Aufsteigerung** f, **Aufstrich** m) *(econ)* etwa common auction, auction
  vgl. Auktion auf Abstrich
Auktionator m *(econ)* auctioneer
auktionieren v/t *(econ)* to auction, to auction off, to sell at auction, to sell by auction, to put up for auction, to put up to auction
Auktionsgebühr f *(econ)* auction fee, auction charge
Auktionshaus n *(econ)* auction house, auction company, auctioneer
Auktionspreis m *(econ)* auction price
AUMA m abbr Ausstellungs- und Messe-Ausschuß der Deutschen Wirtschaft e.V.
Ausbesserung f (**Wartung** f) (bei Plakaten in der Außenwerbung) outdoor service, renewal, renewals pl, renewal service
  The maintenance of and repairs to outdoor advertising posters.
Ausbeutung f **fremden Rufs**
→ Rufausbeutung
Ausbeutung f **durch Nachahmung**
→ Nachahmung

ausbinden *(print)* v/t (Schriftsatz) to tie up
Ausbindeschnur f (**Ausbindschnur** f) *(binding)* page cord, string
ausbleichen 1. v/i (Farben) to bleach, to fade, to grow pale **2.** v/t to bleach, to fade, to discharge, to bleach out, (Kopierwerk) to bleach
Ausbleichen n (**Ausbleichverfahren** n) *(phot)* bleachout process
  A technique of making line drawings on photographs and silverprints with waterproof inks, the image serving as a guide to the artist, and afterwards removed by bleaching, leaving only the drawing on the surface of the paper.
Ausblende f
→ Ausblendung
ausblenden v/t *(film/TV/radio)* to fade, to fade out, to fade to black
→ abblenden
Ausblendregler m *(film/TV)* fader
→ Abblendregler
Ausblendung f (**Ausblenden** n) *(film/TV/radio)* fade-out, fading-down, fade, (mit der Kamera) out-of-focus dissolve, (langsam) sneak, (Licht) dimming, dimming-out, (Objektiv) stopping-down, (Ton) sound fade
Ausbreitung f
→ Diffusion
Ausbreitungszone f
→ Empfangsbereich
ausbringen *(print)* v/t to space out, to overrun, to run over
Ausbringen n *(print)* spacing-out, driving-out
Ausdeckung f
→ Haushaltsabdeckung, Reichweite
aus dem Passer attr *(print)* out of register, off register
  The state in colorwork when the constituent negatives or plates of a color set are not of identical size or when they do not superpose in proper relation to each other.
Ausfall m (**Ausfälle** m/pl) *(survey res)* nonresponse, non-response, (Stichprobenausfälle) sampling loss
Ausfallbogen m (**Aushängebogen** m) *(print)* clean proof, clean machine proof, advance sheet, green copy
Ausfallfehler m (**Verzerrung** f **durch Ausfälle**) *(survey res)* nonresponse bias
Ausfallgage f (**Ausfallhonorar** n) cancellation fee, payoff fee

Ausfallmuster n outturn sample, *brit* out-turn sample
Ausfallquote f (**Ausfallrate** f, **Verweigerungsrate** f) *(survey res)* nonresponse rate
ausflecken
→ abdecken
Ausflugsfahrt f
→ Kaffeefahrt
ausfräsen v/t *(print)* to rout, to rout out, to cut away, *colloq* to dig out
  To remove a portion of a plate, usually by hand.
Ausfräsung f (**Ausfräsen** n) *(print)* routing
  The removal of nonessential or dead metal from nonprinting parts of a plate.
Ausfressen n (**Überbelichtung** f) *(phot)* burning up, blocking up
  Overexposure to an extent that highlights in a photograph appear to be "burned up" with the effect that no definition or detail is to be seen.
Ausfuhr-
→ Export
Ausführpunkt m *(print)* leader, *meist pl* leaders
Ausführstrich m *(print)* stroke leader
Ausfüllungslinie f *(print)* catchline, catch line
Ausgabe f (einer Zeitung/einer Zeitschrift) issue, number, copy
  A single, assembled unit of a periodical publication.
Ausgaben-Nachlaß m (**Ausgaben-Rabatt** m) (für Anzeigen) combination discount
→ Kombinationsrabatt
Ausgabenstruktur f *(econ)* spending pattern
Ausgabenuntersuchung f
→ Haushaltsbudget-Studie
Ausgang m *(print)* break, (Ausgangszeile) breakline, broken line, last line
Ausgangsgesamtheit f *(stat)* parent population, population, universe
→ Grundgesamtheit, Gesamtheit
Ausgangsgewicht n (**Basisgewicht** n) *(stat)* base weight
  The weights of a weighting system for an index number computed according to the information relating to the base period instead, for example, of the current period.
Ausgangsseite f *(print)* short page

Ausgangsstichprobe f **(Brutto-Stichprobe** f) *(stat)* master sample, master frame
→ Erhebungsrahmen
Ausgangszeile f
→ Ausgang
ausgebleicht *adj (phot)* bleached, bleached-out
ausgedünntes Heft n *(media res)* stripped magazine issue, thinned-out issue
ausgegangen *attr (print)* (Schriftgarnitur) out of sorts
ausgewogen (ausgeglichen) *adj* balanced
ausgewogene Stichprobe f *(stat)* balanced sample
  If the mean value of some characteristic is known for a population and the value of the characteristic can be ascertained for each member of a sample, it is possible to choose the sample so that the mean value of the characteristic in it approximates to the parent mean. Such a sample ist said to be balanced.
ausgewogene experimentelle Anlage f **(ausgewogener Versuchsplan** m) *(res)* balanced design, balanced experimental design
ausgewogenes Vermengen n *(stat)* balanced confounding
Ausgewogenheit f **(der Gestaltung)** balance (of design)
Ausgewogenheitsgrundsatz m **(Ausgewogenheit** f) *(radio/TV) etwa* fairness doctrine, equal time, equal opportunity
  The legal requirement that German broadcasting stations must afford a reasonable opportunity for a discussion of conflicting views on issues of public importance.
ausgießen *v/t (print)* to cast, to mold, to mould, to fill
Ausgleich m balance, adjustment, equalization, equilibration
→ Artikelausgleich, Produktausgleich, zeitlicher Ausgleich
ausgleichen *(print) v/t* **1.** (Satz) to underlay **2.** (Zwischenräume) to letterspace, to space, to space equally, to equalize **3.** (Typen) to range
Ausgleichen n *(print)* **1.** (Satz) underlaying **2.** (Zwischenräume) letterspacing, spacing **3.** (Typen) ranging
Ausgleichsanspruch m
→ Handelsvertreterausgleich

Ausgleichsbeleuchtung f *(film/phot)* balancing light, fill light, flat light
Ausgleichsentwickler m *(phot)* compensating developer
Ausgleichskalkulation f
→ kalkulatorischer Ausgleich
Ausgleichstück m *(print)* leveling piece, *brit* levelling piece
Aushangdauer f *(outdoor advtsg)* (Plakate) posting period
→ Anschlagdauer
Aushängebogen m **(Aushänger** m) *(print)* clean sheet, advance sheet, specimen sheet, advance proof, last proof, green copy
  A printer's proof having no errors.
Aushängekasten m bulletin board, *brit* notice board
Aushängeschild n *(outdoor advtsg)* signboard, sign, shop sign, store sign
ausklappbare Beilage f **(ausklappbare Werbebeilage** f) (Zeitschrift) pullout insert
→ aufklappbare Beilage
ausklinken *v/t (print)* (Buchstaben) to mortise, (unterschneiden) to kern
Ausklinken n *(print)* mortising
  The operation by which sections of mounted printing plates are cut out either by means of a drill or a jigsaw.
Ausklinkung f **(Ausfräsung** f, **ausgefräste Stelle** f) *(print)* mortise
  An open space in a plate into which smaller cuts of type matter may be inserted. More in general, an area cut out of a printing plate to allow insertion of other elements.
Auskunftsgespräch n
→ Interview
Auskunftsperson f **(Befragter** m) *(survey res)* informant
Auskunftsvergleich m **(Auskunftsverlangen** n) *etwa* comparative advertising upon request
Auslage f **1.** display, window display
  A device or accumulation of devices which in addition to identifying and/or advertising a company and/or a product, may also merchandise, either by actually offering the product for sale or by indicating its proximity. A display characteristically bears an intimate relationship with the product, whereas a sign is more closely related to the name of the manufacturer, the retailer, or the product.
2. exhibit, goods *pl* exhibited
→ Schaufensterauslage, Warenauslage

Auslagegestell 46

Auslagegestell n (**Auslagegerüst** n) (POP advtsg) gazebo
A freestanding display fixture.
Auslagekarton m (**Auslagepackung** f) (POP advtsg) display package, prepack display carton, display case, display outer, display bin
Auslagekiste f (**Auslagebehälter** m) (POP advtsg) display bin, dump bin, dumper
Auslagenfenster n (POP advtsg) display window
→ Schaufenster
Auslagengestaltung f (POP advtsg) display work
Auslagenregal n (POP advtsg) display rack, display shelf
Auslagenvitrine f (POP advtsg) display case, case
A cabinet with glass panels allowing the contents to be displayed while remaining protected.
Auslagenwerbung f merchandise display advertising, display advertising
→ Schauwerbung
Auslagenzettel m (**Auslagenwerbezettel** m) display card
Auslagepackung f display package
Auslageregal n (**beidseitig offenes Warenregal** n) (POP advtsg) gondola
An island of shelving, open on two or all sides, to display merchandise in retail stores.
Auslagetisch m (POP advtsg) display stand, display table, (für Sonderangebote) dump table
Auslandsauflage f (Zeitung/Zeischrift) foreign circulation
Auslandsfactoring n (econ) export factoring
Auslandslizenz f (econ) foreign license, brit licence
Auslandsmarkt m (econ) foreign market
Auslandsmarktforschung f international market research, market research in foreign countries
Auslandsmesse f (econ) foreign trade fair
Auslandspresse f foreign press
Auslandswerbung f
→ Werbung im Ausland
Auslassungszeichen n (**Einschaltungszeichen** n) (print) caret
auslegen v/t **1.** (Waren) to display, to expose, to lay out, to exhibit **2.** (print)

(Druckbogen) to deliver, to take off **3.** (Projektor) to unlace **4.** (Kamera) to unload, to unthread
Ausleger m **1.** (print) fly, flier, flyer **2.** (studio) jib arm, jib
Auslegestab m (print) flyer stick, flier stick
Auslegevorrichtung f (print) delivery device, delivery station
ausleuchten v/t (phot/film/TV) to illuminate, to light, to floodlight
Ausleuchtung f (**Ausleuchten**n) (phot/film/TV) lighting, illumination
Ausleuchtungszone f (phot/film/TV) (im Studio) lit area
Auslieferer m (econ) distributor, supplier
ausliefern v/t (econ) to deliver, to supply, (vertreiben) to distribute
Auslieferung f (econ) delivery, delivery service, supply, (Vertrieb) distribution
Auslieferungsabteilung f
→ Vertriebsabteilung
Auslieferungslager n (**Auslieferungsgroßhandel** m) (econ) delivery stores pl, supply depot, despatch warehouse
Auslieferungsstelle f (econ) distribution center, brit centre
Auslieferungstag m (**Auslieferungstermin** m) (econ) day of delivery
Auslieferungswagen m (bei Zeitungen) newspaper delivery truck
ausliegen v/i (Ware) to be displayed, to be laid out, to be exhibited, (Zeitungen/Zeitschriften) to be laid out, to be kept available
ausloben v/t to promise a reward in public
Auslobung f etwa public promise of a reward
→ Preisausschreiben, Wettbewerb
Auslobungspreisausschreiben n
→ Auslobung
Auslöseknopf m
→ Auslöser
auslösen v/t (phot) (Verschluß) to trigger, to release
Auslöser m (phot) release
Auslösetaste f release button, operational key
Auslösezeichen n release signal, starting blip
Ausmelkungsstrategie f (marketing) milking strategy
→ Absahnplan, Abschöpfungsstrategie

Ausmustern v/t (Waren) to reject, to discard
Ausmusterung f **1.** (Handelsvertreter) → Musterung **2.** (von Tagesmustern) selection process, daily selection
Ausreißer m (**Extremwert** m) (stat) maverick, outlier, discordant value, straggler, sport, wild shot
   In a sample of n observations it is possible for a limited number to be so far separated in value from the remainder that they give rise to the question whether they are not from a different population, or that the sampling technique is at fault. Such values are called outliers.
Ausreißertest m (**Dixonscher Ausreißertest** m) (stat) outlier test, Dixon test for outliers
   A statistical test to determine whether an extreme score in a distribution differs sufficiently from the main body of scores to justify the conclusion that it comes from a different population. The test statistic consists of a ratio formed by the difference between the outlier and the main body of scores divided by an approximation of the range of the entire distribution.
ausrichten (print) v/t **1.** (Schrift) to align, to straighten **2.** (Papierbogen) to jog
Ausrichtung f (print) **1.** (der Schrift) alignment, straightening **2.** (Papierbogen) jogging
ausrücken v/t (print) to run out, to set out (in the margin)
Ausrufer m barker, tout
Aussagenanalyse f
→ Inhaltsanalyse
Aussatz m (print) evenness of print
ausschalten
→ abschalten
ausschießen (print) v/t **1.** (Kolumnen) to impose **2.** (Makulaturbogen)
→ durchschießen
Ausschießen n (print) imposition
Ausschießschema n (print) imposition sheet, imposition layout, pull for position, position pull
Ausschießplatte f (**Schießplatte** f **Metteurtisch** m) (print) imposing table, imposition table, imposing stone, imposition stone
ausschlachten (print) v/t (Satz nach dem Druck) to pick up, to break up (the form to pieces)

ausschlagbare Anzeige f (**ausschlagbare Seiten** f/pl) gatefold, French door, pullout insert
   A magazine unit of advertising space comprising at least one full page with a second full or partial page folding from the outside margin.
(nach rechts/links ausschlagbar) fold-in page, (in der Heftmitte) centerfold, (Altarfalzanzeige) Dutch door, Dutch door ad(vertisement), Dutch door spread, (ausschlagbare Titelseite) gatefold cover
ausschließen (print) v/t (Zeilen) to adjust, to justify, to space, to space out
Ausschließen n (**Ausschließung** f) (print) adjustment, justification, spacing, word spacing
Ausschließlichkeitsbindung f
→ Vertriebsbindung
Ausschließlichkeitsvertrieb m
→ Alleinvertrieb, Exklusivvertrieb
Ausschließlichkeitsklausel f (econ) noncompete agreement, exclusivity agreement
Ausschluß m (print) spacing material, spaces pl, (großer Ausschluß) quad, mut, nut
Ausschlußkasten m (print) space and quad case
Ausschlußtaste f (print) spacing key
Ausschneidebild n (**Ausschneidefigur** f) cutout, brit cut-out
Ausschneidebogen m cutout sheet, brit cut-out sheet
Ausschneidekunst f cut-paper work, silhouetting
ausschneiden v/t to cut, to cut out, to clip, to excise
Ausschnitt m **1.** (aus einer Zeitung/Zeitschrift) clip, clipping, cut, press clipping, press cutting **2.** (eines Bildes) detail **3.** (phot) cropped negative area, trimmed negative area **4.** (aus einem Text) excerpt, extract
Ausschnittbüro n (**Zeitungsausschnittbüro** n) clipping agency, clipping bureau, press clipping agency, press clipping bureau, press cutting agency
   A business organization that peruses magazines and newspapers, and clips articles, references, or allusions of interest to its clients from them.
Ausschnittdienst m
→ Ausschnittbüro

Ausschnittvergrößerung f *(phot)* selective enlargement
Ausschöpfung f **(einer Stichprobe)** *(stat)* coverage (of a sample) The extent to which all elements in a population, (→) Grundgesamtheit have been included in the sampling frame.
ausschreiben v/t **1.** (bekanntgeben) to announce, to advertise, to invite tenders, to invite bids for **2.** to transcribe
Ausschreibung f **1.** (einer Stelle) advertisement (of a vacancy) **2.** *(econ)* (Submission) call for tenders, call for bids, invitation to tender, **3.** *(econ)* (Angebote aufgrund einer Ausschreibung) bid, tender
Ausschreier m **(Ausrufer** m**)** barker, tout
Ausschuß m **1.** (Komitee) committee, commission, board, panel **2.** *(econ)* (Ausschußwaren) substandard goods *pl*, substandard products *pl*, substandard articles *pl*, rejects *pl*, waste **3.** *(print)* (Abfall) waste, scrap, junk
Auschußanteil m **(Ausschußquote** f**)** *(stat)* fraction defective
Außenanschlag m outdoor advertisement, outdoor advertising poster, outdoor poster
→ Außenwerbemittel
Außenanschlagwerbung f
→ Außenwerbung
Außenantenne f *(radio/TV)* outdoor antenna, *brit* outdoor aerial
Außenaufnahme f **(Außenübertragung** f **) 1.** *(phot)* outdoor photo(graph), outdoor shot, outdoor picture **2.** *(radio/TV)* nemo, nemo broadcast, outside broadcast, remote pickup, exterior broadcast, exterior shot, exteriors *pl* **3.** *(film)* location shot(s) *(pl)*, exterior shot(s) *(pl)*, outside shot(s) *(pl)*
Außenaufnahmetage m *(film/TV/radio)* day on location
Außenaufzeichnung f **(Außenübertragung** f *(radio/TV)* outside recording, OB recording
Außenbau m *(film/TV)* location set, exterior set
Außenbetriebstechnik f *(radio/TV/film)* outside operations, *pl*, outside broadcasts *pl* (OBs)

Aussendewelle f **(Aussendungswelle** f **)** *(direct advtisg)* mailing, direct mail shot
aussenden v/t (Werbesendung) to mail out, to dispatch, to despatch
Außendienst m **(die Außendienstmitarbeiter)** field force, field representatives *pl*
Außendienstbericht m **(Vertreterbericht** m**)** call report, contact report A salesperson's report to a supervisor of calls made to prospects or customers during a given time or in a specific market.
Außendienstler m **(Außendienstmitarbeiter** m**)** field man, field representative, member of the field force
Außendienstorganisation f organization of the field force, *brit* organisation of the field force, field force organization
außengeleitetes Verhalten n other-directed behavior, *brit* behaviour, outer-directed behavior (David Riesman)
Außenhandel m foreign trade, external trade
→ Export
Außenkante f *(print)* outer edge, outside edge
Außenlenkung f other-directedness, outer-directedness (David Riesman)
Außenproduktion f *(radio/TV)* OB production, outside broadcast production
Außenrand m **(Außensteg** m**)** *(print)* outside margin, outer margin, fore edge, side stick
Außenreportage f *(radio/TV)* OB commentary, OB broadcast, OB report
Außenrequisiteur m *(film/TV)* property buyer, props buyer
Außenreklame f
→ Außenwerbung
Außensteg m
→ Außenrand
Außenstudio n *(radio/TV)* regional studio, local studio
Außentitel m (Zeitschrift) cover title, outside front cover
→ Titelseite
Außenübertragung f *(radio/TV)* outside broadcast (OB), remote broadcast, remote pickup, nemo broadcast, field pickup

Außenübertragungsort m *(radio/TV)* outside broadcast location, OB location, OB point
Außenwerbeflächenkäufer m outdoor space buyer
Außenwerbemittelkontakt m *(media res)* outdoor advertising exposure
→ Plakatkontakt
Außenwerbemittel-Reichweite f **(Plakatreichweite** f**)** *(media res)* outdoor circulation, outdoor audience, effective circulation, daily effective circulation (DEC)
Außenwerbeunternehmen n outdoor advertising plant, outdoor advertising plant operator
  A business organization that builds, maintains and sells the space of outdoor advertising displays consisting of billboards, poster panels, or painted bulletins.
Außenwerbung f outdoor advertising, outdoor poster advertising, out-of-home media advertising
  Display-type advertising (billboards, posters, signs, etc.) placed out-of-doors, along highways and railroads, or on walls and roofs of buildings.
Außer-Haus-Lesen n *(media res)* out-of-home reading, away-from-home reading
Außer-Haus-Leser m **(Leser** m **außer Haus)** *(media res)* out-of-home reader
Außer-Haus-Leserschaft f **(Leser** m/pl **außer Haus)** *(media res)* out-of-home readers pl, out-of-home audience
aussetzen *(print)* v/t to complete setting, to set in full
Ausspannen n
→ Abwerbung
aussparen *(print)* v/t to leave blank
Aussparung f *(print)* blank space, free space, blank
aussperren *(print)* v/t (Zeilen) to space (out), (Satz) to lead (out), to white
→ sperren
Ausspielung f lottery, raffle
→ Tombola
Ausstaffierung f
→ Dekoration
ausstanzen v/t to punch, to cut
Ausstanzstück n **(Stanzschnitt** m**)** die cut
Ausstatter m *(film/TV)* furnisher, set dresser, designer

Ausstattung f 1. → Warenausstattung
2. (eines Buchs) getup, *brit* get-up
3. *(film/TV)* decor and makeup, mounting, costumes pl
Ausstattungsfilm m **(Ausstattungssendung** f**)** spectacular, spectacular film
Ausstattungsschachtel f **(Austattungskarton** m**)** *(POP advtsg)* fancy box, fancy carton
Ausstattungsschutz m
→ Warenzeichenschutz
Ausstattungsgrad m
→ Haushaltsabdeckung, Haushaltsausstattung
Ausstattungsingenieur m installation engineer
Ausstattungskosten pl design cost(s) *(pl)*
Ausstattungsleiter m head of design
Ausstattungsmaterial n
→ Auslagematerial
Ausstattungsstab m design team
Ausstattungstechnik f design planning and installation
Ausstattungstest m *(market res)* design test, test of product design
ausstellen v/t (Waren etc) to display, to exhibit, to show
Aussteller m exhibitor, exhibiting company
Ausstellerbefragung f
→ Messebefragung
Ausstellkarton m
→ Auslagekarton
Ausstellung f exhibition, show, fair
→ Messe
Ausstellungsbau m exhibition stand construction
Ausstellungsfläche f exhibition space, exhibition area
Ausstellungsgegenstand m exhibit, showpiece, exhibited object
Ausstellungsgelände n exhibition grounds pl, exhibition site, fair grounds pl, fair site
Ausstellungsgüter n/pl exhibits pl, exhibited articles pl
Ausstellungshalle f exhibiton hall
Ausstellungskarton m
→ Auslagekarton
Ausstellungsjahr n exhibition year
Ausstellungskatalog m exhibition catalog, *brit* catalogue
Ausstellungsmaterial n
→ Auslagematerial

Ausstellungspavillon m exhibition pavilion
Ausstellungsplakat n exhibition poster
Ausstellungsraum m showroom, exhibition room, display room, exhibition hall
Ausstellungsrecht n exhibition rights pl
Ausstellungsstand m exhibition stand, exhibition booth, display booth
Ausstellungsständer m **(Aufsteller** m) *(POP advtsg)* floor stand
Ausstellungsstück n
→ Ausstellungsgegenstand
Ausstellungs- und Messeausschuß m der Deutschen Wirtschaft (AUMA) Exhibition and Trade Fair Committee of German Industry
Ausstellungsvitrine f *(POP advtsg)* showcase, display case
Ausstellungswagen m exhibition van
Aufstellungswerbung f exhibition advertising, trade fair advertising
Ausstellungszug m exhibition train
aussteuern *(radio/TV/tape)* v/t to modulate, to control, (Tonbandgerät) to control the recording level (of a tape)
Aussteuerung f *(radio/TV/tape)* modulation, control, level control
Aussteuerungsanzeiger m *(radio/TV/tape)* recording level indicator
Aussteuerungsbereich m *(radio/TV/tape)* modulation range, level control range
Aussteuerungsgrad m *(radio/TV/tape)* depth of modulation, modulation index
Aussteuerungsmesser m *(radio/TV/tape)* program meter, volume indicator, level indicator, program-volume indicator
Aussteuerungsregler m *(radio/TV/tape)* (Tonband) recording level control
ausstrahlen (senden) v/t + v/i *(radio/TV)* to broadcast, to radiate
Ausstrahlung f *(radio/TV)* broadcast
Ausstrahlungseffekt m *(res)* halo, halo effect, spillover effects pl
 The extension from an impression to an individual's perception and interpretation of stimuli. Also, the subjective reaction to an individual feature of a product or an advertisement, conditioned by attitudes toward the whole.
→ Irradiation
ausstreichen v/t (Geschriebenes) to cross out, to delete, to cancel
Ausstreichung f
→ Streichung
austasten v/t *(TV)* to blank, to gate, to black out
Austasten n **(Austastung** f) *(TV)* blanking, black-out
Austastgemisch n *(TV)* mixed blanking signal, mixed blanking pulses pl
Austastimpuls m **(A-Impuls** m) *(TV)* blanking pulse
Austastlücke f **(Bildlücke** f) *(TV)* blanking interval, field blanking interval
 The brief moment, measured in microseconds, during which the television receiver scanning beam is suppressed by a blanking pulse while it returns to the left side of the screen to retrace the next horizontal scan line — or to the top of the picture tube to begin another field.
Austastpegel m **(Austastniveau** n, **Austastwert** m, **Schwarzpegel** m) *(TV)* blanking level, black level
Austastpegelfesthaltung f *(TV)* blanking level stability
Austastsignal n **(A-Signal** n) *(TV)* blanking signal
Austastung f
→ Austasten
Austastverstärker m *(TV)* blanking amplifier
Austastwert m
→ Austastpegel
Austausch m exchange
→ Tausch
Austauscharten f/pl **(Austauschmodi** m/pl)
→ Transaktion
Austauschtheorie f exchange theory, theory of exchange
austragen v/t (Zeitungen) to deliver
Austräger m
→ Zeitungsausträger
austreiben v/t *(print)* (Satz) to set (type) to full measure
Austrittblende f *(phot)* field stop, exit slit
Ausverkauf m **(Räumungsverkauf** m)
1. clearance sale, sell out, close-out sale, closing-down sale, winding-up sale, sell-out

The sale of goods at a reduced price to clear surpluses or end of season stock on the grounds of incomplete assortment, error in judging demand, or space priorities. The loss of profit is balanced by the increase in liquidity.
2. (liegengebliebener Waren) rummage sale, *brit* jumble sale
→ Sonderveranstaltung, Saisonausverkauf

Ausverkaufspreis *m* bargain price
→ Sonderangebotspreis

ausverkauft *attr/adv* out of stock, sold out

Auswahl *f* 1. → Warenangebot 2. → Muster 3. → Markenwahl 4. *(stat)* (Stichprobenauswahl) sampling, (Stichprobe) sample

Auswahl *f* **aufs Geratewohl**
→ willkürliche Auswahl

Auswahl *f* **mit replizierten Ziehungen (Parallelauswahl** *f*) *(stat)* replicated sampling (Vorgang/Verfahren), replicated sample (Stichprobe)

Auswahl *f* **mit Zurücklegen** *(stat)* sampling with replacement

Auswahl *f* **nach dem Konzentrationsprinzip (Abschneideverfahren** *n*) *(stat)* (Vorgang/Verfahren) cut-off sampling, cut-off sample (Stichprobe)

Auswahl *f* **ohne Zurücklegen** *(stat)* sampling without replacement

Auswahlabstand *m* *(stat)* sampling interval

Auswahlbasis *f*
→ Grundgesamtheit, Ausgangsstichprobe

Auswahleinheit *f*
→ Erhebungseinheit

Auswahlfehler *m* **(Stichprobenfehler** *m*, **Zufallsfehler** *m*) *(stat)* sampling error, sample error, (systematischer Fehler) sample bias, sampling bias
  The discrepancy, due to random sampling, between the true value of a parameter and the sample estimate thereof. The expected magnitude of the sampling error is shown by the standard deviation, (→) Standardabweichung, of the sampling distribution of the statistic used to estimate the parameter value.

Auswahlfeld *n* *(marketing)* selection field (Philip Kotler)

Auswahlfrage *f* **(Mehrfach-Auswahlfrage** *f*, **Selektivfrage** *f*) *(survey res)* multiple-choice question, cafeteria question, forced-choice question, multiple-response question,
multiple choice, *auch* answer question
  A structured survey question in which the respondent chooses one or several of a given number of response alternatives, even though he might not "like" any of the alternatives. Respondents are usually asked to choose the alternative that is closest to their views, even though no alternative may exactly express their opinion.

Auswahlgrundlage *f* **(Auswahlbasis** *f*, **Stichprobenrahmen** *m*) *(stat)* sampling frame

Auswahlmuster *n*
→ Muster

Auswahlplan *m* **(Stichprobenplan** *m*) *(stat)* sampling plan, sample design, sample plan, sampling scheme

Auswahlsatz *m* *(stat)* sampling fraction, sampling ratio
  The proportion of the total number of sampling units in the population within which simple random sampling is made.

Auswahlsendung *f*
→ unbestellte Waren

Auswahlsortiment *n* *(retailing)* assortment
→ Sortiment

Auswahlstreuung *f* *(media planning)* selective advertising, selective media planning, selective planning, rifle approach
→ Allgemeinstreuung, Einzelstreuung, Gruppenstreuung; *vgl.* Zufallsstreuung

Auswahltest *m* *(market res)* choice test

Auswahlumfang *m*
→ Stichprobenumfang

Auswahlumwerbung *f*
→ Auswahlstreuung

Auswahlverfahren *n* **(Auswahltechnik** *f*) *(stat)* sampling, sampling technique, sampling method, sampling procedure
  The statistical technique used to select a part of a population, (→) Grundgesamtheit, for some investigative purpose.

auswechselbares Objektiv *n* *(phot)* interchangeable lens

auswerten *v/t* to analyze, *brit* to analyse, to evaluate

Auswertung *f*
→ Datenauswertung

Auswurfbogen *m* **(Auswechselbogen** *m*) *(print)* replacement sheet

auszählen v/t (Daten) to tally,
(Manuskript) to cast off, to make a
character count, to copycast
Auszählen n **(Auszählung f)** (Daten)
tally, tallying, (Anschläge) character
count, copycasting, casting off
Auszahlungsmatrix f pay-off matrix
auszeichnen v/t **1.** *(econ)* (Waren) to
mark out, to label, to tag, to ticket
2. *(print)* (Text partien) to accentuate,
to display, to mark up **3.** *(print)* (Satz)
to spec type, to type spec
  To specify the typefaces and sizes to be
  used in printing a piece of copy.
Auszeichnung f **1.** *(econ)* (Waren)
marking out, labeling, tagging, tag,
branding → Markierung **2.** *(print)*
accentuation, display **3.** *(print)* spec
type, type spec
Auszeichnungsschrift f **(Akzidenzschrift** f, **Plakatschrift** f **)** *(typ)* display
face, display type
  A type of a larger size than in the body
  copy, used for headlines and
  subheadlines for its greater attentiongetting value.
Ausziehfeder f **(Reißfeder** f **,
Zeichenfeder** f **)** drawing pen, ruling
pen
Auszeichnungszeile f *(typ)* display
line, displayed line of type
Ausziehtusche f drawing ink, India
ink
  A heavy, black waterproof ink used in
  drawings.
Auto n
→ Autotypie
Autobushäuschen n *(transit advtsg)*
bus shelter
Autobuswerbung f **(Omnibuswerbung**
f **)** bus advertising, car advertising
Autobusplakat n **(Omnibusplakat** n**)**
bus card, car card
  A small card generally with poster-like
  design placed in buses, street cars and
  subways.
Autochroma n (MAZ) automatic
chroma control
Autochromdruck m **(Autochromverfahren** n**)** *(phot)* autochrome
process, autochrome printing
Auto-Cue m *(film/TV)* autocue
Autokino n drive-in, drive-in movietheater, *brit* drive-in cinema
Autokorrelation f **(Eigenkorrelation**
f **)** *(stat)* autocorrelation, serial
correlation
  The correlation of each error term in a
  regression model with a preceding error
  term; autocorrelation can bias linearity
  estimates prepared by ordinary least
  squares estimation.
Autokorrelationsfunktion f *(stat)*
autocorrelation function
Autokorrelationskoeffizient m *(stat)*
coefficient of autocorrelation, autocorrelation coefficient
Autokovarianz f *(stat)* autocovariance
Automat m **(Verkaufsautomat** m,
Warenautomat m**)** automat, vending
machine, automatic vending machine,
vendor, slot machine
→ Verkaufsautomat
Automatenverkauf m **(automatischer
Verkauf** m**)** *(retailing)* automatic
vending, automatic selling
  The retail sale of goods or services
  through currency operated machines
  activated by the ultimate consumerbuyer. Most, if not all, machines now
  used in automatic selling are coin
  operated.
automatische Entfernungsmessung f
(automatische Scharfeinstellung f **)**
(phot) automatic focusing,
autofocusing, autofocus
automatische Lautstärkeregelung
(ALR) f *(radio/TV)* automatic volume
control (AVC)
automatischer Zugriff m **(auf Daten)**
automatic retrieval, automatic data
retrieval
Automobilwerbung f **(Autowerbung** f **)**
car advertising
Autoradio n car radio
Autoraster m
→ Autotypie-Raster
Autoregression f **(Eigenregression** f **)**
(stat) autoregression
autoregressive Reihe f *(stat)*
autoregressive series
autoregressiver Prozeß m *(stat)*
autoregressive process
autoregressives Modell n *(stat)*
autoregressive model
Autorenexemplar n **(Autorenbeleg** m**)**
author's copy
Autorenkorrektur f *(print)* author's
alteration(AA), author's
correction(AC)
Autorenzeile f (bei Artikeln) byline,
by-line
  The name of the journalist usually
  printed below the headline of a report he
  has written.

Autoritätswerbung f
→ allegatorische Werbung, Leitbildwerbung, Testimonialwerbung
Autostart m *(film)* autostart
Auto/Strich m
→ Auto-Strich-Kombination
Auto-Strich-Kombination f **(Auto/Strich** m, **Kombi** n, **Kombinationsätzung** f **)** *(print)* combination cut, combination plate, combined line and halftone block, combined line and halftone plate
A printing plate in which line or solid and halftone images are combined, both for monochrome or multicolor effects.
Autotypie f *(print)* halftone, halftone block, halftone plate, halftone engraving
An engraving made by photographing through a screen which breaks up the subject into small dots of varying size, reproducing intermediate shades or tones.
Autotypieätzung f *(print)* halftone etching
The process of etching halftone images into relief on metal plates.
Autotypiepunkt m *(print)*
→ Rasterpunkt
Autotypieraster m *(print)* halftone screen

A grating of ruled, etched and pigmented lines on two glass plates, each plate bearing a series of parallel lines of a definite number per inch, the two plates cemented together so that the lines cross each other at right angles and produce transparent apertures between the intersecting lines.
autotypischer Tiefdruck m autotypography
Autowerbung f
→ Automobilwerbung
AV *abbr* audiovisuell, Audiovision
AV-Medien n/pl
→ Audiovisionsmedien
Average-Linkage-Methode f *(stat)* average-linkage method
Aversion f aversion
AWA f *abbr* Allensbacher Werbeträger-Analyse
Axiom n axiom
Azetat n **(Azetatfolie** f, **Azetatfilm** m**)** acetate, acetate film
A slow-burning transparent chemical substance used as a film base.
Azetatabzug m *(print)* acetate proof, cellophane proof, celluloid proof
Azetathülle f **(Plastikhülle** f **)** acetate sleeve

B

B-Geschäft n
→ Bedienungsgeschäft
B-Welle f (**Feinwelle** f) *(packaging)* B flute, fine flute
B-Wicklung f (**B-Rolle** f) *(film)* B roll, B winding
vgl. A-Wicklung
Babyspot m (**Babyspotlampe** f) baby spotlight, baby spot, *brit* baby pup, pup
Baby-Stativ n *(phot)* pup stand, baby legs *pl*, small lighting stand, *colloq* turtle
Background m
→ Hintergrund, Rückprojektion
Bad n *(phot)* bath
Badwill m badwill
Bädertank m *(phot)* developing tank, processing tank
Bahn f *paper* pack, web
Bahnabriß m *(paper)* breakage of the paper web
Bahnbreite f *(paper)* width of the web
Bahnhofsbuchhandel (BB) m *etwa* transit station book trade, station newsstand book trade, station kiosk book trade
Bahnhofsbuchhändler m station bookseller
Bahnhofsbuchhandlung f station bookstand, station bookshop, station kiosk
Bahnhofshallenwerbung f station display advertising, transit station display, depot advertising, depot display advertising
Bahnhofsplakat n station poster, transit station poster, depot display poster, station display poster, transportation display poster
    An advertising poster appearing on walls of stations or passenger platforms serving subway or surface rail lines.
Bahnhofswerbung f transit station advertising, station advertising, railway station advertising
    Advertising in stations and on passenger platforms of public transportation companies.
Bahnlänge f **der Walze** *(paper)* face length of the roll

Bahnsteigplakat n (**Perronanschlag** m, **Perronplakat** n) railroad platform poster, railway platform poster, track poster, cross tracks poster
Bajonettfassung f bayonet fitting, snap-on fitting
Bajonettsockel m bayonet socket, (Röhre) bayonet cap(BC)
Bajonettverschluß m *(phot)* bayonet mount, snap-on mount, bayonet connection
    A device used on some cameras to facilitate the exchange of lenses. The lens has prongs fitting into the camera, and a lever locks them in place from within.
Bakenantenne f beacon antenna, *brit* beacon aerial
Bakenfrequenz f *(Sat)* beacon frequency
bakterizider Packstoff m bactericidal packaging material
Balanceregelung f *(radio/TV)* balance adjustment
Balancetheorie f (Fritz Heider) theory of balance, balance theory
Balgen m *(phot)* bellows *pl* (*construed as sg or pl*)
    The folding portions which unite the front and back sections of process cameras.
Balgenkamera f *(phot)* bellows camera
Balgenkompendium n
→ Kompendium
Balken m *(print)*
Balkendiagramm n *(stat)* horizontal bar chart, bar chart
vgl. Stabdiagramm (Säulendiagramm)
Balkengeber m *(TV)* bar generator
Balkenüberschrift f banner headline, banner head, banner, ribbon, line screamer, streamer headline, streamer, (über mehrere Artikel) binder line, blanket headline, blanket head
    A large headline stretching over the top of one page.
Ballaströhre f ballast tube
Ballasttriode f ballast triode

Ballempfang m *(radio)* relay reception, rebroadcasting reception (RBR), rebroadcast
Ballempfänger m *(radio)* relay receiver, rebroadcast receiver, repeater receiver
Ballen m *(paper)* bale, ten reams *pl*
Ballenbrett n baling board
Ballenpresse f (für Abfälle) baler, baling press, scrap baler
Ballenumreifung f bale hooping, bale strapping
Ballonfrage f *(survey res)* balloon cartoon question
Ballonleinen n balloon linen
Ballontest m balloon test
Ballonwerbung f balloon advertising
Ballsendung f **(Relaisübertragung** f) *(radio)* relay broadcast, rebroadcast
Band n 1. (Ton-, Video-, Magnet-) tape 2. (Frequenzband) (frequency) band 3. (um Ballen) hoop 4. *(print)* tape
Bandabheber m tape lifter
Bandandruck m (MAZ) tape pressure
Bandandruckfehler m (MAZ) tape pressure fault
Bandantenne f *(radio)* tape antenna, band antenna, *brit* tape aerial, band aerial
Bandantriebswelle f drive capstan, drive shaft
Bandarchiv n tape library
Bandaufnahme f tape recording
Bandbearbeitung f *(radio/TV)* tape editing
Bandbegleitkarte f VT log
Bandbeitrag m tape insert, (Bild) VT insert
Bandbeschichtung f tape coating
Bandbreite f 1. *(econ)* spread, range, scope 2. *(radio)* band-pass width, bandwidth, frequency range
  The number of frequencies contained in one designated channel.
3. (Magnetband) tape width
Bandbreitenregler m *(radio)* bandwidth control
Bändchenmikrophon n (-mikrofon n) ribbon microphone
  A high-velocity microphone.
Banddiagramm n **(Bandgraphik** f, **Bänderschaubild** n, **Schichtenkarte** f) *(stat)* band chart, band graph, band curve chart
  An instrument of graphical representation used for comparing and summing the values or measures of a set of constituents or components over a period of time. The constituents or components are plotted above each other, so that the chart consists of a set of bands.
Bandenwerbung f etwa sports field advertising, advertising in sports fields
Banderole f package band, banderole
  A band wrapped around a retail package, frequently with an advertising message or a promotional offer printed on it.
Banderolenzugabe f **(Banderolengutschein** m, **Banderolenkupon** m) package band premium, banded premium, package band
  A package band that serves either as an advertising premium or a coupon.
Bandfehler m **(Bandfehlstelle** f) *(TV)* (MAZ) drop-out, tape error
  A horizontal television picture playback streak, reflecting a momentary lack of video information caused by irregularities on the tape surface when recording.
Bandfilter m **(Bandpaßfilter** m) *(radio)* band-pass filter, band pass, waveband filter
Bandfluß m tape flux
Bandführung f tape guide, tape guidance, (Bandführungsvorrichtung) tape guides *pl*
Bandgerät n tape recorder, tape machine, tape deck
Bandgeschwindigkeit f tape speed
Bandgeschwindigkeitsumschalter m speed selector
Bandkassette f tape cassette, tape cartridge
Bandkleber m taping machine, taper
Bandkontrollkarte f VT log
Bandkopie f tape copy
Bandlauf m tape run
Bandleitung f *(radio)* band lead, twin lead, ribbon feeder
Bandmikrofon n (-mikrophon n)
→ Bändchenmikrofon
Bandmusik f taped music, *colloq* canned music
Bandpaßfilter m
→ Bandfilter
Bandrauschen n tape noise
Bandreportage f *(radio)* recorded report, *colloq* canned report, (als Sendung) delayed broadcast, pre-recorded report
Bandriß m tape break

Bandsäge

Bandsäge f band saw, belt saw, ribbon saw
Bandschnitt m (**Bandschneiden** n) tape editing, tape edit
Bandsendung f *(radio/TV)* pre-recorded broadcast, pre-recorded program, brit programme, transmission of pre-recorded material, (zeitversetzt) delayed broadcast (DB)
Bandsperre f band-stop filter, band-rejection filter
Bandspieler m tape recorder
Bandspreizung f *(radio)* band spreading, band spread
Bandspule f tape reel, tape spool
Bandstahl m (für Stanz- und Rillformen) cutting and creasing rule, die rule
Bandteller m tape plate
Bandtransport m tape transport
Bandtransportrolle f capstan
Bandtrieb m tape drive capstan
Bandwickelfehler m *(phot)* cinch, cinch mark
Bandzählwerk n position indicator
Bandzuführung f tape feed
Bandzug m tape tension
Bandzugfeder f (**Breitfeder** f) broad-point pen
Bandzugregelung f regulation of tape tension
Bang-Tail-Rückumschlag m *(direct advtsg)* bangtail
BA-Regler m *(TV)* variable video attenuator
Bankenwerbung f (**Bankwerbung** f) bank advertising, advertising of banks
Bankmarketing n bank marketing
Bankpostpapier n bank paper, bank post
Bannerschlepp m banner trailing
Bargain-Store m (**Kaufhaus** n **für Gelegenheiten**) bargain store
Bargaining-Forschung f bargaining research
Barometertechnik f *(res)* barometer technique
barometrische Prognose f barometer forecast, barometer prognosis
Barpreis m cash price, cash rate
Barrabatt m (**Skonto** n) cash discount
  An allowance given by a seller to a buyer provided the invoice is paid within the time limits specified in the terms of sale. Its purpose is to induce quicker payment of the invoice.

Bartschatten m *(phot)* beard line
Barwert m (**einer Investition**) cash value (of an investment), cash equivalent, value in cash
Barytabzug m (**Barytpapierabzug** m) *(print)* reproduction proof, repro proof, repro pull
Barytpapier n (**Kreidepapier** n)
Barzahlungsnachlaß m (**Barzahlungsrabatt** m)
→ Barrabatt
Baseline f (**Unterzeile** f) base line, baseline
Basement Store m *(retailing)* basement store, auch budget store, budget department
  Any part of a store which specializes in merchandise priced to go easy on the budget of average consumers.
Basis f (**Basiswert** m) 1. *(stat/math)* base 2. *(econ)* basis
Basisbreite f stereo sound-stage width
Basisdaten n/pl *(stat)* base data pl, basic data pl
Basiseinspeisung f base feeding
Basiserhebung f (**Standarderhebung** f, **Strukturerhebung** f) standard survey, general survey, survey of structural data
Basisgewicht n
→ Ausgangsgewicht
Basislinie f *(stat)*
→ Grundlinie
Basismedium n basic advertising medium, primary medium
Basispanel n *(survey res)* basis panel
Basisperiode f (**Basiszeitraum** m) *(stat)* base period
  The period of time for which data used as the base of an index number or other ratio, have been collected. This period is frequently one of a year but it may be as short as one day or as long as the average of a group of years.
Basispreis m
→ Grundpreis
Basissortiment n basic assortment
vgl. Impulssortiment
Basisumkehrtest m (**Umkehrprobe** f **für Indexbasen**) *(stat)* base reversal test
  Usually applied for staple items, it is the assortment plan of items to be kept continuously on hand for a period usually of at least one year. Brand identification generally is of considerable significance. It includes a list of items to be carried in stock, reorder points, (→)

Bestellpunkt, and reorder quantities, (→)
Bestellmenge. Non-staple items can become basic while, for fashion or fad reasons, they enjoy intensified customer demand.
vgl. Zeit-Umkehr-Probe
Basiszeitraum m
→ Basisperiode
Basrelief n (**Flachrelief** n) *(print)* low relief, bas-relief
Baßanhebung f *(radio)* bass boost
Baßlautsprecher m low-frequency loudspeaker unit, *colloq* woofer
Baßregelung f bass control
Bastardschrift f (**Bastarda** f) *(typ)* bastard typeface, bastard type, bastard face, bastard
   An unusual typeface that does not conform to the standard font system.
Bastardformat n 1. *(print)* bastard size 2. → Flexformanzeige
Bastpapier n manila paper, manilla paper, manila, manilla
Batterie f
→ Fragenbatterie, Testbatterie
Batussi f *(studio)* baffle
Bau m **und Ausstattung** f *(studio)* scenery and furnishing
Baubühne f 1. (Raum) scenic dock 2. (Gruppe) scenery operatives *pl*, scene hands *pl*
Baubühnenarbeiter m scene hand
Bauch m *(typ)* belly
Bauchbinde f (**Bauchstreifen** m, **Bauchband** n) bookband, advertising band, advertising strip, jacket band, jacket flap, jacket blurb
Baueinheit f (Dekoration) scenic unit, solid piece, built piece
Bauelement n 1. component 2. (Dekoration) stage flat, flat
Baufluchtlinie f building line
Baufundus m scenery stock
Bauhöhe f hight of construction, construction depth, limiting height
Baukastensystem n modular design construction, unit construction principle, unitized construction principle, unit principle
Baulicht n *(studio)* working light, houselight
Baumanalyse f (**AID**, **Segmentation** f, **Kontrastgruppenanalyse** f) *(res)* tree analysis, Automatic Interaction Detection (AID), segmentation

Baumdiagramm n (**Kontrastgruppendiagramm** n) *(res)* tree diagram
→ Dendogramm
Bauordnungsrecht n building regulations *pl*
Bauten m/pl 1. setting, scenery 2. (Filmtitel) art direction
Bauzaun m *(outdoor advtsg)* hoarding, hoarding site, billboard
Bayes-Analyse f (**Bayes'sche Analyse** f) (Thomas Bayes) *(stat)* Bayesian analysis, Bayes analysis, Bayesian decision analysis
Bayes-Formel f (**Bayes'sche Formel** f) *(stat)* Bayes' formula, Bayesian formula
Bayes-Postulat n (**Bayes'sches Postulat** n) *(stat)* Bayes' postulate
Bayes-Regel f (**Bayes-Theorem** n) *(stat)* Bayes' theorem, Bayesian theorem
Bayes-Statistik f (**Bayes'sche Statistik** f) Bayesian statistics *pl (construed as sg)*
BB *abbr* Bahnhofsbuchhandel
BDG m *abbr* Bund Deutscher Grafik-Designer e.V.
BDP m *abbr* Berufsverband Deutscher Psychologen
BDS m *abbr* Bund Deutscher Schauwerber e.V.
BDVT m *abbr* Bund Deutscher Verkaufsförderer und Verkaufstrainer e.V.
BDW Deutscher Kommunikationsverband m *etwa* Association of German Communications Experts
BDZV m *abbr* Bundesverband Deutscher Zeitungsverleger
Beachtung f (**Beachtungswert** m) *(media res)* noting, noted score, noting claim
   The percentage or absolute number of respondents who recognize a particular advertisement or adpage when interviewed in a Starch test, (→) Starch-Test, irrespective of any other association or involvement with the content of the ad.
Beachtung f **pro Anzeige** *(media res)* ad noting, noting (of an advertisement), *brit* eyes open in front of advertisement (E.O.F.A.), noting per advertisement
Beachtungswert m **pro Seite** *(media res)* page traffic, reader traffic per

Beanschriftung

page, noting per page, reading/noting per page, noted score per page
Beanschriftung f
→ Adressierung
Beantwortung f
→ Antwort
bearbeiten v/t **1.** (Text) to adapt, to edit, to prepare **2.** (Auftrag) to handle, to process, to deal with, to work on **3.** *(phot/print)* to process, to treat **4.** *(music)* to arrange
Bearbeiter m **1.** (Text, Manuskript) adapter, revisor, editor **2.** (Auftrag) handler **3.** *(music)* arranger
Bearbeitung f **1.** (Text) adaption, adaptation, revision **2.** (Auftrag) handling, processing **3.** *(phot/print)* processing, treatment **4.** *(music)* arrangement
Bearbeitungsgebühr f *(econ)* handling charge, fee for handling
Bearbeitungshonorar n **1.** (Buch) adaptation fee **2.** (Musik) arranging fee
beauftragen v/t to commission, to charge, to instruct, to entrust
bebildern v/t to illustrate
Bebilderung f illustration
Becher m cup, mug, (aus Plastik) beaker
Bedarf m (**Nachfrage** f) *(econ)* demand
vgl. Bedürfnis, Kaufkraft
Bedarfsanalyse f (**Nachfrageanalyse** f) *(econ)* analysis of demand, demand analysis
Bedarfsartikel m (**Bedarfsgegenstand** m, **Bedarfsgüter** n/pl)
→ Gebrauchsgut, Convenience Goods
Bedarfsbeobachtung f observation of demand, demand observation
Bedarfsberater m (Erich Schäfer/ Hans Knoblich) *etwa* supply consultant
Bedarfsdeckung f *(econ)* supply, coverage of demand, supply of demand
Bedarfsdeckungsanalyse f *(market res)* analysis of household supply
Bedarfsdichte f
→ Nachfragedichte
Bedarfselastizität f
→ Nachfrageelastizität
Bedarfsfaktor m *etwa* factor of demand, demand factor, factor determining demand

Bedarfsfeld n (**Bedarfskomplex** m) *etwa* complementary goods pl
Bedarfsforschung f *etwa* research into demand, demand research
Bedarfsgebiet n
→ Nachfragegebiet
Bedarfsgegenstand m
→ Bedarfsartikel
Bedarfsgruppe f *(econ)* group of persons (households) with an identical demand structure
Bedarfsgüter n/pl
→ Bedarfsartikel
Bedarfshäufigkeit f *(econ)* frequency of demand, demand frequency
Bedarfsintensität f *(econ)* intensity of demand, demand intensity
Bedarfskennzahl f
→ Kaufkraftkennziffer
Bedarfslenkung f *(econ)* consumption control, consumer guidance, controlled distribution of supply
Bedarfslücke f
→ Marktlücke, Nachfragelücke, Marktnische
bedarfsorientiertes Fenster n *(POP advtsg) etwa* related-item display window, setting display window
Bedarfsprognose f
→ Nachfrageprognose
Bedarfsstruktur f (**Nachfragestruktur** f) *(econ)* structure of demand, demand structure
Bedarfsuntersuchung f
→ Nachfrageuntersuchung
Bedarfsverschiebung f
→ Nachfrageverschiebung
Bedarfsvorhersage f
→ Nachfrageprognose
Bedarfsweckung f (**bedarfsweckende Werbung** f)
→ Bedürfnisweckung (bedürfnisweckende Werbung)
bedeutsam adj *(attitude res)* salient
Bedeutsamkeit f **1.** *(attitude res)* (Stellenwert, Wichtigkeit) salience, *auch* saliency
   The importance of the topic or question to the respondent, as indicated by the thought that has been given to it by the respondent prior to the interview. Personal and family concerns are generally more salient than public issues.
2. *(stat)* → Signifikanz
Bedeutungsanalyse f
→ Inhaltsanalyse

Bedeutungsäquivalenz f (der Fragen im Fragebogen) *(survey res)* equivalence of meaning (of questionnaire questions)
Bedeutungslehre f
→ Semantik
bedienen v/t (Kunden) to serve, to attend to, to wait (upon)
Bediengerät n control device, control unit, control box
Bedienpult n control desk
Bedienung f **1.** (Service) service, counter service, service selling
  The activities of salespersons satisfying customer requirements, handing over merchandise, providing counsel, helping them choose products and retaining their goodwill.
2. (die Verkäufer) sales clerk, clerk, *brit* shop assistent **3.** (von Geräten) operation attendance, maintenance, control
Bedienungsanleitung f operating instructions *pl*, service instructions *pl*
Bedienungsaufschlag m extra charge for service, service charge
Bedienungsfeld n *(tech)* control panel
Bedienungsform f **(Bedienungssystem** n, **Verkaufsform** f) service system, type of service
vgl. Bedienung, Selbstbedienung, Teilselbstbedienung
Bedienungsgeschäft n (B-Geschäft n, **Bedienungsladen** m) *(retailing)* service shop, service retailer, service store
  A retail store in which buyers are served by sales clerks.
Bedienungsgroßhandel m service wholesaling
Bedienungsgroßhändler m service wholesaler, regular wholesaler
  A merchant selling to retailers, industrial users, and other wholesalers, and performing the usual complete services of such a merchant. These services include credit, delivery, redress for faulty or damaged merchandise, significantly large variety and assortment, information and education through salesmen, and assistance with dealer aids and displays.
Bedienungsknopf m control button, control knob
Bedienungspult n control desk
Bedienungsraum m control room, operations area, maintenance area
Bedienungsverkauf m
→ Bedienung 1.

Bedienungsvorschrift f operating instructions *pl*, service instructions *pl*
Bedienungswanne f studio console
bedrucken v/t **1.** to print on, to imprint on, to impress something with, to overprint **2.** (prägen) to stamp
Bedrucken n printing, imprinting, impressing, overprinting
Bedruckmaschine f overprinting machine
Bedruckstoff m (**Bedruckmaterial** n) printing stock
Bedürfnis n *(econ)* need, want
  The desire by an individual to possess an object, e.g. a product or a service. Also, the internal tension or forces that cause activity toward specific satisfaction.
vgl. Bedarf, Nachfrage
Bedürfnisausgleichsgesetz n
→ Gossensche Gesetze
Bedürfnisbefriedigung f *(econ)* satisfaction of needs, satisfaction of wants
Bedürfniserweckung f **(bedürfniserzeugende Werbung** f) want-creating advertising (John Kenneth Galbraith)
  Any advertising the central function of which it is to bring into being wants that previously did not exist.
Bedürfnisforschung f
→ Wohlfahrtsforschung
Bedürfnishierarchie f (Maslowsche Bedürfnishierarchie f) hierarchy of needs, Maslow's hierarchy of needs (Abraham H. Maslow)
  The theory that all behavior is the result of unsatisfied needs which create tension, (→) Bedürfnisspannung, and then activity to satisfy them. Maslow has defined a five-level hierarchy: (1) Physiological needs, or those most basic, necessary to sustain life and well-being; (2) Safety needs, or protection from the world around us, physical and mental security; (3) Social needs, or love, friendship, companionship, and acceptance by others; (4) Esteem needs, or recognition, self-confidence, self-respect, appreciation; (5) Self-actualization needs, or the fulfillment of one's potential in life.
Bedürfnismatrix f matrix of needs
Bedürfnispyramide f
→ Bedürfnishierarchie
Bedürfnisreduktion f (**Bedürfnisreduzierung** f) *(psy)* need reduction
Bedürfnissättigungsgesetz n
→ Gossensche Gesetze

Bedürfnisspannung

Bedürfnisspannung f *(psy)* need tension
→ Bedürfnishierarchie
Bedürfnisweckung f
→ Bedürfniserweckung
Beeinflussung f
→ Einfluß
Beeinflußbarkeit f persuasibility, suggestibility, influenceability
Beeinflusser m *(econ)* influencer (Philip Kotler)
Beeinflussung f **(Beeinflussungswirkung** f) persuasion, influence
  Any communication process with the aim of changing a person's opinion, attitude or behavior with respect to some object. In marketing, the development in a person of the desire to acquire the perceived benefit of a product or a service.
→ Einfluß
befeuchten (anfeuchten) v/t to damp, to dampen, to humidify, to moisten, to wet
Befeuchter m humidifier, spray dampener, spray damp
Beflockung f **(Velourtierung** f) flocking
Before-after-Design n **(Before-after-Experiment** n)
→ Experiment in der Zeitfolge
Befragter m **(Auskunftsperson** f, **Respondent** m) *(survey res)* respondent, interviewer, informant
  The individual interviewed or subjected to test in marketing and advertising research.
Befragung f **(Interview** n) *(survey res)* sample survey, survey, interview, poll
Befragung f **am Kaufort** *(market res)* point-of-purchase interview, POP interview, intercept interview
Befragungsexperiment n *(survey res)* survey experiment
Befragungsgespräch n
→ Interview
Befragungsmethode f **(Befragungstechnik** f, **Interviewtechnik** f) *(survey res)* interview technique, interviewing technique
Befragungsstrategie f *(survey res)* interviewing strategy
Befragungstaktik f *(survey res)* interviewing tactics pl *(construed as sg)*
Befragungstyp m *(survey res)* type of interviewing technique

Befragungszeit f *(survey res)* time of interviewing, duration of interview
Befund m finding, findings pl, data pl
beglaubigte Auflage f certified circulation, audited circulation, (beglaubigte Nettoverkaufsauflage) audited net circulation, audited net sale
begleitende Werbung f **(flankierende Werbung** f) tie-in advertising
  Any advertising effort made in addition to the basic advertising campaign.
→ Referenzwerbung
Begleitmaterialien n/pl *(advtsg)* tie-ins pl, tie-in material
Begleitmusik f incidental music, accompanying music
Begleittext m 1. accompanying text, accompanying copy 2. *(radio/TV)* exposition, narration, accompanying script, (Nachrichten) dope sheet
Begleitton m
→ Echoton
Begleitung f *(music)* accompaniment
Begrenzer m *(radio)* limiter, clipper
Begrenzung f *(radio)* limiting, clipping
Begriffsabgrenzung f **(Begriffsbestimmung** f)
→ Definition
begründende Werbung f reason-why advertising, reason why, reason-why approach, factual approach, long-circuit appeal
  An advertising statement or advertisement offering specific, objectively stated arguments in support of claimed benefits.
begründender Werbetext m reason-why copy
Begründungszusammenhang m (Arnold Brecht) context of justification
vgl. Entdeckungszusammenhang
Begutachtung f
→ Gutachten
behalten v/t to remember, to retain, to keep (in mind)
Behalten n remembrance, retention
Behaltensprüfung f
→ Erinnerungsprüfung
Behälter m **(Behältnis** n) Am container, brit case, box, (für Flüssigkeiten) tank, vessel, fountain
Behaviorismus m *(psy)* behaviorism, brit behaviourism
behavioristisch adj behavioristic, brit behaviouristic

Behinderung f (**Behinderung** f von **Konkurrenten, Behinderungswettbewerb** m) *etwa* hindrance of competitors, obstruction of competitors
Behördenhandel m
→ Belegschaftshandel
Behördenrabatt m
→ Großverbraucherrabatt
Behörden- und Belegschaftshandel m
→ Belegschaftshandel
Beiblatt n (**Beilagenzettel** m) inserted leaf, enclosed leaf, insert, loose insert, stuffer, newspaper stuffer, stuffer
  A separately printed, unbound section of a periodical that is tucked into its regular pages.
beidseitig beschichtet (beidseitig gestrichen) *adj* double-coated
Beifilm m *(Kino)* supporting film, featurette, B picture, short subject
Beiheft n 1. supplement 2. special issue, theme issue
Beihefter m (**Einhefter** m, **Durchhefter** m) bound insert, bound-in insert, (in der Mitte des Bogens eingeheftet) inset, (in den Bogen gesteckt) wrap, (außen) outside wrap, outsert, (innen) inside wrap, (Beikleber) tip-in
  A separately printed section of a magazine or an advertisement that is bound into its regular pages.
Beikleber m (**Einkleber** m) tip-in
  A separately printed advertising page or card that is pasted into a magazine either by a strip of paste along one edge or, if the insert is folded, along the edge of the fold.
Beilage f (**Werbebeilage** f) loose insert, insert, (vom Inserenten vorgedruckt) pre-print insert, preprint, (Endlos-Farbbeilage) continuous roll insert, hifi insert, *brit* wallpaper
  A separate advertising sheet or folder that is tucked into the regular pages of a periodical.
→ Fremdbeilage, Verlegerbeilage
Beilagenhinweis m insert notice
Beilagenzettel m
→ Beiblatt
beilegen *v/t* to insert, to attach, to enclose
Beipack m (**Packungsbeigabe** f, **Packungsbeilage** f) (Innenbeilage) package insert, insert, insert, in-pack, stuffer, package enclosure, (als Zugabe) in-pack premium, container premium, factory-pack premium, boxtop offer (Außenbeilage) package outsert, outsert, out-pack, zip ad, (Beipack von Werbedrucksachen) envelope stuffer
  Advertising material or a premium either put into or onto a package, frequently to promote a different product, or containing printed instructions explaining the operation and care of the product (Beipackzettel).
Beiprogramm n *(film)* supporting program, *brit* supporting programme
Beirat m advisory board, advisory panel
Beischaltblatt n outsert, zip ad
  Separate printed matter attached to the outside of a package.
Beißen n
→ Reflexlicht
Beiwerk n accessories *pl*, embellishments, *pl, colloq* frills *pl*, (überflüssiges Textbeiwerk) padding
Beize f 1. *(phot)* (Flüssigkeit) mordant, (Bad) mordant bath 2. *(print)* aqua fortis, etchant
beizen
→ ätzen
Beizendruck m *(phot)* mordant printing
Bekanntgabe f announcement, public announcement, pronouncement
bekanntgeben *v/t* to announce, to make public, to make known, to divulge, to proclaim
Bekanntheit f (**Bekanntheitsgrad** m, **Bewußtheit** f) *etwa* awareness, (einer Marke) brand awareness, (der Werbung) advertising awareness
→ aktiver Bekanntheitsgrad, passiver Bekanntheitsgrad
Bekanntheitsgradmessung f measurement of awareness, (einer Marke) measurement of brand awareness, (eines Produkts) measurement of product awareness, (der Werbung) measurement of advertising awareness
Bekanntmachung f announcement, public announcement, public notice, (schriftlich) notification
Beklebemaschine f pasting machine, (in der Wellpappenanlage) combiner, double facer, double backer, double facing unit
Beklebepapier n lining paper

bekleben v/t to paste, to paste over, (Plakat an die Wand) to paste a poster on something, to post a poster on something, to stick a poster on something, (eine Flasche mit einem Etikett) to label a bottle, to paste a label on a bottle
Beklebepapier n lining paper, pasting paper
Beklebezettel m gummed label, stick-on label, paste-on label
Bekräftigungstheorie f
→ Verstärkerhypothese
belästigende Werbung f (**Belästigung** f) badgering, molestation, molesting advertising
Beleg m (**Belegexemplar** n, **Belegstück** n) 1. (econ) (Quittung) voucher, receipt 2. (media) (Vollbeleg) checking copy, voucher copy, voucher (Agenturbeleg) agency copy, advertising agency copy, (Beleg für den Werbungtreibenden) advertiser's copy, (Korrespondentenbeleg) correspondent's copy, (Autorenbeleg) author's copy (Einzelbeleg) tear sheet, tearsheet
  A copy of a publication delivered to an agency, correspondent or advertiser to verify insertion of an advertisement or an article as ordered or agreed upon.
Belegheft n
→ Beleg (Vollbeleg)
Beleggleser m (EDP) optical reader
Belegnummer f
→ Beleg
Belegschaftshandel m (**Behörden- und Belegschaftshandel** m) (econ) company trade, company trading
Belegschaftsladen m (**Industrieladen** m) company store, company-owned store, industrial store, commissary store
  A retail store which sells exclusively to the employees of the company or governmental unit which owns it. It is usually owned and operated by a company or governmental unit to sell primarily to its employees. Many of these establishments are not operated for profit. The matter of the location of the control over and responsibility for these stores rather than the motive for their operation constitutes their distinguishing characteristic.
Belegseite f (**Einzelbeleg** m) tear sheet, tearsheet
  A single page upon which an advertisement appears, torn or cut out of

publications, sent to the client as proof of insertion.
Belegstück n
→ Beleg
Belegung f (**von Werbezeiten, Werbeflächen, Anzeigenraum**) booking, placing, (Anzeigenraum) space buying, (Plakatflächen) posting, space buying, (Werbezeit in Hörfunk und Fernsehen) air-time buying, time buying
Belegungskombination f (**Mediakombination** f) combination buy, (obligatorisch) forced combination, forced combination buy
  A special-rate purchase of advertising space or time either offered or required by two or more advertising media, often newspapers, magazines or broadcasting stations, usually under the same ownership or just collaborating in the field of advertising.
→ Kombinationsrabatt, Kombinationstarif
Belegungsdauer f
→ Anschlagdauer
beleuchten v/t to illuminate, to light, to light up
Beleuchter m (film/TV) studio electrician, lighting electrician, lighting man, colloq spark
Beleuchterbrücke f (**Beleuchterbühne** f) (film/TV) lighting bridge, gantry
Beleuchterfahrzeug n (film/TV) lamp trolley
Beleuchtergalerie f (film/TV) lighting gallery
Beleuchtergang m (film/TV) gallery, catwalk
Beleuchtertrupp m (film/TV) lighting crew, colloq sparks pl
Beleuchtung f (**Beleuchten** n) (phot/film/TV) illumination, lighting, (Geräte) lights pl, light fittings pl, lighting equipment, lighting installation, (mit Schlagschatteneffekt) lighting with hard-shadow effect
Beleuchtungsanlage f (phot/film/TV) lighting equipment, lighting installation
Beleuchtungsdienst m (film/TV) lighting department
Beleuchtungseinrichtung f
→ Beleuchtungsanlage
Beleuchtungsfeuer n (film/TV) beacon
Beleuchtungskontrast m (phot/film/TV) lighting contrast

Beleuchtungskörper m *(phot/film/TV)* lighting unit
Beleuchtungslinse f *(phot/film/TV)* illumination lens, condenser, *colloq* bull's eye
Beleuchtungsmaterial n *(phot/film/TV)* lighting equipment
Beleuchtungsmeister m *(film/TV)* lighting supervisor
Beleuchtungspult n **(Lichtregelanlage** f, **Lichtsteuerpult** n**)** *(film/TV)* lighting-control console
Beleuchtungsrampe f **(Lichtrampe** f**)** *(film/TV)* float(s) *(pl)*, footlights pl, footlight
Beleuchtungsraum m **(Lichtsteuerraum** m**)** *(film/TV)* lighting control room
Beleuchtungsreflektion f *(phot/film/TV)* catchlight, flare, camera flare, flare spot, lens flare
  Catchlights are reflections in a subject's eye that come from the light sources used for illumination. Flare is the appearance of a circular disc of light in the center of photographic images when viewed on a focusing screen, the defect due either to optical errors in the camera lens or to mechanical causes. The condition known as "camera flare" is due to scattered light within the apparatus and causes fogged images, particularly in the shadow areas of halftone negatives.
Beleuchtungsscheinwerfer m *(film/TV)* basher, scoop, camera light, floodlight
  A 500-watt circular floodlight.
Beleuchtungsstärke f *(phot/film/TV)* lighting level, lighting intensity, (als Meßgröße) lux
Beleuchtungsstärkemessung f *(phot/film/TV)* measurement of lighting level, measurement of lighting intensity, lux measurement
Beleuchtungssteuerung f **(Lichtregelung** f, **Lichtregie** f**)** *(film/TV)* lighting control
Beleuchtungsumfang m *(phot/film/TV)* lighting-level range, range of lighting level
Beleuchtungsverhältnis n *(phot/film/TV)* lighting contrast ratio
Beleuchtungswerkstatt f lighting workshop
Beleuchtungstechnik f **(Beleuchtungswesen** n, **Lichttechnik** f**)** lighting, light engineering, lighting engineering

belichten *(phot)* v/t + v/i to expose
Belichtung f *(phot)* exposure
  The action of light upon the sensitive film. It is a function of time, controlled by the camera shutter and of intensity, controlled by the lens aperture. The necessary exposure will vary with the prevailing lighting conditions, type of subject, and the sensitivity of the film.
Belichtungsangaben f/pl *(phot)* exposure data pl
Belichtungsanzeige f *(phot)* exposure indicator
  A device attached to plate-holders to show that the plate has been exposed.
Belichtungsautomat m *(phot)* automatic exposure control, (Dunkelkammeruhr) darkroom timer, automatic exposure timer, *(print)* (im Lichtsatz) photo unit
Belichtungsautomatik f *(phot)* automatic exposure control
Belichtungsfaktor m
  → Verlängerungsfaktor
Belichtungsindex m *(phot)* exposure index
Belichtungsintensität f *(phot)* intensity of exposure to light
Belichtungskeil m *(phot)* sensitometric step wedge, step wedge, step tablet
  The length of a motion picture negative for processing control. Each frame is progressively darker.
Belichtungsmesser m **(Lichtmeßgerät** n**)** *(phot)* exposure meter, lightmeter, light meter, photometer
  An electrical or optical device that measures the amount of light reflected from or directed on a subject. This is done by converting or translating light energy to exposure units, thus indicating lens aperture, (→) Blende, and shutter speed, (→) Verschlußgeschwindigkeit.
Belichtungsmessung f **(Lichtmessung** f**)** *(phot)* measurement of exposure, photometry
Belichtungsprobe f *(phot)* exposure test
Belichtungsrechner m *(phot)* exposure calculator
Belichtungsregler m **(Belichtungsregelung** f**)** *(phot)* exposure control
Belichtungsreihe f
  → Blendenreihe
Belichtungsschablone f *(phot)* punched tape
Belichtungsschaltuhr f *(phot)* exposure timer

Belichtungsspielraum m (phot) latitude of exposure, latitude, range of exposure, exposure latitude
    The range of exposures, from underexposure to overexposure, that still produces an acceptable picture.
Belichtungssteuerung f
→ Belichtungsregelung
Belichtungstabelle f (phot) exposure table, exposure chart, exposure scale
Belichtungsuhr f
→ Belichtungsschaltuhr
Belichtungsumfang m (phot) exposure ratio
→ additive Belichtung
Belichtungswert m (phot) exposure value (EV)
→ additive Belichtung
Belichtungszeit f (phot) exposure time, period of exposure, exposure period
Belohnung f
→ Anreiz
bemalte Anschlagwand f (bemalter Anschlag m, Hausbemalung f) (outdoor advtsg) painted bulletin, painted display, painted wall
    An outdoor panel on which an advertisement is manually painted on a wall or a bulletin structure.
bemalter Bus m
→ Rundumbemalung
bemustern v/t (econ) to supply samples (of), to attach samples, to sample
Bemusterung f (econ) sampling, supply of samples
    The technique by means of which a market is exposed to new products, packages, or package sizes through the sending or giving to prospects of a miniature or an actual unit.
Bemusterungsgroßhandel m sample wholesaling, sample wholesale trade
→ Katalogladen; vgl. Lagergroßhandel, Streckengroßhandel
benetzbar adj (phot/print) wettable
Benetzbarkeit f (phot/print) wettability
benetzen v/t (phot/print) to wet, to moisten, to sprinkle
Benetzungsmittel n (phot/print) wetting agent
    A chemical substance which reduces the surface tension of a liquid, thereby promoting smoother and more uniform results when added to photographic solutions.

Benutzer m
→ Nutzer
Benutzergruppe f (Btx) user group, (abonnierte Benutzergruppe) syndicated closed user grup, (geschlossene Benutzergruppe) closed user group, (private Benutzergruppe) private closed user group
Benutzungsanalyse f
→ Nutzwertanalyse
beobachten v/t to observe
Beobachter m observer
Beobachtung f (Beobachtungsmethode f, wissenschaftliche Beobachtung f) observation, observational method
→ strukturierte Beobachtung, nichtstrukturierte Beobachtung, direkte Beobachtung, indirekte Beobachtung, teilnehmende Beobachtung, nichtteilnehmende Beobachtung, Laboratoriumsbeobachtung, Feldbeobachtung, offene Beobachtung, verdeckte Beobachtung, biotische Beobachtung, nichtbiotische Beobachtung, persönliche Beobachtung, unpersönliche Beobachtung, Fremdbeobachtung, Selbstbeobachtung
Beobachtungsabstand m observation distance
Beobachtungseffekt m (res) observation effect, observation bias
Beobachtungsexperiment n (res) observation experiment
Beobachtungsfehler m (res) observation error, (systematischer Fehler) observation bias
Beobachtungsgenauigkeit f accuracy of observation, observational accuracy
Beobachtungslernen n, **Imitationslernen** n, **Modellieren** n (Albert Bandura) (psy) observational learning, modeling
Beobachtungsmethode f (res) observational method, method of observation
Beobachtungsplan m (Beobachtungsschema n) (res) observation schedule, observation plan
Beobachtungsprotokoll n (res) observation protocol
Beobachtungszeitraum m period of observation, observation period

Bequemlichkeitsbedarf m **(Kleinbedarf** m, **Bedarfsgüter** n/pl) convenience goods pl
→ Convenience Goods
beratender Ingenieur m consulting engineer
Berater m adviser, *auch* advisor, counselor, *brit* counsellor, consultant
Beraterhonorar n service fee
Beratung f advice, counsel, consultancy
→ Marketingberatung, Werbeberatung
Beratungsagentur f
→ Marketingberater, Werbeberater
Beratungsfirma f consulting agency
Beratungsvertrag m
→ Werbevertrag
berechnen v/t **1.** to compute, to calculate **2.** *(print)* (Satzumfang) to cast off, to cast, to copycast
Berechnung f **(Berechnen** n, **Kalkulation** f) *(print)* (des Satzumfangs) casting off, copycasting, copy fitting, fitting copy, copy scaling
berechnete Auflage f *(Zeitung/Zeitschrift)* invoiced circulation
Berechtigungsschein m *(econ)* (im Kaufscheinhandel) warrant, certificate
Bereich m *(radio)* band
Bereichsantenne f *(radio)* band antenna, *brit* area aerial
Bereichssperrkreis m *(radio)* band-stop filter
Bereichsumschalter m *(radio)* band selector
Bereichsverstärker m *(radio)* band amplifier
bereinigte Stichprobe f *(stat)* adjusted sample, corrected sample
Bericht m report, account, (Zeitungsbericht) newspaper report
berichten v/t to report (on)
Berichterstatter m reporter, newsman, newspaperman, *brit* pressman, *(radio/TV)* reporter, commentator
Berichterstattung f coverage, news coverage, reporting, report
berichtigen v/t to correct
Berichtigung f correction
Berichtigungsanzeige f **(Gegendarstellungsanzeige** f) corrective advertisement, corrective ad
  An advertisement designed to correct an erroneous or misleading impression conveyed in an earlier advertisement.
Berichtigungswerbung f corrective advertising
Berichtsperiode f **(Berichtszeitraum** m) *(stat)* (bei der Indexbildung) given period
vgl. Basisperiode
Berliner Format n *etwa* tabloid size, tabloid-size newspaper
  One of three German standard newspaper sizes, the Berlin size being the smallest one. The dimensions of its type area measure 410 × 275 millimeters (minimum) and 440 × 310 millimeters (maximum).
vgl. Nordisches Format, Rheinisches Format
Berner Übereinkunft f Berne Convention, Convention of Berne
Bernouillis Gesetz n **der großen Zahlen** (Jakob Bernouilli) *(stat)* Bernouilli's law of large numbers
Bernouilli-Polynom n **(Bernouillisches Polynom** n) (Jakob Bernouilli) *(stat)* Bernouilli polynomial
Bernouilli-Streuung f **(Bernouilli-Variation** f, **binomiale Streuung** f) (Jakob Bernouilli) *(stat)* Bernouilli variation
Bernouilli-Stichprobe f **(Bernouillische Stichprobe** f) *(stat)* Bernouillian sample
Bernouilli-Theorem n **(Bernouilli-Prinzip** n, **Bernouillisches Theorem** n, **Bernouillischer Lehrsatz** m (Jakob Bernouilli) Bernouilli's theorem, Bernouilli theorem
Bernouilli-Zahlen f/pl **(Bernouillische Zahlen** f/pl) (Jakob Bernouilli) *(stat)* Bernouilli numbers pl
Berücksichtigungsfeld n (Philip Kotler) *(econ)* consideration frame, brand set, evoked set
→ relevante Vergleichsprodukte
Beruf m occupation, trade, *colloq* job
Berufsfachzeitschrift f
→ Berufszeitschrift
Berufsgruppe f **(Berufsklasse** f, **Berufskategorie** f) occupational class
Berufsgruppenzeitschrift f horizontal magazine, horizontal paper, horizontal publication
  A business or trade periodical that covers the interests or activities of a number of different trades or industries and does

Berufs-Interessen-Test

not cater to one single business interest and function.
→ Berufszeitschrift; *vgl.* Branchenzeitschrift
Berufs-Interessen-Test *m* **(BIT)** *(psy)* occupational interest test
Berufsklassifizierung *f* **(berufliche Gliederung** *f,* **Berufsgruppengliederung** *f*) occupational classification
Berufsprestige *n* occupational prestige
Berufsprestige-Skala *f* occupational prestige scale
Berufspresse *f*
→ Berufszeitschrift
Berufsschicht *f*
→ Berufsgruppe
Berufsstatistik *f* occupational statistics *pl (construed as sg)*
berufstätig *adj* gainfully employed, economically active, working, employed
Berufstätiger *m* gainfully employed person, economically active person, employed person
Berufstätigkeit *f* gainful employment, employment, economical activity
Berufsverband *m* (**Berufsvereinigung** *f*) professional association, professional organization, *brit* organisation
Berufsverband *m* **des Rundfunkgewerbes** broadcast trade organization, *brit* organisation
Berufsverband *m* **Deutscher Markt- und Sozialforscher e.V. (BVM)** Professional Association of German Market and Social Researchers
Berufswahl *f* occupational choice, choice of an occupation, vocational choice
Berufszeitschrift *f* (**Berufsfachzeitschrift** *f*) professional journal, professional magazine, (Zeitung) professional newspaper, professional paper, (Publikation) professional publication, horizontal magazine, horizontal paper, horizontal publication
→ Berufsgruppenzeitschrift; *vgl.* Branchenzeitschrift
berühmte Marke *f* famous brand
Berühmtheit *f* (**berühmte Persönlichkeit** *f*) celebrity
beschädigen *v/t (print)* to batter (the type)

beschädigte Letter *f* (**beschädigte Type** *f*) *(print)* battered type
beschädigtes Plakat *n* (**beschädigter Anschlag** *m*) *(outdoor advtsg)* damaged poster
Beschaffenheitsangaben *f/pl*
→ Gattungsbezeichnung
Beschaffung *f (econ)* buying, procurement, acquisition, corporate purchasing
 The marketing function consisting of the efficient acquisition of materials and services for the operation of a business. It comprises the determination of the suitability of goods, the proper price, an adequate source, an economic order and inventory quantities.
Beschaffung *f* **von Investitionsgütern** *(econ)* procurement of investment goods
Beschaffungsentscheidung *f (econ)* buying decision, corporate purchasing decision
Beschaffungsentscheidungsprozeß *m (econ)* buying decision making, process of making buying decisions
Beschaffungsfunktion *f (econ)* buying function, procurement function
→ Beschaffung
Beschaffungskooperation *f (econ)* cooperative buying group, cooperative buying, buying cooperation, buying syndicate, supply cooperative, supply cooperation
 A cooperative mainly concerned with buying products its members need and reselling these to them.
Beschaffungsmarketing *n* supply marketing, procurement marketing
Beschaffungsmarkt *m (econ)* supply market
Beschaffungsmarktanalyse *f* analysis of supply market, supply market analysis
Beschaffungsmarktbeobachtung *f* observation of supply market, supply market observation
Beschaffungsmarktforschung *f* research into the supply market, supply market research
Beschaffungsmenge *f (econ)* supply, quantity of supply
Beschaffungsorganisation *f (econ)* organization of supply, *brit* organisation of supply, supply organization
Beschaffungsplan *m (econ)* supply plan, procurement plan

Beschaffungsplanung f *(econ)* supply planning, procurement planning
Beschaffungspolitik f
→ Beschaffungsmarketing
beschaffungspolitisches Instrumentarium n **(beschaffungspolitische Instrumente** n/pl*) etwa (econ)* instruments pl of supply policy, instruments pl of supply marketing
Beschaffungsprogramm n *(econ)* supply program, *brit* programme, procurement program, buying program
Beschaffungs- und Vorratspolitik f
→ Marketinglogistik
Beschaffungsverhalten n *(econ)* buying behavior, *brit* behaviour, procurement behavior, organizational buying behavior, *brit* organisational buying behaviour
Beschaffungsweg m *(econ)* supply channel, buying channel, procurement channel
Beschaffungswerbung f *(econ)* supply advertising, procurement advertising
Beschaffungsziel n *(econ)* supply objective, procurement objective, buying objective
beschallte Anzeige f sound advertisement, sound ad
Beschallungsanlage f
→ Lautsprecheranlage
beschichten v/t to coat
beschichteter Karton m coated board
Beschichtung f *(phot/print)* coating, backing, emulsion layer, (außerhalb der Maschine) off-machine coating, (innerhalb der Maschine) on-machine coating, (durch Extrusion) extrusion coating, (durch Eintauchen) dip coating, (mittels Schlepprakel) trailing blade coating, (mit gravierten Walzen) gravure coating, (zum Verhindern des Gleitens) antislip surfacing, non-skid coating, non-slip coating, (zum Verhindern des Haftens) release coating
Beschichtungsmaschine f coating machine, coater, (nach dem Extrudierverfahren) extrusion coater, coating machine
Beschichtungsstoff m coating
beschildern v/t
→ plakatieren
Beschilderung f
→ Plakatierung

Beschneidebank f *(print)* dressing bench, rule cutter
Beschneidelinie f *(print)* trimming line
Beschneidemaschine f *(paper)* trimming machine, trimmer, cutter
beschneiden v/t *(print)* to trim, to cut, to exact size
→ anschneiden
Beschnitt m
→ Anschnitt
Beschnitt m **im Bundsteg**
→ Anschnitt
beschnitten
→ angeschnitten
Beschnittgröße f **(Größe** f **nach Beschnitt)** *(print)* trim size
  The size of a page after the surplus edges required in printing are trimmed off.
Beschnittkante f
→ Anschnittkante
Beschnittrand m *(print)* bleeding, bleed border, bleed margin, trim edge
→ Anschnittrand
Beschnittsteg m *(print)* side stick, side margin
Beschnittzugabe f *(print)* bleed difference, trim
Beschnittzuschlag m *(advtsg)* additional charge for bleeding, bleeding surcharge
Beschreibungsmodell n
→ deskriptives Modell
beschriften v/t to label, to letter, to mark, to ticket
Beschriftung f labeling, lettering, marking, *brit auch* labelling
Beschwerde f
→ Reklamation
beschwertes Kraftpapier n filled kraft paper
Besenkeil m *(TV)* wedge, resolution wedge, (Testbild) test wedge
besetzen *(film/TV)* v/t (Rollen) to cast (the parts), to choose the cast, to cast (a film)
Besetzung f **(Rollenbesetzung** f**)** *(film/TV)* casting, cast
Besetzungsbüro n *(film/TV)* booking section, artists' bookings pl
Besetzungsdirektor m **(Besetzungsleiter** m**)** *(film/TV)* casting director
  The executive responsible for auditioning and selecting talent for parts in radio or TV programs.

Besetzungskartei

Besetzungskartei f (**Besetzungsliste** f) (film/TV) artists' index, artists' file, cast list
bespielen v/t to record, to make a recording of, to record something (on tape)
Besprechungsexemplar n (**Besprechungsstück** n) review copy, reviewer's copy, press copy
Bespurung f (**Bespurungsverfahren** n) (film) striping, striping process
 The process of coating a film print with a narrow oxide band for track recording on single-system playback.
Bestandsaufnahme f (**im Haushalt**)
→ Speisekammertest
Bestandsaufnahme f **nach dem Kauf** inventory taking, stock taking
Bestandsaufnahme f **in Testläden**
→ Ladentest
Bestandsmanagement n (econ) stock management, inventory management, inventory control
Bestandsprüfung f (econ) audit, stock check, inventory control, shop audit
 The use of a system or mechanism to maintain stocks of goods at desired levels. Such control is usually exercised to maintain stocks that are (a) representative in that they include all the items the customer group served expects to be able to buy from the firm involved, (b) adequate in that a sufficient quantity of each item is included to satisfy all reasonably foreseeable demands for it, and (c) economical in that no funds of the firm are held in inventory beyond those needed to serve purposes (a) and (b) and in that it facilitates savings in costs of production.
Bestätigung f
→ Auftragsbestätigung
Bestellabschnitt m (**Bestellgutschein** m) order coupon, order slip
Bestellbuch n
→ Auftragsbuch
Bestellbrief m order letter
bestellen v/t to order, to book
Besteller m
→ Abonnent, Käufer
Bestellformular n order form, order blank
Bestellkarte f order card, reply card
Bestellkosten pl (econ) ordering costs pl, cost per order (cpo)
 The total cost incurred in placing orders.
Bestellkupon m
→ Bestellabschnitt

Bestellmenge f (econ) order quantity, order size
 The quantity of product units ordered.
(**optimale**) economic order quantity (EOQ)
 The number that minimizes the total cost of placing an order and of holding the item in inventory.
Bestellnummer f (econ) order number, order code
Bestellpunkt m (econ) reorder point
 In inventory management, the point at which reordering becomes necessary to avoid stockouts.
Bestellpunktverfahren n (**Bestellpunktmodell** n) (econ) reorder point system, economic order quantity (EOQ) model, EOQ model
 A system of inventory management to determine the point in time at which reordering becomes necessary.
Bestellschein m
→ Bestellformular
Bestellung f (econ) order
Bestellvertrag m
→ Werkvertrag
Bestellzeitpunkt m (econ) reorder time, reorder period
Bestellzettel m
→ Bestellabschnitt
Bestimmtheitskoeffizient m (**Bestimmtheitsmaß** n) (stat) coefficient of determination
 The square of the correlation coefficient.
 vgl. Korrelationskoeffizient
bestoßen v/t to plane, (Druckstock) to dress
Bestoßhobel m (print) dresser, trimming plane, shaving plane
bestrahlen v/t
→ anstrahlen
Bestseller m bestseller
Besuch m (Vertreterbesuch, Interviewerbesuch) call, (Kino) attendance, audience attendance
Besucher m
→ Kinobesucher
Besucherbefragung f 1. (Kino) survey of movie-goers, interviews pl among moviegoers, survey of cinema-goers, interviews pl among cinema-goers 2. (Messen und Ausstellungen) survey among trade fair attendants, interviews pl among trade fair attendants
Besucherfrequenz f **der Filmtheater** frequency of movie-theater

attendance, frequency of cinema attendance
Besucherzahlen *f/pl* **(in Filmtheatern)** movie-theater attendance, movie-theater audience figures
Besucherzählung *f* (Messen und Ausstellungen) count of trade fair attendants
Besuchsauswertung *f* (Vertreter) call analysis, post call analysis
   The study of a sales representative's customer calling patterns.
Besuchsbericht *m* (Vertreter) call report
→ Vertreterbericht
Besuchseffizienz *f* (Vertreter) order/call ratio
Besuchserfolgskontrolle *f* (Vertreter) post call analysis, analysis of call effectiveness
→ Besuchsauswertung
Besuchshäufigkeit *f* (Vertreter) call frequency
   The frequency with which sales representatives visit or contact customers or prospects.
Besuchsplan *m* (Vertreter) call schedule, call frequency schedule, *brit* journey plan
Besuchsplanung *f* (Vertreter) call scheduling, *brit* journey planning
Besuchsquote *f* (Vertreter) call rate
   The number of personal contacts or visits a sales representative makes with customers or prospective customers within a given period of time.
Besuchswahrscheinlichkeit *f (media res)* (Kino) probability of movie attendance, probability of movie-theater attendance, *brit* probability of cinema-attendance
Beta-Koeffizient *m* (β-**Koeffizient** *m*) *(stat)* beta coeffient, β coefficient
Beta-Fehler *m* (β-**Fehler** *m*)
→ Fehler 2. Art
Betamax *m* betamax
beteiligte Verkehrskreise *m/pl*
→ Verkehrsauffassung
Beteiligungsmedium *n* (**Beteiligungsprogramm** *n*, **Beteiligungssendung** *f*) audience-participation medium, participation medium, audience-participation program, *brit* programme, audience-participation broadcast, participation program, participation broadcast

A medium, usually a radio or television broadcast, which depends on the participation of its audience.
Beteiligungsuntersuchung *f* (**Beteiligungsumfrage** *f*) *(survey res)* tack-on survey, tack-on investigation, multi-client survey, multi-sponsor survey
vgl. Mehrthemenumfrage
betiteln *v/t* (mit einem Titel versehen) to title, to entitle, (Kapitel) to head
Betitelung *f* title, heading, head
Betrachter *m* (**Betrachtungsgerät** *n*) *(phot)* (für Dias) viewer, table viewer, viewing cabinet
   An illuminated desk, table or cabinet whereon colorfilm transparencies and photographic images can be viewed and examined by transmitted light.
Betrachtungsabstand *m* viewing distance
Betrachtungsschirm *m* viewing screen, oscilloscope screen
Betrachtungswinkel *m* view angle, viewing angle
Betrachtungszeit *f (media res)* noting time, reading time, time spent reading
→ Lesedauer
betreiben *v/t* (Werbung)
→ treiben
Betreuungsbesuch *m*
→ Besuch
betriebliche Marktforschung *f* (**interne Marktforschung** *f*) *etwa* company-based market research, company market research
vgl. Institutsmarktforschung
Betriebsanalyse *f (econ)* operational analysis
Betriebsanleitung *f* (**Betriebsanweisung** *f*) operation instruction(s) *(pl)*, operating instruction(s) *(pl)*
→ Gebrauchsanweisung
Betriebsartenschalter *m (radio)* function selector switch, selector switch, mode selector
Betriebsartenwahl *f (radio)* function selection
Betriebsbeobachtung *f (econ)* operational observation
Betriebsberatung *f* industrial consultation, managerial consultation, business consultation
Betriebserde *f (radio)* service earth, operational earth
Betriebsfernsehen *n* (**Drahtfernsehen** *n* **für begrenzten Teilnehmerkreis**)

Betriebsform

closed-circuit television (CCTV, C.C.T.V.), closed-circuit TV, non-broadcast television, non-broadcast TV, narrowcasting
   A television signal limited to an immediate area, e.g. a classroom, building, a cable system, etc. Signals are transmitted via wire, not over-the-air.
Betriebsform f **(Betriebstyp** m) *(econ)* etwa type of company, type of business, type of firm
Betriebsfrequenz f *(radio)* operating frequency, nominal frequency, working frequency
Betriebsführung f
→ Management
Betriebsgröße f *(econ)* company size, size of company
Betriebshandel m **(Betriebs- und Belegschaftshandel** m**)**
→ Belegschaftshandel, Kaufscheinhandel
Betriebshandelsspanne f
→ Handelsspanne
Betriebskosten pl *(econ)* operating expenses pl, working costs pl, running costs pl
Betriebsleitung f
→ Management
Betriebsmittel n/pl *(econ)* operation stock, working material, working stock, working capital, working funds pl
Betriebsoszillograph m *(radio)* service oscilloscope
Betriebsspanne f
→ Handelsspanne
Betriebsstatistik f business statistics pl *(construed as sg)*, industrial statistics, company statistics
Betriebssystem n operating system
Betriebstechnik f engineering operations pl and maintenance, *(TV)* television engineering operations, *(film)* film operations pl
Betriebstyp m
→ Betriebsform
Betriebstypendynamik f
→ Dynamik der Betriebsformen
Betriebsvergleich m *(res)* interfirm comparison, inter-company comparison
Betriebswirtschaftslehre f business administration, business economics pl *(construed as sg)*, business management

Betriebszeitschrift f company magazine, company journal, internal house organ, house organ
→ Werkzeitschrift
Betriebszeitung f company newspaper, company paper, internal house organ, house organ
→ Werkzeitung
betrügerische Werbung f fraudulent advertising
Bett n
→ Druckformbett, Formbett
Beugung f (des Lichts) diffraction, ray diffraction
Beugungsstrahl m diffracted ray
Beugungswinkel m diffraction angle
Beurteilung f
→ Evaluierung
Beurteilungsstichprobe f *(stat)* judgment sample, *brit auch* judgement sample
vgl. bewußte Auswahl
Beurteilungstest m **(Beurteilungsverfahren** n**)** discrimination test
Beutel m bag, sack
Beutelblitz m
→ Kapselblitz
Beutelverschließgerät n bag sealer
Bevölkerungshochrechnungsfaktor m *(media res)* population projection factor
   The factor by which audience percentages ascertained in sample surveys are transformed into absolute population numbers.
Bevölkerungsschicht f social class, population stratum
Bevölkerungsstichprobe f **(Bevölkerungsumfrage** f**)**
→ repräsentative Stichprobe
bevorzugte Plazierung f **(Plazierungsvorschrift** f**)** (einer Anzeige) preferred position, premium position, special position
   Any advertisement position in publications for which the advertiser must pay a premium when specifically ordered.
Bevorzugung f **(einer Marke)**
→ Markenpräferenz
Bevorzugungstest m
→ Präferenztest
bewegliche Requisite f *(film/TV)* hand prop
Bewegtbildübertragung f *(TV)* transmission of moving pictures, moving picture transmission,

transmission of motion pictures, motion picture transmission
vgl. Festbildübertragung
Bewegung f movement, motion
Bewegungsaufnahme f *(film/TV)* moving shot, action shot
→ Fahrtaufnahme, Kamerafahrt
Bewegungsprobe f *(film/TV)* (Zeichentrick) animatic, animatic test, limited animation, limited animation test, mechanical animation, mechanical animation test
bewerben v/refl (sich bewerben) to apply (for), (um einen Auftrag) to make a bid, to submit a tender, to tender
Bewerber m **(Bewerberin** f**)** applicant, (bei Kaufangeboten) bidder, (bei Ausschreibungen) tenderer
Bewerbung f application, (bei Kaufangeboten) bid, (bei Ausschreibungen) tender
bewerten v/t to evaluate, to appraise, to assess
Bewertung f evaluation, appraisal, assessment
→ Evaluierung, Produktbewertung
Bewertungsmatrix f
→ Produktbewertung
Bewertungsmethode f
→ Evaluierung
Bewertungsmuster n evaluative pattern, pattern of evaluation
Bewertungsphase f (bei Innovationen) evaluation stage, evaluation phase
Bewertungsschema n **(für neue Produkte)**
→ Produktbewertung
Bewertungsverhalten n (von Konsumenten) evaluative behavior, *brit* behaviour, evaluation behavior
Bewirtung f **(Bewirtungskosten** pl**)** expenses pl
bewußte Auswahl f *(stat)*
1. (Stichprobe) purposive sample, non-random sample, non-probability sample **2.** (Verfahren) purposive sampling, non-random sampling, non-probability sampling
  A sampling technique in which the individual sample units are selected by some purposive, and therefore, nonrandom method.
vgl. Zufallsauswahl
bewußter Hauptleser m **(bewußter Erstleser** m**)** (Jean-Michel Agostini)

(media res) intentional primary reader
Bewußtseinsschwelle f *(psy)* limen
Bezahlfernsehen n
→ Münzfernsehen
bezahlte Auflage f
→ Verkaufsauflage
beziehen v/t (Waren) to get, to be supplied with, to obtain, to buy, (Zeitung/Zeitschrift) to subscribe to, to take (in), to have a subscription (for, to)
Bezieher m **1.** (von Waren) buyer, customer **2.** (Zeitung/Zeitschrift) subscriber, buyer
Bezieheranalyse f analysis of subscribers, subscriber study
Bezieherkartei f **(Bezieherliste** f**)** mailing list, list of subscribers
Bezieherwerber m
→ Abonnementswerber
Bezieherwerbung f
→ Abonnementswerbung
Beziehungsanalyse f
→ Relationsanalyse
Beziehungshandel m **(Beziehungskauf** m**)** direct sale (of wholesalers or producers) to private households
Beziehungslinie f *(stat)*
→ Regressionslinie (Regressionsgerade)
Beziehungszahl f **(Beziehungskennziffer** f**)** *(stat)* quotient, rate
→ Kennzahl
Bezirksausgabe f **(Regionalausgabe** f **)** (Zeitung) regional issue, regional edition, regional market issue, local issue, local edition, local market issue
  An edition of a newspaper distributed within one regional or local market.
Bezirksprovision f
→ Gebietsprovision
Bezirksschutz m
→ Gebietsschutz
Bezirksvertreter m
→ Gebietsvertreter
Bezirksvertretung f
→ Gebietsvertretung
Bezug m **1.** (Waren, Dienstleistungen) buying, purchase, ordering **2.** (Periodikum) subscription
bezugnehmende Werbung f etwa advertising using personal reference to competitors (or to competitors' brands), direct-comparison advertising

Bezugsband *n (TV)* calibration tape, standard tape, standard magnetic tape, test tape, reference tape, line-up tape
Bezugsbedingungen *f/pl* 1. *(econ)* terms *pl* of delivery, delivery conditions 2. (Zeitungen/Zeitschriften) subscription terms *pl*
Bezugsbindung *f*
→ Absatzbindung
Bezugsdauer *f* (bei Abonnements) subscription period
Bezugsgeld *n* (bei Abonnements) subscription fee
Bezugsgenerator *m (radio)* reference generator, standard signal generator
Bezugsgenossenschaft *f*
→ Einkaufsgenossenschaft
Bezugsgruppe *f (soc)* reference group
Bezugsjahr *n (stat)* base year
→ Basisperiode
Bezugskante *f (radio)* reference edge
Bezugsoszillator *m (radio)* reference oscillator
Bezugspegel *m (radio)* reference level
Bezugsperiode *f* (**Bezugszeitraum** *m*) *(stat)* base period
→ Basisperiode
Bezugsperson *f (soc)* reference person
Bezugsphase *f* reference phase
Bezugspreis *m* 1. *(econ)* purchase price, advertised price 2. (bei Abonnements) subscription rate, subscription price
Bezugspunkt *m* (**Richtwert** *m*, **Richtgröße** *f*) benchmark, reference point
Bezugsquelle *f (econ)* source, source of supply
Bezugsquellennachweis *m* (**Bezugsquellenverzeichnis** *n*) list of suppliers, directory of suppliers
Bezugsschwarz *n (TV)* reference black
 The darkest part of a television picture.
Bezugsspannung *f* reference voltage
Bezugsstoff *m*
→ Einbandmaterial
Bezugssystem *n* (**Bezugsrahmen** *m*) reference system, frame of reference
Bezugsweiß *n (TV)* reference white
 The brightest part of a television picture.
Bezugswert *m (stat)* base
BFF *m abbr* Bund Freischaffender Foto-Designer e.V.
Bias *m*
→ systematischer Fehler

Bibeldruckpapier *n* (**Bibelpapier** *n*) Bible paper, India paper, India
Bichromat *n* (**Dichromat** *n*) bichromate
bichromatisch (**bichrom, zweifarbig**) *adj (print)* bichrome
Bichromatkolloid *n (print)* bichromated colloid
Bichromatkolloidverfahren *n (print)* chromatype
Bichromatkopie *f (print)* chromatype
bichromatischer Fischleim *m (print)* bichromate fish glue
Bierdeckel *m* beer mat, drip mat, beer coaster
Bierdeckelwerbung *f* (**Bierfilzwerbung** *f*) advertising on beer drip mats, advertising of beer coasters, advertising on beer mats
Bierwerbung *f* beer advertising, advertising for beer
bikonkav *adj (phot)* concavo-concave, biconcave
Bikonkav-Linse *f* (**Zerstreuungslinse** *f*) *(phot)* concavo-concave lens, biconcave lens
bikonvex *adj (phot)* convexo-concave, biconvex
Bikonvex-Linse *f* (**Sammellinse** *f*) *(phot)* convexo-convex lens, biconvex lens
Bild *n* 1. picture, (gedruckt) print, illustration 2. *(phot)* photo, photograph, picture, (auf dem Film) frame, (Papierbild) print 3. (reproduktionstechnisch) image 4. (Szene) scene, take 5. → Bildzeichen
Bildablenktransformator *m (TV)* frame-scan transformer
Bildablenkung *f (TV)* frame scan, picture scan, vertical sweep
Bildabtaster *m (TV)* scanner, scanning device, television scanning device, television scanner
Bildabtastung *f (TV)* picture scanning, image scanning
Bildabzug *m*
→ Papierphoto
Bildagentur *f* (**Photoagentur** *f*) picture agency, photo agency
Bildamplitude *f (TV)* picture amplitude
Bildandruck *m* (**Klischeeandruck** *m*) *(print)* illustration proof, picture proof, repro proof

Bildanpaßmonitor m *(TV)* picture matching monitor
Bildanzeige f illustrative ad(vertisement), illustrated ad(vertisement), pictorial ad(vertisement)
Bildarchiv n picture library, photo library, picture archives *pl*, photo archives *pl*, picture files *pl*, photo files *pl*, art library
Bildarchivar m picture librarian
Bild-Assoziationstest m
→ Assoziationstest
Bildauflösung f **(Auflösungsvermögen** n) *(print/phot/film/TV)* picture resolution, picture definition, resolving power
→ Auflösung
Bildaufnahme f *(phot/film/TV)* take, shot, picture recording, visual recording, video recording
Bildaufnahmeröhre f *(TV)* camera tube, pick-up tube, image pick-up tube, iconoscope, vidicon, image orthicon, orthicon, (Markenname) Plumbicon
Bildaufnahmewagen m
→ Aufnahmewagen
Bildaufzeichnung f picture recording, picture record, image recording, image record, visual recording, vision recording, *(TV)* kinescope recording, kine, film transfer, television recording (TVR), video recording, transfer
Bildaufzeichnungsgerät n *(TV)* telerecorder, television recording equipment, video recorder
Bildausfall m *(TV)* blackout, image blackout, image dropout, vision break
Bildausgangssignal n *(TV)* picture output signal
Bildauskippen n *(TV)* line tearing, line pulling
Bildausreißen n *(TV)* picture break-up
Bildausschnitt m 1. detail 2. *(phot)* cropping 3. *(film/TV)* image area, picture area, camera shot, view
Bildausschnittsmarkierung f *(phot/print)* crop mark
  A line or any other mark on a photograph indicating where it is to be cropped.
Bildausschnittsucher m *(film/TV)* director's finder, gonoscope
Bildaussteuerung f *(TV)* picture control

Bildaustastsignal n **(BA-Signal** n) *(TV)* picture and blanking signal, blanked picture signal, video signal without sync pulse
Bildaustastsynchronsignal n **(BAS-Signal** n) *(TV)* composite signal, composite video signal, composite picture signal
Bildaustastsynchronsignal n **mit Prüfzeile (BASP-Signal** n) *(TV)* composite video signal with insertion test signal, *colloq* composite signal with test line
Bildband n *(TV)* videotape, *(film)* film strip, (Kopierwerk) grading strip; Bildband und Tonband auf gleiche Länge ziehen: to sync up, to lip-sync, to bring into lip sync
Bildbandarchiv n video tape library, tape store
Bildbandbreite f video tape bandwidth, picture bandwidth
Bildbandgerät n video tape recorder (VTR), video tape machine
Bildbandkassette f video tape cassette, video tape cartridge
Bildbandkassettengerät n cassette video tape recorder
Bildbegrenzung f *(film)* framing, *(TV)* frame limiting
  The subject area recorded by a camera.
Bildbeilage f **(Bilderbeilage** f) (einer Zeitung) illustrated supplement, pictorial supplement (Tiefdruckbeilage) roto section, rotogravure supplement
Bildbericht m photoreport, picture report, photographic report, picture story, pictorial record, pictorial report
Bildberichterstatter m (Presse) photo reporter, photo journalist, press photographer, *colloq* still man, *(TV)* cameraman, news cameraman
Bildberichterstattung f (Presse) photo journalism, photo reporting, picture coverage, visual coverage, *(TV)* television coverage, visual coverage
Bildbetrachter m (für Dias) film viewer, slide viewer, viewer, *Am* editola
Bildbreitenregler m *(TV)* width control
Bildbrumm m *(TV)* picture hum
→ Brumm
Bilddauer f *(film)* frame duration, picture duration

Bilddauerleitungsnetz n permanent vision network
Bilddetail n (Bildausschnitt m) picture detail, image detail, detail
Bilddiagramm n (stat) pictorial diagram, pictogram
  Any pictorial representation of statistical data.
Bilddruckstock m
→ Klischee
Bild-Dup n
→ Dup-Negativ, Dup-Positiv
Bilddurchlauf m (TV) frame roll, picture roll, picture slip
Bildebene f (Kamera) image plane, (Objektiv) focal plane
Bildeinstellung f 1. focusing, *auch* focussing, image focusing **2.** framing, centering-up
Bildeinzelheit f
→ Bilddetail
Bildelement n pictorial element, visual element
Bild-Endkontrolle f final picture quality check, picture quality check
Bild-Enttäuschungstest m (Rosenzweig-Test m, Rosenzweig-P.F.-Test m) (Paul Rosenzweig) *(psy)* picture-frustration test, Rosenzweig test, Rosenzweig picture frustration test, Rosenzweig P.F. test
Bilder n/pl pro Sekunde (film) frames *pl* per second(fps), pictures *pl* per second(pps)
  The speed with which a film runs through the camera or the projector gate.
Bilderbogen m (print) picture sheet
Bilderdienst m
→ Bildagentur, Bildarchiv
Bilderdruck m (Illustrationsdruck m) 1. picture printing, art printing **2.** picture print, art print
Bilderdruckpapier n (Illustrationsdruckpapier n) art paper, art matt paper, art mat paper, art matte paper
Bilderergänzungstest m (Bildlückentest m) *(psy)* picture completion test
Bilderheft n
→ Comic-Heft
Bilderscheck m picture check, picture premium check
Bildertest m (Bildertestverfahren n) picture probe, picture test, picture test technique
Bildfang m (Bildfangregler m) (TV) hold control, framing control, frame hold, vertical hold, vertical lock

Bildfeld n (phot/film) image field, image area, picture area, field of vision, field of view, frame, picture screen
  The amount of the scene recorded on the sensitive film, usually expressed as an angle. A normal camera lens will embrace a field of view of about 45°.
  (TV) picture screen, frame
Bildfeldgröße f (phot/film) width of the field
  The horizontal size of a picture.
Bildfenster n film gate, picture gate, gate, (Kamera) camera aperture, (Projektor) projection aperture, projection gate
Bildfensterabdeckung f (Bildfenstereinsatz m) film gate mask, (Kamera) taking mask
Bildfensterplatte f (phot) aperture plate
Bildfernsprechen n (Bildtelefonie f) picture telephony, video telephony
Bildfernsprecher m (Bildtelefon n) picture telephone, video telephone
Bildfilm m picture film
Bildfläche f (film) picture screen, screen
Bildfolge f sequence of pictures, sequence of frames, series of pictures, series of frames
Bildfolgefrequenz f picture repetition frequency, scanning rate, number of frames per second
Bildformat n size of a picture, picture size, dimension of picture, frame size, image size, aspect ratio(AR), picture ratio, picture shape
  The relationship of width to height of any picture.
Bildfortschaltzeit f film sequencing time, film pulldown time, pulldown period
Bildfrequenz f (TV) (Vollbild) picture frequency, (Teilbild) vertical frequency, field frequency, *(film)* frame frequency
Bildfrequenzkanal m (Fernsehkanal m) video channel
Bildführung f
→ Kameraführung
bildfüllend adj full-frame
Bildfunk m (Bildtelegraphie f, Photofax n, Bildfernübertragung f) picture telegraphy, facsimile broadcasting (fax broadcasting),

facsimile transmission, picture
transmission
　The transmission of words or pictures by
　radio.
Bildfunkempfänger *m* facsimile
receiver, picture receiver
Bildfunkgerät *n* (**Bildfunktelegraph**
m, **Photofax** *n*) facsimile telegraph
Bildfunksender *m* (**Bildgeber** *m*)
picture transmitter, facsimile
transmitter, TV vision transmitter
Bildfunkstrecke *f* vision radio link
Bildfunkübertragung *f*
→ Bildfunk
Bildgeber *m* facsimile transmitter,
picture transmitter
Bildgeometrie *f* picture geometry
Bildgestaltung *f* picture composition,
pictorial composition
Bildgleichlaufimpuls *m* *(TV)* picture
synchronising pulse, vertical
synchronising pulse
Bildgröße *f* size of a picture, picture
size
Bildgüte *f* (**Bildqualität** *f*) picture
quality, quality of a picture
Bildhelligkeit *f* picture brightness,
brightness of an image
Bildhintergrund *m* picture
background, background of a picture
Bildhöhe *f* picture height, image
height, frame height
Bildhöhenregler *m* height control
Bildideengestalter *m* (**Layouter** *m*,
Visualizer *m*) visualizer
　An advertising creative whose
　responsibility consists of outlining
　visualizations of advertising and/or
　marketing strategies or campaigns.
Bildideengestaltung *f* (**Layouten** *n*,
Visualisierung *f*) visualizing
　The creative process of developing
　sketches and outlines of advertising and/
　or marketing strategies or campaigns.
Bild-in-Bild-Technik *f* *(TV)*
composite-shot technique, side-by-
side shot technique, split-screen
technique
Bildinformation *f* picture information
Bildingenieur *m* *(TV)* vision control
engineer, senior television engineer,
video engineer
Bildinhalt *m* picture content, content
of a picture
Bildintermodulation *f* *(TV)* crossview
Bildjournalismus *m*
→ Photojournalismus

Bildjournalist *m*
→ Photojournalist, Pressephotograph
Bildkante *f* picture edge, frame edge
Bildkarte *f*
→ Fensterkarte
Bildkassette *f* (**Videokassette** *f*) video
tape cassette, video tape cartridge
Bildkennung *f* *(TV)* picture
identification, picture I.D., vision
identification, identification caption,
station identification, station I.D.
→ Senderkennung
Bildkippen *n* *(TV)* frame roll, picture
roll, loss of picture lock
Bildkippgerät *n* *(TV)* frame sweep
unit
Bildkomposition *f* *(phot)* picture
composition, pictorial composition
Bildkontrast *m* (**Kontrast** *m*) *(phot)*
image contrast, picture contrast,
contrast
Bildkontrolle *f* (**Bildüberwachung** *f*)
(TV) picture control, vision control,
video monitoring, picture monitoring
Bildkontrolleitung *f* *(TV)* vision
control circuit, video monitoring
circuit
Bildkontrollempfänger *m* *(TV)* vision
check receiver, picture monitor,
monitor, picture monitoring receiver,
television monitor
Bildkontrollgerät *n* *(TV)* picture and
waveform monitor
Bildkontrollraum *m* *(TV)* vision
control room
Bildkontur *f* picture contour
Bildkopie *f* copy, print
Bildkorrekturzeichen *n* *(print)*
picture proofmark, picture
proofreaders' mark, proofreaders'
mark for pictures
Bildkreis *m* *(phot)* covering power
　The capacity of a lens to give a sharply
　defined image to the edges of the plate it
　is designed to cover, when focused with
　the largest stop opening.
Bildlage *f* frame position, picture
position
Bildlegende *f*
→ Bildunterschrift
Bildleitung *f* (**BL**) *(TV)* video circuit,
vision circuit
Bildleitungsnetz *n* *(TV)* vision
network, vision circuit network
Bildlinie *f* *(phot)* focal line, image line

Bildmarke f (**Bildzeichen** n) logograph, logo, picture trademark, pictorial trademark
Bildmaske f framing mask, film-gate mask
Bildmaterial n (**Anschauungsmaterial** n, **Illustrationsmaterial** n) picture material, visual material, illustrations pl, visual material, pictures pl, visual aids pl
Bildmischer m (**Videomixer** m) *(TV)* 1. (Gerät) video mixer 2. (Person) vision mixer, vision switcher
Bildmischpult n (**Bildmischer** m) *(TV)* video mixer, video mixing desk, video monitoring and mixing desk
Bildmischung f (**Bildmischen** n, **Videomischen** n) *(TV)* video mixing, vision mixing
Bildmitte f (**Bildmittelpunkt** m) 1. *(phot/film)* center of frame 2. *(TV)* center of picture; aus der Bildmitte setzen: to off-center the picture, to compose off center, *brit* off centre; in die Bildmitte setzen: to frame to center, *brit* to centre
Bildmonitor m *(TV)* vision check receiver, picture monitor, monitor, picture monitoring receiver, television monitor
Bildmontage f (**Photomontage** f, **Filmmontage** f, **Montage** f) *(phot)* montage, picture montage, photomontage
Bildmuster n/pl (**Bildkopien** f/pl) *(film/phot)* picture rushes pl, rushes pl, daily rushes pl, dailies pl
Bildnachweis m (**Quellenangabe** f **für Illustrationen**) *(print)* illustration credits pl, photo credits pl
Bildnegativ n *(phot)* picture negative, negative picture, negative
Bildnegativbericht m negative report
Bildoperateur m *(film/TV)* camera control operator
Bildoriginal n *(phot)* picture original, original of a picture
Bildpegel m *(TV)* picture level
Bildpegeländerung f *(TV)* change of picture level
Bildpegelschwankung f *(TV)* fluctuation of picture level
Bildpegelsprung m *(TV)* sudden change of picture level, sudden picture-level change
Bildperiode f picture period

Bildplakat n *(outdoor advtsg)* picture poster
Bildplatte f (**Videoplatte** f) *(TV)* video disk, videodisk, video disc, videodisc
   A disc of phonograph record size on which video and audio signals are recorded for playback only in consumers' homes.
Bildpositiv n *(phot)* picture positive, positive picture, positive
Bildpostkarte f picture postcard
Bildpresse f illustrated press, picture press, picture papers pl, picture magazines pl, illustrated papers pl, illustrated magazines pl, tabloid papers pl, tabloids pl
Bildprojektor m still projector, overhead projector, (für Dias) slide projector, (für Papierbilder) opaque projector, episcope
Bildprojektion f still projection, overhead projection, projection of pictures, picture projection
Bildpunkt m image point, picture point, *(TV)* scanning point, scanning spot, picture element
Bildpunktebene f *(phot)* focal plane
   The position in the camera on which the lens is sharply focused and occupied by the film or plate.
Bildpunktfrequenz f *(TV)* video frequency, picture point frequency, scanning point frequency, vision frequency
Bildpunktzahl f *(TV)* number of picture points, number of scanning points, number of scanning spots, number of picture elements
Bildqualität f quality of (the) picture, picture quality, (beim Druck) quality of reproduction, reproduction quality
Bildquellenverzeichnis n
→ Bildnachweis
Bildrand m *(phot/print)* margin of (the) image, picture margin, *(TV)* contour
Bildrandverschärfer m *(TV)* contour correction unit
Bildraster m (**Raster** m) *(TV)* raster, picture raster
→ Raster
Bildrauschen n (**Grieß** m, **Schnee** m) *(TV)* picture noise, video noise, granulation effect, *colloq* sand, snow
   An extraneous picture signal interference.
Bildrechte n/pl reproduction rights pl, copyright

Bildredakteur m picture editor, photo editor
Bildreflektion f *(phot)* burn
Bildregie f *(TV)* vision control, video control
Bildregiepult n *(TV)* vision control desk
Bildregieraum m *(TV)* vision control room
Bildregisseur m
→ Regisseur
Bildregler m *(TV)* fader, vision fader, video attenuator
Bildreportage f picture feature, picture story
Bildreporter m press photographer, photojournalist, *colloq* stills man, *(TV)* TV reporter
Bildröhre f **(Fernsehbildröhre** f, **Fernsehröhre** f**)** picture tube, television tube, tube, (Kathodenstrahlröhre) cathode-ray tube, *Am* kinescope
Bildrücklauf m **(Rückwärtsgang** m**)** *(film/TV)* picture flyback, frame flyback, reverse motion, return movement, rewind, reverse shot (RevS)
Bildschallplatte f
→ Bildplatte
Bildschaltraum m *(TV)* vision switching center m, *brit* centre
Bildschärfe f *(phot)* picture definition, image definition, (Randschärfe) picture sharpness, image sharpness, (Auflösung) picture resolution, image resolution, *colloq* pluckiness
Bildscherz m *obsol*
→ Cartoon
Bildschirm m screen, television screen, picture screen, video display screen, display screen
Bildschirmformat n **(Bildseitenverhältnis** n**)** aspect ratio (AR), screen size, picture aspect ratio
The relationship of width to height of a television screen.
Bildschirmgerät n **(Bildschirmterminal** m, **Bildsichtgerät** n**)** *(TV)* video display terminal (VDT), video display unit, video display screen
Bildschirmspiel n
→ Videospiel
Bildschirmtelefon n **(Bildtelefon** n**)** videotelephone, videophone, picture telephone, visphone

Bildsignal

Bildschirmtext m **(Btx)** video text, *brit* viewdata, *(TM)* Prestel
The display of textual information on a specially adapted television set. Information is transmitted via conventional telephone lines from a computer data bank. It has two-way capability.
Bildschirmtext-Informationsabruf m message retrieval, retrieval
Bildschirmtextseite f video text frame, frame
Bildschirmtext-Seitenkennziffer f video text frame number, frame number
Bildschirmtext-Seitennutzungszahl f video text frame count, frame count
Bildschirmtext-Seitenpreis m video text frame charge, frame charge
Bildschirmtext-Zentrale f retrieval center, *brit* centre
Bildschirmübertragung f **(Fernsehübertragung** f**)** television transmission
Bildschirmzeitung f electronic newspaper, newspaper on the air, vidnews *pl (construed as sg)*, (Eigennamen) Ceefax, Oracle
Bildschnitt m **(Lichtschnitt** m, **Filmschnitt** m**)** 1. (Tätigkeit) cutting and editing, picture cutting and editing, (beim Film) film cutting and editing, (beim Fernsehen) vision switching
The arrangement of picture scenes already on film into a desired sequence, timing and synchronization with the sound track.
2. (einzelner Schnitt) cut, picture cut, (beim Film) film cut, (beim Fernsehen) vision switch
The transition from one motion picture or television scene to another.
Bildschramme f *(phot/film)* scratch, film scratch
Bildschreiber m
→ Bildfunkgerät
Bildschritt m **(Filmschritt** m**)** frame gauge, frame pitch
Bildschwarz n *(TV)* picture black
Bildscript n *(film/TV)* camera script
Bildseitenverhältnis n
→ Bildschirmformat
Bildsender m
→ Bildfunksender
Bildsignal n **(B-Signal** n, **Videosignal** n, **Tonsignal** n**)** *(TV)* video signal, picture signal, vision signal, modulation signal, (mit Austast- und

Bildsignalabgleich 78

Synchronsignal) picture and blanking signal, blanked picture signal, video signal without sync pulse
Bildsignalabgleich m *(TV)* video adjustment
Bildsignalverstärkung f *(TV)* video gain, picture signal gain, video signal gain
Bildsortiertest m **(Bilderreihentest** m, **Bilderordnungstest** m) *(res)* picture arrangement test
Bildsprung m **(Sprung** m) *(film/TV)* jump, break of picture sequence, (Schnitt) jump cut
Bildspur f **(Videospur** f) *(TV)* video track
Bildstand m *(TV)* picture steadiness, picture stability
Bildstandfehler m *(TV)* picture instability
Bildstandschwankung f *(TV)* picture jitter
Bildstärke f *(typ)* point size
Bildstart m **(Startmarkierung** f, **Bildstartmarke** f) *(film/TV)* picture start, picture start mark, sync cross, *colloq* envelope
Bildsteg m *(phot)* spacing, picture spacing, *(TV)* frame bar, *(film)* frame line, rack line
Bildstern m **(Bildsternpunkt** m) *(TV)* vision switching center, *brit* centre
Bildsteuersender m *(TV)* vision pilot frequency, video pilot frequency
Bildsteuerung f **(Bildkontrolle** f)
1. camera mixing 2. picture control, video control, video monitoring, vision control
Bildstock m *(print)*
→ Klischee
Bildstörung f *(TV)* picture interference, picture disturbance, picture breakdown, vision interference, vision disturbance, vision breakdown
Bildstreifen m
1. → Bildspur
2. → Cartoon
Bildstrich m *(phot/film)* frame line
Bildstricheinstellung f *(phot/film)* framing
Bildstruktur f picture structure, structure of (the) picture, picture grain
Bildsucher m *(phot)* viewfinder, finder

An eyepiece for observing what is being photographed through the camera lens and thus facilitating aiming.
bildsynchron adj *(film/TV)* picture-phased, in-sync, in-synchronization
Bildsynchronimpuls m *(TV)* frame sync, frame synchronization pulse, vertical synchronization pulse, vertical sync pulse
Bildsynchronisation f *(film/TV)* frame synchronization, picture synchronization, *brit* synchronisation, vertical hold
Bildtäuschung f
→ optische Täuschung
Bildtechnik f *(TV)* video engineering
Bildtechniker m *(TV)* video engineer, vision controller
Bildtelefon n
→ Bildschirmtelefon
Bildtelefonie f picture telephony, video telephony
Bildtelegramm n picture telegram, phototelegram, wire photo
Bildtelegraph m picture telegraph, picture transmission, facsimile broadcast (fax broadcast), facsimile transmission
Bildtelegraphie f
→ Bildfunk
Bildtext m
→ Bildunterschrift
Bildton m *(phot)* tone
Bild-Ton- adj picture-and-sound, audiovisual
Bild-Ton-Kamera f *(film/TV)* double-headed camera
Bild-Ton-Platte f picture-and-sound disc, picture-and-sound disk
Bild-Ton-Synchronisierung f
→ Lippensynchronisierung
Bild-Ton-Versatz m *(TV)* (beabsichtigt) sound track advance, sound advance, sync advance, (unbeabsichtigt) slippage of sound to picture
Bildträger m 1. *(TV)* video carrier, vision carrier, picture carrier 2. *(phot)* film strip carrier, slide carrier
Bildträgerfrequenz f *(TV)* vision frequency, video frequency
Bildüberblendung f **(Bildüberblenden** n) *(film/TV)* cross fade, cross fading, dissolve, lap dissolve, mix, mix-through, superimposure, superimposition, super-imp

A television control technique by which a picture on the air is gradually faded out as a picture from another camera is comes into full view.
Bildüberblendzeichen n *(film/TV)* changeover cues *pl*, cue dots *pl*, cue marks *pl*
Bildübersprechen n *(film/TV)* crossview
Bildübertragung f **1.** → Bildfunk **2.** *(TV)* picture transmission, video transmission
Bildüberwachung f
→ Bildkontrolle
Bild- und Tonschaltraum m *(TV)* vision and sound switching area, central apparatus room (CAR)
Bildungsfernsehen n educational television (ETV, E.T.V.), educational TV
Bildungsfunk m **(Bildungshörfunk** m**)** educational broadcasting, educational radio
Bildungsgrad m level of education, educational level, formal education
Bildungsprogramm n educational program, *brit* programme
Bildunterkleber m film tape join, perforated transparent tape
Bildunterschrift f **(Bildtext** m**, Bildlegende** f**, Bildzeile** f**)** *(print)* caption, cut line, cutline, underline, legend
The explanatory text accompanying an illustration.
Bildverdrängung f *(film/TV)* picture displacement
Bildverschiebung f *(film/TV)* image shift
Bildverstärker m *(TV)* video amplifier
Bildverstellung f (Projektor) picture framing
Bildverzeichnis n
→ Abbildungsverzeichnis
Bildverzerrung f *(phot)* picture distortion, image distortion
Bildvorlage f
→ Original, Reproduktionsvorlage
Bildwand f screen, viewing screen, projection screen, cinema screen, theater screen
Bildwandhelligkeit f screen brightness, screen luminance
Bildwandler m **1.** image converter **2.** *(TV)* picture transformer, video transformer, picture tube, image tube

Bildwandlerröhre f **(Ikonoskop** n**)** *(TV)* image converter tube, iconoscope, *colloq* ike
Bildwandlerschärfe f *(TV)* image converter sharpness
Bildwechsel m
1. (Vollbild) picture frequency
2. → Bildschnitt
3. → Szenenwechsel
Bildwechselfrequenz f
→ Bildwechsel 1.
Bildwechselimpuls m *(TV)* frame sync, frame synchronization pulse, vertical synchronization pulse, vertical sync pulse
Bildweiß n *(TV)* picture white
Bildweite f *(phot)* image distance, distance from image to lens
Bildwerfer m
→ Bildprojektor
Bildwerbung f pictorial advertising
Bildwiedergabe f picture reproduction, image reproduction
Bildwiedergabe f
→ Bildröhre
Bildwinkel m *(phot/film/TV)* angle of vision, angle of view, visual angle, angle of image, picture angle, angular field of (the) lens, shooting angle
Bildwinkelanzeige f *(phot)* zoom angle indication
Bildwinkelanzeiger m *(phot)* zoom indicator
Bildzahl f **1.** *(phot/film)* number of frames **2.** → Bildfrequenz
Bildzähler m **(Bildzählwerk** n**)** *(phot/film)* frame counter, film counter, exposure counter
Bildzeichen n
→ Bildmarke
Bildzeile f *(TV)* scanning line, picture line
Bildzeilenstandardzahl f **(Bildzeilenstandard** m**)**
→ Fernsehnorm
Bildzeitung f **(illustrierte Zeitung** f**)** picture paper, illustrated paper, illustrated newspaper, (kleinformatige Bildzeitung) tabloid paper, tabloid
Bildzerlegung f *(print/TV)* scanning
Billigabonnement n **(Werbeabonnement** n**)** cut-rate subscription
Billigmarke f
→ Zweitmarke
Billigpreis-(Billig-) *adj (econ)* cut-rate, price-off

Billigprodukt n (**Billigware** f, **Schleuderartikel** m) *(econ)* catchpenny product, catchpenny, *colloq* schlock merchandise
Billings pl
→ Honorarumsatz
Bimetallkontakt m bimetallic contact
Bimetallplatte f *(print)* bimetal plate
Bindeart f (**Einbandart** f, **Bindeverfahren** n, **Heftart** f) binding method, binding technique, type of binding
Bindeauflage f (**Bindequote** f) *(print)* bindung-up, pl bindings-up
Bindeauftrag m binding order
Bindemaschine f
→ Buchbindemaschine
Bindematerial n
→ Einbandmaterial
Bindemittel n binding agent, binder, (Klebstoff) adhesive material, adhesive, (zum Kaschieren) laminating compound
binden (einbinden) v/t *(print)* to bind
Binden n (**Einbinden** n, **Heften** n) binding
Bindequote f
→ Bindeauflage
Binder m
→ Buchbinder
Binderand m
→ Falzkante
Binderei f
→ Buchbinderei
Bindung f
→ Binden, Abnehmerbindung, Absatzbindung, Vertriebsbindung
Binnenhandel m *(econ)* domestic market trade, domestic trade, home market trade, home trade
Binnenhandelspolitik f *(econ)* domestic market policy, home market policy
Binnenmarkt m *(econ)* domestic market, home market
Binnenmarktforschung f *(econ)* domestic market research, market research on the domestic market
Binokulartest m *(res)* binocular test
binomial (binomisch) adj *(stat)* · binomial
Binomialtest m (**binomialer Test** m) *(stat)* binomial test
Binomialverteilung f (**Bernouilli-Verteilung** f) *(stat)* binomial distribution, binomial frequency distribution, Bernouilli distribution, Bernouilli frequency distribution
  If an event has probability p of appearing at any one trial, the probability of r appearing in n independent trials is $\binom{n}{r} q^n - p^r$, where $q = 1 - p$. This term involves p^r in the binomial expansion of $(q+p)^n$ and is known as the binomial distribution.
Bionik f bionics pl *(construed as sg)*
Bioskop n *(phot)* bioscope
biotisches Experiment n (**biotische Situation** f) biotic experiment, biotic test situation, biotic experimental design, biotic test design
Bipack m (**Bipackfilm** m, **Zweischichtfilm** m) *(phot)* bipack, bipack film
Bipackverfahren n (**Zweipackverfahren** n, **Kaschverfahren** n) *(phot)* bipack procedure, bipack technique
bipolar adj bipolar
bipolare Adjektiva n/pl *(res)* bipolar adjectives pl
→ semantisches Differential
bipolare Skala f bipolar scale
Birne f *(phot)* bulb, light bulb
bis auf weiteres (bei Werbeaufträgen) till forbid (T.F., TF), till cancelled, *Am* till canceled, till countermanded
  Instructions to a medium to continue running an advertisement as scheduled until further notice.
Bisektion f bisection
biserielle Korrelation f *(stat)* biserial correlation
  A measure of correlation between two continuous variables, when one has been reduced to a dichotomy. The statistic estimates what the correlation coefficient would be if the second variable had not been dichotomized.
bivariat adj *(stat)* bivariate
bivariate Daten n/pl *(stat)* bivariate data pl
bivariate Häufigkeitsverteilung f (**bivariate Verteilung** f) *(stat)* bivariate frequency distribution, bivariate distribution
  The joint distribution of pairs of observations on the same subject or on subjects matched in some manner. It is usually assumed that the pairs of values are sampled from a bivariate normal distribution, meaning that for any selected value of one variable, the values of the other variable are normally distributed.

bivariate Normalverteilung f *(stat)* bivariate normal distribution
bivariate Statistik f **(Bivariat-Statistik** f) bivariate statistics pl *(construed as sg)*
　Descriptive and inferential statistical procedures, such as correlation, designed for use when the analysis involves two dependent measures on each subject, or one measure on a matched pair of subjects.
bivariate Tabelle f **(zweidimensionale Tabelle** f) *(stat)* bivariate table
bivariater Vorzeichentest m bivariate sign test
bivariates Experiment n **(zweidimensionales Experiment** n) *(stat)* bivariate experiment
BL *abbr* Bildleitung
Black-Box-Modell n **(S-R-Modell** n) *(psy)* black box model, black-box model
Blankdruck m *(print)* blanking
Blankfilm m **1.** *(phot)* film base, film support **2.** *(film)* blank film, clear film, spacing, (Start) clear leader, (Blankfilm mit Bildstrich) clear film with frame
Blankieren n polishing
Blankiermaschine f polishing machine
Blankoauftrag m **(Blankobestellung** f) blanket order
Blankobogen m *(print)* blank sheet
Blankoprospekt m blank leaflet
blankschlagen (freischlagen) v/t *(print)* to blank out, to leave blank
Blankschramme f *(phot)* celluloid scratch, scratch on base side
Blankseite f **(Glanzseite** f) *(phot)* base side, shiny side
Bläschen n *(phot)* blister
Blase f
→ Sprechblase
Blasen f/pl *(print)*
→ Ätzrückstand
Blatt n **1.** (Blatt Papier) leaf, sheet, (Seite) page **2.** (Zeitung) paper, newspaper, (Zeitschrift) magazine, journal **3.** (Kunstdruck) art print
Blattbreite f *(print)* page width
Blättchen n
→ Lokalzeitung, Vereinsblatt
Blattfilm m sheet film
Blattfolie f foil, leaf
Blattgold n gold leaf, leaf gold, gold foil

Blatthalter m *(print)* catch, jigger, visorium, retinaculum
Blattheber m *(print)* fly
Blattnumerierung f **(Paginierung** f, **Blattzahl** f) *(print)* foliation
Blattrand m margin, sheet margin
Blauabzug m *(print)* blueline, blue
Blaudruck m **(Blaupausverfahren** n, **Zyanotypie** f) *(phot)* blueprint process, cyanotype process, blueprinting, cyanotyping, cyanotypy
Blaufilter m *(phot)* blue filter
Blaupause f *(print)* blueprint, blue, cyanotype
Blaupauspapier n blueprint paper
Blauplatte f *(print)* blue plate
Blaustanzverfahren n **(Blue-Box** f, **Blue-Box-Verfahren** n) *(film/TV)* blue screen, blue matting color separation overlay, chroma key
　A matting technique, usually with a vast difference in size relationships; the subject matted is placed against a background (usually blue) and the signal is mixed with that particular color channel suppressed.
Blaustich m *(phot)* blue cast, bluish cast
Blaustift m blue pencil, blue crayon
Blechdruck m **1.** *(print)* tin-plate printing, tin printing **2.** *(phot)* (Ferrotypie) ferrotype, tintype
Blechplakat n **(Blechschild** n)
→ Emailplakat
Blei n *(print)* lead
bleibt *imp (print)* (Satzanweisung) stet
　The instruction to a typesetter or printer to ignore an alteration originally called for in a proof.
Bleichbad n *(phot)* bleaching bath, bleach bath
bleichen v/t **1.** *(phot)* to bleach **2.** *(paper)* to poach
Bleichen n **(Bleiche** f) **1.** *(phot)* bleaching
　The process of whitening photographic images during intensification.
2. *(paper)* poaching
Bleichfixierbad n **(Blix** n) *(phot)* combined bath
Bleichholländer m *(papermaking)* poacher
Bleichmittel n *(phot)* bleaching agent
Bleifuß m *(print)* metal mount
Bleilegierung f lead alloy, alloy of lead

Bleiletter f (**Handsatztype** f) foundry type, hand type
A letterpress type of individually cast metal characters set by hand.

bleiloser Satz m
→ Schreibsatz, Kaltsatz, Photosatz (Lichtsatz)

Bleisatz m *(print)* hot type, hot-metal typesetting, hot-metal composition
A system of setting type which uses relief images made from molten metal. Examples include Linotype, Monotype, and hand composition, (→) Handsatz. In contrast, cold type is composition made directly on paper without any casting of metal.
vgl. Schreibsatz, Kaltsatz, Photosatz (Lichtsatz)

Bleischnitt m *(print)* lead engraving

Bleisetzmaschine f *(print)* hot-metal machine, hot-metal typesetter, hot type machine

Bleistereo n *(print)* lead stereo
→ Stereo

Bleistift m lead pencil, pencil

Bleistiftskizze f (**Bleistiftzeichnung** f) rough, pencil test, pencil drawing

Blende f **1.** *(phot)* diaphragm, f-stop, light stop, stop, (die Öffnung) aperture, (Objektiv) lens stop, iris
In photography, the light-gathering capacity of the lens, usually expressed as an f/number, obtained by dividing the diameter of the lens opening image focal length of the lens.
2. (Scheinwerfer) lantern, barndoor, diffuser, douser
3. (Lichtblende, Schallblende) gobo, gobbo, flag, nigger, blade, dot, baffle, barndoor, blind **4.** (Trick) dissolve, (Schiebeblende) wipe, wipe-off

Blendenband n (**Lichtband** n) *(phot)* (Kamera) exposure control band, exposure control strip, (Kopierung) printing control band, printing control strip

Blendenbandkopiermaschine f *(phot)* control band printer

Blendeneinstellung f *(phot)* diaphragm setting, aperture setting, stop setting, iris setting, setting

Blendenflügel m *(phot)* shutter blade, blade, mirror shutter

Blendenklammer f *(phot)* cleat, flat clamp

Blendennachdrehvorrichtung f *(phot)* inching knob, shutter-phasing device

Blendenöffnung f *(phot)* aperture, stop, lens aperture, shutter aperture, working aperture, aperture of diaphragm, iris aperture, shooting aperture

Blendenraste f *(phot)* click setting

Blendenrechner m *(phot)* aperture computer

Blendenring m *(phot)* diaphragm ring

Blendenschablone f *(film/TV)* camera matte, effects matte

Blendenskala f *(phot/film/TV)* diaphragm scale

Blendenstütze f (**Blendenstrebe** f) *(phot/film/TV)* brace, stay

Blendenvorwahl f *(phot/film/TV)* presetting of aperture, preset diaphragm mechanism

Blendenweite f
→ Blendenöffnung

Blendenzahl f
→ Blendeneinstellung

Blendlaterne f *(phot/film/TV)* dark lantern, (mit Konvexlinse) bull's eye lantern, bull's eye

Blendschutz m
→ Schirmblende

Blickaufzeichnung f (**Blickregistrierung** f) *(res)* eye-movement registration, eye-flow registration, eye-direction registration, gaze-motion registration, direct eye movement observation

Blickaufzeichnungsgerät n (**Augenkamera** f, **Blickregistrierungskamera** f) *(res)* eye-movement camera, eye camera, eye-movement observation camera, direct eye movement observation camera

Blickaufzeichnungsmethode f (**Blickregistrierungsverfahren** n) *(res)* eye camera technique, eye-flow observation technique, gaze-motion observation technique, gaze-motion registration technique, direct eye movement observation system (D.E.M.O.S.)

Blickfang m *(advtsg)* eye catcher, eye stopper, attention getter, hook

Blickfanganzeige f eye-catching advertisement, eye-catching ad

Blickfangpunkt m (**fettgedruckter Punkt** m) *(typ)* bullet

Blickfangwerbung f (**Blickfangreklame** f) eye-catching advertising, attention getting advertising

Blickfangzeile f (auffällige Überschrift f) (print) catchline, catch line
Blickfeld n (phot) field of vision, field of view, range of vision, range of view, visual field; im Blickfeld sein: to be in frame, to be in shot
Blickregistrierung f
→ Blickaufzeichnung
Blickrichtung f (res) eye direction, gaze direction, eye gaze, eyegaze
Blickverlauf m (res) eye flow, gaze motion, eye movement
Blickwinkel m (phot) angle of view, view angle, visual angle
Blimp m (film/TV) blimp
Blimp-Kamera f (film/TV) blimp camera, blimped camera
blind adj (print) blind, dead, blank
Blindband m (Blindmuster n, Blindexemplar n) (print) dummy, blank dummy, dummy copy, (Zeitschrift) dummy magazine, experimental magazine
Blinddruck m (Blindprägung f, Blindexemplar n) (print) blind blocking, blind embossing, blind stamping, blind tooling
Blindfilm m blind film
blindgeprägt (blindgedruckt) adj (print) blind-stamped, blind-blocked, blind-tooled, blind-embossed
Blindmaterial n (print) spacing material, metal furniture, quotation furniture, wood furniture, dead metal, leading
→ Durchschuß, Regletten, Ausschuß
Blindmuster n
1. → Blindband
2. → Attrappe
blindprägen (blind prägen, blind pressen, blindpressen) v/t (print) to blind emboss, to blind-stamp, to blind-tool
Blindprägung f (Blindpressung f)
→ Blinddruck
blindschlagen v/t (print) to blank, to leave blank, to blank out
Blindschlagzeile f (Blindüberschrift f) blind headline, blind head
Blindtest m (Blindversuch m, blinder Produkttest m) blind test, blind analysis, blind assessment, blind procedure, blind scoring, blind product test, (einfacher Blindtest) single-blind test, (Doppelblindtest) double-blind test

In marketing research, a product test in which the test persons are unaware of the product's brand that is tested. More in general any procedure designed to ensure that subjects and/or experimenters are not aware of the true nature of the treatment being administered or assessed. The procedure is designed to reduce the influence of experimenter or subject bias, or placebo effects. In a single-blind procedure, the subjects remain uninformed about the purpose of the experiment and particular treatment given them. In a double-blind procedure, (→) Doppel-Blindtest, neither the subject nor the experimenter(s) administering the treatment or assessing its effect knows the assignment of subjects to treatments.
Blindzeile f (print) blank line, blind line, white line
Blinker m blinker
Blinkgeber m blinker unit
Blinklichtwerbung f
→ Leuchtwerbung
Blinzelgeschwindigkeit f (Blinzelhäufigkeit f) (res) frequency of blinking, blink rate
Blinzelmeßgerät n
→ Augenkamera
Blinzeltest m (res) eye-blink test
Blitz m (phot) flash
Blitzanschluß m (Blitzkontakt m) (phot) (innen) flash contact, (außen) flash socket
Blitzaufhellung f (phot) synchrosunlight technique, synchro-sunlight
Blitzaufnahme f (Blitzphotographie f, Blitzphoto n) flashlight photo, flash photo, flashlight shot, flashlight exposure, flash exposure
Blitzbelichtung f (phot) flash exposure
Blitzbirne f
→ Blitzlampe
Blitzdauer f (phot) flash duration
Blitzgerät n (Blitzleuchte f, synchronisierter Blitzlichtanschluß m) (phot) flash gun, flash unit
Blitzkabel n (phot) flash cable
Blitzkontakt m
→ Blitzanschluß
Blitzlampe f (Blitzlicht n) (phot) flashbulb, flash bulb, flashlamp, flash lamp, flashlight, flash light
A glass bulb containing magnesium or aluminum foil in an atmosphere of oxygen. When electrically ignited, the metal burns almost instantaneously, giving a brilliant but brief light.

Blitzlampenanschluß

Blitzlampenanschluß m (**Blitzlichtanschluß** m) *(phot)* flashbulb holder
Blitzlicht n
→ Blitzlampe
Blitzlichtaufnahme f
→ Blitzaufnahme
Blitzlichtlampe f
→ Blitzlampe
Blitzlichtröhre f (**Blitzröhre** f) *(phot)* flash tube
Blitzmeldung f news flash, snap
Blitznachrichten f/pl flash news, spot news pl *(construed as sg)*
Blitzsynchronisation f *(phot)* flash synchronization
Blitzwürfel m *(phot)* flash cube, flashcube, cube
Blix n
→ Bleichfixierbad
Block m
→ Schreibblock, Zeichenblock, Klischeefuß, Szenenaufbau
Blockade f *(print)* turned letters pl
Blockbuchen n *(film)* block booking
  The practice of requiring an exhibitor to book films other than the ones he wants.
Blockbuchstabe m block capital
Blockdiagramm n
→ Säulendiagramm
Blockheftmaschine f *(binding)* side-stitching machine, flat-stitching machine
Blockheftung f *(binding)* side stitching, flat stitching
→ Seitenheftung, Durchheftung
Blocksatz m *(type)* justified style
  Any type arranged in such a manner so that each line is set flush left and right, aside from specified indentations, and with words and letters evenly spaced.
vgl. Flattersatz
Blocksatz m **ohne Einzug** *(typ)* book style, block paragraph, flush paragraph
Blockschrift f block letters pl, block capitals pl, (Satzanweisung) all in capital letters, all in caps
Blooming n (**Nachzieh-Effekt** m)
→ Kometeneffekt
Blow-up m
→ Aufblasen, Vergrößerung
Blue-Box f
→ Blaustanzverfahren
Bobine f (**Bobby** m) *(film)* bobbin, spool, hub, core
Bodenbeutel m (mit Seitenfalten) gusset bag, gusseted bag

Bodenfunkstelle f (**Bodenstation** f) *(radio/TV)* terrestrial broadcasting station, earth station
  A broadcast receiving facility for satellite transmissions.
Bodenstativ n *(phot)* floor stand
Bodenwelle f ground wave, surface wave, direct wave
  In broadcasting, signal waves distributed through the conducting earth and not subject to transmission variations because of upper atmosphere conditions.
Body Copy f
→ Haupttext, Textteil
Bogen m (**Druckbogen** m) sheet, sheet of paper, (signierter Bogen) signature
Bogenablage f (**Bogenauslage** f) *(print)* delivery, sheet delivery
Bogenableger m *(print)* sheet deliverer, layboy, laying machine
Bogenanleger m (**Bogenanlage** f) sheet feeder, sheet feed, feeder, sheet feeding mechanism, sheet feeding unit
Bogenanschlag m (**Bogenanschlagwerbung** f, **Plakatanschlag** m, **Plakatanschlagwerbung** f, **Anschlagwerbung** f) billposting, bill posting, poster advertising
vgl. Daueranschlag
Bogenausrichtung f *(print)* sheet registration, sheet imposition
Bogenkaschierung f (**Bogenbeklebung** f) sheet lining
Bogendicke f (**Bogenhöhe** f)
→ Papierdicke
Bogeneinführungsvorrichtung f *(print)* sheet feeder, board feeder
Bogen-Einsteckmaschine f *(print)* sheet inserter
Bogenfalzmaschine f *(print)* sheet folding machine
Bogenfalzung f *(print)* sheet folding
Bogenfilm m *(print)*
→ Offsetlitho
Bogenformat n (**Bogengröße** f) size of sheet, sheet size, sheetage
Bogengeradleger m *(print)* jogger, jogger-up
Bogenhalter m *(print)* blanket pin, pin
Bogenhöhe f
→ Papierdicke
Bogenkalander m *(paper)* sheet calender

84

Bogenkante f *(print)* edge of a sheet, sheet edge
Bogenlampe f *(phot/film/TV)* arc lamp, arc, kleig light, klieg light, broad
   A powerful illuminant in which an electric current is passed through a pair of slightly separated electrodes or carbons, causing combustion of the carbons and emission of intensely bright light.
Bogennorm f *(print)* signature mark
Bogenpapier n paper in sheets
   vgl. **Rollenpapier**
Bogenpreis m price per sheet
Bogenrotationspresse f *(print)* sheet-fed rotary press
Bogensatz m *(paper)* stand of paper
Bogenscheinwerfer m *(film/TV)* brute, 10k
Bogenschneider m (**Bogenzuschneider** m) *(print)* sheet cutter, trimmer
   → Papierschneidemaschine
Bogenschneiden n
   → Bogenzuschneiden
Bogenschwenk m *(film/TV)* fan wipe
   A camera wipe in the form of a radially moving line so as to pass through an arc.
Bogensignatur f *(print)* signature, signature mark
   The sections for printing and binding into which magazines or books are divided.
   → Signatur
Bogenstapler m (**Bogenstapelvorrichtung** f) sheet stacker
Bogentagpreis m *etwa* one-day outdoor poster rate, basic outdoor advertising rate (for one sheet per day)
Bogenzähler m *(print)* sheet counter
Bogenzeichen n (**Bogenziffer** f)
   → Bogensignatur
Bogenzuführung f *(print)* sheet feeding, *(Maschine/Person)* sheet feeder
Bogenzusammentragmaschine f (**Zusammenträger** m) *(print)* gatherer
Bogenzuschneiden n (**Bogenschneiden** n) *(print)* sheet cutting, (Schneiden der gefalzten Bogen) trimming, sheet trimming
Bon m
1. → Gutschein
2. → Gratisgutschein
Bondpapier n bond paper, bond

Bonus m bonus
   An incentive payment for above-the-norm achievement.
Bonuspackung f bonus pack, merchandise pack
Bordfernsehen n (**Schiffsfernsehen** n) ship television, ship's television
Bordkino n (**Schiffskino** n) ship cinema, ship's cinema, *Am* ship's theater
Bordmagazin n (**Bordzeitschrift** f) inflight magazine, inflight magazine
Bordüre f
   → Einfassung
Bordzeitung f (**Schiffszeitung** f) ship's newspaper, ship's paper
Börse f exchange, (Effektenbörse) stock exchange, bourse, (Warenbörse) commodity exchange
   → Devisenbörse, Dienstleistungsbörse
Börsenzeitung f
   → Finanzzeitung
Boston-Effekt m
   → Erfahrungskurveneffekt
Bostonpresse f *(print)* jobbing handpress, handpress, lever press
Botschaft f message
   → Werbebotschaft
Boulevardblatt n (**Boulevardzeitung** f) mass-circulation paper, popular paper, penny paper, yellow paper, (Bildzeitung) tabloid paper, tabloid, *contempt* gutter paper, rag
Boulevardpresse f (**Sensationspresse** f) mass-circulation press, popular press, penny press, yellow press, *contempt* gutter press, rags *pl*
Boutique f *(retailing)* boutique
   A highly specialized and high-quality retail store, particularly in the field of high fashion or mod.
Box-Jenkins-Modell n *(stat)* Box-Jenkins model
Brainstorming n brainstorming (Alex F. Osborn)
Brainwriting n brainwriting
Brainwriting-Pool m brainwriting pool
Branche f line of business, trade
Branchenadreßbuch n (**Branchenadreßverzeichnis** n) trade directory, commercial directory, classified directory
branchengleiche Agglomeration f
   → Agglomeration (im Einzelhandel)

Branchen-Handelsspanne f
(**Branchenspanne** f) line of business margin, trade margin
Branchenimage n image of a line of business, line of business image, trade image
vgl. Markenimage, Produktimage
Branchen-Panel n *(marketing res)* trade panel
Branchenspanne f
→ Handelsspanne
Branchentelefonbuch n trade telephone directory, commercial telephone directory, classified telephone directory
→ Gelbe Seiten
branchenübergreifende Zeitschrift f horizontal publication, horizontal magazine, horizontal paper
  A periodical devoted to men or officials of similar responsibilities and functions regardless of the business or industry in which they are engaged; contrasted with vertical publication.
→ Berufsgruppenzeitschrift; vgl. Branchenzeitschrift
branchenungleiche Agglomeration f
→ Agglomeration (im Einzelhandel)
Branchenwerbung f
→ Gemeinschaftswerbung
Branchenzeitschrift f trade magazine, trade journal, vertical publication, vertical magazine, vertical journal, vertical paper
  A business publication with its editorial focus on the needs, interests, and activities of a specific trade or industry.
vgl. branchenübergreifende Zeitschrift
Brand-
→ Marken-
braunfleckig adj *(paper)* foxed
Braunpause f sepia print
  A photographic print in brown tones.
Braunsche Röhre f
→ Kathodenstrahlröhre f
Braunschliff m brown mechanical pulp, leather board pulp
Braunschliffpappe f brown mechanical pulp board, leather board, pulp board
Bravais-Pearsonscher Korrelationskoeffizient m *(stat)*
→ Produkt-Moment-Korrelation
Break m (**Breakdown** m)
→ demographische Aufgliederung

Break-Even m (**Break-even-Punkt** m)
→ Gewinnschwelle
Break-even-Analyse f *(econ)* break-even analysis
  The systematic examination of the relationships between sales revenue, fixed costs, and variable costs to determine the most profitable level of output or the most profitable product mix. An original German term does not exist.
brechen v/t **1.** *(phot)* (Licht) to diffract, to refract, to break **2.** *(print)* (Papier) to fold, to crease
Brechkraft f *(phot)* refractive power, refracting power, focal power
Brechung f *(phot)* (Licht) refraction
  The deviation of a light ray from a straight path when passing obliquely from one medium into another of different density, or in traversing a medium whose density is not uniform.
Brei m
→ Papierbrei
Breitbahn f *(print)* grain short
vgl. Schmalbahn
Breitband n *(radio)* broad band, wide band
Breitbandabstimmung f *(radio)* broad tuning, wide-band tuning
Breitbandantenne f *(radio)* wide-band antenna, brit wide-band aerial
Breitbanddialog m *(radio)* wide-band dialog, brit dialogue
→ Bildfernsprechen, Bildfernsprechkonferenz, Videokonferenz
Breitbandkabel n wide-band cable
Breitbandkommunikation f wide-band communication, broad-band communication
Breitbandkreis m wide-band circuit
Breitbandmikrofon n (**Breitbandmikrophon** n) wide-response microphone
Breitbandtechnik f wide-band technique
Breitbandverstärker m wide-band amplifier
Breitbild n
→ Breitwandbild
Breitbildfilm m
→ Breitwandfilm
Breite f (**Weite** f) *(print)* width (of a column, of the page, of type; volle Satzbreite: full measure, full out
Breitenwinkel m *(TV)* azimuth, wide angle

The perpendicular relationship of the magnetic head gap to the tape travel direction. The angle should be exactly 90°.
Breitfeder f
→ Bandzugfeder
Breitfilm m wide-gauge film, 70 mm film
vgl. Schmalfilm, Kinofilm
Breitformat n
→ Querformat
Breitwand f (Kino) wide screen, large screen, (Fernsehen) giant screen, eidophor screen
Breitwandbild n (**Breitbild** n) widescreen picture, large-screen picture
Breitwandfilm m (**Breitbildfilm** m, **Breitwand-Theaterkopie** f) widescreen film, large-screen film
Breitwandfilmprojektion f (**Breitwandverfahren** n) wide-screen projection, wide-screen projection technique
Breitwandfilmvorführung f widescreen film presentation
Brennachse f (phot) focal axis
Brenndauer f
→ Blitzdauer
Brennebene f (**Brennfläche** f, **Brennpunktebene** f) (phot) focal plane
The plane surface on which the image transmitted by a lens is brought to sharpest focus. The focal plane on process cameras is the position interchangeably occupied by the focusing screen and the photographic plate or film.
Brennpunkt m (phot) focus, focal point
Brennweite f (**Brennpunktabstand** m) (phot) focal distance, focal length
The distance of the principal focus of a lens from its optical center.
Brennweitenänderung f (phot) change of focus, change of focal length
Brennweitenband n focus calibration tape
Brennweitenbereich m (phot) range of focus
Brennweitenbügel m (phot) zoom handle
Brennweitenring m (phot) focus ring, focusing ring
Brennweitenverlängerung f (phot) range extender
Brett n
→ Anschlagbrett

Bretterwand f (**Plakatwand** f) (outdoor advtsg) billboard, board, brit hoarding, billboard hoarding
Briefing n briefing
briefliche Befragung f (**postalische Befragung** f)
→ schriftliche Befragung
Briefumschlagwerbung f advertising on envelopes, envelope advertising, corner card advertising
Briefumschlagwerbematerial n (**Briefwerbematerial** n) (Einzelstück) mailer
Briefwerbeaktion f (**Postwurfsendung** f) direct mailing
Briefwerbeunternehmen n (**Briefwerbefirma** f, **Briefwerber** m) direct-mail advertiser, direct-mail advertising company, direct-mail advertising agency
Briefwerbetest m (**Direktversandtest** m) direct-mail test, (gegabelter Briefwerbetest) direct-mail split test
Briefwerbung f direct-mail advertising
That advertising which asks for the order to be sent by mail. Delivery of the order is by mail. Also the medium which delivers the advertising message by mail. Provides greatest control of direction to a market, flexibility of materials and processes, timeliness of scheduling, and personalization.
Brillantpapier n (**satiniertes Papier** n) glazed paper
Brillantsucher m (phot) brilliant viewfinder, reflector viewfinder
bringen (**veröffentlichen, senden**) v/t to bring, to present, to print, to publish, to carry, to feature, to run
Bristolkarton m (**Isabykarton** m, **Einlagekarton** m) Bristol board, bristol board
Bristolpapier n (**Isabeypapier** n) Bristol paper, bristol paper
Bromdruck m (**Bromsilberphoto** n, **Bromsilberdruck** m) bromide print
A photograph printed on bromide paper.
Bromdruck m (**Bromsilberphotographie** f) bromide printing
Bromöldruck m (**Bromölphoto** n) bromoil photo, bromoil print
Bromöldruck m (**Bromölphotographie** f) Bromoil printing, bromoil process
Bromsilberpapier n (**Bromidpapier** n) (phot) bromide paper
Bronze f (**Bronzefarbe** f) bronze
Bronzeabzug m (print) bronze proof

Bronzedruck *m* **1.** (Produkt) bronze print, metallic print **2.** (Verfahren) bronze printing
bronzefarben (bronzen) *adj* bronze, bronzy
Bronzepapier *n* bronze paper
Bronzepulver *n* bronze powder
Bronzeschrift *f* bronze type
bronzieren *v/t* to bronze
Bronzieren *n* (**Bronzierung** *f,* **Behandlung** *f* **mit Bronze**) bronzing
broschieren *v/t* to stitch, to sew, to bind
broschiert *adj* stitched, sewed, sewn
Broschur *f* **1.** (Verfahren) binding in paper covers **2.** (broschiertes Buch) bound book, book bound in paper covers
Broschüre *f* pamphlet, folder, booklet, brochure
  A booklet or pamphlet used in sales solicitation or promotional activities.
  → Werbebroschüre, Prospekt
Broschürenmaschine *f* brochure binding machine
Brotsatz *m* (**Brotschrift** *f,* **Werkschrift** *f*) *(typ)* body type, book type, text type, body, book face
  The type commonly used for the reading matter in newspapers, magazines, or in an advertisement, as distinguished from the display type in headlines.
  vgl. Akzidenzschrift, Auszeichnungsschrift
Bruch *m* *(print)* fold
  The point at which the newspaper page is folded in half.
  → Falzbruch, Falz
Bruchschrift *f* *(typ)*
  → gebrochene Schrift
Brücke *f* **1.** *(print)* (an der Presse) till, shelves *pl* *(radio/TV)* **2.** (Klangbrücke etc.) bridge
Brückenschaltung *f* *(radio/TV)* bridge circuit, bridge connection
Brückenstanze *f* up-and-down slotter
Brückenwerbung *f* advertising on bridges, outdoor advertising on bridges
Brumm *m* (**Brummton** *m,* **B-Spannung** *f*) *(radio/TV)* hum, buzz, humming noise, ripple
brummen *(radio/TV)* *v/i* to hum, to buzz
Brummer *m* *(radio/TV)* buzzer
Brummspannung *f* *(radio/TV)* hum voltage, ripple voltage, ripple

Brummstör-Amplitudenmodulation *f* *(radio/TV)* hum amplitude modulation
Brummstreifen *m* *(TV)* hum bar
Brummüberlagerung *f* *(TV)* hum bars *pl,* hum superimposition
Brummunterdrückung *f* *(TV)* hum suppression
Brustbild *n* *(phot)* shoulder shot, bust shot
Bruststativ *n* *(phot)* chestpod
Brute *m* *(TV)* brute, 10k
  A 10,000-watt carbon arc spotlight, used for poorly lit locations.
brutto *adj* gross
Brutto für Netto (**brutto für netto**) gross for net
Brutto-Anzeigenpreis *m*
  → Grundpreis
Brutto-Einschaltpreis *m*
  → Grundpreis, Einschaltpreis
Bruttoeinkommen *n* *(econ)* gross income, income before tax
Bruttoeinnahmen *f/pl* *(econ)* gross receipts *pl,* gross revenue
Bruttoertrag *m*
  → Bruttogewinn
Bruttogewinn *m* *(econ)* gross profit, gross profits *pl*
  The value of the difference between the cost of purchase and the selling price of a product, i.e. without allowance for overheads, promotion or other expenses.
Bruttogewinnspanne *f* *(econ)* gross margin of profit(s) *(pl),* gross margin
  The difference between the quantity of goods sold at net selling prices in total and the same quantity of goods at total cost.
Bruttohörer *m/pl* (**Bruttohörerschaft** *f*) *(media res)* gross audience, gross number of listeners, (Reichweite) gross rating points *pl* (GRPs, G.R.P.s), radio rating points *pl,* duplicated audience
  The gross total of the number of households or individuals counted in radio audiences during two or more time periods. Thus, if a household or an individual appears in audiences during two or more time periods, that household or individual is counted two or more times in computing the gross audience total. One may compute a gross audience figure for time periods during the same day, on different days within a week, or over a period of several weeks. In any case, a gross audience figure reflects both reach and frequency; that is, it reflects the number of different members in audiences and the average frequency

with which these members are in audiences. It expresses in terms of households or individuals what gross rating points expresses in percentage terms.

Brutto-Inlandsprodukt *n (econ)* gross domestic product (GDP)
The total output of goods and services by a country's national economy in one full year, i.e. the gross national product (G.N.P.), (64) Bruttosozialprodukt, minus net foreign investment.

Bruttokontaktsumme *f* **(Bruttokontakte** *m/pl*) *(media res)* gross audience, gross impacts *pl*, gross impressions *pl*, gross opportunities *pl*, to see, gross OTS (O.T.S.), duplicated audience, *(outdoor advtsg)* gross circulation
The total number of exposures, (→) Kontakt, to an advertising medium.

Bruttoleser *m/pl* **(Bruttoleserschaft** *f*) *(media res)* gross audience, gross number of readers, duplicated audience, accumulated audience, cumulated audience ("cume")
The total audience of a newspaper or magazine as counted in surveys of several publications at one time and surveys of one such medium at several times without regard to repeated counting of individual readers.

Bruttopreis *m (econ)* gross price, gross
A price without any discounts or allowances.
(für Werbung) gross rate, gross cost, gross, (Grundpreis) base rate, basic rate, card rate, flat rate, full rate-card cost, one-time rate, open rate
The published rate for advertising space or time without regard to commissions or discounts.

Bruttopreissystem *n* **(Bruttopreisbildung** *f*) gross pricing, gross billing

Brutto-Reichweite *f (media res)* gross audience, gross coverage, gross cover, gross reach, combined audience, audience combination ("combo"), combination of audiences, *(radio/TV)* gross rating points *pl* (GRPs, G.R.P.s)
The total coverage, *cf.* (→) Reichweite, of an advertising medium without regard to duplications.

Brutto-Sozialprodukt *n (econ)* gross national product (GNP, G.N.P.)
The total market value of the output of goods and services of a nation's economy at selling prices.

Bruttospanne *f* **(Brutto-Handelsspanne** *f*, **Brutto-Gewinnspanne** *f*) *(econ)* gross margin of profit, gross margin, gross merchandising margin
The difference between the cost or purchase price and the selling price for a particular piece of merchandise.

Brutto-Stichprobe *f (stat)*
→ Ausgangsstichprobe *f*

Bruttotarif *m*
→ Bruttopreis

Brutto-Umsatz *m*
→ Honorarumsatz

Bruttovolumen *n* gross volume

Brutto-Werbeaufwendungen *f/pl* advertising input, advertising expenditure, advertising outlay

Brutto-Werbeeinnahmen *f/pl* advertising output, advertising receipts *pl*, advertising payout, advertising payback, advertising revenue

Bruttozuschauer *m/pl* **(Bruttozuschauerschaft** *f*) *(media res)* gross audience, gross number of viewers, (Reichweite) gross rating points *pl* (GRPs, G.R.P.s), television rating points *pl*, television audience, TV audience
The gross total of the number of households or individuals counted in television audiences during two or more time periods. Thus, if a household or an individual appears in audiences during two or more time periods, that household or individual is counted two or more times in computing the gross audience total. One may compute a gross audience figure for time periods during the same day, on different days within a week, or over a period of several weeks. In any case, a gross audience figure reflects both reach and frequency; that is, it reflects the number of different members in audiences and the average frequency with which these members are in audiences. It expresses in terms of households or individuals what gross rating points expresses in percentage terms.

Btx *abbr* Bildschirmtext

BuBaW-Verfahren *n* (Johannes Bidlingmaier) *(res) abbr* **B**estellung **u**nter **B**ezugnahme **a**uf **W**erbung etwa coupon redemption test procedure, redemption rate investigation, redemption test technique

Buch *n* book

Buchabnahme f (Buchannahme f)
(radio/TV)
→ Drehbuchannahme
Buchanzeige f book advertisement, book ad
Buchbauchbinde f (Buchbinde f) bookband, jacket band
Buchbindemaschine f bookbinding machine, bookbinder, binder
Buchbinder m bookbinder, binder
Buchbinderahle f bodkin, bookbinder's awl, awl
Buchbinderei f **1.** (Tätigkeit) bookbinding, binding **2.** (Abteilung) bookbinding department, binding department, book bindery, bindery **3.** (Werkstatt) book bindery, bindery, binder's workshop
Buchbinderfarbe f bookbinder's ink, binder's ink
Buchbindergalvano n bookbinder's electro, bookbinder's electrotype, binder's electrotype, binder's electro
Buchbindergeselle m journeyman bookbinder
Buchbinderhammer m **(Buchrückenhammer** m**)** backing hammer
Buchbinderhandwerk n
→ Buchbinderei 1.
Buchbinderleim m bookbinder's glue, binder's glue, bookbinding glue, bookbinder's size, binder's size
Buchbinderleinen n **(Buchbinderleinwand** f**)** book cloth, bookbinder's cloth, binder's cloth, bookbinder's linen, binder's linen
Buchbindermesser n bookbinder's knife, binder's knife
Buchbinderstempel m **(Prägestempel** m**)** bookbinder's brass, bookbinder's stamp, bookbinder's tool
Buchbinderpappe f **(Buchbinderkarton** m**)** bookbinding board, binder's board, binder's millboard, binder's cardboard
Buchbinderpresse f bookbinding press, binding press, bookbinder's press, screw press
Buchdecke f
→ Einbanddecke
Buchdeckel m book cover, cover
Buchdeckelpappe f millboard, pasteboard, board, (Graupappe) grayboard, *brit* greyboard
Buchdeckenmaschine f
→ Einhängemaschine

Buchdruck m **(Hochdruck** m**) 1.** (Produkt) letterpress print, letterpress **2.** (Verfahren) letterpress printing
Direct printing from raised surfaces consisting of type, line plates and halftone engraving.
→ Trockenoffsetdruck (indirekter Buchdruck)
Buchdrucker m **(Hochdrucker** m**)** letterpress printer
Buchdruckerlehrling m
→ Setzerlehrling
Buchdruckerpresse f **(Buchdruckmaschine** f**)** letterpress printing machine
→ Tiegeldruckpresse, Schnellpresse, Rotationsmaschine
Buchdruckfarbe f
→ Druckfarbe
Buchdruckgewerbe n
→ Druckereigewerbe
Buchdruckrotationspresse f **(Hochdruckrotationspresse** f**)** letterpress rotary press, letterpress rotary
Bucheinband m book cover, cover, binding
Bucheinhängemaschine f
→ Einhängemaschine
buchen v/t to book, (Sendezeit) to book airtime, (Anzeigen- bzw. Werbefläche) to book space
Büchergutschein m book token
Büchermarktforscher m
→ Buchmarktforscher
Büchermarktforschung f
→ Buchmarktforschung
Buchfachzeitschrift f **(Buchzeitschrift** f, **Buchhandelszeitschrift** f**)** book trade journal, book trade magazine
Buchfadenheftmaschine f
→ Fadenheftmaschine
Buchfadenheftung f
→ Fadenheftung
Buchheftmaschine f
→ Fadenheftmaschine
Buchhülle f **(Buchumschlag** m, **Schutzhülle** f**)** book jacket, dust cover, dust jacket, book wrapper, jacket wrapper
Buchleinen n **(Buchleinwand** f**)**
→ Buchbinderleinen
Buchmarkt m book market, market for books
Buchmarktforscher m book market researcher
Buchmarktforschung f book market research

Buchmesse f (**Buchhandelsmesse** f, **Buchhändlermesse** f) book fair
Buchpapier n book paper, book printing paper, plate paper vgl. Zeitungspapier
Buchrücken m book spine, spine, backstrip, shelfback, backbone
Buchrückenpresse f backing press
Buchscheck m
→ Buchgutschein
Buchschnitt m (**Buchkante** f) book edge
Buchschrift f
→ Brotschrift
Buchstabe m
→ Letter
Buchstaben-Bildzeichen n logotype
Buchstabenprägestempel m
→ Patrize
Buchsteindruck m *(print)* typolithography, lithotypy
Buchstreifen m
→ Buchbauchbinde
Buchumschlag m
→ Buchhülle
Buchumschlagklappe f (**Buchklappe** f, **Klappe** f) jacket flap, book jacket flap
Buchung f (**Buchen** n) booking
Buchungstermin m
→ Annahmeschluß
Buchwerbeagentur f book advertising agency
Buchwerbekampagne f (**Buchwerbefeldzug** m) book advertising campaign, book campaign
Buchwerbeplakat n book poster, book advertising poster
Budget n (**Etat** m) budget
  The estimate of future sources of income and expenditure including the statement of intentions within a given period of time.
Budgetallokation f budget allocation, allocation of (marketing) expenditure, allocation of (advertising) expenditure
Budgetierung f (**Budgetplanung** f) budgeting
Budgetkontrolle f (**Etatkontrolle** f) budget control, budgetary control, budget check
  The methodical monitoring of planned income and expenditure by issuing sales targets, placing orders, and authorizing payments within the context of a previously approved and detailed budget.
Buffalo-Methode f
→ kreatives Problemlösen

Bühne f *(film/TV)* **1.** (im Studio) stage, set, scene **2.** (Hebevorrichtung) elevating platform, feeding platform **3.** (kleine Hebeplattform im Studio) riser, apple box, half apple
Bühnenarbeiter m *(film/TV)* stage hand, stagehand, scene shifter, sceneshifter, *colloq* grip, (Baubühne) scene hand, (Drehbühne) scenic service man
Bühnenbauten m/pl
→ Bauten
Bühnenbild n (**Bühnenausstattung** f) *(film/TV)* set, decor, scenery, stage setting, setting, set design, (im Filmbild) art direction
Bühnenbildner m (**Bühnenbildnerin** f) *(film/TV)* stage designer, set designer, scenewright, scenery designer, scenic designer, art director
Bühnendekoration f *(film/TV)* stage decorations pl, décor, setting, set dressing
Bühnenpersonal n (**Bühnenarbeiter** m/pl) *(film/TV)* stage hands pl, scene shifters pl
Bühnenprobe f (**Studioprobe** f) *(film/TV)* stage rehearsal
Bühnenrequisite f
→ Requisite
Bulkware f *(econ)* bulk commodity, bulk goods pl
→ Schüttware
Bulletin n bulletin
Bumerang-Effekt m boomerang effect
Bumerang-Methode f boomerang method
Bund m (**Heftbund** m, **Bundsteg** m) *(print)* gutter, gutter margin, gutter stick, (Zeitung) gutter column
  The inside margins of facing pages, the edge along which the publication is bound.
Bund m **Deutscher Grafik-Designer e.V. (BDG)** Association of German Graphic Designers
Bund m **deutscher Konsumgenossenschaften e.V. (BdK)** Association of German Consumer Cooperatives
Bund m **Deutscher Schauwerber e.V. (BDS)** Association of German Display Artists
Bund m **Deutscher Verkaufsförderer und Verkaufstrainer e.V. (BDVT)** Association of German Sales Promoters and Sales Trainers

Bund

Bund *m* **Freischaffender Foto-Designer e.v.** (BFF) Association of Freelance Photo Designers
Bunddurchdruck *m (print)* bridge, gutter bleed, bleed in the gutter
    The run of an advertisement in a magazine across the gutter of a spread.
→ angeschnittene Anzeige
Bündel *n* bundle, package
Bündeldurchschnitt *m*
→ Strahlquerschnitt (Strahlbreite)
Bündeleinschlagen *n packaging* bundle wrapping, (in Kraftpapier) bundle wrapping in kraft paper, (in Folie) bundle wrapping in film
Bündelmaschine *f (packaging)* bundler, tying machine
bündeln *(packaging) v/t* to bundle, to bundle up, to tie in bundles, to tie up into bundles
Bündelpresse *f (packaging)* bundling press, baling press
Bundesfachvereinigung *f* **Deutscher Werbemittelverteiler e.V.** (BDWV) Federal Association of German Direct Advertising Distributors
Bundesverband *m* **Deutscher Kundenzeitschriftenverleger e.V.** Federal Association of German Customer Magazine Publishers
Bundesverband *m* **Deutscher Zeitungsverleger e.V.** (BDZV) Federal Association of German Newspaper Publishers
Bundesverband *m* **Druck e.V.** Federal Association of the German Printing Industry
Bündezange *f* **(Bundzange** *f*) band nippers *pl*
bündig *adj (print)* flush; bündig setzen: to set flush
    Type matter lined up and set even with the edge of a page or block of printed matter.
→ linksbündig, rechtsbündig

Bundsteg *m*
→ Bund
bunt *adj*
→ farbig, mehrfarbig
Buntdruck *m*
→ Farbendruck, Mehrfarbendruck
Buntfarbendruck *m*
→ Farbendruck
Buntfilm *m*
→ Farbfilm
Buntpapier *n*
→ Tonpapier
Buntstift *m* crayon, color pencil, *brit* colour pencil
Bürofernschreiben *n* teletex
Bürofernschreiber *m* teletex
Burst *m*
→ Farbsynchronsignal
Bürstenabzug *m (print)* brush proof, galley proof, galley, (erster Probeabzug) green proof, green copy, proof
    The first proof pulled after type has been set and taken of type matter while it is still on a galley, before it has been made up into pages.
Bus-
→ Autobus-, Omnibus-
Bustest *m*
→ Caravan-Test
Bütte *f (paper)* vat, pan
Büttenpapier *n* **(Bütten** *n***)** handmade paper, deckle-edged paper, hand paper, deckle-edge paper
Büttenpresse *f* vat press
Büttenrand *m* deckle edge, rough edge, deckle
Buygrid-Modell *n* buygrid model
Buying Center *n*
→ Einkaufsgremium
Buy-Response-Funktion *f*
→ Kurve der Kaufwahrscheinlichkeit
BVM *m abbr* Berufsverband Deutscher Markt- und Sozialforscher e.V.

C

C *abbr* Copyright
C-Welle *f* **(Mittelwelle** *f*) *(paper)* C flute, medium flute
C & C-Großhandel *m* **(C & C-Betrieb** *m*)
→ Cash-and-Carry-Großhandel
Caravan-Test *m* **(Bus-Test** *m*) *(market res)* mobile shop test, merchandising bus test, caravan test
Caran-Testverfahren *n* **(Caravan-Testtechnik** *f*) *(market res)* mobile shop technique, merchandising bus technique, caravan test technique
A research technique employing a mobile shop in the area under investigation, usually to test a new product, its package and advertising. Copies of papers, magazines or leaflets are distributed in the area, and when the mobile shop tours the area, it is investigated whether the new product or competing brands are purchased.
Carry-over-Effekt *m* **(Übertragungseffekt** *m*, **Wirkungsverzögerung** *f*) *(res)* carryover effect
In the most general sense, any future effect that a marketing or advertising effort of today exerts.
Cartoon *m* **(Bildstreifen** *m*, **Streifenbild** *n*) cartoon
Cartoonanzeige *f* **(Bildstreifenanzeige** *f*, **Streifenbildanzeige** *f*) cartoon advertisement, cartoon ad
An advertisement using a cartoon or a series of cartoons. The English expression has become a household term in German.
Cartoon-Werbung *f* **(Werbung** *f* **mit Cartoons**, **Streifenbildanzeigenwerbung** *f*, **Bildstreifenanzeigenwerbung** *f*) cartoon advertising
Cash-and-Carry-Betrieb *m* **(Cash-and-Carry-Großhandel** *m*, **Abhollagergroßhandel** *m*, **Lagergroßhandel** *m*, **Selbstbedienungsgroßhandel** *m*) cash-and-carry wholesaler, cash-and-carry warehouse, self-service wholesaler, self-service warehouse
A limited-service wholesaler who offers no credit and no transportation and sells for cash a variety of fast moving, high-turnover merchandise. In common usage, the English term prevails over the original German expressions.
Cash Flow *m* **(Kapitalfluß** *m* **aus Umsatz)** *(econ)* cash flow
The change in cash position during a given period resulting from cash receipts and disbursements for that period. In general, it is equivalent to net profit plus all non-cash charges such as depreciation. In marketing terminology, the English is generally prevailing over the German term.
Cash-Flow-Analyse *f* **(Analyse** *f* **des Kapitalflusses aus Umsatz)** *(econ)* cash-flow analysis
Catalog Showroom *m*
→ Katalogladen (Katalogschauraum)
CC-Vertrieb *m* qualified circulation, controlled circulation (CC, C.C.)
The circulation of vocational publications delivered free, or largely free, to individuals selected by job category or other relevant criteria. There is no original German expression.
CC-Zeitschrift *f* qualified circulation magazine, controlled circulation magazine, qualified circulation publication, controlled circulation publication, free publication
→ CC-Vertrieb
CCD-Bildwandler *m* *(TV)* charge coupled device
Census *m*
→ Zensus
Centrale Marketinggesellschaft *f* **der deutschen Agrarwirtschaft e.V. (CMA)** Central Marketing Organization of German Agriculture
Charge *f* *(stat)*
→ Los
Charge *m* **(Chargenspieler** *m*) *(film/TV)* bit actor, bit player, bit-part actor
A performer who plays a very small part (a "bit") in a dramatic program.
Chargennummer *f* *(film/TV)* batch number
Charting-System *n* charting system
Checkfrage *f*
→ Kontrollfrage
Checkliste *f*
→ Prüfliste

Checklisteneffekt m *(res)* check list effect
Checklistenverfahren n
→ Prüflistenverfahren
Chef m **vom Dienst (CvD)** *(Zeitung/Zeitschrift)* managing editor, *(radio)* senior duty editor, *(TV)* editor for the day, (Studio) managing director
Chefansager m **(Chefsprecher** m**)** *(radio/TV)* chief announcer, chief newsspeaker
Chefgraphiker m **(Chefgrafiker** m**)**
→ Art Direktor
Chefinterviewer m **(Gebietsinspektor** m**)** *(survey res)* supervisor, field supervisor
Chefkameramann m *(film/TV)* director of photography, lighting cameraman
Chefredakteur m *(print media)* editor, editor-in-chief, *(radio/TV)* news director, head of news
Cheftexter m *(advtsg)* copy chief, copy supervisor
  The head of the copy department in an agency or advertising department, the supervisor of copywriters.
→ Texter
Chemigraph m *(print)* blockmaker, process engraver, photoengraver
Chemiegraphie f *(print)* blockmaking, process engraving, photoengraving
  The process and technique of making relief printing plates by photographing a picture on sensitized metal and then etching it chemically or electrolytically.
chemigraphische Anstalt f
→ Klischeehersteller, Klischeeanstalt
Chi-Quadrat n **(χ-Quadrat** n, **χ²** n, **Chi-Quadrat-Meßzahl** f**)** *(stat)* chi square, chi-squared, chi-square statistic, chi-squared statistic (χ^2)
  The sum of the form
  $$\chi^2 = \frac{(O_{ij} - E_{ij})^2}{E_{ij}}$$
  where i = 1, ..., m and j = 1, ..., n and where for a two-way classification O_{ij} is the observed frequency, and E_{ij} the expected (theoretical) frequency under the working hypothesis.
Chi-Quadrat-Test m *(stat)* chi-square test, chi-squared test
  A test of significance for discontinuous data consisting of mutually exclusive categories or attributes. The test is based on the chi-square statistic, (→) Chi-Quadrat, and occurs either as a goodness-of-fit test, (→) Gütetest, or a hypothesis test, (→) Hypothesenprüfung.
Chi-Quadrat-Verteilung f *(stat)* chi-square distribution, chi-squared distribution
  The distribution of the sum of squares of ʋ independent normal variates expressed in standard normal form; ʋ is the number of degrees of freedom, (→) Freiheitsgrad.
Chiffre f **(Kennziffer** f, **Ziffer** f, **Chiffrenummer** f**)** (bei Anzeigen) key number, box number
Chiffreanzeige f **(Kennzifferanzeige** f, **Ziffernanzeige** f**)** keyed advertisement, keyed ad, box number advertisement, box number ad
Chiffregebühr f **(Kennzifferanzeigengebühr** f**)** box number adrate
chiffrieren v/t 1. *(data analysis)* to code, to encode
→ kodieren, verschlüsseln
2. (Anzeigen) to key (an advertisement)
Chinapier n Chinese paper, China paper
Chipboard n
→ Schachtelpappe
Chromakey m
→ Blaustanzverfahren, Farbstanze, Farbstanztrick
chromatische Aberration f **(Farbabweichung** f**)** *(phot)* chromatic aberration
  A lack of color correction consisting in the inability of a photographic lens to bring yellow and red rays to the same focus of blue and violet.
Chromatizität f **(Farbigkeit** f, **Farbcharakter** m**)** chromaticity
→ Farbwert
Chrombad n *(phot)* chrome bath
Chrominanz f *(TV)* chrominance
  The color camera channels for television's red, green and blue signals (RGB signals). The colorimetric difference between one color and reference white, (→) Bezugsweiß, of the same luminance, (→) Leuchtdichte (Luminanz).
Chrominanzkanal m *(TV)* chrominance channel
Chrominanzkomponente f *(TV)* chrominance component
Chrominanzmodulator m *(TV)* chrominance modulator
Chrominanzsignal n *(TV)* chrominance signal, *colloq* chrom. sig.
→ Chrominanz

Chromoduplexkarton m chromo duplex board, chromolitho duplex board
Chromoersatzkarton m bleached lined folding boxboard, imitation chromo board
chromogen adj (phot) chromogenic
Chromogen n (phot) chromogen
chromogene Entwicklung f (phot) chromogenic development
Chromokarton m **(Chromokartonpapier** n) cast-coated paper board, brit chromo-board paper, chromoboard
Chromolithographie f
→ Farblithographie
Chromopapier n cast-coated paper, brit chromo-paper
Chromoskop n
→ Farbenmischer
Chromoskopie f
→ Farbenmischung
Chromotypie f
→ Farbphotographie
C.I.-Wert m
→ Corporate-Identity-Wert
Cicero f (typ) etwa pica, twelve-point type
Cinéast m
→ Filmschaffender
Cinemascope n cinemascope
Cinemathek f
→ Kinemathek
Cinerama n cinerama
City-Block-Distanz f **(Manhattan-Distanz** f) (stat) city-block distance, city-block metric, Manhattan distance, taxi-cab metric
Clair-obscur-Druck m **(Hell-Dunkel-Druck** m) chiaroscuro, clair-obscure, claire-obscure
    The effect of the distribution of light and shadow in a picture.
Cliché n
→ Klischee
Close-up m
→ Nahaufnahme
Cloze-Verfahren n **(Lückentest** m) (readership res) cloze procedure
    A technique of measuring readability. It is related to the term closure (Geschlossenheit) in gestalt psychology. The test consists of dropping out a sample of words from a context and having test persons guess the exact words which have been deleted.

Cluster n **(Klumpen** m, **geschlossene Erfassungsgruppe** f) (stat) cluster
    A group or collection of elements.
Clusteranalyse f **(Klumpenanalyse** f) (stat) cluster analysis
    A technique for grouping together data on products or people into clusters with similar characteristics. Any one unit in a cluster is more similar to the other units in the cluster than it is to units in other clusters.
Cluster-Bildung f **(Klumpenbildung** f) (stat) clustering
Cluster-Sampling n
→ Klumpenauswahl
CMA f abbr Centrale Marketing-Gesellschaft der deutschen Agrarwirtschaft e.V.
Cochran-Kriterium n **(Cochransches Kriterium** n) (stat) Cochran's criterion
Cochran-Test m **(Cochran-Q-Test** m, **Cochranscher Q-Test** m) (stat) Cochran's Q test, Cochran's test
    A nonparametric test of significance, (→) Signifikanztest, for differences among a set of items when each subject gets a score of 1 or 0 on each item. It is an adaptation of the chi-squared statistic test, (→) Chi-Quadrat-Test, for significant differences between three or more sets or samples of matched observations and a generalization of the (→) McNemar test.
Code m
→ Kode
Code-
→ Kode-
codieren
→ kodieren
cognitive Dissonanz f
→ kognitive Dissonanz
Collective-Notebook-Methode f collective notebook method
Colley's Stufenmodell n **der Werbewirkung**
→ DAGMAR-Modell
Color-
→ Farb-
Colorama n colorama
Colorkiller m color killer, brit colour killer
Color-Matching n
→ Farbangleichung
Colorseparation f
→ Farbauszug
Colortran-Lampe f **(Colortran-Licht** n) colortran lamp, colortran light

Combination Store *m*
→ Verbrauchermarkt
Combipack *m*
→ Verbundpackung
Comic-Heft *n* **(Comic-Buch** *n***)** comics book, comics *pl (construed as sg)*, comic strip
Comics-Zeitschrift *f* **(Comics-Heft** *n***)** comics magazine
Communicator-Effekt *m*
→ Kommunikator-Effekt, Kommunikationseffekt
Community Center *n*
→ Einkaufszentrum
Community Relations *f/pl*
→ Kommunalmarketing
Complete-Linkage-Methode *f* **(Maximum-Distanz-Verfahren** *n***)** *(stat)* complete linkage
vgl. Average-Linkage-Methode, Single-Linkage-Methode
Compurverschluß *m (phot)* compur shutter
computergestützte Telefonbefragung *f (survey res)* computer-assisted telephone interviewing (CATI)
A telephone interviewing method in which a printed questionnaire is not used; instead, the questions appear on a cathode-ray terminal, and the answers are entered directly into a computer via a keyboard attached to the terminal. The major advantages of the procedure are that it allows a researcher to design a questionnaire with very complex skip instructions, provides for instant feedback to the interviewer if an impossible answer is entered, and speeds up data processing by eliminating intermediate steps.
Computergraphik *f* computer graphics *pl (construed as sg)*
The systems and techniques which use computers to produce graphic artwork.
Computersatz *m* computer-controlled typesetting (CCT), computer-aided type-setting, computer-aided composition
Conjoint-Analyse *f* **(Conjoint Measurement** *n***)** *(stat)*
(→) konjunkte Analyse
Consumerismus *m*
→ Konsumerismus
Container *m* container
Content-Analyse *f* **(Aussagenanalyse** *f***)**
→ Inhaltsanalyse
Controlled-Circulation *f* **(CC)**
→ CC-Vertrieb

Convenience Goods *n/pl* **(Klein- und Bequemlichkeitsbedarf** *m***, Güter** *n/pl* **des täglichen Kleinbedarfs)** *(econ)* convenience goods *pl*, red goods *pl*
Those consumers' goods which the customer usually purchases frequently, immediately, and with the minimum of effort in comparison and buying. Examples of merchandise customarily bought as convenience goods are: tobacco products, soap, newspapers, magazines, chewing gum, small packaged confections, and many food products. These articles are usually of small unit value and are bought in small quantities at any one time, although when a number of them are bought together as in a supermarket, the combined purchase may assume sizeable proportions in both bulk and value. The convenience involved may be in terms of nearness to the buyer's home, easy accessibility to some means of transport, or close proximity to places where people go during the day or evening, for example, downtown to work.
vgl. Shopping Goods, Specialty Goods
Convenience-Laden *m*
→ Nachbarschaftsladen
Coop-Mailing *n*
→ Gemeinschaftsversand
Coop-Werbung *f*
→ Gemeinschaftswerbung, Verbundwerbung
Coplanarkassette *f* coplanar cassette, coplanar cartridge
Coproduktion *f*
→ Koproduktion
Copy *f* 1. → Werbetext 2. → Heft
Copy-Card *f*
→ Duplizierkarte
Copy Chief *m* **(Copy Director** *m***)**
→ Cheftexter
Copy-Plattform *f* copy platform, copy plan, copy outline, copy policy, copy approach, strategy platform
The description and rationale of the basic ideas for an advertising campaign, usually based on an established creative strategy. It describes the major selling points, their importance and considerations to carry them out. It is the copythinking phase in the creation of advertisements.
Copy-Preis *m*
→ Einzelheftpreis
Copyright *n* (©) copyright
The legal right to the sole use of original writing or art work. No publication may be copyrighted before it is printed, and every different issue requires a separate

copyright and a separate application with fee.
Copyright-Vermerk *m* copyright notice, notice of copyright
Copy-Strategie *f* (**Textstrategie** *f*, **Werbetextstrategie** *f*) copy strategy
→ Copy-Plattform
Copy-Test *m* copy test
In advertising research, a test of the effectiveness of an advertisement with the target audience. Alternative advertisements are shown to test persons in the sample; for print ads the folder technique, (→) Folder-Technik, is most common, for TV commercials the in-theater test, (→) Labortest.
Copytesten *n* (**Copy-Testforschung** *f*) copy testing
The process of measuring the effectiveness of an advertising campaign, an advertisement, or elements of an advertisement.
Copy-Test-Stichprobe *f* copy-testing panel
Cordband *n*
→ Magnetfilm
Cordmaschine *f* (**Cordspieler** *m*) magnetic film recording machine, magnetic film recorder
Cornell-Technik *f* (**der Einstellungsmessung, der Skalenanalyse**) Cornell technique (of attitude measurement, of scale analysis)
Corporate Advertising *n*
→ Unternehmenswerbung, Firmen-Imagewerbung
Corporate Communication *f* corporate communication, corporate communications *pl* (*construed as sg*)
→ Corporate Identity, Unternehmenswerbung
Corporate Design *n* (**Corporate-Identity-Design** *n*) corporate design
The outward appearance of a corporation in its architecture, product presentation, media etc. that, taken together, convey the impression of a corporate style. The German word "Unternehmensgestalt" is barely used and understood.
Corporate Identity *f* (**C.I.**) corporate identity, corporate image
→ Unternehmensidentität
Corporate-Identity-Wert *m* (**C.I.-Wert** *m*) corporate identity value
Corporate Image *n* (**Firmen-Image** *n*, **Unternehmens-Image** *n*)
→ Unternehmensidentität
Corporate-Philantropie *f* (**unternehmerische Philantropie** *f*) corporate philantropy, business philantropy
Corrigenda *n/pl* (**Druckfehlerverzeichnis** *n*, **Setzfehlerverzeichnis** *n*) *(typ)* corrigenda *pl*, errata *pl*, errata sheet
Cost Center *n*
→ Profit Center
Cost-plus-System *n*
→ Pauschalpreis plus Kosten
Countermarketing *n*
→ Kontramarketing
Countervailing Power *f*
→ gegengewichtige Marktmacht
Coupon *m*
→ Gutschein, Kupon
Coupon-
→ Gutschein-, Kupon-
Couponanzeige *f*
→ Kuponanzeige
Courtage *f* (**Kurtage** *f*) brokerage commission, brokerage fee, brokerage
A charge, sometimes in the form of a commission, made by a functional middleman for bringing buyer and seller together. Usually applied to the side for whom the middleman is working, sometimes both the buyer and the seller pay.
Coverage *f*
→ Reichweite, Haushaltsabdeckung
Cox-Box *f* (Michael Cox) *(media res)* Cox box
CPM *abbr* Critical-Path-Methode
CpO-Wert *m* *(econ)* cost-per-order value, cost per order
→ Bestellkosten
Crab-Dolly *f* *(TV)* crab dolly
A hand-propelled camera and operator mount on which all wheels can be swivelled synchronously for sideways movement.
Crayonmanier *f*
→ Kreidemanier
Cream-Plan *m*
→ Abschöpfungsstrategie
Creativ-Abteilung *f*
→ Kreativabteilung
Creative-Director *m* (**CD**)
→ Kreativdirektor
Critical-Path-Methode *f* (**CPM**) (**Methode** *f* **des kritischen Pfades**) critical path method (CPM)
A planning technique derived from network analysis, (→) Netzplantechnik, usually applied to complex projects with a large number of interrelated variables. Any step in the process whose timing is critical to the whole project is

Cue

represented in a diagram that shows which jobs must be completed before others can be started. The series thus forms a linear sequence, the critical path, from which the minimum time for the project can be calculated.
Cue m **(Cue-Marke** f**)**
→ Startmarkierung (Schnittmarke)
Cue-Track m
→ Hilfstonspur
Cut m
→ Schnitt
Cut-off-Verfahren n *(stat)*
→ Auswahl nach dem Konzentrationsprinzip (Abschneideverfahren)
cutten *v/t (film/TV)* to cut, to edit
 To rearrange motion picture or television scenes into a desired sequence, timing, and synchronization with the sound track.
Cutten n **(Lichtschnitt** m**)** *(film/TV)*
cutting and editing, cutting, film cutting and editing, editing, film editing
 The process of selecting and arranging motion picture or television scenes into a completed film.
Cutter(in) *m(f)* **(Schnittmeister(in)** *m(f))* *(film/TV)* cutter, cutter and editor, editor, film editor, (Band) tape editor
 The technician who carries out the actual rearranging of motion picture or television scenes or sequences on a tape into a desired sequence until the finished picture or tape is completed.
Cutterassistent(in) *m(f)* *(film/TV)* assistant film editor, assistant editor
Cutterbericht m **(Cutterzettel** m**)** *(film/TV)* editor's report (ER), film editor's report (FER)
Cyanotypie f
→ Zyanotypie

D

D²-Abstandsmaß n
→ Mahalanobis-Distanz
D-Welle f (**übergroße Welle** f) *(paper)*
D flute
Dachantenne f *(radio/TV)* roof antenna, *brit* roof aerial
dachförmige Antenne f *(radio/TV)* roof-shaped antenna, *brit* roof-shaped aerial
dachförmige Welle f (**V-förmige Welle** f) *(paper)* V-shaped flute
Dachinformationsanbieter m *(Btx)* umbrella information provider
Dachkampagne f umbrella campaign
Dachmarke f (**Markenfamilie** f) umbrella brand, family brand
   A single brand name that is applied to a large number (or all) of the products of one producer or seller, so that, ideally, all products, and particularly product innovations, profit from the goodwill built up for the brand.
Dachschild n (**Dachplakat** n) *(outdoor advtsg)* roof panel
   A poster panel or painted bulletin placed in a roof or gable-end position.
Dachposition f (**Giebelposition** f) *(outdoor advtsg)* roof position, gable-end position
Dachprisma n
→ Umlenkprisma
Dachrinnenantenne f *(radio)* eaves antenna, *brit* eaves aerial
Dachspiegel m
→ Umlenkspiegel
Dachwerbung f *(outdoor advtsg)* roof advertising, roof panel advertising, gable advertising, gable-end advertising
Dachzeile f *(print)* overline, deck head, deck, *colloq* kicker
   An overline over the main head of an article or advertisement.
DAGMAR-Formel f (**DAGMAR-Modell** n) *(advtsg res)* DAGMAR model, DAGMAR formula (Russell H. Colley)
   An acronym for: Defining Advertising Goals for Measured Advertising Results, a controversial concept advanced in 1961 by the Association of National Advertisers in a paper authored by Russell H. Colley.
daktyloskopische Methode f (**Fingerabdruckverfahren** n) *(media res)* dactyloscopic method, dactylogram method, fingerprint method
Dampfbehandlung f (**eines Liners**) *(paper)* water finish, water finishing, *brit* steam finish, steam finishing
dämpfen v/t to attenuate, to damp, (Licht) to soften
Dampfradio n *colloq* blind radio, steam radio
Dämpfung f (**Dämpfen** n) damping, attenuation
Dankschreiben n (in der Werbung) testimonial, testimonial letter
   A letter of recommendation for a product or service by a user for advertising purposes.
Darsteller m
→ Schauspieler
Darstellerbesetzung f *(film/radio/TV)* casting
   The process and/or result of putting together the group of actors and actresses (the cast) or announcers in a motion picture, a radio or television program, or a commercial.
Darstellerliste f *(film/radio/TV)* cast list
Datei f data file, file, data set
Dateianalyse f data file analysis, file analysis
Datel m (**Datel-Dienst** m) *abbr* Data Telecommunication Service
→ Datenfernübertragung
Daten n/pl data pl
   Any information which is given or provided for the solution of a problem. Because more than one unit of information is necessary for solving every problem, the word is plural. Data must be quantified and structured before being usable for the solution of a statistical problem. They are measured in statistical units, which must be:
(1) relevant to the enquiry or problem;
(2) homogeneous (i.e. of the same type); and (3) stable.
In accounting statistics a measure of homogeneity is often achieved by comparing dissimilar units, for example,

Datenanalyse

the standard hour, a measure of work which a typical individual performs in an hour. Data are often divided into two categories, primary and secondary indicating nearness to source or otherwise. For example, data collected by means of experiment, interview, observation, questionnaires or survey are primary, while items of data obtained by the researcher from a previous source or publication are secondary.

Datenanalyse f (**Datenauswertung** f) data analysis
The statistical techniques of testing hypotheses and estimates following data reduction.

Datenaufbereitung f (**Datenreduktion** f, **Datenverdichtung** f) data processing, data reduction
The statistical techniques of obtaining raw scores from the raw data collected in an investigation through consolidation, organization, tabulation and computation.

Datenauswertung f
→ Datenanalyse

Datenbank f data bank, data archive(s) *(pl)*
A comprehensive file of data, usually stored on a direct-access storage device. In the specific computing sense, a data bank is usually a file stored on a direct-access storage device. It can thus be available to different users, often remotely situated from the data bank, and can be accessed by means of terminals, and updated by using a real time system. Airline booking systems often use this kind of data bank.

Datenbankmarketing n data bank marketing

Datenbereinigung f (**Cleanen** n **von Daten, Plausibilitätskontrolle** f) data cleaning, data editing, editing of data
The elimination of obvious inconsistencies and mistakes in raw data.

Datenbeschaffung f (**Datenerhebung** f, **Datengewinnung** f) data collection

Datenbestand m data base
A small-scale file of data. A file of data which is designed so that it can satisfy any of a number of different purposes. It is structured in such a way that it may be accessed and updated, but these processes do not modify or limit its content or design.

Datenblatt n data sheet
A leaflet containing classified factual information.

Datenendgerät n (**Daten-Terminal** m, **Datenstation** f) data terminal

Datenerfassung f data acquisition

Datenerhebung f
→ Erhebung

Datenfeld n **der Preispolitik** (Heribert Meffert) *etwa* data field of price policy, data field of pricing
vgl. Aktionsfeld, Erwartungsfeld

Datenfernübertragung f (**Datenübertragung** f) data transmission, remote data transmission

Datenfernverarbeitung f teleprocessing, data teleprocessing, teleprocessing of data

Datenfusion f
→ Fusion

Datengewinnung f
→ Erhebung

Datenkommunikation f data communication, data communications *pl (construed as sg)*
→ Mensch-Maschine-Kommunikation, Maschine-Maschine-Kommunikation

Datenmatrix f data matrix
→ Matrix

Datenplan m (**der Anzeigen**) schedule of insertions, schedule of insertions
→ Mediaplan, Terminplan

Datenplatte f data disc, data disk

Datenreduktion f (**Datenverdichtung** f)
→ Datenaufbereitung

Datensammlung f data collection, collection of data

Datensatz m data set, set of data

Datenschutz m data protection, protection of data privacy

Datenspeicher m
→ Datenbank, Datenbestand, Datenträger

Datenstation f
→ Datenendgerät

Datenträger m data store, data storage medium, data medium, data carrier

Datenübertragung f
→ Datenfernübertragung

Datenverarbeitung f data processing (DP)
The arrangement of statistical data into some systematic form for further analysis.

Datenverarbeitungsanlage f (**Datenverarbeitungssystem** n) data processing equipment, data processing system, data processing center, *brit* data processing centre

Datenverknüpfung f
→ Fusion
Datex-Dienst m data exchange service
Datumsangabe f (wie Frischestempel) code date, date
→ Frischestempel, Verfalldatum
Daueranschlag m **(Dauerplakat** n) *(outdoor advtsg) etwa* long-term poster, painted bulletin, painted display, painted wall
Dauereinkommenshypothese f *(econ)* permanent income hypothesis (Milton Friedman)
vgl. relative Einkommenshypothese
Dauerfalzfestigkeit f **(Falzwiderstand** m) *(paper)* folding endurance, folding strength
Dauerfalzprüfung f *(paper)* folding endurance test
Dauergruppenbefragung f *obsol*
→ Panel
Dauerkunde m
→ Stammkunde
Dauerleitung f *(radio/TV)* permanent circuit
Dauerleitungsnetz n *(radio/TV)* permanent-circuit network, permanent network
Dauerstörung f *(radio/TV)* continuous interference
Dauerwerbung f *etwa* long-term posting, long-term outdoor advertising, permanent posting, permanent outdoor advertising
→ Dachwerbung, Giebelwerbung, Leuchtwerbung
Dauerwirkung f long-range effect, long-term effect, lasting effect
Daunendruckpapier n **(Federleichtpapier** n) featherweight paper, featherweight antique
db *abbr* Dezibel
DBGN n *abbr* Deutsches Bundesgebrauchsmuster
→ Gebrauchsmuster
DBPa *abbr* Deutsches Bundespatentamt angemeldet
Debriefing n debriefing
Decision-Calculus-Ansatz m **(Decision-Calculus-Methode** f, **Decision-Calculus-Modell** n) *(marketing)* decision-calculus approach, decision-calculus method, decision-calculus model (John D. C. Little)

Decision-Support-System n **(DSS)** *(marketing)* decision-support system
Deckblatt n *(print)* 1. (Vorsatzblatt) flyleaf, fly leaf, *brit* fly title 2. (Korrekturblatt) change sheet, correction sheet 3. (durchsichtig) overlay, transparent guardsheet 4. (Zurichtebogen) overlay, top drawsheet
Deckbogen m
→ Deckblatt 4.
Decke f
→ Einbanddecke, Deckenbahn
Deckel m
→ Buchdeckel, Einbanddeckel
Deckelbezug m covering
Deckelklappe(n) f*(pl)* package top flap(s) *(pl)*
Deckelschachtel f lidded box
Deckelsatinage f board glazing
Deckenanhänger m **(Deckenhänger** m, **Deckenaufhänger** m) *(POP advtsg)* dangler, mobile, pelmet, wobbler
→ Mobile
Deckenbahn f **(Decke** f) *(paper)* liner, liner board, liner web, facing
Deckeneinband m
→ Einbanddecke
Deckengestänge n **(Deckengitter** n) *(POP advtsg)* aisle jumper
   An overhead wire or grid reaching across the aisles in a retail store. Signs or banners may be hung on it or flags and pennants draped on it.
Deckenherstellung f
→ Einbandherstellung
Deckenpapier n **(Deckenpappe** f)
→ Umschlagpapier
Decker m
→ Deckblatt
Deckfähigkeit f **(Deckkraft** f) *(print/phot)* (Farbe) opacity, opaqueness, body
   The characteristic of not permitting the passage of light.
Deckfarbe f *(print)* body color, *brit* colour, opaque color, *brit* colour, opaque ink
Deckfolie f *(print/phot)* acetate overlay, overlay
→ Abdeckfolie
Decklage f *(paper)* liner, liner board, facing
Decklack m
→ Abdecklack
Deckplatte f
→ Abdeckplatte

Deckung *f* 1. *(econ)* (des Bedarfs) supply 2. *(TV)* (Raster) registration, convergence, (Negativ) density
Deckungsauflage *f*
Deckungsbeitrag *m (econ)* etwa direct cost
Deckungsbeitragsrechnung *f* (DBR) *(econ)* etwa direct costing
 A method of applying costs directly to a particular brand, product, or function.
Deckungsfehler *m (TV)* (Raster) convergence error, registration error, (Negativ) error in density
Deckweiß *n (print/phot)* opaque white, zinc white
Decoder *m* decoder
decodieren (dekodieren) *v/t* to decode
Deduktion *f* **(Schlußfolgerung** *f*, **Folgerung** *f***)** deduction
vgl. Induktion
deduktive Methode *f* **(Methode** *f* **der Deduktion)** deductive method
 The method and process of logically deriving a specific prediction from a set of general principles or axioms of a theory.
vgl. induktive Methode
defekt *adj (print)* battered, damaged, defective, bad
Defektbuchstabe *m* **(Defektletter** *f*, **Defekte** *m/pl*) *(print)* battered letter, battered type, batter, (Reservelettern) sorts *pl*
Defektbogen *m (print)* spoilage, overplus sheet, overplus, imperfect sheet
 A sheet of paper that was wasted during the printing process.
Defektenkasten *m* **(Defektkasten** *m*, **Zeugkasten** *m*) *(print)* hellbox, hell
 In hot-metal composition, (→) Bleisatz, a box in the composing room wherein discarded type and other lead to be remelted may be thrown.
Deflationsmethode *f* **(Deflationsverfahren** *n*) *(advtsg res)* deflation technique, deflation
 A number of techniques of eliminating false claims of having seen advertisements that had never been published.
Deformationsverfahren *n* **(Zerfallsverfahren** *n*) *(advtsg res)* distortion technique
 A technique of testing the form quality, (→) Gestaltfestigkeit, of advertisements, product designs, and packages by distorting them to find out whether test persons are able to recognize the original.
Degenerationsphase *f* **(Schrumpfungsphase** *f* **(im Produktlebenszyklus)** decline stage, decline, obsolescence
 The last of four stages in the product life cycle (→) Produktlebenszyklus. Sales turn downward, profits decrease, competitors leave the market.
vgl. Einführungsphase, Wachstumsphase, Reifephase
Dehnfolieneinschlag *m (packaging)* stretch wrapping
Dehnfolienpackung *f (packaging)* stretch pack, stretch package
Dehnrichtung *f (paper)* cross grain, cross direction, against-the-grain direction
vgl. Laufrichtung
Dekoder *m*
→ Decoder
Dekodierung *f*
→ Decodierung
Dekor *n*, *auch m (film/TV/phot)* set, scenery, set, setting, décor, decor
Dekorateur *m* decorator, display artist, window dresser, set designer, scene painter
→ Schauwerber, Schaufenster-Dekorateur
Dekoration *f* **(Dekorieren** *n*) *(POP advtsg)* decoration, decorating, display work, window dressing, design, *(film/TV/phot)* scenery set, scenery, setting and properties, set
Dekorationsabbau *m (film/TV/phot)* set striking
Dekorationsaufbau *m (film/TV/phot)* set construction, set erection
Dekorationshilfen *f/pl*
→ Händlerhilfen
Dekorationslicht *n (film/TV/phot)* set light, background light
Dekorationsmaler *m (film/TV/phot)* scene painter
Dekorationsmaterial *n (POP advtsg)* display material, displays *pl*
 Any promotional material used or installed in retail stores for display or visual embellishment in windows, on floors, on walls, or counters.
vgl. Händlerhilfen
Dekorationsrabatt *m* display discount, display allowance
 A promotional allowance granted by vendors to retailers to offset the added

costs of making special efforts in displaying their products.
Dekorationsrequisiten *n/pl (film/TV/phot)* set dressings *pl*
Dekorationsstück *n* (**Dekorationsteil** *m*) *(POP advtsg)* display piece, show piece
Dekorationsstoff *m (film/TV/phot/POP advtsg)* decorative material, decoration material, display material
dekorativ *adj* decorative
dekorieren *v/t* to decorate, to dress
Delaminierung *f* delamination
Delayed-response-Effekt *m*
→ Wirkungsverzögerung
Delay-Line *f*
→ Verzögerungsfilter
deleatur *imp (typ)* delete, dele, deleatur
  The instruction to a typesetter to remove part of a manuscript, or copy that has been set in type.
Deleaturzeichen *n* (**Deleatur** *n*, **Tilgungszeichen** *n*) *(typ)* deletion mark, dele mark
Delkredere *n* (**Delkrederegeschäft** *n*) *(econ)* del credere, del credere business
  The acceptance of responsibility by an agent for the payment of money due to a principal for an increased commission (→) Delkredereprovision, in return for the additional risk involved.
Delkredereprovision *f (econ)* del credere commission
Delphi-Befragungsmethode *f* (**Delphi-Methode** *f*, **Delphi-Technik** *f*) *(marketing res)* Delphi technique, Delphi interviewing technique, Delphi method, Delphi interviewing method
  A research technique based on interviews with experts of the field under investigation. First, they are asked individually by personal interview or mail questionnaire to express their judgments. After compilation, the results are given to the participants, who may revise their estimates. At no time do the participants meet together. The process may be repeated a number of times. Usually a consensus is reached which can then be used as a basis for decision-making.
→ Expertenbefragung
Demand-Pull-Theorie *f*
→ Pull-Theorie
Demarketing *n*
→ Reduktionsmarketing
Demodulation *f* demodulation

Demodulator *m* demodulator
demographisch *adj* demographic(al)
demographische Analyse *f (res)* demographic analysis
demographische Aufgliederung *f* (**demographische Zusammensetzung** *f*) *(res)* demographic breakdown, breakdown, *colloq* break
  The formation of an analysis group, or the group itself, broken down by demographic characteristics, (→) demographische Merkmale.
demographische Marktsegmentierung *f (marketing res)* demographic market segmentation
  A technique of market segmentation, (→) Marktsegmentierung, on the basis of demographics, (→) demographische Merkmale.
  vgl. psychographische Marktsegmentierung
demographische Merkmale *n/pl* (**demographische Struktur** *f*) *(res)* demographic characteristics *pl*, demographics *pl*, demographic structure
  Objective statistical characteristics of a population, (→) Grundgesamtheit, such as sex, age, household size, income, occupation, religion, marital status, or social class.
demographische Segmentierung *f*
→ demographische Marktsegmentierung
demographischer Analogieschluß *m (media planning)* etwa demographic analogy
demographische Struktur *f*
→ demographische Merkmale
DEMON *n* (**DEMON-Modell** *n*) *(marketing)* DEMON model
Demonstration *f* (**Vorführung** *f*) demonstration, sales demonstration, presentation, *colloq* demo, (im Laden) in-store demonstration
  The act of showing how a product works.
Demonstrationsauslage *f* (**Vorführauslage** *f*) *(POP advtsg)* demonstrator display
  A point-of-purchase display that shows the functioning of a product.
Demonstrationsfilm *m* (**Musterfilm** *m*, **Vorführrolle** *f*) demonstration recording, demonstrational film, demo reel, demo, sample reel
  A film recording that shows samples of television or motion picture commercials.
Demonstrationsmaterial *n*
→ Anschauungsmaterial

Demonstrationsplatte *f* (**Demo-Platte** *f*, **Vorführplatte** *f*) demonstration recording, demo record, demo
A recording used for demonstration purposes.

demonstrative Muße *f* (**ostentative Muße** *f*, **demonstratives Freizeitverhalten** *n*) conspicuous leisure (Thorstein Veblen)

demonstrativer Konsum *m* (**Geltungskonsum** *m*, **ostentativer Konsum** *m*) conspicuous consumption (Thorstein Veblen), (demonstrative Verschwendung) conspicuous waste

demonstrieren *v/t* to demonstrate, to present

Demoskop *m* 1. (Umfrageforscher) survey researcher 2. (Meinungsforscher) public opinion researcher

Demoskopie *f* 1. survey research, survey research methodology, *obsol* demoscopy
An empirical social research technique based on scientific sampling, experimental design and interviewing, usually with questionnaires. The term demoscopy was originally coined in the U.S., and has gained general acceptance in Germany.
2. public opinion research, opinion research
The use of survey research methodology to investigate public opinion.

demoskopische Marktforschung *f* (Karl Christian Behrens) *etwa* demoscopic market research, subject-centered market research, demographically oriented empirical market research
vgl. ökoskopische Marktforschung

demoskopisches Befragungsexperiment *n* (zur Messung des Umsatzerfolgs von Marketing) (Johannes Bidlingmaier) *etwa* controlled survey experiment (to measure sales effectiveness of marketing), split-run test, split-run survey

demoskopisches Interview *n*
→ Interview

Dendrogramm *n* (**Baumdiagramm** *n*) *(stat)* dendrogram

Denken *n*
→ Kognition

Denkpsychologie *f* (**Psychologie** *f* **des Denkens**) psychology of thought, psychology of thinking, psychology of thought perception

Densitometer *n* (**Schwärzungsmesser** *m*, **Dichtemesser** *m*) *(phot)* densitometer
A photoelectric device for measuring the density of photographic negatives and positives.
→ Schwärzungsdichte

Densitometrie *f* (**Schwärzungsmessung** *f*, **Dichtemessung** *f*) *(phot)* densitometry

densitometrisch *adj (phot)* densitometric(al)

Departmentsystem *n*
→ Abteilungsorganisation

Dependenzanalyse *f* (**Abhängigkeitsanalyse** *f*) dependence analysis (Raymond Boudon)
vgl. Interdependenzanalyse

Depothandel *m (econ)* silent trade, silent barter

Deprivation *f*
→ relative Deprivation

Desensibilisierung *f* (**Herabsetzung** *f* **der Lichtempfindlichkeit**) *(phot)* desensitization
The process of reducing the sensitivity to light of films or plates.

Design *n* (**Gestaltung** *f*, **Formgebung** *f*, **Formgestaltung** *f*) design
The visual and artistical plan determining the outward appearance and form of an object, e.g. a product, an advertisement. The English word has become a generally accepted household term in German.

Designer *m* (**Formgestalter** *m*) designer
An artist who creates and executes designs.

Desk-Research *m*
→ Sekundärforschung

deskriptive Forschung *f* (**deskriptive Marktforschung** *f*) descriptive research, descriptive market research
Gathering information from surveys, polling, or public records. The research does not attempt to establish cause-and-effect relationships.

Deskriptivstatistik *f* (**deskriptive Statistik** *f*, **beschreibende Statistik** *f*) descriptive statistics *pl (construed as sg)*
That field of statistics that is concerned with the description of characteristics of data as well as the measures and techniques used for describing them.

Dessin *n* pattern, design, ornament, ornamental style

Dessinateur m
→ Musterzeichner
Detailaufnahme f **(Ganzgroß-
aufnahme** f **(Makro-Aufnahme** f**)**
(phot/film/TV) extreme close-up (ECU,
E.C.U.), big close-up (BCU, B.C.U.),
extra close-up
 A close-up showing limited to a detail of
 an object.
Detailgeschäft n
→ Einzelhandelsgeschäft
Detailhandel m
→ Einzelhandel
Detailhändler m
→ Einzelhändler
Detailleur m **(Detaillist** m**)**
→ Einzelhändler
Detailwiedergabe f *(phot/print)* detail
reproduction
 The degree of fidelity in rendering the
 minute subdivisions of an original.
Detailzeichnung f detail drawing
Determinante f determinant
 The difference between cross-product
 elements, or the sum of differences
 between corresponding cross-product
 elements of a matrix expressed as a
 scalar, or matrix.
 vgl. Resultante
Determination f *(stat)* determination
→ Bestimmtheit, Bestimmtheitskoeffizient
deterministische Beziehung f
determinate relationship
 vgl. stochastic relationship
deterministischer Fall m
→ Entscheidung unter Sicherheit
deterministisches Experiment n
(determiniertes Experiment n**)**
determinate experiment (Johan
Galtung)
 vgl. stochastisches Experiment
deterministisches Modell n
determinate model, deterministic
model
 A mathematical model or theory that
 specifically predicts which one response
 from two or more responses will occur.
 For example, a deterministic choice
 model may predict which of several
 objects will be chosen on a given
 occasion.
 vgl. stochastisches Modell
Deutsche Eisenbahn-Reklame f
GmbH (ERG) German Railroad
Advertising Inc.
Deutsche Gesellschaft f **für
Kommunikationsforschung e.V.**

(DGfK) German Association of
Communications Research
Deutsche Marketing Vereinigung f
e.V. **(DMV)** German Marketing
Association
Deutsche Postreklame f **GmbH**
German Post Advertising Inc.
**Deutsche Public Relations
Gesellschaft** f **(DPRG)** German Public
Relations Society
**Deutsche Werbewissenschaftliche
Gesellschaft** f e.V. **(DWG)** German
Society for Advertising Research
Deutscher Designertag m e.V.
Congress (Confederation) of German
Designers
Deutscher Franchise-Verband m e.V.
German Franchise Association
Deutscher Kommunikationstag m
e.V. German Congress of
Communication
Deutscher Kommunikationsverband
m
→ BDW Deutscher Kommunikations-
verband
Deutscher Presserat m German Press
Council
Deutscher Werbefachverband m e.V.
(DWF) Federation of German
(regional) Advertising Associations
Deutscher Werberat m German
Advertising Review Board, German
Advertising Standards Authority
deutsches Abrechnungsverfahren n
(advtsg) cost-and-commission system,
cost and commission
 The system of advertising agency
 remuneration under which the agency
 charges the cost incurred in producing
 advertising in addition to its commission.
Deutsches Institut n **für Public
Relations (DIPR)** German Institute of
Public Relations
Devisenbörse f *(econ)* foreign
exchange market, foreign exchange
Dezibel n **(dB)** decibel
Dezibelmesser m decibel meter
Dezile f **(Zehntelwert** m**, Zehntelstelle**
f**)** *(stat)* decile
 A quantile, (→) Quantile, which divides
 the total frequency of a set of variate
 values into ten equal partitions.
dezile Spannweite f **(Spannweite** f
einer Dezile) *(stat)* decile range
Dezistrecke f **(Mikrowellen-Relais** n**)**
(radio) microwave link
Dia n short for Diapositiv

Dia

Dia n auf Film
→ Filmdia
Diaabtaster m
→ Diageber
Diabetrachter m (**Dia-Betrachter** m)
(phot) transparency viewer, slide viewer
Diageber m (**Diaabtaster** m) *(TV)* slide scanner, (Titel) caption scanner
Diagnose f diagnosis
Diagonalblende f (**Diagonalschwenk** m) *(film/TV)* diagonal wipe, fan wipe
→ Bogenschwenk
Diagonale f *(stat)* diagonal line, diagonal
diagonale Zelle f (**diagonales Feld** n) *(stat)* (einer Matrix) diagonal cell
Diagonalklebestelle f *(film)* diagonal splice, diagonal join
Diagramm n *(stat)* diagram, graph, chart
Diagrammpapier n *(stat)* graph paper
Dia-Kopie f *(phot)* transparency duplicate, positive made from transparency (PMT)
Dialog m dialog, dialogue
Dialogautor m *(film/radio/TV)* dialoguist, writer of dialogs, author of dialog scripts
Dialogbuch n (**Dialog-Drehbuch** n) *(film/radio/TV)* dialog script, dialogue script
Dialogdatenstation f *(EDP)* interactive data terminal, interactive terminal
Dialogfrage f *(survey res)* dialog question, *brit* dialogue question
Dialogführung f
→ Dialogregie
Dialog-Marketing n interactive marketing, direct-response marketing
Dialogregie f (**Dialogführung** f) *(film/radio/TV)* dialog direction, dialogue direction
Dialogregisseur m *(film/radio/TV)* dialog director, dialogue director, (Synchronisation) dubbing director
Dialogszene f *(film/radio/TV)* dialog scene, dialogue scene
Dialogwerbung f (**Rücklaufwerbung** f, **Direct-Response-Werbung** f) direct-response advertising, direct-response marketing, direct response
  A variety of advertising and marketing techniques that encourage and expect a responsive action, such as coupon returns, inquiries, or buys, on the part of target persons. No German term has gained general acceptance, but "Direkt-Response-Werbung" has.
Dialogzeitschrift f (**Dialogzeitung** f) *etwa* interactive magazine, interactive (news)paper
Diapositiv n (**Dia** n, **Durchsichtbild** n, **Durchscheinbild** n) **1.** (Photographie) transparency **2.** (gerahmt) slide, lantern slide, film slide
Diapositiv-Wechselschlitten m slide carrier, slide changer
Diaprojektor m (**Diapositivprojektor** m) slide projector
Diarahmen m slide mount, transparency mount
Dia n **viva** slidefilm, film strip, filmstrip, stripfilm, slide motion picture
  A sequence of still pictures that were photographed on a motion picture film to give the effect of quasi motion.
Diawerbung f **1.** slide advertising, film slide advertising, cinema slide advertising **2.** (Werbemittel) slide advertisement, film slide advertisement, cinema slide advertisement, *(TV)* slide commercial
→ stummes Dia, tönendes Dia, Dia viva, Film-Dia
Diazofilm m diazo film
Diazokopie f (**Diazopause** f) *(phot)* diazo print, dye-line copy, white print
Diazokopieverfahren n (**Diazotypie** f, **Diazokopie** f) *(phot)* diazo printing, diazo process
Diazoverbindung f *(phot)* diazo compound
Diaphragma n
→ Blende
dichotom *adj* dichotomous
  Describing a set of stimuli, events, etc., that are divided or classified into two mutually exclusive categories.
dichotome Frage f
→ Alternativfrage
dichroitischer Filter m *(phot)* dichroic filter
dichroitischer Nebel m *(phot)* dichroic fog, red fog
  A condition in a negative where the film or plate looks red when seen by light coming through, and green by light reflected from it.
Dichromat m
→ Bichromat
Dichte f **1.** *(stat)* density **2.** *(phot)* (Schwärzungsdichte) density

The degree of opaqueness of the negative or positive print.
→ Schwärzung
Dichtefilter *m* **(Neutralfilter** *m*, **ND-Filter** *m) (phot)* neutral density filter, neutral filter
Dichtefunktion *f (stat)* density function
→ Häufigkeitsverteilung
Dichtekurve *f*
→ Schwärzungskurve
dichtester Wert *m (stat)*
→ häufigster Wert (Modus)
Dichteumfang *m* **(Schwärzungsumfang** *m) (phot)* density range
Dichteziffer *f*
→ Beziehungszahl
Dickte *f (typ)* set, set-width, set size, width, brass width
The width of a typeface.
Dicktentabelle *f (typ)* brass width table
Dienstleistung *f (econ)* service
Services are activities, benefits, or satisfactions which are offered for sale, or are provided in connection with the sale of goods. Examples are amusements, hotel service, electric service, transportation, the services of barber shops and beauty shops, repair and maintenance service, the work of credit rating bureaus, etc.
Dienstleistungsanzeige *f* service advertisement, service announcement
Dienstleistungsunternehmen *n (econ)* service company, service-rendering enterprise
Dienstleistungsbörse *f (econ)* service exchange market
Dienstleistungsbranche *f* **(Dienstleistungsgewerbe** *n) (econ)* service industry, services industry, services trade
The industry or trade consisting of suppliers of services, (→) Dienstleistung, not directly involved with manufacturing, e.g. insurance, consultancy, professional and personal treatment, health, travel, etc.
Dienstleistungsmarke *f (econ)* service mark
A trademark, (→) Warenzeichen, registered for a service.
Dienstleistungsmarketing *n* service marketing, marketing of services
Dienstleistungsprobe *f (econ)* service sample
A sample, *cf.* (→) Warenprobe, of a service.

Differenzenschätzung *f (stat)* difference estimation
Differenzmethode *f* **(Methode** *f* **des Differenztests)** *(stat)* difference method, variate-difference method
diffus *adj (phot)* diffuse, diffused
Diffusorlinse *f (phot)* diffusing lens, diffuser lens, diffusor lens, soft-focus lens
→ Diffusionsscheibe
Diffusion *f* **1.** *(econ)* (Ausbreitung) diffusion
In sociology, the communication process through which social ideas, attitudes, cultural values etc. spread in a society. In marketing, the process by which new products and services, innovations, behavior patterns etc. spread in an economic system.
2. *(phot)* diffusion, soft focus, diffusion of focus, soft definition
The lack of sharpness in the picture image due to a defective lens, imperfect focusing, or a special lens made to give soft effects.
Diffusionsfilter *m (phot)* diffusing filter, diffuser, diffuser, soft-focus filter, *colloq* romanticizer, (Beleuchtung) scrim
In photography, motion pictures and television a translucent screen or the like used to soften shadows and highlights created by bright lights. Also, a device used to blur the focus of a camera image.
→ Diffusion 2., Diffusionsscheibe
Diffusionsforschung *f (econ)* diffusion research
→ Diffusion 1.
Diffusionskurve *f (econ)* diffusion curve, curve of diffusion
→ Diffusion 1.
Diffusionsmodell *n (econ)* diffusion model
→ Diffusion 1.
Diffusionsprozeß *m (econ)* diffusion process
→ Diffusion 1.
Diffusionsrate *f* **(Diffusionsgeschwindigkeit** *f) (econ)* diffusion rate
The speed with which the diffusion process progresses.
Diffusionsscheibe *f* **(Diffusionsvorsatz** *m*, **Softscheibe** *f*, **Weichstrahler** *m) (phot)* diffusor, diffuser, diffusion disk, soft-focus disk
A disk, or a net, a piece of cloth, a glass or a mesh stretched on a frame and used

Diffusionstheorie

to diffuse or soften harsh light and reduce contrast.
Diffusionstheorie f *(econ)* diffusion theory
Diffusions-Übertragungs-Verfahren n **(Diffusionsverfahren** n) *(phot)* diffusion-transfer process
Diffusor m
→ Diffusionsscheibe
Digest m digest
Digital-Marketing n
→ Dialog-Marketing; *vgl.* Analog-Marketing
Dimension f **(Maß** n, **Ausmaß** n, **Grad** m) dimension
  The measurable quantity, used in marketing research, to compare responses at different levels or in regard to platforms.
Dimmer m dimmer
DIN *abbr* Deutsche Industrie-Norm German Standards Association
DIN-Format n **(DIN-Papierformat** n) German standard paper size
Diode f **(Gleichrichter** m) *(electr.)* diode
Diodenanschluß m *(electr.)* diode terminal
Dioptrie f **(dptr)** *(optics)* diopter, *brit* dioptre
Dioptrieausgleich m *(optics)* diopter correction, *brit* dioptre correction
Diorama n *(phot/film/TV)* diorama
  1. A mockup of a scene shot built with a three-dimensional foreground blending into a two-dimensional background.
  2. A specially lighted, often animated, three-dimensional advertising display.
Dipol m *(radio/TV)* dipole, doublet
Dipolantenne f *(radio/TV)* dipole antenna, *brit* dipole aerial, doublet, dipole
Dipolebene f *(radio/TV)* broadside array, dipole array
Dipolfeld n *(radio/TV)* dipole panel
Dipolgruppe f *(radio/TV)* dipole array, group antenna, *brit* group aerial
Dipolreihe f *(electr.)* collinear array of dipoles
DIPR *abbr* Deutsches Institut für Public Relations e.V.
DIR-Kuppler m **(Developing-Inhibitor-Releasing-Kuppler** m) developing inhibitor releasing coupler
Direct Costing n
→ Teilkostenrechnung
Direct Mail n
→ Briefwerbung

Direct-Response-Marketing n
→ Dialogmarketing (Rücklaufmarketing)
Direct-Response-Werbung f
→ Dialogwerbung (Rücklaufwerbung)
Direktabsatz m 1. direct sale 2. direct selling
  The process whereby the firm responsible for production sells to the user, ultimate consumer, or retailer without intervening middlemen.
Direktansage f **(Direktvorspann** m) *(radio/TV)* live tag
  A live announcement added to a recorded broadcast.
Direktansprache f **(Methode** f **der direkten Ansprache)** (in der Werbung) you approach, "you" attitude
  The personalized form of directing the advertising message at an individual target person.
Direktaufnahme f *(film)* direct recording
  The simultaneous recording of sound and film.
Direktausblendung f **(Live-Ausblendung** f) *(radio/TV)* live fade
  A sound fade created in the transmission studio.
Direktbefragung f **(Direktbefragungsmethode** f) *(market res)* direct survey, direct-survey method
  vgl. BuBaW-Verfahren, demoskopisches Befragungsexperiment, Gebietsverkaufstest, Netapps-Methode, Noreensches Modell
Direktbeleuchtung f **(Direktbelichtung** f) *(phot/film/TV)* front lighting
Direktbestellung f *(econ)* direct order
Direktbezug m **(Direkteinkauf** m, **Direktkauf** m) 1. direct purchase, direct buy 2. direct purchasing, direct buying, buying direct, industrial buying, industrial purchasing
  The process of purchasing directly from a producer.
  3. (Abonnement) direct subscription
  A subscription made directly with the publisher. Wholesalers, retailers or the postmaster are not part of the process.
Direktbildfilm m **(Polaroidfilm** m, **Sofortbildfilm** m) *(phot)* direct image film, polaroid film
Direktbildkamera f **(Polaroidkamera** f, **Sofortbildkamera** f) *(phot)* direct image camera, polaroid camera

direkte Frage f *(survey res)* direct question
direkte Preiselastizität f
→ Preiselastizität
Direkteinkauf m
→ Direktkauf
Direktempfang m *(radio/TV)* direct reception
Direktexport m *(econ)* direct export, direct exporting
  A type of direct selling, (→) Direktabsatz in which a manufacturer perform all required tasks to export his product himself and without intermediaries.
Direktivinterview n **(direktives Interview** n) *(survey res)* directive interview
Direktkauf m **(Direkteinkauf** m)
→ Direktbezug 1. und 2.
Direktklischee n **(Photoklischee** n) *(print)* direct halftone
  A halftone for which the screen negative was made by photographing the original, instead of a picture of the object.
Direktklischierung f **(Direktklischeeverfahren** n) *(print)* automatic engraving, direct halftone process, direct process
  The production of relief printing plates from photographic images by means of automatical engraving machines and the direct production of color separation negatives from originals through color filters and a halftone screen.
Direktmarketing n direct marketing
  The marketing of goods or services directly to the ultimate consumers by a manufacturer, without the involvement of retail outlets.
Direktmarketingagentur f **(Direktmarketing-Unternehmen** n) direct-marketing agency, direct-marketing company
Direktsatellit m **(Direktsendesatellit** m) direct broadcast satellite (DBS)
Direktschaltung f *(radio/TV)* direct relay, direct hook-up
Direktsendung f **(Live-Sendung** f, **Direktübertragung** f) *(radio/TV)* live broadcast, live transmission, remote pickup, remote
  A broadcast originating outside the regular studios.
Direktstreuung f
→ Direktwerbung
Direktsucher m *(phot)* optical viewfinder
Direktübertragung f
→ Direktsendung

Direktverkauf m 1. direct sale 2. direct selling
→ Direktabsatz
3. (ab Hersteller) industrial selling 4. (Haustürverkauf an den Endverbraucher) house-to-house sale, house-to-house selling, door-to-door sale, door-to-door selling 5. (per Post) (→) Versandhandel
Direktverkaufspreis m *(econ)* direct-sale price, direct-sale rate
Direktversand m **(Postversand** m)
→ Versandhandel
Direktvertrieb m **(Direktverteilung** f) direct distribution, direct-channel distribution
→ Direktabsatz
Direktvertriebsweg m **(Direktvertriebskanal** m) direct distribution channel, direct channel of distribution, direct channel
  A distribution channel in which no intermediaries are used.
Direktvertriebssystem n direct distribution system, direct-channel distribution system
Direktwerbeaktion f **(Direktwerbekampagne** f) direct-advertising campaign
Direktwerber m 1. direct advertiser, direct-advertising agent, direct-advertising man 2. (Kundenbesucher) canvasser, house-to-house salesman, door-to-door salesman (Abowerber) subscription canvasser, magazine subscription canvasser, subscription agent, subscription salesman
Direktwerbesendung f direct mailing, mailing
Direktwerbeunternehmen n **(Direktwerbeagentur** f) direct advertising agency, direct advertising company, direct advertiser
Direktwerbung f direct advertising
  All forms and techniques of advertising issued directly by the advertiser and distributed directly to customers or prospects, either by mail, house-to-house delivery, bag stuffers etc., but not in an advertising medium.
→ Briefwerbung, Drucksachenwerbung, Dialogwerbung, Versandhauswerbung
Direktwerbung f **durch die Post**
→ Briefwerbung, Drucksachenwerbung
Direktzugabe f **(Sofortzugabe** f) direct premium

Diskont

A premium, (→) Zugabe, that is offered together with the product unlike indirect premiums that are available through coupon redemption and the like.
Diskont *m* **(Discount** *m***, Diskonto** *m***)** discount, discounting *(retailing)*
The term in German only refers to retail trading at a relatively low markup.
Diskonter *m* **(Discounter** *m***, Diskontgeschäft** *n***, Diskonthaus** *n***)** *(retailing)* discounter, discount house, discount store
A retailing business unit, featuring consumer durable items, competing on a basis of price appeal, and operating on a relatively low markup and with a minimum of customer service.
Diskonthandel *m* **(Discounthandel** *m***)**
1. (Institution) discount trade
2. (Funktion) discount selling
A method of retailing which involves the sale of merchandise at less than list price or the regular advertised price.
Diskontpreis *m* **(Discount-Preis** *m***)** discount price
Diskontpreiswerbung *f* **(Discount-Preis-Werbung** *f***)** discount price advertising, advertising with discount prices
Diskont-Warenhaus *n* discount department store
vgl. Verbrauchermarkt
diskrete Daten *n/pl* **(unstetige Daten** *n/pl***, ganzzahlige Daten** *n/pl***)** *(stat)* discrete data *pl*
Data that can only take on certain fixed values, e.g. a number of fixed integers.
vgl. kontinuierliche Daten (stetige Daten)
diskrete Häufigkeitsverteilung *f* **(unstetige Häufigkeitsverteilung** *f***, diskrete Verteilung** *f***, unstetige Verteilung** *f***)** *(stat)* discrete frequency distribution, discrete distribution, discrete series
vgl. kontinuierliche Häufigkeitsverteilung
diskrete Skala *f* **(unstetige Skala** *f***)** *(stat)* discrete scale
vgl. kontinuierliche Skala
diskrete Variable *f* **(unstetige Variable** *f***)** *(stat)* discrete variable
A variable that only takes on certain fixed values.
vgl. kontinuierliche Skala
diskrete Zufallsgröße *f* **(unstetige Zufallsgröße** *f***)** *(stat)* discrete variate, discrete random variable
vgl. kontinuierliche Zufallsgröße

Diskriminanzanalyse *f* **(Diskriminantanalyse** *f***, Trennverfahren** *n***)** *(stat)* discriminant analysis, discriminatory analysis
A multivariate statistical procedure for describing the classification of individuals into two groups. Multiple discriminant analysis is used for classification into three or more groups. The analysis yields one or more equations (discriminant functions), similar to regression equations. In stepwise discriminant analysis, one or more predictor variables are added or omitted at each step to determine which combination of variables provides the best discrimination among the groups.
Diskriminanzfunktion *f* **(Trennfunktion** *f***, Entscheidungsfunktion** *f***)** *(stat)* discriminant function, discriminatory function
Diskriminationsvermögen *n* **(Diskriminationsfähigkeit** *f***)** *(psy)* discrimination
Diskriminationstechnik *f*
→ Skalendiskriminationstechnik
Diskriminierung *f* discrimination
Dispergiermittel *n* **(Dispergator** *m***)** *(phot/print)* dispersing agent, dispersant, dispersing medium
Dispersion *f*
1. → Streuung 1.
2. (Farbzerstreuung) dispersion
Dispersionsklebstoff *m* *(phot/print)* emulsion adhesive
Display *n* display
→ Warenauslage, Auslage
Displayartikel *m* display product
→ Auslageware
Displaygestalter *m*
→ Schauwerber
Displaygestaltung *f*
→ Schauwerbung
Displaymaterial *n* **(Displaymittel** *n/pl***)** *(POP advtsg)* display material, displays *pl*
→ Auslagematerial, Dekorationsmaterial, Händlerhilfen, Warenauslage
Display-Werbung *f* **(Auslagenwerbung** *f***, Verkaufsauslagenwerbung** *f***, Schauwerbung** *f***)** display advertising
→ Schauwerbung
disponibles Einkommen *n* **(verfügbares Einkommen** *n***)** *(econ)*
1. discretionary income, discretionary buying power, discretionary spending

power, discretionary purchasing power
That part of a consumer's or household's income which he has the choice of spending or saving. Usually considered to be that portion above an amount required for the "necessities of life".
2. disposable income, personal disposable income
That part of a consumer's or household's income that is left over after taxes and forced savings.

Disposition f disposition

Dispositionswerbung f **(Goodwillwerbung** f**, einstimmende Werbung** f**)** indirect-action advertising
All advertising that aims at creating a favorable attitude toward the product or service through long-range planning of frequent exposure over a period of time, so that at a particular time when the prospect is ready, the impact already made will impel a decision favorable to the seller.
vgl. Aktionswerbung

Dispositionszentrale f **(Dispositionszentrum** n**)** *(retailing)*
→ Einkaufszentrale, Großhandelszentrum, Trade Mart

disproportional geschichtete Auswahl f **(disproportional geschichtete Stichprobe** f**)** *(stat)* disproportionate stratified sample, disproportional stratified sample

disproportional geschichtetes Auswahlverfahren n **(disproportional geschichtetes Stichprobenverfahren** n**)** *(stat)* disportionate stratified sampling, disproportional stratified sampling
A type of stratified sampling, (→) geschichtete Auswahl, that is characterized by disproportionate allocation of the strata, i.e. the use of different sampling fractions, (→) Auswahlsatz, in each stratum.

disproportionale Auswahl f **(disproportionale Stichprobe** f**)** *(stat)* disproportionate sample, disproportional sample
A method of drawing a sample from a population which consists of a number of groups the importance of which to the validity of the study is each not directly related to relative size. The basis for the allocation of numbers from each group must be specially determined for each study requiring this procedure.

disproportionales Auswahlverfahren n **(disproportionales Stichprobenverfahren** n**, disproportionale Stichprobenbildung** f**)** *(stat)* disproportionate sampling, disproportional sampling
→ disproportional geschichtetes Auswahlverfahren; optimale Allokation

Dissimulation f *(survey res)* dissimulation

Dissonanz f *(psy)* dissonance
→ kognitive Dissonanz

Dissonanztheorie f *(psy)* dissonance theory
→ kognitive Dissonanz

Distanz f **(Abstand** m**)** *(stat)* distance
The closest proximity of points in a space.

Distanzhandel m
→ Streckenhandel

Distanzmaß n **(Ähnlichkeitsmaß** n**)** *(stat)* measure of distance, distance measure
→ City-Block-Distanz, Euklidische Distanz, Proximitätsmaß, Tanimoto-Koeffizient

Distanzrating n **(Distanzskalierung** f **)** *(stat)* distance rating, distance scaling (Clyde H. Coombs)

Distorsion f *(phot/print)* distortion
Any departure from the proper perspective of an image. In photography and platemaking, the departure in size or change of shape of a negative or reproduction as compared to the original, due to lack of parallelism in the camera equipment, or errors in stripping and handling of negatives and printing plates.

Distribution f distribution
→ Absatzweg(e), Vertrieb

Distributionsanalyse f *(market res)* distribution analysis, analysis of distribution, distribution check
The systematic examination of the quality, organization, performance, and number of outlets and channels of distribution, (→) Absatzwege, for a company's products.
→ Vertriebsanalyse

Distributionsauslese f
→ selektiver Vertrieb (selektive Distribution)

Distributionsdaten n/pl
→ Vertriebsdaten

Distributionsdichte f **(Vertriebsdichte** f**)** *(marketing)* distribution density

Distributionseffizienz f *(marketing)* distribution efficiency, efficiency of distribution

Distributionsgrad *m*
→ Distributionsquote
Distributionsindex m *(marketing)* index of distribution, distribution index
Distributionskanal m
→ Absatzweg, Vertriebsweg
Distributionskette f *(marketing)* distribution chain, chain of distribution
→ Absatzweg, Beschaffungsweg, Vertriebsweg
Distributionskosten pl *(marketing)* distribution cost, cost of distribution
Distributionskostenanalyse f *(marketing)* distribution cost analysis (DCA)
  An accounting system for determining the profit contribution of a company's individual products. It takes into account channels of distribution, geographic variables, handling peculiarities and other differences among the product cost factors.
Distributions-Mix n **(Distributionspolitik** f, **Absatz-Mix** n) *(marketing)* distribution mix, distribution policy
→ Absatzwegepolitik, Vertriebspolitik
Distributionsorgan n *(marketing)* distribution organ
Distributionsquote f **(Distributionsgrad** m, **Distributionsgrad** m) *(marketing)* distribution quota, distribution rate
Distributionssystem n
→ Absatzsystem, Vertriebssystem
Distributionsweg m
→ Absatzweg, Beschaffungsweg, Vertriebsweg
Distributor m distributor, service wholesaler
→ Vertriebsunternehmen
Diversifizierung f **(Diversifikation** f) *(marketing)* diversification
  The policy and process of adding new products to an already existing line of products to extend life cycles, offset decline, and spread risk.
→ horizontale Diversifizierung, vertikale Diversifizierung, laterale Diversifizierung
DNS-Verfahren n **(dynamisches Rauschunterdrückungsverfahren** n) dynamic noise suppression
Dokudrama n
→ Dokumentarspiel n
Dokumentalist m **(Bibliothekar** m) librarian

Dokumentarbericht m **(Tatsachenbericht** m) documentary report, documented report, documentary feature, documentary
  A report that presents actual events and factual background information.
Dokumentarfilm m **(Dokumentationsfilm** m) documentary film, documentary, *Am auch* fact film
  A film based on real life made in the actual setting and without professional actors.
dokumentarisch *adj* documentary
Dokumentarsendung f **(Dokumentationssendung** f) *(radio/TV)* documentary broadcast, documentary feature, documentary
  A broadcast presenting actual events and factual background information.
Dokumentarspiel n **(Dokudrama** n) *(radio/TV)* documentary drama, docudrama, dramatized documentary, semi-documentary
  A presentation in the form of a play, a film, a radio or television broadcast, etc., in which historical events are dramatized and sometimes fictionalized.
Dokumentation f **1.** documentation documentary evidence
  The creating, gathering, organizing, distributing, etc. of documents and the information recorded therein.
2. *(radio/TV)* documentary, documentary report, *(film)* documentary film, documentary, (Bericht) documentary report, documentary
→ Dokumentarbericht, Dokumentarfilm, Dokumentarsendung
Dokumentationsaufnahme f **(Dokumentationsphoto** n) documentary photo(graph), news photo(graph)
Dokumentationsphotographie f documentary photography, news photography
Dokumentenfilm m *(phot)* document film, high-contrast film, document-copying stock
Dolby n **(Dolby-Verfahren** n, **Dynamik-Verbesserungsverfahren** n) *(film)* Dolby, Dolby sound, Dolby technique (Ray M. Dolby)
Dolly m
→ Kamerawagen
dominante Werbung f
→ Intensivwerbung; *vgl.* flankierende Werbung

Dope-Sheet n
→ Aufnahmebericht, Kamerabericht
Doppelacht m **(Doppelachtfilm** m,
Doppel-8mm-Film m**)** double-eight film, double run 8mm film, double eight
Doppelausgabe f
→ Doppelheft
Doppelbelegung f **(Zweifachbelegung** f**)** *(transit advtsg)* double-carding
  An inside transit advertising arrangement wherelly two displays are specified in each vehicle.
Doppelbelichtung f *(phot)* double exposure, superimposition, super-imp
  The photographing of two different objects or scenes on the same film.
Doppelberstung f *(paper)* double pop
Doppelbild n **(Geisterbild** n, **Doppelkontur** f**)** *(TV)* double image, ghost image, ghost, double-path effect, echo effect, echo
  An offset secondary, weaker picture tube image on a television screen, caused by an earlier or later reflected transmission signal imitating the principal image.
Doppelblattsperre f *(print)*
→ Vorlagensperre
Doppelblindtest m **(Doppelblindversuch** m**)** *(res)* double blind test, double blind experiment
vgl. Blindtest
Doppelbogen m **(Doppelblatt** n**)** *(print)* double sheet
Doppelbrechung f *(phot)* birefringence, birefraction, double refraction
Doppelbünde m/pl *(binding)* double cords pl
Doppeldecker m *(print)* two-magazine composing machine, double-decker
Doppeldeckerplakat n *(outdoor advtsg)* double-decker, golden showcase
  Two outdoor advertising panels sited one above the other in two separate tiers.
→ Doppelplakat
Doppel-Doppel-Wellpappe f
→ zweiwellige Wellpappe
Doppeldruck m *(print)* mackle, blur, double impression, slur
  Blurred or imperfect impressions as a result of uneven pressure or movement of the plate or paper during proving or printing.
Doppelfalz m *(print)* double fold
Doppelfalzmaschine f *(print)* two-sheet folder

Doppelfrage f *(survey res)* double-barreled question, double-barrelled question
  A wide-spread question error that consists in really putting two questions into one survey question.
Doppelheft n **(Doppelausgabe** f**)** *(Zeitschrift)* double issue, combined edition
Doppelheftung f *(binding)* double-stitch joint
Doppelhörer m
→ Mehrfachhörer
Doppelkontakt(e) m(pl)
→ Mehrfachkontakt(e)
Doppelkontur f
→ Doppelbild
Doppelkreuz n *(typ)* double dagger, double obelisk, diesis
Doppelleser m
→ Mehrfachleser
Doppellinie f **(Doppelstrich** m**)** *(typ)* double rule, Oxford rule, Scotch rule
Doppelnummer f
→ Doppelheft
Doppelnutzer m
→ Mehrfachnutzer
Doppelnutzung f
→ Mehrfachnutzung
Doppelpackung f **(Zweierpackung** f**)** twin pack, *auch* double-sized package
  A package containing two product units sold as one at a promotional discount price.
Doppelplakat n *(outdoor advtsg)* double-decker, *auch* center spread, golden showcase, *(transit advtsg)* (an der Verkehrsmittelfront) double front
→ Doppeldecker
Doppelpostkarte f double post card, double postal card
Doppelseite f *(magazine)* double page, spread, double-page spread (DPS), (newspaper) double truck, (in der Heftmitte) center spread, (ohne Beschnitt) two pages facing pl
  A single sheet of paper that forms the two facing pages in the center of a publication and permits printing across the fold, or gutter.
→ doppelseitige Anzeige
Doppelseitenbandmodulation f *(radio)* double-sideband modulation, dsb modulation
Doppelseitenkontakt(e) (DSK) m(pl) **(Doppelanzeigenseitenkontakt** m, **Kontakte** m/pl **pro Doppelseite)**

doppelseitig

(media res) double-page spread exposure, double-page exposure
The exposure, (→) Kontakt, of readers to a double-page spread advertisement.
→ doppelseitige Anzeige
doppelseitig *adj* double-page, spread, double-page spread
doppelseitige Anzeige *f* double-page spread (DPS), double truck, double spread, two-page spread, advertising spread, (in der Heftmitte) center spread, *brit* centre spread, (im Bundsteg beschnitten) bridge
A magazine advertisement appearing on two facing pages.
Doppelspalte *f* **(doppelte Spalte** *f* **)** *(print)* double column (dc)
Doppelspielband *n* (Ton) double-play tape
Doppelspur *f (tape)* twin track, double track, double-head, double system
Doppelspur-Tonbandgerät *n* twin-track recorder, two-track recorder, dual-track recorder
Doppelstichprobe *f*
→ Zweiphasenstichprobe (Mehrphasenstichprobe)
Doppelstichprobenverfahren *n* **(Doppelauswahl** *f* **)**
→ Zweiphasenauswahl (Mehrphasenauswahl)
doppelt durchschossen *adj (typ)* double-leaded
→ doppelter Durchschuß
doppelte Brennweite *f (phot)* double focal length
doppelte Beschichtung *f* **(Doppelbeschichtung** *f* **)** *(paper/phot)* double coating
The coating of a film with two emulsions. One is a slow-speed and the other a high-speed emulsion. The slow emulsion provides correct exposure of the highlights, (→) Spitzlicht, and the fast emulsion provides detail in the shadows. The effect is to increase both the latitude and the tone scale of the film.
doppelte Trennlinie *f* **(doppelter Trennstrich** *m*, **zweifacher Trennstrich** *m*) *(typ)* double cutoff rule, double cutoff
doppelter Durchschuß *m* **(doppelter Zwischenschlag** *m*) *(typ)* double leading
The use of two leads, instead of one, between the slugs in a newspaper or magazine article.

doppelter Kameraauszug *m (phot)* double extension
A camera or bellows which allows a distance between the lens and focusing screen about double the focal length of the lens.
Doppeltondruck *m* **(Doppeltondruckverfahren** *n*) **1.** (Produkt) doubletone print, duotone print, duotone **2.** (Verfahren) doubletone printing, duotone printing, duotone
A type of printing produced by two plates, one with dark ink, the other with light ink, that results in a third color.
Doppeltonfarbe *f (print)* doubletone ink, duotone ink
Doppeltonmaterial *n (print)* doubletone
A drawing material or surface originally intended for the preparation of comic cartoons.
Doppelweggleichrichter *m (electr.)* full-wave rectifier
Dorfman-Steiner-Modell *n* **(Dorfman-Steiner-Theorem** *n*) *(marketing res)* Dorfman-Steiner model, Dorfman-Steiner theorem (R. Dorfman/P.O. Steiner)
Dose *f* box, container, can, *brit* tin
Dosierleiste *f* **(Dosierrakel** *m*) *(print)* metering bar
Dosierung *f* **(Regenierung** *f* **)** dosage, dosing
Dosierungsgerät *n* flowmeter, dosimeter
doubeln *v/t + v/i (film/TV)* to dub, (Darsteller) to stand in, to double
Doubeln *n (film/TV)* dubbing, post-synching, voice dubbing, (Kopierwerk) duping
Double *n (film/TV)* double, stand-in
Doublette *f* **(Doppelstück** *n*, **Dublette** *f* **)** *(print)* double, doublet, dupe
An item, word or passage accidentally set twice and repeated in the same copy.
Dow-Verfahren *n*
→ Einstufenätzverfahren
Doxologie *f*
→ Demoskopie, Meinungsforschung
DPRG (dprg) *f abbr* Deutsche Public Relations-Gesellschaft
Draht *m (binding/packaging)* wire, (zum Heften) stitching wire, sewing wire, (zum Bündeln) tying wire, (zum Umreifen) strapping wire
Drahtauslöser *m (phot)* cable release, antinous release

Drahtblockheftmaschine f *(print)* side-wire stitcher, side-wire binder
Drahtblockheftung f *(seitliche Drahtheftung* f*) (binding)* side-wire stitching, side-wire binding
Drahtfernsehen n cable television (CATV), wired television, closed-circuit television (CCTV)
→ Kabelfernsehen
Drahtfunk m **(Kabelfunk** m**)** cable broadcasting, wired broadcasting, wired radio, closed-circuit broadcasting
drahtgeheftet adj *(binding)* wire-stitched, stapled, wired
drahtgeheftete Pappeschachtel f *(binding)* wire-stitched cardboard box
Drahthefter m *(binding)* wire stitcher, wire stapler
Drahtheftmaschine f *(binding)* wire stitcher, wire stapler, wire-stitching machine, stapling machine, stapler, (Drahtblockheftmaschine) side-wire stitcher, (Drahtrückstichheftmaschine) saddle wire stitcher, (mit Doppelheftkopf) double-headed stapler, twin-head(ed) stapler
Drahtheftung f *(binding)* wire stitching, stapling, (Drahtblockheftung) side-wire stitching, (Drahtrückstichheftung) saddle wire stitching
 A method of binding a publication, usually a magazine or a periodical, by fastening the pages through the middle fold of the sheets with wire.
Drahtklammer f **(Drahtheftklammer** f**)** *(binding)* wire staple, staple
drahtlos adj wireless
drahtlose Bildtelegraphie f
→ Bildfernübertragung
drahtloser Hörfunk m **(Netzfunk** m**)**
→ Rundfunk
drahtloses Fernsehen n **(Netzfernsehen** n**)** wireless television, open-circuit television (OCTV), broadcast television, radiovision
→ Rundfunk
drahtloses Mikrofon n **(schnurloses Mikrofon** n**)** cordless microphone, cordless mike
Drahtrückenheftung f **(Drahtrückstichheftung** f, **Drahtrückstichbroschur** f**)** *(binding)* saddle wire stitching, saddle stitching
→ Rückenheftung

Drahtspiralheftung f **(Drahtspiralbindung** f**)**
→ Spiralbindung
Drahttongerät n **(Drahtmagnetophon** n, **Stahldrahtmagnetophon** n**)** wire recorder, wire sound recorder
Drahttonaufnahme f wire recording
 A magnetic audio recording made on wire.
Dramaturg m *(radio/film/TV)* script editor, scenario editor, continuity editor
Dramaturgie f *(radio/TV)*
1. dramaturgy 2. (Abteilung) script department, script unit
Draufgabe f
→ Naturalrabatt m
Draufsicht f **(Draufsichtaufnahme** f**)** *(phot)* tilt shot
Dreharbeiten f/pl *(film/TV)* shooting, filming
Drehbeginn m *(film/TV)* start of shooting, start of filming
Drehbericht m *(film/TV)* shooting record, report sheet, dope sheet
 The camera operator's take-by-take record of shooting with instructions to the film laboratory.
Drehblende f *(phot)* rotating stop plate
Drehbuch n **(Skript** n, **Script** n**)** *(radio/film/TV)* scenario, script, shooting script, (technisches Drehbuch) continuity, (Filmdrehbuch) film script, (Hörfunkdrehbuch) radio script
 The detailed shot-by-shot and sequence-by-sequence written guide to the making of a film, a commercial, a radio, or a television program.
Drehbuchautor m *(radio/film/TV)* script-writer, scenario writer, screenwriter, screen writer, scenarist, (Filmdrehbuchautor) filmwright, screen writer, screen author, continuity writer, film script writer, (Hörfunkdrehbuchautor) radio script writer, radio script author
 A writer who develops the dramatic, musical and other entertainment portions of a film, a commercial, a radio, or a television program.
Drehbuchentwurf m
→ Rohdrehbuch
Drehbühne f *(film/TV)* revolving stage, *(studio)* scenic service crew
Dreheinschlagpapier n twisting paper

drehen v/t + v/i *(film/TV)* to film, to shoot
Dreherlaubnis f *(film/TV)* filming permission, shooting permission
Drehfolge f *(film/TV)* shooting order, shot list
→ Drehplan
Drehort m *(film/TV)* location, lot
→ Aufnahmestandort
Drehplan m **(Drehübersicht** f) *(film/TV)* shooting plan, shooting schedule, schedule
 The list of motion picture, television, or commercial scenes in the order they are to be shot, rather than in the sequence they will be in the finished production.
Drehprisma n deviating prism, prism attachment
→ Umkehrprisma
Drehprobe f *(film/TV)* dry rehearsal, dry run rehearsal, runthrough, run-through, read-through
 The initial rehearsal without cameras, in or outside the film or television studio.
Drehsäule f **(Drehturm** m) *(POP advtsg)* carrousel, carrousel display, rotating tower, revolving tower
Drehscheiben-Display n **(Drehscheibenauslage** f) *(POP advtsg)* lazy Susan display
Drehstab m **(Drehteam** n) *(film/TV)* production team
Drehtag m *(film/TV)* shooting day, filming day
Drehverhältnis n *(film/TV)* shooting ratio
Drehzeit f *(film/TV)* shooting time, shooting period, filming time, filming period
Dreibein n **(Dreibeinstativ** n)
→ Dreifuß
3-D-Verfahren n **(dreidimensionales Verfahren** n) *(film/TV/print)* three-dimensional technique, tridimensional technique, 3D technique
3-D-Werbemittel n **(dreidimensionales Werbemittel** n) dimensional advertisement, dimensional ad, 3D advertisement, 3D ad, *(POP advtsg)* (Auslage) dimensional display, 3D display, three-dimensional
dreidimensionaler Film m **(3D-Film** m) three-dimensional film, 3D film, *colloq* deepie
dreidimensionaler Ton m **(3-D-Klang** m, **Raumton** m, **Stereoton** m) three-dimensional sound

Drei-Dimensionen-Test m *(media res)* trivariant dimension test (Dik Warren Twedt), trivariant analysis
Drei-Assoziations-Test m **(Dreier-Assoziations-Methode** f) *(market res)* triple associates test, triple associates method, triple association (Henry C. Link)
Dreifarbenätzung f *(print)* three-color etching, *brit* three-colour etching, process etching
Dreifarbendruck m **(Dreifarbendruckverfahren** n) three-color printing, *brit* three-colour printing, three-color process printing, three-color process, *brit* three-colour process, trichromatic
 A method of printing in which all hues, (→) Farbton, of an original are considered possible of reproduction by use of three separate printing plates, each plate used for printing or recording one of the primary colors of the original. The plates usually are made by recourse to three-color photography and the employment of halftone separation negatives.
Dreifarbenphotographie f three-color photography, *brit* three-colour photography, trichromatic photography
 A field of photography in which colored originals are reproduced by making color separation negatives through proper color filters, the negatives dividing the hues, (→) Farbton, of the original into the three primary colors, and making printing plates from them to be printed in yellow, red and blue inks.
dreifarbig (trichromatisch, Dreifarben-) adj *(print/phot)* three-color, *brit* three-colour, trichromatic, tricolor, *brit* tricolour
Dreifarbigkeit f *(print/phot)* trichromatism, trichroism
Dreifuß m **(Dreifußstativ** n, **Dreibein** n, **Dreibeinstativ** n) *(phot)* tripod, (ausziehbar) collapsible tripod, extensible tripod
Drei-Komponenten-Theorie f **(Drei-Komponenten-Modell** n) *(attitude res)* three-component theory (of attitude), three-component model
 The theory that attitudes have one affective (emotional), one cognitive, and one behavioral component.
→ Affekt, Kognition, Verhalten

dreimal wöchentlich (dreimal in der Woche) adv/adj triweekly, three times a week
dreimal wöchentlich erscheinende Zeitung f triweekly newspaper, triweekly paper
Dreimessermaschine f **(Dreischneider** m, **Dreimesserschneider** m) *(print)* three-knife trimmer
Dreingabe f
→ Naturalrabatt
Dreipack m **(Tripackfilm** m, **Dreischichtfilm** m) *(phot)* tripack
30-Sekunden-Spot m **(30-Sekunden-Werbesendung** f) *(TV)* 30-second commercial, thirty, -30-, :30
Dreiviertelband m *(print)* three-quarter binding
Dreizeilenfall m *(typ)* three-deck headline
Dressman m male fashion model
dritte Umschlagseite f **(U 3** f) inside back cover (IBC, I.B.C.), third cover (3C)
Drittelbogen m *(print)* one third of a sheet, one-third sheet
Drittelseite f one-third page, one third of a page
drittelseitige Anzeige f one-third page advertisement, one-third page ad
Drittes Programm n *(TV)* Third Programme, Channel Three
Drittleser m **(Mitleser** m **andernorts)** *(readership res)* tertiary reader, out-of-home pass-along reader
  A pass-along reader, cf. (→) Zweitleser, who reads a publication in public places, such as waiting rooms, trains, airplanes, libraries etc.
Drive-in-Filmtheater n **(Drive-in-Kino** n) drive-in movietheater, *brit* drive-in cinema, drive-in
Drive-in-Geschäft n *(retailing)* drive-in store, (Restaurant) drive-in restaurant, drive-in
  A service or customer sales facility equipped to accomodate buyers in their cars. An original German term does not exist.
Drop-out m (Ton) drop-out, (Film) scratch
Drop-out-Kompensation f **(Drop-out Unterdrückung** f) (Ton) drop-out suppression, (Film) anti-scratch treatment
Drossel f **(Drosselspule** f) *(electr.)* inductance coil, inductance, reactance coil, choke

Druck m 1. (Produkt) print
2. (Abdruck) impression, print
3. → Schriftart 4. (Vorgang/Verfahren) printing im Druck sein: to be in the press; in Druck geben: to send to (the) press, to send to the printer(s); in Druck gehen: to got to press, to go to the printer
Druckabsteller m **(Absteller** m) *(print)* throwoff
Druckanzeige f **(gedruckte Anzeige** f, **Printanzeige** f)
→ gedruckte Anzeige
Druckapparat m
→ Druckmaschine
Druckanstalt f
→ Druckerei
Druckarbeit(en) f(pl) **(Druckereiarbeiten** f/pl) presswork, printing
Druckart f
→ Druckverfahren
Druckauflage f **(gedruckte Auflage** f) *(Zeitung/Zeitschrift)* print run, press run, pressrun, total print run
  The total number of copies of a publication that are printed and bound.
Druckauftrag m printing order, print order, commission to print
Druckausfall m
→ Druckqualität
Druckautomat m
→ Druckmaschine
Druckbalken m crosspiece, cross piece
druckbar adj printable, fit to be printed
→ druckreif (druckfertig)
Druckbeginn m start of printing
Druckberichtigung f
→ Korrektur
Druckbewilligung f
→ Druckerlaubnis
Druckbild n
1. → Typographie
2. → Druckträger
Druckblende f *(phot)* automatic diaphragm control, automatic diaphragm pre-setting mechanism, pressure-release diaphragm control
Druckbogen m printed sheet, press sheet
Druckbuchstabe m **(Blockbuchstabe** m) printed letter
→ Letter
Druckdublee n *(print)* mackling
Druckelement n printing area, printing image

drucken v/t to print
Drucken n printing
Drucker m 1. (Person) printer, press man 2. (Gerät) printer, printing machine, small printer
Druckerarbeit f
→ Druckarbeit
Druckerei f 1. (Firma) printer, printing plant, printing office, printing shop, printing house, printing business, printing company 2. (Abteilung) pressroom, press room 3. (Druckereiwesen) printing 4. → Akzidenzdruckerei
Druckereibesitzer m printer, owner of a printing plant
Druckereianstalt f
→ Druckerei 1.
Druckereigewerbe n
→ Druckgewerbe
Druckerfarbe f
→ Druckfarbe
Druckerfaktor m
→ Faktor
Druckergeselle m journeyman, journeyman printer
Druckerlaubnis f (**Druckbewilligung** f, **Druckgenehmigung** f)
→ Imprimatur
Druckerlehrling m (**Setzerlehrling** m, **Setzerjunge** m) printer's devil
Druckermarke f (**Druckerzeichen** n) printer's mark, printer's emblem, printer's device
Druckermeister m master printer
Druckerpresse f
→ Druckmaschine
Druckerschwärze f
→ Druckfarbe
Druckerzeugnis n
→ Druck 1. + 2.
Druckfachmann m printing expert
Druckfachzeitschrift f printing journal, printing trade journal
druckfähig adj
→ druckreif
Druckfähigkeit f
→ Druckreife
Druckfahne f (**Fahne** f, **Fahnenabzug** m) proof, galley proof, galley, brush proof, hand proof, machine proof, page proof, press proof, proof impression
→ Abzug, Bürstenabzug, Fahne, Korrekturfahne
Druckfarbe f (**Druckerschwärze** f) printer's ink, printing ink, printer's color, brit printer's colour, printing color, brit printing colour
Druckfehler m 1. printer's error (P.E.), misprint
Any error appearing in print that is deemed to be the fault of the printer and is therefore not charged to the publisher or author in correction. The German term is commonly used interchangeably for misprints and for typographical errors.
2. → Setzfehler
Druckfehlerverzeichnis n
→ Corrigenda
druckfertig adj
→ druckreif
druckfertiges Manuskript n
→ druckreifes Manuskript
Druckfirnis m printer's varnish, litho varnish
Druckfläche f printing surface
Druckform f (**Druckplatte** f) printing form, brit printing forme, form, brit forme, printing plate, plate
Any material used to make a printed impression by letterpress, gravure, or lithography. In letterpress, plates and type locked in the chase for printing or stereotyping.
Druckformbett n bed
The flat surface on which a printing form lies on a press during printing.
Druckformular n (**gedrucktes Formular** n) printed form, preprinted form
Druckgang m printing operation, printing step, printing
Druckgenehmigung f
→ Imprimatur
Druckgewerbe n (**Druckereigewerbe** n, **Druckindustrie** f) printing industry, printing trade
Druckgradientenempfänger m (**Druckgradientenmikrofon** n) pressure-gradient microphone
Druckgraphik f (**Druckgrafik** f) 1. (Produkt) art print, art pull, fine-art print 2. (Kunst) art printing, fine-art printing
Druckindustrie f
→ Druckgewerbe
Druckingenieur m printing engineer
Druckjahr n year of printing, year of publication
Druckkapazität f (**Druckleistung** f, **Druckleistungsfähigkeit** f) printing capacity
Druckkosten pl printing cost(s) (pl)

Druckkunst f (**schwarze Kunst** f) (the) art of printing, printer's art, printmaking, printing
Drucklegung f printing, printing time, press time
Druckleiste f bearer, bed bearer
  The margin of metal around an engraving. Used to evenly distribute the pressure of molding.
Drucklizenz f license to print, *brit* licence to print, permission to print, printing license, *brit* printing licence
Druckmaschine f (**Druckpresse** f, **Druckerpresse** f) printing machine, printing press, press, printer
  A machine that holds a printing form, inks and makes an impression on paper.
Druckmaterial n printing material, printing stock
Druckmedium n (**Printmedium** n) print medium (*pl* print media), printed-word medium
  An advertising medium prepared by printing.
Druckmedienanzeige f (**Printmedienanzeige** f, **Printanzeige** f) print advertisement, print ad, press advertisement, press ad, printed-word advertisement, printed-word ad
Druckmedienwerbung f (**Printmedienwerbung** f, **Werbung** f **in Printmedien**) print advertising, advertising in print media, press advertising, publication advertising
Druckmikrofon n (**Druckmikrophon** n) pressure microphone
Druckort m place of publication, place of printing
Druckpapier n printing paper, printings *pl*, paper stock, stock
Druckperforation f rule perforation, press perforation
Druckplatte f (**Platte** f)
→ Druckform, Klischee, Stereo
Druckplattenherstellung f
→ Klischeeherstellung, Klischierung
Druckpresse f
→ Druckmaschine
Druckprobe f
→ Druckfahne, Andruck, Probeabzug, Probedruck
Druckqualität f (**Qualität** f **des Drucks**) print quality, quality of print
Druckraster m printer's screen, screen, halftone screen, line screen
druckreif (**druckfertig, druckbar**) *adj* 1. (Text) ready for the press, fit for printing, printable 2. (Satzanweisung) O.K. to print, (nach Korrektur) O.K. with corrections (O.K. w/c) 3. (reproduktionsfähig) camera-ready (CR)
druckreifer Abzug m (**druckfertiger Abzug** m, **korrigierter Abzug** m) O.K. proof, fair proof
druckreifes Manuskript n (*print*) fair copy
Drucksache f printed matter, (als Postsache) *Am* third-class mail, second-class mail
Drucksachenbeilage f (**Beipack** m **in einer Werbedrucksache**) (*direct advtsg*) envelope stuffer
  A printed advertising message or product sample enclosed in a mailing envelope.
Drucksachenwerbung f
→ Briefwerbung
Drucksatz m
→ Satz
Druckschrift f 1. publication, printed publication 2. (Blockschrift) block letters *pl*, print hand, capital letters *pl*, upper-case letters *pl*, (Satzanweisung) all in caps, caps
Druckseite f printing page, printed page
Druckspiegel m
→ Satzspiegel
Druckstelle f (*phot/print*) stress mark
  A mark on a print due to mechanical contact or pressure.
Druckstempel m printing stamp
Druckstock m
→ Klischee
Drucktechnik f
→ Druckverfahren
Drucktiegel m (**Tiegel** m) platen
Druckträger m
1. → Druckform 2. printing material, printing stock, paper stock, stock
Drucktype f
→ Letter
Drucktypenkörper m
→ Kegel
Drucküberschuß m overprint, overprints *pl*, overissue, overruns *pl*, overrun
  The number of pieces of printed material in excess of the specified quantity. Advertisers usually accept up to 10 percent overrun at pro rata cost.
Druckunterlage f
→ Druckvorlage, Manuskript, Druckmaterial, reproduktionsfähiger Abzug

Druckverfahren

Druckverfahren *n* printing technique, printing process
Druckvermerk *m* imprint, printer's imprint
    The name or symbol of a printer, publisher, or dealer printed on a folder, broadside, etc. to identify the firm producing and/or distributing it.
Druckvorlage *f* copy, (für eine Anzeige) advertisement copy, advertising copy, (Manuskript) manuscript, (Anzeigenvorlage mit gesetztem Text und reprofähigen Vorlagen) art-type mechanical, mechanical, keyline
→ Layout, Reinzeichnung, Reproduktionsvorlage
Druckwalze *f* printing cylinder, cylinder, printing roller, printing roll, presser, (Gegendruckzylinder) impression cylinder, (Farbwalze) ink roller, roller, roll, inker, waver
Druckwerk *n* printed publication, printed work, print
Druckwesen *n*
→ Drucken
Druckzeile *f* print line, printed line, line of type
Druckzeit *f* printing time
Druckzeitschrift *f*
→ Druckfachzeitschrift
Druckzylinder *m*
→ Druckwalze
Dualdistribution *f* (**duale Distribution** *f*) dual distribution, two-channel distribution
    The practice of some manufacturers of planning channels of distribution, (→) Absatzwege, through both wholly owned and independent establishments at the same time.
vgl. Monodistribution
duale Ökonomie *f* dual economy
Dubbing *n*
→ Nachsynchronisieren
Dublette *f*
→ Doublette
dublieren
→ schmitzen
Duktor *m* (**Farbenzufuhrwalze** *f*) *(print)* ductor, drop roller
Dumping *n (pricing)* dumping
    The practice of selling products in foreign countries at a price much lower than the equivalent in the market of origin, frequently even below cost, to dispose of surplus.

Dumpingpreis *m (econ)* dumping price
Dunkelkammer *f (phot)* darkroom, *brit* dark-room
    A room that is free from actinic light, so that photographic operations can be carried out with light-sensitive materials.
Dunkelkammerausrüstung *f (phot)* darkroom equipment
Dunkelkammerfilter *m (phot)* darkroom safelight filter
Dunkelkammerlampe *f* (**Dunkelkammerleuchte** *f*) *(phot)* safelight, safe light
    A darkroom light that does not affect light-sensitive photographic materials.
Dunkelpause *f (film/TV)* blackout, black-out, black-out period
Dunkelphase *f* dark period
Dunkelsack *m (phot)* changing bag
    A portable cloth bag serving as a darkroom with armholes for loading film magazines on location without any risk of fogging.
Dunkelton *m* (**Dunkeltonlicht** *n*, **Low-Key-Licht** *n*) *(phot)* low-key light
    A key light of low intensity.
Dunkeltonphoto *n* (**Dunkeltonphotographie** *f*, **Low-Key-Photo** *n*) low-key photo, low-key photograph
    A photo that is predominantly dark in value.
dunkler Hintergrund *m (film/phot/TV)* limbo
    A neutral background for a shot.
Dünndruckausgabe *f* (**Dünndruck** *m*) *(print)* India paper edition, Bible paper edition
Dünndruckpapier *n (print)* India paper, Bible paper, catalog paper, onionskin paper
Dunning-Verfahren *n*
→ Wandermasken-Verfahren
Dünnschichtfilm *m (phot)* thin-emulsion film, polyester film
Dup *n colloq (film)* duplicate, dupe, dub
Dup-Negativ *n* (**Duplikatnegativ** *n*) *(film)* dupe negative
    A commercial or motion picture negative made from a fine grain positive print.
Dup-Positiv *n* (**Duplikatpositiv** *n*, **Lavendel** *n*, **Zwischenpositiv** *n*) *(film)* dupe positive
Duplex *m (print)* duplex, duotone
Duplex-Autotypie *f (print)* duplex halftone block, duplex halftone cut, duotone

A halftone block used for the reproduction of a one-color picture in two colors, or different shades of the same color.

Duplexdruck m **(Duplexdruckverfahren** n**)** duplex printing, duotone printing, duoblack printing
A two-color printing technique in which the effect of black-and-white halftone illustration printing is enriched by adding an additional color from a second halftone plate.

Duplexkarton m **(Duplexpappe** f**)** duplex board, two-layer board

Duplexraster m **(Hochlichtraster** m, **Kombinationsdruckraster** m**)** *(print)* duplex screen
A special type of halftone screen for the production of highlight effects and combination line-halftone negatives.

Duplikat n *(print/film/phot)* duplicate, *colloq* dupe, ditto, dup
A tape or film which has been printed or copied from the original.

Duplikatfilm m *(film)* (Rohfilm) duplicating film, duplicating stock, (entwickelt) duplicated film

Duplikation f
→ Duplizierung

Duplikatnegativ n **(Dup-Negativ** n**)** *(film)* (Rohfilm) duplicating negative, (entwickelt) duplicated negative, dupe negative

Duplikatplatte f *(print)* duplicate plate
A replica of an original engraving prepared for distribution to a number of publications, or for gang printing.

Duplikatpositiv n **(Dup-Positiv** n**)** *(film)* (Rohfilm) duplicating positive, (entwickelt) duplicated positive, dupe positive, lavender print, lavender

Duplikatprozeß m *(film/print)* duplicating process, duping process, duping

Duplikatumkehrfilm m *(film)* (Rohfilm) duplicated reversal stock, duplicated reversal film (entwickelt) duplicate reversal, dupe reversal

Duplikatvorlage f
→ Duplikatpositiv

Duplizierfilm m
→ Kopierfilm

Duplizierung f *(media res)* duplication ("dupe"), audience duplication, duplicate exposure, duplicated audience
The amount of exposure of the known audience of a medium to another medium of the same type carrying the same advertising, or to more than one appearance of the same advertising in the same medium, e.g., successive issues of the same magazine.
→ Mehrfachnutzung, Mehrfachkontakt, externe Überschneidung

duppen colloq v/t *(film)* to duplicate, to dupe

durchblättern v/t (Zeitschrift/Zeitung) to leaf through, to page through, to skimp, to thumb through, to skim (over)

durchblenden v/t *(film/TV)* to superimpose, to super-imp, to dissolve, to mix

Durchblendung f *(film/TV)* superimposition, super-imp, superimposure, dissolve, lap dissolve, mix

Durchblickspiegel m
→ Spionspiegel

Durchblicksucher m
→ Rahmensucher

Durchdringung f **(Penetration** f**)** penetration
The degree of effectiveness of marketing or advertising activities in terms of their impact on the target audience, usually expressed as a percentage. Also, the extent to which a product has been accepted by, or has registered with the total of prospective buyers.

Durchdringungsmodell n **(Parfittsches Modell** n**)**
→ Marktdurchdringung

Durchdruck m
→ Siebdruck, Schablonendruck

Durchgang m
→ Druckgang

durchgeschlagener Druck m blotted print, strike-through, show-through, embossment
The condition of a sheet of paper where print on one side can be seen through from the other side.

durchgestrichener Preis m ("Anstatt"-Preis m, "Jetzt"-"Früher"-Preis m) *(econ)* was-is price
A reduced price comparing the present price with the previous price, crossed out on the price tag.

Durchhefter m
→ Beihefter

Durchklatschen n *(print)* print-through, show-through
→ durchgeschlagener Druck

Durchlaßbandbreite f *(radio)* filter passband

Durchlässigkeit

Durchlässigkeit f transmittance, transmission
Durchlässigkeitsbereich m *(radio)* pass-band, band-pass width
Durchlauf m *(film/TV)* (Probe) runthrough, (Kopierwerk) run, clear run, (Wobbler) sweep
Durchlaufgeschwindigkeit f (Band) tape speed, (Wobbler) sweep
Durchlaufkamera f rotary camera
Durchlaufkopiermaschine f continuous film printer, continuous rotary printer, continuous printer
  A film laboratory machine used to print optical track negatives.
vgl. Schrittkopiermaschine
Durchlaufverfilmung f rotary filming
Durchlaufzeit f transit time, *(tape)* playing time
Durchprojektion f
→ Rückprojektion
Durchreißversuch m *(paper)* tear test
Durchsage f
→ Ansage
Durchscheinbild n
→ Leuchtbild
durchscheinen v/i *(print)* to show through, to strike through
durchschießen v/t *(print)* to interleave
Durchschlag m copy, manifold
Durchschnitt m
→ Mittelwert
durchschnittliche Abweichung f
→ arithmetisches Mittel
durchschnittliche Auflage f
→ Durchschnittsauflage
durchschnittliche Einschaltzahl f *(media res)* average households set tuning pl
  The average number of households whose radio or television set is tuned to a specific program or channel at a given time period.
vgl. Einschaltzahl
durchschnittliche Kontaktzahl f *(media res)* average number of exposures, average frequency, (Kontaktchance) average opportunity to see, average OTS
  The average number of times an individual is exposed to an advertising medium or an advertisement.
vgl. Kontakt
durchschnittliche Konsumneigung f *(econ)* average propensity to consume
→ Konsumneigung
durchschnittliche Kontaktzahl f pro Leser *(readership res)* average number of exposures per reader, average frequency
  The average number of times a reader, (→) Leser, is exposed to an issue of an advertising medium or to an advertisement.
vgl. durchschnittliche Leserzahl, Durchschnittskontakte, Kontakthäufigkeit

durchschnittliche Leserzahl f (einer Ausgabe) *(readership res)* average-issue audience (AIA), average-issue readership (A.I.R.)
  The estimated number of persons reading an average issue of a publication, as measured by the method of actual issue recognition, (→) Originalheftmethode, (→) Wiedererkennungsverfahren, the reading frequency method, (→) Lesehäufigkeit, or combinations of these. In the recency method, average issue audience is estimated by calculating the number of people who read any issue of the publication in the publication interval, (→) Erscheinungsintervall.

durchschnittliche Nutzungswahrscheinlichkeit f (durchschnittliche Lesewahrscheinlichkeit f) *(readership res)* average reading probability
→ Durchschnittskontakte

durchschnittliche Verkaufsauflage f (Zeitung/Zeitschrift) average net paid circulation, average net paid, average paid
  The average paid circulation per issue of a periodical, established by dividing the total number of paid copies, i.e. gross circulation less leftover, unsold, returned, file, sample, exchange, advertisers', and special edition copies, during a specified period of time, by the total number of issues during the same period.

durchschnittliche Zahl f **der Hörer** *(audience res)* average number of listeners, average audience (AA)
  The average number of listeners tuned in during a specified interval of time, e.g. for the length of a program or for a 1, 15, or 30 minute period, for a radio broadcast.

durchschnittliche Zahl f **der Leser** *(readership res)* average number of readers, average audience (AA)
→ durchschnittliche Leserzahl

durchschnittliche Zahl f **der Kontakte pro Seite** *(readership res)*

average page exposure (apx), ad-page exposure (apx)
→ Anzeigenseitenkontakt, Seitenkontakt
durchschnittliche Zahl f **der Prüfstichproben** *(stat)* average run length (ARL)
durchschnittliche Zahl f **der Zuschauer** *(audience res)* average number of viewers, average audience (AA), (Reichweite) average audience rating
 The average number of viewers tuned in during a specified interval of time, e.g. for the length of a program or for a 1, 15, or 30 minute period, for a television broadcast.
durchschnittlicher Stichprobenumfang m **(mittlerer Stichprobenumfang** m**)** *(stat)* average sample number (ASN)
Durchschnittsabsatz m *(econ)* average sales pl
Durchschnittsauffassung f
→ Verkehrsauffassung
Durchschnittsauflage f (Zeitung/Zeitschrift) average circulation, (Druckauflage) average print run, average press run, (Verkaufsauflage) average net paid circulation, average net paid, average paid
→ durchschnittliche Verkaufsauflage
Durchschnittsformat n average size
Durchschnittshonorar n
→ Standardhonorar
Durchschnittskontakte m/pl *(media res)* average number of exposures, average frequency
 The average number of times a target person is exposed to an advertising medium or an advertising message, i.e. the ratio
$$\text{the ratio average number of exposures} = \frac{\text{gross number of exposures}}{\text{audience}},$$
$$\text{or} \frac{\text{sum of exposures}}{\text{net coverage}}.$$
Durchschnittskosten pl *(econ)* average cost(s) *(pl)*
 The total cost divided by the related quantity.
Durchschnittsleser m *(readership res)* average reader
Durchschnittsrabatt m *(econ)* average discount
Durchschnittsverkaufsauflage f

→ durchschnittliche Verkaufsauflage
Durchschnittszeichnung f
→ Aufrißzeichnung
durchschossen *adj (print)* leaded, spaced-out
durchschossener Satz m *(print)* leaded matter
Durchschuß m **(Zwischenschlag** m**)** *(print)* interlinear space, spacing, leading, (Regletten) lead, furniture, slug
 In hot-metal composition, the insertion of metal strips, or leads, between lines of type to provide greater space and improve readability and appearance. In cold composition, any measure to provide greater space between the lines.
Durchschußblatt n *(print)* interleave, slip sheet
Durchschußlinie f *(print)* space line, white line
Durchsetzung f **im Verkehr**
→ Verkehrsauffassung, Verkehrsgeltung
Durchsetzungswerbung f penetration advertising
→ Marktdurchsetzung (Marktpenetration)
Durchsichtbild n **(durchscheinendes Bild** n**, Transparentbild** n**)**
1. translucency, translucent picture
 A photographic positive or dye transfer print on a clear or transparent base, usually for display.
2. → Dia(positiv)
durchsichtig (durchscheinend) *adj* translucent, transparent
Durchsichtigkeitsgrad m **(der Druckfarbe)** *(print)* ink density, density
Durchsichtvorlage f
→ Durchsichtbild
durchspielen v/t *(radio/film/TV)* (Szene) to run through
Durchzeichnung f 1. (Pause) tracing
2. *(phot)* definition, detail recording
DWF m *abbr* Deutscher Werbefachverband e.V.
DWG f *abbr* Deutsche Werbewissenschaftliche Gesellschaft e.V.
Dye Transfer m **(Dye-Transfer-Vorlage** f**)** *(phot)* dye transfer, dye transfer print
 An opaque color print made from a photographic transparency.
Dynamik f **der Betriebsformen (im Einzelhandel)** wheel of retailing, the wheel of retailing, retail institution cycle, dynamics pl *(construed as sg)* of

Dynamikbereich

retailing
The cyclical pattern of evolutionary changes in retailing, which according to a hypothesis originally advanced by Malcolm P. McNair is characterized by the fact that new types of retailers usually enter the market as low-status, low-margin, and low-price operators. Gradually they acquire more elaborate establishments and facilities, with both increased investments and higher operating costs. Finally they mature as high-cost, high-price merchants, vulnerable to newer types who, in turn, go through the same pattern.

Dynamikbereich m (**Dynamikumfang** m) dynamic range
dynamische Motivtheorie f
→ Bedürfnishierarchie
dynamisches Modell n dynamic model
Dyopol n *(econ)* dyopoly
Dysfunktion f dysfunction
Dysstruktur f dysstructure

E

E-Kamera f
→ elektronische Kamera
E-Leser m
→ Einzelverkaufsleser, A + E-Leser
E-Musik f (ernste Musik f) serious music, classical music
E-Welle f (Feinstwelle f) (paper) E flute, micro flute
EAN-Code m (EAN-Strichcode m, Europäische Artikelnumerierung f) European Product Code
The type of product code generally accepted in Europe. It consists of an arrangement of light and dark bars which can be read by an optical scanner. The pattern combinations are unique for certain products and makers, so that identification is unambiguous.
EB abbr Elektronische Berichterstattung
Eau de Javelle n
→ Javellewasser
ebenerdige Warenauslage f (POP advtsg) floor display, (pyramidenförmig) floor pyramid
A merchandise display arranged on the floor of a retail outlet.
eben merklicher Unterschied m (Unterschiedsschwelle f) (psy) just noticeable difference (JND), difference threshold, liminal difference
Eberhard-Effekt m (phot) Eberhard effect
EC-Anlage f (E-CAM, EC-Kamera f) video-film equipment
Echo n (Hall m, Nachhall m) echo, (im Studio erzeugtes Echo) reverberation, reverb
Echo-Effekt m (radio/TV) reverb effect, reverberation effect, echo effect
A multiple effect added electronically or acoustically to an audio signal.
Echogerät n (Echokammer f, Echomaschine f) (radio/TV) reverberator, echo chamber, reverberation room, echo room
In broadcasting, a device used to produce a hollow sound or echo effect.
Echoton m (radio/TV) ambient sound

Eckanzeige f (Titelboxanzeige f) (Zeitung) ear, ear space advertisement, earlug, title corner ad(vertisement), title corner
A special advertising position on the front page of a newspaper left or right of the masthead.
Eckenabstoßmaschine f (Eckenrundungsmaschine f,
Eckenrundstoßmaschine f) (print) beveling machine, brit bevelling machine, cornering machine
Eckenheftung f (binding) corner stapling, corner stitching
Eckfläche f (Eckflächenanschlag m) (transit advtsg) square end, square-end display
An inside transit advertising display located near the doors.
eckige Klammer f (typ) bracket, square bracket
Eckplatz m (Eckposition f) (Anzeige) ear space position, ear position, earlug position,
→ Eckanzeige
Eckstück n (Eckverzierung f) corner piece
Edition f
→ → Ausgabe, Veröffentlichung
EDR abbr elektrodermale Reaktion
Edwards-Skala f
→ Paarvergleich
EFA abbr Emnid Faktorielle Anzeigenanalyse
Effekt m effect, (film/TV) (Trickeffekt) special effect, (optischer) optical effect, optical (Geräusch) sound effect, sound
→ Wirkung, Geräuscheffekt, optischer Effekt
Effektbeleuchtung f 1. (film) special effect(s) lighting, effect(s) lighting 2. (phot) decorative lighting
Effektbogenlampe f (film/TV/studio) flame arc lamp, carbon arc lamp
Effektenbörse f (econ) stock exchange
Effektgesetz n (psy) law of effect (Edward L. Thorndike)
Effekthascherei f (effekthascherische Werbung f) claptrap

effektive Abdruckhöhe f
→ Abdruckhöhe
effektive Blendenzahl f *(phot)*
effective aperture
  The diameter of the diaphragm of a lens, as measured through the front lens element.
effektive Nachfrage f *(econ)* effective demand
  Demand supported by purchasing power.
→ Kaufkraft
effektive Reichweite f **(wirksame Reichweite** f**)** *(media res)* effective coverage, effective cover, effective audience, *(radio/TV)* full attention rating (FAR) *(outdoor/transit advtsg)* effective circulation *(magazine/newspaper advtsg)* effective circulation
  That part of an audience, (→) Reichweite, that consists of persons who are part of an advertising message's target group and devote sufficient attention to its content.
effektive Spannweite f *(stat)* effective range
effektiver Nettopreis m (für Werbung) earned rate
  The rate an advertiser pays for space or time actually used within a specific time period.
effektiver Stichprobenumfang m **(effektive Stichprobengröße** f**)** *(stat)* effective sample size, effective sample base (ESB)
Effektivität f effectiveness
Effektlicht n **(Effektspitze** f**)** *(phot/film/TV)* effect(s) lighting, effect(s) light
Effektmikrofon n **(Effektmikrophon** n**)** effect microphone
Effektmusik f *(film)* effect music, mood music
Effektscheinwerfer m *(phot/film/TV)* effects spot, profile spot
Effektspitze f
→ Effektlicht, Effektbeleuchtung 1.
Effizienz f efficiency
Egalisierrakel m *(print)* doctor blade, smoothing blade
Ego-Involvement n
→ Ich-Beteiligung
Egoutteur m *(paper)* dandy roll, dandy roller, dandy
EH *abbr* Einzelhandel
eichen v/t to calibrate, to gauge, to standardize, *brit* to standardise
Eichmarke f calibration mark

Eichung f calibration, standardization, *brit* standardisation
Eidophor m
→ Großbildprojektor, Fernseh-Großbild-Projektion
Eigenanzeige f **(Eigenwerbemittel** n**)** house advertisement, house ad
  An advertisement of an advertiser, frequently a publisher, appearing in an advertising medium he owns.
Eigenbeilage f **(Eigensupplement** n**)** individual supplement
vgl. Fremdbeilage
Eigenfrequenz f *(electr.)*
eigenfrequency, natural frequency, characteristic frequency
Eigengeräusch n residual noise, inherent noise, (Plattenspieler) surface noise, (film) inherent film noise
Eigenheimbesitzer-Zeitschrift f home-owner magazine
Eigenimage n **(Selbstimage** n, **Selbstbild** n**)** mirror image, self-image, self-concept
  In multiple-image research, the image an individual or a corporation has of itself.
Eigenkorrelation f
→ Autokorrelation
Eigenmarke f **(Hausmarke** f, **Handelsmarke** f, **Verteilermarke** f**)**
1. house brand, private brand, private label, dealer's brand, (eines Großhändlers/einer Handelskette) controlled brand, controlled label
2. (die Waren) private-label goods *pl*, private brand goods *pl*
  Goods produced for exclusive labeling by distributors, retailers, or other middlemen.
→ Handelsmarke (Händlermarke)
Eigenmodulation f self modulation
Eigenprogramm n **(Eigensendung** f**)** *(radio/TV)* (eines Senders) station-produced broadcast, station-produced program, house program, house show, (einer Agentur) agency-produced program
  An unsponsored broadcast program.
Eigenrauschen n ground noise, (Verstärker) internal noise
Eigenregression f
→ Autoregression
Eigenresonanz f self-resonance, natural resonance, resonant property
Eigenschaft f
→ Merkmal

Eigenschaftszuordnung f (**Merkmalszuordnung** f) (res) allocation of attributes
Eigenschwingung f natural oscillation, characteristic oscillation
Eigensendung f
→ Eigenprogramm
Eigenspur f home track
Eigenstreuung f (**Eigenstreuwege** m/pl) etwa advertising in house organs vgl. Fremdstreuung
Eigensynchronisation f self-synchronization, brit self-synchronisation
Eigenvergleich m (in der Werbung) etwa self-comparison, comparison advertising with own products
Eigenverzerrung f inherent distortion
Eigenwerbeträger m house organ, advertiser-owned advertising medium
Eigenwerbung f
→ vgl. Fremdwerbung, Gemeinschaftswerbung, Sammelwerbung
Eigenwert m (**charakteristische Wurzel** f) (stat) eigenvalue, characteristic root
einäugige Spiegelreflexkamera f (phot) single-lens reflex camera, SLR camera
Einbad-Entwicklung f (**Monobadentwicklung** f) (phot) monobath processing, unibath processing
Einband m binding, case, cover
Einbandart f (**Einbandform** f) type of binding, binding
Einbanddecke f 1. (Einbanddeckel) cover 2. binding case, binder, easibinder, binder's case, case
Einbandgestaltung f cover design
Einbandleinen n (**Buchleinen** n) binding cloth, binder's cloth, bookbinder's cloth, book cloth, bookbinder's linen, binder's linen
Einbandmaterial n (**Einbandstoff** m, **Einbandgewebe** n) binding material, covering material, binding fabric
Einbandkarton m (**Einbandpappe** f)
→ Buchbinderpappe
Einbandstativ n (phot) unipod, monopod
Einbildbelichtungskamera f (**Spaltbildkamera** f) (phot) one-shot camera
Ein-Bild-Test m
→ Thematischer Apperzeptions-Test (TAT)

einbinden v/t
→ binden
Einbindenadel f
→ Buchbinderahle
Einblattdruck m broadsheet, broadside
    A promotional flier consisting of a single sheet, printed on one side only and folded for mailing.
einblenden v/t (film/TV/radio) to fade in, to dub in, (dazwischenblenden) to cross-fade, (Zweitbild) to superimpose, (sich einblenden) to cut in, (abrupt einblenden) to pop in, (ganz langsam einblenden) to sneak in
Einblender m (film/TV) (Person) vision mixer, mixer
Einblendtitel m (film/TV) caption, title
Einblendung f (**Einblenden** n) (film/TV/radio) fade-in, fading-in, cut-in, cross-fade, (langsam) sneak in, sneaking-in, (abrupt) pop-in, pop on, (Zweitbild) superimposition, superimp, superimposure, super
einbrennen v/t (Farben) to burn in
Einbrennen n 1. (Farben) burning-in 2. (TV) sticking, (Röhre) warm-up
Einbrennfleck m (TV) ion spot
einbringen v/t (print) (Zeile) to take in, to break in, to take back
Einbringen n (print) taking back, taking in
Einbruchfalz m (**Einbruch** m) folding in half
Eindringungspreisstrategie f
→ Penetrationsstrategie
Eindruck m 1. (psy) impression 2. (print) imprint
    Printing of additional copy on previously printed material
Eindrückdeckel m (packaging) plug-in lid, press-in lid
Eindrucken n (**Herstellung** f **von Werbeeindrucken**) imprinting
Eindruckfeld n
→ Eindruck 2., Händlereindruck, Firmeneindruck
Einergang m (film/TV)
→ Zeitraffer
Einfachkorrelation f (**einfache Korrelation** f) (stat) simple correlation
Einfachstruktur f (stat) simple structure
einfärben (einschwärzen) v/t (print) (die Druckwalze) to ink

Einfärben

Einfärben n (**Einschwärzen** n, **Einfärbung** f)
The process of applying ink to metal plates with a roller, either for the purpose of creating an acid resist, or for depositing ink on the surface of a printing plate to take an impression therefrom.
Einfarbendruck m *(phot)* **1.** (Produkt) monochrome print, monochrome copy, monochrome
A photograph, picture or reproduction in a single color.
2. (Verfahren) monochrome printing, monochrome printing, monochromy
Einfarbenkopie f
→ Einfarbendruck 1.
einfarbig (monochrom, monochromatisch) adj *(phot/print)* monochrome, monochromic(al), monochromous
Ein-Firmen-Handelsvertreter m **(Ein-Firmen-Vertreter** m)
manufacturer's agent
An agent who generally operates on an extended contractual basis, often sells within an exclusive territory, handles goods of a single manufacturer and possesses limited authority with regard to prices and terms of sale. He may be authorized to sell a definite portion of his principal's output.
Einfluß m influence
Einfluß-Matrix-Projektmanagement n **(Einfluß-Projektmanagement** n)
→ Projektmanagement
einfügen v/t **1.** (Text einschieben) to insert, to put in, to interpolate, to fill in **2.** *(print)* to run in, to insert **3.** (zusätzlichen Text z.B. in eine Anzeige zwängen) to shoehorn
Einfügung f **1.** (Einschub) insertion, filling-in, interpolation **2.** *(print)* (das Eingefügte) run-in, insert, insertion, inserted word(s) *(pl)* (zwischen zwei Zeilen) interlineation, (zwischen zwei Zeilen eingefügter Satz) interlinear matter
einführen v/t **1.** *(econ)* to import **2.** *(marketing)* (Neuerung) to introduce, to adopt, to initiate, to innovate, to launch **3.** *(print)* (Bogen in die Maschine) to feed into, to insert into
Einführer m
→ Innovater
Einführung f **1.** (Einleitung) introduction, lead-in **2.** *(radio/TV)* (einleitende Ansage) lead-in, lead-in program, lead-in show **3.** *(econ)* (eines Produkts) (new product) launch, introduction
→ Produkteinführung
Einführungsaktion f
→ Einführungskampagne
Einführungsangebot n introductory offer, launch offer
A special offer designed to stimulate interest in and promote sales of a new product.
Einführungsanzeige f launch advertisement, launch ad, introductory advertisement, introductory ad, (Ankündigung) announcement advertisement, announcement ad
An advertisement designed to announce, to launch, or to support the launch of a new product or service.
→ Einführungsphase
Einführungskampagne f **(Einführungsaktion** f) launch campaign, launch advertising campaign, introductory campaign
Einführungsnummer f **(Einführungsausgabe** f) (Zeitschrift) pilot issue, pilot number
A demonstration issue of a new magazine used to provide a sample of its content and editorial policy.
Einführungsphase f **(im Produktlebenszyklus)** *(marketing)* pioneering stage (in the product life cycle), introduction stage, introductory phase, primary stage
The first stage in the product life cycle. It begins at its first appearance in the markeplace, when sales are zero, profits negative, expenses for promotion and distribution activities high, and initial revenues low.
vgl. Wachstumsphase, Reifephase, Marktsättigung, Degenerationsphase.
Einführungspreis m *(econ)* launch price, introductory price
Depending on price policy, a particularly low, occasionally also a particularly high price, cf. (→) Abschöpfungspreis, designed to support a company's marketing strategy in the introduction stage of a new product.
Einführungsrabatt m introductory allowance, launch discount
A allowance or discount, (→) Rabatt, granted to promote sales of a new product in the introductory stage of its life cycle.

Einführungswerbung *f* introductory advertising, launch advertising, pioneer advertising
 Advertising in the pioneering stage of a newly launched product or service aiming at making it known to prospects and at spreading awareness of its benefits.
 vgl. Durchsetzungswerbung, Erhaltungswerbung, Fortführungswerbung, Erinnerungswerbung, Verdrängungswerbung, Verstärkungswerbung, Expansionswerbung, Wettbewerbswerbung
eingebaute Obsoleszenz *f*
 → geplante Obsoleszenz
eingeblendet *f adj (TV)* fade-in, faded-in, cut-in, blended
 A commercial that is inserted into a program during the broadcast.
 → programmunterbrechende Werbesendung
eingedruckte Händleranschrift *f*
 → Händlereindruck, Firmeneindruck
eingedruckter Gutschein *m* **(eingedruckter Kupon** *m***)** on-page coupon, boxed-in coupon
 A coupon which is part of a printed advertisement
eingedruckter Rücksendegutschein *m* **(eingedruckter Rücksendekupon** *m***)** on-page return coupon, boxed-in return coupon
eingehefteter Gutschein *m* **(eingehefteter Kupon** *m***)** bound-in coupon
 → Beihefter
eingeheftete Antwortkarte *f* **(eingeheftete Rückantwortkarte** *f***)** bound-in return card
 → Beihefter
eingeheftete Beilage *f*
 → Beihefter (Durchhefter)
eingehen *v/i* **1.** *(econ)* (Firma) to close down, to cease to exist **2.** (Zeitung/Zeitschrift) to cease publication, to cease to appear, to perish
eingeklebt *adj* tipped-in, tip-in
eingeklebter Gutschein *m* **(eingeklebter Kupon** *m***)** tip-in coupon, tipped-in coupon, tip-in
 → Beikleber
eingeklebter Rücksendegutschein *m* **(Rücksendekupon** *m***)** tip-in return coupon, tipped-in return coupon, tip-in
 → Beikleber
eingeklebtes Bild *n* tip-in picture, tip-in illustration, tip-in

eingepackter Gutschein *m* in-pack coupon, in-pack
 → Beipack
eingeplante Veralterung *f*
 → Obsoleszenz
eingerahmte Anzeige *f* **(Anzeige** *f* **im Kasten)** box advertisement, box ad, boxed advertisement, boxed ad
eingerückt (eingezogen) *adj (print)* indented
eingerückte Überschriftszeile *f (print)* cut-in head, cut-in headline
eingerückter Brotsatz *m* **(hängender Einzug** *m***)** *(print)* hanging indent, hanging indentation, hanging indention, (Satzanweisung) flush and hang, flush and indent
 A way of typesetting a paragraph with the first line being set full measure and all other lines indented. This paragraph is set with a hanging indentation.
eingeschoben *(print)* inserted, run-in
eingeschossene Blätter *n/pl (print)* interleaves *pl*
 Flat sheets that are placed together before binding.
eingetragenes Gebrauchsmuster *n* registered design
 A design, (→) Gebrauchsmuster, which is legally registered thus providing protection against its unauthorized use.
eingetragenes Warenzeichen *n* registered trademark ®
 A legally registered trademark, thus protected against its unauthorized use.
eingezogen *adj*
 → eingerückt
eingipflig *(stat) adj* unimodal
eingipflige Kurve *f* **(unimodale Kurve** *f***)** *(stat)* unimodal curve
eingipflige Häufigkeitsverteilung *f* **(eingipflige Verteilung** *f***)** *(stat)* unimodal frequency distribution, unimodal distribution
Eingipfligkeit *f* **(Unimodalität** *f***)** *(stat)* unimodality
Einhängemaschine *f (print)* casing-in machine, book casing machine
einhängen *v/t (print)* to case in, to case, to attach
Einhängen *(print)* casing-in, book casing
Einhänger *m (print)* (bei der Linotype) pi matrix
einheben *v/t (print)* to lay on, to put into the press
einheften *v/t* to bind in, to stitch in, to sew in

Einhefter m
→ Beihefter m
Einheftkante f binding edge
Einheitscontainer m *(packaging)* unit container, standard-size container
Einheitsformat n standard size
Einheitsformular n (für Werbeaufträge) standard order blank
Einheitsfragebogen m
→ standardisierter Fragebogen
Einheitsmaß n standard measure
Einheitspreis m **(Festpreis** m, **Grundpreis** m) *(econ)* standard price, standard rate, fixed price, fixed rate *(advtsg)* single rate, flat rate, flat price, base rate, basic rate, card rate, full rate-card cost, one-time rate, open rate, transient rate
Einheitspreisgeschäft n
→ Kleinpreisgeschäft
Einheitspreisliste f **(Einheitstarifliste** f) *(advtsg)* single rate card
Einheitsskala f
→ Intervallskala
einhüllen v/t
→ einpacken, einschlagen, einwickeln
einkanalig v/t single-channel, monaural, monophonic, mono
Einkauf m *(econ)* 1. purchase, buy 2. (das Einkaufen) purchasing, buying, (Einkaufengehen) shopping
→ Beschaffung
einkaufen v/t + v/i
→ kaufen
Einkäufer m buyer, buying agent, purchasing agent, *brit* purchasing officer
 1. In a department store, the key person who is really a department head responsible in his department for buying, selling, pricing, and controlling his lines of goods, as well as managing his area and his personnel. Also, the person authorized to acquire materials needed for operation and maintenance of the premises. 2. In an industrial firm, an employee who is delegated the authority to commit the firm for the acquistion of materials and equipment. 3. In a multi-unit retailing business, a person responsible for buying certain goods for resale. Separated from the selling function.
→ Käufer
Einkäuferverhalten n buyer behavior, industrial buyer behavior, *brit* behaviour
 The behavior of industrial or corporate buyers.
→ Einkäufer, Beschaffungspolitik
Einkaufsabteilung f buying department, purchasing department
→ Einkäufer
Einkaufsanalyse f *(market res)* purchase analysis, purchasing analysis, buying analysis
→ Beschaffungsanalyse
Einkaufsausweis m
→ Kaufschein
Einkaufsbeobachtung f *(market res)* purchasing observation, buying observation
Einkaufsentscheidung f
→ Kaufentscheidung
Einkaufsforschung f purchase research, purchasing research, buying research
→ Beschaffungsmarktforschung, Kaufverhaltensforschung, Konsumforschung
Einkaufsfrequenz f
→ Einkaufshäufigkeit
Einkaufsgemeinschaft f **(Einkaufsinigung** f) voluntary group, voluntary association, retailer-owned voluntary association, retailer-owned voluntary group, informal buying group, pooled buying group
 A group of retailers each of whom owns and operates his own store and is associated with a wholesale organization or manufacturer to carry on joint merchandising activites and who are characterized by some degree of group identity and uniformity of operation. Such joint activities have been largely of two kinds, cooperative advertising, (→) Gemeinschaftswerbung, and group control of store operation. An "Einkaufsvereinigung" is usually sponsored by a wholesaler.
→ freiwillige Handelskette
Einkaufsgenossenschaft f **(EKG)** retailer cooperative, buying cooperative, purchasing cooperative, cooperative retailer organization, retailer-sponsored cooperative, retailers' cooperative
 A group of independent retailers organized to buy cooperatively either through a jointly owned warehouse or through a buying club. Their cooperative activities may include operating under a group name, joint advertising and cooperative managerial supervision.

Einkaufsgewohnheit f
→ Kaufgewohnheit
Einkaufsgremium n **(Einkaufskern**
m, **Buying Center** n) buying center
(Frederick E. Webster Jr./Yoram
Wind)
  The individuals or groups of individuals within an organization who are responsible for a purchase decision.
Einkaufsgutschein m
→ Kaufgutschein
Einkaufshäufigkeit f **(Einkaufsfrequenz** f) shopping frequency, buying frequency
  The rate at which consumers tend to go shopping within a specified period of time.
→ Kaufhäufigkeit
Einkaufshäufigkeitsanalyse f **(Einkaufsfrequenzanalyse** f) *(market res)* analysis of shopping frequency, analysis of buying frequency
Einkaufskartell n
→ Einkaufsgemeinschaft
Einkaufskern m
→ Einkaufsgremium
Einkaufskomitee n
→ Einkaufsgremium
Einkaufskommission f buying commission
Einkaufskommissionär m buying agent, purchasing agent
  A functional middleman who works as a representative of a buyer.
Einkaufskooperation f buying cooperation, cooperation in buying, buying group
→ Einkaufsgemeinschaft (Einkaufsvereinigung), Einkaufsgenossenschaft, Einkaufsring, freiwillige Handelskette
Einkaufslimitrechnung f
→ Limitrechnung
Einkaufsliste f **(Einkaufszettel** m) shopping list
Einkaufslistenverfahren n **(Einkaufszettelverfahren** n) *(market res)* shopping list technique, shopping list test (Mason Haire)
Einkaufsmarktforschung f buying market research
→ Beschaffungsmarktforschung, Konsumforschung
Einkaufsorganisation f
→ Einkaufsgremium
Einkaufsort m
→ Kaufort
Einkaufspolitik f
→ Beschaffungspolitik

Einkaufspreis m **(Einkaufsrechnungspreis** m)
purchase price, stock price, trade price
  The price a middleman pays to a manufacturer.
Einkaufsquelle f
→ Kaufort
Einkaufsring m retailer-owned wholesaler, purchasing group, voluntary chain of retailers, buying syndicate
Einkaufsstatistik f purchasing statistics *pl (construed as sg)*
Einkaufsstätte f
→ Kaufort
Einkaufsstraße f **(Fußgängerzone** f) shopping mall, mall, shopping strip, strip center
  A type of shopping center (→) Einkaufszentrum, which may be a number of shopping blocks closed to vehicular traffic, or shopping center of the usual type but with walkways entirely closed against the weather and airconditioned, or the same in the form of a building with inside parking provided, sometimes near a particular department area.
Einkaufstagebuch n *(market res)* purchase diary, buying diary, shopping diary
→ Haushaltsbuchforschung, Tagebuchmethode
Einkaufstasche f shopping bag, (Papier) paper bag
Einkaufstechnik f
→ Beschaffungstechnik
Einkaufstest m
→ Ladenbeobachtung, Store-Test, Testkauf
Einkaufsvereinigung f
→ Einkaufsgemeinschaft
Einkaufsverhalten n shopping behavior, *brit* behaviour, buying behavior, purchasing behavior
vgl. Kaufverhalten
Einkaufswagen m *(retailing)* shopping cart, cart
Einkaufswagenplakat n *(POP advtsg)* cart wrap
  A printed advertising message made of paper, designed to go around shopping carts.
Einkaufsverband m
→ Einkaufsgemeinschaft

Einkaufsvertreter

Einkaufsvertreter *m* purchasing agent, purchasing representative
→ Einkaufskommissionär
Einkaufszentrale *f*
→ Einkaufsgremium
Einkaufszentrum *n (retailing)* shopping center, shopping mall, *brit* shopping centre, (einzelne Gebäude) shopping plaza, (durch Planung entstanden) planned shopping center, controlled shopping center, major retail center, mall center
A geographical cluster of retail stores, collectively handling an assortment of goods varied enough to satisfy most of the merchandise wants of consumers within convenient travelling time, and thereby attracting a general shopping trade. It is planned, developed and controlled by one organization, which may be a major department store or an individual investor. The center is built to be free of traffic congestion in a convenient location outside the inner city, and to have a wide variety of stores to meet the needs of the market it serves. Usually, a shopping center has at least one major department store as its focus and a variety of limited-line and specialty stores.
→ Nachbarschaftszentrum, Gemeindezentrum, Regionalzentrum
Einkaufszentrum *n* **mit offener Ladenstraße** *(retailing)* open-mall shopping center
Einkaufszentrum *n* **mit überdachter Ladenstraße** *(retailing)* enclosed-mall shopping center
Einkaufszentrum *n* **mit Ladenstraßen auf mehreren Ebenen** *(retailing)* multiple-level shopping center
Einkaufszetteltest *m*
→ Einkaufslistenverfahren
Einkaufszusammenschluß *m*
→ Einkaufsgemeinschaft
Einklappbild *n* **(Klapptafel** *f,* **Flip-Chart** *f)* flip chart, flip card
Einklebebuch *n* **(Sammelbuch** *n)* scrapbook
einkleben *v/t* **1.** to stick in, to paste in, to glue in, to tip in **2.** *(print)* (Vorsatz) to paper up
Einkleben *n* tipping-in, tipping
Einkleber *m*
→ Beikleber
Einkommen *n (econ)* income, earnings *pl*
Einkommen-Konsumfunktion *f*
→ Engel-Kurve

Einkommenseffekt *m* (der Werbeausgaben) income effect (of advertising expenditure)
Einkommenselastizität *f* **der Nachfrage (Einkommensnachfrageelastizität** *f)* *(econ)* income elasticity of demand
The percentual change in quantity demanded which is to be expected from a one percent change in income.
Einkommensgruppe *f* **(Einkommensklasse** *f)* *(econ)* income bracket, income group
Einkommensstatistik *f (econ)* income statistics *pl (construed as sg)*
Einkommensverteilung *f (econ)* income distribution, distribution of income
The national income divided among households for an average comparison with other markets.
Ein-Komponenten-Entwicklung *f (phot)* one-component development
einkopieren *v/t* **1.** *(print)* to overprint **2.** *(TV)* to superimpose, to super
Einkopieren *n* **(Einkopierung** *f)*
1. *(print)* overprinting **2.** *(TV)* superimposition, superimposure, super-imp
Einkreisempfänger *m* **(Einkreiser** *m)* *(radio)* single-circuit receiver
Einlage *f* **1.** (Kissen, Polster) cushion, pad fitment, fitting, inset, insert **2.** → Zwischenlage
Einlagekarton *m*
→ Bristolkarton
Einlaufrille *f* (in der Schallplatte) lead-in groove, run-in groove
Einlaufzeit *f (TV)* warm-up time, running-up time
Einlegeapparat *m* **(Einleger** *m)* *(print)* feeder
Einlegeblatt *n*
→ Loseblatt
Einlegemarke *f (film/phot)* start mark
einlegen *v/t* **1.** (Kamera) to load, to thread up **2.** (Projektor, Band) to lace up **3.** (beilegen) to insert
Einleitung *f* introduction, lead-in, *colloq* intro
einleuchten *(phot/film/TV) v/i* to set the lighting
Einleuchtung *f (phot/film/TV)* setting of the lighting, lighting setting
Einleuchtzeit *f (phot/film/TV)* lighting setting time

Ein-Licht-Kopie f *(film)* rushprint, one-light print
Ein-Licht-Kopierung f *(film)* rush printing, one-light printing
einlösen *v/t* (Gutschein) to redeem (a coupon)
 To fulfill the requirements of a promotional offer by returning a coupon or a trading stamp in order to obtain a premium or a discount.
Einlösung f **(von Gutscheinen)** redemption, coupon redemption
→ einlösen
Einlösungsquote f **(Einlösungsrate** f**)** (bei Gutscheinen) redemption rate, coupon redemption rate
 The percentage of coupons, trading stamps or similar promotional offers that is returned in order to obtain goods at a discount, or premiums, or cash.
Einmalbad n **(Einmalentwickler** m, **Monobad** n**)** *(phot)* unibath, monobath
 A combined developing and fixing process for film with only one bath. Every grain of silver in the emulsion is either used in forming the image or discarded.
einmalige Vergütung f
→ Pauschalhonorar
einmalige Befragung f **(Querschnittsbefragung** f**)** *(survey res)* one-shot interview, one-shot survey, single-shot survey, single-shot interview
→ Querschnittsanalyse; *vgl.* Panelbefragung, Wiederholungsbefragung, Trenduntersuchung
einmaliger Rabatt m *(econ)* temporary allowance, one-time discount
Einmalkontakt m **(einmaliger Kontakt** m**)** *(media res)* single exposure, exposure
vgl. Mehrfachkontakt
Ein-Minuten-Film m **(einminütige Einblendung** f**)** minute movie
einmischen *v/t*
→ einblenden
einpacken *v/t* to pack, to wrap, to package
Einpackpapier n
→ Packpapier
einlassen *v/t*
→ Register machen
einpegeln *v/t (radio/TV)* to line up, to adjust
Einpegeln n *(radio/TV)* line-up, level adjustment

Einpegelzeit f *(radio/TV)* (Übertragung) lineup period, line-up period
Einpersonenhaushalt m single-adult household, single-person household
Einplanung f
→ Zuteilung von Sendezeit
Ein-Produkt-Unternehmen n *(econ)* one-product enterprise
Einreichungsfrist f *(econ)* (bei Ausschreibungen) tender period, closing date
einrichten *v/t*
→ zurichten
Einrichtung f
→ Zurichtung
einrücken *v/t* **1.** *(print)* (Zeile) to indent **2.** (Anzeige) → einschalten, schalten
Einrückung f
→ Einzug
eins zu eins (1 : 1, Originalformat n, **Originalgröße** f**)** same size (s/s, SS, S.S.), as is
Einsägemaschine f *(print)* notching machine
einsägen *v/t (print)* to saw in
Einsammelinterview n
→ Filter-Interview
Einsammeln n
→ Screening
Einsatz m **1.** *(promotion)* (Gewinnspiel) stake, stakes *pl* **2.** *(packaging)* (Einlage) fitting, fitment, insert, inset, inner packing form, partition **3.** *(film)* release **4.** *(film/TV)* (Stichwort) cue, film cue
→ Einsatzsignal
Einsatzphase f **(Einsatzperiode** f, **Aktionszeitraum** m**)** (bei Werbung/ Verkaufsförderung) drive period, promotion drive period, promotion time
 The limited period of time during which a manufacturer or a wholesaler makes particular efforts of promoting a product and grants deal and promotional terms to consumers and/or retailers.
Einsatzsignal n **(Stichwort** n**)** *(radio/ film/TV)* cue, film cue
 A verbal, visual, or printed signal used to guide some action of a performer.
Einschaltauftrag m
→ Anzeigenauftrag, Mediavertrag, Werbeauftrag

Einschaltbeleg

Einschaltbeleg *m*
(Einschaltbestätigung *f*)
→ Beleg
Einschaltbrumm *m* **(Einschaltbrummton** *m*) *(radio/TV)* starting hum
einschalten *v/t* **1.** *(advtsg)* (Anzeige) to insert, to run, to place, to schedule **2.** *(print)* (Text) to insert, to interpolate, to interline, to intercalate **3.** *(radio/TV)* (Gerät) to switch on, to turn on, (Sender) to tune in **4.** *(electr.)* (Spannung) to switch in **5.** *(phot)* (Kamera) to start
Einschalten *n* **(Einschaltung** *f*)
1. *(advtsg)* (Anzeige) insertion, placing, advertising, scheduling **2.** *(print)* (Text) insertion, interpolation, interlining, interlineation, intercalation **3.** *(radio/TV)* (Gerät) switching-on, switching, turning-on, (Sender) tuning-in, tuning, set tuning **4.** *(electr.)* (Spannung) switching in **5.** *(phot)* (Kamera) start, starting
Einschalter *m*
→ Schalter
Einschaltfrequenz *f*
→ Werbehäufigkeit
Einschaltjahr *n* **(Geschäftsjahr** *n*) *(advtsg)* contract year
  The year during which a contractual relationship exists betwen an advertiser and an advertising medium. It need not correspond to the calendar year.
Einschaltplan *m* **(Schaltplan** *m*) advertising schedule, insertion schedule
→ Mediaplan
Einschaltpreis *m* **(Anzeigenpreis** *m*, **Werbepreis** *m*) advertising rate, insertion rate, adrate rate, (bei Werbung, deren Preis in Flächeneinheiten berechnet wird) space rate, (bei Werbung, deren Preis in Zeiteinheiten berechnet wird) time rate
  The amount of money that an advertising medium charges per unit of space or time purchased by an advertiser.
Einschaltquote *f (auch* **Einschaltrate** *f*) *(audience res)* (Anteil der Hörer/ Zuschauer) audience rating, rating (the ratings *pl*), broadcast rating, share-of-audience rating, share of audience, audience share, (beim Fernsehen) television rating, TV rating, (beim Radio) radio rating, (Anteil der eingeschalteten Geräte) sets-in-use rating, S.I.U. rating, SIU rating, sets in use *pl*, tune-in, (Anteil der Haushalte, in denen ein Gerät eingeschaltet ist) homes-using-sets rating, homes using sets *pl*, households using sets *pl*, (beim Fernsehen) homes-using-television rating, homes-using-TV rating, HUT rating, households-using-television rating, households-using-TV rating, households using television, (beim Radio) homes-using-radio rating, HUR rating, households-using-radio rating, homes using radio *pl*, households using radio *pl*, (Anteil der Personen, die hören/zuschauen) (beim Fernsehen) individuals-using-television rating, individuals using television *pl*, (beim Radio) individuals-using-radio rating, individuals using radio *pl*, (Anteil der Hörer/Zuschauer, die ein bestimmtes Programm eingeschaltet haben) program rating, tune-in audience rating, tune-in audience, (Anteil der Hörer/Zuschauer, die ein bestimmtes Programm eines bestimmten Senders eingeschaltet haben) program station rating, program station basis (P.S.B.), P.S.B. rating, (Einschaltquote eines Sendernetzes) network rating, network audience rating, (Einschaltquote eines Einzelsenders) station rating, station audience rating, (Einschaltquote eines einzelnen Werbespots) commercial rating, commercial audience rating, commercial audience, (Einschaltquote einer programmunterbrechendenden Werbesendung) commercial break audience rating, commercial break audience, (durchschnittliche Einschaltquote) average audience rating, AA rating, A.A. rating, aa rating, (Bruttoeinschaltquote, Bruttoreichweite) gross rating points *pl*, GRPs *pl*, G.R.P.s. *pl.*, cumulative gross rating points *pl*, (Beliebtheitsquote) popularity rating (Einschaltquote in einem designierten Marktgebiet) designated market area rating, DMA rating
  A panel survey or one-shot survey estimate of the size of a television or

radio audience expressed in relative or percentage terms. It represents a percentage of some base. The base may be a number of households or a number of individuals. A number of different types of ratings are widely used. First of all, there are several alternative criteria used for counting a household or an individual in, or out of, a television or radio audience. Second, ratings may measure the audience of a network (or station), or of a program, or of a group of stations or programs. Third, ratings may represent only audience in homes, or audience in homes and away from home as well - for example, radio audience in automobiles. Fourth, ratings may reflect audience at an instant in time, average audience over several points in time, or an accumulation of audiences over several points in time. Hence, any rating must be accompanied by a careful definition of the nature of the audience it measures.

Einschaltquote f **pro Minute** (im Minutentakt gemessene Einschaltquote) *(audience res)* minute-by-minute audience rating, minute-by-minute audience, average minute rating, audience minute rating

Einschaltseite f *(print)* insert, inserted leaf
An extra page placed in a magazine or a book

Einschaltung f
→ Einschalten

Einschaltungszeichen n
→ Auslassungszeichen

Einschaltverhalten n *(media res)* set-tuning behavior, *brit* behaviour
The overall pattern of how radio or television users tend to tune in and listen to or watch the program.

Einschaltzahl f *(audience res)* audience score, audience, broadcast audience, (beim Fernsehen) television audience, TV audience, (beim Radio) radio audience, (Zahl der eingeschalteten Geräte) sets in use *pl*, tune-in, (Zahl der Haushalte, in denen ein Gerät eingeschaltet ist) homes using sets *pl*, households usings sets *pl*, (beim Fernsehen) homes using television *pl*, households using television *pl*, homes using TV *pl*, households using TV *pl*, (beim Radio) homes using radio *pl*, households using radio *pl*, (Zahl der Personen, die hören/zuschauen) individuals using television *pl*, individuals using TV *pl*, individuals using radio *pl*, (Zahl der Hörer/Zuschauer, die ein bestimmtes Programm eingeschaltet haben) program audience, tune-in audience, (Zahl der Hörer/Zuschauer, die ein bestimmtes Programm eines bestimmten Senders eingeschaltet haben) program station audience, (Einschaltzahl eines Sendernetzes) network audience, network audience score, (Einschaltzahl eines Einzelsenders) station audience, (Einschaltzahl eines einzelnen Werbespots) commercial audience, (Einschaltzahl einer programm-unterbrechenden Werbesendung) commercial break audience, (durchschnittliche Einschaltzahl) average audience
The estimate of the size of a radio or television audience expressed in absolute terms, and counted according to any one of several alternative criteria. Audience measurements represent either a number of households or a number of individuals. When audience is expressed on a household basis, one commonly-used criterion for whether to count a household in an audience is whether there is evidence that at least one of the television sets or radios in the household was tuned to some station. An alternative criterion involves counting a household in an audience if at least one individual member of the household is reported to have viewed or watched television, or to have listened to or heard radio. In addition, different operational definitions of viewing or listening result in different definitions of audience. When audience is measured on an individual basis, the criterion normally used for whether to count an individual in an audience is whether that individual is reported to have viewed or watched television, or to have listened to or heard radio. In this case also, different operational definitions of viewing or listening result in different definitions of audience. Television and radio audience may be located in households where so-called in-home listening or viewing takes place. These audiences may also be located outside of households, in public places or in automobiles. For example, radio audiences may include a number of persons listening to automobile or to portable radios away from home. Audience figures may reflect only in-home audiences, or they may reflect both in-home and away-from-home audiences, depending on their intent. The

Einschaltzeichen

measurement of audiences also has a time dimension. An instantaneous audience represents households or individuals in the audience at a given instant, or point in time. Audience data may represent an average of these instantaneous audience figures. Alternately, audience figures can represent an accumulation of the instantaneous audience over a number of points in time. Such an accumulation may or may not duplicate households or individuals that are in the audience during two or more points in time. Irrespective of the criterion, when audience is expressed on a household basis, a household should be counted in a given television or radio audience only once in a given instant no matter how many sets in the household are in use, or no matter how many members of the household are in the audience.

Einschaltzeichen *n*
→ Auslassungszeichen
Einschätzungsskalierung *f*
→ Rating, Ratingskala
Einschießbogen *m* (**Einschießpapier** *n*) *(print)* slip sheet, slipsheet, interleaves *pl*
einschießen *v/t (print)*
1. (Makulaturbogen) to slip-sheet
2. → durchschießen
einschlagen *v/t*
→ einwickeln
Einschlagklappe *f*
→ Umschlagklappe
Einschlagmaschine *f*
→ Einwickelmaschine
Einschlagpapier *n*
→ Einwickelpapier
Einschreibung *f* (**Einschreibeverfahren** *n*)
Einschub *m* (**Einschiebsel** *n*, **Einschiebung** *f*) *(print)* insertion, insert, interpolation
    Any printed matter or copy intended to be incorporated within the body of an existing manuscript or other text.
einschweißen *v/t (packaging)* (in Schrumpffolie) to shrink-wrap
Einschweißen *n* (**Einschweißung** *f*) *(packaging)* (in Schrumpffolie) shrink wrapping
Einschwingung *n (radio)* build-up, rise
Einschwingzeit *f (radio)* build-up time, rise time
Einseitenband *n* (**ESB**) *(tape)* single-side band (SSB)
einseitig beklebt *adj* single-faced

136

einseitig gefärbt *adj (paper)* single-side colored, *brit* coloured
einseitig gestrichenes Papier *n* single-side coated paper
einseitig glattes Papier *n* machine-glazed paper, M.G. paper, M.G.
einseitige Anzeige *f*
→ ganzseitige Anzeige
einseitiger Test *m* (**Ein-Segment-Test** *m*) one-tailed test, one-tail test, one-sided test, (Test des linksseitigen Segments) lower-tail test, (des rechtsseitigen Segments) upper-tail test
    A hypothesis test, in which the critical region of the test statistic is located in only one tail of the distribution, so that the null hypothesis is rejected only if the test statistic is greater than the critical value that cuts off the most extreme values in the lower or in the upper tail.
vgl. zweiseitiger Test
einspaltig *adj (print)* single-column, one column wide
einspaltige Anzeige *f* single-column advertisement, single-column ad
Einspiegelung *f*
→ Spiegeltrickverfahren
einspielen *v/t* (Platte, Band) to record, (Gewinn) to bring in, to make, (zuspielen) to inject, to feed to, to insert, to play in
Einspielergebnis *n (film)* box office returns *pl*, *brit* box-office receipts *pl*
Einspielung *f*
→ Filmeinspielung
einstampfen (makulieren) *v/t (paper)* to pulp, to repulp
Einstampfung *f* (**Einstampfen** *n*, **Makulierung** *f*) *(paper)* pulping
Einstandspreis *m* (**Selbstkostenpreis** *m*) *(econ)* cost price; zum Einstandspreis verkaufen: to sell at cost
einstarten *v/t (film)* to cue in, to make start marks, to place cue marks
Einstechbogen *m (print)* tympan sheet, tympan
    The paper that covers the platen or impression cylinder of a letterpress.
Einsteckbogen *m (print)* inset
    Pages that are cut off in folding and placed in the middle of the sheet.
Einstecksockel *m (POP advtsg)* crow's feet
Einstellbild *n (TV)*
→ Einstelltestbild, Testbild

Einstellebene f
→ Schärfenebene
einstellen v/t **1.** (regulieren) to adjust, to regulate, to set **2.** *(radio/TV)* to tune, to tune in, to modulate **3.** *(phot)* to focus (the camera), to adjust (the distance), to rack focus **4.** (Kamera) to set up, to aim, to point, to rack focus **5.** (Bild) to frame **6.** (Erscheinen einstellen) to to discontinue publication, to cease to appear, to cease publication
Einstellen n **(Einstellung** f**) 1.** *(print/phot)* (Regulierung) adjustment, adjusting, setting **2.** *(radio/TV)* → Einschaltung **3.** *(phot)* focusing **4.** *(phot/film/TV)* (Kamera) setting, aiming, pointing **5.** *(phot)* (Bild) framing **6.** (Aufhören) discontinuation **7.** *(film/TV)* (der Bildfrequenz) picture-frequency setting, picture-frequency adjustment, (der Zeilenfrequenz) line-frequency adjustment, line-frequency setting
Einstellfassung f *(phot)* focusing mount
Einstellring m *(phot)* (am Objektiv) focusing ring, (am Kameragehäuse) focusing knob
Einstellscheibe f *(phot)* focusing screen, focusing glass, swingback
Einstelltestbild n **(Einstellbild** n**)** *(TV)* (Kamera) test card, (Gerät) test pattern
→ Testbild
Einstellung f
1. → Einstellen 1. - 7.
2. *(film)* take **3.** *(soc res)* Haltung, Attitüde) attitude
  A general orientation or way of thinking. An attitude gives rise to many specific "opinions", cf. (→) Meinung, a term often used with regard to a specific issue or object.
→ Drei-Komponenten-Theorie
Einstellungsanalyse f *(market res)* attitude analysis, analysis of attitude
→ Einstellungsforschung
Einstellungsänderung f **(Einstellungswandel** m**)** *(social res)* attitude change
  The extent to which attitudes vary, usually as a result of external stimuli.
Einstellungsanweisung f (bei irreführender Werbung) cease and desist order

Einstellungsbatterie f **(Batterie** f **von Einstellungsfragen)** *(survey res)* attitude battery
Einstellungsbildung f *(psy)* attitude formation
Einstellungsbündel n **(Einstellungs-Cluster** n**)** *(psy)* attitude cluster
Einstellungsdissonanz f *(psy)* attitude dissonance
→ kognitive Dissonanz
Einstellungsdynamik f *(psy)* attitude dynamics pl *(construed as sg)*
Einstellungsfolge f **(Folge** f **von Einstellungen)** *(film)* sequence of shots
Einstellungsforschung f **(Attitüdenforschung** f**)** *(psy)* attitude research
  The scientific analysis of attitudes toward organizations, products, services, values, etc. by means of sample surveys with the goal of recognizing their implication for consumers' behavior.
Einstellungsfrage f *(survey res)* attitudinal question, attitude question
vgl. Verhaltensfrage
Einstellungskonditionierung f *(psy)* attitude conditioning
Einstellungskonsonanz f *(psy)* attitude consonance
→ Konsonanz
Einstellungskontinuum n attitude continuum
Einstellungsmessung f *(res)* attitude measurement
Einstellungsmodell n *(market res)* attitudinal model, attitude model
Einstellungsobjekt n attitude object
Einstellungssegmentierung f *(market res)* attitude segmentation
Einstellungsskala f **1.** *(social res)* attitude scale
  A research instrument for the systematic measurement of attitudes, by means of which respondents are usually asked to express agreement or disagreement with a series of verbal statements concerning some issue, product, advertisement, person, etc.
2. *(phot)* lens scale
  The scale mounted above process lenses on the camera as an aid in quick and accurate setting of iris diaphragm apertures, particularly in halftone photography.
Einstellungsuntersuchung f **(Einstellungsstudie** f**)** *(res)* attitude investigation, attitude study

Einstellungswandel

Einstellungswandel
A social or market research model trying to establish the nature of the relationship between attitudes toward an object and behavior.
Einstellungswandel *m*
→ Einstellungsänderung
Einstellungswechsel *m* **1.** *(film)* change of angle, changeover **2.** *(phot)* change of focus
einstrippen *v/t (print)* to strip in, to strip
  Combining two or more negatives in the making of a single plate.
einstudieren *v/t (radio/TV)* (Rolle) to rehearse, to get up
Einstudierung *f*
→ Probe
Einstufenätzverfahren *n* **(Dow-Verfahren** *n***)** *(print)* Dow etch process
Ein-Stufen-Fluß *m* (der Kommunikation) **(einstufiger Kommunikationsfluß** *m***)** one-step flow (of communication)
  The early theory of communication which assumes that there is an immediate influence between a communicator's message and its influence on recipients.
vgl. Zwei-Stufen-Fluß
Einthemenbefragung *f*
→ Spezialbefragung; *vgl.* Mehrthemenbefragung
Eintourenmaschine *f* **(Eintourenpresse** *f* **)** *(print)* single-revolution machine, single-revolution press
Einwegflasche *f* one-way bottle, nondeposit bottle, no-return bottle, expendable bottle, nonreturnable bottle, *brit* non-returnable bottle
Einweg-Spiegel *m*
→ Spionspiegel
Einwegpackung *f* **(Einwegverpackung** *f***)** one-way pack, one-way package, single-service pack, single-service package, disposable pack(age), no-return pack(age), nonreturnable pack(age), one-trip pack(age), single-trip pack(age), single-use pack(age), throwaway pack(age)
vgl. Mehrwegpackung
einwellige Wellpappe *f (paper)* single-flute corrugated board, single-wall corrugated board
einwickeln (einpacken, einschlagen) *v/t (packaging)* to wrap, to wrap up
Einwickelpapier *n* **(Einwickelstreifen** *m*, **Einwickelmaterial** *n***)** *(packaging)* wrapping paper, kraft paper, case wraparound
→ Packpapier
Einwohneradreßbuch *n* **(Einwohnerverzeichnis** *n***)** city directory, directory
Einzelaufhängung *f (phot/film/TV)* (Scheinwerfer) single-suspension unit, single-lamp suspension unit
Einzelaufnahme *f* **(Einzelbild** *n***)** *(phot)* single frame, frame, still, (aus einem Film) motion picture still, cinema still
Einzelaufnahmebelichtung *f (phot)* single-frame exposure
Einzelauslage *f (POP advtsg)* spot display
  An individual piece of retail display in an island position.
→ alleinstehende Auslage
Einzelbeleg *m* tearsheet, tear sheet
  A page containing an advertisement, clipped from a publication and sent to the advertiser for checking purposes.
Einzelbild *n*
→ Einzelaufnahme
Einzelbildaufnahme *f (film)* single-frame exposure, frame-by-frame exposure, single-frame shooting, stop-frame shooting
→ Zeitraffer
Einzelbildmotor *m (film)* stop-frame motor, single-frame motor, animation motor
Einzelbildschaltung *f (film)* single-frame mechanism, single-frame control, single-picture mechanism, single-picture control, stop-frame mechanism, stop-frame control
→ Zeitraffer
Einzelexemplar *n* **(Einzelheft** *n*, **Einzelausgabe** *f* **)** (einer Publikation) individual copy, single copy
Einzelfilm *m* **(Einzelsendung** *f* **)** *(radio/TV)* one shot, one time only, one-time-only, OTO, O.T.O., non-serial
  A non serialized broadcast.
Einzelgeschäft *n* **(Filiale** *f* **)** sales outlet, outlet
  A single retail selling or trading unit.
Einzelhandel (EH) *m* **1. (Institution)** retail trade, the retailers *pl* **2. (Funktion)** retailing, retail trading
  All business activities involved in selling goods and services directly to ultimate or final users for personal, nonbusiness consumption or use.

Einzelhandelsanzeige f
(Einzelhandelswerbemittel n) retail
advertisement, retail ad, local
advertisement, local ad
Einzelhandelsbefragung f
→ Einzelhändlerbefragung
Einzelhandelsbestandsprüfung f
(market res) retail audit, shop audit,
dealer audit
  A type of sample survey conducted
  among retail outlets with the aim of
  collecting information on sales volume,
  stock levels, promotional effectiveness of
  brands, displays used, etc.
→ Händlerbefragung
Einzelhandelsbetrieb m
→ Einzelhandelsgeschäft
Einzelhandelsbindung f
→ Geschäftsbindung, Ladenbindung
Einzelhandelsdynamik f
→ Dynamik der Betriebsformen (im Einzelhandel)
Einzelhandelsfiliale f retail outlet, outlet
→ Verkaufsfläche
Einzelhandelsforschung f retail trade research, retail research, dealer research
→ Handelsforschung
Einzelhandelsgeschäft n **(Einzelhandelsbetrieb** m, **Einzelhandelsunternehmen** n) retail establishment, retail shop, retail store, retail business, independent store
  A retailing business unit which is
  controlled by its own individual
  ownership or management rather than
  from without, except insofar as its
  management is limited by voluntary
  group arrangements.
Einzelhandelskette f
→ freiwillige Handelskette
Einzelhandelskunde m retail customer
Einzelhandelsmarketing n retail marketing
  The application of marketing
  management concepts and strategy to
  retailing.
Einzelhandelsmarktforschung f retail marketing research, dealer marketing research, dealer research
→ Handelsmarktforschung
Einzelhandelspanel n *(market res)* retail panel survey, retail panel
→ Handelspanel, Händlerpanel
Einzelhandelspreis m **(Ladenpreis** m) retail price

Einzelhandelspreispolitik f retail pricing
Einzelhandelsrabatt m
(Wiederverkäuferrabatt m) retail discount, (für besondere Werbeaktivitäten) performance allowance, promotional discount
Einzelhandelsreisender m
→ Handelsreisender
Einzelhandelsspanne f
→ Handelsspanne
Einzelhandelsspezialisierung f retail specialization, *brit* specialisation
Einzelhandelsstatistik f
→ Handelsstatistik
Einzelhandelsstruktur f retail structure
Einzelhandelsstrukturanalyse f retail structure analysis, analysis of retail structure
Einzelhandelsumsatz m retail sales *pl*, retail turnover, stockturn
Einzelhandelsunternehmen n
→ Einzelhandelsgeschäft
Einzelhandelsverkauf m 1. (einzelner Verkaufsakt) retail sale 2. (das Verkaufen) retail selling, retail sales *pl*
Einzelhandelsverkaufspreis m
→ Einzelhandelspreis
Einzelhandelsvertreter m
→ Handelsvertreter
Einzelhandelsvertrieb m retail distribution
Einzelhandelswerbetarif m
(Einzelhandelswerbepreis m) retail rate, local rate
  A special adrate offered only to local
  advertisers by newspapers and broadcast
  media, ostensibly because they do not
  benefit from coverage which extends
  beyond the central market area. Local
  rates are not common in Germany.
Einzelhandelswerbung f 1. (die Werbung örtlicher Einzelhändler) retail advertising, local advertising 2. (Gemeinschaftswerbung örtlicher Einzelhändler) dealer cooperative advertising 3. (eines einzelnen Händlers) store advertising, dealer advertising
Einzelhandelszeitschrift f
(Einzelhändlerzeitschrift f) dealer magazine, retail magazine
  A business magazine catering to the
  reading needs and information interests
  of retailers.

Einzelhandelszentralität f
→ Zentralität
Einzelhandelszentrum n
→ Einkaufszentrum
Einzelhändler m retailer, retail dealer, dealer, (in einer Vertriebsorganisation) distribution outlet
   A merchant, or occasionally an agent, whose main business is selling directly to the ultimate consumer. The retailer is to be distinguished by the nature of his sales rather than by the way he procures the goods in which he deals. The size of the units in which he sells is an incidental rather than a primary element in his character. His essential distinguishing mark is the fact that his typical sale is made to the ultimate consumer.
Einzelhändlerbefragung f *(market res)* retail survey, dealer survey
→ Händlerbefragung
Einzelhändlergenossenschaft f
→ Einkaufsgenossenschaft
Einzelheft n **(Einzelnummer** f**)** single copy, single issue
Einzelheftpreis m **(Heftpreis** m**)** *(Zeitschrift)* single-copy price, single-issue price, single-number price
Einzelinterview n
→ Exploration
Einzelkontakt m *(media res)* single exposure, one-time exposure
→ Kontakt; *vgl.* Mehrfachkontakt
Einzelpackung f unit pack, primary package
Einzelpersonenpanel n
→ Personenpanel
Einzelpersonenstichprobe f
→ Personenstichprobe
Einzelplakat n **(Nicht-Serie** f**)** *(outdoor advtsg)* etwa non-serial poster, single poster
Einzelpreis m
→ Einheitspreis
Einzelprodukttest m **(Einzeltest** m**)** *(market res)* single product test
vgl. Mehrfachprodukttest (Mehrfachtest)
Einzelreichweite f
→ Reichweite
Einzelsendung f
→ Einzelfilm
Einzelspalte f *(print)* single column
Einzelstreuung f *obsol* (Rudolf Seyffert)
→ Direktwerbung

Einzelumwerbung f *obsol* (Rudolf Seyffert) individual advertising, personal advertising, mouth-to-mouth advertising, face-to-face advertising
→ Direktwerbung; *vgl.* Mengenumwerbung
vgl. Mengenumwerbung
Einzelverkauf m **(Apartverkauf** m, **Einzelverkaufsexemplare** n/pl**)** *(Zeitung/Zeitschrift)* single copy sales pl, newsstand sales pl, counter sales pl, (abzüglich der Remittenden) net single copy sales pl, (durch Straßenverkäufe) street sales pl, (durch Zeitungsjungen) newsboy sales pl, boy sales pl
   The number sales of a periodical made through retail outlets, including newsstands and newsboys and including single copies sold by mail, with the returns deducted.
vgl. Abonnementsverkauf
Einzelverkaufsauflage f *(Zeitung/ Zeitschrift)* single copy circulation, single copy sales pl, newsstand circulation, newsstand sales pl, (abzüglich der Remittenden) net single copy circulation, net single copy sales pl
→ Einzelverkauf
Einzelverkaufsleser m **(E-Leser** m**)**
→ A + E-Leser
Einzelverkaufszeitschrift f
→ Kaufzeitschrift
Einzelwerbebrief m individual advertising letter, personal advertising letter
Einzelwerbung f
→ Alleinwerbung; *vgl.* Gemeinschaftswerbung, Sammelwerbung
einziehen v/t *(print)*
→ einrücken
Einziehen n
→ Einzug
einzigartiges Verkaufsversprechen n
→ U.S.P.
Einzug m *(print)* indent, indentation, indention
   Type matter in which the first line of a paragraph begins with a blank space. (Einzug nach überstehender Kopfzeile) flush and indent, flush and hang, hanging indent, hanging indentation, hanging indention, (ohne Einzug) flush, full-out, bookstyle, justified style

Einzugsbereich m **(Einzugsgebiet** n**)**
1. *(retailing)* (im Einzelhandel) trading area, trading zone, retail trading zone, shopping radius
The entire geographical area around a retail outlet or a shopping district, the residents of which patronize the outlet or district to a relevant degree.
2. *(radio/TV)* (Marktvorherrschaftsbereich eines Radio- oder Fernsehsenders) area of dominant influence, A.D.I., ADI, designated market area, D.M.A., DMA, dominant area, exclusive coverage area
→ Sendebereich, Empfangsbereich
3. *(outdoor advtsg)* circulation area
The geographical area in which a transit or outdoor advertising operator is active.
4. (Zeitung) coverage area
Einzugswalze f *(print)* feed roll
Eisbrecherfrage f **(Kontaktfrage** f**, Einleitungsfrage** f**)** *(survey res)* rapport builder, warm-up question, warm-up
Eisenbahnplakat n *(transit advtsg)* railroad poster, railway poster, railroad showing
An advertising poster placed either in a railroad station or along the right-of-way for exposure to train passengers.
Eisenbahnwerbung f **(Eisenbahnreklame** f**)** railroad advertising, railway advertising
All advertising involving facilities of railroads, in Germany the package of advertising opportunities offered by (→) Deutsche Eisenbahnreklame.
→ Bahnhofswerbung, Verkehrsmittelwerbung, Fahrkartenwerbung
EKG *abbr* Einkaufsgenossenschaft
elektrische Methode f (der Werbebudgetierung) eclectic method (of advertising budget determination), composite method
The method of taking recourse to several of the generally accepted techniques of advertising bugdet determination.
Ektachrom m **(Ektachromfilm** m**, Ektachrome** m**)** *(phot)* Ektachrome
Ektacolorfilm m **(Ektacolor** m**)** *(phot)* Ektacolor
Ela f *short for* Elatechnik
elastische Nachfrage f **(elastischer Bedarf** m**)**
→ Nachfrageelastizität
Elastizität f **(Elastizität** f **der Nachfrage)** *(econ)* elasticity, elasticity of demand

In the most general sense, a measure of the degree of responsiveness of a dependent variable to changes in an independent variable, between which a causal relationship is known to exist.
→ Preiselastizität der Nachfrage, Einkommenelastizität, Verbrauchselastizität; Absatzelastizität, Angebotselastizität, Bedarfselastizität, Kreuzpreiselastizität
Elastizitätskoeffizent m
→ Triffinscher Koeffizient
Elastizitätsmethode f (der Werbebudgetierung) elasticity method (of advertising budget determination)
Elatechnik f **(Ela** f**, Elektroakustik** f**)** electro-acoustics *pl (construed as sg)*
elektrodermale Reaktion f **(EDR)**
→ pschogalvanische Reaktion (PGR)
Elektroenzephalogramm n **(EEG)** *(market res)* electroencephalogram
Elektrolyse f electrolysis
elektromechanische Einschaltquotenmessung f *(media res)* mechanical recorder method, mechanical recorder technique
The generally accepted method of making measurements of audience ratings by equipping a panel of household with electromechanical recording devices.
elektromechanische Reproduktion f electromechanical reproduction
elektrolytisches Bad n *(print)* electrolytic bath, eletrolye
Elektronenkanone f **(Elektronenstrahlsystem** n**, Strahlerzeuger** m**)** electron gun
Elektronenblitz m *(phot)* electronic flash
A high speed light source used as a substitute for flash blubs.
elektronische Berichterstattung f **(EB)** electronic news gathering (ENG)
elektronische Bildaufzeichnung f electronic video recording (EVR)
elektronische Datenverarbeitung f **(EDV)** electronical data processing (EDP)
elektronische Kommunikation f electronic(al) communication(s) *(pl)*
elektronische Medien n/pl electronic(al) media pl
elektronische Reproduktion f electronic(al) reproduction
elektronische Zeitung f
→ Bildschirmzeitung

elektronischer Filmabtaster *m*
electronic(al) scanner, color scanner,
brit colour scanner
elektronischer Schnitt *m*
(elektronisches Schneiden *n) (film/
TV)* electronic editing
   The process wherein different live or
   prerecorded inputs (picture and sound)
   are edited together electronically, that is,
   without manual cutting and splicing.
elektronischer Sucher *m (phot)*
electronic viewfinder, electronic
finder
**elektronisches Datenvermittlungs-
system** *n* **(EDS)** electronic(al) data
transmission system
elektronisches Editieren *n*
→ elektronischer Schnitt
elektronisches Schneiden *n*
→ elektronischer Schnitt
elektronisches Testbild *n*
→ Testbild
Elektronovision *f* electronovision
Elektrotype *f*
→ Galvano
Elektrotypie *f*
→ Galvanoplastik
Element *n (stat)* element, elementary
unit, *auch* elementary element
   A unit in a set of data, a statistical
   aggregate or collection of items that
   cannot be further subdivided into
   constituents that could legitimately be
   regarded as members of the set.
Elementauswahl *f* **(Elementen-
auswahl** *f,* **Element-Stichprobe** *f)*
(stat) element sample
→ Elementenauswahlverfahren
Elementenauswahlverfahren *n*
(Elementauswahl *f,* **Element-Stich-
probenverfahren** *n,* **Element-
Stichprobenbildung** *f) (stat)* element
sampling
   In contrast to cluster sampling,
   (→) Klumpenauswahl, all sampling
   techniques in which the sampling unit
   contains only one element.
Elementenpsychologie *f* psychological
elementalism
Elfenbeinkarton *m* ivory board
Elfenbeinpapier *n* ivory paper
Eliminationsverfahren *n (advtsg res)*
elimination technique
   A method of testing the form quality,
   (→) Gestaltfestigkeit, of advertisements,
   or product packages by eliminating parts
   from them to see whether informants
   recognize the original.
vgl. Substitutionsverfahren

Emaille *f* **(Emaillearbeit** *f*) enamel
Emailledruck *m* **(Kaltemailledruck**
m) enamel print, photoresist
Emailleschild *n* **(Emailleplakat** *n*)
(outdoor advtsg) enamel plate, enamel
sign
Emanzipationswerbung *f* (Karl
Christian Behrens) etwa
emancipatory advertising
vgl. Kontinuitätswerbung,
Synchronisationswerbung
Emblem *n* emblem
Emnid Faktorielle Anzeigenanalyse *f*
(EFA) *(advtsg res) etwa* Emnid Impact
Test, Emnid Recall & Recognition
Test
Emotion *f* **(Gefühl** *n,*
Gemütsbewegung *f) (psy)* emotion
Emotional-Quotient-Skala *f*
→ EQ-Skala
emotionale Konditionierung *f*
emotional conditioning
emotionale Werbung *f* emotional
advertising, short-circuit appeal
   Advertising aimed at appealing to
   psychological rather than to utility needs.
vgl. rationale Werbung
emotionales Engagement *n* emotional
involvement
Emotionsforschung *f (psy)* emotions
research
Empfang *m (radio/TV)* reception
empfangen *v/t (radio/TV)* (Sender) to
receive
Empfänger *m* 1. *(communication)*
(Rezipient) recipient 2. *(direct advtsg)*
addressee 3. *(radio/TV)* receiver,
receiving set, set
Empfänger *m* **im Betrieb** *(media res)*
call-at-office subscriber
Empfängeranalyse *f (media res) etwa*
mailing-list analysis, analysis of
adresses in the mailing list, mail
address analysis
   A type of readership analysis based on
   an examination of data available from
   information gained from a publisher's
   mailing list.
Empfängerröhre *f (radio/TV)* receiving
valve
Empfängerseite *f (communication)*
receiving end
Empfänger-Strukturanalyse *f (media
res)* analysis of readership structure
   A type of readership analysis aimed at
   gaining structural data, (→)
   Strukturanalyse, on a publication's
   audience as a result of survey interviews

using self-administered questionnaires mailed out or otherwise addressed to subscribers.

Empfangsantenne f *(radio/TV)* receiving antenna, *brit* receiving aerial

Empfangsbereich m **(Empfangsgebiet** n) *(radio/TV)* service area, reception area, coverage area, signal area, *(electr)* tuning range, frequency range
The geographic area within which a television or radio station can be received. One commonly used criterion for inclusion in such a coverage area is whether at least some specified percentage, e.g., 5 or 10 percent of the households can receive a station's program. A coverage area is defined on a "can-receive" basis and should not be confused with a circulation area which is defined on a "do-receive" basis. Another method of defining a coverage area is in terms of certain geographic contours, which are determined on the basis of engineering calculations about which areas are within range of a broadcast signal of specified strength. When one refers to a geographic area defined on this basis it should be referred to as "signal coverage area".

Empfangsbereichskarte f *(radio/TV)* coverage map
A map showing the geographical area reached by transmission from a broadcast station. Usually divided into primary, cf. (→) Nahempfangsbereich, and secondary coverage areas, cf. (→) Fernempfangsbereich, for both day and night.

Empfangsfrequenz f *(radio)* receiving frequency, incoming frequency

Empfangsgerät n *(radio/TV)* receiver, receiving set, *(TV)* kinescope

Empfangsgüte f **(Empfangsqualität** f) *(radio/TV)* reception quality

Empfangsstation f *(radio/TV)* receiving station

Empfangsstörung f *(radio/TV)* interference, interference of reception, distortion

Empfehlung f recommendation

Empfehlungsschild n recommendation sign

Empfehlungsschreiben n **(Anerkennungsschreiben** n) letter of recommendation, testimonial letter, testimonial
→ Dankschreiben

empfindlich adj *(phot)* sensitive, (Kopierwerk) high-speed
→ lichtempfindlich

Empfindlichkeit f *(phot)* sensitivity, (film) speed, emulsion speed
→ Lichtempfindlichkeit

Empfindlichkeitsmesser m **(Sensitometer** n) *(phot)* sensitometer

Empfindlichkeitsregelung f *(phot)* sensitivity control

empfohlener Preis m
→ Richtpreis

empirische Auswahl f **(empirische Wahrscheinlichkeitsauswahl** f) *(stat)* empirical sampling

empirische Methode f **(Empirie** f) empirical method, empiricism

empirische Sozialforschung f empirical social research

empirische Wirtschaftsforschung f empirical economics pl *(construed as sg)*, empirical economic research

empirische Standardabweichung f **(empirische Häufigkeitsverteilung** f) *(stat)* empirical distribution, empirical frequency distribution

empirischer Test m *(res)* empirical test

empirisches Anfangsmoment n *(stat)* empirical initial moment

empirisches Moment n *(stat)* empirical moment

empirisches zentrales Moment n *(stat)* empirical central moment

Emulsion f *(phot)* emulsion
The light-sensitive coating on films, papers, and plates. It consists of a silver salt or salts suspended in gelatin.

Emulsionschargennummer f **(Emulsionsnummer** f) *(phot)* emulsion batch number
A number placed on the label of film and paper packages which identifies the batch from which it was made.

Emulsionsebene f **(Schichtseite** f, **Schichtlage** f) *(phot)* (des Films) emulsion side, sensitized side, *brit* sensitized face

Emulsionsschicht f *(phot)* emulsion coating, emulsion layer

Emulsionsträger m **(Schichtträger** m) *(phot)* emulsion carrier

Endabhörkontrolle f *(radio/TV)* (Sender) output monitoring

Endabnahme f *(radio/TV)* acceptance, continuity acceptance, continuity clearance

Endabnehmer

The process of declaring a script of a program or a commercial to be suitable for broadcast.
Endabnehmer *m*
→ Endverbraucher
Endabnehmerpreis *m*
→ Endverbraucherpreis, Ladenpreis, Einzelhandelspreis
Endabschaltung *f*
→ Sendeschluß
Endband *n (TV)* (Regie) outgoing picture
Endbogen *m (print)* final signature, final section, last section
Endfassung *f* final version
Endfertigung *f* (**Endkonfektionierung** *f*) finishing
Endformat *n* (**Beschnittformat** *n*) *(print)* trim size
The actual size of a periodical or book page after trimming.
→ Beschnitt
Endgerät *n* terminal
Endkontrolle *f (radio/TV)* main control (MC), master control (MC) broadcast operations control (BOC), (Raum) central control room, master control room (MCR), main control room (MCR)
Endkorrektur *f*
→ Schlußkorrektur
endliche Grundgesamtheit *f (stat)* finite population, finite universe
Endlichkeitskorrektur *f* (**Endlichkeitsfaktor** *m*) *(stat)* finite population correction (fpc), finite population factor, finite sampling correction, finite multiplier, finite population multiplier
In case a sample of *n* values is drawn without replacement (→) Auswahl ohne Zurücklegen, from a population of limited size *N* the sampling variance depends on *N* as well as *n*. The variance of the sample-mean $\bar{x}$ may be written as:

$$\text{Var } \bar{x} = \frac{\sigma^2}{n}\left(1 - \frac{n}{N}\right)$$

where σ^2 is the population variance and *n* the sample size. The factor $(1 - \frac{n}{N})$ is the fpc.
→ Yates-Korrektur
Endlos-Bandkassette *f* tape loop cassette, tape loop cartridge

Endlosdruck *m* continuous roll printing, wallpaper printing, hifi printing, Hi-fi printing, hifi, Hi-Fi
A printing process in which color ads are pre-printed on newspaper-size rolls and sent to papers for insertion in their regular issues. Only one side is printed with the ad, and the paper uses the other for editorial or other copy. Pre-printing costs paid for separately by the advertiser, and most papers charge standard black-and-white rates for running the ads.
→ Endlos-Farbanzeige
endlose Bahn *f (paper)* continuous web
endloses Band *n* (**endloser Gurt** *m*) continuous belt
Endlos-Farbanzeige *f* (**HiFi-Anzeige** *f*) continuous roll insert, hifi insert, hifi color ad(vertisement), hifi, wallpaper, Hi-Fi insert, Hi-Fi color ad(vertisement), Hi-Fi color, spectacolor
In newspaper advertising preprinted color advertisements which feed into the press like wallpaper so that the paper may be cut at any point without damaging the effect of the ad.
→ Endlosdruck
Endlospapier *n* reel paper, continuous roll, web paper, endless paper
Endlosschleife *f* (**Filmschleife** *f*) *(film)* film loop, loop
Endlosvordruck *m*
→ Endlosdruck
Endmischband *n* master tape
Endpunkt *m* (**Endstelle** *f*) *(radio/TV)* (Leitung) terminal, terminating point, terminal point
Endschwärzung *f (TV)* maximum density
Endtitel *m (film/TV)* end titles *pl*, closing titles *pl*, trailer
→ Absage
Endverbraucher *m* (**Verbraucher** *m*) *(econ)* end consumer, final consumer, ultimate consumer, consumer
A consumer who buys and/or uses goods or services to satisfy personal or household wants rather than for resale or for use in business, institutional, or industrial operations. A vital difference exists between the purposes motivating the two types of purchases wich in turn results in highly significant differences in buying methods, marketing organization, and selling practices.
Endverbraucher-Panel *n*
→ Verbraucher-Panel

Endverbraucher-Preis m
→ Einzelhandelspreis, Ladenpreis
Endverbraucherwerbung f
(Letztverbraucherwerbung f**)**
consumer-directed advertising, consumer advertising
→ Publikumswerbung
Endverstärker m *(radio/TV)* final amplifier, output amplifier
Endverstärkerstufe f *(radio/TV)* final amplifier stage, output amplifier stage
Endzeit f finishing time, end time, out time
Endzifferneffekt m *(econ)* (in der Preispolitik) odd-price effect, odd-number price effect, odd-ending number price effect, odd-pricing effect, odd-number effect
A psychological effect which results from the fact that the price for a product is set at any amount except even Deutschmarks.
Engel-Blackwell-Kollat-Modell n **(Engel-Kollat-Blackwell-Theorie** f**)** (der Konsumentenentscheidungen) *(market res)* Engel-Blackwell-Kollat model, Engel-Blackwell-Kollat theory of consumer decisions (James F. Engel/Roger D. Blackwell/David T. Kollat)
Engelsches Gesetz n **(Engel-Schwabesches-Gesetz** n, **Engelkurve** f**)** (Ernst Engel) *(econ)* Engel's law, Engel's income-consumption function
The regularity that food expenditure of private households increases in terms of absolute figures with increasing income, while it decreases in terms of percentage of total expenditure.
enggesetzt *adj*
→ kondens
Engländern n **(Buchfadenheftung** f**)** *(binding)* smyth-sewing, Smyth sewing
englische Linie f *(typ)* French line rule, plain swelled rule
Engroshandel m
→ Großhandel
Engroshändler m
→ Großhändler
enkodieren
→ kodieren
Enkodierung f
→ Kodierung
Enquete f **(Enquête** f**)**
→ Erhebung
Ensemble-Auslage f *(POP advtsg)* ensemble display
A type of merchandise display in retail stores that shows together all products which are suggested to be used together.
Entbrummer m *(radio)* anti-hum potentiometer
Entdeckungszusammenhang m (Arnold Brecht) context of discovery
vgl. Begründungszusammenhang
Ente f
→ Zeitungsente
Entfaltung f **(Entfaltungstechnik** f, **Unfoldingtechnik** f**)**
→ Verfahren der transferierten Rangordnungen
entfärben *v/t (print)* (die Walzen) to deink, to de-ink
Entfärber m **(Entfärbungsmittel** n**)** *(print)* deinking agent, de-inking agent
Entfernung f **(Entfernungsmaß** n**)**
→ Distanzmaß
Entfernungseinstellung f *(phot)* focus setting, distance setting, focusing, focal length
The determination of the correct position of the focal plane on cameras, i.e. the distance a lens must be placed from a surface to form on it a sharp image of a subject at infinite distance.
Entfernungsmesser m *(phot)* range finder, rangefinder, telemeter
An optical device for measuring distance by a triangulation method based on a view of the subject from two separated lenses, whose images are combined in a single field. Rangefinders may be of the split-image type, in which the field is divided horizontally into two parts, one of which can be adjusted relative to the other by a calibrated control. When vertical lines appear unbroken across the field, the distance can be read from a scale. Other rangefinders use the coincidence method, in which two images appear superimposed until the correct distance is set, when they combine into one. Rangefinders can be directly coupled to the camera focusing control.
Entfernungsskala f *(phot)* focusing scale, distance scale
A graduated scale on process cameras for bringing the images to correct size without image measurement and ocular focusing.
Entgelt n **(Entgeltpolitik** f, **Entgelt-Mix** n**)**
→ Kontrahierungs-Mix
Entladepolitik f
→ Fuhrparkpolitik

Entlohnung *f* (für Werbung)
→ Abrechnungsverfahren
entsättigen *v/t* to desature, to pale out
Entsättigung desaturation, paling-out
Entscheidung *f* decision
 The determination of the course of action to be taken in solving a problem.
Entscheidung *f* **bei Risiko (Entscheidung** *f* **unter Risiko, stochastischer Fall** *m***)** *(stat)* decision making under conditions of risk
Entscheidung *f* **bei Sicherheit (Entscheidung** *f* **unter Sicherheit, deterministischer Fall** *m***)** *(stat)* decision making under conditions of certainty
Entscheidung *f* **bei Unsicherheit (Entscheidung** *f* **unter Unsicherheit, probabilistischer Fall** *m***)** *(stat)* decision making under conditions of uncertainty
Entscheidungsalternative *f* alternative decision
Entscheidungsanalyse *f* decision analysis, formal decision analysis, analysis of decision making
Entscheidungsbaum *m (stat)* decision tree, decision network
 In formal decision theory, the diagram of the decision process.
Entscheidungsbaumanalyse *f (stat)* decision-tree analysis
Entscheidungseinheit *f* **(bei Kaufentscheidungen)** *(econ)* decision-maker, decision-making unit (DMU)
 Both in consumer and in industrial marketing, the group of persons who together are actively involved in making a decision on whether or not, and what to purchase.
Entscheidungsfehler *m*
→ Fehler, Fehler 1. Art, Fehler 2. Art
Entscheidungsfeld *n* decision field
Entscheidungsforschung *f* decision-making research
Entscheidungshilfe *f(pl)* decision-making aid(s) *(pl)*, decisions aid(s) *(pl)*
Entscheidungskriterium *n* decision-making criterion, decision criterion
Entscheidungslogik *f*
→ Entscheidungstheorie
Entscheidungsmatrix *f (stat)* decision matrix
Entscheidungsmethode *f* decision-making method, decision-making technique

Entscheidungsmodell *n* decision model, decision-making model
→ heuristisches Modell, Optimierungsmodell
Entscheidungsnetz *n*
→ Entscheidungsbaum
Entscheidungsparameter *m*
→ Aktionsparameter
Entscheidungsprämisse *f* decision premise
Entscheidungsprinzip *n*
→ Entscheidungsregel
Entscheidungsprozeß *m* decision-making process, process of decision making
Entscheidungsregel *f (stat)* decision rule, decision-making rule
Entscheidungsraum *m (stat)* decision space
Entscheidungstheorie *f (stat)* decision theory, formal decision theory, decision-making theory, theory of decision making
Entscheidungsträger *m (econ)* decision-maker
→ Entscheidungseinheit
Entscheidungsverfahren *n* decision-making procedure, decision procedure
Entscheidungsverhalten *n* decision-making behavior, *brit* behaviour, decision behavior, decision making
Entscheidungsziel *n* goal of decision making
Entschichtung *f (film)* emulsion stripping
entschlüsseln (dekodieren) *v/t (res)* to decode
Entschlüsselung *f* **(Dekodierung** *f* **)** *(res)* decoding
Entspiegelung *f* **(Entspiegeln** *n***)** *(phot)* reduction of reflection, *brit* reflexion, anti-reflection coating, lens correction, coating of lens
 The coating of a very thin film of evaporated metallic fluorides on the uncemented glass elements of a lens, the coating tending to increase the speed of the objective and reduce reflections from glass to air surfaces.
entstören *(radio/TV) v/t* to suppress interference, to clear interference, to eliminate interference, to suppress noise
entwerfen *v/t* (Text, Illustration) to design, to sketch, to sketch out, to outline, to draft, to draw up

entwickeln v/t **1.** *(econ)* (Verfahren) to develop, to work out, to evolve **2.** *(phot)* to develop, to process
Entwickler m **(Entwicklersubstanz f)** *(phot)* developer, developing agent, *colloq* soup
  Die chemical agent used to bring out the image on an exposed film.
Entwicklerbad n **(Entwicklerlösung f, Entwicklungsbad** n) *(phot)* developing bath
Entwicklerdose f *(phot)* developing tank
Entwicklerflüssigkeit f *(phot)* developer, developing liquid
Entwicklerschale f **(Entwicklungsschale f)** *(phot)* developing tray, developing dish
Entwicklersubstanz f **(Entwicklungssubstanz f)** *(phot)* developer, developing agent
→ Entwickler
Entwicklung f **1.** *(econ)* (Verfahren) development **2.** *(phot)* development, processing, developing
  In photography, a process whereby an invisible, or latent, image, formed by brief exposure in the camera, is made visible on the film by chemical treatment.
→ Produktentwicklung
Entwicklung f **(neuer Erzeugnisse, neuer Produkte)**
→ Produktentwicklung
Entwicklungsabteilung f **1.** *(econ)* (im Unternehmen) research and development (R & D), research and development department, R & D department, research department **2.** *(film)* (Kopierwerk) film-processing department
Entwicklungsanlage f *(phot)* developing equipment, developing plant
Entwicklungsanstalt f **(Entwicklungslabor** n, **Photolabor** n) *(film/phot)* film laboratory
Entwicklungsingenieur m *(econ)* development engineer, research engineer
Entwicklungskosten pl *(econ)* development cost(s) *(pl)*
Entwicklungsmarketing n developmental marketing (Philip Kotler)
  Marketing activities designed to turn latent demand into patent demand.

vgl. Konversionsmarketing, Anreiz-Marketing, Revitalisierungsmarketing, Synchro-Marketing, Erhaltungsmarketing, Reduktionsmarketing, Kontramarketing
Entwicklungsmaschine f *(phot)* developing machine, processing machine
Entwicklungsschleier m *(phot)* darkroom fog
Entwicklungssubstanz f
→ Entwicklersubstanz
Entwicklungszeit f **(Entwicklungsdauer** f) *(phot)* developing time
Entwurf m **1.** design **2.** (Konzept) draft, outline **3.** (Zeichnung) sketch, outline, draft, (Rohentwurf) rough, rough drawing, rough outline, visual **4.** layout, rendering, comprehensive layout
Entwurfsfarbe f draft color, *brit* draft colour
Entwurfszeichner(in) m(f)
→ Konzipist(in)
entzerren v/t *(radio/film/phot)* (Bild/Ton) to correct, to equalize, *brit* to equalise, to eliminate distortion, *(phot)* to rectify, (Kopierwerk) to grade, to time
Entzerrer m *(radio/film/phot)* (Bild/Ton) equalizer, *brit* equaliser, corrector, distortion corrector, *(phot)* rectifier, (Kopierwerk) grader, timer
Entzerrer f *(radio/film/phot)* (Bild/Ton) equalization, *brit* equalisation, correction, elimination of distortion, *(phot)* correction of distortion, (Kopierwerk) grading, timing
Entzerrungslinse f **(Entzerrlinse f)** *(phot)* anamorphic lens, shrink lens
→ Anamorphot
EPF
→ *abbr* Erste Private Fernsehgesellschaft
Epidiaskop n *(phot)* epidiascope
Episkop n episcope, opaque projector
Episodenfilm m serial film, serial
Episodenreihe f **(Serienfilm m)** *(film/TV)* series, serial
→ Serie
EPS-Kurve f *(communication res)* EPS curve (Richard Maisel), curve of elite media, popular mass media and special-interest media
EQ-Skala f EQ scale, emotional quotient scale (William D. Wells)

Equity-Theorie f *(econ)* equity theory, theory of equity
Equivalent Billings *pl*
→ Honorarumsatz
Erbauungsnutzen m (Wilhelm Vershofen) *(econ)*
→ Zusatznutzen
Erdanschluß m (**Erde** f) *(electr.)* earth connection, earth, ground connection, grounding, ground
Erdantenne f *(electr.)* ground antenna, buried antenna, *brit* buried aerial
Erdefunkstelle f (**Erdstation** f) *(radio/TV)* ground signal station, ground station, earth station
  A parabolic antenna (dish) and associated electronic equipment used by a cable operator to receive and transmit signals from or to a satellite.
erden v/t *(electr.)* to ground, *brit* to earth
Erdkabel n *(electr.)* underground cable
Erdleitung f *(electr.)* earth connection, earth wire, ground connection, ground wire
Erdstation f
→ Erdefunkstelle
Erdung f *(electr.)* grounding, ground, *brit* earthing, earth
Erfa-Gemeinschaft f (**Erfa-Gruppe** f) *(econ) short for* Erfahrungs-Austauschgemeinschaft experience-exchanging group
Erfahrung f experience
Erfahrungskurve f *(market res)* experience curve
  A curve taking into account the combined effect of learning, specialization, investment, and scale, the plot of the decline in product cost relative to volume.
Erfahrungskurveneffekt m (**Boston-Effekt** m) *(market res)* experience curve effect (Boston Consulting Group), Boston Consulting Group approach
Erfahrungstest m (**Erprobungstest** m) *(market res)* experience test, trial test
Erfolgsanalyse f (**Erfolgskontrolle** f)
→ Marketingkontrolle, Werbeerfolgskontrolle
Erfolgsprämie f (**für Einzelhändler**) *(promotion)* push money (P.M.), spiff
  A special reward given by manufacturers or service sources for encouraging the sale of their goods.

erforschen v/t to research into, to investigate, to examine
ERG *abbr* Deutsche Eisenbahn-Reklame GmbH
Ergänzungsfarben f/pl
→ Komplementärfarben
Ergänzungstest m (**Geschlossenheitstest** m)
→ Lückentest
Ergänzungswerbung f
→ flankierende Werbung
Erhaltungsmarketing n maintenance marketing (Philip Kotler)
  The effort of maintaining an existing level of full demand.
  vgl. Konversionsmarketing, Anreiz-Marketing, Entwicklungsmarketing, Revitalisierungs-Marketing, Synchro-Marketing
Erhaltungswerbung f (**Stabilisierungswerbung** f, **Festigungswerbung** f) maintenance advertising, sustaining advertising, reinforcement advertising
  Advertising aiming at the stabilization of a position already reached.
  vgl. Erinnerungswerbung, Expansionswerbung, Reduktionswerbung
Erhebung f (**Enquete** f, **Enquête** f, **Datenerhebung** f) *(social res)* investigation, inquiry, enquiry, survey, data collection
Erhebungsauswahl f
→ Auswahlverfahren
Erhebungsbogen m
→ Fragebogen
Erhebungsdauer f (**Erhebungszeit** f, **Erhebungszeitraum** m) *(market res)* element, investigation element, investigation unit, sampling element, sampling unit, sample unit
Erhebungsfehler m
→ Fehler, Auswahlfehler, Zufallsfehler, systematischer Fehler
Erhebungsgrundlage f *(stat)* base, sampling base
→ Auswahleinheit
Erhebungshäufigkeit f *(stat)* frequency of investigation, sampling frequency
Erhebungsmaterial n (**Erhebungsdaten** n/pl) primary data *pl*, primary data material
Erhebungsmerkmal n
→ Merkmal

Erhebungsmethode f *(market res)* investigation method, method of investigation, method of data collection
Erhebungsobjekt n investigation object
Erhebungstechnik f
→ Erhebungsverfahren
Erhebungsumfang m
→ Stichprobenumfang; vgl. Teilerhebung, Totalerhebung
Erhebungsverfahren n **(Erhebungstechnik** f**)** *(stat)* investigation method, data investigation method
Erhebungswelle f
→ Panelwelle, Umfragewelle
Erhebungszeitpunkt m
→ Untersuchungszeitpunkt
erhöhte Werbungskosten pl
→ Werbekosten
Erinnerung f **(Recall** m**)** *(psy)* recall
The experiencing or evoking of a representation of something which an individual had experienced previously. In research, more specifically, the ability of a respondent to remember previous exposure to an advertising medium or advertisment, or elements of their content.
vgl. Gedächtnis, Wiedererkennung; gestützte Erinnerung, ungestützte Erinnerung
Erinnerung f **(an Werbung, Werbeerinnerung** f**)** *(res)* **1.** (an den Inhalt der Werbung) advertising recall, advertising playback, ad playback **2.** (an den Werbeträger) advertising media recall
Erinnerungsanzeige f reminder advertisement, reminder ad
→ Erinnerungswerbung
Erinnerungsbefragung f
→ Erinnerungsinterview (Recall-interview)
Erinnerungsbild n *(psy)* memory image
Erinnerungserfolg m
→ Gedächtniserfolg
Erinnerungsfehler m **(Erinnerungsverzerrung** f**)** *(survey res)* recall error, recall bias, memory error, memory bias, (vollkommener Erinnerungsverlust) recall loss, (zeitliche Erinnerungsverzerrung) telescoping, telescoping of time, telescoping of error
A nondeliberate error in respondents' reporting of a behavior, caused either by forgetting that the event occurred or misremembering some details of the event.
Erinnerungsfrage f **(Recallfrage** f**)** *(survey res)* recall question
A survey question asking about respondent behavior that occurred in the past. Particularly in media and advertising research a question about past exposure to an advertising medium or an advertisement.
Erinnerungsfunktion f (der Werbung) reminder function
Erinnerungshilfe f *(survey res)* recall aid
→ Gedächtnisstütze
Erinnerungsimpulskauf m reminder impulse buy, reminder impulse buying
A type of impulse buying where the customer is reminded in the store of the need to replenish his stock by the visual prod alone.
Erinnerungsmethode f **(Erinnerungsverfahren** n**)** *(survey res)* recall method, time method
→ Erinnerungstest
Erinnerungstest m **(Recalltest** m**)** *(survey res)* recall test, (gestützt) aided-recall test, (ungestützt) unaided-recall test, pure recall test
A survey technique of testing advertising copy, advertising effectiveness, and media exposure by asking respondents to tell which advertisement or which parts of the editorial section they remember having seen, read, or heard.
Erinnerungswerbekampagne f **(Erinnerungsaktion** f**)** reminder advertising campaing, reminder campaign
→ Erinnerungswerbung
Erinnerungswerbemittel n **(Erinnerungsanzeige** f**)** reminder advertisement, reminder ad
→ Erinnerungswerbung
Erinnerungswerbung f **(Verstärkungswerbung** f**)** reminder advertising, name advertising, reinforcement advertising, retentive advertising, follow-up advertising, remembrance advertising, name advertising
Advertising designed to remind an audience of a product's or service's benefits in a phase subsequent to the introduction of the product, service, or the advertising campaign.
Erinnerungswert m *(media res)* recall value, retention value, *auch* reminder

Erinnerungswirkung
value, memory value, remembrance value
Erinnerungswirkung f (von Werbung) reminder effect, recall effect (of advertising)
Erkennungsmelodie f (**Erkennungszeichen** n) *(radio/TV)* signature tune, signature, theme song, theme, station indentification signal, station I.D. music, station I.D. song
→ Kennung
Erklärung f (**Explanation** f)
explanation
Erklärungsmodell n *(market res)* explanatory model
Erklärungsvariable f explanatory variable
→ unabhängige Variable
Erlaubniskartell n *(econ)* lawful cartel, cartel permitted by law
Erlebnismagazin n (**Erlebniszeitschrift** f) true story magazine
Erlös m **1.** *(econ)* profit(s) *(pl)*, net profit(s) *(pl)*, revenue **2.** *(promotion)* (eines Gewinnspiels) proceeds *pl*
Erlösfunktion f
→ Umsatzfunktion
Erlöskurve f (**monetäre Nachfragekurve** f) *(econ)* monetary demand curve
Erlösmaximierung f
→ Gewinnmaximierung, Grenzerlös
ermäßigter Grundpreis m (für Werbung) reduced basic rate, reduced base rate, reduced flat rate, reduced one-time rate
ermäßigter Preis m **1.** (für Werbung) reduced rate **2.** *(econ)* reduced price
Ermäßigung f
→ Preisermäßigung
Ermittlungsfrage f
→ Informationsfrage
Ermüdung f *(survey res)* (des Befragten) respondent fatigue, (des Interviewers) interviewer fatigue
  A source of error in surveys, particularly in media research interviews, ascribable to excessive length of interviews and tedious questions.
Ernährer m *(econ)* (einer Familie) provider, breadwinner
Erneuerungsbedarf m
→ Ersatzbedarf
Eröffungsangebot n
Eröffnungspreis m
→ Einführungspreis

Eröffnungswerbung f
→ Einführungswerbung
Erprobungskauf m
→ Erstkauf
Erprobungstest m
→ Erfahrungstest
Errata n/pl *(print)* errata *pl*, corrigenda *pl*
Erregerlampe f (**Lichttonlampe** f) *(film/TV/studio)* exciter lamp
  A light bulb in a projector which projects light through the film to the photoelectric cell.
Ersatzanzeige f makegood (MG), make-good, makegood advertisement
  An advertisement repeated without charge as compensation for an advertisement omitted, improper, or containing a significant error.
Ersatzbedarf m (**Ersatznachfrage** f, **Erneuerungsbedarf** m, **Erneuerungsnachfrage** f) *(econ)* replacement demand, after-market, after-demand, aftermath market, aftermath demand
  The demand, and potential sales, associated with the requirements of consumers or industrial users after they have bought a piece of equipment.
  vgl. Neubedarf
Ersatzeinschaltung f
→ Ersatzanzeige, Ersatzsendung, Ersatzwerbemittel
Ersatzkauf m (**Nachkauf** m) *(econ)* replacement purchase
→ Ersatzbedarf
Ersatzlieferung f *(econ)* replacement delivery
Ersatzmedium n (**Ersatzwerbeträger** m) replacement medium
Ersatznachfrage f
→ Ersatzbedarf
Ersatzsender m *(radio/TV)* standby transmitter
Ersatzsendung f (**Ersatzwerbesendung** f) *(radio/TV)* makegood (MG), make good, makegood commercial, make-good commercial, bonus spot
  A broadcast announcement accepted by an advertiser as a replacement for a commercial which did not appear as scheduled, was transmitted improperly or was placed too close to a competitive product's advertising message.
Ersatzverkauf m *(econ)* replacement sale

Ersatzwerbemittel *n* makegood (MG), make good, makegood advertisement, makegood ad
→ Ersatzanzeige, Ersatzsendung
Ersatzwerbespot *m*
→ Ersatzsendung
erscheinen *v/i* (Zeitung/Zeitschrift) to appear, to be published, to come out, to be brought, to be issued
Erscheinen *n* (Zeitung/Zeitung) appearance, publication, issuance
Erscheinen einstellen
→ einstellen
Erscheinungsbild *n*
→ Image
Erscheinungsdatum *n* (**Erscheinungstermin** *m*) *(Zeitung/Zeitschrift)* date of publication, publication date
   The date on of actual appearance printed on the cover or masthead of a publication.
Erscheinungshäufigkeit *f*
→ Erscheinungsweise
Erscheinungsintervall *n* (**Erscheinungsrhythmus** *m*) (Zeitung/Zeitschrift) interval of publication, publication interval, publishing interval, issue period
   The time period regularly lying between the appearance of one issue of a periodical and the next.
Erscheinungsjahr *n* (Zeitschrift) year of publication, publication year
Erscheinungsort *m* (Zeitung/Zeitschrift) place of publication
Erscheinungsrythmus *m*
→ Erscheinungsintervall, Erscheinungsweise
Erscheinungstag *m* (Zeitung/Zeitschrift) day of publication, publication day, publishing day
Erscheinungstermin *m*
→ Erscheinungsdatum
Erscheinungsvermerk *m*
→ Impressum, Verlegervermerk
Erscheinungsweise *f* (**Erscheinungshäufigkeit** *f*) (Zeitung/Zeitschrift) frequency of publication, publication frequency, frequency of appearance, frequency of issuance
   The number of publication intervals characteristic for a periodical.
Erscheinungszeitraum *m*
→ Erscheinungsintervall
Erschließung *f* **neuer Märkte**
→ Markterschließung
Erschließungsbedarf *m*
→ latenter Bedarf

erschöpfende Klassifizierung *f* (**erschöpfende Kategorisierung** *f*) *(res)* exhaustive categorization, exhaustive classification, exhaustive set
Erstanmutung *f*
→ Anmutung
Erstargumenthypothese *f* (**Primateffekthypothese** *f*) *(communication res)* primacy effect hypothesis, primacy hypothesis
vgl. Letztargumenthypothese (Recency-Hypothese)
Erstaufführung *f (film)* first performance, first night, first run, premiere
Erstaufführungskino *n* (**Erstaufführungstheater** *n*) first-run theater, *brit* theatre
Erstauflage *f*
→ Startauflage
Erstausgabe *f* (**erste Ausgabe** *f*) (Zeitung/Zeitschrift) first edition, pilot edition, first issue, pilot issue
Erstauslieferungstag *m*
→ Erstverkaufstag
Erstausrüstungsgeschäft *n* (**Erstausrüstung** *f*) *(econ)* original equipment manufacturing
Erstausstrahlung *f*
→ Erstsendung, erster Sendetermin
Erstbedarf *m* (**Erstnachfrage** *f,* **Neubedarf** *m*) *(econ)* original demand
vgl. Ersatzbedarf
Erstbefragungseffekt(e) *m(pl)* *(panel res)* first-time effect(s) *(pl)*
Erstdruck *m* first printing
erste Morgenausgabe *f* (Zeitung) bulldog edition
erste Seite *f* (**Titelseite** *f,* **Kopfseite** *f*) first page, cover page, front cover, outside front cover(C), title page
erste Sonntagsausgabe *f* (Zeitung) bullpup
erste Umschlagseite *f* (**U 1** *f,* **Titelseite** *f*) front page, front cover, outside front cover(C), first cover, title page
Erstellungspreis *m*
→ Einstandspreis
Erstempfänger *m (media res)* first reader, first-time reader, buyer-reader
Erstentwickler *m*
→ Schwarzweißentwickler
erster Eindruck *m* first impression

erster Entwurf

erster Entwurf m first draft, rough draft, rough
→ Rohentwurf

erster Grenzwertsatz m **(erstes Grenzwerttheorem** n) *(stat)* first limit theorem

erster Korrekturabzug m **(erster Abzug** m, **erste Korrekturfahne** f) *(print)* first proof, green proof, green copy
→ Bürstenabzug

erster Sendetermin m **(Zeitpunkt** m **der Erstausstrahlung)** *(TV)* first telecast (F.T.)
  The first day on which a series of commercials or a serial program is to be broadcast.

Erstinnovation f
→ Innovation

Erstkauf m **(Probekauf** m) *(econ)* trial purchase, initial purchase, trial
  The first time an individual buys a product to see if it should be used regularly
  vgl. Wiederholungskauf

Erstkäufer m *(econ)* **1.** (Probekäufer) trial buyer, trier **2.** → Konsumpionier, Innovator

Erstkontakt m *(media res)* first exposure, first time exposure
  vgl. Wiederholungskontakt, Gesamtkontakte pro Nummer

Erstkopie f **(Nullkopie** f, **Abnahmekopie** f, **Schnittkopie** f) *(film/TV)* answer print (AP), first proof print, optical answer print (A.P.O.)
  The first composite print of a commercial, with both picture and sound track on the same film, prepared for review before being aired.

Erstleser m *(media res)* primary reader, buyer-reader, claimed buyer-reader, first-time reader
  An individual reached by a magazine or newspaper who resides in a household where a family member purchased or subscribed to the publication. Those who come from "non-purchase" households are called pass-along readers, *cf.* (→) Zweitleser. Primary readers are a magazine's hard-core audience and will usually be exposed to more issues than any other group. They also tend to be "better" readers in terms of interest and time spent with the issue.

Erstleserhaushalt m **(Primärleserhaushalt** m) *(media res)* primary household, buyer household
→ Erstleser

Erstleserschaft f **(Erstleser** m/pl, **Primärleser** m/pl) *(media res)* primary audience, primary readers pl, primary readership, buyer-readers pl, claimed buyer-readers pl, first-time readers pl, first-time audience
  The entire audience of primary readers.
→ Erstleser; *vgl.* Folgeleser

Erstmappe f (Lesezirkel) *etwa* first set of magazines (in a Lesezirkel)
→ Lesezirkel

Erstsendung f *(radio/TV)* first broadcast, *(TV)* first showing, first telecast(F.T.)

Erstübernehmer m *(econ)* early adopter, early acceptor
→ Innovator

Erstverkauf m *(econ)* initial sale

Erstverkaufstag m **(Erstauslieferungstag** m) *(econ)* day of delivery, delivery day

Erstverwender m *(econ)* trial user, first user, first-time user
→ Erstkäufer

Ertragszentrum n **(Profit Center** n) *(econ)* profit center
  vgl. Kostenzentrum

Erwartung f expectation

Erwartungseffekt m **(Hawthorne-Effekt** m) *colloq* guinea pig effect, *(social res)* expectation effect, anticipation effect, Hawthorne effect
  A source of error in tests that is the effect of informants' knowledge that they are participants in a test and behave differently.

Erwartungsfehler m **(Erwartungsverzerrung** f) *(social res)* expectation bias, expectation error, anticipation error
→ Erwartungseffekt

Erwartungsfeld n **der Preispolitik** (Heribert Meffert) *(econ)* expectations pl of price policy, expectation field of pricing
  vgl. Aktionsfeld, Datenfeld

Erwartungstreue f **(Konsistenz** f, **Unverzerrtheit** f) *(stat)* unbiasedness, consistency, unbiased estimate

erwartungstreue Schätzfunktion f *(stat)* unbiased estimator

erwartungstreue Schätzung f *(stat)* unbiased estimate

Erwartungswert *m* **(Erwartung** *f* **)**
(stat) expected value, expectation, mathematical expectation
Erweiterungsbedarf *m*
→ Neubedarf
Erweiterungswerbung *f*
→ Festigungswerbung
Erwerbsperson *f* **(Erwerbstätiger** *m***)** *(econ)* gainfully employed person, economically active person
Erwerbstätigkeit *f (econ)* gainful employment
Erzähler *m* **(Off-Sprecher** *m***)** *(radio/TV)* narrator
Erzähltest *m* **(Geschichtenerzählen** *n***)** *(res)* storytelling
Erzeugergemeinschaft *f* **(Erzeugervereinigung** *f* **)** *(econ)* producers' association, farmers' production association, agricultural association
Erzeugergenossenschaft *f (econ)* producers' cooperative, farmers' cooperative, agricultural cooperative
  A cooperative organization, (→) Genossenschaft, formed by a number of small farmers to enable them to achieve some of the competitive advantages of larger scale marketing.
Erzeugerpreis *m (econ)* producer's price
Erziehungsfilm *m* educational film, instructional film, training film
ESOMAR *f abbr* European Society for Opinion and Marketing Research
Esparto *n* esparto
Espartogras *n* **(Halfagras** *n***)** esparto grass
Espartopapier *n* **(Halfapapier** *n*, **Alfapapier** *n***)** esparto paper, alfalfa paper
Etat *m* **(Budget** *n*, **Haushalt** *m***)** budget, account
→ Marketingetat, Werbeetat, Kunde
Etataufteilung *f* **(Budgetaufteilung** *f* **)** budget allocation
  The process of distributing a given budget on various accounts.
Etatbestimmung *f*
→ Etatfestsetzung
Etatdirektor *m* account executive, account manager, account supervisor, account representative, senior account executive, senior account manager, account controller, contact executive
  A member of an advertising agency staff primarily responsible for interpreting a client's needs to the agency and the agency's ideas to the client.
Etatfestsetzung *f* **(Etatbestimmung** *f* **)** budget determination
Etatkonflikt *m* account conflict
  A conflict of interest for an advertising agency that works for competing clients.
Etatkontrolle *f (econ)* budgetary control, budget check
  The methodical monitoring of planned income and expenditure by issuing sales targets, placing orders, and authorizing payments within the context of a previously approved budget.
Etatplan *m* budget plan, account plan
Etatplanung *f* budget planning, account planning
Etatstrategie *f* budget strategy, account strategy
ethische Werbung *f*
→ Arzneimittelwerbung, Heilmittelwerbung
ethisches Produkt *n*
→ Arzneimittel
Etikett *n* label, tag, card, slip, ticket
→ Preisschild
etikettieren *v/t* to label, to tag, to provide with a label, with a tag, with a price tag
Etikettiermaschine *f* **(Etikettiergerät** *n***)** labeling machine
Etikettierung *f* labeling, *auch* labelling
Et-Zeichen *n* **(Und-Zeichen** *n***)** *(typ)* ampersand (&)
Euklidische Distanz *f* **(Euklid-Distanz** *f* **)** *(stat)* Euclidean distance
  The most commonly used distance measure in cluster analysis. In terms of the Minkowski metric, the distance d_{ij} between two points i and j is expressed as:

$$d_{ij} = \left[\sum_{q=1}^{p} (x_{ik} - x_{jk}^2) \right]^{\frac{1}{2}}$$

Euro *short for* Eurovision
Europäische Arbeitsgruppe *f* **der Werbewirtschaft (EAG)** Advertising Information Group (AIG)
Europäischer Verband *m* **der Werbewirtschaft (EAG)** Advertising Information Group (AIG)
Europäischer Verband *m* **der Lichtwerbung (EVL)** European Association for Electric Sign Advertising
Eurovision *f* **(Euro)** Eurovision

Europäische Gesellschaft f für Meinungs- und Absatzforschung European Society for Opinion and Marketing Research (ESOMAR)
EV-Lieferung f (**Einzelverkaufslieferung** f, **Apartlieferung** f)
→ Einzelverkauf
EV-Stück n
→ Einzelverkauf
EV-Verkauf m
→ Einzelverkauf
EVA abbr Entscheidung - Verbrauch - Anschaffung
Evaluierung f (**Evaluation** f) evaluation
Evaluierungsmodell n (**Evaluationsmodell** n) (media planning) evaluation model
Evaluierungsprogramm n (media planning) evaluation program, brit programme
Evaluierungsverfahren n (media planning) evaluation technique
Eventualplan m contingency plan
Evoked Set m (**Brand Set** m)
→ relevanter Produktmarkt
Exemplar n (Zeitung/Zeitschrift) copy, issue, number
exklusiv adj exclusive
Exklusivagent m (**Alleinagent** m) (econ) exclusive agent
→ Alleinvertreter
Exklusivagentur f (**Alleinagentur** f) exclusive agency
Exclusivbeitrag m (**Exklusivbericht** m) exclusive contribution, exclusive article
Exklusivität f exclusiveness, exclusivity
→ Konkurrenzausschluß
Exklusivitätsklausel f exclusive agency agreement
→ Konkurrenzausschluß
Exklusivleser m (**Alleinleser** m) (media res) exclusive reader
Exklusivvertrieb m (**Alleinvertrieb** m) (econ) exclusive distribution, exclusive dealing, exclusive selling, exclusive outlet selling, exclusive agency method of distribution, appointed dealer distribution
  That form of selective selling, (→) selektiver Vertrieb, whereby sales of an article or service or brand of an article to any one type of buyer are confined to one retailer or wholesaler in each area, usually on a contractual basis.
Exklusivware f (econ) exclusive merchandise
Expander m (Ton) volume expander, expander
Expansionswerbung f expansion advertising
  vgl. Einführungswerbung, Erhaltungswerbung, Reduktionswerbung, Verdrängungswerbung
Experiment n experiment
  → Feldexperiment, Laborexperiment
Experiment n **in der Zeitfolge** (**Zeitfolgenexperiment** n) (res) before-after experiment, preposterior experiment
  An experimental design that involves relevant observations on one or more groups both before and after the experimental treatment.
Experimentalfilm m experimental film
Experimentanlage f
  → experimentelle Anlage
Experimentdaten n/pl (res) experimental data pl
Experimentdesign n
  → experimentelle Anlage
experimentelle Anlage f (**experimentelle Versuchsanlage** f)
  The general plan of an experiment, including the number and arrangement of independent variables as well as plans for controlling possible confounding variables.
experimentelle Einheit f (**Experimentaleinheit** f) (res) experimental unit
experimentelle Gruppe f (**Experimentalgruppe** f) (res) experimental group
  That group in a controlled experiment which is assigned to receive some value of an independent variable as an experimental treatment.
  vgl. Kontrollgruppe
experimentelle Manipulation f (**Experimentalhandlung** f) (res) experimental treatment, treatment, experimental manipulation
experimentelle Methode f (**Experimentalmethode** f) (res) experimental method
  The method of conducting scientific investigations characterized by active manipulation of independent variables, control of extraneous variables, and observation of the resulting changes in the dependent variables.

experimentelle Variable f **(Experimentalvariable** f**)** *(res)* experimental variable
Experimenter-Effekt m
→ Versuchsleitereffekt
Experimentkontrolle f *(res)* experimental control
→ kontrolliertes Experiment
Experte m **(Fachmann** m**)** expert
Expertenbefragung f *(market res)* experts' survey, survey among experts, experts' jury, experts' panel survey
→ Delphi-Befragungsmethode
Explanandum n explanandum
Explanans n explanation, explanans
Explanation f explanation
Exploration f exploration
→ Explorationsstudie
Explorationsforschung f exploratory research
Explorationsgespräch n **(Explorationsinterview** n**)** *(survey res)* exploratory interview
Explorationsleitfaden m
→ Leitfaden
Explorationsstudie f **(Explorationsuntersuchung** f**)** exploratory investigation, exploratory study
  A preliminary investigation designed either to verify the existence of a phenomenon or to identify potential independent variables for further investigation.
→ Leitstudie, Vorstudie (Voruntersuchung)
Explosion f explosion
Explosionsblende f *(film)* explosions shutter
Explosionsschwenk m **(Schwenk** m**)** *(film/TV)* explosion wipe
  A very sudden optical wipe effect bursting from the center of the frame outwards.
Exponat n exhibit
Exponentialfunktion f **(Exponentialkurve** f**)** *(stat)* exponential function
  A function representing the continuous or limiting form of an exponential series and a relationship between two variables x and y that can be represented by a curve whose equation has the general form $y = ae^{bx} + c$, where a, b, and c are constants and e is the base of the natural logarithms.
Exponentialtrend m
→ exponentieller Trend

exponentielle Glättung f *(stat)* exponential smoothing
  A technique of removing random fluctuations from time series.
exponentielle Regression f *(stat)* exponential regression
exponentieller Trend m *(stat)* exponential trend
→ Exponentialfunktion
Exportgemeinschaft f *(econ)* export association
Exportkatalog m export catalog, *brit* catalogue
Exportmarketing n export marketing
Exportmarktforschung f export market research
Exportmusterschau f export fair
Exportwerbung f export advertising
Exportzeitschrift f export magazine
Exposé n expose, exposition, draft, outline
Exposition f
→ Kontakt
Ex-post-facto-Experiment n *(res)* after-only experiment, after-only design
  A type of experimental design in which relevant observations of the experimental group, (→) experimentelle Gruppe, and the control group, (→) Kontrollgruppe, are confined to the situation after the experimental treatment, (→) experimentelle Manipulation.
Ex-post-Kontrolle f
→ Marketingkontrolle
Extensivwerbung f
→ akzidentelle Werbung
externe Konsumeffekte m/pl
→ Nachfrageeffekt
externe Marktforschung f
→ Institutsmarktforschung
externe Überschneidung f **(Quantuplikation** f, **Duplikation** f**)** *(media res)* audience duplication, duplication ("dupe"), quantuplication
  The "overlap" of audiences to different media, showing how many people reached by one media vehicle are *also* reached by another. The number of duplicate exposures is frequently expressed as a percentage of the total. In advertising research, the term describes the number of households or individual listeners, readers, viewers exposed more than once to the same advertising message through various media.
vgl. interne Überschneidung

externe Validität f (externe Gültigkeit f, extrinsische Validität f)
→ Kriteriumsvalidität
Extraausgabe f (Extrablatt n) special edition, special issue, (Zeitung) extra, chaser
extrafett adj (typ)
→ fett

Extrapolation f (stat) extrapolation
Extrembereich m
→ Spannweite
Extremwert m
→ Ausreißer
Exzeß m (stat)
→ Wölbung

F

F-Quotient m **(F-Verhältnis** n**,
F-Wert** m**, Maßzahl F** f**)** *(stat)* F ratio,
variance ratio
  The ratio of two variances or two sample variance estimates used to test the hypothesis that the samples come from populations white equal variances.
F-Signal n
  → Farbsignal
F-Test m **(Varianz-Verhältnis-Test** m**)** *(stat)* F test, variance-ratio test
  A test based on the ratio of two independent statistics, (→) F-Quotient, each of which is distributed as the variance in samples from normal populations with the same parent variance. The test is employed in variance-analysis to test the homogeneity of a set of means.
F-Verteilung f **(Fishersche Verteilung** f**)** *(stat)* F distribution, F-distribution, variance-ratio distribution
  A probability distribution defined as the distribution of the ratio of two chi-square (χ^2) variables each divided by its degrees of freedom, (→) Freiheitsgrad, or the ratio of two estimates of population variances (s^2) each divided by the true population variance (σ^2).
  → F-Quotient
Fabrikabgabepreis m
  → Fabrikpreis
Fabrikat n *(econ)* make
Fabrikhandel m
  → Belegschaftshandel, Betriebshandel
Fabrikladen m
  → Belegschaftsladen
Fabrikmarke f
  → Herstellermarke
Fabrikpreis m **(Fabrikabgabepreis** m**)** *(econ)* manufacturer's price, price ex works, factory price, prime cost
  The basic price of a product at the point of its manufacture, excluding delivery, insurance, and sometimes packaging.
Fabrikverkauf m
  → Belegschaftshandel
Fabrikware f *(econ)* **1.** manufactured goods *pl*, manufactured products *pl*, factory-made goods *pl*, factory-made products *pl*, factory products *pl*,

factory goods *pl* **2.** mass merchandise, mass-produced merchandise
Face-to-face-Kommunikation f
  → persönliche Kommunikation (direkte, persönliche Kommunikation)
Face-to-face-Verkauf m
  → persönlicher Verkauf
Facette f *(print)* (des Klischees) bevel, bevel edge, beveled edge
  The flange of the printing plate.
facettieren v/t *(print)* to bevel
Facettiergerät n **(Facettierhobel** m**)** *(print)* beveler, *brit* beveller, beveling plane
Facettierung f **(Facettieren** n**)** *(print)* beveling, milling
Fach n *(print)* (des Setzkastens) box
Fachadreßbuch n
  → Branchenadreßbuch
Fachausstellung f special exhibition, specialized exhibition
Fachblatt n
  → Fachzeitschrift, Fachzeitung
Fachblattanzeige f
  → Fachzeitschriftenanzeige
Facheinzelhandel m *(econ)* special-line retailing, special-line retail trade, specialty retailing, specialty retail trade
Fächerblende f *(film)* fan wipe
Fächerregal n rack
Fachgeschäft n *(econ)* specialty store, special-line store, specialty shop
  A relatively small-scale retail store which makes its appeal on a broad selection of a restricted class of merchandise.
Fachgroßhandel m *(econ)* special-line wholesaling, special-line wholesale trade, specialty wholesaling, specialty wholesale trade
Fachgroßhändler m *(econ)* special-line wholesaler, specialty wholesaler
  A wholesaler who carries a limited number of items within one field.
Fachhandel m *(econ)* specialty trade, special-line trade
Fachhandelspanel n
  → Einzelhandelspanel
Fachhandelstreue f **(Fachhandelsloyalität** f**)** specialty store loyalty

Fachjournalist m specialized journalist
Fachmann m
→ Experte
Fachmarkt m *(econ)* specialty market, specialty warehouse, special-line market
Fachmesse f *(econ)* specialized trade fair, specialized fair
Fachperiodikum n
→ Fachzeitschrift
Fachpresse f *etwa* business press, trade press, specialized press
  The periodical publications that are addressed to people working in trade (merchandising trade papers and magazines), in production (industrial and vertical papers and magazines), in professions (professional papers and magazines), in executive or managerial positions (executive and horizontal papers and magazines), and in institutions (e.g. universities, school, etc.).
Fachpromoter m
→ Promoter
Fachschule f
→ Werbefachschule
Fachverband m **Außenwerbung e.V. (FAW)** Outdoor Advertising Association
Fachverband m **Film- und Diapositiv-Werbung e.V. (FDW)** Association of Screen and Slide Advertisers
Fachverband m **Kalender und Werbeartikel e.V.** Association of Calendar and Specialty Advertisers
Fachverband m **Lichtwerbung e.V. (FVL)** Association for Electric Sign Advertising
Fachverband m **Medienberater e.V. (FDM)** Association of Media Consultants
Fachverband m **Messe- und Ausstellungsbau e.V. (FAMAB)** Association of Fair and Exhibition Construction Companies
Fachverband m **Messen und Ausstellungen e.V. (FAMA)** Association of Trade Fairs and Exhibitions
Fachversandhandel m *(econ)* specialty mail order trade, special-line mail order trade
Fachwerbung f **(Werbung** f **in Fachkreisen)** business advertising, trade advertising, industrial advertising, professional advertising
  Advertising directed at wholesalers or retailers.
vgl. Publikumswerbung (Sprungwerbung)
Fachzeitschrift f periodical, technical journal, trade magazine, trade journal, professional magazine, professional journal, scientific journal, scientific magazine, specialist magazine, specialized magazine, special magazine, specialist journal, specialized journal, special journal, nonfiction magazine, non-fiction magazine
  A periodical publication dealing with special fields of interest such as management, manufacturing, sales or operation of industries or busines, or some specific industry, occupation, or profession, and which is published to interest and assist persons actively engaged in the field it covers.
vgl. Publikumszeitschrift
Fachzeitschriftenanzeige f trade advertisement, trade ad, advertisement in a trade magazine, technical magazine, specialized magazine
Fachzeitschriftenwerbung f advertising in specialized magazines, advertising in trade magazines
Fachzeitung f trade (news)paper, technical (news)paper, professional (news)paper, specialist (news)paper, specialized (news)paper, special (news)paper
→ Fachpresse
Factor m *(econ)* factor
  A specialized financial institution engaged in factoring accounts receivable and lending on the security of inventory.
Factoring n *(econ)* factoring
  A specialized financial function whereby producers, wholesalers, and retailers sell their accounts receivable to financial institutions, including factors and banks, often on a non-recourse basis. Commercial banks as well as factors and finance companies engage in this activity.
Faden m
→ Heftfaden
Fadenbuchheftmaschine f
→ Fadenheftmaschine
Fadenheftung *(binding)* thread-stitching machine, Smyth sewing

machine, Smyth sewer, Smyth book sewer
Fadenheftung f *(binding)* thread-stitching, Smyth sewing, (Fadenrückstichbroschur) saddle sewing, (seitliche Fadenheftung) side-sitching, side sewing
Fadenkreuz n *(phot)* crosshairs pl, reticule
fadenlose Bindung f
→ Klebebindung
Fadenzähler m *(phot/print)* linen tester, magnifier
  A small magnifying glass mounted at a distance above its base equal to the focal length of the lens. Originally designed for counting threads in linen, they are now used for examination of negatives, plates and proofs.
Fading n **(Schwund** m) *(radio)* fading
Fähnchen n
→ Werbefähnchen
Fahne f
→ Korrekturfahne, Fahnenziehen
Fahnenabzug m
→ Korrekturfahne, Abzug, Bürstenabzug
Fahnenkorrektur f
→ Korrektur
Fahnenziehen n *(TV)* streaking, afterglow
  A picture distortion as a result of which objects are extended horizontally beyond their normal boundaries.
Fahraufnahme f **(Fahrt** f, **Fahrtaufnahme** f) *(film/TV)* dolly shot, trucking shot, truck shot, traveling shot, tracking shot, track, moving shot, action shot
  A camera shot in which the camera itself follows the action.
fahrbare Verkaufsstelle f *(retailing)* mobile shop, merchandising bus
Fahreffekt m *(film/TV)* zooming-in effect, varifocal lens effect, zoom effect
Fahrgast m **(Passagier** m) *(transit advstg)* rider, passenger
Fahrseite f *(transit advtsg)* traffic side
  The side of a bus which faces the street. vgl. Gehseite
Fahrstativ n **(fahrbares Stativ** n) *(film/TV)* rolling tripod, dolly, crab dolly, fearless dolly
Fahrt f **(Fahraufnahme** f)
→ Fahraufnahme
Fahrverkauf m *(retailing)* mobile shop selling

Faksimile n
→ Funkbild
Faksimile-System n **(Fax-System** n)
→ Bildfernübertragung
Faksimilie-Zeitung f
→ Bildschirmzeitung
Faktor m **1.** *(factoring)* factor **2.** *(soc res)* factor **3.** *(print)* (Setzereileiter) overseer, foreman, (Obersetzer) clicker
→ Faktorenanalyse
Faktorenanalyse f **(Faktoranalyse** f) *(stat)* factor analysis, factorial analysis
  A multivariate method of data analysis that describes relationships among a large number of variables in a correlation matrix by reducing them to a small number of relatively independent, conceptually meaningful composite variables (the factors).
Faktorenladung f **(Faktorladung** f) *(stat)* factor loading
Faktorenextration f **(Extraktion** f **von Faktoren)** *(stat)* factor ectraction
Faktorenmatrix f **(Faktormatrix** f) *(stat)* factor matrix
Faktorenrotation f *(stat)* factor rotation
Faktorenwert m **(Faktorenzahl** f) *(stat)* factor score
faktorielle Anzeigenanalyse f
→ Emnid Faktorielle Anzeigenanalyse
faktorielle Versuchsanlage f **(faktorieller Versuchsplan** m) *(stat)* factorial experimental design, factorial design
Fallmethode f **(Einzelfallmethode** f) *(res)* case method, case rate method
  A research approach trying to extract monothetic findings from the intensive investigation of particular cases.
Fallstudie f *(res)* case study, case history
→ Fallmethode
Fallzahl f
→ Stichprobenumfang
falsche Angaben f/pl
1. → irreführende Werbung
2. *(media res)* false claiming, false claims pl
→ Fehlangaben
Fälscherfrage f **(Fangfrage** f) *(survey res)* cheater question
Fälscherproblem n *(survey res)* cheating, cheater problem

Falsifikation f (**Falsifizierung** f)
(hypothesis testing) falsification
vgl. Verifikation
Faltblatt n folded page, folded sheet, folder
Falte f
→ Falz
falten v/t to fold
Faltkalender m folding calender, pocket calender
Faltprospekt m
→ Prospekt
Faltschachtel f folding box, folding carton, slotted container, *brit* onepiece case
Faltseite f (**faltbare Seite** f) fold-in page, fold-out page
Faltung f 1. folding 2. *(stat)* convolution
Falz 1. (Faltstelle) fold, crease 2. (Falzbruch) fold 3. (der Buchdecke) hinge, joint, (zum Einkleben) guard, slipfold
  The point at which the newspaper page is folded in half.
4. (Bundsteg) back 5. (Innenkante) binding edge, edge
Falzbein n (**Falzmesser** n) folder, bone folder, paper folder
Falzbruch m
→ Falz 2.
falzen v/t to fold
Falzen n (**Falzung** f) folding
Falzkante f (**Faltkante** f, **innere Heftkante** f) binding fold, binding edge, folding edge
Falzmaschine f (**Faltmaschine** f) folder, folding machine
Falzmesser n
→ Falzbein
FAMA m *abbr* Fachverband Messen und Ausstelllungen e.V.
FAMAB m *abbr* Fachverband Messe- und Ausstellungsbau e.V.
→ Familienanzeige
Familienblatt n
→ Familienzeitschrift
Familieneinkaufsentscheidung f
(econ) family buying decision, buying decision within the family, family purchasing decision, purchasing decision-making within the family
  There is growing awareness that in addition to knowing who in the family makes a purchase, it is even more important who actually decides what products to buy. In general, the process has become more specialized and involves increasingly more joint decision making.
Familieneinkommen n *(econ)* family income
  The total income of people who live together and are legally related.
Familienentscheidung f
→ Familieneinkaufsentscheidung
Familienkino n (**Familien- und Stammkino** n) *etwa* family movie theater, family cinema
Familien-Lebensstil m *(econ)* family life-style
→ Lebensstil
Familien-Lebenszyklus m (**Familienzyklus** m) *(econ)* family life cycle, family cycle
  The subsequent stages and ensuing changes in behavior that are associated with the typical changes of an individual's family situation - a segmentation variable which combines the characteristics of age, marital status, presence and age of children, and survivor status of spouse to explain family purchasing behavior,
  (→) Familieneinkaufsentscheidung.
Familienpackung f (**Großpackung** f) family package, family pack, economy-size pack, economy-size package
Familienprogramm n *(radio/TV)* general-audience program, *brit* programme, family program, *brit* programme, general-interest program
Familienserie f *(radio/TV)* family series, comedy drama, comedy show
Familienstand m marital status
Familienzeitschrift f
1. → Publikumszeitschrift
2. family magazine
Familienzeitung f family paper, family newspaper
Familienzyklus m
→ Familien-Lebenszyklus
Fangbereich m *(TV)* interception area, lock-in range, pull-in range
Fangfrage f *(survey res)*
→ Fälscherfrage
Fantasiefenster n
→ Phantasiefenster
Fanzeitschrift f fan magazine, pop music magazine, rock music magazine
Farbabgleich m (**Farbabstimmung** f, **Farbbalance** f) *(TV)* color balance, *brit* colour balance
  The proper selection of color elements to give a satisfying picture.
→ Hauteffekt

Farbabschalter m (**Color-Killer** m) (TV) color killer, brit colour killer
Farbabstimmung f
→ Farbabgleich
Farbabstufung f (**Farbabtönung** f, **Farbgradation** f) (print/phot) color gradation, brit colour gradation, color graduation, brit colour graduation
 The tonal color range in prints and negatives.
Farbabtaster m (**Farbabtastgerät** n, **Farbscanner** m) (print/phot) color scanner, brit colour scanner
 Any of various photoelectrical or electronic devices for the production and automatic color correction of continuous tone sparation negatives made from multi-color originals, the devices intended for more accurate balancing of a set of four-color images.
Farbabtastung f (**Farbabtasten** n, **Farbscanning** n) (print/phot) color scanning, brit colour scanning
Farbabweichung f (print/TV) 1. colour deviation, brit colour deviation, color distortion, brit colour distortion, hue error 2. (phot) (einer Linse) → chromatische Abberration
Farbabzug m (**Farbandruck** m) (print) color proof, brit colour proof, color print, brit colour print, progressive proof, colloq progressive, prog
 A progressive proof is one of a set of engraver's proofs used in color process printing, showing each color plate separately and in combination.
Farbanalyse f (print/phot) color analysis, brit colour analysis
Farbanalysegerät n (print/phot) color analyst, brit colour analyst
 A device operating on the principle of additive synthesis, (→) additive Synthese, designed to show full-color pictures from monochrome color separation prints or halftone proofs.
Farbandruck m
→ Farbabzug
Farbangleichung n (**Farbanpassung** f) (print/phot/TV) color matching, brit colour matching, color matrixing, brit colour matrixing
Farbanordnung f (print/phot/TV) coloration, coloring, brit colouring, color scheme, brit colour scheme
Farbanzeige f (**farbige Anzeige** f, **mehrfarbige Anzeige** f) color advertisement, brit colour advertisement, color ad, brit colour ad

Farbart f
→ Chromatizität
Farbart-Signal n (**F-Signal** n) (TV) chrominance signal
→ Chrominanz, Chrominanzsignal
Farbätzung f (print) color process etching, brit colour process etching, process engraving
Farbaufbrechen n (TV) color break-up, brit colour break-up
Farbauflösung f (TV) chrominance resolution
→ Auflösung
Farbauflösungsvermögen n (phot) acuity of color image, brit acuity of colour image, chromatic resolution
Farbaufnahme f
→ Farbphoto
Farbaufschlag m
→ Farbzuschlag
Farbaufteilung f (phot) chromatic separation, chromatic splitting
Farbausbleichprozeß m (print) dye-bleach process
Farbausgleich m
→ Farbabgleich
Farbauszug m (print) color separation, brit colour separation, separation
 In full-color printing, either a black-and-white negative of one primary color in the full-color original, or the process of breaking down full-color copy into its primary color components.
Farbauszugsnegativ n (print) color separation negative, brit colour separation negative, separation negative
Farbbalance f
→ Farbabgleich
Farbbalken m (TV) color bar, brit colour bar
 An electronically generated, bar-shaped video tape leader color pattern designed to match playback to the original recording levels and phasing.
Farbbalkentestbild n (TV) color bar test pattern, brit colour bar test pattern, standard test bars pl, SMPTE standard test bars pl
→ Farbbalken
Farbballen m (print) dab, dabber, inking ball, ink ball
Farbbeilage f 1. color insert, brit colour insert 2. (Supplement) color supplement, brit colour supplement

Farbbereich

Farbbereich m *(print/phot/TV)* color range, *brit* colour range
→ Farbskala

Farbbestimmungsprobe f *(TV)* color cinex test, *brit* colour cinex test, *brit* colour pilot test
    A test using fifteen-frame laboratory strips of key film scenes, each frame printed with slightly differences for the final release print color selections.

Farbbezugspunkt m *(phot/print/TV)* color reference, *brit* colour reference

Farbbild n
→ Farbphotographie

Farbbildaustastsynchronsignal n **(FBAS-Signal** n) *(TV)* composite color video signal, comp. sig., *brit* composite colour video signal, color video signal, *brit* colour video signal, composite color signal, *brit* composite colour signal

Farbbildkontrollgerät n *(TV)* color picture and waveform monitor, *brit* colour picture and waveform monitor

Farbbildner m **(Farbkuppler** m, **Farbkomponente** f) *(phot)* coupler

Farbbildröhre f *(TV)* color picture tube, *brit* colour picture tube, color tube, *brit* colour tube, chromoscope, Am color kinescope

Farbbildsignal n *(TV)* color picture signal, *brit* colour picture signal

Farbbildsignalgemisch n
→ Farbbildaustastsynchronsignal

Farbbuch n
→ Farbmusterbuch

Farbbüchse f *(print)* ink box

Farbcoder m **(Farbkoder** m) *(TV)* color coder, *brit* colour coder, color encoder, *brit* colour encoder

Farbdecker f *(print/TV)* registration
→ Passer

Farbdecoder m **(Farbdekoder** m) *(TV)* color decoder, *brit* colour decoder

Farbdemodulator m *(TV)* color demodulator, *brit* colour demodulator, chrominance demodulator

Farbdia n **(Farbdiapositiv** n) *(phot)* color transparency, *brit* colour transparency, (gerahmt) color slide, *brit* colour slide
    A full-color positive image on screenplates or colorfilms, or any other transparent support.

Farbdichte f **(Farbstoffdichte** f) *(phot)* color density, *brit* colour density, ink density, colorimetric purity

Farbdifferenz f *(phot)* color difference, *brit* colour difference, chromatic difference

Farbdifferenzsignal n *(TV)* color difference signal, *brit* colour difference signal

Farbdimension f *(phot/print/TV)* color dimension, *brit* colour dimension

Farbdreieck n **(Farbendreieck** n, **Farbtafel** f, **Spektralfarbenzug** m) *(phot/print)* chromaticity diagram, color triangle, *brit* colour triangle, Maxwell triangle
    The triangle showing the tree dimensions of color, i.e. value, chroma, hue, and the relations that can be produced between the different types of color by means of additive color mixing, (→) additive Farbmischung.

Farbdruck m
→ Farbendruck

Farbduplikatnegativ n *(phot)* color duplicate negative, *brit* colour duplicate negative, color dupe neg., *brit* colour dupe neg., internegative, interneg

Farbe f **1.** *(phot/print/TV)* color, *brit* colour **2.** → Farbton **3.** → Farbkörper
    The representation of hues other than white.
4. *(print)* ink, printer's ink, printing ink **5.** → Farbstoff

farbecht adj
→ orthochromatisch

Farbeffekt m
→ Farbenwirkung

Farbeneindruck m *(phot/print/TV)* color effect, *brit* colour effect

Farbeisen n **(Farbenspachtel** m) *(print)* slice, ink slice

Farbelektronik f color electronics pl *(construed as sg)*, *brit* colour electronics

Farbempfang m *(TV)* color reception, *brit* colour reception

Farbempfänger m
→ Farbfernsehgerät

Farbempfinden n **(Farbenwahrnehmung** f) *(psy)* color perception, *brit* colour perception, color sensation, *brit* colour sensation

farbempfindlich adj *(phot)* color-sensitive, *brit* colour-sensitive

farbempfindlich machen v/t *(phot)* to color-sensitize, *brit* to colour-sensitise

To increase the sensitivity of emulsions for color by adding a special, sensitizing dye.
Farbempfindlichkeit f *(phot)* color sensitivity, *brit* colour sensitivity, sensitivity to color, *brit* sensitivity to colour, chromatic sensitivity, spectral response
Farbempfindung f
→ Farbempfinden
färben v/t to color, *brit* to colour, to dye, *(phot)* to tone
→ kolorieren, tönen
Farbenabstufung f
→ Farbabstufung
Farbenanordung f
→ Farbanordnung
Farbenbrechung f *(opt)* color refraction, *brit* colour refraction
Farbendiagramm n
→ Farbdreieck
Farbendruck m **(Farbdruck** m) **1.** (Verfahren) color printing, *brit* colour printing **2.** (Produkt) color print, *brit* colour print
→ Mehrfarbendruck, Vierfarbendruck
Farbendrucker m color printer, *brit* colour printer
Farbendruckmaschine f color printing machine, *brit* colour printing machine
Farbendruckpresse f color printing press, *brit* colour printing press, chromatic printing press
farbempfindlich adj
→ farbempfindlich
Farbenempfindlichkeit f
→ Farbempfindlichkeit
Farbenfotografie f
→ Farbphotographie
Farbenharmonie f *(phot/print)* color harmony, *brit* colour harmony
Farbenkombination f *(phot/print)* color combination, *brit* colour combination
Farbenkonstanz f *(phot/print)* color constance, *brit* colour constancy
Farbenkreis m
→ Farbkreis
Farbenkunstdruck m
→ Farbkunstdruck
Farbenlehre f **(Farbenstudie** f) chromatics pl *(construed as sg),* theory of colors, *brit* theory of colours
Farbenlichtdruck m *(print)* collotype
Farbenlithographie f
→ Farblithographie

Farbenmeßapparat n **(Farbenmesser** m) *(phot/print)* colorimeter, chromoscope, chromometer
Farbenmessung f **(Farbmetrik** f, **Kolorimetrie** f) *(phot/print)* colorimetry, chromatometry
Farbenmischapparat m **(Farbenmischer** m, **Farbenmischgerät** n) *(phot/print)* color mixer, *brit* colour mixer, chromoscope
Farbenmischer m *(phot/print)*
1. → Farbenmischapparat 2. (Person) color mixer, *brit* colour mixer, ink man
Farbenmischung f **(Chromoskopie** f) *(phot)* color mixing, *brit* colour mixing, chromoscopy, *(print)* ink mixing, color blending, *brit* colour blending
Farbenordnung f
→ Farbsystem
Farbenpsychologie f psychology of color, *brit* psychology of colour
Farbenreinheit f
→ Farbreinheit
Farbensehen n **(Farbwahrnehmung** f) *(psy)* color vision, *brit* colour vision
Farbenskala f
→ Farbskala
Farbenspachtel m **(Farbenspatel** m)
→ Farbeisen
Farbenspektrum n
→ Farblithographie
Farbensymbolik f *(psy)* color symbolism, *brit* colour symbolism
Farbensystem n
→ Farbsystem
Farbentafel f
→ Farbtafel
Farbentest m
→ Farbtest
Farbentisch m
→ Farbtisch
Farbentopf m **(Farbtopf** m) *(print)* ink pot
Farbenentwickler m *(phot)* color developer, *brit* colour developer
Farbentwicklung f *(phot)* color development, *brit* colour development, color developing, *brit* colour developing
Farbenwertskala f
→ Farbskala
Farbenwirkung f **(Farbwirkung** f) *(print/phot)* color effect(s) *(pl),* *brit* colour effect(s) *(pl),* effect(s) *(pl)* of color

Farbenzufuhrwalze f
→ Farbzufuhrwalze
Farberinnerungsvermögen n (**Farberinnerung** f) (psy) color memory, brit colour memory
Farbetisch m (**Farbtisch** m, **Farbstein** m) (print) inking stone, inkstone, ink stone, inking table, ink table, inking slab, ink slab
Farbfehler m (phot/print) chromatic defect, color error, brit colour error, color defect, brit colour defect
Farbfernsehempfänger m
→ Farbfernseher
Farbfernsehen n color television, brit colour television, color TV, brit colour TV
Farbfernsehkamera f color television camera, brit colour television camera, color TV camera, brit color TV camera
Farbfernseher m (**Farbfernsehgerät** n, **Farbvernsehempfänger** m) color television set, brit colour television set, color TV set, brit colour TV set, color television receiver, brit colour television receiver, color TV receiver, brit colour TV receiver, color set, brit colour set
Farbfernsehröhre f color television tube, brit colour television tube, color TV tube, brit colour TV tube, color tube, brit colour tube
Farbfilm m (**Kolorfilm** m) 1. (phot) color film, brit colour film, colorfilm 2. (Kino) color film, brit colour film, film in color, brit film in colour, technicolor film
Farbfilmverfahren n (phot) color film system, brit colour film system
Farbfilter m (phot/TV) color filter, brit colour filter, colored filter, brit coloured filter, color screen
1. A tinted transparent camera lens covering used in photography to absorb certain colors to allow better rendering of others, or to eliminate undesirable colors in a subject, or to produce color separation negatives, (→) Farbauszugnegativ. 2. An electronic camera tube sensitive to one of three ranges of hues. The camera contains three tubes, which together produce the full color image by superimposing the three primary color signals.
Farbgrauwerttafel f (**Farbgrauskala** f) (phot/print) color gray scale chart, brit colour grey scale chart

Farbhilfsträger m (TV) color subcarrier (CSC), brit colour subcarrier, colloq color carrier, brit colour carrier
farbig adj colored, brit coloured, color, brit colour
farbiges Rauschen n
→ Farbrauschen
Farbigkeit f (phot/print) chromaticity, chromatism
Farbillustration f (**farbige Illustration** f) color illustration, brit colour illustration, colored illustration, brit coloured illustration
Farbflimmern n (TV) color flicker, brit colour flicker
Farbfolie f colored foil, brit coloured foil
Farbfoto n
→ Farbphoto
Farbfotografie f
→ Farbphotographie
Farbgebung f (phot/print) coloration, brit colouration, coloring, brit colouring
Farbgestaltung f color design, brit colour design
Farbgleichgewicht n (**Farbbalance** f) (phot/print/TV) color balance, brit colour balance
→ Farbabgleich
Farbgraphik f (**farbige Graphik** f) color artwork, brit colour artwork
Farbinformation f (phot/print/TV) color information, brit colour information, chrominance information
→ Farbwertsignal, Chrominanzsignal
Farbintensität f (**Farbstärke** f) (phot/print/TV) chromatic intensity, chroma
Farbkamera f (film/TV) color camera, brit colour camera
Farbkanalentzerrer m (TV) chrominance equalizer, brit chrominance equaliser
Farbkasten m (print) ink duct, duct, ink fountain, fountain trough, pan trough
Farbkegel m (phot/print) color solid, brit colour solid, color space, brit colour space
Farbkennung f (TV) color identification, brit colour identification, color ID
Farbkinematographie f (film) color cinematography, brit colour cinematography

Farbkissen *n* **(Stempelkissen** *n*)
(print) ink pad
Farbklischee *n (print)* color plate, *brit*
colour plate, color block, *brit* colour
block, color engraving, *brit* colour
engraving, color cut, *brit* colour cut,
process block, process plate
 A printing plate used in combination
 with others to print one of a desired
 number of colors for color illustration,
 usually the four colors yellow, red, blue,
 and black.
Farbklischeehersteller *m (print)*
process engraver
Farbklischeeherstellung *f (print)*
process engraving, colorwork
 The production of photoengravings in
 two or more colors.
Farbklischeesatz *m*
→ Farbsatz
Farbkoder *m*
→ Farbcoder
Farbkoeffizient *m (phot/print/TV)*
chromatic coefficient
Farbkompensationsfilter *m (phot/
print)* color compensation filter, color
compensating filter, *brit* colour
compensation filter
Farbkomponente *f (phot/print)* color
component, *brit* colour component
Farbkontrast *m (phot/print/TV)* color
contrast, *brit* colour contrast
Farbkontrolle *f (phot)* control process,
color control process
Farbkonturschärfe *f* **(Farbkontur** *f*)
(phot/print/TV) chromatic resolution
Farbkoordinate *f (phot/print/TV)*
chromaticity coordinate
Farbkopie *f (phot)* color print, *brit*
colour print
 A color photograph printed on paper.
Farbkopiermaschine *f (phot)* color
printer, *brit* colour printer
Farbkopierung *f* **(Farbkopieren** *n*)
(phot) color printing, *brit* colour
printing
Farbkörper *m* **(Pigment** *n*) pigment
Farbkorrektor *m (phot/print/TV)*
color corrector, *brit* colour corrector
Farbkorrektur *f (phot/print/TV)* color
correction, *brit* colour correction
 The improvement of color rendition by
 masking of the separation negatives, or
 by treatment of the printing plates, or by
 eliminating chromatic aberration in the
 camera lens.

Farbkorrekturfilter *m (phot/print)*
color-correction filter, *brit* colour-
correction filter
Farbkorrekturmaske *f (phot/print)*
color-correction mask, *brit* colour-
correction mask
farbkorrigiert *adj (phot/print/TV)*
color-corrected, *brit* colour-corrected
farbkorrigierte Filmkopie *f*
(farbkorrigiertes Photo *n*) *(phot/film)*
color corrected print, *brit* colour-
corrected print
 A black and white photograph made
 from a color photograph or drawing by
 using filters to give more nearly perfect
 separation between colors; or a motion
 picture color print in which the colors
 were corrected to true values.
Farbkreis *m* **(Farbtonkreis** *m*) *(phot/
print)* color circle, *brit* colour circle,
color cycle, *brit* colour cycle
Farbkreisel *m (phot/print)* color
sensitometer, *brit* colour sensitometer
Farbkunstdruck *m* color print, *brit*
colour print
Farbkuppler *m* **(Kuppler** *m*) *(phot/
print)* color matcher, *brit* colour
matcher
Farbläufer *m* **(Reiber** *m,* **Reibstein** *m*)
(print) color grinder, *brit* colour
grinder, ink block
Farblavendel *m (film)* color lavender,
brit colour lavender
Farblehre *f*
→ Farbenlehre
Farblichtbild *n*
→ Farbphoto
Farblineal *n* **(Farbmesser** *n*) *(print)*
ink knife
Farblithographie *f* **(Farbsteindruck**
m) *(print)* color lithography, *brit*
colour lithography, chromo-
lithography
Farbmatrix *f (film)* (Technicolor)
color matrix, *brit* colour matrix
Farb-MAZ-Wagen *m (TV)* color
mobile video tape recorder (CMVTR),
brit colour mobile video tape recorder
Farbmessung *f*
→ Farbenmessung
Farbmetrik *f (phot/print)*
chromatometry, colorimetry
farbmetrisch *adj (phot/print)*
colorimetric, chromatometric
Farbmischung *f*
→ Farbenmischung

Farbmodulator m *(TV)* color modulator, *brit* colour modulator, chrominance modulator
Farbmuster n **(Farbprobe** f**)** *(phot/print)* color pattern, *brit* colour pattern, color sample, *brit* colour sample, color swatch
Farbmusterbuch n *(print)* ink sample book, paint-swatch book
Farbnachlauffilm m *(film/TV)* color tail leader, *brit* colour tail leader, color run-out leader, *brit* colour run-out leader
Farbnegativfilm m *(phot)* color negative film, *brit* colour negative film
Farbort m *(phot/print)* point on the color triangle, *brit* point on the colour triangle
Farbortmessung f *(phot/print)* measurement of color coordinates, *brit* measurement of colour coordinates
Farbpasser m **(Farbpasserkreuz** n**)** *(print)* color register, *brit* colour register, color register mark, *brit* colour register mark
→ Passer
Farbphoto n **(Farbfoto** n**, Farbphotographie** f, **Farbbild** n**)** color print, *brit* colour print, color photo, *brit* colour photo, color photograph, *brit* colour photograph, color photoprint, *brit* colour photoprint
Farbphotographie f **(Farbfotografie** f **)** color photography, *brit* colour photography
Farbpigment n
→ Farbkörper
Farbplatte f *(print)* color plate, *brit* colour plate
→ Farbklischee
Farbpositiv n
→ Farbphoto
Farbpositivfilm m *(phot)* color positive film, *brit* colour positive film
Farbpreis m **(Preis** m **für eine Farbanzeige, Farbanzeigentarif** m**)** color rate, *brit* colour rate, color advertisement rate, *brit* colour advertisement rate
Farbqualität f *(phot/print)* color quality, *brit* colour quality
Farbrand m **1.** *(phot)* chromatic halo **2.** *(TV)* color fringe, *brit* colour fringe
Farbraster m *(print)* tint screen

Farbrasterverfahren n *(phot)* color screen process, *brit* colour screen process
Farbrauschen n
→ Bildrauschen
Farbreibemaschine f **(Farbreiber** m**)**
→ Farbläufer
Farbreinheit f **(Farbreinheitsgrad** m**)** *(phot/print)* chroma
Farbreiz m *(psy)* color stimulus, *brit* colour stimulus
Farbreproduktion f *(print)* color reproduction, *brit* colour reproduction
Farbreservoir n **(Füllreservoir** n**)** *(print)* ink fountain, fountain
Farbretusche f **(Farbretuschieren** n**)** *(phot)* color retouching, *brit* colour retouching
Farbsättigung f *(TV)* color saturation, *brit* colour saturation
Farbsättigungsregelung f *(TV)* color saturation adjustment, *brit* colour saturation adjustment
Farbsättigungsregler m *(TV)* color saturation control, *brit* colour saturation
Farbsättigungsregler m *(TV)* color saturation control, *brit* colour saturation control
Farbsatz m **(Farbklischeesatz** m**)** *(print)* set of color plates, *brit* set of colour plates, process plates *pl*
Farbsaum m **(Farbrand** m**)** *(film/TV)* color fringe, *brit* colour fringe, color fringing, *brit* colour fringing
Farbschablonentrick m
→ Farbstanztrick
Farbschattierung f *(phot/print)* color shade, *brit* colour shade, hue
→ Farbton
farbschön adj *(phot) colloq* snappy
Farbschwelle f *(phot/print/TV)* color threshold, *brit* colour threshold
Farbsehen n **(Farbsehvermögen** n**)**
→ Farbensehen
Farbseite f **(farbig gedruckte Seite** f **)** color page, *brit* colour page
farbselektiv adj color-selective, *brit* colour-selective
Farbsendung f **(Farbfernsendung** f **)** color transmission, *brit* colour transmission, color program, *brit* colour programme, color broadcast, *brit* colour broadcast, colorcast
Farbsensitiser m **(Colorsensitiser** m**)** *(phot)* color sensitizer, *brit* colour sensitiser

Farbsignal n **(F-Signal** n, **Farbwertsignal** n) *(TV)* color signal, chrominance signal, *brit* colour signal
Farbskala f **(Farbenskala** f) *(print)* chromatometer, color scale, *brit* colour scale, color range, *brit* colour range, gray scale, *brit* grey scale
→ Graukeil
Farbsperre f *(TV)* color killer, *brit* colour killer
Farbstärke f color intensity, *brit* colour intensity
Farbstärkeregler m *(TV)* color intensity control, *brit* colour intensity control
Farbstein m
→ Farbetisch
Farbsteindruck m **(farbiger Steindruck** m)
→ Farblithographie
Farbstich m **1.** (falsche Farbwiedergabe) *(phot)* color cast, *brit* colour cast, cast, color tinge, *brit* colour tinge, color dash, *brit* colour dash **2.** *(print)* color print, *brit* colour print, colored print, *brit* coloured print, (Farbradierung) colored engraving, *brit* coloured engraving, copperplate color print, *brit* copperplate colour print
Farbstift m **(Buntstift** m**)** crayon, colored pencil, *brit* coloured pencil
Farbstoff m **1.** (Färbungsmittel) dye, dyestuff, coloring matter, *brit* colouring matter **2.** → Farbkörper
Farbstrahldruck m ink-jet printing
Farbsynchronsignal n **(Farbsynchronisiersignal** n, **Burst** m**)** *(TV)* color burst, *brit* colour burst, burst, color synchronizing burst, *brit* colour synchronising burst, color synchronizing signal, *brit* colour synchronising signal
A sub-carrier frequency color information sample at the back porch of each scan line, synchronizing transmitted color signals to a receiver.
Farbsynthese f *(phot/print)* color synthesis, *brit* colour synthesis
Farbsystem n **(Farbensystem** n, **Farbordnungssystem** n) *(phot/print)* color system, *brit* colour system
Farbtafel f **(Farbtabelle** f, **Farbentafel** f) **1.** → Farbskala **2.** → Farbplatte

Farbtemperatur f *(phot)* color temperature, *brit* colour temperature
The color value, (→) Farbwert, of a light source, measured in degrees Kelvin.
Farbtemperaturmesser m **(Lichtfarbmeßgerät** n) *(phot)* color temperature meter, *brit* colour temperature meter, Kelvinmeter
Farbtest m **(Farbentest** m) *(market/res)* color test, *brit* colour test
Farbtiefdruck m *(print)* color gravure, *brit* colour gravure
Farbtisch m
→ Farbetisch
Farbton m **(Farbtönung** f, **Farbtonintensität** f) **1.** *(print)* color shade, *brit* colour shade, shade, tint **2.** *(phot)* tone
Farbtoneffekt m *(phot)* tonal effect
Farbtonknopf m *(TV)* color intensity control, *brit* colour intensity control
farbtonrichtig adj *(phot/print)* orthochromatic
Farbträger m *(TV)* color subcarrier (CSC), *brit* colour subcarrier, *colloq* color carrier, *brit* colour carrier
Farbträgermoiré n *(TV)*
→ Moiré
Farbtrennung f
→ Farbauszug
Farbtreue f
→ Farbwiedergabe
Farbtripel f *(TV)* color triad, *brit* colour triad
Farbübergang m *(phot/print/TV)* color transition, *brit* colour transition
Farbübertragung f *(TV)* color transmission, *brit* colour transmission
→ Farbsendung
Farbumkehrduplikat n *(phot)* color reversal print, *brit* colour reversal print
Farbumkehrfilm m *(phot)* color reversal film, *brit* colour reversal film, reversal color film, *brit* reversal colour film
Farbumkodierer m *(TV)* color transcoder, *brit* colour transcoder, transcoder
Farbumschlag m *(phot/print)* color change, *brit* colour change
Farbunterscheidungsvermögen n *(psy)* color difference sensitivity, *brit* colour difference sensitivity
Farbunterschied m *(phot/print/TV)* color difference, *brit* colour difference

Farb-U-Wagen *m* (**Farbübertragungswagen** *m*) *(TV)* color OB vehicle, *brit* colour OB vehicle, color mobile control room (CMCR), *brit* colour mobile control room
Farbvalenz *f (phot/print)* chromaticness
Farbvalenzflimmern *n*
→ Farbflimmern
Farbverfahren *n (print)* color process, *brit* colour process
Farbvorlage *f (print)* colored copy, *brit* coloured copy
Farbvorlauffilm *m* color film leader, *brit* colour film leader, color head leader, *brit* colour head leader
Farbwalze *f (print)* ink roller, inking roller, inker, waver
Farbwerk *n (print)* inking apparatus, inking mechanism, inker mechanism, inker unit, inking unit, ink rollers *pl*
Farbwert *m (phot/print)* chromaticity, chromaticity value, chromatic value, color value, *brit* colour value, value
  The quality of a color by which it is seen as light or dark.
farbwertrichtig *adj*
→ farbtonrichtig
Farbwertsignal *n*
→ Farbsignal
Farbwiedergabe *f* (**Farbreproduktion** *f*) *(phot/print)* color rendering, *brit* colour rending, color rendition, *brit* colour rendition, color reproduction, *brit* colour reproduction
Farbwirkung *f*
→ Farbenwirkung
Farbzufuhr *f* (**Farbzuführung** *f*) *(print)* ink feed, ink feeding, ink supply
Farbzufuhrwalze *f* (**Farbenzuführwalze** *f*, **Duktor** *m*) *(print)* ink ductor, ductor
Farbzurichtebogen *m* (**Farbzurichtungsbogen** *m*) *(print)* color overlay, *brit* colour overlay, color guide, *brit* colour guide, guide sheet
  A transparent paper overlay on a black an white drawing on which colors are indicated as guide for reproduction
Farbzuschlag *m* (**Farbaufschlag** *m*) *(advtsg)* color surcharge, *brit* colour surcharge, additional color charge, *brit* additional colour charge
  The additional amount charged for color advertisements in print media.

Farbzwischenpositiv *n (phot)* color intermediate positive, *brit* colour intermediate positive
Farbzylinder *m (print)* inking cylinder, inking roller
Faser *f (paper)* fiber, *brit* fibre
Faserbrei *m*
→ Papierbrei
Faserlaufrichtung *f*
→ Laufrichtung
Faseroptik *f* fiber optics *pl (construed as sg)*, *brit* fibre optics
Faserrichtung *f* (**Faserung** *f*)
→ Laufrichtung
Fashion Center *n (retailing)* fashion center, *brit* fashion centre
Fashion Leader *m*
→ Modeführer
Fassade *f* façade, wall
Fassadenbemalung *f (outdoor advtsg)* painted wall, painted bulletin, painted display
  An outdoor advertisement in which the elements of copy and art are manually painted on the wall of a building.
Fassadenwerbung *f (outdoor advtsg)* painted wall advertising, painted bulletin advertising, wall advertising
Fassung *f* **1.** (Version) version **2.** *(phot)* (in der Kamera) bed, fitting, socket
FAT *m abbr* Filmabtaster
Faustskizze *f*
→ Rohentwurf
FAW *m abbr* Fachverband Außenwerbung e.V.
FAZ *f abbr* Filmaufzeichnung
FAZ-Anlage *f* (**Filmaufzeichnungsanlage** *f*) film recorder, telerecording equipment, film transfer equipment, *Am* kinescope
  An equiment to make records or film copies of live television programs or commercials.
FAZ aufzeichnen (fazen) *v/t* to record on film, to film-record, to kine
FDM *m abbr* Fachverband der Medienberater e.V.
FDW *m abbr* Fachverband Film- und Diapositivwerbung e.V.
Feasibility-Studie *f* (**Durchführbarkeitsstudie** *f*) *(market res)* feasibility study, feasibility investigation
→ Machbarkeitsstudie
Feature *n* feature, feature story, feature article, featuresque article

federführende Agentur f
(Hauptagentur f) captain agency, master agency, parent agency
 Under a master contract, the advertising agency responsible for placing the advertising of one of several advertisers by two or more agencies.
federführendes Unternehmen n *(econ)* (beim Konsortialgeschäft) pilot contractor
federleicht *adj*
→ Daunendruckpapier
Federleichtpapier n
→ Daunendruckpapier
Federzeichnung f pen-and-ink drawing, pen drawing, pen-and-ink sketch
Feedback n
→ Rückkoppelung
Feedbackschlaufe f **(Feedbackschleife** f)
→ Rückkoppelungsschleife
Feeder Jobber m
→ Rack Jobber
Fehlabsorption f
→ Maskierung, Nebenfarbdichte
Fehlangaben f/pl *(survey res)* (in einer Befragung) false claims *pl*, false reports *pl*, (übertriebene Angaben) overclaims *pl*, overreports *pl*, (untertriebene Angaben) underclaims *pl*, underreports *pl*
 Respondents may report that they have bought more or done someting more frequently than they actually have, or they may underreport their activities. Overreporting tends to occur in responses to questions about socially desirable activities, and underreporting tends to be in response to questions about threatening topics.
Fehlangabenmachen n *(survey res)* (in einer Befragung) false claiming, false reporting, (übertriebene Angaben) overclaiming, overreporting, (untertriebene Angaben) underclaiming, underreporting
Fehlbelichtung f *(phot)* incorrect exposure, faulty exposure
Fehlbesetzung f *(film/TV)* miscast, miscasting
Fehlbogen m *(print)* spoiled sheet, imperfect sheet, faulty sheet, (*pl* Fehlbögen; Vorkommen von Fehlbögen) spoilage
 A sheet of paper wasted in the printing process.

Fehldruck m
→ Druckfehler
Fehler m **(Erhebungsfehler** m) *(res)* error, (Erhebungsfehler) error in survey, (Beobachtungsfehler) error in observation
 The difference between an occurring value and its true or expected value.
Fehler m **1. Art (Fehler** m **der ersten Art, Typ-I-Fehler** m) *(stat)* error of the first kind, error of the first type, type I error, α error, alpha error
 In hypothesis testing, (→) Hypothesenprüfung, the rejection of a true null hypothesis, (→) Nullhypothese.
Fehler m **2. Art (Fehler** m **der zweiten Art, Typ-II-Fehler** m) *(stat)* error of the second kind, error of the second type, type II error, ß error, beta error
 In hypothesis testing, (→) Hypothesenprüfung, the failure to reject a false null hypothesis, (→) Nullhypothese.
Fehlerbereich m **(Fehlerintervall** n) *(stat)* error band
 The range of values within which an estimated or predicted value in statistical prediction or estimation may be supposed to lie with a certain probability.
→ Mutungsbereich
Fehlerberichtigung f
→ Korrektur
fehlerfrei *adj* correct, faultless, flawless
Fehlerfunktion f *(stat)* error function
fehlerhaft *adj* faulty, imperfect, defective
fehlerhafte Bildeinstellung f *(TV)* bad framing, bad centering, (Empfänger) mistuning
Fehlerhäufigkeit f
→ Fehlerquote
Fehlerintervall n
→ Mutungsbereich
Fehlerquelle f *(stat)* source of error
Fehlerquote f **(Fehlerrate** f) *(stat)* error rate
Fehlerspanne f
→ Irrtumsbereich
Fehlertabelle f **(Fehlertafel** f)
→ Genauigkeitstabelle
Fehlervarianz f *(stat)* error variance
 The variance, (→) Varianz, of error, (→) Fehler, in repetitions of an experimental situation, regardless of whether the error is due to sampling effects or not.
Fehlerverteilung f *(stat)* distribution of error, error distribution

Fehlerverzeichnis n (print) errata pl (construed as sg), list of errata, errata sheet, errata slip, corrigenda, list of corrigenda
→ Korrekturverzeichnis
Fehler-Wahl-Methode f (**Fehler-Wahl-Technik** f, **Fehler-Wahl-Verfahren** n) (res) error-choice technique (Philip E. Hammond)
A method of test construction, under which test persons are forced to choose between several wrong items as an indication of attitudinal bias.
Fehlerwahrscheinlichkeit f (stat) error probability, probability of error
Fehlmaß n (typ) bastard measure, bastard
A typographical measure that does not conform to standard sizes.
Fehlschluß m fallacy, false conclusion, false inference
→ statistischer Fehlschluß
Fehlstreuung f (media res) circulation waste, waste circulation
That portion of advertising which cannot be considered to reach its logical target group, (→) Zielgruppe.
→ Streuverlust
fein (hochfein) adj(typ) (Linie) hairline, fine-line, hair stroke, fine-stroke
Feindruckpapier n fine printing paper, fine paper
Feineinstellung f (print/phot) fine adjustment, fine setting, fine control, (radio/TV) fine tuning
feines Briefpapier n (**feines Schreibpapier** n) Bath paper, Bath post
feingekörnt adj (phot)
→ feinkörnig, Feinkorn-
feingerastert (Feinraster-) adj (print) fine-screen
Feinkarton m (**Feinpappe** f) fine cardboard
Feinkorn n (**feines Korn** n) (phot) fine grain
The characteristic of photographic material that provides for positives free of any textural effects except for those provided by the subjects.
Feinkornkopie f (**feinkörniges Papierbild** n, **Marronkopie** f, **Zwischenkopie** f) (phot) fine-grain print
A photographic positive that is free of textural effects other than those provided by the subjects.

Feinkornentwickler m (phot) fine-grain developer
Feinkornfilm m (phot) fine-grain stock, fine-grain film
→ Feinkorn
Feinpapier n
→ Feindruckpapier
Feinpappe f
→ Feinkarton
Feinschnittkopie f (**Feinschnitt** m) (film/TV) fine cut
A fully edited, finished work print that is ready for reproduction and distribution after its final approval.
Feinstreuung f (media planning) rifle approach, selective advertising
Feinstwelle f (paper)
→ E-Welle
Feinwelle f (paper) B-Welle
Feld n 1. field 2. (print) (auf Papier) square, panel 3. (phot) frame
Feldanteil m (**Verbraucheranteil** m) (Bernt Spiegel) (market res) etwa field share, consumer share
The percentage of the total number of persons having demand for a product, a brand, a service, etc., who actually buy it, or are customers of the company.
Feldarbeit f (survey res) field work, fieldwork, (die Feldarbeiter m/pl) field force, field staff, fieldworkers pl
In survey and market research, the process whereby interviewers are sent out to gather information by conducting interviews, making observations or checks.
Feldarbeiter m/pl (**Feldorganisation** f) (survey res) field force, field staff, field organization, brit field organisation
The team of interviewers used for gathering information directly from respondents.
Feldbeobachtung f (survey res) field observation
Felderhebung f field survey
Feldexperiment n (survey res) field experiment
Feldforschung f (survey res) field research
→ Primärforschung
Feldlinse f (phot) field lens, field flattener
Feldmodell n (market res) field model
Feldpsychologie f (**Vektorpsychologie** f, **topologische Psychologie** f) field psychology

Feldstudie f (**Felduntersuchung** f)
(survey res) field study, field
investigation
Feldtheorie f (Kurt Lewin) *(psy)* field
theory
→ Feldpsychologie
Feldverschlüsselung f (**Feldkodierung**
f) *(survey res)* field coding
The coding of open questions, (→) offene
Frage, by interviewers during the
interview. In a field-coded question, the
question itself usually is identical to that
of an open-answer format. Instead of a
blank space for the interviewer to record
the respondent's answer verbatim, a set
of codes is printed. Interviewers simply
check each topic that is mentioned.
FEM n *abbr* Filmmeßgerät
Fenster n window
→ Schaufenster
Fensterantenne f *(electr.)* window-
frame antenna, *brit* window-frame
aerial, window-mounted antenna,
brit window-mounted aerial
Fensteraufkleber m (**Fenster-
aufklebestreifen** m) *(POP advtsg)*
window streamer, window strip
A narrow point-of-purchase poster
gummed on the printed side for
attachment inside a dealer's store
window.
Fensterbriefumschlag m (**Fenster-
briefhülle** f, **Fensterkuvert** n) window
envelope
An envelope with a transparent panel on
the address side permitting the address
on the enclosure to show through.
Fensterfalz m (**Fensterfalzung** f)
window fold, window folding
→ Altarfalz
Fernaufnahme f *(film/phot/TV)*
distance shot, *(phot)* telephoto,
telephoto picture, *(film/TV)* long shot
(LS), long-distance shot, *Am* vista
shot
A camera shot showing the entire person
or any other object from a certain
distance and, therefore, in full view
against the background or set.
Fernauge n closed-circuit TV camera,
closed-circuit camera
Fernauslöser m *(phot)* remote control
release, remote release
Fernbedarf m
→ Shopping Goods
Fernbedienung f *(electr.)* remote
control
Fernbildlinse f
→ Teleobjektiv

Fernempfangsgebiet n
(**Fernempfangsbereich** m) *(radio)*
secondary service area, secondary
signal coverage area, sky-wave
service area, *(TV)* grade B coverage
area, grade B signal coverage area
The area in which the reception of a
radio station is generally fair, but subject
to variation.
vgl. Nahempfangsgebiet
Fernkopieren n (**Telefax-Dienst** m)
telecopying
→ Bildfunk
Fernkopierer m (**Telefaxgerät** n)
telecopierer
→ Bildfunk
Fernlinse f
→ Teleobjektiv
Fernmeldeamt n telecommunication
office
Fernmeldesatellit m
telecommunications satellite,
communications satellite
Fernmeldetechnik f
telecommunications *pl (construed as
sg)*, telecommunications engineering,
communications *pl (construed as sg)*
Fernmeldetechniker m
telecommunications engineer,
communications engineer
Fernmeldewesen n telecommunications *pl (construed as sg)*
Fernmeldezentrum n telecommunications center, *brit* centre
Fernmeßdaten n/pl telemetrical data
pl
Fernphotographie f telephotography
Fernsatz m *(print)* remote-control
composition, teletypesetting
Fernsatzgerät n *(print)* teletypesetter
Fernschreiben n teleprint message,
teleprinter message, teletyped
message, teletype message, telex
message, telex
Fernschreiber m 1. (Gerät)
teletypewriter, teleprinter, telex,
teletyper, *colloq* teletape, ticker
2. (Person) teletypist, teletype
operator, telex operator
Fernschreiberwerbung f teleprinter
advertising, teletypewriter
advertising, telex advertising
Fernschreibnetz n teletypewriter
network, teleprinter network,
teletyper network, telex network
Fernsehaufführung f television
performance

Fernsehansager(in) *m(f)* television announcer, TV announcer, television speaker, TV speaker
Fernsehansprache *f* television address, TV address
Fernsehanstalt *f* television station, TV station, television corporation, TV corporation, television network, TV network
Fernsehantenne *f* television antenna, *brit* television aerial
Fernsehapparat *m*
→ Fernseher
Fernseharchiv *n* television archives *pl*, TV archives *pl*, television library
Fernsehaufnahme *f*
→ Fernsehaufzeichnung
Fernsehaufnahmekamera *f* television camera, TV camera
Fernsehaufnahmewagen *m* television camera truck, pick-up truck, video bus, remote pickup mobile station, television OB van, television car, mobile video tape recorder (MVTR)
→ Übertragungswagen
Fernsehaufzeichnung *f* telerecording (TR), kinescope recording, video recording, television pickup, television recording (TVR), kinescope recording, kinescope, kine, teletranscription, transfer, teletranscription
  A film record of a live TV program or commercial obtained from a station broadcast signal or a receiver and intended for possible rebroadcasting.
Fernsehausstrahlung *f* television transmission, TV transmission
Fernsehautor *m*
→ Drehbuchautor
Fernsehband *n* television band, television frequency band
Fernsehbearbeitung *f* television adaptation, television version
Fernsehbeirat *m* television advisory board, television advisory council
Fernsehbericht *m* television report, TV report
Fernsehberichterstattung *f* television coverage, TV coverage
Fernsehbild *n* television image, TV image, television picture, TV picture, telepicture
Fernsehbildprojektor *m* television picture projector, TV picture projector
Fernsehbildröhre *f*
→ Fernsehröhre

Fernsehbildschirm *m*
→ Fernsehschirm
Fernsehdauer *f* (**Dauer** *f* **des Fernsehens, Sehdauer** *f*) *(media res)* time spent viewing
  The number of hours over a given period that a TV set-owning household or any of its members spends in watching TV.
Fernsehdienst *m* television service
Fernsehdirektor *m* director of television, managing director of television
Fernsehdirektübertragung *f* live television broadcast, live broadcast, live television relay
  A TV transmission presented directly from the actual event or performance.
Fernsehdiskussion *f* television panel discussion, television debate
Fernsehdrehbuch *n* television script, TV script, (technisches Drehbuch) television continuity, TV continuity
→ Drehbuch
Fernseheinschaltquote *f*
→ Einschaltquote
Fernsehempfang *m* television reception, TV reception
Fernsehempfänger *m* (**Fernsehempfangsgerät** *n*)
→ Fernseher
fernsehen *v/t* to watch television, to teleview
Fernsehen *n* **1.** (Institution) television, TV, *Am auch* video **2.** (Tätigkeit) televiewing, watching television, watching TV
Fernseher *m*
→ Fernsehgerät
Fernsehfassung *f* television version, TV version, video version
Fernsehfilm *m* television film, TV film, telefilm, telecine, *Am auch* video film
Fernsehfilmkassette *f* television film cassette, television film cartridge, TV film cassette, TV film cartridge, video film cassette, video film cartridge
Fernsehfilmkassettenwiedergabegerät *n* television cassette player, teleplayer, video cassette player
Fernsehforschung *f* television audience research, TV audience research, television research, TV research
→ Zuschauerforschung
Fernsehfüllsender *m* (**Fernsehumsetzer** *m*) television relay station,

TV relay station, television translator station, TV translator station, television translator, TV translator
A television station whose purpose it is to receive and pass on the signal from a feed point in order to expand the coverage area of this station.

Fernsehgebühr *f* television license fee, *brit* television licence fee, TV license fee, *brit* TV licence fee

Fernsehgenehmigung *f* **(Sendelizenz** *f*) television license, *brit* television licence

Fernsehgerät *n* **(Fernsehempfänger** *m*, **Fernseher** *m*, **Fernsehapparat** *m*) television set, TV set, television receiver, TV receiver, set

Fernsehgesellschaft *f* television corporation, TV corporation, television company, TV company, television network, TV network

Fernsehgewohnheiten *f/pl (audience res)* TV viewing habits *pl*, TV watching habits *pl*, viewing habits *pl*

Fernsehgroßbildprojektion *f* large-screen television projection, giant-screen television projection, projection television, *(TM)* eidophor screen projection
The method of using a giant television screen for the magnification of a video picture by projecting either a simultaneously photographed or an existing video tape on it.

Fernsehgroßbildprojektor *m* large-screen television projector, giant-screen television projector, television projector, eidophor screen projector

Fernsehhaushalt *m* **1.** *(media res)* television household (TVHH), TV household (TVHH), television home, TV home
A household equipped with at least one television set.
2. television budget

Fernsehinszenierung *f* television production, TV production

Fernsehinterview *n* television interview, TV interview

Fernsehjournalist *m* television journalist, TV journalist

Fernsehkanal *m* television channel, TV channel, video channel

Fernsehkanalumsetzer *m* television transposer, television translator

Fernseh-Kasch *n* television graticule

Fernsehkassette *f* **(Videokassette** *f*) television cartridge, TV cartridge, television cassette, TV cassette, video cassette, video cartridge

Fernsehkonferenz *f* video conference

Fernsehkofferempfänger *m*
→ tragbares Fernsehgerät

Fernsehkopie *f* television film, TV film

Fernsehleitung *f* television circuit, TV circuit

Fernsehlivesendung *f* **(Fernsehliveübertragung** *f*) live television transmission, live TV transmission, live television broadcast, live TV broadcast
→ Fernsehdirektübertragung, Direktübertragung

Fernsehlizenz *f* television franchise, TV franchise

Fernsehnachrichten *f/pl* television news *sg*, TV news *sg*, television news show, TV news show

Fernsehnetz *n* television network, TV network

Fernsehnorm *f* television standard, picture line standard

Fernsehnutzung *f (audience res)* television consumption, TV consumption

Fernsehoper *f* television opera, TV opera

Fernsehpreis *m* television award, TV award

Fernsehproduktion *f* television production, TV production

Fernsehproduzent *m* television producer, TV producer

Fernsehprogramm *n* **1.** *allg* television program, *brit* television programme
2. (Kanal) television channel, TV channel, channel
3. (Sendung) → Fernsehsendung

Fernsehprogrammgestaltung *f* television programming, TV programming

Fernsehpublikum *n* **(Fernsehzuschauerschaft** *f*, **Fernsehzuschauer** *m/pl*) television audience, TV audience
→ Zuschauer, Zuschauerschaft

Fernsehrat *m* television program committee, *brit* television programme committee, television council, TV council

Fernsehraster *m* **(Bildraster** *m*) television raster, TV raster, raster

Fernsehregisseur *m* television director, TV director

Fernsehreklame *f*
→ Fernsehwerbung
Fernsehreportage *f* television report, TV report
Fernsehreporter *m* television reporter, TV reporter
Fernsehröhre *f* **1.** (in der Kamera) television tube, pickup tube, *brit* pickup tube, TV tube, iconoscope **2.** (im Fernsehgerät) picture tube, television tube, viewing tube, kinescope
Fernsehrundfunk *m* television broadcasting, TV broadcasting, broadcast television, broadcast TV
Fernsehsatellit *m* television satellite, telecommunication satellite
Fernsehschaltraum *m* television switching area, TV switching area
Fernsehschirm *m* (**Bildschirm** *m*, **Fernsehbildschirm** *m*) television screen, TV screen, telescreen, video screen
Fernsehsender *m* **1.** (einzelne Sendestation) television station, TV station, telestation **2.** (Sendernetz) television network, TV network **3.** (Übertragungssender) television transmitter, TV transmitter
Fernsehsendung *f* television broadcast, TV broadcast, telecast, television show, TV show, television transmission, TV transmission, video transmission, television program, *brit* television programme, TV program, *brit* TV programme
Fernsehserie *f* television series, TV series, television serial, TV serial
Fernsehsignal *n* television signal, TV signal, signal
Fernsehspiel *n* television play, TV play, television drama, TV drama, teleplay, featurette
Fernsehspot *m* (**Werbespot** *m*) television commercial, TV commercial, commercial
Fernsehspot-Test *m* (*advtsg res*) television commercial test, TV commercial test
Fernsehstation *f*
→ Fernsehsender
Fernsehstrecke *f* television link, television relay link
Fernsehstudio *n* television studio, TV studio
Fernsehtechnik *f* **1.** television engineering, TV engineering, television technology, TV technology **2.** video technique
Fernsehteilnehmer *m*
→ Fernsehzuschauer
Fernsehtelefon *n* video telephone, videophone, television telephone
→ Bildschirmtelefon
Fernsehtelefonie *f* video telephony, videophony, television telephony
Fernsehturm *m* television tower, TV tower, *brit* television aerial mast
Fernsehübertragung *f* television transmission, TV transmission
Fernsehunterhaltung *f* television entertainment, TV entertainment
Fernsehveranstaltung *f* television show, TV show, television performance, TV performance, television event, TV event
Fernsehversion *f*
→ Fernsehfassung
Fernsehversorgung *f* television coverage, TV coverage
   The geographical area, or the number or percentage of homes in that area either reached by a station's signal or equipped with television sets.
Fernsehverteilersatellit *m* television distribution satellite, TV distribution satellite
Fernsehwerbung *f* television advertising, TV advertising
Fernsehwettbewerb *m* television contest, TV contest
Fernsehzeitschrift *f* (**Fernseh-Programmzeitschrift** *f*) TV guide, television guide, television magazine, TV magazine
→ Programmzeitschrift
Fernsehzeitung *f*
→ Fernsehzeitschrift, Programmzeitschrift
Fernsehzentrum *n* television center, *brit* television centre
Fernsehzuschauer *m* **1.** television viewer, TV viewer, viewer, *Am* video viewer, televiewer **2.** (Zuschauerschaft) television audience, TV audience
→ Zuschauer, Zuschauerschaft
Fernsehzuschauerforschung *f*
→ Zuschauerforschung
Fernsetzmaschine *f* (*print*) teletype setting machine, teletypesetter
Fernsetzverfahren *n*
→ Fernsatz

Fernsprechbuch n (**Fernsprechteilnehmerverzeichnis** n)
→ Telefonbuch
Fernsprechbuchwerbung f
→ Telefonbuchwerbung
Fernsteuerung f *(electr.)* remote control, telecontrol
fertig gesetzt *attr (typ)* all up
fertiggepackt *adj* (Ware) packaged
Fertigmacher m *(print)* adjuster, *auch* adjustor
Fertigpackung f prepack, prepackage
Fertigwaren f/pl *(econ)* packaged goods *pl*, package goods *pl*
  Merchandise delivered to retailers in some sort of package or container designed for practical handling and display at the point-of-purchase.
Festabonnement n (**Festauftrag** m, **Festbestellung** f, **Festbezug** m) (Zeitung/Zeitschrift) firm order
Festbildkommunikation f (**Festbildübertragung** f) transmission of still picture, still picture transmission *vgl*. Bewegtbildübertragung
Festeinstellung f *(phot)* fixed angle
feste, zahlende Einzelbezieher m/pl (Zeitung/Zeitschrift) paid subscribers *pl*, net paid circulation
Festgröße f
→ Anzeigengröße; *vgl*. Abdruckhöhe
Festhonorar n
→ Pauschale
Festigungswerbung f (**Verstärkungswerbung** f)
→ Erhaltungswerbung
Festival n festival
Festobjektiv n *(phot)* fixed-angle lens, fixed lens
Festplazierung f (**Dauerplazierung** f, **feste Position** f) fixed position, fixed advertising position, fixed location, fixed advertising location, *(radio/TV)* (selbe Stelle, selbe Welle) across the board
  A preferred position, (→) Plazierungsvorschrift, in a periodical publication occupied for advertising by one advertiser for two or more consecutive periods, or a time specified on a radio or television station reserved for a commercial for the duration of the agreement.
Festpreis m *(econ)* fixed price, protected rate, (Mindestpreis) pegged price
  A cost for goods or services which a supplier agrees to maintain for a purchaser, despite later cost increases for other purchasers.
Festpreisabonnement n (Zeitschrift/Zeitung) charter subscription
Festpreisabonnent m (Zeitung/Zeitschrift) charter subscriber
Festzeit f *(radio/TV)* (Rundfunkwerbung) fixed time
fett *adj* **1.** (halbfett) *(typ)* boldface (b.f., bf, B.F., BF), bold face, boldfaced, bold-faced, bold **2.** *(typ)* extra bold, extra-bold, full-faced, full-faced, heavy, thick
  The characteristic of any type face heavier than lightface, (→) mager, giving an overall effect of blackness, heaviness, and boldness. Usage in German is equivocal: formally halbfett is the equivalent for boldface, and fett for extra bold, but fett is widely used as a synonym for halbfett.
3. (fettig) greasy
Fett n grease
Fettdruck m **1.** *(typ)* (halbfett) bold print, boldface print, bold type **2.** extra bold type, full-faced type, full-face print, heavy-faced print
→ fett
Fettfarbe f *(print)* greasy ink
fettfeine Linie f *(typ)* Oxford rule, double rule, Scotch rule
fettgedruckter Punkt m *(typ)* bullet
Fettstift m grease pencil, chinagraphic pencil
Feuchtkopierung f (**Naß-in-Naß-Druck** m) *(phot)* wet printing, wet color printing, wet-on-wet printing, immersion printing
  A printing process for which it is characteristic that successive colors are laid down before the preceding colors are dry.
Feuchtverfahren n *(phot)* wetplate process
Feuilleton n **1.** feuilleton, feature section, feature supplement, literary section **2.** (Einzelbeitrag) feuilleton, feature article, essay
Feuilletonist m (**Feuilletonredakteur** m) feuilletonist, feature writer, feature article writer, literary editor, culture editore, cultural editor, arts feature editor, cultural affairs editor
Feuilletonwerbung f (**feuilletonistische Werbung** f) advertising in short-story style, narratory copy advertising

FFF-Berater

FFF-Berater m **(FFF-Fachmann** m, **FFF-Gestalter** m) etwa film, broadcast and television advertising adviser, screen and broadcast media advertising adviser
FFF-Werbung f advertising in film, broadcast and television media, advertising in screen and broadcast media
FiFo-Prinzip n **(FiFo-Verfahren** n) (econ) fifo, fifo principle, first-in, first out
Figurentrick m **(Sachtrick** m) (Trickfilm) live animation
 A limited-animation technique by which motion is imparted on photographed objects.
Figur-Grund-Differenzierung f (psy) figure-ground discrimination
Figur-Grund-Täuschung f (psy) figure-ground illusion
Filiale f **(Filialbetrieb** m) **1.** (eines Herstellers) manufacturer's sales branch, manufacturer's sales office, manufacturer's store, branch store, branch house, branch office, branch establishment, sales outlet, outlet
 A retail store owned and operated by a manufacturer, sometimes as outlets for his goods, sometimes primarily for experimental or publicity purposes.
2. (eines Handelsunternehmens) retail store, retail outlet, sales outlet, outlet, branch store
 A subsidiary retailing business owned and operated at a separate location by an established store.
3. (einer Handelskette) chain store
 An establishment maintained by a manufacturer, detached from the headquarters establishment and used for the purpose of stocking, selling and delivering his products, or providing service. A subsidiary retailing business owned and operated at a separate location by an established store. One of a group of retail outlets of similar type and under single ownership, (→) Handelskette, each offering a wide variety of merchandise according to local demand.
Filialunternehmen n **(Filialist** m) (econ) (Unternehmen mit Filialbetrieben) branch establishment, multiple-store company, multiple-store enterprise, store chain
 The organization owning and operating chain stores.
Filigranpapier n watermarked paper, laid paper, laid finish
 Paper with watermarked parallel lines made by means of a dandy roll and running at equal distances apart.
Fill-in-Booklet n (direct advstg) fill-in booklet
Fill-in-Brief m (direct advtsg) fill-in letter
 In fluent advertising German, a direct-mail letter to which the salutation and other insertions are added after printing to personalize it.
Film m **1.** (im Photoapparat) film **2.** (Spielfilm) motion picture, picture, movie **3.** (Kino) cinema, cine, colloq the flicks pl, flicker **4.** (Filmmaterial) film stock, stock, film **5.** → Filmbranche **6.** → Filmwesen **7.** → Filmkunst **8.** (Beschichtung) film, coating
 A thin layer on paper, photographic material, lenses, etc. The transparent photographic material chemically coated with a thin layer of light-sensitive silver emulsion to produce images when exposed to lighted subjects.
Filmabtaster m **(FAT) (Filmgeber** m) film scanner, telecine machine, telecine
Filmabtasterraum m **(Filmgeberraum** m) telecine area
Filmabtastung f film scanning, scanning
Filmagentur f **(Werbefilmagentur** f) film studio
 An agency which specializes in arranging the production of movies or commercials.
Filmamateur m film amateur, amateur filmmaker, amateur cinematographer
Filmandruck m **(Filmkopie** f) film print, film copy, proof of (a) film
 A motion picture film reproduction, complete with all visual and audio components, for projection or transmission.
Filmandruckplatte f **(Platine** f) film flat, flat
Filmapparat m
 → Filmkamera
Filmarchitekt m set designer, art director
Filmarchiv n **(Filmothek** f) film library, film archives pl
Filmarchivar m film librarian
Filmatelier n **(Filmstudio** n, **Studio** n, **Filmaufnahmestudio** n) film studio, studio

Filmaufnahme f (**Aufnahme** f)
1. (Vorgang) shooting, filming
2. (Einstellung) film shot, shot, film take, take 3. (Standbild) film still, still, still picture
Filmaufzeichnung f (**FAZ**) electronic film recording (EFR), telerecording, Am kinescope recording, kine, colloq canned drama, film transfer, video recording, transfer
  A television film made from videotape.
Filmaufzeichnungsgerät n electronic film recorder, film recorder, Am kinescope, kine
Filmauslauf m film run-out
Filmausschnitt m film clip, clip, film excerpt, film sequence
  A short section of film footage.
Filmautor m (**Film-Drehbuchautor** m) film author, film script writer, filmwright, screen author, screenwriter, screenplay writer, scenarist, continuity writer
  → Drehbuchautor
Filmband n (**Filmführungsschiene** f) film path
Filmband n film strip, strip of film, film
  A motion picture film composed of a number of still photographs that are shown sequentially.
Filmbearbeitung f film adaptation, filmization, cinematization, cinemazation, screen adaptation
Filmbauten pl
  → Bauten
Filmbehälter m (**Filmdose** f, **Filmbüchse** f) film case, can
Filmbehandlung f (**filmische Behandlung** f) film treatment
Filmbeitrag m film sequence, film item, film inject
Filmbericht m 1. film report, film story 2. (TV) film telecording, video recording, video tape recording (VTR)
Filmbesuch m
  → Kinobesuch
Filmbesucher m
  → Kinobesucher m
Filmbewertung f (**Prädikat** n) film rating, movie rating
Filmbewertungsstelle f film rating board, movie rating board
Filmbild n film image, motion picture, (Einzelbild) frame, film element, element, (Standbild) film still, still

Filmbranche f (**Filmindustrie** f) film business, film industry, motion picture industry, the movies pl, the screen pl, the pictures pl, (die Welt des Films) screenland
Filmbreite f film width
Filmbüchse f
  → Filmbehälter
Filmbüro n film service
Filmcutter(in) m(f) (**Schnittmeister(in)** m(f) film editor, film cutter, film cutter and editor, cutter
  → Cutter
Film-Dia n (**Film-Diapositiv** n, **Kino-Dia** n, **Lauf-Dia** n) cinema slide, film slide, filmslide, cinema slide advertisement, advertising film slide, film strips pl, filmstrips pl, slidefilm
  In motion-picture advertising, (→) Kinowerbung, a film sequence of individual 35 mm frames, shown singly in a special projector and with or without a separate synchronized soundtrack.
Film-Diawerbung f
  → Kino-Diawerbung
Filmdichte f (phot) film density
Filmdrehbuch n film script, motion-picture script, (Drehplan) shooting script, (technisches Drehbuch) continuity
  → Drehbuch
Filmdrehbuchautor m
  → Filmautor, Drehbuchautor
Filmeinblendung f underlay, floater
Filmeinfädelung f (**Einfädeln** n **des Films**) (im Projektor) lacing-up (of the film)
Filmeinlegen n (Kamera) loading, film loading, threading, (Projektor) lacing-up
Filmeinspielung f (**Einspielung** f) film insert, telecine insert
Filmeinzeichnung f (**Schnittmarkierung** f) cutting mark
Film-E-Kamera f
  → Videokamera
Filmemacher m film maker, film-maker, moviemaker
filmen 1. v/t to film, to shoot, to take 2. v/i to be filming, to take shots, to shoot; bei Außenaufnahmen: to be on location
Filmen n filming, shooting
Filmentwickler m Entwickler
Filmerzählung f film narrative, film narration

Filmfassung 178

Filmfassung *f* (**Filmversion** *f*) film version, motion picture version
→ Filmbearbeitung
Filmfenster *n* (**Bildfenster** *n*) film gate, picture window, projection aperture
Filmfestspiel *n* (**Filmfestival** *n*) film festival
Filmformat *n* film size, film gauge, film format
→ Bildformat
Filmfortschaltung *f* film feed, intermittent movement, intermittent meachanism, pulldown movement
Filmfortschaltzeit *f* pulldown time
Filmführung *f* film guide
Filmführungsrolle *f* *(phot)* film take-up spool, take-up spool, take-up sprocket, sprocket
Filmgalgen *m* trims bin
Filmgeber *m*
→ Filmabtaster
Filmgeberraum *m*
→ Filmabtastraum
Filmgelände *n*
→ Aufnahmegelände
Filmgeschäft *n*
→ Filmbranche
Filmgeschwindigkeit *f*
→ Laufgeschwindigkeit
Filmgesellschaft *f* film company, motion-picture company
Filmhersteller *m*
→ Filmemacher, Filmproduzent
Filmherstellung *f*
→ Filmproduktion
Filmhobel *m* film scraper, scraper
Filmholographie *f* cineholography
Filmindustrie *f*
→ Filmbranche
Filminsert *m*
→ Filmeinspielung
filmisch *adj* cinematographic(al), motion-picture
Filmkamera *f* film camera, cinecamera, motion-picture camera, movie camera
Filmkameramann *m*
→ Kameramann
Filmkassette *f* (**Filmmagazin** *n*) film cassette, film cartridge, film magazine
Filmkern *m* film bobbin, film core, hub, center, *brit* centre, core
Filmkitt *m* film cement, splicing cement, joining cement
Filmklappe *f*
→ Klappe

Filmkleben *n* film splicing, film joining
Filmkleber *m* 1. (**Filmklebepresse**) film joiner, joiner, film splicer, splicer 2. (Person) negative cutter, *colloq* neg cutter, (Kleberin) splicing girl
Filmklub *m* (**Filmclub** *m*) film club, cineclub
Filmkomödie *f* film comedy
Filmkonserve *f* canned drama, canned film
Filmkopie *f*
→ Filmandruck
Filmkopierer *m* (**Filmkopiermaschine** *f*) film printer, film printing device
Filmkopierung *f* (**Filmkopieren** *n*) film printing
Filmkopierwerk *n*
→ Kopierwerk
Filmkorn *n* film grain
→ Korn
Filmkritik *f* film review, film criticism
Filmkritiker *m* film critic
Filmkunde *f* filmology
Filmkunst *f* cinematography, cinematics pl *(construed as sg)*
Filmkunsttheater *n* art cinema, *Am* art house
Filmlabor *n* film laboratory
Filmladekassette *f*
→ Filmkassette
Filmlager *n* film stock
Filmlagerung *f* film storage
Filmlänge *f* film footage, footage, (Spieldauer) film duration, duration, running time
Filmlängenmeßuhr *f* (**Filmzähler** *m*) footage counter, film counter, frame counter, film footage counter
Filmlauf *m* film run, film travel, (kontinuierlicher Filmlauf) continuous run
Filmlaufgeschwindigkeit *f* (**Filmlaufzeit** *f*)
→ Aufnahmegeschwindigkeit, Projektionsgeschwindigkeit
Filmleinwand *f* projection screen, screen, film screen, cinema screen, motion-picture screen, movie-theater screen
Filmlet *n* filmlet, minute movie, short film
→ Kurzfilm

Filmliebhaber m **(Filmfan** m, **Cinemast** m, **Kinofan** m) cinephile, cineast
Filmlustspiel n
→ Filmkomödie
Filmmagazin n 1. → Filmkassette 2. → Filmzeitschrift
Filmmaß n film dimension
Filmmaterial n film stock, raw stock, (belichtet) film material
Film-Mattiermaschine f film-polishing machine
Filmmeßgerät n **(FEM)** film sensitometer
Filmmontage f *(print)* film stripping, stripping, stripping in, montage
 The process of mounting a photographic negative, or a piece of camera-ready copy on a sheet containing similar material before they are reproduced on a printing plate.
Filmmusik f screen music, film music, movie music
Filmnachrichten f/pl (im Kino) newsreel, newsfilm
Filmnegativ n
→ Negativ
Filmologie f
→ Filmkunde
Filmothek f **(Filmesammlung** f)
→ Filmarchiv
Filmpack m **(Packfilm** m) *(phot)* pack of films, film pack
Filmpalast m motion-picture palace, *brit* super-cinema
Filmpatrone f film chamber
→ Filmkassette
Filmperforation f **(Perforationslinie** f) film perforation, perforation
Filmplakat n **(Kinoplakat** n) cinema poster, film poster, movie poster
Filmpoliermaschine f film-polishing machine
Filmprädikat n movie rating
→ Filmbewertung
Filmpreis m film award, movie award
Filmpremiere f
→ Erstaufführung
Filmpresse f **(Filmfachpresse** f) film-trade press
Filmprobe f film test strip
Filmproduktion f film production
Filmproduzent m film producer, producer, moviemaker, movie producer
Filmprogramm n
→ Kinoprogramm

Filmprojektion f film projection, motion-picture projection, cineprojection
Filmprojektor m film projector, motion-picture projector, movie projector, cineprojector
Filmpublikum n
→ Kinopublikum
Filmraster m
→ Raster
Filmrauschen n
→ Rauschen
Filmrechte n/pl film rights pl, movie rights pl, motion picture rights pl
Filmregie f film direction, screen direction
Filmregisseur m film director, screen director
Filmreklame f
→ Filmwerbung
Filmriß m break, tear
Filmrolle f 1. (Kamera) roll of film, film roll, roll 2. (beim Kleinbildfilm) film spool 3. (Projektor) reel film reel 4. (eines Schauspielers) part, film part, role
Filmsalat m (in der Kamera) camera buckle, film jam, *colloq* pile-up, spaghetti, (Projektor) *colloq* rip-up
Filmschauspieler(in) m(f) screen actor (actress), motion-picture actor (actress), movie actor (actress)
Filmscheinwerfer m **(Fernsehschein-werfer** m) broad
Filmschleife f **(Filmschlaufe** f) (Projektor) film loop, loop
 A piece of motion picture film spliced end to end for continuous, unending projection.
Filmschneidegerät n film editing machine, film cutting machine
Filmschneidetisch m
→ Schneidetisch
Filmschnitt m **(Filmschneiden** n, **Lichtschnitt** m, **Cutten** n) film editing, film cutting and editing
→ Schnitt
Filmschrank m film cabinet, film-storage cabinet
Filmschritt m
→ Bildschritt
Filmschrumpfung f
→ Schrumpfung
Filmsprecher m narrator
Filmspule f
→ Filmrolle 1., 2., 3.

Filmstanzung

Filmstanzung f
→ Stanzverfahren
Filmstar m (**Filmstern** m) film star, screen star, movie star, motion-picture star
Filmsternchen n starlet, film starlet, movie starlet, screen starlet, motion-picture starlet
Filmstreifen n (**Bildstreifen** m, **Stehfilm** m) cinestrip, film strip, film, (beim Filmschnitt) reel, Am trailer
Filmstudio n 1. film studio, motion-picture studio, movie studio
 A studio in which motion picture films are recorded.
 2. → Studiofilmtheater
Filmsynchronisation f (**Filmsynchronisierung** f)
→ Synchronisation
Filmszene f scene, film scene, (Einstellung) take
Filmtechnik f filming technique, shooting technique
Filmtext m narrative, commentary, script
Filmtheater n
→ Lichtspieltheater
Filmtheaterbesuch m
→ Kinobesuch
Filmtheaterkategorie f movie-theater category, type of cinema, picture theater category, type of movie theater, type of motion picture theater
→ Action-Kino, City-Kino, Familientheater, Filmkunstkino, Studiotheater, Programmkino, Autokino, Truppenkino, Sex- und Pornokino
Filmtheaterwerbung f
→ Filmwerbung, Kinowerbung
Filmtitel m film title, motion-picture title, movie title
Filmton m (**Lichtton** m) sound on film (S.O.F.), sound track
 The audio portion of a film or a video tape.
Filmträger m (**Filmunterlage** f) film support, film carrier, film base, backing film
Filmtransport m 1. (Vorgang) film transport, film winding, pulldown, film travel, film advance, film drive
2. (Mechanismus) film transport mechanism, film transport, film winding mechanism

180

Filmtransportrolle f (**Filmtransporttrommel** f) film-feed sprocket, feed sprocket, sprocket
Filmtrupp m camera crew
Filmübertragung f (**Filmüberspielung** f) (TV) film pickup, pickup, brit film pick-up
Filmübertragungsanlage f telecine(TK)
Filmumroller m film rewind
Film- und Diapositivwerbung f
→ Filmwerbung, Kinowerbung
Filmunterlage f
→ Filmträger
Filmveranstaltung f
→ Filmvorführung
Filmverleih m 1. (Verleihvorgang) film distribution 2. (Verleihfirma) film distributor, film distributing company, film distributors pl
Filmverleiher m
→ Filmverleih 2.
Filmversion f
→ Filmfassung
Filmvertrieb n
→ Filmverleih
Filmvorführapparat m
→ Filmvorführgerät
Filmvorführer m film projectionist, projectionist, cinematographer, cinema operator
Filmvorführgerät n (**Filmvorführapparat** m) action-picture projector, film projector, cinematograph
→ Filmprojektor
Filmvorführraum m film booth, projection booth
Filmvorführung f (**Filmvorstellung** f, **Kinovorstellung** f) film performance, film projection, film screening, cinema performance, movie performance, motion-picture performance, picture show, movie house show
Filmvorführraum m film booth, projection booth
Filmvorführung f (**Filmvorstellung** f, **Kinovorstellung** f) film performance, film projection, film screening, cinema performance, movie performance, motion-picture performance, picture show, movie house show
Filmvorführwagen m cinemobile, cinema van
Filmvorschau f film preview

Filmvorspann m **(Vorspanntitel** m**)** opening titles pl, titles, opening credits pl, opening captions pl, (Startband) leader, head leader, (standardisiert) Am Academy leader
Filmvorstellung f
→ Filmvorführung, Kinovorstellung
Filmwagen m
→ Kamerawagen
Filmwerbespot m
→ Kinowerbespot
Filmwerbung f **(Film- und Diawerbung** f, **Kinowerbung** f**)** 1. (Werbemittel) cinema advertisement, cinema ad, cinema announcement, film commercial, screen advertisement, movie-theater advertisement, theater-screen advertisement 2. (Reklame) cinema advertising, screen advertising, film advertising, film commercial advertising, in-theater advertising, theater advertising, theater-screen advertising
Filmwesen n the movies pl, the screens pl, (die Welt des Films) screenland, the film world, filmland, filmdom, screendom, movieland, colloq the flicks pl, the flickers pl
Filmwirtschaft f
→ Filmbranche
Filmwochenschau f
→ Filmnachrichten
Filmzähler m
→ Filmlängenmeßuhr
Filmzeitschrift f film magazine, cinema magazine, movie magazine, screen magazine
Filmzuschauer m
→ Kinopublikum
Filmzuschauerschaftsforschung f
→ Kinopublikumsforschung
Filter m 1. (optisch/akustisch) filter
  A device to simulate a voice over the telephone or a public address system. In the production of color plates, a transparent device that absorbs certain colors and permits transmission of other. In photography, a disc or square of colored glass or colored gelatin, used to affect the tonal rendering of colored objects in a black and white photograph. Used with an orthochromatic or panchromatic film, the filter will darken the rendering of objects of a complementary color. Thus, a yellow filter will darken the rendering of a blue sky, heightening the contrast between sky and clouds.
2. (media res) filter, filter question, screen, hurdle question
  A question process, usually short, used to determine whether respondents or households have certain characteristics that would make them eligible for a full-scale interview. Also a question asked to determine which, if any, subsequent questions will be asked.
Filterband n **Kopierfilterband** n**)** (film) (Kopiermaschine) printer charge-band
Filtereingang m (film) filter input, (Kamera) filter slot
Filterfaktor m (phot) filter factor, filter coefficient
Filterfolie f **(Kopierfilter** m**)** (phot) filter foil
Filterfrage f (survey res) filter question, hurdle question
Filterhalter m **(Filterhalterung** f**)** (phot) filter holder
Filterinterview n (survey res) filter interview, screening interview
Filterkreuzschiene f (TV) video matrix
Filtermikrophon n **(Filtermikrofon** n**)** filter microphone, filter mike
  A microphone modified to produce certain sound effects, such as the simulated sound of a telephone voice.
filtern v/t to filter
Filternetz n filter network
Filterphase f **(Screeningphase** f**)** (survey res) screening stage, screening phase
→ Filter 2.
Filterrad n **(Filterrevolver** m**)** filter wheel, filter turret
Filterrahmen m filter frame
Filterrand m filter border
Filterschicht f filter layer
Filz m 1. (paper) felt 2. → Bierfilz
Filzpapier n felt finish, felt finish paper
  A rough textured antique paper, (→) Antikdruckpapier, with a surface of an unusual character.
Filzröllchen n (print) felt roller
Filzscheibe f (print) felt mat, felt washer
Filzseite f **(Schönseite** f**)** (print) felt side
  The top side of the sheet when manufacturing, the correct side for printing.
vgl. Siebseite
Finanzanzeige f financial advertisement, financial ad

Finanzjahr

Finanzjahr n
→ Haushaltsjahr
Finanzmarketing n 1. finance marketing 2.
→ Bankmarketing
Finanzmarktforschung f finance market marketing research, marketing research on the finance market
finanzmittelbezogene Werbebudgetierung f affordable method, all-you-can-afford method, affordable budgeting method, what-can-be-afforded method
A method of advertising budget determination in which an advertiser allocates to advertising whatever money is left after all fixed and necessary expenses have been allotted money and a predetermined profit level has been established.
Finanzwerbung f finance advertising, financial advertising
The advertising efforts undertaken by organizations or companies, such as banks, insurance, unit trusts, building societies, etc., who are inolved in financial markets.
→ Bankenwerbung
Fingerabdruckmethode f **(Fingerabdruckverfahren** n**)**
→ daktyloskopische Methode
firmenbetonte Werbung f
→ Firmenwerbung
Firmenbild n
→ Firmenimage
firmeneigene Werbeagentur f
→ Hausagentur
Firmeneindruck m **(Firmenaufdruck** m**)**
→ Händlereindruck
Firmenimage n **(Corporate Image** n**)**
corporate image (C.I.)
→ Unternehmensimage
Firmenimage-Werbemittel n
corporate advertisement
Firmenimagewerbung f corporate image advertising, institutional advertising
→ Unternehmensimagewerbung, Unternehmenswerbung
Firmenmarkt m
→ akquisitorisches Potential
Firmenphilosophie f
→ Unternehmensphilosophie
Firmenschild n nameplate, signboard, facia, shingle
Firmenstil m
→ Werbestil

Firmen-Vertrauenswerbung f
patronage institution advertising
→ Unternehmens-Vertrauenswerbung
Firmenvertreter m
→ Handelsreisender
Firmenwerbung f **(firmenbetonte Werbung** f**)** institutional advertising, corporate advertising
→ Unternehmenswerbung
Firmenwert m **(Geschäftswert** m**)**
goodwill (of a company)
That part of a company's value that reflects its reputation, image, and established market connections, all of which form that portion of its purchase price, in the case of a sale, that is not accounted for by its total net assets.
Firmenzeichen n **(Firmensignet** n**)**
company signature, signature, company logo, logotype, logograph
The standard name or signature plate of a company.
Firmenzeitschrift f
→ Kundenzeitschrift
Fisch m *(print)*
→ Zwiebelfisch
Fischauge n *(phot)* fish-eye lens
Fishbein-BI-Modell n **(Fishbein-Ajzen-Modell** n**)** *(market res)*
Fishbein BI model, Fishbein behavioral intention model, Fishbein-Ajzen model (M. Fishbein/J. Ajzen)
Fishbein-Modell n *(market res)*
Fishbein model (M. Fishbein)
Fisher-Yates-Test m **(exakter Test** m**, von Fisher, exakter χ^2-Test** m**)** *(stat)*
Fisher-Yates test, Fisher's exact test, Fisher exact probability test
A test of independence for frequency data arranged in a fourfold table, (→) Vierfeldertafel, used for small samples for which the chi-squared test of independence, (→) Chi-Quadrat-Test, cannot be applied. The test statistic is:

$$P = \frac{(a + b)!(c + d)!(a + c)!(b + d)!}{n!a!b!c!d!}$$

where a,b,c,d are the cell frequencies, and n is the total number of observations.
Fishers F-Verteilung f
→ F-Verteilung
Fishers z-Transformation f
→ z-Transformation
Fishers z-Verteilung f *(stat)* Fisher's z distribution, z distribution
Fixfokus-Objektiv n **(Fixfokus** m**)**
(phot) fixed focus, fixed-focus lens
Fixfokuskamera f *(phot)* fixed-focus camera

Fixierentwicklung f
→ Einbad-Entwicklung
Fixierlösung f **(Fixiermittel** n**)** *(phot)* fixing agent, fixer
Fixiernatron n *(phot)* sodium thiosulphate, *auch* thiosulflate, hypo
Fixiersalz n *(phot)* fixing salt, fixative salt
Fixiertank m *(phot)* fixing tank
Fixierung f
→ Fixieren
Fixkosten pl *(econ)* fixed cost(s) *(pl)*
   That portion of a company's total costs that remains the same, regardless of business volume or production level.
FKM f *abbr* Gesellschaft zur freiwilligen Kontrolle von Messe- und Ausstellungszahlen
Flachbettbuchdruck m **1.** (Produkt) flatbed letterpress print, flatbed print **2.** (Verfahren) flatbed letterpress printing, flatbed printing
   A letterpress printing technique, (→) Buchdruck (Hochdruck), with a printing press with a flat base on which the page forms are locked, and ink and paper are conveyed to the type form by rollers.
Flachdruck m **1.** (Produkt) planographic print, planograph, lithoprint, offset print **2.** (Verfahren) planographic printing, flat printing, lithographic printing, lithoprinting, planography, offset printing
   Any printing from a plane surface, wheter direct or offset.
vgl. Hochdruck (Buchdruck)
Fläche f **1.** area, surface **2.** *(print)* face
   That part of the type that makes the impression.
3. (Licht) *colloq* broad
flache Beleuchtung f *(film/phot/TV)* flat lighting
Flächenantenne f *(radio)* flattop antenna, sheet antenna, *brit* flat-top aerial, sheet aerial
Flächenauswahl f
1. → Flächenstichprobe
2. → Flächenauswahlverfahren
Flächenauswahlverfahren n **(Flächenauswahl** f, **Bildung** f **von Flächenstichproben)** *(stat)* area sampling, area sampling procedure, block sampling, *selten* areola sampling
   A probability sampling technique, (→) Wahrscheinlichkeitsauswahl, which divides the total geographical area under study into a number of smaller areas, and then uses random selection,

(→) Zufallsauswahl, usually a random-route technique, (→) Random-Walk, to determine the specific areas or specific respondents to be interviewed. Area sampling is a special case of cluster sampling, (→) Klumpenauswahl.
Flächendiagramm n **(Flächengraphik** f**)** *(stat)* area diagram, area chart, area graph
   A form of graphic respresentation, (→) graphische Darstellung, where the areas are proportional to frequencies or quantities.
Flächendruck m
→ Reliefdruck
Flächengewicht n *(paper)* area weight, basic weight, basis weight, substance number
Flächenleuchte f *(film/phot/TV)* bank of lamps, soft source
Flächenhistogramm n *(stat)* area histogram
Flächenstichprobe f **(Flächenauswahl** f**)** *(stat)* area sample
→ Flächenauswahlverfahren
Flächenstichprobenverfahren n
→ Flächenauswahlverfahren
flachgeätzte Autotype f **(flachgeätzte Strichätzung** f**)** *(print)* flat plate, shallow halftone block, shallow plate, shallow-etched plate
   An etched, but not re-etched or finished halftone
Flachheftung f *(binding)* flat stitching
Flachkabel n *(electr)* twin lead, ribbon feeder
Flachrelief n *(print)* low relief, bas-relief
Flachstereo n *(print)* flat stereotype, flat stereo
flackern v/i *(film/TV)* to flicker, to flutter, to jitter
Flackern n *(film/TV)* flicker, flutter, jitter
Flaggschiff n **(Flaggschiffprodukt** n**)** *(econ)* flagship, flagship product
flankierende Werbung f **(akzidentelle Werbung** f, **Extensivwerbung** f**)** complementary advertising, accessory advertising, collateral advertising
   In general, any advertising that is not the focus of a specific campaign, e.g. advertising in print media when the focus of a campaign is on television commercials. More specifically, below-the-line advertising with noncommissionable collateral materials, such as brochures, letters, broadsides, staffers, premiums, sales sheets, etc.

Flaschenanhänger *m* (**Flaschenaufhänger** *m*) *(POP advtsg)* (als Werbemittel) bottle hanger, *colloq* bottle glorifier
A paper or cardboard advertisement hung around the neck of a bottle.

Flaschenaufsatz *m* (**Flaschenaufstecker** *m*) *(POP advtsg)* (als Werbemittel) bottle topper, *colloq* bottle glorifier
An advertising display designed to fit on a bottle.

Flaschenkragen *m* (**Flaschenkrause** *f*, **Flaschenring** *m*) *(POP advtsg)* (als Werbemittel) bottle collar, *colloq* bottle glorifier
A cardboard display designed to fit around the neck of a bottle and to carry an advertising message.

Flattermarke *f (print)* collation mark, collation mark, back mark

Flattersatz *m (typ)* unjustified style, unjustified matter, ragged type
Arranging the spacing between letters and words in such a way that all spaces are equal, so that the right-hand edge of the column is not flush, while the left-hand edge is.

flau *adj(phot)* (kontrastarm) flat, weak, low-contrast

Flauheit *f (phot)* (Kontrastarmut) flatness, low contrast

Fleck *m* (**Schmutzfleck** *m*) *(print)* stain, blot, spot, blur, mottle

Fleisch *n (typ)* (Achselfläche der Type) shoulder, shoulder of type, beard, beard of type
The beveled space below the face of a type.

Flexformanzeige *f* (**Flexform** *f*) flexform advertisement, flexform ad, bastard size advertisement, bastard size ad, bastard size, special shape advertisement, spezial shape ad

flexibel *adj* flexible

Flexibilität *f* flexibility

Flexichromie *f (phot)*
1. (Flexichromphoto) flexichrome
2. (Flexichromieverfahren) flexichrome process
A process, similar to color toning, for converting a black and white photograph into a color photo by hand coloring.

Flexodruck *m* (**Gummidruck** *m*)
1. (Produkt) flexographic print, aniline print 2. (Verfahren) flexography, flexographic printing, aniline printing
→ Anilindruck

Fliegenkopf *m* (**Blockade** *f*) *(typ)* turned letters *pl*, turn

Fließsatz *m* (**glatter Satz** *m*) *(typ)* solid matter, set solid

Fließsatzanzeige *f* (**reine Textanzeige** *f*) all-copy advertisement, all-copy ad, solid matter advertisement, solid-matter ad, undisplay advertisement, undisplay ad, *contempt* tombstone advertisement, tombstone ad
An advertisement in a newspaper or magazine that uses small print only without any display type or artwork.

Fließsatzanzeigenwerbung *f* all-copy advertising, solid-matter advertising, undisplay advertising, *contempt* tombstone advertising

Flimmerkasten *m* (**Flimmerkiste** *f*)
→ Glotze

flimmern *v/i (film/TV)* to flicker, to sparkle

Flimmern *n (film/TV)* flicker, flickering

Flop *m (econ)* flop

Floprate *f (econ)* flop rate

flüchtiger Leser *m (media res)* inlooker

Flugblatt *n* (**Handzettel** *m*, **Werbezettel** *m*) handbill, leaflet, flyer, flier, fly sheet, dodger, giveaway, throwaway
A promotional sheet handed out to shoppers on the street, in the store, or in a shopping center.

Flügelblende *f* (**Sektorenblende** *f*) *(phot)* rotary disc shuter, rotating shutter

Flughafenwerbung *f* airport advertising

Fluglinienwerbung *f* airline advertising

Flugzettel *m*
→ Flugblatt

Flugzeugwerbung *f* (**Flugzeugreklame** *f*)
→ Luftwerbung

Fluktuation *f* **1.** *(econ)* fluctuation, turnover
The measure of the staff mobility in an organization.

2. *(audience res)* turnover
The ratio of a cumulative audience over several periods of time (e.g., four weeks) to the average audience per period of time (e.g., per week). This ratio serves as an indication of the relative frequency with which the audience of a program, or of a station, changes over a period of time. The greater the turnover in audience, the higher is the ratio.
3. *(survey res)* panel turnover
Fluktuationsbereitschaft f
→ Markenwechsel
Fluktuationstabelle f *(panel res)* turnover table
Fluktuationsuntersuchung f **(Fluktuationsstudie** f**)** *(survey res)* turnover investigation, turnover study
→ Flußstudie
Fluoreszenz f *(phot)* fluorescence
Fluoreszenzlampe f *(phot)* fluorescent lamp, *Am* fluorescent tube
Flußdiagramm n **(Ablaufdiagramm** n**)** *(stat/econ)* flow chart, flow diagram
The graphical presentation of turnover in a flow study, (→) Flußstudie, or of stages in a critical path procedure.
Flüssigkeitsblende f *(phot)* fluid iris
Flüssigkeitsentwicklung f *(phot)* wet processing
Flüssigkeits-Kopierfenster n *(phot)* liquid gate
Flüssigkeitsmengenmesser m *(phot)* flowmeter, liquid meter
Flußkarte f *(econ/stat)* flow map
Flußmatrix f **(Ablaufmatrix** f**)** *(stat/econ)* flow matrix
Flußstudie f *(stat/econ)* flow study, flow investigation, *(media res)* (Zuschauer-, Hörerflußstudie) audience flow study, audience flow investigation
In economics and statistics, the graphical presentation of the logical sequence of events in the form of a diagram, in which the stages are connected in a flow sequence. In broadcasting research, the graphical presentation of household audience "carry-over" between programs aired in successive time periods on the same network. Audience flow is an important factor in program scheduling, since the number of viewers a program inherits from its lead-in show often means the difference between success and failure.
Flüsterkampagne f whispering campaign
Flüsterpropaganda f whispering propaganda

Flutlicht n **(Fluter** m**)** *(phot/film/TV)* floodlight, floodlamp, flood, scoop, photoflood
A cameraman's light, able to illuminate a wide area. It is a form of electric light bulb run from a voltage high enough to cause it to give out a very bright light, but with a greatly reduced lifte.
Flutlichtscheinwerfer m *(phot/film/ TV)* floodlight projector, floodlight
Flying-Spot-Abtaster m
→ Punktlichtabtaster
FMA f *abbr* Funkmedien-Analyse
Fokus m **(Brennpunkt** m**)** *(phot)* focus, focal point
Fokusdifferenz f *(phot)* depth of focus, depth of field
→ Schärfentiefe (Tiefenschärfe)
fokussieren v/t *(phot)* to focus
To adjust the lens in a camera so as to sharpen the image.
→ einstellen
Fokussierung f **(Fokussieren** n**)** *(phot)* focusing
The adjustment of the lens in a camera so as to give a sharp rendering of the subject on the film. It is usually done by moving the lens towards or away from the film, depending upon whether the subject is far or near.
Folder m folder
Foldertest m **(Foldertestverfahren** n**)** *(media res)* folder test, folder test technique, folder technique, portfolio test portfolio technique
A field research technique, in which a sample of respondents in a copy test, (→) Copy-Test, or advertising pretest are shown alternative advertisement or mastheads of periodical publications presented in a little folder.
Folge f **1.** (Aufeinanderfolge) sequence, succession **2.** (Reihenfolge) order, sequence **3.** (Serie, Reihe) series **4.** (Fortsetzung) continuation, installment, instalment, sequel **5.** (Lieferung, Heft) number, issue, sequel
Folgeanzeige f
→ Anschlußanzeige
Folgeauftrag m **(Anschlußauftrag** m**)** follow-on order, follow-up order
Folgebedarf m *(econ)* etwa follow-up and replacement demand
→ Erneuerungsbedarf
Folgebedürfnis n *(econ)* etwa follow-up and replacement need
Folgefrequenz f repetition frequency

Folgeleser *m*
→ Zweitleser
Folgeprogramm *n* (**Folgesendung** *f*)
→ Nachfolgeprogramm
Folgerecht *n* (**Folgeschutzrecht** *n*)
consequential right, droit de suite
Folgeschaltung *f* sequence control, sequence operation
Folgeware *f* (Bruno Tietz)
→ Erneuerungsbedarf; *vgl.* Grundware
Folie *f* foil, leaf, sheet, sheeting, film
→ Plastikfolie
Folienblende *f (phot)* silver-foil reflector
Folienfilter *m*
→ Gelatinefilter
Folienschlag *m* (**Folienpackung** *f*) *(packaging)* film wrap
folienkaschiert *adj*
→ glanzfolienkaschiert
Folienraster *m*
→ Rasterfolie
foliieren *v/t (print)* to folio, to foliate
Follow up *m*
→ Nachfaßaktion
Fond *m*
→ Hintergrund
Foodwerbung *f*
→ Lebensmittelwerbung
fördern *v/t* (finanziell unterstützen) to sponsor, to patronize
forensische Marktforschung *f etwa* survey research in court procedures, forensic market research
Form *f* shape, form, format
→ Druckform
Format *n* 1. size, format, gauge, dimension
    The size, shape, style, and appearance of a publication, printed page, or advertisement.
2. *(print)* form, *brit* forme
    A metal square chase into which the type to be used on a particular page is placed.
3. → Bildschirmformat
Format ändern *v/t (print)* (Anzeige, Druckvorlage) to rescale, to resize
    To redesign and proportion an advertisement to fit into a larger or smaller space.
Formatänderung *f* (**Formatändern** *n*) *(print)* rescale, rescaling, resizing, scaling
    The production of an advertisement in various sizes for different units of space.

Formatanzeige *f* (**Eckanzeige** *f*) position ad, full position advertisement, full
    A special preferred position for a newspaper advertisement, either next and following reading matter, or top of column next to reading matter.
Formatberechnung *f*
→ Satzumfangsberechnung
Formatblende *f*
→ Kaschblende
Format machen *v/t (print)* to impose, to gauge (the form), to make up the margin
    The arrangement of pages in a form, (→) Druckform, for printing.
Formatmarkierung *f (phot/print)* dimension mark
    Dimension marks are points indicated on an original outside image area to be reproduced, between which the size of reproduction is marked and focusing is performed.
Formbett *n* (**Druckformbett** *n*) *(print)* type bed, plate base, plate bed, bed
    A metal plate for supporting and registering unmounted printing plates while taking proofs therefrom.
Formenanalyse *f*
→ Inhaltsanalyse
Formgebung *f* (**industrielle Formgebung** *f*)
→ Design
Formgebungstest *m*
→ Produktgestaltung
Formgestalter *m*
→ Industriedesigner
Formgestaltung *f*
→ Industriedesign
Formsatz *m (typ)* run-around type, run-around
    A block of type that is set to less than full measure, (→) volle Spaltenbreite, around an odd-measure cut in order to leave space for an illustration, or a large initial, and the like.
Formschließen *n* (**Schließen** *n* der **Druckform**) *(print)* lockup, *brit* lock-up, locking up
    The process of locking type matter and cuts into a rigid form for printing, matting, or electrotyping.
Formschließer *m (print)* lockup man, lock-up man, stone hand, stone man, stonehand, stoneman
Formular *n* form, printed form, blank, blank form
Formzylinder *m*
→ Zylinder

forschen *v/i* to research
Forscher *m* researcher
Forschung *f* research
Forschung *f* **und Entwicklung** *f (econ)* research and development (R & D)
Forschungs- und Entwicklungsabteilung *f (econ)* research and development department, research and development, R & D department, R & D
Forschungsbericht *m* (**Bericht** *m*) research report, report
Fortdruck *m (print)* run-on, offprint vgl. Auflagendruck
fortdrucken *(print) v/t* to run off, to run on
Fortdruckkosten *pl (print)* run-on cost
Fortführungswerbung *f* (Karl Christian Behrens) follow-up advertising, continuation advertising, expansion advertising
  Any advertising activities subsequent to the introductory campaign, cf. (→) Einführungswerbung, for a new product or service.
fortgesetzt *attr* continued, cont'd; (Fortsetzung folgt) to be continued, cont'd
fortlassen *v/t*
→ weglassen
fortlaufend gesetzt *adj (typ)* run-on, run-in
  A piece of copy that is set without beginning a new paragraph and as an immediate continuation of the preceding copy.
Fortschreibung *f* (**Fortschreibungsmittel** *n*)
→ Extrapolation, Trendextrapolation
Fortschritts- und Systemvergleich *m* (**Fortschrittsvergleich** *m*)
→ Systemvergleich
fortsetzen *v/t* to continue
Fortsetzung *f* continuation, (eines Textes) installment, instalment, sequel, part, continuation
Fortsetzungsanzeige *f* follow-on, advertisement, follow-on ad, continuity series
Fortsetzungsauftrag *m (econ)* continuation order, standing order (S.O.), follow-up order
  An order to supply a specified quantity of merchandise or advertising space or time till forbid (T.F.) as available or at regular intervals.

Fortsetzungsgeschichte *f* serialized story, serial story
Fortsetzungslieferung *f* (**Nachlieferung** *f*) follow-up delivery
Fortsetzungsrabatt *m* continuing discount, continuity discount
  A discount that is granted for advertisements that are run for an extended period of time or have a heavy schedule during a limited period of time.
Fortsetzungsreihe *f* (**Fortsetzungsserie** *f*) serial, serialized article, serialized articles *pl*
Fortsetzungsroman *m* serialized novel, serial novel, novel in installments, instalments
Foto *n*
→ Photo
Foto-
→ Photo-
Fourieranalyse *f*
→ Spektralanalyse
Frage *f (survey res)* question
Frage *f* **mit Antwortvorgabe** *(survey res)*
→ Vorgabefrage
Frage *f* **nach dem letzten Lesen (nach dem letzten Kontakt)** *(media res)* recency question, recent reading question
  A method of readership measurement that contends that the audience of an average issue of a publication can be measured by establishing through a survey question ("When did you last read or leaf through...?") how many people have read or paged through the publication in a time interval, equal to the publishing interval, (→) Erscheinungsintervall, by measuring the lapsed time between the last reading event and the day of the interview.
Frage- und Antwortspiel *n* (in einem Werbemittel) question and answer (q and a, q & a)
  A popular technique of using dialogs in advertising copy, in which consumers ask questions which advertisers or spokesmen answer.
Frageart *f* (**Fragetyp** *m*) *(survey res)* type of question
Fragebogen *m* (**Erhebungsbogen** *m*) *(survey res)* questionnaire, *ungebr* questionary, opinionaire
  The complete data collection instrument used by an interviewer and/or respondent during a survey. It includes not only the questions and space for answers but also interviewer instructions, the introduction, and cards

Fragebogen

used by the respondent. Traditionally, the questionnaire has been printed, but more recently nonpaper versions are being used on computer terminals.
Fragebogen m **für schriftliche Befragungen** *(survey res)* self-administered questionnaire, self-completion questionnaire
   A questionnaire which is completed by respondents and not by interviewers, as is the rule in survey research.
Fragebogenaufbau m **(Fragenbogenkonstruktion** f**)** *(survey res)* questionnaire construction, questionnaire design
Fragebogeninterview n *(survey res)* questionnaire interview
 → standardisiertes Interview
Fragenbogenitem m *(survey res)* questionnaire item
Fragebogenrücklauf m **(Rücklauf** m **bei schriftlichen Befragungen)** *(survey res)* questionnaire return, (Rücklaufquote) questionnaire return rate, return rate
 → Rücklaufquote
Fragefehler m
 → Interviewfehler
Frageform f
 → Frageart
Frageformulierung f **(Fragenformulierung** f**)** *(survey res)* wording of question, question wording
Fragen-Reihenfolge f
 → Reihenfolgeeffekt
Franchise f **(Franchise-System** n**, Franchising** n**)** *(econ)* franchising, franchise system
   A special form of exclusive distribution, (→) Alleinvertrieb, which consists in an arrangement whereby an organization (franchisor) which has developed a successful retail product or service extends to another organization (franchisee) for a fee the right to engage in the business, provided they agree to follow the established pattern.
Franchise-Circulation f
 → Privilegvertrieb
Franchisegeber m *(econ)* franchisor
 → Franchise
Franchisenehmer m *(econ)* franchisee
 → Franchise
fräsen *(print)* v/t to rout, to mill
 → ausfräsen

Fräsmaschine f *(print)* routing machine, router, milling machine, miller, cutting machine
   A device used to cut away surplus metal from printing plates.
Frauenbeilage f womens's supplement, women's service supplement, ladies' supplement
Frauenblatt n
 → Frauenzeitschrift
Frauenfunk m *(radio/TV)* women's service broadcasting, women's service program
Frauenpresse f women's publications pl, women's service programm
Frauenpresse f women's publications pl, women's magazines pl, women's service publications pl, women's service magazines pl
Frauenseite f women's page, women's service page
Frauenzeitschrift f women's magazine, women's service magazine, ladies magazine, service magazine, *colloq* women's service book
   A magazine the editorial focus of which is largely concentrated on the interests of homemakers and women in general.
Freeze m
 → Standbild
frei verfügbares Einkommen n **(verfügbares Einkommen** n**)** *(econ)* disposable income, discretionary income
 → disponibles Einkommen
Freiabonnement n **(Freistücke** n/pl, **Freieinweisung** f, **Gratisabonnement** n**)** (Zeitung/Zeitschrift) complimentary subscription, free subscription, free copies pl
Freianschlag m **(Gratisanschlag** m**)** *(outdoor advtsg)* free posting
Freianschlagstelle f **(Gratisanschlagstelle** f**)** *(outdoor advtsg)* free billboard, free poster panel
Freibrufler m freelancer, freelance
   A self-employed person, e.g. an independent artist, journalist, writer, etc., whose services can be contracted for on a single assignment.
freiberuflich adj freelance
freiberuflicher Graphiker m **(freischaffender Künstler** m**)** freelance artist
 → Freiberufler
freie Benutzung f
 → gemeinfreie Werke

freie Marktwirtschaft *f (econ)* free market economy, free-enterprise economy
freie Plazierung *f* **(ohne Plazierungsvorschrift** *f***)** (Anzeige in einer Zeitung) run-of-paper position, run-of-paper, ROP, R.O.P., ROP position, R.O.P. position, run-of-press position, run-of-press, (Anzeige in einer Zeitschrift) run-of-book position, run-of-the-book position, run-of-book, run-of-the-book, ROB, R.O.B., ROB position, R.O.B. position, (Radio/Fernsehen) (ohne Vereinbarung über die Sendezeit) run-of-schedule, run-of-station, ROS., R.O.S., (freie Plazierung im Jahresverlauf) run-of-year, R.O.Y., ROY, (freie Plazierung im Laufe des Monats) run-of-month, R.O.M., ROM, (freie Plazierung im Laufe der Woche) run-of-week, ROW, R.O.W., (freie Plazierung im Laufe des Tages) run-of-day, ROD, R.O.D.
  Any arrangement between an advertiser and an advertising medium whereby the exact position of an advertisement is at the medium's discretion.
freies Gespräch *n* **(freies Interview** *n***)**
→ Gruppendiskussion, Intensivinterview, Tiefeninterview
Freiexemplar *n* **(Freistück** *n,* **Gratisexemplar** *n***)** (Zeitung/ Zeitschrift) free copy, unbilled copy, unpaid copy, complimentary copy, specimen copy, sample copy, courtesy copy
Freigabe *f* **1.** release
2. (urheberrechtlich geschütztes Material) clearance
  A signed statement by a person quoted or photographed, authorizing use of the statement or photograph for advertising purposes. Also, the authorization to the medium for the insertion of advertisement.
Freigabedatum *n* **(Freigabetermin** *m***)** release date
  The date and time after which a news release may be used for publication.
Freigutschein *m*
→ Gratisgutschein
freihändige Vergabe *f*
→ Ausschreibung
Freihandmethode *f (stat)* free-hand method, freehand method
  A method of describing the relationship in a series of data, ordered in time or space, particularly in regression analysis, (→) Regressionsanalyse, or in correlation analysis, (→) Korrelationsanalyse, whereby the general trend is estimated by drawing in line freehand through or near the series of plotted observations.
Freihandzeichnung *f* **(Freihandskizze** *f***)** free-hand drawing, free-hand sketch, free-hand copy
  Any sketch, visual image, design, layout, rough, etc., outlined without mechanical guides by hand.
Freihauslieferung *f* **(Lieferung** *f* **frei Haus, Gratiszustellung** *f***)** *(econ)* free delivery, house delivery
Freiheitsgrad *m (stat)* degree of freedom (d.f., df)
  The number of observations on which a statistic is based minus the number of restrictions existing for the freedom of these observations to vary.
Freilichtaufführung *f* open-air performance
Freilichtaufnahme *f*
→ Außenaufnahme
Freilichtkino *n* open-air cinema, open-air theater, open-air movie-theater, outdoor theater
→ Autokino
freischaffender Künstler *m*
→ freiberuflicher Graphiker
freischlagen *v/t*
→ blankschlagen
freistehend *adj* **1.** *(print)* (Autotypie) blocked-out, outline, outlined, silhouette **2.** *(typ)* (Initiale) cock-up, stick-up **3.** *(typ)* (hängender Einzug) flush-and-hang, hanging indent **4.** *(print advtsg)* (Anzeige) island, solus **5.** *(outdoor advtsg)* (Anschlag) island, solus
freistehende Anzeige *f* island advertisement, island ad, solus advertisement, solus ad
→ alleinstehende Anzeige
freistehende Autotypie *f (print)* blocked-out halftone, outline halftone, outlined cut, silhouette halftone
  A halftone in which the background has been removed (cut out).
  vgl. rechteckige Autotypie
freistehende Position *f* **(freistehende Plazierung** *f***)** *(advtsg/merchandise display)* island position, solus position
→ alleinstehende Position
freistehende Warenauslage *f (POP advtsg)* island display
→ alleinstehende Warenauslage

freistehende Werbesendung f *(radio/ TV)* isolated commercial, island position commercial
→ alleinstehende Werbesendung
freistellen v/t *(print)* (Autotypie freistehend machen) to cut out, to drop out, to silhouette
 To cut or etch away the screen (→) Raster, surrounding any part of the image from a halftone.
Freistellen n **(Freistellung** f)
→ Alleinstellung 1., 2.
Freistück n
→ Freiexemplar
freiverkäufliches Arzneimittel n **(apothekenpflichtiges Arzneimittel** n) *(econ)* patent medicine, proprietary medicine, O.T.C., OTC
 Those items of medicinal use which may be sold over the counter (OTC) by pharmacists without a doctor's prescription.
Freiversand m
→ Gratisversand
Freiwahl f
→ Teilselbstbedienung (Selbstauswahl)
freiwillige Gruppe f **(freiwillige Handelsgruppe** f) *(retailing)* voluntary group, informal buying group, pooling buying group
 A loosely connected group of independent middlemen who combine their buying activities informally.
→ Einkaufsgemeinschaft
freiwillige Kette f **(freiwillige Handelskette** f) *(retailing)* voluntary chain, wholesale sponsored voluntary chain
 A group of retail stores organized by a wholesaler around a common interest in the goods or services the wholesaler can provide. The wholesaler usually owns the common name under which the stores operate, and the relative responsibilities of the stores and the wholesaler are delineated in a written contract. The wholesaler most often provides private label, (→) Hausmarke, merchandise.
Freizeichen n *(econ)* secondary meaning, secondary meaning mark
Freizeit f leisure time
Freizeitforschung f leisure time research
Fremdbedienung f **(Bedienung** f) *(retailing)* service, service selling, counter service
→ Bedienung

Fremdbedienungsgeschäft n
→ Bedienungsgeschäft
Fremdbedienungseinzelhandel m
→ Bedienungsgeschäft
Fremdbedienungsgroßhandel m
→ Bedienungsgroßhandel
Fremdbeilage f
→ Beilage; *vgl.* Verlegerbeilage
Fremdbild n *(TV)*
→ Bildintermodulation
Fremdenverkehr m tourism
Fremdenverkehrsmarketing n tourism marketing, tourist marketing, travel marketing
Fremdenverkehrswerbung f tourism advertising, tourist advertising, travel advertising
Fremdfilmmaterial n **(Archivmaterial** n, **Archivaufnahmen** f/pl) *(phot)* stock shots pl, library material, non-original material
Fremdstreuung f **(Fremdstreuwege** m/pl) *etwa* advertising in external media, paid advertising
vgl. Eigenstreuung
Fremdwerbung f *etwa* paid advertising
vgl. Eigenwerbung
Frequenz f **1.** *(electr.)* frequency
2. *(stat)* → Häufigkeit
Frequenzabstimmung f *(electr.)* frequency tuning
Frequenzabweichung f *(electr.)* frequency drift
Frequenzänderung f *(electr.)* (Schwankung) frequency variation, frequency fluctuation, (absichtlich herbeigeführt) frequency change
Frequenzband n *(electr.)* frequency band
Frequenzbandbreite f *(electr.)* frequency bandwidth
Frequenzbereich m **(Frequenzumfang** m) *(electr.)* frequency range
Frequenzdrift f *(electr.)* frequency drift
Frequenzgang m *(electr.)* frequency response, amplitude frequency response
Frequenzfrage f *(survey res)*
→ Häufigkeitsfrage
Frequenzmodulation f **(FM)** *(electr.)* frequency modulation (FM)
 A method of modulating tone in broadcasting by frequency of waves rather than their amplitude.

Frequenzplan m **(Wellenplan** m, **Frequenzverteilung** f) *(radio/TV)* frequency allocation plan, frequency plan
Frequenzskala f
→ Häufigkeitsskala
Frequenztestbild n *(TV)* frequency test pattern
Frequenzumfang m
→ Frequenzbereich
Fresnel-Linse f **(Fresnelsche Linse** f, **Stufenlinse** f) *(phot)* Fresnel lens
Friedman-Test m **(Friedmanscher Chi-Quadrat-Test** m, **Friedman-**χ^2**-Test** m) *(stat)* Friedman's test, Friedman χ^2 test
An adaption of the chi-squared test, (→) Chi-Quadrat-Test, to compare three or more matched samples. The test statistic for analysing variance of ranked data is obtained by squaring rank totals. The formula reads:

$$\chi^2 = \frac{12R}{Nk(k+1)} - 3N(k+1),$$

where R is the sum of squares of ranks, k the number of observations, N the number of values of each observation, and χ^2 the rank chi-squared coefficient.
Friktion f *(phot)* friction
Friktionsantrieb m *(phot)* friction drive
Friktionskalander m *(paper)* friction calender
Friktionskupplung f *(phot)* friction clutch
Frischestempel m *(econ)* (auf Warenpackungen) fresh sales life date
The indication of fresh sales life on a package, as stipulated for many food products under German law.
Frontalauslage f
→ Vollsichtauslage
Frontalbeleuchtung f **(Frontalbelichtung** f) *(phot/film/TV)* front lighting
The direct lighting of a scene or photographic object from the direction of the camera.
Frontlicht n *(phot/film/TV)* front light
→ Frontalbeleuchtung
Frontplakat n **(Frontseitenplakat** n) *(transit advtsg)* front-end display, headlight display
An outside display placed on the front of a public transportation vehicle.
vgl. Heckplakat

Frontseite f (eines Verkehrsmittels) *(transit advtsg)* front end, (als Werbefläche) front-end space, (beim Doppeldeckerbus) double front
vgl. Heckseite
Frosch m *(print)* (am Winkelhaken) slide, sliding bar, adjustable slide, sliding head, knee
Frühausgabe f **(Morgenausgabe** f) (Zeitung) early morning edition
Frühstücksfernsehen n **(Vormittagsprogramm** n) breakfast television, breakfast TV
Führung f
→ Management
Führungslicht n **(Führung** f) *(phot/film/TV)* key light, key lighting, main light
The major source of lighting for a scene.
Füllanzeige f **(Füllinserat** n, **Füller** m) filler, fill, stop-gap advertisement, stop-gap ad
An advertisement, regularly a house advertisement, placed somewhere on a newspaper or magazine page to fill empty space.
Füller m **(Füllprogramm** n) *(radio/TV)* filler, fill-up, cushion, plug, squib, stretch
That portion of a program that can be lengthened or shortened so that the full program fits correctly into the allotted time.
Füllhaltermikrofon n **(Füllhaltermikrophon** n) pencil microphone, pencil mike
Füllinserat n
→ Füllanzeige
Fülllicht n **(Füll-Licht** n) *(phot/film/TV)* fill light, fill-in light, filler
Füllmaterial n *(print)*
→ Blindmaterial
Füllmenge f **(Füllinhalt** m) *(packaging)* filling quantity
Füllprogramm n **(Füllsendung** f)
→ Füller
Füllsender m *(radio/TV)* low-power transmitter, standby transmitter
Full Service m **(Vollservice** m) *(econ)* full service
Full-Service-Agentur f **(Full-Service-Werbeagentur** f) full service agency, full service advertising agency
An advertising agency that offers its clients a full range of staff service activities and expertise over and above the normal creative and media facilities, including marketing planning and

Full-Service-Genossenschaft

management, creative, media, research, accounting, merchandising, below-the-line activities, such as sales promotion, public relations, packaging, and advertising-related legal counsel.
Full-Service-Genossenschaft f **(Universalgenossenschaft** f) *(econ)* full service cooperative
Full-Service-Konzeption f *(econ)* full-service concept
→ Full-Service-Agentur
Fundus m **(Fundusbestand** m) *(film/ TV)* properties pl in stock, props pl in stock
fungibel adj *(econ)* fungible
Fungibilität f *(econ)* fungibility
Funk m broadcasting
→ Rundfunk
Funk-
→ Hörfunk, Rundfunk
Funkbild n **(Funkphoto** n) photoradiogram
Funkmedium n broadcast medium
Funkmedien-Analyse f **(FMA)** Broadcast Media Analysis
Funkmedienforschung f broadcast media research
→ Hörerforschung, Zuschauerforschung
Funkspot m
→ Hörfunkspot
Funktion f function
funktionaler Einzelhandel m
→ Einzelhandel 2.
funktionaler Großhandel m
→ Großhandel 2.
Funktionalqualität f **(Grundqualität** f) (Werner Pfeiffer) *(econ)* functional quality
→ Grundnutzen; vgl. Integralqualität
Funktionen f/pl **des Handels**
→ Handelsfunktionen
Funktionsanalyse f **(funktionale Analyse** f) *(res)* functional analysis
In general, the analysis of a structure or organization that reveals the functional interdependence of its elements. In marketing research, a technique of creative problem solving that develops innovation on the basis of an analysis of functions that require a solution.
Funktionsmanagement n *(econ)* functional management
Funktionsorganisation f **(funktionsgliederung** f) *(marketing)* functional organization, brit organisation
Funktionsrabatt m **(Händlerrabatt** m, **Wiederverkäuferrabatt** m) *(econ)*

functional discount, trade discount, handling allowance
A discount granted to a buyer, usually a retailer or wholesaler, that is granted as a reward for the marketing activities the buyer performs for the seller.
Funkwagen m
→ Aufnahmewagen, Übertragungswagen
Funkwerbung f
→ Hörfunkwerbung, Rundfunkwerbung
Furcht f *(psy)* fear
furchterregende Werbung f **(furchteinflößende Werbung** f) scare copy, fear-instilling advertising
Fusion f **(Fusionierung** f, **Datenfusion** f, **Umfragefusionierung** f) *(survey res)* marriaging, data marriaging
Fuß m *(print)* 1. (einer Seite) bottom (of a page), tail
→ Fußsteg
2. (Klischeefuß) base, mount, block
The wood or metal base on which a printing plate is fastened for use on a press.
3. (der Kolumne) foot 4. (der Letter) foot, *meist* pl feet
Fußgänger m **(Passant** m) *(outdoor advtsg)* pedestrian
Fußgängerfluß m **(Passantenfluß** m) *(outdoor advtsg)* pedestrian traffic flow, pedestrian traffic
Fußgängerkontakt m **(Passantenkontakt** m) *(outdoor advtsg)* pedestrian exposure
Fußgängerzone f *(retailing)* mall, shopping mall
Fußleiste f *(print)* tailpiece
Fußnote f *(print)* footnote
Fußnummer f *(film)* key number, footage number, edge number
Fußrampe f *(film/TV)* (Licht) footlights pl, striplights pl
Fußsteg m *(print)* tail margin, foot stick
Both the margin at the bottom edge of a printed page and, in hot-metal typesetting, the heavy metal bar at the bottom of a chase, used in locking it.
Fußtitel m
→ Untertitel
Fußzeile f
→ Unterzeile
Futurologie f **(Zukunftsforschung** f) futurology
FVL m *abbr* Fachverband Lichtwerbung e.V.

G

G-Faktor m **(genereller Faktor** m**, Generalfaktor** m**)** *(factor analysis)* G factor, g factor
vgl. S-Faktor
Gabelung f **(Gabelungsfrage** f**)**
→ gegabelte Befragung
Gag m gag, gimmick
Any humorous trick device intended to gain attention. There is no original German term. On the contrary, *der Gag* is in the process of being superseded by *der Gimmick.*
Gage f fee, honorarium, royalty
Gain-Loss-Analyse f **(Zu- und Abwanderungs-Analyse** f**)** *(econ)* gain-and-loss analysis
Galerie f gallery
Galgen m *(radio/film/TV)* (Ton) microphone boom, sound boom, boom, (Schneideraum) trims bin, cuts rack
A boom from which a microphone is suspended, so that it can be lowered, raised or otherwise moved about to keep it near the actors (or near the action) as they move about in the studio.
→ Scheinwerfergalgen
Galgenschatten m *(film/TV)* boom shadow
Galvaniseur m
→ Galvanoplastiker
galvanisieren v/t *(print)* to electroplate, to electrotype, to galvanize
→ Galvano
Galvanisieren n *(print)* electrotyping, electroplating, galvanizing, galvanic etching
→ Galvano
Galvano n **(Elektrotype** f**)** *(print)* electrotype, electroplate, electro, galvanograph
A duplicate of an engraving or type form made by electrolytically depositing metal on a wax, lead, or plastic mold made from the original plate.
Galvanometer n *(psy)* galvanometer
→ Psychogalvanometer
galvanometrische Methode f **(galvanische Hautreaktion** f**)** *(res)* arousal method, galvanic skin response (G.S.R.)

G.S.R. is the result of the decreased electrical resistance of the skin due to physiological activity of the autonomic nervous system, following sensory or ideational stimulation. Its intensity can be measured by the degree of skin conductivity created by varying perspiration rates. It is used in advertising research to determine the arousal potential and emotional quality of advertising.
→ psychogalvanische Reaktion
Galvanoplastik f *(print)* electrotyping, electrotypy, galvanography
Galvanoplastiker m **(Galvaniseur** m**)** *(print)* electrotyper, electrotypist
Gamma n **(Gammawert** m**, Schwärzungsumfang** m**)** 1. *(phot)* gamma, gamma value
The degree of contrast or gradation in a negative.
2. *(stat)* → Goodman & Kruskals Gamma, Gammaverteilung
Gammaentzerrung f **(Gradationsentzerrung** f**)** *(phot)* gamma correction, *Am* log masking
Gamma-Koeffizient m **(γ-Koeffizient** m**)**
→ Goodman & Kruskals Gamma
Gammaverteilung f *(stat)* gamma distribution, γ distribution
Gammawert m
→ Gamma
Gamma-Zeit-Kurve f **(Gradationskurve** f**)** *(phot)* gamma characteristic, Hurter and Driffield curve
ganz seltener Leser m *(media res)* seldom reader
Ganzbemalung f
→ Rundumbemalung
ganze Seite f (Zeitung/Zeitschrift) full page
Ganzgroßaufnahme f
→ Großaufnahme, Makroaufnahme
Ganzheftremission f **(Vollremission** f**)** full-copy return, copy return, return copies *pl*
vgl. Kopfremission
Ganzheitslehre f **(Ganzheitspsychologie** f**, Leipziger Schule** f**)** *(psy)* holism, holistic psychology

Ganzsäule

Ganzsäule f
→ Ganzstelle
ganzseitig adj full-page
ganzseitige Anzeige f (Zeitung/ Zeitschrift) full-page advertisement, full-page ad, spread advertisement, spread ad, spread, full-page spread, *obsol* single truck
Ganzstelle f (**Ganzsäule** f) *(outdoor advtsg)* bulletin board, solus site
  A large bulletin board reserved for the posters of one single advertiser.
  vgl. Allgemeinstelle
Ganzzeug n (**Ganzstoff** m) *(paper)* pulp, stuff
  The mass of material used to make paper.
Garantie f *(econ)* guarantee, guaranty, warranty, *auch* money-back guarantee
  A formal commitment by a seller, supplier, or manufacturer that his product performs as specified and that, if it should not or prove to be defective, some form of compensation or corrective action will be provided.
Garantiefrist f (bei Werbung) rate protection
  The contractual guarantee that an agreed-upon advertising rate will be continued for a specific advertiser for the time of the contract's duration even if the communication medium raises its rates while the contract is in effect.
Garantiegemeinschaft f
→ Gütegemeinschaft
Garantiepreis m (**Preisgarantie** f) *(econ)* guaranteed price, price guarantee, guaranty against price decline, price protection
  An agreement on the part of a seller to make a proportionate refund to the buyer on all applicable items in the buyer's inventory at the time of a price reduction. Price guarantees are usually qualified for a specified time after the purchase.
garantieren v/t to guarantee, to warrant
garantierte Auflage f (**garantierte Mindestauflage** f) (Zeitung/ Zeitschrift) rate base, guaranteed circulation, guaranteed minimum circulation, minimum circulation
  The minimum guaranteed circulation of a publication serving as the basis for its advertising rates.
garantierte Einschaltquote f (**garantierte Reichweite** f) *(radio/TV)* rate base, guaranteed home impacts

(GHIs) *pl,* guaranteed home impressions *pl*
  The minimum size of audience or number (percentage) of homes reached by a commercial or program in return for the stated airtime rate.
garantierter Anzeigenpreis m guaranteed advertising rate, guaranteed rate
→ Garantiefrist
Garantieschein m (**Garantiebrief** m) *(econ)* guarantee, guaranty, warranty
  An in-pack or on-pack coupon, (→) Beipack, containing a warranty, (→) Garantie.
Garnitur f
→ Schriftgarnitur
Gastspiel n *(radio/TV)* guest performance
Gatekeeper m
→ Pförtner (Türhüter, Informationsselektierer)
Gattungsbezeichnung f *(econ)* generic label, generic term, generic name
  A product or service label that applies to an entire category of goods. When a product or trademark name becomes descriptive of a product or service category, it is generic.
  vgl. Herkunftsbezeichnung
Gattungsimage n
→ Produktimage
Gattungsmarke f *(econ)* generic brand, generic name, generic brand name, generic-labeled product, generic, *meist pl* generics
  An unbranded product sold under its generic name, (→) Gattungsbezeichnung, at a low price and with no frills.
Gattungswerbung f
→ Produktwerbung
Gaufrage f (**Gaufrieren** n) *(paper)* goffering, gauffering, gofering
gaufrieren v/t *(paper)* to goffer, to gauffer, to gofer
Gaufrierkalander m *(paper)* goffering calender, gauffering calender, gofering calender
Gauß-Kurve f (**Gauß'sche Kurve** f)
→ Normalverteilung
gautschen v/t *(paper)* to couch
Gautschpresse f *(paper)* couch press, couching rolls *pl*
Gebietsanalyse f
→ Regionalanalyse
Gebietsausgabe f
→ Regionalausgabe

Gebietsschutz m
→ Ortsexklusivität
Gebietsverkaufstest m **(Gebietstest m)** *(market res)* area sales test
A test of marketing and advertising effectiveness in different sales areas which relates sales to planned variations in marketing and/or sales expenditure between areas.
Gebrauchsanweisung f **(Gebrauchsanleitung** f) operation instruction(s) *(pl)*, instruction(s) *(pl)*, instructions sheet, instructions slip
Gebrauchsartikel m
→ Gebrauchsgüter
Gebrauchsgraphik f **(Gebrauchsgrafik** f) commercial art, creative art, advertising art
Gebrauchsgraphiker m **(Gebrauchsgrafiker** m) commercial artist, creative artist, advertising artist
Gebrauchsgüter n/pl **(langlebige Konsumgüter** n/pl) *(econ)* durable goods *pl*, durable consumer goods *pl*, consumer durables *pl*, durables *pl*, hard goods *pl*, yellow goods *pl*, white goods *pl*
Those consumer goods that provide a service over an extended period of time rather than being extinguished at the moment of consumption. They are seldom consumed and replaced, require relatively high levels of service and have a relatively high gross margin, (→) Stückspanne.
Gebrauchsgüter-Panel n *(market res)* consumer durables panel
Gebrauchsmuster n *(econ)* registered design
A technical innovation of devices, tools, hard goods, or parts thereof that is legally registered in accordance with the stipulations of the German (→) Gebrauchsmustergesetz thus providing protection against unauthorized use.
Gebrauchsmustergesetz n *(econ)* registered design law, registered design legislation
→ Gebrauchsmuster
Gebrauchsmusterrolle f *(econ)* design registration roll, design register
→ Gebrauchsmuster
Gebrauchsmusterschutz m etwa registered design protection
→ Gebrauchsmuster
Gebrauchsnutzen m **(Gebrauchswert m)** *(econ) etwa* functional value, functional utility, functional product value, functional product utility

That part of a product's or service's utility, (→) Nutzen, which is confined to its performing a prescribed function.
vgl. Geltungsnutzen, Zusatznutzen
Gebrauchsprodukt n
→ Gebrauchsgüter
Gebrauchstest m *(market res)* usage test, product use test
A type of product test, (→) Produkttest, intended to examine consumers' experience with a product over an extended period of time to find ways of improving its design or use of materials.
Gebrauchswerbung f
→ Schauwerbung
Gebrauchswert m
→ Gebrauchsnutzen
Gebrauchtwarenhandel m *(retailing)* second-hand trade
gebrochener Preis m *(econ)* odd price
A form of psychological price that is set at any amount of money except even Deutschmarks.
Gebühr f fee, charge
Gebührenverein m
→ Abmahnverein
gebunden adj *(binding)* bound, (in Leinen gebunden) clothbound, cloth-bound
gebundener Preis m *(econ)* regulated price, maintained resale price, fixed price
→ Preisbindung
gebundener Prospekt m **(gehefteter Prospekt** m) brochure
An elaborate booklet or pamphlet bound with a special cover, and usually designed with special care.
Geburtstagsverfahren n **(Geburtstags-Stichprobenbildung** f) *(stat)* birthday sampling procedure, birthday sampling
Geburtstagswerbung f etwa advertising directed to people who celebrate their birthday
Gedächtnis n *(psy)* memory
The capacity of an individual to retain, to recall, to reorganize, and to reproduce past experiences, events, and ideas.
vgl. Erinnerung, Wiedererkennung
Gedächtniserfolg m **(Erinnerungserfolg** m) *(advtsg)* recall effect
Gedächtnisstütze f **(Erinnerungsstütze** f) *(survey res)* recall aid
→ gestützte Erinnerung
Gedächtnistest m
→ Erinnerungstest
Gedächtniswirkung f
→ Erinnerungswirkung

gedehntes Lesen *n* **(gedehntes und wiederholtes Lesen** *n*) *(media res)*
replicated reading, replication
　The reading of a periodical publication repeatedly over time and thus extending into other issue periods of the publication. Re-reading of old issues leads to the statistical probability of a single reader being counted twice or more as an average-issue reader, (→) Leser pro Ausgabe (LpA), resulting in inflated readership figures that do not truly represent additional readers, but double counts of the same readers.
vgl. **gehäuftes Lesen**
gedruckt *adj* printed, print
gedruckte Auflage *f*
→ Druckauflage
gedruckte Kommunikation *f* printed communication
Gefälligkeitsantwort *f (survey res)*
courtesy reply
Gefälligkeitsfehler *m (survey res)*
(der durch Gefälligkeitsantworten bewirkte Fehler) courtesy effect, courtesy bias
Gefälligkeitsanzeige *f* courtesy advertisement, courtesy ad
Gefühl *n*
→ Emotion
gefühlsbetonte Werbung *f*
→ emotionale Werbung
Gefühlston *m* feeling tone
gegabelte Befragung *f* **(Methode** *f* **der gegabelten Befragung)** *(survey res)*
split-ballot survey, split-ballot technique, split-ballot
　The use of an experimental design for determining the effects of question wording or placement. Alternate forms or placements of questions are randomly assigned to portions of the sample. Usually, each half of the sample gets one of two forms or placements of the split questions, but the technique can be expanded to accommodate a larger number of experimental treatments, where each form or placement of the question is considered a treatment.
gegabelter Anzeigentest *m* **(gegabelter Werbetest** *m*) split-ballot advertising test, split-run advertising test, split-run test, split-run inquiry test, split-run test, split run
　An advertising research technique based on the use of two or more advertisements of the same size in the same position in different copies of the same issue of a publication. Serves to test different versions of an advertisement, or to feature different products in the regional editions of a national magazine.
Gegenabdruck *m* **(Gegenabzug** *m*) *(print)* counterproof
Gegendarstellung *f* corrective statement, correction
　A statement designed to correct an erroneous impression created by an earlier publication in the editiorial section of a medium. It is required by the German state laws governing the press under specified conditions.
Gegendarstellungsanzeige *f* corrective advertisement, corrective ad
→ Berichtigungsanzeige
Gegendruckzylinder *m* **(Preßwalze** *f*) *(print)* impression cylinder
Gegeneinstellung *f* **(Gegenschuß** *m*) *(film/TV)* reverse shot (RevS), reverse angle shot, reverse angle, reaction shot
→ Achsensprung
Gegenfarbe *f*
→ Komplementärfarbe
Gegengeschäft *n* **(Kompensationsgeschäft** *n*) *(econ)* barter, barter transaction, barter business
　A transaction in which goods or services are exchanged directly and in an agreed-upon ratio without the use of money.
Gegengeschäftsanzeige *f* barter advertisement, barter ad, exchange advertisement, exchange ad
Gegengeschäftsmittler *m* **(Gegengeschäftsmakler** *m*) *(econ)* barter broker
Gegengeschäftsplan *m* **(Tauschvereinbarung** *f*) *(econ)* barter plan
Gegengeschäftsvereinbarung *f* **(Gegengeschäftsanerkenntnis** *f*) *(econ)* due bill
　An agreement or statement for the barter of products or services.
Gegengeschäftswerbung *f* barter advertising
gegengewichtige Marktmacht *f (econ)* countervailing power (John Kenneth Galbraith)
Gegenkoppelung *f (cybernetics)* negative feedback, reverse feedback, antiphase feedback
Gegenlicht *n (phot)* contre jour, reverse lighting, backlighting, back lighting, back light
　A style of lighting which illuminates the side of an object opposite the camera, resulting in a halo, (→) Lichthof, around the edges of the object.

Gegenlichtaufnahme f (**Gegenlichtphotographie** f) *(phot)* contre-jour picture, contre-jour exposure
Gegenlichtblende f *(phot)* lens hood, lens shade, sunshade, lens screen, flag
Gegenmaske f reverse mask
Gegenprogramm n
→ Konkurrenzprogramm
Gegenprogrammgestaltung f (**Konkurrenzprogrammgestaltung** f) *(radio/TV)* counterprogramming, counter programming
> The practice by competing channels of scheduling a program with specific demographic appeal in direct competition with others which draw their audience from a completely different segment of the population.

Gegenschuß m
→ Gegeneinstellung
Gegenseite f
→ gegenüberliegende Seite
Gegenseitigkeitsgeschäft n
→ Kompensationsgeschäft
Gegenstreiflicht n *(phot/film/TV)* kicker light, kicker
gegenüber *prep (advtsg)* facing, next to, opposite
gegenüber den Geleisen *(transit advtsg)* cross tracks
> A poster site on the wall opposite the platform on which passengers wait, thus facing them.

gegenüber Inhaltsverzeichnis *(advtsg)* facing contents
> A preferred position, (→) Vorzugsplazierung, predominantly in magazine advertising on the page opposite the list of contents, usually at a premium rate.

gegenüber redaktionellem Text (**gegenüber Text**) *(advtsg)* facing matter (FM), facing editorial matter, facing text matter
> A preferred position, (→) Vorzugsplazierung, in newspaper or magazine advertising opposite editorial matter.

gegenüberliegende Seite f *(print)* opposite page
Gegenwahrscheinlichkeit f
→ Irrtumswahrscheinlichkeit
Gegenwerbung f
→ Anti-Werbung
gegenzyklische Werbung f counter-cyclical advertising
> The scheduling of advertising in such a manner that the bulk of advertisements are run at periods when sales are usually low, and few or none are run during normally large-volume periods.

gehäuftes Lesen n (**paralleles Lesen** n) *(media res)* parallel reading
> The reading of two or more separate issues of a periodical publication within one publication interval, (→) Erscheinungsweise, prior to the interview. It leads to the statistical probability of a reader being counted only once (instead of twice or more times) as an average-issue reader, (→) Leser pro Ausgabe (LpA), resulting in deflated readership figures.

vgl. gedehntes Lesen
geheftet
→ fadengeheftet, drahtgeheftet
geheftete Beilage f
→ Beihefter
geheime Verführer m/pl hidden persuaders pl (Vance Packard)
Gehirnforschung f brain research
→ Zwei-Hemisphären-Theorie
gehren v/t *(print)* to miter
Gehrfuge f *(print)* miter joint
Gehrung f *(print)* print miter, (Facette) bevel, (Eckstück) corner
Gehseite f *(transit advtsg)* curb side, *brit* kerb side
> That side of a bus or streetcar which loads and discharges passengers, i.e. the door side.

vgl. Fahrseite
Geisterbild n (**Doppelbild** n) *(TV)* ghost image, ghost, double image, echo, double-path effect
> An offset unwanted secondary picture tube image reflected on the screen and caused by an earlier or later transmission signal.

Geisterzeitung f
→ Phantomzeitung (Phantomzeitschrift)
geklebter Karton m
→ Pappe
geknickte Nachfragekurve f (**geknickte Preis-Absatz-Funktion** f) *(econ)* kinked demand curve
> A characteristic demand curve, (→) Preis-Absatz-Kurve, in an oligopoly, (→) Oligopol; this curve is down-sloping at about the expected angle until a certain price-quantity relationship is reached, after which the angle changes sharply and becomes very steep. The kink represents that point beyond which competition will not allow any one competitor to drop the price in an attempt to increase his market share without immediately meeting the new price in an effort to retain customers.

→ akquisitorisches Potential

gekoppelter Entfernungsmesser *m*
(phot) coupled range finder
Gelände *n*
→ Aufnahmegelände
Gelatine *f* **(Gel** *n*) *(phot)* gelatine,
gelatin, *colloq* gel
Gelatinefilter *m* **(Folienfilter** *m*)
(phot) gelatine filter, gelatin filter,
gelatin, *colloq* gel, jellies *pl*
   A translucent color filter for a camera or
   a spotlight.
Gelatineschicht *f (phot)* gelatine
coating, gelatin coating, gelatine film,
gelatin film
gelatinieren *v/t (phot)* to gelatinize, to
gel
Gelatinierung *f (phot)* gelatinization,
gelatination
Gelbe Seiten *f/pl* **(Branchenseiten** *f/
pl* **im Telefonbuch)** yellow pages *pl*
Gelbfilter *m* **(Gelbscheibe** *f*) *(phot)*
yellow filter
Gelbplatte *f (print)* yellow plate
   In four-color printing, that plate which
   prints yellow.
Gelbschleier *m (phot)* yellow fog
Geldrabatt *m*
→ Barrabatt
Gelegenheit *f* **(Gelegenheitskauf** *m*)
(retailing) bargain
→ Sonderangebot
Gelegenheitsanzeige *f*
→ Sonderangebotsanzeige,
Kleinanzeige
Gelegenheitsdruck *m*
→ Akzidenzdruck
Gelegenheitsdrucker *m*
→ Akzidenzdrucker
Gelegenheitskauf *m*
→ Sonderangebotskauf
Gelegenheitspreis *m*
→ Sonderangebotspreis
Gelegenheitsstichprobe *f*
→ willkürliche Auswahl
Gelegenheitsstichprobenverfahren *n*
→ willkürliche Auswahl
gelegentlicher Hörer *m (media res)*
occasional listener
gelegentlicher Leser *m (media res)*
occasional reader
   A reader with the reading probability of
   between 0.42 and 0.58, i.e. a reader who
   has read between 3 to 5 of 12 subsequent
   issues of a paper or a magazine.
gelegentlicher Zuschauer *m (media
res)* occasional viewer
geleimtes Hochglanzpapier *n*
→ satiniertes Hochglanzpapier

geleimtes Papier *n* sized paper
Geltungsbedürfnisse *n/pl (psy)*
esteem needs *pl*
→ Bedürfnishierarchie
Geltungsnutzen *m* **(Prestigenutzen** *m*)
(Wilhelm Vershofen) *(econ)* prestige
value, prestige utility
   That portion of a product's or service's
   utility that imparts prestige on its owner
   and goes beyond its mere functional
   utility, (→) Gebrauchsnutzen.
vgl. Gebrauchsnutzen, Zusatznutzen
gelumbeckt *adj (bookbinding)*
perfect-bound, adhesive-bound
→ Lumbecken
GEMA *f abbr* Gesellschaft für
musikalische Aufführungs- und
mechanische Vervielfältigungsrechte
GEMA-frei *adj*
→ gemeinfreie Werke
gemalter Hintergrund *m (TV)* oleo
   A painted backdrop.
Gemeine *m/pl (typ)*
→ Kleinbuchstabe
gemeinfreie Werke *n/pl* public
domain, PD, P.D.
   Those creative or artistic works that are
   not, or no longer, protected by copyright.
Gemeindezentrum *n* **(Community-
Center** *n*) *(retailing)* community
center, community shopping center
   A type of shopping center that includes
   one or two department stores and some
   specialty and convenience stores. The
   center serves a larger geographical area
   and draws customers who are looking for
   shopping and specialty goods unavailable
   in neighborhood shopping centers,
   (→) Nachbarschaftszentrum. Consumers
   drive longer distances to community
   centers.
vgl. Einkaufszentrum
Gemeinkosten *pl (econ)* overhead
cost(s) *(pl)*, overhead
   Those expenses of a general nature that
   are not attributable to a specific product
   or service, but apply to a business as a
   whole.
gemeinnütziges Unternehmen *n*
→ öffentlicher Versorgungsbetrieb
gemeinsamer Merkmalsraum *m*
→ Merkmalsraum
Gemeinschaftsantenne *f* **(Gemeinschaftsantennenanlage** *f*) **(GA)**
(radio/TV) community antenna, *brit*
community aerial
   A common antenna for a larger number
   of households in a geographical area
   designed to provide a radio or, more
   commonly, a television reception service,

direct by wire transmission, to connected households.

Gemeinschaftsantennen-Fernsehen n
→ Kabelfernsehen

Gemeinschaftsanzeige f **(Gemeinschaftswerbemittel** n**)** cooperative advertisement, cooperative ad, co-op advertisement, co-op ad, (zweier Werbungtreibender) crossruff advertisement, crossruff ad
→ Gemeinschaftswerbung

Gemeinschaftsausstellung f cooperative exhibition

Gemeinschaftsbezug m *(retailing)* pooled buying, cooperative buying, cooperative purchasing
The informal combination of orders by functional middlemen who join their efforts in an informal buying group, (→) Einkaufsgemeinschaft.

Gemeinschaftsforschung f syndicated research
Any research sponsored or conducted jointly by several clients who in one way or another collaborate in the investigation.

Gemeinschaftshandelsgesellschaft f *(econ)* manufacturer's sales office, manufacturer's wholesaler
An establishment owned and operated by a manufacturer apart from his plants out of which his salesmen may work, and which houses stocks from which deliveries may be made to customers.

Gemeinschaftsmarke f *(econ)* cooperative brand

Gemeinschaftsmarketing n cooperative marketing
The process by which independent producers, wholesalers, retailers, consumers, or combinations of them act collectively in buying or selling or both. In German, the term is practically synonymous with what in English is producers' cooperative marketing, i.e. that type of cooperative marketing which primarily involves the sale of goods or services of the associated producing membership. It may perform only an assembly or brokerage function but in some cases, notably in milk marketing, it extends into processing and distribution of the members' production.

Gemeinschaftsmarktforschung f cooperative market research, syndicated market research
→ Gemeinschaftsforschung, Gemeinschaftsstudie

Gemeinschaftspreis m **(Gemeinschaftstarif** m**)** (für Werbung) joint rate

Gemeinschaftsproduktion f *(econ)* coproduction, joint production

Gemeinschaftsprogramm n **(Gemeinschaftssendung** f**)** *(radio/TV)* joint program, *brit* programme, national program, *brit* programme, (im gesamten Sendernetz) full-network program, full net program, syndicated program

Gemeinschaftsstudie f **(Gemeinschaftsuntersuchung** f**)** *(res)* syndicated study, syndicated investigation, syndicated analysis, syndicated survey, (Leserschaftsuntersuchung) syndicated readership survey, syndicated readership investigation, syndicated readership study, *(radio/TV)* (Einschaltquotenuntersuchung) syndicated rating survey, syndicated rating study
Any research study which is shared by at least two, regularly more clients is a syndicated investigation, i.e. by being shared in terms of payment and results it becomes the property of the syndicate. Most syndicated research is indeed marketing to a number of clients, none of whom retains exclusive rights to it.

Gemeinschaftsunternehmen n **(Gemeinschaftsprojekt** n**)** *(econ)* joint venture
An enterprise in which two or more investors share ownership and control over property rights and operation.

Gemeinschaftsversand m **(Gemeinschaftswerbeversand** m**)** cooperative mailing, group mailing
The inclusion of several messages from different advertisers in the same envelope in a mass mailing, whereby addressing, postage, and cover costs are shared.

Gemeinschaftsvertrieb m *(econ)* cooperative distribution
Channel cooperation between two or more business organizations in the field of distribution.

Gemeinschaftsvertriebsgesellschaft f *(econ)* cooperative distributor

Gemeinschaftswarenhaus n **(Kollektivwarenhaus** n**, Kaufmannswarenhaus** n**, Ladengemeinschaft** f**)** *(retailing) etwa* planned shopping center, controlled shopping center, shopping plaza

Gemeinschaftswerbekatalog 200

A shopping center, (→) Einkaufszentrum, that is constructed by noncompeting private owners to contain a complementary mix of stores that provide one-stop shopping for family and household needs.

Gemeinschaftswerbekatalog m (**Gemeinschaftskatalog** m) file catalog, *brit* catalogue, combination catalog
A reference medium made up of standardized catalogs of different individual advertisers in a single bound volume.

Gemeinschaftswerbung f (**Kollektivwerbung** f) cooperative advertising, co-op advertising, (horizontale Gemeinschaftswerbung) horizontal cooperative advertising, (vertikale Gemeinschaftswerbung) vertikal cooperative advertising
The German term is about as equivocal as its English counterpart(s). It is most commonly used to refer to horizontal cooperative advertising, i.e. joint advertising of a group of independent local advertisers, or trade advertising. But it is also used to refer to vertical cooperation, i.e. advertising paid for jointly by a national advertiser and his wholesalers or retailers.
vgl. Gattungswerbung, Gruppenwerbung, Sammelwerbung, Verbandswerbung, Verbundwerbung

Gemischtwarengeschäft n (**Gemischtwarenhandlung** f) *(retailing)* general store, country general store
A small retailing business unit, not departmentized, usually located in a rural community and primarily engaged in selling a general assortment of merchandise of which the most important line is food, and the more important subsidiary lines are notions, apparel, farm supplies, and gasoline.

Gemischtwarenhandel m *(econ)* general goods trade, variety trade
→ Gemischtwarengeschäft

Gemischtwarenladen m
→ Gemischtwarengeschäft

Genauigkeit f (**Akkuranz** f, **Treffgenauigkeit** f) *(stat)* accuracy, unbiasedness
→ Akkuranz; *vgl.* Präzision

Genauigkeitstabelle f (**Genauigkeitstafel** f, **Fehlertabelle** f, **Fehlertafel** f) *(stat)* accuracy table

Generalanzeiger m *etwa* nonpartisan newspaper, bipartisan paper, apolitical newspaper

Generalanzeigerpresse f *etwa* nonpartisan press, bipartisan press, apolitical press
vgl. Meinungspresse

Generalisierung f (**Generalisation** f) generalization

Generalklausel f (**des Wettbewerbsrechts**) *(econ)* general clause of the German Unfair Competition Act
The stipulation of §1 of the German Unfair Practice Act, (→) Gesetz gegen den unlauteren Wettbewerb (UWG) that unfair practice (Verstoß gegen die guten Sitten) may justify claims for damages and result in a cease and desist order.

Generalprobe f *(radio/film/TV)* dress rehearsal, dress *(film/TV)* camera rehearsal
The last rehearsal, in full dress, before shooting.

Generalunternehmer m *(econ)* general contractor, prime contractor

Generalvertreter m *(econ)* general sales representative, general representative
vgl. Bezirksvertreter, Versandhandelsvertreter

Generation f *(film)* generation
1. Generation (Original): first generation 2. Generation (Kopie von Original): second generation 3. Generation (Kopie von der 1. Kopie): third generation

Generator m *(electr.)* generator

generisches Marketing n generic marketing, generic concept of marketing (Philip Kotler)
→ Metamarketing

generische Marke f
→ Gattungsmarke

Genetischer Motivationstest m (**GMT**) (Otto Walter Haseloff) *etwa* genetic motivation test

Genomotiv n genomotive (William Stern)
An innate, unconscious motive.
vgl. Phänomotiv

genormte Verpackung f (**genormte Packung** f) *(econ)* standardized package, standard package

Genossenschaft f *(econ)* cooperative
A voluntary organization set up by consumers and/or producers to serve their needs and distribute profit according to purchases, sales, or fixed return on capital.

Genre n genre, style

Genremusik f genre music

Genußgüter n/pl **(Genußmittel** n)
→ Luxusgüter
geographische Angabe f
(geographische Warenbezeichnung f)
→ Herkunftsangabe
geographische Verbreitung f
geographic distribution
geographische Verbreitungsanalyse f
geographic distribution analysis
geographischer Split m **(geographischer Anzeigensplit** m) geographic split run, split run
A split run, (→) Anzeigensplit, in periodical advertising on an area basis.
Geometrietestbild n *(TV)* geometrical test pattern, linearity test pattern
geometrische Verteilung f *(stat)* geometric distribution
A distribution in which the frequencies fall off in geometric progression as the variate values increase. The term is usually confined to discontinuous distributions.
geometrischer gleitender Durchschnitt m *(stat)* geometric moving average
geometrischer Trend m
→ logarithmischer Trend
geometrisches Mittel n *(stat)* geometric mean
A measure of central tendency consisting of the nth root of the product of the n values in a distribution of scores, i.e.

$$G = \sqrt[N]{\prod_{i=1}^{N} x_i}$$

geometrisches Mittel n **der Extremwerte (geometrische Spannweite** f) *(stat)* geometric range
geplante Obsoleszenz f **(geplante Veralterung** f) planned obsolescence, managed obsolescence, (eingebaute Obsoleszenz) built-in obsolescence
The intentional effort on the side of producers to make an existing product out of date in order to increase the market for replacement products. The term has been used in three ways:
1. *Technological* or *functional obsolescence:* Significant technological improvements result in a more effective product.
2. *Postponed obsolescence:* Technical improvements are available, but they are not introduced until demand for the existing product decreases and a new market stimulus is needed.
3. *Style obsolescence* or *psychological* or *fashion obsolescence:* Superficial characteristics of the product are altered, while it basically remains the same, to make people feel out of date if they continue to use old models.
gerade *adj* **1.** *(typ)* (normal, nicht kursiv) roman type, roman, rom.
2. (linke Seite) even (page) **3.** (Satz) flush
→ bündig
geradeschneiden *v/t (print)* to trim flush
geradestoßen (ausrichten) *v/t (print)* to jog
Geradestoßen n **(Ausrichtung** f) *(print)* jogging
Geradestoßmaschine f *(print)* jogging machine, jogger
gerastert *adj (print)* screened, screen, halftone
→ Raster
Geräteeinschaltquote f **(Quote** f **der eingeschalteten Geräte)** *(media res)* sets-in-use rating, S.I.U. rating, SIU rating
The percentage of some specified group of television sets or radios that are being used during a specified period of time. Similarly, the term "sets in use", (→) Geräteeinschaltzahl, should be used to refer to the actual number of television sets or radios in audiences. The term has sometimes been used to mean the percentage of a group of households estimated to be in the audience of any one of a group of television or radio stations over a specified period of time. However, such a quantity is more precisely called a "households-using-television rating" or a "households-using-radio rating", (→) Haushaltseinschaltquote. The term "sets-in-use rating" used in this way may be misleading because some households may have two or more television sets or radios in use at a given time. Particularly in view of the large number of multi-set households, it should no longer be used as a synonym for either "households-using-television rating" or "households-using-radio rating".
Geräteeinschaltzahl f **(Zahl** f **der eingeschalteten Geräte)** *(media res)* sets-in-use *pl,* S.I.U., SIU
→ Geräteeinschaltquote
Geräusch n noise
Geräuscharchiv n **(Tonarchiv** n) *(radio/film/TV)* sound effects library
geräuscharm *adj* low-noise

Geräuschaufnahme f *(radio/film/TV)* sound effects recording
Geräuschband n *(radio/film/TV)* sound effects track, sound effects tape, sound on tape (S.O.T.)
Geräuscheffekt(e) *m(pl)*, **(Toneffekt(e)** *m(pl)*, **Klangeffekt(e)** *m(pl))* *(radio/film/TV)* sound effect(s) *(pl)*, S.E., S.F.X., SFX *pl*, music and sound effects *pl*, M. and E. effects *pl*, M. and E., M & E
   Special audio effects produced in the studio for a dramatic performance, creating an illusion of lifelike sounds.
Geräuschemacher m **(Tontechniker** m**)** *(radio/film/TV)* sound effects man, sound man, sound effects technician, effects operator, sound mixer
   The technician responsible for producing sound effects.
Geräuschmikrofon n *(radio/film/TV)* effects microphone, effects mike, audience microphone
Geräuschpegel m noise level
Geräuschspannung f noise voltage
Geräuschstudio n *(radio/film/TV)* sound effects studio
Geräuschsynchronisation f *(radio/film/TV)* sound synchronization, sound sync, dubbing of sound effects
Geräuschtechniker m
   → Geräuschemacher
gerechter Preis m *(econ)* fair price
   Fair price is a theory, rather than a real phenomenon, that implies that among many people there seems to have developed a kind of social learning which causes them to judge the propriety of a price for an item so that they buy more of it and more willingly at that price than at a lower or higher price.
geriffelt (gewellt) *adj (paper)* corrugated
geriffeltes Papier n unlined corrugated board
Geringstkosten *pl (econ)* minimum cost
gerippt *adj (paper)* laid
geripptes Papier n **(gestreiftes Papier** n**)** laid finish, laid paper
   → Filigranpapier
Geruchstest m
   → Geschmacks- und Geruchstest
Gesamtaufhellung f *(film/TV)* general lighting, overall lighting, general ambient light, overall ambient light

Gesamtauflage f (Zeitung/Zeitschrift) total circulation, total print run, print run
   The full number of a publication's copies printed and distributed, including subscription, newstand sales, and free copies.
Gesamtaufnahme f **(Totale** f, **Entfernungsaufnahme** f**)** *(film/TV)* long shot (L.S., LS), establishing shot, master shot, *Am auch* vista shot
   → Totale
Gesamterhebung f
   → Vollerhebung
Gesamtfehler m *(stat)* total error
Gesamtheit f *(stat)*
   → Grundgesamtheit
Gesamtkontake *m/pl* **(Gesamtzahl** f **der Kontakte)** *(media res)* total number of exposures, total effective exposure, TEE, *(radio/TV)* total audience rating, total audience impressions *pl*, audience rating
   The number of exposures, (→) Kontakt, of an audience with an advertising medium or an advertisement.
   vgl. Gesamtreichweite
Gesamtkosten *pl (econ)* total cost
Gesamtkostenverfahren n *(econ)* total cost approach
   An analytical approach to profit decisions which recognizes that distribution decisions have a critical impact on total business costs and that, therefore, analysis of various alternate distribution plans involving channels of distribution, warehouses, rail versus air versus truck versus water shipping systems, is crucial to the maximizing of profit within each firm's internal and external constraints.
Gesamtmodell n
   → Totalmodell
Gesamtreichweite f *(media res)* total audience rating, total coverage, *auch* total reach, total effective exposure (TEE), total number of exposures
   The percentage of households or individuals, ascertained by means of a survey, who form the audience of an advertising medium. To be counted in the audience for purposes of a total audience rating, a household or an individual must be in the audience for some consecutive period of time during the interval (e.g., for five consecutive minutes or more). To calculate a total audience rating, the number of households or individuals that are counted in the audience is expressed as a percentage of some specified base. The

base may be a group of households, or a group of individuals. A total number of exposures is commonly interpreted as a cumulation of instantaneous exposures.
→ Bruttoreichweite

Gesamtszenenbeleuchtung f *(film/TV)* production lighting

Gesamtumsatz m *(econ)* total sales *pl*, total business, total turnover

Gesamtumsatzrabatt m *(econ)* total sales discount, volume discount, patronage discount, (bei Werbung) bulk discount
A type of quantity discount, (→) Mengenrabatt, allowed on the basis of the amount of business with one firm.

Gesamtvarianz f
→ Varianz

Gesamtverband m **Werbeagenturen e.V. (GWA)** German General Association of Advertising Agencies

Gesamtwerbeaufwand m total advertising expenditure, total advertising

Gesamtzahl f **der Hörer** *(media res)* total number of listeners, total listeners *pl*, total audience (T.A., TA)
An estimate of the number of net, unduplicated radio households or individuals tuned to a particular program for at least a specified minimum period of time.

Gesamtzahl f **der Kontakte** *(media res)*
→ Gesamtkontakte

Gesamtzahl f **der Leser** *(media res)* total number of readers, total readers *pl*, total audience (T.A., TA)
An estimate of the number of persons who read or look into an issue of a publication, regardless of how they obtained their copy or where they read it. Magazine total audiences include both primary, (→) Erstleser, and pass-along readers, (→) Zweitleser.

Gesamtzahl f **der Zuschauer** *(media res)* total number of viewers, total viewers *pl*, total audience (T.A., TA)
→ Gesamtzahl der Hörer

Gesamtzahl f **der eingeschalteten Geräte** *(media res)*
→ Geräteeinschaltzahl

Geschäftsabzeichen n corporate logotype, corporate logograph, name flag, nameplate, name slug, logo
→ Firmenzeichen

Geschäftsanzeige f business advertisement, business ad

Geschäftsbezeichnung f corporate name
→ Firmenbezeichnung

Geschäftsbindung f **(Geschäftstreue** f, **Geschäftsloyalität** f**)**
→ Ladentreue

Geschäftsfläche f *(retailing)* gross leasable area (GLA)

Geschäftsgestaltung f *(retailing)* store engineering, store design
The design of the architectural character or decorative style of a store, in which the intended projected image of the store should play a large part.

Geschäftsimage n
→ Ladenimage

Geschäftsjahr n contract year (CY)
In advertising a contractual relationship of one full year from the first insertion under the contract.

Geschäftskarte f **(Visitenkarte** f **)** business card

Geschäftstreue f
→ Ladentreue

Geschäftswerbung f business advertising
→ Wirtschaftswerbung

Geschäftswert m
→ Firmenwert

Geschäftszentrum n **(gewachsenes Einkaufszentrum** n**)** *(retailing)* central business district (CBD), central shopping district
The downtown area in a city which has traditionally been the hub of retailing, the location of the main units of department stores, major apparel specialty stores, jewelry stores, and other shopping goods stores.
vgl. Einkaufszentrum

Geschenk n
→ Werbegeschenk

Geschenkabonnement n (Zeitung/ Zeitschrift) gift subscription
A subscription purchased for persons other than the purchaser himself or his employees.

Geschenkartikel m
→ Werbeartikel, Werbegeschenk

Geschenkartikelhändler m **(Werbeartikelvertrieb** m**)** advertising specialty distributor
A distributing firm handling advertising specialties on a wholesale basis.

Geschenkartikelwerbung f **(Geschenkwerbung** f**)** specialty advertising, novelty advertising, gift advertising

Geschenkbon
A type of remembrance advertising with products which bear the name and address or slogan of a business firm and which are given away free by the advertiser to prospective and to present customers. Specialty advertising can provide reinforcement for other forms of communication done by a company.

Geschenkbon m
→ Geschenkgutschein

Geschenkgutschein m **(Geschenkkupon** m, **Geschenkbon** m) gift coupon, gift voucher, gift certificate
A promotional voucher which is given with products, when purchased. They are redeemed for goods.

Geschenkgutschein-System n gift coupon system, gift couponing

Geschenkpackung f **(Geschenkverpackung** f) gift package, gift pack, gift wrapper, gift box

Geschenkwerbung f
→ Geschenkartikelwerbung

Geschichtenergänzungstest m (res) story-completion test

geschichtete Auswahl f **(geschichtete Stichprobe** f) (stat) stratified sample

geschichtetes Auswahlverfahren n **(geschichtetes Stichprobenverfahren** n) (stat) stratified sampling, stratification
Stratification is the division of a population into strata, particularly for the purpose of drawing a sample. Proportional stratified sampling is any sampling procedure that draws elements in proportion to their frequency in the subgroups that make up the population to be sampled; cf. (→) disproportional geschichtete Auswahl. The process of stratification may be undertaken on a geographical basis, e.g. by dividing up the sampled area into sub-areas on a map, or some other quality, e.g. by sex or according to whether people belong to upper-, middle- or lower-income groups.

geschichtete Zufallsauswahl f **(geschichtete Zufallsstichprobe** f) (stat) stratified random sample
A type of stratified sample, (→) geschichtete Auswahl, where a random sample, (→) Zufallsauswahl, is drawn from each stratum.

geschichtetes Zufalls-Auswahlverfahren n **(geschichtetes Zufallsstichprobenverfahren** n) (stat) stratified random sampling

geschlossene Benutzergruppe f (Btx) closed user group

geschlossene Frage f (survey res) closed question, closed-end question, closed-ended question, closed alternative question, auch selective answer question
Closed questions give the alternative answers to the respondent, either explicitly or implicitly. Closed questions may have two alternatives (dichotomous questions), (→) Alternativfrage, such as "yes" or "no" or "male" or "female,", or they may have multiple choices, (→) Auswahlfrage, such as "strongly agree," "agree," "disagree," and "strongly disagree." In contrast, an open question does not provide answer categories to the respondent.
· vgl. offene Frage

geschlossene Warenauslage f (POP advtsg) closed display, closed assortment display
The display of merchandise in showcases or behind glass, often kept locked.

geschlossener Kreislauf m **(geschlossener Stromkreis** m) (electr.) closed circuit

geschlossener Markt m (econ) closed market

Geschlossenheitstest m
→ Lückentest

Geschmack m taste

Geschmacksführer m (res) taste maker
An opinion leader, (→) Meinungsführer, in the area of taste and style.
→ Modeführer

Geschmacksmuster n (econ) etwa registered design
→ Gebrauchsmuster

Geschmacksmusterschutz m (econ) etwa registered design protection

Geschmackstest m (market res) taste test

geschöpftes Papier n
→ handgeschöpftes Papier

geschweifte Klammer(n) f(pl) (typ) brace(s) (pl), curly bracket(s) (pl), bow bracket(s) (pl), brace bracket(s) (pl)

Gesellschaft f **der PR-Agenturen e.V. (GPRA)** Association of Public Relations Agencies

Gesellschaft f **für musikalische Aufführungs- und musikalische Vervielfältigungsrechte (GEMA)** etwa German Society of Composers and Publishers
The organization which protects the rights and copyrights of its members and collects royalties on their behalf.

Gesellschaft f **zur freiwilligen Kontrolle von Messe- und Ausstellungszahlen e.V. (FKM)** Society for the voluntary control of trade fair and exhibition audience figures
Gesellschaft f **Werbeagenturen e.V. (GWA)** obsol German Association of Full-Service Advertising Agencies
→ Gesamtverband Werbeagenturen (GWA)
gesendet werden v/i to be broadcast, to be aired, to be on the air
Gesetz n **der Agglomeration im Einzelhandel** (econ) law of retail gravitation (William J. Reilly)
A formula for determining the interchange of retail trade between cities that purports to tell at what distance from one city a consumer would be indifferent to going to either city. Applicable to cities of rather large size and quite far apart.
Gesetz n **der großen Zahlen** (stat) law of large numbers
The general form of this fundamental form reads: If x_k is a sequence of mutually independent variates with a common distribution and if the expectation $\mu = E(x_k)$ exists, then for every $\epsilon > $ as $n \to \infty$ the probability

$$P\left\{\left|\frac{X_1 + ... + X_n}{n} - \mu\right| > \epsilon\right\} \to 0.$$

Gesetz n **gegen den unlauteren Wettbewerb (UWG)** (econ) German Unfair Practice Act
Gesetz n **gegen Wettbewerbsbeschränkungen (Kartellgesetz) (GWB)** (econ) German Cartel Law, Anti-Trust Act
Gesetz n **von Engel**
→ Engelsches Gesetz
Gesetz n **von Schwabe**
→ Engelsches Gesetz
Gesetz n **zur Regelung des Rechts der Allgemeinen Geschäftsbedingungen**
→ AGB-Gesetz
gesetzliche Schutzrechte n/pl
→ gewerblicher Rechtsschutz
Gesichtsfarbe f (TV) flesh tone
→ Hauteffekt
Gesichtsfeld n (phot) visual field, field of view
Gesichtswinkel m (phot) angle of view, camera angle, viewing angle
The viewpoint from which the camera photographs the scene.
Gesinnungspresse f
→ Meinungspresse
gesperrt adj (typ) spaced, letter-spaced, spaced-out
gesperrter Satz m (typ) spaced type, letter-spaced type, space type
Type with more blank units between characters than normal type.
Gesprächsleitfaden m
→ Leitfaden, Interviewerleitfaden
Gestalt f 1. shape, form 2. (psy) gestalt
gestalten v/t to form, to frame, to design, to shape, to create, to fashion
Gestalten n
→ Gestaltung
Gestalter m creative artist, creative, designer, visualizer, artist, artsman, draftsman, draftswoman, auch draughtsman, draughtswoman
gestalterisch adj creative
Gestaltfestigkeit f (psy) form quality
→ Gestaltpsychologie
Gestaltgesetz n **(Gestaltfaktor** m) (psy) gestalt law
→ Gestaltpsychologie
Gestaltpsychologie f **(Berliner Schule** f, **Gestalttheorie** f) gestalt psychology, gestalt theory, gestaltism, form psychology
A school of thought in contemporary psychology whose advocates protest against reductive analysis and emphasize the entity of total configurations (gestalt). They see the individual as an organized whole formed by integration and not an addition of parts. The nature of the part depends on the whole rather than vice versa.
Gestaltqualität f (psy) gestalt quality, form quality
Gestaltung f **(Gestaltungsarbeit** f) design, artistic design, creative design, creative work, creation, production, print presentation
→ Werbemittelgestaltung
Gestaltung f **einer Anzeige**
→ Anzeigengestaltung
Gestaltungsabteilung f creative department, creative group, art department
→ Kreativabteilung
Gestaltungsgesetz n **(Gestaltungsgrundsatz** m) design rule, creative rule

Gestaltungsgrundlage f (Copy-Platform f, Gestaltungskonzept n) (für ein Werbemittel) copy platform
→ Copy-Platform
Gestaltungskosten pl art and mechanical costs pl, A & M costs pl
The costs incurred in producing graphic materials, type, and other artwork required for the production and design of advertisements.
Gestaltungskunst f (künstlerische Gestaltung f) creative art, art design, arts and crafts pl
Gestaltungsmaterial n (Gestaltungsmittel n/pl) art and mechanical, A & M
The graphic material, type, and other artwork required for the production and design of advertisments.
Gestaltungsstrategie f (Copy-Strategie f) copy strategy
Gestehungskosten pl
→ Selbstkosten
gestochen adj 1. (print) engraved 2. (TV) pin sharp
gestorben (film/TV) (Aufnahme) in the can! wrap it up! (Dekoration) strike!
gestreiftes Papier n
→ geripptes Papier
gestrichelte Linie f (print) broken line, dashed line
gestrichenes Papier n coated paper, (maschinengestrichenes Papier) process-coated paper, coated stock, process-coated stock, (gestrichenes Offsetpapier) coated offset paper, coated offset, (gestrichenes Umschlagpapier) coated cover paper, coated cover, (einseitig gestrichenes Papier) enameled paper
Paper which has been chemically treated to provide a smooth surface suitable for printing fine-screen halftones.
gestrichener Karton m
→ Kunstdruckkarton
gestürzte Letter f (gestürzter Buchstabe m) (typ) kerned letter
gestützte Erinnerung f (Erinnerung f mit Gedächtnisstütze) (survey res) aided recall
A research technique used to provide one or more memory cues to respondents when behavior or knowledge questions are asked. Specific procedures include the use of lists, pictures, households inventories, and specific detailed questions. The method is frequently used to measure the impression made by an advertisement or other communication, and in which the interviewer shows the respondent an advertisement, program log, or other aid to memory.
→ passiver Bekanntheitsgrad
gesungener Werbespruch m jingle
Music and rhyme, sung, and forming an integral part of a commercial.
geteiltes Bild n (zweigeteiltes Bild n) (film/TV) half-lap, halflap, split screen, side-by-side shot, split shot, split frame
A shot in which two or more independently taken images appear simultaneously on the screen, one on each half.
getöntes Papier n tinted paper
Geviert n (typ) quad, quadrat, em quadrat, em quad, em, m, mutton, mut
The square of any type size. The English term is derived from the letter M, which is as wide as it is high.
vgl. Halbgeviert, Viertelgeviert
Geviertreglette f (Geviertsteg m) (typ) quotation quad
Geviertstrich m (typ) em rule, em dash, (Korrekturzeichen)

$$\frac{1}{M}, \frac{1}{m}, \frac{1}{em}$$

Gewährleistung f
→ Garantie
Gewebeeinband m cloth binding
gewellt adj
→ geriffelt
Gewerbefachzeitschrift f (gewerbliche Fachzeitschrift f)
→ Branchenzeitschrift
gewerbliche Anzeige f
→ Geschäftsanzeige
Gewerkschaftspresse f (Arbeitnehmerpresse f) labor union press, union press, brit trade union press
Gewerkschaftszeitschrift f (Arbeitnehmerzeitschrift f) labor union journal, labor union magazine, union journal, union magazine, brit trade union magazine, trade union journal
Gewerkschaftszeitung f (Arbeitnehmerzeitung f) labor union paper, union paper, brit trade union paper
Gewicht n (stat) weight
The importance of an object in relation to a set of objects to which it belongs, usually a numerical coefficient attached to an observation (frequently by multiplication) in order that it shall

assume a desired degree of importance in a function of all the observations of the set.

gewichteter Index *m* **(gewogener Index** *m***)** *(stat)* weighted index number, weighted index
An index number in which the components items are weighted according to some system of weights reflecting their relative importance.

Gewichtsfaktor *m* *(stat)* weighting factor

Gewichtsfunktion *f* *(stat)* weighting function, weight function
A nonnegative function used for weighting purposes, particularly in the theory of decision functions, (→) Entscheidungsfunktion, where the word is used as a synonym for loss function.

Gewichtskoeffizient *m* *(stat)* weighting coefficient
The coefficient attached to an observation as its weight, (→) Gewicht, in a procedure involving weighting, (→) Gewichtung

Gewichtung *f* **(Gewichten** *n***)** *(stat)* weighting
The statistical procedure by which raw data, (→) Rohdaten, are assigned weights, (→) Gewicht, to give them the required measure of importance in relationship to other values. Weighting is used in the calculation of index numbers, (→) Index, averages, (→) gewogener Durchschnitt, and in sampling, (→) Auswahlverfahren, particularly in cases where a sample is deliberately biased toward one group of the population or to solve the problem of not-at-homes, (→) Gewichtung der Nichtangetroffenen (Nonresponse-Gewichtung).

Gewichtung *f* **der Nichtangetroffenen (Nonresponse-Gewichtung** *f***)** *(survey res)* weighting for not-at-homes, Politz-Simmons method

Gewinn *m* **(Profit** *m***)** *(econ)* profit

Gewinnanalyse *f* *(stat)* gain analysis

Gewinnanteilsmethode *f* (der Werbebudgetierung) percentage-of-profit method, (projektiv) percentage-of-anticipated-profit method, percentage-of-expected-profit method, (historisch) percentage-of-last-year's-profit method, percentage-of-previous-profit method
The method of determining advertising expenditure as a percentage of either past or expected profits. The method is based on the same, faulty philosophy as the percentage-of-sales method,

(→) Umsatzanteilsmethode, because it interprets advertising as a function of sales and not vice versa.

Gewinngutschein *m*
→ Einkaufsgutschein

Gewinnmaximierung *f* *(econ)* maximization of profits

Gewinnmaximum *n* *(econ)* profit maximum, maximum profit

Gewinnschwelle *f* **(Break-even-Punkt** *m*, **Breakeven** *m***)** *(econ)* breakeven point, break-even
The point at which sales revenue exactly covers all expenditure and neither profit nor loss is being made. The time required to reach this point is the payout period, and the return on investment thereafter is known as payout or payback.

Gewinnschwellenanalyse *f*
→ Break-even-Analyse

Gewinnspanne *f* **(Gewinnmarge** *f***)** *(econ)* margin of profit, profit margin

Gewinnspiel *n* sweepstakes *pl*, short sweeps *pl*
A type of promotion which awards substantial prizes on the basis of a chance drawing. No element of skill is involved, nor is an order or a purchase necessary. There are few legal restrictions for sweepstakes in Germany.

Gewinn- und Verlustrechnung *f*
→ Gain-und-Loss-Analyse

gewogene Zeitreihe *f* **(gewichtete Zeitreihe** *f***)** *(stat)* weighted time series

gewogener Durchschnitt *m* **(gewogenes Mittel** *n***)** *(stat)* weighted average, weighted mean
A weighted sum divided by the sum of weights, (→) Gewicht.

gewogener Index *m*
→ gewichteter Index

gewogenes Mittel *n*
→ gewogener Durchschnitt

Gewohnheit *f* habit
A pattern of behavior that occurs consistently and without specific consideration. Once established, it usually requires repetition in order to persist for any significant period of time.

Gewohnheitskauf *m*
→ Wiederholungskauf

Gewohnheitskaufverhalten *n*
→ habituelles Kaufverhalten

gewölbter Bogen *m* **(gekrümmter Bogen** *m***)** *(paper)* warped sheet

gezeichneter Artikel *m* **(Artikel** *m* **mit Autorenzeile)** bylined article

gezielte Streuung *f* (von Werbemitteln) **(Richtstrahlansatz** *m***)** selective advertising, rifle approach
A type of advertising and media planning that tries to reach an advertising goal by scrupulous aiming of efforts to the selected target group.
vgl. ungezielte Streuung
Giebel *m* **(Giebelspitze** *f*) *(outdoor advtsg)* gable end, gable, *brit* gable-end
Giebelwerbung *f (outdoor advtsg)* gable-end advertising, gable advertising, gable-end publicity, gable publicity, wall advertising, wall publicity
Poster or painted advertising at sites located on the end walls of buildings.
Gießapparat *m* **(Gießmaschine** *f,* **Gießgerät** *n***)** *(print)* (bei der Monotype) casting machine, caster, casting box
Gießbach *m* **(Rinnsal** *n***)** *(print)* river of white, river, pigeonhole
gießen *v/t (print)* to cast, to found
Gießer *m (print)* (Arbeiter am Gießapparat) caster, caster operator, casting man, founder, type founder
Gießerei *f (print)* foundry, type foundry
Gießform *f* **(Gußform** *f***)** *(print)* mould, mold, casting mold, casting mould
A wax, lead or plastic impression used in making electrotypes.
Gießkannenansatz *m* **(Gießkannenstreuung** *f,* **Streuung** *f* **nach dem Gießkannenprinzip)** *(advtsg)* shotgun approach
→ ungezielte Streuung; *vgl.* gezielte Streuung (Richtstrahlansatz)
Gießlöffel *m (print)* casting ladle
Gießmaschine *f*
→ Gießapparat
Giffen-Effekt *m* **(Giffen-Fall** *m,* **Giffen-Paradox** *n***)** *(econ)* Giffen effect (Sir R. Giffen)
The paradoxical movement of demand in the same direction as price, instead of following the classical laws of supply and demand.
→ externe Konsumeffekte
Giganto *n* **(Gigantographie** *f,* **Gigantografie** *f***)** *(print) etwa* giant coarse-screen halftone
Gini-Koeffizient *m* **(Ginis Konzentrationsmaß** *n***)** *(stat)* Gini coefficient (G), Gini coefficient of concentration, coefficient of concentration

Giraffe *f*
→ Hebebühne
Gitter *n (film/TV)* lattice, grid, grille, grating, (Orthikon) mesh
Gitterantenne *f (electr.)* umbrella-type antenna, *brit* umbrella-type aerial
Gitterblende *f (film/TV)* venetian blind, venetian-blind shutter
Gitterdecke *f (film/TV)* (Beleuchtung) lighting grid
Gitterrostdecke *f (film/TV)* lighting suspension grid, lighting grid, grid
Gitterschrift *f (typ)* black-letter type, text type, text
Gittertestbild *n (TV)* grid test pattern
Glacépapier *n*
→ Hochglanzpapier
Glamourlicht *n (film/TV)* (Beleuchtung) glamor light, *brit* glamour light
Glanz *m* gloss, brilliance, brightness, shine
glänzen *v/i* to shine, to glitter, to be glossy, to be bright
glänzend *adj* glossy, shiny, brilliant, bright
Glanzfarbe *f (print)* gloss ink
A printing ink that gives the effect of a glossy finish.
Glanzfolie *f* glossy foil, transparent foil, anti-dim foil, (zum Kaschieren) glassine, lamination
glanzfolienkaschiert (laminiert) *adj* laminated
Glanzfolienkaschierung *f* **(Laminierung** *f***)** lamination
The process or the result of coating printed sheets of paper with cellophane or acetate, to impart a high gloss or soil-resistant quality.
Glanzkarton *m* **(Glanzpappe** *f***)** glazed board, (gestrichen) coated board
Glanzkopie *f*
→ Hochglanzkopie
Glanzlicht *n* highlight
Glanzlichtautotypie *f* **(Spitzlichtautotypie** *f***)** *(print)* blowout
A halftone made from a highlight negative.
glanzlos *adj* → matt
Glanzpapier *n*
→ Hochglanzpapier
Glanzschnitt *m* **(Achatschnitt** *m***)** *(bookbinding)* burnished edge
Glanzseite *f*
→ Blankseite
Glasfaserkabel *n* glass fiber cable, *brit* glass fibre cable

Glashaut f *(TV)* (Orthikon) storage plate
Glasraster m *(print)* glass screen
glatt adj **1.** (paper) smooth, glazed, calendered, coated **2.** *(print)* (Satz) straight, plain, solid, run-on
Glätte f (**Glattheit** f) *(paper)* smoothness
glatte Bahn f *(paper)* liner web
glätten v/t → satinieren, kalandrieren
Glätten n (**Glättung** f)
→ Satinage, Kalandrieren
Glättung f **von Zeitreihen**
→ exponentielle Glättung
glatter Satz m *(typ)* run-on matter
→ Brotsatz, Gließsatz
Glättungsfaktor m *(stat)* smoothing factor
Glättzahn m (**Glättbein** n, **Glättwerkzeug** n) *(print)* burnisher, tooth burnisher, burnishing tool, polishing tool
Glaubwürdigkeit f credibility, believability, (der Werbung) advertising credibility, credibility of advertising, advertising believability, believability of advertising, (des Kommunikators) communicator credibility, communicator believability, (eines Werbeträgers) media credibility, media believability, (einer Quelle) source credibility, source believability
 The degree of trustworthiness or truth an audience ascribes to a message, such as an advertisement or an editorial article or a broadcast, or its communicator, such as a newspaper, a magazine, radio, or television.
gleicherscheinende Intervalle n/pl *(stat)* equal-appearing intervals pl
→ Thurstone-Skala (Skala der gleicherscheinenden Intervalle)
Gleichgewichtstheorie f
→ Konsistenztheorie
Gleichkanalbetrieb m common-channel service, co-channel service
Gleichlauf m (Bewegung) ganging, (Platte) regular rotational movement, no flutter and wow, (Synchronlauf) synchronism, tracking
Gleichlaufsignal n synchronising signal
Gleichrichter m *(electr.)* rectifier, detector, straightener

Gleichverteilungskurve f *(stat)* line of equal distribution
vgl. Lorenzkurve
gleitender Durchschnitt m (**gleitendes Mittel** n) *(stat)* moving average
 A statistical smoothing technique used to make long-term trends easier and more clearly discernible by reducing the significance of wide seasonal and other variations.
Gleitpreis m *(econ)* flexible price, moving price
Gliederungszahl f (**Gliederungsziffer** f) *(stat)* ratio
 An expression of the relative magnitude between two or more values or elements in a series and their total.
Gliedzahl f (**Gliedziffer** f) *(stat)* link-relative
 The value of a magnitude in a given period divided by the value in the previous period.
Gliedzahlenmethode f (**nach Persons**) *(stat)* link-relative method of seasonal adjustment, method of link-relatives
Glimmlampe f *(phot)* glow lamp, glow-discharge lamp, ready light
Globalanalyse f global analysis
Globalansatz m global approach
globale Marke f
→ Weltmarke
Globalmarketing n (**globales Marketing** n) global marketing (Theodore E. Levitt)
 The application of a uniform worldwide marketing strategy by companies that sell a fairly standard product or service in markets all over the world.
globale Marktforschung f global market research
Globalmerkmal n *(res)* global characteristic (Paul F. Lazarsfeld/Herbert Menzel)
Globovision f
→ Mondovision
Glockeisen n
→ Gaufriermaschine
Glockenkurve f (**Gauß'sche Glockenkurve** f)
→ Normalverteilung, Normalkurve
Gloriole f *(phot/film/TV)* (Licht) rim light, halation, halo
 The circle of light around an object due to reflection or dispersal of light.
Glotze f (**Glotzkiste** f, **Pantoffelkino** n) *colloq* *(TV)* boob tube, the tube, idiot box, idiot's box, idiot's lantern, gogglebox, goggle

Glückslos *n*
→ Los
Glücksspiel *n (promotion)* game of chance, gamble
Glühlampe *f* (**Glühlicht** *n*) *(phot)* incandescent lamp
Glühlichtscheinwerfer *m (film/TV)* inky, baby spotlight, inky dink, dinky inkie, inkie
  A tiny 250-watt spotlight.
GMT *abbr* Genetischer Motivationstest
Goldener Schnitt *m* the golden section, the extreme and mean ratio
Goldfolie *f* gold foil, gold leaf, leaf gold
Gompertzfunktion *f (stat)* Gompertz function
  An exponential growth function (curve) the dependent variable of which is a double exponential function of the independent variable: Y = ab^{cx}, where a, b, and c are three separate parameters.
Gompertzkurve *f (stat)* Gompertz curve
→ Gompertzfunktion
Gompertz-Modell *n (stat)* Gompertz model
Goodman und Kruskals Gamma *n* (**Goodman und Kruskals γ** *n*, **Goodman-Kontingenz** *f*) *(stat)* Goodman and Kruskal's gamma, Goodman and Kruskal's γ
Goodman und Kruskals Tau *n*, **Goodman und Kruskals τ** *n*, **Goodman-Kruskal-Korrelationskoeffizient** *m*) *(stat)* Goodman and Kruskal's tau, Goodman and Kruskal's τ
Goodman und Kruskals Lambda *n* (**Goodman und Kruskals λ** *n*) *(stat)* Goodman and Kruskal's lambda, Goodman and Kruskal's λ
Goodwill *m* goodwill
→ Firmenwert
Goodwill-Effekt *m* goodwill effect
Goodwill-Werbung *f* (**Vertrauenswerbung** *f*, **Prestigewerbung** *f*)
1. goodwill advertising, indirect-action advertising 2. (Goodwill-Werbetext) goodwill copy, indirect-action copy
→ Dispositionswerbung
Gossensche Gesetze *n/pl*
→ Bedürfnissättigungsgesetz (1. Gossensches Gesetz), Bedürfnisausgleichsgesetz (2. Gossensches Gesetz)

Gossenzeitschrift *f* (**Gossenzeitung** *f*, **Gossenblatt** *n*) pulp magazine, gutter paper, rag
GPRA *f abbr* Gesellschaft PR-Agenturen e.V.
Grabbelkiste *f* (für Sonderangebote)
→ Wühlkiste (Wühltisch)
Grabstichel *m (print)* burin, graver's chisel, graving tool, engraver's burin, graver
  A steel graver or cutting tool with a lozenge-shaped point, used for line engraving on metal.
Gradation *f (phot/print)* gradation
  The tonal range in negatives or prints, i.e. the variation in intensity of color or tone.
Gradationsentzerrung *f*
→ Gammaentzerrung
Gradationskurve *f* (**Gradationsverlauf** *m*)
→ Gamma-Zeit-Kurve
Gradientenmikrofon *n* pressure-gradient microphone, pressure-gradient mike
Gradientenmodell *n*
→ Aufforderungsgradient
Grafik *f*
→ Graphik
Grain *m*
→ Narbung, Korn, Körnung
Graph *m (stat)* graph
Graphentheorie *f* (**Theorie** *f* **der Graphen**) *(stat)* graph theory, theory of graphs
Graphik *f* (**Grafik** *f*) 1. (graphische Kunst) graphic art, graphic arts *pl*, graphics *pl (construed as sg)*, creative art, artwork, creative copy and art, creative work, arts and crafts *pl*
2. (graphische Gestaltung) creative art, artwork, creative work, creative copy and art, creative design
3. (Kunstdruck) art print, print, artwork, graphic picture 4. *(stat)* (graphische Darstellung) diagram, graph, graphic presentation
5. → graphische Abteilung
Graphikblatt *n* (**Grafikblatt** *n*)
→ Graphik 3.
Graphik-Designer *m* (**Grafik-Designer** *m*)
→ Graphiker
Graphiker(in) *m(f)* (**Grafiker(in)** *m(f)*) graphic artist, artist, (Gebrauchsgraphiker) commercial artist, (Werbe-

graphiker) advertising artist, (Chef-graphiker) art director, art editor
graphische Abteilung f **(Graphik** f**)** (in einer Werbeagentur) art department, commercial art department, art studio, *colloq* bull pen
 That department in an advertising agency whose major function it is to translate copywriters' ideas into layouts, package design, corporate logotypes, trademarks, symbols, and storyboards. The artists specify style and size of typography, paste the type in place, and arrange all other details of an advertisement, so that it can be reproduced by engravers and printers.
graphische Darstellung f **(Graphik** f**)** *(stat)* diagram, graph, chart, graphic representation, graphic presentation
 The presentation of statistical data in geometric form to facilitate the comprehension of the pattern of distribution of a variable or the relationship of two or more variables. Differences in quantities are represented by area, shape, color, distances, or other differentiating characteristics of the design.
graphisches Archiv n
→ Bildarchiv
graphisches Gewerbe n
→ Druckgewerbe
graphisches Material n **(Material** n **für Graphiker)** artists' medium, art and mechanical, A & M
graphische Ratingskala f **(graphische Bewertungsskala** f**)** *(stat)* graphic rating scale, graphic scale
→ Ratingskala
graphologischer Test m *(psy)* graphological test
Grat m *(typ)* (einer Type) beard
Gratifikation f gratification
Gratifikationsmuster n gratification pattern, pattern of gratification
Gratifikationsprinzip n gratification principle, principle of gratification
Gratisabonnement n
→ Freiabonnement
Gratisangebot n *(econ)* free offer, gratuitous offer
Gratisankündigung f **(Gratisansage** f, **Gratisanzeige** f**)** puff notice, free puff, free mention, puff, plug, editorial mention, deadhead
 An advertisement or a commercial printed or aired free of charge.
Gratisanschlag m
→ Freianschlag

Gratisanschlagstelle f
→ Freianschlagstelle
Gratisanzeige f
→ Gratisankündigung
Gratisanzeiger m **(Gratisblatt** n**)**
→ Anzeigenblatt
Gratisexemplar n
→ Freiexemplar
Gratisgutschein m **(Freigutschein** m**)** gratuitous coupon
Gratislieferung f
→ Freihauslieferung
Gratismuster n **(Gratisprobe** f**)** *(econ)* free sample, gratuitous sample
→ Muster
Gratispresse f
→ Anzeigenblätter
Gratisprobe f
→ Gratismuster
Gratisverlosung f
→ Verlosung
Gratisversand m **(Freiversand** m**)** free mailing
Gratiswerbesendung f **(Gratissendung** f**)** *(radio/TV)* bonus spot, plug
 A commercial aired free of charge.
Gratiszustellung f
→ Freihauslieferung
Grauentzerrung f *(TV)* gray-scale correction, *brit* grey-scale correction
graue Wickelpappe f millboard
→ Buchbinderpappe
grauer Markt m *(econ)* gray market, *brit* grey market
→ Direktabsatz
grauer Preis m *(econ)* gray market price, *brit* grey market price
Graufeld n *(phot)* gray patch, *brit* grey patch
Graufilter m *(phot)* gray filter, *brit* grey filter
Graukarte f *(phot)* gray chart, *brit* grey chart
Graukeil m **(Grauskala** f, **Grautafel** f**)** *(phot/print/TV)* gray wedge, gray scale, neutral wedge, step wedge, *brit* grey wedge, grey scale
 A ten-step intensity scale used to judge tonal values ranging from black to white, placed at the side of colored originals during photography and printing, or used in evaluating the shading of the black-and-white television picture for balance and uniformity of tone.
Graupappe f
→ Buchbinderpappe

Grauschleier *m (phot)* gray fog, *brit* grey fog
Graustufe *f (phot)* gray step, shade of gray, *brit* grey step, shade of grey
→ Graukeil
Grauwert *m*
→ Halbton
Graveur *m (print)* engraver, graver
 Anyone who engraves or makes engravings.
gravieren *v/t (print)* to engrave, to enchase
 To cut or incise lines or designs in metal, wood and other surfaces by manual use of tools.
Graviermaschine *f*
→ Klischee-Graviermaschine
Graviernadel *f (print)* engraving needle
Gravierung *f* (**Gravieren** *n*) *(print)* engraving
Gravur *f* (**Gravüre** *f*) *(print)* gravure, engraving
 A printing process which transfers images to paper with ink retained in depressions in plate.
Greifbühnentest *m* (**Schnellgreiftest** *m*, **Greiftest** *m*, **Schnellgreifbühnentest** *m*) *(market res)* pickup test, pick-up test, product pickup test, product pick-up test
 A studio test designed to examine the immediate attraction of products, product packages, or the effect of advertising. Test persons are briefly exposed to products and invited to spontaneously pick out the ones they like.
Greifer *m* 1. *(print)* gripper, (Zeilensetzmaschine) elevator 2. *(phot)* (Zahnrad) claw, (Justiergreifer) register pin, pilot pin, moving pin
Greiferkante *f (print)* gripper margin, gripper edge, lay edge, lay margin
 A device on printing presses that picks up the sheet of paper from the paper table and holds it in position while it receives the impression.
Greiftest *m*
→ Greifbühnentest
Grenzanbieter *m* (**Grenzbetrieb** *m*) *(econ)* marginal enterprise
Grenzerlös *m (econ)* marginal revenue (MR)
 The increment in total revenue resulting from the sale of one additional unit of a product, considered from the point of view of sliding down the demand curve.
Grenzkosten *pl (econ)* marginal cost (MC)
 The addition to total cost resulting from the production of one additional unit of a product.
Grenzkostenpreis *m (econ)* marginal cost price, marginal cost
→ Grenzkosten
Grenzkostenrechnung *f (econ)* marginal costing
 The pricing of additional sales on the basis of merely the direct costs with overhead costs, (→) Betriebsunkosten, being recovered from existing sales.
Grenznutzen *m (econ)* marginal utility
 The amount of increased satisfaction an individual consumer gains from the purchase of an additional unit of a product or service.
Grenzpreis *m (econ)* marginal price
 A price based on marginal cost.
Grenzrate *f* **der Substitution** *(econ)* marginal rate of substitution
 The differential quotient indicating the amount of a product x_2 a consumer has to give up to obtain the same utility, (→) Nutzen, by increasing the number of units purchased of a product x_1.
Grenzwert *m (econ)* marginal value
Grenzwertbetrachtung *f*
→ Marginalanalyse
Grenzwertsatz *m (stat)* marginal value theorem
griechisch-lateinisches Quadrat *n (stat)* Graeco-Latin square
Grieß *m (TV)* (Bild) shot noise, random noise, Johnson noise, *colloq* grass
grob *adj (print)* (Raster) coarse
Grobeinstellung *f (phot)* rough focusing, coarse setting, rough adjustment
grobkörnig *adj (phot)* coarse-grained
Grobraster *m* (**grober Raster** *m*) *(print)* coarse screen
Grobrasterautotypie *f* (**Grobrasterklischee** *n*) *(print)* coarse-screen halftone, coarse-screen engraving
 A halftone, (→) Autotypie, with a comparatively low screen suitable for newsprint.
Grobwelle *f*
→ A-Welle
Grobstreuung *f (media planning)* shotgun approach
→ ungezielte Streuung
Groschenheft *n* (**Groschenroman** *m*, **Groschenromanheft** *n*) dime novel
Groschenpresse *f* penny press

Groschenzeitung f (billiges Massenblatt n, **Boulevardzeitung** f) penny paper
Großabnahmerabatt m *(econ)* patronage discount
→ Funktionsrabatt
Großabnehmer m *(econ)* bulk purchaser, bulk buyer
Großanschlag m (**Großanschlagfläche** f) *(outdoor advtsg)* bulletin board, supersite
→ Großfläche
Großanschlagwerbung f (**Großanschlagflächenwerbung** f) *(outdoor advtsg)* bulletin board advertising, supersite advertising
→ Großflächenanschlagwerbung
Großanzeige f
→ Formatanzeige
Großanzeigenwerbung f
→ Formatanzeigenwerbung
Großauflage f
→ Massenauflage
Großaufnahme f (**Nahaufnahme** f) *(film/TV/phot)* close-up (CU), close shot (CS), close-up view
A shot in which the details of an object are discernible, because the object dominates the image.
Großbetrieb m *(econ)* large-size enterprise, large-scale enterprise
Großbildprojektion f *(phot)* large-screen projection, giant-screen projection, wide-screen projection, eidophor screen projection
Großbildprojektor m *(phot)* large-screen projector, giant-screen projector, wide-screen projector, eidophor screen projector
Großbuchstabe m (**Versal** n) *(typ)* capital letter, capital, uppercase letter (UC, uc), cap
vgl. Kleinbuchstabe
Großdia n (**Großdiapositiv** n) *(phot)* super slide
Größe f size, format, dimension, (Umfang) volume
Größe f **nach Beschnitt**
→ Beschnittgröße
große Brennweite f *(phot)* long focal length, long focus
Großeinkauf m *(econ)* large-scale purchase, large-quantity purchase, bulk purchase
Großeinkäufer m *(econ)* large-scale purchaser, large-scale buyer, large-quantity purchaser, large-quantity buyer, bulk purchaser, bulk buyer
Großfläche f *(outdoor advtsg)* bulletin board, large panel, magna panel, supersite
A large solus advertising site, cf. (→) Ganzstelle, located on private ground.
vgl. Allgemeinstelle, Spezialstelle
Großflächenanschlag m (**Großflächenplakat** n) *(outdoor advtsg)* bulletin board poster, bulletin board, large panel poster, magna panel poster, supersite poster
Großflächenanschlagwerbung f, **Großflächenwerbung** f) *(outdoor advtsg)* bulletin board advertising, large-panel poster advertising, magna panel advertising, supersite poster advertising
Großflächensender m *(radio/TV)* wide-coverage transmitter, main station
Großformat n large size, large format
Großgemeinschaftsantenne f (**Gemeinschaftsantenne** f) community antenna, *brit* community aerial, community antenna relay station, *brit* community aerial relay station
Großgemeinschaftsantennenanlage f (**GGA**)
→ Großgemeinschaftsantenne, Gemeinschaftsantennenanlage
Großhandel m *(econ)* 1. (Institution) wholesale trade, the wholesalers pl
All establishments or places of business primarily engaged in selling merchandise to retailers; to industrial, commercial, institutional, farm, or professional users; or to other wholesalers; or acting as intermediaries, i.e. agents or brokers, in buying merchandise for or selling merchandise to such persons or companies.
2. (Funktion) wholesaling, wholesale trading
All activities involved in selling goods or services to those who are buying for the purpose of resale, or business or institutional use.
Großhandelsbetrieb m (**Großhandelsfirma** f, **Großhandelsunternehmen** n) *(econ)* wholesaler, wholesale business, wholesale merchant, wholesale company, *auch* jobber, distributor, supply house (Filiale) wholesale outlet
A business unit which buys and resells merchandise to retailers and other merchants and/or to industrial,

Großhandelsdispositionszentrum

institutional, and commercial users but which does not sell in significant amounts to ultimate consumers. In the basic materials, semi-finished goods, and tool and machinery trades, merchants of this type are commonly known as "distributors" or "supply houses." Generally, these merchants render a wide variety of services to their customers. Those who render all the services normally expected in the wholesale trade are known as service wholesalers; those who render only a few of the wholesale services are known as limited function wholesalers. The latter group is composed mainly of cash and carry wholesalers who do not render the credit or delivery service, drop shipment wholesalers who sell for delivery by the producer direct to the buyer, truck wholesalers who combine selling, delivery, and collection in one operation, and mail order wholesalers who perform the selling service entirely by mail.

Großhandelsdispositionszentrum n **(Trade Mart** m**)** *(econ)* trade mart, mart, trade center
A relatively permanent facility that firms can rent in order to exhibit products year round. In them, products such as furniture, home decorating supplies, toys, clothing, and gift items are sold to wholesalers and retailers.

Großhandelsfläche f
→ Verkaufsfläche

Großhandelsformat n **(Großhandelspackung** f, **Großverbraucherpackung** f**)** *(econ)* institutional size, bonus pack size, extra size pack
A package or product size intended to satisfy the needs of institutions, such as hospitals, hotels, plants, restaurants, or wholesalers rather than that of private households or individual consumers.

Großhandelsindex m **(Großhandelspreisindex** m**)** *(econ) obsol* wholesale price index (WPI)

Großhandelskette f *(econ)* wholesale chain, chain of wholesalers

Großhandelslager n *(econ)* wholesale store, wholesale warehouse

Großhandelsmarketing n *(econ)* wholesale marketing

Großhandelsmarkt m
→ Großmarkt

Großhandelsmarktforschung f wholesale market research

Großhandelspanel n *(market res)* wholesaler panel survey, wholesaler panel study, wholesaler panel investigation, wholesaler panel

Großhandelspreis m *(econ)* wholesale price

Großhandelspreisindex m
→ Großhandelsindex

Großhandelsrabatt m *(econ)* wholesale discount

Großhandelsreisender m
→ Reisender

Großhandelsspanne f *(econ)* wholesale margin

Großhandelsunternehmen n
→ Großhandelsbetrieb

Großhandelswerbung f wholesale advertising, wholesaler advertising

Großhandelszentrum n **(Standortzentrum** n, **Kooperationszentrum** n**)** *(econ)* wholesale center, wholesaling center, trade center, mart, trade mart

Großhändler m *(econ)* wholesaler, wholesale dealer, wholesale merchant, distributor, *auch* jobber
→ Großhandelsbetrieb

Großhändlerwerbung f
→ Großhandelswerbung

Großhandlung f
→ Großhandelsbetrieb, Großhändler

Grossierer m *obsol* → Großhändler

Grossist m
→ Großhändler, Pressegrosso

Großkopie f **(Großphotokopie** f**)** *(phot)* jumbo stat

Großkunde m **(Großauftrag** m, **großer Etat** m**)** (einer Werbeagentur) key account
A major client (with a sizable account) of an advertising agency.

Großkundenbetreuung f key account management
Giving particular care to key accounts is frequently considered a vital task in advertising agencies, since these clients account for a significant part of an agency's billings.

Großmarkt m **(Erzeugergroßmarkt** m, **Versorgungsgroßmarkt** m**)** *(econ)* wholesale market, central market, trade center, merchandise mart

Grosso n
→ Pressegrosso

Grossorabatt m
→ Großhandelsrabatt

Großplakat n *(outdoor advtsg)* king-size poster, magna poster
vgl. Großfläche

Großraumladen m
→ Discountbetrieb, Supermarkt, Verbrauchermarkt

Großschreibung f capitalization, *brit* capitalisation

Großsender m *(radio/TV)* high-power transmitter, high-power station, *(radio)* powerhouse station, clear-channel station

Großstadtpresse f big city press, metropolitan press

Großstadtrandzone f suburban zone

Großsupermarkt m *(retailing)* supersupermarket, hypermarket, hypermarché, superstore
A low-cost, high-volume, limited-service retail operation that in addition to the services provided by a supermarket fills such routine purchasing needs as personal-care products, alcoholic beverages, tobacco products, some apparel, low-priced housewares, hardware items, gasoline, consumable lawn and garden products, stationery and sewing supplies, some leisure-time products, and household services.

Großtafel f
→ Großfläche

Großverbraucher m *(econ)* institutional consumer, large-scale consumer

Großverbrauchergeschäft n *(econ) etwa* large-scale consumption dealer, institutional consumer dealer

Großverbraucher-Rabatt m *(econ)* bonus, bonus discount

Großverlag m large-size publisher, large-size publishing company

Großverpackung f
→ Familienpackung, Großhandelsformat

Großzahlmethode f **(Großzahlforschung** f) *obsol*
→ quantitative Analyse

grotesk (serifenlos) *adj (typ)* sanserif, sans serif, Gothic, Doric, *selten* grotesque

Groteskschrift f **(serifenlose Schrift** f) *(typ)* sanserif type, sans serif type, sanserif, sans serif, Gothic type, Doric type, *selten* grotesque type
A typeface that has no cross strokes (serifs) at the top or bottom of the characters.

Grund m *(print)* (aus Tratantgummi) bed

Grundaufforderungswert m
→ Aufforderungswert

Grundaussage f **(Grundbotschaft** f) basic message

Grundausschluß m *(print)* standard spacing

Grundauszählung f *(stat)* basic frequency count

Grundbedarf m **(Primärbedarf** m) **(Wilhelm Vershofen)** *(econ)* basic demand, primary demand
The demand suited to satisfy basic physiological needs such as hunger, thirst, shelter, etc. In economics, the demand for a type of product without regard to a specific brand.
vgl. Zusatzbedarf

Grundbedürfnis n **(Primärbedürfnis** n) *(econ)* basic need, primary need
The need for satisfaction of basic physiological necessities.

Grundeinheit f (von Maßsystemen) basic unit, base

Grundfarbe f **(Primärfarbe** f) elementary color, *brit* elementary colour, primary color, *brit* primary colour, salient color, *brit* salient colour
The fundamental colors for explaining the process of color vision, and for reproduction of colored originals. Applied to light, the true primary colors are violet, red and green; the primary colors of printing inks are termed yellow, red and blue — with green being formed by a mixture of blue and yellow.

Grundformat n *(paper)* basic size, basic area

Grundfrequenz f *(radio/TV)* fundamental frequency

Grundgage f basic fee

Grundgeräusch n **(Grundrauschen** n) background noise, (Platte) surface noise

Grundgesamtheit f **(Gesamtheit** f, **Population** f, **statistische Masse** f) *(stat)* universe, population, (Grundgesamtheit für die Ziehung) sampled population, sampled universe
The entire set or collection of objects, people, events, etc., of interest in a particular context of investigation. More specifically, the total number of units from which a sample is taken.

Grundhelligkeit f *(phot)* background brightness

grundieren *v/t (print)* to size

Grundierung f **(Grundieren** n) *(print)* sizing

Grundinteresse *n* (**Minimalinteresse** *n*) base-line involvement, baseline involvement
  Involvement in a product or service prior to advertising exposure.
Grundkonzept *n* (**Grundkonzeption** *f*) basic concept
Grundlagenforschung *f* basic research
  vgl. angewandte Forschung
grundlegende Werbebotschaft *f* basic advertising message, basic message
Grundleuchtdichte *f* base-light intensity
gründlicher Leser *m (media res)* thorough reader
gründliches Leser *n (media res)* thorough reading
Gründlichkeit *f* **des Lesens** *(media res)* thoroughness of reading
Grundlicht *n* base light, foundation light
Grundlinie *f* (**Schriftlinie** *f*) *(typ)* base line
  That line on which the base of all capital letters of a font, (→) Schriftart, and the bodies of its lower-case letters align.
Grundnachfrage *f*
  → Grundbedarf
Grundnutzen *m* (Wilhelm Vershofen) *(econ)* basic utility
  The technical and functional utility of a product or a service.
  vgl. Zusatznutzen
Grundpreis *m* **1.** *(econ)* base price, basic price, advertised price
  The standard price at which a product or a service, or a publication, may be purchased by anyone.
2. *(advtsg)* base rate, basic rate, card rate, flat rate, full rate-card cost, one-time rate, open rate, transient rate, standard rate
  A uniform rate for advertising space or time, with no discounts for volume or frequency.
Grundrauschen *n*
  → Grundgeräusch
Grundschleier *m (phot)* base veil, background fog
Grundschrift *f (typ)* body type, text type, main type, body text, body copy
  The type used for body copy in the editorial section of a publication or in an advertisement, in contrast to display type, (→) Auszeichnungsschrift, used for headlines and subheads.
Grundstrich *m (typ)* main stroke, thick stroke
  → Abstrich 1.

Grundstücksanzeige *f* real estate advertisement, real estate ad
Grundtenor *m* (**Grundthema** *n*) (eines Werbetextes) copy theme, theme
  The central idea of an advertisement, campaign, or program.
Grundtrend *m*
  → Trend
Grundware *f (econ)* basic product, primary product
  → Erstausstattung; *vgl.* Folgeware
Gruppendiskussion *f* (**Gruppengespräch** *n*, **Gruppeninterview** *n*) *(survey res)* group discussion, focus group interview, focused group interview
  A research technique using interviews in which a small group of persons (six to fifteen) are brought together for a group discussion about a selected topic under the direction of a discussion leader. Group discussions are frequently used in the pilot stage of a study in order to establish the range of people's attitudes or to recognize the gamut of a problem.
Gruppendynamik *f (soc)* group dynamics *pl (construed as sg)*
Gruppeneinstellung *f* (**Gruppenaufnahme** *f*) *(phot)* group shot, crowd shot
Gruppenentscheidung *f* (**kollektive Entscheidung** *f*) *(econ)* group decision, collective decision
  vgl. Individualentscheidung
Gruppengespräch *n* (**Gruppeninterview** *n*)
  → Gruppendiskussion
Gruppenmarketing *n* group marketing, horizontal marketing, horizontal marketing cooperation
  A type of cooperative marketing whose cost is shared by two or more marketers at the same level in the channel of distribution.
Gruppenorganisation *f* (**Gruppensystem** *n*) (Agenturorganisation) group system, group organization system, creative groups organization system
  A type of advertising agency organization, in which specific individuals are assigned to a team which does the planning, creative contact, and similar work for accounts turned over to the group. Other groups in the agency handle different accounts. In effect, several small agencies are created within the framework of the large agency.
  vgl. Abteilungsorganisation, spezialisierte Organisation

Gruppenwerbung f group advertising, horizontal advertising, horizontal advertising cooperation
A kind of cooperative advertising that is jointly financed by two or more advertisers at the same level in the channel of distribution, e.g. by a group of local retailers.

Gruppenwettbewerb m group contest

Gruppierung f (**Gruppieren** n) *(stat)* grouping, grouping of data, data grouping
The arrangement of raw statistical data in class intervals.

Gruselfilm m *(film/TV)* suspense-mystery drama

Guasch f (**Guaschbild** n, **Guaschzeichnung** f) gouache, gouache painting
A method of painting with opaque colors which have been ground in water and mixed with a preparation of gum.

Guaschfarbe f gouache color, *brit* gouache colour

Guckkasten m
→ Glotze

Gültigkeit f (**Validität** f) *(res)* validity
The ability of a measure or a test to in fact measure what it purports to measure. Validity is to be contrasted with consistency, (→) Konsistenz, which is concerned with the internal agreement of data or procedures among themselves. vgl. Zuverlässigkeit (Reliabilität)

Gültigkeitskoeffizient m (**Validitätskoeffizient** m) *(res)* validity coefficient, coefficient of validity

Gültigkeitsprüfung f (**Validitätsprüfung** f, **Validierung** f) *(res)* validity check, validation
A procedure which provides, by reference to independent sources, evidence that an enquiry is free from bias or otherwise conforms to its declared purpose.

Gummiarabikum n (**Gummi arabicum** n) gum arabic
A substance used as vehicle in photoengraving, and rendered sensitive in solution by the addition of ammonium bichromate.

Gummidruck m
→ Flexodruck

Gummierkalander m (**Schlichtmaschine** f) sizing machine

Gummiklischee n *(print)* rubber block, rubber plate
A printing plate consisting of an engraved or molded surface of rubber, made either by manual engraving or by molding from relief etchings.

Gummileim m (**Gummilösung** f, **Kautschukkitt** m, **Fixogum** n) rubber cement
An adhesive made with a rubber base, used widely in the graphic arts. It does not wrinkle or stain paper and is removable.

Gummilinse f (**Vario-Objektiv** n, **Zoom** m, **Zoom-Objektiv** n) *(phot/film/TV)* zoom, zoom lens, zoomar lens, varifocal lens, vario lens;
Gummilinse zuziehen: to zoom in;
Gummilinse aufziehen: to zoom out
A special camera lens with an adjustable focal length, (→) Brennweite, used to achieve zoom shots that impart the impression of movement without having to move or dolly the camera.

Gummilinsenaufnahme f (**Zoomaufnahme** f) *(phot/film/TV)* zoom shot
A shot taken with a varifocal lens, (→) Gummilinse. Also, a rapid change of focus which makes the image grow larger (zoom in) or smaller (zoom out).

Gummirakel m *(print)* squeegee
Gummischnitt m *(print)* rubber cut
Gummistereo n *(print)* rubber duplicate plate
Gummituch n *(print)* rubber blanket
Gummizylinder m *(print)* rubber-blanketed cylinder, rubber-covered offset cylinder

Guß m 1. *(phot)* coating
→ Beschichtung
2. *(print)* → Schriftguß

gußgestrichener Karton m (**gußgestrichenes Papier** n) cast-coated paper, cast-coated paper board, chromo-board paper, chromo-board

Gußnummer f
→ Emulsionschargennummer

Gutachten n expert opinion, expert advice, expertise

Gutachter m (**Sachverständiger** m) expert, referee

Güte f (**Gütefunktion** f) *(stat)*
→ Trennschärfe

gute Sitten f/pl etwa business practice

Gütefunktion f
→ Trennschärfe

Gütegemeinschaft f *(econ)* etwa grade label association, certification mark association, quality label association

Gütekriterium n *(res)*
→ Objektivität, Zuverlässigkeit (Reliabilität), Gültigkeit (Validität)

Güter *n/pl (econ)* goods *pl*
In economics, any tangible things which people consider useful and are willing to exchange for other merchandise or products.
Güter *n/pl* **des gehobenen Bedarfs**
→ Shopping Goods
Güter *n/pl* **des täglichen Bedarfs**
→ Convenience Goods
Güterklassifikation f **(Gütertypologie** f**)** *(econ)* classification of goods, typology of goods
Güterstrom *m (econ)* flow of goods
Gütertest *m*
→ Warentest
Gütertypologie f
→ Güterklassifikation
Gütesiegel *n*
→ Testsiegel
Gütetest *m (stat)*
→ Anpassungstest, Trennschärfetest
Gütezeichen *n (econ)* grade label, certification mark, quality label
Gutschein *m* **(Kupon** *m,* **Coupon** *m***)** coupon
A certificate that carries an offer of a cash reduction in the price of an item in a retail store.
→ Kupon
Gutscheinanzeige f
→ Kuponanzeige
Gutscheinausschneiden *n* **(Kuponausschneiden** *n***)** coupon clipping
Gutscheinblock *m* **(Kuponblock** *m,* **Gutscheinabreißblock** *m***)** coupon pad
Gutscheineinlösung f **(Kuponeinlösung** f**)** coupon redemption
→ Einlösung
Gutscheineinlösungsrate f **(Kuponeinlösungsrate** f**)** coupon redemption rate
→ Einlösungsrate
Gutscheineinlösungsverhalten *n* **(Kuponeinlösungsverhalten** *n***)**
coupon redemption behavior, *brit* coupon redemption behaviour

→ Einlösungsverhalten
Gutscheinrücklauf *m* **(Kuponrücklauf** *m***)** coupon returns *pl*, coupon redemption rate, redemption rate
→ Einlösungsrate
Gutscheinwerbung f **(Kuponwerbung** f**)** coupon advertising, couponing
The use of coupons in the promotion of a product. This is a way of offering consumers a special, temporary price reduction on an item without actually changing the regular market price. A coupon good for a specified cents off on the purchase of a product is mailed to the consumer, placed in the package of another product, or published in advertisements in print media. Its promotional value is determined by its ability to induce consumers to purchase the product.
Guttman-Skala f **(Guttman-Skalogramm** *n,* **Skalogramm** *n***)** *(res)*
Guttman scale, Guttman scalogram, scalogram (Louis Guttman)
A scale that uses the method of cumulative ratings. It is based on the hypothesis that the universe of items forms a scale for all members of the population if it is possible to rank people on their attitude and to reproduce, from their rankings, their responses to each of the items.
Guttman-Skalierung f **(Guttman-Methode** f, **Guttman-Technik** f, **Guttman-Verfahren** *n,* **Guttman-Skalierungsverfahren** *n***)** *(res)*
Guttman scaling, Guttman method, Guttman scalogramn technique, Guttman scalogram analysis, scalogram analysis (Louis Guttman)
Guttmans Lambda *n* **(Guttmans λ** *n***)**
→ Goodman und Kruskals Lambda
GWA *m abbr* Gesamtverband Werbeagenturen
GWA-Effie *m* GWA effie award, GWA Effie Award
GWB *n abbr* Gesetz gegen Wettbewerbsbeschränkungen

H

H₀-Hypothese f
→ Nullhypothese
Hₐ-Hypothese f (**H₁-Hypothese** f)
→ Arbeitshypothese
Haarspatium n *(print)* hair space
  A half-point or one-point space used to letterspace words and to justify lines of type.
Haarspieß m *(print)* → Spieß
Haarstrich m **(hochfeine Linie** f)
(typ) hairline, hairline rule, hair stroke, fine line
  A fine and delicate line in a type face design or in an illustration. Also, the narrowest or finest black or white line capable of being etched or engraved on a relief printing plate; a black finishing line bordering the edges of a square finished halftone plate.
habituelles Kaufverhalten n *(econ)* habitual buying behavior,
brit habitual buying behaviour
  A pattern of buying behavior that occurs routinely and consistently without specific consideration.
vgl. impulsives Kaufverhalten
Hadern m/pl *(paper)* rags pl
Hadernfaser f **(Hadernstoff** m)
(paper) rag fiber, *brit* rag fibre, rag substance
Haderngehalt m *(paper)* rag content
Hadernpapier n rag paper, rag bond, rag
Haftetikett n adhesive label, self-adhesive label, pressure-sensitive label
Haftfolie f **(Haftklebepapier** n, **Selbstklebepapier** n) pressure-sensitive adhesive, pressure-sensitive adhesive paper
Haftschicht f
→ Substratschicht
Halbbelegung f *(outdoor & transit advtsg)* half showing, 50 showing, 50 showing, half run, half service, number 50 showing, minimum coverage
  The number of poster panels approximating one-half of the number included in a full showing, (→) Ganzbelegung, for the area. Sometimes defined as: a number of posters sufficient to reach about 85% of the people in the market every other day.
Halbbild n *(TV)* field
  One half of a television picture scanning cycle. There are two interlaced fields to each frame.
Halbbilddauer f *(TV)* field period, field duration
Halbbildfrequenz f *(TV)* field frequency
halbe Doppelseite f **(halbe Doppelseitenanzeige** f) half-page spread, junior spread, pony spread, Scotch spread
  An arrangement for an advertisement consisting of the upper or lower half of each of two facing pages.
Halbfaltschachtel f half-slotted container with separate cover (HSC)
Halbfabrikat n **(Halbfertigware** f)
(econ) semifinished product, *brit* semi-finished product, semifinished goods pl, *brit* semi-finished goods pl, semi-manufactured goods pl, fabricating materials pl
  Raw material which has been processed into a stable form which requires only dimensional changes to permit its incorporation into a product, including raw materials which have gone through some stages of manufacturing but require more processing before they can be used. In other words, those industrial goods which become a part of the finished product and which have undergone processing beyond that required for raw materials but not as much as finished parts.
halbfett (fett) adj *(print)* boldface, bold face, (b.f., bf, BF, B.F.), boldfaced, boldfaced, bold
→ fett
halbfette Schrift f **(fette Schrift** f,
halbfette Type f) *(print)* boldface type, bold-face type, bold-faced type, boldface, bold face (b.f., bf, B.F., BF)
  Type that is heavier in strokes than other designs of the same type family, or heavier than text type with which it is used.
→ fette Schrift
Halbfettdruck m **(Fettdruck** m) *(print)* bold type

halbfrontale Aufnahme f *(phot)* three-quarter shot
halbgeleimtes Papier n half-sized paper, soft-sized paper, medium-sized paper
Halbgeviert n *(typ)* en quad, en quadrat, n-quadrat, en, nut
One half of the width of an em.
vgl. Geviert, Viertelgeviert
Halbgeviertstrich m *(typ)* en quad dash, en dash, n dash
Halbierungskorrelation f *(stat)* split-half correlation
The correlation measuring split-half reliability, (→) Halbierungsreliabilität.
Halbierungsmethode f **(Halbierungsverfahren** n, **Split-half-Verfahren** n) *(survey res)* split-half method, split-half technique, split-half reliability test, split-halves reliability test, split-test method, split-test technique
A technique used to ascertain the degree to which a given measurement procedure elicits the same results each time it is applied under identical circumstances. It consists of dividing a particular scale into equivalent halves, e.g. by assigning even numbers to one and odd numbers to the other half.
Halbierungsreliabilität f **(Halbierungszuverlässigkeit** f) *(survey res)* split-half reliability, split-halves reliability
Halbjahresschrift f **(Halbjahres-Zeitschrift** f, **Sechsmonats-Zeitschrift** f, **halbjährlich erscheinende Zeitschrift** f) bi-annual journal, bi-annual magazine, bi-annual publication, semi-annual journal, semi-annual magazine, semi-annual publication, biyearly journal, biyearly magazine, biyearly publication
Halbkarton m paperboard, thin cardboard
Halbleinen n **(Halbleinenband** m) half-cloth
halbmonatlich (vierzehntäglich) adj semi-monthly, fortnightly, (doppeldeutig) bi-weekly, *adv* twice a month, every two weeks
Halbmonatszeitschrift f **(vierzehntäglich erscheinende Zeitschrift** f) semi-monthly magazine, fortnightly magazine, (doppeldeutig) biweekly magazine
Halbnahaufnahme f **(Halbnahe** f) *(phot)* medium close-up (M.C.U., MCU), medium shot (MS), mid-shot (MS), semi-close-up (SCU), close medium shot (CMS), bust shot
A camera shot that focuses on a person or object and shows a limited amount of background.
halboffene Frage f *(survey res)*
→ geschlossene Frage
Halbschatten m *(phot)* penumbra, penumbral shadow, half-shadow, half-shade
halbseitige Anzeige f half-page advertisement, half-page ad
Halbselbstbedienung f
→ Teilselbstbedienung (Selbstauswahl)
halbspaltig *adj (print)* half-measure, half-column measure, half-column, half-stick
halbstandardisiertes Interview n
→ zentriertes Interview
halbstrukturiertes Interview n **(teilstrukturiertes Interview** n) *(survey res)* semi-structured interview, partially structured interview
An interview that involves the predetermination of the general course, but not the details.
Halbtitel m
→ Schmutztitel
Halbton m **(echter Halbton** m) *(print/phot)* continuous tone
Prints or photographs with a continuous shading rather than a shading rendered with halftone dots, hatching, the use of screens, etc.
Halbtonbild n *(phot)* continuous-tone picture, continuous tone
→ Halbton
Halbtondruck m **(echter Halbtondruck** m) continuous-tone printing
→ Halbton
Halbtonphotographie f continuous-tone photography
→ Halbton
Halbtonpunkt m
→ Rasterpunkt
Halbtonvorlage f *(phot/print)* continuous-tone copy, continuous tone
→ Halbton
Halbtonwiedergabe f **(Halbtonreproduktion** f) *(phot/print)* continuous-tone reproduction, continuous-tone rendering
→ Halbton
Halbtotale f *(phot/film/TV)* medium long shot (MLS), full-length shot (FLS)

A camera shot showing several objects from a certain distance and, therefore, with their background.
Halbwelle f half wave
halbwöchentlich adj semi-weekly, half-weekly, (doppeldeutig) bi-weekly adv twice a week
halbwöchentlich (zweimal wöchentlich) erscheinende Zeitschrift f **(Zeitung** f**)** semi-weekly magazine, semi-weekly paper, half-weekly magazine, half-weekly paper, (doppeldeutig) bi-weekly magazine, bi-weekly paper
Halfagras n
→ Espartogras
Hall m **(Echo** n, **Nachhall** m) (radio/film/TV) echo, (im Studio erzeugt) reverb, reverberation
→ Echo
Hallanteil m (radio/film/TV) degree of echo
Hallgenerator m (radio/film/TV) reverberation generator, echo source
→ Echogerät
Hallraum m
→ Echogerät (Echokammer)
Halo n **(Haloeffekt** m**)**
→ Ausstrahlungseffekt, Lichthofeffekt
Halogenlampe f **(Halogenlicht** n**)** (phot) halogen light, halogen lamp
Haltestellenplakat n (transit advtsg) transit station poster, transportation display poster
Haltung f
→ Einstellung
Hamburger Format n
→ Nordisches Format
Handabzug m (print) hand proof, hand pull
An impression taken from a printing plate on a hand press, (→) Handpresse.
Handauswertung f **(Handauszählung** f, **manuelle Auszählung** f**)** (survey res) tallying, tallysheet analysis, manual analysis, pencil-and-paper computation
The process of aggregating and disaggregating survey data by hand, i.e. the questionnaires are physically counted and the answers recorded one by one on summary sheets.
Handbeschriftung f **(manuelle Beschriftung** f**)** hand lettering
Lettering drawn by hand, in contrast to that set in type.
vgl. Handsatz

Handbütten n
→ handgeschöpftes Papier
Handdruck m **(Handdrucken** n**)** hand printing
Handel m (econ) 1. (Funktion) trade, trading, commerce 2. (Institution) distributive trades pl, the trades pl
A collective term designating the institution and the function of both wholesalers and retailers, particularly those involved in selling directly to consumers.
Handelsadreßbuch n trade directory, commercial directory
A directory for a particular line of trade.
Handelsaktivität f (econ) trade activity
Handelsbefragung f
→ Händlerbefragung, Einzelhandelsbefragung, Großhandelsbefragung
Handelsbetrieb m
→ Handelsunternehmen
Handelsblatt n
→ Handelsfachzeitschrift
Handelsbrauch m **(Handelsusance** f**)** (econ) trade practice, commercial practice, commercial usage, practice of trade
→ Usance
Handelsdynamik f
→ Dynamik der Betriebsformen
Handelsfachzeitschrift f **(Handelszeitschrift** f, **Handelsblatt** n**)** commercial magazine, trade magazine, commercial journal, trade journal
A magazine catering to the information needs of retailers and/or wholesalers, or a particular line of trade.
Handelsfirma f
→ Handelsunternehmen
Handelsforschung f trade research
Handelsfunktion f (econ) trade function, function of trade
Handelsgewohnheit f
→ Handelsbrauch
Handelsgut n **(Handelsware** f**)** (econ) merchandise, (pl Güter) commercial goods pl, commodity
Handelshof m **(Abholgroßhandlung** f**)**
→ Cash-and-Carry-Betrieb
Handelskette f (Rudolf Seyffert) 1. trade chain, chain of distribution, dealer chain, chain of dealers
→ Absatzweg
2. → freiwillige Handelskette
Handelskettenmethode f **(Handelskettenanalyse** f**)** (Rudolf Seyffert)

Handelskettenspanne 222

(econ) etwa trade chain analysis, chain of distribution analysis, dealer chain analysis
Handelskettenspanne f
→ Distributionskosten
Handelsklasse f (**Güteklasse** f) *(econ)* quality grade, market grade, grade label, grade
  A predetermined standard of quality classification applied to individual units or lots of a commodity.
Handelsklausel f *(meist pl* **Handelsklauseln)** International Commercial Terms *pl* (incoterms)
Handelslager n *(econ)* trade warehouse
Handelsmakler m *(econ)* merchant broker
Handelsmanagement n **Unternehmensführung f im Handel)** *(econ)* (im Einzelhandel) retail management, (im Großhandel) wholesale management
Handelsmanager m *(econ)* (im Einzelhandel) retail manager, (im Großhandel) wholesale manager
Handelsmarke f (**Händlermarke** f) *(econ)* dealer's brand, dealer brand, private brand, private label, private distributor brand, middleman's brand, retailer's brand
  A brand sponsored by a merchant or agent as distinguished from a brand sponsored by a manufacturer or producer.
Handelsmarketing n *(econ)* dealer marketing, dealers' marketing, trade marketing
→ Einzelhandelsmarketing, Großhandelsmarketing
Handelsmesse f
→ Messe
Handelspanel n
→ Einzelhandelspanel, Großhandelspanel
Handels-PR f (**Pflege** f **der Beziehungen zum Handel)** dealer relations *pl oder sg*
Handelsreisender m
→ Reisender
Handelssortiment n
→ Sortiment
Handelsspanne f *(econ)* gross margin, gross profit, trade margin of profit, trade margin, (Einzelhandelsspanne) retail trade margin of profit, retail trade margin, (Großhandelsspanne) wholesale trade margin of profit, wholesale trade margin, (Betriebsspanne) dealer's margin of profit, dealer margin, (Stückspanne) per product margin of profit, per product trade margin, (Artikelgruppenspanne) product group margin of profit, product group trade margin, (Branchenspanne) trade branch margin of profit, trade branch margin
  The difference between the quantity of goods sold at net selling prices in total and the same quantity of goods at total cost, in other words:
  GM = Net Sales − Cost of Goods Sold.
Handelsspannenmethode f (der Werbebudgetierung) gross margin method (of advertising budget determination)
  A method of advertising appropriation as a percentage of the residuum after the deduction of production and distribution costs.
Handelsstatistik f *(econ)* trade statistics *pl (construed as sg)*
Handelsstruktur f *(econ)* trade structure, commercial structure
Handelsstufe f *(econ)* trade level
Handelsstufenrabatt m *(econ)* trade discount, dealer discount
→ Funktionsrabatt
Handelsteil m (der Zeitung) commercial section, commercial pages *pl*
→ Wirtschaftsteil
Handelsunternehmen n (**Handelsfirma** f, **Handelsbetrieb** m) *(econ)* commercial enterprise, trade company
Handelsusance f
→ Handelsbrauch
Handelsverband m *(econ)* trade association, dealer association, dealers' association
Handelsverkehr m *(econ)* trade, commerce
Handelsvermittlung f *(econ)* trade brokerage
Handelsvermittlungshandel m *(econ)* brokerage trade
Handelsvertreter m (**Handelsagent** m) sales representative, commercial representative, sales agent, selling agent, commercial agent, trade representative, trade agent
  An agent or representative who operates on an extended contractual basis. He often sells all of a specified line of

merchandise or the entire output of his principal, and frequently has full authority with regard to prices, terms, and other conditions of sale.

Handelsware f (*oft pl* **Handelswaren**) *(econ)* commercial goods *pl*, commercial product, merchandise, commodity
→ Handelsgut
Handelswerbung f
→ Händlerwerbung
Handelswettbewerb m
→ Händlerwettbewerb
Handelswissenschaft f
→ Handelsforschung
Handelszeitschrift f
→ Handelsfachzeitschrift
Handelszone f
→ Einzugsbereich 1.
handfalzen *v/t* to hand-fold, to handfold
Handfalzen n (**Handfalzung** f) hand folding, handfolding
Handfarbwalze f (**Farbläufer** m) *(print)* brayer, hand ink-roller
handgeschöpftes Papier n (**geschöpftes Papier** n) handmade paper, deckle-edge paper, deckle-edged paper
handgesetzt *adj (typ)* handset, handset, foundry
→ Handsatz
Handgießform f (**Handgießmaschine** f) *(print)* hand mold, hand mould, handcasting machine
Handhabungstest m *(market res)* handling test
  A product test designed to establish whether a new product is easy to handle.
handheften (manuell heften) *v/t (binding)* to handsew, to hand-sew
Handheften n (**Handheftung** f) *(binding)* hand sewing, (mit Heftlade) loom sewing
Handkabel n hand cable
  A camera without a tripod, or a dolly, or any other support.
handkolorieren *v/t (phot/print)* to hand-tint, to hand-color, *brit* to colour by hand
Handkolorierung f *(phot/print)* hand-tinting, hand-coloring, *brit* hand-colouring
Händler m *(econ)* dealer, merchant
  A firm that buys and resells merchandise at either retail or wholesale. The term is naturally ambiguous. For clarity, it should be used with a qualifying adjective, such as "retail" or "wholesale."
→ Einzelhändler, Großhändler
Händlerbefragung f *(market res)* dealer survey, dealer interview
Händlerdichte f *(econ)* dealer outlet density, outlet density
Händlereindruck m (**Firmeneindruck** m) *(advtsg)* dealer imprint, imprint, *colloq* hooker
  A dealer's name and address, or other identification, placed on material produced by a national advertiser.
Händlerfachzeitschrift f
→ Handelsfachzeitschrift
Händlerhilfen f/pl (**Verkaufshilfen** f/pl für Händler) *(promotion)* dealer aids *pl*, sales aids *pl*, merchandising materials *pl*, point-of-purchase material, *auch* dealer helps *pl*, promotional material, (Paket von Materialien) promotional kit, promotional package
  Any promotional material furnished by manufacturers to retail outlets.
Händlerkatalog m *(promotion)* dealer catalog, *brit* dealer catalogue
Händlermarke f
→ Handelsmarke
Händlerpanel n *(market res)* dealer panel, dealer panel investigation
→ Einzelhandelspanel, Großhandelspanel
Händler-Promotions f/pl
→ Verkaufsförderung
Händlerrabatt m *(econ)* dealer allowance, trade discount, (für Verkaufsförderungsmaßnahmen) promotion allowance, merchandising allowance
→ Funktionsrabatt
Händlerumwerbung f
→ Fachwerbung
Händlerwerbehilfen f/pl
→ Händlerhilfen
Händlerwerbung f (**Handelswerbung** f) dealer advertising, (Gemeinschaftswerbung) dealer cooperative advertising, cooperative dealer advertising
vgl. Fachwerbung
Händlerwettbewerb m *(promotion)* dealer contest, contest
Händlerzeitschrift f dealer magazine
  An external house magazine published to provide information about a company and its products or services for distributors.
→ Handelsfachzeitschrift

Handleuchte f (**Handlampe** f) (film/
TV) hand lamp, inspection lamp
Handlungsablauf m (radio/TV) plot,
story line
Handlungsintention f
→ Verhaltensintention
Handlungskosten pl (**Handlungsunkosten** pl)
→ Gemeinkosten, Vertriebskosten
Handlungsreisender m
→ Reisender
Handmikrofon n (**Handmikrophon** n)
hand-held microphone
Handmuster n
→ Attrappe
Handpapier n
→ handgeschöpftes Papier
Handpresse f (print) hand press
   A hand-operated proof press, (→)
   Abzugspresse
Handpressendruck m hand press
printing
Handsatz m (typ) hand composition,
hand setting, manual typesetting,
casework
   Setting type by hand, in contrast to
   setting it by machine, (→) Maschinensatz.
Handsatzschrift f (typ) foundry type,
hand-set type
Handwerkerzeitschrift f craftsman's
trade magazine, craftsmen's trade
magazine
Handzeichen n (**Verweiszeichen** n)
(print) index, fist
Handzeichnung f
→ Freihandzeichnung
Handzettel m handbill, dodger,
giveaway, throwaway
   A small form of direct advertising or
   sales promotion distributed by hand.
Handzuführung f (print) hand feeding
Hängegitter n (phot/film/TV) (im
Studio) hanging grid
Hängeplakat n (promotion) hanger
card
Hänger m (film/TV) (Scheinwerfer)
hanger
Hängestück n (promotion) suspension
unit
Harmonikafalz m
→ Leporellofalz
harmonisches Mittel n (stat)
harmonic mean
   The reciprocal of the arithmetic mean,
   (→) arithmetisches Mittel, of the
   reciprocals of a set of observations. In
the discrete case for n quantities $x_1, x_2, ..., x_n$, it is written as:

$$\frac{1}{H} = \frac{1}{n} \sum_{i=1}^{n} \left(\frac{1}{x_i}\right).$$

In the continuous case, as

$$\frac{1}{H} = \int_{-\infty}^{\infty} \frac{f(x)}{x} dx,$$

where f(x) is the frequency function.
Härtebad n (phot) hardening bath
   A solution used to toughen photographic
   images, specifically baths for negatives
   and chromic acid or bichromate mixtures
   for glue prints on zinc.
Härtefixierbad n (phot) fixing-hardening bath
   A bath in which films, plates, or prints
   are freed from the unaltered silver
   bromide and at the same time the gelatin
   film is toughened.
härten v/t (phot) to harden
→ Härtebad
hartgewickelte Rolle f hard roll, tight
roll
Hartkautschuk m (**Ebonit** n) (phot)
ebonite
Hartschaumverpackung f rigid-foam
package
Hartzeichner m (phot) sharp-focus
lens, high-definition lens
Harz m resin
häufiger Leser m (readership res)
frequent reader
   A reader with a reading probability of
   between 0.5 and 0.75, i.e. a reader who
   had read between 6 and 9 of 12
   subsequent issues of a paper or a
   magazine.
häufiges Lesen n (readership res)
frequent reading
Häufigkeit f (**Frequenz** f) (stat)
frequency
   The number of times a given type of
   event occurs or the number of members
   of a population falling into a specified
   class, or the proportion of the total
   number of occurrences or the total
   number of members (the relative or
   proportional frequency).
Häufigkeit f **des Erscheinens**
→ Erscheinungsweise
Häufigkeitsanalyse f (stat) frequency
analysis
Häufigkeitsauszählung f (**Häufigkeitszählung** f) (stat) frequency count

Häufigkeitsfrage f (**Frequenzfrage** f, **Frage** f **nach der Kontakthäufigkeit**, **Frage** f **nach der Häufigkeit des Lesens etc.**) *(media res)* frequency question
→ Häufigkeitsmethode
Häufigkeitskurve f (**Frequenzkurve** f) *(stat)* frequency curve, frequency distribution curve
The graphic representation of a continuous frequency distribution, (→) Häufigkeitsverteilung.
Häufigkeitsmethode f (**Frequenzmethode** f, **Frequency-Methode** f) *(media res)* frequency method (of audience measurement)
A method of readership measurement, in which the respondents are asked to classify themselves into a specific reading frequency category for a particular publication. The researcher then allocates an average reading probability to each frequency group for every publication.
Häufigkeitsmoment n (**Moment** n **einer Häufigkeitsverteilung**) *(stat)* frequency moment
Häufigkeitspolygon n (**Frequenzpolygon** n, **Treppenpolygon** n) *(stat)* frequency polygon
A diagram showing the form of a frequency distribution.
Häufigkeitstabelle f (**Frequenztabelle** f) *(stat)* frequency table
A table drawn up to show the distribution of the frequency of occurrence of a given characteristic according to some specified set of class intervals.
Häufigkeitsverteilung f *(stat)* frequency distribution
A tabulation which shows the number, or the proportion, of times that given values or characteristics occur in a set of statistical observations.
Häufigkeitsziffer f
→ Beziehungszahl
häufigster Wert m (**dichtester Wert** m, **Modus** m, **Modalwert** m, **Dichtemittel** n, **Gipfelwert** m) *(stat)* mode, modal value
A value of x for which

$$\frac{df(x)}{dx} = 0, \quad \frac{d^2f(x)}{dx^2} < 0,$$

if f(x) is a frequency function. It is the score or category in a frequency distribution, (→) Häufigkeitsverteilung, that has the greatest frequency of occurrence.

Hauptabsatzgebiet n *(econ)* major sales area, sales area, primary marketing area (P.M.A.), primary market area (P.M.A.), heartland
The principal area of sale for a product or service.
Hauptachsenmethode f
→ Hauptkomponentenanalyse
Hauptagentur f
→ federführende Agentur
Hauptartikel m
→ Aufmacher
Hauptausgabe f (Zeitung) main edition
vgl. Lokalausgabe, Regionalausgabe
Hauptaussagentest m (**Werbeaussagentest** m) *(advtsg res)* proposition test
Hauptbeleuchtung f (**Hauptlichtquelle** f)
→ Führungslicht
Hauptdarsteller(in) m(f) *(film/TV)* principal actor, principal actress, leading actor, leading actress, lead
Hauptempfangsbereich m (**Hauptempfangsgebiet** n) *(radio/TV)* dominant service area, dominant area, primary service area, *(TV)* A contour, grade A coverage area, grade A signal area
The area in which the reception of a radio or television station is consistently good to excellent.
Hauptfilm m (**Spielfilm** m) *(Kino)* feature film, full-length film
Hauptfarbe f
→ Grundfarbe
Hauptgeschäft n *(retailing)* main store, parent store, flagship store
The central store of a retailer operating two or more branch stores.
Hauptgeschäftszeit f (**Hauptgeschäftsstunden** f/pl) *(econ)* peak hours pl, peak business hours pl, main business hours pl
Hauptkomponentenanalyse f (**Hauptkomponentenmethode** f) *(stat)* principal components analysis, principal components method, principal axes method, principal axes analysis, principal components technique, principal components model
Hauptleitung f *(electr.)* mains pl
Hauptleser m (**bewußter Hauptleser** m)
→ Erstleser

Hauptlicht

Hauptlicht n
→ Führungslicht
Hauptmonitor m *(TV)* transmission monitor
Hauptnegativ n **(Matrize** f) *(phot)* master negative
Hauptphase f *(film)* (Zeichentrick) key animation
Hauptphasenzeichner m *(film)* (Zeichentrick) key animator
Hauptrolle f *(film/TV)* leading part, leading rôle, leading role, principal part, principal rôle, principal role, lead, lead part, lead rôle, lead role
Hauptschriftleiter m
→ Chefredakteur
Hauptsendezeit f **(Sendezeit** f **mit den höchsten Einschaltquoten)** *(TV)* prime time, *brit* peak time, peak viewing hours *pl*
 The evening hours of broadcasting, generally from 8:00 to 11:00 p.m. when the ratings, (→) Einschaltquote, are highest.
Hauptsender m *(radio)* main transmitter, master transmitter, main transmitting station, master transmitting station
Hauptstudio n main studio
Hauptteil m **(Body Copy** f, **Haupttext** m) (einer Anzeige) body copy, body matter, body
 The main part of a printed advertisement, as opposed to its headline or baseline.
Hauptüberschrift f **(Hauptschlagzeile** f, **Haupttitel** m) main headline, main head
Hauptverbreitungsgebiet n **(Kernverbreitungsgebiet** n) (Zeitung/Produkt) primary marketing area (P.M.A.), sectional center
 1. *(econ)* → Hauptabsatzgebiet 2. The central area in which a newspaper is circulated.
Hauptverkaufsargument n focus of sale
 The basic claim(s) made by a brand in its advertising strategy, together with supportive material designed to insure the believability of the claims.
Hauptverkehrsroute f **(Hauptverkehrsweg** m) *(outdoor advtsg)* primary route of travel
 vgl. Nebenverkehrsroute (Nebenverkehrsweg)

Hauptware f **(Hauptprodukt** n) *(econ)* (im Gegensatz zur Zugabe) basic product
Hauptwerbemittel n basic advertisement
Hauptwerbeträger m basic advertising medium, basic medium, primary medium
Hausagentur f (*auch* **Haus-AE** f) *(advtsg)* house agency
 1. An advertising agency controlled by a single advertiser. 2. An advertising agency which offers full or limited service capabilities and is owned wholly or in part by an advertiser who typically is the agency's only or most important advertising client.
Hausbemalung f **(bemalte Häuserwand** f, **Hausbemalungswerbung** f) *(outdoor advtsg)* painted wall, painted wall advertising
Hausbesuch m **(Kontaktbesuch** m) call, canvas, canvass
 The visit of a sales representative to a customer or prospective customer or that of an interviewer in survey research to the home of an interviewee.
Hauseigentümer-Zeitschrift f **(Eigenheimbesitzerzeitschrift** f) homeowner magazine
Hausfarbe f **(Hausausstattung** f) *(econ)* house style
 The typical style and colors that characterize a firm and its products.
Hausfrauenzeitschrift f
→ Frauenzeitschrift
Haushalt m 1. (privater Haushalt) household, private household
 A dwelling unit occupied by one or more persons living together under a single roof which constitutes a housing unit.
 2. → Etat
 3. → öffentlicher Haushalt
Haushaltsabdeckung f
→ Haushaltsreichweite
Haushaltsbefragung f survey of households
 vgl. Personenbefragung
Haushaltsbuch n household book
Haushaltsbuchforschung f *(market res)* household book research
Haushaltsbudget n **(Etat** m **eines Haushalts)** *(econ)* household budget
Haushaltseinkommen n *(econ)* household income
Haushalts-Einschaltquote f *(media res) (radio/TV)* homes-using-sets rating, households-using-sets rating, homes per rating point (HPRP), share

of audience (beim Fernsehen) homes-using-television rating (HUT rating), households-using-television rating (HUT rating), homes-using-TV rating, households-using-TV rating, (beim Radio) homes-using-radio rating (HUR rating), households-using-radio rating, Nielsen rating, Hooperating
A type of rating, (→) Einschaltquote, for radio and television in general, rather than for a specific network, station, or program. The base is households with one or more radio or television sets, in a specified area. A households-using-radio or television rating shows the percentage of these households that are estimated to be in the audience of any one of a group of radio or television stations, at a specified time. A household should be counted as using radio or television only once in the computation of this type of rating even if it is using two or more radios or television sets simultaneously.

Haushalts-Einschaltzahl f *(media res) (radio/TV)* homes using sets *pl*, households using sets *pl*, household audience (beim Fernsehen) homes using television *pl*, households using television *pl*, homes using TV *pl*, households using TV *pl*, (beim Radio) homes using radio *pl*, households using radio *pl*
The actual (absolute) number of households with one radio or television set tuned in any program in a specified time. It is a tabulation of the number of households where one or more family members were reached by radio or television. These statistics indicate that someone in the household was exposed, but do not say who or how many were in the audience. Because any family member can qualify his entire household as "reached", analysis of household-audience characteristics can be completely misleading.

Haushaltsentscheidung f
→ Familieneinkaufsentscheidung

Haushaltsgröße f *(econ)* household size

Haushalts-Investitionsgüter n/pl
→ Gebrauchsgüter

Haushaltsjahr n *(econ)* fiscal year (FY)

Haushaltsmanagement n (**Haushaltsführung** f) household management

Haushaltsnettoeinkommen n *(econ)*
→ verfügbares Einkommen

Haushaltspackung f
→ Familienpackung

Haushaltspanel n *(survey res)* panel of households
vgl. Personenpanel

Haushaltsplan m *(econ)* budget

Haushaltsreichweite f *(econ/media res)* household coverage, auch households reached *pl*, household reach, audience of households, household audience, accumulated households *pl*, (Druckmedien) circulation-to-household coverage
The percentage of households reached by an advertising medium.
→ Reichweite

Haushaltssättigung f
→ Sättigung

Haushaltsstichprobe f *(stat)* sample of households
A sample whose sampling units, (→) Erhebungseinheit, are households.
vgl. Personenstichprobe

Haushaltstheorie f (**mikroökonomische Haushaltstheorie** f) *(econ)* microeconomic theory

Haushaltsvorstand m *(stat)* head of household, household head, family head, householder, (alleinstehend) primary individual
The person responsible for the management of a household. The term has been replaced by "Bezugsperson" for anyone who either gives himself that name or is given it by other members of the household in an interview.

Haushaltswerbung f (**Haushaltsumwerbung** f) direct household advertising, door-to-door advertising, canvassing

Haushaltszusammensetzung f *(stat)* household composition
Information about the number of household members, their ages, sexes, and relation to one another. This information is obtained from a household enumeration or listing. Names (or the first names) of household members are usually obtained, so that specific questions can be asked about each member individually or so that one or more household members can be selected for further interviewing. A household may consist of only one person or of unrelated individuals. A family consists of two or more related individuals.

Haushaltszuschauerschaft f (**Haushaltszuschauer** m/pl) *(media res)* audience of households, household audience
→ Haushaltseinschaltzahl

Haushaltung f
→ Haushalt 1.
Hausierhandel m **(Hausiergewerbe** n) *(econ)* door-to-door selling, house-to-house selling, hawking, peddlery, peddling
Hauskorrektor m printer's proofreader, printer's reader
Hauskorrektur f printer's proofreading, first proofreading
Hausmarke f
→ Eigenmarke
Hauszeitschrift f **(Hausmitteilung** f)
house organ, house publication, house magazine, internal house organ, internal house magazine, internal house publication, staff magazine, company magazine, company organ, company journal
  A publication issued regularly by a business firm for its employees, dealers, prospects, or other groups.
vgl. Kundenzeitschrift
Hausschild n door sign
Hauteffekt m **(Skin-Effekt** m) *(TV)* skin effect
hautenge Verpackung f skin-tight package
Hautwiderstandsmessung f
→ psychogalvanische Reaktion
Hawthorne-Effekt m **(Versuchskanincheneffekt** m) *(res)* Hawthorne effect, guinea pig effect, reactive effect, reactivity, reactivity effect
  The influence that participating in an experiment may have upon the subjects' behavior.
Headline f
→ Schlagzeile
Hebebühne f *(film/TV)* stage lift, lifting platform, platform lift, elevating platform, feeding platform
Hebekran m *(film/TV)* derrick, crane
Heckantenne f *(electr.)* rear antenna, *brit* rear aerial
Heckfläche f *(transit advtsg)* rear end, tail end, (beim Doppeldeckerbus) double back
Heckflächenplakat n **(Heckfläche** f) *(transit advtsg)* rear-end display, rear end, tail-light display, tail-light poster
  An outside advertising display placed on the rear end of public transportation vehicles.
Heft n **(Zeitschriftenexemplar** n) copy, *colloq* the book
Heftalter n *(media res)* age of an issue

Heftchenroman m
→ Groschenroman
Heftdraht m *(binding)* stapling wire, stitching wire, wire
heften v/t *(binding)* (mit Faden) to sew, (mit Draht) to stitch
Hefter m
→ Heftmaschine
Heftfaden m *(binding)* sewing thread, binding thread, stitching thread
Heftgaze f *(binding)* mull, scrim, crash
Heftkante f **(innere Heftkante** f)
→ Falzkante
Heftklammer f *(binding)* wire staple, staple
Heftlade f *(binding)* sewing loom, sewing frame
Heftmaschine f **(Hefter** f) *(binding)* stapling machine, stapler, (Buchheftmaschine) book sewing machine, stitching machine
Heftnadel f *(binding)* stitching needle
Heftpreis m
→ Einzelheftpreis
Heftschnur f *(binding)* sewing cord, cord
Heftstich m *(binding)* stitch
Heftung f **(Heften** n) binding
Heftvorlage f
→ Originalheftvorlage
Heilmittelwerbung f **(Pharmawerbung** f) pharmaceutical advertising, (für rezeptpflichtige Heilmittel) ethical advertising, (für nichtrezeptpflichtige Heilmittel) patent medicine advertising, OTC advertising
Heimatpresse f
→ Lokalpresse, Regionalpresse
Heimatsender m
→ Lokalsender
Heimatzeitung f
→ Lokalzeitung, Regionalzeitung
Heimdienst m *(distribution)* home-delivery service
Heimvideorecorder m home video recorder
heißabbindender Klebstoff m hot-setting adhesive
heiße Probe f
→ Generalprobe
Heißklebefolie f heat-seal foil
heißprägen v/t *(print)* to hot stamp
Heißprägung f hot stamping, hot die stamping
→ Blindprägung, Reliefprägung

Heißschmelzkleber m (**Hot-Melt-Kleber** m, **Schmelzkleber** m) hot melt adhesive
Heliogravüre f (**Photogravüre** f, **Fotogravüre** f) (print) heliogravure, photogravure
　Any of several processes by which an intaglio engraving is made in a metal plate by photographic means. When this type of plate is covered by ink and then scraped off, the ink remaining in the depressed lines and areas makes the printed image on the paper.
hell adj (Farbe) light, (Licht) bright
Helldunkel n chiaroscuro, clair-obscure
Hellempfindlichkeit f (phot) light sensitivity, sensitivity to light
Helligkeit f (phot) lightness, (Leuchtdichte) luminosity, intensity, (TV) brightness, brilliance
Helligkeitsbereich m (TV) brightness range
Helligkeitseindruck m (TV) brightness impression, sensation of brightness
Helligkeitseinstellung f (**Helligkeitssteuerung** f) (TV) brightness control
Helligkeitsflimmern n
Helligkeitskontrast m (phot) brightness contrast
Helligkeitskreis m (phot) circle of illumination
Helligkeitssignal n (TV) brightness signal, luminance signal
Helligkeitsüberstrahlung f (TV) white crushing
Helligkeitsumfang m (phot/TV) brightness range, contrast range
Helligkeitswert m (phot) brightness value (BV), density value
Hellphase f (TV) light period
Hellspannung f (**Hellspannungswert** m) (TV) bright level, light level
Helmert-Pearson-Verteilung f
→ Chi-Quadrat-Verteilung
Hemisphärenforschung f (**Hirnhälftenforschung** f) brain hemisphere research
→ Zwei-Hemisphären-Theorie
herabgesetzter Preis m (econ) reduced price
herabsetzende Werbung f (**herabsetzende Bezugnahme** f) denigratory advertising, mudslinging, knocking copy, disparaging advertising
→ diffamierende Werbung

herausbringen v/t (Publikation) to bring out, to put out, to publish
Herausgabe f putting out, publishing, editing, publication, bringing out
herausgeben v/t (Publikation) to publish, to edit, to put out, to issue
Herausgeber m editor, publisher
herausklappbare Anzeige f
→ ausschlagbare Anzeige
Herkunftsangabe f (**Herkunftsbezeichnung** f) (econ) mark of origin, mark of geographical origin
Herkunftstäuschung f deceptive mark of origin, misleading mark of origin
Herrenzeitschrift f (**Herrenmagazin** n)
→ Männermagazin
Hersteller m (**Produzent** m) producer, manufacturer
herstellereigene Verkaufsfiliale f (econ) manufacturer's sales branch, branch house, branch store, branch office, manufacturer's sales outlet, manufacturer's sale office
　An establishment maintained by a manufacturer, detached from the headquarters establishment and used for the purpose of selling his products or providing service.
Herstellerhaftung f
→ Produzentenhaftung
Herstellermarke f (**Industriemarke** f) (econ) producer's brand, manufacturer's brand, national brand, manufacturer brand
　A manufacturer's or producer's brand, usually enjoying wide territorial distribution.
vgl. Händlermarke
Herstellermarkensystem n
→ Markenartikelsystem
Herstellerwerbung f
→ Unternehmenswerbung
Herstellerzugabe f (promotion) factory-pack premium
　A direct premium, (→) Direktzugabe, which is attached in some way (e.g. as an in-pack, an on-pack, a container premium) to the product as it is delivered by the producer.
Herstellung f (**Produktion** f) 1. (econ) production, manufacture, manufacturing
　In an advertising agency or advertising department, those persons responsible for the conversion of copy and art work into printed advertising material. In broadcasting, those responsible for the

Herstellungskosten

production and presentation of a program.
2. (Herstellungsabteilung) production department
Herstellungskosten *pl* **(Produktionskosten** *pl*) *(econ)* production costs *pl*, manufacturing costs *pl*, cost of production, cost of manufacture, *(advtsg)* (für Werbung) art and mechanical costs *pl*, A & M costs *pl*, (im Agenturbudget) above-the-line cost, above the line
Herstellungsleiter *m (econ/advtsg)* production manager
Hertz *m* **(Hz)** cycles *pl* per second(cps)
Herzaufsteller *m (promotion)* A board, "A" board, A frame, "A" frame
Herzfrequenzmessung *f* **(Herzschlagfrequenzmessung** *f*) *(res)* measurement of heart frequency, heart frequency measurement
heterograde Fragestellung *f* **(heterograder Fall** *m*, **heterograde Statistik** *f*)
→ quantitative Statistik
heulen *v/i* to howl
Heulen *n* howling
Heuristik *f (res)* heuristics *pl (construed as sg)*
    A strategy or rule of thumb that frequently is helpful in achieving a goal, but is not guaranteed to be successful.
heuristische Hypothese *f*
→ Arbeitshypothese
heuristisches Modell *n (res)* heuristic model
HF-Kanal *m*
→ Hochfrequenzkanal m
HF-Signal *n*
→ Hochfrequenzsignal
HI *abbr* Hochintensität
HI-Scheinwerfer *m*
→ Hochintensitätsscheinwerfer
Hierarchy-of-effects-Modell *n* **(Lavidge-Steiner-Modell** *n*) *(advtsg)* hierarchy-of-effects model (Robert J. Lavidge/Gary A. Steiner)
HiFi-Anzeige *f* **(HiFi-Endlosfarbanzeige** *f*) hifi, hi-fi, Hi-Fi, hifi insert, continuous roll insert, wallpaper, preprint
    A full-page, high-quality, four-color rotogravure advertisement that is preprinted on coated stock and furnished to a newspaper in roll form for insertion during regular run. As the roll is fed into the press, editorial copy or other

advertising is printed on the reverse side, and, in some cases, a column of type is imprinted on the hi-fi insert itself.
High-Assay-Verfahren *n (media planning)* high assay model, high assay iteration model
High Key *m (phot)* high key (HK)
→ Spitzlicht
High-key-Bild *n (phot)*
→ Spitzlichtphoto
Hilfsbetriebe *m/pl* **des Marketing** facilitating agencies *pl* of marketing
    Those agencies which perform or assist in the performance of one or a number of the marketing functions but which neither take title to goods nor negotiate purchases or sales. Common types are banks, railroads, storage warehouses, commodity exchanges, stock yards, insurance companies, graders and inspectors, advertising agencies, firms engaged in marketing research, cattle loan companies, furniture marts, and packers and shippers.
Hilfskanal *m (radio/TV)* auxiliary channel, (Sender) sub-channel
Hilfssynchronsignal *n (radio/TV)* equalizing pulse, *brit* equalising pulse, blip
Hilfstonspur *f* **(Cue-Track** *m*) cue track, guide track, pilot tone track
    The auxiliary audio recording area on a video tape.
Hilfsträger *m (radio/TV)* subcarrier
Hilfsvariable *f* **(Scheinvariable** *f*) *(res)* dummy variable
Himmelsschreiben *n* **(Himmelsschrift** *f*) *(advtsg)* skytyping, skywriting
Himmelswerbung *f* sky advertising, aerial advertising
hinstimmende Werbung *f* mood advertising, mood copy
    Any type of advertising which is deliberately aimed at putting its recipients into a frame of mind conducive to acceptance of a product or service.
Hintereinanderschaltung *f (electr.)* series connection, tandem connection, *Am* serial hookup
Hintergrund *m (phot/film/TV)* background, backdrop
    Music or sound effects used as accompaniment to a radio or television program. Also, the set or scene in a television program.
Hintergrundausleuchtung *f (film/TV)* background lighting, background illumination

Hintergrunddekor n *(film/TV)* backing
Hintergrunddekoration f *(film/TV)* background setting, background set
Hintergrundlicht n *(film/TV)* background light, background mood light
Hintergrundmusik f mood music, background music
Hintergrundprojektion f
→ Rückprojektion
Hintergrundprojektor m *(film/TV)* background projector, *colloq* vizmo
   An optical device capable of generating graphic images on a rear-projection screen.
Hintergrundsprecher m **(Narrator** m, **Off-Sprecher** m) *(film/TV/radio)* narrator, off-camera announcer, off-camera speaker
Hinterlicht n *(phot)* back light, backlight
   Any illumination from behind, separating the camera subject from the background.
Hinterlinse f *(phot)* back combination
   The half of a doublet lens nearest the film.
Hintersetzer m backing, set-in
Histogramm n **(Blockdiagramm** n, **Staffelbild** n, **Treppendiagramm** n) *(stat)* histogram
   The graphical presentation of the frequency distribution, (→) Häufigkeitsverteilung, of a discrete series of categories in which rectangles proportional in area to the class frequencies are erected on sections of the horizontal axis, the width of each section representing the corresponding class interval of the variate.
historische Methode f (der Werbebudgetierung) historical method (of advertising budget determination), (auf den letzten Jahresumsatz bezogen) percentage-of-last-year's sales method, (bezogen auf die Überschüsse des letzten Jahres) percentage-of-last-year's surplus method, percentage-of-previous-year's surplus method
   Any of a variety of methods by which the advertising budget is established on the basis of past performance, be it last year's sales, surplus or the like.
Hochantenne f *(electr.)* overhead antenna, elevated antenna, outdoor antenna, *brit* overhead aerial, elevated aerial, outdoor aerial, *Am* roof antenna
hochätzen v/t *(print)* to etch in relief

Hochätzung f *(print)* relief printing from an etched plate, relief etching, ectotypography
Hochdruck m **(Hochdruckverfahren** n) letterpress printing, relief printing, surface printing
   A method of printing in which the ink is carried on a raised, or relief, surface.
Hochdruckmaschine f **(Hochdruckpresse** f) relief printing press
Hochdruckraster m
→ Raster
hochempfindlich adj *(phot)* high-speed, fast
Hochformat n upright size, vertical size, portrait format, portrait
hochformatig adj upright, high, portrait
hochformatiges Bild n **(hochkantformatiges Bild** n) upright picture, vertical picture, portrait format picture, panel photo, panel
hochfrequent adj *(radio)* high-frequency, radio-frequency
Hochfrequenz f **(HF)** *(radio)* high frequency (HF), radio frequency (RF)
   Any sound frequency from 15,000 hertz to 20,000, far above the hearing threshold.
Hochfrequenzbild n radio-frequency television signal
Hochfrequenz-Filmkamera f **(Hochfrequenzkamera** f) *(phot)* high-speed camera, rapid-sequence camera
Hochglanz m **(Glanz** m) *(phot/print)* gloss
Hochglanzabzug m **(Hochglanzkopie** f) *(phot/print)* glossy print, high gloss print, glossy photograph, glossy photo, glossy photostat, slick, enamel proof
   A photograph with a smooth glossy surface for better reproduction.
hochglanzkaschiert adj → laminiert
Hochglanzkaschierung f *(print)* high gloss lamination
→ Laminierung
Hochglanzkopie f
→ Hochglanzabzug
Hochglanzpapier n (satiniert) super-calendered paper, (reibungskalandriert) friction-glazed paper, friction-calendered paper, (gestrichen) coated paper, coated stock, process coated paper, cast-coated paper, (für Illustrierte) slick-finished paper, slick paper
Hochglanzzeitschrift f slick magazine, slick, glossy magazine

Hochintensitätslampe f (**HI-Lampe** f) *(film/TV)* high-intensity arc lamp, high-power arc lamp
Hochlaufzeit f *(film/TV)* (Kamera) run-up time
The time required to bring a film or television camera to normal operating speed.
Hochlicht-Autotypie f
→ Spitzlicht-Autotypie
Hochlichtblende f
→ Spitzlichtblende
Hochpaß m (**Hochpaßfilter** m) *(radio/TV)* high-pass filter
hochprägen (erhaben prägen) v/t *(print)* to emboss
To raise portions of the surface of a sheet of paper, plastic, or metal, in order to form a design by pressing the material between concave and convex dies.
Hochprägung f (**Hohldruck** m, **Prägedruck** m, **Reliefdruck** m, **erhabener Prägedruck** m) *(print)* embossing
Hochprägeplatte f (**Prägeplatte** f) *(print)* embossing plate
Hochprägepresse f (**Prägepresse** f) *(print)* embossing press
Hochpreispolitik f *(econ)* high-price policy, skimming policy
The policy of setting a price high initially with the objective of getting the best out of the market rather than the most. The intent is to appeal to those persons in the market who are interested in innovations and are little, if at all, conscious of price.
→ Marktabschöpfung
Hochrechnung f (**Projektion** f) *(stat)* projection
Hochrechnungsfaktor m (**Projektionsfaktor** m) *(stat)* projection factor, raising factor
hochsatiniert (hochgeglättet) adj *(paper)* supercalendered, *colloq* supercal, super
hochsatiniertes Papier n (**hochgeglättetes Papier** n) supercalendered paper, *colloq* supercal, super
A type of paper that in its manufacture is run between heated calender rolls, after sizing has been added to the pulp. The better grades of super stock will carry 120-line halftones acceptably.
hochstehend (hochgestellt) adj *(typ)* (Zahl/Buchstabe) superior
Höchstformat n (**Höchstgröße** f) maximum size, (in Zeilen) maximum linage, *auch* maximum lineage
Höchstpreis m 1. *(econ)* maximum price 2. *(advtsg)* (für Anzeigen) maximil rate (höchster Zeilensatz), *colloq* maximil, maxiline
Höchstpreisberechnung f (für Werbung) charging the top of the rate card
Höchstrabatt m *(econ)* maximum discount
Hochton m *(acoustics)* high pitch, treble
Hochton-Lautsprecher m high-frequency loudspeaker, treble loudspeaker, *colloq* tweeter
Hochzahl f (**hochgestellte Zahl** f) *(typ)* superior figure, superior, superscript
Hochzeilen-Fernsehen n high-definition television, high-definition TV
Hochzeit f *(print)* double
→ Doublette
Höhe f 1. *(print)* (des Satzes) depth
→ Schrifthöhe
2. *(acoustics)* (Ton) pitch
Höhenabschwächung f *(acoustics)* treble cut, treble attenuation, top cut
Höhenanhebung f *(acoustics)* treble boost, high-frequency emphasis
Hohlkehle f *(POP advtsg)* channel strip, case strip, shelf strip
An extruded molding covering the front edge of a retail display shelf, used to exhibit price data or hold point of purchase advertising.
Hohlprägung f
→ Hochprägung
Hohlspiegel m *(phot)* concave reflector, reflector
Hökerhandel m *(econ)* street trade, street trading, huckstering
Hologramm n (**Holograph** m, **Holographon** n, **Hologrammplatte** f) *(phot)* hologram, holograph
A photograph produced by holography, (→) Holographie.
Holographie f (**Laserphotographie** f) *(phot)* holography
A photographic technique on the basis of laser technology. It consists in coding film without using lenses, so that a light beam applied at the proper angle will show a three-dimensional image. Some use of this technique is being made to produce illustrations for advertisements, but this has the disadvantage of requiring a source of a relatively small beam of light to make the picture understandable to the human eye.
holographisch adj *(phot)* holographic
Holophon n holophone

Holoskop *n* holoscope
holoskopisch *adj* holoscopic
holzfrei (holzschlifffrei) *adj (paper)* without wood-pulp, free from groundwood, delignified
Holzgehalt *m* **(Holzschliffgehalt** *m)* *(paper)* groundwood content, lignin content
holzhaltig *adj (paper)* would-pulp, containing wood pulp, groundwood
Holzschliff *m (paper)* groundwood pulp, woodpulp, pulp
  A mechanically-prepared coarse woodpulp used chiefly in the manufacture of newsprint.
Holzschliffgehalt *m*
→ Holzgehalt
Holzstativ *n (phot)* wooden tripod
homograde Fragestellung *f* **(homograde Statistik** *f*, **homograder fall** *m)*
→ qualitative Statistik
homöostatischer Trieb *m*
→ Primärbedürfnis
Honorar *n (advtsg)* (einer Agentur/ eines Instituts) service fee
  A fee paid by an advertiser to an advertising agency as a retainer for general services or a compensation for special services or by a client to a research institute for its general services.
Honorarpauschale *f*
→ Pauschalhonorar
Honorarumsatz *m* billing, billings *pl*
  The total amount of money charged to clients by an advertising agency, including media bills, production costs, and service charges.
Hörbeteiligung *f (radio)* audience rating, share-of-audience
→ Einschaltquote; *vgl.* Sehbeteiligung
Hörbild *n* sound picture, *(radio)* feature
Hörer *m* **(Radiohörer** *m)* *(media res)* listener, radio listener
  A person whose radio is tuned to a particular program or radio station at a specified time.
→ Hörerschaft
Hörer *m/pl* **pro Stunde** *(media res)* listeners *pl* per hour
Hörer *m/pl* **pro Tag** *(media res)* listeners *pl* per day
Hörerakzeptanz *f (media res)* radio program acceptance, radio acceptance
Höreranalyse *f* **(Hörerschaftsanalyse** *f) (media res)* radio audience analysis, audience analysis, broadcast audience analysis, listenership analysis
Hörerbefragung *f (media res)* radio audience survey, survey among radio listeners, audience survey, broadcast audience survey
Hörerdaten *n/pl (media res)* radio audience data *pl*, broadcast audience data *pl*, listener data *pl*
Hörerfluß *m (media res)* audience flow
  The gain or loss in audience during a radio program, or from one program channel to another.
Hörerforschung *f (media res)* radio audience research, listener research, radio listener research, broadcast audience research, audience research
Hörergemeinde *f*
→ Hörerschaft
Hörerschaft *f* **(Hörer** *m/pl*, **Hörergemeinde** *f) (media res)* radio audience, radio listeners *pl*, audience, listenership, circulation
  The number of households or individuals that are estimated to be in the audience of a given radio program or station at least once during a specified period of time
Hörerschaftsmessung *f* **(Hörerschaftsermittlung** *f) (media res)* radio audience measurement, audience measurement
Hörerschaftspanel *n (media res)* panel of listeners, panel of radio listeners
Hörerschaftsstruktur *f (media res)* audience composition, radio audience composition, radio audience structure, audience structure, listener characteristics *pl*
  The classification of the individuals or the households in a radio audience into various categories. Common categories for individuals are age and sex groupings (e.g., men, women, teenagers, and children). Common categories for households are based on the number of members of the household, age or education of the head of household, household income.
Hörer-Strukturanalyse *f (media res)* structure analysis of radio audience, radio audience structure analysis
Hörertagebuch *n* **(Hörerschaftstagebuch** *n) (media res)* radio-listening diary, radio diary, radio listener diary, listener diary

Hörerzahl

A method of research in which respondents maintain a continuing record of listening. Diaries are not used in present-day German radio audience research.
→ Tagesablaufschema, Tagebuchmethode
Hörerzahl f *(media res)* radio audience, size of radio audience, radio audience figure
→ Hörerschaft
Hörfolge f feature series, radio feature series, radio series
Hörfunk m **(Radio** n**)** radio broadcasting, sound broadcasting, sound radio, radio
Hörfunkaufnahme f radio recording
Hörfunkdienst m radio service
Hörfunkgebühr f radio license fee, *brit* radio licence fee
Hörfunkgenehmigung f radio license, *brit* radio licence
Hörfunkhörer m **(Radiohörer** m**)**
→ Hörer
Hörfunklizenz f radio franchise, radio broadcasting franchise
Hörfunkmagazin n
→ Programmzeitschrift
Hörfunknachrichten f/pl **(Hörfunknachrichtensendung** f**)** radio news *sg*, radio newsbroadcast, radio news bulletin
Hörfunknetz n radio network
Hörfunkprogramm n **(Hörfunksendung** f**)** radio program, *brit* radio programme, radio broadcast
Hörfunkreihe f radio serial
Hörfunksendung f **(Radiosendung** f**)** radio broadcast, radiocast
Hörfunkspot m **(Hörfunkwerbespot** m**, Hörfunkwerbesendung** f**)** radio commercial, radio announcement
Hörfunkstudio n radio studio
Hörfunkübertragung f radio transmission, radio broadcast
Hörfunkwerbung f **(Radiowerbung** f**)** radio broadcast advertising, radio advertising, broadcast advertising
Hörgewohnheit f *(media res)* listening habit
Horizontalauflösung f *(TV)* horizontal definition, horizontal resolution
Horizontalbalken m *(TV)* horizontal bar, strobe line
Horizontalfrequenz f *(TV)* line frequency

Horizontalschwenk m *(film/TV)* horizontal pan
Hörrundfunk m
→ Hörfunk
Hörspiel n radio play, radio drama
Hörspielautor m radio playwright
Hörspielmanuskript n radio drama script
Hörspielregisseur m radio drama director
Horrorfilm m suspense-mystery film
Horrorwerbung f
→ angsterzeugende Werbung
Hörstunden f/pl **pro Kopf** *(media res)* man-hours *pl* of listening
Hotelexemplar n (Zeitschrift) hotel copy
Hotmeltkleber m
→ Heißschmelzkleber
Howard-Sheth-Modell n *(advtsg res)* Howard-Sheth model (John A. Howard/Jagdish Sheth)
Hülle f *(packaging)* wrapper, wrap
humanes Marketing n human concept of marketing
Human Relations pl **(Human-Relations-Arbeit** f**)** human relations pl *(construed as sg)*
→ werbende Führung
Humor m humor
Hurenkind n *(typ)* widow
A single word or short line of type at the end of a paragraph, particularly at the top of a column or page.
Hydrasystem n
→ Schneeballverfahren
hyperbolischer Trend m *(stat)* hyperbolic trend
hypergeometrische Verteilung f *(stat)* hypergeometric distribution
Hypodermic-Needle-Modell n
→ Injektionsmodell
Hypothese f *(res)* hypothesis
An empirically testable proposition regarding the relationships believed to prevail between two or more phenomena.
Hypothesenprüfung f **(Hypothesentest** m**)** *(res)* hypothesis test, hypothesis testing
The process of determining whether a hypothesis is correct.
Hypothesentheorie f **der Wahrnehmung** *(psy)* hypothesis theory of perception (Leo J. Postman/Jerome S. Bruner)
hypothetisches Konstrukt n **(theoretisches Konstrukt** n**)** *(res)* hypothe-

hypothetisches Konstrukt

tical construct, theoretical construct, construct

A mediating construct whose reality cannot be directly observed, but is thought to be probable.

I

Ich-Beteiligung f (**Ego-Involvement** n) *(psy)* ego involvement
  A behavior, (→) Verhalten, attitude, (→) Einstellung, or motive, (→) Motiv, that is primarily concerned with an individual's defense or enhancement of his image in the eyes of others.
Idealimage n ideal image, image ideal, ideal self-image
  A view of how one would like to be.
Ideal-Modell n **von Trommsdorf**
  → Trommsdorf-Modell
Idealprodukt n *(market res)* ideal product
Idealproduktmodell n *(market res)* ideal product model
Idealpunktmodell n *(market res)* ideal-point model
Idealtypus m (Max Weber) ideal type
Idealvektormodell n *(market res)* ideal vector model
Ideenentwicklung f (**Ideenentwicklungsinterview** n) idea development interview (IDI), idea generation interview
Ideenfenster n
  → Phantasiefenster
Ideenfindungsmethode f
  → Kreativitätstechnik
Ideenproduktion f generation of ideas, idea generation
Ideenskizze f
  → Rohentwurf
Identifikation f identification
identische Nachbildung f
  → sklavische Nachahmung
Identitätspolitik f corporate communication, corporate communications pl *(construed as sg)*
  → Unternehmenswerbung
IDFA f abbr Interessengemeinschaft Deutscher Fachmessen und Ausstellungsstädte
Illustration f illustration, picture
Illustrationsdruck m
  → Bilderdruck
Illustrationsdruckpapier n
  → Bilderdruckpapier
Illustrator m illustrator
illustrieren v/t to illustrate, to picturize

Illustrierte f (**illustrierte Zeitschrift** f) picture magazine, magazine, illustrated magazine
illustrierte Anzeige f illustrated advertisement, illustrated ad
Illustriertenleser m
  → Zeitschriftenleser
Illustriertenstand m
  → Kiosk
Illustriertenverlag m magazine publisher, magazine publishing company
Illustriertenverleger m magazine publisher
im Kasten *(film/TV)* in the can
  A colloquial expression used to indicate that film scenes are shot and that recorded broadcast material is complete and ready for being aired.
im Satz *(typ)* all in hand
  All copy has been given to the typesetters.
Image n (**Vorstellungsbild** n) image
  The total perception of an object, such as a product, a brand, a company, a personality, etc., shared by other persons.
Image-Aktion f
  → Imagekampagne
Imageanalyse f image analysis
Image-Aufbau m (**Image-Entwicklung** f, **Imagepflege** f) image building
Imageforschung f image research, multiple image research
Imagekonzept n image concept, concept of image
Image-Marketing n (H.J. Richter) image marketing
Imagemessung f measurement of image, image measurement
Image-Modell n image model
Image-Optimierung f optimization of image, image optimization
Image-Orthicon n (**IO**)
  → Bildaufnahmeröhre
Imagepolitik f image policy
Image-Stabilität f stability of image, image stability
Image-Theorie f image theory, theory of image

Imagetransfer *m* image transfer, transfer of image
Image-Untersuchung *f* **(Imagestudie** *f*) image investigation, investigation of (an) image, image study
Imageverstärker *m* (Uwe Johannsen) *etwa* image factor, image reinforcer
Imagewerbung *f* image advertising
Advertising aimed at reinforcing or changing an image.
Imagewirkung *f* image effect, image impact
Imitation *f* 1. *(econ)* → Nachahmung 2. *(psy)* imitation
Imitationslernen *n (psy)* → Beobachtungslernen
imitieren *v/t* to imitate
IMMA *f abbr* Infratest-Multi-Media-Analyse
Immobilienanzeige *f* real estate advertisement, real estate ad
Immobilienwerbung *f* real estate advertising
Immunisierung *f* (gegenüber beeinflussender Kommunikation) → Inokulation, Inokulationstheorie
Impacttest *m* **(Impactverfahren** *n*, **Impacttestverfahren** *n*) *(advtsg res)* impact test, impact testing, impact test procedure
A test designed to measure the intensity of the effect advertising has on target persons. An original German term does not exist.
Impactwert *m* **(Impact-Wert** *m*) impact value
A measure of the degree to which an advertisement, an advertising campaign, or a medium affects the audience receiving it.
Impedanz *f (electr)* impedance
Imperative *m* → Intensivnutzer, Vielnutzer
Implosion *f (TV)* implosion
Importagent *m (econ)* import agent, import agency
Import-Factoring *n (econ)* import factoring
Importmarketing *n (econ)* import marketing
Importmarktforschung *f* import market research
Imprägnierlack *m* **(Absorptionsmittel** *n*) *(phot)* dope
A varnish used on a negative to facilitate retouching.

Impressum *n* imprint, publisher's imprint, printer's imprint, masthead statement, flag
Imprimatur *n (print)* imprimatur, pass for press, ready for press
imprimieren *v/t (print)* to pass (a manuscript, a proof) for press
Impulsgüter *n/pl* **(Impulswaren** *f/pl,* **Impulssortiment** *n*) *(econ)* impulse goods *pl*, impulse items *pl*
Products that are purchased without careful prior consideration; the decision to buy them is typically made spontaneously, at the point of purchase.
Impulskauf *m* **(impulsive Kaufentscheidung** *f*) *(econ)* impulse purchase, impulsive buying decision
An unpremeditated purchase of consumer goods, motivated by chance rather than plan.
Impulskaufen *n* **(impulsiv Kaufen** *n*, **impulsive Kaufentscheidungen** *f/pl*) *(econ)* impulse buying, impulse purchasing
The act of purchasing, the buying decision being made on the spur of the moment and without previous intention, impelled by some impulse occurring at the point of purchase.
Incentive *f* incentive, incentive item → Anreiz
Incentive-Reise *f* incentive travel → Anreiz
Index *m* **(Indexzahl** *f,* **Indexziffer** *f*) *(stat)* index, index number
A quantity which, by its relation to a standard quantity determined at a base period, (→) Bezugszeitraum, measures variation over time or space of a magnitude which is not susceptible of direct measurement in itself or of direct observation in practice.
Index *m* **der sozialen Stellung (Index** *m* **der sozialen Schichtzugehörigkeit)** *(social res)* Index of Class Position (I.C.P., ICP) (Robert A. Ellis), Index of Social Position (I.S.P., ISP) (August B. Hollingshead/J. Myers), Index of Status Characteristics (I.S.C., ISC) (William L. Warner)
One of a variety of systems for assigning persons to social classes or categories in survey research. The basis usually is occupation, education, income of the head of household.
Index *m* **für die Lebenshaltung** → Preisindex für die Lebenshaltung
Indexbildung *f (stat)* index construction, indexing → Index

Indifferenzgesetz n *(econ)* law of indifference
Indifferenzkurve f *(econ)* curve of indifference
Indifferenz-Präferenz-Theorie f *(econ)* indifference-preference theory (J.R. Hicks/F.Y. Edgeworth)
Indikator m *(res)* indicator
  A characteristic that can be directly observed, but is highly correlated with another characteristic that cannot be directly observed, so that it may serve as an indication of the correctness of a hypothesis.
Indikatorensystem n *(res)* system of indicators, indicator system
Indikatorfunktion f *(res)* indicator function
Indikatorfrage f *(survey res)* indicator question
Indikatorvariable f *(res)* indicator variable
indirekte Frage f *(survey res)*
→ projektive Frage
indirekte Befragung f *(survey res)*
→ projektive Technik
indirekte Beleuchtung f *(phot/film/TV)* indirect lighting, indirect light
indirekte Suggestion f indirect suggestion
indirekte Werbung f indirect advertising
→ Dispositionswerbung
indirekter Test m
→ projektiver Test
Individualentscheidung f **(individuelle Kaufentscheidung** f**)** *(econ)* individual decision
vgl. Gruppenentscheidung (Kollektiventscheidung)
individualisierter Werbebrief m individual advertising letter
Individualkommunikation f individual communication
vgl. Massenkommunikation
Individualmarke f *(econ)* individual brand
  In contrast to a family brand, (→) Markenfamilie, a distinctive identification for a single product.
Individualmerkmal n
→ Merkmal
Individualpanel n
→ Personenpanel
Individualstichprobe f
→ Personenstichprobe
Individualumwerbung f
→ Einzelumwerbung

Individualwerbung f
→ Einzelumwerbung
Induktion f **(Induktionsschluß** m**)** *(stat)* induction
  In philosophic discourse as well as in statistics, the process of reasoning from the particular to the general, i.e. the logical process in which generalizations are inferred from individual instances.
induktive Statistik f **(Induktionsstatistik** f**)** inductive statistics pl *(construed as sg)*
→ Inferenzstatistik
Induktor m inductor
Industrial Relations f/pl industrial relations pl *(construed as sg)*
Industrie-Design n
→ industrielle Formgebung
Industriefachzeitschrift f **(Industriezeitschrift** f**)** industrial magazine, industrial journal, industrial publication
  A business periodical addressed to persons engaged in manufacturing and industry.
Industriefilm m **(industrieller Dokumentationsfilm** m**)** industrial film, business film, sponsored film, theatrical film
Industriegüter n/pl **(industrielle Güter** n/pl**)** industrial goods pl
  Goods which are destined to be sold primarily for use in producing other goods or rendering services as contrasted with goods destined to be sold primarily to the ultimate consumer. They include equipment (installed and accessory), component parts, maintenance, repair and operating supplies, raw materials, fabricating materials. The distinguishing characteristic of these goods is the purpose for which they are primarily destined to be used, in carrying on business or industrial activities rather than consumption by individual ultimate consumers or resale to them. The category also includes merchandise destined for use in carrying on various types of institutional enterprises. Relatively few goods are exclusively industrial goods. The same article may, under one set of circumstances, be an industrial good, and under other conditions a consumers' good.
Industriegüterwerbung f **(Investitionsgüterwerbung** f**)** industrial goods advertising, industrial advertising, capital goods advertising
  Advertising goods or services to businesses for use in the production or distribution of other goods and services.

The term usually refers to industrial or technical products.
Industrieladen m
→ Belegschaftsladen
industrielle Formgebung f (**Industrie-Design** n) industrial design
industrielle Kaufentscheidung f (*econ*) industrial buying decision, buying decision
→ Beschaffungsentscheidung, Einkaufsentscheidung
industrielle Werbung f
→ Industriegüterwerbung
Industriemarke f
→ Herstellermarke
Industriemarketing n industrial marketing (E. Raymond Corey)
Industrieverpackung f 1. industrial package 2. industrial packaging
Industriewerbung f
→ Industriegüterwerbung
ineinanderschneiden (mischen) v/t *(film/TV)* to crosscut
Ineinanderschneiden n (**Mischen** n) *(film/TV)* crosscutting
The rapid picture-to-picture alternation.
Inferenz f *(stat)* inference
A process of reasoning in which existing knowledge is used to derive new knowledge.
Inferenzstatistik f (**schließende Statistik** f, **analytische Statistik** f) inferential statistics *pl (construed as sg)*
The area of statistics concerned with deriving general statements, i.e. inferences, about a population, (→) Grundgesamtheit, from information available from a sample, (→) Stichprobe, of that population. The two basic types of inference, (→) Inferenz, in statistics are estimation, (→) Schätzung, and hypothesis testing, (→) Hypothesentest.
→ induktive Statistik; *vgl.* deskriptive Statistik
inferiore Güter n/pl *(econ)* inferior goods *pl,* Giffen goods *pl*
Goods that either do not satisfy a required standard or the demand for which tends to fall as the incomes of their buyers rise and, more paradoxically, tends to rise as the incomes of their purchasers fall.
→ Giffen-Effekt
Influenz f *(electr.)* static induction
Informatik f theory of information processing, computer science
Information f (**Informationen** f/pl) information

Informationsanalyse f (**Informationsauswertung** f) analysis of information, information analysis
Informationsbank f
→ Datenbank
Informationsbewertung f evaluation of information, information evaluation
Informationsblatt n (**Informationszettel** m) fact sheet
An outline of key product facts supplied to copywriters, or to broadcast announcers who use it as a basis for ad-libbed rather than prepared commercials.
Informationsdienst m (**Nachrichtendienst** m, **Informationsbulletin** n) newsletter, news bulletin, information bulletin
Informations-Display-Matrix f (**IDM**) information display matrix
Informationsfilm m information film, informative film
Informationsfluß m flow of information, information flow
Informationsfrage f (**Ermittlungsfrage** f) *(survey res)* information question
An interview question in a survey exclusively intended to obtain information from a respondent, or to separate informed from uninformed respondents in an opinion interview.
Informationsgemeinschaft f **zur Feststellung der Verbreitung von Werbeträgern e.V.** (**IVW**) German Audit Bureau of Circulations (ABC)
An independent, non-profit organization of advertisers, agencies, and publishers which provides verified audits of the circulation of business publications, general magazines, customer magazines, giveaway papers and newspapers.
Informationsgewinnung f
→ Datenbeschaffung
Informationsgrad m level of information
Informationskanal m channel of information, information channel
Informationsmarkt m information market
Informationsnachfrage f demand for information, information demand
Informationspolitik f information policy
Informationsprogramm n (**Informationssendung** f) *(radio/TV)* news broadcast, news program, *brit* news programme, current affairs program,

Informationsquelle 240

brit current affairs programme, current affairs broadcast
Informationsquelle f source of information
Informationsselektion f selection of information, information selection
Informationssendung f
→ Informationsprogramm
Informationssystem n information system, data information system
Informationstheorie f information theory, theory of information
  The statistical theory of selective information.
Informationsträger m
→ Datenträger
Informationsüberlastung f (**Informationsüberflutung** f) information overload
  An excess of information for interpretation or for processing.
Informationsübermittlung f (**Informationsübertragung** f) transfer of information, information transfer
Informationsverarbeitung f (**Nachrichtenverarbeitung** f) information processing, processing of information
Informationsverarbeitungstechnologie f information-processing technology
Informationsverbreitung f (**Informationsdiffusion** f) diffusion of information, information diffusion
Informationsverhalten n information-getting behavior, *brit* behaviour, information-gathering behavior, information behavior
informative Etikettierung f (**Informative Labeling** n) informative labeling, *auch* informative labelling
  Affixing labels that provide technical and how-to information and/or facts about ingredients of a product.
informative Werbung f informative advertising, information advertising, informative product advertising, factual approach (in advertising), reason-why advertising, reason-why approach (in advertising), (einzelner Werbetext) informative copy, reason-why copy
  A rational copy approach stressing the technical facts about a product or service to prove the logic of the benefits for which the market should buy the product or service; it is typical in the pioneering stage, (→) Einführungsphase, of the product life cycle, (→) Produktlebenszyklus.
informelle Befragung f (**informelle Ermittlung** f)
→ offene Befragung
Infrarot-Filter m *(phot)* infrared filter, infra-red filter
Infrarotphotographie f infrared photography, infra-red photography
Infratest-Anzeigenkompaß m
→ Anzeigenkompaß
Infratest-Multi-Medianalyse f (**IMMA**) Infratest Multi-Media Analysis
Inhaltsanalyse f (**Aussagenanalyse** f, **Bedeutungsanalyse** f, **Textanalyse** f, **Dokumentenanalyse** f, **Content-Analyse** f) *(res)* content analysis
  "A research technique for the objective, systematic, and quantitative description of the manifest content of communication." (Bernard Berelson)
Inhaltsvalidität f (**Kontentvalidität** f, **inhaltliche Gültigkeit** f, **inhaltliche Validität** f) *(res)* content validity, internal validity, intrinsic validity
  The degree to which the items of a test are representative of the variable to be measured.
Initial n (**Initiale** f) *(typ)* initial, initial letter
  The first character in a block of copy, particularly if set in a larger size and different type face.
Initiator m initiator
Inkongruenz f (**Inkongruität** f) incongruity
  vgl. Kongruenz
Inkonsistenz f inconsistency
  vgl. Konsistenz
Inlandsauflage f *(Zeitung/Zeitschrift)* domestic market circulation, national market circulation, home circulation
Inlandsmarkt m *(econ)* domestic market, home market
Inlandsmarktforschung f domestic market research, national market research, home market research
Inlandswerbung f domestic market advertising, national advertising, home market advertising
Innenanschlag m (**Innenplakat** n) *(poster & transit advtsg)* indoor panel, indoor poster, inside advertisement, inside poster, interior poster, (Verkehrsmittel) inside transit poster, baby billboard, inside car card, inside bus bard

Any poster or transit advertisement placed in the interior of buildings or of buses, commuter trains, subway or surface vehicles of public transportation.
Innenanschlagwerbung f **(Innenplakatwerbung** f) *(poster & transit advtsg)* (in Verkehrsmitteln) inside transit advertising, inside car card advertising, inside bus card advertising, inside advertising
Innenantenne f *(electr.)* indoor antenna, *brit* indoor aerial, internal antenna, *brit* internal aerial
Innenaufnahme f *(phot/film/TV)* interior shot, interior, interior shooting, indoor shot, studio shot
  Any scene shot indoors.
Innenauslage f **(Ladenauslage** f) *(POP advtsg)* interior display, in-store display
  The exhibit of advertised goods or of promotional material inside a retail or a wholesale outlet, as distinguished from window display, (→) Schaufensterauslage.
Innenbelegung f *(transit advtsg)* (Belegung der Innenanschläge) basic bus
  The arrangement under which an advertiser has a car card placed inside every vehicle of a fleet.
Innenkante f *(print)* inside edge, inner edge
Inneplakat n
  → Innenanschlag
Innenrand m *(print)* inside margin, inner margin, back margin, fold margin
  → Bundsteg
Innenseite f *(print)* inside page, inside, inner side, inner page
Innenspalte f *(print)* gutter column
Innenspiegel m *(print)* paste-down, lining paper
innerbetriebliche Werbung f
  → werbende Führung
Innovation f **(Innovationsprozeß** m) *(econ)* innovation
  In the most general sense, the development or recognition of new elements or material as well as immaterial patterns in a culture. As a broad term, innovation includes both discovery and invention.
Innovationsbereitschaft f *(econ)* innovativeness
Innovationsdiffusion f diffusion of innovation, diffusion, innovation diffusion

The general process by which an innovation becomes adopted for regular use. Sometimes this process is divided into the stages of awareness, interest, evaluation, trial, and adoption.
  → Diffusion
Innovationsforschung f innovation research
Innovationsrate f *(econ)* rate of innovation, innovation rate
Innovationsrisiko n *(econ)* innovation risk
Innovationsverhalten n *(econ)* innovation behavior, *brit* innovation behaviour
innovatives Marketing n innovative marketing
innovatives Verhalten n *(econ)* innovative behavior, *brit* innovative behaviour
Innovativität f **(Innovationseffizienz** f) *(econ)* innovative efficiency
  That aspect of marketing efficiency that is manifest in the willingness of offering products and services demanded by and supplied to the market by activities which together with the offerings are the most appropriate which can be brought into being under our present knowledge of markets and technology.
Innovator m *(econ)* innovator
  A person who by his personality and mentality is particularly open-minded toward innovations and, therefore, tends to be among the first to adopt a new product, service, habit, or idea.
Inokulation f **(Beeinflussung** f **mit immunisierender Wirkung)** *(communication)* inoculation (William J. McGuire)
Input-Output-Analyse f *(econ)* input-output analysis (Wassilij Leontieff)
  The use of tables showing the quantity or monetary value of goods flowing from one industry to another.
Input-Output-Methode f *(econ)* input-output-method
Input-Output-Tabelle f *(econ)* input-output table
Inselanzeige f **(Insel-Form-Anzeige** f)
  → alleinstehende Anzeige
Inserat n
  → Anzeige
Inseratenagentur f
  → Anzeigenagentur, Annoncen-Expedition
Inseratenreisender m
  → Anzeigenvertreter

Inseratenstatistik f
→ Anzeigenstatistik
Inseratenteil m
→ Anzeigenteil
Inserent m **(Werbungtreibender** m**)**
advertiser
Inserentenbeleg m advertiser's copy
→ Einzelbeleg
inserieren v/t to advertise
Insert m *(film/TV)* insert, (Schriftbild) caption
→ Einblendung
Insertabtaster m *(TV)* caption scanner
Insertion f
→ Anzeigenschaltung
Insertionsanweisung f *(advtsg)* scheduling instruction(s) *(pl)*
Insertionsauftrag m
→ Anzeigenauftrag
Insertionskosten pl
→ Anzeigenkosten, Werbekosten
Insertionsplan m *(advtsg)* space schedule
Insertionsvertrag m
→ Anzeigenvertrag, Werbevertrag
Insertionsvolumen n
→ Anzeigenvolumen
Insertpult n *(TV)* caption desk, caption easel, caption stand
institutionelle Kommunikation f institutional communication
institutionelle Werbung f **(firmenbetonte Werbung** f**)** institutional advertising, corporate image advertising, corporate advertising
 A type of goodwill advertising whose objective it is to enhance the prestige of a company or institution rather than its specific products.
→ Unternehmenswerbung
institutioneller Einzelhandel m
→ Einzelhandel 1.
institutioneller Großhandel m
→ Großhandel 1.
Institutionenmarketing n institutional approach in marketing, institutional marketing approach
Instrumentaldefinition f
→ operationale Definition
Instrumentalinformation f **(Instrumentalvariable** f**)** *(res)* instrumental information, instrumental variable
instrumentelle Frage f *(survey res)* instrumental question
inszenieren v/t to produce, to direct, to stage

Inszenierung f production, direction, staging
Integralqualität f **(integrale Qualität** f **)** (Werner Pfeiffer) *(econ)* integral quality
 The ability of a product to be integrated into a production system.
 vgl. Funktionalqualität
Integration f integration
Integrationsmanager m integration manager
Integrationssystem n **(Integrationsmanagement** n**)**
→ Produktmanagement
integrierte Globalplanung f integrated global planning
integrierte Kommunikation f integrated communication
integrierte Schaltung f **(integrierter Baustein** m**)** *(electr.)* integrated circuit (IC)
integriertes Kommunikations-Mix n integrated communication mix
integriertes Marketing n integrated marketing
Intelligenzzyklus m **der Marketingforschung** (Heribert Meffert) intelligence cycle of marketing research
Intendant m *(radio/TV)* director-general
Intendanz f **(Intendantur** f **)** *(radio/TV)* director-general's office
Intensität f intensity
Intensitätsfrage f *(survey res)* intensity question
→ Skalafrage
Intensitätsskala f **(Magnitudeskala** f**)**
→ Ratingskala
Intensivinterview n **(Intensivgespräch** n**)** *(survey res)* intensive interview, unstructured interview
 A research instrument in empirical social research and in market research designed to discover more precisely what respondents really think or do (have done) by a process of continued and patient probing, usually done by a highly trained interviewer, into belief and desires. Intensive interviews are, for the most part, conducted without any structured questionnaires, but with an interviewer's manual, (→) Leitfaden.
intensive Distribution f **(Intensivvertrieb** m**)** *(econ)* intensive distribution, broadcast distribution
 A method of providing maximum exposure of goods to buyers in the market, by using as many different types

of retailers and retail locations as possible for distribution.
Intensivkampagne f (**Intensivwerbekampagne** f) *(advtsg)* saturation campaign
Intensivleser m
→ häufiger Leser
Intensivwerbung f (**Sättigungswerbung** f) saturation advertising, satiation advertising, supersaturation advertising
Any advertising well above the normal level of coverage, (→) Reichweite, frequency, and impact.
Intention f (**Absicht** f) intention
intentionales Lesen n (**absichtsvolles Lesen** n) *(media res)* intentional reading
vgl. inzidentelles Lesen
Interaktiogramm n (Peter Atteslander) *(social res)* interactiogram
Interaktion f interaction
In general, the dynamic interplay and relationship of reciprocal determination between two variables. In communication, any process in which the action of one entity causes an action by or a change in the other entity.
Interaktionismus m interactionism
Interaktionsanalyse f (**Interaktionsprozeßanalyse** f) *(social res)* interaction analysis, interaction process analysis (Robert F. Bales)
Interaktionsmodell n interactive model
Interaktionsprozeß m interaction process
interaktive Kommunikation f
→ Zwei-Weg-Kommunikation
interaktive Werbung f
→ Rücklaufwerbung
interaktives Kabelfernsehen n
→ Zweiweg-Kabelsystem
Intercarrier m (**Differenzträger** m) *(TV)* intercarrier
Intercarrierbrumm m *(TV)* intercarrier hum
Interdependenz f interdependence, *auch* interdependency
Interdependenzanalyse f *(stat)* interdependence analysis
vgl. Dependenzanalyse
interdisziplinäre Zeitschrift f interdisciplinary magazine, interdisciplinary journal
Interesse n interest, *auch* involvement

Interessengemeinschaft f **Deutscher Fachmessen und Ausstellungsstädte (IDFA)** Association of German Specialized Trade Fairs and Exhibition Cities
Interessent m
→ Kaufinteressent
Interessengruppe f
→ Zielgruppe
Interessentenvorführung f *(TV)* trade showing
Interesseweckung f *(advtsg)* arousal of interest, interest arousal
Interessenweckungserfolg m (Folkard Edler) *(advtsg)* interest arousal effect
vgl. Bedürfnisweckungserfolg
Interferenz f *(electr.)* interference
Interferenzfilter m *(electr.)* interference filter
Interferenzringe m/pl (**Newtonsche Ringe** m/pl) *(phot)* Newton's rings pl, Newtonian rings pl
The rainbow-like rings or formations of color occurring when negatives are locked into contact with sensitized metal plates in printing frames; they are caused by interference of light waves.
Interlock n *(film/TV)* interlock
Intermed-Negativ n (**Internegativ** n) *(phot)* internegative, intermediate negative, *colloq* interneg
A negative made from a color transparency or color print in order to produce a color print of the original transparency or print.
Intermed-Positiv n (**Interpositiv** n) *(phot/film)* interpositive, intermediate positive, *colloq* interpos
1. In photography, an intermediate photographic or photostatic positive produced to permit the further reduction or enlargement of the image size beyond that possible in one original exposure.
2. In motion pictures, a positive prepared for use in optical effects, while permitting the original negative to be preserved unchanged.
Intermediaforschung f intermedia research
The comparative research into the communicative and advertising characteristics of different media types aimed at gaining methods and data for an objectification of media comparisons, (→) Medienvergleich.
Intermediaplanung f intermedia planning, mixed-media planning
Intermediaselektion f intermedia selection, intermedia choice

Intermediate-Negativ n
→ Intermed-Negativ
Intermediate-Positiv n
→ Intermed-Positiv
Intermediavergleich m intermedia comparison
 The comparison of one medium or media type against another or others according to cost, characteristics of the audience, coverage, advertising effectiveness etc.
intermittierende Werbung f
→ pulsierende Werbung
Intermodulation f intermodulation
Internal Relations pl
→ Human Relations
Internationale Fernmeldeunion f International Telecommunication Union (ITU)
Internationale Handelskammer f International Chamber of Commerce (ICC)
 An organization which since 1920 has worked across national lines to improve conditions for international business. Its policies favor the free movement of persons, goods, services, and capital between countries, at all levels of development. It has members in more than 80 countries, comprising about 6,000 companies and some 1,600 economic organizations, some of which themselves represent thousands of companies. Among its practical services are a Court of Arbitration, the International Council on Advertising Practice, and work on the standardization of documents and practices.
internationale Marke f international brand, international trademark, worldwide brand, global brand
internationale Marktforschung f (**Auslandsmarktforschung** f) international market research, market research in foreign countries
Internationale Verhaltensregeln f/pl **für die Verkaufsförderungspraxis** International Code of Sales Promotion Practice
Internationale Verhaltensregeln f/pl **für die Werbewirtschaft** International Code of Advertising Practice
Internationaler Code m **der Markt- und Meinungsforschung** International Code of Market and Opinion Research
internationale Werbung f international advertising, multinational advertising

internationales Marketing n international marketing, multinational marketing
interne Kommunikation f (**innerbetriebliche Kommunikation** f) internal communications pl (construed as sg), internal relations pl (construed as sg)
interne Marktforschung f
→ betriebliche Marktforschung
interne Überschneidung f (**Kumulation** f) (media res) audience cumulation, cumulation ("cume"), audience accumulation, accumulation, reach
 The process of adding new audiences to a media vehicle's total reach as successive issues or broadcasts are used. This takes place because media audiences constantly expand from a fixed base (the single-issue or telecast level). As time goes by, new audiences are reached, while old ones are "lost." Since old audiences remain reached, from the advertiser's point of view, the new ones are accumulated, providing him with an ever-expanding number of people who have seen his ad message at some time during the campaign.
vgl. externe Überschneidung
interne Validität f
→ Inhaltsvalidität
Internegativ n
→ Intermed-Negativ
interpersonale Kommunikation f interpersonal communication
Interpolation f (stat) interpolation
 The process and technique of drawing conclusions from known data.
vgl. Extrapolation
interpolieren v/t + v/i (stat) to interpolate
vgl. extrapolieren
Interpositiv n
→ Intermed-Positiv
Intervall n interval
Intervallprognose f (stat) interval prognosis, interval forecast, interval prediction
Intervallschätzung f (stat) interval estimate, interval estimation
 The estimation of a population parameter, (→) Parameter, by specifying a range of values bounded by an upper and a lower limit, within which the true value is asserted to lie, as distinct from point estimation, (→) Punktschätzung, which assigns a single value to the true value of the parameter. The unknown value of the population parameter is presumed to lie

within the specified interval either on a stated proportion of occasions, under conditions of repeated sampling, or in some other probabilistic sense.
Intervallskala f **(Einheitsskala** f**)** *(stat)* interval scale
A scale of measurement, (→) Skala, on which the scores are based on equal units of measurement. It is possible, therefore, to compare scale scores not merely in terms of the order of the scores but also in terms of the distances between them.
intervenierende Variable f *(res)* intervening variable, intervening variate
A hypothetical construct that can only be observed in an indirect sense.
(in der Panelforschung) intervening qualifier, intermittent qualifier
Interview n interview
→ Befragung
interviewen v/t to interview
Interviewer(in) m(f) interviewer, field investigator
Intervieweranleitung f **(Intervieweranweisung** f**)** *(survey res)* interviewer instructions pl, interviewer brief, interviewer manual, interviewing manual, assignment sheet
Instructions to interviewers, such as which questions to ask or skip and when to probe, which are included in the questionnaire but not read to the respondent.
Interviewer-Ausbildung f **(Interviewertraining** n**)** *(survey res)* interviewer training
Interviewereinfluß m **(Interviewereffekt** m**)** *(survey res)* interviewer effect
The totality of errors in survey responses due to the interviewer, they include both interviewer bias, (→) Interviewerfehler, and interviewer variance.
Interviewer-Erfahrungsbericht m *(survey res)* interviewer report, call report, interviewer call report, interviewer report form
Interviewerfehler m **(Interviewer-Bias** m**)** *(survey res)* interviewer error, interviewer bias, (Bruttofehler) gross interviewer error, (Nettofehler) net interviewer error
That type of bias, (→) systematischer Fehler, in a survey interview, (→) Befragung, which results directly from an interviewer's behavior. This bias may be due to failure to contact the right persons, the failure to establish proper relations with the informant, with the result that imperfect or inaccurate information is offered, or to systematic errors in recording the answers received from the respondent, or to outright cheating, (→) Fälscherproblem.
Interviewerkontrolle f **(Feldarbeitskontrolle** f**)** *(survey res)* interviewer control, supervision of interviewers
Interviewerleitfaden m
→ Intervieweranleitung
Interviewerorganisation f *(survey res)* field force organization, brit field force organisation, interviewer organization
Interviewerschulung f
→ Interviewerausbildung
Interviewfälschung f
→ Fäschung
Interviewleitfaden m **(Gesprächsleitfaden** m**)** *(survey res)* interview guide, interview outline, interview schedule, interview manual
→ Interviewanleitung
Interviewtechnik f
→ Befragungsmethode (Befragungstechnik)
Intervision f **(IV)** Intervision (IV)
Intramediaplanung f intramedia planning
vgl. Intermediaplanung
Intramediaselektion f *(media planning)* intramedia selection, intramedia choice
vgl. Intermediaselektion
Intramediavergleich m intramedia comparison
The comparison of various media of one media type according to cost, characteristics of the audience, coverage, advertising effectiveness etc.
vgl. Intermediavergleich
intrinsische Validität f
→ Inhaltsvalidität
Introduktionsanalyse f (Rudolf Seyffert) *(econ)* introduction analysis, product introduction analysis
vgl. Ökonomisierungsanalyse
Intuition f intuition
intuitive Methode f (der Werbebudgetierung) arbitrary method (of advertising budget determination)
The widespread "method" of subjective advertising budgeting on the basis of intuition rather than analysis, the funds available, or other considerations of the task of advertising.

Inventurausverkauf *m* (**Inventurverkauf** *m*)
→ Saisonschlußverkauf
Inversion *f* (**Umkehrung** *f*) *(stat)* inversion
Inversionsfilter *m*
→ Konversionsfilter
Investitionsgüter *n/pl* (**gewerbliche Gebrauchsgüter** *n/pl*) *(econ)* investment goods *pl*, capital goods *pl*, capital investment goods *pl*
All types of goods of relatively long life, for industry and commerce, which are to be used for a long period of time or to remain permanent or long-term fixtures, e.g. plant and machinery. Those industrial goods that do not become part of the physical product and which are exhausted only after repeated use, such as machinery, installed equipment and accessories, or auxiliary equipment. Installed equipment includes such items as boilers, linotype machines, power lathes, bank vaults. Accessories include such items as gauges, meters, and control devices. Auxiliary equipment includes such items as trucks, typewriters, filing cases, and industrial hoists.
Investitionsgütermarketing *n* (**Invest-Marketing** *n*) *(econ)* investment goods marketing, capital goods marketing
Investitionsgütermarkt *m* *(econ)* investment goods market, market for investment goods, capital goods market
Investitionsgütermarktforschung *f* (**Investmarktforschung** *f*) investment goods market research, capital goods market research
Investitionsgüternachfrage *f* *(econ)* demand for investment goods, demand for capital goods
Investitionsgütertypologie *f* *(econ)* typology of investment goods, typology of capital goods
Investitionsgüterwerbung *f* **Investwerbung** *f*) investment goods advertising, advertising for investment goods, capital goods advertising
Investment Center *n*
→ Ertragszentrum
IO *abbr* Image-Orthikon
Ionenfleck *m* *(TV)* ion spot, ion burn
Irisblende *f* (**Kreisblende** *f*) *(phot)* iris diaphragm, (Trick) iris fade, iris wipe
The adjustable diaphragm, (→) Blende, in front of the camera lens. It is an aperture consisting of overlapping metal leaves controlling the admission of light.
Irisdruck *m* (**Regenbogendruck** *m*)
1. (Produkt) iris print 2. (Verfahren) iris printing
Irradiation *f* 1. *(psy)* irradiation
In psychology, originally the stage at which any stimulus may elicit the response which at a later stage in the conditioning process, will be elicited by the conditioned stimulus alone. In marketing, the concept is also known as the "price-aura effect": Inasmuch as a customer usually buys an assortment of satisfaction bundles at the same time and place, he tends to judge the suitability of the price of any one item by his judgment of the prices of other items of high importance to him which are in the assortment purchased.
2. *(phot)* → Überstrahlung
Irradiationsphänomen *n* *(psy)* irradiation phenomenon, phenomenon of irradiation
irradiierender Faktor *m* *(psy)* irradiating factor
irreführende Angaben *f/pl*
→ irreführende Werbung
irreführende Werbung *f* (**irreführende Reklame** *f*) deceptive advertising, misleading advertising
All advertising the message of which possesses the capacity to deceive a substantial portion of the relevant population.
Irreführung *f* deception
Irrtum *m* *(stat)* → Fehler
Irrtumswahrscheinlichkeit *f* (**Gegenwahrscheinlichkeit** *f*) *(stat)*
→ Fehler 1. Art
Isogewinnkurve *f* *(econ)* isoprofit curve
Isopräferenzlinie *f* *(econ)* isopreference line
Isomorphie *f* (**Gestaltgleichheit** *f*) *(psy)* isomorphism, isomorphy
Isomorphieprinzip *n* (**Isomorphietheorie** *f*, **Isomorphiehypothese** *f*) *(psy)* isomorphism hypothesis, isomorphism principle
IT-Band *n* Internationales Tonband *n* international sound tape
Item *m* item
Itemanalyse *f* (**Aufgabenanalyse** *f*, **Indikatorenanalyse** *f*) *(res)* item analysis
The determination of item discriminability in tests. In general, the term refers to the determination of test item characteristics, such as difficulty

level, clarity level, time limit, and other aspects of item selection. More specifically, it refers to the determination of item discriminability. Since a test as a whole is expected to discriminate between various degrees of the attribute it measures, the items that comprise it should do the same.

Itemskala f item scale, itemized rating scale
In attitude research, (→) Einstellungsforschung, a scale calling for respondents to select one of a given number of categories applying to a phenomenon being on a given attribute.

Iteration f *(math/stat/media planning)* iteration
In general, a trial and error system for finding a mathematical solution to a problem for which a formula cannot be constructed in advance. The procedure is used in media planning to find out which of a given list of media will give the widest reach at the lowest cost.

Iterationsmodell n *(media planning)* iteration model, iterative model
An operational model of media planning. The underlying concept of the iteration approach is to try to bring one vehicle into the solution at a time. The vehicle with the highest value is selected first. The list is then re-examined, and the vehicle with the next highest value is selected. This process is repeated until

IVW-Meldung f (**Auflagenmeldung** f)
etwa publisher's statement, sworn statement, six-month statement
IVW-Prüfung f
→ IVW-Auflagenkontrolle
enough media vehicles have been selected to exhaust the budget. Often values of the remaining vehicles are recomputed after every selection, and any duplication in values of the remaining vehicles is subtracted. Such recomputing ensures that the vehicles with the largest unduplicated value are selected.

Iterationstest m *(stat)* iteration test, runs test, run test
→ Wald-Wolfowitz-Test
Iterationsverfahren n (**Iterationsmethode** f) *(media planning)* iteration model (of media selection), media schedule iteration
→ Iterationsmodell
iteratives Verfahren n
→ Iterationsverfahren
IVW f *abbr* Informationsgemeinschaft zur Feststellung der Verbreitung von Werbeträgern e.V.
IVW-Auflagenkontrolle f (**IVW-Prüfung** f) *etwa* A.B.C. circulation audit, audit of circulation, certified audit of circulation, verified audit of circulation

J

J-förmige Kurve f (**J-Kurve** f) *(stat)* J-shaped curve, J curve, J frequency distribution curve
A graphic presentation of an extremely skewed unimodal distribution with the mode at one end. It is characteristic of data with marked floor or ceiling effect.
J-Skala f **(gemeinsames Kontinuum** n) *(stat)* J scale, joint scale
Ja-Nein-Frage f *(survey res)* quantal question, yes-no question
→ Alternativfrage
Jahrbuch n annual publication, annual book, annual yearbook
Jahresabonnement n annual subscription
Jahresabonnementspreis m **(Jahresbezugspreis** m) annual subscription rate
Jahresrabatt m **(Jahresnachlaß** m) annual discount
Jahresstreuplan m **(Jahresmediaplan** m) annual media plan, annual space schedule, schedule of annual insertions
Jalousie f *(phot/film/TV)* venetian blind
Jalousienblende f **(Klappblende** f) *(phot)* multi-flap shutter, venetian shutter
Japanpapier n Japanese paper, Japan paper
Jaulen n howl, howling, wow
Javellewasser n **(Eau de Javelle** n) *(phot/print)* eau de Javelle, Javelle water, Javel water
"Jetzt"-Preis m **("Jetzt"-"Früher"-Preis** m) *(econ)* was-is price
→ durchgestrichener Preis
Jingle m jingle
Jittern n jitter
Jobfernverarbeitung f remote job entry
Joint-Venture n **(Gemeinschaftsunternehmen** n) *(econ)* joint venture

Journal n journal, magazine
Journalismus m journalism
Journalist(in) m(f) journalist
Journalistenausbildung f education in journalism, journalistic education
Journalistik f journalism
Jubiläumsschrift f anniversary publication
Jubiläumsverkauf m anniversary sale
Jugendfernsehen n
→ Jugendprogramm
Jugendfilm m youth film
jugendfrei adj *(film)* U-certificate, Am etwa PG(general audience, parental guidance) oder G(general audience)
Jugendfunk m
→ Jugendprogramm, Jugendsendung
Jugendmedium n youth medium
Jugendpresse f youth press, youth papers and magazines pl
Jugendprogramm n youth program, brit youth programme, youth broadcast
Jugendsendung f *(radio/TV)* youth broadcast, youth program, brit youth programme
Jugendzeitschrift f youth magazine
Jugendzeitung f youth paper, youth newspaper
Jungfer f *(print)* perfect page
Juniorwarenhaus n
→ Kleinpreisgeschäft
Jupiterlampe f *(film/TV)* floodlight, floodlamp, sun light
Justierblock m *(print)* adjusting block
justieren v/t *(stat/print)* to adjust, to justify
To arrange the spacing between letters and words in such a way that lines of type are of equal length, so that the right hand edge of the column is flush, just as the left edge is.
Justieren n adjustment, justification
Justierkeil m *(print)* adjusting wedge
Justierung f *(stat/print)* adjustment, justification

K

K-Markt *m*
→ Konsumentenmarkt
KA (K.A.) *abbr* Keine Antwort, Keine Angabe *(survey res)* D/K(Don't Know), NR(no response)
 "Don't know" answers are given by respondents to indicate that they would be willing to answer the question but are unable to do so because of lack of information. In difficult or sensitive questions about behavior, a "don't know" may also be a polite refusal to answer. A "no opinion" response to an attitude question indicates that the respondent has not yet formed an opinion on the issue. An "undecided" answer indicates that the respondent cannot choose between two or more alternatives to a closed question. A "no answer" typically is caused by a refusal to answer the question, although it might also result from an interviewer error in skipping the question or because the respondent broke off the interview at some earlier point.
K₁ *m* **(K₁-Wert** *m) (media res)* average-issue audience(AIA, A.I.A.), average-issue readership
Kabel *n* cable, cord, flex
Kabelbericht *m* cabled dispatch
Kabelfernsehen *n* cable television, cable TV, community-antenna television(CATV), community-antenna TV, cablevision, closed-circuit television(CCTV), cablecasting
 Originally, a system for extending the coverage of TV stations through the use of coaxial cable connections to subscribers in weak viewing areas. Today, a wire television service which uses elaborate antennas to transmit TV signals to subscribing households via cable.
Kabelfernsehgemeinschaftsantenne *f*
→ Großgemeinschaftsantenne
Kabelfernsehsystem *n* cable television system, cable TV system, cablevision system
 A television system employing a single antenna to pick up broadcast signals, which are amplified and distributed to local individual sets via direct cable.
Kabelfernsehunternehmen *n* **(Kabelfernsehsendernetz** *n*) cable television system operator, cable television network, cable TV network, cable network
Kabelfernsehzuschauer *m* **(Kabelzuschauer** *m*) cable viewer, cable television viewer, cable TV viewer
Kabelfernsehzuschauerhaushalt *m* **(Kabelhaushalt** *m*) cable television household, cable TV household, cable household
Kabelfernsehzuschauerschaft *f* **(Kabelfernsehzuschauer** *m/pl*) cable television audience, cable audience, cable TV audience
Kabelfernsehzuschauerschaftsmessung *f* **(Kabelzuschauerschaftsmessung** *f*) cable television audience measurement, cable audience measurement
Kabelkanal *m* cable duct
Kabelkern *m* cable core
Kabel-Kleinanzeige *f* **(Kabel-Gelegenheitsanzeige** *f*) cable classified advertisement, cable classified ad, cable classified
Kabel-Kleinanzeigenwerbung *f* **(Kabel-Gelegenheitsanzeigenwerbung** *f*) cable classified advertising
Kabelkommunikation *f* cable communication
Kabelleitung *f* cable circuit
Kabelnetz *n* **(Kabelfernsehsendernetz** *n*) cable television network, cable network, cable television system, cable TV network, cablevision system
Kabelrundfunk *m* **(Kabelfunk** *m*) cable broadcasting, cablecasting
Kabelsatellit *m* cable satellite
Kabeltext *m* cable text, wide-band cable text
Kabelwerbung *f* **(Kabelfernsehwerbung** *f*, **Werbung** *f* **im Kabelfernsehen**) cable advertising, cable TV advertising, (Kleinanzeigenwerbung) cable classified advertising
Kabelzuschauer *m*
→ Kabelfernsehzuschauer
Kabelzuschauerhaushalt *m*
→ Kabelfernsehzuschauerhaushalt

Kabelzuschauerschaft f
→ Kabelfernsehzuschauerschaft
Kabelzuschauerschaftsmessung f
→ Kabelfernsehzuschauerschaftsmessung
Kader m **(Bildfeld** n**)** *(phot/film)* frame
    A single image of a motion picture or television film.
Kaffeefahrt f **(Fahrt** f **ins Grüne)** *etwa* sales excursion
Kakographie f *(print)* cacography
Kalander m **(Glättmaschine** f, **Satiniermaschine** f**)** *(paper)* calender, calender roller, rolling machine, roller, plate calender, plater, plate glazing calender, plater
    A papermaking machine with rollers to give the finish to paper.
kalandern v/t → kalandrieren
Kalanderwalze f **(Kalanderrolle** f**)** *(paper)* roll, calender roll, calender roller, *brit auch* bowl
kalandrieren(kalandern) v/t *(paper)* to calender, to plate
Kalandrieren n **(Kalandern** n, **Glätten** n, **Satinieren** n**)** *(paper)* calendering, plate finish, plater finish
kalandriertes Papier n **(Glanzpapier** n, **geglättetes, satiniertes Papier** n**)** calendered paper, plated paper, plated stock
    Paper with a hard, smooth surface and a high gloss, the result of rolling between calender rolls or of pressing between polished sheets of metal.
Kalender m calendar
Kalenderwerbung f calendar advertising
kalibrieren v/t → eichen
Kalibrieren n **(Kalibrierung** f**)**
→ Eichung
Kaliko m **(Buchbinderkaliko** m, **Buchbinderleinwand** f**)** calico, cloth binding
Kalkulationsauflage f **(kalkulierte Auflage** f**)** rate base, circulation rate base
    In periodical publishing, a minimum guaranteed circulation used as a basis for determining advertising space rates.
Kalkulationsaufschlag m *(econ)* markup, *brit* mark-up
    An amount added to a purchase price to provide a selling price.
kalkulatorischer Ausgleich m **(Ausgleichskalkulation** f, **Mischkalkulation** f, **preispolitischer Aus-**

gleich m**)** *(econ) etwa* leader pricing, loss-leader pricing, leader-pricing strategy, loss-leader pricing strategy
    A pricing policy under which some products or services are offered at unusually low prices, frequently below cost, to induce a larger customer traffic, while others are offered at higher prices to set off the reduction in revenue as a result of the lower prices.
kalkulierte Auflage f
→ Kalkulationsauflage
Kalligraph m calligrapher, calligraphist
Kalligraphie f calligraphy
    A lettering or type style derived from writing with a broad tipped pen.
kalligraphisch adj calligraphic, calligraphical
kaltabbindender Klebstoff m coldsetting adhesive
kalte Nadel f
→ Kaltnadel
kalte Probe f *(radio/film/TV)* cold rehearsal
Kaltemaille n **(Kaltemail** n**)** *(print)* cold enamel
    A photoengraving sensitizer for metal plates consisting of a solution of bichromated shellac, the image being ready for etching after development and drying of the print.
Kaltemailledruck m enamel print
Kaltlicht n *(phot)* cold light
Kaltnadel f **(kalte Nadel** f, **trockene Nadel** f**)** *(print)* drypoint, dry point
Kaltnadelmanier f **(Kaltnadelradierung** f**)** *(print)* drypoint engraving, drypoint, drypoint technique
Kaltprägung f **(Kaltprägedruck** m**)** *(print)* cold embossing, cold stamping, cold blocking, ink stamping
vgl. Heißprägung
Kaltsatz m **(kalter Satz** m**)** *(typ)* cold type, cold composition, cold-type composition
    All types of modern-day direct-impression composition produced, not with the casting of metal, but rather directly on paper by a typewriter device, and used for photographic reproduction. In contrast, hot-metal typesetting, (→) Bleisatz, is made with metal being cast.
Kaltsatzgerät n *(typ)* cold-type machine, cold-type device
Kamera f *(phot/film/TV)* camera, *short* cam.
Kameraachse f *(phot)* camera axis

Kameraarm m *(film/TV)* camera boom arm, pan bar
  A cantilevered camera mount.
Kameraassistent m *(film/TV)* camera assistent, assistent cameraman, focus puller; erster Kameramann: camera operator, zweiter Kameramann: focus operator, second cameraman
Kameraaufnahme f *(phot)* camera shooting, camera shot, *(TV)* recording
Kameraausrüstung f **(Kamerakette** f **)** *(film/TV)* camera equipment, camera chain, film chain
  The entire set of equipment for motion picture or live television pickup, including the camera, monitor, and in-studio control equipment, i.e. cables, controls, and power supply.
Kameraauszug m **(Kameraauszugslänge** f**)** *(phot)* camera extension
  The distance between the exit node of the lens and the focal plane, (→) Brennebene, in which the film lies. When focused on infinity the camera extension equals the focal length, (→) Brennweite, of the lens.
Kamerabericht m *(film/TV)* dope sheet, shot list, film report, (Kamerazustand) camera report
  The camera operator's take-by-take record with instructions to the film laboratory.
Kamerabewegung f *(film/TV)* camera movement
Kamerablende f *(film/TV)* camera fade
  → Blende
Kameradeckel m *(phot/film/TV)* camera cover, camera door
Kameraeinrichtung f *(phot/film/TV)* camera setup, camera set-up
Kameraeinstellung f *(phot/film)* camera alignment, *(TV)* camera placing, (Aufnahme) shooting angle, camera angle, view angle, viewpoint
  The position of the camera and point of view from which a subject is photographed or filmed.
Kamerafahrer m *(film/TV)* tracker, helmsman, grip, steerer
Kamerafahrgestell n **(Kamerawagen** m**)** *(film/TV)* camera dolly, dolly, camera truck, camera pedestal, pedestal, rolling tripod, crab dolly, velocilator
  A truck or mobile platform for television or motion picture cameras.
Kamerafahrplan m *(MAZ)* camera script, shooting script

Kamerafahrt f *(film/TV)* camera tracking; Kamerafahrt vorwärts: tracking in; Kamerafahrt rückwärts: tracking out, tracking back, backtrack, back-track; seitliche Kamerafahrt: crabbing
  vgl. Fahrtaufnahme
Kamerafilm m
  → Aufnahmefilm
Kameraführung f *(phot/film/TV)* camerawork, photography
Kameragehäuse n *(phot)* camera barrel
Kameragewichtsausgleich m *(film/TV)* camera weight adjustment, counterbalance weight
Kameragrundplatte f *(film/TV)* camera base-plate, camera mounting-plate
Kameraheizung f *(film/TV)* camera heating
Kamerakabel n *(film/TV)* camera cable, camera lead
Kamerakette f
  → Kameraausrüstung
Kamerakoffer m *(phot/film/TV)* camera case
Kamerakontrolle f *(film/TV)* camera control
Kamerakontrollgerät n **(KKG)** *(film/TV)* camera control unit (CCU), camera monitor
Kamerakontrollverstärker m *(film/TV)* camera control amplifier
Kamerakopf m *(film/TV)* camera head
Kamerakran m *(film/TV)* camera crane, crane, camera boom, camera derrick
Kamera-Lesebeobachtung f *(media res)* camera observation of reading, camera observation of reading behavior
  → Blickregistrierung
Kameraleute pl *(film/TV)* cameramen pl
Kameralicht n **(Kameraleuchte** f **)** *(film/TV)* camera light
Kameralupe f **(Okular** n**)** *(phot/film/TV)* eyepiece
Kameramann m *(film/TV)* cameraman, camera operator; erster Kameramann: *(film)* director of photography, lighting cameraman, cinematographer, *(TV)* senior cameraman

Kameramischen n (Kameramischung f)
→ Bildsteuerung 1.
Kameranotiz f (Aufnahmelicht n, Aufnahmewarnlicht n) *(film/TV)* camera cue, cue light, tally light, warning light
Kameraplakat n (Kameranotiz f) *(film/TV)* camera card, camera cue card
Kameraprobe f (Kamerastellprobe f) *(film/TV)* camera rehearsal
  Any motion picture or television rehearsal in which the camera follows the action.
Kameraprüfzelle f *(TV)* camera test line
Kameraröhre f *(film/TV)* camera tube
Kameraschwenk m
→ Schwenk
Kameraschwenkkopf m
→ Schwenkkopf
Kamerascript n
→ Kamerafahrplan
Kamerasignal n *(film/TV)* camera signal, camera pulse
Kamerasignalüberwachung f *(film/TV)* camera signal control, vision control, pulse monitoring, *colloq* racks *pl*
Kamerastand m *(film/TV)* camera stand, camera mounting
Kamerastandort m *(film/TV)* camera position, camera setup, camera set-up
  The angle and distance relationship of the subject to the camera.
Kamerastativ n *(film/TV)* camera tripod
Kamerastecker m *(film/TV)* camera plug
Kamerastellprobe f
→ Kameraprobe
Kamerasucher m (Bildsucher m) *(phot/film/TV)* viewfinder, finder
Kameratage m/pl *(film/TV)* camera days *pl*, shooting days *pl*
Kamerateam n *(film/TV)* camera crew, film crew, camera team
Kameratechniker m *(film)* camera maintenance man, *(TV)* camera maintenance engineer, racks engineer, vision control operator, vision operator
Kameraverschluß m *(phot)* camera shutter, shutter
Kameraverstärker m *(film/TV)* camera amplifier

Kamerawagen m
→ Kamerafahrgestell
Kamerawagen m **mit kurzem Kranausleger** *(film/TV)* fearless dolly
  A camera dolly mounted on a short crane boom.
Kameraweg m *(film/TV)* tracking line
Kamerazentralbedienung f *(TV)* central apparatus room(CAR), camera operations center, *brit* centre
Kamerazubehör n *(film/TV)* camera accessories *pl*
Kamerazug m *(film/TV)* camera channel
Kammerzeitschrift f chamber journal, chamber magazine, chamber publication
Kampagne f (Feldzug m) campaign
  A program of coordinated advertisements and/or promotional activities, intended to accomplish a specific marketing or sales objective.
Kampagnenevaluierung f (Kampagnenbewertung f) campaign evaluation
Kanal m channel, (Sendekanal) broadcasting channel, (Fernsehprogramm) channel, service
  The frequency, (→) Frequenz, in the broadcast spectrum assigned to a station for its transmissions.
Kanalantenne f *(electr.)* single-channel antenna, *brit* single-channel aerial
Kanalfunktion f channel function
Kanalgruppe f group of channels
Kanalisierung f canalization
  In psychology, the process by which a need, (→) Bedürfnis, becomes focused upon a particular stimulus or class of stimuli. In selling, the building by a salesperson or advertiser on some association, fear, or bit of information possessed by a prospect or customer and thereby bringing about a dramatic behavior change.
Kanalkapazität f channel capacity
Kanalkapitän m *(marketing)* channel captain, channel leader
  A member of a channel of distribution, (→) Absatzweg, which because of its position or economic power can stipulate marketing policies to other channel members, in effect exercising control over some or all of their decisions and activities. More specifically, the term ist used to designate a firm acting in leadership of a trade channel which has become a single, integrated system. The position is earned by leadership ability

and market power, rather than by appointment by anyone.
Kanalmeßsender m *(radio/TV)* channel signal generator
Kanalschalter m **(Kanalwähler** m**)** *(radio/TV)* channel selector, channel selector switch
Kanalsperrkreis m *(radio/TV)* channel rejector circuit
Kanaltrennung f *(radio/TV)* channel separation
Kanalverstärker m *(radio/TV)* channel amplifier
Kanalwähler m **(Kanalwählschalter** m**)**
→ Kanalschalter
Kanalweiche f *(radio/TV)* channel diplexer, channel combining unit
Kandidatenliste f *(media planning)* list of candidate media, candidate media, candidate list, basic media list, list of basic media, basic media schedule
Kandidatenmedien n/pl *(media planning)* basic media pl, basic advertising media pl
Kannibalisierung f **(Kannibalisierungseffekt** m**)** *(econ)* cannibalization, cannibalizing, market cannibalization, cannibalizing a market
  The practice or process of drawing sales away from another product of the same manufacturer in a manner diminishing the maker's profit. This happens when a new form of a product, instead of producing new business from market segments not before reached, eats into the volume already enjoyed from the existing product, so that no sales increase occurs.
kanonische Analyse f **(kanonische Korrelationsanalyse** f**)** *(stat)* canonical analysis, canonical correlation analysis
  A technique of multivariate data analysis (MDA), (→) multivariate Datenanalyse, that correlates two sets of variables with each other. One set, consisting of two or more independent variables, are considered predictor variables, and the other set, consisting of two or more dependent variables, are considered criterion variables. Canonical correlation analysis finds the pairs of linear combinations of these two sets of variables that are maximally correlated. Each linear combination is called a canonical variate.

kanonische Korrelation f *(stat)* canonical correlation
→ kanonische Analyse
kanonische Matrix f *(stat)* canonical matrix
Kante f 1. *(print)* edge 2. *(phot)* (Licht) rim, rim light
→ Gloriole
Kantenlicht n
→ Kante 2.
Kantenschärfe f *(phot)* edge sharpness, definition, contour sharpness
Kapazität f *(econ)* capacity
  The productive potential of an economy, an industry, or a firm.
Kapazitätsengpaß m *(econ)* bottleneck
Kapazitätsnutzungsgrad m *(econ)* capacity utilization rate
  The proportion of an economy's, an industry's or firm's capacity in actual use or, more precisely, the ratio of actual output to full-capacity output.
Kapazitätsprinzip n *(econ/ communication)* capacity principle, principle of capacity
Kapitalband n
→ Kaptalband
Kapitälchen n *(pl)* *(typ)* small capital letter(s) *(pl)*, small caps pl, SC, s.c.
  Capital letters that are smaller than the regular full-size caps for a given type font.
Kapitalertrag m **(Kapitalertragszahl** f **)** *(econ)* return on investment(s) (ROI), return on capital employed (ROCE)
  The ratio of profits to invested capital, usually expressed in percentage terms. It is the ultimate measure of business performance. It may refer to a measure profitability against total assets, employed net worth, or working capital.
Kapitalgüter n/pl
→ Investitionsgüter
Kapitalkasten m **(oberer Schriftkasten** m**)** *(print)* upper case
Kapitalrentabilität f *(econ)* return on assets managed (ROAM)
  The ratio of profits to total assets, usually expressed in percentage terms.
Kapitalwiedergewinnungszeit f *(econ)* return on time invested (ROTI)
  A measure of the productivity achieved by calling on accounts in a sales territory, (→) Absatzgebiet. By calculating this for each of a salesperson's accounts, the optimum

Kapitel

allocation of time and the optimum number of calls for each account can be determined.

Kapitel n **(Abschnitt** m**)** chapter
Kapitelüberschrift f chapter head, chapter heading, chapter headline
Kappenschachtel f *(packaging)* capped box
Kaptalband n **(Kaptal** n**, Kaptitalband** n**, oberes Kaptalband** n**)** *(print)* headband
vgl. unteres Kaptalband
Karduspapier n **(Linienpapier** n**)** cartridge paper
Karenz f **(Karenzfrist** f, **Karenzzeit** f **)** (für Werbepreise) rate protection, (in der Außen- und Verkehrsmittelwerbung) posting leeway
  The guarantee of continuation at a former rate, made to an advertiser having a contract with a communications medium that raises its rates while the contract is in effect.
Karikatur f cartoon, *auch* caricature
Karikaturist m **(Trickzeichner** m**)** cartoonist
karitative Organisation f
→ Wohlfahrtsverband
Karte f
→ Postkarte, Graphik, Visitenkarte
Kartell n *(econ)* cartel, *auch* kartel, trust
  The organization of a number of firms operating jointly in one market with the intention of minimizing competition.
Kartellamt n **(Kartellbehörde** f**)** *(econ)* anti-cartel authority, anti-trust authority, fair trade commission
Kartellgesetz n
→ Gesetz gegen Wettbewerbsbeschränkungen (GWB)
Kartellrecht n *(econ)* anti-trust legislation
Kartenspiel n *(survey res)* set of cards, cards *pl,* deck of cards, card deck
  Material handed the respondent by the interviewer during the interview, generally on a cardboard card. The card might contain a list of answer categories when there are too many for the respondent to remember, or it might show a picture or diagram to which a reaction is required. Cards are usually numbered or lettered and placed on a ring, so that the interviewer can find the proper card easily.
Kartenvorlage f **(Kartensortieren** n**)** *(survey res)* card sorting
  A procedure for obtaining answers that requires the respondent to place answers printed on cards into two or more piles.
Kartogramm n **(statistische Karte** f**)** cartogram
  A device for displaying statistical information of a descriptive nature by means of (a) symbol(s) on a map. The symbolism may take various forms, such as dots or circles of varying density, shading in black and white, or the use of a full range of colors. Cartograms are particularly convenient for portraying data according to geographical distribution.
Karton m *(packaging)* **1.** (dünne Pappe) cardboard, pasteboard, paperboard, board **2.** (Schachtel) box, cardboard box, carton, container **3.** *(print)* → Auswechselblatt
Kartonage f **1.** *(packaging)* cardboard cover, pasteboard box **2.** (Produkte) cardboard products *pl,* cardboard goods *pl,* cardboard-box products *pl,* cardboard-box goods *pl* **3.** *(bookbinding)* board binding, binding in boards
Kartonagenpappe f
→ Kartonage 1.
kartonieren v/t to bind in boards, (in Karton einpacken) to pack in paperboard
kartoniert *adj* bound in boards, paperbound, bound in paper covers
Kartonpapier n **(dünne Pappe** f **)** fine cardboard
Kartonpappe f box board
Kartuschpapier n **(Kartuschpappe** f **)**
→ Karduspapier
Kasch m *(film/TV)* matte, matt, mat, cover, vignette, (äußerer Kasch) cut-off area, (innerer Kasch) distortion area
  The technique of optical or electronic insertion of an image against a selected background.
Kaschaufnahme f *(film/TV)* mat shot, matt shot, matte shot, process shot
  The imposition of a title, artwork element, or scene over another scene with complete exclusion of background. A matte shot should be carefully distinguished from a superimposition in which the background is kept intact and from a blend in which the background, though not excluded, loses its identity as it is mixed with what is imposed over it.
→ Kasch

Kaschblende f **(Formatblende** f**)** (film/TV) mat diaphragm, matt diaphragm, matte diaphragm
Kaschhalter m (film/TV) mat box, matt box, matte box, mat holder, matt holder, matte holder
kaschieren v/t (print) to laminate, to double, to cover
  To bond or compact materials in layers, as a printed sheet to acetate for strength and permanence.
Kaschieren n (print) lamination, laminating
Kaschierpapier n (phot/print) lining paper, facing paper
kaschiertes Papier n laminated paper, lined paper
Kaschierung f
→ Kaschieren
Kaschverfahren n
→ Bipackverfahren
Käseblatt n **(Käsblättchen** n**)**
→ Gossenzeitung
Kaskadeur m **(Stuntman** m**)** (film/TV) stuntman, stunt man
Kassamarkt m (econ) cash bargain market, cash market
  That part of the market for a commodity in which orders are accepted for delivery at once.
Kassapreis m
→ Barpreis
Kasse f **1.** (Registrierkasse) cash register **2.** (Kino) box office, box-office
Kassenauslage f **(Kassen-Verkaufs-förderungsauslage** f**)** (POP advtsg) cash register display
Kassenerfolg m **(Kassenschlager** m**)** (film) box office hit, box office draw, draw
Kassenterminal n (POP advtsg) cash register terminal
Kassette f **1.** (film/video/phot) cassette, cartridge, auch magazine **2.** (phot) (für Platten) cassette, dark slide, plateholder **3.** (Schuber) case, box, slipcase, slipcover **4.** (Platte) album **5.** (Geschenkkassette aus Karton) gift carton
Kassettenfernsehen n
→ Audiovision
Kassettenfilm m (phot) cartridge film, cartridge roll film
  A roll of sensitized film wound on a metal spool, the roll being encased in a metal casing (cassette) for protection against light and dampness. The cassette protects the film from light and thus it can be loaded into the camera in daylight. The name was given from its similarity in shape to a shot-gun cartridge and its ease of loading into the camera.
Kassetteninsert n audiovision commercial, AV commercial
Kassettenrahmenträger m slide cassette, transparency cassette
Kassettenrekorder m **(Kassetten-recorder** m**)** cassette recorder, cartridge recorder
Kassettentonband n **(Kassettenaufnahme** f, **Aufnahme** f **auf Kassette)** cassette recording, recording
Kästchen n (typ) box, little box
  A portion of a printed message set off from the rest by a border.
Kasten m **1.** (typ) box, copy box
  A satellite copy and/or art element within ruled lines to set it apart from the rest of editorial copy or an advertisement.
2. (packaging) (Karton) box
→ Behälter, Schaukasten, Setzkasten
Kastenanzeige m **(Anzeige** f **im Kasten)** boxed advertisement, box advertisement, boxed ad, box ad
Kastenkamera f (phot) box camera
Kastenoberlicht n (film/TV) (studio) battens pl, overhead lighting, magazine battens pl
Katalog m catalog, brit catalogue
  A buying guide intended for long use, which so completely describes the merchandise it presents that a person can make ordering decisions directly from it.
→ Industriekatalog, Händlerkatalog, Versandkatalog, Einzelhandelskatalog
Kataloggeschäft n
→ Katalogladen
Kataloggestaltung f catalog design, brit catalogue design
Katalogladen m **(Kataloggeschäft** n, **Katalogschauraum** m, **Katalogbüro** n**)** (retailing) catalog showroom, catalog warehouse
  A retailer operating from a warehouse to which customers come prepared to purchase and take away items which they have already selected from the retailer's catalog. Items on display are not available to customers, but are brought from the warehouse section which is often two-thirds of the outlet's space. It rarely deals in anything other than appliances, jewelry and other hard goods. It was originally conceived as a

Katalogpapier

low-cost operation to rival discount houses, (→) Diskonter.
Katalogpapier n catalog paper, *brit* catalogue paper
Katalogpreis m *(econ)* catalog price, *brit* catalogue price, list price
→ Listenpreis
Katalogschauraum m
→ Katalogladen
Katalogversandhandel m catalog retailing, catalog mail-order retailing, catalog selling, catalog sales *pl*
> Offering products or services to consumers in a catalog from which orders are placed to be delivered using an appropriate transportation mode.

Kategorie f **(Begriffsklasse** f**)** category
> A homogeneous class or group of a population of objects or measurements.

Kathode f *(electr.)* cathode
Kathodenbasis f **(KB) (Kathodenbasisschaltung** f**)** *(electr.)* earthed cathode circuit, grounded cathode circuit
Kathodenstrahloszilloskop n *(electr.)* cathode ray oscilloscope (CRO)
Kathodenstrahlröhre f **(Kathodenstrahlmaschine** f, **Kathodenstrahlrohr** n**)** *(electr.)* cathode-ray tube (CRT), CRT machine
Katzenauge n **(Rückstrahler** m**)** reflector button, reflection button
> A small glass or plastic reflector, used in combination with others to create letters or designs in unilluminated outdoor advertisements.

Kauf m **(Einkauf** m**)** *(econ)*
1. (Kaufakt) purchase, buy
2. (Kaufvorgang) purchasing, buying

Kaufabsicht f **(Kaufintention** f, **Kaufplan** m**)** buying intention, buying intent, purchase intention, purchase intent, purchasing intention, purchasing intent
Kaufakt m **(Kaufhandlung** f**)** act of purchase
Kaufaktmarketing n direct-sale marketing, direct-action marketing
Kaufangebot n *(econ)* bid, offer, offer to buy
Kaufanreiz m buying incentive
Kaufausweis m
→ Kaufschein
Kaufbeeinflusser m
→ Beeinflusser
Kaufbereitschaft f
→ Kaufabsicht

Kaufbeweggrund m
→ Kaufmotiv
Kaufeinfluß m buying influence, purchasing influence
Kaufeinstellung f buying attitude, purchasing attitude
kaufen v/t to buy, to purchase
Kaufeintrittsmodell n
→ Durchdringungsmodell
Kaufentscheidung f **(Kaufentschluß** m**)** (bei Konsumenten) buying decision, purchasing decision, purchase decision, consumer decision, consumer choice
Kaufentscheidungsprozeß m **(Kaufentschlußprozeß** m**)** buying decision process, process of making buying decisions, purchasing decision process, purchase decision process, process of making purchasing decisions
> The decision process ending and culminating in the act of buying. Very generally speaking, consumers go through a five-stage process when they buy something:
> 1. **problem recognition:** The individual recognizes come need, (→) Bedürfnis, desire, (→) Wunsch, or problem.
> 2. **information search:** The consumer begins to collect information about purchase alternatives.
> 3. **altervative evaluation:** The consumer evaluates the various purchase alternatives in the light of certain criteria.
> 4. **choice:** The consumer makes a selection from among the purchase alternatives.
> 5. **outcome:** The consumer experiences some degree of satisfaction or dissatisfaction with his purchase decision.

Kaufentscheidungstyp m type of buying decision, type of purchasing decision, type of consumer decision
Kaufentschlußanalyse f **(Kaufentschlußforschung** f**)** *(market res)* activation research, activation analysis
> A technique of obtaining testimony from new buyers of brands and products under which consumers in a probability sample of households are asked in detail about circumstances surrounding recent product brands purchased for the first time. Questioning goes from the purchase to the advertising, and advertising is treated as a cause for action, hence the name. The technique was developed by George H. Gallup.

Käufer *m (econ)* 1. buyer, purchaser, (Konsument) consumer, shopper 2. (Kunde) customer 3. *(media res)* single-copy buyer
Käuferbeobachtung *f (market res)* buyers' observation, consumer observation
Kauferfolg *m* **(Kaufwirkung** *f*) (von Werbung) sales effect, sales effectiveness (of advertising), conversion rate
  The effectiveness of an advertisement or an advertising campaign in stimulating sales of a product or a service.
  → Verkaufserfolg
Käuferkategorie *f*
  → Konsumentenkategorie
Käufermarkt *m (econ)* buyer's market, *auch* loose market
  A condition of the market in which buyers are able to bargain and to be selective because there is an overabundance of goods available as the result of an imbalance between supply and demand.
  vgl. Verkäufermarkt
Käuferpanel *n (market res)* consumer-purchase panel
Käuferrente *f*
  → Konsumentenrente
Käufersegment *n*
  → Marktsegment
Käufersouveränität *f*
  → Konsumentensouveränität
Käuferstudie *f* **(Käuferuntersuchung** *f*) *(market res)* purchaser study, purchaser investigation
Käufertyp *m*
  → Konsumententyp
Käufertypologie *f*
  → Konsumententypologie
Käuferverhalten *n* buyer behavior, *brit* buyer behaviour, purchaser behavior, *brit* purchaser behaviour, (Einkaufsverhalten) shopping behavior, *brit* shopping behavior
  → Konsumentenverhalten
Käufer-Verkäufer-Beziehung *f*
  → Verkäufer-Käufer-Beziehung
Käuferwanderungsanalyse *f (market res)* buyer flow analysis, analysis of buyer flow
Käuferzeitschrift *f* **(Kundenzeitschrift** *f* **des Handels)** buyer's guide
  → Kundenzeitschrift
Kauffrequenz *f* **(Kaufhäufigkeit** *f*) *(market res)* buying frequency, purchasing frequency, frequency of buying, frequency of purchasing, (Einkaufsfrequenz) shopping frequency, frequency of shopping
Kaufgewohnheit *f* buying habit, purchase habit, purchasing habit, shopping habit
Kaufhandlung *f*
  → Kaufakt
Kaufhäufigkeit *f*
  → Kauffrequenz
Kaufhaus *n (retailing) etwa* departmentized specialty store
  A type of retail store between a specialty store, (→) Fachgeschäft, and a department store, (→) Warenhaus. If the term is not used as a synonym for Warenhaus, it describes, in essence, a specialty store which has become large and in which the various types of merchandise carried are accounted for separately for profit knowledge and general managerial decision making.
Kaufhaus *n* **für Gelegenheiten (Bargain-Store** *m) (retailing)* bargain store
Kaufhemmung *f* buyer's resistance, buying resistance
Kaufintensität *f* buying intensity, purchasing intensity
Kaufintention *f*
  → Kaufabsicht
Kaufinteressent *m* **(potentieller Käufer** *m*) prospective buyer, prospective customer
Kaufkraft *f (econ)* buying power, purchasing power, *auch* spending power
  The capacity to purchase possessed by an individual buyer, a group of buyers, or the aggregate of the buyers in an area or a market.
Kaufkraft-Elastizität *f (econ)* elasticity of buying power, elasticity of purchasing power
Kaufkraftindex *m*
  → Kaufkraftkennziffer
Kaufkraftkarte *f (market res)* buying power map, purchasing power map
Kaufkraftkennziffer *f* **(Kaufkraftkennzahl** *f,* **Kaufkraftindex** *m) (econ)* buying power index (B.P.I., BPI), buying power quota (B.P.Q., BPQ), purchasing power index
  Any weighted index that converts specific basic elements, e.g. population, effective buying income, retail sales, etc. into a comparable measurement of a market's ability to buy, and expresses it as a percentage of the national potential.

Kaufkraftschwelle f *(econ)* threshold level of buying power, threshold level of purchasing power
käufliches Warenmuster n *(econ)* saleable sample, salable sample
Kaufmann m business man, businessman, merchant, dealer, trader
Kaufmannsmarke f
→ Händlermarke
Kaufmannswarenhaus n
→ Gemeinschaftswarenhaus
Kaufmotiv n buying motive, purchasing motive
 One of a variety of factors within a person or organization which combine to create a desire to purchase. Such factors are usually complex and comprise both objective criteria such as price, quality, service, delivery, etc., and subjective criteria such as prestige, brand image, color, shape, packaging, and the like.
Kaufmotivation f buying motivation, purchasing motivation
Kaufmotivationsforschung f **(Kaufmotivforschung** f**)** buying motivation research, purchasing motivation research
Kaufmuster n **(Muster** n **des Kaufverhaltens)** buying pattern, purchase pattern, spending pattern
 The regularity that can be observed in overt buying behavior.
Kaufneigung f *(econ)* propensity to buy, propensity to purchase, buying propensity, purchasing propensity
→ Konsumneigung
Kaufort m **(Einkaufsort** m, **Verkaufsort** m**)** point of purchase (P.O.P., POP), point of sale (P.O.S., POS)
 The actual place at which a purchase (sale) is made, in general, the retail sales outlet. Logically, the P.O.P. and the P.O.S. may be different in one act of purchase, e.g. in mail order.
Kaufphase f buying phase, buying stage, buy phase
Kaufplan m buying plan, purchase plan
Kaufprozeß m buying process, purchasing process
→ Kaufentscheidungsprozeß
Kaufprozeßanalyse f buying process analysis, purchasing process analysis
Kaufquote f **(Kaufrate** f**)** *(econ)* conversion rate
 The rate of conversion of inquiries or replies to an advertisement into sales.
Kaufreaktion f **(Konsumreaktion** f**)** purchase response, consumer reaction

 The behavioral response of the consuming public on exposure to a particular stimulus, as manifested in purchasing activities.
Kaufreaktionsmuster n purchase-response pattern
Kaufreue f **(Nachkaufreue** f**)** postdecisional regret, post-purchase doubt, postpurchase cognitive dissonance, cognitive dissonance, buyer's remorse
 The experience a buyer may make, particularly after high-cost purchases, questioning the wisdom of the purchase. The negative factors associated with the purchase seem greater, the disadvantages of the options not taken appear less important. If this condition continues, it is quite likely that a consumer will never be satisfied with the product's usage.
Kaufrisiko n consumer-perceived risk, purchase risk
 In making product decisions, the consumer usually considers these uncertainties: *functional risk* (perhaps the product will not do what it is said to be able to do); *physical risk* (could it do injury to the physical self of someone?); *financial risk* (the product may not be worth its cost); *social risk* (could it cause embarrassment?); and *psychological risk* (danger of bruised ego).
Kaufsituation f buying situation, purchase situation
Kaufstatistik f purchasing statistics *pl (construed as sg)*
Kaufstätte f
→ Kaufort
Kaufstruktur f
→ Ausgabenstruktur
Kaufverhalten n buying behavior, *brit* buying behaviour, purchasing behavior, *brit* purchasing behaviour
→ Konsumentenverhalten
Kaufverhaltensbeobachtung f
→ Käuferbeobachtung
Kaufverhaltensmodell n model of buying behavior, model of purchasing behavior
→ Konsumentenverhaltensmodell
Kaufverzicht m
→ Konsumverzicht
Kaufvorgang m
→ Kaufprozeß
Kaufvorhaben n
→ Kaufplan
Kaufwahrscheinlichkeit f buying probability, probability of buying,

purchasing probability, probability of purchase
The percentage of individual consumers or households in a target group, (→) Zielgruppe, who will buy a product or brand within a given period of time. In market research practice, buying probabilities are determined by means of surveys, (→) Befragung, of buying intentions, (→) Kaufabsicht.
Kaufwerbemittel *n* direct-action advertisement
Kaufwerbung *f* **(Kaufaktwerbung** *f*) direct-action advertising
Kaufwunsch *m* buying desire, purchasing desire
Kaufzeitschrift *f* **(Einzelverkaufszeitschrift** *f*) store-distributed magazine, newsstand magazine, kiosk magazine
Kaufzeitung *f* **(Straßenverkaufszeitung** *f*) newsstand newspaper, newsstand paper
A newspaper that is exclusively or overwhelmingly sold through newsstands or newsboys rather than being subscribed to.
Kaufzwang *m*
→ moralischer Kaufzwang, psychologischer Kaufzwang
Kausalanalyse *f* **(kausale Abhängigkeitsanalyse** *f*)
→ Pfadanalyse
Kausalanalyse-Diagramm *n*
→ Pfaddiagramm
Kausalhypothese *f* causal hypothesis
Kausalität f causality, causal relationship
The state in which some condition produces, or always results in, a particular consequence.
Kausalmodell *n* causal model
Kausalprognose *f* causal forecast, causal prognosis, causal prediction
KB *abbr* Kathodenbasis
Keep-out-Preis *m*
→ Abwehrpreis
Kegel *m* **(Schriftkegel** *m*) *(print)* shank, type body, body of the type
The main body or stem of a unit of type.
Schrift auf anderem Kegel: bastard type, bastard typeface, bastard size, bastard
Kegelgröße *f* **(Kegelstärke** *f*) *(print)* body size, body
The size of type from the bottom of the descenders, (→) Oberlänge, to the top of the ascenders, (→) Unterlänge, excluding leading, (→) Durchschuß.
Kegelhöhe *f* *(print)* body height

Kehlkopfmikrophon *n* **(Kehlkopfmikrofon** *n*) throat microphone, throat mike
Keil *m* **1.** *(film)* (Kopierwerk) optical wedge **2.** *(print)* sliding quoin, quoin, sliding coign, (bei einer Zeilensetzmaschine) space band
A small wedge or expanding device used for locking type forms in chases in letterpress.
Keilentfernungsmesser *m* *(phot)* wedge range-finder
Keilspatium *n* *(print)* quoin space
Keilvorlage *f* *(phot)* density wedge, sensitometric wedge, step wedge
Kendalls Tau *n* **(Kendalls τ** *n*) *(stat)* Kendall's tau, Kendall's τ, tau coefficient, Kendall's rank correlation coefficient
A measure of agreement between two separate rankings based on the number of inversions. The tau coefficient is computed by taking 1 minus the proportion of inversions.
Kennimpuls *m* *(tape)* blip, *(film)* sync plop, sync pip
Kennlinie *f* characteristic curve; fallende Kennlinie: falling characteristic curve, steigende Kennlinie: rising characteristic line
Kennmelodie *f* *(radio/TV)* musical signature, signature tune, signature theme, theme
zur Kenntnis (zur Kenntnisnahme) for your information (FYI)
Kennung *f* **(Kennungssignal** *n*) *(radio/TV)* identification, ID identification signal, *colloq* ident, (Kennbuchstaben) call letters *pl*
A brief announcement or sign by which a radio or television station identifies itself.
→ Kennmelodie, Senderkennung
Kennzahl *f* **(Kennziffer** *f*)
1. *(stat)* ratio, quota
2. → Chiffre
Kennzeichen *n*
→ Markierung
Kennzeichenanzeige *f*
→ Chiffre-Anzeige
kennzeichnen *v/t* → markieren
Kennzeichnung *f*
→ Markierung
Kennziffer *f*
→ Kennzahl, Chiffre
Kennzifferanzeige *f*
→ Chiffre-Anzeige

Kennzifferdienst m
→ Leserdienst
Kennziffergebühr f
→ Chiffre-Gebühr
Kennzifferkarte f
→ Chiffre-Karte
Kennziffermethode f (**Kennwortmethode** f) (in der Anzeigenwerbung) keying of an advertisement, keying of an ad
 Inserting in the address or coupon a different code for each medium used, so that inquiries can be traced and media effectiveness compared.
Kennzifferwerbung f keying of advertisements
Kennzifferzeitschrift f etwa controlled circulation magazine, qualified circulation magazine
 A controlled circulation periodical in which all advertisements and most parts of the editorial section are keyed, so that readers can send inquiries to the publisher who forwards them to the advertiser.
Kernleser m (**Stammleser** m) (media res) regular reader, primary reader
 A reader with a reading probability (→) Lesewahrscheinlichkeit, between 0.83 and 1.00, i.e. a reader who has read at least 10 out of 12 subsequent issues of a periodical.
Kernleserschaft f (**Kernleser** m/pl) (media res) regular readers pl, regular audience, primary readers pl, primary audience
Kernmaß n (print) gauge, gage
 An electrotype of the same thickness as an engraving.
Kernprodukt n (econ) core product
Kernschatten m complete shadow, deep shadow
Kernsortiment n
→ Basissortiment, Standardsortiment
Kernverbreitungsgebiet n
→ Hauptverbreitungsgebiet
Kettenanzeige f
→ Serienanzeige
Kettengeschäft n (**Kettenladen** m) (retailing) chain store
 A group of retail stores of essentially the same type, centrally owned and with some degree of centralized control of operation. The term may also refer to a single store as a unit of such a group.
→ Ladenkette
Kettenindex m (**Kettenindexziffer** f, **Gliedziffer** f) (stat) chain index, chain index-number, chain-relative
 An index number in which the value at any given period is related to a base in the previous period in contrast to an index which is related to a fixed base. The comparison of nonadjacent periods is usually made by multiplying consecutive values of the index numbers, which, as it were, form a chain from one period to another. In practice, chain index numbers are usually formed from weighted averages of link-relatives, i.e. the values of magnitudes for a given period divided by the corresponding values in the previous period.
Kettenladen m
→ Kettengeschäft n
Kettenstich m (**Kettstich** m) (bookbinding) kettle stitch
Keule f (radio) lobe
Key Light n
→ Spitzlicht
Kilohertz n (**KHz**) kilocycle (kc), kilocycle per second
Kilometerdruck m
→ Bromdruck (Bromsilberdruck)
Kinderfernsehen n children's television, children's TV, children's television program, brit programme, children's television broadcast, children's TV broadcast, colloq kidvid
 Television programming intended to appeal exclusively to children.
Kinderfilm m children's film, children's movie
Kinderfunk m children's broadcasting, children's program, brit programme
 Radio programming intended to appeal exclusively to children.
Kinderprogramm n (radio/TV) children's program, brit children's programme, children's broadcast, children's hour
Kinderserie f (radio/TV) child serial, children's serial
Kinderwerbung f advertising to children
Kinderzeitschrift f children's magazine
Kinefilm m
→ Kinofilm
Kinemathek f (**Cinemathek** f) film library, cinematheque
Kinematograph m cinematograph
Kinematographie f cinematography
kinematographisch adj cinematographic
Kino n 1. (Institution) cinema, motion pictures pl, movies pl, pictures pl,

colloq the flicks *pl*, the flickers *pl*
2. (Vorstellung) film, picture, movie
3. → Lichtspieltheater (Filmtheater)
Kinobesuch *m (media res)* cinema attendance, film attendance, motion-picture attendance, movie attendance, movietheater attendance
  The absolute number or percentage of persons attending a movietheater within a given period of time.
Kinobesucher *m (media res)* cinemagoer, cinema-goer, filmgoer, film-goer, picture goer, moviegoer, movie-goer
Kino-Dia *n* (**Kino-Diapositiv** *n*)
→ Film-Dia
Kino-Diawerbung *f*
→ Diawerbung
Kinofilm *m* (**Kinefilm** *m*, **Cinefilm** *m*) cinefilm, cinema film, motion picture, movie
  A sequence of photographs recorded in a manner permitting restoration of images of the subjects filmed, in motion. Also, a photographic transparency film used to photograph or print motion pictures.
→ Film 2., 3.
Kinokasse *f* cinema box office, movie theater box office
Kinomobil *n* (**Filmvorführwagen** *m*) cinemobile, cinema van
Kinoplakat *n* cinema poster, film poster, movie poster
Kinoreklame *f*
→ Kinowerbung
Kinovorstellung *f* (**Kinovorführung** *f*)
→ Filmvorführung
Kinowerbeansage *f* cinema announcement
Kinowerbefilm *m* (**Kinowerbespot** *m*) advertising film, cinema advertising film, advertising picture, (Kurzfilm) advertising filmlet
Kinowerbung *f* (**Filmwerbung** *f*, **Filmtheaterwerbung** *f*, **Lichtspieltheaterwerbung** *f*, **Film- und Dia(positiv)werbung** *f*) screen advertising, theater-screen advertising, cinema advertising, film advertising, in-theater advertising, theater advertising
Kintopp *m* (*colloq* für Kino) the flicks *pl*, the flickers *pl*, the movies *pl*
Kiosk *m* newsstand, kiosk, *auch* kiosque, *brit* bookstall, *brit* news stall
Kioskplakat *n* (**Kioskposter** *n*) newsstand poster, kiosk poster

Kioskwerbung *f* (**Werbung** *f* **am Zeitungsstand**) newsstand advertising, kiosk advertising
kippen *v/t (film/TV)* (Bild) to tilt
Kippschwenk *m (film)* flip wipe
Kirchenblatt *n*
→ Kirchenzeitung, Kirchenzeitschrift
Kirchenfernsehen *n* religious television program, *brit* programme, religious TV program, church television, church television program, *brit* programme, church TV program
Kirchenfunk *m* church broadcasting, religious broadcasting
Kirchenpresse *f* religious press, church press
Kirchenzeitschrift *f* church magazine, church periodical
Kirchenzeitung *f* church newspaper, church paper, (Gemeindemitteilungsblatt) parish paper, parish magazine, parish journal
Kiste *f (packaging)* container, box, *brit* case
KKG *n abbr* Kamerakontrollgerät
KLA *f abbr* Kundenzeitschriften Leseranalyse
Klammer *f* 1. *(typ)* paranthesis, (eckige Klammer) bracket, (geschweifte Klammer) brace
2. → Heftklammer
Klammerheftung *f* (**Klammerheften** *n*)
→ Drahtheftung
Klammerteil *m (film)* crop
Klang *m* sound, (Tonqualität) tone
Klangbild *n* sound pattern, acoustic pattern
Klangblende *f*
→ Tonblende
Klangbrücke *f (radio/TV)* bridge
  A short phrase of transitional music or sound effects used to connect two dramatic sequences in a program.
Klangeffekt *m*
→ Geräuscheffekt
Klangeindruck *m* sound impression
Klangfarbe *f* tone color, *brit* tone colour, tone quality, tonality, tone, timbre
Klangfarbenkorrektur *f* **Klangfarbenregelung** *f*) *(radio/TV)* tone correction, tone control
Klangfarbenmodulation *f (radio/TV)* tone modulation
Klangfilter *m* sound filter

Klangfülle f sound volume, (Musik) richness of tone, fullness of tone
Klanggemisch n sound spectrum
Klappblende f
→ Jalousienblende
Klappdeckel m *(bookbinding)* hinged lid, hinged cover, hinged flap, hinged lid
Klappdeckelschachtel f *(packaging)* flip-top box
Klappe f **1.** *(bookbinding)* (eines Buchumschlags) jacket flap, flap
→ Umschlagklappe
2. *(film)* (Synchronklappe) clapstick, clap stick, slate, clapper board, clapper
 A device used at the start of a take, (→) Einstellung, in motion picture or TV commercial production for a guide to synchronize sound and picture.
Klappenliste f *(film/TV)* camera sheet, camera notes pl, magazine card, rushes log
Klappenschläger(in) m(f) *(film)* clapper boy, clapper girl
Klappentext m (Buchwerbung) flap blurb, jacket blurb, blurb
 A short piece of promotion copy printed on the jacket flap, (→) Umschlagklappe, of a book.
Klappkamera f *(phot)* folding camera
Klapp-Plakat n (**Klappschild** n) *(POP advtsg)* A frame, "A" frame, A board, "A" board
 A two-sided sign shaped as the letter A, enabling it to stand on its own.
Klappschwenk m *(film)* flip wipe
Klappstativ n *(phot)* folding tripod
Klapptafel f (**Flip-Chart** n) flip card, flip chart
 A tablet sheet bearing one of a sequence of messages for use in a presentation.
Klapptitel m *(TV)* flip caption, flip titles pl
 The titles or illustrations produced on cards for use in sequence in a television program or commercial.
Klappwand f flipper
Klärbad n *(phot)* clearing bath, washer bath
 A bath used to remove veil, fog, scum or stains from photographic negatives, especially wet collodion images.
Klarschriftbeleg m (**Klarschrift** f) (beim Photosatz) hard copy
Klarsichtfolie f acetate foil, acetate overlay, acetate film, transparent foil, transparent overlay, transparent film
 A thin plastic, used in clear or translucent sheet form for various purposes in packaging or in advertising graphics, as for overlays and repro proofs.
Klarsichtpackung f (**Klarsichtschachtel** f) transparent box, transparent package, transparent pack
Klassenstatistik f
→ homograde Fragestellung
Klassenzimmerbefragung f *(survey res)* group interview, structured closed-group interview
 An interview with self-administered questionnaires where a single interviewer provides instructions and may present visual material to multiple respondents in a school classroom, a work place, or some other central location. Interviews with several members of a household would not normally be considered group interviews.
Klassifikation f (**Klassifizierung** f) classification
klassische Werbung f
→ Mediawerbung
klassisches Medium n traditional medium
Klatschkopie f *(phot)* direct print, slash print, slash dupe
Klatschspalte f (Zeitung/Zeitschrift) gossip column
Klatschzeitung f (**Klatschzeitschrift** f, **Klatschblatt** n) gossip paper, gossip magazine
Klebeapparat m *(print)* gummed tape sealer
Klebeband n **1.** adhesive tape, pressure-sensitive tape, (zum Umreifen) strapping tape **2.** *(film)* splicing tape, joining tape, adhesive tape **3.** (MAZ) strip of foil, foil
Klebebindemaschine f (**Klebebindeapparat** m) *(bookbinding)* perfect binder
klebebinden v/t → lumbecken
Klebebindung f (**Klebebroschur** f, **Lumbecken** n) *(bookbinding)* perfect binding, adhesive binding, thermoplastic binding, threadless binding, check binding
 A type of binding in which the binding edges of signatures are scuffed and then glued to the backbone or binding edge of a periodical or book, thus eliminating wire staples.
Klebeetikett n
→ Aufkleber

Klebefolie f
→ Klebeband, Klebestreifen
klebegebunden (klebegeheftet, gelumbeckt) adj *(bookbinding)* perfect-bound, adhesive-bound
Klebeheftung f
→ Klebebindung
Klebekarton m pasteboard
Klebekolonne f *(outdoor advtsg)* group of billstickers, billstickers pl
Klebelade f
→ Klebepresse
Klebemuster n
→ Klebeumbruch
kleben v/t **1.** to glue, to stick, to paste, to gum, to post, to size **2.** *(film/tape)* to splice, to join
   To cement two pieces of film or tape together.
Kleben n **(Klebung** f**) 1.** pasting, glueing, sticking, gumming, posting, sizing **2.** *(film/tape)* splicing, joining, sizing, *(tape)* blooping
Klebepresse f **(Klebelade** f**)** *(film/tape/TV)* joiner, jointer, splicer, splicing press
   A device for accurate joining of edited film frames with transparent tape or cement.
Klebespiegel m **(Klebeumbruch** m**, Klebemuster** n**)** *(print)* pasteup, brit paste-up, pasteup layout, brit paste-up layout
   A layout in which illustration and type material are combined on one sheet for reproduction as a single engraving.
Klebestelle f *(film/tape)* join, joint, splice
   The joint that results from cementing two pieces of film or tape together.
Klebestellenlack m *(film/tape)* blooping ink
   A type of ink used for patching the sound track on a film print or a tape to eliminate bloops.
Klebestreifen m **(Klebefolie** f**)** adhesive foil, adhesive-backed acetate, adhesive film, adhesive strip, adhesive tape, paster
Klebetisch m *(film/tape)* splicing table, splicing bench
Klebeumbruch m *(print)*
1. (Klebeumbrechen) pasting-up, pasteup, brit paste-up, pasting on **2.** → Klebespiegel
   The assemblage of type proofs, art work, etc. pasted on paperboard.

Klebeumbruch machen v/t *(print)* to paste up (the pages), to paste on
Klebeverschluß m adhesion seal, bond seal
Klebezettel m
→ Aufkleber
Klebstoff m **1.** (Leim) glue, gum, mucilage **2.** *(print)* paste **3.** (Papierleim) size **4.** *(phot)* (zum Aufkleben von Bildern) mountant
Klecksographie f **(Klecksographientest** m**)**
→ Rorschach-Test
Kleidungslicht n *(film/TV)* cloth light
Kleinanzeige f **(Gelegenheitsanzeige** f**, Rubrikanzeige** f**)** classified advertisement, classified ad, small-space advertisement, small-space ad, small advertisement, small ad
   A small-size advertisement in a newspaper or magazine, usually appearing under distinctive headings, with special rates for insertion and, in general, in uniform and specified type of a single size. Help wanted, positions wanted, family announcements are typical classified ads. They normally apply to the sale of a single item or service and are not an instrument of mass product promotion.
Kleinanzeigenrubrik f **(Gelegenheitsanzeigenrubrik** f**, Kleinanzeigenspalte** f**, Gelegenheitsanzeigenspalte** f**, Anzeigenrubrik** f**)** classified column, classified advertising column
Kleinanzeigenwerbung f **(Gelegenheitsanzeigenwerbung** f**, Rubrikanzeigenwerbung** f**)** classified advertising, *auch* small-space advertising, (Werbung mit rubrizierten Formatanzeigen) classified display advertising, semi-display advertising
   Advertising arranged according to the product or service advertised, and usually restricted in size and format. Some newspapers offer special sections devoted to only one product or service, in which the layout and the elements of the advertisement are virtually unlimited, as in other parts of the paper. Advertising in these sections combines the freedom of display advertising with the grouping advantages of classified advertising.
Kleinbedarf m **(Klein- und Bequemlichkeitsbedarf** m**)**
→ Convenience Goods
Kleinbild n *(phot)* 35mm picture
Kleinbildfilm m *(phot)* 35mm film

Kleinbildkamera f *(phot)* 35mm camera
Kleinbuchstabe m *(typ)* lower-case letter, lower case (l.c., lc, L.C., LC), small letter, *auch* minuscule, miniscule
   Small letters, in contrast to capital letters.
Kleindarsteller m
→ Charge (Chargenspieler)
Kleindruck m *(print)* small type, small print, minuscules *pl*, miniscules *pl*
kleine Stichprobe f *(stat)* small sample
Kleinfläche f **(Kleintafel** f**)** *(outdoor advtsg)* junior panel
   A small-size outdoor advertising panel measuring between 180 × 120 cm and 260 × 120 cm.
Kleinflächenplakat n **(Kleinflächenanschlag** m**)** *(outdoor advtsg)* junior panel poster
Kleinformat n (Anzeige) small size, junior size
   A unit of space that permits an advertiser to use the same plates for large- and small-page magazines. Plates prepared for full-page space in the smaller magazine appear in the larger one with editorial material on two or more sides.
(Zeitung) tabloid size
→ kleinformatige Zeitung
kleinformatig *adj* small-size, small
kleinformatige Zeitung f **(Kleinformatzeitung** f**)** tabloid newspaper, tabloid paper, tabloid
   A newspaper usually about one half the standard size.
Kleingedrucktes n **(das Kleingedruckte** n**)** (in Verträgen, Geschäftsbedingungen) the fine print, the mouse print
   The very small typeface used in contracts, on food packages, etc., to specify conditions, describe the contents, ingredients, and potential harm, as required by law.
Kleingruppe f *(soc)* small group
Kleingruppenforschung f *(soc)* small-group research
Kleinkatalog m condensed catalog, *brit* condensed catalogue
   An abbreviated catalog with a price list of leaders in the product line with only brief, highspot descriptions.
Kleinhandel m
→ Einzelhandel

Kleinhandelsgeschäft n
→ Einzelhandelsgeschäft
Kleinoffset m **(Kleinoffsetdruck** m**)** office duplicating, office duplication
Kleinoffsetdruckmaschine f **(Kleinoffsetdrucker** m**)** offset duplicator, office offset duplicator
Kleinplakat n advertising card, quarter-size poster, small poster
Kleinpreisgeschäft n **(Juniorwarenhaus** n**)** *(retailing)* low-price store, low-margin, low-price store, penny store, mass merchandiser, junior department store
   A type of retailer who tends to offer fewer customer services, (→) Kundendienst, than a department store, who focuses his attention on low prices, high turnover, and large sales volumes, thus appealing to a large heterogeneous target market.
Kleinschreibung f *(typ)* lowercasing, noncapitalization, *brit* non-capitalisation
   Using small letters as opposed to capital letters.
vgl. Großschreibung
Kleinsender m *(radio/TV)* low-power transmitter, low-power station, *(radio)* daytime station, limited-time station, daytimer
Kleinstativ n *(phot/film/TV)* baby legs *pl*
   A low camera tripod.
Kleinstbildkamera f *(phot)* candid camera, miniature camera
   A small camera taking negatives of small format. The 35mm film camera, popularised in the 1920s after the introduction of the Leica camera in 1925, influenced the development of small roll film cameras in the 1930s.
Kleinste-Quadrate-Schätzung f
→ Methode der kleinsten Quadrate
Kleinstichprobe f
→ kleine Stichprobe
Kleintafel f
→ Kleinfläche
Kleister m paste, size, sizing, (sehr dünner Kleister) paste wash
→ Leim
kleistern *v/t* → kleben
Kleistern n
→ Kleben (Klebung)
Klemmbacke f **(Preßlade** f**)** book clamp
Kliegscheinwerfer m
→ Aufheller, Bogenlampe

Klirrfaktor m *(radio)* distortion factor, coefficient of harmonic distortion, nonlinear distortion coefficient
Klischee n **(Druckstock** m) *(print)* printing block, block, cut, printing cut, plate, printing plate, engraving
  An original printing plate produced by engraving and intended for use on a printing press.
  → Autotypie (Rasterklischee), Strichklischee, Galvano, Stereoklischee, Negativklischee
Klischeeabzug m **(Klischeeandruck** m) *(print)* engraver's proof, blockmaker's proof, block pull
  A carefully executed impression of a line, (→) Strichätzung, or halftone etching, (→) Autotypie, on quality paper.
Klischeeanstalt f **(Klischeehersteller** m) *(print)* blockmaking establishment, blockmaker, engraver, photoengraver, plate maker
Klischeeanzeige f *(print)* block advertisement, block ad
Klischeeätzung f *(print)* blockmaking, block making, engraving, block engraving
  A method of reproducing a design for printing by etching metal plates.
Klischeeaufbewahrung f *(print)* block storage, storage of blocks
Klischeefacette f
  → Facette
Klischeefuß m *(print)* block base, base, block mount, block, mount, patent block, patent base
  The support for a printing plate.
Klischeegraviermaschine f **(Graviermaschine** f) *(print)* platemaker, engraving machine, (elektronische Graviermaschine) scan-a-graver, photoelectric engraver, scanner
Klischeehersteller m **(Klischeur** m) *(print)* blockmaker, block maker, engraver, process engraver, platemaker, photoengraver
Klischeeherstellung f **(Klischierung** f) *(print)* blockmaking, platemaking, engraving
Klischeekosten pl **(Klischierkosten** pl) *(print)* cost of blockmaking, cost of platemaking, cost of process engraving, engraving costs pl
Klischeelayout n **(Klischee-Entwurf** m) *(print)* engraver's spread
Klischeesatz m
  → Farbsatz (Farbklischeesatz)
Klischeevorlage f *(print)* copy

Any type of material (words, pictures, designs) used in the production of printing.
Klischeur m
  → Klischeehersteller
klischieren v/t *(print)* to make a block, to make a plate, to engrave
Klischiermaschine f
  → Klischeemaschine
Klischierung f
  → Klischeeherstellung
Klischierverfahren n *(print)* blockmaking technique, engraving process, engraving technique
Klischograph m *(print)* photoengraving machine
Klopfbürste f *(print)* dabber, dapper, type brush, molding brush, *brit* moulding brush
klopfen v/t *(print)* (Druckform) to plane, to plane down
Klopfholz n *(print)* planer
Klotzen n *colloq (advtsg)* flight saturation, (massierter Werbeeinsatz) heavy-up, heavying up
  Maximum concentration of spot advertising in a short time period.
Klotzpresse f *(print)* blocking press, block press
Klumpen m **(Cluster** n, **geschlossene Erfassungsgruppe** f) *(stat)* cluster
  A group of contiguous elements of a statistical population, such as a group of people living in a single house, a consecutive run of observations in an ordered series, or a set of adjacent plots in one part of a field.
Klumpenanalyse f
  → Clusteranalyse
Klumpenauswahl f **(Klumpenauswahlverfahren** n, **Klumpenstichprobenbildung** f) *(stat)* cluster sampling
  A sampling technique, (→) Auswahlverfahren, in which the sampling unit, (→) Auswahleinheit, contains more than one population unit, i.e. the sampling unit is a cluster of elements. Cluster sampling is used when the basic sampling unit in the population is only to be found in groups or clusters (e.g. human beings in households).
Klumpeneffekt m **(Klumpungseffekt** m) *(stat)* cluster effect
Klumpenstichprobe f **(Klumpenauswahl** f) *(stat)* cluster sample, *auch* clustered sample
  → Klumpenauswahl

Klumpenverfahren *n*
→ Clusteranalyse, Klumpenauswahlverfahren
Klumpung *f*
→ Klumpeneffekt
Klumpungsanalyse *f*
→ Clusteranalyse
Klumpungseffekt *m*
→ Klumpeneffekt
Knacken *n* (**Knackgeräusch** *n,* **Knacklaut** *m*) *(film/tape)* crackle, crackling noise, bloop
 A noise caused by a splice across the sound track of a film or a tape.
Knick *m*
→ Falz
knicken *v/t* (Papier) to fold, to crease, to bend
Kniehebelpresse *f (print)* fly press
Knittelvers *m* (**holpriger Vers** *m*) doggerel
Knopflochmikrofon *n* lapel microphone, clip-on microphone, button microphone
Koaxialkabel *n (electr.)* coaxial cable, coaxial line, *colloq* coax
 A special type of cable used to transmit telephone, telegraph, and television impulses.
Kodachrom *m* (**Kodachrom-Umkehrfarbfilm** *m*) *(phot)* Kodachrome
Kodacolor *m* (**Kodacolor-Farbnegativfilm** *m*) *(phot)* Kodacolor
Kode *m* (**Code** *m*) code
Köder *m* (**Köderangebot** *n,* **Warenköder** *m*) *(econ)* bait
→ Lockangebot
Köderwerbung *f*
→ Lockangebotswerbung
Kodebuch *n* (**Code-Buch** *n*) *(survey res)* codebook, code book
 A list of each of the codes used to record the answers to questions in quantitative form on a punch card or other machine-readable storage. Usually this is done by giving each item a location designated by column and deck numbers of a punch card (or "card image").
Kodeplan *m* (**Codeplan** *m,* **Kodierplan** *m,* **Verschlüsselungsplan** *m*) *(survey res)* code plan, coding sheet
 The form on which the codes for the responses to a survey schedule are written in preparation for punching.
→ Kodebuch
kodieren (codieren, verkoden) *v/t*
→ verschlüsseln

Kodierung *f* (**Codierung** *f,* **Verschlüsselung** *f,* **Verkodung** *f*) *(survey res)* coding
 The processing of survey answers into numerical form for entry into a computer, so that statistical analyses can be performed. Coding of alternative responses to closed questions, (→) geschlossene Frage, can be performed in advance, so that no additional coding is required (precoding). If the questionnaire is mostly precoded, coding refers only to the subsequent coding of open questions, (→) Feldverschlüsselung.
Kodierung *f* **und Klassifizierung** *f* (**Verkodung** *f* **und Verschlüsselung** *f*) *(survey res)* coding and classifying, coding and classification
Koeffizient *m (math/stat)* coefficient
 A scalar constituent of a term used in a multinominal expression, a dimensionless statistic, a summarizing measure that provides in one mathematical value information about the relationship between two or more variables.
Koffergerät *n (radio/TV)* portable set, portable receiver, portable receiving set
Kofferradio *n* portable radio, portable radio receiver, portable radio set
Kognition *f* (**Erkennen** *n*) *(psy)* cognition
 The mental process by which an individual comes to perceive, know, and interpret his environment, relating it to previous knowledge or experience, remembering, wondering, imagining, generalizing, judging, and understanding what is perceived.
kognitiv *adj (psy)* cognitive
kognitive Dissonanz *f (psy)* cognitive dissonance (Leon Festinger)
→ kognitive Dissonanzhypothese
kognitive Dissonanzhypothese *f* (**Theorie** *f* **der kognitiven Dissonanz**) *(psy)* cognitive dissonance hypothesis (Leon Festinger)
 The theory that an individual strives for internal harmony and consistency, (→) kognitive Konsistenz, within himself, so that his attitudes, values, beliefs, and opinions are consonant with each other and with his behavior, because the psychological discomfort resulting from inconsistencies will typically motivate him to seek balance and to reduce dissonance through changes in behavior or cognition, (→) Kognition.
kognitive Funktion *f (psy)* cognitive function

kognitive Inkonsistenz f *(psy)*
cognitive inconsistency
kognitive Konsistenz f *(psy)* cognitive
consistency, cognitive consonance
kognitive Kontrolle f *(psy)* cognitive
control
kognitive Landkarte f **(kognitive
Karte** f**)** *(psy)* cognitive map (Edward
C. Tolman)
  A mental image of an external object
kognitive Selektivität f *(psy)* cognitive
selectivity
  The tendency of an individual to include
  among his cognitions those items of
  knowledge that are in agreement with
  his convictions, beliefs, attitudes,
  opinions, values, needs, and behavior,
  and to exclude those that are not.
kognitive Struktur f *(psy)* cognitive
structure
kognitiver Prozeß m *(psy)* cognitive
process
→ Kognition
kognitives Einstellungsmodell n
(kognitives Attitüdenmodell n**)** *(psy)*
cognitive attitude model, cognitive
model of attitude
  A theoretical approach in attitude
  research, (→) Einstellungsforschung, that
  emphasizes the role of cognition, (→)
  Kognition, in attitudes, (→) Einstellung,
  and behavior, (→) Verhalten, and that
  regards the cognitive processes as
  important foci of attitude analysis.
kognitives Entscheidungsmuster n
(psy) cognitive pattern of decision-
making, cognitive decision-making
pattern
kognitives Gleichgewicht n *(psy)*
cognitive balance
kognitives Programm n *(psy)*
cognitive program, *brit* cognitive
programme
kognitives Ungleichgewicht n (psy)
cognitive imbalance
Kohlebogen m **(Kohlelichtbogen** m**)**
(electr.) carbon arc
Kohledruck m **(Karbondruck** m,
Kohlelichtdruck m**)** *(phot)* carbon
print
  A photograph made on carbon tissue.
Kohlemikrofon n **(Kohlemikrophon**
n**)** carbon microphone
Kohlestift m charcoal pencil, charcoal
  A pencil of fine charcoal used for
  drawing.
Kohlezeichnung f charcoal drawing,
charcoal, fusain
  An illustration done in charcoal.

Kohorte f *(stat)* cohort
  Any aggregate of individual elements
  each of which experienced a specified,
  common significant event in its life
  history during the same chronological
  interval, e.g. the persons who were born
  in the same year.
Kohortenanalyse f *(stat)* cohort
analysis
  The analysis of the characteristics,
  differences, and/or similarities of cohorts,
  (→) Kohorte, over a long period of time.
Koinzidenz f coincidence
Koinzidenzbefragung f **(Koinzidenzinterview** n**)** *(media res)* coincidental
survey, coincidental interview,
coincidental, *auch* concurrent survey,
concurrent interview, (telefonisch)
coincidental telephone survey,
coincidental telephone interview,
coincidental telephone test, *auch*
concurrent telephone survey,
concurrent telephone interview,
concurrent telephone test, (zur
Messung von Einschaltquoten)
coincidental audience rating,
coincidental audience measurement,
auch concurrent audience rating,
concurrent audience measurement
  In general, a survey research technique
  based on interviews conducted while an
  event takes place. In media research, a
  procedure which measures the time or
  duration of reading, viewing, or listening
  by ascertaining what activity was going
  on during the time of the check, which is
  usually done by telephone.
Koinzidenzmethode f **(Koinzi-
denzverfahren** n, **Koinzidenztechnik**
f**)** *(media res)* coincidental method,
coincidental technique, coincidental
interview method, coincidental
interview technique, coincidental
testing, *auch* concurrent method,
concurrent technique, duplex method,
duplex technique
→ Koinzidenzbefragung
Kollation f **(Kollationieren** n,
Kollationierung f**)** *(print)* collation,
collating
  Assembling all pages or elements of a
  publication after they have been printed.
kollationieren v/t *(print)* to collate
  To assemble the pages or signatures of a
  book or the like in the proper final order.
Kollegenrabatt m **(Verlegerrabatt** m**)**
publisher's discount

Kollektion f (**Produktrange** f) (econ) product range, range
The full list of products made by one firm.
Kollektionstest m (market res) product range test, range test
A technique used to predict product acceptability. Respondents are selected from consumers who intend to buy such a product. Preference ratings are taken at three stages: 1. On first appearance of a new product. 2. After closer examination. 3. After prices have been revealed. Further ratings may assess features of the product.
Kollektivanzeige f (**Kollektivseite** f)
→ Anzeigenkollektiv
kollektive Kaufentscheidung f (**Gruppenentscheidung** f)
→ Familieneinkaufsentscheidung
Kollektivseite f
→ Anzeigenkollektiv
Kollektivwarenhaus n
→ Gemeinschaftswarenhaus
Kollektivwerbung f
→ Gemeinschaftswerbung, kooperative Werbung, Sammelwerbung, Verbundwerbung
Kollodium n (phot) collodion
A mixture of pyroxylin in a solution of alcohol and ether.
Kollodialemulsion f (phot) collodion emulsion
Negative collodion emulsified with silver bromide.
Kollodiumlauge f (phot) collodion base
Plain or weakly iodized negative collodion.
Kolmogorov-Smirnov-Test m (stat) Kolmogorov-Smirnov test, Kolmogorov-Smirnov D test
A nonparametric test of significance for comparing frequency distributions.
Kolmogorov-Test m (stat) Kolmogorov test
→ Kolmogorov-Smirnov test
kolorieren v/t (phot) to color, brit to colour
Kolorierung f (phot) coloration, brit colouration, color toning, brit colour toning
A method for coloring a black and white photography by the use of bleaches and dyes.
Kolorimetrie f
→ Farbmetrik
Kolorit n 1. (Farbgebung) color, brit colour, coloration, brit colouration, coloring, brit colouring, color tone, brit colour tone, shade
2. → Klangfarbe
Kolumne f
1. → Spalte
2. → Kommentar, Leitartikel
Kolumnenbreite f
→ Spaltenbreite
Kolumnenhöhe f (**Kolumnentiefe** f)
→ Spaltenhöhe (Spaltentiefe)
Kolumnenlinie f
→ Spaltenlinie
Kolumnenmaß n
→ Spaltenmaß
Kolumnenschnur f (print) page cord, string
Kolumnentitel m
→ Spaltenüberschrift
Kolumnenunterschlag m
→ Unterschlag
Kolumnist m (**Kolumnenschreiber** m)
→ Leitartikler
Koma n (phot) coma
Kombi n (**Kombinationssätzung** f)
→ Auto-Strich-Kombination
Kombination f (**Kombinationsbelegung** f, **Medienkombination** f) (advtsg) combination buy, media combination, combined media scheduling, combined scheduling, (obligatorisch) forced combination
A special, combination rate purchase of advertising time, or space (→) Kombinationspreis, offered or required ("forced") by two or more broadcasting stations or publishers, usually, but not necessarily, under the same ownership.
Kombinationssätzung f
→ Auto-Strich-Kombination
Kombinationsbad n
→ Bleichfixierbad (Blix)
Kombinationsbelegung f
→ Kombination
Kombinationsdruck m (**Überdruck** m) double print, combination print
Kombinationsdrucken n (**Überdrucken** n) double printing, combination printing
Kombinationsmethode f (**Mischmethode** f) (der Werbebudgetierung) composite method (of advertising budget determination)
→ eklektische Methode
Kombinationspackung f (**Sammelpackung** f, **Verbundpackung** f) (packaging) combined pack,

combipack, composite package, composite container, combination sale An item of merchandise together with a premium, (→) Zugabe, offered at a combination price, (→) Kombinationspreis. Sometimes the premium part of the offer is self-liquidating.

Kombinationspreis m **(Kombinationstarif** m) *(advtsg)* (bei Kombinationsbelegung) combination rate, combined rate A special rate for advertising in two or more publications under the same ownership or with a special cooperation agreement.

Kombinationsprodukt n **(Warenkombination** f, **kombiniertes Produktangebot** n) *(marketing)* combination feature, combination sale
→ Kombinationspackung

Kombinationsrabatt m **(Kombinationspreisnachlaß** m) *(advtsg)* combination discount, media combination discount, combined scheduling discount, group discount, continuity-impact discount rate (CID), combination buy discount The discount, (→) Rabatt, granted in case of a combination buy, (→) Kombinationsbelegung.

Kombinationszeichen n *(labeling)* arbitrary mark, coined word An invented and originated arbitrary combination of letters or syllables to form a new word, as opposed to a dictionary word, for a trademark, (→) Warenzeichen, or brand name, (→) Markenname.

Kombinatorik f *(math/stat)* theory of combinations, combinatorics pl *(construed as sg)*

kombiniert adj combined

kombinierte Kopie f **(Filmkopie** f **mit Bild und Ton)** *(film/TV)* composite print, composite, brit combined print A "married" film print containing both a picture and a sound track.

kombinierte Reichweite f
→ Bruttoreichweite

kombinierte Strich- und Tuschezeichnung f
→ lavierte Strichzeichnung

kombinierte Umfrage f
→ Mehrthemenbefragung

kombinierte Werbung f
→ Verbundwerbung

kombiniertes Muster n
→ kombinierte Kopie

Kometeneffekt m **(Nachzieheffekt** m, **Blooming** n) *(TV)* blooming A type of television picture halation caused by excessive light saturation.

Kommando n **(Kommandozeichen** n) *(radio/film/TV)* (Regie) cue Any visual or audible signal used to direct the start or end of a program, music, action, etc.

Kommentar m commentary, comment, news commentary, news analysis

Kommentator m commentator, news analyst

kommentieren v/t to comment on

kommerzieller Rundfunk m
→ privater Rundfunk

kommerzielles Fernsehen n
→ privates Fernsehen

Kommission f *(econ)* commission
→ Provision

Kommissionär m **(Kommittent** m) *(econ)* commission agent, commission merchant, commission house An agent who usually exercises physical control over and negotiates the sale of the goods he handles. The commission house usually enjoys broader powers as to prices, methods, and terms of sale than does the broker although it must obey instructions issued by the principal. It generally arranges delivery, extends necessary credit, collects, deducts its fees, and remits the balance to the principal.

Kommissionshandel m *(econ)* commission business, commission agency business
→ Kommissionär

Kommissionsvertreter m **(Kommissionsagent** m)
→ Kommissionär, Provisionsvertreter

kommunale Werbung f etwa community advertising, advertising activities of communities

Kommunalfernsehen n community television, community TV, community station television, community station broadcasting
→ Lokalfernsehen

Kommunalität f *(stat)* communality In factor analysis, (→) Faktorenanalyse, that proportion of the total variance, (→) Varianz, which is attributable to the factor(s) it has in common with other variates, the remainder being due to specific factors or error terms.

Kommunalmarketing n **(Marketing** n **für die Kommune)** community marketing, local community marketing

Kommunikation f communication, communications pl *(construed as sg)*
The process, the means, and the relevant results of the process of conveying, transferring or transmitting information from one person, group, place, or unit to another.

Kommunikationsakt m **(Kommunikationshandlung** f) communication act
A process of social interaction in which messages are exchanged between a source and a recipient.

Kommunikationsberufe m/pl **(Kommunikationsgewerbe** n) communications arts pl
The many professions which are actively involved in the exchange of messages, ideas, attitudes or feelings, e.g. journalism, advertising, marketing, film, television, theater, music, literature, public forum, and graphic and fine arts.

Kommunikationsbeziehung f communicative relationship

Kommunikationsbudget n **(Kommunikationsetat** m) communication budget, budget for communication activities

Kommunikationsdichte f communication density, density of communication(s)

Kommunikationseffekt m **(Kommunikationswirkung** f) communications effect, communication effect

Kommunikationserfolg m **(Kommunikationswirksamkeit** f) communications effectiveness, communication effectiveness

Kommunikationsevaluation f **(Kommunikationsevaluierung** f) evaluation of communication(s), communication(s) evaluation

Kommunikationsfähigkeit f ability to communicate

Kommunikationsfilter m communication filter

Kommunikationsfluß m flow of communication, flow of communication(s)
→ Ein-Stufen-Fluß, Zwei-Stufen-Fluß (der Kommunikation)

Kommunikationsform f form of communication, type of communication

Kommunikationsforschung f communications research, communication research
The systematic scientific investigation of the communication process, including the content of the message, the means of transmission, feedback, the message received, the recipients, and the effect as well as the effectiveness of the message.

Kommunikationsfunktion f **(kommunikative Funktion** f) (der Werbung) communicative function (of advertising), communication function (of advertising)

Kommunikationshelfer m **(Kommunikationsmittler** m) agent of communication, intermediary of communication

Kommunikationsinhalt m content of communication(s), communication(s) content

Kommunikationsinstrument n instrument of communication(s), means of communication(s)

Kommunikationskanal m channel of communication, communication channel
The relatively regularized relationship of communication established between two or more persons, groups, units, or places.

Kommunikationskette f chain of communication, chain of communications

Kommunikationskonzept n concept of communication(s), communication(s) concept

Kommunikationskosten pl cost of communication(s), communication(s) cost(s) *(pl)*

Kommunikationslücke f communications gap, communication gap

Kommunikationsmanager m communication manager

Kommunikations-Marketing n message marketing, communication(s) marketing, communicative marketing

Kommunikationsmedium n **(Kommunikationsmittel** n) communication medium, medium of communication(s)

Kommunikationsmethode f method of communication(s), communication method

Kommunikationsmittel n
→ Kommunikationsmedium

Kommunikationsmittler m
→ Kommunikationshelfer

Kommunikations-Mix n **(Kommunikationspolitik** f**)** communications mix, communication mix
One of the four components of a company's marketing mix (→) Marketing-Mix. It consists of the combination of different media in a specific marketing, advertising, or promotional campaign to reach a predetermined target audience.

Kommunikationsmodell n communication model
The representation, in model form, of the steps of communication.

Kommunikationsmodell n **der Werbung** communication model of advertising

Kommunikationsmuster n **(Muster** n **des Kommunikationsablaufs)** communication pattern, communicative pattern, pattern of communication(s)

Kommunikationsnetz n communication network, communication net, communication grid

Kommunikations-Persuasions-Matrix f *(psy)* communication-persuasion matrix (William J. McGuire)

Kommunikationsplanung f communications planning, communication planning

Kommunikationspolitik f
→ Kommunikations-Mix

Kommunikations-Portfolio n communications portfolio, communication portfolio

Kommunikationsprozeß m communications process, communication process, communicative process

Kommunikationsqualität f quality of communication

Kommunikationsquelle f source of communication, communication source

Kommunikationsrückkoppelung f feedback of communication, communication feedback

Kommunikationssatellit m **(Nachrichtensatellit** m**)** *(radio/TV)* communications satellite, *colloq* bird
An electronic retransmission vehicle located in space in a fixed geosynchronous orbit, 22,300 miles above the earth. Used by the cable industry for the transmission of its network programming.

Kommunikationssituation f communication situation, communicative situation

Kommunikations-Spektrum n spectrum of communications, communications spectrum, communicative spectrum

Kommunikationsstörung f **(Kommunikationsverzerrung** f**)** disturbance of communication, communication disturbance, communication distortion
The tendency for information to become changed in content or partially lost in the communication process.

Kommunikationsstrategie f strategy of communication(s), communication(s) strategy, communicative strategy

Kommunikationsstrom m
→ Kommunikationsfluß

Kommunikationsstruktur f communication structure, communications structure

Kommunikationssubjekt n
→ Kommunikator

Kommunikationssystem n communication system, communications system, system of communication(s)
The interrelated organization of communication channels, (→) Kommunikationskanal.

Kommunikationstaktik f tactics pl *(construed as sg)* of communication(s), communication tactics pl *(construed as sg)*

Kommunikationstechnik f
→ Kommunikationsmethode

Kommunikationstechnologie f communications technology, communication technology, communications

Kommunikationstheorie f communications theory, communication theory, *auch* information theory, mathematical theory of communication
A theoretical orientation to symbolization stressing the development of principles or models that are so generally applicable that they can be used as a basis for understanding all forms of communication, including written or spoken words, pictures, music, codes, etc.

Kommunikationsumfeld n
communications environment,
communicative environment
Kommunikationsverhalten n
communicative behavior, brit
behaviour, communication behavior
Kommunikationsweg m
→ Kommunikationskanal
Kommunikationswirksamkeit f
→ Kommunikationserfolg
Kommunikationswirkung f
→ Kommunikationseffekt
Kommunikationswissenschaft f
communication science, communications science, communications sg
 The science concerned with the research into the origination, sending, receiving, and interpreting of messages.
Kommunikationsziel n objective of communication, communications objective
kommunikative Dissonanz f
communicative dissonance
kommunikative Integration f
communicative integration
 The degree to which a common communication network, (→) Kommunikationsnetz, is operative throughout a communication system.
kommunikative Phase f
communicative phase
kommunikatives Handeln n
communicative action
Kommunikator m communicator
 The sender of a message in a communication process.
Kommunikatoranalyse f
communicator analysis
Kommunikatoreffekt m
communicator effect
 Any effect the characteristics or behavior of a communicator have on the communication process.
Kommunikatorglaubwürdigkeit f
communicator credibility,
communicator believability
→ Glaubwürdigkeit
Kommuniqué n communiqué, bulletin
kommunizieren v/i to communicate
Komödie f **(Lustspiel** n) *(radio/TV)*
comedy, comedy play
Kompakt-Kamera f *(phot)* compact camera
Kompaktwerbung f
→ Intensivwerbung
Komparativreklame f **(Komparativwerbung** f)
→ vergleichende Werbung

Komparse m **(Statist** m) *(film/TV)*
extra, supernumerary, super, walk-on, bit player
 An actor in a motion picture, television show or commercial who has no spoken lines, and whose performance is confined to making an appearance which will enhance the realism of the scene.
Komparsengage f *(film/TV)* walk-on fee, extra's fee
Komparserie f *(film/TV)* extras pl, crowd, supers pl
kompatibel adj compatible
Kompatibilität f compatibility
 The adaptability of a device to another system, as a color television signal to black and white reception or a quadraphonic record to playing on a stereophonic record player.
Kompendium n *(phot)* compendium, matte box, effects box
Kompensation f *(psy/econ)*
compensation
 1. A psychological defense mechanism used unconsciously to overcome feelings of inadequacy, inferiority, or frustrated motive. Important to the seller because some people compensate by buying flashy or expensive things. 2. Any remuneration in money or benefits for work assigned.
Kompensationsfarbe f compensatory color, brit compensatory colour
Kompensationsgeschäft n *(econ)*
barter business transaction, barter business, barter trade, barter, compensation deal
 The direct exchange of one good or service for another good or service in an agreed-upon ratio. Particularly in international trade, a transaction involving payment in goods and cash.
→ Gegengeschäft
Kompensationsmikrofon n
(Kompensationsmikrophon n)
balancing microphone, differential microphone
Komplementärfarbe f complementary color, brit complementary colour
 One of any pair of chromatic color stimuli which give rise to an achromatic color, when mixed additively. They have the property of producing the sensation of white when superposed optically in proper proportion in the form of colored lights and consist of the hues or colors which, combined with others, complete the spectrum.
Komplementärgüter n/pl
(komplementäre Güter n/pl) *(econ)*
complementary goods pl

Any products or services that are related in use so that an increase in the quantity demanded by the market of one results in or accompanies an increase in the quantity demanded of the other, assuming prices remain the same. The cross-elasticity value, (→) Kreuzpreiselastizität, if algebraically negative, is usually considered evidence that two goods or services are complementary, provided no change in the real income of the buyer has occurred.

Komplementarität f *(econ)* complementarity
→ Komplementärgüter

Komplementärwerbung f **(flankierende Werbung** f**)** complementary advertising, collateral advertising
→ Verbundwerbung

Komponentenanalyse f **(Komponentenzerlegung** f**)** *(stat)* component analysis
A technique of multivariate data analysis (MDA), (→) Mehrvariablenanalyse, which represents k-dimensional variations as due to a number of orthogonal components in such a way that a few components account for as much of the variation as possible.

Komponentengeschäft n
→ Produktgeschäft

Komponentenmethode f
→ Komponentenanalyse

Kompositphoto n composite photograph, composite photo, composite
A photographic print produced by stripping two or more negatives together.

Kompositphotographie f composite photography

kompreß (kompreß gesetzt) adj *(print)* solid, set solid, unleaded, close, compact

kompresser Satz m *(print)* solid matter, unleaded matter, close matter
Lines of type set without leading.

Konation f *(psy)* conation
A social effort or striving under the stimulus of desire.

konative Einstellungskomponente f *(psy)* conative component of attitude
→ Drei-Komponenten-Hypothese

Kondensator m *(electr.)* capacitor, condenser

Kondensatorantenne f *(electr.)* condenser antenna, brit condenser aerial

Kondensatormikrofon n **(Kondensatormikrophon** n**)** condenser microphone, electrostatic microphone

Kondensor m *(phot)* condenser, condenser lens, condensing lens

Kondition f *(meist pl* **Konditionen)** *(econ)* terms pl

Konditionen-Mix n **(Konditionenpolitik** f**)**
→ Kontrahierungsmix (Kontrahierungspolitik)

Konditionierung f **(Konditionieren** n**)** *(psy)* conditioning
The process of learning by association, either as classical conditioning (klassische Konditionierung) or as operant conditioning (operante Konditionierung). In the first, a stimulus that normally evokes a particular response is repeatedly paired with another stimulus that does not normally evoke the response; in the latter, the subject engages in various random acts, one of which is reinforced.

Konferenz f **(Tagung** f**)** conference

Konferenzschaltung f **(Konferenzleitung** f**)** conference circuit, multiplex, hook-up

Konferenzsendung f multiplex transmission, hookup broadcast

konfessionelle Presse f
→ Kirchenpresse

Konfidenzintervall n
→ Mutungsbereich, Vertrauensbereich

Konflikt m conflict

Konfliktmanagement n conflict management
The social control of conflict so as to maximize its beneficial effects.

Konfliktvermeidung f avoidance of conflict, conflict avoidance

Konformität f
→ Marktkonformität

Konfusionskontrolle f *(media res)* confusion control, confusion control technique, confusion control procedure, deflation technique
Any of a variety of techniques used to check false claiming of respondents, because they confound e.g. the issue of a publication under investigation with another issue, or one publication with a similar publication. The most common technique is to present advance copies in the interview.

konglomerative Diversifikation f **(Diversifizierung** f**)** *(marketing)* conglomerative diversification

Kongreß *m* congress, convention
Kongreßagentur *f* congress agency
Kongruenz *f* (**Kongruität** *f*) *(psy)* congruity, congruence
Kongruenzprinzip *n* (**Kongruitätsprinzip** *n*) *(psy)* principle of congruity, (Charles E. Osgood/Percy H. Tannenbaum)
  A theory of attitude change, (→) Einstellungsänderung, which suggests that when a message is received which relates two or more objects of judgment, via an assertion in a particular communication situation, evaluative behavior is always in the direction of increased congruity with the existing frame of reference.

konjunkte Analyse *f* (**Verbundmessung** *f,* **Conjoint Measurement** *n*) *(stat)* conjoint analysis, conjoint measurement, multidimensional measurement
  A set of analysis techniques, similar to multidimensional scaling (MDS), (→) multidemensionale Skalierung, for relating preference rankings, which are usually ordinal, to a set of attribute levels which are presented to respondents. Used in marketing and consumer research to represent the structure of consumer preferences and to predict consumers' behavior toward new stimuli.

Konkavkonvex-Linse *f* (**hohlerhabene Linse** *f*) *(phot)* concavo-convex lens
  A lens, one surface of which is a concave spherical surface and the other a convex spherical surface.

Konkordanzkoeffizient *m* *(stat)* coefficient of concordance (W), Kendall's coefficient of concordance, Kendall coefficient of concordance W
  A measure of agreement between several different rankings of a number of objects. The formula reads:

$$W = \frac{12 \sum T^2}{m^2 N(N^2 - 1)} - \frac{3(N + 1)}{N - 1},$$

  where m is the number of judges, N the number of objects being ranked, and the Ts are the sums of the ranks for each of the objects.

Konkurrent *m* (**Mitbewerber** *m*) *(econ)* competitor
  A business rival who offers similar or identical products or services.

Konkurrenz *f (econ)* **1.** (Wettbewerb) competition
  The presence and activities of rival products, brands, or services within one market.
2. (die Konkurrenten) the competition, the competitors *pl*, rival companies *pl*, rival firms *pl*, (die Konkurrenzmarke) brand X
  The rival firms of a company in a market, taken as a whole.
Konkurrenzanalyse *f* (**Konkurrenzuntersuchung** *f*) *(market res)* analysis of the competition, competition analysis
Konkurrenzausschluß *m* *(advtsg)* exclusive agency agreement, exclusivity clause
  An agreement between an advertiser and an advertising agency under which the agency commits itself not to work for the advertiser's competitors.
Konkurrenzbeobachtung *f (market res)* observation of the competition, competition observation
Konkurrenzbetrieb *m*
  → Konkurrenzunternehmen
Konkurrenzdynamik *f (econ)* dynamics *pl (construed as sg)* of competition
Konkurrenzforschung *f (market res)* competition research
Konkurrenzimage *n* image of competitor(s)
Konkurrenzintensität *f (econ)* intensity of competition
Konkurrenzklausel *f*
  → Konkurrenzausschluß
Konkurrenzmarke *f* (**Konkurrenzprodukt** *n*) competitor's brand, brand X
Konkurrenzmethode *f* (der Werbebudgetierung) competitor's advertising method, competitive-parity method, competition-matching approach (to advertising appropriations), competitors' expenditure method
  A method of determining an advertising budget to match past, present or anticipated expenditures of competitors.
Konkurrenzprogramm *n (radio/TV)* **1.** (Programm eines konkurrierenden Senders) program opposite, competing program **2.** (bewußt gestaltetes Gegenprogramm) counter program
  → Gegenprogramm
Konkurrenzpublikation *f* competitive publication, competing publication, rival publication

Konkurrenzreaktion f *(econ)* competitor's reaction, competitors' reaction, competitor's response, competitors' response
Konkurrenzsender m **(Konkurrenzkanal** m, **Konkurrenzprogramm** n) *(radio/TV)* competing station, competing channel, competing program, station opposite, channel opposite, program opposite
Konkurrenzspanne f *(econ)* competitors' margin, competitor's margin
Konkurrenzuntersuchung f
→ Konkurrenzanalyse
Konkurrenzverhalten n
→ Wettbewerbsverhalten
Konkurrenzvorteil m *(econ)* competitive edge, competitive advantage
 Any benefit or value provided by a product, a service, or company, often unique to the organization concerned, that gives it superiority in the marketplace.
Konkurrenzwerbung f **(Wettbewerbswerbung** f) (Rudolf Seyffert) competitive advertising
 An aggressive type of advertising aimed more or less directly at competing products, services, brands, or organizations.
Konkurrenzzeitschrift f competitive magazine, competing magazine, rival magazine
Konkurrenzzeitung f competitive (news)paper, competing (news)paper, rival paper
Konnotation f connotation
 Those characteristics by virtue of which a term is applied to a thing.
Konsequenzenmatrix f
→ Ergebnismatrix
Konserve f **(Sendekonserve** f) *(radio/TV)* canned program, (Musik) canned music, (Hörspiel) canned drama
 A recorded or transcribed program.
Konsignatant m **(Konsignant** m) *(econ)* consignor, consigner
 The holder of the title to goods that are shipped under consignment terms, (→) Konsignationssystem.
Konsignatar m *(econ)* consignee
 The holder of goods that are shipped under consignment terms, (→) Konsignationssystem.
Konsignation f **(Konsignationsgeschäft** n, **Konsignationshandel** m) *(econ)* consignment, consignation, consignment deal, consignment dealing, consignment buying
 A business transaction under which a stock of merchandise is advanced to a dealer and located at his place of business, while the title remains with the vendor until the merchandise has been sold.
Konsignationslager n *(econ)* consignment store, consignment warehouse, consignment
Konsignationssystem n *(econ)* consignment system, consignment terms *pl*
→ Konsignation
konsistente Schätzfunktion f **(asymptotisch treffende Schätzfunktion** f) *(stat)* consistent estimator
 An estimator which converges in probability, as the sample size increases, to the parameter of which it is an estimator.
konsistenter Test m **(asymptotische treffender Test** m) *(stat)* consistent test
 A test of a hypothesis, (→) Hypothesentest, is consistent with respect to a particular alternative hypothesis, (→) Alternativhypothese, if the power, (→) Trennschärfe, of the test tends to unity as the sample size tends to infinity.
Konsistenz f *(stat)* consistency, *auch* consistence
 The internal agreement of data or procedures among themselves.
→ Erwartungstreue
Konsistenzforschung f *(survey res)* consistency research
Konsistenzkoeffizient m **(Kendallscher Konsistenzkoeffizient** m) *(stat)* coefficient of consistence
Konsistenzkontrolle f **(Konsistenzprüfung** f, **Datenbereinigung** f) *(survey res)* consistency check, consistency control, (Durchführung) consistency checking, consistency control
 That part of the editing process in the preparation of survey data for analysis that consists in checking whether the answers given to different questions are consistent with one another.
Konsonanz f *(psy)* consonance
vgl. Dissonanz
Konsonanztheorie f *(psy)* theory of consonance, consonance theory
vgl. Dissonanztheorie
Konsortium n *(econ)* syndicate, consortium

Konstant-Summen-Spiel

A group of companies, national or international, working together as a joint venture, sharing resources and having interlocking financial agreements.

Konstant-Summen-Spiel n *(game theory)* constant-sum game

konstanter Einflußfaktor m *(panel res)* constant qualifier

konstanter Fehler m *(stat)* constant error, persistent error, bias
→ systematischer Fehler; vgl. Zufallsfehler

Konstanz f constancy, constance

Konstrukt n *(soc res)* construct
→ hypothetisches Konstrukt (theoretisches Konstrukt)

Konstruktvalidierung f *(soc res)* construct validation
The validation, (→) Validierung, of a hypothetical construct, (→) hypothetisches Konstrukt.

Konstruktvalidität f **(Aussagegültigkeit** f **eines Konstrukts)** *(test theory)* construct validity
The degree to which posited underlying, but unmeasured variables, (→) hypothetisches Konstrukt, can logically explain variation in a measurement instrument.

Konsum m **(Verbrauch** m**, privater Verbrauch** m**)** *(econ)* consumption
The use of a product or a service by a consumer, (→) Konsument, in a private household eventually ending in the destruction of the utility, (→) Nutzen, the product or service embodies.

Konsumangebot n **(Angebot** n **an Konsumgütern)** *(econ)* supply of consumer goods, consumer goods supply

Konsumartikel m
→ Konsumgüter

Konsumdaten n/pl **(Konsuminformationen** f/pl**, Verbrauchsdaten** n/pl**)** *(market res)* consumption data pl

Konsument m **(Verbraucher** m**)** *(econ)* consumer
An individual, a household, or family who purchases and uses a product or a service for personal or household use, as distinguished from an industrial user (who buys industrial goods for remanufacture) or a distributor (who buys for resale).

Konsumentenbefragung f **(Verbraucherbefragung** f**)** *(market res)* consumer survey, consumer jury test, consumer panel test, consumer opinion test, consumer interview, (Wiederholungsbefragung) consumer tracking
A survey of consumer attitudes, (→) Konsumenteneinstellung, buying habits (→) Kaufgewohnheit, etc., conducted among the actual or potential customers of a consumer product, (→) Konsumgüter.

Konsumenteneinstellung f **(Verbrauchereinstellung** f**)** *(market res)* consumer attitude

Konsumentenforschung f **(Verbraucherforschung** f**)** consumer research, consumer analysis
That branch of marketing research that describes, analyzes, and applies attitudes, motives, the behavior, reactions, and preferences of purchasers and prospective purchasers of consumer goods, (→) Konsumgüter.

Konsumentengesellschaft f **(Konsumgesellschaft)** f**)** *(econ)* consumer society

Konsumentenhandel m *(econ)* consumer trade

Konsumenteninformation f **(Verbraucherinformation** f**)** *(econ)* consumer information

Konsumenteninteresse n
→ Verbraucherinteresse

Konsumentenjury f **(Verbraucherjury** f**)** *(market res)* consumer jury, consumer panel
A sample, (→) Stichprobe, of actual and/or prospective consumers who are asked, in a pretest, (→) Vorstudie, to judge a product, a service, or the effectiveness or creative quality of an advertisement.

Konsumentenkredit m **(Konsumtivkredit** m**, Konsumkredit** m**)** *(marketing)* consumer credit
A loan to consumers granted by a vendor as a marketing instrument to enable them to buy his products or services, either directly through a bank or another intermediary.

Konsumentenloyalität f
→ Geschäftstreue, Produkttreue, Markentreue

Konsumentenmarkt m **(K-Markt** m**)** *(econ)* consumer market, C market (Philip Kotler)
vgl. Produzenten-Markt (P-Markt), Wiederverkäufer-Markt (W-Markt), Ö-Markt (Markt der öffentlichen Betriebe)

Konsumentenmerkmale *n/pl* (**Verbrauchermerkmale** *n/pl*) *(market res)* consumer characteristics *pl*
→ Merkmale
Konsumentennachfrage *f* (**Verbrauchernachfrage** *f*) *(econ)* consumer demand
Konsumenten-Ombudsmann *m* consumer ombudsman
Konsumentenpanel *n*
→ Verbraucherpanel
Konsumentenpsychologie *f* consumer psychology
Konsumentenrabatt *m* (**Verbraucherrabatt** *m*) *(econ)* consumer discount, patronage discount
Konsumentenreaktion *f*
→ Kaufreaktion
Konsumentenrente *f* (**Käuferrente** *f*) *(econ)* consumer's surplus, consumer surplus, consumer's rent
In economic theory, the difference between the actual price of a product or service and its utility, (→) Nutzen, for its buyer, the consumer.
Konsumentenrisiko *n* (**Verbraucherrisiko** *n*) *(stat)* consumer's risk, consumer's risk point (CRP)
In quality control, (→) Qualitätskontrolle, the risk which a consumer takes that a defective lot will be accepted by a sampling plan. It is usually expressed as a probability of acceptance, and is equivalent to an error of the second kind, (→) Fehler 2. Art, in the theory of testing hypotheses, (→) Hypothesenprüfung, in the sense of corresponding to the acceptance of a hypothesis when an alternative is true.
vgl. Produzentenrisiko
Konsumentenschutz *m*
→ Verbraucherschutz
Konsumentenschutzgesetzgebung *f*
→ Verbraucherschutzgesetzgebung
Konsumentensouveränität *f* (**Verbrauchersouveränität** *f*, **Käufersouveränität** *f*) *(econ)* consumer sovereignty
The theory that all economic processes are ultimately focused toward satisfying the wants to the final consumer, including even those of investment goods manufacturers and that, therefore, the performance of any economy ought to be evaluated in terms of how well it satisfies the wants of its consumers.
Konsumentensozialisation *f* (**Verbrauchersozialisation** *f*) consumer socialization
The social process by which children acquire knowledge, attitudes, and skills pertinent to their effective functioning as consumers.
Konsumentenstadt *f* (**Verbraucherstadt** *f*) consumer city
Konsumentenstimmung *f* (**Verbraucherstimmung** *f*) *(market res)* consumer sentiment
A more or less enduring pattern of emotional dispositions held by the consumers or groups of consumers in an economy, influencing their consumption behavior, (→) Konsumverhalten.
Konsumentenstimmungsindex *m* (**Index** *m* **der Verbraucherstimmung**) *(market res)* index of consumer sentiment
Konsumententreue *f* (**Verbrauchertreue** *f*)
→ Geschäftstreue, Produkttreue, Markentreue
Konsumententyp *m* (**Verbrauchertyp** *m*, **Käufertyp** *m*) *(market res)* consumer type
Konsumententypologie *f* (**Verbrauchertypologie** *f*) *(market res)* consumer typology
→ Typologie
Konsumentenunzufriedenheit *f* (**Verbraucherunzufriedenheit** *f*) *(econ)* consumer dissatisfaction
vgl. Konsumentenzufriedenheit
Konsumentenverhalten *n* (**Verbraucherverhalten** *n*, **Käuferverhalten** *n*) *(econ)* consumer behavior, *brit* consumer behaviour
The behavioral manifestations of the search and information activities, buying habits and patterns of consumers in the acquisition and consumption of goods and services.
Konsumentenwerbung *f* (**Verbraucherwerbung** *f*)
→ Publikumswerbung
Konsumentenwettbewerb *m*
→ Verbraucherwettbewerb
Konsumentenzufriedenheit *f* (**Verbraucherzufriedenheit** *f*) *(econ)* consumer satisfaction
The fulfillment of consumer want, which is the essential objective of all marketing operations.
Konsumentenzuversicht *f* (**Verbraucherzuversicht** *f*) *(econ)* consumer confidence
Konsumentscheidung *f*
→ Kaufentscheidung

Konsumerismus 278

Konsumerismus *m (econ)*
consumerism, consumers' rights movement, consumers' movement
  The public movement and social trend that favors the protection of the consumer from improper marketing practices through examination of product performance, advertising and sales practices, etc. The English term has been integrated into German to differentiate it from (→) Verbraucherschutz.
Konsumforschung *f*
→ Verbrauchsforschung
Konsumfreiheit *f (econ)* consumer freedom, consumers' freedom
Konsumfunktion *f (econ)* consumption function
Konsumgenossenschaft *f* (**Konsumverein** *m*) *(retailing)* consumer cooperative, *brit* consumer co-operative, *colloq* coop, co-op, *auch* retail cooperative
  A retail business owned and operated by ultimate consumers to purchase and distribute goods and services to the membership. Cooperatives are a type of cooperative marketing institution. Through federation, retail units frequently acquire wholesaling and manufacturing institutions.
Konsumgesellschaft *f*
→ Konsumentengesellschaft
Konsumgewohnheit *f* (**Muster** *n* **des Konsumverhaltens**) *(econ)* consumption pattern, consumption habit
Konsumgüter *n/pl* (**Konsumartikel** *m/pl*, **Konsumtivgüter** *n/pl*) *(econ)* consumer goods *pl*, consumers' goods, consumer products *pl*, (dauerhafte) durable consumer goods *pl*, durable consumer products *pl*, consumer durables *pl*, durables *pl*, consumer hardgoods *pl*, (nicht dauerhafte) non-durable consumer goods *pl*, non-durable consumer products *pl*, non-durables *pl*
  Goods destined for use by ultimate consumers or households and in such form that they can be used without commercial processing. Certain articles, e.g. typewriters, may be either consumer goods or industrial goods depending upon whether they are destined for use by the ultimate consumer or household or by an industrial, business, or institutional user.
Konsumgüterindustrie *f (econ)* consumer goods industry, consumer products industry

Konsumgütermarketing *n* (**Konsumtivgütermarketing** *n*) consumer goods marketing, consumer products marketing
Konsumgütermarkt *m (econ)* consumer goods market, consumer products market
Konsumgütermarktforschung *f* consumer goods market research, consumer products market research
Konsumgütertypologie *f (market res)* typology of consumer goods, typology of consumer products, consumer goods typology, consumer products typology
Konsumgüterwerbung *f* consumer goods advertising, consumer products advertising
Konsumklima *n (econ)* consumption climate, climate of consumption
Konsumkredit *m*
→ Konsumentenkredit
Konsumleitbild *n (market psy)* consumption model
Konsummarkt *m*
→ Käufermarkt
Konsummotiv *n* (**Konsummotivation** *f*)
→ Kaufmotiv
Konsummuster *n* (**Verbrauchsmuster** *n*) *(econ)* consumption pattern, pattern of consumption behavior, *brit* behaviour
Konsumnachfrage *f* (**Konsumgüternachfrage** *f*) *(econ)* demand for consumer goods, demand for consumer products
Konsumneigung *f (econ)* propensity to consume, consumption propensity
  The total value of consumer expenditure on consumer goods and services divided by the national income.
Konsumniveau *n (econ)* level of consumption
Konsumnorm *f*
→ Konsumstandard
Konsumpionier *m* early adopter consumption pioneer
→ Geschmacksführer, Meinungsführer, Innovator, Modeführer
Konsumpolitik *f*
→ Verbrauchspolitik
konsumrelevanter Persönlichkeitsfaktor *m (market psy)* consumption-relevant personality factor
Konsumsoziologie *f* sociology of consumption

Konsumstandard m **(Konsumnorm** f)
(market psy) consumption standard
Any social or ethical norm or goal of
consumption behavior to be striven for,
maintained, or regained.
Konsumstil m (market psy)
consumption style
Konsumstruktur f (econ)
consumption pattern, consumption
structure, structure of consumption
Konsumsymbol n (econ) consumption
symbol
Konsumtheorie f (econ) theory of
consumption, consumption theory
Konsumtion f (**Konsumption** f)
→ Konsum
Konsumtionskredit m
→ Konsumentenkredit
Konsumtivbedarf m
→ Konsumgüternachfrage
Konsumtivgüter n/pl
→ Konsumgüter
Konsumverein m
→ Konsumgenossenschaft
Konsumverhalten n (market res)
consumption behavior, brit
consumption behaviour
→ Käuferverhalten, Kaufverhalten,
Konsumentenverhalten
Konsumverhaltensforschung f
consumption behavior research, brit
consumption behaviour research
Konsumwunsch m
→ Kaufwunsch
Konsumzwang m
→ Kaufzwang
Kontakt m (media res) exposure
A key term of media research, (→)
Mediaforschung, and media planning,
(→) Mediaplanung. It designates any
visual or audio contact of an individual
or household with a communication
medium or an advertisement, ranging,
e.g. in readership research, from just
leafing through a publication to thorough
reading.
→ Werbemittelkontakt,
Werbeträgerkontakt
Kontakt m **pro Anzeigenseite** (media
res) advertising page exposure (apx),
ad-page exposure
→ Anzeigenseitenkontakt
Kontakt m **pro Doppelseite** (media
res) double-page spread exposure,
DPS exposure
→ Doppelseitenkontakt

Kontaktabzug m (**Kontaktkopie** f)
(phot) contact print, contact sheet,
direct print
A photographic print made directly by
superimposing a negative on print paper
in the darkroom; since they are the same
size as the negatives, they are used
mainly for the selection of one or more
photographs from a large number.
Kontaktbericht m
(**Kontaktmemorandum** n) (eines
Vertreters/Interviewers) call report,
contact report
→ Besuchsbericht, Vertreterbericht,
Interviewerbericht
Kontaktbewertungsfunktion f
(**Kontaktbewertungskurve** f) (media
res) response function
→ Reaktionsfunktion
Kontaktchance f
→ Kontaktwahrscheinlichkeit
Kontaktdosierung f (media planning)
exposure dosage
Kontakter m (advtsg) account
representative, account executive,
contact executive, contact man
The member of an advertising agency
who supervises the planning and
preparation of advertising for one or
more clients, and who is responsible for
the primary liaison between agency and
advertiser.
Kontaktfaktor m (media res)
exposure factor
An estimate indicating the proportion of
television viewers or magazine readers
who will have a physical opportunity to
see the average advertising message.
Kontaktforschung f (media res)
exposure research
Kontaktfrage f
→ Eisbrecherfrage
Kontaktfrequenz f
→ Kontakthäufigkeit
Kontaktgewichtung f (media res)
exposure weighting
Kontaktgruppe f
→ Kontaktklasse
Kontaktgruppenleiter m (**Kontakt-
gruppenmanager** m) (advtsg) account
supervisor, group head
An executive employee in an advertising
agency responsible for supervising the
work of account executives, (→)
Kontakter, and for maintaining liaison
with his client counterparts.
Kontakthäufigkeit f (**Kontakt-
frequenz** f) (media res) frequency of
exposure, exposure frequency,

Kontaktintensität

frequency, (Leserschaftsforschung) frequency of reading, (Hörerschaftsforschung) frequency of listening, (Zuschauerschaftsforschung) frequency of viewing
 The number of times an advertising message is delivered within a set period of time. It is, the number of times or time periods in which households or individuals are in the audience of a given television or radio station, or program or a publication. This type of frequency rating is normally computed only for those households or individuals that are in the audience during at least one of the time periods.

Kontaktintensität f *(media res)* intensity of exposure, depth of exposure

Kontaktintervall n *(media res)* exposure interval, interval of exposure

Kontaktinterview n *(survey res)* screening interview
→ Filter

Kontaktkleben n contact bonding

Kontaktkopie f
→ Kontaktabzug m

Kontaktkosten pl **(Kontaktpreis** m) *(media res)* cost per exposure

Kontaktmenge f
→ Kontaktzahl

Kontaktmessung f *(media res)* measurement of exposure, exposure measurement, audience measurement

Kontaktmuster n *(media res)* pattern of exposure, exposure pattern

Kontaktpapier n *(phot)* contact paper
→ Kontaktabzug

Kontaktpreis m
→ Kontaktkosten

Kontaktqualität f *(media res)* quality of exposure, exposure quality

Kontaktraster m *(print)* contact screen

Kontaktstrecke f *(outdoor advtsg)* approach to billboard, approach
 The distance on the line of travel between the point where the poster first becomes comprehendible to the point where the copy ceases to be readable.

Kontaktstreuung f **(Kontaktvarianz** f) *(media res)* exposure variance, variance of exposure

Kontaktverfahren n **(Kontaktkopierverfahren** n, **Kontaktkopieren** n) *(phot)* contact printing, contact

280

printing process, contact printing method, contact process
→ Kontaktabzug

Kontaktversuch m **(Kontaktbesuch** m) *(survey res)* (des Interviewers beim Befragten) call
→ Besuch

Kontaktverteilung f *(media res)* exposure distribution, distribution of exposures
 A distribution that indicates how many people or households are exposed to an advertising medium or advertising message and how many times they are.

Kontaktverteilungskurve f *(media res)* exposure distribution curve, curve of exposure distribution

Kontaktwahrscheinlichkeit f **(Kontaktchance** f) *(media res)* probability of exposure, exposure probability, opportunity of exposure, opportunity for exposure, probability of receiving an impression (P.R.I., PRI), (bei Druckmedien, Fernsehen) opportunity to see (O.T.S., OTS), (beim Hörfunk) opportunity to hear (O.T.H., OTH)
 The estimated average number of times the audience of an advertising medium, (→) Werbeträger, or advertisement, (→) Werbemittel, is expected to be exposed to that particular medium or ad.

Kontaktzahl f **(Kontaktmenge** f) *(media res)* number of exposures, audience figure, coverage figure

Kontaktzone f
→ Kontaktstrecke

Konterbild n **(Konter** n) *(print)* flop, reverse print, lateral reversal print
 A laterally reversed photo, picture, or other piece of artwork, so that a mirror image of the original form results.

Konterdruck m **(Kontern** n) lateral reversal printing, reverse printing, flop printing
→ Konterbild

kontern v/t *(print)* to flop, to make a lateral reversal print
→ Konterbild

Kontern n
→ Konterdruck

Konterpresse f *(print)* offset flatbed machine

Kontextanalyse f **(Milieuanalyse** f) *(res)* contextual analysis (Paul F. Lazarsfeld)
 A research technique aimed at isolating the significant forms of communicative

behavior and at gaining, in separate research operations, perspective upon the nature of the level of context in which these forms function.

Kontingenz f *(stat)* contingency
The interrelationship or association existing between any of two variables such that the presence, form, or magnitude of one variable is dependent upon the presence, form, and magnitude of the other variable.

Kontingenzanalyse f *(stat)* contingency analysis (Charles E. Osgood), contingent analysis
The analysis of contingency, (→) Kontingenz, using contingency measures, such as the contingency coefficient (C), (→) Kontingenzkoeffizient, and contingency tables, (→) Kontingenztabelle.

Kontingenzkoeffizient m *(stat)* coefficient of contingency, coefficient of contingency (C), contingency coefficient, contingency coefficient C
A measure of contingency, (→) Kontingenz, between two variables used as a test of independence for a two-way contingency table, (→) Kontingenztafel. Its formula reads:

$$C = \sqrt{\frac{\chi^2}{N + \chi^2}}$$

where N is the total number of observations and χ^2 the computed value of the chi-squared statistic, (→) Chi-Quadrat.

Kontingenztabelle f **(Kontingenztafel** f) *(stat)* contingency table, *auch* contingent table
The tabular representation of the two-dimensional frequency distribution, (→) Häufigkeitsverteilung, of nominal scale data, (→) Nominalskala. The table shows the number or frequency of observations in each of the cells formed by the intersection of different levels of two or more classification variables.

kontinuierliche Daten n/pl **(stetige Daten** n/pl) *(stat)* continuous data *pl*
Those statistical data for which, at least theoretically, any of an infinite number of values can be obtained, so that no number, amount, degree, value, or subvalue is ruled out.
vgl. diskrete Daten (unstetige Daten)

kontinuierliche Grundgesamtheit f **(stetige Grundgesamtheit** f, **stetige statistische Masse** f) *(stat)*
continuous universe, continuous population
A population that is continuous in regard to some variate.
vgl. diskrete Grundgesamtheit (stetige Grundgesamtheit)

kontinuierliche Häufigkeitsverteilung f **(stetige Häufigkeitsverteilung** f) *(stat)* continuous frequency distribution, continuous distribution, continuous series
A frequency distribution, (→) Häufigkeitsverteilung, with an infinite number of values between the highest and the lowest value.
vgl. diskrete Häufigkeitsverteilung (unstetige Häufigkeitsverteilung)

kontinuierliche Skala f **(stetige Skala** f) *(stat)* continuous scale
A scale, (→) Skala, with an infinite number of values between the highest and the lowest value.
vgl. diskrete Skala (unstetige Skala)

kontinuierliche Variable f **(stetige Variable** f) *(stat)* continuous variable
A quantitative variable that, at least theoretically, can increase or decrease continuously, with an uninterrupted series of gradations of possible values. Between the highest and the lowest value any of an infinite number of values or fractional values may occur.
vgl. diskrete Variable (unstetige Variable)

kontinuierliche Werbung f
continuous advertising
The extended and uninterrupted use of advertising, especially the repetition of the same basic theme, layout, or commercial format over a longer period of time.
vgl. periodische Werbung (phasenweise Werbung)

kontinuierliche Zufallsgröße f **(stetige Zufallsgröße** f) *(stat)*
continuous variate, continuous random variate
A variate, (→) Zufallsgröße, that may take an infinite number of values in a continuous range.
vgl. diskrete Zufallsgröße (unstetige Zufallsgröße)

Kontinuität f **(Stetigkeit** f) *(stat)* continuity
The characteristic of a parameter, (→) Parameter, a variable, (→) Variable, or a variate, (→) Zufallsgröße, that may take an infinite number of values in a continuous range. A frequency or probability distribution is sometimes said

Kontinuitätskorrektur 282

to be continuous when it relates to a continuous variate, and sometimes when the function itself is continuous.
Kontinuitätskorrektur *f*
→ Yates'sche Kontinuitätskorrektur
Kontinuum *n* continuum
An uninterrupted series of an infinite number of gradual changes in the magnitude of a characteristic.
Kontorhandel *m*
→ Streckenhandel
Kontrahierungs-Mix *n* (**Konditionen-Mix** *n,* **Kontrahierungspolitik** *f,* **Konditionenpolitik** *f*) *(marketing) etwa* terms mix, terms policy, mix of general business terms, general business terms policy
That ingredient of the marketing mix, (→) Marketing-Mix, that consists of pricing, (→) Entgeltmix, (→) Preispolitik, discount policy, (→) Rabatt, general business terms, (→) Konditionen, including terms of delivery and payment, (→) Lieferungs- und Zahlungsbedingungen, and loan policies, (→) Kreditpolitik.
Kontraktmarketing *n* (**Bruno Tietz**) *etwa* contractual marketing, contract buying
vgl. Kaufaktmarketing
Kontramarketing *n* counter marketing (Philip H. Kotler)
Kontrast *m (phot/film/print/TV)* contrast
The degree of difference between the highlights and the darkest shadows in a piece of artwork, motion picture, or television image.
kontrastarm *adj (phot/print/TV)* flat, low-contrast, soft
vgl. kontrastreich
Kontrastarmut *f* (**Kontrastmangel** *m,* **Kontrastlosigkeit** *f*) *(phot/print/TV)* flatness, lack of contrast
The lack of tonal gradation between highlights and shadows in prints or negatives, generally due to flat, even lighting, overexposure, or incorrect concentration of developer.
Kontrastbereich *m*
→ Kontrastumfang
Kontrasteffekt *m (TV)* contrast effect
Kontrastfaktor *m (phot/print/TV)* contrast factor
One of a variety of factors contributing to contrast, (→) Kontrast, in a photographic image, a motion picture, a television image, a piece of artwork, a print, etc., such as e.g. the exposure given the negative, the filter used, the kind of film, the duration of development, the duration of exposure and development in printing, the paper used in printing, and the developer used both for the negative and the print.
Kontrastfarbe *f (phot/print/TV)* contrasting color, *brit* contrasting colour
Kontrastfilter *m (phot)* contrast filter
Kontrastgleichgewicht *n (phot/print/ TV)* contrast balance
Kontrastgrad *m*
→ Gamma
Kontrastgruppenanalyse *f* (**Kontrasttypenanalyse** *f*) *(res)* tree analysis (John A. Sonquist/James N. Morgan)
→ Segmentation
kontrastieren *v/t* to contrast
kontrastlos *adj (phot/print/TV)* no-contrast, lacking contrast
→ kontrastarm
Kontrastlosigkeit *f (phot/print/TV)* lack of contrast
→ Kontrastarmut
Kontrastprogramm *n (radio/TV)* counter program, *brit* counter programme
The practice of scheduling a television or radio program that is deliberately designed to appeal to the audience of a specific competing program on another channel during the same time period.
Kontrastregelung *f (TV)* contrast control
kontrastreich (kontraststark) *adj (phot/print/TV)* contrasty, high-contrast, hard, *colloq* snappy
The quality of a photographic image, a print, a motion picture, a television image, a negative, or a piece of artwork with very dark shadows and white highlights, due to underexposure or overdevelopment of the negative.
Kontrastübertragungsfunktion *f* (**KÜF**) *(TV)* transmission gamma
Kontrastumfang *m* (**Kontrastspielraum** *m,* **Kontrastbereich** *m*)
1. *(TV)* contrast range, contrast ratio, acceptable contrast ratio (ACR)
The (acceptable) degrees of difference between lightest and darkest areas of a television picture.
2. *(phot)* → Objektumfang
Kontrastverhältnis *n (TV)* contrast ratio
→ Kontrastumfang
Kontrastwerbung *f* contrast advertising

A technique in advertising which attempts to emphasize how two products differ from one another in a way that is commercially beneficial to the advertiser's product.

Kontrollautsprecher *m* control loudspeaker, monitoring loudspeaker

Kontrollbefragung *f* **(Kontrollinterview** *n*) *(survey res)* control interview

Kontrolle *f* control

Kontrollfrage *f* *(survey res)* control question, check question, checking question

Kontrollgruppe *f* *(res)* control group
In experimental design, (→) experimentelle Anlage, a group of subjects selected in a way that makes them comparable to subjects in the experimental group(s), except that they are not exposed to the experimental treatment, (→) Experimentalhandlung.

Kontrollicht *n* **(Kontroll-Licht** *n*) *(film/TV)* indicator light, (Studio) cue light

kontrollieren *v/t* to control, to check

kontrollierte Beobachtung *f* *(res)* controlled observation, *auch* contrived observation

kontrollierte Verbreitung *f*
→ CC-Zeitschrift

kontrollierte Wiedererkennung *f* **(überprüfte Wiedererkennung** *f*) *(media res)* controlled recognition
→ überprüfte Wiedererkennung

kontrollierter Markttest *m* *(market res)* controlled market test
→ kontrolliertes Experiment

kontrolliertes Experiment *n* *(res)* controlled experiment
An experiment designed in advance, (→) experimentelle Anlage, and conducted under conditions in which it is possible to control relevant factors while measuring the effects of the experimental variable. The subjects are divided into an experimental group, (→) Experimentalgruppe, and a control group, (→) Kontrollgruppe, and the variable that is hypothesized to be the independent variable, (→) unabhängige Variable, is introduced into the experimental group. The groups are compared after the experimental treatment, (→) Experimentalhandlung, to determine whether there are significant differences between them in regard to the dependent variable, (→) abhängige Variable.

kontrolliertes Wiedererkennungsverfahren *n*
→ kontrollierte Wiedererkennung

Kontrollinterview *n*
→ kontrollierte Befragung

Kontrollpult *n* **(Steuerpult** *n*) *(radio/TV)* control desk, control console

Kontrollraum *m* **(Steuerraum** *m*) *(radio/TV)* control room, monitoring room, control booth, *(radio)* cubicle
A room or booth adjoining a radio or television studio wherein video and audio switching and other functions of a TV or radio production are controlled and balanced by engineers and directors.

Kontrollschirm *m* **(Kontrollbildschirm** *m*) *(TV)* monitor screen, monitoring screen, monitor
A television receiver to check video recording in process.

Kontrollspur *f* *(film/TV)* control track, guide track
A secondary motion picture sound track, (→) Tonspur, or section of the video tape signal used to control either timing or volume of sound by affecting playback synchronization.

Kontrollsystem *n* control system

Kontrollvariable *f* *(stat)* control variable

Kontur *f* *(phot/print/TV)* contour, outline, border

Konturendeckung *f* *(TV)* contour convergence

Konturenplatte *f* *(print)* key plate
In color-process printing, the plate with maximum detail to which other plates must be registered.

Konturenschärfe *f* **(Konturschärfe** *f*) *(phot/print/TV)* definition, contour sharpness, edge sharpness
The clarity of contour in the objects of a photographic image, a print, or a television picture.

Konturentzerrung *f* *(TV)* contour correction

Konturschrift *f*
→ lichte Schrift

Konturverstärkung *f* *(TV)* contour accentuation, crispening

Konturzeichnung *f* outline drawing, outline

Konus *m* *(print)* bevel
The edge of a printing plate, trimmed on an angle, by which it can be clamped to a press bed or cylinder.

Konuslautsprecher *m* cone speaker

Konvergenz *f* convergence

Konvergenztestbild n *(TV)* convergence test pattern, grille
Konversionsfilter m *(TV)* conversion filter
Konversions-Marketing n conversional marketing (Philip H. Kotler)
vgl. Anreiz-Marketing, Reduktionsmarketing, Entwicklungsmarketing, Erhaltungsmarketing, Kontramarketing, Revitalisierungsmarketing, Synchro-Marketing
Konversionsrate f conversion rate
  The rate at which marketing efforts, including advertising, sales promotion, salesmanship, etc. are turned into actual orders of a product or service.
Konversionstabelle f conversion table
Konverter m converter
Konvex-Beleuchtungslinse f *(print)* bull's eye
  A magnifying lens mounted on a stand and used by finishers for concentrating light on any area of the printing plate.
Konvexkonkav-Linse f **(Zerstreuungslinse** f**)** *(phot)* convexo-concave lens
  → Konkavkonvex-Linse
Konzentration f *(psy/stat)* concentration
Konzentrationsauswahl f
  → Auswahl nach dem Konzentrationsprinzip
Konzentrationskoeffizient m **(Gini-Koeffizient** m**)** *(stat)* coefficient of concentration, coefficient of concentration (G)
  A coefficient designed to measure the extent of disproportion in the dispersion, (→) Streuung, of some variables. If a variable X can take values $x_1, x_2 \ldots x_n$ with frequencies $f_1, f_2 \ldots f_n$, the sum of the last m units as compared with the total sum obeys the inequality

$$\frac{\sum\limits_{i=n-m+1}^{n} f_i x_i}{\sum\limits_{i=1}^{n} f_i x_i} > \frac{\sum\limits_{n-m+1}^{} f_i}{\sum\limits_{i=1}^{n} f_i}$$

  and the extent to which these two expressions depart from equality is taken as a measure of concentration.
Konzentrationskurve f
  → Lorenzkurve
Konzentrationsprinzip n
  → Auswahl nach dem Konzentrationsprinzip
Konzentrationsverfahren n
  → Auswahl nach dem Konzentrationsprinzip
Konzept n concept
Konzeptanalyse f *(advtsg res)* concept analysis, conceptual analysis
Konzeption f conception
Konzeptionstest m **(Konzepttest** m**)** *(advtsg res)* concept test, conception test
  A variety of research methods aimed at measuring the viability of new ideas in product design, advertising copy, or marketing approaches prior to conducting product or market tests.
Konzept-Segmentation f *(advtsg res)* concept segmentation, conceptual segmentation
Konzernrabatt m *(econ)* group discount
Konzession f *(econ)* license, *brit* licence
  A legal arrangement that transfers the right to manufacture or to market a product to a licensee.
Kooperation f *(econ)* cooperation, *brit* co-operation
Kooperationsform f *(econ)* form of cooperation, type of cooperation, *brit* co-operation
Kooperationssystem n *(econ)* cooperation system, *brit* co-operation system
Kooperationstyp m
  → Kooperationsform
Kooperationsvereinbarung f *(econ)* cooperative agreement, *brit* cooperative agreement, cooperation agreement, *brit* co-operation agreement
Kooperationswerbung f **(kooperative Werbung** f**)** cooperative advertising, *brit* co-operative advertising
  → Gemeinschaftswerbung
kooperatives Marketing n cooperative marketing, *brit* co-operative marketing
  → Gemeinschaftsmarketing
Koordinate f *(stat)* coordinate, *brit* co-ordinate
Koordinatensystem n *(stat)* coordinate system, *brit* co-ordinate system
Koordination f **(Koordinierung** f**)** coordination, *brit* co-ordination
Koordinationszentrale f **(Koordinierungszentrale** f**)** coordination center, *brit* co-ordination centre

Koordinator *m* coordinator, *brit* co-ordinator
Koordinierungsentfernung *f (sat)* coordination distance, *brit* co-ordination distance
Koorganisation *f* coorganization, *brit* co-organisation
Kopenhagener Wellenplan *m (radio/TV)* Copenhagen plan
Kopf *m* **1.** (Überschrift) head, heading, headline **2.** (Briefkopf) letterhead **3.** (Zeitungskopf) masthead, logotype, logo
  The name of a newspaper, usually at the top of the first page and generally in a distinctive typographic style or arrangement.
4. (einer Tabelle) head, heading, table head **5.** *(typ)* (einer Drucktype) beard
  The beveled space below the face of a type.
Kopfblatt *n* **(Kopfausgabe** *f* **)** *(Zeitung)* ring paper
  A local edition of a regional daily newspaper with local news coverage.
Kopfbeleg *m*
  → Kopfremission
Kopfhörer *m* headphone, earphones *pl*, head receiver, headset, *colloq* cans *pl*
  A listening device that is worn over both ears and used to convert electrical signals into sound that is audible only to its wearer.
Kopfleiste *f* **(Kopfvignette** *f* **)** *(print)* headpiece, flourish
Kopfnote *f* **(Vorbemerkung** *f* **)** *(print)* headnote
Kopfremission *f* **(Titelkopfremission** *f*, **Titelremission** *f* **)** returns *pl* of cover pages, cover returns *pl*
Kopfsteg *m (print)* headstick, head stick, head margin, top margin
Kopfzeile *f (print)* catch line, catchline
Kopie *f* **1.** copy, duplicate, manifold
  Anything that was printed or otherwise duplicated from an original.
2. *(phot/print)* photographic print
3. → Arbeitskopie, Filmkopie, Dup-Negativ, Internegativ
Kopierapparat *m* **(Kopiergerät** *n***)** copier, printer, copying machine, copying device, printing machine, duplicator, duplicating machine, manifolder
Kopierdruck *m* copying print

Kopiereffekt *m (film)* accidental printing, spurious printing, *(tape)* magnetic transfer
kopieren *v/t* **1.** *(phot/print)* to copy, to duplicate, to print
2. → plagiieren
Kopieren *n* **1.** *(phot/print)* copying, duplicating, printing
2. → Plagiieren
Kopierer *m*
  → Kopierapparat m
Kopierfilm *m* **(Duplizierfilm** *m***)** printer stock, printing stock
Kopierfilter *m*
  → Filterfolie
Kopierfilterband *n*
  → Filterband
Kopiergerät *n*
  → Kopierapparat
Kopierkontrast *m (film)* printing contrast
  → Kontrast
Kopierlänge *f (film)* printing length
Kopierlicht *n (film)* printer light
Kopierlichtschaltung *f (film)* printer-light setting
Kopiermaschine *f*
  → Kopierapparat
Kopiermeister *m (film)* film grader
Kopierung *f*
  → Kopieren
Kopierverfahren *n (phot)* copying process, printing process
Kopiervorlage *f* copy
  → Original
Kopierwerk *n* **(Kopieranstalt** *f* **)** *(film)* printing laboratory, printing lab, film-processing laboratory, film laboratory, film lab
Kopierwert *m* **(Kopierlichtwert** *m***)** *(film)* printer-light value, printer-light strength
Koppelanzeige *f*
  → Referenzanzeige
Koppelgeschäft *n*
  → Kopplungsgeschäft
Koppeln *n* **(Kopplung** *f* **)** *(film)* coupling
Koppelschleife *f (film/TV)* coupling loop, loop
  A piece of television commercial or motion picture film spliced end to end for continuous projection.
Koppelzeichen *n (film/TV)* changeover cues *pl*, cue dots *pl*, cue marks *pl*

Kopplungsgeschäft

Kopplungsgeschäft
The projectionist's changeover warning, consisting of several frames of a tiny white triangle, circle, or the like in advance of a film's beginning or end.

Kopplungsgeschäft n **(Koppelangebot** n) *(econ)* package deal
The combination of a number of product units or range of services into one salable unit.

Kopplungswerbung f
→ Referenzwerbung

Koproduktion f **(Co-Produktion** f)
(film/TV) coproduction,
brit co-production
A motion picture or television program produced by two or more producers.

Koproduzent m *(film/TV)* coproducer, *brit* co-producer

Korn n **(Körnigkeit** f) *(film/phot)* grain, *(TV)* granule
The distribution of silver particles in photographic emulsions and images.

Kornätzung f **(Kornautotypie** f, **Kornrasterklischee** n) *(print)* grain halftone, mezzograph, metzograph
A halftone reproduction made with either a dust grain or by means of a grain screen, (→) Kornraster.

Kornflimmern n *(TV)* granule

Kornraster m *(print)* grain screen, mezzograph screen, metzograph screen
A halftone screen, (→) Autotypieraster, embodying a grain rather than a ruled line formation.
vgl. Linienraster, Punktraster

Kornrasterklischee n
→ Kornätzung

Körperfarbe f body color, *brit* body colour

körperliche Remission f (Zeitung/Zeitschrift) full-copy returns pl

körperlose Remission f **(KR-Verfahren** n) (Zeitung/Zeitschrift) returns pl of cover pages or logos

Korrektor m *(print)* proofreader, *brit* proof-reader
A person who corrects mistakes in typesetting by reading proofs and sending them back to the printer for revision.

Korrektorat n **(Korrektursaal** m, **Korrekturraum** m) *(print)* proofroom, proofreaders' room

Korrektur f **(Korrigieren** n) *(print)* correction, correcting, proofing

Korrekturabzug m **(Korrekturfahne** f, **Korrekturbogen** m)** *(print)* proof,
galley, proof, flat proof, proof sheet, press proof, pull
A rough proof for checking taken from type still on the compositor's bench, in contrast to a press proof made after type has been adjusted to take the best possible impression.

Korrekturanweisung f
→ Korrekturvorschrift

Korrekturband n correction tape

Korrekturbank f **(Korrekturtisch** m) ring bank

Korrekturbogen m
1. → Korrekturabzug
2. → Korrekturseite

Korrekturfahne f **(Fahne** f)
→ Fahnenabzug

Korrekturfaktor m *(stat)* correction factor

Korrekturfilter m *(phot)* correction filter, trimming filter

Korrekturgehilfe m **(Korrekturhilfe** f) *(print)* copy holder, copyholder
An assistant in the proofroom who holds the copy and reads it aloud to the proofreader, (→) Korrektor, for comparison purposes.

Korrekturkopie f *(film)* first release print
vgl. Nullkopie

Korrekturlesen n *(print)* proofreading, *brit* proof-reading, proofing
Reading a printer's proof or document for the purpose of checking the correctness of the typesetting or page makeup, and of adding corrections and alterations.

Korrekturstellenanzeiger m
→ Lichtgriffel

Korrekturvorschrift f **(Korrekturanweisung** f) *(print)* proofreader's instructions pl, proofreading instructions pl

Korrekturzeichen n *(print)* proofreader's mark, proof mark
The standardized signs used by proofreaders to denote errors and corrections to be made.

Korrekturzettel m *(print)* errata slip, errata sheet, corrigenda slip, list of corrigenda

Korrelation f *(stat)* correlation
In the most general sense, the interdependence between quantitative or qualitative data. In this sense, it would include the association of dichotomised attributes, (→) Assoziation, and the contingency of multiply-classified attributes, (→) Kontingenz. In a narrower sense, the

relationship between measurable variates or ranks.

Korrelationsanalyse f *(stat)* correlation analysis
A class of statistical techniques designed to measure the degree of correlation, (→) Korrelation, between sets of measurement.

Korrelationsbündel n **(Bündel** n **von interkorrelierten Variablen)** *(stat)* correlation cluster

Korrelationsdiagramm n *(stat)* correlation diagram

Korrelationsfrage f **(analytische Frage** f**)** *(survey res)* correlation question, analytical question

Korrelationskoeffizient m *(stat)* correlation coefficient, coefficient of correlation
A statistical measure of the interdependence between two variates. It is usually a pure number which varies between -1 and $+1$ with the intermediate value of zero indicating the absence of correlation, but not necessarily the independence of the variates. The limiting values indicate perfect negative or positive correlation.
→ Kendalls Tau, Produkt-Moment-Korrelation, Rangkorrelation

Korrelationsmatrix f *(stat)* correlation matrix

Korrelationstabelle f *(stat)* correlation table
A frequency table of a bivariate distribution.

Korrelationsverhältnis n *(stat)* correlation ratio, eta coefficient, η coefficient
A measure of correlation, symbolized by the coefficient eta (η), used when the relationship between two variables is curvilinear (nonlinear) rather than linear. The correlation ratio may be used for any pattern of curvilinear relationship, and it may be used not only for the association of two quantitative variables, as is the case for most measures of correlation, but also when one variable is quantitative and one is qualitative.

Korrelogramm n *(stat)* correlogram
Korrespondent m correspondent
Korrespondentenbeleg m (Zeitung/Zeitschrift) correspondent's copy
Korrespondenzbüro n
→ Ausschnittbüro
korrigieren v/t to correct

korrigierte Fahne f **(korrigierter Abzug** m**)** *(print)* O.K. proof, final proof
→ endgültiger Abzug

Kosten pl *(econ)* cost, costs pl, (Ausgaben) expenses pl

Kosten pl **pro Anfrage** cost per inquiry
The cost of producing one inquiry about the product from an advertisement or an advertising campaign. When direct mail advertising is used for the purpose of developing leads for salespersons to follow up, this is often a tentative measure of selling expense and a base for estimating the probable final cost of a sale.

Kosten pl **pro Rückantwort** cost per return, cost per reply, cost per conversion, conversion rate
The cost of achieving either a sale or any other intended economic result from an inquiry to an advertisement based on the cost of the advertisement divided by the number of resulting sales.

Kosten pl **pro Verkauf** *(econ)* cost per sale, cost per order
The cost of making one sale or obtaining one order through advertising, computed by dividing the total cost of advertising by the total number of sales achieved or orders received.

Kosten pl **pro Tausend**
→ Tausenderpreis

Kostenanalyse f *(econ)* cost analysis
Kostenbudgetierung f *(econ)* cost budgeting
kostendeckend adj *(econ)* cost-covering
Kostendeckung f *(econ)* cost coverage, coverage of cost
Kosteneffizienz f *(econ)* cost efficiency, *auch (falsch)* cost effectiveness
Kostenelastizität f *(econ)* cost elasticity
→ Elastizität
Kostenfaktor m *(econ)* cost factor
Any factor contributing to cost rather than profit.
kostenfrei adj → kostenlos
Kostenfunktion f *(stat)* cost function
In sampling theory, a function giving the cost of obtaining the sample as a function of the relevant factors affecting cost.
Kostenkontrolle f *(econ)* cost control
kostenlos (kostenfrei) adj free, free of charge, gratuitous

kostenlose Werbung *f*
→ Gratiswerbung, Schleichwerbung
kostenloser Versand *m*
→ Gratisversand (Freiversand)
Kosten-Mix *n (econ)* cost mix, mix of costs
Kosten-Nutzen-Analyse *f (econ)* cost-benefit analysis
 The investigation of the relationship existing between the economic and social cost and the economic and social benefits of an investment.
Kosten-Nutzen-Verhältnis *n (econ)* cost-benefit-ratio, cost-benefit relationship
 The relationship between the social or economical costs and the benefits of any investment project.
Kosten-Plus-System *n*
→ Pauschalpreis plus Kosten
Kostenpreis *m (econ)* cost-oriented price, cost-plus price
vgl. Selbstkostenpreis
Kostenpreiskalkulation *f* (**Kostenprinzip** *n*) *(econ)* cost-oriented pricing, cost-plus pricing
 A way of arriving at a selling price by taking the invoice cost of an item and adding a certain percentage to it. It is a pricing method whereby actual production costs, or an estimate thereof, is added to a profit figure to arrive at a selling price. Originally used for war contracts, the system is still used in development work where eventual costs cannot be realistically estimated. The principle is used widely in industry but as a princing policy where historical costs, together with agreed profit margin, give the selling price.
Kostenquote *f* (**Kostenverhältnis** *n*, **Preisquote** *f*, **Preisverhältnis** *n*) *(econ)* cost ratio
 A measure for evaluating sources of supply whereby all identifiable purchasing and receiving costs are related to the value of the shipments. The result is a quality-cost ratio found by dividing for any one supplier the associated costs by the total value of purchases.
Kostenrangordnung *f*
→ Preisrangordnung
Kostenschätzung *f (econ)* estimation of cost, cost estimation
Kostenvoranschlag *m* (**Kostenanschlag** *m*) *(econ)* cost estimate
Kostenzentrum *n (econ)* expense center, cost center, *brit* centre

A collection of controllable costs which are related to one particular job of work or kind of service, a unit or center of activity.
vgl. Ertragszentrum
Kostprobe *f*
→ Warenprobe
Kovarianz *f (stat)* covariance
 A measure of the joint variance, (→) Varianz, of two or more variables. Each deviation from the arithmetic mean, (→) arithmetisches Mittel, of one variable is multiplied by the corresponding deviation from the mean of the other variable. The mean of the resulting products is the covariance.
Kovarianzanalyse *f (stat)* analysis of covariance (ANCOVA), covariance analysis
 An extension of the analysis of variance, (→) Varianzanalyse, to cover the case where members falling into the classes bear the values of more than one variate. Interest centers on one of these, chosen as the dependent variate and the question is whether variation between classes is due to class effects or to dependence on other variates which themselves vary among classes. This is discussed by considering the regression of the dependent variate on the other variates and the variation of the regressions, or of covariances, among classes.
Kovarianzfunktion *f (stat)* covariance function
Kovarianzkern *m (stat)* covariance kernel, mean value function
Kovarianzmatrix *f (stat)* covariance matrix, variance-covariance matrix
Kovariation *f*
→ Kovarianz
kovariierender Einflußfaktor *m (panel res)* covariant qualifier
KR-Verfahren *n*
→ körperlose Remission
Kramladen *m*
→ Gemischtwarengeschäft
Kran *m (film/TV)* crane, boom
Kran-Dolly *f (film/TV)* crane dolly
Kratzer *m* (Platte) scratch, (Geräusch) scratching noise
kräuseln (sich kräuseln) *v/refl (phot)* to frill
Kräuseln *n (phot)* frill, frilling
 A defect in which the emulsion separates from the plate or film in folds and wrinkles. It is caused by differences of temperature between solutions during fixing.

Krayonmanier f crayon engraving, chalk manner
Krayonzeichnung f (**Pastellzeichnung** f) crayon drawing, line drawing
kreativ adj creative
Kreativagentur f creative boutique, boutique, hot shop
  A small advertising agency differing from a full service agency in that its work is primarily confined to creative services, on a job-by-job or continuing basis with its clients.
Kreativdirektor m *(advtsg)* creative director (C.D.), (stellvertretender) associate creative director, (leitender) executive creative director
  An executive advertising agency employee responsible for managing the operations and personnel of a creative group, (→) Kreativgruppe, or department.
Kreativer m (**kreativer Mitarbeiter** m, **Kreativmitarbeiter** m) agency creative, creative artist, creative man
  An artist in an advertising agency who develops, or helps develop, advertising messages and advertising art, such as a copy writer, (→) Texter, layout man, (→) Layouter, or continuity writer, (→) Drehbuchautor.
kreatives Problemlösen n (**Buffalo-Methode** f) *(innovation)* creative problem solution, Buffalo method (Sydney J. Parnes)
Kreativgruppe f *(advtsg)* creative group
  A department in a large advertising agency, comprising copywriter(s), visualizer(s), storybord artist(s), etc., who work on one or more accounts, (→) Kundenetat, under a creative director, (→) Kreativdirektor.
Kreativität f creativeness, *auch* creativity
Kreativitätsmethode f (**Kreativitätstechnik** f, **Ideenfindungsmethode** f) *(innovation)* idea development method, creative idea development, idea generation method, creative idea generation
Kreativstrategie f *(advtsg)* creative strategy
  The statement of the communications goal and basic message to be used in an advertising campaign, usually consisting of a stated intent, target prospect description, the benefit or benefits to be promised, and the facts to be used to support the believability of the benefits promised.

Kreide f
  → Kreidestift, Kreidezeichnung
Kreidemanier f
  → Krayonmanier
Kreidepapier n chalk overlay paper, coated paper
  → Barytpapier
Kreidestift m chalk, crayon
Kreidezeichnung f
  → Krayonzeichnung
kreiern (schaffen, schöpfen) v/t to create, to design, to develop
Kreisauflage f (**Summe** f **der Auflagen in Gemeinden**) *(newspaper)* district circulation
Kreisblende f (**Irisblende** f) *(phot)* iris diaphragm, iris
  → Irisblende
Kreisdiagramm n (**Kreisgraphik** f, **Tortendiagramm** n) *(stat)* circular chart, circular diagram, *colloq* pie chart pie diagram, pie graph
  A type of graphical representation in the form of an area diagram, (→) Flächendiagramm, whereby the components of a single total can be shown as sectors of a circle. The angles of the sectors are proportional to the components of the total.
Kreiselkopf m *(phot)* gyroscopic head
Kreiselstativ n *(phot)* gyroscopic tripod, gyro-tripod
Kreisfahrt f *(film)* track-round
Kreisraster m *(print)* circular screen
  A circular-shaped halftone screen, (→) Autotypieraster, which enables the camera operator to move without disturbing the copy, (→) Vorlage, thereby obtaining the proper screen angles, (→) Rasterwinkel, for color halftones.
Kreuz n (**Kreuzzeichen** n) *(typ)* dagger (†), obelisk
Kreuzauswertung f (**Kreuztabulierung** f, **Kreuztabellierung** f) *(stat)* cross tabulation, *brit* cross-tabulation, *short* cross tab, cross tabbing
  A technique of joint tabulation of data with regard to two or more variables, each of which is divided into two or more categories. The cross tabulation indicates the number of cases that occur jointly in each combination of categories of the variables under investigation.
Kreuzband n
  → Streifband
Kreuzbruchfalz m (**Kreuzbruch** m) right-angle fold, French fold
  A type of fold, (→) Falz, used for four-page leaflets made from sheets, printed

Kreuzelastizität

on one side only, in which pages one and four are printed on one half of the leaflet upside-down, and pages two and three on the other half upside-up. A transverse fold is followed by a vertical one.

Kreuzelastizität f *(econ)* cross-elasticity
→ Kreuzpreiselastizität

Kreuzfalz m
→ Kreuzbruchfalz

Kreuzklassifikation f **(Kreuzklassifizierung** f) *(stat)* cross classification, crossed classification, *brit* cross-classification
   A subclassification of data following an initial classification.

Kreuzlicht n *(phot/film/TV)* crosslighting, crosslight, crossed spots pl
   The lighting of a photographic object, a motion picture or television scene from two sides.

Kreuzlinienraster m *(print)* cross-line screen

Kreuzlinientestbild n *(TV)* cross-line test pattern

Kreuzmodulation f *(radio/TV)* cross modulation

Kreuzpreiselastizität f **(Preiskreuzelastizität** f, **Substitutionselastizität** f, **Triffinscher Koeffizient** m) *(econ)* cross elasticity of demand, cross price elasticity
   The response of demand, (→) Nachfrage, for one product or service to a change in the price of another. Where the ratio is high, e.g. a small change in the price of product A results in a large change in the sales of product B, the product involved may be construed to be substitutional, (→) Substitutionsgüter. Where the ratio is low, the possibility of substitution is so remote that the products must be regarded as being in separate markets.

Kreuzraster m
→ Kreuzlinienraster

Kreuzschiene f *(TV)* matrix, cross bar, crossbar, *brit* cross-bar

Kreuzsteg m
→ Bundsteg

Kreuztabellierung f **(Kreuztabulierung** f)
→ Kreuzauswertung

Kreuzvalidierung f *(test theory)* cross validation
   The evaluation of a prediction equation, discriminant function, etc., in a different sample than the one used for deriving the equation. A single sample may be randomly divided into two groups, with each group serving as the cross-validation sample for the other, or a new independent sample obtained for the purpose.

Kreuzvalidität f **(Kreuzgültigkeit** f) *(test theory)* cross validity

Kreuzverweis m
→ Querverweis

Kreuzworträtselzeitschrift f **(Kreuzworträtselzeitung** f) crossword puzzle magazin, crossword puzzle paper

Kreuzzeichen n
→ Kreuz

Krimi m **(Kriminalfilm** m) detective film, suspense thriller, mystery show, *colloq* whodunit

Kristallmikrofon n **(Kristallmikrophon** n) crystal microphone, piezoelectric microphone

Kristalloszillator m crystal oscillator

Kriterium n *(test theory)* criterion

Kriteriumsvalidität f **(Kriteriumsgültigkeit** f) *(test theory)* criterion-oriented validity, criterion-related validity, empirical validity

Kriteriumsvariable f *(test theory)* criterion variable
   1. In hypothesis testing, the measure taken as the standard against which other measures (e.g., a new test) of the construct are validated. 2. A measure to be predicted from one or a combination of several predictor variables. 3. In experimental design, the dependent variable.

kritischer Bereich m **(kritische Region** f, **Ablehnungsbereich** m, **Zurückweisungsbereich** m) *(stat)* critical region, region of rejection, rejection region
   In statistical hypothesis testing, (→) Hypothesentest, one of two mutually exclusive regions into which the sample space is divided, the other being the region of acceptance, (→) Annahmebereich. If the sample point falls into the region of acceptance, the hypothesis is accepted. If it falls in the region of rejection, it is rejected.

kritischer Quotient m **(kritischer Bruch** m) *(stat)* critical ratio (C.R.), z value, Z measure

kritischer Wert m *(stat)* critical value, critical value of t

Krümmung f curvature, bend

Kruskal-Wallis-Test m *(stat)* Kruskal-Wallis test, Kruskal-Wallis procedure

A nonparametric test of differences in location for two or more independent samples.

Kruskals Stress *m (stat)* Kruskal stress, Kruskal's stress

KÜF *abbr* Kontrastübertragungsfunktion

Kugelmikrofon *n* (**Kugelmikrophon** *n*, **Kugel** *f*) omnidirectional microphone

Kulisse *f (film/TV/studio)*
1. (einzelne) flat, set flat, stage flat
An upright, two-dimensional unit of scenic background.
(Seitenkulisse) wing
2. set, scenery

Kulissenfundus *m (film/TV/studio)* scenery store

Kulissenklammer *f (film/TV/studio)* cleat, flat clamp

Kulissenschieber *m*
→ Bühnenarbeiter

Kulissenwand *f (film/TV/studio)* flat, set flat, stage flat

Kuller *m*
→ Titelkuller

Kulturfilm *m* cultural film, cultural documentary

Kulturredakteur *m*
→ Feuilletonredakteur

Kulturvergleich *m* (**kulturvergleichende Untersuchung** *f*) *(survey res)* cross-cultural research, cross-cultural investigation, cross-cultural study

Kulturzeitschrift *f* cultural magazine, cultural journal

Kumulation *f* 1. *(stat)* cumulation, accumulation
The process of progressive, additive change in two or more variables resulting from their interrelationship. It occurs when two or more variables are so related that a change in one results in a change in the same direction in the second.
2. *(media res)* accumulation, accumulation of audiences, audience accumulation, cume
→ interne Überschneidung

Kumulationseffekt *m* (**Kumulationswirkung** *f*) *(media res)* cumulative effect, cumulation effect, accumulation
→ interne Überschneidung

Kumulationsskala *f* (**kumulative Skala** *f*) *(stat)* cumulative scale
→ Guttman-Skala

kumulative Reichweite *f (media res)* cumulative coverage, cumulative reach, cumulative audience
→ interne Überschneidung

kumulieren 1. *v/t* to cumulate, to accumulate 2. *v/refl* (sich kumulieren, kumuliert werden) to cumulate, to accumulate

kumulierte Hörerschaft *f* (**kumulierte Hörerzahl** *f*) *(media res)* accumulated audience, cumulated audience, cumulated listeners *pl*, accumulated listers *pl*
→ interne Überschneidung

kumulierte Leserschaft *f* (**kumulierte Leserzahl** *f*) *(media res)* accumulated audience, cumulated audience, cumulated readers *pl*, accumulated readers *pl*, cumulated readership, accumulated readership
→ interne Überschneidung

kumulierte Zuschauerschaft *f* (**kumulierte Zuschauerzahl** *f*) *(media res)* accumulated audience, cumulated audience, cumulative audience, *colloq* cume, cumulated viewers *pl*, accumulated viewers *pl*, net audience, unduplicated audience
The net size of a television audience during two or more time periods. That is, a household or an individual will be counted as part of a cumulative audience only once even though the household or the individual appears in audiences during two or more time periods. One may compute a cumulative audience figure for time periods during the same day, on different days within a week, or over a period of several weeks. Cumulative audience figures are often used as a measure of the circulation of a network or a station and as a measure of the reach of a television program, or group of programs. The concept of cumulative audience also may be used for different combinations of media. In all cases duplications are eliminated in the computations.
→ interne Überschneidung

kumulierte Häufigkeitsverteilung *f* (**kumulative Häufigkeitsverteilung** *f*)
→ Summenhäufigkeitsverteilung

kumulierte Nettoreichweite *f (media res)* cumulative net coverage, accumulative net reach, cumulative net audience, accumulative net audience, net unduplicated audience
→ interne Überschneidung

kumulierte Reichweite *f (media res)* cumulative coverage, accumulative coverage, cumulative reach, accumulative reach, cumulative audience, accumulative audience, audience accumulation, audience cumulation, *colloq* cume
→ interne Überschneidung

kumulierte Werbewirkung *f* (**kumulative Werbewirkung** *f*) cumulative advertising effect, cumulated advertising effect
   The progressive, additive buildup of goodwill and/or desire for a product, a service, a firm, or organization, etc. through the successive stages of an advertising campaign or a series of advertisements.

Kunde *m* customer, client, buyer, (einer Werbeagentur) account
   A person or organization who actually makes the decision to buy a certain product or service from a source. Also, an advertiser with whom business is done.

Kundenanreißer *m* (**Kundenfänger** *m*) puller-in

Kundenausweis *m*
→ Kaufschein

Kundenberatung *f* customer advisory service

Kundenbesuch *m* 1. (einzelner Besuch) call, call on a customer, customer call, canvass 2. (Vorgang) canvassing, detailing

Kundenbesucher *m* canvasser, detailer
   A sales representative, (→) Handelsvertreter, or selling agent, (→) Reisender, who calls direct on customers.

Kundenbeziehungen *f/pl* customer relations *pl*
   Those public relations activities intended to maintain good relations with customers and to establish or stabilize their loyalty.

Kundenbindung *f*
→ Geschäftstreue, Ladentreue, Markentreue, Produkttreue

Kundendienst *m* (**Kundendienstleistung** *f*, **Kundendienstleistungen** *f/pl*) *(econ)* service, customer service, (nach dem Kauf) after-sales service, (vor dem Kauf) pre-sales service
   The total range of activities and privileges extended to the customers of a firm beyond the merchandise itself, such as pleasant general business conditions, consumer credit, (→) Konsumentenkredit, returns, delivery, wrappings, etc.,
to maintain the utility of products sold and establish customers' loyalty.

Kundendienstpolitik *f* (**Kundendienst-Mix** *n*) *(econ)* service policy

Kundenetat *m* (einer Werbeagentur) account
   The client of an advertising agency.
→ Etat

Kundenfang *m* touting, pulling-in of customers

Kundenfänger *m* (**Kundenschlepper** *m*) tout, puller-in

Kundenforschung *f (market res)* intercept interviewing, exit interviewing

Kundenfrequenzanalyse *f*
→ Kundenlaufstudie

Kundenkartei *f* list of buyers, list of customers, mailing list

Kundenlaufanalyse *f* (**Kundenlaufstudie** *f,* **Kundenstromanalyse** *f,* **Kundenfrequenzanalyse** *f*) *(market res)* customer flow analysis, customer flow investigation, store traffic analysis, store traffic investigation
   The analysis of the flow of customers into and throughout a store. Placement of merchandise in various store areas must take into account the natural and the desired pattern of customer movement to and from these areas.

Kundenlayout *n* comprehensive layout, comprehensive, comp
   An advertising layout with illustration and lettering done almost as expertly as in finished art, complete in detail, with component parts accurately proportioned, copy scaled and measured, photostats of artwork and illustrations pasted in position, for presentation to the client.

Kundenmanagement *n (advtsg/ marketing)* account management

Kunden-Netto *n (advtsg)* net cost, net, net plus
   The amount of a bill made to an advertising agency client after the deduction of all applicable discounts, (→) Rabatt, but before the agency commission, (→) Agenturprovision, is added.

Kundenplazierung *f (retailing)* customer spotting

Kundenprofil *n (market res)* customer profile
   The demographic and socioeconomic description of a company's customers.

Kundenrabatt *m*
→ Rabatt

Kundenservice m
→ Kundendienst
Kundenstromanalyse f
→ Kundenlaufanalyse
Kundenstruktur f *(market res)* customer structure, customer characteristics *pl*
→ Kundenprofil
Kundentreue f
→ Geschäftstreue, Ladentreue, Markentreue, Produkttreue
Kundentyp m *(market res)* customer type, type of customer
Kundentypologie f *(market res)* customer typology, typology of customers
Kundenverhalten n customer behavior, *brit* customer behaviour, client behavior, *brit* client behaviour
Kundenwerbung f
→ Publikumswerbung
Kundenzeitschrift f customer magazine, external house organ, customers' free magazine, customers' free journal, *auch* shopping news, sales bulletin, buyer's guide, buyers' guide
A publication issued periodically by a business company to further its own interests with actual and prospective customers or others outside the company, to maintain ties with customers and to establish or stabilize loyalty.
Kundenzeitschriften Leseranalyse f **(KLA)** Readership Analysis of Customer Magazines
Kundenzeitung f customer newspaper, external house organ, customers' free paper, *auch* shopping news, sales bulletin
→ Kundenzeitschrift
Kundenzufriedenheit f customer satisfaction, buyer satisfaction, (nach dem Kauf) postdecisional satisfaction, post-buy satisfaction
→ Konsumentenzufriedenheit
Kundenzuschrift f
→ Anerkennungsschreiben
Kunstabteilung f
→ graphische Abteilung
Kunstdruck m art print
Kunstdruckabzug m **(Abzug** m **auf Kunstdruckpapier, Bildandruck** m**)** *(print)* art pull

Kunstdruckkarton m art board, coated board, (doppelt gestrichen) cast-coated board
→ Bristolkarton
Kunstdruckpapier n art printing paper, art paper, (matt) art mat paper, art matt paper, art matte paper, art mat, art matt, art matte
Kunstgewerbeschule f **(Kunstschule** f, **Kunstfachschule** f**)** art school
Kunsthochschule f **(Kunstfachhochschule** f**)** arts college
Kunstharz m synthetic resin
Kunstharzlack m synthetic resin varnish
Künstler m
→ Graphiker, Gebrauchsgraphiker, Gestalter, Designer, Layouter, Illustrator, Photograph
Künstlerabzug m *(print)* artist's proof
Künstleragentur f talent agency, art representative
An agency for a studio, a group, or an individual artist or photographer.
Künstlerdruck m fine-art print, artist's print
künstlerische Gestaltung f
→ Gestaltung
künstliche Veralterung f
→ geplante Obsoleszenz
Kunstlicht n *(phot/film/TV)* artificial light, tungsten light
Kunstlichtemulsion f *(phot)* emulsion for artificial light, artificial light emulsion
Kunstlichtfilm m *(phot)* artificial light film
Kunstlichtfilter m **(Korrekturfilter** m**)** *(phot)* artificial light filter
Kunststoffeinband m
→ Plastikeinband
Kunststoffklischee n
→ Plastikklischee
Kunststoffmater f
→ Plastikmater
Kunststoffstereo n
→ Plastikstereo
Kunststoffstereotypie f
→ Plastikstereotypie
Kunstwort n **(Phantasiemarke** f**)** *(branding)* arbitrary mark, coined word
→ Kombinationszeichen
Kunstzeitschrift f art magazine, fine-art magazine
Kupferätzung f *(print)* copper etching, engraving on copper

Both the act of etching line and halftone images in relief on copper and the copper plate, (→) Kupferplatte, so etched.

Kupferautotypie f *(print)* copper halftone
A halftone, (→) Autotypie, with a fine screen, (→) Raster, on a copper plate, (→) Kupferplatte.

Kupferdruck m **1.** (Verfahren) copperplate printing, copperplate printing, plate printing, intaglio printing, copperplate engraving
The process of intaglio printing, (→) Tiefdruck, in which ink is transferred to the paper from depressions etched into a copper plate. The ink on the completed job appears intense in color, and stands out from the surface of the paper or card.
→ Kupfertiefdruck
2. (Produkt) copper-plate print, copperplate print, intaglio print

Kupferdrucker m copper-plate printer, copperplate printer

Kupferdruckpapier n plate paper, copperplatte paper, etching paper
→ Tiefdruckpapier

Kupferdruckpresse f copper-plate press, copperplate press, copper-plate printing press, copperplate printing press, rolling press

Kupferemailverfahren n *(print)* copper enamel process

Kupferhaut f **(Kupferhäutchen** n) *(print)* galvanic shell, electro shell, copper shell

kupfern (abkupfern) *colloq* v/t to crib
→ plagiieren

Kupferplatte f *(print)* copperplate, copper plate, plate
An engraved die made of copper and used as a printing plate, (→) Druckplatte, for copper-plate printing.

Kupferstechen n *(print)* copperplate engraving, copper engraving, engraving on copper

Kupferstecher m *(print)* copperplate engraver, engraver, burinist, chalcographer, chalcographist

Kupferstich m *(print)* copperplate engraving, engraving, copper engraving, copperplate printing, copperplate

Kupfertiefdruck m
→ Flachbettiefdruck, Rotationstiefdruck, Rakeltiefdruck

Kupfertiefdruckbeilage f
→ Tiefdruckbeilage

Kupon m **(Gutschein** m, **Coupon** m) *(advtsg)* coupon
A detachable part of a publication advertisement, a product wrapper, container, or label, designed to encourage consumers to return it to the advertiser or his representative, sometimes by providing a reduction in the regular price or by giving the product or a sample thereof away free of charge, to purchase the product or to secure a premium. In a wider sense, any certificate exchangeable for a premium, (→) Zugabe.

Kuponanzeige f **(Couponanzeige** f, **Gutscheinanzeige** f) coupon advertisement, coupon ad
→ Kupon

Kuponausschneiden n
→ Gutscheinausschneiden

Kuponblock m
→ Gutscheinblock

Kuponeinlösung f
→ Gutscheineinlösung

Kuponeinlösungsverhalten n
→ Gutscheineinlösungsverhalten

Kuponrücklauf m
→ Gutscheinrücklauf

Kupon-Test m **(Coupon-Test** m) *(res)* coupon test
→ Anfragenkontrolltest

Kuponwerbung f **(Gutscheinwerbung** f, **Coupon-Werbung** f) coupon advertising, couponing
The use of coupons, (→) Kupon, in the promotion of a product or a service or in advertising.

Kuppler m
→ Farbkuppler

kursiv *adj (typ)* italic, Italic

Kursive f **(Kursivschrift** f) *(typ)* italic type, Italic type, (Satzanweisung) in italics, itals *pl*
A variation of a Roman typeface that is slanted to the right.

Kursivsatz m **(Kursivdruck** m) *(typ)* italic print

kursiv setzen (kursiv drucken) v/t *(typ)* to italicize

Kurtosis f
→ Wölbung

Kurve f *(stat)* curve

Kurvendiagramm n **(Kurvengraphik** f)
→ Liniendiagramm

kurvilinear *adj (stat)* curvilinear

kurvilineare Aktivierungshypothese f
→ umgekehrte u-Hypothese

kurvilineare Korrelation f (nicht-lineare Korrelation f) *(stat)* curvilinear correlation
kurvilineare Regression f (nichtlineare Regression f) *(stat)* curvilinear regression
kurvilinearer Trend m (nichtlinearer Trend m) *(stat)* curvilinear trend
Kurzansage f (**Kurzwerbesendung** f, **Kurzeinblendung** f) *(radio/film/TV)* short announcement, pop-in, *auch* filmlet, minute movie, short film, quickie
kurze Brennweite f *(phot)* short focus, short focal length
kürzen v/t (Text) to abridge, to cut, to cut down, to shorten
Kurzfassung f (**Kurzversion** f) short version, abridged version
Kurzfilm m short film, short, *auch* filmlet, minute movie, quickie
kurzlebige Gebrauchsgüter n/pl *(econ)* nondurable consumer goods *pl*, nondurables *pl*, orange goods *pl*
   Any goods that are consumed and replaced at moderate rates; ususally they are in fairly broad distribution, require moderate service, and have a moderate to good gross margin (e.g., dress clothing).
kurzlebige Konsumgüter n/pl *(econ)* nondurable consumer goods *pl*, nondurables *pl*, red goods *pl*
   Goods that are consumed immediately and, therefore, replaced at fast rates.
   vgl. langlebige Konsumgüter
Kurznachricht f news flash
Kurznachrichten f/pl news summary, news headlines *pl*, news flash
Kurzspielfilm m short feature film, short film, short
Kurz-Spot m *(TV)* quickie
Kurztitel m short title
Kurzwelle f (**KW**) short wave
Kurzwellensender m short-wave transmitter, high-frequency transmitter
Kurzwerbefilm m advertising filmlet, advertising minute movie
Kurzzeittest m *(market res)* short-exposure test
Kustode f catchword, catch word
   → Stichwort
Kustos m catch word, catch word, catchline, catch line
   A guideline or slugline used to identify a story before the type is set in page form.
   → Stichzeile
Kybernetik f cybernetics *pl* *(construed as sg)*
kybernetisches Modell n cybernetic model
kybernetisches System n cybernetic system

L

L-Form-Anzeige f (**L-förmige Anzeige** f) L-shaped advertisement, L-shaped ad
LA f abbr Leseranalyse
LA Kinderpresse f abbr Leseranalyse Kinderpresse
LA-Med f abbr Leseranalyse medizinischer Zeitschriften
Labor n (**Laboratorium** n) (res) laboratory, colloq lab
Laborbeobachtung f (**Laboratoriumsbeobachtung** f) (res) laboratory observation
→ Laborexperiment
Laborexperiment n (**Laboratoriumsexperiment** n) (res) laboratory experiment
  A type of controlled experiment, (→) kontrolliertes Experiment, in which the experimenter (investigator) creates the entire experimental situation, thus enabling him to determine and manipulate the experimental conditions as required.
Labortest m (**Laboratoriumstest** m, **Laborversuch** m) (res) laboratory test, studio test, auditorium test, in-theater test, theater test, hall test
  A product or advertising test designed as a laboratory experiment, (→) Laborexperiment.
Lack m lacquer, varnish, enamel, dope
Lackfarbe f (print) lacquer ink
lackieren v/t (print) to lacquer, to varnish
Lackieren n (**Lackierung** f) (print) lacquering, varnishing, doping
  The process or result of coating applied to a surface of a finished printed job for protectiveness as well as improving the appearance.
Lade f
→ Heftlade
Laden m (**Geschäft** n) (retailing) store, shop
  A business establishment into which customers and prospects are invited to visit and to select purchases.
Ladenaufseher m (retailing) (im Warenhaus) floorwalker, brit shopwalker

A store security officer who usually mixes with customers trying to spot shoplifters.
Ladenausstattung f (retailing) store layout, store design, store atmosphere
  The architectural character, equipment or decorative style and atmosphere of a retail store including the allocation and arrangement of space to each selling and nonselling department.
Ladenbau m (retailing) store construction
Ladenbeobachtung f (market res) store observation, shop observation, in-store observation
Ladenbesitzer m (**Ladeninhaber** m, **Geschäftsinhaber** m) (retailing) storekeeper, brit shopkeeper
Ladendesign n (**Ladengestaltung** f) (retailing) store design, brit shop design
Ladeneinrichtung f (retailing) store fittings pl, store equipment, brit shop fittings pl, shop equipment, store fixtures pl
Ladenfenster n
→ Schaufenster
Ladenfront f (retailing) store front, brit shop front
Ladenfunk m (retailing) storecasting
  Broadcasting, or to be more accurate, narrowcasting, (→) Netzfunk, at the point-or-purchase, usually offering music and news as well as commercials.
Ladengemeinschaft f
→ Gemeinschaftswarenhaus
Ladengeschäft n (retailing) store, retail store, shop, retail shop
→ Geschäft
Ladengestaltung f
→ Ladendesign
Ladenhandel m (**seßhafter Handel** m, **stationärer Handel** m) (econ) store trade, retail trade, store business, store retailing, shop trade, stationary trade
Ladenhüter m (retailing) shelf warmer, deadwood, dead stock, sticker
  An item in the inventory of a store for which there is no demand.
Ladenimage n (**Geschäftsimage** n) (retailing) store image

The way in which a store is defined in shoppers' minds partly by its functional qualities and partly by its aura of psychological attributes. It is thus defined as the total conceptualized or expected reinforcement that an individual associates with shopping at a particular store.
Ladeninhaber m
→ Geschäftsinhaber
Ladenkasse f **(Registrierkasse** f**)** *(retailing)* cash register
Ladenlayout n **(Geschäftslayout** n**)** *(retailing)* store layout, *brit* shop layout
→ Ladenausstattung
Ladenöffnungszeit f **(Geschäftsöffnungszeit** f**)** *(retailing)* store opening time, opening time, business hours *pl*
Ladenpreis m **(Einzelhandelspreis** m, **Endverbraucherpreis** m**)** retail price, consumer price, (Listenreis) list price, (Zeitschriften) cover price, single-copy price
   The basic recommended or actual price without allowance for any possible discounts.
Ladenschild n *(POP advtsg)* store sign, shop sign, sign, signboard, *colloq* shingle
Ladenschluß m **(Ladenschlußzeit** f**)** *(retailing)* store closing time, closing time, shop closing time
Ladensendung f **(Ladenfunk** m**)** storecast
→ Ladenfunk
Ladentest m **(Ladenbeobachtung** f**)** *(market res)* store test, in-store test
   Any test that is carried out in a retail outlet, e.g. comparing the level of consumer sales resulting from different pricing policies, the effect of merchandising material, or packaging, or brand names.
Ladentheke f **(Ladentisch** m**)** *(retailing)* store counter, counter
Ladentischauslage f **(Thekenauslage** f**)** *(POP advtsg)* counter display, counter display piece, counter dispenser
Ladentreue f **(Geschäftstreue** f, **Ladenloyalität** f, **Geschäftsloyalität** f**)** *(retailing)* store loyalty, single-store loyalty
   A type of store-customer relationship that is characterized by giving customers reasons to keep coming back to a store, gaining their confidence and establishing good rapport, so that customers are more likely to patronize the store.
Ladenverkauf m
→ Ladenhandel
Ladenverschleiß m *(retailing)* store erosion
Ladenwerbung f
→ POP-Werbung
LAE f *abbr* Leseranalyse Entscheidungsträger in Wirtschaft und Verwaltung
lädiert *adj* → beschädigt
Lag n *(stat)* lag
Lag-Korrelation f *(stat)* lag correlation
Lag-Regression f *(stat)* lag regression
Lage f **1.** → Standort **2.** (Papier) quire, (Pappe) ply, layer **3.** (bookbinding) section, gathering
Lageparameter m **(lagetypischer Mittelwert** m, **Mittelwert** m **der Lage)** *(stat)* parameter of location, location parameter, parameter of central tendency
Lageplan m site plan, layout plan
→ Standortskizze
Lager n *(econ)* **1.** (Vorrat) stock, store, supplies *pl* **2.** (Gebäude) warehouse, storehouse, storage room, stock room
Lagerbestand m
→ Lager 1.
Lagerbestandsaufnahme f *(econ)* stocktaking, stock inventory, inventory, stock audit
   The process and procedure of physical or manual counting of trading stock.
Lagerbestellung f **(Lagerauftrag** m**)** *(econ)* stock order
Lagerdauer f *(econ)* (im Einzelhandel) shelf life
   The length of time that is generally accepted as the maximum that a certain product may remain in stock before serious enough deterioration takes place that the product should not be sold.
Lager-Discounter m *(econ)* warehouse discounter
Lagerergänzung f *(econ)* warehouse replenishment
Lagergeschäft n **(Lagerhandelsgeschäft** n**)** *(retailing)* warehouse store, box store
   A stripped-down retail food operation offering a limited assortment at discount prices mainly of foods obtained from producers on special deals. Items are often stacked on the floor in original cut-open boxes.

Lagerhaltung f *(econ)* storage, stockkeeping, warehouse policy
　The marketing function that involves holding goods between the time of their production and their final sale. It is characterized by the creation of time utility by holding and preserving goods for varying periods of time. Storage is inherent in all goods handling except in those few instances where the item is put into its next use immediately upon being produced.
Lagerhandel m *(econ)* warehouse selling, store retailing
　vgl. Streckengeschäft
Lagerhaus n
　→ Lager 2.
Lagerkosten pl **(Lagerhaltungskosten** pl) *(econ)* warehouse charges pl, warehouse expenses pl, storage charges pl, storage expenses pl, cost(s) *(pl)* of storage
lagern v/t *(econ)* to stock, to store
Lagerpolitik f **(Lagerhaltungspolitik** f) *(econ)* storage policy, stockkeeping policy, warehouse policy
　→ Lagerhaltung
Lagerraum m *(econ)* stock room, storage room, store room
Lagerschein m *(econ)* warehouse receipt
　A receipt given by a warehouseman to the owner of goods deposited in the warehouse.
Lagerstatistik f *(econ)* inventory statistics pl *(construed as sg)*
Lagerumschlag m **(Lagerumschlagshäufigkeit** f, **Lagerumschlagsgeschwindigkeit** f) *(econ)* stock rotation, speed of stock rotation, frequency of stock rotation, warehouse replenishment, warehouse replenishment time,
　The rapidity with which items sold from a warehouse can be replaced from the factory.
　(retailing) stockturn
　The rate at which trading stock is sold and replaced.
Lagerung f
　→ Lagerhaltung
Lagerwirtschaft f
　→ Lagerhandel, Lagerhandelspolitik;
　vgl. Streckenhandel
Lagerzyklus m *(econ)* stock cycle, storage cycle
lagetypischer Mittelwert m
　→ Lageparameter

Lahiri-Verfahren n *(stat)* Lahiri procedure, Lahiri sampling, Lahiri multi-phase sampling
Laienwerbung f
　→ Publikumswerbung
Laienwerber m
　→ Sammelbesteller
Lambda-Koeffizient m **(Guttmans Lambda** n) *(stat)* lambda coefficient, lambda, Goodman and Kruskal's lambda, coefficient of predictability
laminieren v/t *(print)* to laminate
　To coat a printed sheet of paper with acetate or cellophane to impart a high gloss or soil-resistant quality.
Laminiermaschine f **(Glanzfolienkaschiermaschine** f) *(print)* laminating machine
laminiert (glanzfolienkaschiert) adj *(print)* laminated
　→ laminieren
laminiertes Papier n **(glanzfolienkaschiertes Papier** n) laminated paper
　→ laminieren
Laminierung f **(Glanzfolienkaschierung** f) *(print)* lamination
　→ laminieren
Lampe f **(Beleuchtungslampe** f) lamp
Lampenfieber n *(film/TV)* stage fright
Landfunk m *(radio/TV)* agricultural broadcasting program, brit programme, agricultural program, farm program
Landfunksendung f *(radio/TV)* agricultural broadcast, agricultural program, brit programme, farmers' broadcast, farmers' broadcast, farmers' program, brit programme
Landhandel m *(econ)* agricultural trade, farm trade, rural trade
ländlicher Rundfunksender m *(radio/TV)* rural broadcasting station, rural station
landwirtschaftliche Fachzeitschrift f agricultural journal, farm journal, agricultural publication, farm publication, agricultural periodical, farm periodical
landwirtschaftliche Zeitschrift f agricultural magazine, farm magazine, farmers' magazine
landwirtschaftliche Zeitung f agricultural newspaper, agricultural paper, farm paper, farm newspaper
Landwirtschaftsmarketing n **(Agrarmarketing** n) agricultural marketing

Länge f length
→ Filmlänge
lange Brennweite f *(phot)* long focus, long focal length
Langformat n **(Längsformat** n, **längliches Format** n, **rechteckiges Format** n) *(phot/print)* oblong size, *auch* portrait format, hypotenuse
A size with width greater than depth. *vgl.* Querformat
langfristige Reaktion f
→ Wirkungsverzögerung
langlebiges Konsumgut n
→ Gebrauchsgut
Langsamverkehr n **(langsam vorbeifließender Verkehr** m) *(outdoor advtsg)* slow travel
Längsbahn f **(Schmalbahn** f) *(paper)* long grain
Längslinie f
→ senkrechte Linie
Langspielplatte f **(LP)** long-playing record (LP), long play disc
Längsrichtung f
→ Längsbahn
Längsschnitt m longitudinal section *vgl.* Querschnitt
Längsschnittanalyse f **(Langzeitstudie** f, **Langzeituntersuchung** f, **Longitudinalstudie** f) *(res)* longitudinal analysis, longitudinal study, longitudinal investigation
The analysis and study of one or more variables over time in order to determine change or stability. The variable(s) may be undergoing experimental manipulation by the investigator or it (they) may be experiencing certain changes in its natural setting.
→ Kohortenanalyse, Zeitreihenanalyse, Trendanalyse, Panel, Quasi-Panel; *vgl.* Querschnittanalyse
Langwelle f **(LW)** *(electr.)* long wave (LW), low frequency (LF), kilometric waves *pl*
vgl. Kurzwelle, Mittelwelle
Langwellenbereich m *(electr.)* long-wave band, low-frequency band
Langwellensender m *(electr.)* long-wave transmitter, low-frequency transmitter
lasieren v/t *(print)* to glaze
Lasierfarbe f **(Lasurfarbe** f, **Lasurlack** m) *(print)* glazing color, *brit* glazing colour, transparent ink, clear varnish, transparent color, *brit* transparent colour

Laspeyre-Index m **(Laspeyrescher Index** m) *(econ)* Laspeyre's index, Laspeyre index
A type of index number which, if the prices of a set of commodities in a base period are p_o, p_o', p_o'', etc. and those in a given period p_n, p_n', p_n'', etc.; and if q_o, q_o', q_o'' are the quantities sold in the base period, is written

$$I_{on} = \frac{\sum(p_n q_o)}{\sum(p_o q_o)},$$

where the summation takes place over commodities, i.e. the prices are weighted by quantities in the base period.
Lassoband n *(film)* camera tape, adhesive tape, gaffer tape
A strong, extremely adhesive aluminized-surface, pressure-sensitive tape for temporary set rigging.
Lasswell-Formel f *(communication)* Lasswell formula (Harold D. Lasswell)
The postulate that for every communication process an answer must be given to the question: "Who says what to whom and with which effect."
Lasur f *(print)* glaze
lateinisches Quadrat n *(test theory)* Latin square, (experimentelle Anlage mit lateinischen Quadraten) Latin square design
A type of experimental design which aims at removing from the experimental error the variation from two sources, which may be identified with the rows and columns of the square. The allocation of k experimental treatments in the cells is such that each treatment occurs once in each row or column. A design for a 5 × 5 square with five treatments, A, B, C, D and E would be:

A	B	C	D	E
B	A	E	C	D
C	D	A	E	B
D	E	B	A	C
E	C	D	B	A

Latensifikation f *(phot)* latensification
The process of increasing the sensitivity of a photographic emulsion after exposure.
latente Nachfrage f *(econ)* latent demand
→ latenter Bedarf
latente Strukturanalyse f **(Skalierung** f **latenter Strukturen)** *(res)* latent structure analysis (Paul F. Lazarsfeld/Samuel A. Stouffer)

latenter Bedarf

A procedure that is designed to ascertain the structure of attitudes or other unobservable entities that can only be observed through their probabilistic connection with observed data.

latenter Bedarf m **(Erschließungsbedarf** m) *(econ)* latent demand, hidden demand, unsought goods *pl*
A situation in which a significant segment of a market exhibits a preference for a product which is not being offered.

latentes Bedürfnis n *(econ)* latent need

latentes Bild n *(phot)* latent image, latent picture
The image existing on an exposed film before it is developed.

latentes Kontinuum n latent continuum

Latte f *(studio)* lath, batten, strip board

Laufbild n
→ Filmbild

Lauf-Dia n
→ Film-Dia

laufende Erhebung f
→ kontinuierliche Erhebung

laufende Kosten pl *(advtsg)* below-the-line-cost

laufender Kolumnentitel m *(print)* running head
The title of a magazine, a magazine section, or a book printed at the head of each page.

laufendes Heft n **(aktuelles Heft** n, **laufende Ausgabe** f) (Zeitschrift) current issue

Laufgeschwindigkeit f **(Filmgeschwindigkeit** f) film speed, operation speed, running speed, speed
The standard operating speed or acknowledged variations therefrom for film, tape, or disc in the recording and reproducing of scenes and sound.

Laufkran m *(film/TV)* overhead crane, mobile hoist

Laufkunde m *(retailing)* chance customer, chance buyer, transient customer, transient buyer
vgl. Stammkunde

Laufkundschaft f *(retailing)* chance customers *pl*, chance buyers *pl*, transient business, transient customers *pl*, transient buyers *pl*

Laufrichtung f *(paper)* grain of paper, grain direction, paper grain, grain, machine direction
In machine-made paper, the predominant direction of the fibers. Paper is stronger across the grain and folds more easily with the grain.

Laufrolle f guide roller, idler

Laufschiene f guide rail, track

Lauftitel m *(TV/film)* crawl, creeping title, rolling title
The drum or scroll-mounted program credits or titles the position of which can be continuously altered in printing on successive frames, usually by being superimposed over a picture, thus creating a creeping title.

Laufwerk n *(phot/film)* transport mechanism, drive mechanism

Laufzeit f **1.** (Werbung) advertising time, advertising period, (bei Plakatwerbung) posting period **2.** *(film/TV)* screen time, running time, length, duration, (Signal) delay time, phase delay **3.** (eines Vertrags) contract period

Laut m sound, tone

Lautarchiv n
→ Geräuscharchiv

lauterer Wettbewerb m fair competition, fair trade

Lauterkeit f **in der Werbung** fair practice in advertising

Lautsprecher m loudspeaker

Lautsprecheranlage f loudspeaker system, public address system (P.A. system)

Lautsprecheranordnung f loudspeaker layout

Lautsprecherbox f loudspeaker case, loudspeaker box

Lautsprecherschallwand f
→ Schallwand

Lautsprecherübertragungsanlage f
→ Lautsprecheranlage

Lautsprecherwagen m sound truck

Lautsprecherwagenwerbung f sound truck advertising, mobile advertising

Lautstärke f sound volume, sound intensity, volume

Lautstärkemesser m volume indicator, sound level meter

Lautstärkenregler m **(LR)** **(Potentiometer** n) potentiometer, volume control, *colloq* pot

Lautstärkepegel m sound level, volume level

Lautstärkeregelung f volume control, sound volume control

Lautstärkeumfang m volume range, dynamic range, loudness range

Lavallier-Mikrofon n **(Lavallier-Mikrophon** n) lavalier microphone, lanyard microphone
A microphone that is hung around the neck, leaving a performer's or speaker's hands free.
Lavendel m **(Lavendelkopie** f)
→ Duplikatpositiv
Lavidge-Steiner-Modell n **der Werbewirkung**
→ Hierarchy-of-effects-Modell
lavierte Strichzeichnung f **(kombinierte Strich- und Tuschezeichnung** f, **aquarellierte Strichzeichnung** f) line and wash drawing
→ aquarellierte Strichzeichnung
Lawinensystem n
→ Schneeballverfahren
Layout n layout, makeup
The arrangement of type and plates in page form for printing. Also, the arrangement of advertising and editorial material for the page of a publication.
Layouter m layout man, layouter, make-up man, makeup man, maker-up
The person responsible for the arrangement of typographic and illustrative elements on a printed piece as an advertisement or a complete magazine.
Layoutpapier n **(durchsichtiges Layoutpapier** n) layout paper
A translucent paper used to superimpose different versions of a sketch until a satisfactory design is produced.
Layoutskizze f *(print)* visual, visualization
A preliminary rough sketch showing a variety of ways in which elements in the makeup of a page or an advertisement can be arranged.
Layout-Test m *(advtsg res)* layout test, makeup test, make-up test
Layout-Typograph m *(print)* layout typographer
Layoutzeichner(in) m(f) *(print)* layouter, layout man, draftsman, draftswoman, *brit auch* draughtsman, draughtswoman
Leaderfilm m
→ Vorspannfilm
Leader-Panel n *(market res)* leader panel
Leased-department-Prinzip n *(retailing)* leased department principle, concession principle
The principle of leasing a business operated within the physical space of another business, usually on a rental agreement based on sales.
Leasing n *(econ)* leasing
A business practice whereby a firm may acquire the use of equipment or other plant without the necessity of purchasing it.
lebende Kolumne f **(lebender Kolumnentitel** m)
→ laufender Kolumnentitel
Lebensdauer f **1.** *(econ)* (eines Produkts) product life, entire life
→ Produktlebenszyklus
2. *(media res)* (Zeitschrift/Zeitung) issue life, entire life
The length of time it takes a publication to reach a maximum measurable audience. Research institutes measure an issue's total audience after the publication has been in circulation long enough for most of its readers to have seen it, but before enough time has elapsed for them to forget it. The issue life of a weekly is considered to be five weeks and that of a monthly about 10 to 12 weeks.
Lebenshaltungskosten pl **(Lebenshaltungskostenindex** m)
→ Preisindex für die Lebenshaltung
Lebenshilfezeitschrift f **(Lebenshilfepublikation** f) service magazine, service publication
Lebensmittelanzeige f food advertisement, food ad
Lebensmitteleinzelhandel m
1. (Institution) food retail trade, food retailers pl **2.** (Funktion) food retailing
Lebensmitteleinzelhandelswerbung f food retail trade advertising, food retail advertising
Lebensmitteleinzelhändler m food store detailer, food detailer, food store, grocery, grocer
Lebensmittelgesetz n **(Gesetz** n **zur Neuordnung und Bereinigung des Rechts im Verkehr mit Lebensmitteln, Tabakerzeugnissen, kosmetischen Mitteln und sonstigen Bedarfsgegenständen)** German Food, Drug and Cosmetic Act
Lebensmittelpackung f food package, food pack
Lebensmittel-SB-Laden m **(Lebensmittelselbstbedienungsladen** m) *(retailing)* food self-service store, food self-service shop

Lebensmittel-SB-Markt m (**Lebensmittelselbstbedienungsmarkt** m)
→ Lebensmittel-SB-Laden
Lebensmittelwerbung f food advertising, foodstuff advertising
Lebensphase f
→ Familien-Lebenszyklus (Familienzyklus)
Lebensqualität f quality of life, life quality
Lebensstandard m *(econ)* standard of living
  For an individual or household, the availability of goods and services within his income; for a community, the quality of life related to its income and wealth.
Lebensstil m *(econ)* life style
  The characteristic mode of living in its broadest sense of a household or an individual, a segment of or the whole of a society, especially as it is concerned with those unique qualities which distinguish one group or culture from others.
Lebensstilanalyse f (**Lebensstilstudie** f, **Lebensstiluntersuchung** f) *(market res)* life-style analysis, life-style study, life-style investigation
→ Lebensstil
Lebenszyklus m
→ Familien-Lebenszyklus, Produktlebenszyklus
leer (unbedruckt) adj *(print)* blank
Leerband n blank tape, clean tape
Leerbandteil m yellow
Leerblatt n (**leere Seite** f, **unbedruckte Seite** f) *(print)* blank leaf, blank sheet
Leerinterviews n/pl
→ Überrepräsentation, Überquote
Leermuster n
→ Blindmuster
Leerpackung f dummy package, dummy
→ Attrappe
Leerzeile f *(print)* white line, blank line
  A line of unprinted space, usually between paragraphs.
Legende f legend
  A piece of descriptive writing used as a picture caption or the explanation of symbols on a map or chart.
Legetrick m (**Schiebetrick** m) (Trickfilm) mechanical animation, limited animation
  Animation by the actual movement of drawings.

Lehrfernsehen n (**Fernsehuniversität** f, **Funkuniversität** f) educational television, educational TV, ETV, E.T.V.
Lehrfilm m instructional film, educational film, nontheatrical film
Leiche f *colloq* 1. *(typ)* out 2. (Briefwerbung) *colloq* nixie, nix
leichte Unterhaltung f (**leichte Unterhaltungsmusik** f) easy listening
leichtes Streifleinen n *(bookbinding)* art canvass
Leim m glue, mucilage, paste, (Papierleim) size
leimen v/t to glue, to paste, (Papier) to size
Leimpresse f size press
Leimung f (**Leimen** n) gluing, glueing, pasting, (Papier) sizing
Leinen n (**Leinwand** f) *(bookbinding)* cloth, bookcloth, linen
→ Leinenpapier
Leineneinband m *(bookbinding)* cloth binding
Leinenkarton m *(bookbinding)* cloth-lined board
leinenkaschiert adj *(bookbinding)* cloth-lined
Leinenpapier n (**Leinwandpapier** n) *(bookbinding)* linen paper, linen finish, cloth-lined paper, reinforced paper
  A paper finished with a surface similar to linen.
Leinwand f 1. *(film)* screen 2. *(print)* → Leinen
Leipziger Schule f
→ Ganzheitslehre (Ganzheitspsychologie)
Leiste f *(print)* 1. border, flourish, flower 2. → Kopfleiste, Fußleiste
Leistenanzeige f
→ Streifenanzeige
Leistungsmotivation f *(psy)* achievement motivation, motivation to achieve (David C. McClelland)
  The sociopsychological explanation of human behavior as dependent for its motivational strength on the expectation that the activity will produce a particular consequence of recognized benefit to the individual while at the same time avoiding negative consequences.
Leitartikel m editorial column, column, *brit* leading article, leader
leitartikeln v/i to editorialize, *brit* to editorialise
  To express an opinion in an editorial column or to write an editorial column.

Leitartikler *m* **(Leitartikelschreiber** *m*) editorial writer, editorialist, *brit* leader writer, leader-writer
Leitbild *n (psy)* model, (Person) model person, model, (Leitbildgruppe) model group
  A person or group either imitated or regarded as a reference, (→) Bezugsperson, (→) Bezugsgruppe, or an ideal or value.
Leitbildmarketing *n* model marketing
Leitbildwerbung *f* model advertising
Leiter *m* **1.** (eines Unternehmens, einer Agentur) manager, managing director, head **2.** (einer Abteilung) head (of a department, department head) **3.** → Leiterskala
Leiter *m* **der Textabteilung**
→ Cheftexter
Leiterfrage *f* **(Leiterskalenfrage** *f,* **Leiterskala** *f*) *(survey res)* ladder question, ladder scale question, ladder scale (Hadley Cantril)
Leitfaden *m* **1.** (Handbuch) manual, guiding manual, guide, guide book, handbook, (Lehrbuch) textbook **2.** → Interviewleitfaden
Leitfadengespräch *n* **(Leitfadeninterview** *n*) *(survey res)* directed interview, directed conversation → halbstrukturiertes Interview
Leitpunkte *m/pl (typ)* leaders *pl, auch* ellipsis
  A series of dots or dashes used to guide the reader's eye across a page, or from one part of an advertisement to another. Also, a series of three or four periods used to indicate omission of words, or to carry emphasis over to the succeeding words.
Leitstudie *f* **(Pilotstudie** *f,* **Vorstudie** *f*) *(res)* pilot study, pilot survey, pilot test, exploratory study, pre-survey, test-tube survey
  A preliminary, small-scale research investigation conducted for the purpose of providing information intended to improve the planned large-scale study, testing and perfecting research technique and questionnaire, etc.
Leontieff-Modell *n*
→ Input-Output-Analyse
Leporellofalz *m* **(Leporellofalzung** *f,* **Zickzackfalz** *m*) accordion fold, accordion folding, concertina fold, concertina folding, natural fold, natural folding

  A zigzag, accordion-like fold in a sheet of material, permitting it to be extended to its full breadth with a single pull.
Lerneffekt *m* (des Befragten)
→ Ausstrahlungseffekt
Lernen *n (psy)* learning
Lernkurve *f (psy)* learning curve, curve of learning
Lernprozeß *m (psy)* learning process
Lernpsychologie *f* **(Psychologie** *f* **des Lernens)** learning psychology, psychology of learning
Lerntheorie *f* **(Theorie** *f* **des Lernens)** *(psy)* learning theory, theory of learning
Lesbarkeit *f* **(Verständlichkeit** *f*) readability, reading ease
  The ease with which a particular piece of printed communication is understood and read by an audience.
Lesbarkeitstest *m (media res)* readability test, reading ease test
  A test technique intended to help editors and publishers judge the difficulty of a particular piece of printed communication and to estimate the type and size of audiences that can readily understand the message. It is a technique to test those factors of writing style that can be measured to check the complexity of writing and increase the probability of comprehension for specific audiences, e.g., sentence length, long words, familiar words, abstract words, personal references, strong verb forms, simple sentences, etc.
Leseanreiz *m* reading incentive, incentive
Lesebeobachtung *f* **(Beobachtung** *f* **des Leseverhaltens)** *(media res)* observation of reading behavior, *brit* behaviour, reading observation
Lesedauer *f* **(Lesezeit** *f*) *(media res)* time spent reading, reading time
  The amount of time that a particular magazine's audience devotes to reading the issue. It is useful as a guide in establishing relative intensity or thoroughness of reading, and many monthlies have a market superiority over weeklies in this respect.
Lesefrequenz *f*
→ Lesehäufigkeit
Lesegeschwindigkeit *f (media res)* speed of reading, reading speed
Lesehäufigkeit *f* **(Häufigkeit** *f* **des Lesens, Lesefrequenz** *f*) *(media res)* frequency of reading, reading frequency, frequency

Leseintensität

The estimate of the frequency of exposure to a printed publication, (→) Kontakt, (→) Lesen. Measurement techniques include verbal frequency scales or categories ("How often do you read or skim through ...?"), numerical frequency scales or categories, mixtures of both, and recognition, (→) Wiedererkennung, of a series of publications.
→ Nutzungshäufigkeit, Kontakthäufigkeit

Leseintensität f (Nutzungsintensität f) *(media res)* intensity of reading, reading intensity, thoroughness of reading, reading thoroughness
The intensity and thoroughness of reading a publication are vital indicators of advertising effectiveness or interest in a publication. However, from a research point of view, measurement of thoroughness often causes problems.

Lesemappe f (Lesezirkelmappe f) *etwa* magazine portfolio, magazine folder
→ Lesezirkel

Lesen n reading, act of reading
→ Leser

Leseort m *(media res)* place of reading, reading place
The location at which a publication is read, be it at home (which is rated as an indication of thoroughness of reading and an extended time of reading, (→) Lesedauer) or away from home, e.g. in waiting rooms, airplanes, etc.

Lesephase f *(media res)* phase of reading, stage of reading, reading phase, reading stage

Leseprobe f *(film/TV)* read-through, first reading, reading
A preliminary reading aloud of a script by a cast of performers before actual rehearsals.

Leser m *(media res)* reader
In audience research, any person who says in a readership survey interview that he or she was exposed to a publication or a part thereof, regardless whether reading was thorough or whether the publication was just leafed through.

Leser m einer Ausgabe *(media res)* issue reader

Leser m im Betrieb
→ Mitleser

Leser m im weitesten Sinn *(media res)* noter
→ Leser

Leser m/pl pro Ausgabe (LpA m, LpA-Wert m, Leser m/pl im Erschei-nungsintervall, relativer K_1-Wert m) *(media res)* issue audience, average-issue audience (A.I.A., AIA), average-issue-readership (A.I.R., AIR), readers pl per issue (rpi)
The computed number of persons who read an issue of a magazine or newspaper in its publication interval, (→) Erscheinungsintervall, i.e.:

$$\text{rpi} = \frac{\text{reading probability}}{\text{number of issues}}.$$

Leser m/pl pro Exemplar (LpE, LpE-Wert m, Leserauflage f) *(media res)* average-issue audience (A.I.A., AIA), average-issue readership, primary and secondary audience, readers pl per copy (rps)
The computed number of persons who read an average issue of a periodical publication in its publication interval, i.e.:

$$\text{rpc} = \frac{\text{total audience}}{\text{known circulation}}.$$

Leser m/pl pro Nummer (LpN m, LpN-Wert m) *(media res)* readers pl per copy, rpc, RPC, R.P.C., readers pl per single copy
The estimated number of people, as ascertained in a readership survey, reading one average issue or copy of a publication.

Leser-pro-Nummer-Preis m (LpN-Preis m)
→ Tausend-Leser-Preis

Leser m/pl pro Woche *(media res)* weekly readers pl, number of readers pl per week, weekly readers pl

Leseranalyse f (Leserschaftsanalyse f) readership analysis, audience analysis

Leseranalyse f Entscheidungsträger in Wirtschaft und Verwaltung (LAE) Readership Analysis Decision-Makers in Industry and Administration

Leseranalyse f Kinderpresse (LA Kinderpresse) Readership Analysis Children's Press

Leseranalyse f medizinischer Fachzeitschriften (LA-Med) Readership Analysis of Medical Journals

Leseranalyse f Roman- und Rätselhefte Readership Analysis of Fiction and Puzzle Magazines

Leseranalyse f Spezialzeitschriften (LASI) Readership Analysis of Special-Interest Magazines

Leserauflage *f*
→ Leser pro Exemplar (LpE)
Leserbefragung *f* **(Leserumfrage** *f*)
(media res) readership survey, audience survey, (mit eingedrucktem Fragebogen in der Zeitschrift/Zeitung) coupon survey
Leser-Blatt-Bindung (LBB) *f* reader involvement, reader loyalty, reader confidence
> The allegiance, loyalty and support regular readers display for a particular publication. It is usually measured by means of questions such as: "If for one reason or another, publication X were to cease publication, would you regret this or not?"

Leserdienst-Karte *f* reader service card, reader service inquiry card
Leserbrief *m* letter to the editor
Leserfluktuation *f (media res)* (von Heft zu Heft) issue-audience turnover, audience turnover
> A measurement of the frequency with which a periodical's audience changes from one issue to the next. More specifically, the ratio of the net unduplicated cumulative audience to the average audience.

Leserforschung *f* **(Leserschaftsforschung** *f*) audience research, readership research, reader research
> The systematic analysis of periodical publications' audience characteristics, reading behavior, and attention given to the publication or any of its elements.

Leser-Konsumenten-Untersuchung *f (market & media res)* reader-consumer investigation, reader-consumer study, reader-buyer investigation, reader-buyer study
Leserkontakt *m*
→ Kontakt
Leserkreis *m*
→ Weitester Leserkreis (WLK), Leserschaft
Leserkreisanalyse *f*
→ Leseranalyse
Leserschaft *f* **(Leser** *m/pl*) *(media res)* audience, readership, readers *pl*, number of readers, total number of readers, audience score
> The total number of individuals exposed to any part of a publication's content in contrast to circulation. Also, the number of persons who recall a specific advertisement or editorial item in a given issue of a publication.

Leserschaftanalyse *f*
→ Leseranalyse
Leserschaftsforschung *f*
→ Leserforschung
Leserschaftsmessung *f (media res)* audience measurement, readership measurement
Leserschaftspanel *n (media res)* panel of readers
Leserschaftsprofil *n (media res)* audience profile, reader profile, readership profile
→ Leserschaftsstruktur
Leserschaftsstruktur *f* **(Leserschaftszusammensetzung** *f*) *(media res)* audience characteristics *pl*, audience composition, audience comp, audience breakdown, audience setup, demographic audience characteristics *pl*, demographics *pl*, audience profile, audience structure, readership characteristics *pl*, reader characteristics *pl*, readership composition, readership breakdown, readership setup
> The demographic and statistical characteristics, e.g. age, sex, education, income, occupation, marital and family status, household equipment, habits, and lifestyles of the readers of a periodical publication.

Leserschaftsumfrage *f*
→ Leserbefragung
Leserschaftsuntersuchung *f* **(Leserschaftsstudie** *f*) *(media res)* audience investigation, audience study, readership investigation, readership study
> An investigation of the characteristics of the readership of a periodical or of the attention given to a periodical or any of its elements by its readership.

Leserservice *m* reader service
> The special service publishers of some periodicals provide to readers who request information on products or services mentioned in the editorial section of the publication or in advertisements.

Leser-Strukturanalyse *f (media res)* analysis of readership structure, analysis of audience structure, audience structure analysis
Leserumfrage *f*
→ Leserbefragung
Leseruntersuchung *f*
→ Leserschaftsuntersuchung
Leserwerbung *f*
→ Abonnentenwerbung

Leserzahl f (**Leserschaftsumfang** m) *(media res)* audience score, number of readers, audience size, size of audience
→ Leserschaft
Leserzuschrift f
→ Leserbrief
Lesestoff m reading, reading matter
Lesestunden f/pl *(media res)* reading hours pl, hours pl spent reading
Lesestunden f/pl **pro Kopf** (**Pro-Kopf-Lesestunden** f/pl) *(media res)* man-hours pl of reading
Lesetage m/pl *(media res)* reading days pl
  A reading day is any day when a primary, (→) Erstleser, or pass-along reader, (→) Folgeleser, looks into a copy of a particular magazine issue. Monthly magazines generally have more reading days than weeklies. This gives them a substantial edge in generating multiple ad-page exposures, (→) Mehrfachkontakt, since their audiences look into the same issue many times over a 10- to 12-week period.
Lesetage m/pl **pro Heft** *(media res)* reading days pl of issue exposure
Leseverhalten n reading behavior, *brit* reading behaviour
Leseverhaltensbeobachtung f (**Beobachtung** f **des Leseverhaltens**) *(media res)* observation of reading behavior, *brit* behaviour
Lesevorgänge m/pl (**Lesegeschehen** n, **Nutzungsvorgänge** m/pl) *(media res)* reader traffic, reading/noting traffic, reading and noting (Daniel Starch), editorial traffic
  The general pattern of attention shift from one page to the next or one part of a periodical to another on the part of its readers.
Lesewahrscheinlichkeit f (**Nutzungswahrscheinlichkeit** f) *(media res)* reading probability, probability of reading, adult probability
  For a given publication, reading probabilities are calculated for people falling within each claimed reading frequency group. The probability may be calculated in two ways, either on the claimed frequency or as an "observed frequency". The former is straight arithmetic, e.g. reading 3 out of 6 is a probability of 0.5 for the average issue. Observed frequency is a cross-tabulation, and the probability is the proportion within the frequency grouping who in fact qualified as average-issue-readers in answer to a recent-reading question.
Lesezeit f
→ Lesedauer
Lesezirkel m (**LZ**) *etwa* magazine club, deferred subscription club, clubbing
  A unique institution on the German magazine market for which there is no counterpart in the English-speaking world. A number of general-interest magazines is bound together in so-called Lesemappen. They are delivered to households on a subscription basis, with subscription rates being highest for those receiving the current issues and becoming lower for those subscribing to the issues that are one week old, two weeks old, etc.
Lesezirkelwerbung f *etwa* magazine club advertising, advertising in magazine club portfolios
Letter f (**Type** f, **Drucktype** f) *(typ)* type
  Printers' letters having a character cast or cut in relief at one end.
Letternart f
→ Schrifttype (Schriftart)
Letterngießmaschine f
→ Gießmaschine
Letterngut n (**Letternmetall** n)
→ Schriftmetall
Letternkopf m *(type)* beard, face
  That part of a type that makes the impression.
Letternmetall n
→ Schriftmetall
Letternsatz m
→ Bleisatz, Handsatz
Letternsortiment n
→ Schriftbestand
Letztargumenthypothese f (**Recency-Effekt-Hypothese** f) recency effect hypothesis, recency hypothesis
  The hypothesis that the most recent argument in persuasive communication is the most effective argument.
  vgl. Erstargumenthypothese
letzte Seite f *(print)* last page
letzte Umschlagseite f
→ Umschlagseite
letzte Zeile f (**Ausgangszeile** f) *(print)* last line
letzter Lesevorgang m *(media res)* recent reading
  The time lapsed between the last reading event and the day of interview, as ascertained in a readership survey. The recency method of readership measurement contends that the audience

of an average issue of a publication can be measured by establishing how many people have read it in a time interval equal to the publication interval.

letzter Sendetermin *m* (Werbe- oder Programmsendung) last telecast (L.T., L.T.C.)
The last date on which a commercial or program is scheduled for television broadcast.

Letztkäufer *m* **(Letztnachfrager** *m*, **Letztverbraucher** *m*)
→ Endverbraucher

Letztverbraucherbefragung *f*
→ Verbraucherbefragung

Letztverbraucherwerbung *f*
→ Verbraucherwerbung, Endverbraucherwerbung

Letztverkaufsstelle *f*
→ Verkaufsstelle

Leuchtbild *n* backlighted transparency, translight
A full color advertisement printed on a translucent sheet rather than on paper or card stock. Special lighting behind the sheet turns it into a dramatic color slide.

Leuchtdichte *f* **(Luminanz** *f*) *(TV)* luminous density, luminance, brightness
The amount of brightness, as measured on a gray scale.

Leuchtdichtemesser *m* **(Luminanzmesser** *m*) *(TV)* brightness meter, lumen meter

Leuchtdichtepegel *m* **(Luminanzpegel** *m*) *(TV)* luminance level, brightness level

Leuchtdichtesignal *n* **(Luminanzsignal** *n*) *(TV)* luminance signal

Leuchtdichtestruktur *f* **(Luminanzstruktur** *f*) *(TV)* luminous texture

Leuchtdichteumfang *m* **(Luminanzumfang** *m*, **Luminanzspektrum** *n*) *(TV)* contrast range, range of luminance

Leuchte *f* **(Lampe** *f*) lamp, light

Leuchtfarbe *f* **(Reflexfarbe** *f*) *(print)* luminous paint
Any paint or other substance used for lettering or tinting advertisements, particularly on billboards, in such a way that they appear vividly under street lighting, blacklight, in the light of automobile headlights in the night.

Leuchtfeld *n* indicator panel, light display panel

Leuchtfleck *m* *(TV)* bright spot, hot spot

Leuchtfleckabtaster *m* *(TV)* flying spot scanner
A film-to-video transfer technique utilizing an electronic shutter.

Leuchtplakat *n* **(Leuchtposter** *n*) *(outdoor advtsg)* glow bulletin, glow bulletin board, glow panel, *(TM)* Dayglo poster, (neonbeleuchtet) neonized bulletin
An outdoor advertisement with a translucent surface and backlighting.

Leuchtpult *n* **(Leuchttisch** *m*) *(print/ film)* illuminated desk, luminous desk, lining-up desk, stripping desk, stripping table, light table
A glass-topped table, with a light source beneath the glass, on which a stripper works.

Leuchtschicht *f* luminous coating, luminous film

Leuchtschild *n* *(transit advtsg)* busorama
A transit advertisement with a translucent surface and backlighting for use on public transportation vehicles.

Leuchtschirm *m* **(Leuchtstoffschirm** *m*) luminous screen

Leuchtschrift *f* luminous letters *pl*, (TM) lumitype
Any letters used on signs and bulletins to intensify light and color especially by reflection at night.

Leuchtschriftband *n* **(Leuchtschriftnachrichten** *f/pl*) *(outdoor advtsg)* newscaster
An electronically operated moving light sign spelling out newsflashes, sometimes interspersed with advertisements.

Leuchtstofflampe *f* **(Leuchtstoffröhre** *f*) fluorescent lamp, fluorescent tube, discharged lamp

Leuchttransparent *n*
→ Leuchtbild

Leuchtwerbemittel *n*
→ Lichtwerbemittel

Leuchtwerbung *f*
→ Lichtwerbung

licht *adj (typ)* outline, contour, open

lichter Satz *m* **(durchschossener Satz** *m*) *(typ)* open type, open matter
→ Durchschuß

Licht *n* light

Lichtabdeckschirm *m* *(phot/film/TV)* flag, French flag
A square shade, usually made of black cloth, attached to the metal support in front of a camera to protect the lens from stray light.
→ Lichtblende

Lichtband

Lichtband *n* light-control tape
lichtbeständig *adj* → lichtecht
Lichtbestimmer *m* (phot/film) timer, grader
Lichtbestimmung *f* (phot/film) grading, timing
 The alteration of printing light intensities and color filters to achieve a balanced film positive from unbalanced negative material.
Lichtbestimmungskopie *f* (phot/film) grading copy, grading print
 An initial married print made from a completed film negative, used for evaluation and corrections.
Lichtbestimmungstisch *m* (phot/film) grading bench
Lichtbeugung *f* (optics) diffraction of light, diffraction
 The deviation of light rays from a straight course when partially cut off by an obstacle, or in passage near the edges of a small opening or through a small hole.
Lichtbild *n*
→ Photographie, Dia(positiv)
Lichtbildner *m*
→ Photograph
Lichtbildwerbung *f*
→ Diawerbung, Film- und Diawerbung
Lichtbildwerk *n*
→ Photographie
Lichtblende *f* (**Lichtschirm** *m*, **Lichtschutz** *m*) (phot/film/TV) gobbo, gobo, flag, French flag, *colloq* nigger, Frenchman, barndoor, *brit colloq* cookie
 A small black screen used to keep stray light from striking the lens of a camera.
Lichtbogen *m* (film/TV) electric arc, arc, carbon arc
 A high-intensity light source, used in motion picture photography and in projection.
Lichtbogenlampe *f*
→ Bogenlampe
Lichtdiffusion *f* (optics) diffusion of light, diffusion
 The reflection of light by a mat surface, or the transmission of light through glass, or the scattering caused by particles in the atmosphere.
Lichtdruck *m* 1. (Verfahren) collotype, collotype printing, collotype procedure, photogelatin printing, photogelatin, collotypy
 A high-quality method of printing for reproducing artwork or photographs by using a gelatin-coated plate.

2. (Produkt) collotype print, collotype, photogelatin print
lichte Schrift *f* (**Konturschrift** *f*) (typ) outline type, outline, inline type, in-line type, inline face, in-line face, inline, open type, open face, contour face, contour type
 A category of display type, (→) Auszeichnungsschrift, with an unprinted inner part showing white against the contour of black.
lichtecht (**lichtbeständig**) *adj* fadeless, resistant to light, lightfast, *brit* fadeproof
 The quality of a print, an ink, or any other material not to lose color.
Lichtechtheit *f* (**Lichtbeständigkeit** *f*) fadelessness, resistance to light, lightfastness
→ lichtecht
Lichteffekt *m* lighting effect
lichtempfindlich (phot) *adj* light-sensitive, photosensitive, sensitive, sensitized
 Affected by the incidence of light.
Lichtempfindlichkeit *f* (phot) sensitivity to light, light sensitivity, photosensitivity, sensitivity
→ lichtempfindlich
lichtempfindliches Papier *n* (phot) sensitized paper
lichtempfindlich machen (**sensibilisieren**) (phot) *v/t* to sensitize
 To render photographic material, e.g. film or paper, sensitive to light.
Lichtempfindlichmachen *n* (**Lichtempfindlichmachung** *f*) (phot) light sensitization, optical sensitization, optical sensitizing, photosensitization, photosensitizing, sensitization, sensitizing
Lichtfarbe *f* color of light, *brit* colour of light
Lichtfarbmeßgerät *n*
→ Farbtemperaturmesser
Lichtfilter *m* (phot) light filter, ray filter
Lichtfleck *m* (TV) light spot
Lichtführung *f* (film/TV) direction of lighting, light direction
Lichtgestalter *m* (film/TV) lighting cameraman, director of photography, lighting director, director of cinematography
Lichtgestaltung *f* (film/TV) direction of lighting, light direction

Lichtgitter n (**Beleuchtungsgitter** n) (film/TV) lighting grid, light grid
The metal girders or lattice suspending lights over a set.
Lichthof m (phot/film/TV) halation, halo, blur circle
The ring of light surrounding a bright object, producing a blurred image as a result of the dispersal of light.
Lichthofbildung f (**Überstrahlung** f) (phot/film/TV) halation
The spreading of light action beyond proper boundaries in photographic negatives, particularly around the highlights of the image.
→ Lichthof
Lichthofeffekt m (phot/film/TV) halo effect
→ Lichthof
lichthoffrei adj (phot/film/TV) antihalation, antihalo
Lichthofschutz m (phot/film/TV) antihalation, antihalo base
Lichthofschutzschicht f (phot/film/TV) antihalation backing, antihalo backing, antihalation layer, antihalo layer, film backing
Lichtingenieur m (**Beleuchtungsingenieur** m) (film/TV) lighting engineer
Lichtintensität f (phot) intensity of light, light intensity, light level
Lichtkasten m (film/TV) light box, spotting box
An illuminated, translucent rotating desk used in cartoon animation for preparing animation artwork.
Lichtkegel m cone of light, light cone
Lichtmarke f (TV) light spot
→ Lichtpunkt
Lichtmeßgerät n
→ Belichtungsmesser
Lichtmessung f
→ Belichtungsmessung
Lichtmodulation f (TV) light modulation
A recorded visual signal pattern
Lichtorgel f (Studio) lighting console
Lichtpausanstalt f
→ Kopieranstalt
Lichtpause f (phot) blueprint, photoprint, copy, whiteprint
A photographic print that reproduces lines and solid shapes in white on a dark blue or black background.
→ Photosatzkorrekturabzug, Blaupause, Braunpause
Lichtpausgerät n (phot) blueprinter, photocopier, copier, photoprinter

Lichtpausverfahren n (phot) blueprinting, blueprinting process, photocopying, copying, photoprinting, whiteprinting
Lichtpunkt m (TV) light spot, bright spot, luminous spot
Lichtquelle f (phot) source of light, light source, luminous source
Lichtreflektor m light reflector, reflector, colloq light stealer
Any object which has no illumination of its own, but appears to be illuminated because it is made of materials which reflect light derived from other sources.
Lichtreflektion f light reflection, brit light reflexion, reflection
Lichtregelung f
→ Beleuchtungssteuerung
Lichtregie f
→ Beleuchtungssteuerung
Lichtregler m (**Beleuchtungsregler** m) dimmer
A device used for varying the intensity of light.
Lichtreklame f
→ Lichtwerbung
Lichtsatz m
→ Photosatz
Lichtschleier m (phot) light fog, (Schleierbildung) light fogging
A defect in which the photographic image is completely or locally veiled by a deposit of silver of varying density, due either to the action of extraneous actinic light or to improper chemical action.
Lichtschleuse f (phot) light trap, light lock
Any arrangement for preventing light passage through an opening which must admit a moving part such as the felts on plate holders. In particular, a baffle type of entrance to photographic darkrooms, preventing entry of stray light during traffic from the chamber.
Lichtschnitt m
→ Cutten
Lichtschranke f (phot) light barrier
Lichtsetzanlage f (**Lichtsetzgerät** n)
→ Photosatzanlage
Lichtspalt m light gap, light slit
Lichtspiel n
→ Film, Kino, Kinofilm
Lichtspieltheater n (**Filmtheater** n, **Lichtspielhaus** n) cinema, cinema theater, brit theatre, motion-picture house, movie theater, picture house
Lichtspieltheaterwerbung f
→ Kinowerbung

lichtstark *adj (phot)* fast, rapid, high-speed

Lichtstärke f 1. *(optics)* (Lichtintensität) light intensity, luminous intensity, candle power, intensity of light, brightness
  The level of light a light source emits.
2. *(phot)* (Objektiv) speed, f number, lens speed
  The relative aperture of a camera lens, i.e. the number obtained by dividing the focal length, (→) Brennweite, of a lens by its effective diameter.

Lichtstärkewert *m (phot)* brightness value (BV)

Lichtsteuerband *n*
→ Blendenband

Lichtsteuerpult *n*
→ Beleuchtungspult

Lichtsteuerraum *m*
→ Beleuchtungsraum

Lichtsteuerung *f*
→ Beleuchtungssteuerung

Lichtstrahl *m* light beam, light ray

Lichtstrahlenmesser *m* (**Aktinometer** *n*) *(phot)* actinometer
  A device used for measuring the actinicity or chemical power of light.

Lichtstrahlenmessung *f* (**Aktinometrie f**) *(phot)* actinometry

Lichtstrom *m* luminous flux, light flux, lamp current

Lichttechnik *f*
→ Beleuchtungstechnik

Lichtton *m (film)* sound on film (S.O.F., SOF), optical sound, photographic sound
  In broadcasting, film footage with a sound track, usually recorded simultaneously.

Lichtton-Aufzeichnung *f* (**Lichtton-Aufzeichnungsverfahren** *n*) sound on film (S.O.F., SOF), optical sound recording, photographic sound technique

Lichttonkamera *f (film)* optical sound recorder

Lichttonkopie *f (film)* optical sound print

Lichttonlampe *f (film)* exciter lamp, optical sound lamp
→ Erregerlampe

Lichtton-Negativ *n* (**Lichtton-Duplikatnegativ** *n*) *(film)* optical sound negative, optical negative

Lichtton-Positiv *n* (**Lichtton-Duplikatpositiv** *n*) *(film)* optical sound positive, optical positive

Lichttonspur *f (film)* optical track, optical sound track
  A final soundtrack printing negative.

Lichttonverfahren *n*
→ Lichttonaufzeichnung

Lichtübergang *m (film/TV)* light crossover

lichtunechte Farbe *f* (**lichtunbeständige Farbe** *f*) *(print)* fugitive color, fugitive ink, *brit* fugitive colour
  A color or ink which is not permanent, but fades or changes when exposed to light.

Lichtverlust *m (phot)* loss of light, light loss

Lichtverteilung *f (phot)* distribution of light, light distribution

Lichtvorhang *m (film/TV)* light curtain

Lichtwagen *m (film/TV)* lighting truck, lighting vehicle, lighting van, (im Studio) lighting trolley

Lichtwand *f (phot/film/TV)* (Studio) baffle
  A panel used for light adjustment.

Lichtwanne *f (film/TV)* lighting float, broad source, broad, lighting trough
  A box-shaped 2.000-watt floodlight providing a flat, even illumination of the set.

Lichtwerbeanlage *f* light advertising equipment

Lichtwerbung *f* (**Leuchtwerbung f**) electric sign advertising, electric light advertising, light advertising, lightbox advertising, signpost advertising

Lichtwert *m (phot/film/TV)* (Beleuchtung) light-value level, light value
→ Belichtungswert

Lichtwurflampe *f*
→ Projektorlampe

Lichtzeichen *n (film/TV)* light signal, cue light
  A visual signal to commence or to cease action.

Lichtzerlegung *f (optics)* dispersion of light, dispersion
  The separation of light into the components of its spectrum.

Lieferant *m (econ)* supplier

Lieferantentreue *f (econ)* supplier loyalty

Lieferbedingungen *f/pl* (**Lieferungsbedingungen f/pl**) *(econ)* terms *pl* of delivery

Lieferbereitschaft f **(Servicegrad** m) (econ) serviceability
The ratio of satisfied demand and total demand.
Lieferhäufigkeit f **(Lieferfrequenz** f) (econ) frequency of delivery
Liefermenge f (econ) quantity delivered
liefern v/t (econ) to supply, (ausliefern) to deliver
Lieferpreis m (econ) delivery price, delivered price
The ex-works selling price which includes freighting or transportation charges to the buyer's establishment.
Lieferschein m **(Lieferzettel** m) (econ) delivery ticket, bill of delivery, delivery note
The document accompanying goods on delivery to the buyer, used as a means of checking orderly delivery, dealing with claims for damage, shortage and empties.
Lieferservice m (econ) delivery service
Liefertermin m (econ) delivery date, date of delivery
Lieferung f (econ) delivery
Lieferung f **frei Haus**
→ Freihauslieferung
Lieferungsgeschäft n
→ Lokogeschäft
Lieferwagen m delivery truck, brit delivery van
Lieferzeit f (econ) lead time, delivery period, delivery time, time of delivery
The expected time interval between the day of placing an order and the day of arrival of the items.
Lieferzuverlässigkeit f (econ) reliability of delivery, delivery reliability
Life-Style-Studie f
→ Lebensstilanalyse
LIFO-Verfahren n **(LIFO)** (econ) LIFO procedure, last-in, first-out procedure, last-in, first-out, LIFO
A method of inventory valuation and costing under which merchandise received last is always sold first.
vgl. FIFO-Verfahren (FIFO), LOFO-Verfahren (LOFO)
Ligatur f (typ) ligature, double letter
Two or more letters tied together and cast in one piece of type, as e.g. fi, ff, fl.
Lignin n **(Holzstoff** m) (paper) lignin
ligninfrei adj → holzfrei
Ligningehalt m (paper) lignin content
Likelihood f **(Mutmaßlichkeit** f) (stat) likelihood

A measure of the plausibility of a postulated population structure, given values of observations on a random sample form that population.
Likelihood-Funktion f (stat) likelihood function
Likelihood expressed as an algebraic function of possible values of parameters for a particular population distribution and the observed set of sample data.
Likelihood-Matrix f (stat) likelihood matrix
Likelihood-Verhältnis n **(Likelihood-Quotient** m, **Likelihood-Ratio** f) (stat) likelihood ratio
The ratio of the likelihood of one postulated population structure to another for a given set of sample data.
Likelihood-Verhältnis-Test m **(Likelihood-Quotienten-Test** m, **Likelihood-Ratio-Test** m) (stat) likelihood ratio test
A test of a null hypothesis H_0 against an alternative hypothesis H_1, based on the ratio of two likelihood functions, one derived from each of H_0 and H_1.
Likert-Skala f **(Punktsummenskala** f, **Methode** f **der summierten Einschätzungen)** Likert scale, Likert-type scale, Likert technique, summated scale, method of summated ratings, method of internal consistency (Rensis Likert)
A summated attitude scale consisting of a series of items (attitude statements) each of which is rated by the respondent to indicate his degree of agreement or disagreement. Typically each statement has five possible responses: strongly agree, agree, uncertain, disagree, strongly disagree. The responses are assigned weights, for example, strongly agree, 1, agree, 2, uncertain, 3, etc. A total score for each respondent is obtained by summing his scores on all the individual items. Item analysis may then be used to compare scores on individual items with total scores, or factor analysis to analyze interrelationships among the items. Those items that are most consistent with each other are included in the final scale.
Liliput m **(Babyspot** m, **kleiner Spotscheinwerfer** m, **Pipifax** m) (film/TV) baby spotlight, baby spot, baby pup, auch dinky inky, dinkie inkie
A small theatrical spotlight of 500 to 750 watts.
Liliputformat n (print) miniature size
Lineal n ruler

linear

linear *adj* linear
Involving one dimension only.
lineare Funktion f *(stat)* linear function
lineare Korrelation f *(stat)* linear correlation
A correlation in which there is a constant ratio between the rates of change of two or more quantitative variables.
Lineare Programmierung f **(Lineare Planungsrechnung** f) linear programming (LP)
A group of mathematical techniques used to optimize a linear form subject to linear restraints with the additonal restraint that only nonnegative results are permissible. LP techniques are used in economics to allocate limited resources among alternative uses, and to select optimum decisions that simultaneously satisfy a number of requirements. In media planning, LP models enable media planners to specify reach, frequency, seasonal and demographic goals for a given advertising campaign. The computer examines costs and audience data and produces the plan and schedule that comes closest to achieving the stated goals at the budget level. Also provided is a detailed analysis which lets the planner examine each variable to determine how it affects the findings and make modifications where necessary.
lineare Regression f *(stat)* linear regression
The regression of one variable on one or more other variable(s) in a constant ratio, so that each unit of increase or decrease in the independent variable(s) is associated with a fixed number of units of change in the dependent variable.
lineare Struktur f *(stat)* linear structure
lineare Trennfunktion f **(lineare Diskriminanzfunktion** f) *(stat)* linear discriminant function
A discriminant function, (→) Diskriminanzfunktion, which is a linear function of observed variate values or frequencies.
linearer Prozeß m linear process
linearer Trend m *(stat)* linear trend
A trend in which the rate of change is constant.
lineares Modell n *(stat)* linear model
A model in which the equations connecting the variates or variables are in a linear form.
Linearität f linearity
Linearitätsfehler m *(phot)* linearity error, linearity defect

Linearitätsspektrum n
→ Linienspektrum
Linearitätsraster m
→ Linienraster
Linearitätstestbild n *(TV)* linearity test pattern
Linie f **1.** *(print)* line, rule
A metal strip with a line or lines on its face, used to print borders or to separate elements in printed material.
2. (redaktionelle Linie) editorial policy
3. (graphische Darstellung) line, curve
4. *(econ)* (im Gegensatz zum Stab) line
In an organization, e.g. a firm, those positions assigned the responsibilities and the authority to act directly to achieve its defined goals.
Linienblatt n
→ liniiertes Papier
Liniendiagramm n **(Kurvendiagramm** n, **Kurvengraphik** f) *(stat)* line diagram, line graph
Linieneinfassung f **(Linieneinrahmung** f, **Kasten** m) *(print)* line border, rule border, line box, box, rule box
Linienmaß n *(print)* line gauge
Linienorganisation f **(Liniensystem** n) *(econ)* line organization, *brit* line organisation, line system
→ Linie 4.
Linienrand m
→ Linieneinfassung
Linienraster m
→ Strichraster
Linienrasterfilm m
→ Strichrasterfilm
Linie-Stab-Organisation f **(Linie-Stab-System** n)
→ Stab-Linien-Organisation
Liniensystem n
→ Linienorganisation
Linienumrandung f
→ Linieneinfassung
liniieren (linieren) v/t to line
Liniierfeder f **(Linierfeder** f, **Ausziehfeder** f) *(print)* ruling pen
Liniiergerät n **(Liniiermaschine** f) *(print)* ruling machine
Liniierung f **(Liniieren** n) *(print)* ruling
Linkage-Analyse f *(stat)* linkage analysis
→ Average-Linkage-Analyse, Complete-Linkage-Analyse, Single-Linkage-Analyse

linke Seite f *(print)* left page, left-hand page
linksbündig *adj (print)* flush left
  The characteristic of type set without indention on the left side (and with a ragged ending of lines to the right).
links oben
  → oben links
links von der Kamera *(film/TV)* camera left
  vgl. rechts von der Kamera
Linse f *(phot)* lens
  The curved-glass eye through which pictures are photographed by the camera.
Linsenantenne f lens antenna, *brit* lens aerial
Linsenblende f **(Linsenschirm** m, **Linsenschutz** m) *(phot)* gobbo, gobo
  → Lichtblende
Linsendurchmesser m *(phot)* lens diameter
Linseneffekt m **(Linsenreflektion** f) *(phot)* lens flare, flare, flare spot, camera flare
  A light-flash on the film caused by using a very fast lens at a very small diaphragm stop.
Linsenfehler m *(phot)* lens flaw, lens aberration, lens error, lens impairment
Linsenrasterfilm m *(phot)* lens screen film
Linsensatz m *(phot)* set of lenses
Linsenschirm m
  → Lichtblende
Linsenschutzglas n *(phot)* safety glass
Lippenmikrofon n **(Lippenmikrophon** n) lip microphone
lippensynchron *adj (film/TV)* lip-sync, lip sync
Lippensynchronisierung f **(Lippensynchronisation** f) *(film/TV)* lip synchronization, *brit* lip synchronisation, lip sync
  In television and motion pictures, the synchronization of an actor's lip movements with separately recorded spoken lines.
List-Broking n
  → Adressenhandel
Liste f list
Listenauswahl f 1. *(stat)* (Listenstichprobenverfahren) list sampling
  A random sampling technique, (→) Zufallsauswahl, using random number tables, (→) Zufallszahlentabelle.
Listenfrage f *(survey res)* list question, card question

Listenpreis m 1. *(econ)* list price, advertised price
  A manufacturer's or wholesaler's recommended retail price, before any applicable discounts.
  2. (für Werbung) card rate, flat rate, basic rate, base rate
  The standard rate charged for a specified quantity of advertising space or time by a communication medium without regard to any discounts, as listed on the rate card.
Listenstichprobe f
  → Listenauswahl 2.
Listenstichprobenbildung f
  → Listenauswahl 1.
Listenstichprobenverfahren f
  → Listenauswahl 1.
Litfaßsäule f *(outdoor advtsg)* poster pillar
  A cylindrical pillar used for posting outdoor advertisements.
Litho n **(Offsetfilm** m) *(print)* offset film, litho
Lithograph m **(Steindrucker** m) *(print)* lithographer, lithographic artist, lithographic printer, litho-printer, litho printer
Lithographie f **(Steindruck** m) *(print)*
  1. (Verfahren) lithography, litho printing, litho
  Any form of printing from a plane surface, including offset printing and planographing. Lithographic plates have neither raised nor recessed areas; the antagonism of grease and water is the principle involved in separating the printing areas from the nonprinting areas. The image is laid down in a greasy substance, dampness is applied to the plate and then the ink. The ink adheres only to the greasy area. In lithography the printed image is generally first applied to a rubber blanket, (→) Gummituch, and transferred or offset from this to the paper.
  2. (Produkt) lithograph, lithoprint, litho print
Lithographiestein m **(Maschinenstein** m, **lithographischer Stein** m) *(print)* lithographic limestone, lithographic stone
lithographisch (Steindruck-) *adj (print)* lithographic, litho
lithographischer Kreidestift m **(Farbstift** m) *(print)* lithographic crayon, crayon
lithographieren (im Steindruck herstellen) v/t *(print)* to lithograph

Lithostein m
→ Lithographiestein
Live-(live) adj *(radio/TV/film)* live
Presented directly from an actual performance or event.
Live-Aufnahme f *(radio/TV/film)* live reporting, live coverage, camera reporting
Liveproduktion f
→ Livesendung
Liveprogramm n
→ Livesendung
Livereportage f
→ Live-Aufnahme, Livesendung
Livesendung f **(Live-Sendung** f**)** *(radio/TV)* live broadcast, live transmission, live program, *brit* programme, (zeitversetzte Livesendung) deferred broadcast, live-time delay broadcast, clock-hour delay broadcast
An instantaneous broadcast presented directly from an actual event or performance in contrast to a broadcast by delayed recording or on a film.
Live-Spot m *(radio/TV)* live-action commercial
In TV commercial production, shooting actual people or things, rather than using artwork or animation.
Livestudio n *(radio/TV)* live studio
Liveübertragung f
→ Livesendung
Lizenz f *(econ)* license, *brit* licence
A legal arrangement by which the right to manufacture, or to market a product is transferred from the owner of the right, the licenser, to another person or organization, the licensee.
Lizenzabkommen n *(econ)* license agreement, *brit* licence agreement
Lizenzdauer f *(econ)* license period, *brit* licence period
lizenzfrei adj public domain (P.D.)
→ gemeinfrei
Lizenzgeber m *(econ)* licenser, *auch* licensor, *brit* licencer
Lizenzgebühr f *(econ)* license fee, *brit* licence fee
lizenzieren (lizensieren, Lizenz verleihen) v/t *(econ)* to license, *brit* to licence, to grant a license, *brit* to grant a licence
Lizenzierung f **(Lizensierung** f, **Lizenzverleihung** f) *(econ)* licensing, *brit* licencing
Lizenzinhaber m
→ Lizenznehmer

Lizenznehmer m *(econ)* licensee, *brit* licencee
Lizenzpolitik f *(econ)* licensing policy, *brit* licencing policy, licensing
Lizenzprodukt n *(econ)* licensed product, license product, *brit* licenced product
Lizenzrecht n
→ Lizenz
Lizenzträger m
→ Lizenznehmer
Lizenzvergabe f
→ Lizenzierung
Lochkamera f **(Camera obscura** f) *(phot)* pinhole camera, camera obscura
Lockangebot n **(Lockvogelangebot** n, **Köder** m, **Warenköder** m) *(econ)* bait, nailed down
A product offered at a low price to bring customers into a store or in contact with the promotion or selling sphere of an advertiser.
Lockangebotswerbung f **(Lockvogelwerbung** f, **Köderwerbung** f) bait advertising, bait-and-switch advertising, bait-and-switch selling, bait-and-switch-tactics *pl (construed as sg)*, bait-and-switch, switch selling
Advertising that offers a sale item at a low price to entice buyers, although the cost of an actual purchase is intended to be higher.
Lockartikel m **(Loss Leader** m, **Zugartikel** m) *(econ)* loss leader, price leader
A product of known or accepted quality priced at a loss or no profit for the purpose of attracting patronage to a store.
Lockartikelwerbung f loss leader advertising
Lockvogel m **(Lockvogelangebot** n)
→ Lockangebot
Lockvogelwerbung f
→ Lockangebotswerbung
LOFO-Verfahren n **(LOFO)** *(econ)* LOFO procedure, last-out, first-out procedure, last-out, first-out, LOFO
A method of inventory valuation and costing under which merchandise received last is always sold last.
vgl. FIFO-Verfahren (FIFO), LIFO-Verfahren (LIFO)
logarithmische Darstellung f **(logarithmische Graphik** f) *(stat)* logarithmic chart, logarithmic graph

logarithmischer Trend *m (stat)*
logarithmic trend
Logistik *f* logistics *pl (construed as sg)*
→ Marketinglogistik (physische Distribution)
logistische Funktion *f (stat)* logistic function, growth function
logistische Kurve *f (stat)* logistic curve, growth curve
  A curve used to describe the normal progress of growth.
logistische Verteilung *f (stat)* logistic distribution
logistischer Prozeß *m (stat)* logistic process
logistischer Trend *m (stat)* logistic trend
logistisches Modell *n (stat)* logistic model, normal ogive model
Lokalanzeiger *m* **(Lokalblatt** *n)* local advertiser, local paper, local newspaper
Lokalausgabe *f* (einer Zeitschrift) spot market edition, local edition, (Zeitung) slip edition
Lokalbericht *m* local report, spot report, local
Lokalberichterstatter *m*
→ Lokalreporter
Lokalberichterstattung *f* local coverage, spot news coverage, local reporting
Lokalblatt *n*
→ Lokalanzeiger
lokale Fernsehwerbung *f* **(örtliche Fernsehwerbung** *f*) spot television advertising, spot TV advertising, spot television, spot TV, localized time
lokale Radiowerbung *f* **(lokale Hörfunkwerbung** *f*) spot radio advertising, spot radio, localized time
lokale Werbung *f* **(Werbung** *f* **des örtlichen Einzelhandels)** local advertising, retail advertising
  Any advertising appearing only in one or more specific localities, usually advertising by local retailers, as distinguished from advertising appearing regionally or nationally.
lokale Wochenzeitung *f* **(örtliche Wochenzeitung** *f*) local weekly paper, local weekly
lokaler Werbungtreibender *m* **(regionaler Werbungtreibender** *m*) local advertiser

lokales Fernsehen *n* **(Lokalfernsehen** *n*) local television, local TV, nonnetwork television, nonnetwork TV
Lokalhandel *m (econ)* local trade, local business
Lokalnachrichten *f/pl* local news *sg*
Lokalpresse *f* local press, community press
Lokalseite *f* local page, regional page
Lokalsender *m* **(Regionalsender** *m*) local-channel station, community station, (eines Sendernetzes) O. & O. station (O and O station, O. and O. station), owned and operated station
Lokalsendung *f* local broadcast, local program, *brit* local programme, local-origination broadcast, local origination program, spot broadcast, spot program, spot
Lokaltarif *m* (Preis für örtliche Werbung) local rate, retail rate
Lokalteil *m* **(lokale Seiten** *f/pl*) (Zeitung) local section, local pages *pl*
Lokalwerbung *f*
→ lokale Werbung
Lokalzeitung *f* local newspaper, local paper
Lokogeschäft *n (econ)* spot business, spot transaction, spot deal
  A business transaction involving the immediate delivery of a commodity.
Lokohandel *m (econ)* spot trade
Longitudinalstudie *f* **(Longitudinaluntersuchung** *f*)
→ Längsschnittanalyse
Lorenzkurve *f* **(Konzentrationskurve** *f,* **Einkommensverteilungskurve** *f*) *(stat/econ)* Lorenz curve, curve of income distribution, income distribution curve
  A graphic representation that shows the extent of inequality in the distribution of a variable throughout a population. In the graph percentiles of the population are plotted against percentiles of the variable concerned. More specifically, in economics, a method for showing the concentration of ownership of economic quantities, such as income or wealth.
Los *n* **1.** *(promotion)* (Lotterielos) lottery ticket **2.** *(stat/econ)* (Warenposten) lot, batch, charge
  In quality control, a group of units of a product produced under similar conditions and therefore, in a sense, of homogeneous origin. It is sometimes implicit that the lot is for inspection.

Löschdrossel f (**Löschgerät** n) *(tape)* bulk eraser

löschen v/t to erase
To remove electronically, or degauss, all previously recorded picture and sound signals from a tape for reuse, or to delete parts of a manuscript, of copy, or an illustration.

Löschkopf m *(tape)* erasing head, erase head, wiping head

Löschung f (**Löschen** n) *(tape)* erasing, erasure, erosion, wiping

lose Beilage f (**Losebeilage** f) loose insert
→ Beilage

Loseblatt- *adj* loose-leaf

Loseblatthefter m
→ Schnellhefter

Loseblattkatalog m loose-leaf catalog, *brit* catalogue

Losgröße f *(stat)* lot size
→ Los 2.

Losung f
→ Slogan

Lotterie f *(promotion)* lottery
A promotional scheme in which making a required purchase gives a person a chance to win a prize which is awarded at random. Lotteries are prohibited in Germany.

Lotterieauswahl f 1. *(stat)* (Lotterieauswahlverfahren) lottery sampling
A method of drawing random samples, (→) Zufallsauswahl, from a population by constructing a miniature of the population, e.g. by inscribing the data of each member on a card and drawing members at random from it, e.g. by shuffling the cards and dealing a set haphazardly or using a random number table, (→) Listenauswahl.

Lotteriespiel n
→ Glücksspiel

Low-interest-Produkt n *(econ)* low-interest-product

Low-involvement-Produkt n *(econ)* low-involvement product

Low-Key m
→ Dunkelton

LpA m *abbr* Leser pro Ausgabe

LpE m *abbr* Leser pro Exemplar

LpN m *abbr* Leser pro Nummer

Lückenergänzungstest m (**Lückentest** m) 1. *(survey res)* completion technique, completion test
→ Argument-Ergänzungs-Test, Satzergänzungstest, Bilderergänzungstest, Rorschachtest, Rosenzweigtest, TAT-Test

2. (Leseverständnistest) cloze procedure, cloze test
A method of measuring readability based on gestalt psychology and its notion that humans tend to perceive a familiar pattern as a whole even when parts of it are missing or distorted. Mutilated passages are used which have had deleted words replaced by blank spaces. Subjects are asked to guess the missing words and the "cloze score" for any passage is the total number or percentage of its missing words filled in correctly.

Luftballon m balloon

Luftballonwerbung f balloon advertising

Luftbläschen n (**Luftblase** f) *(phot)* airbell, *meist pl* airbells
Small bubbles of air occurring in glass and film supports, or forming on photographic surfaces during development.

Luftpackung f
→ Mogelpackung

Luftpinsel m (**Spritzpistole** f) *(phot/print)* airbrush, air brush

Luftpinseltechnik f (**Luftpinselverfahren** n) airbrush technique, airbrushing
A commercial art method of painting by use of a fine spray to produce tonal gradations and to retouch photographs.

Luftpostausgabe f (Zeitung) airmail edition

Luftreklame f (**Luftwerbung** f) air advertising, aerial advertising, sky advertising

Luftschiff-Werbung f airship advertising

Luftverkehrslinienwerbung f airline advertising

Lügendetektor m lie detector
Any of the sensitive instruments for indicating, during the course of an examination, physiological changes correlated with marked changes in emotional tension.

Lumbeckeinband m *(bookbinding)* perfect binding, adhesive binding

lumbecken (klebebinden) v/t *(bookbinding)* to perfect bind

Lumbecken n (**Klebebindung** f, **Lumbeckverfahren** n) *(bookbinding)* perfect binding, adhesive binding, check binding

Luminanz f
→ Leuchtdichte

Luminanzsignal n
→ Leuchtdichtesignal

Luminanzspektrum n
→ Leuchtdichteumfang
Lumineszenz f luminescence
Lustspiel n
→ Komödie f
Lustspielfilm m
→ Filmkomödie
Lux (lx) n lux
The metric measurement of one lumen per square meter of surface.
Luxmeter n luxometer, lux meter, illumination photometer
A photoelectric device for controlling the duration of camera exposures according to actinicity and fluctuation of camera lamps.

Luxusbedarf m *(econ)* demand for luxury goods, luxury goods demand
Luxusgüter n/pl **(Luxuswaren** f/pl**)** *(econ)* luxury goods pl, luxury products pl
Luxusgüterwerbung f **(Luxuswarenwerbung** f**)** luxury goods advertising, luxury product advertising
lx *abbr* Lux
LZ *abbr* Lesezirkel
LZ-Leser m *(media res) etwa* magazine-club subscriber, magazine-club reader

M

M-Quadrat n
→ Geviert
MA f abbr Media-Analyse
Machbarkeit f (econ) feasibility
  The degree of practicality of a planned new product or any other business venture's success, usually in economic, financial, or technical terms.
Machbarkeitsstudie f (econ) feasibility study, feasibility investigation
→ Machbarkeit
Macht f eines Tests
→ Trennschärfe
Machtpromoter m (E. Witte) power promoter
vgl. Fachpromoter
Madrider Markenabkommen n (**Madrider Abkommen** n) Madrid Convention
  A European convention intended on granting automatic trademark protection, (→) Warenzeichenschutz, for all members through the Bureau for International Registration of Trademarks.
Magazin n
1. → Lager
2. → Zeitschrift
Magenta f (print) magenta
mager adj (print) lightface (l.f., lf), light-face, light-faced, lean
vgl. halbfett, fett
magere Schrift f (print) lightface type, lightface (l.f., lf), light-face type, lightfaced type, light-faced type, lean type
  A type design that has thin, light lines, in contrast to boldface.
vgl. halbfette Schrift, fette Schrift
Magnesiumfackel f (phot) magnesium flare, magnesium torch, magnesium flash
  Magnesium powder, if blown through a hot flame such as that of a spirit lamp, will ignite and burn very rapidly, giving a brilliant white light. Such flash lamps were widely used in the 1880s and 1890s. Alternatively, the magnesium powder could be mixed with other chemicals, called oxidising agents, which enabled it to be ignited very readily by a taper, sparks from a flint wheel or by percussion caps. Flash lamps using this explosive mixture were popular during the earlier part of this century, until the advent of the flash bulb.
Magnetaufzeichnung f (**MAZ**) magnetic recording
  A video or audio recording effected by the changing polarity of microscopic particles of metallic oxide on film or tape base passing across the modulated gap of a magnetic head, (→) Magnetkopf.
Magnetaufzeichnungstechnik f (**MAZ-Technik** f) magnetic recording technique
→ Magnetaufzeichnung
Magnetausgleichsspur f magnetic balance track, balance stripe, balancing magnetic stripe, balancing stripe
  The extra strip on a magnetic-striped film, opposite the main stripe, to avoid uneven winding.
Magnetband n magnetic tape
Magnetbandgerät n magnetic tape recorder
Magnetbandkassette f (**Kassette** f) magnetic tape cassette, cassette, tape cartridge
Magnetbild n magnetic picture, magnetically recorded image
Magnetbildaufzeichnung f (**MAZ**) video tape recording (VTR), videotape recording, video cassette recording (VCR)
→ Magnetaufzeichnung
Magnetbildaufzeichnungsanlage f (**MAZ**) video tape recorder (VTR), video cassette recorder (VCR), video recorder, television tape recorder, colloq ampex
Magnetfilm m (**Magnettonfilm** m) magnetic sound film
magnetische Bildaufzeichnung f
→ Magnetbildaufzeichnung
Magnetkopf m (**Magnettonkopf** m) magnetic head, magnetic sound head
  One out of three magnetic gaps, i.e. the erase head, the record head, and the playback head, that are in contact with the tape in audio recording.
Magnetperfoband n (**Perfoband** n, **Perfomagnetband** n) perforated

magnetic tape, perforated magnetic film, magnetic film
Magnetplatte f magnetic disk, magnetic disc
Magnetrandspur f (**Magnetspur** f) magnetic track, sound track, mag track
  Any magnetically recorded sound track.
Magnetton m magnetic sound
Magnettonaufnahme f magnetic sound recording
Magnettonband n magnetic sound tape, magnetic tape
Magnettongerät n magnetic tape recorder, magnetic recorder, tape recorder
Magnettonkamera f sound camera, magnetic sound camera
Magnitude-Skalierung f *(social res)* magnitude scaling, magnitude estimation, magnitude production
  A direct scaling method in which it is the subjects' task to assign numbers to objects under investigation, so that they are proportional to the subjective magnitudes.
Mag-Optical-Kopie f magoptical copy, magoptical print, combined print
Mahalanobis-Distanz f (**D²-Abstandsmaß** n) *(stat)* Mahalanobis distance, Mahalanobis generalized distance, Mahalanobis D^2, D^2 statistic
  A measure of the distance between two populations with differing means but identical dispersion matrices.
Mailing n
  → Aussendung, Postaussendung
Mail-order-
  → Versand-, Versandhandels-
MAIS n *abbr* Marketing-Informations-System
Majuskel f
  → Großbuchstabe (Versal)
Make-or-buy-Entscheidung f *(econ)* make-or-buy decision, make or buy
  The general decision-making dilemma for a manufacturer facing the alternative of whether a product that is needed should be made or bought. There is no German equivalent for the English term.
Makler m *(econ)* broker, agent, middleman, go-between
  A functional middleman whose services to a principal are intermittent, he has limited authority to make terms, and he finances his principal only under unusual circumstances. He may represent either the buyer or the seller.

Maklergebühr f (**Maklerprovision** f, **Maklerlohn** m, **Courtage** f) *(econ)* broker's fee, broker's commission, broker's charge, brokerage, brokerage fee, brokerage commission
  A charge, sometimes in the form of a commission, (→) Provision, made by a functional middleman for bringing buyer and seller together. Usually applied to the side for whom the middleman is working, sometimes both buyer and seller pay. A broker does not have direct physical control of the goods in which he deals but represents either buyer or seller in negotiating purchases or sales for his principal. The broker's powers as to prices and terms of sale are usually limited by his principal. The term is often loosely used in a generic sense to include such specific business units as free-lance brokers, manufacturer's agents, selling agents, and purchasing agents.
Maklergewerbe n (**Maklerhandel** m) *(econ)* brokerage
  The trade whose primary function it is to bring buyers and sellers together.
Maklerprovision f
  → Maklergebühr
Maklerwerbung f broker's advertising, brokers' advertising, brokerage advertising
Makroaufnahme f (**Makro** f) *(film/TV)* extreme close-up (E.C.U., ECU), extra close-cup, big close-up (B.C.U., BCU), tight close-up (T.C.U., TCU), macro shot
  A camera shot limited to one part of an object to show maximum detail.
Makrofotographie f
  → Makrophotographie
Makrokilar m *(phot)* pack-shot lens
Makromarketing n macromarketing, macro-marketing
  Marketing from the overall view of the aggregate activity in the economy for meeting society's objectives and needs of a proper flow of goods and services.
  vgl. Mikromarketing
Makro-Marketing-System n macromarketing system, macromarketing system
  vgl. Mikro-Marketing-System
Makromodell n (**makroökonomisches Modell** n) macro model, macroeconomic model
  vgl. Mikromodell (mikroökonomisches Modell)
Makrophotographie f macrophotography

Makrosegmentierung f *(market res)* macro segmentation
Makro-Umwelt f *(marketing)* macro environment
Makulatur f **(Makulaturpapier** n**)** *(print)* wastepaper, waste, spoilage, spoiled sheets *pl,* spoiled copies *pl, auch* maculature
   The amount of paper stock that is wasted in a printing job.
Makulaturbogen m *(print)* spoil sheet, waste sheet
→ Einschießbogen
makulieren (einstampfen) v/i *(paper)*
1. to print waste 2. v/t to pulp, to repulp
   To reduce something to pulp for making paper or cardboard.
Makulierung f **(Einstampfung** f**)** *(paper)* pulping, repulping
Malkarton m **(Zeichenkarton** m**)** illustration board, illustrator's board
   A heavy board or paper, finished on one side, used for wash and tempera drawings.
Mall f **(Mall-Zentrum** n**)**
→ Einkaufszentrum
Malrabatt m **(Wiederholungsrabatt** m**)** frequency discount, time discount, series discount, consecutive-weeks discount (C.W.D., CWD), vertical discount
   A discount, (→) Rabatt, granted on the cost of advertising on the basis of the number of insertions or commercial broadcasts in a specified period of time.
vgl. Mengenrabatt
Malstaffel f **(Wiederholungsrabattstaffel** f**)** frequency discount rate, time discount rate, series discount rate, consecutive-weeks discount rate, C.W.D. rate, CWD rate
→ Malrabatt
Mammutplakat n *(outdoor advtsg) etwa* magna panel poster, magna panel, supersite panel, supersite poster
Management n *(econ)* management
   1. The directors or owner-directors of a firm. 2. Those executive tasks in a business firm which ensure that resources are utilized to achieve economic objectives.
Management n **durch Delegation** *(econ)* management by delegation
Management n **durch Entscheidungsregeln** *(econ)* management by decision rules

Management n **durch Innovation** *(econ)* management by innovation
Management n **durch Kommunikation** *(econ)* management by communication
Management n **durch Motivation** *(econ)* management by motivation
Management n **durch Systemorientierung (systemorientiertes Management** n**)** *(econ)* management by systems
Management n **durch Verstärkung** *(econ)* management by reinforcement
Management n **nach Ausnahmeprinzipien** *(econ)* management by exception
   A management technique by which the attention and energies of management are focused on those activities where performance is significantly different from goals, to establish why, and to attempt corrective measures whenever large enough deviations are recorded.
Management n **nach Ergebnissen** *(econ)* management by results
Management n **nach Organisationen** *(econ)* management by organization, *brit* organisation
Management n **nach Zielvorgaben** *(econ)* management by objectives (MBO)
   A management technique by which each management function is required to define the objectives it is set to achieve. Supervisors on all levels are drawn into the process, and a mechanism is arranged so that any superior and his subordinates may contribute mutually discussed inputs. Four aspects are generally regarded as fundamental: the objectives must be stated clearly, the time factor must be set as an established schedule of events to occur, subordinates must be given a significant participatory role in designing the objectives, and motivation must be activated by providing a high level of job satisfaction.
Management-Informations-System n **(MIS)** *(econ)* management information system (MIS)
   An information system in which data from a firm's market environment are collected in computers in a systematic and comprehensive manner, evaluated in terms of relevance and accuracy, transformed to make them useful and usable, and conveniently stored or expeditiously transmitted to the user.

Managementwissenschaft f *(econ)* management science, operations research (OR)
An approach to management that emphasizes the application of scientific methods for the improved understanding and practice of management.
→ Operations Research
Manilapapier n
→ Packpapier
Manipulation f **(Manipulieren** n**)** manipulation
manipulieren v/t to manipulate
Mann-Whitney-Test m **(Mann-Whitneyscher Rangsummentest** m, **Mann-Whitney-U-Test** m, **U-Test** m**)** *(stat)* Mann-Whitney test, Mann-Whitney U test, U test
A test of significance, (→) Signifikanztest, applicable to two independent samples.
Mannequin n model, mannequin
manuelle Datenaufbereitung f manual data processing
manuelle Datenauszählung f manual data counting, tallying
Manuskript n manuscript (MS, pl MSS), typescript, script
→ Drehbuch
Manuskriptabteilung f **(Drehbuchabteilung** f**)** *(radio/TV)* continuity department, continuity acceptance, department, continuity clearance department
Manuskriptberechnung f **(Satzumfangsberechnung** f**)** *(print)* copy casting, casting, casting off, castoff
The use of mathematical computations to estimate the space a piece of copy will occupy when set in a specific type and line length.
Manuskripthalter m *(print)* copyholder, copy holder
→ Korrekturgehilfe
Marginalanalyse f **(Grenzwertanalyse** f**)** *(econ)* marginal analysis
Marginalie f **(Randbemerkung** f**)** *(print)* marginal note, side note, *brit* side-note
Marginalien f/pl *(print)* marginal notes pl, side notes pl, *brit* side-notes pl, marginalia pl
Marginalverteilung f
→ Randverteilung
Marginalzahl f **(Marginalziffer** f**)**
→ Randziffer

Marke f 1. *(econ)* (Markenname) brand, brand name, *auch* trade name, (Auto, Radio) make
A name, term, sign, symbol, or design, or a combination of them which is intended to identify the goods or services of one seller or group of sellers and to differentiate them from those of competitors. A brand may include a brand name, a trade mark, or both. The term is sufficiently comprehensive to include practically all means of identification except perhaps the package and the shape of the product. All brand names (→) Markenbezeichnung, and all trade marks, (→) Warenzeichen, are brands or parts of brands but not all brands are either brand names or trade marks. Brand is the inclusive general term. The others are more particularized.
2. → Markenartikel (Markenware)
3. → Markenzeichen
4. → Markierung
5. → Warenzeichen
6. → Rabattmarke
Markenakzeptanz f **(Markenartikelakzeptanz** f**)** brand acceptance
Markenartikel m, **Markenprodukt** n**)** *(econ)* brand article, branded article, branded goods pl, brand product, branded product, branded merchandise
All goods that are identified with a proprietary name and are normally prepacked by a manufacturer for promotional, security, or trading purposes.
Markenartikelanzeige f **(Markenartikelwerbemittel** n**)** brand advertisement, brand product advertisement, brand ad, brand product ad
Markenartikelbewußtsein n
→ Markenbewußtsein
Markenartikelhersteller m **(Markenartikelprodukt** m**)** *(econ)* brand producer, brand article producer, branded goods producer, brand product manufacturer
Markenartikelkäufer m
→ Markenkäufer m
Markenartikelpräferenz f
→ Markenpräferenz
Markenartikelpreis m
→ Markenpreis
Markenartikelprofil n
→ Markenprofil
Markenartikelsystem n **(Markenartikelabsatzsystem** n**)** *(econ)*

branded goods, system, branded merchandise system, brand product distribution system
Markenartikeltreue f
→ Markentreue
Markenartikelvertrieb m *(econ)* brand distribution, branded merchandise distribution, brand product distribution, branded goods distribution
Markenartikelwerbung f brand advertising, branded goods advertising, brand product advertising, branded merchandise advertising
Markenassoziation f *(market res)* brand association, (Assoziation mit einer Gebrauchsgüterkategorie) commodity-brand association, (mit einer Produktkategorie) product-brand association
>The association of a specific brand with its general product category or with an unsatisfied want, used to measure the share of mind, (→) Markenbekanntheit, the brand enjoys.

Markenausdehnungsstrategie f *(marketing)* brand extension strategy, brand extension
>A competitive tactic that involves the addition of (a) new product(s) to the existing products of a company, all of which are marketed under a single brand name.

Markenauswahl f (**Markenauswahlentscheidung** f, **Markenwahl** f) brand choice, interbrand choice
Markenbarometer n (**Markenindex** m) *(market res)* brand barometer, brand trend survey
>The continuous observation of brand developments in a market.

Markenbekanntheit f *(marketing)* brand awareness, share of mind, (Bekanntheitsgrad) brand rating, share of mind rating
>The extent to which consumers are aware of a particular brand. More specifically, the percentage of all brand awareness or brand advertising awareness for a given category of product or service that ist enjoyed by a particular brand in that category.

Markenbekanntheitsindex m *(market res)* brand rating index (BRI)
>A service which measures the marketing and media exposure patterns of adults on a national basis in the fall of each year. BRI interviewers personally place and retrieve self-administered questionnaires with a sample of approximately 15,000 adults. These call for the respondent's estimate of frequency of consumption for a large number of products or services, information on brands purchased, and detailed definitions of exposure to all major magazines and network TV shows (along with more generalized data on radio and newspapers). BRI provides definitions of audience and marketing by demographics and the relationships that exist between media and marketing behavior. It is useful for direct comparisons of audience levels among heavy or light product user groups or buyers of individual brands.

Markenbekanntheitstest m *(market res)* brand awareness test, share-of-mind test
Markenbevorzugung f
→ Markenpräferenz
Markenbewußtsein n (**Markenartikelbewußtsein** n) *(marketing)* brand consciousness, brand product consciousness
>The degree to which (a) consumer(s) is (are) determined to buy branded rather than unbranded goods.

Markenbezeichnung f
→ Markenname
Markenbild n
→ Markenimage, Markenprofile
Markenbildung f *(econ)* branding
Markenbindung f
→ Markentreue
Markendesign n *(marketing)* brand design
Markendifferenzierung f *(econ)* brand differentiation
>The strategy of establishing a brand image as unique or, as a result thereof, the degree to which the uniqueness of a brand's image is established.

Markenentscheidung f
→ Markenauswahl, Markenwahl
Markenerzeugnis n (**Markenfabrikant** n)
→ Markenartikel
Markenfamilie f *(econ)* family of brands, brand family
→ Familienmarke
Markenfenster n *(POP advtsg)* brand product display window
Markenfigur f (**Markensymbol** n, **Symbolfigur** f) trade character
>An animated object, an animal, or an invented person designed to personify and identify a product or an advertiser.

Markenführer m *(econ)* brand leader

That brand among a number of competing brand products that holds the greatest single share of a market, (→) Markanteil.
Markenführung f *(econ)* brand leadership
Markenfunktion f *(econ)* brand function
Markengebrauchsgut n *(econ)* branded commodity, branded durable consumer product, branded consumer durable
Markenidentität f *(econ)* brand identity
Markenimage n **(Markenvorstellungsbild** n**)** brand image
The pattern of associations, thoughts, feelings, and atmosphere the general public of consumers holds in regard to a particular brand.
Markenimagewerbung f **(Imagewerbung** f **für eine Marke)** brand image advertising
Markenindex m *(market res)* brand index
→ Markenbarometer
Markeninformation f brand information, (Markeninformationen pl) brand intelligence
Markenkäufer m **(Markenartikelkäufer** m**, Markenwarenkäufer** m**)** *(econ)* brand buyer, brand purchaser
Markenloyalität f
→ Markentreue
Markenmanagement n
→ Produktmanagement
Markenname m **(Markenbezeichnung** f**)** *(econ)* brand name, trade name
A brand or part of a brand consisting of a word, letter, group of words or letters comprising a name which is intended to identify the goods or services of a seller or a group of sellers and to differentiate them from those of competitors. The brand name is that part of a brand which can be vocalized – the utterable.
Markenpersönlichkeit f *(econ)* brand personality
→ Produktpersönlichkeit
Markenpiraterie f *(econ)* brand piracy
Markenpolitik f **(Markierungspolitik** f**)** *(econ)* brand policy, policy of branding, branding, branding policy
Markenpotential n
→ Marktpotential (einer Marke)

Markenpräferenz f **(Markenproduktpräferenz** f**)** *(econ)* brand preference
The degree to which prospects consider a brand acceptable or unacceptable, especially relative to competitive brands.
Markenprägnanz f *(marketing)* brand-product association, brand association, brand impression
→ Markenassoziation
Markenpreis m **(Markenproduktpreis** m**)** *(econ)* brand price
Markenprodukt n
→ Markenartikel
Markenprofil n **(Profil** n **einer Marke)** *(marketing)* brand profile
Markenqualität f *(marketing)* brand quality, quality of brand products
Markenstil m
→ Werbestil
Markenstrategie f *(marketing)* branding strategy, brand strategy
Markentest m *(market res)* brand product test, brand test
→ Produkttest
Markentrend m *(market res)* brand trend
Markentreue f **(Markenartikeltreue** f**, Markenbindung** f**, Markenloyalität** f**)** *(econ)* brand loyalty, (vollkommene Markentreue) brand insistence
The faithfulness a user displays toward a brand, as measured by the relative length of time or regularity with which he uses the item.
Markenverband e.V. m German Brand Producers' Association
Markenverbund m
→ Komplementarität
Markenvergleich m **(Vergleich** m **von Markenartikeln)** *(market res)* brand comparison
Markenvertrieb m **(Markenartikelvertrieb** m**)** *(econ)* brand distribution
Markenwahl f **(Markenwahlentscheidung** f**, Markenauswahl** f**, Markenauswahlentscheidung** f**)** *(econ)* brand choice
The gamut of decision alternatives ranging from brand insistence or loyalty, (→) Markentreue, to brand switching, (→) Markenwechsel.
Markenwahrnehmung f **(Markenperzeption** f**)** *(market res)* brand perception
Markenware f
→ Markenartikel
Markenwarenwerbung f
→ Markenartikelwerbung

Markenwechsel m *(econ)* brand switching
The decision of a consumer to select among the available brand products or services of the like type one that differs from that he bought before.
Markenwechselmodell n **(Modell** n **des Markenwechsels)** *(market res)* brand-switching model, model of brand switching
Markenwechsler m *(econ)* brand switcher
Markenwerbung f
→ Markenartikelwerbung
Markenzeichen n
→ Marke, Warenzeichen, Bildzeichen
Marketing n *(econ)* marketing
The total system of interacting business activities designed to plan, price, promote, and distribute want-satisfying products and services to present and potential customers. In a narrower sense, the performance of business activities that direct the flow of goods and services from producer to consumer or user. It includes such facilitating activities as marketing research, transportation, certain aspects of product and package planning, and the use of credit as a means of influencing patronage.
Marketing n **der öffentlichen Hand**
→ Öffentliches Marketing
Marketingabteilung f *(econ)* marketing department
A department in a business firm, a manufacturer or mass service organization responsible for the development, implementation, and review of its marketing strategy and marketing plans.
Marketingagentur f **(Marketingmittler** m**)** *(econ)* marketing agency, marketing agent
Marketingaktivität f *(econ)* marketing activity, marketing effort
Marketinganalyse f *(econ)* marketing analysis
Marketing-Assessment n
→ Marketing-Folgenbewertung
Marketingassistent(in) m(f) *(econ)* marketing assistant
Marketing-Audit n
→ Marketingrevision
Marketingaufgabe f *(econ)* marketing task
Marketingausgabe f *(econ)* marketing expenditure
Marketingberater m *(econ)* marketing adviser, marketing consultant

Marketingberatung f *(econ)* marketing advice, advisory marketing, marketing consultancy
Marketingberufe m/pl marketing professions pl
Marketingbriefing n marketing briefing
Marketingbudget n **(Marketingetat** m**)** *(econ)* marketing budget
A statement of the planned monetary sales and planned marketing cost for a specified future period. The term Marketingbudget is usually confined to an estimate of future sales, while the term Marketingetat includes schedules of both receipts and expenditures.
Marketingbudgetallokation f **(Marketingbudgetaufteilung** f**)** *(econ)* marketing budget allocation, allocation of marketing budget
Marketing-Club m marketing club
Marketingdirektor m *(econ)* marketing manager, marketing executive, marketing director
→ Marketingleiter
Marketingdynamik f *(econ)* marketing dynamics pl *(construed as sg)*, dynamics pl *(construed as sg)* of marketing
Marketingeffektivität f *(econ)* marketing effectiveness, effectiveness of marketing, marketing efficiency
Marketingentscheidung f *(econ)* marketing decision
Marketing-Entscheidungskriterium n *(econ)* criterion of marketing decision, criterion of marketing decision-making
Marketing-Erfolgskontrolle f *(econ)* marketing effectiveness control, measurement of marketing performance
Marketingetat m
→ Marketingbudget
Marketing-Ethik f ethics pl *(construed as sg)* of marketing, marketing ethics pl *(construed as sg)*
Marketingforscher m marketing researcher
Marketingforschung f marketing research
The systematic gathering, recording and analyzing of data about problems relating to the marketing of goods and services. Such research may be undertaken by impartial agencies or by business firms or their agents for the solution of their marketing problems.

Marketing research is the inclusive term which embraces all research activities carried on in connection with the management of marketing work. It includes various subsidiary types of research, such as (1) market analysis, (→) Marktanalyse, which is a study of the size, location, nature, and characteristics of markets (2) sales analysis (or research), (→) Umsatzanalyse, which is largely an analysis of sales data; (3) consumer research (→) Konsumentenforschung, of which motivation research, (→) Motivationsforschung, is a type, which is concerned chiefly with the discovery and analysis of consumer attitudes, reactions, and preferences, and (4) advertising research, (→) Werbeforschung, which is carried on chiefly as an aid to the management of advertising work.
→ Absatzforschung, Marktforschung

Marketingführerschaft f (Marketingführung f) *(econ)* marketing leadership

Marketingfunktion f *(econ)* marketing function
A major specialized activity or group of related activities performed in marketing. There is no generally accepted list of marketing functions, nor is there any generally accepted basis on which the lists compiled by various writers are chosen.

Marketinggebiet n (Marketingbereich m) *(econ)* marketing area, marketing territory

Marketinggemeinschaft f
→ Gemeinschaftsmarketing

Marketinggenossenschaft f (Erzeugergemeinschaft f) *(econ)* marketing cooperative, *brit* co-operative
An organization formed by a group of farmers who have joined together to sell their produce more efficiently. As a group they can hire specialized managers, advertise and promote with greater impact, control handling and grading quality so that consumer demand may be enhanced.

Marketinginformation f *(econ)* marketing information, (Marketinginformationen f/pl) marketing intelligence
A marketing function, (→) Marketingfunktion, characterized by the accumulation and dissemination of intelligence concerning market developments and other market data.

Marketing-Informations-System n (MAIS) *(econ)* marketing information system (MAIS), marketing intelligence system
The means by which a business firm or mass service organization coordinates its various marketing functions, (→) Marketingfunktion, and integrates the activities of the marketing department, (→) Marketingabteilung, with those of the company as a whole through the collection of relevant data.

Marketinginstrument n *(econ)* marketing instrument, instrument of marketing, marketing tool
Any one of the variety of activities, processes, and techniques used for implementing marketing strategies or tactics.

Marketingkommunikation f *(econ)* marketing communication(s) *(pl)*
The routes and methods by which a business firm or mass service organization communicates with its market(s) by means of the press, television, radio, advertising and all other forms of nonpersonal promotion. A wider understanding of the term holds that it also covers factors such as price, outlet, branding and packaging, all of which serve to communicate an impression or a piece of information about the product(s) or service(s).

Marketingkontrolle f *(econ)* marketing control

Marketingkonzept n (Marketingkonzeption f) *(econ)* marketing concept, marketing philosophy
The consumer-oriented management philosophy which holds that all marketing activities should develop from or be designed to meet the needs of the consumer and that this is the best means to satisfy corporate objectives.

Marketingkooperation f
→ Gemeinschaftsmarketing

Marketingkoordination f (Marketingkoordinierung f) *(econ)* marketing coordination, coordination of marketing, *brit* co-ordination

Marketingkosten pl *(econ)* marketing cost(s) *(pl)*

Marketingkostenanalyse f *(econ)* marketing cost analysis
The study and evaluation of the relative profitability or cost of different marketing operations in terms of customers, marketing units, commodities, territories, or marketing activities. One of its tools is marketing cost accounting, (→) Marketingkostenrechnung.

Marketingkostenrechnung f (econ) marketing costing, marketing cost accounting
> The branch of cost accounting which involves the allocation of marketing costs according to customers, marketing units, products, territories, or marketing activities.

Marketingleiter m (econ) head of marketing department, marketing department head, marketing director, director of marketing, marketing executive, marketing manager
> An executive employee of a manufacturer or mass service organization responsible for its marketing management, (→) Marketingmanagement. In most firms the person who performs these functions is a member of its top management in that he or she plays a part in determining company policy, in making product decisions, and in coordinating marketing operations with other functional activities to achieve the objectives of the company as a whole.

Marketinglogistik f (**physische Distribution** f) (econ) marketing logistics pl (construed as sg), physical distribution
> The management of the movement and handling of goods from the point of production to the point of consumption or use.

Marketingmanagement n (econ) marketing management
> The planning, direction and control of the entire marketing activity of a firm or division of a firm, including the formulation of marketing objectives, policies, programs and strategy, and commonly embracing product development, organizing and staffing to carry out plans, supervising marketing operations, and controlling marketing performance.

Marketing-Management-System n (econ) marketing management system

Marketingmanager m
→ Marketingleiter

Marketing-Mix n (econ) marketing mix (Neil H. Borden)
> The unique combination of a firm's controllable marketing variables, in particular its product policy,
> (→) Produkt-Mix, distribution,
> (→) Distributions-Mix, communication,
> (→) Kommunikations-Mix, and pricing,
> (→) Kontrahierungs-Mix.

Marketing-Mix-Instrument n
→ Marketinginstrument

Marketing-Mix-Modell n
→ Marketingmodell

Marketingmodell n (econ) marketing model
> A model that is a device for simulating not only a market, cf. (→) Marktmodell, but also the manner in which the individual supplier to the market obtains his share of it.

Marketingökologie f (econ) marketing ecology
→ Ökomarketing

Marketingoperation f (econ) marketing operation

Marketingorganisation f (econ) marketing organization, brit marketing organisation

marketingorientiert adj (econ) marketing-minded, marketing-oriented

Marketingorientierung f (econ) marketing orientation
> The general orientation of a business firm's policy toward consumer needs, in contrast to production orientation.

Marketingphilosophie f (econ) marketing philosophy
→ Marketingkonzept

Marketingplan m (econ) marketing plan
> Both the implicit strategy for marketing a product or service and the comprehensive document explicitly formulating the strategy, background and supportive detail regarding a marketer's objectives.

Marketingplanung f (econ) marketing planning
> The work of setting up objectives for marketing activities and of determining and scheduling the steps necessary to achieve such objectives. This understanding of the term includes the work of deciding upon the goals or results to be attained through marketing activity and the determination in detail of exactly how they are to be accomplished.

Marketingpolitik f (econ) marketing policy
> A course of action established to obtain consistency of marketing decisions and operations under recurring and essentially similar circumstances.

marketingpolitische Instrumente n/pl (econ) instruments pl of marketing policy, marketing policy instruments pl, tools pl of marketing policy
→ Marketinginstrument; vgl. absatzpolitische Instrumente

Marketingprogramm n *(econ)*
marketing program, *brit* marketing
programme
　The coordination of all the elements of
　the marketing mix, (→) Marketing-Mix,
　for the company as a whole toward the
　attainment of a particular goal.
Marketingprozeß m *(econ)* marketing
process
Marketingpsychologie f marketing
psychology
→ Marktpsychologie
Marketingrecht n marketing
legislation, marketing regulations pl
Marketingrevision f *(econ)* marketing
audit
　A rigorous scrutiny of the marketing
　system within a firm to determine its
　efficiency, the strengths and weaknesses
　of the system's parts and how well the
　parts are performing their assigned
　tasks.
Marketing-Service m *(econ)*
marketing services pl
　A collective term used to cover all
　marketing activities other than sales, i.e.
　marketing communications,
　(→) Marketingkommunikation, including
　advertising and public relations.
Marketingsituation f *(econ)*
marketing situation
Marketingsoziologie f marketing
sociology, sociology of marketing
Marketingstatistik f marketing
statistics pl *(construed as sg)*
Marketingsteuerung f *(econ)*
marketing control
Marketingstrategie f *(econ)*
marketing strategy
　The explicit or implicit plan describing
　or underlying all activities involved in
　achieving a particular marketing
　objective, and their relationship to one
　another in time and magnitude.
Marketingsystem n *(econ)* marketing
system
Marketingtheorie f *(econ)* marketing
theory, theory of marketing
Marketingumwelt f *(econ)* marketing
environment, environment of
marketing
Marketingziel n **(absatzpolitisches
Ziel** n) *(econ)* marketing objective
Marketingzyklus m *(econ)* marketing
cycle
markierte Ware f
→ Markenartikel
Markierung f *(econ)* 1. (Waren)
branding 2. (Kennzeichnung)

marking, (Etikettierung) labeling,
brand labeling
Markierungspolitik f **(Markenpolitik**
f) *(econ)* branding policy
Markovkette f **(Markoff-Kette** f,
Markovsche Kette f) *(stoch)* Markov
chain
　A system of a set of events in which each
　event depends upon the outcome of the
　preceding event.
Markovmodell n **(Markoff-Modell** n,
Markovsches Modell n) *(stoch.)*
Markov model
Markov-Prozeß m **(Markoff-Prozeß**
m, **Markovscher Prozeß** m) *(stoch)*
Markov process
Markt m *(econ)* market, marketplace,
brit market-place
　In the most general sense, the economic
　place where supply, (→) Angebot, and
　demand, (→) Nachfrage, come together.
　More specifically, the aggregate of forces
　or conditions within which buyers and
　sellers make decisions that result in the
　transfer of goods and services; or the
　aggregate demand of the potential
　buyers of a commodity or service.
Marktabdeckung f *(econ)* market
coverage, market coverage intensity
　The extent to which sales and marketing
　activities succeed in reaching a target
　market.
Marktabgrenzung f *(econ)* market
zoning
Marktabschöpfung f **(Marktabschöpfungspolitik** f)
→ Abschöpfung (Abschöpfungsstrategie)
Marktakzeptanz f *(econ)* market
acceptance
　The condition in which a product or
　service satisfies a sufficient proportion of
　its market.
Marktanalyse f *(market res)* market
analysis
　A sub-division of marketing research,
　(→) Marketingforschung, which involves
　the measurement of the extent of a
　market and the determination of its
　characteristics.
Marktanpassung f *(marketing)*
market adjustment, adjustment to the
market
Marktanteil m *(econ)* market share,
share of market, (eines Marken-
artikels) brand share, brand share of
market, (einer Produktgruppe)
category development, market
development, category development

index, market development index, (einer Marke pro 1000 Einwohner) brand development (B.D.), brand development index (B.D.I., BDI)
   The ratio of a company's actual sales to the total industry sales, expressed as a percentage.
   vgl. Marktpotential
Marktatomisierung f (**Atomisierung** f **des Marktes**) *(econ)* market atomization, *brit* market atomisation
Marktaufbaumethode f *(marketing)* buildup method, market buildup method
Marktausschöpfung f
→ Abschöpfung
Marktausweitung f *(econ)* market extension
Marktbefragung f (**Marktumfrage** f) *(market res)* market survey
Marktbeherrschung f *(econ)* market domination
Marktbeobachtung f *(market res)* market observation
Marktcharakter m (Ernst Fromm) *(psy)* market character
Marktdaten n/pl *(econ)* market data pl
Marktdiagnose f
→ Marktanalyse
Marktdifferenzierung f *(econ)* market differentiation
Marktdurchdringung f *(econ)* market penetration
   The extent to which a firm supplying a market with a product or service has realized its market potential, (→) Marktpotential.
Marktdurchdringungspolitik f *(marketing)* market penetration policy
Marktdurchsetzung f (**Marktgeltung** f) *(econ)* market acceptance
→ Marktakzeptanz
Markteinführung f *(econ)* market launch, launch
→ Produkteinführung
Markteintritt m *(econ)* market entry
Marktentscheidung f *(econ)* market decision
Markterkundung f *(market res)* market exploration
Markterschließung f
→ Einführung neuer Produkte
Marktexpansion f (**Marktausweitung** f) *(econ)* market expansion
Marktexperiment n *(market res)* market experiment

Marktfähigkeit f *(econ)* marketability
Marktfaktor m *(econ)* market factor
Marktfeld n *(econ)* market field
Marktform f *(econ)* form of the market, type of market, market structure
Marktforscher m market research
Marktforschung f market research
   The gathering, recording, and analyzing of all facts about problems relating to the transfer and sale of goods and services from producer to consumer.
Marktforschungsabteilung f market research department, market research
Marktforschungsberater m market research adviser, market research consultant
Marktforschungsbericht m (**Marktforschungsreport** m) market research report
Marktforschungsbriefing n market research briefing
Marktforschungsbudget n (**Marktforschungsetat** m) market research budget
Marktforschungsdaten n/pl market research data pl
Marktforschungsdesign n
→ experimentelle Anlage
Marktforschungsinformationen f/pl market research intelligence
Marktforschungsinstitut n market research institute
Marktforschungsorganisation f organization of market research, *brit* organisation of market research, market research organization
Marktforschungsplan m market research design, design of market research investigation
Marktforschungspräsentation f
→ Präsentation
Marktforschungsreport m
→ Marktforschungsbericht
Marktforschungsverband m (**Marktforscherverband** m) market research association, association of market researchers
Marktforschungsverfahren n (**Marktforschungstechnik** f) market research technique
Marktfragmentierung f (**Marktparzellierung** f) *(econ)* market fragmentation
Marktführer m *(econ)* market leader
   The brand, product or service, or the company which markets it, scoring the

largest market share, (→) Marktanteil, within its field, i.e. in comparison with its competitors.
Marktführerschaft f **(Marktführung** f**)** *(econ)* market leadership
Marktgebiet n *(econ)* trading area, trading zone
→ Absatzgebiet, Einzugsbereich
Marktgeltung f
→ Marktdurchsetzung
Marktgröße f **(Marktvolumen** n**)** *(econ)* market size, size of market, market volume, volume of market
  The actual volume of total sales of products, services, firms in one market.
Markthandel m **(Meßhandel** m**)** *(econ)* marketplace trade, local market trade, public market trade
Marktherausforderer m *(econ)* market challenger
Marktindex m *(econ)* market index
Marktindikator m *(econ)* market indicator
Marktinformation f *(econ)* market information, (Informationen pl) market intelligence
Marktinstrument n *(econ)* market instrument
→ Marketinginstrument
Marktinvestition f *(econ)* market investment
Marktkanal m *(econ)* market channel
→ Absatzkanal, Absatzweg, Beschaffungskanal, Beschaffungsweg
Marktkapazität f *(econ) etwa* market want, want
Marktkapital n (Herbert Gross)
→ akquisitorisches Potential
Marktkette f
→ Absatzkette
Marktkommunikation f market communication, market communications pl (construed as sg)
→ Marketingkommunikation
Marktkonstellation f *(econ)* market configuration
Marktkontrolle f *(econ)* market control
Marktlage f
→ Marktposition
Marktleistung f *(econ)* market performance
Marktlogistik f
→ Marketinglogistik

Marktlücke f **(Marktnische** f**)** *(econ)* niche in the marketplace, market niche
Marktmacht f *(econ)* market power
  The ability of a market partner to control the activities in which it engages in the market, e.g. determining prices, acquiring sources of supply, controlling that part of the trade channel which is its concern; in short, market power is an indication to the absence of competition.
Marktmachtverteilung f *(econ)* distribution of market power
Marktmanagement n
→ Marketingmanagement
Marktmanager m
→ Marketingmanager
Markt-Mix n
→ Marketing-Mix
Marktmodell n *(econ)* market model
  A model that simulates the functioning of a market.
Marktmorphologie f **(Marktformenlehre** f**)** *(econ)* market morphology, theory of market structure
Marktnachfrage f
→ Nachfrage
Marktneuheit f **(Marktinnovation** f**)** *(econ)* market innovation, innovation
→ Innovation
Marktnische f (Bernt Spiegel)
→ Marktlücke
Marktordnung f *(econ)* market organization, *brit* market organisation, market regulations pl
Marktorganisation f *(econ)* organization of the market, *brit* organisation of the market
Marktorientierung f *(econ)* market orientation
→ Marketingorientierung
Marktphase f *(econ)* market phase
Marktplanung f *(econ)* market planning
Marktpolitik f *(econ)* market policy
Marktposition f **(Marktstellung** f**)** *(econ)* market position, position in the marketplace, market standing
Marktpositionierung f
→ Positionierung
Marktpotential n **(MP)** *(econ)* market potential, market sales potential, total market (einer Marke) brand potential
  A calculation of maximum possible sales opportunities for all sellers of a good or service during a stated period.

Marktpotentialanalyse f *(market res)* market potential analysis, analysis of market potential, (einer Marke) brand potential analysis, analysis of brand potential
Marktpreis m *(econ)* market price
  The ruling price at which a product or service ist exchanged in the marketplace.
Marktprofil n *(econ)* market profile
  A collection of facts about the prospects, or an analysis by age, sex, income, possessions, etc., of people who constitute the market for a product or service.
Marktprognose f *(market res)* market prognosis, market forecast
Marktprojektion f *(market res)* market projection
Marktpsychologie f market psychology
Marktreaktion f *(econ)* market response
  Any of the consequences, particularly in terms of sales, marketing activities may stimulate.
Marktreaktionsfunktion f **(Marktreaktionskurve** f**)**
  → Reaktionsfunktion
Marktregion f
  → Marktgebiet
Marktreichweite f *(marketing)* market reach
  The total number of prospects it is possible to reach in a marketing campaign.
Marktreife f *(econ)* marketability
Marktsättigung f *(econ)* market saturation, market satiation
  The level at which any further expansion of distribution in a market can no longer be achieved.
Marktsättigungsfunktion f
  → Sättigungsfunktion
Marktsättigungsphase f
  → Sättigungsphase
Marktschreierei f **(marktschreierische Werbung** f**)** puffing advertising, puffery, puffing, puff, ballyhoo, tum-tum
Marktschreier m **(marktschreierischer Kundenwerber** m**)** barker
Marktschwankung f *(econ)* market fluctuation, (stärker) market vacillation
Marktsegment n *(market res)* market segment

Marktsegmentierung f **(Marktsegmentation** f**)** *(market res)* market segmentation, *auch* market cleavage
  The theory and practice of dividing the market for a product into defined, homogeneous subsections in order that each segment may be treated in the most appropriate manner, because different segments of a market may display individual behavior patterns and, therefore, a different approach.
Marktseitenverhältnisse n/pl (Paul Theisen) *(econ) etwa* market partner relationships pl
Marktselektion f
  → Marktsegmentierung
Marktsimulation f *(market res)* market simulation
  → Marktmodell, Simulation
Marktsimulationsmodell n *(market res)* market simulation model
Marktsituation f *(econ)* market situation
Marktsoziologie f **(Soziologie** f **der Marktbeziehungen)** market sociology
Marktspaltung f **(Marktteilung** f**)** *(marketing)* market split, split of the market, split market
Marktspanne f *(econ)* market margin
  The average margin of profit, (→) Gewinnspanne, in a specific market.
Marktstatistik f market statistics pl (construed as sg)
Marktstellung f
  → Marktposition
Marktstrategie f *(marketing)* market strategy
  → Marketingstrategie
Marktstruktur f *(econ)* market structure, market composition
  The pattern of characteristic features of a market that are so significant economically that they affect the behavior of the firms in the industry supplying the market, such as the number and size distribution of buyers and sellers, the type and importance of product differentiation, and the conditions of entry of new sellers.
Marktstudie f **(Marktuntersuchung** f**)** *(market res)* market study, market investigation
  A research study which seeks to isolate demographic, attitudinal or similar factors which determine the patterns of consumer behavior toward a category of goods or services or seeks to depict key groupings of consumers.
Marktteilung f
  → Marktspaltung

Markttheorie f *(econ)* market theory
Markttransaktion f *(econ)* market transaction
Markttransparenz f *(econ)* openness of the market
Markttyp m *(econ)* type of market, market type
Marktüberschwemmung f (**Marktübersättigung** f, **Marktverstopfung** f) *(econ)* glut of the market
Marktunifizierung f *(marketing)* market unification
Marktuntersuchung f
→ Marktstudie
Marktveranstaltung f *(econ)* etwa regular market event, regularly convened market
Marktverhalten n *(econ)* market behavior, *brit* market behaviour
Marktverhaltensanalyse f *(market res)* analysis of market behavior, *brit* analysis of market behaviour, market behavior analysis, *brit* marketbehaviour analysis
Marktverstopfung f
→ Marktüberschwemmung
Marktvolumen n *(econ)* size of the market, market size, market volume
→ Marktgröße
Marktwachstum n *(econ)* market growth
Marktwachstums-Marktanteils-Portfolio n *(marketing)* market growth - market share portfolio
→ Portfolio-Management
Marktwachstumsrate f *(econ)* rate of market growth, market growth rate
  The rate of present or forecast market growth.
Marktwert m *(econ)* market value
  The price at which a product or service is valued at the market, (→) Marktpreis.
Marktwiderstand m *(econ)* market resistance, (der Käufer) buyers' resistance
Marktwirkung f
→ Marktreaktion
Marktwirkungsfunktion f
→ Reaktionsfunktion (Wirkungsfunktion)
Marktwirtschaft f market economy, free market economy
marmorieren v/t *(print)* to marble
Marmorierung f (**Marmorieren** n) *(print)* marbling

Marmorpapier n (**marmoriertes Papier** n) marble paper, marbled paper
Marronkopie f
→ Feinkornkopie
Mart m (**Trade Mart** m)
→ Großhandelszentrum
maschinegestrichenes Papier n (**maschinell gestrichenes Papier** n) machine-coated paper
maschinelle Ätzung f (**Maschinenätzung** f) *(print)* machine etching
  The process of etching printing plates in a machine by the mechanical application of the mordant to the metal surface, or by electrical action.
maschinelle Datenaufbereitung f (**maschinelle Tabulierung** f) *(stat)* machine tabulation of data, machine data tabulation, machine tabulation
  vgl. manuelle Datenaufbereitung
maschinelle Glättung f *(paper)* machine finish (M.F., MF)
→ maschinenglattes Papier
Maschinenabzug m (**Maschinenbogen** m) *(print)* machine proof, press proof
  A proof made on the regular printing press before or during the actual press run.
Maschinenfalz m (**Maschinenfalzung** f) machine fold, machine folding
maschinengestrichenes Papier n
→ maschinegestrichenes Papier
maschinenglatt (**maschinell geglättet**) *adj (paper)* machine-finished (M.F., MF), mill-finished
maschinenglattes Papier n machine-finished paper (M.F., MF), mill finished paper
  An uncoated, smooth paper for printing books; it has been sized but not ironed and takes halftones.
Maschinenpapier n machine-made paper
Maschinenpappe f machine-made board
Maschinenrevision f *(print)* machine revise, final proof
→ Maschinenabzug
Maschinenrichtung f
→ Laufrichtung
Maschinensatz m (**maschineller Satz** m) *(print)* machine composition, mechanical composition
  Type set mechanically, or machine-set in contrast to hand-set.
  vgl. Handsatz

Maschinensaal m (Druckerei f, Druckereiraum m) *(print)* press room
Maschinensetzer m *(print)* machine compositor, machine typesetter, machine operator
Maschinenstein m
→ Lithographiestein
Maske f **1.** *(phot/film/print)* (Abdeckmaske) mask, frisket
  A sheet of paper or other material used to cover part of an area to help it free from ink, paint or air-brush action and to take a particle proof of type matter or engraving.
2. *(phot)* (Kamera) mask, matte, matt, mat, vignette, border
  A cutout or shield fitted to a camera lens to reduce or give a specific shape to the camera's field.
3. (Make-up) mask, makeup, make-up
4. → Auflegemaske
Maskenbildner(in) m(f) *(film/TV)* make-up artist, makeup artist, makeup man, makeup woman
Maskenbildnerei f **(Maskenbildnerwerkstatt** f) *(film/TV)* make-up department, make-up room
Maskenröhre f *(TV)* shadow mask tube
Maskentrick m
→ Kaschtrick (Kaschverfahren)
maskieren v/t → abdecken
maskierte Anzeige f **(abgedeckte Anzeige** f) *(advtsg res)* masked advertisement, masked ad, masked copy
Maskierungstest m **(Werbemitteltest** m **mit Maskierung)** *(advtsg res)* masked-identification test, masked copy-identification test, masked copy identification, masked copy test
  A print copy test using advertisements in which the brand or company name is masked for the purpose of measuring association with the advertiser.
Maskierung f **(Maskieren** n)
→ Abdeckung (Abdecken)
Maslows Bedürfnishierarchie f
→ Bedürfnishierarchie
Masse f **(statistische Masse** f)
→ Grundgesamtheit
Massenartikel m
→ Massenprodukt, Massenware
Massenauflage f mass circulation
Massenaussendung f **(Massenversand** m) *(direct marketing)* mass mailing, blanket mailing, bulk mailing

Massenbedarfsgut n *(econ)* mass commodity, mass consumer good, *meist pl* goods, mass product, bulk commodity
Massenblatt n **(Zeitung** f **mit Massenauflage)** mass-circulation paper, (Zeitschrift) mass-circulation magazine
Massendrucksache f
→ Massenaussendung
Massenfenster n
→ Stapelfenster
Massenfertigung f **(Massenproduktion** f) *(econ)* mass production
Massengüter n/pl
→ Massenware
Massenkommunikation f mass communication, mass communications *pl (construed as sg)*
  The delivery of large numbers of identical messages simultaneously by communication organizations, or media, in contrast to personal or individual communication.
Massenkommunikationsforschung f mass communication research, mass communications research
Massenkommunikationsmittel n
→ Massenmedium
Massenkomparserie f *(film/TV)* crowd supers *pl*, crowd extras *pl*
Massenkopie f
→ Verleihkopie
Massenkultur f masscult
Massenmarkt m *(econ)* mass market
Massenmedium n mass medium
  A communication and advertising medium directed to and intended to attract the general public.
Massenpresse f mass-circulation press, popular press
Massenprodukt n
→ Massenbedarfsgut
Massenproduktion f
→ Massenfertigung
Massenpsychologie f **(Psychologie** f **der Masse)** mass psychology
Massenstreuung f
→ Allgemeinstreuung
Massensuggestion f mass suggestion
Massenumwerbung f
→ Mengenumwerbung
Massenverbrauchsgut n
→ Massenbedarfsartikel
Massenversand m
→ Massenaussendung
Massenvertrieb m *(econ)* mass distribution

Massenware *f*
→ Massenbedarfsartikel
Massenwerbung *f*
→ Mengenumwerbung
Massenzeitschrift *f* mass-circulation magazine, popular magazine
Maßkorrelation *f*
→ Korrelation
Maßstabsfrage *f*
→ Ergebnisfrage
Maßzahl *f* statistic
Mast *m* mast, pylon
Masterkopie *f*
→ Dup-Positive
Master Sample *n*
→ Ausgangsstichprobe
Matched Groups *pl*
→ parallelisierte Gruppen
Matching *n*
→ Parallelisierung
Mater *f* **(Matrize** *f*) *(print)* matrix, mat, mold, *brit* mould, (Maternpappe) flong
  A mold of impregnated paper pulp, plastic, or other substance taken from type or plates. Molten lead cast in this mold produces a stereotype, (→) Stereotypie. Also, a brass mold used in typesetting machines.
matern *v/t (print)* to make a mat, to make a matrix, to mold, *brit* to mould
Materndienst *m (print)* matrix service, mat service
  A commercial organization supplying advertisers, publications, and printers with ready-made mats (→) Mater, and illustrations through a subscription service.
Maternkarton *m* **(Maternpappe** *f*) *(print)* flong
  A paper used for matrix making.
Maternklischee *n (print)* pattern plate
  An electrotype with an extra heavy shell backed with hard metal used for producing mats and additional electrotypes.
Maternpappe *f*
→ Maternkarton
Maternpresse *f (print)* matrix press, mat press
Materplatte *f (print)* boilerplate, boiler plate
  A prepared section of news matter and features offered to newspapers by syndicates in the form of thin metal plates which are attached to metal bases when it is desired to print them.

mathematisches Modell *n*
mathematical model
  An attempt to describe a phenomenon by means of mathematical expressions specifying the relationships among the elements that are related to that phenomenon.
mathematische Programmierung *f*
mathematical programming
  A mathematical technique used to find the optimum relationship between a number of interdependent variables, also a means of obtaining the very best course of action where many courses of action exist.
mathematische Statistik *f*
mathematical statistics *pl (construed as sg)*
Matinée *f (film)* morning performance, matinee
Matrix *f (stat/radio)* matrix
  1. In *statistics*, a grid system of squares for the presentation of data which can be manipulated as if the table were one single element. **2.** In *broadcasting*, a quadrosonic FM broadcast and recording/playback system used to encode quadriphonic signals into a pair of audio channels.
Matrixmanagement *n (marketing)*
matrix management
Matrixorganisation *f* **(Matrixsystem** *n*) *(marketing)* matrix organization, *brit* matrix organisation, matrix system
  A mode of organizing large-scale projects that includes persons having both task and function assignments and as a consequence being attached to two units of the organization at one time. The organization diagram has functional units across the top and task units down the side with entries indicating persons from various functions assigned to a given task.
Matrix-Projekt-Management *n*
(marketing) matrix project management
→ Matrixorganisation
Matrixsystem *n*
→ Matrixorganisation
Matrize *f* **1.** → Mater
  2. (Schablone) stencil
  1. A sheet of paper or other material from which certain portions have been removed so as to form designs, letters, etc.; **2.** A fibrous, waxed sheet used in mimeographing, etc.; a stylus or typewriter removes the wax so as to leave designs or lettering, and ink can

Matrizenpapier

pass through these areas to a sheet of paper beneath.
Matrizenpapier n
→ Maternpapier
matt (mattiert) adj **1.** *(paper)* matte, matt, mat, dull-coated, dull-finish **2.** *(print)* (Farbe) dull **3.** *(phot)* (Licht) soft, subdued
Mattaufnahme f (**Mattbild** n, **Mattphoto** n) dead matte, dead matt, dead mat, dull finish, matte finish, matt finish, mat finish, matte surface, matt surface, mat surface
 A photographic print or photostat having a dull finish so as to be easily marked with pencil or pen.
Matteverfahren n (**Mattaufnahme** f)
→ Kaschverfahren
Mattdruck m (**Mattdruckverfahren** n) dull-finish printing
Mattglanz m (**Mattierung** f) *(paper)* eggshell finish, English finish (E.F., EF), dull enamel
Mattglanzpapier n (**mattglänzendes Papier** n) eggshell paper, eggshell, English finish paper, English finish (E.F., EF), dull enamel
 A smooth-finished, machine-made and calendered book paper with an even surface.
Mattglanzpaste f *(print)* encaustic paste
 A wax paste used to impart a slight gloss to matte or semi-matte prints.
mattieren v/t to matte, to matt, to mat, to dull
Mattierung f (**Mattieren** n) dull finish, matte finish, matt finish, mat finish, matting
Mattkunstdruckpapier n (**mattes Kunstdruckpapier** n) mat art paper
Mattscheibe f **1.** groundglass, ground glass, ground-glass, groundglass screen, ground-glass screen, ground-glass plate, ground-glass plate
 A sheet of glass ground to a matte surface.
2. *(phot)* focusing screen
 The surface on which camera images are viewed and brought to correct size and sharpness, usually consisting of a sheet of groundglass.
3. *(TV)* screen
Maueranschlag m
→ Wandanschlag
Mauerbemalung f
→ Wandbemalung

Mäusezähnchen n/pl *(TV)* jitters pl, mouse's teeth pl, serrations pl
 A small, vibrational malfunction of the television picture.
maximal adj maximum
Maximalbildfeld n *(phot)* maximum field of view
Maximalfeldwinkel m *(phot)* maximum field angle
Maximax-Entscheidung f (**Maximax-Kriterium** n, **Maximax-Regel** f) *(stat)* maximax decision, maximax criterion, maximax rule
 A decision that maximizes the maximum gain.
 vgl. Maximin-Entscheidung, Minimax-Entscheidung
Maximierung f *(econ)* maximization, brit maximisation
Maximin-Entscheidung f (**Maximin-Kriterium** n, **Maximin-Regel** f) *(stat)* maximin decision, maximin criterion, maximin rule
 A decision that maximizes the minimum gain.
 vgl. Maximax-Entscheidung, Minimax-Entscheidung
Maximum n (**Höchstwert** m, **Maximumstelle** f, **Scheitelwert** m, **Scheitelstelle** f) *(stat)* maximum
Maximum-Likelihood-Methode f (**Maximum-Likelihood-Schätzung** f, **Maximum-Likelihood-Verfahren** n, **Methode** f **der größtmöglichen Mutmaßlichkeit** f, **Methode** f **der größten Dichte**) *(stat)* maximum-likelihood method, method of maximum likelihood, maximum-likelihood estimation, maximum-likelihood technique, method of ml
 A method of estimating (a) parameter(s) of a population by that value (s) which maximise(s) the likelihood, (→) Mutmaßlichkeit of a sample.
Maximumstelle f
→ Maximum
maya-Maxime f (**Maya-Prinzip** n) *(econ)* maya principle ("most advanced yet acceptable" principle) (Richard Loewy)
maz abbr Meldestelle für das Anzeigenwesen von Zeitschriftenverlegern e.V.
MAZ abbr Magnetbandaufzeichnung, Magnetbildaufzeichnung
MAZ-Band n
→ Magnetband

MAZ-Cutter m videotape cutter, VT cutter
mazen v/t to videotape, to VTR, to VT, to tape
MAZ-Kontrolle f VTR control, VT control
MAZ-Schnitt m **(MAZ-Cutten** n**)** videotape editing, videotape cutting, VTR editing, VTR cutting, VT editing, VT cutting
MAZ-Techniker m videotape operator, videotape engineer, VTR operator, VT operator, VT engineer/ editor
MAZ-Wagen m mobile videotape recorder (MVTR)
McNemar-Test m *(stat)* McNemar test, correlated proportions test, test for significance of changes
A test of significance, (→) Signifikanztest, for paired samples classified on the same dichotomous variable.
MDS *abbr* Multidimensionale Skalierung
Me-too-Produkt n *(econ)* me-too product
Me-too-Werbung f me-too advertising
mechanische Kommunikation f mechanical communication
mechanischer Schnitt m **(Filmschnitt** m**, Schnitt** m**)** *(film/TV)* mechanical cut, mechanical cutting
mechanischer Spilt m
→ Anzeigensplitting
Media n/pl
→ Medium
Media- *adj* media
Media-Abteilung f media department
A department, usually in full-service advertising agencies, responsible for maintaining and collating media statistics.
Media-Agentur f **(Streuagentur** f**)** media agency, media buying agency, media buying service, media services agency, media buying shop, media broker
An agency which specializes in purchasing print space or broadcast time for an advertiser. Its services may include media planning or other support services.
Mediaanalyse f **(Werbeträgeranalyse** f**)** media analysis
Media-Assistent(in) m(f) media assistant
Media-Auswahl f
→ Mediaselektion

Mediaforschung

Mediaberater m media consultant
Mediaberatung f media consultancy
Mediabindung f **(Leser-Blatt-Bindung** f**)** media involvement, media loyalty, media confidence, (Senderbindung) *(radio/TV)* channel loyalty
Mediabriefing n media briefing
Media-Buyer m
→ Mediaeinkäufer
Mediadaten n/pl **(Media-Unterlagen** f/pl**)** media data pl, rate book, media data card
Media-Direktor m **(Leiter** m **der Media-Abteilung)** media director, media manager
An advertising agency executive responsible for the selection, the purchase of space or time and the scheduling of advertising media.
Mediadisponent m
→ Mediaeinkäufer, Anzeigenkäufer
Media-Einkauf m **(Streuplanung** f**)** media buying, *(print media)* space buying, *(radio/TV)* airtime buying
The function, skill and responsibility of those members of an advertising agency's staff who are in charge of presenting advertising messages in media for communicating at the right time to the largest number of greatest possible effect.
Media-Einkäufer m **(Streuplaner** m**, Mediadisponent** m**)** media buyer, *(print media)* space buyer, *(radio/TV)* airtime buyer, time buyer
An advertising agency employee who helps plan both printed advertising campaigns and campaigns in broadcast media, and who selects and buys space in publication, outdoor, and transit media or radio and television time.
Media-Einsatz m **(Media-Einsatzplan** m**)** *(media planning)* flow chart
A scheduling calendar which plots the media elements of an advertising campaign as they will be used across a period of time. It shows when the ads or commercials will be used and helps the advertiser to relate his activity to seasonal or other problems.
→ Mediaplan
Media-Entbehrlichkeit f
→ Leser-Blatt-Bindung, Mediabindung
Media-Experte m **(Medienfachmann** m**)** media expert, media man
Mediaforscher m media researcher
Mediaforschung f **(Werbeträgerforschung** f**)** media research

Mediafunktion

The systematic investigation and analysis of audience and circulation data of communications media, their characteristics, both qualitative and quantitative factors, cost factors and mechanical data with regard to their suitability as advertising vehicles.

Mediafunktion f
→ Werbeträgerfunktion

Mediagattung f (**Werbeträgergattung** f) media type

Mediagewicht n (**Werbeträgergewicht** n) *(media planing)* media weight, media vehicle weight
An instrument of media planning used for weighting, (→) Gewichtung, advertising expenditure according to the value of particular media characteristics, particularly qualitative factors, as a reflection of the expected effectivenees with which advertising will work in a particular medium.

Mediagewichtung f (**Werbeträgergewichtung** f) *(media planning)* media weighting, media vehicle weighting
→ Mediagewicht

Mediaglaubwürdigkeit f (**Werbeträgerglaubwürdigkeit** f) media credibility, media believability
→ Glaubwürdigkeit

Media-Image n
→ Medienimage

Mediakandidatenliste f
→ Kandidatenliste

Mediakombination f (**Belegungskombination** f, **Werbeträgerkombination** f) media combination, advertising media combination, combination, combination buy, combined media scheduling
Advertising in two or more media at a combination rate, (→) Kombinationstarif.

Mediakonsumgruppe f media consumption group

Medialeiter m
→ Mediadirektor m

Media-Mann m
→ Media-Experte

Mediamanager m
→ Mediadirektor

Mediamarketing n media marketing

Mediamathematik f media mathematics *pl (construed as sg)*

Mediamarkt m
→ Medienmarkt

Media-Mix n media mix, *auch* media support

That part of the communication mix which consists of the entire complex of advertising media that are used in marketing, advertising and promotion campaigns.

Media-Mix-Planung f
→ Mediaplanung

Median m (**Zentralwert** m, **zentraler Wert** m) *(stat)* median
That value in a given set of values above which and below which half of the values in the set fall. It is the "middle" value when the values in the set are arrayed in order of magnitude. The median can be readily computed when the number of values in the set is odd. When the number is even, the median is, by convention, the mean of the two middle values.

Mediantest m (**Zentralwerttest** m) *(stat)* median test

Medianutzer m
→ Mediennutzer

Medianutzung f
→ Mediennutzung

Media-Overlapping n
→ Überschneidung

Mediapanel n *(media res)* media panel, media panel survey
A panel survey, (→) Panel, conducted to investigate the media consumption behavior of a target group over a longer period of time.

Mediaplan m (**Streuplan** m) media plan, media schedule, schedule of insertions, schedule, space plan, space schedule, timetable, *colloq* sked
A listing of proposed advertisements, by specific media, with dates of appearance, amount of space or time, etc.

Mediaplaner m (**Streuplaner** m) media planner, media man
An advertising agency employee who applies expert knowledge of media and statistical data from media analyses to the planning and implementation of media schedules, (→) Mediaplan, to obtain maximum coverage of a target audience at minimum cost.

Mediaplanung f (**Streuplanung** f) media planning, media scheduling, media buying, media distribution of advertising (Einsatzplanung) media phasing
→ Mediaplan, Mediaplaner

Mediaplanungsabteilung f
→ Media-Abteilung

Mediapräsentation f media presentation

Mediaprestige n
→ Werbeträgerprestige
Mediarecht n
→ Medienrecht
Mediareichweite f **(Reichweite** f
eines Werbeträger) *(media res)* media
coverage
  The reach of an advertising schedule that
  employs one or more media vehicles. It is
  usually expressed as a percentage of the
  population group which the advertiser
  has targeted as his prime marketing
  prospects.
→ Reichweite
Mediaselektion f **(Media-Auswahl** f,
Werbeträgerauswahl f) *(media
planning)* media selection, media
choice, advertising media selection
  The process of deciding which are the
  appropriate advertising media to achieve
  advertising objectives in line with a
  given media strategy and evaluation and
  of allocating the given advertising budget
  to the various media types and individual
  media.
Mediaselektionsentscheidung f
(Werbeträgerauswahl f) *(media
planning)* media selection choice,
media choice, media choice decision,
media selection decision
Mediaselektionsmodell n **(Modell** n
der Werbeträgerauswahl) *(media
planning)* media selection model
Mediaselektionsprogramm n **(Media-
Auswahlprogramm** n) *(media
planning)* media selection program,
brit programme
Mediaselektionsverfahren n
(Methode f **der Mediaselektion)**
(media planning) media selection
procedure, medie selection technique,
method of media selection
Mediastrategie f
→ Medienstrategie
Mediastreuplan m
→ Mediaplan
Media-Terminplan m **(Terminplan** m
des Werbeträgereinsatzes) *(media
planning)* media timetable, media
schedule, schedule, *colloq* sked
→ Mediaplan
Media-Unterlagen f/pl
→ Mediadaten
Mediavergleich m *(media planning)*
media comparison
→ Intermediavergleich, Intramedia-
vergleich

Mediaverhalten n
→ Mediennutzung, Medienverhalten
Mediavertrag m media agreement,
advertising agreement
→ Werbevertrag
Mediawahl f
→ Mediaselektion
Mediawerbung f **(klassische Werbung**
f, **Werbung** f **in Werbeträgern)** media
advertising, media-vehicle advertising,
above-the-line advertising, theme
advertising
  Any traditional commission paying
  advertising in communication media, in
  contrast to direct-mail advertising, POP
  advertising, etc.
Media-Wirkungsforschung f
→ Wirkungsforschung
Mediaziel n **(Mediaplanziel** n) media
objective
  One of a variety of specific media goals
  for an advertising campaign, such as the
  desired reach of key target groups,
  media-mix combinations, the
  compatibility of copy to media, obtaining
  proper frequency levels, and seasonal
  and timing factors.
Medien n/pl **(Werbeträger** m/pl)
media *pl*
Medienanalyse f
→ Mediaanalyse
Medienangebot n
→ Werbeträgerangebot
Medienausstattung f **(Ausstattung** f
der privaten Haushalte mit Medien)
media household penetration
Medienbindung f
→ Mediabindung
Medienduplikation f
→ externe Überschneidung
Medienforscher m
→ Mediaforscher
Medienforschung f
→ Mediaforschung
Medienfunktion f
→ Werbeträgerfunktion
Mediengattung f
→ Mediagattung
Mediengewicht n
→ Mediagewicht
Mediengewichtung f
→ Mediagewichtung
Medienimage n **(Media-Image** n,
Image n **eines Werbeträgers)** media
image, media image profile
  The attitudes and opinions users or
  prospective users have with reference to
  a medium.

Medienkombination f
→ Mediakombination
Medienkontakt m **(Werbeträgerkontakt)** m, **Kontakt** m **mit einem Werbeträger)** *(media res)* media exposure, advertising media exposure
→ Kontakt; *vgl.* Werbemittelkontakt
Medienkultur f media culture
Mediennutzer m **(Nutzer** m **eines Werbeträgers)** media consumer, media user
Mediennutzung f **(Werbeträgernutzung** f, **Medienkonsum** m) media consumption
Mediennutzungsverhalten n media consumption behavior, *brit* behaviour
Medienpanel n
→ Mediapanel
Medienpolitik f media policies *pl*, media policy, media legislation
Medienpräferenz f **(Werbeträgerpräferenz** f) media preference
Medienrecht n **(Mediengesetzgebung** f) media legislation, media law, media regulations *pl*
Mediensoziologie f media sociology
Medienstatistik f **(Werbeträgerstatistik** f) media statistics *pl (construed as sg)*
Medienstrategie f media strategy
  The general method applied to achieve the advertising plan's media objectives, (→) Mediaziel. It is the plan of action or final blueprint for bringing the advertising message to the consumer.
Medienverbund m **(Medienverbundsystem** n) multimedia system
Medienvergleich m
→ Mediavergleich
Medienverhalten n
→ Mediennutzungsverhalten
Medienvertrieb m **(Pressevertrieb** m) media distribution
Medienwerbung f
→ Mediawerbung
Medienwirkungsforschung f
→ Wirkungsforschung
Medien-Zeitbudget n *(media res)* media time budget
  The time budget, (→) Zeitbudget, for media consumption.
Medium n *(pl* **Medien) (Werbeträger** m**)** medium, advertising medium, media vehicle, advertising vehicle
  Any vehicle used to convey advertising messages, such as television, magazines, or direct mail.

Mehrauflage f overprint, overrun, overissue, surplus copies *pl*, surplus
→ Drucküberschuß
Mehrbedarf m
→ Zusatzbedarf
Mehrbereichantenne f multichannel antenna, *brit* multi-channel aerial
mehrdeutige Angaben f/pl **(Mehrdeutigkeit** f**) (in der Werbung)**
→ irreführende Angaben
mehrdeutige Frage f **(Doppelfrage** f**)** *(survey res)* double-barreled question, double-barreled question
mehrdimensionale Morphologie f multidimensional morphology
→ Morphologie.
mehrdimensionale Skalierung f
→ Multidimensionale Skalierung (MDS)
Mehrdimensionalität f **(Multidimensionalität** f**)** multidimensionality
Mehrdruck m
→ Fortdruck
Mehrebenenanalyse f
→ Multivariate Datenanalyse
Mehrfachabzug m **(Mehrfachkopie** f**)**
→ Verleihkopie
Mehrfachangaben f/pl **(Mehrfachnennungen** f/pl**)** *(survey res)* multiple replies *pl*, multiple responses *pl*
Mehrfachfrage f **(Mehrfachauswahl** f**)**
→ Auswahlfrage
Mehrfachbelichtung f **(Simultanbelichtung** f**)** *(phot)* multiple exposure
Mehrfachbelichtungskamera f **(Doppelbelichtungskamera** f**)** *(phot)* multiple exposure camera
  A process camera, (→) Reprokamera, fitted with an attachment of shutters or flaps to permit up to four exposures being made on a plate or film.
Mehrfachecho n multiple echo, flutter echo
Mehrfachkabel n multiple cable
Mehrfachkontakt m **(Wiederholungskontakt** m**)** *(media res)* multiple exposure
→ externe Überschneidung, interne Überschneidung
Mehrfachkontur f *(TV)* multiple ghosting
Mehrfachkorrelation f
→ multiple Korrelation

Mehrfachleser m *(media res)* multiple reader, (Zeitschriften) multi-magazine reader
vgl. **Exklusivleser**
Mehrfachmeßgerät n multimeter
Mehrfachmodulation f multichannel modulation, multi-channel modulation, multiplex modulation
Mehrfachnennungen f/pl
→ Mehrfachangaben
Mehrfachpackung f (**Mehrstückpackung** f) masterpack, multipack, multiple-unit package, multiple-unit packaging, combination pack
A package containing a number of smaller or individual packages.
Mehrfachregression f
→ multiple Regression
Mehrfachtest m (**Mehrfachprodukttest** m) *(market res)* multiple-product test
Mehrfaktorenanalyse f
→ multiple Faktorenanalyse
Mehrfarben-(mehrfarbig) adj *(print)* multi-color, *brit* multi-colour, multiple color, *brit* multiple-colour, full-color, *brit* full-colour
Mehrfarbanzeige f (**mehrfarbige Anzeige** f) color advertisement, *brit* colour advertisement, color ad
Mehrfarbendruck m 1. (Verfahren) multicolor printing, *brit* multi-colour printing, multiple color printing, *brit* multiple-colour printing, polychrome printing, process printing
Printing in which one color is printed over another with transparent inks to produce different hues.
2. (Produkt) multicolor print, *brit* multi-colour print
Mehrfarbendruckmaschine f (**Mehrfarbendruckpresse** f)
multicolor printing press, multicolor printing machine, *brit* multi-colour printing press, *brit* multi-colour printing machine
Mehrfarbenklischee n
→ Farbklischeesatz
Mehr-Firmen-Handelsvertreter m (**Mehr-Firmen-Vertreter** m) vgl. Ein-Firmen-Handelsvertreter (Ein-Firmen-Vertreter)
Mehrgitterröhre f multi-grid valve, multi-grid tube
Mehrheit f majority, *(marketing)* (frühe Mehrheit, Frühadopter) early majority, early adopters pl, (späte

Mehrheit, Spätadopter) late majority, late adopters pl
Mehrheitsirrtum m (**Mehrheitstrugschluß** m) *(marketing)* majority fallacy
The fundamental error made in launching new products or in marketing that anything which pleases the majority of consumers will gain acceptance or be successful in the marketplace.
Mehrheitsumwerbung f
→ Mengenumwerbung
Mehrkomponentenpackung f
→ Mehrfachpackung
Mehrpersonenentscheidung f
→ Gruppenentscheidung
Mehrphasenauswahl f *(stat)* 1. (Stichprobenverfahren) multi-phase sampling, multiple sampling, double sampling 2. (Stichprobe) multi-phase sample, multiple sample, double sample
Mehr-Produkt-Unternehmen n multiple-product enterprise
vgl. Ein-Produkt-Unternehmen
Mehrschichtenfarbfilm m *(phot)* multi-layer color film, *brit* multi-layer colour film
Mehrschichtenpappe f multi-ply board
Mehrstückpreis m *(econ)* multiple-unit price
Mehrstückpreisgebung f (**Mehrstückpreispolitik** f) *(econ)* multiple-unit pricing
A pricing method involving the combination of a number of product units into one wrapping or container, (→) Mehrfachpackung, and selling them at a lower price than the total number of units would cost, if sold individually.
Mehrstufenauswahl f (**mehrstufige Auswahl** f) *(stat)* 1. (mehrstufiges Stichprobenverfahren) multi-stage sampling, multiple-stage sampling, double sampling, multiple sampling 2. (mehrstufige Stichprobe) multi-stage sample, multiple-stage sample, double sample, multiple sample
A sampling procedure, (→) Auswahlverfahren, in which groups of units are sampled at one stage and then units taken from each selected group at the next stage.
Mehrstufenfluß m der Kommunikation (mehrstufige

Kommunikation f) multiple-step flow of communication(s)
→ Zweistufenfluß der Kommunikation
Mehrthemenbefragung f (Mehrthemenumfrage f)
→ Omnisbusbefragung
Mehrvariablenanalyse f (multivariate Analyse f, mehrdimensionale Analyse f) *(res)* multivariate analysis, multivariate data analysis (MDA), multivariate statistical analysis
    Techniques suited for the analysis and interpretation of the interrelationships of three or more variables.
Mehrvariablenexperiment n (multivariates Experiment n) *(res)* multivariate experiment
    An experiment in which two or more variables are allowed to vary simultaneously.
Mehrvariablenstatistik f (multivariate Statistik f) multivariate statistics *pl (construed as sg)*
Mehrwegpackung f (Mehrwegverpackung f) dual-use package, reuse package, re-use package, (Strategie/Vorgang) reuse packaging, re-use packaging, dual-use packaging
vgl. Einwegpackung
Mehrzweckpackung f (Mehrzweckverpackung f) multi-purpose package, multi-purpose pack, double-duty package, double-duty pack
Mehrzweckstudie f (Mehrzweckuntersuchung f, Mehrzweckumfrage f) *(survey res)* multiple-purpose study, multiple-purpose investigation
Meinung f opinion
Meinungsbefragung f public opinion survey, opinion survey
→ Befragung
Meinungsbildner m
→ Meinungsführer
Meinungsbildung f opinion formation
Meinungsblatt n opinion paper, opinion magazine
vgl. Nachrichtenblatt
Meinungsfluß m flow of opinion, opinion flow
Meinungsforschung f public opinion research, opinion research
vgl. Demoskopie, Umfrageforschhung
Meinungsführer m (Meinungsbildner m) opinion leader
    An individual within a community who has a strong impact on others, who tend to look to him for information and advice. In the two-step-flow-of-communication theory, (→) Zwei-Stufen-Fluß der Kommunikation, opinion leaders function as the mediators between the news media and the general public. They are of considerable interest to marketers because successful appeals to these people have the effect of successful appeals to the group, thereby reducing the cost of the promotional campaign and the time of securing acceptance for the product.
Meinungsführerschaft f (Meinungsführung f) opinion leadership
→ Meinungsführer
Meinungsumfrage f
→ Meinungsbefragung
Meistbegünstigungsklausel f (im Mediavertrag) favored-nations clause
    The agreement made by a medium with an advertiser that no comparable purchase shall be made by another advertiser on more advantageous terms without an adjustment in the original terms of purchase.
Meldeleitung f control circuit, control line
Meldestelle f im Anzeigengeschäft von Zeitschriftenverlagen e.V. (maz) German Publishers' Association for the Prevention of Rate Cutting
Meldung f news item, news report, information, news announcement
Mengenabonnement n
→ Sammelabonnement, Gruppenabonnement
Mengenrabatt m (Mengennachlaß m) *(econ/advtsg)* quantity discount, volume discount, space discount, case rate discount, (für Mehrfachschaltungen) bulk discount
    Any discount, (→) Rabatt, granted on the basis of quantity or size of orders. In advertising, a schedule of payment for advertising set by a publisher, in which the charge per unit of space or time decreases as the total units accumulate to specified amounts.
Mengenstaffel f *(advtsg)* quantity discount rate, volume discount rate, space discount rate, case rate, (für Mehrfachschaltungen) bulk discount rate
Mengenumwerbung f (Rudolf Seyffert) mass advertising, media advertising
vgl. Einzelumwerbung
Merchandiser m *(econ)* merchandiser

Merchandising n *(econ)* merchandising
The planning and supervision involved in marketing the particular merchandise or service at the places, times, and prices and in the quantities which will best serve to realize the marketing objectives of the business. The English term has been integrated into German, an original German expression does not exist.
Merkblatt n
→ Schreibregeln
Merkmal n *(res)* characteristic
Merkmalsausprägung f **(Merkmalseigenschaft** f**)** *(res)* property, trait, characteristic
Merkmalsraum m **(Eigenschaftsraum** m**)** *(res)* property space
Merkspur f *(TV)* cue track, control track
An auxiliary audio recording area on a video tape.
Meßbarkeit f mensurability
Meßbereich m measurement range
Messe f trade fair, fair, trade show
An exhibition organized in a large, central place which allows a large number of suppliers to convene at one time to show their wares to customers and prospects.
Messebau m exhibition stand construction, exhibit design and construction
Messebauer m exhibition constructor, exhibit constructor, exhibition designer, exhibit designer, exhibit producer
Messebesuch m trade fair attendance, trade show attendance, fair attendance, show attendance
Messebesucher m trade fair attendant, trade show attendant, fairgoer, showgoer
Messeerfolg m trade fair effectiveness, trade show effectiveness
Messeerfolgskontrolle f trade fair effectiveness control, trade show effectiveness control, (Untersuchung) trade fair audit, trade show audit
Messegelände n trade fair site, trade fair ground, trade show site, trade show ground, fairground, showground
Messemarketing n trade fair marketing, trade show marketing
Messemarktanalyse f trade fair market analysis, trade show market analysis

Messen n **(Messung** f**)** *(res)* measurement, measuring, *auch* mensuration
Messeplanung f trade fair planning, trade show planning
Messerfalzmaschine f knife folder
Messestand m **(Stand** m**, Ausstellungsstand** m**)** exhibition stand
Messetest m trade fair test, trade show test, trade fair audit, trade show audit
Messeumsatz m trade fair sales *pl*, trade show sales *pl*
Messewerbung f **(Messe- und Ausstellungswerbung** f**)** trade fair advertising, trade show advertising
Messeziel n trade fair objective, trade show objective
Meßfehler m *(stat)* measurement error, error in measurement
→ Beobachtungsfehler
Meßfilm m calibration film, test film
Meßgenauigkeit f
→ Zuverlässigkeit (Reliabilität)
Messinglinie f **(Messingreglette** f**)** *(print)* brass rule
Messingstempel m *(print)* brass die
Meßniveau n
→ Skalenniveau
Meßsignal n
→ Testsignal
Meßskala f **(Meßskala** f**)** *(stat)* measurement scale
Meßtechnik f **(Meßverfahren** n**)** *(res)* measurement technique, technique of measurement, measurement procedure, method of measurement, measurement method
Meßtheorie f **(Theorie** f **des Messens)** *(res)* theory of measurement, measurement theory
Meßton m line-up tone
Messung f
→ Messen
Meßverfahren n
→ Meßtechnik
Meßzahl f **(Meßziffer** f**)**
→ Kennzahl
Metakommunikation f meta-communication
Metalldruckstock m metal printing plate
Metallfolie f *(print)* metal foil
Metallfuß m **(Bleifuß** m**, Klischeefuß** m**)** *(print)* metal mount, metal base

Metallklischee

A block of solid type metal on which relief plates are mounted type high in substitution of a wooden base.

Metallklischee n *(print)* metal cut, metal block, metal plate

Metallpresse f *(print)* metal press

Metamarketing n metamarketing, meta marketing (Philip Kotler)
An approach to the study of marketing and its relationship to every aspect of life by focusing all social, ethical, scientific, and business experience on marketing, thus establishing a body of knowledge based on the integration of every facet of experience with the human personality.

Metawerbung f meta advertising

Methode f method

Methode f der Direktbefragung
→ Direktbefragung

Methode f der exponentiellen Glättung
→ exponentielle Glättung

Methode f der gleitenden Durchschnitte
→ gleitender Durchschnitt

Methode f der gleicherscheinenden Intervalle *(scaling)* method of equal-appearing intervals, method of mean gradations
→ Thurstone-Skala

Methode f der größte Dichte
→ Maximum-Likelihood-Methode

Methode f der größten Mutmaßlichkeit
→ Maximum-Likelihood-Methode

Methode f der Halbreihenmittelwerte (Methode f der halben Durchschnitte) *(stat)* method of semi-averages

Methode f der kleinsten Quadrate *(stat)* method of least squares, least-squares method
A technique of estimation by which the quantities under estimate are determined by minimising a certain quadratic form in the observations and those quantities.

Methode f der nachträglich bestimmten Abstände *(stat)* method of graded dichotomies

Methode f der paarweisen Assoziation
→ paarweise Assoziation

Methode f der sukzessiven Intervalle
→ Methode der nachträglich bestimmten Abstände

Methode f der summierten Einschätzungen *(scaling)* method of summated ratings
→ Likert-Skala

Methode f der Teilgruppen
→ gegabelte Befragung

Methode f der transferierten Rangordnungen (Entfaltungstechnik f) *(scaling)* unfolding technique, unfolding

Methode f der Wettbewerbsparität (der Werbebudgetierung) competitive-parity method (of advertising budget determination)
→ konkurrenzorientierte Budgetierung

Methode f des absoluten Urteils *(scaling)* method of absolute judgment

Methode f des kritischen Pfades critical path method (CPM), critical path analysis
A diagrammatic technique of analyzing the scheduling of projects with multiple subactivities, using diagrams that represent the component activities. The time required to complete each activity is analyzed, and the earliest and latest date for beginning each activity is specified. Finally the longest path through the sequence of activities, i.e. the critical path, is identified.

Methode f des Paarvergleichs
→ Paarvergleich

Methodenbank f *(survey res)* method bank, bank of methods

Methodologie f methodology
The logic of scientific investigation, the procedures of research, including the methods of data gathering, handling and analyzing.

Mettage f *(print)* makeup, *brit* make-up
The process of assembling type and plates into complete pages.

Mettageabteilung f *(print)* make-up department

Metteur m *(print)* makeup man, *brit* make-up man, clicker, (Formschließer) lockup man, *brit* lock-up man, stonehand, stone hand
The printer who assembles pages.

Mezzotinto n
→ Schabkunst

Mikrofon n **(Mikrophon** n**)** microphone, *colloq* mike

Mikrofonangel f **(Mikrophonangel** f, **Tongalgen** m**)** hand boom, mike boom, microphone boom

Mikrofonie f (Mikrophonie f)
microphony
Mikrofonprobe f (Mikrophonprobe f)
(radio/TV) voice test
→ Sprechprobe
Mikromarketing n micromarketing
Marketing from the marketing manager's point of view, the specific objectives and activities of the individual firm. The process of formulating and implementing a product development, distribution, pricing and communication strategy that enables an individual company to earn a profit in the marketplace.
Mikrosegmentierung f *(market res)*
micro segmentation
vgl. Makrosegmentierung
Mikrowelle f *(electr.)* microwave
Mikrowellensender m *(radio/TV)*
microwave relay, microwave link
A method of relaying television signals by use of ultra high frequency relay stations at high topographic locations or in mobile equipment.
Mikrowellen-Münzfernsehvertrieb m *(TV)* multi-point distribution system(MDS)
Mikrozensus m (Teilerhebung f)
(stat) sample census
A survey investigation providing census material collected from a sample and not from the universe.
vgl. Vollerhebung
Milieuanalyse f
→ Kontextanalyse
Millimeterpreis m (Millimetertarif m)
(advtsg) (allg) lineage, linage, line rate, Am etwa agate line, column inch, inch, column millimeter rate
Minderheitenpresse f minority press, (ethnische Minderheiten) ethnic press
Minderheitenprogramm n *(radio/TV)* minority program, *brit* minority programme, (ethnische Minderheiten) ethnic program
Mindestabschluß m (Mindestbelegung f) *(advtsg)* etwa minimil rate, minimil, back-up space, back-up page
The minimum amount of advertising space or time an advertising medium is willing to accept.
Mindestanschlagdauer f (Mindestanschlag m) *(outdoor advtsg)* minimum display period, minimum posting period

Mindestauflage f (Minimalauflage f)
minimum circulation, circulation rate base
→ garantierte Mindestauflage
Mindestbelegung f (Minimalbelegung f) *(outdoor advtsg)* minimum showing, quarter showing, *(print advtsg)* back-up space, back-up page
→ Mindestabschluß
Mindestbreite f minimum width
Mindesteinkommen n *(econ)*
minimum income, minimum wage
Mindesteinschaltquote f *(radio/TV)*
minimum audience rating, minimum rating
Mindestgröße f (Mindestformat n)
minimum size
Mindesthöhe f *(print)* minimum depth, minimum depth of space, minimum depth of column, minimum height, minimum column height
The minimum depth acceptable for an advertisement in a publication.
Mindestpreis m (Minimalpreis m)
(econ) minimum price, *(advtsg)* minimum rate, end rate
The lowest possible rate an advertiser can qualify for after every maximum earned discount has been applied.
Mindestrabatt m *(econ)* minimum discount
Mindestzahl f der Kontaktchancen
(media res) minimum frequency (of exposure)
The level of exposure to advertising that is believed to represent the lowest level at which the advertising will be effective in attaining its ends.
Minimarkttest m *(market res)*
minimarket test
Mini-Rolle f
→ Charge
Miniseite f (verkleinerte Seite f)
(print) junior page, pony page minipage, *brit* mini-page
An advertising size of the same proportions as a full page, but scaled down to about two-thirds of the total page.
Miniserie f (kleine Fortsetzungssendung f, kleine Fernsehserie f)
(TV) miniseries
A made-for-television movie of long duration (e.g. 15 hours) that is broken down into a series of episodes presented on different days.
Minimax-Entscheidung f (Minimax-Kriterium n, Minimax-Regel f, Wald-

Regel f) *(stat)* minimax decision, minimax criterion, minimax rule
A decision which minimizes the maximum loss.
vgl. Maximax-Entscheidung, Maximin-Entscheidung
Minimax-Regret-Regel f (Savage-Niehans-Regel f, Regel f des geringsten Bedauerns) *(stat)* minimax regret decision rule, minimax regret rule
The principle of making a decision which minimizes maximum regret.
Minimumstelle f
→ seltenster Wert
Minitestmarkt m *(market res)* mini test market
Minkowski-Metrik f *(stat)* Minkowski metric
Minuskel f
→ Kleinbuchstabe
MIS *n abbr* Management-Informations-System
Mischatelier n *(radio/TV)* mixing studio, mixing room, reduction room
A recording facility equipped to combine electronically two or more audio elements into a single final soundtrack, usually against picture projection.
Mischband n *(radio/TV)* mixing material, reduction material
mischen v/t *(radio/TV)* (Ton) to mix, (Bild) to mix, to crossfade, to blend, to overlap
To rerecord the several separate sound tracks, voice, music, sound effects, etc., into a single sound track.
→ überblenden
Mischen n *(radio/TV)* (Ton) mixing, (Bild) mixing, crossfading, blending, overlapping
→ mischen
Mischer m *(radio/TV)* mixer, *brit* recordist
A sound-recording engineer who handles the mix control console.
Mischfarbe f *(print/phot)* mixed color, *brit* mixed colour
Mischfrequenz f (Pfeifton m, Überlagerungsfrequenz f) *(radio/TV)* beat frequency
Mischkalkulation f
→ kalkulatorischer Ausgleich
Mischkopf m *(film/TV)* mixing head, superimposing head
Mischlicht n *(phot)* mixed light

Mischplan m *(film/TV)* cue sheet, *brit* dubbing chart
The written collection of sequential cues, usually for audio mixing.
Mischpult n *(radio/TV)* mixing console, mixing desk, control console control desk, mixer
The panel for the control and blending of sound or pictures picked up by multiple microphones or cameras
Mischröhre f mixer valve, mixer tube, converter tube
Mischstudio n *(radio/TV)* mixing studio, mixing suite, dubbing theater
→ Mischatelier
Mischstufe f *(radio/TV)* mixer stage, converter stage
Mischtechnik f
→ Kombinationsdruck
Mischtisch m
→ Mischpult
Mischtonmeister m *(radio/TV)* dubbing mixer
Mischung f
→ Mischen
Mitarbeiterabonnement n *(Zeitschrift/Zeitung)* call-at-office subscription
Mitarbeiterzeitschrift f
→ Werkzeitschrift
Mitbewerber m
→ Konkurrent
Mitbewerberanalyse f
→ Konkurrenzanalyse
Mitbewerberbeobachtung f
→ Konkurrenzbeobachtung
Mitgliederstück n *(Zeitung/Zeitschrift)* association member copy
→ Mitgliedsabonnement
Mitgliederzeitschrift f (Mitgliedszeitschrift f) association magazine, association journal
→ Verbandszeitschrift
Mitgliedsabonnement n *(Zeitung/Zeitschrift)* association subscription
A subscription sale of a periodical publication received because of membership in an association, in which the membership fee includes the cost of subscription.
Mitläufereffekt m (Bandwagon-Effekt m) *(econ)* bandwagon effect, *brit* bandwaggon effect
One of several effects resulting from a pattern of consumer behavior that deviates from the assumptions underlying the law of demand, because people buy a product because others are buying it. Demand is increased by the

desire to conform or to be fashionable. The slope of the demand curve may be positive if this effect continues through a situation of rising price of the product.

Mitleser m **(Folgeleser** m, **Zweitleser** m, **Sekundärleser** m) *(media res)* pass-along reader, pass-on reader, non-buyer-reader, claimed non-buyer reader, secondary reader
→ Folgeleser

Mitleserschaft f **(Mitleser** m/pl, **Folgeleser** m/pl) *(media res)* pass-along audience, pass-along readership, pass-on audience, pass-on-readership, secondary audience, secondary readership
→ Folgeleserschaft

mitschneiden v/t *(radio/TV)* (Sendung) to record, to record off

Mitschnitt m **(Mitschneiden** n) *(radio/TV)* (Sendung) recording, simultaneous recording, recording off the air

Mitschwenk m *(film/TV)* follow shot, following shot, moving shot
  A shot in which the camera moves to follow the action of a scene situation.

Mittagsausgabe f **(Mittagsblatt** n) (Zeitung) noon edition

Mitte f center, *brit* centre; auf Mitte setzen: to center, *brit* to centre

mitteilen v/t to communicate

Mitteilung f communication, message, information

Mitteilungsblatt n
→ Bulletin, Vereinsblatt

Mittel-Zweck-Analyse f *(econ)* means-end analysis

Mittel-Zweck-Beziehung f **(Mittel-Zweck-Relation** f) *(econ)* means-end relation

mittelbare Marktforschung f **(mittelbare Forschung** f) (Karl Christian Behrens)
→ Sekundärforschung

mittelbare Frage f
→ projektive Frage

Mittellänge f *(typ)* x-height
  The standard height of lower-case letters in a given font, as measured by the height of the letter x.

Mittelstand m middle class

Mittelton m **(Halbton** m) *(phot)* middletone
  The range between highlights and shadows of a photograph.

Mitteltonblende f *(phot)* middletone stop
  The lens aperture used in halftone photography to register the middletones, the diameter of which is midway between that of the highlight and detail stops.

Mittelwelle f **(MW) 1.** *(radio)* medium wave, medium frequency
2. *(paper)* → C-Welle

Mittelwellenbereich m *(radio)* medium-wave band, medium-wave frequency, medium-frequency band (MF band)

Mittelwellensender m *(radio)* medium-wave transmitter, medium-frequency transmitter

Mittelwert m **(Mittel** n) *(stat)* mean, average
  There are several kinds of averages, but unless otherwise noted, this term is to be taken to refer to an arithmetic mean, (→) arithmetisches Mittel.

Mittelwert m **der Lage**
→ Lageparameter

Mittler m *(econ)* broker, middleman, functional middleman, go-between
  A business concern that specializes in performing operations or rendering services directly involved in the purchase and/or sale of goods in the process of their flow from producer to consumer. Middlemen are of two types, merchants and agents. The essence of the middleman's operation lies in the fact that he plays an active and prominent part in the negotiations leading up to transactions or purchase and sale.

mittlere Abweichung f **(durchschnittliche Abweichung** f) *(stat)* mean deviation (MD), mean variation
  A measure of dispersion (→) Streuungsmaß, derived from the average deviation of observations from some central value, such deviations being taken absolutely, i.e. without reference to sign.

mittlere quadratische Abweichung f **(mittleres Abweichungsquadrat** n) *(stat)* mean square deviation, standard deviation, variance, mean square (MS)
  The arithmetic mean of the squares of the differences in a set of values from some given value, i.e. their second moment about that value. When regarded as an estimator, (→) Schätzfunktion, of certain parental variance components the sum of squares about the observed means is usually divided by the number of degress of freedom, (→) Freiheitsgrad, not the number of observations.
→ Standardabweichung

mittlere Spannweite f *(stat)* mean range
mittlerer Quartilabstand m (**mittleres Quartil** n, **Quartilabweichung** f, **Interquartilabstand** m) *(stat)* interquartile range
Mittlervergütung f (**Mittlungsvergütung** f, **Mittlerprovision** f)
→ Agenturprovision
Mittlervergütung f **plus Honorar**
→ Pauschale plus commission
Mitverfasser m
→ Ko-Autor
Mix n (**Mixen** n)
→ Mischen
Mobile n *(POP advtsg)* mobile, dangler, wobbler
    An advertising device suspended from the ceiling at points-of-purchase.
Mobile Datenerfassung f mobile data acquisition
Mobilität f mobility
Modalwert m (**Modus** m)
→ häufigster Wert
Mode f fashion
Mode-Akzeptanz f fashion acceptance, acceptance of fashion
Modeartikel m *(econ)* fashion article, fashion goods pl
    A type of product whose major appeal is the frequent change of its design.
Modebeilage f (**Modesupplement** n) fashion supplement
Modeblatt n
→ Modejournal (Modezeitschrift)
Modeforschung f fashion research
Modefotograf m
→ Modephotograph
Modeführer m *(econ)* fashion leader
    An opionion leader, (→) Meinungsführer, in the field of fashion.
Modeführerschaft f (**Modeführung** f) *(econ)* fashion leadership
→ Modeführer
Modejournal n (**Modezeitschrift** f) fashion magazine, fashion journal
Modell n **1.** *(econ)* (Muster) model, sample **2.** *(econ)* (Ausführung) model, type, design **3.** (theoretisches Modell) model
    A representation of a specific reality, usually chosen to be broadly relevant in portraying some aspect in which the model constructor will be interested as an ongoing device.
4. (Mannequin) model **5.** *(econ)* (Produktmodell) model, prototype, (Nachbildung) mockup, mock-up
    A first wirking model or initially constructed version of a product.
6. *(print)* (Gußmodell) pattern
7. *(print)* print
Modellagentur f model agency, talent agency
Modellbank f model bank
Modellbau m model making, model construction
Modellbauer m model maker, model constructor
Modellbroschüre f (**Modellprospekt** m) composite
    A model's brochure, depicting appearance and other vital data.
Modellernen n (**Modellieren** n, **Modellierung** f)
→ Beobachtungslernen
Modellperson f
→ Leitbild, Vorbild
Modellsendung f
→ Pilotsendung
Modelltrick m
→ Figurentrick
Modem n modem (modulator - demodulator)
Modephotograph m (**Modefotograf** m) fashion photographer
Modephotographie f (**Modefotografie** f) fashion photography
Moderation f *(radio/TV)* moderation, presentation, *(TV)* anchoring
Moderator(in) m(f) *(radio/TV)* moderator, presenter, *(TV)* anchorman
moderieren v/t *(radio/TV)* to present, to anchor, to moderate
modern adj modern, (modisch) fashionable
Modeschau f (**Modenschau** f) fashion show, fashion parade
Modewerbung f fashion advertising
Modezeitschrift f
→ Modejournal
Modezyklus m *(econ)* fashion cycle
    The process whereby basic fashion styles move in and out of popularity in a society.
Modifikation f (**Modifizierung** f) modification
Modul n module
Modulation f modulation
Modulationsbeleuchtung f (**Modulationslicht** n) *(phot/film)* modeling light

A light cast on a subject for the purpose of giving emphasis to its general form or to prevent excessive light-and-shade contrast.
Modulationsfrequenz f **(MF)** *(electr.)* modulation frequency (MF)
Modulationsgrad m **(Modulationstiefe** f**)** *(electr.)* modulation depth, modulation ratio, modulation factor
Modulationsklirrfaktor m *(electr.)* modulation distortion
Modulationsrauschen n *(electr.)* modulation noise
Modulationssignal n *(electr.)* modulation signal, program signal, *brit* programme signal
Modulationsübertragung f *(electr.)* modulation transfer
Modulationsübertragungsfunktion f **(Modulationskontrastübertragungsfunktion** f**) (MÜF)** *(electr.)* modulation transfer curve
Modulator m *(electr.)* modulator
modulieren v/t *(electr.)* to modulate
Modus m **(Modalwert** m**)**
→ häufigster Wert
Mogelpackung f slack filling, deceptively oversized package, deceptive package, deceptive packaging
  An oversized package that creates the impression of containing more of a product than it actually contains.
Moiré n *(print/TV)* moiré, moiré pattern, moire, moire pattern, *(TV)* watered silks *pl*
  1. In *printing*, an undesirable effect exactly like the pattern in moire silk that occurs when halftone screens are superimposed on one another with the incorrect degree of tilt. If the screen is not tilted at exactly the right angle, the dots in the new halftone may coincide with those in the old, resulting in a wavy, blurred effect. 2. In *television*, an undesirable optical effect caused by one set of closely spaced lines improperly imposed over another. It is usually caused by the interference of similar frequencies.
Moiré-Effekt m **(Moirébildung** f**)** *(print/TV)* moiré effect, moiré, *(TV)* watered silks effect
→ Moiré
Moment n *(stat)* moment, moment coefficient
Momentaufnahme f *(phot)* instantaneous shot, instantaneous photograph

Momentesystem n **(System** n **der Momente)** *(stat)* moment system
monatlich *adj* monthly, *adv/attr* every month
Monatsblatt n
→ Monatszeitschrift
Monatszeitschrift f **(monatlich erscheinende Zeitschrift** f**)** monthly magazine, monthly publication, monthly journal, monthly
Mönchsbogen m *(print)* friar, blank sheet
→ Schimmelbogen
Monitor m *(TV)* monitor
  A television receiver in the control room or studio used by production personnel or performers to follow the action of a program.
Monitoring n *(TV)* monitoring
Monobad n *(phot)* monobath
→ Einbadentwicklung
monochrom (monochromatisch) *adj (print/phot)* monochrome, monochromatic
→ einfarbig, Einfarb-
Monodistribution f *(econ)* monodistribution, one-channel distribution
vgl. Dualdistribution
Monoempfänger m mono receiver
Monopack n *(phot)* monopack
  A film combining three colors in one layer of emulsion.
monophon *adj* monaural, monophone, mono
Monopol n *(econ)* monopoly
  A market condition in which there is but one source of supply for a given good or class of product, and there are no acceptable substitutes.
monopolistischer Bereich m **(monopolistischer Spielraum** m**)**
→ akquisitorisches Potential
Monopolpreis m **(monopolistischer Preis** m**)** *(econ)* monopolistic price, monopoly price
monopolistischer Wettbewerb m *(econ)* monopolistic competition
  A structure of a market in which many firms offer items of a similar but not identical nature. Each firm tries to differentiate its offering in such a way as to win acceptance over competitors. Generally characterized by a down-sloping demand curve.
Monopolzeitung f non-competitive newspaper, monopoly newspaper

Montage

Montage f **1.** *(print)* assembly, assembling, mounting, montage, (Offsetmontage) stripping, montage
In the most general sense, the operation of attaching by pasting or otherwise layouts, photos, prints or proofs on a backing. Also, the combination of several negatives of different pieces of art work for production as a single engraving. Or, the combination of several drawings or photographs into a single illustration.
2. *(film)* → Filmschnitt

Montagefilm m **(montierter Offsetfilm** m, **Stripping-Film** m**)** *(print)* flat, mechanical, stripfilm, stripping film
In offset lithography, the negatives or positives properly assembled on a lithographic layout and ready for plate making.

Montagefolie f *(print)* goldenrod paper, goldenrod, masking paper
A support for negatives used by a stripper in making flats, (→) Montagefilm, for the albumin process of platemaking in offsetlithography to prevent the exposure of the plate in the blank areas.

Montagetisch m
→ Leuchttisch

Montagevorlage f
→ Montagefilm

Monte-Carlo-Methode f **(Monte-Carlo-Verfahren** n**)** *(stoch.)* Monte-Carlo method, Monte-Carlo procedure

montieren v/t **1.** *(print)* to assemble, to mount, (Offsetfilme) to strip
2. *(film)* → cutten
→ Montage

Montierung f **(Montieren** n**)**
→ Montage

moralischer Kaufzwang m *(marketing/advtsg)* etwa moral coercion to buy

Morgenausgabe f (Zeitung) morning edition, early morning edition

Morgenzeitung f morning newspaper, morning paper

Morphem m morpheme

morphologische Analyse f **(morphologische Methode** f, **diskursive Problemlösungsmethode** f**)** (Fritz Zwicky) *(econ)* morphological analysis

morphologische Matrix f *(econ)* morphological matrix, morphological grid

morphologischer Kasten m *(econ)* morphological box

Moses-Test m *(stat)* Moses test, Moses test of extreme reactions
A nonparametric test of significance, (→) Signifikanztest, use to compare the span of the scores in two samples. The test indicates whether one sample has significantly more extreme scores than the other.

Motiv n **1.** *(psy)* (Motivation) motive, motivation **2.** *(phot)* (photographisches Motiv) motif

Motivanalyse f **(Motivationsanalyse** f **)** *(psy/market res)* motivation analysis, analysis of motives, motive analysis

Motivation f *(psy)* motivation

Motivationsauslösung f
→ Motivation

Motivationsforschung f **(Motivforschung** f**)** *(psy/market res)* motivation research (MR), motivational research
Research which attempts to relate behavior to underlying desires, emotions, and intentions, in contrast to research which merely enumerates behavior or describes a situation; it relies heavily on the use of techniques adapted from psychology and other social sciences. MR consists of a group of techniques developed by the behavioral scientists which are used by marketing researchers to discover factors influencing marketing behavior. These techniques are widely used outside the marketing sphere, for example, to discover factors influencing the behavior of employees and voters.

Motivationsfunktion f motivational function, motivation function

Motivationslage f *(psy)* motivational state

Motivationsmanagement n
→ Management durch Motivation

Motivationsmodell n *(psy)* motivational model, motivation model, pattern of motivation, motivation pattern

Motivationstheorie f *(psy/market res)* motivational theory, theory of motivation

Motivforschung f
→ Motivationsforschung

Motivkonflikt m *(psy)* motivational conflict

Motivkontrast m
→ Objektkontrast

Motivsuche f *(phot/film)* lining-up, location burst, recce, reccy

Motivsucher m
→ Sucher
Motivtheorie f
→ Motivationstheorie
Motorpresse f
→ Automobilpresse
Motto n *(advtsg)* motto, slogan
Mülleimerkontrolle f *(market res)* dustbin check
  A market research survey conducted at the consumer level to establish objective data on the level of household purchases over a period of time according to brand and pack. Emptied containers are retained in a dustbin.
Multidimensionale Skalierung f **(MDS) (mehrdimensionale Skalierung** f**)** *(stat)* multidimensional scaling (MDS)
Multidimensionalität f
→ Mehrdimensionalität
Multifokusobjektiv n *(phot)* multifocus lens, variable focus lens, varifocal lens, zoom lens, zoom
→ Gummilinse
Multifunktionalität f multifunctionality
Multi-Kanal-Kommunikation f **(Mehrkanalkommunikation** f**)** multichannel communication, multichannel communication
Multikollinearität f *(stat)* multicollinearity
Multimarkenstrategie f *(econ)* multiple brand entries strategy, strategy of multiple brand entries
  A competitive strategy which aims to exclude others from a market by producing the same product or the applicable variants of the product under different brands.
Multi-Media-Analyse f multimedia analysis
Multi-Media-Plan m **(Multi-Media-Kampagne** f**)** *(advtsg)* multimedia plan, multimedia campaign, multimedia schedule
  Any advertising campaign which takes place in several media types.
Multi-Media-Planung f *(advtsg)* multimedia planning, multimedia campaign planning, multimedia scheduling
Multi-Media-System n
→ Medienverbund
Multipack m
→ Mehrfachpackung

multiple Auswahl f **(Mehrfachauswahl** f**)**
→ Auswahlfrage
multiple Diskriminanzanalyse f *(stat)* multiple discriminant analysis
multiple Faktorenanalyse f **(Mehrfachfaktorenanalyse** f**)** *(res)* multiple factor analysis
multiple Klassifikationsanalyse f **(Mehrfach-Klassifikations-Analyse** f**)** *(stat)* multiple classification analysis (MCA)
multiple Korrelation f **(Mehrfachkorrelation** f**)** *(stat)* multiple correlation(R)
multiple Regression f **(Mehrfachregression** f**)** *(stat)* multiple regression
Multiplexer m *(TV)* diplexer, multiplexer, dividing filter
  Equipment permitting the transmission of television sound and picture signals from the same antenna.
Multiplexsignal n *(TV)* multiplex signal
Multiplikationstheorem n **(Multiplikationsregel** f**)** *(prob)* multiplication theorem, multiplication rule
Multiplikator m *(communication)* multiplier
multistrategisches Marketing n multistrategic marketing
multivariate Analyse f **(multivariate Auswertung** f**)**
→ Mehrvariablenanalyse
Multivision f *(TV)* multivision, multiscreen technique
mündliche Befragung f **(mündliches Interview** n**, direktes persönliches Interview** n**)** *(survey res)* face-to-face interview, personal interview
Mundwerbung f **(Mundreklame** f**)** word-of-mouth advertising, advertising by word of mouth
  The advocacy of action regarding a product or service which is passed from one person to another without a sponsor's paid support. Plays an important part in the two-step-flow-of-communication theory, (→) Zwei-Stufen-Fluß der Kommunikation.
Münzfernsehen n **(Abruffernsehen** n**, Abonnentenfernsehen** n**, Abonnementfernsehen** n**, Bezahlfernsehen** n**)** pay TV, pay television, subscription television, subscription TV, premium television, premium TV,

Musik

see-fee television, see-fee TV, pay cable television, pay cable TV
　A type of home television programming for which the viewer pays, usually by the program or by the month, and that is distributed by cable or broadcast decoder.

Musik f music
Musikaufnahme f music recording, *(film)* scoring
Musikaufnahmeatelier n (**Musikaufnahmestudio** n) music studio, *(film)* scoring stage
Musikberieselung f (**musikalische Berieselung** f) piped music, nonstop background music, background musik, *colloq* muzak
Musikeinblendung f
→ Kennmelodie
Musiksendung f (**Musikprogramm** n) *(radio/TV)* music broadcast, music program, *brit* music programme, music show, *colloq* platter program
Musikstudio n
→ Musikatelier
Musikspur f (**Tonspur** f **mit Musik**) music track
Musiktonmeister m music mixer, music and sound effects mixer, M. and E. mixer, M & E mixer
Muster n *(econ)* sample
　A representative item or portion used by salesmen or promoters to convince prospective buyers of the product's or service's qualities.
→ Gebrauchsmuster, Geschmacksmuster, Warenmuster, Dienstleistungsmuster, Musterkopie, Warenprobe, Probeexemplar

Musterband m
→ Blindband, Probeband
Musterbogen m *(print)* sample sheet
Musterbuch n
→ Schriftmusterbuch

Musterexemplar n
→ Probeexemplar
Musterfilm m (**Musterkopie** f) *(film)* sample reel, demo reel
　A film showing samples of television commercials or motion picture work.
Musterlager n *(econ)* stock of samples, depot of samples, store of samples
Mustermesse f *(econ)* samples fair, samples trade fair, samples trade show, samples exhibition
Musterschutz m
→ Gebrauchsmusterschutz, Geschmacksmusterschutz
Musterseite f *(print)* sample page, specimen page
Mustertest m
→ Konsumentenjury
Musterung f *(econ)* stockless purchasing
　A system of buying in which the financial responsibility for inventory remains with the vendor. The inventory may remain at he vendor's location or may be placed at the buyer's location, in which case it is called consignment buying, (→) Konsignation.
Musterzeichner m draftsman, draughtsman
Musterzeichnung f draft, design, pattern
Mutterband n master copy, master tape
Mutterfrequenz f *(electr.)* master frequency
Muttersender m *(radio/TV)* parent station, master station, master transmitter
Mutterstein m
→ Lithographiestein
Mutungsbereich m (**Mutungsintervall** n)
→ Vertrauensbereich
Mutungsgrenzen f/pl
→ Vertrauensgrenzen

N

nachahmen v/t to imitate, to copy, (Patente, Gebrauchsmuster etc.) to pirate, to counterfeit
→ plagiieren
Nachahmer m imitator, (Patent, Gebrauchsmuster) pirate, counterfeiter
Nachahmung f imitation, (Patent, Gebrauchsmuster) piracy, counterfeiting, (nachgeahmtes Produkt) counterfeit
→ Plagiat, sklavische Nachahmung
nacharbeiten
→ nachbehandeln
Nacharbeitung f (**Nacharbeit** f)
→ Nachbehandlung
nachätzen v/t (print) to reetch, to rebite
Nachätzung f (**Nachätzen** n) (print) reetching, brit re-etching, rebiting, final etching
The process of supplementary or local etching of halftone plates to satisfactorily render the detail, tones and color values of the original in the printed reproduction. Lightening a tone or local area by additional etching.
Nachaufführungstheater n (**Nachaufführungskino** n) (film) second-run theater, brit second-run theatre
vgl. Erstaufführungstheater
Nachauflage f
→ Nachdruck
Nachaufnahme f (**Nachdrehaufnahme** f, **Neuaufnahme** f, **Retake** m) (film/TV) retake, re-take
The refilming of a motion picture scene or the refilmed scene itself.
nachaufnehmen (nachdrehen) v/t (film/TV) to retake
To rephotograph a scene in a motion picture.
Nachaustastung f (TV) final blanking, post-blanking
Nachbarkanal m (radio/TV) adjacent channel
Nachbarprogramm n (**Nachbarsendung** f) (radio/TV) adjacent program, brit adjacent programme, adjacency
A program following or preceding another on the same television or radio station.
Nachbarschaftsladen m (**Convenience Store** m, **Bequemlichkeitsladen** m) (retailing) convenience store, convenience goods store, bantam store, vest-pocket supermarket, (für Lebensmittel) convenience food store
A small, supermarket type store established to serve the convenience wants, (→) Klein- und Bequemlichkeitsbedarf, of its area.
Nachbarschaftssender m (**Lokalsender** m) (radio/TV) community broadcasting station, community station, local broadcasting station, local station
Nachbarschaftszentrum n (retailing) neighborhood center, neighborhood cluster, neighborhood shopping center
A type of shopping center, (→) Einkaufszentrum, which consists of a group of several stores in an otherwise residential district of a city. Mainly found are convenience goods stores such as grocery, drug, and baked goods stores, and service establishments such as dry cleaners and barber shops. Patronage comes essentially from residents of the area immediately surrounding the location.
Nachbarspot m (**angrenzende Werbesendung** f) (radio/TV) adjacent commercial, adjacency
A broadcast commercial following or preceding another on the same radio or television station.
nachbearbeiten
→ nachbehandeln
nachbehandeln (nachbearbeiten) v/t (phot/print) to finish
→ retuschieren
Nachbehandlung f (**Nachbearbeitung** f) (phot/print) finishing
The final work performed on a printing plate or a photograph for removal of defects and to promote the best possible reproduction.
→ Retusche
Nachbelastung f (**Rückbelastung** f)
→ Rabattnachbelastung (Rabattrückbelastung)

nachbelichten
→ aufhellen
Nachbelichtung f
→ Aufhellen
nachbestellen *(econ)* v/t to reorder
Nachbestellung f *(econ)* reorder, reordering, (Anschlußauftrag) follow-on order
Nachbild n **(Nachbildeffekt** m, **Nachbildwirkung** f) *(psy)* afterimage, *brit* after-image, aftersensation, *brit* after-sensation, aftereffect
The illusory visual image remaining with a spectator after the actual image is no longer visible.
Nachbildung f
→ Nachahmung
Nachdruck m **(Sonderdruck** m, **unveränderte Neuauflage** f) *(print)*
1. (Produkt) reprint, reissue
2. (Vorgang) reprinting
The process of unaltered reproduction of a printed publication.
nachdrucken (unverändert neu auflegen) v/t *(print)* to reprint, to reissue
Nachdruckerlaubnis f
→ Abdruckererlaubnis, Druckerlaubnis
Nachdruckgebühr f
→ Reproduktionsgebühr
Nachdruckrecht n
→ Abdruckrecht, Reproduktionsrecht
nachentwickeln v/t *(phot)* to redevelop
Nachentwicklung f **(Nachentwickeln** n) *(phot)* redevelopment
Nachentzerrung f **(NE)** *(radio/TV)* de-emphasis(DE), post equalization, *brit* post-equalisation
Nachfaßbesuch m *(econ/survey res)* (Vertreter/Interviewer) follow-up call, callback, call-back, follow-up
1. A sales visit to a prospective customer who has expressed interest in a product or service when he or she was visited first. 2. The visit of an interviewer to a household or individual he or she was unable to reach at the first time.
Nachfaßbrief m follow-up letter
In direct-mail advertising, (→) Briefwerbung, a mailing to a potential customer who has expressed interest in a product or service, or more generally, a letter subsequent to the first letter or other action in the introduction of a new product or advertising campaign.

Nachfaßinterview n *(survey res)* callback, call-back
→ Nachfaßbesuch 2.
Nachfaßwerbung f 1. (Werbemittel) follow-up advertisement, follow-up ad, follow-up, (Kampagne) follow-up campaign, follow-through 2. follow-up advertising, follow-through advertising
All advertising actions subsequent to the introductory campaign, (→) Einführungswerbung.
→ Erinnerungswerbung, Verstärkungswerbung
Nachfrage f 1. *(econ)* demand
The quantity of a product or service a market will absorb at a given time under conditions of specified price, income, promotional activity, and environmental factors.
2. *(survey res)* follow-up question, probe
Questions or statements made by the interviewer to the respondent to obtain additional information to a question when the initial answer appears incomplete. The researcher sometimes specifies when to use probes and what to say, but their use is often left to the interviewer's judgment. A key problem for the interviewer is to avoid leading probes that put words into the respondent's mouth.
Nachfrageanalyse f **(Bedarfsforschung** f) *(econ)* analysis of demand, demand analysis
The systematic study of demand for a product or service in order to establish reasons for its success or failure, or to determine how sales can be increased.
Nachfragedichte f **(Bedarfsdichte** f) *(econ)* density of demand, density of consumer demand
Nachfrageeffekt m **(externer Konsumeffekt** m) *(econ)* etwa consumer behavior effect on demand, behavioral effect on demand, psychological demand effect
→ Mitläufereffekt, Giffen-Effekt, Snob-Effekt, Veblen-Effekt
Nachfrageelastizität f **(Absatzelastizität** f **der Nachfrage)** *(econ)* elasticity of demand, demand elasticity
Demand is considered elastic when a reduction in unit price, (→) Stückpreis, increases total revenue from a product or service. Demand is inelastic when a reduction in unit price produces a decline in total revenue. It is unitary

when a reduction in price produces just enough increase in volume so that total revenue from the product or service remains the same.

Nachfrageforschung f
→ Bedarfsforschung

Nachfragefunktion f **(Nachfragekurve** f**)** *(econ)* demand function
The formal relationship existing between demand, (→) Nachfrage 1., and its determinants such as price, substitute goods, income, etc.
→ Nachfragekurve; *vgl.* Preis-Absatz-Funktion

Nachfragegebiet n **(Bedarfsgebiet** n**)** *(econ)* demand area

nachfragekonforme Preispolitik f *(econ)* demand-oriented pricing
A way of setting price that takes into account the nature and quality of market demand for the offering.

Nachfragekonzentration f *(econ)* concentration of demand, demand concentration

Nachfragekurve f *(econ)* demand curve
The plot of the demand function, (→) Nachfragefunktion, which shows for all possible prices within the relevant range the quantity of goods the market will absorb.

Nachfragelücke f **(Bedarfslücke** f**)**
→ Marktlücke

Nachfragemacht f *(econ)* power of demand, buyer power, *auch* buying power
A type of market power, (→) Marktmacht, which is the result of an organization's, a firm's, a trade's or industry's capacity to purchase in large quantities and thereby obtain concessions in price, deliveries, packaging, and other marketing-related advantages.

Nachfragemessung f *(econ)* measurement of demand

Nachfragemodell n *(econ)* demand model

Nachfrageprognose f **(Bedarfsprognose** f**)** *(econ)* demand prognosis, demand forecast, demand prediction
Any attempt at undertaking a series of value forecasts at different selling prices for a product or service to determine the point of optimum profit opportunity, usually on the basis of a given demand function, (→) Nachfragefunktion

Nachfragereaktion f *(econ)* demand response

Nachfrageschätzung f *(econ)* demand estimate

Nachfragesog m *(econ)* pipeline effect, surge of demand, demand pull *(econ)*
The resultant of demand stimulants applied in marketing.

Nachfragestruktur f
→ Bedarfsstruktur

Nachfragetheorie f *(econ)* theory of demand, demand theory
That branch of economic theory which is devoted to the analysis of the determinants of demand.

Nachfrageüberhang m *(econ)* overfull demand
The market condition existing when demand significantly exceeds supply.

Nachfrageverschiebung f **(Bedarfsverschiebung** f**)** *(econ)* shift of demand, demand shift, change of demand

Nachhall m
→ Echo

nachhallen v/i to reverberate, to reverb, to echo

Nachhallzeit f reverberation time (RT)
The time that passes until a signal has died away to one-millionth of its original intensity.

Nachholbedarf m *(econ)* pent-up demand, *auch* backlog demand, backlog

Nachinterview n
→ Nachfaßinterview

Nachkauf m
→ Ersatzkauf

Nachkaufreue f
→ Kaufreue

Nachkaufwerbung f after-sales advertising, post-buy advertising, post-sales advertising, post-purchase advertising
All advertising aimed at preventing or softening cognitive dissonance, (→) kognitive Dissonanz, among buyers in the wake of a purchase, (→) Kaufreue.

Nachlaß m
→ Preisnachlaß, Rabatt

Nachlassen n **der Gedächtnisleistung** *(psy)* memory decay, memory lapse
1. In surveys, the inability of respondents to recall past events, e.g. past behavior, clearly or accurately. **2.** The loss of brand recollection among consumers, potentially causing a significant loss in sales volume if not set off by expenditure

Nachlassen

on reminder advertising, (→) Erinnerungswerbung.
Nachlassen n der Werbewirkung (Decay-Effekt m, Wearout m) advertising wearout, wearout, advertising decay, decay effect
The point at which an advertisement loses its sales effectiveness due to excessive exposure and consequent disregard. Decay effects explain the need for continuous advertising to maintain a current market share.
Nachlaßstaffel f
→ Rabattstaffel
Nachleuchten n *(phot/film/TV)* afterglow
A glow which remains after the source of light has gone.
Nachlieferung f
→ Fortsetzungslieferung
Nachmittagsausgabe f (einer Zeitung) afternoon edition, afternoon issue
Nachmittagsfernsehen n (Nachmittagsprogramm n) daytime television, daytime TV, afternoon television, afternoon TV, afternoon program, *brit* afternoon programme
Nachmittagszeitung f afternoon newspaper, afternoon paper
Nachrabatt m (nachträglich eingeräumter Rabatt m) *(econ)* retroactive discount, retroactive rebate
Nachricht f news *sg*, news item, news information
Nachrichten f/pl news, news report, (Sendung) news broadcast, newscast
Nachrichtenabteilung f news department
Nachrichtenagentur f (journalistischer Nachrichtendienst m) news agency, press agency, news bureau, wire agency, wire service
Nachrichtenbeschaffung f news gathering, information gathering
Nachrichtenblatt n information newspaper, information paper *vgl.* Meinungsblatt
Nachrichtenbüro n
→ Nachrichtenagentur
Nachrichtendienst m
→ Nachrichtenagentur
Nachrichtenfilm m newsfilm
Nachrichtenindikativ n
→ Vorspann
Nachrichtengewinnung f
→ Nachrichtenbeschaffung

354

Nachrichtenmagazin n newsmagazine, news magazine
Nachrichtenmaterial n news material, information material
Nachrichtennetz n communications network, newsgathering network
Nachrichtenquelle f (Informationsquelle f) news source, source of information, information source
Nachrichtenraum m
→ Nachrichtenredaktion
Nachrichtenredakteur m news reporter, newswriter, sub-editor, news editor
Nachrichtenredaktion f newsroom, news department
Nachrichtensatellit m communications satellite, broadcast, satellite, *colloq* bird
Nachrichtensendung f *(radio/TV)* news broadcast, newscast, news program, *brit* news programme, news transmission, news show, radio news, TV news
Nachrichtensperre f news blackout, news ban
Nachrichtensprecher(in) m(f) *(radio/TV)* news announcer, announcer, newscaster, newsreader
Nachrichtenstudio n news studio
Nachrichtensystem n
→ Kommunikationssystem
Nachrichtentechnik f communication engineering
Nachrichtenträger m (Nachrichtenmedium n) news medium
Nachrichtenübersicht f (Nachrichtenüberblick m) news summary, news wrapup
Nachrichtenübertragung f (Nachrichtenübermittlung f) news transmission
Nachrichtenverarbeitung f
→ Informationsverarbeitung
Nachrichtenwesen n communications *pl (construed as sg)*
The entirety of technical systems and methods used for communicating information.
Nachschieben n (Nachschieben n von Ware) *(retailing)*
nachschneiden *v/t (print)* (Klischee) to finish, to handtool, *brit* to hand-tool
Nachschneiden n (Nachschnitt m)
1. *(print)* (Klischee) finishing, finish, handtooling, *brit* hand-tooling

The particular treatment that ist given to the outer edges of printing plates, e.g. ovaling, hairline finish, square finish, vignetted finish, etc.

2. *(film)* (Kopierwerk) negative cutting, chequerboard cutting
Nachsehbogen m
→ Revisionsabzug
Nachspann m **(Endtitel** m) *(film/TV)* end titles *pl*, end captions *pl*, end credits *pl*, closing titles *pl*, closing credits *pl*, closing captions *pl*, trailer
  The sign or title at the end of a motion picture or television film that lists the contributions of the production's various participants.
nachstellen v/t *(phot/film)* (Szene) to reset, to readjust
Nachsynchronisation f **(Nachsynchronisierung** f) *(film/TV)* post-synchronization, post-synching, post-sync, postscoring, *brit* post-synchronisation
  The later addition of synchronous sound to a silent picture.
Nachsynchronisationsstudio n *(film/TV)* post-synchronization studio, *brit* post-synchronisation studio, post-sync studio, postscoring studio
nachsynchronisieren v/t *(film/TV)* to postsynchronize, *brit* to post-synchronise, to post-sync
Nachtaufnahme f *(phot)* night exposure, night shot, night photo, night photograph
Nachtausgabe f (Zeitung) night edition, late evening edition, night issue, late evening issue
Nachteffektaufnahme f *(phot)* day-for-night shot
Nachtest m
→ Posttest
Nachtprogramm n **(Nachtsendung** f) *(radio/TV)* night program, *brit* night programme, night broadcast, *colloq* late-late show
Nachverkauf m **(Nachverkäufe** m/pl)
→ Ersatzverkauf
Nachwerbung f
→ Nachfaßwerbung
Nachwickelrolle f **(Nachwickelspule** f) *(phot/film/tape)* take-up spool, take-up reel, take-up
  A reel used for spooling up tape or film from the feed reel.
Nachziehen n **(Nachzieheffekt** m) *(TV)* streaking, smearing effect,

transparency effect, afterglow, comet tail
  A television picture distortion by which objects are horizontally extended beyond their normal boundaries.
Nachziehtestbild n *(TV)* streaking test pattern
Nadel f **(Ätznadel** f, **Radiernadel** f) *(print)* stylus, needle
Nahaufnahme f **(Naheinstellung** f) *(film/TV)* close-up(CU), close-up view, close shot(CS), (Ton) close-perspective recording, *(phot)* bust shot, *colloq* mug shot
  A camera shot to show a single object or part of it at close range.
Nahaufnahme-Objektiv n *(phot)* portrait attachment, portrait lens
  A supplementary lens which shortens the focal length, (→) Brennweite, so that near objects may be brought into sharp focus.
Nahbedarf m
→ Convenience Goods
Nahempfangsgebiet n **(Nahempfangsbereich** m) *(radio)* primary service area, ground-wave service area
vgl. Fernempfangsgebiet
Näherung f *(math/stat)* approximation
Näherungsfehler m *(stat)* approximation error, error in approximation
Nahkontrast m close contrast
Nahpunkt m **(Perigäum** n) *(phot)* near point
  The nearest object point lying between the camera and the object in critical focus which is reproduced without perceptible unsharpness.
(Sat) perigee
Nahschwund m **(Nahfading** n) *(radio)* short-range fading, local fading
Nahschwundzone f **(Nahfadingzone** f) *(radio)* close-range fading area, short-range fading area, local fading area
Nahverkehr m **(öffentlicher Nahverkehr** m) mass transit
  The public method of moving people from point to point within an urban area by means of public transportation.
namenlose Ware f **(namenloses Produkt** n) *(econ)* no-name product, unbranded product
→ Gattungsmarke

Namensanzeige f open
advertisement, open ad
  An advertisement which indicates the
  advertiser's name.
vgl. anonyme Anzeige
Namensartikel m **(Artikel** m **mit
Autorenzeile)** bylined article
Namensnachspann m
→ Nachspann
Namensvorspann m
→ Vorspann
Namenszug m name slug, flag,
logotype, logo
  The signature plate or standard name
  plate of an advertiser.
Napf m **(Näpfchen** n**)**
→ Rasternapf
Narbe f **(Narbung** f**)**
→ Korn
Narkotisierung f narcotization
narkotisierende Dysfunktion f **(der
Massenmedien)** narcotizing
dysfunction (of the mass media) (Paul
F. Lazarsfeld/Robert K. Merton)
Narrator m
→ Hintergrundsprecher
Nasenschild n *(POP advtsg)* vertical
store sign
Naß-in Naß-Druck m *(print)* wet-on-
wet printing, wet printing, wet color
printing, *brit* wet colour printing
  Color printing on high speed presses,
  with one color following another before
  the ink left by the previous plate has
  dried.
Naßkleben n wet bonding
Naßkopieren n **(Naßkopierverfahren**
n**, Naßverfahren** n**)** *(phot)* wet process,
diffusion transfer copying, diffusion
transfer process
Naßkopiergerät n **(Naßkopierer** m**)**
(phot) wet process copier, diffusion
transfer copier
Natronpapier n
→ Sulfatpapier
Naturalrabatt m *(econ)* discount in
kind, bonus goods *pl*
  Any goods given to a buyer, normally by
  a manufacturer to a retailer, as a reward
  for a large purchase.
Naturaltausch m *(econ)* barter
  The exchange of goods and services
  without the use of money.
Naturalwirtschaft f *(econ)* barter
economy
Naturkarton m **(gelaufener Karton**
m**)** single-ply paperboard

natürliche Falzung f **(natürlicher
Falz** m**)**
→ Leporellofalz
natürliche Sendeunterbrechung f
(radio/TV) (für Werbesendung)
natural break
  A noninterrupting pause a commercial.
Naturselbstdruck m *(print)*
1. (Produkt) nature print 2. (Technik)
nature printing
ND-Filter m
→ Dichtefilter (Neutralfilter)
Nebelmaschine f *(film/TV)* fog
machine
neben Text (textanschließend)
(advtsg) (Anzeigenposition) next to
reading (N.R., NR), next to reading
matter, full position, following and
next to reading matter, following or
next to reading, following reading
  A preferred position, (→) Plazierungsvorschrift, for newspaper and magazine
  advertisements either next to or
  following reading matter, or top of the
  column next to reading matter, usually
  charged for extra when demanded.
Nebenabdruck m
→ Separatdruck
Nebenabsorption f **(Fehlabsorption** f**)**
→ Nebenfarbdichte
Nebenfarbdichte f **(Fehlabsorption** f**,
Nebenabsorption** f**)** *(phot)*
misabsorption
Nebenfilm m *(film)* supporting film,
program picture
Nebengeräusch n **(Begleitton** m**)**
(film/radio/TV/tape) ambient noise,
ambient sound, wild noise,
atmosphere, *colloq* atmo, (parasitär)
electrical interference, interference
  The sound reflected from interior
  surfaces rather than direct from a sound
  source.
Nebenlicht n **(Streulicht** n**, Überstrahlung** f**)** *(phot)* spill light, spill,
stray light
  The marginal rays radiating from a
  photographic light.
Nebenregie f *(film/TV)* sub-control
room, *colloq* sub CR
Nebenrolle f (für einen Schauspieler)
supporting part, supporting role, small
part
Nebenschluß m *(electr.)* shunt, by-
pass
Nebensortiment n *(econ)* nonbasic
assortment, nonbasic merchandise
assortment, nonbasic stock

Negativ n (**Negativbild** n, **Kehrbild** n) (phot) negative
A developed photographic film with its image reversed, i.e. mirror-wise, left for right, type matter reading backward, and black for white, white for black, serving as the source for the positive.
vgl. Positiv
Negativabziehen n (**Negativcutten** n) (film/TV) negative cutting, negative pulling
The process of matching film negative material to an edited work print, (→) Schnittkopie.
Negativabzieher m (**Negativcutter** m) (film/TV) negative cutter
Negativabziehraum m (film/TV) negative cutting room
Negativabziehtisch m (film/TV) negative cutting bench, negative synchronizer, brit negative synchroniser
Negativabzug m 1. (film/TV) negative cut, negative pull 2. (print) Van Dyke
A proof from an offset negative for checking before making the printing plate.
Negativätzung f (**Negativklischee** n, **Negativplatte** f) (print) reverse plate, reverse block, reverse photoengraving
An engraving or plate opposite in value to the original, such as white on black.
Negativbild n (phot) negative picture, reverse picture, picture negative, negative image, reverse image
Negativdruck m (print) 1. (Produkt) reverse print 2. (Verfahren) reverse printing
vgl. Konterdruck
Negativentwicklung f (phot) negative developing, negative development
negative Option f (econ) inertia selling
The delivery of goods to prospects upon a sale-or-return basis without the previous consent or knowledge of the prospect.
Negativfarbfilm m (phot) negative color film, brit negative colour film
Negativfilm m (phot) negative film, negative stock
Negativklischee n
→ Negativätzung
Negativmaterial n (phot) negative material, negative stock, negatives pl
Negativplatte f
→ Negativätzung
Negativ-Positiv-Prozeß m (phot) negative-positive process

Negativschnitt m (film) negative cutting
Negativschrift f (print) negative type
Neger m colloq (film/TV) 1. → Lichtblende 2. (optisches Souffliergerät) idiot card, idiot board, crib card
A large card containing the lines to be spoken by a performer.
Neobehaviorismus m (psy) neobehaviorism, brit neobehaviourism
Neon n neon
Neonbeleuchtung f (**Neonlicht** n) neon light, neon lighting, strip lighting, neonization
Neonlampe f (**Neonröhre** f) neon lamp, neon light, neon tube
A gas-filled glass tube bent in shape of letters or designs and used as a means of electrical illumination on displays and outdoor signs.
Neonplakat n (**neonbeleuchtetes Plakat** n) (outdoor advtsg) neonized bulletin
An outdoor advertising display using neon tubes.
Neon-Leuchtschild n (**Neonreklame** f) (outdoor advtsg) neon sign
Neophiler m (market res) neophile
→ Innovator
Neopositivismus m neopositivism
Nest n (film/TV/studio) (Beleuchtung) lighting nest
netto (**Netto-**) adj net, (auf Gewinne/Verluste bezogen) bottom-line
Referring to any quantity remaining from a gross amount after deductions.
vgl. brutto
Nettoauflage f (Zeitung/Zeitschrift) net circulation
→ Nettoverkaufsauflage
Nettobetrag m (econ) net amount
Any quantity remaining from a gross amount after deductions.
vgl. Bruttobetrag
Nettodruckauflage f (**Vertriebsauflage** f) net press run, net print run
The total number of a newspaper's, a magazine's or other printed publication's copies that are for distribution.
Nettogewinn m (econ) net profit
Profit after payment of all costs of operation. Net before taxes is profit after payment of all operating costs except taxes.
vgl. Bruttogewinn
Nettohaushaltsreichweite f (media res) net household coverage, net

Nettoleserschaft

household reach, net audience of households, net households audience
The unduplicated percentage of homes, or of readers, viewers, or listeners, reached over a period of time, or by a combination of different media.

Nettoleserschaft f (**-Hörerschaft** f, **-Zuschauerschaft** f) *(media res)* net audience, net unduplicated audience, net readership
The unduplicated number of individuals or households reached by a communications medium over a specified period (each being counted only once regardless of the number of exposures).
vgl. Bruttoleserschaft

Nettopreis m *(econ)* net cost, net price, *(advtsg)* net rate, net cost
1. The final price of a product or service after all discounts, (→) Rabatt, and allowances, (→) Nachlaß, have been deducted.
2. A medium's published rate less agency commission.
→ Agentur-Netto; *vgl.* Bruttopreis

Nettopreissetzung f (**Nettopreissystem** n) *(econ/advtsg)* net pricing, net costing

Nettoreichweite f *(media res)* net coverage, net rating points *pl* (NRPs *pl*), net cover, reach, cumulative audience, net unduplicated audience, *(radio/TV)* cumulative reach, net rating, net ratings points *pl* (NRPs *pl*), *(outdoor advtsg)* net advertising circulation (N.A.C., NAC), net circulation
The total unduplicated coverage, (→) Reichweite, of an advertising medium, an advertisement or an advertising campaign, i.e. the percentage of the target audience who receive at least one exposure, (→) Kontakt. Also, the total number of persons or homes reached by a number of successive issues of a publication or successive broadcasts.
vgl. Bruttoreichweite

Nettosozialprodukt n *(econ)* net national product (NNP)

Nettoumsatz m *(econ)* (Nettoverkäufe) net sales *pl,* net orders processed *pl* (N.O.P.), (Zeitung/Zeitschrift) (Netto-Einzelverkäufe) net single copy sales *pl*
1. The quantity of items sold, or more precisely the amount received for these items, after all adjustments and returns.
2. The total number of a publication's sales through retail outlets, including newsstands, newsboys, mail, but excluding returns, (→) Remittenden.
→ Honorarumsatz, Nettoverkaufsauflage

Nettoverkaufsauflage f (Zeitung/Zeitschrift) net paid circulation, net paid, primary circulation, total net paid circulation, total net paid
The average number of copies of a publication sold per issue through subscription, newsstand sales, newsboys, or otherwise.

Netzanschlag m *(outdoor advtsg)* full showing, full run, full run showing, full service, number 100 showing, 100 showing, one hundred showing, representative showing, (Zahl der dafür erforderlichen Plakate) requirements *pl*
A standard showing of outdoor posters by which a message is placed on each unit of the system.

Netzfernsehen n (**Betriebsfernsehen** n) closed-circuit television (CCTV, C.C.T.V.), closed-circuit TV, non-broadcast television, non-broadcast TV, narrowcasting
A television signal limited to an immediate area, e.g. a classroom, a ship, a building, etc. Signals are transmitted via wire, not over-the-air. Reception is controlled, limited, and not available to the public at large. Sales, educational, and medical conventions and major sports events are frequently transmitted on closed circuit.

Netzfunk m (**Drahtfunk** m) *(radio/TV)* closed-circuit broadcasting, narrowcasting, wired broadcasting, *(radio)* closed-circuit radio, wired radio, *(TV)* closed-circuit television, cablecasting
A television or radio system for the distribution of video and/or audio signals to specific receivers connected to a closed circuit, rather than for broadcasting; often on a one-time basis.

Netzmittel n *(phot/print)* wetting agent

neuauflegen (neu herausgeben) *v/t* to reissue, *brit* to re-issue, to reedit, *brit* to re-edit
vgl. nachdrucken

Neuauflage f (**Neuausgabe** f) reissue, *brit* re-issue, new edition, revised edition
vgl. Nachdruck

Neuaufnahme f
→ Nachaufnahme

neu ausschießen v/t (print) to reimpose, brit to re-impose
Neubedarf m **(Neunachfrage** f**)** (econ) original product demand, new product demand, primary demand
→ Erstausstattungsbedarf; vgl. Ersatzbedarf
neubesetzen v/t (film/TV) to recast
neubestellen
→ nachbestellen
Neubestellung f
→ Nachbestellung
Neudruck m
→ Nachdruck
Neueinführung f
→ Einführung 3.
Neue Medien n/pl **(neue Medien** n/pl **)** new media pl
Neuerscheinung f new publication
Neugeschäft n **(Neukunden** m/pl**)** (advtsg/econ) new business
Those prospective or recently acquired clients, (→) Klient, (→) Kunde, or accounts, (→) Etat, purchasing through a single supplier, as an advertising agency or distributor.
Neugeschäftskontakter m (advtsg/econ) new business man, new business executive, pioneer salesman
Either an advertising agency employee or principal responsible for developing new agency clients, or a sales person who is responsible for making initial sales.
neugiererregendes Werbemittel n **(neugiererregendes Werbeelement** n**)** teaser
Any advertisement designed to stimulate curiosity, particularly one withholding identification of the advertiser or product, but promising more information in future messages.
Neuheit f
→ Innovation, Produktinnovation
Neuherausgabe f
→ Neuausgabe
Neuigkeit f
→ Nachricht
Neukunden m/pl
→ Neugeschäft
Neunachfrage f
→ Neubedarf
Neupositionierung f
→ Umpositionierung
Neuprodukteinführung f (econ) new product launch, product launch
→ Produkteinführung

Neuproduktentwicklung f (econ) new product development, product development
→ Produktentwicklung
Neuproduktidee f (econ) new product idea
→ Produktidee
Neuproduktmodell n (econ) new product model
Neuproduktplanung f (econ) new product planning
→ Produktplanung
Neuprodukttest m
→ Produkttest
Neusatz m **(Neusetzen** n**)** (typ) recomposition, resetting (of type), reset
Neutralfilter m **(ND-Filter** m**)**
→ Dichtefilter m
Neutralgraufilter m
→ Dichtefilter
Neutralisieren n
→ Maskieren
neu umbrechen v/t (print) to remake, to repaste, to repage
Neuumbruch m (print) remake-up, remakeup, reimposition
Neuverfilmung f remake
Newtonsche Ringe m/pl
→ Interferenzringe
NF abbr Niederfrequenz
nicht abbrechen (typ) (Satzanweisung) run on, run in
To set a piece of copy as a direct continuation of the previous copy, without beginning a new paragraph.
nicht im Passer (print) out of register, off register
→ aus dem Passer
nichtaktinisch adj (phot) nonactinic, brit non-actinic
The quality of light rays which do not affect photographic surfaces during a given or reasonable length of time.
vgl. aktinisch
nichtangeschnittene Anzeige f **(Anzeige** f **ohne Beschnitt)** non-bleed advertisement, non-bleed ad
An advertisement in a publication, usually a full-page or double-page ad, that does not bleed off, i.e. extend flush with the edges of the page, but rather has white space margins.
vgl. angeschnittene Anzeige
Nichtauslieferung f **(Nichtzustellung** f **)** (econ) non-delivery

Nichtbeantwortung f *(survey res)* nonresponse
→ Ausfälle
nichterwerbswirtschaftliches Versorgungsunternehmen n *(econ)* public utility, public service
  A business organization deemed by law to be vested with public interest, usually because of monopoly privileges or a publicly owned enterprise (waterworks, telephone company, etc.) conducted for the benefit of the community as a whole.
Nicht-Fernsehzuschauer m **(Nichtfernseher** m, **Nichtzuschauer** m) *(media res)* nonviewer
Nichthörer m *(media res)* non-listener
Nichtkäufer m *(econ)* nonbuyer
nichtkommerzielles Unternehmen n *(econ)* nonbusiness enterprise, public utility
→ nichterwerbswirtschaftliches Versorgungsunternehmen
nichtkommerzielle Werbung f nonbusiness advertising, noncommercial advertising
  Advertising placed by government agencies, charitable institutions, religious organizations, or by political groups for informational purposes or in order to attempt to create support for causes or for persons running for office.
vgl. Wirtschaftswerbung
nichtkommerzieller Rundfunk m *(radio/TV)* public broadcasting, nonbusiness broadcasting
nichtkommerzielles Marketing n **(Non-Business-Marketing** n) nonbusiness marketing, not-for-profit marketing
  All marketing activities conducted by individuals and organizations to chieve some goal other than ordinary business goals such as profit, market share, or return on investment.
Nichtkopierer m **(NK)** *(film)* NG take, NG
Nichtleser m *(media res)* nonreader
nichtlinear adj
→ kurvilinear
nichtlokale Werbung f **(überörtliche Werbung** f) nonlocal advertising
nichtneutraler Ausfall m
→ systematischer Fehler
nichtparametrisch
→ parameterfrei
nichtperiodisch (nicht periodisch erscheinend, unregelmäßig) adj nonperiodical

nichtreaktive Messung f **(nichtreaktives Verfahren** n) *(res)* nonreactive measurement, nonreactive technique, nonreactive method, unobtrusive measurement
  A measure of behaviors that minimizes the subjects' awareness of being studied and, thus, their tendency to react in ways that produce artifacts or other distortions of the data.
vgl. reaktive Messung
nicht remissionsberechtigt (nicht remittierbar) adj (Zeitung/Zeitschrift) nonreturnable
  Not subject to credit on being returned; applies to periodical or nonperiodical publications under sales plans in which dealers or other distributors purchase their copies with the understanding that they must pay for all copies purchased regardless whether they sell them or not.
nicht remittierbares Exemplar n (Zeitung/Zeitschrift) nonreturnable copy
→ nicht remissionsberechtigt
nicht repräsentativ adj *(stat)* (Erhebung) nonrepresentative
vgl. repräsentativ
nichtverbale Kommunikation f nonverbal communication
vgl. verbale Kommunikation
nichtvergütungsfähige Werbung f **(nichtkommissionsfähige Werbung** f) below-the-line advertising, scheme advertising
  All advertising activities which do not normally make provision for a commission, (→) Provision, to be payable to an advertising agency, e.g. direct mail, exhibitions, demonstrations, P.O.P. advertising, etc.
vgl. vergütungsfähige Werbung
nichtveröffentlichte Ausgabe f **(unveröffentlichte Ausgabe** f) *(media res)* (Konfusionskontrolle) advance copy, unpublished issue
nichtveröffentlichte Anzeige f **(unveröffentlichte Anzeige** f) *(media res)* (Konfusionskontrolle) unpublished advertisement, unpublished ad
Nickelgalvano n *(print)* nickeltype, nickel electro, nickel-faced electrotype, nickel-faced plate
  An electrotype, (→) Galvano, on which the first deposit is of nickel to increase its durability on the press as to the number of impressions obtained during a press run, and the remainder of the shell is copper.

Nicosia-Modell n (des Konsumentenverhaltens) *(res)* Nicosia model (of consumer behavior)
NiE *abbr* Nutzer im letzten Erscheinungsintervall
Niederfrequenz f **(NF)** *(electr.)* low frequency (LF), audio frequency (AF), audio, audible frequency
An audible sound frequency in the range of 15 to 15,000 hertz.
vgl. Hochfrequenz
Niederlassung f
→ Filiale
Niederstrich m
→ Abstrich
Niedrigpreis m *(econ)* bottom price, low price, cut price, cut rate
Niedrigpreisabonnement n
→ Billigabonnement (Werbeabonnement)
Niedrigpreispolitik f *(econ)* low price policy, bottom price policy, cut-price policy, cut-rate policy
Niedrigpreiswarenhaus n
→ Kleinpreiswarenhaus
Nielsen-Ballungsraum m *(market res)* Nielsen conurbation
Nielsen-Gebiet n *(market res)* Nielsen area
Nielsen-Index m *(market res)* Nielsen index, (Lebensmittelindex — NLI) Nielsen Food Index, (Drogerien-/Apothekenindex — NKI) Nielsen Drug Index
Nielsen-Panel n *(market res)* Nielsen panel
Nierenmikrofon n **(Niere** f, **Nierenmikrophon** n) cardioid microphone
A microphone with a heart-shaped (kidney-shaped) pickup sensitivity area.
Nipkowsche Scheibe f *(TV)* scanning disk
Nische f
→ Marktnische
Nischenstrategie f **(Nischenpolitik** f) *(econ)* nicher strategy, market nicher strategy, nicher policy, market nicher policy
Nitraphotlampe f *(phot/film/TV)* tungsten lamp
NK *abbr* Nichtkopierer
nochmal (nochmal von vorn) *(radio/film/TV)* (Regieanweisung) from the top, take it from the top
Start rehearsing again from the very beginning of a performance.

Nominalskala f *(scaling)* nominal scale
A scale derived from the arbitrary assignment of numbers to objects, which separates data into categories by naming only.
Nomogramm n nomogram, nomograph
A type of multiple line diagram.
No-Name-Produkt n
→ anonyme Ware, Gattungsmarke, namenlose Ware, markenlose Ware
nonparametrisch (nichtparametrisch)
→ parameterfrei
Non-response-Problem n
→ Ausfälle
Nonsense-Korrelation f **(unsinnige Korrelation** f) *(stat)* nonsense correlation
Nonstop-Kino n *(film)* nonstop cinema, nonstop movietheater
nonverbale Kommunikation f
→ nichtverbale Kommunikation
Nordisches Format n
→ Hamburger Format
Norm f 1. → Fernsehnorm
2. *(print)* signature title
Normal-8-Film m
→ Doppelacht
normale Faltkiste f *(packaging)* regular slotted container (RSC)
Normalfilm m standard-gauge film, standard-gauge stock
Normalbildformat n *(film)* standard gauge
Normalformat n **(Standardgröße** f) (bei Zeitungen) standard size
Normalfrequenz f *(electr.)* standard frequency, reference frequency
Normalgleichung f *(stat)* normal equation
One of a set of simultaneous equations arrived at in estimation by the method of least squares, (→) Methode der kleinsten Quadrate.
Normalhöhe f
→ Schrifthöhe
Normalkurve f **(Normalverteilungskurve** f) *(stat)* normal curve, normal frequency distribution curve
The graphic representation of a continuous frequency distribution of infinite range represented by the equation

$$dF = \frac{1}{\sigma\sqrt{(2\pi)}} e^{-\frac{1}{2}\left(\frac{x-m}{\sigma}\right)^2} dx, \quad -\infty \leqslant x \leqslant \infty,$$

.mwhere m is the mean, (→) arithmetisches Mittel, and σ the standard deviation, (→) Standardabweichung.

Normalmaß *n* **(Einheitsmaß** *n*) standard measure

Normalobjektiv *n (phot)* normal lens
A type of camera lens, (→) Objektiv, with an angle of acceptance of scenes, and consequent perspective, close to that of the unaided human eye.

Normalpapier *n* standard paper

Normalpapierformat *n* **(Papiernormalformat** *n*) standard paper size

Normalpreis *m (econ)* standard price, *(advtsg)* standard rate
→ Grundpreis

Normalrabatt *m* **(Einheitsrabatt** *m*) *(econ)* standard discount

Normalschrift *f (typ)* standard typ, standard tapeface, medium face
→ Brotschrift, Grundschrift

Normalschriftlinie *f*
→ Schriftlinie

Normalsortiment *n*
→ Grundsortiment

Normaluhrwerbung *f (outdoor & transit advtsg)* clock spectacular advertising
Advertising on the accompanying backlighted display of a large clock, usually in transit stations and railway terminals.

Normalverbraucher *m (econ)* average consumer

Normalverteilung *f* **(Gauß'sche Normalverteilung** *f***)** *(stat)* normal frequency distribution, Gaussian normal distribution
→ Normalkurve

Normalzeitung *f* **(Zeitung** *f* **im Einheitsformat)** standard-size newspaper, standard newspaper

Normband *n* **(Normbezugsband** *n*) standard tape, reference tape

Normenwandler *m* **(Normwandler** *m*) standards converter, standard conversion equipment

Normenwandlung *f* **(Normwandlung** *f* **)** standards conversion

Normformat *n*
→ Normalformat

Normierung *f* standardization, *brit* standardisation
The establishment of criteria of limits to which grades of goods are expected to conform. May be internal for just one firm, applicable to an industry as a whole, or apply across all activities of a certain kind in the economy.

North-Hatt-Prestige-Skala *f (social res)* North-Hatt scale of occupational prestige, North-Hatt scale (C. C. North/P. Hatt)

Notverkauf *m (econ)* emergency sale

Nullausgabe *f*
→ Nullnummer

Nullerde *f (electr.)* neutral

Nullhypothese *f (stat)* null hypothesis
A particular hypothesis under test, as distinct from the alternative hypotheses, (→) Alternativhypothese, which are under consideration. It is therefore the hypothesis which determines the type 1 error, (→) Fehler 1. Art.

Nullkopie *f (tape/film)* first release, release print, *brit* show print
A duplicate film or tape for air use.

Nullkorrelation *f (stat)* zero-order correlation
No correlation at all.

Nullnummer *f* **(Nullausgabe** *f,* **Nullheft** *n*) (Zeitung/Zeitschrift) dummy magazine, dummy copy, dummy, experimental magazine, pilot issue, pilot number
The simulation of a finished periodical publication prepared prior to the printing of multiple copies, and indicating the finishing characteristics of any of a number of design and production factors (e.g., size, content, weight, etc.), used for demonstration purposes.

Nullsummenspiel *n (game theory)* zero-sum game
A game played by a number of persons in which the winner takes all the stakes provided by the losers so that the algebraic sum of gains at any stage is zero. Many decision problems may be viewed as zero-sum games between two persons.

Nullzeit *f*
→ Sendebeginn

numerieren *v/t* to number
→ paginieren

Numeriermaschine *f*
→ Paginiermaschine

Numerierung *f* numbering
→ Paginierung

numerische Skala *f (stat)* numerical scale
A discontinuous rating scale consisting of scale numbers with or without descriptions of intensities.
vgl. verbal scale

Nummer *f* **(Zahl** *f*) number
→ Heft, Exemplar, Ausgabe

Nut *f* **(Nute** *f*) groove

Nuten *n* scoring

Nutzauflage f
→ Deckungsauflage

Nutzen m *(econ)* utility
In the most general sense, the capacity of a good or service to satisfy a human want.

Nutzen m/pl *(print)* number of copies

Nutzenansatz m **1.** *(econ)* utility approach **2.** *(communications)* uses-and-gratifications approach (Elihu Katz)
→ Nutzen

Nutzenerwartung f *(econ)* utility expectation

Nutzenfilm m (**Repetierkopie** f)
(print) gang negative, group negative
A negative, (→) Negativ, bearing a number of properly positioned duplicate images, produced either from a pasted-up original, by assembling and stripping duplicate negatives, or by direct printing from a single negative on a plate or film with a photocomposing machine, (→) Photosatzgerät.

Nutzenfunktion f *(econ)* utility function

Nutzenmaximierung f *(econ)* utility maximization, *brit* utility maximisation
In microeconomic theory, (→) Haushaltstheorie, the assumed striving of private households to maximize utility, (→) Nutzen, which is viewed as being the correlate of a business firm's striving to maximize profits, (→) Gewinnmaximierung.

Nutzenmaximierungshypothese f *(econ)* hypothesis of utility maximization, *brit* maximisation, theorem of utility maximization

Nutzenmessung f *(econ)* measurement of utility

Nutzenprofil n *(econ)* utility profile

Nutzensegmentierung f *(market res)* benefit segmentation
The breaking down of a market into groups, (→) Marktsegmentierung, based upon the benefits purchased, the values received, and the needs or wants matched.

Nutzentheorie f (Wilhelm Vershofen) *(econ)* theory of utility, utility theory

Nutzer m **1.** *(econ)* user
An industrial or institutional "consumer" or purchaser of a product or service.

2. *(media res)* user, exposed person, consumer, pl audience, users pl, exposed persons pl, consumers pl
Any individual who is or was exposed, (→) Kontakt, to a communication medium or an advertising message.
→ Hörer, Leser, Zuschauer

Nutzer m **im letzten Erscheinungsintervall (NiE)** *(media res)* user during the last publication interval

Nutzer m/pl **pro Ausgabe (NpA)**
→ Leser pro Ausgabe (LpA)

Nutzeranalyse f *(media res)* audience analysis

Nutzerstruktur f *(media res)* audience composition, audience comp
A term describing the kinds of people reached by a media vehicle or advertising campaign in terms of sex, age, income and other demographic groupings.

Nutzer-Strukturanalyse f *(media res)* audience structure analysis, audience composition analysis, audience comp analysis

Nutzung f (**Mediennutzung** f) *(media res)* coverage, media consumption

Nutzungsanalyse f *(media res)* coverage analysis, audience analysis, media consumption analysis

Nutzungsgewohnheit f *(media res)* media consumption habit

Nutzungshäufigkeit f (**Nutzungsfrequenz** f) *(media res)* frequency of media consumption, frequency of exposure

Nutzungsintensität f *(media res)* quality of media exposure, quality of exposure, exposure intensity, depth of exposure, thoroughness of media consumption
→ Kontaktqualität

Nutzungsvorgänge m/pl *(media res)* traffic, (Lesevorgänge) reader traffic
A measure of the number or percentage of persons (readers or other media consumers) who are exposed to the different sections and pages of a publication's issue, thus revealing the pattern of attention shift from one part to another.

Nutzungsvorgänge m/pl **pro Seite** *(media res)* reader traffic per page
The pattern of readers' attention shift on the different parts of a publication's page.

Nutzungswahrscheinlichkeit f *(media res)* probability of exposure, exposure probability, opportunity to see (O.T.S.,

Nutzwert

OTS), (Lesewahrscheinlichkeit) probability of reading, reading probability
→ Kontaktwahrscheinlichkeit

Nutzwert m (**Gebrauchswert** m) *(econ)* use value
The specific characteristics of a product or service which enable it to accomplish a particular function and thereby make it desirable from the viewpoint of value analysis, (→) Nutzwertanalyse.

Nutzwertanalyse f (**Benutzungsanalyse** f) *(econ)* analysis of use value, value analysis, value control, value engineering
The systematic investigation of the performance of a material or a part in terms of its function and its unit price aimed at developing the most effective specifications at the lowest ultimate product cost, including the consideration of the effects of various substitutes, different manufacturing methods, real labor cost, source factors, etc.

Nylonklischee n *(print)* nylon block, nylon plate
→ Plastikklischee

O

Ö-Markt m (Markt m der öffentlichen Hand) *(econ)* public utilities market (Philip Kotler)
oben links top left; (Anzeigenposition links oben) top left position
oben rechts top right; (Anzeigenposition rechts oben) top right position
oberer Eckplatz m **der Titelseite** (Anzeigenposition) ear position, ear, (rechts) right ear, (links) left ear
Oberflächenbeschaffenheit f **(Oberflächenglätte** f) *(paper)* finish
 The textural quality of the surface a sheet of paper.
Oberflächenentwickler m *(phot)* surface developer
Oberflächenentwicklung f *(phot)* surface development
 A type of photographic development, (→) Entwicklung, characteristic of fine-grain developers, in which only the superficial layers of silver in the emulsion are acted upon.
Oberkasten m *(print)* (Setzkasten) upper case, uppercase
 vgl. Unterkasten
Oberlänge f *(typ)* ascender
 That part of a lowercase letter, (→) Kleinbuchstabe, (b, d, f, h, k, l, or t) that rises above the main body of the letter. (Buchstabe mit Oberlänge) ascending letter
 vgl. Mittellänge, Unterlänge
Oberlicht n *(phot/film/TV)* top lighting, top light, (natürliches Oberlicht) sky light, sky lighting
Oberlichtscheinwerfer m *(phot/film/TV)* boom light
 Light on a long arm or spar that is easily adjusted over a model or set up at a height of several feet from the floor.
Obertitel m **(Haupttitel** m) main title, main head
 The principal display head of a body of printed matter.
Oberton m overtone, harmonic
Objekthelligkeit f
 → Objektumfang
Objektiv n **(Linse** f, **Linsensystem** n) *(phot)* lens, *auch* objective lens, *ungebr* objective

Objektivanzeiger m *(phot)* lens indicator
Objektivbeschichtung f **(Coating** n) *(phot)* lens coating
Objektivblende f **(Blende** f, **Objektivöffnung** f) *(phot)* lens aperture, lens opening, diaphragm
 The opening in a camera lens at which each frame stops during exposure, (→) Belichtung, and which permits the passage of light rays.
Objektivdeckel m *(phot)* lens cap, lens cover
 A dust cover for the protection of a camera lens.
Objektiveinstellung f *(phot)* lens adjustment
Objektivfassung f **(Objektivhalterung** f, **Objektivtubus** m) *(phot)* lens mount, lens barrel, objective mount
Objektivrevolver m **(Revolverkopf** m) *(TV)* lens turret, cine turret
 An obsolete rotatable television camera mount holding up to five lenses; nowadays turrets are obsoleted by zoom lenses, (→) Gummilinse.
Objektivring m *(phot)* lens ring, focusing ring, focusing mount, lens adapter
 The lens mount which permits the lens to be moved toward or away from the film in order to focus it accurately on given distances.
Objektivsatz m **(Satz** m **von Objektiven)** *(phot)* lens set, set of lenses
Objektivstütze f *(phot)* lens plate
Objektivtubus m
 → Objektivfassung
Objektkontrast m
 → Objektumfang
Objektmessung f *(phot)* reflected light measurement, reflected light reading, measuring reflected light
 vgl. Lichtmessung
Objektumfang m **(Objektkontrast** m, **Kontrastumfang** m, **Motivkontrast** m) *(phot)* contrast range of the object, brightness range of the object

**obligatorische Kombinations-
belegung** f *(advtsg)* forced
combination buy, forced combination
→ Kombinationsbelegung
Oblimax m **(Oblimax-Methode** f)
(stat) oblimax, oblimax method,
oblimax technique
Oblimin m **(Oblimin-Methode** f)
(stat) oblimin, oblimin method,
oblimin technique
oblique Rotation f **(schiefwinklige
Rotation** f) *(stat)* oblique rotation,
oblique factor rotation
Obsoleszenz f **(Veralterung** f,
Produktveralterung f) *(econ)*
obsolescence
  The loss in value of merchandise due to
  the advent of superior technology, a
  better product, or a change of style or
  fashion.
vgl. geplante Obsoleszenz
OC-Kurve f **(OC)**
→ Operationscharakteristik
Off n **(im Off)** *(TV)* off, off camera
  Outside the image field of a motion
  picture or television camera.
vgl. On (im On)
Off-Kommentar m *(TV)* voice over
(V.O., VO), off-camera commentary,
narration, off-screen narration, out-
of-vision commentary
  A commentary spoken by a person
  whose voice is heard but who does not
  appear on camera.
vgl. On-Kommentar
Off-Sprecher m *(film/TV)* off-screen
narrator, off-camera narrator, voice-
over (V.O., VO)
  An announcer whose voice is heard but
  who does not appear on screen.
vgl. On-Sprecher
Off-Stimme f *(film/TV)* off-screen
voice (OSV), voice-over (V.,O., VO)
  Narration with the narrator not being
  visible on the screen.
Off-Text m *(film/TV)* off-screen
narration script, voice-over script
→ Off-Kommentar
offene Auslage f **(offene Warenauslage** f) *(POP advtsg)* open display,
open assortment display, assortment
display
  A type of merchandise display that
  enables shoppers to come in direct
  contact with the merchandise, to pick it
  up, feel it, try it on, etc. In a more
  specific sense, it is a display that has the
  look of being unstructured and fluid,
  appearing to be placed almost at random,
  rather than being lined up or set up in
  predictable patterns on shelves and
  fixtures.
vgl. geschlossene Auslage
offene Frage f *(survey res)* open-
ended question, open-end question,
open question
  An interview question in which the
  respondent is not restricted in his
  answer to a choice of predetermined
  categories, but is allowed to give a full
  answer of his own choosing.
vgl. geschlossene Frage
offener Kanal m **(Offener Kanal** m)
(TV) open channel, public access
channel, access channel, (für die
allgemeine Öffentlichkeit) public
access channel, (für Bildungsein-
richtungen) educational access
channel, (für die Kommunen) local
government access channel, (für
bezahlende Bürger oder Gruppen)
leasing channel
offener Verkaufskarton m *(POP
advtsg)* cut-case display
  A shipping carton so designed that when
  cut as indicated on it a shelf tray is
  formed which shows the names of the
  variety and producer.
öffentlich *adj* public
öffentliche Meinung f public opinion
öffentlicher Anzeiger m
→ Mitteilungsblatt
öffentliches Marketing n **(Marketing
n der öffentlichen Hand)** public
service institutional marketing
  The marketing activities of public service
  institutions, e.g. governments,
  organizations and public utility
  enterprises.
Öffentlichkeitsarbeit f **(Public
Relations** f/pl) public relations pl
(often construed as sg) (PR, P.R.),
publics sg
  Any communication created primarily to
  build prestige or good will for an
  individual or an organization.
Öffentlichkeitsarbeiter m **(PR-
Arbeiter** m) public relations man,
public information officer (P.I.O.),
public relations officer (PRO, P.R.O.)
Öffentlichkeitsarbeitsberater m
→ PR-Berater
Öffentlichkeitsarbeitsberatung f
→ PR-Beratung
Öffentlichkeitsmarketing n public
marketing
Öffentlichkeitswerbung f public
service advertising, public service

institutional advertising, (einzelnes Werbemittel) public service announcement (P.S.A.)
Any advertising placed by a medium without charge in the interest of promoting the general welfare and good will of its audience.

öffentlich-rechtlicher Rundfunk m *(radio/TV)* public service broadcasting
The type of broadcasting typical of the German broadcast networks ARD and ZDF, as stipulated by law, free of political domination or commercial ownership, and based on obligatory license fees.

Offerte f
→ Angebot, Anzeige

Offertenblatt n freesheet, free sheet, *colloq* freebee
→ Anzeigenblatt

Offertengebühr f
→ Chiffregebühr

Office-Test m *(market res)* office test
The most simple type of a product test, (→) Produkttest, which consists of having the manufacturer's staff test a new product.

Öffnungsfehler m **(Zonenfehler** m**)** *(phot)* aperture defect, aperture error

Öffnungsverhältnis n *(phot)* aperture ratio, relative aperture
The ratio between the effective aperture, (→) Blende, of a lens and its focal length, (→) Brennweite, usually given in numbers.

Öffungswinkel m *(phot)* aperture angle

Öffnungszahl f *(phot)* aperture number
→ Blendenzahl

Öffnungszeit f *(phot)* aperture time

Offsetdruck m *(print)*
1. (Offsetverfahren) offset printing process, offset printing, offset lithography, photo-offset printing
A lithographic printing process, (→) Flachdruck, in which the image is first transferred to a rubber roller, or blanket, (→) Gummituch, which in turn makes the impression on the paper.
2. (Produkt) offset print, lithography, litho

Offsetdrucker m *(print)* offset printer, offset lithographer

Offsetdruckerei f *(print)* offset printing plant, offset printer

Offsetdruckmaschine f **(Offsetpresse** f **)** *(print)* offset printing machine, offset printing press, offset machine

Offsetdruckfarbe f **(Offsetfarbe** f **)** *(print)* offset printing ink, offset ink

Offsetfilm m *(print)* offset film, (eingeklebt) stripped-in film, (Montage) flat, (Offsetlitho) film negative
→ Litho

Offsetlithographie f *(print)* offset lithography, offset lithographic printing

Offsetmaschine f
→ Offsetdruckmaschine

Offsetmontage f
→ Offsetfilm

Offsetpapier n *(print)* offset paper, litho paper, litho stock
A smooth, coated or uncoated type of paper, bulkier than most book papers, with a surface quite similar to that of bond paper in appearance, but not as hard, properly sized, to resist the effect of water and entirely free from fluff or fuzz, for use in offset printing.

Offsetplatte f *(print)* offset plate

Offsetpresse f
→ Offsetdruckmaschine

Offsetrotationsdruck m *(print)* offset rotary printing, offset rotary

Offsetrotationspresse f *(print)* offset rotary press, offset rotary

Offsetverfahren n
→ Offsetdruck

Ogive f **(Galtonsche Ogive** f**, Summenpolygon** n**, Summenkurve** f **)** *(stat)* ogive, Galton ogive
The graphic representation of a cumulated frequency distribution, (→) Häufigkeitsverteilung.

ohne Einzug *(typ)* (Satzanweisung) full-out, set flush, (flush, bookstyle,) justified style
Not indented.

ohne Platzvereinbarung (ohne Plazierungsvorschrift) *(advtsg)* (Zeitungsanzeige) run-of-paper (R.O.P., ROP), run-of-press (R.O.P., ROP), (Zeitschriftenanzeige) run-of-book (R.O.B., ROB), run-of-the book (R.O.B., ROB), (Radio-, Fernsehwerbung) run-of-station (R.O.S., ROS), run-of-schedule (R.O.S., ROS)
An advertisement the position of which is allocated at the advertising medium's discretion, i.e. either a newspaper or magazine ad which can be run anywhere in the edition at the publisher's discretion or a spot commercial bought

for placement anywhere within a station's schedule.
→ freie Plazierung
Ökologie f ecology
ökologischer Fehlschluß m **(Gruppenfehlschluß** m) *(res)* ecological fallacy
ökologisches Marketing n **(Öko-Marketing** n) ecological marketing, eco-marketing
Ökonometrie f *(econ)* econometrics pl *(construed as sg)*
The systematic study of the applications of mathematics, statistics and other quantitative techniques to economic problems.
ökonometrisches Modell n econometric model
Ökonomisierungsanalyse f (Rudolf Seyffert) *etwa* analysis of economization
vgl. Introduktionsanalyse
Ökoskopie f **(ökoskopische Marktforschung** f) (Karl Christian Behrens) *etwa* ecoscopical market research, market research based on primary statistical data
vgl. demoskopische Marktforschung
Ökosystem n ecosystem
Okular n
→ Kameralupe f
Ölbad n oil bath
Ölfarbe f oil paint, oil, oil color, *brit* oil colour
A paint using oil, often linseed oil, as a vehicle in which to suspend pigment.
Öldruck m **(Öldruckverfahren** n) *(phot)* oil transfer process, oleography
A photographic process in which the pigmented image produced in the oil process is transferred to another support by means of pressure.
Ölpapier n oil paper
Oligopol n *(econ)* oligopoly
A condition of a market in which there are only a few sources of supply for a given product or class of products or service(s).
oligopolistische Konkurrenz f **(oligopolistischer Wettbewerb** m) *(econ)* oligopolistic competition
vgl. monopolistischer Wettbewerb
Omega-Quadrat-Test m **(Omega-Test** m) *(stat)* omega squared test, ω^2 test, Cramér-von Mises test
A test of significance, (→) Signifikanztest, for the difference between an observed distribution function and a hypothetical distribution function. If F(x) is the observed distribution function and F(x) its hypothetical counterpart, the criterion is

$$\omega^2 = \int_{-\infty}^{\infty} \{F_n(x) - F(x)\}^2 dx.$$

Omnibusbefragung f **(Mehrthemenumfrage** f) *(survey res)* omnibus survey, omnibus, multi-client survey
A regularly conducted survey which is used to a number of topics at the same time thus enabling different clients to ask a limited number of questions (tack-on questions), sharing the overall cost.
Omnibustest m *(survey res)* omnibus test
On n **(im On)** *(film/TV)* on, on camera (O.C., OC)
Inside the image field of a motion picture or television camera.
vgl. Off (im Off)
On-Kommentar m *(TV)* on-camera commentary
A commentary spoken by a person who is actually picked up by the camera and can be seen on the screen.
vgl. Off-Kommentar
On-Sprecher m
→ Sprecher; *vgl.* Off-Sprecher
One-Stop-Shopping n *(econ)* one-stop shopping
opak *(phot/print) adj* opaque
The state or condition of not permitting the passage of light.
opake Kopie f *(phot)* opaque copy, opaque print
Opazität f **(Deckfähigkeit** f, **Absorptionsfähigkeit** f) *(phot/print)* opacity, opaqueness
The property of paper which obstructs light or prevents printed matter from showing through from the reverse side or from the next or preceding sheet. In photographic negatives, the suppression or absorption of light by the silver deposit of the image, i.e. the percentage of light transmitted by the image.
operationale Definition f *(res)* operational definition
The definition of an abstract concept in terms of observable procedures (operations) for research purposes.
Operationalisierung f *(res)* operationalization, *brit* operationalisation
Substituting an operational definition, (→) operationale Definition, of a term for

a conceptual definition (Begriffs-
definition).
Operationscharakteristik *f* **(OC-
Kurve** *f,* **Prüfplankurve** *f*) *(stat)*
operating characteristic (OC),
operating-characteristic curve (OC
curve), *auch* performance
characteristic
In the theory of decisions, (→)
Entscheidungstheorie, and especially in
quality control, (→) Qualitätskontrolle,
and sequential analysis, (→) sequentielle
Analyse, a description of the behavior of
a decision rule, (→) Entscheidungsregel,
which provides the probability of
accepting alternative hypotheses when
some null hypothesis is true.
Operations Research *m* **(Operations-
forschung** *f,* **unternehmerische
Entscheidungsforschung** *f,* **wissenschaftliche Unternehmensforschung**
f) *(econ)* operations research (OR,
O.R.)
An interdisciplinary approach to
marketing and marketing research, using
physical or mathematical models which
are subjected to possible courses of
action.
operative Marktforschung *f* operative
market research
Optik *f* optics *pl (construed as sg),
(phot)* (Objektiv) optical system, lens
system
optimale Allokation *f* **(bestmögliche
Aufteilung** *f* **nach Schichten, Yates-
Zakopanaysche Aufteilung** *f*) *(stat)*
optimum allocation
In general, the allocation of numbers of
sample units to various strata,
(→) Schicht, so as to maximize some
desirable value such as precision for
fixed cost. More specifically, the
allocation of numbers of sample units to
individual strata for a given size of
sample if it affords the smallest value of
the variance of the mean value of the
characteristic under consideration.
Optimum allocation in this sense for
unbiassed estimators requires that the
number of observations from every
stratum be proportional to the standard
deviation, (→) Standardabweichung, in
the stratum.
optimale Bestellmenge *f (econ)*
optimum order quantity
→ Bestellpunkt
Optimalfarbe *f (phot/print)* optimum
color, *brit* optimum colour
optimieren *v/t* to optimize, *brit* to
optimise
Optimierung *f* optimization,

brit optimisation, optimizing,
brit optimising, satisficing
Any formal decision procedure designed
to find optimum solutions for a given
problem on the basis of defined marginal
conditions.
Optimierung *f* **des Werbebudgets**
advertising budget optimization,
brit optimisation
Optimierungskriterium *n*
optimization criterion,
brit optimisation criterion
Optimierungsmodell *n* optimization
model, *brit* optimisation model
Optimierungsprogramm *n*
optimization program,
brit optimisation programme
Optimierungsverfahren *n*
optimization technique, *brit*
optimisation technique, optimization
procedure, *brit* optimisation
procedure
Optimum-Allokation *f*
→ optimale Allokation
Option *f* option, choice
Optionsgeschäft *n (econ)* option
business
optische Achse *f* **(Sehachse** *f*) optical
axis, principal axis
The imaginary line joining the centers of
the two spherical surfaces of a lens.
A ray of light entering the lens along this
path will continue through the lens and
emerge without being bent or refracted.
optische Bank *f (film)* optical bench,
aerial-image printer
optische Dichte *f* optical density
optische Fahrt *f* **(optische Fahrtaufnahme** *f*) *(film/TV)* zoom shot,
zoom
A camera shot made with a zoomar lens,
(→) Gummilinse, creating the impression
as if the camera made an extremely fast
dolly into a scene or back from it,
without requiring the camera to move or
dolly.
optischer Trick *m (film/TV)* optical
effect, optical
A special effect, (→) Trick, for the
transition between scenes, such as a fade,
dissolve, wipe, etc. Optical effects are
made mechanically on motion picture
film and electronically in television.
optisches Feld *n* optical field
ordern
→ bestellen
Ordinalskala *f* **(Rangordnungsskala** *f,*
Rangskala *f*) *(stat)* ordinal scale, rank
order scale, ranking scale

Ordinate

A scale, (→) Skala, in which the categories have an inherent order of magnitude according to which they are arranged. The categories represent degrees of magnitude of a given characteristic, and may be ranked from greatest to least, highest to lowest, or first to last. There is no implication that there is an equal distance between succeeding categories or that the categories represent a uniform rate of increase or decrease. That is, there may be twice as great a distance between the first and second categories as there is between the second and third categories. An ordinal scale provides only a rank order of categories. Most attitude scales and scales of socioeconomic status are ordinal scales.

Ordinate f *(stat)* ordinate, y-axis
Organ n organ
Organisationsmarketing n organization marketing, *brit* organisation marketing
A collective term designating all marketing activities in the service of an entire (business or nonbusiness) organization rather than a single product or service.

Organisationsmodell n *(econ)* organization model, *brit* organisation model
Organisationsstruktur f organizational structure, *brit* organisational structure
Orientierungsreaktion f **(Orientierungsreflex** m, **Was-Ist-Das-Reflex** m) *(psy)* orienting reaction, orientation reaction, orienting response, orientation response, orienting reflex, orientation reflex, what-is-that-reaction
Original n **(Vorlage** f) *(phot/print/ film/TV/tape)* original, copy
A photograph, drawing, painting, design, print or other matter submitted for photomechanical reproduction, also the first recording on videotape, before any post-production work has been done.

Originalaufzeichnung f **(Originalband** n) *(TV/tape)* master tape, original recording, original tape
A tape or videotape accepted for reproduction or transmission.

Originalausgabe f **(Originalband** m) *(print)* original edition, original issue
Originalband n
→ Originalaufzeichnung
Originalband m
→ Originalausgabe

370

Originalbeitrag m original contribution, *(radio/TV)* live contribution
A contribution, e.g. a performance or presentation given at the present moment and in-person, as distinguished from one which is recorded on tape, film, or disc.

Originalbildnegativ n *(film)* original picture negative
Originalbrief m original letter
Originalfassung f **(Urfassung** f) original version
Originalfilm m **(Kopiervorlage** f, **Schnittkopie** f) *(film)* answer print (AP), optical answer print (A.P.O., APO), first proof print
A film print in which all color corrections and optical effects have been incorporated; used to obtain final approvals of a production.

Originalformat n **(Originalgröße** f, 1:1) *(phot/print)* original size, same size (s/s, S.S., SS), as is
Originalheftmethode f **(Originalheftverfahren** n) *(media res)* through-the-book method (TTB method, TTB), through-the-book technique (TTB technique, TTB), through-the-book (TTB), editorial-interest method, editorial-interest technique, issue-recognition method, issue-recognition technique, issue recognition, issue method, issue technique
A method of measuring readership that consists of showing respondents an actual issue, or a stripped issue, of a periodical publication and then asking them whether they remember having read or seen that particular issue before. The method is generally recognized as one of the most accurate ones, and its data are frequently adduced for validation, (→) Validierung, of data ascertained by other methods.

Originalheft-Wiedererkennung f *(media res)* actual issue recognition, issue recognition
→ Originalheftmethode
Originalklischee n *(print)* original block, original cut, original plate, pattern plate, original engraving, master plate, caster plate, caster
An original plate used for producing mats, (→) Mater, and additional electrotypes, (→) Galvano.

Originalkopie f *(phot)* master print, master copy
→ Musterkopie

Originalmanuskript n **(Original** n,
Originaltext m) *(phot/print)* original
copy, original manuscript, original
text
→ Original
Originalnegativ n *(phot)* master
negative, original negative
Originalschauplatz m *(radio/film/TV)*
location; am Originalschauplatz
drehen: to film on location
Originalsendung f *(radio/TV)* original
broadcast, live broadcast
→ Direktsendung, Livesendung
Originaltext m
→ Originalmanuskript
Originaltitel m original title
Originalton m **(O-Ton** m) original
sound, original version
Original-Tonnegativ n original sound
negative
Originalübertragung f
→ Live-Übertragung
Originalvorlage f
→ Originalheft-Methode
Originalzeichnung f original drawing,
key drawing
→ Musterzeichnung
Orthikon n **(Orthicon** n) *(TV)*
orthicon, image-orthicon tube, image
orthicon
**orthochromatisch (farbwertrichtig,
farbrichtig)** *adj (phot)* orthochromatic
  The quality of a negative or reproduction
  of a vari-colored original showing correct
  monochrome rendition of the color
  values and natural tones of the subject.
orthochromatische Emulsion f **(farbwertrichtige Emulsion** f) *(phot)*
orthochromatic emulsion
orthochromatischer Film m **(farbwertrichtiger Film** m) *(phot)*
orthochromatic film
  A film that is sensitive to blue and green,
  but not to red and orange.
orthogonale Rotation f **(orthogonale
Faktorenrotation** f) *(stat)* orthogonal
rotation, orthogonal factor rotation
orthogonaler Test m *(stat)* orthogonal
test
Orthogonalität f *(stat)* orthogonality
orthopanchromatisch *adj (phot)*
orthopanchromatic
örtliche Werbung f
→ lokale Werbung
örtlicher Einzelhandel m (Institution)
local retail trade, local retail business,
local retailers *pl,* (Funktion) local
retailing
örtlicher Großhandel m (Institution)
local wholesale trade, local wholesale
business, local wholesalers *pl,*
(Funktion) local wholesaling
Ortsantennenanlage f
→ Großgemeinschaftsantenne
Ortsbatterie f **(OB)** local battery (LB)
Ortsbedarf m *(econ)* local demand
→ Convenience Goods
Ortsgeschäft n *(econ)* local business,
(in der Werbung) local advertising
Ortsleitung f *(electr.)* local line, local
circuit, local end
Ortsmarketing n
→ Kommunalmarketing
Ortssender m
→ Lokalsender
ostentativer Konsum m
→ demonstrativer Konsum
Oszillation f **(Schwingung** f)
oscillation
Oszillator m oscillator, generator
Oszillogramm n oscillogram
Oszillograph m **(Oszillograf** m)
oscillograph, oscilloscope
OTC-Produkt n *(econ)* OTC
pharmaceutical, patent medicine,
proprietary medicine
  Derived from the English abbreviation
  for over-the-counter, the word is used in
  German to apply to items of medicinal
  use which may be sold without
  prescription.
Overhead-Projektor m
→ Arbeitsprojektor

P

P-Markt m (**Produzenten-Markt** m) (econ) producer market, industrial market, business market (Philip Kotler)

p-Maßzahl f (**Maßzahl p** f, **p-Wert** m)
→ Signifikanzwahrscheinlichkeit

Paarassoziationen f/pl (Hermann Ebbinghaus) (psy) paired associates pl

Paarassoziationslernen n (Hermann Ebbinghaus) (psy) paired associates learning
Learning of pairs of items in the way one learns a foreign language vocabulary.

Paarvergleich m (**Methode** f **des Paarvergleichs**) (res) paired comparison, method of paired comparison
A scaling technique, (→) Skalierung, wherein judges, using a particular value as a point of reference, rate two stimuli relative to one another in a series of comparisons within pairs; the technique is frequently used to establish preference relationships: A preferred to B or B preferred to A, neither preferred to the other. The method is used where order relations are more easily determined than measurements, e.g. in investigating taste preferences. More generally, the expression is used to denote the comparison of two samples of equal size where members of one can be paired off against members of the other.

Paarvergleichsbewertung f (**paarweise Werbemittelbewertung** f) (res) paired comparison rating, paired comparison test
→ Binokulartest, Paarvergleich

paarweise Parallelisierung f (**paarweises Matching** n) (stat) paired matching, matched samples design, precision matching
A pair of matched samples are those in which each member of a sample is matched with a corresponding member in every other sample by reference to qualities other than those immediately under investigation. The object of matching is to obtain better estimates of differences by removing the possible effects of other variables.

Paasche-Index m (**Paasche-Indexzahl** f, **Paasche-Indexziffer** f) (stat/econ) Paasche index
A type of index number which, if the prices (quantities) of a set of commodities in a base period are p_0, p_0', p_0'' etc. (q_0, q_0', q_0'' etc.) and those in the given period are p_n, p_n', p_n'' etc. (q_n, q_n', q_n'' etc.), is written as

$$I_{on} = \frac{\sum(p_n q_n)}{\sum(p_o q_n)},$$

(price index) where the summation takes place over commodities, i.e. the prices are weighted by the quantities of the given period.

packen v/t to pack, to package
→ verpacken

Packfilm m
→ Filmpack

Packgut n (**Packgüter** n/pl) (econ) package goods pl, packaged goods pl
Products, such as food, soap, laundry detergents and bleaches, paper goods and similar household goods that are wrapped, packaged, or put in containers by the manufacturer, especially small items used broadly and frequently consumed and typically sold through food, drug, and mass merchandiser retail stores.

Packmaterial n (**Packmittel** n)
→ Verpackungsmaterial

Packpapier n packing paper, wrapping paper, manilla paper, manila paper, manilla, manila, kraft paper, kraft, (Papiersorte) brown paper
A strong brown paper made from unbleached sulphite wood pulp and used to wrap or bag retail parcels.

Packung f pack, package, packet, wrapping, wrapper
The exterior part of a single unit of a product which serves as a protective device as well as a vehicle to carry the brand and the label.

Packungsanhänger m (**angehängte Packungszugabe** f) on-pack premium, on-pack, banded premium, package outsert, outsert

A package premium consisting of a display card, suitable for hanging on hooks, which has been affixed to the product without any covering.

Packungsattrappe *f*
→ Attrappe

Packungsbanderole *f* (**Banderole** *f*) package band
A band wrapped around a retail package and printed with a promotion offer or other announcement.

Packungsbeilage *f* (**beigegebene Packungszugabe** *f,* **Beipack** *m*) near-pack premium, near-pack, package outsert, outsert
A piece of printed material or a premium attached to, rather than inserted into, a package; often promotion material to advertise a different product.
vgl. Packungseinlage

Packungsdesign *n* (**Packungsgestaltung** *f*) package design, packaging design
Both the graphic design employed on a package for a unit of a product and the marketing services professional specialty, consisting of the art and study of creating effective product packages.

Packungseinlage *f* (**eingelegte Packungszugabe** *f*) in-pack premium, in-pack, package enclosure, package insert, boxtop premium, box-top premium, boxtop offer, box-top offer
A premium or a piece of printed material inserted into a package.
vgl. Packungsbeilage

Packungsentwurf *m colloq* ticky-tack
A very rough permanent model constructed just to provide a basis for judging size and general appearance.

Packungsgestaltung *f*
→ Packungsdesign

Packungsgröße *f* package size, size of package

Packungsgutschein *m* (**Packungskupon** *m*) package coupon, boxtop coupon, box-top coupon, boxtop offer, box-top offer
An offer of a premium based on return of the box top from the package or other proof of purchase.

Packungsmaterial *n*
→ Verpackungsmaterial

Packungstest *m* (**Verpackungstest** *m*) package test, packaging test; Packungstests durchführen, Durchführung von Packungstests: package testing

Packungszugabe *f* package premium, factory-pack premium, factory pack, in-pack, on-pack, container premium
A direct premium which comes attached in some way to the product, be it as a container premium, an in-pack, or an on-pack.
→ Packungsanhänger, Packungsbeilage, Packungseinlage

Pagina *f (print)* folio, page number

paginieren *v/t (print)* to page, to paginate, to folio, to foliate
To number the pages of a piece of printed matter.

Paginieren *n*
→ Paginierung

Paginiermaschine *f (print)* paging machine, paginating machine, numbering machine
A type-high printing machine which is locked with type in regular printing forms, and prints numbers in constructive order, forward or backward as wanted.

Paginierung *f (print)* paging, pagination, foliation, folio
→ paginieren

PAL-Farbträger *m (TV)* PAL color subcarrier, *brit* PAL colour subcarrier

PAL-Jalousieeffekte *m/pl (TV)* PAL venetian-blind effect, *colloq* Hanover bars *pl*

PAL-Verfahren *n (TV)* PAL technique (Phase Alternation Line)

Panchromatik *f (phot)* panchromatism
→ Panchromatismus

panchromatisch (panchro) *adj (phot)* panchromatic, pan
Registering all visible colors in gray values falling between white and black.

panchromatische Emulsion *f (phot)* panchromatic emulsion

panchromatische Reproduktion *f (phot)* panchromatic reproduction, panchromatic
A black and white photograph or print of color artwork made from a color-sensitive negative in which the various colors are shown as shades of gray.

Panchromatismus *m (phot)* panchromatism

Panel *n* (**Panelerhebung** *f,* **Panelbefragung** *f,* **Panelstudie** *f*) *(survey res)* panel, panel investigation, panel survey, panel study, (in der Hörerforschung) board
A data collection procedure in which information is obtained from the sample

units two or more times. Since panels can track individual changes, they provide more reliable as well as more detailed information over time than independent samples do, but they are more difficult to recruit and maintain. Particularly in market and media research, a panel is a group of respondents that are surveyed continuously over time, or perhaps periodically over time, rather than only once. The use of a panel particularly facilitates the study of changes and trends in behavior or attitudes. If, as an alternative to a panel, different groups of individuals are selected at different times for comparison, it is more difficult to ascertain whether observed changes represent actual change or merely reflect sampling error, (→) Zufallsfehler. A panel is a continuing sample in the sense that its members are, by and large, the same from one time to another. However, some turnover in the membership of a panel naturally occurs over time. Some members are added to replace others that drop out for one reason or another, (→) Panelmortalität, or simply to bring some newly-formed households into the panel. Often part of an existing panel is deliberately replaced with new members periodically with the intent of keeping the panel up-to-date.

Panelanalyse f *(survey res)* panel analysis
→ Panel

Panelbefragung f **(Panelumfrage** f**)** *(survey res)* panel survey
→ Panel

Paneldaten n/pl *(survey res)* panel data pl

Paneldatenbank f *(survey res)* panel data bank

Paneleffekt m **(Lerneffekt** m **bei Panelbefragungen)** *(survey res)* panel effect, panel participation effect, participation effect, (systematischer Fehler) panel bias
 The effect of participation in a panel survey, (→) Panel, on the nature of the participant's behavior and for responses.

Panelerhebung f
→ Panel

Panelforschung f *(survey res)* panel research, panel survey research, *colloq* panel polling
→ Panel

Panelinterview n *(survey res)* panel interview
→ Panel

Panelmitglied n *(survey res)* panel member, panelist, panel participant

Panelmortalität f **(Panelsterblichkeit** f**)** *(survey res)* panel mortality
 The cumulative loss of members of a panel, (→) Panel, because they die, move away, refuse to continue participating in the panel, etc.

Panelrekrutierung f **(Rekrutierung** f **von Panelmitgliedern)** *(survey res)* panel recruitment, recruitment of panel members
→ Panel

Panelrotation f *(survey res)* panel rotation

Panelsterblichkeit f
→ Panelmortalität

Panelstudie f **(Paneluntersuchung** f**)** *(survey res)* panel study, panel investigation
→ Panel

Paneltechnik f **(Panelverfahren** n, **Panelmethode** f**)** *(survey res)* panel technique, panel polling technique, panel survey technique
→ Panel

Panelumfrage f
→ Panelbefragung

Panlicht n *(phot/film/TV)* tungsten light

Panographie f **(Panografie** f, **Xographie** f**)** *(print)* **1.** (Verfahren) xography
 A printing technique that produces pictures which appear to be three-dimensional. Xographs have been used to good effect in advertisements, and as cover pictures for some magazines.
2. (Produkt) xograph

Panorama-Anzeige f bleed in the gutter, gutter bleed double spread advertisement, double-page spread, double spread, double-truck advertisement, double truck
 A double-page advertisment that is run in such a way that it passes uninterrupted through the gutter, (→) Bundsteg, into the binding edge of the sheet.

Panoramaaufnahme f *(phot/film/TV)* pan shot, pan, panning shot, panoramic shot
 A shot of a scene or sequence made by rotating or swiveling the camera along a horizontal arc, as distinguished from a dolly shot, (→) Kamerafahrt, where the whole camera is moved on a platform to follow the action.

Panoramabreitwand f *(film)* panoramic screen
Panoramaeffekt m *(film/TV)* panoramic effect
→ Panoramaaufnahme
Panoramakamera f *(film/TV)* panoramic camera
Panoramakopf m *(film/TV)* panning head, pan head, pam head, panoramic head
The mechanism at the top of a tripod, (→) Stativ, which permits the camera to be moved in horizontal or vertical planes.
Panoramaschwenk m *(film/TV)* pan shot, pan, panning shot, panoramic shot, panoramic movement
→ Panoramaaufnahme
panoramieren v/t + v/i *(film/TV)* to pan, to chinese
To swivel the camera in a horizontal arc.
Panoramierung f (**Panoramieren** n) *(film/TV)* panning
→ Panoramaaufnahme
panoramisch adj panoramic(al)
Panscheibe f *(film/TV)* pan filter
Pantoffelkino n *(derog for television)* home movie
Pantograph m (**Storchschnabel** m) pantograph
A mechanical device for reproducing, enlarging or reducing a line figure when the figure is traced with a stylus.
Paperback n paperback
A book with a paperlike covering or binding as contrasted with the standard hardcover book. The English expression is a household term in German.
Papier n paper, (bestimmte Papierart) stock, paper stock, stocks pl
Papierabfall m (**Papierabfälle** m/pl, **Papierausschuß** m) waste paper, trimmings pl, defective sheets pl
Papierabzug m *(phot)* paper print, print
Papierart f paper stock, stock, sort of paper
Papierbahn f paper web, web, paper strip, length of paper
A roll of printing paper that allows continuous and repeated printing on a rotary press; used especially for newspapers, magazines and long run collateral pieces.
Papierbeschneider m
→ Papierschneidemaschine
Papierbogen m sheet of paper
The unit of paper printed by the form on a printing press during the press run.

Papierbogenformat n (**Bogenformat** n) sheet size
Papierbrei m (**Faserbrei** m, **Papierfaserbrei** m, **Pulpe** f) paper pulp, pulp
Any disintegrated fibrous material, such as wood or cloth, used for making paper.
Papierdehnung f paper stretch
Papierdichte f density of paper
Papierdicke f (**Papierstärke** f) thickness of paper, paper thickness, caliper of paper, caliper, (relative Papierstärke) bulk, bulkiness
The degree of thickness a particular type of paper has.
→ Papiergewicht
Papiereigenschaft(en) f(pl) quality of paper, characteristics pl of paper
Papiereinband m *(bookbinding)* paper cover
Papiereinführung f (**Papierzuführung** f) *(print)* feeding of paper, paper feeding
→ Bogenzuführung
Papiereinkauf m paper purchase
Papierfabrik f
→ Papiermühle
Papierfabrikant m (**Papierhersteller** m) paper manufacturer, papermaker
Papierfabrikation f (**Papierherstellung** f) paper manufacturing, papermaking
Papierfalzmaschine f folding machine, folder
Papierfaser f paper fiber, brit paper fibre
Papierfaserbrei m
→ Papierbrei
Papierformat n size of paper, paper size, (Grundformat) basic size
→ Papiernormalformat
Papierführung f
→ Papiereinführung
Papiergewicht n weight of paper, weight, (Grundgewicht) basis weight, basic weight, basic substance weight, substance number
A standardized system used by paper manufacturers for identifying paper weights, in Germany the basis is gramms per square meter (g/m^2).
Papierglanz m (**Papierglätte** f) brightness of paper, glaze, gloss, glossiness, shininess, smoothness
Papiergradation f *(phot)* paper grades pl
Papierhersteller m
→ Papierfabrikant

Papierherstellung f
→ Papierfabrikation
Papierindustrie f paper industry
Papierkorbwerbung f (**Werbung** f **an Papierkörben**) *(outdoor advtsg)* litter bin advertising
Papierlaufrichtung f
→ Laufrichtung
Papierleim m paper size, size
  A type of glue or starch used for filling the pores of paper to give it a coated finish.
Papierleimung f paper sizing, sizing
  The process of filling the pores of paper to give it a coated finish.
Papierlieferant m (**Papierhändler** m) paper supplier, paper merchant
Papierlieferung f paper supply
Papiermaché n (**Pappmaché** n) paper-mâché, paper-mache, paper maché
  A mixture of wood and paper fibers, (→) Papierfaser, with a paste of clay and resin, molded into various forms and used for making matrixes.
Papiermaschine f papermaking machine
Papiermaß n
→ Papierformat
Papiermasse f
→ Papierbrei
Papiermater f (**Papiermatrize** f) *(print)* paper mold, *brit* paper mould, flong, paper matrix
  A matrix, (→) Mater, made of papier-mâché, (→) Papiermaché, used in stereotyping, (→) Stereotypie.
Papiermesser n paper knife, paper cutter
Papiermühle f (**Papierfabrik** f) paper mill
Papiernormalformat n standard paper size
Papieroberfläche f paper surface
→ Oberflächenbeschaffenheit
Papierplakat n *(poster advtsg)* paper poster
Papierpreis m paper price
Papierrolle f reel of paper, mill roll
Papierschild n (**Papieretikett** n) paper label
Papierschneidemaschine f paper cutter, guillotine cutter, guillotine, paper trimmer, trimmer
  A machine comprising a heavy treadle-operated steel blade, used for cutting sheets of paper.

Papierschneiden n (**Papierbeschnitt** m) paper cutting, paper trimming, trimming
Papiersorte f (**Papierart** f) type of paper, paper stock, stock
Papierstärke f
→ Papierdicke
Papiertüte f (**Papiertasche** f, **Papierbeutel** m) paper bag
Papierumschlag m
→ Schutzumschlag
Papier-und-Bleistift-Test m *(res)* paper-and-pencil test, pencil-and-paper test
Papier-und-Bleistift-Testmethode f *(res)* paper-and-pencil test method, paper-and-pencil method
Papiervolumen n bulk of paper
→ Papierdicke
Papierwahl f (**Papierauswahl** f) paper selection
Papierzuschuß m *(print)* overplus of paper, overplus
Pappband m
1. → Paperback
2. → Pappeinband
Pappdeckel m (**Buchbinderpappe** f) *(bookbinding)* paperboard, binder's board, cardboard, board
Pappe f pasteboard, paperboard, board, (dünne Pappe) cardboard, (dicke Pappe) millboard
  Any heavy paper-like material made from wood pulp, waste paper, or straw.
Pappeinband m *(bookbinding)* cardboard binding, pasteboard binding, cardboard cover, pasteboard cover
Pappkarton m (**Pappschachtel** f) *(packaging)* cardboard box, cardboard container
Pappmatrize f
→ Papiermater
Parabelfunktion f (**parabolische Funktion** f) *(stat)* parabolic function
parabolische Regression f *(stat)* parabolic regression
parabolischer Trend m *(stat)* parabolic trend
Parabolsignal n *(radio/TV)* parabolic signal
Parabolspiegel m *(radio/TV)* parabolic reflector, parabolic mirror
Parabolspiegelantenne f (**Parabolantenne** f) *(radio/TV)* parabolic reflector antenna, *brit* parabolic

reflector aerial, parabolic mirror antenna, brit parabolic mirror aerial
Parabolstrahler m *(radio/TV)* parabolic radiator, paraboloid
Paradigma n paradigm
Generally, a model or schema. The term has been used by Robert K. Merton to refer to a device for presenting a succinct codification of an area of research analysis. A paradigm is a compact outline of the major concepts, assumptions, procedures, propositions, and problems of a substantive area or a theoretical approach in research analysis.
Parallaxe f parallax
The optical displacement of one object with respect to another when viewed from different positions; also the angle of divergence between a camera lens, (→) Objektiv, and its viewfinder, (→) Sucher.
Parallaxenausgleich m *(phot)* parallax compensation, parallax correction
Parallaxensucher m *(phot)* parallax viewfinder
Parallelbruch m **(Parallelfalz** m, **Parallelfalzung** f) parallel fold, parallel folding
paralleles Lesen n
→ gehäuftes Lesen
Parallelfahrt f **(Parallelfahrtaufnahme** f) *(film/TV)* running shot, crab shot, lateral dolly shot
A shot of a subject in motion from a camera maintaining a constant, parallel position relative to the subject.
Parallelfalz m
→ Parallelbruch
Parallelformmethode f *(res)* parallelforms method
Parallologrammanalyse f *(res)* parallelogram analysis (Clyde H. Coombs)
Parallelkreis m *(electr.)* parallel circuit
Parallelschaltung f *(electr.)* parallel connection, shunt connection
Paralleltest m *(stat)* parallel test
Paralleltestmethode f *(stat)* paralleltest method
The use of alternate forms of the same test comprised of items selected from one pool. The distributions of scores yielded thus have comparable means, (→) Mittelwert, standard deviations, (→) Standardabweichung, and correlations with criterion measures.
Paralleltonverfahren n parallel sound system

Parameter m *(stat)* parameter, parametric constant, population parameter, universe parameter
A summary measure of a characteristic of a population, (→) Grundgesamtheit. A parameter may be a measure of central tendency, (→) Lageparameter, such as a mean, (→) arithmetisches Mittel, a median, (→) Median, or a mode, (→) häufigster Wert, a measure of dispersion, (→) Streuungsmaß, such as a standard deviation, (→) Standardabweichung, a measure of association between two variables such as a coefficient of correlation, (→) Korrelationskoeffizient, or any other measure of the distribution of one or more characteristics in a population. It is important to note that a parameter is a measure of an entire population, or universe, and not a measure of a sample, (→) Stichprobe. Since most social research deals with samples, true parameters are usually unknown and must be estimated from sample data.
parameterfrei (nonparametrisch, verteilungsfrei) *adj (stat)*
nonparametric, brit non-parametric, distribution-free
parameterfreie Statistik f **(nonparametrische Statistik** f, **nichtparametrische Statistik** f, **verteilungsfreie Statistik** f) nonparametric statistics *pl (construed as sg)*, nonparametric statistics, distribution-free statistics
That branch of statistics comprising techniques of statistical analysis that do not entail assumptions about the exact form of the distribution of the population, (→) Grundgesamtheit. The use of nonparametric statistical tests does not require that the sample, (→) Stichprobe, being analyzed be from a population with a normal distribution or with any other specified distribution, i.e. the exact shape of the distribution of the population need not be known. The term nonparametric itself refers to the fact that these techniques do not make stringent assumptions or assertions about population parameters, (→) Parameter, but only some limited, less restrictive assumptions about the nature of the population, and deal primarily with the sample data. Moreover, whereas data must be in the form of absolute scores or values to be used in parametric statistics, (→) parametrische Statistik, there are nonparametric techniques that may be used with data in the form of ranks, (→) Ordinalskala, ordinal scale techniques for use with data classified as plus or minus (higher or lower), and

techniques for data simply in categories nominalscale, (→) Nominalskala.
parameterfreier Test *m* **(nonparametrischer Test** *m*, **nichtparametrischer Test** *m*, **verteilungsfreier Test** *m*) *(stat)* nonparametric test, distribution-free test
A significance test, (→) Signifikanztest, for any null hypothesis, (→) Nullhypothese, that is not a statement about a parameter, (→) Parameter, of a distribution, or about randomness or trend.
vgl. parametrischer Test
parameterfreies Modell *n* **(nonparametrisches Modell** *n*, **nichtparametrisches Modell** *n*, **verteilungsfreies Modell** *n*) *(stat)* nonparametric model, distribution-free model
Parameterschätzung *f (stat)*
1. (einzelne Schätzung) parameter estimate 2. (Schätzen von Parametern) parameter estimation
Parametertest *m* **(parametrischer Test** *m*) *(stat)* parametric test
A statistical test of significance, (→) Signifikanztest, for any null hypothesis, (→) Nullhypothese, that requires assumptions about (a) parameter(s), (→) Parameter, of the underlying population.
vgl. parameterfreier Test
parametrisch (Parameter-) *adj (stat)* parametric
parametrische Statistik *f* parametric statistics *pl (construed as sg)*
That branch of statistics comprising techniques of statistical analysis which require that the data being analyzed be drawn from a population distribution with a specified form. Usually parametric techniques assume that the population, (→) Grundgesamtheit, from which the sample, (→) Stichprobe, was drawn has a normal frequency distribution, (→) Häufigkeitsverteilung, in addition, parametric techniques require that each case included in the sample has been included independently of every other case, i.e. the inclusion of one case does not automatically lead to the inclusion of another case, that when samples have been drawn from two or more populations these populations have the same variance, (→) Varianz, or in some cases a known ratio of variances, (→) Varianzverhältnis, and that the data be in arithmetic form (so that they can be added, divided, multiplied) and not in the form of ranks.
parametrischer Test *m*
→ Parametertest

parametrisches Modell *n* **(Parametermodell** *n*) *(stat)* parametric model
Parteipresse *f* partisan press, political party press, party press
Parteizeitung *f* partisan newspaper, partisan paper, party paper
Partialanalyse *f* partial analysis
Partialbelichtungsmesser *m (phot)* spot photometer
Partialkorrelation *f* **(partielle Korrelation** *f*) *(stat)* partial correlation
A measure of the amount of variation caused by one independent variable when the effects of all other relevant variables are controlled. Also, the degree of the strength of relationship between two variables when other relevant variables are held fixed, the index of relationship generally being the product-moment correlation coefficient, (→) Produkt-Moment-Korrelation.
Partialmodell *n* partial model
vgl. Totalmodell
Partialregression *f* **(partielle Regression** *f*) *(stat)* partial regression
Partie *f (econ/stat)* lot, batch
→ Los
partielle Korrelation *f*
→ Partialkorrelation
partielle Regression *f*
→ Partialregression
Partil *n* **(Partile** *f*) *(stat)* partile
Partizipationseffekt *m*
→ Paneleffekt
Partneragentur *f (advtsg)* partner agency
Partner-Split *m* **(Anzeigen-Split** *m* **zwischen mehreren Werbungtreibenden)** omnibus cooperative advertisement
Typically, a full-page advertisement placed by a retailer over his own name, which consists of mats, (→) Mater supplied by manufacturers of different products. The retailer will bill each manufacturer a pro rata share of the cost of the whole advertisement in accordance with the provisions of the various cooperative advertisement agreements with the manufacturers.
Partyverkauf *m (marketing)* party selling, party-plan selling
A form of house-to-house selling in which a hostess is persuaded through the promise of a gift to invite her friends to an afternoon or evening gathering at which the salesman can demonstrate his wares.

Pascaldreieck n **(Pascalsches Dreieck** n) *(math/stat)* Pascal triangle
Pascalverteilung f *(Pascalsche Verteilung* f, **negative Binomialverteilung** f) *(stat)* Pascal distribution, negative binomial distribution
Passage f **1.** (Textstelle) passage **2.** (Szenenüberbrückung) bridge
Passagier m *(transit advtsg)* passenger, car passenger
Passant m *(outdoor advtsg)* transient, passer-by, pl (Passanten) passers-by, (Fußgänger) pedestrian
Passantenbefragung f **(Straßenbefragung** f) *(survey res)* street-corner survey
Passantenfluß m *(outdoor advtsg)* pedestrian traffic flow
    The number of pedestrians using a certain route, as ascertained by a traffic count, (→) Passantenzählung.
Passantenzählung f **(Verkehrszählung** f) *(outdoor advtsg)* traffic count
    The evaluation of outdoor poster readers by an actual count of traffic passing the poster.
passen (Register halten, im Passer sein) v/i *(print)* to register, to hold register
    Printing in which the impression is made in the precise spot desired, as in the accurate superimposition of color plates.
Passer m **(Register** n) *(print)* register; im Passer sein, Passer halten, Register halten: to register, to be on register; aus dem Passer sein, nicht im Passer sein, nicht Register halten: to be out of register, to be off register
    The correct alignment of successive plates in printing more than one color. The print is said to be in register if properly printed and out of register if not.
Passerdifferenz f *(print)* register difference, color fringing, *brit* colour fringing
    Printing in which the type or plates do not make the impression in the exact spot desired, or in which color plates do not overprint accurately.
Passerkreuz n **(Paßkreuz** n) *(print)* register mark, color register, *brit* colour register
    A guide in the form of a small cross or mark placed or drawn on an original before photography to facilitate registration in platemaking and proving.

Passerprobe f *(print)* register check, checking of register
passiver Bekanntheitsgrad m **(gestützte Erinnerung** f) *(survey res)* aided recall
    Any recall measured by means of a test using recall aids, (→) Gedächtnisstütze.
    vgl. aktiver Bekanntheitsgrad, Wiedererkennung
Paßkreuz n
    → Passerkreuz
Passus m
    → Passage 1.
Pastellfarbe f pastel color, *brit* pastel colour, pastel
    Soft chalks used by artists, especially for drawings in color.
Pastellton m **(Pastellfarbton** m) pastel tone, pastel shade
Pastellzeichnung f pastel drawing
    An illustration made with colored chalk crayons, made of ground color paste, marked by a soft effect. It is easily marred because of its grained surface, unless fixed with a fixative.
Patent n *(econ)* patent
    The grant by a government authority, (→) Patentamt, of the exclusive right to produce, or to license the production of, an invention for a certain period; in Germany the period is 18 years.
Patentamt n *(econ)* patent office
Patentanmeldung f *(econ)* application for a patent, patent application
Patentanwalt m *(econ)* patent attorney, patent lawyer, patent agent
Patenteintragung f *(econ)* patent registration, registration of a patent
Patentgebühr f *(econ)* **1.** (Anmeldungsgebühr) patent filing fee, filing fee **2.** (Erteilungsgebühr) patent fee **3.** (Jahresgebühr) patent annuity, patent renewal fee, renewal fee
Patentgesetz n *(econ)* patent law
Patentgesetzgebung f **(Patentrecht** n) *(econ)* patent legislation, patent law, patent regulations pl
Patentinhaber m *(econ)* patent holder
Patentrecht n
    → Patentgesetzgebung
Patrize f **(Prägestempel** m, **Schriftstempel** m) punch, counter-die
Patronatsfirma f **(Sponsorfirma** f) *(print/radio/TV advtsg)* broadcast-program sponsor, sponsor
    The firm or individual or organization that pays for the cost of talent and/or time for a broadcast feature, or the advertisement in print media, and who is

Patronatsgemeinschaft 380

identified as such. In a strict sense, one who pays for program time as distinguished from an advertiser who pays only for announcement or commercial time.

Patronatsgemeinschaft f **(Sponsorengemeinschaft** f) *(radio/TV advtsg)* cosponsorship, *brit* co-sponsorship

Patronatssendung f **(gesponserte Programmsendung** f) *(radio/TV)* sponsored broadcast, sponsored program, *brit* sponsored programme, sponsored radio program, *brit* sponsored radio programme, sponsored television program, *brit* sponsored television programme, sponsored radio, sponsored television, commercial program, (mit mehreren Sponsoren) participation program
 A radio or television program fully or partly financed by a sponsor, (→) Patronatsfirma. Also, a regularly scheduled program on which advertisers may place spot announcements, (→) Werbespot, without any responsibility for program content.

Pauschale f **(Pauschalhonorar** n) **1.** *(econ)* global amount, lump sum, global sum **2.** *(advtsg)* fee basis, fee, agency fee
 A type of down payment made to an advertising agency by an advertiser either as an agreed-upon alternative to commission compensation, or in situations where commission, (→) Provision, is not provided by the agency's supplier.

Pauschale f **plus Kosten (Kosten** pl **plus Pauschale, Pauschal-Kosten-Verfahren** n) *(advtsg)* (Agenturvergütung) cost plus fee, cost plus
 → Kosten plus Pauschale

Pauschale f **plus Provision** *(advtsg)* (Agenturvergütung) fee plus commission
 A method of advertising agency remuneration which consists of both a charge rendered by the agency for its services (frequently, 17.65 percent on outside purchased materials and or services, negotiable in connection with creative, media, and other services) and the usual 15 percent agency commission.

Pauschalgebühr f *(econ)* flat rate, flat fee
 A uniform rate charged for a service without allowing for any discounts, (→) Rabatt.

Pauschalhonorar n
 → Pauschale

Pauschalhonorierung f *(econ)* (Agenturvergütung) flat fee only
 → Pauschale 2.

Pauschalvergütung f
 → Pauschale

Pause f *(radio/TV)* **1.** (Unterbrechung) intermission, interval, break, (Programmunterbrechung) program break, (Lokalsender) station break, (Sendernetz) chain break **2.** *(phot)* (Lichtpause) blueprint, tracing, traced design
 A copy of a mechanical or architectural drawing.

pausen v/t to trace, to copy

Pausenbild n *(film/TV)* interval slide, interval caption, interlude slide
 → Senderkennung

Pausenfüller m *(radio/TV)* filler, fill-up, fill
 Any optional material for use in broadcasting if a program runs short.

Pausensignal n **(Pausenzeichen** n) *(radio/TV)* interval signal
 → Senderkennung

Pauspapier n tracing paper, pounce paper, traceoline
 A transparent film with a granular surface, used for drawing.

Pay-TV n
 → Münzfernsehen

Pearson-Korrelation f **(Pearsonsche Korrelation** f)
 → Produktmomentkorrelation

Pearson-Kurve f **(Pearsonsche Kurve** f) *(stat)* Pearson curve

Pearson-Schiefemaß n **(Pearsonsches Schiefemaß** n) *(stat)* Pearson measure of skewness
 → Schiefe

Pearson-Verteilung f **(Pearsonsche Verteilung** f) *(stat)* Pearson distribution

Pegel m *(electr.)* level

Penetration f *(market & media res)* penetration
 The percentage of households or individuals in a market or a target group that own a given product or, in media research, the percentage of households or individuals that are exposed, (→) Kontakt, to a medium or to advertising.
 → Durchdringung, Haushaltsabdeckung, Marktdurchdringung, Reichweite

Penetrationspolitik f
 → Marktdurchdringungspolitik

Penetrationspreispolitik f
→ Marktdurchdringungspolitik
Penetrationstest m *(res)* penetration test
→ Penetration
Penetrationsuntersuchung f *(res)* penetration study, penetration investigation
→ Penetration
Perfoband n **(Perfomagnetband** n**)**
→ Magnetperfoband
Perforation f **(Perforierung** f**)** perforation, perforating, (Perforationslöcher) sprocket holes *pl*
The process or result of piercing a sheet, a film, or multiple sheets with small, closely-spaced dots or slits to facilitate tearing, as in printed advertising pieces having reply forms, coupons, etc., or to make holes in the edge of a film that engage the sprockets in the camera and the projector.
Perforationsmarkierung f *(film)* punch marks *pl*
Perforator m perforator
perforieren v/t to perforate, to punch
→ Perforation
Perforiermaschine f perforating machine
Perforierung f
→ Perforation
Perigäum n
→ Nahpunkt
Periodenauflage f (Zeitung/ Zeitschrift) seasonal circulation
Perioden-Werbeplan m **(Phasen-Werbeplan** m**)** *(advtsg)* flighting schedule, flight schedule, blinking schedule, pulsation schedule, wave schedule, (mit Klotzphase) burst schedule, (mit großen Pausen) drip schedule
Periodenwerbung f **(phasenweise Werbung** f**, pulsierende Werbung** f**)** flight advertising, flighting, blinking, pulsation advertising, pulsation, pulsing, wave scheduling, waving, (Periodenwerbung mit Phasen intensiver Klotzwerbung) burst advertising, flight saturation advertising, flight saturation, (Periodenwerbung mit langen Werbepausen) drip scheduling
An advertising scheduling technique that alternates periods of advertising with periods of inactivity. Flighting is employed by smaller advertisers to concentrate their effort and maximize frequency, while others use it to synchronize their advertising with special promotions or to solve seasonal marketing problems. In the most common form, it is a technique of having several short but intensive periods of advertising during the year, interspersed with hiatuses, periods with little or no advertising. Some firms use a large smash at a certain time of the year, followed by a spotty cadence. Others use a more regular cadence of heavy then light or none at all. A widespread variant is flight saturation, i.e. the maximum concentration of spot television or radio advertising within a short period, to a point at which any further advertising would presumably have diminishing or negative effects, followed by a long hiatus and one or more flights.
vgl. kontinuierliche Werbung
Periodikum n **(periodische Druckschrift** f**)** periodical, periodical publication, *auch* serial, serial publication
Any regularly issued publication appearing less frequently than daily, as distinguished from newspapers, and more frequently than annuals.
periodischer Bedarf m
→ saisonaler Bedarf
Perlleinwand f **(Perlenleinwand** f**)** *(film/TV)* beaded screen
Perlonklischee n *(print)* perlon block, perlon cut, perlon plate
→ Plastikklischee
Permastat m **(Permastatdruck** m**, Permastatkopie** f**)** *(phot)* permastat
A photostat print on a special antique finish paper with a soft tonal effect.
Permutation f *(math/stat)* permutation
The arrangement of objects in a particular order. Each possible ordering of a number of objects is a permutation. The permutations of a given set of objects are all the possible sequences of those objects. Thus ABC is one permutation of the letters A, B, and C. The other permutations are ACB, BAC, BCA, CAB, and CBA.
Permutationsverfahren n **(permutatives Verfahren** n**)** *(media planning)* permutation method, permutation technique
Perronanschlag m **(Perronplakat** n**, Perronschild** n**)** *(transit advtsg)* station display poster, depot display poster, platform advertising poster, dash sign, two-sheet poster, railroad platform poster, railway platform

Perronfläche

poster, track poster, cross tracks poster
    A poster appearing on the wall of passenger platforms serving subway or surface rail lines.
Perronfläche f (**Perronanschlagfläche** f) (*transit advtsg*) platform advertising poster panel, railroad platform poster panel, railway platform poster panel, track poster panel, cross tracks poster panel, station display poster panel
Perronschild n
    → Perronanschlag
Personalbeschaffungsmarketing n
    → Personalmarketing
Personalkauf m
    → Belegschaftshandel
Personalmarketing n (**Personalbeschaffungsmarketing** n) personnel marketing, recruitment marketing
Personalrabatt m (*econ*) staff discount
Personalstück n (*meist pl* **Personalstücke**) (Zeitung/Zeitschrift) staff copy (*pl* staff copies)
Personalwerbung f personnel advertising, staff advertising, recruitment advertising
    All advertising activities aimed at recruiting staff of any kind.
Personen f/pl **mit Kontakt** (**mit Werbeträger- oder Werbemittelkontakt**) (*media res*) exposed people pl, exposed persons pl
    → Kontakt
Personen f/pl **ohne Kontakt** (**ohne Werbeträger- oder Werbemittelkontakt**) (*media res*) unexposed people pl, unexposed persons pl
Personeneinschaltquote f (*radio*) individuals-using-radio rating, persons-using-radio rating, (*TV*) individuals-using-television rating, persons-using-television rating
    A type of rating, (→) Einschaltquote, for television and radio. The base is all individual persons, or perhaps some specified group of individual persons, e.g. those who have attained a specified age, in a specified area. An individuals-using-television or radio rating shows the percentage of the individuals included in the base that are estimated to be in the audience of any one of a group of television or radio stations at a specified time. An individual should be counted only once in the computation of this type of rating even if he or she has been counted in the audience of two or more television stations during the specified time.
Personengewicht n (*media planning*) individual weight
Personengewichtung f (*media planning*) weighting for individuals
Personenmarketing n (**Marketing** n **für ein Individuum**) person marketing
    The marketing activities directed to modify public attitudes and behavior regarding a specific person, such as a political candidate, celebrity, or prospect for a position.
Personenmerkmal n
    → Merkmal
Personenpanel n (**Einzelpersonenpanel** n, **Individualpanel** n) (*survey res*) panel of individuals
    vgl. Haushaltspanel
Personenreichweite f (*media res*) individuals pl reached, persons pl reached
    The number of individuals that are estimated to be in the audience of a communication medium during a specified period of time, regardless of where located.
Personenstandsanzeige f (**Familienanzeige** f) family announcement, family advertisement, family ad
Personenstichprobe f (**Einzelpersonenstichprobe** f, **Individualstichprobe** f) (*survey res*) sample of individuals
    vgl. Haushaltsstichprobe
Personen-Zuordnungstest m
    → Szondi-Test
Personenzuschauerschaft f (**-leserschaft** f, **-hörerschaft** f) (*media res*) audience of individuals, individuals reached pl, persons reached pl
    → Personenreichweite
persönliche Akquisition f (**persönliche Anzeigenakquisition** f)
    → Anzeigenakquisition
persönliche Gleichung f (**Beobachtungsfehler** m) (*survey res*) personal equation
    The factors in the investigator tending to distort his observations or his judgment.
persönliche Werbung f (**persönlich bezugnehmende Werbung** f) person-related advertising
    → bezugnehmende
persönlicher Einfluß m (*communication*) personal influence
    The patterns of personal, face-to-face interactions of individuals, e.g. prospects,

which bear directly on their behavior, e.g.
purchase decision, such as personal sales
contacts, opinion leader influences, and
word-of-mouth advertising.
persönlicher Verkauf m *(econ)* **1.**
(einzelner Verkaufsakt) personal sale
2. (persönliches Verkaufen) personal
selling, face-to-face selling, *colloq*
belly-to-belly selling
The oral presentation in a conversation
with one or more prospective purchasers
for the purpose of making sales. The
presentation may be either formal, (as a
"canned" sales talk), or informal,
although it is rather likely to be informal,
either in the actual presence of the
customer or by telephone although,
usually the former, either to an
individual or to a small group, although
usually the former.
persönliches Einkommen n *(econ)*
personal income, (persönlich
verfügbar) personal disposable
income
persönliches Interview n **(persönliche
Befragung** f**)** *(survey res)* personal
interview
An interview in which the interviewer
both asks the questions and records the
answers. Such interviews may be
conducted face to face or by telephone.
Group interviews, (→) Klassenzimmerbefragung, and self-administered
questionnaires, (→) schriftliche
Befragung, are not considered personal
interviews even if an interviewer is
present.
Persönlichkeitsmerkmal n
→ Merkmal
Persönlichkeitsrecht n right of
privacy, privacy
perspektivische Zeichnung f
perspective drawing
A drawing creating the illusion of depth
in a flat visual presentation by use of a
system of vanishing points or lines to
which depicted objects or lines regularly
diminish or converge as receding.
Persuasibilität f *(communication)*
persuasibility
Persuasion f
→ Überredung
Persuasionskraft f
→ Überredungskraft,
Überzeugungskraft
Perzentil n **(Perzentile** f, **Hunderter-
stelle** f**)** *(stat)* percentile
One of one hundred points dividing a
frequency distribution, (→) Häufigkeitsverteilung, into one hundred equal parts.
A particular percentile tells the percent
of the total number of cases in the
distribution that fall below that point.
Perzeption f
→ Wahrnehmung
P-F-Test m
→ Bildenttäuschungstest
Pfadanalyse f **(Dependenzanalyse** f**)**
(stat) path analysis
The analysis of causal relationships
among a series of variables attempting to
determine the plausibility of a causal
ordering among variables, based upon
regression analysis. In a simplified
example, variable b may be dependent on
variable a, and variable c, in turn, may be
dependent on variable b. The models
developed in path analysis are usually
presented diagrammatically and are
referred to as path diagrams.
Relationships between independent and
dependent variables are asymmetric
(one-way) and are shown by an arrow.
(Independent variables may be
symmetrically related to each other and
this is shown by a two-way arrow.) Path
analysis can be particularly useful in
analyzing causal relationship among
variables over a prolonged period of time.
Pfaddiagramm n *(stat)* path diagram
→ Pfadanalyse
Pfadmodell n *(stat)* path model
→ Pfadanalyse
Pfeifen n **(Pfeifton** m**)**
→ Mischfrequenz
Pfuscher m (in der Werbung)
huckster
PGR *abbr* Psychogalvanische
Hautreaktion
Phänomotiv n *(psy)* phenomotive
(William Stern)
A motive of which the individual is
conscious.
vgl. Genomotiv
Phantasiefenster n **(Fantasiefenster**
n, **Ideenfenster** n**)** *(POP advtsg)* etwa
imaginative window display, creative
window display
Phantasie-Markenzeichen n
(Phantasiezeichen n**)** *(econ)* arbitrary
mark, coined word
An invented or dictionary word used as a
brandname which effects no connotation
about the product it is to identify.
Phantasiename m **(Phantasie-
Markenname** m**)** *(econ)* coined word,
arbitrary word
Phantasiepreis m
→ Mondpreis
Phantasiewort n
→ Phantasiename

Phantomzeitung f bogus paper
Pharmawerbung f pharmaceutical advertising, (für ethische Produkte) ethical advertising
→ Arzneimittelwerbung, Heilmittelwerbung
pharmazeutische Industrie f pharmaceutical industry
Phase f 1. phase, stage 2. *(electr.)* phase 3. → Phasenbild
Phasenänderung f
→ Phasenverschiebung
Phasenbild n *(film)* (Trick) animation phase, *(video)* phase diagram, phase pattern
Phasenblatt n
→ Phasenbild 1.
Phaseneinstellung f *(TV)* phasing, phase adjustment
  The standard process of television camera and VTR alignment.
Phasenfehler m *(TV)* phase error
Phasenmodell n phase model
Phasentrick m *(film)* stop-frame animation
→ Standbildverlängerung
phasenweise Klotzwerbung f burst advertising, burst phasing, flight saturation advertising
  An advertising scheduling technique concentrating advertising activities on a sequence of phases with hiatuses between the phases.
phasenweise Werbung f (**Phasenwerbung** f)
→ Periodenwerbung
Phasenzeichner m *(film)* animator
→ Trickzeichner
Phi-Koeffizient m (**Punkt-Vierfelder-Korrelationskoeffizient** m) *(stat)* phi coefficient, φ coefficient
  A statistic used to determine whether there is a significant association between two dichotomous variables in a fourfold table. The formula is:

$$\emptyset = \frac{ad - bc}{\sqrt{(a+b)(+d)(a+c)(b+d)}} = \sqrt{\frac{\chi^2}{N}},$$

  where a, b, c, and d are the cell frequencies and the sums in the denominator are the marginal totals.
Phonem n phoneme
Photo n (**Foto** n, **Photoghraphie** f, **Fotographie** f) photo
Photoagentur f
→ Bildagentur

Photochemie f (**Fotochemie** f)
photochemistry
  That branch of chemistry which treats of photographic effects and the production of images on sensitized surfaces by the action of light.
Photochemigraph m (**Fotochemigraf** m, **Chemigraph** m) photoengraver, engraver, process engraver
Photochemigraphie f (**Fotochemigrafie** f) photoengraving, engraving, process engraving, processwork
  The process and technique of making relief printing plates by a photochemical process.
Photochromie f (**Fotochromie** f)
1. (Verfahren) photochromy
  A formerly used process of color photography in which a silver chloride emulsion layer assumes approximately the color of the exposing light.
2. (Produkt) photocrome
Photoelement n
→ Photozelle
Photofax m facsimile telegraph, fax telegraph, fax
→ Fax
Photogramm n (**Fotogramm** n)
photogram
  A positive photographic print of objects in silhouette form made by placing the objects on the paper and exposing it to light, so that the shadows of the objects are cast directly onto positive photographic paper.
Photograph m (**Fotograf** m)
photographer, *short* photog
Photographie f (**Fotografie** f)
1. (Verfahren) photography 2. (Bild) photograph, photo, photography
photographieren (fotografieren) v/t to take a photo, to photograph, to shoot, to take a shot
photographisch (fotografisch) adj
photographic(al)
photographischer Farbdruck m (**fotografischer Farbdruck** m) chromatone process, chromatone
  A photographic color process in which three colored images are formed separately by toning, stripped from their special paper, and superimposed in register.
photographische Schicht f
→ lichtempfindliche Schicht
Photogravüre f (**Fotogravüre** f)
→ Heliogravüre

Photokopie f (**Fotokopie** f)
photocopy, photostat, stat, photostatic copy, xerox copy, xerox
An expensive and quickly made photographic reproduction, usually in the form of a positive print, made with a special camera apparatus.
photokopieren (**fotokopieren, kopieren**) v/t to photocopy, to photostat, to xerox
Photokopierer m (**Fotokopierer** m, **Photokopiergerät** n, **Fotokopiergerät** n) photocopier, photostat, xerox machine
Photolithograph m (**Fotolithograf** m) photolithographer
Photolithographie f (**Fotolithografie** f, **Lichtsteindruck** m) photolithography
→ Lithographie
photomechanisch (**fotomechanisch**) adj photomechanical
photomechanisches Verfahren n photomechanical process
Any process in which printing surfaces are produced by photography.
Photomodell n (**Fotomodell** n) photo model, model
Photomontage f (**Fotomontage** f) photomontage, montage, composite picture
The process and the result of combining or blending several photographic images or portions thereof into a single print.
Photooffset m (**photographischer Offsetdruck** m) photooffset printing, photooffset, photo-offset
Offset printing using a photolithographic printing plate.
Photooffsetlithographie f (**Fotooffsetlithografie** f) photooffset lithography
Photopapier n (**Fotopapier** n, **photographisches Papier** n, **fotografisches Papier** n) photopaper, photo paper, photographic paper
A paper sensitized with a photographic emulsion and intended for either contact or projection printing.
Photoreportage f (**Fotoreportage** f)
→ Bildreportage
Photoreporter m (**Fotoreporter** m)
→ Bildreporter
Photosatz m (**Fotosatz** m, **Lichtsatz** m) (print) photocomposition, phototypesetting, photosetting, photographic composition, phototypography, phototype, phototexttyping
The transference of print onto film or sensitized paper to be used for reproduction. The term often refers to the more specific terms phototypesetting or phototypography, i.e. the photographic method of setting type, which today is the most widespread method in newspaper and other printing production.
Photosatzgerät n (**Fotosatzgerät** n, **Photosetzmaschine** f)
phototypesetter, photocomposition machine, photocomposing machine
A machine used in phototypesetting, (→) Photosatz, to choose and assemble the characters or type, as distinguished from photolettering typesetting, (→) Phototitelsatz, where the composition is done by hand.
Photosetzer m (**Fotosetzer** m) photocomposer, phototypesetter, photosetter
Photosetzgerät n
→ Photosatzgerät
Photosetzmaschine f
→ Photosatzgerät
Photostudio n (**Fotostudio** n, **Photoatelier** n, **Fotoatelier** n, **photographisches Atelier** n, **fotografisches Atelier** n) photo studio, photographer's parlor, brit photographer's parlour
Phototitelsatz m (**Fototitelsatz** m, **Photoakzidenzsatz** m, **Fotoakzidenzsatz** m) photolettering, photolettering typesetting
A technique for producing display and headline type through manual selection and assemblage of characters and photographic reproduction, as distinguished from phototypesetting, (→) Photosatz, which produces the type through mechanical devices.
Phototrick m
→ Phasentrick
Photozelle f (**Fotozelle** f) photocell, photoelectric cell (P. E. cell), electric eye
A photoelectric device which converts light into electric current proportionate to the amount of light that falls on it. It is a layer of a light-sensitive metal, usually selenium, coated on an insulating base. When light falls on the cell, it generates an electric potential in proportion to the brightness of the illumination. This voltage can be measured by a galvanometer or meter to provide a basis for exposure calculation in photography.
Photozuordnungstest m
→ Bildzuordnungstest
physiologische Methode f (**der Einstellungsmessung**) (res) physiological method (of attitude measurement)

physische Distribution

The branch of attitude research, (→) Einstellungsforschung, that studies the relationship between organic processes, e.g. neural stimulation, visceral activity, psychogalvanic skin response, hormonal secretions, etc., and psychological processes, and particularly attitudes, (→) Einstellung.

physische Distribution f **(physischer Vertrieb** m) *(econ)* physical distribution
→ Marketing-Logistik; *vgl.* akquisitorische Distribution

Piepton m beep

Pigment n pigment
A natural or synthetic substance that imparts a color to other materials; in printing, the substance used for coloring ink.

Pigmentdruck m **(Kohlepigmentdruck** m) *(print)* pigment process, carbon printing, carbon print
A photographic printing process in which the image consists of a black or colored pigment distributed as gelatin in a collodial medium.

Pigmentfarbe f *(print)* pigment color, *brit* pigment colour, pigment dye

Pigmentpapier n *(print)* pigment paper, carbon paper

Pigmentschablone f
→ Siebdruckschablone

Piktogramm n pictogram, *auch* pictograph
1. A pictorial representation of some object or process used to symbolize it.
2. In *statistics*, a diagram representing data by pictorial forms which can be varied in color, size, or number to indicate different dimensions or change.

Pilotinterview n **(Pilotgespräch** n)
→ Probeinterview

Pilotprojekt n pilot project

Pilotprogramm n *(radio/TV)* pilot program, *brit* pilot programme, pilot
→ Pilotsendung

Pilotsendung f **(Probesendung** f) *(radio/TV)* pilot broadcast, pilot transmission
In broadcasting, a representative program from a projected series, produced either for the purpose of pretesting audience reaction or as a sample for prospective sponsors.

Pilotsignal n *(radio/TV)* pilot signal, pilot

Pilotstudie f
→ Leitstudie

Pilotton m *(radio/TV)* pilot tone

Pilottonverfahren n *(radio/TV)* pilottone process

Pilzmethode f
→ Schirmmethode

Pingpongblitz m **(indirekte Reflektionsbelichtung** f) *(phot)* bounce light
A softer light than a regular flash or flood, produced by reflecting the light from a ceiling, wall, or other surface. The additional exposure required depends on the color and distance of the reflecting surface, it is usually between 3 to 5 times the regular exposure.

Pionierstadium n **(Pionierphase** f)
→ Einführungsphase (im Produktlebenszyklus)

Pipeline-Effekt m *(econ)* pipeline effect
→ Nachfragesog

Pipifax m *colloq (studio)* baby spotlight, baby spot, dinky inky, dinky inkie, dinkie inkie, inky dink, inkie dink
A small theatrical spotlight.

Piratensender m *(radio/TV)* pirate station

placieren
→ plazieren

Placierung f
→ Plazierung

Plagiarismus m **(Plagiat** n, **Plagiieren** n) plagiarism, *auch* plagiary, cribbing
The habit, act or instance of stealing the ideas or words of another person and passing them of as one's own.

Plagiator m plagiarist, plagiator, plagiarizer, cribber

plagiieren v/t to plagiarize, *brit* to plagiarise, to crib

Plakat n **(Poster** n) poster, advertising poster, bill, advertising bill, *auch* billposter, billboard, placard, (klein) sticker, *ungebr* affiche
An advertising message printed on large sheets of paper and pasted on boards or panels.

Plakatankleber m
→ Plakatkleber

Plakatanschlag m **(Anschlag** m, **Bogenanschlag** m) billposting, bill posting, poster advertising, billsticking, billboard advertising, billing, posting
→ Anschlagwerbung

Plakatanschläger m
→ Plakatkleber

Plakatanschlagfläche f
→ Anschlagfläche
Plakatanschlaginstitut n
→ Plakatanschlagunternehmen
Plakatanschlagkontrolle f
→ Anschlagkontrolle
Plakatanschlagstelle f **(Anschlagstelle** f) *(outdoor advtsg)* poster site, site, advertising poster site, posting site, billboard site
A flat, upright structure for the display of outdoor advertising in printed paper sheets rather than being painted.
→ Allgemeinstelle, Ganzstelle, Großfläche, Kleintafel, Spezialstelle
Plakatanschlagunternehmen n *(outdoor advtsg)* poster plant, outdoor poster plant, plant, poster plant operator, billposting agency, billposting company, billposter, poster plant, outdoor advertising plant, outdoor advertising plant operator, outdoor advertising contractor
→ Anschlagunternehmen
Plakatanschlagwerbung f **(Anschlagwerbung** f, **Plakatwerbung** f) *(outdoor advtsg)* poster advertising, billboard advertising, billposting, billsticking, billboard advertising
→ Anschlagwerbung
Plakataufkleber m **(Plakatüberkleber** m, **Aufklebestreifen** m) poster overlay, overlay, paster, snipe
A strip of copy pasted over a poster to add something new or special to the message.
Plakatbeobachtung f **(Reichweitenbeobachtung** f) *(media res)* poster circulation observation, circulation observation, poster audience observation
The observation of exposure, (→) Kontakt, to poster message in outdoor and transit advertising.
Plakatentwurf m poster design
Plakatformat n **(Plakatgröße** f) poster size
plakatieren 1. v/i to post bills, to stick bills **2.** v/t to post, to stick, to billpost
Plakatierung f **(Plakatkleben** n, **Plakatanschlagen** n) posting, billposting, billsticking
The physical placement of (an) outdoor or transit advertisment(s).
Plakatierungsauftrag m billposting order, posting order
Plakatkleben n
→ Plakatierung

Plakatkleber m **(Plakatanschläger** m, **Plakatankleber** m) billposter, billsticker, poster sticker, bill poster, bill sticker
Plakatkontakt m **(Plakatanschlagkontakt** m, **Anschlagkontakt** m) *(media res)* poster exposure, poster advertising exposure, outdoor advertising exposure
Plakatkontrolle f
→ Anschlagkontrolle
Plakatmaler m poster painter, poster artist, poster designer, sign painter
Plakatpächter m
→ Anschlagflächenpächter
Plakatrahmen m **(fester Plakatanschlagrahmen** m) poster frame
A framed panel structure used in outdoor and transit advertising for holding a poster on or in a bus, terminal, station, store, etc.
Plakatreichweite f *(media res)* advertising poster circulation, outdoor circulation, effective circulation, (tägliche effektive Reichweite) daily effective circulation (DEC), (absolut) advertising poster audience, outdoor poster audience, poster audience, outdoor audience, outdoor-panel audience
An estimate of the percentage (or absolute number) of the passers-by or of any other given target audience of a poster site or a transit poster who might reasonably be considered of being exposed, (→) Kontakt, to its advertising message.
Plakatsäule f **(Litfaßsäule** f)
→ Anschlagsäule
Plakatreichweitenuntersuchung f *(media res)* poster audience investigation, poster audience survey, circulation study, circulation investigation
Plakatschrift f display face, display type, poster type, poster lettering
→ Auszeichnungsschrift
Plakatstatistik f **(Anschlagstatistik** f) poster advertising statistics pl *(construed as sg)*, outdoor advertising statistics
Plakatstelle f
→ Anschlagstelle
Plakattafel f
→ Anschlagtafel
Plakattest m **(Anschlagwerbetest** m) poster test, poster advertising test,

Plakattitel 388

billposting test, outdoor advertising test, billboard test
Plakattitel *m* poster title
Plakatträger *m (outdoor advtsg)* sandwich man
  A man, walking in the street with an advertising poster suspended from his shoulders.
Plakatträgerwerbung *f* **(Werbung** *f* **mit Hilfe von Plakatträgern)** *(outdoor advtsg)* sandwich-board advertising
Plakatumrandung *f* **(weißer Plakatrand** *m***)** poster margin, white poster margin
Plakatwand *f* **(Anschlagwand** *f,* **Anschlagzaun** *m***)**
  → Anschlagwand
Plakatwerbung *f* **(Anschlagwerbung** *f* **)** poster advertising, poster-panel advertising, billboard advertising, iron poor man's art gallery
vgl. Außenwerbung, Verkehrsmittelwerbung
Plakatzaun *m* **(Anschlagzaun** *m***)**
  → Anschlagwand
plankonkaves Objektiv *n* **(plankonkave Linse** *f* **)** *(phot)* planoconcave lens
plankonvexes Objektiv *n* **(plankonvexe Linse** *f* **)** *(phot)* plano-convex lens
Planung *f*
  → Marketingplanung, Werbeplanung
Planversand *m ungebr*
  → Wechselversand
Plastikeinband *m* **(Kunststoffeinband** *m***)** *(bookbinding)* plastic-coated binding, plastic cover, plastic case
Plastikfolie *f*
  → Folie
Plastikheftung *f (bookbinding)* plastic binding
  A type of mechanical binding with plastic rings or ring-like fasteners that originally look like a solid back comb rolled to make a cylinder of any thickness. The book is punched with slots along the binding side and the comb is inserted through the slots.
Plastikhülle *f* acetate sleeve
Plastikklischee *n* **(Kunststoffklischee** *n***)** *(print)* plastic block, plastic cut, plastic plate, plastic stereo, (Duplikatätzung) plastic duplicate block, plastic duplicate printing plate
  A relief printing plate or electro made of synthetic material, such as vinylite,
tenaplate, nylon, or perlon, used for making castings.
Platte *f* **1.** → Druckplatte **2.** → Schallplatte **3.** *(phot)* photographic plate, plate, (lichtempfindlich) sensitized plate
  A sensitized sheet of glass on which negatives or positives are made.
4. (Dekor) rostrum, panel
Plattenarchiv *n*
  → Schallplattenarchiv
Plattenbeschichtung *f (print)* plate coating, coating
Plattendruck *m*
  → Klischeedruck
Plattenhalter *m*
  → Plattenkassette
Plattenkamera *f (phot)* plate camera
Plattenkassette *f* **(Plattenhalter** *m***)** *(phot)* plateholder, plate holder, dark slide
  The light-tight frame or case used for transporting photographic plates to and from the camera, and for holding the sensitized material in position during exposure.
Plattenspieler *m* **(Schallplattenspieler** *m***)** record player, record reproducer, pick-up, turntable, phonograph
Plattentiefdruck *m (print)* plate gravure printing, plate gravure
vgl. Rotationsdruck
Plattenunterlage *f* **(Steigetrichter** *m***)** *(print)* patent base, patent block, riser
  Sectional metal blocks used as supports for printing plates and provided with means for holding the plates in position for the press bed so that electros or stereos need not be mounted on wood or a metal base.
Plattenwechsler *m* record changer
Plattenzylinder *m (print)* plate cylinder
  The cylinder on a rotary press which holds the printing plate or curved electros.
vgl. Gegendruckzylinder
Plattformanschlag *m* **(Plattformplakat** *m***)**
  → Perronanschlag
Platz *m* **(Anzeigenraum** *m,* **Anzeigenfläche** *f* **)** *(advtsg)* space
Platzaufschlag *m*
  → Plazierungsaufschlag
Platzvorschrift *f*
  → Plazierungsvorschrift
Plausibilitätskontrolle *f (survey res)* editing of data, data editing

The procedure of ensuring that the data contained on questionnaires, punched cards, or tape are consistent and logical and, therefore, suitable for processing.
→ Datenbereinigung
Playback n **(Playbackverfahren** n**)** playback, playback procedure
In broadcasting, playing a transcription immediately after recording, to check performance or production.
plazieren (placieren) v/t to place, to position
Plazierung f **(Placierung** f**)** *(advtsg)* placement, placing, position, positioning
Plazierung f **oben links (Anzeigenposition** f **oben links)** *(advtsg)* top left position
Plazierung f **oben rechts (Anzeigenposition** f **oben rechts)** *(advtsg)* top right position
Plazierung f **unten links (Anzeigenposition** f **unten links)** *(advtsg)* bottom left position
Plazierung f **unten rechts (Anzeigenposition** f **unten rechts)** *(advtsg)* bottom right position
Plazierungsaufschlag m **(Aufschlag** m **für Vorzugsplazierung)** *(advtsg)* preferred position rate, preferred position surcharge, premium position rate, premium position surcharge
An extra charge or higher total cost for a preferred advertising position, (→) Plazierungsvorschrift.
Plazierungseffekt m **(Positionseffekt** m**)** *(advtsg)* position effect, placement effect
Plazierungsvorschrift f **(bevorzugte Plazierung** f**)** *(advtsg)* position request, placement request, preferred position, premium position, special position, (exklusive Plazierung) franchise position
The request or positive demand by an advertiser for a certain location (preferred position) in a periodical or on a television or radio program, if available.
Plazierungswunsch m
→ Plazierungsvorschrift
Plunder m **(Talmi** m, **Schundware** f**)** borax
Low-quality merchandise.
Podest n *(phot/film/TV)* (im Studio) platform, stage, riser, apple box, apple, half-apple
A riser for a performer or a prop.
Point-of-Purchase m **(POP)**
→ Kaufort (Einkaufsort)

Point-of-Purchase-Material n
→ POP-Material
Point-of-Purchase-Werbung f
→ POP-Werbung
Point-of-Sale m **(POS)**
→ Kaufort (Verkaufsort)
Point-of-Sale-Material n
→ POP-Material (POS-Material)
Point-of-Sale-Werbung f
→ POP-Werbung (POS-Werbung)
Poisson-Verteilung f *(stat)* Poisson distribution, Poisson probability distribution
A limited form of the binomial distribution, (→) Binomialverteilung, that occurs when the number of cases in the sample is large and drawn from a very large universe and the proportion in one of the two categories is very small. It is a discontinuous distribution with relative frequencies at variate-values 0, 1, 2, ... r, ... given by

Pol m pole
Polafilter m
→ Polarisationsfilter
Polarisation f **(Polarisierung** f**)** polarization, brit polarisation
Polarisationsfilter m **(Polafilter** m**)** *(phot)* polarizing filter, pola screen
A neutral gray light filter, transmitting plane polarized light of all visible colors, but absorbing ultraviolet. Used on camera lenses and lights to eliminate or subdue undesirable reflections from originals.
Polarität f polarity
Polaritätenprofil n **(Polaritätsprofil** n**)**
→ semantisches Differential
Polaroidkamera f **(Sofortbildkamera** f**)** *(phot)* polaroid camera, polaroid
polieren v/t to polish, to finish
Polieren n polishing, finishing
politische Anzeige f political advertisement, political ad
politische Kommunikation f political communication
politische Werbung f political advertising, (zur Information der Öffentlichkeit) public service advertising, public-interest advertising, (politisch engagierte Werbung) advocacy advertising, issue-oriented advertising
The use of advertising for political ends, e.g. to influence elections and govern-

politisches Marketing 390

ment, by persuading voters and government officials to behave voluntarily in a recommended manner. Also, advertising concerned with the propagation of political and social ideas and the elucidation of controversial social issues of public importance in a manner that supports the economic and political philosophy of the sponsor. It thus covers a broad spectrum of attempts to change or sustain public opinion and social policy on specific short-term and fundamental long-term values that underlie political and social institutions.
politisches Marketing n **(Politmarketing** n**)** political marketing
→ Soziomarketing
Polychromie f
→ Mehrfarbendruck
Polydistribution f *(econ)* polydistribution
vgl. Dualdistribution, Monodistribution
Polygon n **(Polygonzug** m**)**
→ Häufigkeitspolygon
polytechnische Zeitschrift f polytechnical magazine, polytechnical journal
POP-Material n **(Point-of-Purchase-Material** n**, POS-Material** n**, Point-of-Sale-Material** n**)** point-of-purchase material, P.O.P. material, POP material, point-of-purchase advertising material, P.O.P. advertising material, POP advertising material, point-of-purchase display material, P.O.P. display material, POP display material, dealer aids *pl*, merchandising material, sales aids *pl*, dealer helps *pl*
 The materials, such as displays, signs, banners, etc., used in retailing at one or more in-store locations, e.g. shelf, window, back bar, counter, wall, overwire, island, checkout area, as means of point-of-purchase advertising, (→) POP-Werbung; particularly the type of promotional material furnished by national manufacturers or advertisers to retail outlets.
POP-Werbung f **(Point-of-Purchase-Werbung** f**, POS-Werbung** f**, Point-of-Sale-Werbung** f**)** point-of-purchase advertising, P.O.P. advertising, POP advertising, point-of-sale advertising, P.O.S. advertising, POS advertising
 A collective term for all types of advertising found in retail stores, i.e. the point-of-purchase, (→) Kaufort, which is the last chance in the chain of opportunities where advertising can be addressed to consumers before the actual purchase is made.
Population f
→ Grundgesamtheit
Pornokino n
→ Sex- und Pornokino
Portfolio n *(econ)* portfolio
 Portfolios are sets of strategic business units (SBU) that work together as a team to achieve an organization's overall goals.
Portfolio-Management n *(econ)* portfolio management, portfolio analysis
 A management strategy that bases business decisions within the context of the company viewed explicitly as a portfolio, (→) Portfolio, of individual businesses.
Portfolioplan m *(econ)* portfolio plan
Portfolio-Strategie f *(econ)* portfolio strategy
Portfoliotechnik f **(Portfoliomethode** f **)** *(econ)* portfolio technique, portfolio method
→ Produktportfolio, Portfolio-Management
Portfoliotest m
→ Foldertest
Portion f *(econ)* take
Portrait n
→ Porträt
Porträtaufnahme f **(Portraitaufnahme** f**, Porträtphoto** n**)** *(phot)* portrait shot, *colloq* mug shot
 A close-up shot of a subject's face.
Porträtobjektiv n **(Portraitobjektiv** n**)** *(phot)* portrait lens, (Nahaufnahmeobjektiv für eine Fixfokuskamera) portrait attachment
 A supplementary lens, (→) Objektiv, which shortens the focal length, (→) Brennweite, so that near objects may be brought into sharp focus.
Porträtphotographie f **(Portraitphotographie** f**)** portrait photography, portraiture
Position f *(marketing/advtsg)* position
 In *marketing*, the consumer perception of a product's or service's benefit(s), in comparison to its competition, (→) Positionierung, (→) Produktpositionierung.
 In *advertising*, the placement of an advertisement in a publication or of a commercial in a program, (→) Plazierung.
→ Standort
Positionierung f *(marketing)* positioning

The art and science of creating a distinct identity for a product or service by fitting it to one or more segments of a market in such a way that it is meaningfully set apart from competition products or services, thereby optimizing opportunity for greater sales or profits.
Positionierungsforschung f *(market res)* positioning research
→ Positionierung
Positionsbewertung f **(Positionsevaluierung** f) position evaluation
→ Standortevaluierung
Positionseffekt m **(Plazierungseffekt** m, **Standorteffekt** m) *(advtsg)* position effect
→ Standorteffekt
Positionsmedium n
→ Standortmedium
Positiv n **(Positivbild** n, **Positivabzug** m) *(phot)* positive, positive print, print
A photographic print in which the light and dark values or the colors correspond to those seen by the human eye, as distinguished from a negative, (→) Negativ, in which such values are reversed.
Positivfarbfilm m *(phot)* color print film, *brit* colour print film, color positive film, *brit* colour positive film
Positivfilm m *(phot)* positive film
A non-color-sensitive film, much slower than negative film but faster than positive plates, used as an intermediate in making a copy negative.
Positivfilmmaterial n *(phot)* positive stock, printed material
Positivkopie f *(film)* positive copy, positive print, positive
A motion picture print in which the light and dark values or the colors correspond to those seen by the human eye, as distinguished from a negative copy, (→) Negativkopie, in which such values are reversed.
Positivmuster n *(film)* positive rush print, positive work print, test print
Postabonnement n (Zeitung/ Zeitschrift) postal subscription, mail subscription, (Einzelabonnement) individual mail subscription, (Sammelabonnement) special mail subscription
In Germany, all subscriptions that are served by mail.
postalische Befragung f
→ briefliche Befragung
Postauflage f **(Postbezugsauflage** f) (Zeitung/Zeitschrift) mail circulation, mail distribution

Postauslieferung f
→ Postvertrieb
Postbezieheranalyse f *(media res)* mail address analysis
A type of analysis that reports the number of copies mailed out, to whom they are sent, etc.
Postbezugsauflage f
→ Postauflage
Postbezugskartei f **(Postbezugsliste** f) (Zeitung/Zeitschrift) mailing list
Poster n
→ Plakat
Postkartenbeikleber m **(beigeklebte Antwortpostkarte** f) *(direct-response advtsg)* bound-in return card
Postkäufer m
→ Versandhandelskunde
Postreklame f
→ Deutsche Postreklame, Postwerbung
Posttest m *(res)* post test, *auch* follow-up test, after-test
Any research design in which one or more groups of subjects are observed or measured after an experimental treatment is given, or an event has occurred.
vgl. Pretest
Postversand m **(Versand** m) mailing
Postversandgeschäft n
→ Versandhandel
Postversandwerbung f
→ Versandwerbung, Briefwerbung
Postvertrieb m **(Postauslieferung** f) (Zeitung/Zeitschrift) mail distribution
Postwerbung f **(Postreklame** f) postal advertising
vgl. Briefwerbung, Direktwerbung
Postwurfsendung f
→ Wurfsendung
Postzeitungsdienst m mail-subscription service
Postzeitungsordnung f German Mail Subscription Regulations pl
potentieller Käufer m *(econ)* prospective buyer, prospective purchaser, prospect, potential buyer
Anyone not now using a product or service, who can benefit from owning it and who has the purchasing power to acquire it.
potentieller Konsum m
→ potentieller Verbrauch
potentieller Konsument m **(potentieller Verbraucher** m) *(econ)*

prospective consumer, prospect, potential consumer
→ potentieller Käufer
potentieller Kunde m *(econ)* prospective customer, prospect, potential customer
→ potentieller Käufer
potentieller Markt m *(econ)* prospective market, potential market
potentieller Verbrauch m **(potentieller Konsum** m) *(econ)* prospective consumption, potential consumption
potentieller Verbraucher m
→ potentieller Konsument
Potentiometer n
→ Lautstärkenregler
PR *abbr* Public Relations
PR-Abteilung f public relations department, PR department, public relations office
    The department of an organization responsible for designing, planning and implementing its public relations policy.
PR-Anzeige f PR advertisement, PR ad, public relations advertisement, public relations ad
→ redaktioneller Hinweis
PR-Arbeit f
→ Öffentlichkeitsarbeit
PR-Experte m **(PR-Mann** m)
→ Öffentlichkeitsarbeiter
PR-Berater m **(Öffentlichkeitsarbeitsberater** m**)** public relations consultant, public relations counsellor
    An individual or a firm employed by an organization to provide advice and/or to act on its behalf in the field of public relations.
PR-Beratung f **(Öffentlichkeitsarbeitsberatung** f**)** public relations consultancy, public relations counselling
    The provision of advice and organization of activities by an outside unit, (→) PR-Berater, in the field of public relations for an organization.
PR-Direktor m **(Leiter** m **der PR-Abteilung)** public relations director, publicity director, public relations manager, publicity manager
    An executive in an organization, e.g. a business firm or an advertising agency, responsible for designing, planning, and implementing the public relations policy of the organization itself or of clients.
Präferenz f **(Bevorzugung** f**)** *(econ)* preference
    A favorable consumer attitude toward a specific product or service, normally a brand product, which serves to differentiate otherwise equal goods in the marketplace.
Präferenzkurve f *(econ)* preference curve
Präferenzlandkarte f **(Präferenzkarte** f**)** *(econ)* preference map
Präferenz-Rating n **(Präferenzbewertung** f**)** *(scaling)* preference rating
Präferenzraum m *(scaling)* preference space
Präferenzsegmentierung f *(econ)* preference segmentation
Präferenzskala f *(scaling)* preference scale
Präferenzstruktur f *(econ)* preference structure
Präferenzsystem n *(econ)* preference system
Präferenztest m *(market res)* preference test
Präferenzurteil n *(scaling)* preference judgment, preference rating
Präferenzwahrscheinlichkeit f *(scaling)* preference probability
Prägedruck m **(Prägung** f**)** *(print)*
1. (Produkt) relief print, die-stamp, (Hochprägung) embossed print, (Tiefprägung) tooled print
2. (Verfahren) relief printing, die-stamping, (Hochprägung) embossing, (Tiefprägung) tooling
    Any printing using two dies to raise or recess the printed surface above or below the rest of the sheet.
Prägeeisen n
→ Prägestempel
prägen *(print)* v/t to stamp, to tool, (mit Prägeplatte)to block, (hochprägen) to emboss
Prägeplakat n *(print)* die cut
    A cut-out of any shape in a promotion piece or a sheet of paper cut to any shape other than rectangular.
Prägeplatte f *(print)* embossing plate, relief plate, die plate
    A plate etched or engraved below its surface, into which paper is forced for the production of a raised design on the surface of the sheet.
Prägepresse f *(print)* embossing press, blocking press
Prägestempel m *(print)* relief die, stamping die, die, binder's die, binder's tool

A deeply etched or engraved relief plate on brass or zinc for stamping bookcovers, brass plates being used when the stamping process repuires heat.

Prägnanz f *(psy)* praegnanz, pragnanz, pregnance, precision, **Prägnanzprinzip** n **(Prägnanzgesetz** n) *(psy)* praegnanz principle, pragnanz principle, pregnance principle, law of precision, eidotropic principle
Praktikabel n *(film/TV)* rostrum, riser, apple, half apple
→ Podest
Prämie f *(econ)* premium, bonus, bonus payment, premium money, premium pay, extra pay
An incentive payment granted to salespersons for above-the-norm achievement.
Präsentation f **(Agenturpräsentation** f) presentation, *colloq* pitch
The formal face-to-face exposition of facts, information, figures, plans, ideas, visual material, etc. regarding a subject or a proposed course of action, and used in selling a marketing or advertising campaign to a client or any other service.
Präsentationseffekt m **(Darbietungseffekt** m) presentation effect
The effect a well-done sales presentation has in favor of a product.
Präsenter m *(radio/TV)* presenter
An actor in a television or radio commercial who delivers a sales message, or a compère who presents a television or radio program.
Präsentwerbung f
→ Geschenkwerbung
Präsenzfilter m presence filter
Präzision f **(Treffgenauigkeit** f) *(res)* precision
→ Genauigkeit (Wiederholungsgenauigkeit)
Präzisionsjournalismus m **(sozialwissenschaftlicher Journalismus** m) precision journalism (Philip Meyer)
Preemphasis f pre-emphasis
Preis m *(econ)* 1. (für Waren, Dienstleistungen) price
The amount of money (or in barter trade of something else) for which a product or service can be acquired. It is the representation of the value placed on the product or service for purposes of exchange.
2. (für Werbemittel) rate, cost
The unit cost of space or time for advertising purposes in a communications medium.

Preis m **pro Einschaltprozentpunkt** *(radio/TV advtsg)* cost per gross rating point **(CPGRP)**, cost per cover point, cost per rating point
The price of a single gross rating point (GRP) for a medium serving as a measure of broadcast media efficiency in media planning.
Preis m **pro Werbeminute** *(radio/TV/ advtsg)* cost per commercial minute
The average price for a minute of commercial time in a program, or a media element, or media schedule.
Preisabsatzelastizität f
→ Absatzelastizität, Preiselastizität
Preisabsatzfunktion f *(econ)* demand curve
→ Nachfragekurve
Preisabsprache f **(Preisabrede** f, **Preisabkommen** n) *(econ)* price agreement, price arrangement
Preisaktion f
→ Sonderpreisangebot
Preisanalyse f *(econ)* price analysis
The investigation by a buyer of a supplier's costs to make an item with the objective of assisting the buyer to negotiate a price closely parallel to the supplier's cost to produce.
Preisänderung f *(econ)* change in price
Preisangabe f *(econ)* price quotation, quotation
The verbal or written offer of a price for goods or services.
Preisangabenverordnung f German Price Quotation Decree
Preisanstieg m *(econ)* price increase, increase in price
Preisaufschlag m *(econ)* price markup, markup
The amount added to a purchase price to provide a selling price.
Preisausgleich m *(econ)* price equalization, *brit* price equalisation
A competitive pricing policy that results in a firm's delivered price to a customer consisting of the price of the product at the factory plus the freight cost to the customer as though the shipment originated from the shipping point of the firm's competitor nearest to the firm's customer.
Preisausschreiben n *(promotion)* prize competition, competition, contest
A promotional competition in which prizes are awarded for individuals showing the best performance(s).

Preisauszeichnung f *(econ)* price marking, price labeling
The marking of retail prices on packages or on the box in which the package is sold.

Preisbemessung f
→ Preisbestimmung (Preisfestsetzung)

Preisbereitschaft f (**Preisakzeptanz** f) *(econ)* price acceptance
→ Akzeptanz

Preisbereitschaftstest m (**Preisakzeptanztest** m) *(market res)* price acceptance test

Preisbestimmung f (**Preisfestsetzung** f) *(econ)* price determination, price setting, pricing, price setting
The processes and methods involved in choosing a specific selling price for a product or a service.

Preisbestimmungsfaktor m *(econ)* price determining factor, price determinant
One of a multitude of factors affecting the final selling price of a product or service.

Preisbewußtsein n *(econ)* **1.** (Preiskenntnis) price awareness
The knowledge consumers have of the prices and price levels of products and services they buy.
2. (preisorientiertes Verhalten) price consciousness
A type of consumer buying behavior in which buying devisions are strongly influenced by prices or price levels.

Preisbildung f *(econ)* price formation, price setting, pricing
→ Preisbestimmung, Preispolitik

Preisbindung f *(econ)* price maintenance, price fixing, (Kontrolle) price regulation
1. The establishment of a fixed price between directly competing companies such as two manufacturers or two retailers (horizontal price fixing).
2. The establishment of a fixed price between members of one channel of distribution, (→) Absatzweg, such as would occur if a manufacturer required that a retailer sell the manufacturer's products at a specific price (vertical price fixing), (→) Preisbindung der zweiten Hand.
3. Any legal or governmental constraint preventing the free development of prices on the market.

Preisbindung f **der zweiten Hand** (**vertikale Preisbindung** f) *(econ)* resale price maintenance, vertical price fixing
The control by a supplier of the selling prices of his branded goods at subsequent stages of distribution by means of contractual agreement under fair trade laws or other devices. It was abolished in 1974 in Germany (except for books, magazines and newspapers) and replaced by vertical recommended retail selling prices, (→) Preisempfehlung.

Preisbrecher m *(econ)* price cutter

Preisdifferenzierung f *(econ)* price differentiation, differential pricing
A pricing strategy under which a product or service is offered at different prices in different markets or market segments, each of which has a different elasticity of demand, (→) Preiselastizität der Nachfrage, for the product or service in question. The firm attempts to sell the product at a high price in market segments characterized by inelastic demand and at a low price in the segments charcterized by elastic demand.

Preisdiskriminierung f *(econ)* price discrimination
The practice of selling products or services of like grade and quality at different prices to different purchasers when the effect of this practice lessens or injures competition.

Preis m "**früher — jetzt**"
→ "Jetzt"—"Früher"—Preis, durchgestrichener Preis

Preiseffekt m *(econ)* price effect, price-aura effect
The effect of a certain price level has on consumers' quality notions associated with the product or service.
→ Preis-Qualitäts-Assoziation

Preiselastizität f *(econ)* price elasticity, *auch* price sensitivity
→ Preiselastizität der Nachfrage

Preiselastizität f **der Nachfrage** *(econ)* price elasticity of demand, *auch* price sensitivity of demand
A measure of the responsiveness of consumers in terms of quantity demanded as a result of changes in price of a product or service. Other factors remaining constant, it is defined as the percent change in quantity demanded which may be expected to result from a present change in price. The elasticity between any two points on the demand curve may be measured by this formula:

$$\frac{P + P_1}{P - P_1} \cdot \frac{Q - Q_1}{Q + Q_1} = E$$

Where: P is the price at Q quantitiy
P_1 is the price at Q_1 quantity

The numerical value of E, called the elasticity coefficient, indicates the relative increase or decrease (as E is larger or smaller than 1) in the total revenue effected by changes incorporated into the formula. It is customary to express this value as a positive number, regardless of the sign.

Preisempfehlung f **(empfohlener Preis** m **Richtpreis** m) *(econ)* recommended retail selling price (RRSP) recommended price, price recommendation, suggested retail price
Since the abolition of resale price maintenance in 1974 in Germany, (→) Preisbindung der zweiten Hand, manufacturers are only allowed to make nonobligatory price recommendations to provide consumers with some price standard by which they may judge the value of a product and compare it with competitors.

Preisempfinden n *(econ)* cost-price judgment
The subjective notion consumers have of a fair cost-price relationship. When a consumer feels he knows the approximate cost of a product or service, he may react to the price on the basis of whether or not he feels the mark-up to be reasonable. Regardless of what he might have to pay for the same satisfactions from another source, he will resent the price if he considers the cost-price relationship too great.

Preisendziffer f **(Preisendzifferneffekt** m**)**
→ Endziffer

Preisentscheidung f *(econ)* pricing decision
One in a series of steps in a business firm's overall corporate strategy which results from the definition of its corporate mission and the formulation of marketing objectives and programs. It involves relating the product decisions to pricing and comprises decisions on pricing objectives, pricing policies, and pricing tactics.

Preiserhöhung f *(econ)* price increase, increase in price(s), (beabsichtigt) price raise, raise in price(s)

Preisermäßigung f *(econ)* **1.** price cut, price reduction, reduction in price(s), reduction of price(s) **2.** (Preisrabatt) price discount, price rebate
→ Rabatt

Preisindex

Preiserwartung(en) f *(pl)* *(econ)* price expectation(s) *(pl)*
Preisfaktor m *(econ)* price factor, price determinant
→ Preisbestimmungsfaktor
Preisfixierung f
→ Preisbindung
Preisfindung f
→ Preisbestimmung, Preispolitik
Preisführer m *(econ)* price leader
A business firm whose pricing behavior is followed by other companies in the same industry. The price leadership of a firm may be limited to a certain geographical area or to certain products or groups of products.
Preisführerschaft f **(Preisführung** f**)** *(econ)* price leadership
The emergence of one business firm as dominant in an industry (normally as a result of competition-oriented pricing in an oligopolistic market) with the result that the selling prices set by this firm become the prices for the entire industry or market.
Preisgarantie f *(econ)* price guaranty, price guarantee, price protection
The pledge on the part of the seller to make a proportionate refund to the buyer on all applicable items in the buyer's inventory at the time of a price reduction, usually qualified for a specified time after purchase.
→ Reverssystem
Preisgegenüberstellung f **(Jetzt-Früher-Preis** m**)** *(econ)* was-is price labeling
→ durchgestrichener Preis
Preisgefälle n *(econ)* price differential
Preisgefüge n **(Preisstruktur** f**)** *(econ)* price structure
Preisgestaltung f *(econ)* pricing
→ Preispolitik
Preisgrenze f **(Preislimit** n**)** *(econ)* price limit, (obere Grenze) price ceiling, (untere Grenze) bottomline
Preisherabsetzung f
→ Preisermäßigung
Preisheraufsetzung f
→ Preiserhöhung
Preishöhe f
→ Preisniveau
Preisillusion f *(econ)* price illusion
Preisimage n *(econ)* price image
→ Preis-Qualitäts-Assoziation
Preisindex m *(econ/stat)* price index
An index number which combines several series of price data into a single series expressing an average level of

prices, e.g. of retail prices or of prices of manufactured products.
Preisindex m für die Lebenshaltung (Lebenshaltungskostenindex m) *(econ/stat)* consumer price index (C.P.I., CPI), *brit* cost of living index, retail price index
An index number, (→) Indexzahl, representing the trend of a series of prices paid for a representative sample of consumer goods, revealing the changes in the cost to households of typical purchase needs. It is a relative measure issued by the German Federal Bureau of Statistics, which shows the trend of prices of consumer goods, including food, clothing, shelter, recreational items; of services, including professional fees, repair costs, transportation and utilities costs; and of sales excise, and real estate taxes. A weakness of this index is that its "market basket" (→) Warenkorb, is defined in accordance with the average expenditures of moderate income city dwellers, both single and married, and thus may not adequately reflect the prices paid by nor the expenditure patterns of other population groups. For that reason, five different CPIs are measured in Germany.
Preisinformation f (Preiskenntnis f) *(econ)* price information
→ Preisbewußtsein 1.
Preisintervall n *(econ)* price interval
Preiskalkulation f *(econ)* price calculation, calculation of prices
Preiskartell n (Preisabsprache f, Preisabrede f) *(econ)* price cartel
Preiskenntnis f
→ Preisbewußtsein 1.
Preisklasse f (Preiskategorie f) *(econ)* price category, price class, price range
Preiskonstanz f *(econ)* price constancy
Preiskontrolle f *(econ)* price control, price regulation
→ Preisbindung 3.
Preis-Kosten-Kalkulation f
→ Kostenpreiskalkulation
Preis-Kosten-Relation f
→ Kostenquote
Preislage f
→ Preisniveau
Preis-Leistungs-Verhältnis n *(econ)* cost-benefit relation
→ Kosten-Leistungs-Verhältnis
Preislinienpolitik f
→ Preiszonenpolitik

Preisliste f *(econ)* **1.** (allg) price list, rate book (im Handel) trade list
A sales representative's manual of prices for products and services he sells, or more in general, a card or folder listing the prices for products and services a business firm sells.
(advtsg) **2.** (bei Werbeträgern) advertising rate card, rate card, rate book, adrate card, *(radio/TV)* grid card
A booklet, card or folder issued by a communications medium, such as a newspaper or a magazine, or a magazine, or a broadcasting network, listing its advertising rates, mechanical and related requirements, closing dates, etc.
Preislistentreue f *(advtsg)*
Preismechanismus m *(econ)* price mechanism
The economical system of allocating scarce resources according to the effective demand on the market, as expressed through price and price movements.
Preisminderung f
→ Preisermäßigung
Preismix n (Entgeltpolitik f) *(marketing)* price mix, pricing mix
That part of a business firm's marketing mix, (→) Marketing-Mix, that consists of its policy regarding raising and lowering prices to meet the competition, (→) Preispolitik.
→ Kontrahierungs-Mix
Preismodell n *(econ)* price model
Preisnachfrageelastizität f
→ Preiselastizität der Nachfrage
Preisnachlaß m
→ Rabatt, Nachlaß
Preisniveau n (Preishöhe f) *(econ)* price level
Preisobergrenze f *(econ)* price ceiling
Preisparameter m *(econ)* price parameter
Preisplanung f *(econ)* price planning
→ Preispolitik
Preispolitik f (Preisgestaltung f) *(econ)* pricing, price policy, pricing mix, pricing policy
The complex pattern of policies regarding a business company's price setting strategy and practice. It is the guiding philosophy or course of action designed to influence and determine pricing decisions.
preispolitischer Ausgleich m
→ kalkulatorischer Ausgleich
preispolitischer Spielraum m *(econ)* pricing range, price range

The span of prices, from the lowest to the highest, that are scored for a particular type of product or service and may, therefore, be regarded as the upper and lower limits for the pricing policy of any company trying to market a new product or service.

preispolitisches Modell n *(econ)* pricing model

Preispositionierung f *(marketing)* price positioning
→ Positionierung

Preisprognose f *(econ)* price forecast, price prognosis, price prediction

Preispsychologie f price psychology
The field of applied psychology concerned with the investigation of psychological reactions, with particular emphasis on emotional rather than rational responses to pricing policies and price developments in a market.

Preis-Qualitäts-Assoziation f **(Preis-Qualitäts-Irradiation** f**)** *(econ)* price-quality association, price-quality irradiation

Preis-Qualitäts-Effekt m **(Preis-Qualitäts-Irradiation** f**)** *(econ)* price-quality effect, price-aura effect, price-quality irradiation
One of the most significant psychological aspects of pricing is the fact that consumers rely heavily on price as an indicator of a product's or service's quality, especially when they must make purchase decisions with incomplete information. Studies have consistently shown that consumers' perceptions of product quality vary directly with price: The higher the price, the better the quality is perceived to be — particularly when no other clues to product quality are available.

Preisrangordnung f *(econ)* price rank order, cost rank order

Preisrätsel n *(promotion)* puzzle competition, (Kreuzworträtsel) crossword puzzle competition

Preisreagibilität f *(econ)* price sensitivity
→ Preiselastizität

Preisreaktionsfunktion f *(econ)* price response function
→ Reaktionsfunktion

Preisreaktionskurve f *(econ)* price response curve
→ Reaktionsfunktion

Preisreduzierung f
→ Preisermäßigung 1.

Preisschild n *(econ)* price tag, price label, price ticket
The tag or label with the price on an item.

Preisschleuderei f *(econ)* undercutting of prices, price cutting
Offering merchandise or a service for sale at a price below that recognized as usual or appropriate by its buyers and sellers.

Preisschwelle f *(econ)* price line, price tableau, pricing tableau, price threshold
Usually a round figure for a selling price, above and below which sharply increasing price elasticity, (→) Preiselastizität, tends to occur.

Preisschwelleneffekt m **(Schwelleneffekt** m**)** *(econ)* price line effect, price threshold effect, threshold effect

Preissenkung f *(econ)* price reduction, reduction in prices(s) *(pl)*, price cut, price cutting, markdown
The amount of reduction below an original price, expressed in either a percentage or the amount of money.

Preissetzung f
→ Preisbestimmung, Preisgestaltung, Preispolitik

Preisskala f *(econ)* price scale, scale of prices

Preisspaltung f *(econ)* price splitting, split pricing
A variant of differential pricing, (→) Preisdifferenzierung, consisting of selling a product or service at two different prices to two different market segments.

Preisspanne f *(econ)* price range, price margin
→ preispolitischer Spielraum

Preisstabilität f *(econ)* price stability, stability of price(s)

Preissteigerung f *(econ)* 1. → Preiserhöhung 2. (starke Steigerung) price boost

Preisstellung f *(econ)* pricing
→ Preispolitik

Preisstrategie f *(econ)* pricing strategy, price strategy
The deliberate long-term planning of a business firm's pricing structure in relation to factors such as consumer wants, product attributes, competition, etc., in such a way as to ensure overall profitability.
vgl. Preistaktik

Preisstruktur f
→ Preisgefüge

Preistafel f *(econ)* price board

Preistaktik

Preistaktik f *(econ)* price tactics *pl (construed as sg)*, pricing tactics *pl (construed as sg)*
The short-term manipulation of a product's or service's price made in an effort to adjust to changing market conditions, or to stimulate brand switching, (→) Markenwechsel, or an increase in the market share, (→) Marktanteil.
Preistest m *(market res)* price test, pricing test
A test conducted to ascertain the market acceptance of several alternative prices.
Preistheorie f *(econ)* theory of pricing, price theory
Preis-Umsatz-Funktion f *(econ)* price-turnover function
Preisunterbietung f *(econ)* price cutting, undercutting, underselling
→ Preisschleuderei, Preiswettbewerb
Preisuntergrenze f
→ Preisgrenze
Preisunterschied m *(econ)* price difference
Preisveränderung f
→ Preisänderung
Preisverankerung f *(econ)* price anchoring
Preisvereinbarung f
→ Preisabkommen
Preisvergleich m *(econ)* price comparison
Under the restrictive German legislation on comparison advertising, (→) vergleichende Werbung, price comparisons are not admissible.
Preisverzeichnis n
→ Peisliste
Preisvorschriften f/pl *(econ)* price regulations *pl*, price controls *pl*
Preiswahrheit f *(econ)* truth in pricing
Preiswahrnehmung f *(econ)* price perception
→ Preis-Qualitäts-Assoziation
preiswert *adj (econ)* low-priced, inexpensive
Preiswettbewerb m *(econ)* price competition
In developing its marketing program, the management of a business firm has the choice of emphasizing price competition and nonprice competition; while most of the efforts of modern-day marketing, particularly strategies of market segmentation, (→) Marktsegmentierung, and product positioning, (→) Produktpositionierung, also aim at avoiding

outright price competition, there is still a considerable amount of it. Basically, it means that a business firm effectively engages in competition by regularly offering prices as low as possible either by changing its prices or by reacting to price changes of competitors.
Preiswiderstand m *(econ)* price resistance
Preiswilligkeit f
→ Preisbereitschaft
Preiswirkung f *(econ)* price effect
Preisziel n **(Preissetzungsziel** n**, Ziel** m **der Preispolitik)** *(econ)* pricing objective, price objective
The overall pricing goals or targets that are constituent parts of a business firm's pricing policy, (→) Preispolitik, such as e.g. profit maximization, a satisfactory return, target return on investment, cost-plus pricing, target market share, meeting or matching competition, etc.
Preiszone f **(Preislinie** f**)** *(econ)* price line, price zone
A series of price lines that appeal to one group of a given retail store's customers.
→ Preiszonenpolitik
Preiszonenpolitik f **(Preislinienpolitik** f**)** *(econ)* price lining, price zoning
The practice, used preponderantly by retailers and less by wholesalers or producers, of selecting a limited number of prices at which the store sells its merchandise. The extreme variant of this pricing policy is singular pricing, (→) Einheitspreispolitik.
Premiere f
→ Erstaufführung
Premierenkino n
→ Erstaufführungstheater
Presse f 1. (Zeitungswesen) press, the press, publishing, journalism, the journalists *pl* 2. → Druckerpresse
Presseabteilung f **(Pressestelle** f**)** press relations department, press relations office, publicity department, public relations department, public relations office
The department of an organization responsible for establishing, maintaining and expanding good relations with communication media of all types.
Presseagent m press agent
An individual hired by an organization to establish, maintain and expand good relations with communication media.
Presseagentur f press agency
An independent agency in charge of the responsibility to establish, maintain and

expand an organization's good relations with communication media.
Presseagenturwesen n press agentry
Pressearbeit f press relations pl *(construed as sg)*
That field of public relations practice, (→) PR-Arbeit, which specializes in establishing, maintaining and expanding an organization's good relations with communication media.
Presseartikel m
→ Zeitungsartikel, Zeitschriftenartikel
Presseausschnitt m press clipping, press clip, press cutting, press cut
An item such as an article removed (cut out) from a publication by a reader or a professional clipping service, (→) Ausschnittbüro.
Presseausschnittbüro n
→ Ausschnittbüro
Presseausweis m press card
Pressebericht m press report, news report
Presseberichterstatter m
→ Berichterstatter
Pressebilderdienst m
→ Bildagentur (Photoagentur)
Pressebüro n press office, press bureau
Pressechef m **(Leiter** m **der Presseabteilung)** press chief, head of the press relations department, head of the press relations office
Pressedienst m **(journalistischer Nachrichtendienst** m**)** 1. news agency, news service, information service, newspaper syndicate
An organization that sells news and news items, reports and other information, photographs, columns, comic strips, etc. to a number of newspapers for simultaneous publication.
2. (Produkt) newsletter, news release, (Verlautbarung) press release
A piece of informational material on a recent or current event distributed to broadcast stations, newspapers and magazines, or to individual subscribers or other recipients for public relations purposes.
Presseempfang m press reception
Presseerzeugnis n publication, printed publication
Pressefeldzug m
→ Pressekampagne
Presseforschung f
→ Publizistik, Zeitungswissenschaft

Pressefoto n
→ Pressephoto
Pressefreiheit f
→ freedom of the press
Pressegesetz n
→ jounalists' law, press law
Pressegrosso n **(Pressegroßhandel** m**)** press wholesaling, newspaper and magazine wholesaling
Presseinformation f press release, publicity release, handout for the press
→ Pressemappe, Pressedienst 2.
Pressekampagne f **(Pressefeldzug** m**)**
→ press campaign
Pressekonferenz f press conference, news conference
Pressekonzentration f *(econ)* concentration of the press, press concentration
Presseleute pl **(Pressemenschen** m/pl **)** newspaper men pl, newspaper people pl
Pressemann m **(Pressemensch** m**)** newspaperman, newspaper man, newsman
Pressemappe f **(Mappe** f **mit Presseinformationen)** press kit, press book, pressbook
A portfolio which contains mimeographed newsreleases, pictures, articles, speeches, and background material which is distributed to the press for its free use.
Pressemeldung f
→ Meldung
Pressemitteilung f **(Mitteilung** f **für die Presse)** press release, newsrelease, news release
→ Pressedienst 2.
pressen v/t (paper)
→ kalandrieren
Pressenachricht f
→ Nachricht
Pressenotiz f
→ Meldung
Presseorgan n press organ, organ
Pressephoto n news picture, press picture, news photo
Pressephotograph m news photographer, press photographer
Presserat m press council
→ Deutscher Presserat
Presserecht n **(Pressegesetzgebung** f **)** press law, press legislation
Pressereferent m press and public relations officer, press officer

Presseschau f (**Presserundschau** f, **Pressespiegel** m) press review, newspaper review
Pressestelle f
→ Presseabteilung
Presseverlautbarung f
→ Presseinformation
Pressevertrieb m media distribution, newspaper and magazine distribution
→ Medienvertrieb
Pressewesen n press, journalism, the media pl
Pressezeichner m newspaper cartoonist, cartoonist
Preßform f
→ Prägestempel
Preßrevision f
→ Maschinenrevision
Preßwalze f (**Preßzylinder** m)
→ Gegendruckzylinder
Prestige n prestige
In the most general sense, the social standing and reputation of a participant in a social order; more specifically, the regard or honor associated with a given status in a social organization.
Prestige-Effekt m (**Prestigefehler** m **Prestige-Antwortfehler** m) (survey res) prestige bias, prestige effect
One particular cause of response error that results from a respondent's conscious or unconscious attempt to upgrade his social status or cultural level or image by erroneously reporting what he believes are more desirable activities.
Prestigeführer m prestige leader, cosmopolitan influential
Prestigekonsum m
→ demonstrativer Konsum
Prestigemotiv n (**Prestigemotivation** f) prestige motive, prestige motivation
Prestigenutzen m
→ Geltungsnutzen, Zusatznutzen
Prestigepreis m (**Prestigepreisgebung** f) (econ) prestige price, prestige pricing
A price for a product or service that is deliberately set to attract those who find satisfaction in owning expensive and relatively exclusive items, or those who equate high quality with high price. If the demand is high enough and the product lives up to expectations for the buyer, this practice may prove successful.
Prestigestreben n prestige aspirations pl

Prestigewaren f/pl (**Prestigegüter** n/pl, **Prestigeprodukte** n/pl) (econ) prestige goods pl, prestige products pl
Those products or services the utility, (→) Nutzen, of which consists to a large part of the prestige their purchase imparts on their owners or users.
Prestigewerbung f (**Repräsentationswerbung** f) prestige advertising, goodwill advertising
All advertising intended to change, increase or emphasize an organization's or other advertiser's social reputation.
Prestigezeitschrift f prestige magazine, prestige journal, prestige publication, class magazine, class publication, colloq (wegen ihres Hochglanzpapiers) slick magazine, slick journal, slick, glossy magazine
Any magazine which enjoys above-average esteem of the reading public.
Prestigezeitung f prestige paper, prestige newspaper, prestige publication, class paper, class newspaper
Pretest m (**Vorstudie** f, **Voruntersuchung** f, **Probebefragung** f) (survey res) pretest
A final trial use of a questionnaire prior to its large-scale administration. The pretest usually involves interviewing a relatively few respondents to see if the questions used need revision or additions.
vgl. Posttest
Primäranalyse f (res) primary analysis
→ Primärforschung;
vgl. Sekundäranalyse
Primärbedarf m (**Primärnachfrage** f)
→ Erstbedarf, Grundbedarf
Primärbedürfnis n
→ Grundbedürfnis
primäre Datengewinnung f (social res) primary data gathering, primary data collection
→ Primärforschung
primäre Marktforschung f primary market research
→ Primärforschung
Primäreinheit f (**primäre Erhebungseinheit** f, **primäre Stichprobeneinheit** f) (stat) primary sampling unit (PSU), primary unit
Primärerhebung f (**primäre Datenerhebung** f) (survey res) primary data

survey, primary data research, field investigation, field study
→ Primärforschung
Primärfarbauszug m *(print)* primary color component, *brit* primary colour component
Primärfarbe f **(Primärvalenz** f**)** *(optics/print)* primary color, *brit* primary colour
In light, the colors red, green and blue. In printing, yellow, magenta and cyan.
Primärforschung f *(survey res)* primary research, primary data research
That part of social and market research activities consisting of the application of methods and techniques to collect all data required within the context of an investigation, be it by means of field research, (→) Feldforschung, or laboratory research, (→) Laborforschung. *vgl.* Sekundärforschung
Primärgruppe f **(primäre Gruppe** f**)** *(soc)* primary group (Charles H. Cooley)
A small group of persons who maintain intimate, personal relationships within a large work-oriented environment. Such groups, which are often based upon shared interests or background characteristics, may affect production positively or negatively.
vgl. Sekundärgruppe
Primärkommunikation f **(direkte persönliche Kommunikation** f**)** primary communication, face-to-face communication
vgl. Sekundärkommunikation
Primärleser m
→ Erstleser
Primärleserschaft f
→ Erstleserschaft
Primärmaterial n
→ Erhebungsmaterial
Primärmotiv n **(Primärmotivation** f**)**
→ Grundbedürfnis
Primärnachfrage f
→ Erstbedarf, Grundbedarf
Primärton m primary tone
Primärvalenz f
→ Primärfarbe
Primat m primacy
→ Erstargumenthypothese
Primat m **des Absatzsektors (Primat** m **des Absatzes)** *(econ)* primacy of sales
The characteristic principle of management organization in buyers' markets, (→) Käufermarkt, in which all departments and activities of a business firm are subordinated to the sales sector.
Primateffekt m **(Primateffekthypothese** f**)**
→ Erstargumenthypothese
Prime f **(Primform** f**)** *(print)* first form, first impression
The first in a series of successive printings.
Primitivperson f (Ludwig von Holzschuher) *(psy)* primitive individual
Printer m
→ Drucker, Druckmaschine
Printfilm m
→ Kopierfilm
Printmedium n **(Pressemedium** n**, Druckmedium** n**)** print medium, printed-word medium, press medium
Printwerbung f **(Printmedienwerbung** f**, Werbung** f **in gedruckten Medien)** print advertising, printed advertising *auch* press advertising, publication advertising
Priorität f **(Vorrang** m**)** priority
Prisma n *(phot)* prism
A triangular piece of glass, silvered on one side, and attached to the lens of a process camera as an optical instrument for lateral inversion of the image projected by the lens.
Prismensucher m **(parallaxenfreier Sucher** m**)** *(phot)* prism viewfinder, prismatic viewfinder, prismatic eye
Privatanzeige f **(private Anzeige** f**)** personal advertisement, personal ad, personal announcement
privater Haushalt m
→ Haushalt 1.
privater Verbrauch m **(privater Konsum** m**)** *(econ)* private consumption, private household consumption
Privatfernsehen n commercial television, commercial TV, commercially impelled television
vgl. öffentlich-rechtliches Fernsehen
Privatfunk m **(Privatrundfunk** m**)** *(radio/TV)* commercial broadcasting, commercially impelled broadcasting
vgl. öffentlich-rechtlicher Rundfunk
Privatsender m **(privater Rundfunksender** m**, private Rundfunkstation** f**)** *(radio/TV)* commercial broadcasting station, commercial station
Privilegauflage f **(Privilegvertrieb** m**, Privilegmethode** f**)** *(Zeitschrift)* franchise circulation

That part of a publication's circulation which is obtained through contractual agreement with business firms which provide lists of their customers or prospective customers to whom copies of the publication are sent free of charge.
PR-Leiter *m*
→ PR-Direktor
Probe *f (econ)* **1.** (Erprobung) trial, test tryout
→ Erstkauf
2. → Dienstleistungsprobe, Geschmacksprobe, Warenprobe, Probeexemplar **3.** *(radio/TV)* rehearsal, dry run
The practicing of a performance.
Probeabonnement *n* (Zeitung/Zeitschrift) trial subscription
A test subscription for a short-term period.
Probeabzug *m* (**Probeabdruck** *m*) *(print)* proof, pull, advance proof, green proof, green copy
A trial inked impression of composed type of a plate or of an engraving for inspection.
→ Bürstenabzug, Korrekturabzug
Probeandruck *m*
→ Andruck
Probeaufnahme *f (film/TV)* test take, trial shot, test shot, (Schauspieler) screen test, (Schallplatte) test recording
Probeauftrag *m (econ)* trial order
Probebefragung *f*
→ Pretest
Probenbeginn *m (film/TV)* call
Probebogen *m*
→ Korrekturbogen
Probedruck *m*
→ Andruck, Probeabzug
Probedurchlauf *m* (**Probelauf** *m*, **Probe** *f*) *(film/radio/TV)* run-through, walkthrough, dry run
In motion pictures and television, a first rehearsal of the cast without costumes and camera facilities, etc. In radio, a complete reading of the script.
Probeerhebung *f*
→ Pretest
Probeexemplar *n* (**Probeheft** *n*, **Probenummer** *f*) (Zeitung/Zeitschrift) sample copy, specimen copy, complimentary copy
An inspection copy of a paper or magazine distributed free to prospective subscribers.
Probefarbandruck *m* (**Probefarbtafel** *f*) *(print)* specimen plate

Probefilm *m* test film
Probeheft *n*
→ Probeexemplar
Probeinterview *n (survey res)* test interview, pretest interview
Probekauf *m*
→ Erstkauf
Probekäufer *m*
→ Erstkäufer 1.
proben *v/t + v/i (film/radio/TV)* to rehearse
Probenplan *m* (**Probenübersicht** *f*) *(film/TV/radio)* call sheet
The timetable showing the exact dates and times the actors and crew must report for a motion picture, radio, or television production.
Probenraum *m* (**Probenstudio** *n*) *(film/radio/TV)* rehearsal studio, rehearsal room
Probenummer *f*
→ Probeheft, Nullnummer
Probenzeit *f (film/TV/radio)* rehearsal time, rehearsing time
Probepackung *f* trial package, test package, sample package
Probepackungsformat *n* (**Probepackungsgröße** *f*) trial package size, test package size, sample package size
Probeseite *f* (**Satzprobe** *f*, **Musterseite** *f*) *(print)* specimen page, sample page
Probesendung *f* **1.** *(radio/TV)* (Testsendung) test transmission, test broadcast, pilot broadcast, pilot transmission, pilot, audition
→ Pilotsendung
2. *(econ)* sample mailing, mailing of a sample
Probestreifen *m (phot)* test strip
Probestück *n*
→ Warenprobe
Probierkauf *m*
→ Probekauf
Probierstand *m (POP advtsg)* product demonstration stand, demonstration stand
Problemanalyse *f* problem analysis
Problemlösung *f* (**Problemlösen** *n*) problem solution, problem solving
In decision-making, all phases of action undertaken to reduce the risk to acceptable levels of probability in order to lead to a course of activity designed to attain desired objectives.
Problemlösungstechnik *f* (**Problemlösungsverfahren** *n*) problem-solving technique, problem-solving procedure

Problemlösungsverhalten n problem-solving behavior, *brit* problem-solving behaviour
Problemranganalyse f
→ ABC-Analyse
Problemtreue f **(Bedarfstreue** f**)** (Herbert Gross) *(marketing)* etwa problem-solving consistency
Product Placement n
→ Produktplazierung (Requisitenwerbung)
Produkt n **1.** *(econ)* (Artikel, Ware) product, product item, *auch* produce
 A physical item, especially one to which value has been added, that is offered for sale on the market. It consists of a tangible product, i.e. a physical object, an extended product, i.e. the unseen services and ancillary features such as packaging which accompany the tangible product, and the generic product, i.e. the essential benefit the buyer seeks in the product.
2. → Handelsware
3. *(stat)* product
 The number or magnitude resulting from the multiplication together of two or more numbers or magnitudes, i.e. the result of any kind of multiplication.
Produktabbildung f
→ Attrappe
Produktabsatz m *(econ)* product sale(s) *(pl)*
→ Absatz
Produktakzeptanz f *(econ)* product acceptance
 The degree of acceptance a product, particularly a new product, enjoys among consumers.
→ Akzeptanz
Produktakzeptanztest m *(econ)* product acceptance test (P.A.T.)
 A test of the rate or amount of acceptance a product enjoys among consumers.
Produktanalyse f *(econ)* product analysis
 The investigation by a buyer of a product's performance with the objective of determining an adequate quality at the lowest final cost.
Produktangebot n
→ Warenangebot
Produktart f
→ Produkttyp
Produktattrappe f
→ Attrappe
Produktattribut n *(econ)* product attribute, attribute of a product

Produktauffälligkeit f
→ soziale Auffälligkeit
Produktausstrahlung f **(Produktausstrahlungseffekt** m**)**
→ Ausstrahlung (Ausstrahlungseffekt)
Produktbenennung f
→ Produktbezeichnung
Produktbeschaffenheit f
→ Produktqualität
Produktbewertung f **(Produktevaluierung** f**)** *(econ)* product evaluation, new product evaluation, product screening, new product screening
 That part of the process of new product development, (→) Produktentwicklung, that consists of screening those new product ideas, that do not match a business organization's organizational objectives and/or capabilities or capacities; it involves a general assessment of resources and the firm's ability to produce and market the product.
Produktbewertungsmatrix f **(Produktbewertungsschema** n**)** *(econ)* product evaluation matrix
Produktbezeichnung f **(Produktname** m**)** *(econ)* product name
 It is advisable to distinguish clearly between product name and brand name, (→) Markenbezeichnung.
Produktbotschaft f *(advtsg)* product message
Produktbudget n **(Produktetat** m**)** *(econ)* product budget
 That part of a business firm's total budget in a brand management type of organization, (→) Produktmanagement, that is earmarked (or calculated) for an individual product.
Produktbühne f
→ Greifbühne
Produktcharakteristika n/pl
→ Produktmerkmal(e)
Produktdarbietung f **(Produktpräsentation** f**)** *(econ)* product presentation
Produktdaten n/pl *(econ)* product data
Produktdeckungsbeitrag m
→ Deckungsbeitrag
Produktdesign n
→ Produktgestaltung
Produktdifferenzierung f *(econ)* product differentiation
 A strategy of market splitting under which certain features of a product are changed to distinguish it clearly from similar products. As a result products of similar characteristics and end use, usually made by different producers,

Produktdistribution

acquire divergent images in the minds of segments of the market.
Produktdistribution f
→ Produktvertrieb
Produkteigenschaft(en) f(pl)
→ Produktmerkmal(e)
Produkteinführung f *(marketing)* product launch, new product launch, product introduction, new product introduction
　The process of organizing the market entry of a new product.
Produkt-Einzelkosten pl *(econ)* unit cost, product unit cost
→ Stückkosten
Produkteliminierung f **(Produktelimination** f) *(econ)* product elimination, product abandonment, product deletion
　The decision of a business firm to phase out or to drop a weak product.
Produktenbörse f **(Warenbörse** f) *(econ)* commodity exchange, produce exchange
　An organization usually owned by the member-traders, which provides facilities for bringing together buyers and sellers of specified commodities, or their agents, for promoting trades, either spot or futures or both, in these commodities. Agricultural products or their intermediately processed derivatives are the commodities most often traded on such exchanges. Some sort of organization for clearing future contracts usually operates as an adjunct to or an arm of a commodity exchange.
Produktenttäuschung f
→ Nachkaufreue
Produktentwicklung f *(econ)* product development
　The complex marketing function of planned product improvement and modernization, including the determination of new applications for established products. Within the process of product planning, (→) Produktplanung, it is the stage following product idea generation, (→) Produktideenfindung, and product screening, (→) Produktbewertung, and preceding product testing, (→) Produkttesten.
Produktentwicklung f **(und -forschung** f) *(econ)* product development and research
→ Produktforschung und -entwicklung
Produktentwicklungsprozeß m *(econ)* product development process
→ Produktentwicklung

Produkterneuerung f
→ Produktvariation
Produktfamilie f
→ Produktgruppe
Produktfindung f
→ Produktentwicklung
Produktforschung f **(und -entwicklung** f) *(econ)* product research and development (P.R.D., PRD), research and development (R & D)
　Both the corporate process and personnel group using research into the physical properties and characteristics of product formulations or designs either employed by competitors or being considered for future use to further corporate marketing objectives.
Produktfunktion f *(econ)* function of a product, product function
　The problem-solving offer contained in a product.
Produktgattung f
→ Produktgruppe, Produkttyp
Produktgeschäft n *(econ)* product selling
vgl. Anlagengeschäft, Systemgeschäft
Produktgestaltung f **(Produktdesign** n) *(econ)* product design
→ Design, industrielle Formgebung
Produktgestaltungstest m **(Formgebungstest** m, **Gestaltungstest** m) *(econ)* product design test
→ Designtest
Produktgruppe f **(Produktfamilie** f, **Produktlinie** f) *(econ)* product line, line
　A group of products that are closely related either because they satisfy a class of needs, are used together, are sold to the same customer groups, are marketed through the same type of outlets or fall within given price ranges. Sub-lines of products may be distinguished within a product line.
Produktgruppenleiter m **(Produktgruppenmanager** m) *(econ)* product line manager
→ Produktmanager
Produktgruppenorganisation f *(econ)* product line organization, *brit* organisation
→ Linienorganisation
Produktgruppensegmentierung f *(econ)* product line segmentation
Produktgruppenvergleich m *(econ)* product line comparison
Produktgruppenwerbung f product line advertising, line advertising

Advertising devoted to communicating the benefits of an entire product line, (→) Produktgruppe, rather than those of an individual product or brand.

Produktidee *f (econ)* product idea
Produktideenfindung *f (econ)* product idea finding, product idea development, product idea generation, new-product idea generation
The more or less systematic process by which new product ideas are generated in a business firm. It is the first step in the process of product planning, (→) Produktplanung.

Produktideentest *m (econ)* product idea test
Produktimage *n* **(Gattungsimage** *n*) product image, generic image
The image, (→) Image, a type of product or product lines have conveyed to a brand image or corporate (institutional) image.

Produktinformation *f (econ)* product information
Produktinnovation *f (econ)* product innovation, innovation
→ Innovation
Produktinteresse *n (econ)* product involvement
Produktion *f (econ)* production, manufacturing
1. The economic process of creating utility.
2. The process of rehearsing, filming or recording a motion picture, or a broadcast of a radio or television program.
3. The process of converting an advertising idea or the contents of a manuscript, illustration material, general design, layout or storyboard, etc. into a printed book, magazine, advertisement, script, commercial, etc.
→ Herstellung
2. → Produktionsabteilung
Produktionsablauf *m* **(Produktionsfluß** *m*) *(econ)* flow of production
Produktionsabteilung *f* **(Herstellungsabteilung** *f*) *(econ)* production department, production
→ Herstellung
Produktionsassistent(in) *m(f) (film/TV)* production assistant, *colloq* gopher, gofer
Produktionsbericht *m (film/TV)* data sheet
Produktionschef *m* **(Produktionsleiter** *m*) *(econ/film/TV)* production manager, production director

An executive responsible for production in a business firm, a publishing house, an advertising agency, a motion picture company, or a television station.

Produktionsfaktor *m (econ)* production factor
Produktionsfunktion *f (econ)* production function
A statement of the varying amounts of output per time period which may be expected to result from the application of different levels and combinations of resources.

Produktionsgenossenschaft *f (econ)* producer cooperative
→ Erzeugergemeinschaft
Produktionsgüter *n/pl* **(gewerbliche Verbrauchsgüter** *n/pl***)** *(econ)* producer goods *pl*, producer's goods *pl*, producers' goods *pl*, instrumental goods *pl*, intermediary goods *pl*, auxiliary goods *pl*
Capital goods, (→) Produktivgüter, that are "consumed" in the process of manufacturing other products without remaining durable or permanent fixtures or being used continuously for a long period of time like investment goods, (→) Investitionsgüter.
Produktionsgütermarketing *n* producer goods marketing
Produktionsgütermarktforschung *f* producer goods market research
Produktionsgüterwerbung *f* producer goods advertising
Produktionskapazität *f (econ)* production capacity, productive capacity
Produktionskosten *pl*
→ Herstellungskosten
Produktionsleiter *m* **(PL) 1.** *(econ)* production manager, plant manager, production director **2.** *(film/TV)* executive producer
Produktionsmittel *n/pl (econ)* capital goods *pl*, means *pl* of production
All types of goods such as machinery, materials, and other commodities used to produce other products or services.
Produktionsmittelwerbung *f*
→ Investitionsgüterwerbung
Produktionsorientierung *f (econ)* production orientation
The condition typical of producer's markets, (→) Herstellermarkt, in which a business firm's major concern is coping with problems associated with the production of goods.
vgl. Marktorientierung

Produktionspalette f
→ Produktpalette
Produktionsplan m *(econ)* production plan, production schedule
Produktionsplanung f *(econ)* production planning
Produktionspolitik f *(econ)* production policy
Produktionsprogramm n *(econ)* production program, *brit* programme
Produktionsstatistik f production statistics pl *(construed as sg)*
Produktivgüter n/pl *(econ)* capital goods pl, industrial goods pl
  A collective term used to designate all goods needed for industrial rather than for consumers' use. It includes investment goods, (→) Investitionsgüter, and producer goods, (→) Produktionsgüter.
  vgl. Investitonsgüter (gewerbliche Gebrauchsgüter), Produktionsgüter (gewerbliche Verbrauchsgüter)
Produktivgütermarketing n capital goods marketing
Produktivgüterwerbung f capital goods advertising
Produktivität f *(econ)* productivity
Produktkategorie f **(Produktklasse** f**)** *(econ)* product category
Produktklassifikation f *(econ)* product classification
  → Produktivgüter, Konsumgüter
Produktkonzept n *(econ)* product concept
  A management orientation emphasizing efficiency in producing and distributing goods.
Produktkonzeption f *(econ)* product conception
Produktlebensdauer f *(econ)* product life
  → Produktlebenszyklus
Produktlebenszyklus m **(PLZ)** *(econ)* product life cycle (PLC), life cycle of a product
  The pattern of the sales volume of a product as competion and natural processes e.g., the introduction of a new or better product, bring the product through the stages of its market introduction, from maturity to decline and, eventually, extinction. The time extent of the life cycle varies greatly among products. Increasing emphasis is being placed on the use of this concept to guide decision-making about capital investment planning, advertising and promotion planning, the probability of acceptable return of investment for new products, the elimination of certain products based on a rationale, and to assist in integrating management's thinking in all functional areas. The PLC concept, which has become a major planning tool, contends that all products have a beginning and an end, thus dictating the need for new product development, (→) Produktentwicklung.
Produktleistung f *(econ)* product performance
  The instrinsic attributes of a product.
Produktlinie f
  → Produktgruppe
Produktloyalität f
  → Markentreue
Produktmanagement n **(Produktmanagersystem** n**, Integrationssystem** n**)** *(econ)* product management, brand management, program management, project management
  The planning, direction, and control of all phases of the life cycle of products, including the creation or discovery of ideas for new products, the screening of such ideas, the coordination of the work of research and physical development of products, their packaging and branding, their introduction on the market, their market development, their modification, the discovery of new uses for them, their repair and servicing, and their deletion.
Produktmanager m *(econ)* product manager, brand manager, program manager, project manager, *auch* merchandise manager
  An executive in a business firm responsible for the product management, (→) Produktmanagement, of one product (brand) or a series of related products.
Produktmarke f
  → Gattungsmarke
Produktmarkierung f
  → Markierung
Produktmarkt m *(econ)* product market
Produkt/Markt-Expansionsmatrix f
  → Ansoffsche Matrix
Produkt/Markt-Konzentrationsstrategie f
  → Marktabdeckungsstrategie
Produkt/Markt-Raster m
  → Marktsegmentierung
Produktmerkmal(e) n *(pl)* **(Produkteigenschaft(en)** f *(pl)* *(econ)* product characteristic(s) pl, product feature(s) *(pl)*
Produkt-Mix n *(marketing)* product mix

1. The composite of products and product lines offered for sale by a firm or a business unit.
2. → Produktpolitik
→ Produktpalette
Produktmodell n *(econ)* product modell, prototype
Produktmodifizierung f *(econ)* product modification
A minor adjustment in a physical product to better satisfy the needs of its target market in a repositioning effort, such as a change of product quality, style, or feature.
vgl. Produktvariation
Produktmomentkorrelation f **(Pearsonsche Maßkorrelation** f**)** *(stat)* product-moment correlation, Pearson product-moment correlation
A correlation coefficient that serves as an index of the degree of linear relationship between two variables that are measured on an interval scale, (→) Intervallskala, or a ratio scale, (→) Verhältnisskala.
Produktname m
→ Produktbezeichnung
Produktneueinführung f
→ Produkteinführung
Produktnutzen m *(econ)* product utility
→ Nutzen
Produktnutzung f **(Produktgebrauch** m**)** *(econ)* product usage
Produktnutzungsmethode f **(Produktnutzungstest** m**)** *(econ)* product-user method, product-user test, product-usage segmentation
Produktpalette f *(econ)* product range, product mix
The full list of available products made by one business firm.
Produktpersönlichkeit f **(Markenpersönlichkeit** f**)** *(econ)* product personality, brand personality (Pierre D. Martineau)
The idea that brand products have distinct "personalities" comparable to those of individuals and are more than just aggregates of physical characteristics.
Produktplanung f *(econ)* product planning, *auch* merchandising
The entire set of activities that enable a business firm to determine what products it will market, i.e. all planning activities designed to prepare an assortment of products to meet a market demand. Specifically, product planning comprises the steps of new product idea generation, (→) Produktideenfindung, preliminary screening, (→) Produktbewertung, concept testing, (→) Konzepttesten, business analysis, (→) Wirtschaftlichkeitsanalyse, product and strategy development, (→) Produktentwicklung, market testing, (→) Testmarketing, and commercialization,
Produktplazierung f **(Product Placement** n, **Requisitenwerbung** f**)** product placement
Produktpolitik f **(Produkt-Mix** n**)** *(marketing)* product policy, product mix
That part of a business firm's marketing mix, (→) Marketing-Mix, that comprises product design, (→) Produktgestaltung, particularly, product quality, (→) Produktqualität, packaging, (→) Verpackung, branding, (→) Markenbezeichnung, product range policies and service policies.
Produktportfolio n *(econ)* product portfolio
→ Portfoliomanagement
Produktpositionierung f *(marketing)* product positioning, positioning a product
The attempt made by a business firm's marketing policy to achieve the acceptance by target markets of their products as better fulfilling specific wants, or having specific characteristics superior to and clearly distinguishing them from competing brands. A product's position is the image that the product projects in relation to both competitive products and other products marketed by the company in question. Positioning is a strategy of carving out a niche for a product.
Produktprobe f
→ Warenprobe
Produktprofil n *(econ)* product profile
Produktprogramm n
→ Produktionsprogramm
Produktqualität f *(econ)* product quality
Produktraum m **(Merkmalsraum** m **für ein Produkt)** *(econ)* product space, property space of a product, product property space
The totality of all the dimensions of a product as they might be arranged on a continuum of attributes. The closer two competing products are in the product space, the more alike they will be perceived by the market.
→ Merkmalsraum
Produkt-Segment-Strategie f *(marketing)* product usage

Produktsortiment

segmentation strategy, product usage segmentation
A technique of market segmentation, (→) Marktsegmentierung, which tries to relate observed factors of usage to the ways in which users with certain characteristics react to particular marketing mixes.

Produktsortiment n *(retailing)* product assortment
→ Sortiment

Produktstrategie f *(econ)* product strategy
→ Produktpolitik

Produkttest m *(econ)* product test
A collective term to designate all types of tests related to a product, ranging from tests of physical and technical product characteristics to market tests, (→) Test-marketing, and store tests, (→) Ladentest. The term usually refers to the actual trial of a product by a sample of consumers, including the analysis and evaluation of their reactions.

Produkttesten n *(econ)* product testing
→ Produkttest

Produkttest-Panel n *(econ)* product testing panel
→ Produkttest, Panel

Produkttreue f **(Materialtreue** f**)** (Herbert Gross) *(econ)* product loyalty
vgl. Problemtreue, Wissenstreue

Produkttyp m **(Produktart** f**)** *(econ)* type of product, product type
→ Produktkategorie

Produktvariation f **(Produktrelaunch** m, **Relaunch** m**)** *(marketing)* product variation, product relaunch
One of three alternative strategies of product policy in addition to product innovation, (→) Innovation, and product abandonment, (→) Produkteliminierung. It consists of more or less marked modifications in the physical characteristics of an established product, (→) Produktmodifikation, in an effort to reposition it, (→) Umpositionierung, and to revitalize a mature product. It is an attempt to break out of a stagnant or declining market.

Produktveränderung f
→ Produktvariation

Produktvereinheitlichung f
→ Marktunifizierung

Produktvergleich m *(advtsg)* product comparison, comparison of products
→ vergleichende Werbung

Produktverpackung f
→ Verpackung

Produktversprechen n *(marketing) etwa* product proposition
→ USP

Produktversteinerung f **(Produkt-petrifizierung** f**)** *(econ)* product petrification
The last stage in a product's life cycle, (→) Produktlebenszyklus, which is the prolongation of the decline stage, (→) Degenerationsphase, characterized by rapidly falling sales and profits, with most competitors withdrawing from the market.

Produktverwendungstest m *(market res)* product usage test

Produktwahrnehmung f *(econ)* product perception
→ Wahrnehmung

Produktwerbung f product reputation advertising, product advertising, product copy
All advertising intended to communicate the benefits of (a) product(s) rather than those of a business organization
vgl. Firmenwerbung

Produktziel n *(econ)* product objective

Produzent m **1.** *(econ)* producer, manufacturer
An organization or an individual concerned with the process of creating economic utility, (→) Nutzen, in terms of tangible goods.
2. *(film/radio/TV)* producer
The person endowed with final responsibility for all phases of a motion picture, commercial, or television or radio program. He is primarily concerned with overall administration rather than on-the-air production.

Produzentenhaftung f **(Hersteller-haftung** f**)** *(econ)* product liability, manufacturer's product liability, producer's product liability
The liability of manufacturers for customer injury as a result of negligence.

Produzentenmarkt m
→ P-Markt

Produzentenrente f *(econ)* producer's surplus (Alfred Marshall)
The difference between the amount of money a producer receives for a product and the minimum for which he would be willing to supply it.
vgl. Konsumentenrente

Produzentenrisiko n *(econ/stat)* producer's risk
In statistical quality control, (→) Qualitätskontrolle, the risk which a producer takes that a lot, (→) Los, will be rejected by a sampling plan even though

it conforms to requirements. It is equivalent to an error of the first kind, (→) Fehler 1. Art, in the theory of testing hypotheses, (→) Hypothesenprüfung, in that it corresponds to the probability of rejecting a hypothesis when it is, in fact, true.
vgl. Konsumentenrisiko
Produzentenwerbung f (**Herstellerwerbung** f)
→ Firmenwerbung
Profil n *(psy)* profile
In the most general sense, the detailed description of a subject, e.g. a person, or (a) group(s) of persons. More specifically, a statement of a target group or audience in terms of such characteristics as age, sex, race, location, etc.
Profilanalyse f *(psy)* profile analysis
Profil-Marketing n
→ Corporate Identity
Profit m
→ Gewinn
Profitzentrum n (**Profit Center** n)
→ Ertragszentrum
Profitkauf m *(econ)* most profitable purchase, m. p. purchase
Proformarechnung f *(econ)* pro forma invoice
A document which states the value of a transaction to notify the proposed dispatch of a consignment of goods; frequently used as a means of obtaining prepayment.
Prognose f *(stat/econ)* prognosis, forecast, prediction
In general, the process (or result thereof) of predicting future events on the basis of historical data, opinions, trends and known future variables. In economics and marketing, the process and result of estimating future magnitudes and trends of elements of business activity on the basis of historical data and/or predictions of coming evironmental conditions. Commonly used to help plan the sales and sales-related needs of a business in the following year(s). In statistics, the process of forecasting the magnitude of statistical variates at some future point of time.
Prognosefehler m (**Vorhersagefehler** m) *(stat/econ)* forecasting error, error in prediction
Prognosemodell n *(stat/econ)* prognosis model, forecasting model
Prognosetechnik f (**Prognoseverfahren** n) *(stat/econ)* forecasting technique, prognosis technique, forecasting procedure, prognosis procedure

Program-Analyzer-Verfahren n (**Programmanalysatorverfahren** n) *(media res)* program analyzer technique (Paul F. Lazarsfeld/Frank Stanton)
A type of voting machine which permits groups of radio listeners or television viewers to record continuously, for the duration of a program, the degree to which they like or dislike the parts of the program, including the commercials.
Programm n 1. *(radio/TV)* program, *brit* programme, (Sendekanal) channel
The term in German designates both the schedule of shows or commercials for a network or station and a specific show presented by a television or radio station during a certain time period on a specific day or date.
2. (Programmzettel) playbill, program, *brit* programme
Programmabsage f *(radio/TV)* closing announcement, back announcement
→ Absage
Programmabschaltung f
→ Sendeschluß
Programmanalyse f *(media res)* program analysis, *brit* programme analysis
Programmanalysator m (**Programmanalysiergerät** n)
→ Program-Analyzer-Verfahren
Programmankündigung f *(radio/TV)* promotional announcement, promotional spot, promo, station promo, *colloq* teaser, program announcement, *brit* programme announcement, (Hinweistafel) program billboard
Programmansage f (**Ansage** f) *(radio/TV)* presentation announcement
→ Ansage
Programmanzeige f program billing, *brit* programme billing, program billboard, billboard
Programmausschuß m *(radio/TV)* program committee, *brit* programme committee, programming committee, program board, *brit* programme board
Programmaustausch m *(radio/TV)* program exchange, *brit* programme exchange
Programmbeirat m *(radio/TV)* program advisory council, *brit* programme advisory council

Programmblock

Programmblock m *(radio/TV)*
program block, programming block,
brit programme block
A network television scheduling strategy which groups together programs with similar appeal to form a consecutive programming block. The idea behind block programming is to encourage the carry-over of viewers from program to program and to discourage dial switching.
vgl. Werbeblock
Programmdirektion f *(radio/TV)*
program directorate, *brit* programme directorate
Programmdirektor m *(radio/TV) etwa*
managing program director, program manager, *brit* programme manager
In broadcasting, the person responsible for on-the-air programming,
(→) Programmgestaltung.
Programmeinblendung f *(radio/TV)*
program insert, *brit* programme insert
→ Einblendung, programmunterbrechende Werbung
Programmeinschaltquote f *(radio/TV)*
program rating
The percentage of a sample of radio or TV homes tuned to a specific program at a particular time.
→ Einschaltquote
Programmfahne f **(Programmplan** m**)**
(radio/TV) program schedule, *brit* programme schedule, program sheet, *brit* programme sheet
Programmfolge f *(radio/TV)* sequence of programs, *brit* programmes
Programmfrage f (Elisabeth Noelle) *(survey res) etwa* program question, *brit* programme question
vgl. Testfrage
Programmfüller m **(Füller** m**)** *(radio/ TV)* program fill-up, filler, plug
→ Füller
Programmgestalter(in) m(f) *(radio/ TV)* program maker, *brit* programme maker, programmer
Programmgestaltung f *(radio/TV)*
programming, program planning, *brit* programme planning, program policy, *brit* programme policy, (Ablaufgestaltung) program scheduling, *brit* programme scheduling
Programmheft n *(radio/TV/film)*
program, *brit* programme
Programmhinweis m *(radio/TV)*
promotional program announcement, promotional announcement,

promotional spot, promo, station promo, *colloq* teaser, plug, (am Ende eines anderen Programms) program trailer, trailer announcement, trailer
An announcement designed to promote or build an audience for a specific program.
Programmkino n **(PG)** *(film) etwa*
program cinema, *brit* programme cinema, theme cinema, qualityprogram cinema, quality-program movietheater
Programmkonserve f *(radio/TV)*
canned broadcast, canned program, *brit* canned programme
→ Konserve, Sendekonserve
Programmkoordinierung f **(Programmkoordination** f**)** *(radio/TV)*
program coordination,
brit programme co-ordination
Programmkoordinator m *(radio/TV)*
program coordinator, *brit* programme co-ordinator
Programmpaket n **(Programmkomplex** m**)** *(radio/TV)* program package, *brit* programme package
A combination of broadcast announcements and broadcasts, appearing in a number of different programs.
Programmplan m **(Ablaufplan** m**)**
(radio/TV) program schedule, schedule, *brit* programme schedule
Programmplanung f *(radio/TV)*
programming, program planning, *brit* programme planning, (Ablaufsgestaltung) program scheduling, scheduling, *brit* programme scheduling
Programmpolitik f *(radio/TV)*
programming, programming policy
Programm-Spot m
→ programmunterbrechende Werbesendung
Programm-Supplement n TV guide supplement, radio and TV guide supplement
→ Supplement
Programmtyp m **(Programmtypus** m**)**
(radio/TV) program format, format, *brit* type of programme
The general concept, form, makeup, or style of a television or radio program.
programmunterbrechende Werbesendung f **(programmunterbrechende Werbung** f*,* **programmunterbrechender Werbespot** m**)** *(radio/TV)*
straight commercial, middle commercial, cut-in commercial,

station break commercial, (integrierte Werbesendung) integrated commercial, blended commercial, (mit denselben Schauspielern wie in der Programmsendung) cast commercial, (mit Stars) star commercial
   A type of broadcast advertising that does not exist under the present German system of block programming, (→) Blockwerbung. The term has two definitions. One describes a "cast"-delivered commercial, designed as an integral part of a television show's programming format. The second refers to a multiple-brand announcement, where a number of related products (made by the same corporation) are presented within the framework of a single announcement. These commercial messages are "integrated," with an announcer's voice introducing the second at the conclusion of the first.

Programmunterbrechung f **(für Werbung)** *(radio/TV)* commercial break, break, station break, commercial cut-in, cut-in, commercial slot, commercial unit

Programmvorschau f *(radio/TV)* program preview, preview, *brit* programme preview
→ Programmhinweis, Programmankündigung

Programmwahlanlage f **(PWA)** *(radio/ TV)* program selector, *brit* programme selector

Programmzeitschrift f radio and TV guide, radio and TV magazine, TV guide, TV magazine

progressive Kundenwerbung f
→ Schneeballverfahren (Hydrasystem)

Prohibitivpreis m **(prohibitiver Preis** m**)** *(econ)* prohibitive price

Projektanalyse f *(econ)* project analysis

Projektevaluierung f *(econ)* project evaluation

Projektion f **1.** → Hochrechnung
2. *(phot)* projection
   The act of projecting a photographic image onto a sensitized surface or viewing screen.

3. *(psy)* projection
   A psychological process in which an individual unwittingly attributes his own unacceptable thoughts, shortcomings, fears, desires, attributes, etc. to other persons or objects as a way of protecting himself from guilt and self-blame, and as a way of justifying his behavior. Projection is a type of defense mechanism and a way by which a person escapes the recognition and acceptance of his shortcomings and unacceptable attitudes.

Projektionsapparat m
→ Projektor
Projektionsfläche f
→ Leinwand
Projektionsfrage f
→ projektive Frage
Projektionslampe f **(Projektorlampe** f **)** *(phot/film)* projection lamp
Projektionsraum m *(film/TV)* projection room, (im Kino) projection booth
Projektionsröhre f *(TV)* projection tube, *brit* projection valve
Projektionsschirm m
→ Leinwand
Projektionstechnik f
→ projektive Technik
Projektionswand f *(film)* projection screen, screen, silver screen
projektive Frage f **(Projektivfrage** f **)** *(survey res)* projective question
   An interview question that attempts to determine indirectly what respondents think by asking them about their views of what others think. Such questions are intended to reduce the response effect on embarassing questions (peinliche Fragen).

projektive Technik f **(projektive Methode** f, **projektives Verfahren** n, **Deuteverfahren** n**)** *(survey res)* projective technique, projective method
   Motivational research methods, including thematic apperception tests, used to discover why individuals behave as they do. It is a set of procedures in which subjects are asked to interpret relatively unstructured, ambiguous, or vague stimuli, or to respond to incomplete questions. The theory underlying these techniques is that subjects project their own subconscious desires, motives, wishes into the responses.

projektiver Test m *(survey res)* projective test
→ projektive Technik

Projektleiter *m* (**Projektmanager** *m*)
(*econ*) project manager, venture manager
→ Projektmanager, Projektmanagement

Projektmanagement *n* (*econ*) project management, venture management
An effort by an entrepreneur and a investor to establish a new, profitable business by making use of the expertise of and the capital in money of each of the owners in their joint effort, as the particular contribution of each may be required.
→ Produktmanagement

Projektmanager *m*
→ Projektleiter

Projektor *m* (**Filmprojektor** *m*, **Projektionsapparat** *m*) (*film*) projector, film projector
A device used for casting images on a neutral surface by means of a strong light shining through or creating reflections from a motion picture film, slide, etc.

Projektorbildfenster *n* (**Projektorfenster** *n*) (*film*) projection gate, projection opening

Projektorganisation *f* (*econ*) project organization, *brit* project organisation
→ Produktmanagement

Projektplan *m* (*econ*) project plan

Projektplanung *f* (*econ*) project planning

Projektteam *n* (*econ*) project team, venture team
A group of specialists drawn from all areas of a business firm to work together under the leadership of an appointed manager to develop a new product by working outside divisional lines in an effort to find an inventive approach to an opportunity in a new market.

Pro-Kopf-Einkommen *n* (*econ*) per capita income, income per capita, income per person, income per head
The total income of a nation averaged over its population.

Pro-Kopf-Umsatz *m* (*econ*) per capita sales *pl*, per capita turnover

Pro-Kopf-Verbrauch *m* (*econ*) per capita consumption

Prolongation *f* (*film*) prolongation

Promoter *m*
→ Verkaufsförderer; Fachpromoter, Machtpromoter

Promotion *f*
→ Verkaufsförderung, Absatzförderung

Propaganda *f* propaganda
The conscious, systematic, and organized effort designed deliberately to manipulate or influence the decisions, actions, or beliefs of a large number of people in a specified direction on a controversial issue. Usually propaganda is considered to be an attempt to manipulate group opinion by concealing the true purpose of the propaganda and presenting only one side of debatable issues.

Propagandafilm *m* propaganda film

Propagandist *m* 1. propagandist, propagator
2. → Verkaufsförderer, Vorführer

propagieren *v/t* to propagate, to propagandize

Propergeschäft *n*
→ Eigengeschäft

Properhändler *m*
→ Eigenhändler

proportionale Auswahl *f* (**proportionales Auswahlverfahren** *n*, **proportionales Stichprobenverfahren** *n*, **proportionale Stichprobenbildung** *f*) (*stat*) proportionate sampling, proportional sampling, proportional sample allocation, proportional stratified sampling, proportionate sample allocation
A method of selecting sample numbers from different strata so that the numbers chosen from the strata are proportional to the population numbers in those strata.
→ geschichtete Auswahl

proportionale Stichprobe *f* (**proportionale Auswahl** *f*) (*stat*) proportionate sample, proportional sample

Proportionalisierung *f* (*stat*) proportionalization, *brit* proportionalisation

Propositionstest *m* proposition test
→ USP (Unique Selling Proposition)

pro rata (prorata) *adj* (*econ*) prorata, pro rata
Proportionately divided, distributed or assessed according to some exactly calculable factor.

prorata Rückerstattung *f* (*econ*) prorata refund, pro rata refund

Prospekt *m* (**Werbeprospekt** *m*, **Werbebroschüre** *f*) pamphlet, advertising pamphlet, folder, advertising folder, booklet, advertising booklet, brochure, advertising

brochure, prospectus, handout, giveaway, dodger, flier
  An elaborate advertising booklet whose appearance has been given special design attention, and that is either bound in special cover stock or folded; used particularly in sales solicitation or promotional activities.
→ Flugzettel, Flugblatt, Handzettel, Faltprospekt

Prospektanzeige f free-standing insert, free-standing stuffer, newspaper stuffer, sheridan stuffer, giant insert
  A preprinted advertisement, usually in multiple page form, that is inserted loose into newspapers or magazines.

Prospektausgestaltung f
→ Prospektgestaltung

Prospektbeilage f
→ Beilage

Prospektgestaltung f pamphlet design, advertising pamphlet design, folder design, advertising folder design, advertising booklet design, booklet design, brochure design, advertising brochure design, prospectus design, handout design, giveaway design, dodger design, flier design

prospektive Marktforschung f prospective market research
  Market research focused on investigating future developments, trends, and events.
vgl. adspektive Marktforschung, retrospektive Marktforschung

Prospektständer m (POP advtsg) pamphlet rack, pamphlet stand, folder rack, folder stand, booklet rack, booklet stand

Prospekttest m pamphlet test, brochure test, folder test

Prospektverteilung f pamphlet distribution, folder distribution, booklet distribution, booklet distribution, brochure distribution

Prototyp m (econ) prototype
  A first working model or the first constructed version of a product and all its details, including design, appearance, physical and technical characteristics and performance.

Provinzblatt n
→ Provinzzeitung

Provinzpresse f
→ Regionalpresse, Lokalpresse

Provinzzeitung f (**Provinzblatt** n) provincial newspaper, provincial paper, derog parochial paper
→ Lokalzeitung, Regionalzeitung

Provision f (**Mittlervergütung** f, **Kommission** f) (econ/advtsg) commission
  1. A fee paid as an agreed financial share of a business transaction accruing to a sales representative, sales agent or employee for transacting a piece of business or performing a service.
  2. → Agenturprovision

Provision f plus Skonto (**Agenturprovision** f plus Skonto) (advtsg) fifteen and two, 15 and 2, 15 & 2
  The standard discounts to advertising agencies allowed by most media. Fifteen percent of the gross bill is the commission retained by the agency; 2 percent of the net bill is a cash discount, (→) Skonto, normally passed on to the advertiser.

provisionieren v/t (advtsg) to pay a commission

Provisionsbasis f (**Provisionsgutschrift** f) (advtsg) commission credited
→ Provision

Provisionsnachlaß m (advtsg) commission discount, credit
  A deduction by a medium from the amount charged an advertiser.

Provisionsteilung f (**Aufteilung** f **der Agenturprovision**) (advtsg) split commission

Provisionsvertreter m
→ Handelsvertreter

Proximität f (stat) proximity

Proximitätsanalyse f (stat) proximity analysis

Proximitätsmaß n (stat) proximity measure, measure of proximity
→ Ähnlichkeitsmaß, Distanzmaß, Korrelationsmaß

Prozent n percent, brit per cent

Prozentabweichung f (**prozentuale Abweichung** f) (stat) percentage deviation

Prozentdiagramm n (stat) percentage diagram

Prozenthistogramm n (stat) percentage histogram

Prozentpolygon n (**Prozentpolygonzug** m) (stat) percentage polygon

Prozentpunkt m percentage point

Prozentsatz m percentage

Prozentsatz-des-Gewinns-Methode *f*
(der **Werbebudgetierung**)
→ Gewinnanteilsmethode
Prozentsatz-des-Umsatzes-Methode *f*
(der **Werbebudgetierung**)
→ Umsatzanteilsmethode
Prozentzahl *f* percentage figure, percentage number, percentage
prozyklische Werbung *f* (**zyklische Werbung** *f*) cyclical advertising, procyclical advertising
vgl. antizyklische Werbung, gegenzyklische Werbung
Prüfbild *n*
→ Testbild
Prüffilm *m*
→ Testfilm
Prüffunktion *f*
→ Schätzfunktion
Prüfliste *f* (**Checkliste** *f*, **Merkliste** *f*, **Kontrolliste** *f*) check list, checklist
A comprehensive list of actions to be taken in sequence in order to achieve a given effect with maximum efficiency.
Prüflistenverfahren *n* (**Checklistenverfahren** *n*) checklist technique, check list technique
Prüfposten *m* (**Abnahmeposten** *m*) *(econ/stat)* inspection lot
A lot, (→) Los, presented for inspection, which may be carried out on each member of the lot or on a sample of members only.
Prüfprojektor *m* *(phot)* diascope
Prüfsignal *n*
→ Testsignal
Prüfstück *n*
→ Prüfungsexemplar
Prüfton *m*
→ Testton
Prüfungsexemplar *n* (**Prüfstück** *n*) (Zeitung/Zeitschrift) examination copy, inspection copy
Prüfverfahren *n*
→ Signifikanztest
Prüfverteilung *f*
→ Testverteilung
psychische Distanz *f* psychological distance
psychische Sättigung *f*
→ Reaktanz
psychischer Kaufzwang *m*
→ psychologischer Kaufzwang
Psychoanalyse *f*
→ psychoanalysis

Psychobiologie *f* psychobiology, *auch* ergasiology, objective psychology (Adolf Meyer)
Originally in psychology, the analysis and treatment of psychological disorders through a study not only of the psychology of an individual but also of contributing biological and social factors. Today, also an orientation in consumer research, (→) Konsumforschung, attempting to relate consumer behavior to underlying biological behavior patterns.
Psychodrama *n* psychodrama (Jacob L. Moreno)
psychogalvanische Hautreaktion *f* (**psychogalvanischer Reflex** *m*) *(res)* psychogalvanic response (PGR), psychogalvanic reaction, psychogalvanic skin response, galvanic skin response, basal skin response (BSR), basal skin resistance
The physiological reaction to psychological stimuli, e.g., fear or arousal, the intensity of which is measurable by the degree of skin conductivity created by varying perspiration rates.
→ Psychogalvanometer
Psychogalvanometer *n* (**Galvanometer** *n*) *(res)* psychogalvanometer, galvanometer
An instrument which keeps a record of changes in galvanic responses, (→) psychogalvanische Hautreaktion; it is used in advertising research to measure test persons' reactions to emotional stimuli in advertisements.
psychographische Daten *n/pl* *(social res)* psychographics *pl*, psychographic characteristics *pl*
The categorization of a market or other population groups, e.g. consumers, on the basis of psychological — as distinguished from demographic-dimensions.
cf. (→) demographische Daten, including activities, interests, opinions, values, attitudes, life-styles, personality traits, such as innovativeness, sophistication, etc.
psychographische Marktsegmentierung *f* *(marketing)* psychographic market segmentation
The strategy of segmenting a market by psychographics, (→) psychographische Daten.
vgl. demographische Marktsegmentierung
psychologische Marktanalyse *f* psychological market analysis
psychologische Marktforschung *f* psychological market research

psychologische Nische f
→ Marktnische
psychologischer Kaufzwang m
psychological coercion to buy,
psychological pressure to buy
psychologischer Preis m (econ)
psychological price
Psychological pricing is a pricing policy whereby the price of a product or service is adjusted to reflect emotional buyer reactions rather than strictly rational or economic responses. Some of the psychological pricing strategies are odd-even pricing, (→) gebrochener Preis, customary pricing, prestige pricing, (→) Prestigepreis, or price lining, (→) Preiszonenpolitik.
psychologisches Marktmodell n
psychological market model
Psychometrie f psychometrics pl (construed as sg)
Psychophysik f psychophysics pl (construed as sg)
The study of physical stimuli and the relation to sensory reactions.
Psychophysiologie f psychophysiology
The field of psychology that emphasizes physiological correlates of psychological phenomena.
psychophysiologische Messung f psychophysiological measurement
Psychotechnik f psychotechnology, psychotechnics pl (construed as sg)
The psychological techniques used in controlling or influencing human behavior.
Public Affairs pl public affairs
The communicative aspect of social marketing, (→) Soziomarketing.
Publicity f publicity
Non-personal stimulation of demand for a product, service or business unit by planting commercially significant news about it in a published medium or obtaining favorable presentation of it upon radio, television, or stage that is not paid for by the sponsor. The English term has been integrated into German, but it has a slightly derogatory slant.
Public Relations pl (PR) (**Public-Relations-Arbeit** f)
→ Öffentlichkeitsarbeit
Public-Relations-Abteilung f
→ PR-Abteilung
Public-Relations-Arbeit f (**PR-Arbeit** f)
→ Öffentlichkeitsarbeit
Public-Relations-Berater m
→ PR-Berater

Public-Relations-Chef m
→ PR-Chef
Public-Relations-Fachmann m (**Public-Relations-Experte** m)
→ Öffentlichkeitsarbeiter
Public-Relations-Gesellschaft f (**PR-Gesellschaft** f) public relations association, PR association
Publikation f publication
Any piece of printed matter directed to a specific audience.
Publikationsorgan n publication organ
Publikum n audience, public
Publikumsforschung f audience research
→ Hörerforschung, Leserforschung, Zuschauerforschung
Publikumspresse f consumer press, general-interest press
→ Publikumszeitschrift
Publikumsuntersuchung f (**Publikumsstudie** f) (media res) audience investigation
→ Hörerschaftsuntersuchung, Leserschaftsuntersuchung, Zuschauerschaftsuntersuchung
Publikumswerbung f consumer advertising, consumer-directed advertising, national consumer advertising
The directed effort of advertisers, normally national manufacturers, to influence masses of consumers directly through advertising media to build consumer demand which makes it necessary for local retailers to make the advertised product(s) or service(s) available.
→ Sprungwerbung; vgl. Fachwerbung (Werbung in Fachkreisen)
Publikumszeitschrift f consumer magazine, consumer journal, general-interest magazine, general editorial magazine, general magazine
A magazine which appeals to a broad audience or to an audience with a specific interest (but not as specific as that in a trade magazine).
vgl. Fachzeitschrift, Kundenzeitschrift, Spezialzeitschrift
publizieren v/t + v/i to publish, to publicize
Publizist m journalist, auch publicist
Publizistik f journalism
Publizistikwissenschaft f
→ Zeitungswissenschaft

Publizität *f* publicity
→ Öffentlichkeit, Publicity
Pufferfrage *f* **(Ablenkungsfrage** *f*)
(survey res) buffer question
Pull-Methode *f* **(Pull-Strategie** *f*)
(marketing) pull strategy, pull method, pull distribution strategy, pull method, pull distribution strategy, pull distribution method
  A marketing and/or distribution strategy aimed at building up consumer demand, (→) Nachfragesog, for (a) product(s) or service(s), e.g. through consumer advertising, (→) Publikumswerbung or other forms of promotion with the expectation that the consumer will ask the retailer for the item, who in turn will ask the wholesaler who will order it from the maker.
vgl. Push-Methode (Push-Strategie)
Pulsfrequenzmessung *f (advtsg res)* pulse-frequency measurement, measurement of pulse frequency
pulsierende Werbung *f* **(Pulsation** *f,* **phasenweise Werbung** *f*)
→ Periodenwerbung
Pumpstativ *n (phot)* hydraulic stand
Punkt *m* **(typographischer Punkt** *m*) *(typ)* point (pt.), typographical point
→ Didotpunkt
Punktbewertung *f (stat)* scoring
Punktbewertungsmodell *n (stat)* scoring model
Punktbewertungsverfahren *n (stat)* scoring technique
punktbiserielle Korrelation *f* **(punktbiseriale Korrelation** *f*) *(stat)* point biserial correlation
  A modification of the biserial correlation to the case where one variate, instead of being based on a dichotomy of an underlying continuous variate, is discontinuous and two-valued.
Punktdiagramm *n* **(Stigmogramm** *n*) *(stat)* dot diagram
Punktlichtabtaster *m (TV)* flying spot scanner
Punktlichtabtastung *f (TV)* flying spot scanning
  A technique for the transfer of film to video utilizing an electronic shutter.
Punktlichtmesser *m (phot)* spotlight meter
Punktlichtquelle *f* **(Punktlichtscheinwerfer** *m,* **Punktscheinwerfer** *m*) *(phot/film/TV)* spotlight, spot
  A light with a directed beam.
Punktlinie *f* **(punktierte Linie** *f*) dotted line, dotted rule

Punktmarkt *m (econ)* spot market, cash market
  An economic condition in which commodities are directly available for immediate delivery.
Punktprognose *f* **(Punktvoraussage** *f*) *(stat/econ)* point prognosis, point prediction
→ Punktschätzung
Punktschärfe *f (phot)* spot focus
Punktschätzung *f (stat)* point estimate, point estimation
  One of the two principal bases of estimation, (→) Schätzung, in statistical analysis. It attempts to give the best single estimated value of a parameter (→) Parameter, as compared with interval estimation (→) Intervallschätzung, which proceeds by specifying a range of values.
Punktschraffierung *f (print)* stipple, stippling
  The arrangement of small and individual dots sufficiently close together to afford the effect of a tone or tint.
Punktskala *f (stat)* point scale
Punktsystem *n (typ)* point system (of type)
vgl. Didotsystem
Punktwertsystem *n* **(Punktwertverfahren** *n*)
→ Produktbewertungsverfahren
Punze *f (print)* bodkin, punch, stamp, die
punzen *v/t (print)* to punch, to stamp, to emboss
Pupillometer *n* pupillometer
Pupillometrie *f (advtsg res)* pupillometrics *pl* (construed a *sg*), pupil measurement
  A research technique used to studying the interest-arousing qualities of advertising stimuli based on the finding that there is a relationship between pupil dilation and the interest value of visual stimuli.
Push-Methode *f* **(Push-Strategie** *f,* **Schubstrategie** *f*) *(marketing)* push strategy, push method, push distribution strategy, push distribution method
  A marketing and/or distribution strategy aimed at convincing wholesalers that it will be advantageous for them to carry a product, then they in turn will attempt to convince the retailers, who in turn will attempt to convince the consumer of the product's merit.
vgl. Pull-Methode (Pull-Strategie)
PWA *abbr* Programmwahlanlage

Q

Q-Faktorenanalyse *f* **(Q-Analyse** *f*)
(stat) Q analysis, Q technique, Q factor analysis
Q-Sortierttechnik *f* **(Q-Sort-Methode** *f,* **Q-Sort** *m*) *(social res)* Q-sort, Q-sort technique, Q-sort method
  An attitude research technique (→) Einstellungsforschung, wherein, with a before-after, comparative-group, or similar research design individuals are presented with a large number of cards, each card bearing on it a series of statements believed to express different attitudes toward the subject being studied, they are asked to evaluate the statement on each card and then group the cards into a series of piles made up of cards having statements believed to be similar (relative to the subject being studied), with the proviso that participants must place the cards in a stated number of piles with a stated number of cards in each pile (which proviso contributes to ease of analysis since the numbers of cards and piles are fixed so that when they are sorted by the participants a normal curve, (→) Normalkurve, is physically approximated — i.e., participants may be asked to place only one card on each of two extreme positions, four each on the inner positions next to the extremes, etc.), and finally card-placement is analyzed to show important aspects of personality, particularly with reference to self-image.
Q-Technik *f*
→ Q-Sortiertechnik
Q-Test *m*
→ Cochrans Q-Test (Cochrantest)
Quadrat *n (print)* quad, quadrat
  A blank piece of type at least one en, (→) Halbgeviert, in width, used for spacing out lines of composition or for filling in larger areas of white paper.
→ Geviert
Quadratformat *n* square, square size
quadratische Abweichung *f*
→ Varianz
quadratische mittlere Abweichung *f* **(mittlere quadratische Abweichung** *f*)
→ Standardabweichung
Quadratmetergewicht *n*
→ Papiergewicht
Qualifikation *f* qualification

qualifizierter Empfänger *m*
→ tatsächlicher Empfänger
qualifizierter Hörer *m*
→ tatsächlicher Hörer
qualifizierter Leser *m*
→ tatsächlicher Leser
qualifizierter Zuschauer *m*
→ tatsächlicher Zuschauer
Qualifizierung *f*
→ Kontaktqualität
Qualität *f* quality
qualitative Analyse *f (survey res)*
qualitative analysis
→ qualitative Forschung;
vgl. quantitative Analyse
qualitative Daten *n/pl (survey res)*
qualitative data *pl*
→ qualitative Forschung;
vgl. quantitative Daten
qualitative Forschung *f (survey res)*
qualitative research, *auch* subjective research
  A group of research techniques that attempt to get the qualitative rather than the quantitative dimensions of data, usually from small samples (e.g. group discussions, extended interviews), to develop hypotheses and broaden insight. It is barely possible to draw general conclusions about the universes which such samples describe.
vgl. quantitative Forschung
qualitative Marktorschung *f*
qualitative market research
vgl. quantitative Marktforschung
qualitative Mediaforschung *f*
qualitative media research
vgl. quantitative Mediaforschung
qualitative Methode *f (survey res)*
qualitative method
vgl. quantitative Methode
qualitative Untersuchung *f*
(qualitative Studie *f*) *(survey res)*
qualitative investigation, qualitative study
vgl. quantitative Untersuchung
qualitativer Medienvergleich *m*
(media planning) qualitative media comparison
Qualitätsausrichtung *f* **der Nachfrage**
(econ) quality-orientation of demand

Qualitätsbewußtsein n *(econ)* quality consciousness
Qualitätsbezeichnung f *(econ)* quality label, quality description
Qualitätsdruck m high-quality print, high-quality printing, quality print, quality printing
Qualitätseffekt m *(econ)* quality effect
→ Preis-Qualitäts-Effekt
Qualitätserzeugnis n **(Qualitätsprodukt** n) *(econ)* quality product, quality produce, high-quality product
Qualitätsgarantie f *(econ)* quality guarantee, quality guaranty, quality warranty
→ Garantie
Qualitätsimage n *(econ)* quality image
Qualitätsindex m *(econ)* quality index
Qualitätsindikator m *(econ)* quality indicator
Qualitätskonkurrenz f **(Qualitätswettbewerb** m) *(econ)* quality competition, product quality competition
vgl. Preiskonkurrenz
Qualitätskontrolle f **(statistische Qualitätskontrolle** f) *(stat)* quality control, statistical quality control
A statistical method of controlling the quality of a product which is manufactured in large numbers. It aims at tracing and eliminating systematic variations in quality in a sample, or reducing them to an acceptable level, leaving the remaining variation to chance.
qualitätsneutrale Ausfälle m/pl *(stat)* non-biased nonresponse, non-biased error
→ Zufallsfehler
Qualitätsniveau n *(econ)* quality level
Qualitätspolitik f *(econ)* quality policy, product quality policy
Qualitätsprofil n *(econ)* quality profile
Qualitätsschutz m **(Qualitätssicherung** f) *(econ)* quality protection
Qualitätsstandard m **(Qualitätsgrundsatz** m) *(econ)* quality standard
Qualitätstest m **(Produktqualitätstest** m) *(econ)* quality test, product quality test
Qualitätswahrnehmung f quality perception
Qualitätswettbewerb m
→ Qualitätskonkurrenz
Qualitätszeichen n
→ Qualitätsbezeichnung, Gütezeichen

Qualitätszeitschrift f quality magazine, high-quality magazine, quality journal, high-quality journal
→ Prestigezeitschrift
Qualitätszeitung f quality newspaper, quality paper, high-quality newspaper, high-quality paper
→ Prestigezeitung
quantifizieren *(math/stat)* v/t to quantify
Quantifizierung f **(Quantifizieren** n) *(math/stat)* quantification
Quantilabstand m **(Quantil** n) *(stat)* quantile
The class of (n − 1) partition values of a variate which divide the total frequency of a population or a sample into a given number n of equal proportions.
Quantität f quantity
quantitative Analyse f *(survey res)* quantitative analysis
→ quantitative Forschung;
vgl. qualitative Analyse
quantitative Daten n/pl *(survey res)* quantitative data pl
Data in the form of numerical quantities.
→ quantitative Forschung;
vgl. qualitative Daten
quantitative Forschung f *(survey res)* quantitative research, *auch* objective research
All research techniques aimed at gathering and analyzing data in the form of numerical values such as measurements or counts.
vgl. qualitative Forschung
quantitative Marktforschung f quantitative market research
vgl. qualitative Marktforschung
quantitative Mediaforschung f quantitative media research
vgl. qualitative Mediaforschung
quantitative Methode f *(survey res)* quantitative method
vgl. qualitative Methode
quantitative Untersuchung f **(quantitative Studie** f) *(survey res)* quantitative investigation, quantitative study
vgl. qualitative Untersuchung
quantitativer Medienvergleich m quantitative media comparison
vgl. qualitativer Medienvergleich
Quantuplikation f **1.** *(stat)* quantuplication **2.** *(media res)* multiple overlapping, quantuplication
→ externe Überschneidung

Quantuplikationstabelle f *(media res)* quantuplication table, multiple overlapping table
Quartil n *(stat)* quartile
One of three variate values which separate the total frequency of a distribution into four equal parts.
Quartilabstand m
→ mittlerer Quartilabstand
Quartilsdispersionskoeffizient m *(stat)* quartile variation
Quarzgenerator m **(Quarzoszillator** m **)** crystal oscillator
quasi-biotische Anlage f **(quasi-biotische experimentelle Anlage** f**)** (Bernt Spiegel) *(res)* quasi-biotic experimental design
Quasi-Experiment n *(res)* quasi-experiment
A refinement of the naturalistic observation study in which changes in the independent variable occur in nature and not by the experimenter's manipulation, but which incorporates as many principles of scientific control as possible under the circumstances.
quasi-experimentelle Anlage f **(quasi-experimentelle Versuchsanlage** f**)** *(res)* quasi-experimental design
A research design in which subjects frequently are not assigned randomly to conditions, although the independent variable(s) may be manipulated. The reason for not assigning randomly is usually because it is impossible or not feasible to do so.
Quasi-Panel n **(Quasi-Panelbefragung** f**)** *(survey res)* quasi panel, quasi panel survey
Quasi-Skala f *(stat)* quasi scale
Quecksilberdampf m *(phot)* mercury vapor, *brit* mercury vapour
A form of illuminant comprising a long narrow glass tube in which the vapor of mercury is raised to incandescence by passage of an electric current.
Quelle f source
Querbild n horizontal picture, horizontal image, landscape
vgl. Längsbild
Querformat n horizontal format, oblong format, oblong size, (bei Photos) landscape size, landscape
vgl. Längsformat
querformatige Seite f horizontal page, landscape page, landscape
vgl. längsformatige Seite

Querlinie f **(Querstrich** m**)** *(typ)* cross rule, cross line, (diagonal) diagonal rule, diagonal line
Querschnitt m **(Stichprobe** f **)** *(stat)* cross section
Querschnittsanalyse f **(Querschnittsstudie** f**, Querschnittsuntersuchung** f **)** *(res)* cross-sectional analysis, cross-sectional study, cross-sectional investigation
vgl. Längsschnittanalyse
Querspuraufzeichnung f *(TV)* traverse recording, traverse scan
Querstrich m *(typ)* cross-stroke, serif
Querverweis m **(Kreuzverweis** m**)** cross reference, *brit* cross-reference
Quetschfalte f crinkle, gusset, buckle, calender cut, cockle cut
Quintil n *(stat)* quintile, quintile range
Any one of five parts which divide a complete set of values, arrayed in order of magnitude, into five groups of equal frequency. The first quintile range represents the range of values assumed by the first fifth of the observations, that is, those with the smallest values. The second quintile range represents the range of values assumed by the second fifth of the observations, that is, those with the next-to-smallest values. The third and fourth quintile ranges are similarly defined, and the fifth quintile range represents the range of values assumed by the top fifth of the observations, that is, those with the highest values.
Quintilenanalyse f *(stat/media res)* quintile analysis
In general, any analysis using quintiles, (→) Quintil, to divide a set of quantitative data. In media research, the technique is used to examine frequency of media activity. Viewers or readers are divided into five equal groups ranging from the heaviest to the lightest in media exposure. These are then analyzed in terms of their share of total activity, demographic makeup, etc.
Quizsendung f **(Ratesendung** f**, Ratespiel** n**)** *(radio/TV)* game show, quiz game show
Quote f *(econ/stat)* quota
1. The share or proportion assigned to each in a division or to each member of a body.
2. The physical limit set on the import of a product (Importquote)
3. → Verkaufsquote
4. → Quotenauswahl
Quotenauswahl f **(Quota-Auswahl** f**, Quotenstichprobenverfahren** n**,**

Quotenfitting

Quotenstichprobenbildung f) *(stat)*
quota sampling, quota sampling procedure, quota sampling technique, quota sample selection
   A method of purposive (nonprobability) sampling, (→) bewußte Auswahl, in which interviewers look for specific numbers of respondents with known characteristics. Each unit in the universe does not have a known or equal chance of selection.

Quotenfitting n **(Quotafitting** n) *(stat)*
quota fitting

Quotenstichprobe f **(Quota-Stichprobe** f, **Quotenauswahl** f) *(stat)*
quota sample
   A sample selected by dividing a population into categories on the basis of certain variables and choosing a certain number (a quota) of cases from each category. No attempt is made to select the individual cases within each category (quota) randomly. The quota sample has been most widely used in public opinion sampling. The usual procedure is to select geographic areas on a random basis, assign the interviewers quotas of individuals with specified characteristics within each selected area, and leave the selection of specified characteristics within each selection of specific individuals to fill the quotas to the interviewers' discretion.

Quotenanweisung f
→ Quota

Quotenverfahren n
→ Quotenauswahl

R

® *abbr* registered trademark
The symbol for „registered trademark," meaning that the trademark is registered in the German Federal Patent Office. It is used by advertisers in close juxtaposition to their trademarks to give public notice that their marks are registered and therefore are the private property of the owners.
→ eingetragenes Warenzeichen
R x C-Felder-Tafel *f*
→ Vierfeldertafel, Kontingenztabelle
R-Technik *f* **(R-Analyse** *f***)** *(stat)* R-technique
Rabatt *m (econ)* discount, allowance, price discount
A reduction from a quoted or list price of a product or service which may be stated, usual or expected, usually in the form of a percentage.
Rabattgesetz *n*
→ Gesetz für Preisnachlässe
Rabattgutschein *m (promotion)* cents-off coupon, cents-off store coupon, price-off coupon.
A coupon, (→) Gutschein, promising a reduction from a product's or service's standard retail price, used as a promotional inducement to purchasers.
Rabattkartell *n (econ)* discount cartel, discount agreement
Rabattkombination *f*
→ Kombinationsrabatt
Rabattmarke *f (promotion)* trading stamp, trade stamp, discount stamp
An incentive voucher, usually in the form of a stamp issued by retailers to encourage patronage.
Rabatt-Nachbelastung *f* **(Rabatt-Rückbelastung** *f***)** *(econ)* billback, allowance
A merchandising allowance in which the discount is not given to the purchaser until he provides proof he has complied with the merchandising requirements.
(advtsg) short rate
The higher rate an advertiser must pay if he fails to use the amount of space or time specified in his contract.
Rabattpolitik *f (econ)* discount policy, price discount policy, discounting

Rabattrecht *n (econ)* discount law, discount legislation, discount regulations *pl*
Rabattsatz *m* **(Höhe** *f* **des Rabatts)** *(econ)* discount rate
Rabattschinder *m* (Werbung, die zur Erhaltung eines Rabatts geschaltet wird) rate holder
An advertisement placed only to earn a discount for quantity or frequency from an advertising medium.
Rabattstaffel *f (econ)* discount list, price discount list
Rabattwettbewerb *m (econ)* discount competition, discounting competition, price discount competition
Rack Jobber *m*
→ Regalgroßhändler
Radiernadel *f* **(Nadel** *f***)** *(print)* burin, chisel, etching needle
A tool used by finishers to remove burrs and excrescences from surfaces of printing plates.
Radierung *f (print)* etching
→ Kaltnadelradierung
Radio *n* 1. radio
2. → Radioapparat
3. → Hörfunk (Rundfunk)
Radioapparat *m* **(Radiogerät** *n*, **Radio** *n*, **Radioempfänger** *m***)** radio, radio receiver, radio receiving set, radio set, *brit* wireless set, set
Radiodurchsage *f* radio announcement, radio information, *brit* wireless announcement, wireless information
Radioempfänger *m*
→ Radioapparat
Radiofrequenz *f* **(RF)** **(Radiosendefrequenz** *f***)** radio frequency (RF)
Radioreklame *f*
→ Hörfunkwerbung
Radiosender *m* **(Hörfunksender** *m* **)** radio transmitter
→ Rundfunksender
Radiostation *f*
→ Rundfunkstation
Radiozeitschrift *f* **(Radioprogrammzeitschrift** *f***)** radio guide, radio magazine
vgl. Programmzeitschrift

Rahme f
→ Schließrahmen (Formrahmen)
Rahmen *m (phot/print)* frame, border, frisket, mask
   A rule or design that surrounds an advertisement. Also a finishing line or design around a printing plate.
→ Bilderrahmen, Schließrahmen
Rahmenantenne f *(electr.)* frame antenna, *brit* frame aerial, loop antenna, *brit* loop aerial
Rahmengeber *m (phot/print)* mask generator
Rahmenprogramm *n (radio/TV)* backing program, *brit* programme, (für Werbung) commercial program, *brit* programme, sponsored program, *brit* programme
   A television or radio program paid for by sponsors.
Rahmensucher *m (phot)* frame finder, iconometer
Rahmenvereinbarung f *(econ)* skeleton agreement
Rakel f **(Rakelmesser** *n) (print)* doctor blade, doctor bar, doctor knife, wiper blade *(phot)* squeegee
Rakeltiefdruck *m (print)* photogravure printing, photogravure, rotogravure printing, rotogravure
   Gravure printing done on a web-fed press.
Rampenbeleuchtung f **(Rampenlicht** *n) (film/TV)* footlight, foot lighting, float(s) *(pl)*
Ramschkauf *m* **(Restekauf** *m) (econ)* remainder buy, remainders buy
→ Ramschware
Ramschkiste f
→ Wühlkiste
Ramschmarkt *m* **(Restemarkt** *m) (econ)* remainders market
→ Ramschware
Ramschpreis *m* **(Restwarenpreis** *m) (econ)* remainders price, remainder price
→ Ramschware
Ramschware f **(Restware** f) *(econ)* remainders *pl*
   Products, especially books, remaining unsold at the regular price after demand at that price level has expired; usually sold at a discount.
Rand *m* **1.** *(print)* margin
   The area between the printed area and the edge of a sheet or page.
2. → Umrandung (Einfassung)
3. → Kante, Schnitt

Randaufhellung f *(film/phot/TV)* edge lighting, rim lighting
Randbemerkung f **(Marginalie** f)
marginal note, side note
Randbeschnitt *m*
→ Anschnitt, Beschnitt
Randeffekt *m (film/phot/TV)* edge fringing, fringe effect
Randlinie f
→ Einfassung, Einfassungslinie
Randmarkierung f *(film)* edge marking
Randnumerierung f *(film)* edge numbering, rubber numbering, key number
   The multi-digit identification number film manufacturers apply to each foot of negative raw stock.
Randnummer f **(Randziffer** f)
1. *(survey res)* (am Fragebogen) marginal number, marginal
   One of the numbers along the edge of motion picture film, used for a guide.
2. *(film)* edge number
Random-Ausfallgewichtung f **(Redressement** *n) (stat)* weighting for not-at-homes, nonresponse weighting
   A weighting procedure, (→) Gewichtung, used to avoid callbacks, (→) Wiederholungsbesuch, in cases in which an interviewer does not find a preselected individual at home. One technique is the Politz-Simmons method in which respondents testify to the number of nights in the last six that they were at home. This testimony provides the estimates of the probabilities of being at home, and the reciprocals of these probabilities are the appropriate weights.
Randomauswahl f
→ Zufallsauswahl
Randomisierung f **(Randomisation** f, **Zufallsstreuung** f) *(stat)*
randomization, *brit* randomisation
   The use of chance to control extraneous variables in an experiment. Randomization is often used in addition to matching, (→) Parallelisierung, in controlled experiments. Subjects are matched in pairs on those variables which the experimenter seeks to control and then one member of each pair is assigned to the experimental group and one to the control group on a random basis, such as the toss of a coin. Thus randomization is used to equalize on a chance basis the factors that are not specifically controlled but that might affect the outcome of the experiment. Randomization is also used sometimes without matching. That is, subjects are

assigned to the experimental and control groups on a purely random basis. In addition, it may be possible to use randomization at other points in an experiment to minimize the possibility of bias.
Random-Response-Methode f (Randomized Response-Modell n)
→ Technik der Zufallsantwort
Random-Route-Verfahren n (Random-Walk-Verfahren n) *(stat)* random route technique, random walk technique
  The path traversed by a particle which moves in steps, each step being determined by chance either in regard to direction or in regard to magnitude or both.
→ Zufallsweg
Randomstichprobe f
→ Zufallsauswahl
Randomtabelle f
→ Zufallstafel
Randschärfe f *(phot)* margin definition, edge definition
Randschleier m *(phot)* edge fog
Randsortiment n *(econ)* marginal assortment, marginal merchandise assortment
vgl. Kernsortiment
Randspur f *(film)* edge track
Randsteg m
→ Außensteg
Randüberschrift f *(print)* shoulder heading, shoulder head, side-heading, shoulder note
Randverteilung f *(stat)* marginal distribution
Randwahrscheinlichkeit f (Randsummenwahrscheinlichkeit f) *(stat)* marginal probability
Rang m (Rangplatz m, Rangzahl f) *(stat)* rank
  The ordinal number of a single observation among a set when it is ordered according to some criterion.
Rangfolge f
→ Rangordnung
Rangkorrelation f (Rangordnungskorrelation f) *(stat)* rank correlation, rank order correlation
  The intensity of correlation between two sets of rankings or the degree of correspondence between them.
Rangkorrelationskoeffizient m *(stat)* rank correlation coefficient
→ Kendalls Tau, Spearmans Rho
Rangordnung f (Rangfolge f) *(stat)* rank order

Rangordnungsmaßzahl f *(stat)* rank order statistic
Rangordnungsskala f *(stat)* rank scale, rank order scale, ranking scale
  A comparative rating scale, (→) Ratingskala, used in attitude research, (→) Einstellungsforschung; it requires respondents to rank the units of a set of phenomena relative to a particular attribute.
→ Ordinalskala
Rangordnungstest m (Rangtest m) *(stat)* rank order test, rank test
Rangreihenbildung f (Rangreihenverfahren n) *(media planning)* ranking, rank order method, master newspaper list, mock newspaper schedule
Rangskala f
→ Rangordnungsskala
Rangskalierung f *(stat)* ranking
Rapport m 1. *(survey res)* rapport
  A harmonious relationship between an investigator or interviewer and his subject(s).
2. → Register
Raster m 1. *(print)* halftone screen, screen
  A glass or film through which a photograph is taken to make a halftone negative. The screen, made of two pieces of glass with finely ruled parallel lines — those of one screen horizontal, those of the other vertical — breaks up the continuous tones of the image into dots of varying sizes, the larger ones representing the denser values.
→ Autotypieraster
2. *(print)* (beim Siebdruck) silk screen
  A silk cloth mesh used in serigraphy.
3. *(TV)* raster, screen
  The scanned area of the television picture tube, partly hidden by the receiver mask.
4. *(phot)* screen
Rasterabstand m *(print)* screen distance, screen separation
  The separation or space between the surface of a halftone screen and that of the plate or film during halftone photography, the specific distance varying with screens of different ruling.
Rasterätzung f
→ Autotypie (Autotypieätzung)
Rasterauflösung f *(TV)* raster definition
→ Auflösung
Rasterbild n *(TV)* frame, (Halbbild beim Zeilensprung) field

Rasterfeinheit f
→ Rasterweite
Rasterfolie f (Tonpapier n) *(print)* tint sheet, tinting foil, screen tint, shading film, shading medium, shading tint, Ben Day film, Benday film, benday film, Ben Day screen, Benday screen, benday screen
  An inked relief film used for transferring tints or patterns to metal, paper or other surfaces by pressure.
Rasterfrequenz f *(TV)* scanning frequency
Rasterklischee n
→ Autotypie
Rasterlinie f *(print)* screen ruling, screen line
rastern v/t *(print)* to screen
Rastern n (Rasterung f) *(print)* screening
  The process of stripping a halftone tint on the transparent portions of another negative.
Rasternapf m (Napf m, Rasternäpfchen n, Näpfchen n) *(print)* pit, cell
Rasternegativ n *(print)* halftone negative, screen negative
  The image produced by photography of an original through a halftone screen.
→ Rasterpositiv
Rasterpapier n
→ Rasterfolie
Rasterplatine f *(print)* screen plate, screen lineplate
  A line etching made from a pen drawing and bearing a screen or tint effect in the lines and solids of the design.
Rasterpositiv n *(print)* halftone positive, screen positive
  A positive made in a camera from a continuous tone negative with a screen interposed between the photographic plate and the lens.
vgl. Rasternegativ
Rasterpunkt m *(print)* halftone dot
  The individual formation or element in a halftone negative, printing plate and final impression.
Rasterschärfe f
→ Rasterauflösung
Rasterstärke f (Rasterweite f, Rasterfeinheit f) *(print)* screen definition, fineness of the screen, coarseness of the screen, screen density, screen percentage
  The degree of fineness (or coarseness) of a halftone screen, (→) Raster 1.

Rastertiefdruck m
→ Rotationstiefdruck
Rasterton m (Rastertönung f) *(print)* halftone shading, halftone tint, negative tine, shading tint
Rasterung f
→ Rastern
Rasterweite f
→ Rasterstärke
Rasterwinkel m *(print)* screen angle
  The angle at which a halftone screen or original is placed for each of the colorplates of the set in color reproduction, so as to avoid pattern or moiré, (→) Moiré in the completed impression.
Ratespiel n
→ Quizsendung
Rating n (Einschätzungskalierung f, Zuordnungsskalierung f, Ratingverfahren n, Bewertungsverfahren n) *(res)* rating
  A method used in social research in which persons judge and record the characteristics of others or of themselves. Ratings may be made by specialized judges or observers, by group members of each other, or they may be self-ratings. They are used in a variety of social and psychological studies, including studies of social class, studies of small-group interaction, and personality studies. Raters may be given a prepared form on which they simply check categories or they may be asked to respond in their own words.
Ratingskala f (Einschätzungsskala f, Bewertungsskala f, Zuordnungsskala f, Einstufungsskala f, Notenskala f) *(res)* rating scale
  A graduated series of categories arranged in sequential order, e.g. from highest to lowest, most favorable to least favorable, etc. for use in rating the characteristics of others or oneself. Rating scales may consist of personality traits, social characteristics (such as socioeconomic status), or types of interpersonal relationships (such as friend, acquaintance, etc.). The rating scale may be used by judges or observers to rate subjects or by the subjects to rate each other or themselves.
Ratioskala f (Rationalskala f, Proportionalskala f)
→ Verhältnisskala
rationale Werbung f (begründende Werbung f) 1. (Werbemittel) rational advertisement, argumentative copy, reason-why copy **2. (Werbestrategie)** rational advertising, argumentative advertising, reason-why advertising,

reason-why, long-circuit appeal, factual approach
Rationalisierung f *(econ)* rationalization, *brit* rationalisation
    The concentration of forces and resources on those areas and products or services in a business firm from which a maximum return can be expected and the concomitant elimination of areas and products which yield a minimum or no return.
Rätselmagazin n **(Rätselheft** n**, Rätselzeitschrift** f**)** puzzle magazine, (Kreuzworträtsel) crossword puzzle magazine
Raucherkino n smoker cinema, cinema for smokers, smoker movietheater, smokers' movietheater
Rauchschriftwerbung f **(Himmelsschriftwerbung** f**)** skywriting, skytyping, sky advertising
    Advertising done by producing messages, symbols, etc. in the sky with trails or closely grouped puffs of smoke emitted by an airplane.
→ Luftwerbung
Raum m **(Platz** m**, Fläche** f**)** space
Raumausstattungswerbung f
→ Schauwerbung
Raumklang m
→ Stereoton
räumliche Distanz f **(geographische Distanz** f**)** *(stat)* geographical distance, spatial distance
vgl. soziale Distanz
Raumfilm m
→ dreidimensionaler Film
Raumton m stereo sound
Räumungsverkauf m
→ Ramschverkauf
Raumwelle f **(Himmelswelle** f**)** sky wave, indirect wave, ionospheric wave
Rauschabstand m **(Verhältnis** n **von Signal zu Rauschen)** signal-to-noise ratio (S/N ratio), noise-signal ratio
    The ratio of relevant to irrelevant material in a communication of any kind, as measured by the effect on persons receiving the communication.
Rauschen n **(Fremdgeräusch** n**, Geräusch** n**)** noise
    Any extraneous sound signal interference.
Rauschpegel m noise level
Reaktanz f *(psy)* reactance, psychological reactance (J. W. Brehm)
    The negative response to obtrusively persuasive communication.

Reaktanzeffekt m *(psy)* reactance effect, reactance, psychological reactance effect
Reaktanztheorie f *(psy)* theory of reactance, rectance theory
Reaktion f reaction, response
Reaktionseinstellung f **(Antworttendenz** f**, Response Set** m**)** *(social res)* response set, (Reaktionsstil) response style
    The habits or temporary dispositions that cause subjects to respond to test items differently than they would if the same content were presented in a different form, i.e. response consistencies.
Reaktionsfunktion f **(Responsefunktion** f**)** *(res)* response function
    A subjective value given to an impact (or impacts) to help determine the importance of that impact for the marketer or advertiser. These functions are described in many ways — „step", „s"-shaped, curvex — but there is much dispute as to the theory of the concept and the correctness of the shape of the curve in any given circumstance.
Reaktionsgeneralisierung f *(psy)* response generalization, *brit* generalisation, reaction generalization, *brit* generalisation
Reaktionsschema n
→ Reaktionseinstellung
Reaktionsschwankung f *(social res)* response variance
vgl. Antwortfehler
Reaktionsstil m
→ Reaktionseinstellung
reaktive Messung f **(reaktives Verfahren** n**, reaktive Methode** f**)** *(social res)* reactive measurement, reactive technique, reactive method (of measurement)
vgl. nichtreaktive Messung
Reaktivität f **(Reaktivitätseffekt** m**)** reactivity, reactivity effect
Realeinkommen n *(econ)* real income
    The actual group of products and/or services that a person's money income will permit him to acquire.
Reallohn m *(econ)* real wage
Realtypus m (Max Weber) real type
vgl. Idealtypus
Reason-Why m
→ rationale Werbung, begründende Werbung
Recall m **(Recall-Test** m**, Recall-Verfahren** n**, Recallwert** m**)**

Recency-Effekt

→ Erinnerung, Erinnerungstest, Erinnerungsverfahren, Erinnerungswert
Recency-Effekt m
→ Letztargumenthypothese
Rechenschaftspflicht f **(Verpflichtung** f **zur Rechenschaftslegung)** *(econ)* accountability, obligation to render an account
Recherche f **(journalistische Recherche** f**)** research, research work, researching
recherchieren v/t to research
rechte Seite f **(Schauseite** f**)** *(print)* right page, right-hand page, recto
rechteckige Autotypie f *(print)* square halftone block, square finish halftone
   A halftone illustration trimmed square or rectangular as opposed to a vignetted or outline halftone.
vgl. freistehende Autotypie
rechtsbündig *adj (print)* flush right
rechts oben
→ oben rechts
rechts von der Kamera *(film/TV)* camera right
Rechtsgutachten n legal opinion, legal expert's opinion, counsel's opinion, legal counsel's opinion
Recorder m **(Rekorder** m**)**
→ Aufnahmegerät
Recognition f **(Recognition-Test** m**, (Recognition-Verfahren** n**, Recognitionwert** m**)**
→ Wiedererkennung, Wiedererkennungstest, Wiedererkennungsverfahren, Wiedererkennungswert
Recordimeter n *(media res)* recordimeter
Redakteur(in) m(f) Am reporter, news editor, member of the editorial staff, *brit* sub-editor, (leitender Redakteur) editor, senior editor
Reaktion f **1.** (Redigieren) editing, rewriting, rewrite **2.** (Personal) editorial staff, editors *pl*, editorial board **3.** (Redaktionsräume) editorial department, editorial office **4.** (der Platz, an dem die Manuskripte redigiert werden) copy desk
redaktionell (Redaktions-) *adj* editorial
redaktionell gestaltete Anzeige f **(redaktionelle Anzeige** f**, redaktionell aufgemachte Anzeige** f**)** editorial-style advertisement, editorial-style ad, editorializing advertisement,

editorializing ad, reading notice, reader advertisement, reader ad, *colloq* advertorial
   A publication advertisement set in a type to simulate editorial reading matter and with a format similar to that of editorial matter. Must be identified as paid advertising under German law.
redaktionelle Änderung f **(redaktionelle Korrektur** f**)** *(print)* editorial alteration (E.A.)
   Any alteration made by a publisher other than one made at an author's request or one to correct a printer's error.
vgl. Autorenkorrektur, Druckfehler, Satzfehler
redaktionelle Berichterstattung f editorial coverage, editorial news coverage
redaktionelle Konzeption f **(redaktionelle Ausrichtung** f**, redaktionelle Tendenz** f**)** editorial policy
redaktionelle Werbung f editorial-style advertising, editorializing advertising, editorial publicity, publicity
   A story or message about a product or a company prepared as editorial rather than advertising material.
→ redaktionell gestaltete Anzeige
redaktionelle Zugabe f editorial mention, puff notice, puff
redaktioneller Hinweis m editorial mention, free mention, free puff, puff notice, puff
   A courtesy comment or puff in the editorial section of a magazine or a paper for an advertised product or service.
redaktioneller Teil m (im Gegensatz zum Anzeigenteil) editorial section, editorial content, editorial pages *pl*, editorial matter, (Text) editorial copy
   The news, educational, or entertainment portion of a publication or broadcast, as distinguished from the advertising.
vgl. Anzeigenteil
redaktionelles Umfeld n **(redaktioneller Kontext** m **)** editorial environment, editorial context
   The standard editorial content, tone, and philosophy of a communication medium, which may or may not be potentially supportive or destructive of the effectiveness of advertising.
Redaktionsabteilung f
→ Redaktion 2., 3., 4.
Redaktionsassistent(in) m(f) editorial assistant, assistant editor

Redaktionsgemeinschaft f editorial syndicate, syndicate
Redaktionskonferenz f staff conference, editorial staff conference, conference
Redaktionsleiter m
→ Schriftleiter
Redaktionsleitung f editorial management
Redaktionsschluß m copy deadline, deadline, copy date, closing date, closing time, closing hour
  The final time (day and hour) at which editorial contributions must have reached the editor.
  vgl. Anzeigenschluß
Redaktor m
→ Redakteur
redigieren v/t to edit
Redigieren n
→ Redaktion 1.
redliche Werbung f fair practice advertising, fair advertising practice
Redressement n
→ Random-Ausfallgewichtung
Reduktion f *(econ/phot/print)* reduction
→ Preisermäßigung, Verkleinerung, Datenreduktion
Reduktionsmarketing n demarketing, *brit* de-marketing
  The application of marketing know-how in the process of attempting to diminish the apparent demand for a product or service to the level that the firm can accommodate. There are a number of economic reasons which may prompt this policy in preference to one of expanding to fill the demand. Demarketing can either be general or selective. If it is general, a firm or an industry attempts to reduce overall demand for a product or service. If it is selective, it attempts to limit the demand of only certain segments of the market.
Reduktionswerbung f reductionist advertising
Redundanz f redundancy
  The repetitive part of a message which by virtue of an excess of syntax makes it unlikely that mistakes in reception will occur, thus increasing the probability that the communication will be understood.
Referenzanzeige f **(Verbundanzeige** f, **Koppelungswerbemittel** n, **Koppelanzeige** f) tie-in advertisement, tie-in ad, tie-in, (Werbesendung) tie-in commercial
  Any advertisement making reference to another advertisement or piece of promotion.
Referenzgruppe f
→ Bezugsgruppe
Referenzperson f
→ Bezugsperson
Referenzwerbung f **(Verbundwerbung** f, **Koppelungswerbung** f) tie-in advertising
→ Referenzanzeige
Reflektion f **(Rückstrahlung** f, **Reflexion** f, **Reflektieren** n) reflection, *brit* reflexion
  The change of direction a ray of light experiences when it falls upon a surface and is thrown back.
Reflektionslichtfleck m **(Reflexionslichtfleck** m) *(phot/TV)* flare spot, camera flare, flare
  A burned-out area on a photo or television picture tube created by local light oversaturation.
Reflektionslichthof m **(Reflektionslicht** n)
→ Lichthof
Reflektor m reflector, (Katzenauge) reflector button, reflection button, *collq* light stealer
  A reflecting glass used to form letters and designs in outdoor advertising for night-time visibility.
Reflex m reflex
Reflexbeleuchtung f *(phot/film/TV/ outdoor advtsg)* reflected lighting
Reflexempfänger m *(radio/TV)* reflex receiver
Reflexfolie f reflecting foil
Reflexkamera f *(phot)* reflex camera
→ Spiegelreflexkamera
Reflexkopie f reflex copy
Reflexsucher m *(phot)* reflex viewfinder, reflex finder
Regal n **(Warenregal** n) *(POP advtsg)* rack, shelf, display rack
  A floor stand designed to hold merchandise on shelves, on hooks, or in pockets.
Regalanziehungskraft f *(POP advtsg)* shelf appeal
  The package design of a product that is specifically aimed at appealing to customers at the point of purchase, (→) Kaufort, when they walk through the aisles looking at the merchandise racks; in particular, an instrument of promoting impulse buying, (→) Impulskauf.

Regalaufklebestreifen m
(**Regalaufkleber** m) *(POP advtsg)*
shelf tape, shelf strip
A strip of adhesive paper printed with an advertising message, attached to the front edge of a shelf, designed to fit in the molding or price rail.

Regalauslage f (**Warenauslage** f **im Regal**) *(POP advtsg)* shelf display
The display arrangement of goods on the shelf of the point of purchase.

Regalauszug m (**Auszug** m **für Sonderauslagen**) *(POP advtsg)* shelf extender, extender
A small display tray attached to a retail store shelf, used for special displays or as a means of increasing the regular shelf display into the store aisle at that point.

Regalbrett n *(POP advtsg)* shelf

Regalfläche f (**Regalplatz** m) *(POP advtsg)* shelf space
The amount of selling space, (→) Verkaufsfläche, in a retail store that is occupied by a type of merchandise measured in terms of square meters, linear or number of facings.

Regalgroßhändler m (**Regalgrossist** m) *(retailing)* rack jobber, service merchandiser, feeder jobber
A wholesaling business unit that markets specialized lines of merchandise to certain types of retail stores and provides the special services of selective brand and item merchandising and arrangement, maintenance, and stocking of display racks. The rack jobber usually, but not always, puts his merchandise in the store of the retailer on consignment. Rack jobbers are most prevalent in the food business. The English term is widely accepted in German.

Regalgroßhandel m (**Regalgrosso** n) *(retailing)* rack jobbing, service merchandising, feed jobbing
→ Regalgroßhändler

Regalkapazität f *(retailing)* shelf space capacity
The total amount of shelf space in a retail store that belongs to its selling space.

Regalmakler m
→ Regalgroßhändler

Regalmeterstrecke f (**Regalstrecke** f) *(retailing)* shelf footage

Regalmiete f *(retailing)* shelf rent, display space rent

Regalpackung f *(retailing)* shelf pack, shelf package, (sehr platzsparend) shelf miser, space miser

A container for retail items of a size that permits it to be placed on a shelf with ordinary clearance height.

Regalplakat n *(POP advtsg)* shelf poster, *colloq* shelf talker
A printed advertising poster hung over the edge of a retail store shelf and promoting a particular brand.

Regalplatz m
→ Regalfläche

Regal-Preismarkierung f (**Regal-Preisschild** n) *(POD advtsg)* shelf marker
A tag giving the price of a retail item and placed in, or hung from a channel strip.

Regalprospekt m (**Regalfaltblatt** n) *(POP advtsg)* shelf folder, rack folder

Regalschild n *(POP advtsg)* shelf card
A display card set up on a shelf in a retail store.

Regalstreifen m (**Regal-Werbestreifen** m) *(POP advtsg)* shelf strip, case strip, channel strip
A promotional device designed to fit in the molding or price rail of a shelf to call attention to the product above it.

Regalwipper m *(POP advtsg)* shelf wobbler

Regel f **des geringsten Bedauerns**
→ Minimax-Regret-Regel

Regelkreis m *(cybernetics)* feedback control system

regelmäßige Auflagenkontrolle f *(Zeitung/Zeitschrift)* regular circulation audit, regular audit
→ Auflagenkontrolle

regelmäßiger Hörer m *(media res)* regular listener, regular radio listener

regelmäßiger Leser m (**Kernleser** m) *(media res)* regular reader
A reader, (→) Leser, with a probability of reading, (→) Lesewahrscheinlichkeit, ranging from 0.83 to 1.00, i.e. a reader who reads 10 to 12 issues of a periodical.

regelmäßiger Zuschauer m *(media res)* regular viewer

regelmäßiges Hören n (**Regelmäßigkeit** f **des Hörens**) *(media res)* regular listening, regularity of listening

regelmäßiges Lesen n (**Regelmäßigkeit** f **des Lesens**) *(media res)* regular reading, regularity of reading
→ regelmäßiger Leser

regelmäßiges Zuschauen n (**regelmäßiges Fernsehen** n, **Regelmäßigkeit** f **des Fernsehens**) *(media res)* regular viewing, regular TV watching, regularity of viewing

Regenbogenpresse f yellow press, "rainbow press"
Regenbogentestbild n (TV) rainbow test pattern
Regeneration f **(Regenerierung** f) (film) regeneration, reactivation
Regie f 1. (film/radio/TV) direction, directing 2. (TV) (Bildregie) master control
Regieanweisung f (film/TV) stage direction, stage instruction
Regieassistent(in) m(f) (film/TV) assistant director (AD)
   A person whose job it is to assist in implementing a director's instructions.
Regie-Kameramann m (film/TV) director-cameraman
Regiekanzel f **(Regieraum** m) (radio/TV) control room, colloq gallery
   A small room for the production management separated from the performing studio by a soundproof window.
Regiepult n (radio/TV) control desk, mixing desk, console, panel
   The switching desk in the control room, (→) Regiekanzel.
Regieraum m
→ Regiekanzel
Regiewagen m (radio/TV) mobile control room (MCR)
Regiezentrale f (radio/TV) master control room
Regionalausgabe f (Zeitung/Zeitschrift) regional issue, regional edition, local issue, local edition, regional market edition, regional market issue
Regionalbelegung f **(Belegung** f **regionaler Medien)** (media planning) regional buy, regional media buy
regionale Methode f **(der Werbebudgetierung)** area-by-area allocation (ABA, A.B.A.) (of advertising budget), area allocation method (of advertising budget determination, market-by-market allocation (MBM, M.B.M.)
   A method of assigning an advertiser's media budget on a local basis in a manner proportionate to established or potential local sales of the advertiser's product or service.
regionaler Anzeigensplit m geographic split run
→ Anzeigensplit
regionaler Testmarkt m (market res) regional test market, local test market
→ Testmarkt

Regionalfernsehen n regional television, regional TV, local television, local TV
Regionalmarketing n regional marketing, local marketing
Regionalpresse f regional press, local press, regional newspapers pl
Regionalprogramm n (radio/TV) regional program, brit programme, sectional program, (Eigenprogramm eines Regionalsenders) station-produced program, (vom Sendernetz an Regionalsender zugeliefert) regional feed, sectional feed
Regionalsender m (radio/TV) regional market station, regional station, (regionales Sendernetz) regional network
Regionalwerbeplan m **(regionaler Werbeplan** m) regional advertising plan, regional plan, sectional advertising plan, sectional plan
Regionalwerbung f regional advertising, sectional advertising
Regionalzentrum n **(regionales Einkaufszentrum** n) (retailing) regional shopping center
   The largest among the various types of shopping centers, (→) Einkaufszentrum; in it one or more department stores, (→) Warenhaus, provide the main drawing power, supplemented by many smaller stores. They are set up to serve 100,000 to 250,000 people living in a radius of 10 to 20 kilometers, but may draw from much farther away. They are usually located outside a business district in an area of easy access by roads.
Regionalzeitung f regional newspaper, regional paper, sectional newspaper, sectional paper
   A newspaper intended to appeal to people in one geographical area.
Regisseur m (film/TV) director
Regisseur-Kameramann m (film/TV) director-cameraman
Register n (print) register; Register halten: v/i to register, to be in register, to be in correct alignment
   The perfect correspondence in printing; facing pages register (or are in register when their lines are even).
Registerbogen m (print) register sheet
Registerdifferenz f **(Passerdifferenz** f) (print) register difference
Registerhalten n (print) register, backup of lines, backup
→ Register

Registermachen n *(print)* registering, registration
→ Register
Registrierkasse f *(retailing)* cash register
Reglette f *(print)* lead, slug, (*meist pl* **Regletten**) furniture, metal furniture
Thin metal strips used to space out lines of type.
Regression f (**statistische Regression** f) *(stat)* regression, statistical regression
The correspondence of one of a pair of intercorrelated variables corresponding to a given value of the other variable.
→ Regressionsanalyse
Regressionsanalyse f *(stat)* regression analysis
A general term for the statistical procedures concerned with fitting a regression or prediction equation to data, estimating parameters, and testing hypotheses about the true relationship between the dependent or criterion variables and the independent or predictor variable(s).
Regressionseffekt m *(stat)* regression effect
Regressionsfunktion f *(stat)* regression function
Regressionsgerade f (**Regressionslinie** f) *(stat)* regression line, line of regression
Regressionsgleichung f *(stat)* regression equation
The equation that expresses the functional relationship between the means of a criterion variable and one or more predictor variables in regression analysis, (→) Regressionsanalyse.
Regressionskoeffizient m *(stat)* regression coefficient
In a linear regression between two variables, the average unit of change in the dependent variable associated with each unit of change in the independent variable. The regression coefficient is obtained by dividing the standard deviation, (→) Standardabweichung, of the dependent variable by the standard deviation of the independent variable and multiplying the quotient by the coefficient of correlation, (→) Korrelationskoeffizient. The regression coefficient defines the slope of the regression line, (→) Regressionsgerade, illustrating the relationship between the two variables.
Regressionskurve f *(stat)* regression curve, curve of regression

The curve illustrating the relationship between two variables in a nonlinear (curvilinear) regression equation, (→) Regressionsgleichung.
Regressionslinie f
→ Regressionsgerade
Regressionsmodell n *(econ/stat)* regression model
Regressionsrechnung f
→ Regressionsanalyse
Regressionsschätzung f *(stat)* regression estimate
An estimate of the value of a dependent variate obtained from substituting the known values of the independent variables in a regression equation, (→) Regressionsgleichung. The term has a particular application in sample surveys. If the regression of A on B may be estimated from a sample and the total of B is known for the population, the total of A may be estimated from the regression equation. It is then called a regression estimate.
Reiberdruck m
→ Einblattdruck
Reibungskalander m *(print)* friction calender
Reichweite f 1. *(media res)* coverage, media coverage, *colloq* cover, reach, audience penetration, audience *(radio/TV)* gross rating points *pl* (GRPs, G.R.P.s)
The percentage (proportion) of total households or individuals in a target audience who are estimated to be exposed to, (→) Kontakt, a specific advertising medium or advertisement(s) in a given area. Coverage is measured on the basis of sample surveys.
→ Bruttoreichweite, Nettoreichweite
2. → Sendebereich (Empfangsbereich)
Reichweitenanalyse f *(media res)* coverage analysis
Reichweitenanalytiker m (**Reichweitenforscher** m) *(media res)* coverage analyst, coverage researcher
Reichweitendaten n/pl *(media res)* coverage data *pl*
Reichweitenmessung f *(media res)* measurement of media coverages, coverage measurement
Reichweiten-Tausenderpreis m *(media planning)* cost per thousand exposures, cost per gross rating point (CPGRP, C.P.G.R.P.)
A variant of the cost per thousand, (→) Tausenderpreis, relating the CPM to one thousand exposures.

Reichweitenstudie f (**Reichweitenuntersuchung** f) *(media res)* coverage study, coverage investigation, media coverage investigation, audience study, audience investigation
Reichweitenüberschneidung f *(media res)* overlapping of audiences, overlapping of coverages
→ Überschneidung, externe Überschneidung, interne Überschneidung
Reichweitenuntersuchung f
→ Reichweitenstudie
Reichweitenvergleich m *(media res)* comparison of coverages, coverages comparison
Reichweitenzuwachs m *(media res)* coverage increase, audience increase
Reifephase f *(econ)* (im Produktlebenszyklus) maturity stage, product maturity
 The stage in the product life cycle following the introduction and growth phases. In this stage, the rapid growth of sales begins to slow while profits decline; the product's sales and profit curves reach their peaks. At the beginning of this stage, sales continue to grow (at a very slow rate though), towards the end, when the decline stage, (→) Degenerationsphase, draws nearer, they fall rapidly.
Reihe f 1. *(radio/TV/advtsg)* series, serial
 A sequence of connected dramatic episodes forming a continuous story and presented at regular intervals.
→ Serie
2. *(stat)* series
→ Häufigkeitsverteilung
3. *(print)* row
Reihenbild n *(phot)* sequence photograph, sequence photo, serial photograph, serial photo, mosaic photograph, mosaic photo
Reihenbildkamera f *(phot)* serial camera, automatic serial camera, sequence camera, automatic sequence camera, mosaic camera
Reihenfolge f sequence, order, succession, order of succession
Reihenfolgeeffekt m *(survey res)* order effect, serial effect, question order effect, effect of question order
 A change in the distribution or frequency of responses to a question either by the order in which the alternative answers are given to the respondent or by the position of the question after earlier questions on the topic.
Reihenkorrelation f (**Zweizeilenkorrelation** f) *(stat)* serial correlation
 The correlation, (→) Korrelation, between members of a time series, (→) Zeitreihe, and members of a corresponding time series lagged by a fixed interval of time.
Reihenwerk n
→ Fortsetzungsreihe, Serie, Schriftreihe
Reinabzug m
→ Reproabzug
Reinätzung f *(print)* final etching, clean etching, finishing etching
 An etching ready for printing in the form in which it will appear in print.
Reindruck m clean print, perfect impression, fair proof, clean impression
reine Textanzeige f
→ Textanzeige, Fließsatzanzeige
Reinerlös m *(econ)* net revenue, net proceeds pl
 The revenue, (→) Erlös, after all deductions.
Reingewinn m *(econ)* net profit
Reinschrift f *(print)* clean copy, fair copy
Reinlayout n *(print)* comprehensive layout, comprehensive, comp, master layout, finished layout, finished art, mechanical, keyline, art-type mechanical
 An advertising layout with illustration and lettering done as completely and expertly as in finished art. Also, a complete paste-up of all finished art and type proofs in the exact size of the printing plate.
Reinzeichner(in) m(f) *(advtsg)* draftsman, pl, draftsmen, draftswoman, pl draftswomen, auch draughtsman, draughtwoman, draughtswoman, draughtwomen
Reinzeichnung f *(advtsg)* finished art, finished artwork, finished drawing, final artwork, final drawing, camera-ready artwork
 Any art ready for reproduction in the form in which it will be seen by the public.
Reisebeilage f travel supplement
Reisebericht m (**Reisereportage** f,
Reisefilmbericht m) travelogue
Reisender m (**Handlungsreisender** m) *(econ)* salaried salesman, traveling salesman, manufacturer's agent, manufacturer's salesman,

Reise- und Bewirtungsspesen

manufacturer's salesperson, manufacturer's representative
  A manufacturer's employee fulfilling the function of a sales representative who receives commissions on sales made to wholesalers or retailers in a specified territory.
  vgl. Handelsvertreter
Reise- und Bewirtungsspesen f/pl *(accounting)* travel and entertainment (T and E, T & E)
  Both a type of business expense consisting of employees' expenditure for travel, meals, lodging, and client entertainment for business purposes and the budget an employer has established to pay for such expenses.
Reispapier n *(print)* rice paper, pith paper
Reißbrett n drawing board
reißerische Werbung f hype, hyped-up advertising
Reißfestigkeitstest m *(paper)* pop test
Reißschwenk m **(Wischer** m**)** *(film/ TV)* whip pan, whip shot, zip pan, whiz, swish, blur
  A very rapid form of panning, (→) Schwenk, i.e. a rapid transition shot replacing one image on the screen with another.
Reiz m **(Stimulus** m**)** *(psy)* stimulus
Reizdiskriminierung f **(Reizunterscheidung** f, **Reizdiskrimination** f**)** *(psy)* stimulus discrimination
Reizgeneralisierung f **(Stimulusgeneralisierung** f**)** *(psy)* stimulus generalization, *brit* generalisation
Reizintensität f **(Stimulusintensität** f**)** *(psy)* stimulus intensity
Reiz-Reaktions-Modell n **(S-R-Modell** n**)** *(psy)* stimulus-response model, S-R model
Reiz-Reaktions-Psychologie f **(S-R-Psychologie** f**)** stimulus-response psychology, S-R psychology
  → S-R-Modell
Reiz-Reaktions-Theorie f **(des Lernens)** *(psy)* stimulus-response theory (of learning), S-R theory (of learning)
  The theory that conceives learning to be a modification of the strength of associations, habits, or response tendencies.
  → S-R-Modell
Reizschwelle f **(eben merklicher Unterschied** m, **Unterschiedsschwelle** f**)** *(psy)* just noticeable difference (JND), difference threshold, difference limen (DL) absolute threshold, liminal difference
Reizwortanalyse f **(Reizwortmethode** f**)**
  → Assoziationsanalyse (Assoziationsverfahren)
Reklamation f *(econ)* complaint
Reklame f
  → Werbung
Reklame-
  → Werbe-, Werbungs-
Reklamegegenstand m **(von geringem Wert)**
  → Zugabeartikel
Reklamerummel m *(advtsg)* ballyhoo, boom
Reklamezeitschrift f
  → Anzeigenblatt
Rekompatibilität f reverse compatibility
Rekordationszahl f
  → Gedächtniserfolg
Relais n *(electr.)* relay
Relaissender m **(Relaisstation** f**)** *(radio/TV)* relay station, relay transmitter, rebroadcast transmitter
Relaisübertragung f **(Ballsendung** f**)** *(radio/TV)* rebroadcast
Relation f relation
Relationsanalyse f **(Relationsforschung** f, **Beziehungsanalyse** f**)** *(survey res)* relational analysis
Relationsbefragung f **(Relationsumfrage** f**)** *(survey res)* relational survey
  A survey in which each individual is identified by the specific others with whom he interacts and a sample is set up to include these role partners.
Relationsmerkmal n **(Relationscharakteristikum** n**)** *(survey res)* relational characteristic, relational property
relative Deprivation f **(relative Entsagung** f**)** relative deprivation (Samuel A. Stouffer/Robert K. Merton)
  Deprivation or disadvantage measured not by objective standards but by comparison with the relatively superior advantages of others, such as members of a reference group, (→) Bezugsgruppe, whom one desires to emulate.
relative Einkommenshypothese f *(econ)* relative-income hypothesis (J.S. Duesenberry)
  The hypothesis that consumer utility depends not on absolute amounts of

consumption but on the relation of these amounts to the consumption of others with whom the consumer feels in social competition or under pressure to conform.
vgl. Dauereinkommenshypothese
relative Häufigkeit f *(stat)* relative frequency
The ratio of a particular class frequency or cell frequency to the total number of items in a frequency distribution,
(→) Häufigkeitsverteilung.
relative Standardabweichung f
→ Variationskoeffizient
relative Varianz f *(stat)* relative variance, relvariance
The variance, (→) Varianz, of a distribution divided by the square of the arithmetic mean, (→) arithmetisches Mittel, thus

$$\text{relvariance} = \frac{\text{variance}}{\text{mean}}.$$

relativierter K_1-Wert m
→ Leser pro Ausgabe (LpA)
Relaunch m **(Revitalisierung** f**)**
→ Produktvariation
relevanter Produktmarkt m
(relevante Vergleichsmarken f/pl**)**
(econ) brand set, evoked set, consideration frame
The particular group of brands to which a consumer will limit the consideration of choice for purchase. Usually a small number of familiar, remembered, and acceptable brands, even though the total number of brands in the product category may be very large.
Reliabilität f
→ Zuverlässigkeit
Relief n relief
Reliefätzung f *(print)* relief etching
The process of etching out the nonprinting areas in a relief plate, (→) Reliefplatte.
Reliefdruck m 1. (Verfahren) relief printing, embossing 2. (Produkt) relief print
→ Hochdruck
reliefgeätzt(hochgeätzt) adj *(print)* relief-etched
Reliefplatte f **(Reliefklischee** n**)** *(print)* relief plate, relief-etched block
A printing plate in which the nonprinting areas have been etched or cut below the surface of the material, leaving the relief presentation of the design in positive form.
Reliefprägung f
→ Reliefdruck 1.

Remake n *(film)* remake
Remission f 1. *(media distribution)* returning (of unsold copies), returns pl
Copies of magazines, papers, or books returned to the publisher by a dealer or other distributor for credit. Frequently, to save transportation charges, complete copies are not returned but only paper headings or covers, (→) körperlose Remission.
2. *(radio)* reflectance, reradiation, reemission
remissionsberechtigt(remissionsfähig) adj *(media distribution)* returnable
Pertaining to copies of periodicals subject to credit if unsold and returned (whole copies or covers) by a distributor who purchased on terms of fully returnable (all unsold copies) or limited returnable (certain number or percentage of purchase)
Remissionsexemplar n **(Remissionsstück** n**)**
→ Remittende
Remittende f **(Remissionsexemplar** n**, Remissionsstück** n**)** *(media distribution)* return copy, return
→ Remission
Remittendenauflage f *(media distribution)* returns pl, number of returns, number of return copies
Remittendendurchschnitt m **(Remissionsrate** f**)** *(media distribution)* average number of returns, average number of return copies, return rate, rate of returns
Rentabilität f *(econ)* profitability, auch profitableness, return on investment(ROI)
The quality or state of yielding a profit, (→) Gewinn.
→ Kapitalertrag
Repertoire-Verfahren n *(survey res)* repertory grid technique, repertory grid
Repetierkopie f
→ Nutzenfilm
repliziertes Lesen n
→ gedehntes Lesen
Report m
→ Bericht
Reportage f news report, running commentary, news coverage, eyewitness report, on-the-spot account, spot report

Reportagefahrzeug n
→ Aufnahmewagen, Übertragungswagen
Reportagesendung f *(radio/TV)* on-the-spot broadcast, news report broadcast, live broadcast
→ Direktübertragung
Reportagewagen m
→ Aufnahmewagen, Übertragungswagen
Reporter(in) m(f) reporter, newsreporter, *colloq* legman
Repräsentant m *(econ)* representative
→ Handelsvertreter
Repräsentanz f **(Repräsentativität f)** *(stat)* representativeness
 The quality of a sample of any social aggregate which is sufficiently large and diversified to include all the major characteristics of the individuals composing the aggregate, in approximately the proportions found in the aggregate.
Repräsentationsschluß m **(Rückschluß** m) statistical inference
→ Inferenz, schließende Statistik
Repräsentationswerbung f **(Repräsentativwerbung f)**
→ Firmenwerbung, institutionelle Werbung, Prestigewerbung
repräsentativ adj representative
Repräsentativbefragung f **(repräsentative Befragung** f, **repräsentative Umfrage** f, **Repräsentativerhebung f)** *(survey res)* representative survey, cross-sectional survey
repräsentative Auswahl f **(repräsentatives Auswahlverfahren** n, **repräsentatives Stichprobenverfahren** n, **repräsentative Stichprobenbildung** f) *(stat)* representative sampling technique, representative sampling
 A sampling procedure which insures a high probability that all attributes found in a given sample will not differ significantly in quality or in proportionate quantity from the same attributes in the universe, (→) Grundgesamtheit, from which the sample, (→) Stichprobe, is selected.
repräsentative Stichprobe f **(repräsentative Auswahl** f) *(stat)* representative sample
 A sample that has essentially the same distribution of relevant characteristics as the population from which it was drawn.
repräsentativer Querschnitt m *(stat)* representative cross-section

Repräsentativität f
→ Repräsentanz
Repräsentativstichprobe f
→ repräsentative Stichprobe
Repräsentativwerbung f
→ Repräsentationswerbung
Reprint m **(Reprintausgabe f)**
→ Nachdruck
Reprise f *(film/TV)* rerun, reissue
Reproabzug m **(Repro** n, **reproduktionsfähiger Abzug** m) *(print)* repro proof, repro, reproduction proof, repro pull, etch proof
 A clean, sharp proof of type on fine quality paper used for reproduction by photoengraving or offset or gravure printing.
Reproduktion f *(phot/print)* reproduction
 Both the process of duplicating an original by photographic or photomechanical means and the copy or final impression obtained from the original by photoengraving procedure.
Reproduktionsdruck m reproduction printing
Reproduktionsdrucker m **(Reproduktionsphotograph** m) *(phot/print)* reproductionist
reproduktionsfähig (reprofähig, reproduktionsfertig) adj *(phot/print)* camera-ready (CR)
 Suitable for photographic reproduction on film, a printing plate, or the like.
reproduktionsfähige Vorlage f **(Reprovorlage** f) *(phot/print)* camera-ready copy, camera-ready material
Reproduktionsfilm m **(Reprofilm** m) *(phot)* reproduction film, repro film, (Offset) flat
Reproduktionsphotographie f **(Reproduktionsfotografie** f) reproduction photography
Reproduktionsgebühr f **(Nachdruckgebühr** f, **Abdruckhonorar** n) *(phot/print)* reproduction fee, reprint fee
 A fee that is payable to the owner of a copyright for the publication of a photograph, a cartoon or other piece of artwork.
Reproduktionsgerät n **(Reproduktionsapparat** m) *(phot/print)* reproduction device, reproduction machine
Reproduktionskamera f **(Reprokamera** f) *(phot/print)* reproduction camera, process camera

Reproduktionsrecht n **(Abdruckrecht** n, **Nachdruckrecht** n**)** reproduction right, copyright
reproduktionsreif
→ reproduktionsfähig
Reproduktionstechnik f **(Reproduktionsverfahren** n**)** *(phot/print)* reproduction technique, reproduction procedure, reproduction process
Reproduktionsvorlage f
→ Reproabzug, reproduktionsfähige Vorlage
reproduzieren v/t *(phot/print)* to reproduce, to copy
reprofähig
→ reproduktionsfähig
Reprograph m **(Reprograf** m**)** *(phot/print)* reprographer
Reprographie f **(Reprografie** f**)** *(phot/print)* reprography
Reprokamera f
→ Reproduktionskamera
reproreif
→ reproduktionsfähig
Reprotechnik f **(Reproverfahren** n**)**
→ Reproduktionstechnik
Reprovorlage f
→ Reproduktionsvorlage
Requisit n **(Requisite** f**)** *(film/TV)* property, prop, (Requisiten n + f/pl) properties pl, props pl, set dressings pl
  The physical properties needed for a motion picture, or television or still photograph production, such as room furnishings, paintings or other objects required by the script.
Requisitenfundus m **(Requisitenkammer** f**)** *(film/TV)* property store, property room, *colloq* props room
Requisitenreklame f **(Requisitenwerbung** f**)**
→ Produktplazierung
Requisiteur m *(film/TV)* property master, property man, *colloq* props man
Reservefonds m (für Werbung) advertising reserve, contingency fund
  An advertising budget fund established without a prior specification for its use, to be used subsequently for unanticipated contingencies.
Reservelager n *(econ)* (im Sortiment) reserve stock, back-up merchandise, buffer inventory
  Those goods in a retailer's stock that are held in reserve at some storage point removed from access to customers but available to personnel for restocking purposes.
Residualkategorie f **(Restkategorie** f**)** *(res)* residual category
Residualmethode f **(der Werbebudgetierung)** residual method of advertising budget determination, residual of previous year's surplus method
  A method of appropriating next year's advertising appropriation by taking the funds that are left over from the past year.
Resonanz f 1. *(marketing)* (von Umworbenen, Käufern) response 2. (Akustik) resonance, echo
→ Echo
Resonanzanalyse f **(Resonanzauswertung** f**)** *(market res)* response analysis, response investigation
Response-Funktion f
→ Reaktionsfunktion
Response-Marketing n
→ Direktmarketing
Response Set m
→ Reaktionseinstellung
Response-Werbung f
→ Rücklaufwerbung
Restauflage f 1. remainders pl, overstock, overruns pl
  The number of copies of a magazine, a paper, or a book that are produced in a printing job in excess of those eventually sold.
  2. (Audit Bureau of Circulations) all other, all other circulation (Auflage außerhalb des Kernverbreitungsgebietes)
  vgl. Stadtauflage
Rest-, Archiv- und Belegexemplare n/pl **(Reststücke** n/pl**)** (Zeitung/Zeitschrift) unpaid distribution, unpaid copies pl
  All copies distributed either entirely free or at a price inadequate to qualify them as paid in accordance with the rules.
Resteverkauf m remainders sale, remainders selling
Restexemplar n (Zeitung/Zeitschrift) unpaid copy
Restlicht n *(phot)* available light
Restlichtkamera f *(phot)* available light camera
Restlichtphotographie f *(phot)* available light photography
  A system of photography which uses whatever light happens to be available, without resorting to additional artificial light.

Restlichtverstärker *m (phot)* available light amplifier
Restvarianz *f* (**Residualvarianz** *f*) *(stat)* residual variance
 That part of the variance of a set of data which remains after the effect of systematic elements, such as treatments, is removed. It measures the variability due to unexplained causes or experimental error.
Retake *m*
 → Nachaufnahme
Retest-Methode *f*
 → Test-Retest-Methode
Retouche *f*
 → Retusche
Retouren *f/pl* (unzustellbare Direktwerbeaussendungen) *colloq* nixies *pl*
retrospektive Marktforschung *f* retrospective market research
 Research into past market developments and trends.
 vgl. adspektive Marktforschung, prospektive Marktforschung
Retusche *f* (**Retuschieren** *n*) *(phot)* retouching, retouch
 Correcting or improving photographs or other art work prior to the production of printing plates. It is a corrective treatment performed on photographic negatives and prints with pencils, crayons, airbrush and dyes for the elimination of flaws and imperfections, and for general improvement of the final result before plating.
retuschieren *v/t (phot)* to retouch, to touch up
 To make corrections or revisions on artwork, particularly photographs, by means of an artist's airbrush, handbrush, or other instrument, for better reproduction, (→) Wiedergabe.
Retuschierflüssigkeit *f* (**Retuschefarbe** *f*) *(phot)* retouching dye, retouching ink
 A special black or red dye used for retouching, (→) Retusche, (→) retuschieren, and spotting of negatives and prints.
Retuschierpult *n (phot)* retouching desk, retouching easel, retouching frame
Retuschiertechnik *f* (**Retuschierverfahren** *n*) *(phot)* retouching technique
Retuschierung *f*
 → Retusche
Retuschierverfahren *n*
 → Retuschiertechnik
Reusenantenne *f (electr.)* cage antenna, *brit* cage aerial

Revealed-preference-Theorie *f*
 → Theorie der faktischen Präferenz
Reverssystem *n (econ)* price guaranty system, guaranty against price decline
 → Preisgarantie
revidieren *v/t* to revise
Revision *f*
 → Überarbeitung, Maschinenrevision, Fahnenrevision, Marketingrevision
Revisionsabzug *m*
 → Maschinenrevision
Revisionsbogen *m*
 → Maschinenabzug
Revitalisierungs-Marketing *n* (**Remarketing** *n*) remarketing, revival marketing (Philip Kotler)
 The type of marketing that is required in a market configuration of faltering demand. It usually involves a complete reexamination of the market to be served, the product's or service's distinguishing features and its marketing strategy.
Revolverblatt *n* (**Revolverzeitschrift** *f*) *colloq* gutter paper, rag
 A sensationalist paper.
Revolvergriff *m (phot/film/TV)* pistol grip
Revolverkopf *m* (**Objektivrevolver** *m*) *(phot)* lens turret
Revolverkopfdrehung *f* (**Drehung** *f* **mit dem Objektivrevolver**) *(phot)* lens turret rotation, turret rotation
Rezeption *f (res)* reception
Rezessionsmarketing *n (econ)* recession marketing, anticyclical marketing
Rezipient *m* (**Empfänger** *m*) *(res)* recipient
Rezipientenforschung *f* recipient research
Reziprozität *f* reciprocity, reciprocation
Reziprozitätsgesetz *n (phot)* reciprocity law
 The phenomenon that illumination decreases can be compensated for by proportional increases in exposure time, (→) Belichtungszeit.
RF *abbr* Radiofrequenz
RFFU *f abbr* Rundfunk-Fernseh-Film-Union
Rheinisches Format *n (Zeitung)* etwa medium size
 One of three standard newspaper sizes in Germany, measuring 375 × 540 millimeters.

vgl. **Berliner Format, Nordisches Format**
Richtantenne f
→ Richtfunkantenne
Richtfunk m **(RiFu)** microwave link system, radio-link system, point-to-point radio system
Richtfunkantenne f **(Richtantenne** f**)** directional antenna, *brit* directional aerial, beam antenna, *brit* beam aerial
Richtfunknetz n microwave network, radio-link network, radio-relay network
Richtfunksender m **(Richtfunkstelle** f **)** microwave transmitter, point-to-point transmitter, link transmitter, microwave radio station, point-to-point radio station
Richtfunkstrahl m radio beam
Richtigstellung f **(Berichtigung** f**)** correction, rectification
Richtigstellungsanzeige f
→ Berichtigungsanzeige
Richtmikrofon n **(Richtmikrophon** n**)** directional microphone, unidirectional microphone, highly directional microphone
Richtpreis m **(empfohlener Preis** m**)** *(econ)* recommended price
→ Preisempfehlung
Richtstrahlansatz m
→ gezielte Streuung
Richtzahl f
→ Kennzahl
Ries n *(paper) etwa* ream, printer's ream
One thousand sheets of paper of any size or weight.
Riesenschlagzeile f screamer, banner headline, streamer
A large, bold headline covering all or nearly all of a page.
Rieshänge f *(paper)* peel
Riffel m **(Rille** f**)** *(paper)* flute
Riffelmuster n
→ Moiré 2.
Riffelpappe f **(Rillenpappe** f**)** fluted board, flute
Rille f **1.** *(film/TV)* (Beleuchtung) grid slot **2.** → Riffel **3.** (Schallplatte) groove
Rillendecke f *(film/TV)* (Beleuchtung) slotted grid, grid, *brit* runners pl
The metal girders or lattice suspending lights over a set.
Ringsendung f *(radio/TV)* multiplex broadcast
In broadcasting, the use of special equipment to transmit more than one program service from the same station, such as an FM station storecasting music and commercials to supermarkets and broadcasting regular programs to home listeners.
Rinnsal n
→ Gießbach
Rippe f **(Streifen** m**)** *(paper)* laid line
A watermark made by means of a dandy roller, (→) Egoutteur, with close parallel lines running at right angles to chain marks.
Risiko n risk
The probability of loss. Where a number of possible decisions have a loss function attached, the risk is the expected cost of the experimentation plus the expected value of the loss function.
Risikoanalyse f *(econ)* venture analysis
The analysis of the possible risks incurred in the introduction of a new product or service into the market.
Risikofunktion f *(stat)* risk function
The value of the risk taken for different decision functions, (→) Entscheidungsfunktion, in the theory of statistical decision-making.
Risikomanagement n *(econ)* venture management
The systematic evaluation of a new product idea and, if the product appears to have sufficient profit potential, the process of carrying it through to commercialization.
Risikoreduzierung f risk reduction
The general tendency of individuals to avoid some type of possible loss.
Risikoschub m **(Risikoschubphänomen** n**)** *(res)* risky shift, risky shift effect, risky shift phenomenon
The observation made in laboratory experiments that the integration of individuals in a group increases their willingness to take risks.
Risikoverhalten n *(psy/econ)* risk-taking, risk-taking behavior, *brit* risk-taking behaviour
A marketing function characterized by the presence of the possibility of losses inherent in the nature of economic activity.
Rißschwenk m
→ Reißschwenk
RMS-Körnigkeit f *(phot)* RMS granularity, root-mean-square granularity
Rogers-Skala f *(survey res)* Rogers scale
Rohabzug m
→ Probeabzug

Rohdaten *n/pl* (**unaufbereitete Daten** *n/pl*) *(res)* raw data *pl*
Rohdrehbuch *n* (**Drehbuchentwurf** *m*) *(film/TV)* draft script, preliminary shooting script, draft screenplay
Rohentwurf *m* (**Rohskizze** *f*, **Rohlayout** *n*) *(advtsg)* rough draft, rough, rough drawing, rough sketch, rough layout, raw draft, thumbnail sketch, thumbnail, scamp, (Kundenentwurf) client rough, clean rough
 A preliminary sketch or rough layout submitted for approval before the finished illustration or layout is completed.
Rohfassung *f* rough draft, rough form, (Drehbuch) working script, unpolished script
Rohfilm *m* (**unbelichteter Film** *m*) *(film)* raw stock, stock, raw film
 An unexposed or underdeveloped film.
Rohkopie *f (film)* slop print, *brit* slash print
 A rush print of the completed optical negative picture made to check mechanical errors.
Rohlayout *n*
→ Rohentwurf
Rohmaterial *n (econ)* raw material
Röhre *f* tube, valve
Röhrenblitz *m* (**Strobe** *m*, **Stroboskop** *n*) *(phot)* strobe, stroboscope, stroboscopic flash
 A multiple electronic flash illuminating a moving subject several times for exposure on a single piece of film.
Rohrklammer *f (film/TV)* (Scheinwerfer) scaffold clamp
Rohschnitt *m (film)* rough cut
 An initial assembly of scenes from work pictures in approximate length and order that have not gone through the final cutting process, and with the opticals indicated by china marker.
 vgl. Feinschnitt
Rohskizze *f*
→ Rohentwurf
Rohzahl *f* (**rohe Punktzahl** *f*, **unaufbereitete Punktzahl** *f*) *(stat)* raw score, raw number
Rokeachmodell *n* (**der Einstellungs-Verhaltens-Beziehung**) Rokeach model (of attitude-behavior relationship) (Milton Rokeach)
Rolle *f* **1.** → Papierrolle
2. → Filmrolle
3. → Buchbinderrolle
4. *(print)* (Roulette) roulette
 A finisher's tool comprising a handle bearing on one end a rotating wheel or knurl, thus possessing a serrated cutting pattern corresponding to the ruling of halftone screens.
5. *(film/TV)* (Darsteller) part, rôle, character **6.** (soziale Rolle) role, rôle, social role
Rollenbesetzung *f*
→ Besetzung
Rollenbreite *f (paper)* reel width, width of a reel of paper
Rollendruck *m (print)* roll-fed press printing, roll-fed printing, web-press printing, web printing
Rollendruckmaschine *f (print)* roll-fed press, web press
 A large, high-speed press such as are used for newspaper printing or other long run work. It is fed from rolls of paper instead of sheets, and the paper is festooned in and over and under the cylinders.
Rollenfolie *f (phot)* roll leaf, roll foil
Rollenkonflikt *m* role conflict, conflict of roles
Rollenlänge *f (paper)* roll length, length of a reel of paper
Rollenoffset *n* (**Rollenoffsetdruck** *m*) *(print)* web offset printing, web offset, roll-fed offset printing
Rollenoffsetmaschine *f* (**Rollenoffsetpresse** *f*) *(print)* web offset machine, web offset press
Rollenpapier *n (print)* web paper, reel paper, endless paper, continuous roll, *colloq* wallpaper
Rollenrotationspresse *f (print)* web-fed rotary press, reel-fed rotary press, roll-fed rotary
Rollenstempel *m (print)* roll tool, roulette
→ Rolle 4.
Rollenstruktur *f* (**Rollengefüge** *n*) role structure
Rollentext *m*
→ Rolltitel
Rollfilm *m (phot)* roll film, reel
Rollstativ *n (film/TV)* rolling tripod
Rollstempel *m*
→ Rollenstempel
Rolltitel *m (film/TV)* creeping title, creeper title, rolling title, roll title, rolling caption
 A title whose legends appear to pass into the screened image from the bottom and out through the top, as a result of the movement of a crawl roll, (→) Rolltitelgerät.

vgl. Standtitel
Rolltitelgerät *n* **(Rolltitelwalze** *f,*
Rolltitelmaschine *f) (film/TV)* crawl
roll, title roll
A drumlike mechanism on which the titles and credits of a film are mounted so that their position can be continuously altered in printing on successive frames in order to create a creeping title, (→) Rolltitel.
Romandruckpapier *n*
→ Werkdruckpapier
Rorschach-Test *m* **(Klecksographientest** *m)* (Hermann Rorschach) *(psy)* Rorschach test, Rorschach ink blot test, ink-blot test
A projective technique, (→) projektive Technik, originally used in clinical psychology. A series of standardized ink blots are presented to a subject, and he is asked to interpret what the blots look like. The test is occasionally used in motivation research, (→) Motivforschung.
Rosenzweigtest *m* **(Rosenzweig-P.F.-Test** *m,* **Bildenttäuschungstest** *m)* (Saul Rosenzweig) *(psy)* Rosenzweig picture-frustration test, Rosenzweig P.F. test, Rosenzweig test, picture-frustration test, P.F. test
A projective technique, (→) projektive Technik, originally used in clinical psychology for studying the way a person tends to direct blame and aggression in a frustrating situation. The subject is presented with a series of cartoons, each of which consists of a line drawing of a person in a frustrating situation, with the frustrated person's "balloon" empty, to be filled in by the subject taking the test. The subject fills in what he thinks the cartoon character is saying. Responses are classified according to whether the subject, identifying with the frustrated persons, tends to direct blame and aggression toward an external source (outside himself), blame himself, or be impersonal and objective. The test is occasionally used in motivation research, (→) Motivforschung.
Rost *m (film/TV)* (Gitter) grating, grid
Rotaprint *n*
→ Kleinoffset
Rotation *f (stat)* rotation
Rotationsauswahl *f* **(Rotationsstichprobenbildung** *f,* **Rotationsstichprobenverfahren** *n) (stat)* rotation sampling, rotation
Rotationsstichprobe *f* **(Rotationsauswahl** *f) (stat)* rotation sample

Rotationsdruck *m* **(Rotationsdruckverfahren** *n) (print)* rotary printing
→ Rotationspresse
Rotationsdruckmaschine *f*
→ Rotationspresse
Rotationshochdruck *m* **(Rotationsbuchdruck** *m) (print)* rotary letterpress printing
Rotationshochdruckmaschine *f* **(Rotationsbuchdruckmaschine** *f) (print)* rotary letterpress
Rotationsoffsetdruck *m* **(Rotationsoffset** *m) (print)* rotary offset printing, rotary offset
Rotationsoffsetdruckmaschine *f* **(Rotationsoffsetdruckpresse** *f) (print)* rotary offset printing press
Rotationspresse *f* **(Rotationsdruckmaschine** *f) (print)* rotary press, rotary machine, rotary
A press for high-speed and long-run printing that prints from plates on a revolving cylinder on which the printing surfaces are curved into cylindrical shape, rather than on a flat bed.
Rotationsschema *n* **(Rotationsplan** *m)* (in der Werbung) rotary plan, rotation plan, rotation (Außenwerbung) rotating bulletin boards *pl,* rotary plan, rotation plan, (obligatorisch) captive rotary plan, captive rotation, captive rotary
In general, an advertising scheme which consists of repeating a series of advertisements in the order in which they first appeared, after the entire showing has been run. In outdoor advertising, an arrangement whereby the advertiser's message is moved periodically to different preselected locations, rather than remaining on the same bulletin in one location for a year, to achieve exposure to a more varied audience.
Rotationstest *m (res)* rotation test, rotary test
Rotationstiefdruck *m (print)* rotogravure printing, rotogravure, roto
A high-speed gravure printing technique on a web-fed press using endless rolls of paper.
Rotationstiefdruckmaschine *f* **(Rotationstiefdruckpresse** *f) (print)* rotogravure press, rotary photogravure press
Rotlicht *n* **(Warnleuchte** *f) (radio/film/TV)* red light, warning light
Rotplatte *f (print)* red plate

Rough *m*
→ Rohentwurf
Roulett *n*
→ Rolle 4.
Routinemanagement *n (econ)* routine management
Rubrikanzeige *f* (**rubrizierte Anzeige** *f*, **Kleinanzeige** *f*) classified advertisement, classified ad
  A type of newspaper or magazine advertisement that appears in special columns on pages where the advertising is assembled by product or service. Usually the selection of type faces and sizes is very limited, as is the freedom of layout.
rubrizierte Großanzeige *f* (**rubrizierte Formatanzeige** *f*) classified display advertisement, classified display ad, semi-display advertisement, semi-display ad
  An advertisement combining the grouping advantages of classified advertising with the freedom of display advertising. It appears in the classified section of a newspaper or magazine with lines of type displayed in different widths and in type of different sizes and weights and in a subsection devoted to only one product or service or type of product or service.
rubrizierte Kleinanzeige *f*
→ Rubrikanzeige, Kleinanzeige
Rückantwortkarte *f* (**Antwortkarte** *f*) reply card, return card, *colloq* bingo card
  Usually, a self-addressed postcard sent with advertising to encourage customer inquiries or orders.
Rückantwortschein *m* (**Rückantwortgutschein** *m*) reply coupon, return coupon
→ Kupon
Rückblende *f (film/TV)* flashback, cutback
  The interruption of development of the main action of a drama in the form of an episode or scene from a previous time.
Rückenbeleuchtung *f*
→ Hintergrundbeleuchtung
Rückenheftung *f* (**Rückenbindung** *f*) *(bookbinding)* saddle stitching, saddleback stitching
  A method of binding a publication, usually a magazine or a periodical, by fastening the pages through the middle fold of the sheets either with staples or with wire.
Rückenklappe *f*
→ Umschlagklappe

Rückenplakat *n* (**Rückenschild** *n*) *(POP advtsg)* backer card
Rückenstichheftung *f* (**Rückenstichbroschur** *f*) *(bookbinding)* saddle-wire binding, saddle stitching, (mit Faden) saddle sewing
→ Rückenheftung
Rückerinnerung *f*
→ Erinnerung
Rückerstattung *f* (**Rückvergütung** *f*, **Rückzahlung** *f*) *(econ)* refund, rebate
  The return of some or all of an amount of money exchanged for the purchase of goods or services, issued by the seller.
Rückfahrt *f (film/TV)* tracking back, tracking out, back-track
Rückflächenschild *n* (**Rückflächenplakat** *n*)
→ Heckplakat
Rückfrage *f*
→ Nachfaßfrage
Rückgabegarantie *f* (**Rücknahmegarantie** *f*) *(econ)* money-back guaranty, money-back guarantee, money back, refund offer
  The attempt of assuring customer satisfaction, (→) Käuferzufriedenheit, by pledging the full return of payment if customers are not satisfied with the product or service they purchased.
Rückgangsstadium *n* (**Rückgangsphase** *f*) *(im Produktlebenszyklus)*
→ Degenerationsphase
Rückkoppelung *f* (**Rückkopplung** *f*, **Rückmeldung** *f*) *(cybernetics)* feedback
  In marketing communication, the response or reaction of recipients to a communication which tells the sender how his message is being interpreted.
Rückkoppelungsschleife *f*
(cybernetics) feedback loop
Rücklauf *m* **1.** *(direct marketing)* (Rückläufer) return
  The direct response by a member of a target audience to an advertiser in consequence of an advertisement, a sales offer, contest, or coupon promotion.
→ Rückläufe
2. → Bildrücklauf
Rücklaufausstattung *f* (**Bildrücklaufausstattung** *f*) *(TV)* blanking, flyback suppression
Rückläufe *m/pl (direct marketing/ survey research)* returns *pl*, response
  Both the number of direct responses by members of a target audience to an advertiser in consequence of an advertisement, a promotion campaign, a

sales offer, a contest, or a coupon promotion and the number of persons in a predesignated sample who provide useful imformation.
Rückläufer m
→ Rücklauf 1.
Rücklaufkanal m *(cybernetics)* feedback channel
Rücklaufquote f **(Rücklaufrate** f**)** *(direct marketing/survey res)* return rate, rate of returns
The proportion (percentage) of returns, (→) Rückläufe, in the total number of possible returns.
Rücklaufsignal n *(TV)* (Abtastung) blanking signal, flyback signal
Rücklaufstrahl m *(TV)* flyback beam
Rücklauftrick m **(Bildrücklauftrick** m**)** *(film/TV)* reverse-motion effect, reverse-running effect, reverse-shot effect (RevS effect)
Rücklaufwerbung f **(Direct-Response-Werbung** f**)** direct response advertising
All advertising which attempts to obtain orders for purchase to be made directly to the manufacturer or servicer, rather than through agents, stores, or other dealers, or to encourage other forms of direct response to advertising, such as redeeming coupons, (→) Kupon, sending in return cards or enquiries, etc.
Rückleitung f *(TV)* flyback circuit, return circuit
Rückmeldung f
→ Rückkopplung
Rücknahmeverpflichtung f
→ Rückgabegarantie
Rückpro f
→ Rückprojektion
Rückprojektion f **(Rückpro** f**)** *(film/TV)* rear projection(R.P., RP), rear-screen projection, process-screen projection, background projection(B.P., BP), back projection
The technique of providing a background for a motion picture or television scene by projecting a scene on a screen in the background of the set.
Rückprojektor m *(film/TV)* rear projector, rear-screen projector, process-screen projector, background projector, back projector *(TM)* translux
A rear-screen projector used to project slides or film for background scenes or special effects.
Rückproschirm m **(Rückprowand** f**)** *(film/TV)* rear-projection screen,
background-projection screen, back-projection screen, process-projection screen, translucent screen, background plate
A still or motion picture film prepared especially for projection as the background against which the action in the foreground is photographed.
Rückseite f *(print)* reverse page
Rückseitentext m
→ Umschlagtext
Rücksende-Freiumschlag m self-addressed envelope
Rücksendung f return mailing, return
Rücksetzer m *(film/TV)* backprojected picture
Rückspulung f *(film/phot)* rewinding, rewind
Both the process of transferring film from one reel to another and the winding of the film onto the original reel after screening it.
Rückstand m **(Zahlungsrückstand** m**)** *(econ)* arrears *pl;* im Rückstand sein: to be in arrears
Rückstichheftung f
→ Rückenstichheftung
Rückstrahler m **(Katzenauge** n**)** *(outdoor advtsg)* reflector button, reflection button
→ Reflektor
Rückvergütung f *(econ)* rebate
Any refund of payment, e.g. one made by an advertising medium to an advertiser on account of a discount, (→) Rabatt, earned beyond that originally anticipated.
Rückwärtsgang m
→ Bildrücklauf
Rückwärtsintegration f **(vertikale Diversifikation** f**)** *(econ)* vertical diversification
vgl. Vorwärtsintegration
Ruf m **(Reputation** f**)** reputation, repute
Rumpffläche f *(transit advtsg)* car side, bus side, side panel
Any advertising space outside a vehicle of public transportation.
Rumpfflächenbemalung f *(transit advtsg)* painted bus side, painted car side
→ Rundum-Ganzbemalung
Rumpfflächenposition f *(transit advtsg)* bus side position, bus side, side position

Rumpfflächenwerbung f outside transit advertising, bus side advertising, side panel
→ Rumpffläche
Rundbild n
→ Panoramabild
Rundbrief m (**Rundschreiben** n) circular letter, circular
A printed piece of advertising sent out by mail.
Rundfunk m (**Rundfunkwesen** n) (radio/TV) broadcasting
All transmissions of over-the-air radio or television signals.
vgl. Netzfunk
Rundfunkansage f (**Rundfunkdurchsage** f) (radio/TV) broadcast announcement
→ Ansage
Rundfunkanstalt f
→ Rundfunkgesellschaft
Rundfunkapparat m (**Rundfunkgerät** n) (radio/TV) broadcasting receiver, receiver, set, wireless receiver, wireless set, wireless
Rundfunkarchiv n (radio/TV) broadcasting archives pl, broadcasting library
Rundfunkbranche f (**Rundfunkwesen** n) (radio/TV) broadcasting industry
Rundfunkdurchsage f
→ Rundfunkansage
Rundfunkempfänger m
→ Rundfunkapparat
Rundfunkforschung f (radio/TV) broadcasting research, broadcast research
→ Hörerforschung, Zuschauerforschung
Rundfunkgebühr f (radio/TV) broadcasting reception fee, broadcast receiver license fee, brit licence fee
Rundfunkgerät n
→ Rundfunkapparat
Rundfunkgesellschaft f (radio/TV) broadcasting corporation, broadcasting company
Rundfunkhörer m
→ Hörer
Rundfunkhörerforschung f
→ Hörerschaftsforschung
Rundfunkhörerschaft f
→ Hörerschaft
Rundfunkkommentar n (radio/TV) broadcast commentary
Rundfunk-Kommunikation f (radio/TV) broadcast communication

Rundfunkmedium n (radio/TV) broadcasting medium, broadcast medium
Rundfunknetz n (radio/TV) broadcasting network, broadcasting system
Rundfunkprogramm n (radio/TV) broadcast program, brit programme, broadcast show
Rundfunkrecht n (radio/TV) broadcasting legislation, broadcasting law, broadcasting regulations pl
Rundfunksatellit m (**Sendesatellit** m) (radio/TV) broadcast satellite
→ Nachrichtensatellit
Rundfunksender m (radio/TV) broadcasting station, broadcasting station, broadcaster, (Übertragungssender) broadcasting transmitter, broadcast transmitter
Rundfunksendung f (radio/TV) broadcast program, brit programme, broadcast show, aircast, broadcast transmission
Rundfunkspot m
→ Hörfunkspot
Rundfunksprecher(in) m(f) (**Rundfunkansager** m) (radio/TV) broadcast announcer, broadcast speaker, broadcaster
→ Ansager, Sprecher
Rundfunkstation f
→ Rundfunksender
Rundfunkübertragung f (radio/TV) broadcast transmission, broadcasting transmission
Rundfunkwelle f (**Sendewelle** f) (radio/TV) broadcasting wave, broadcast wave
Rundfunkwerbekampagne f (**Rundfunkkampagne** f) (radio/TV) broadcast media campaign, broadcast advertising campaign
Rundfunkwerbesendung f (radio/TV) broadcast commercial, commercial
→ Werbesendung
Rundfunkwerbung f (**Funkwerbung** f) (radio/TV) broadcast advertising, broadcast media advertising
Rundfunkwerbungtreibender m (radio/TV) broadcast advertiser
Rundfunkzeitschrift f
→ Programmzeitschrift
Rundgalvano n (**Rundstereo** n) (print) curved electrotype, curved electro
→ Rundklischee

Rundhorizont m **(Zyklorama** n,
Rundhintergrund m**)** *(film/TV)*
cyclorama, *colloq* cyc
   A curved backdrop used to give the effect
   of sky or distance.
Rundklischee n *(print)* curved
printing block, curved block, curved
engraving, curved plate, curved cut
   A printing plate, used in letterpress
   printing, which is backed up and curved
   to fit a rotary press, (→) Rotationspresse.
Rundschreiben n
→ Rundbrief

Rundschreibenversand m mailing of
circular letters, circularization

Rundschwenk m
→ Panoramaschwenk

Rundstereo n
→ Rundgalvano
Rundstrahlantenne f *(electr.)* omnidirectional antenna, *brit* omnidirectional aerial
Rundumbemalung f **(Rundumstreifen**
m**)** *(transit advtsg)* waistband
   A narrow band of advertising space
   which goes round the outside of a public
   transportation vehicle.
Rundum-Ganzbemalung f *(transit
advtsg)* transit spectacular, painted
bus
   An advertising display occupying all
   sides on the outside of a public-transit
   vehicle.
Rushprint m
→ Musterkopie

S

S-Faktor m *(spezifischer Faktor* m*)*
(stat) s factor, S factor, specific factor
vgl. G-Faktor
S-Kurve f
→ Ogive
sachbezogene Marktforschung f
→ ökoskopische Marktforschung
Sachgüter n/pl *(econ)* material goods pl
→ Produkt
sachliche Wirkungsübertragung f
→ Spill-over-Effekt
Sachmittelwerbung f *(***Sachwerbung** f*) etwa* above-the-line advertising, advertising media advertising, media advertising, theme advertising
 A collective term for all types of traditional advertising in commission-paying media and advertising using other material advertisements such as posters, flyers, handbills etc., in contrast to all types of personal advertising, (→) persönlicher Verkauf, word-of-mouth advertising, (→) Mundwerbung, and public relations, (→) Öffentlichkeitsarbeit.
Sachtrick m *(film)* live animation
 The imparting of motion to photographed objects.
Sachtrickfilm m *(film)* live animation cartoon, live animation film
→ Sachtrick
saisonale Werbung f *(***Saisonwerbung** f*)* seasonal advertising
saisonaler Marktanteil m *(econ)* seasonal market share
Saisonartikel m *(***Saisongüter** n/pl, **Saisonware** f*) (econ)* seasonal article, seasonal goods pl, seasonal merchandise
 All types of merchandise that serve to meet customer demand at specific seasons of the year, e.g. winter clothing, bikinis, sun tan oil, etc.
Saisonausgabe f *(***Saisonheft** n*)* (Zeitschrift) boom issue
 A special issue of a periodical publication, frequently enlarged with a free supplement or giveaway, devoted to seasonal topics, e.g. gardening in the spring.

Saisonausverkauf m *(***Saisonschlußverkauf** m*) (retailing)* seasonal closing-out sale
Saisonbereinigung f *(***Saisonausschaltung** f*) (stat)* seasonal adjustment
 The elimination of seasonal variation from the trend in a time series, (→) Zeitreihe.
Saisonindex m *(***Saisonindexzahl** f, **Saisonindexziffer** f*) (stat)* seasonal index, seasonal index number, seasonal index figure
Saisonkomponente f *(***saisonale Komponente** f*) (stat)* (einer Zeitreihe) seasonal component, seasonal factor
 The component of a time series, (→) Zeitreihe, that exhibits seasonal variation, (→) Saisonschwankung, which gives rise to this variation.
Saisonkorridor m *(stat)* high-low graph
 A graph used to depict ranges of variation in successive intervals of time.
Saisonpreis m *(econ)* seasonal price
Saisonrabatt m *(econ)* seasonal discount
 A discount offered at seasons of slump to encourage business.
Saisonschlußverkauf m *(***Inventurverkauf** m, **Schlußverkauf** m*)*
→ Saisonausverkauf
Saisonschwankung f *(stat)* seasonal fluctuation, seasonal variation
 That part of the movement in a time series, (→) Zeitreihe, which is assigned to the effect of the seasons of the year, e.g. seasonal variation in sales. Sometimes the term is used in wider sense relating to oscillations generated by periodic external influences.
Saisonverkauf m
→ Saisonausverkauf
Saisonwerbung f
→ saisonale Werbung
Sakkade f *(res)* saccade
→ Blickregistrierung
Salat m *(film) colloq* pile-up, rip-up
Salatschalter m *colloq (film)* cut-out switch

Salesfolder m
→ Verkaufsförderungsmappe
Salesportfolio n
→ Verkaufsförderungsmappe
Sales Promoter m
→ Verkaufsförderer
Sales Promotion f
→ Verkaufsförderung
Sammelabonnement n **(Listenauswahlabonnement** n**)** club subscription, clubbing
A magazine subscription practice which allows potential subscribers to choose several magazines from an inclusive list at reduced rates.
Sammelabonnementswerber m (Zeitschrift) club raiser
Sammelanzeige f
→ Kollektivanzeige
Sammelbefragung f
→ Omnibusbefragung
Sammelbesteller m 1. *(econ)* in-home seller, nonstore retailer, party-plan seller
→ Sammelbestellsystem
2. → Sammelabonnementswerber
Sammelbestellsystem n **(Sammelbestellerverkauf** m**)** *(econ)* in-home selling, in-home retailing, nonstore retailing, party-plan selling, party selling
A type of distribution network through selling agents operating from their homes, taking in orders from neighbors and sending them in to the mail-order house which, in turn, sends the products to the agent who ordered them.
Sammelbezug m (Zeitschrift) bulk subscription, bulk sales *pl,* single copy sales in bulk *pl,* group subscription
The subscription of large quantities of a publication bought for redistribution.
Sammelbezugspreis m (Zeitschrift) bulk rate
Sammelbild n *(promotion)* (Zugabe) continuity picture
Sammelgutschein m *(promotion)* continuity coupon, patronage coupon
Sammelkatalog m collective catalog, *brit* catalogue
Sammellinse f *(phot)* collecting lens, condenser lens, convergent lens, converging lens
Sammelmethode f
→ Sekundärforschung

Sammelpackung f **(Sammelgebinde** n**)** multipack, multi-unit pack, multiple-unit pack, collation pack
→ Mehrproduktpackung
Sammelplakat n collective advertising poster
Sammelpostabonnement n (Zeitschrift) group mail subscription
Subscriptions in quantities to corporations, institutions or individuals for employes, subsidiary companies or branch offices.
Sammelrevers m **(Sammelreverssystem** n**)**
→ Reverssystem
Sammelverkäufe m/pl
→ Sammelbezug
Sammelwerbung f **(offene Kollektivwerbung** f**)** association advertising, collective advertising
→ Kollektivwerbung
Sammelzugabe f *(promotion)* continuity premium
The offering by a retailer of a number of related premiums, (→) Zugabe, at regular intervals over a period of time.
Sample n
→ Stichprobe
Sampling n
→ Auswahlverfahren, Stichprobenbildung
Sandwichmann m
→ Plakatträger
Satellit m satellite
Satellitenantenne f satellite antenna, *brit* satellite aerial
Satellitenbahn f orbit
Satellitenerdverbindung f **(Erdverbindung** f**)** satellite earth-link
Satellitenfernsehen n satellite television, satellite TV
Satellitenkommunikation f satellite communication
Satellitennetz n satellite network
Satellitenrundfunk m **(Satellitenfunk** m**)** broadcasting by satellite, broadcasting via satellite
Satellitensender m satellite transmitter
Satellitenstrecke f **(Satellitenfunkstrecke** f **)** satellite link, satellite circuit
Satellitenübertragung f satellite transmission, transmission by satellite, transmission via satellite
Satinage f **(Satinieren** n, **Satinierung** f **)** *(paper)* calendering, glazing

satinieren v/t (paper) to calender, to glaze

Satinierkalander m **(Satinierpresse** f) (paper) glazing calender, glazing press, calender

satiniert adj (paper) glazed, calendered

satiniertes Papier n glazed paper, calendered paper, sized and calendered paper
 Machine-finished paper that has been given a chemical coating to reduce porosity and extra ironing to insure a smooth surface.

Satinierung f
→ Satinage

Satisfizierung f satisficing
 In general, the search for good rather than for best solutions. More specifically, a policy of management which attempts to achieve results which the company's publics will accept as satisfactory, particularly the stockholders as regards profit and the government as regards market performance. Thus a price may be set which does not maximize profit but does produce a satisfactory one.
→ Optimierung

Satisfizierungsmodell n satisficing model
→ Optimierungsmodell

Sattel m (print) (Schriftguß) bed

Sattelheftung f
→ Rückenstichheftung

Sättigung f (econ) saturation, satiation
 The stage in the market development for a product or service in which the majority of sales are to replace the product owned with a new one of the same kind. Characterized by high segmentation, (→) Segmentation, competitive cost structure, trade-ins, stabilized competition, and high entry barriers. It is a level at which any further expansion of distribution in a market is unlikely to be achieved, and further sales are restricted to the potential arising from replacement needs, (→) Erneuerungsbedarf, or population growth.
→ Sättigungsphase

Sättigungsabsatz m (econ) saturation sales pl, satiation sales pl

Sättigungsfunktion f (econ) growth saturation function, saturation function

Sättigungsgrad m
→ Sättigungsniveau

Sättigungsgrenze f **(Wachstumsgrenze** f) (econ) saturation limit, growth limit, saturation line
→ Wachstumsfunktion

Sättigungskurve f (econ) growth saturation curve, saturation curve
→ Wachstumskurve

Sättigungsmenge f (econ) saturation quantity
→ Sättigung

Sättigungsniveau n **(Wachstumsgrenze** f) (econ) saturation level, growth saturation limit, satiation level
→ Sättigung

Sättigungsphase f **(Phase** f **der Marktsättigung)** (econ) (im Produktlebenszyklus) saturation stage
→ Sättigung

Sättigungsprozeß m (econ) saturation process
→ Sättigung

Sättigungspunkt m (econ) saturation point, growth saturation point

Sättigungsreichweite f **(hundertprozentige Reichweite** f) (media res) saturation coverage, saturation, blanket coverage, satiation coverage, satiation, (outdoor advtsg) saturation, showing, supersaturation showing, 100 showing, one hundred showing, hundred showing, number 100 showing, 150 showing, number 150 showing

Sättigungsreichweitenwerbung f **(Sättigungswerbung** f) saturation advertising, saturation, satiation advertising, satiation
 An amount and intensity of advertising well above the normal levels of frequency and coverage.

Satz m **(Schriftsatz** m) 1. (print) typesetting, setting, type composition, composition, setting-up
 The process and techniques of setting type and assembling it with engravings.
 2. (print) (das Gesetzte) type, matter, live matter
 The composed type.
 3. → Satzvorlage
 4. (Gruppe zusammengehöriger Teile) set
 A collection or group of related items, product units, etc.

Satzabzug m
→ Korrekturabzug

Satzanordnung f (print) typographical arrangement, typographical layout, arrangement of type

Satzanweisung f (**Satzauszeichnung** f) (print) job ticket, typesetting instruction, setting instruction, composition instruction, instruction for the compositor, markup, (für eine Anzeige) copy order;
A card or envelope with complete instructions that accompanies a printing job through all departments and provides records on the progress of the work.

Satzanweisung schreiben: to specify type, to spec type, to type spec
To specify the faces and sizes of type to be used in composition work for a piece of copy or text.

Satzanzeige f publication-set type advertisement, publication-set type ad, paper-set advertisement, paper-set ad, pub-set ad
An advertisement with type or other printing materials set or prepared by the periodical in which it is run rather than supplied in some form by the advertiser or his agency.
vgl. Klischeeanzeige

Satzberechnung f (**Satzumfangsberechnung** f) (print) copy casting, copy fitting, fitting copy, copy scaling, casting off
Counting the number of characters or words in a piece of copy in order to determine how much space it will require if set in a specified type face and size. The same procedure is used to determine the amount of copy needed to fill a fixed amount of space.

Satzbild n
→ Satzanordnung

Satzblock m
→ Textblock

Satzbreite f (**Satzspiegelbreite** f) (print) measure, full measure
vgl. Spaltenbreite

Satzergänzungstest m (res) sentence-completion test
A projective method, (→) projektive Technik, wherein a subject is given the first few words of a possible sentence and is asked to complete it with the first words coming to mind, the idea being that the type of completions to a number of such sentences will supposedly give the researcher clues to the nature of the subject's underlying motivations.

Satzergänzungstestmethode f (**Satzergänzungsmethode** f) (res) sentence-completion technique, sentence completion
→ Satzergänzungstest

Satzfehler m
→ Setzfehler

Satzfläche f
→ Satzspiegel

Satzgestaltung f (print) typographical design

Satzhöhe f (**Satzspiegelhöhe** f) (print) depth of page, depth of type area
The top-to-bottom length of a column in a periodical, measured in centimeters.
vgl. Spaltenhöhe

Satzkosten pl
→ Setzkosten

Satzmuster n (**Satzprobe** f) (print) sample of type, composition sample

Satzprobe f
→ Probeseite

Satzschiff n
→ Setzschiff

Satzskizze f
→ Layout

Satzspiegel m (print) type area, typing area, type page, printing space, printing area
The area of a page that is occupied by type, in other words the page size less margins.

Satzspiegelbreite f
→ Satzbreite

Satzspiegelhöhe f
→ Satzhöhe

Satzstück n
→ Textblock

Satztiefe f
→ Satzhöhe

Satztisch m
→ Setztisch

Satzumfangsberechnung f
→ Satzberechnung

Satzvorbereitung f (print) copy preparation

Satzvorlage f
→ Setzvorlage

Satzvorschrift(en) f(pl)
→ Setzvorschriften

saugfähig adj (paper) absorbent

saugfähiges Papier n (**Saugpost** f, **Saugpostpapier** n) absorbent paper

Säulendiagramm n
→ Stabdiagramm

Säure f acid

Säurebad n (print) acid bath
The solution in which metal gets its "bite" during an etch.

Savage-Niehans-Regel f
→ Minimax-Regret-Regel

Say'sches Theorem n (Theorem n von Say) *(econ)* Say's theory, Say's hypothesis (Jean Baptiste Say)
The theorem that production creates not only the supply of goods but also the demand for them.

SB *abbr* Selbstbedienung

SB-Großhandel m
→ Selbstbedienungsgroßhandel

SB-Laden m
→ Selbstbedienungsladen

SB-Lebensmittelmarkt m **(SB-Markt** m**)**
→ Selbstbedienungsmarkt

SB-Warenhaus n
→ Selbstbedienungswarenhaus, Verbrauchermarkt

SB-Zentrum n
→ Selbstbedienungszentrum

Scanner n scanner
In general, any device that automatically checks a process or condition and may initiate a desired corrective action. More specifically, a photoelectrically operated device for sensing recorded data.

Scanning n scanning
→ scanner

Schabekarton m
→ Schabkarton

Schabemanier f
→ Schabmanier, Schabkunst

Schabemesser n
→ Schabmesser

Schabetechnik f
→ Schabmanier

Schabkarton m **(Schabekarton** m**, Kreideschabpapier** n**)** scratchboard paper, scraper board
A special drawing board coated with India ink, on which the artist scratches his design in white with a stylus.

Schabkunst f **(Schabekunst** f**, Schabmanier** f**, Schabemanier** f**)** scratchboard technique, mezzotinto technique, mezzotinto, mezzotint technique, mezzotinto, mezzotint engraving, mezzotint engraving
A drawing technique in which a white surface is painted black and then scratched to let the white show through.

Schabkunstblatt n **(Schabekunstblatt** n**, Mezzotintoblatt** n**)** mezzotinto print, mezzotinto, mezzotint print, mezzotint, mezzotinto engraving, mezzotint engraving
→ Schabkarton

Schabkunstzeichnung f scratchboard drawing, scraperboard drawing,
mezzotinto drawing, mezzotinto, mezzotint drawing, mezzotint
→ Schabkunst

Schablone f **1.** *(print)* (beim Siebdruck) stencil **2.** (Modell, Muster) model pattern **3.** (Kopierschablone) former plate, master **4.** (zum Zeichnen von Buchstaben) template

Schablonendruck m *(print)* stencil duplicating, stencil printing
→ Siebdruck, Vervielfältigungsverfahren

Schabloneneinblendung f *(TV)* overlay insertion

Schablonenmuster n *(TV)* (für Scheinwerfer) projection cut-out

Schablonentrick m *(film/TV)* overlay
The use of a sheet of acetate, used in animation, on which a motion is drawn subsequent to that shown in the original drawing.

Schabmanier f
→ Schabkunst

Schachbrettanzeige f checkerboard advertisement, checkerboard ad, checkerboard
A special type of flexform advertising whereby magazine advertising units consist of diagonally placed quarter or half pages, alternating with editorial text.

Schachmustertestbild n *(TV)* checkerboard test pattern

Schachtel f *(packaging)* **1.** box **2.** (flache, weiche) pack, packet **3.** (Karton) carton

Schachtelbild n *(film/TV)* composite shot, half-lap, split frame, split screen, split shot
An optical effect in which two or more different but complete scenes are shown simultaneously in different areas of the screen.

Schachtelkarton m **(Schachtelpappe** f **)** *(packaging)* boxboard, box board
A grade of heavy paper suitable for folding into boxes.

Schachtelpappe f *(packaging)* (aus Papierabfällen) chipboard
A coarse grade of cardboard made from paper waste, sometimes covered with a paper of a higher grade.

Schall m **1.** (Ton) sound **2.** (Geräusch) noise **3.** → Klangfülle **4.** → Hall, Widerhall

Schallaufnahme f **(Schallaufzeichnung** f **)**
→ Tonaufnahme

Schallblende f (**Schallschirm** m, **Schallschutz** m) *(radio/TV/film)* gobbo, gobo, baffle, baffle board, acoustic baffle
  A sound-absorbent screen used to deaden echoes while a motion picture, a radio or television program is being made.
Schalldämpfung f sound damping, sound absorption, sound deadening
Schalldichtung f sound insulation
Schalleffekt m
  → Geräuscheffekt
Schallfolie f acetate, cellulose acetate
  An individually recorded phonograph disc, as opposed to one pressed to reproduce a master.
Schallplatte f (**Schallplattenaufnahme** f) record, disc, disk, disc recording, disk recording, recording, grammophone record, phonograph record, *colloq* platter
Schallplattenhülle f record sleeve, disc record sleeve, disk record sleeve, sleeve
  A protective casing for a disk.
Schallplattenmatrize f master matrix
  A disc recording of all elements of a performance in complete and final form to be used as an original for reproduction and release.
Schallplattenmusik f record music, recorded music, disc record music, disk record music, *colloq* platter music, grams *pl*
Schallplattenspieler m
  → Plattenspieler
Schallplattenwerbung f record advertising, disc record advertising, disk record advertising
Schallquelle f sound source, sound generator
Schallträger m sound recording medium
Schallvolumen n sound volume, volume
Schallwand f
  → Schallblende
Schallwelle f sound wave
Schaltbild n (**Schaltplan** m) wiring diagram, circuit diagram, switching diagram
Schaltbrett n *(radio/TV)* switchboard, distribution board, control panel, switch panel
Schalter m *(radio/TV)* switch
Schaltfehler m *(radio/TV)* switching error

Schaltfrequenz f *(radio/TV)* switching frequency, sampling frequency
Schaltgerät n *(radio/TV)* switchgear
Schaltkasten m *(radio/TV)* switch box, switch enclosure
Schaltkonferenz f circuit conference, hook-up
Schaltkreis m *(electr.)* circuit
Schaltplan m
  → Schaltbild
Schaltpult n *(radio/TV)* control desk, switchboard, switch desk
Schaltschema n
  → Schaltbild
Schaltung f **1.** (Schalten von Werbemitteln) placement (of an ad), media buying, media buy, (Werbemittel, die nach Fläche berechnet werden) space buying, (Funkmedien) airtime buying, time buying
  → Medieneinkauf
  2. (Steuerung) control **3.** (Verdrahtung) circuit, connection
Schandblatt n
  → Gossenzeitschrift
scharf *adj* **1.** *(phot)* (Bild) sharp, distinct, clear-cut, well-focused, *colloq* plucky **2.** *(print)* (Schriftbild) sharp, crisp
Scharfabstimmung f
  → Feinabstimmung
Schärfe f **1.** *(phot)* sharpness, distinctness, focus, *colloq* pluckiness
  The focus in which a photographic picture, camera or television image appears clearly with a sharp outline.
  2. *(print)* (Schriftbild) sharpness, crispness
  3. → Auflösungsvermögen
  4. *(phot)* (Linse) clearness, acuity, (Emulsion) acutance
  5. (Ton) sharpness
Schärfeassistent m (**Schärfezieher** m) *(film/TV)* focus puller, focus operator, assistant cameraman, second cameraman
  An assistant cameraman who checks the camera and the focus, changes lenses and magazines, etc.
Scharfeinstellung f (**Schärfeneinstellung** f) *(phot)* focus, focusing, adjustment for definition, (Vorrichtung) focus control
  The position in which a photographic picture, camera or television image appears clearly with a sharp outline, or the act of setting the focus of a camera in order to obtain such a picture quality.

Schärfenband n *(film/TV)* focus calibration tape
Schärfenbereich m *(phot)* zone of sharp focus, zone of sharpness
→ Tiefenschärfe
Schärfenring m
→ Einstellring
Schärfentiefe f
→ Tiefenschärfe
Schärferad n
→ Einstellring
Schärfezieher m
→ Schärfeassistent
Scharfschützenansatz m (in der Werbung) rifle approach (of advertising), selective advertising, highly-selective advertising
   The attempt of reaching an objective by careful aiming of the effort to a selected target.
→ gezielte Streuung
Schatten m *(phot/film/TV)* shadow, shade, (im Bild) shadow areas *pl*, shadow effect, *(TV)* (Schwärzung) black crushing, black-crushing
   The dark area(s) of a picture, a positive or negative photograph, a reproduction or a print.
Schattenbuchstabe m **(Schattenletter** f, **Letter** f **in Schattenschrift)** *(typ)* shaded letter
→ Schattenschrift
Schattendichte f *(phot/film/TV)* shade density
→ Schwärzungsdichte
Schattendruckanzeige f shadow print advertisement, shadow print ad
Schattenmaske f *(TV)* shadow mask
   The perforated mask directly behind the face of the picture tube of a color television set.
Schattenmaskenröhre f *(TV)* shadow mask tube
Schattenraster m *(print)* vignette, gate
Schattenrißfilter m **(Schattenrißscheinwerfer** m) *(film/TV)* cucalorus, cukaloris, cuckoolorus, *colloq* cookie, cuke
   A piece of netting or cardboard with shapes cut out of it, used to cast patterns of light on a flat behind an actor.
Schattenschrift f *(typ)* shaded type face, shaded type, shaded letters *pl*
   A kind of display type, (→) Auszeichnungsschrift, having certain strokes, repeated so that a three-dimensional effect is produced.

Schattenschwärzung f *(TV)* black crushing, black-crushing
Schattenwasserzeichen n *(print)* shaded watermark, shadecraft watermark
Schattenzone f *(radio/TV)* shadow area, shadow zone
schattieren v/t *(print)* to shade
Schattierung f 1. (Tönung) shading
2. *(print)* (Durchschlagen der Typen) embossment
   The result of too heavy a printing impression, so that type and rules can be seen on the reverse side of the paper. It can be the fault of poor makeready, (→) Zurichtung, or of inferior paper.
Schätzfehler m *(stat)* error of estimation
   In general, the difference between an estimated value, (→) Schätzung 1., and the true value. More specifically, in regression analysis, (→) Regressionsanalyse, the difference between the estimated and the observed value of the dependent variate. The standard deviation, (→) Standardabweichung, of these differences in repeated samples is sometimes known as the error of estimate.
Schätzfunktion f *(stat)* estimator
   A rule or method of estimating a constant of a parent population, expressed as a function of sample values.
Schätzskala f
→ Ratingskala
Schätzung f 1. *(stat)* (Schätzwert) estimate
   The particular value yielded by an estimator, (→) Schätzfunktion, in a given set of circumstances. In a wider sense, the rule by which such particular values are calculated.
2. (Vorgang des Schätzens) estimation
   Estimation is concerned with inference about the numerical value of unknown population values from incomplete data such as a sample, (→) Stichprobe. If a single figure is calculated for each unknown parameter, (→) Parameter, the process is called point estimation, (→) Punktschätzung. If an interval is calculated within which the parameter is likely to lie, the process is called interval estimation, (→) Intervallschätzung.
Schätzmethode f **(Schätzverfahren** n) *(stat)* estimation technique, method of estimation, estimating method
Schätzwert m
→ Schätzung 1.
Schaubild n
→ Diagramm

Schaufenster n *(POP advtsg)* shopwindow, *brit* shop window, show window, display window, store window
Schaufensteraktion f *(POP advtsg)* window display action, shopwindow display action, display window action
Schaufensterauslage f **(Schaufensterdekoration** f) *(POP advtsg)* window display
Schaufensterbeleuchtung f *(POP advtsg)* shopwindow illumination, shop-window illumination, window illumination, (beleuchtetes Schaufenster) illuminated window
Schaufensterdekorateur m *(POP advtsg)* window dresser, window trimmer
→ Schauwerber
Schaufensterdekoration f *(POP advtsg)* window dressing, window trimming
Schaufenstergestalter m
→ Schauwerbegestalter
Schaufenstergestaltung f
→ Schaufensterdekoration, Schauwerbung
Schaufensterplakat n *(POP advtsg)* window display poster, window poster, windowcard, display poster, (Klebestreifen) window streamer, window banner, (kleinformatig) window sticker
A promotion piece designed for pasting or taping to a store window; frequently a long narrow strip of paper on which an advertising message is printed.
Schaufensterrotor m *(POP advtsg)* lazy Susan display, lazy Susan
A point-of-purchase unit turned by hand or operated by a push-button motor on a turntable base.
Schaufensterschild n **(Kleinplakat** n) *(POP advtsg)* showcard, show card
Schaufensterware f *(POP advtsg)* window display goods *pl,* window display merchandise
Schaufensterwerbung f *(POP advtsg)* window display advertising, display advertising, shop window advertising, shopwindow display advertising
→ Schauwerbung
Schaufensterwettbewerb m *(POP advtsg)* window dressing contest, shopwindow competition, shop window competition

Schaukasten m **(Auslagenvitrine** f) showcase, display case, exhibition case
A cabinet with glass panels allowing the contents to be protected, to be refrigerated, etc., while remaining on display.
Schaupackung f display package, dummy pack, dummy
→ Attrappe
Schauständer m **(Auslageregal** n) *(POP advtsg)* display rack
Schaustück n **(Ausstellungsstück** n) *(POP advtsg)* exhibit
Schauwerbeassistent m *(POP advtsg)* etwa junior display artist, display artist's assistent
Schauwerbeberater m *(POP advtsg)* freelance display artist, freelance advertising display artist
Schauwerbegestalter m **(Schauwerber** m) *(POP advtsg)* display artist, advertising display artist
Schauwerbegestaltung f **(Schauwerbung** f) *(POP advtsg)* display art, advertising display art
Schauwerbeleiter m *(POP advtsg)* managing display artist, managing advertising display artist
Schauwerber m
→ Schauwerbegestalter
Schauwerbung f
→ Schauwerbegestaltung
Scheibenplakat n **(Seitenscheibenplakat** n) *(transit advtsg)* window poster
A strip of advertising posted on the side window of a public transportation vehicle.
Scheidelinie f 1. (Trennungslinie) dividing line, dividing rule 2. *(print)* separatrix
Scheidewand f *(radio/TV/film)* baffle, baffle board, gobbo, gobo
A movable partition for absorbing sound or light and thus preventing undesirable reflection.
Scheidewert m *(stat)* dividing value
Scheinkäufer m **(Testkäufer** m) *(market res)* (im Ladentest) mystery shopper, test buyer, test shopper
Scheinkorrelation f *(stat)* spurious correlation, illusory correlation, nonsense correlation, (Assoziation) spurious association, (Vorliegen einer Scheinkorrelation) spuriousness
A correlation that is significant without implying a causal connection between

Scheinvariable

two variates. Also, the case where correlation, (→) Korrelation, is found to be present between ratios or indices in spite of the original values being random observations on uncorrelated variates. More generally, correlation may be described as spurious if it is induced by the method of handling the data and is not presented in the original material.

Scheinvariable f (**Hilfsvariable** f) *(stat)* dummy variable
A quantity written in a mathematical expression in the form of a variable although it represents a constant. The term is also used, rather laxly, to denote an artificial variable expressing qualitative characteristics.

Scheinwerfer m *(film/TV/studio)* floodlamp, floodlight, floodlight projector, flood, scoop, basher, (stromstarker Bogenscheinwerfer) brute, 10k, (2000 Watt) broad, (spot) spotlight, spot
A cameraman's or photographer's light, which illuminates a wide area.

Scheinwerferaufhängung f *(film/TV/studio)* lamp suspension

Scheinwerferdichte f *(film/TV)* frequency of lights

Scheinwerfergalgen m *(film/TV)* gallows arm

Scheinwerfergerüst n *(film/TV)* scaffold suspension

Scheinwerfergestänge n *(film/TV)* lighting barrels *pl*

Scheinwerferlampe f
→ Scheinwerfer

Scheinwerferlinse f *(film/TV)* spotlight lens

Scheinwerferschwenk m *(film/TV)* lamp trunnion

Scheinwerferstativ n (**Scheinwerferstand** m) *(film/TV)* lamp stand

Scheinwerfertor n (**Scheuklappen** f/ pl, **Torblende** f) *(film/TV)* barndoor, *meist pl* barndoors
A device consisting of adjustable flaps at the sides of a floodlamp, used to keep the projected light from certain areas.

Scheinwerfervignette f *(film/TV)* vignette
A mask for the lens of a motion-picture or television camera that gives a vignettelike effect to a shot.

Scheitel m (**Scheitelwert** m)
→ Gipfel

Scheitelblende f *(phot)* scissors shutter

Scheitelhänger m *(film/TV/studio)* gobbo arm, gobo arm

Schemabrief m *(advtsg)* form letter

Schenkung f donation

scherzhafte Werbung f (**scherzhafte Reklame** f) humorous advertising
→ humorvolle Werbung, Gagwerbung

Scheuklappe f (**Scheunentor** n)
→ Scheinwerfertor

Schicht f 1. → Beschichtung
2. → soziale Schicht

Schichtband n coated tape

Schichtauswahl f
→ geschichtete Auswahl, geschichtetes Auswahlverfahren

schichten (**stratifizieren**) *v/t (stat)* to stratify
→ geschichtete Auswahl

Schichtenkarte f *(stat)* strata chart, zee chart, Z chart
A chart upon which two or more time series, (→) Zeitreihe, are plotted with the vertical scales arranged so that the curves do not cross. Strata charts are particularly valuable in connection with the presentation of time-series data in which a total can be broken down into its constituent parts.

Schichtenpappe f *(packaging)* pasteboard, multi-ply board

Schichtenplan m
→ geschichtete Auswahl

Schichthärtung f *(phot)* hardening of emulsion

Schichtlage f (**Schichtseite** f) *(phot)* emulsion side, sensitized side
That side on the surface of photographic film, paper, or printing plates containing a light-sensitive coating that develops the image when exposed to light.

Schichtschramme f *(phot)* emulsion scratch

Schichtseite f
→ Schichtlage

Schichtträger m *(film/phot)* emulsion carrier, emulsion support, support, base material, base, film base, *(tape)* tape base, base

Schichtträgerseite f *(film/phot)* base side, celluloid side, *colloq* cell side

Schichtung f (**Stratifizierung** f, **Schichtenbildung** f) *(social res/stat)* stratification, (soziale Schichtung) social stratification, (nachträgliche Schichtung) stratification after sampling, stratification after selection, poststratification, (mit verschiedenen

Stichprobengruppen) stratification with variable sampling fraction
→ geschichtete Auswahl
Schichtungseffekt m **(Stratifizierungseffekt** m) *(stat)* stratification effect
Schichtungsfaktor m **(Schichtungsvariable** f, **Stratifizierungsfaktor** m, **Schichtvariable** f) *(stat)* stratification factor, stratifying factor, stratification variable
Schichtzugehörigkeit f **(soziale Schichtzugehörigkeit** f) class, social class
Schiebeblende f **1.** *(film)* sliding diaphragm **2.** → Schiebetrick
Schiebetrick m *(film)* mechanical animation, limited animation
 The creation of an effect of movement, life, or human character to a drawing by actually moving it.
Schiefe f **(Asymmetrie** f) *(stat)* skewness, asymmetry
 If a unimodal distribution has a longer tail extending towards lower values of the variate it is said to have negative skewness; in the contrary case, it has positive skewness.
schiefe Häufigkeitsverteilung f **(schiefe Verteilung** f) *(stat)* skewed frequency distribution, skew frequency distribution, skewed distribution, skew distribution, asymmetrical frequency distribution, asymmetrical distribution
Schiene f rail
Schienenwagen m **(Kamera- oder Beleuchtungswagen** m **auf Schienen)** *(film/TV/studio)* track dolly
Schießplatte f *(print)* imposing stone, imposing table, imposition stone, imposition table
Schiff n
→ Setzschiff
Schild n **1.** (Ladenschild) shop sign, sign, signboard, *colloq* shingle **2.** (Firmenschild) nameplate, name plate, facia **3.** (Leuchtschild) illuminated sign **4.** (Etikett) label, tag, tab, sticker → Preisschild, Anschlagbrett
Schildermaler m sign painter, signpost writer
Schimmel m **(Schimmeldruck** m) *(print)* blind print
Schimmelbogen m *(print)* blind sheet, blind print page, blank sheet
Schirm m screen, shield

A surface onto which the image of a slide, motion picture or a television program is projected.
→ Bildschirm, Lichtblende, Leuchtschirm
Schirmantenne f *(radio)* umbrella antenna, *brit* umbrella aerial
Schirmbild n *(TV)* screen picture, screen image
Schirmbildröhre f
→ Bildröhre
Schirmgitter n *(TV)* screen grid, screen
Schirmgitterspannung f *(TV)* screen-grid voltage, screen voltage
Schirmhelligkeit f *(TV)* screen brightness
Schirmmethode f
Schirmpreis m
→ Einheitspreis
Schirmröhre f
→ Bildröhre
Schirmwanne f *(TV)* (Bildröhre) screen connection
Schirmwerbung f **(Dachwerbung** f) umbrella advertising
Schläfereffekt m **(Sleeper-Effekt** m)
→ Zeitzündereffekt (Spätzündereffekt)
Schlager m **1.** → Kassenschlager
2. → Lockartikel, Lockangebot
3. *(mus)* popular song, musical hit, hit, pop music hit
Schlagschatten m *(phot)* cast shadow, hard shadow, heavy shadow
Schlagwort n **1.** (Werbeslogan) slogan
 A sentence or phrase used consistently in a series of advertisements to express the central message.
2. (Stichwort) catchword, catch word, catch phrase, keynote
Schlagzeile f **1.** headline, heading, head
 Both the largest display matter of an advertisement, setting the theme of the copy, and the head of a newspaper front page, giving the most important story, or simply the head of a newspaper article, giving its major subject.
2. (groß aufgemachte) banner headline, screamer headline, screamer, shout, streamer
Schleichwerbung f **(getarnte Werbung** f, **Schmuggelwerbung** f) editorial mention advertising, editorial hosting, hosting, editorial mention, covert advertising, (Einzelfall von Schleichwerbung) puff notice, puff, free puff,

Schleier 454

free mention, plug; Schleichwerbung machen für: to plug
Schleier m *(phot)* veil, veiling, fog
→ Nebel
Schleierfilter m *(phot)* fog filter
A diffusion screen rather than a filter, used to give the effect of fog in a picture.
Schleife f **1.** → Bauchbinde **2.** → Rückkoppelungsschleife **3.** → Filmschleife
Schleifkasten m **(Schleifenschrank** m) *(film)* loop cabinet
Schlepptransparent n airplane banner, aircraft trailing banner
Schleuderartikel n **(billige Massenware** f) *(econ)* catchpenny article, catchpenny product, catchpenny, borax goods pl, schlock merchandise, *brit* cut-price merchandise
Shoddy merchandise made so poorly that price appeal may be the determining factor inducing purchase.
Schleuderpreis m *(econ)* giveaway price, cutrate price, cutrate, *brit* cut-rate price
Schlieren f/pl **(Schlierenbildung** f) *(phot)* streamer markings pl
Dark strips in a negative in which the density of some long narrow object in the image is extended to adjacent parts.
schließen v/t **1.** (wegen Geschäftsaufgabe) to close down, to close, to shut down, to close (the shop) **2.** (zum Abschluß bringen) to conclude, to bring sth. to an end, to bring sth. to a close **3.** *(print)* (den Satz im Rahmen) to lock up, (die Druckform) to quoin up, to quoin, to coign up, to coign
schließende Statistik f **(schlußfolgernde Statistik** f)
→ Inferenzstatistik
Schließplatte f *(print)* imposing table, imposing surface, imposing stone
Schließrahmen m *(print)* chase
The frame in which all the metal, such as type or cuts, etc., for a given page is placed.
Schließstege m/pl *(print)* dead metal
Metal which is left in non-printing areas of an original engraving or inserted in type forms, type high, (→) Schrifthöhe, so that pressure used in molding duplicate or printing plates does not break down type or vignetted edges of halftone illustrations.
Schließzeug n *(print)* quoins pl
Schlitzantenne f *(electr.)* slot antenna, slot aerial

Schlitzverschluß m *(phot)* focal-plane shutter, slit-type shutter
Schlupf m *(tape)* slip, drift
Schlußbogen m *(print)* final signature, back matter, *brit* end matter
Schlüsselfrage f *(survey res)* key question
Schlüsselindikator m *(survey res)* key indicator
Schlüsselinformant m *(survey res)* key informant, key informer
Respondents who provide information about the community or institution they are associated with. Key informants are chosen because of their expertise and are usually identified either because of their formal roles or because they are identified by other experts as being knowledgeable.
Schlüsselinformation f *(survey res)* key information
→ Schlüsselinformant
Schlüsselreiz m *(psy)* key stimulus
schlußfolgernde Statistik f
→ Inferenzstatistik
Schlußfolgerung f conclusion, inference
Schlußklappe f **(SK)** *(film/TV)* end board **(EB)**
Schlußkorrektur f **(Endkorrektur** f, **Revision** f) *(print)* final correction, final proof, revise proof, revise
→ Maschinenabzug
Schlußszene f **(Schlußsequenz** f) *(film/TV)* closing scene, final scene, closing, close
The last and concluding shot or sequence of a program or commercial.
Schlußtermin m
→ Anzeigenschluß, Redaktionsschluß, Annahmeschluß
Schlußtitel m *(film/TV)* end titles pl, closing titles pl, end caption, end credits pl
All announcements of who did what on the screen titles which follow the film.
Schlußverkauf m
→ Saisonschlußverkauf
schmal *(print)* (Schrift) condensed
→ kompreß, schmallaufende Schrift; *vgl.* mager
Schmalbahn f *paper)* oblong sheet, grain long
Schmalband n narrow tape, (Frequenz) narrow band
Schmalfilm m *(phot)* narrow-gauge film, narrow gauge, substandard film, substandard, eight millimeter film,

8mm film, 8mm, double-eight film, double run 8mm film, sixteen millimeter film, 16mm film
A motion-picture or television film that is narrower than the width commonly adopted as standard, i.e., 35mm for motion picture and 16mm for television film.

Schmalfilmformat n *(phot)* narrow gauge, substandard
→ Schmalfilm

Schmalformat n
→ Hochformat

schmalformatig
→ hochformatig

schmallaufende Schrift f **(Schmalschrift** f**)** *(print)* condensed type
Any type that is narrower than that of standard width.

Schmelzkleber m **(Hotmeltkleber** m**, Heißschmelzkleber** m**)** hot melt adhesive

Schmierpaper n scratch paper, scribbling paper

Schmierskizze f
→ Rohentwurf

Schmitz m *(print)* blur, slur, mackle

schmitzen v/t + v/i *(print)* to slur, to blur, to mackle

Schmitzleiste(n) f(pl) *(print)* dead metal, bed bearer, bearer

Schmuckfarbe f *(print)* additional color, *brit* colour, second color, accompanying color, spot color
Any color applied for emphasis to areas of a basically black and white advertisement. Spot colors are used in color printing in which solid colors are spotted or located in certain areas, printed from individual color plates, with no blending of colors from two or more plates as in process printing.

Schmuggelwerbung f
→ Schleichwerbung

Schmutzbogen m
→ Abschmutzbogen

Schmutzfleck m *(print)* blot, spot, stain

Schmutzpresse f
→ Gossenpresse

Schnappschuß m *(phot)* snapshot, snap, (ungestelltes Bild) candid photo, candid photograph, candid picture
An unposed photograph.

Schneeballsystem n **(Schneeballverfahren** n**, progressive Kundenwerbung** f**, Hydrasystem** n**)**
1. *(marketing/promotion)* (Kundenwerbung) snowball system, snowball procedure, endless chain method, chain prospecting
A technique of prospecting in which a salesperson seeks the names of one or more prospects from each one approached. Offering discounts or rebates to buyers for a number of new buyers is prohibited under German fair practice legislation.
2. *(stat)* (Stichprobenverfahren) snowball sampling, (Stichprobe) snowball sample
A technique of building up a sample of a special population by using an initial set of its members as informants.

Schneidemarke f
→ Abschneidemarkierung

Schneidemaschine f
→ Papierschneidemaschine

Schneideraum m *(film/TV)* cutting room, editing room
The film editor's workshop.

Schneidetisch m *(film/TV)* cutting bench, cutting table, editing bench, editing table

Schneidezeit f *(film/TV)* editing period

Schnellaufzug m *(phot)* shutter wind

Schnellgreifbühnentest m
→ Greifbühnentest

Schnellhefter m loose-leaf binder, easibinder

Schnellpresse f *(print)* cylinder press, cylinder machine, flatbed press, flatbed cylinder press

Schnellreportagewagen m
→ Übertragungswagen

Schnellschuß m rush job

schnell umschlagende Konsumgüter n/pl *(econ)* fast moving consumer goods pl (FMCG), fast-moving, high-turnover goods pl
Consumer goods of low unit value, for repeat selling, that are normally in universal demand.

Schnellverkehr m *(transit advtsg)* fast travel
vgl. Langsamverkehr

Schnipex m *colloq (film/TV)* baby spotlight, baby spot, dinky inky, dinky inkie, dinkie inkie, inky dink
A small theatrical spotlight.

Schnitt m **1.** *(film/radio/TV)* (Filmschnitt) cut
The transition from one motion picture or television scene to another without an intervening optical effect; also a transition from one sound to another in radio.

Schnittabnahme

2. *(film/radio/TV)* (das Filmschneiden) cutting and editing, editing, cutting
    The process and technique of rearranging motion picture or television scenes already on film into a desired sequence, timing, and synchronization; also, the rearrangement of sound sequences in radio.
3. (Form) shape, form, cut, pattern
4. *(print)* (Beschneiden) cut, (Beschnittkante beim Buch) edge, (Schriftbild) face, version of a typeface, typeface style
    The design or style of a type letter.

Schnittabnahme f *(film)* editing acceptance, final viewing of cutting copy
Schnittbearbeitung f *(film)* editing, cutting and editing, cutting
→ Filmschnitt
Schnittbild n (**Schnittansicht** f, **Aufrißbild** n, **Aufrißzeichnung** f) sectional view, ghosted view, phantom section, x-ray picture, x-ray illustration, cut-in
    An X-ray or cross-section picture to show content or interior design.
Schnittbildentfernungsmesser m *(phot)* split-field range finder, split-image range finder
Schnittfolge f *(film)* cutting order
Schnittkontrolle f *(film)* editing control
Schnittkopie f
→ Arbeitskopie
Schnittmarke f *(TV)* edit pulse, edit cue, frame pulse, cue pulse, cue, *(film)* cutting point
Schnittmaterial n (**Schnittabfall** m, **Schnittreste** m/pl) *(allg)* outtake, *(radio)* tape for editing, uncut tape, *(film)* trims pl, offcuts pl
    Any shot, tape, or footage that is not used in the completed version of a film or a commercial broadcast.
Schnittmeister m *(film)* editor, film editor, *(MAZ)* tape editor, editor
→ Cutter
Schnittmodellzeichnung f
→ Schnittbild
Schnittreste m/pl
→ Schnittmaterial
Schnittschablone f
→ Siebdruckschablone
Schnittstabilität f *(film)* cutting precision, *(MAZ)* editing stability, editing accuracy
Schnittweite f *(phot)* width of cut

Schnittzeichnung f
→ Schnittbild
Schnittzeit f *(film)* cutting time, editing time
Schöndruck m *(print)* first run, first printing, first impression
vgl. Widerdruck
Schöndruckform f (**Schöndruckseite** f) *(print)* first form, brit first forme, prime, felt side
Schön- und Widerdruck m *(print)* perfecting
Schön- und Widerdruckmaschine f *(print)* perfecting machine, perfector press, perfector
schöpferisch adj creative
Schöpfpapier n (**Büttenpapier** n, **handgeschöpftes Papier** n) deckle-edged paper, deckle-edge paper, handmade paper
    A type of paper with a torn effect along the natural, untrimmed edge of a sheet.
Schraffen f/pl
→ Schraffur
schraffieren v/t to hatch, to shade, (kreuzschraffieren) to crosshatch, brit to cross-hatch
    To mark an area of a drawing with closely-spaced lines, in order to indicate modeling or shading, to indicate a material seen in cross-section, etc.
Schraffur f (**Schraffierung** f) hatching, hatches pl, (Kreuzschraffur) crosshatching, brit cross-hatching
→ schraffieren
Schrägaufnahme f (**Halbschräge** f) *(phot)* angle shot
    A camera shot taken from a horizontal position rather than one straight on the subject. Usually, a shot taken after the master scene with the camera in a different position.
Schrägblende f (**Schrägschwenk** m) *(film/TV)* diagonal wipe
Schräghobel m
→ Facettiergerät (Facettierhobel)
Schrägspuraufzeichnung f (**Schrägschriftaufzeichnung** f) *(TV)* helical scan, helical recording, slant track recording
    A system, often used in miniaturized videotape recording systems, using a video tape equipment with one or two recording heads "writing" video information in long parallel slants across the tape. The system uniquely offers a still picture, but is more susceptible than quadraplex to tape stretch and slippage.

Schrägstellung f (**Schrägposition** f)
(outdoor advtsg) angled position
Schramme f (**Kratzer** m) *(film)*
shadow scratch, scar, optical scratch,
(tape) tape scratch, *(disc)* disc scratch,
disk scratch, surface noise
Schraubverschluß m *(phot)* screw
mount
  A mount for a lens or filter which screws into the camera or the lens.
  vgl. Bajonettverschluß
Schreibmaschinenmanuskript n
typescript, typewritten copy, typed-up manuscript
Schreibmaschinensatz m (**Schreibsatz** m) typewriter composition, impact composition, strike-on composition, direct impression composition
Schreibregeln f/pl (**Verzeichnis** n **der Schreibregeln**) style sheet, style book
  The list or book containing the rules of style governing a publication.
Schreibsatz m
→ Schreibmaschinensatz m
Schreibschrift f *(typ)* script
  A face of type that resembles handwriting.
Schreibtischforschung f
→ Sekundärforschung
Schreibtitel m *(film/TV)* lettered title
Schrift f 1. writing, script, (Anschläge) characters *pl* 2. *(print)* (Satzmaterial) type, text type 3. → Veröffentlichung 4. → Broschüre 5. → Schriftart
Schrift f **auf anderem Kegel** (kleinerem oder größerem Kegel) *(print)* bastard type, bastard face, bastard typeface, bastard
  Any type whose size does not conform to standard sizes in typography, periodical make-up, or prescribed advertising space units, i.e. type that is bigger or smaller than the pertinent standard size of shank.
Schriftart f (**Schriftsorte** f, **Schriftgarnitur** f) *(print)* type font, font, *brit* fount, family of type, typographical family, kind of type, type
  A complete assortment of type characters in one face and size, including numbers, punctuation marks, etc.
Schriftauge n *(print)* face of type, type face, face
  The printing surface of a type character.
Schriftaustastung f *(TV)* caption positioning
Schriftbild n *(print)* typeface, type face, face of type, face
  The design style of a type letter.

Schriftblase f
→ Sprechblase
Schrifteinblender m *(TV)* caption mixer, caption inserter
Schrifteinblendung f *(TV)* caption insertion, caption superimposition
Schriftenbuch n
→ Schriftmusterbuch
Schriftenmaler m
→ Schriftmaler
Schriftenreihe f serial publication
Schriftfamilie f *(print)* family of type, type family
  A group of type faces of the same basic design, but with variations in size, width of characters, boldness or lightness of strokes, and the like.
Schriftgarnitur f
→ Schriftart
Schriftgattung f
→ Schriftart
Schriftgestalter m *(print)* type designer, letter designer
Schriftgestaltung f *(print)* letter design, type design, design of letters
Schriftgießen n (**Schriftguß** m) *(print)* typefounding, type casting, letter founding
  The manufacturing of type.
Schriftgießer m *(print)* typefounder, letter founder, foundry man
Schriftgießerei f *(print)* type foundry, letter foundry, foundry
Schriftgießmaschine f *(print)* type casting machine, type caster, caster
Schriftgrad m (**Schriftgröße** f, **Schriftkegelgröße** f) *(print)* type size, point size
  The size of type in the printing industry is measured in typographical Didot points, (→) Punktsystem, with one point in Germany equaling 0.3795 millimeters, or 0.01487 inches, or 1.071 points in the American and British pica system.
Schriftgradunterschied m *(print)* remove
Schriftgraphik f
→ Typographie
Schriftgraphiker m
→ Schriftgestalter, Typograph
Schriftgröße f *(print)* body size
  The length of a typeface, measured from the top of the highest ascender to the bottom of the lowest descender.
→ Schriftgrad
Schriftgruppe f
→ Schriftfamilie

Schriftguß *m*
→ Schriftgießen
Schrifthöhe f *(print)* type height, height to paper, height-to-paper
The standard height all letterpress plates and type must be to print well, in Germany 2.3566 centimeters = 0.92777 inches, in other words: a little higher than in the U.S. or in Britain (= 0.9186 inches).
Schriftkasten *m (print)* letter case, typecase, type case, job case, case
A compartmented tray for holding a font of type for hand setting, the types of each character being in separate compartments.
Schriftkegel *m* (**Kegel** *m*) *(print)* body of type, body of a letter, body, shank
The main body or stem of a unit of type.
Schriftkegelgrad *m* (**Schriftkegelgröße** *f*)
→ Schriftgrad
Schriftkörper *m*
→ Schriftkegel
Schriftkünstler *m*
→ Schriftgestalter
Schriftleiter *m*
→ Chefredakteur
Schriftleitung *f*
→ Chefredaktion
schriftliche Befragung *f* (**postalische Befragung** *f*)
→ briefliche Befragung
schriftlicher Fragebogen *m (survey res)* self-administered questionnaire
A questionnaire that requires respondents to read and/or answer the questions themselves. They are almost all paper-and-pencil forms currently, but computer use should increase in the future; the form is considered to be self-administered even if an interviewer is present to hand it out, to collect it, and to answer questions.
→ briefliche Befragung
Schriftlinie *f (print)* body line, type line, base line
The line on which the base of all the capitals of a font, (→) Schriftart, and the bodies of all its lower-case letters align.
Schriftmaler *m* (**Schriftzeichner** *m*, **Schriftgraphiker** *m*) *(print)* lettering artist, lettering man
Schriftmetall *n* (**Letternmetall** *n*) *(print)* type metal, metal, printer's metal
The alloy used as type metal.
Schriftmontage *f*
→ Filmmontage, Montage

Schriftmusterbuch *n* (**Schriftenverzeichnis** *n*) *(print)* typebook, type specimen book
A book, booklet, or list showing the various families and sizes of type a printer has.
Schriftname *m*
→ Schriftart
Schriftsatz *m*
→ Satz
Schriftschablone *f*
→ Schablone 4.
Schriftscheibe *f* (**Typenträger** *m*) *(print)* font disc, *brit* fount disc, type disc, disk
In photocomposition, a disk carrying a complete assortment of type of one size and face or style. It comprises uppercase and lowercase letters, figures, points, signs, spaces, ems, ens, etc.
Schriftschneider *m (print)* letter cutter, letterer
Schriftschnitt *m (print)* type cutting, letter cutting, cutting
Schriftsetzer *m* (**Setzer** *m*) **1.** *(print)* typesetter, compositor, comp.
A worker who sets type, either by hand or by machine.
2. *(TV)* caption mixer
Schriftstempel *m (print)* punch
Schrifttafel *f (TV)* television billboard, TV billboard, billboard
A panel containing the credits at the opening and/or closing of a television program, giving sponsor identification, talent, writers, directors, producers, etc.
Schrifttype *f* (**Schriftzeichen** *n*)
→ Type
Schriftzeichner *m* (**Schriftenzeichner** *m*)
→ Schriftmaler
Schrittkopieren *n (film)* step printing, intermittent printing
Schrittkopiermaschine *f (film)* step printer, intermittent printer
A film laboratory machine used to print optical picture negatives.
vgl. Durchlaufkopiermaschine
Schrittlauf *m (film)* step-by-step motion, stepping motion
Schrittmotor *m (film)* stepping motor
Schrittschaltung *f (print)* proportional spacing
Schrotflintenansatz *m*
→ ungezielte Streuung
Schrumpffolie *f (packaging)* shrink-wrapping, shrink-wrap
A way of covering or packaging something by using an impervious

material which shrinks tight around the object when heat is applied. An item so covered needs no other weather protection, may be shipped so covered, and attached to a pair of blocks for forklift handling purposes.
Schrumpfung f **(Filmschrumpfung** f**)** shrinkage, shrinking
Schubstrategie f **(Schubmethode** f**)**
→ Push-Methode (Push-Strategie)
Schulfernsehen n
→ Bildungsfernsehen
Schulfilm m
→ Unterrichtsfilm
Schulfunk m
→ Bildungsfunk
Schulterstativ n *(film/TV)* shoulder tripod, shoulder pod
Schulung f training
Schundblatt n
→ Gossenzeitschrift
Schüttware f **(Schüttgüter** n/pl**)** *(econ)* bulk commodity, bulk goods pl
Products which are sold and delivered in loose form, such as coal, gravel, grain. They generally have the common quality of flowability, so that they may be loaded and unloaded by either gravity or blower devices.
Schutzblatt n cover flap, flap, jacket flap
A piece of paper attached to the back of artwork and folded over its face to provide protection.
Schutzfolie f overlay, protective overlay
A piece of tissue or acetate secured over a layout or piece of artwork for protective purposes.
Schutzkappe f *(phot)* (an der Kamera) lens cap, lens cover, lens guard, (am Scheinwerfer) safety mesh
Schutzmarke f
→ eingetragenes Warenzeichen
Schutzpapier n paper overlay, protective paper overlay
Schutzrechte n/pl
→ gewerblicher Rechtsschutz
Schutzschicht f protective coating
Schutzumschlag m book jacket, book wrapper, jacket wrapper, dust jacket, dust cover, jacket, wrapper, cover, protective cover
A protective paper wrapper for a book.
Schutzumschlagtext m
→ Klappentext
Schwabesches Gesetz n
→ Engelsches Gesetz (Engel-Schwabesches Gesetz)

Schwanenhals m goose neck, gooseneck, swan neck
A bendable microphone stand.
Schwankungsbreite f **(Variationsbreite** f**)** *(stat)* variation
The span of differences between individuals or groups in the population, usually measured as a statistical variance, (→) Varianz, or simply by observing the differences between the values for the group.
→ Toleranzintervall, Vertrauensbereich
Schwarzabgleich m **(Schwarzwertsteuerung** f**)** *(film/TV)* black level adjustment
Schwarzblende f *(film/TV)* fade to black, blackout; Schwarzblende ziehen: to fade to black
The gradual disappearance of an image by means of a steadily decreased camera aperture, until only black remains.
Schwärze f *(print)* black dye
schwärzen v/t *(print)* to blacken, to darken
Schwarzer Kasten m **(Black Box** f**)** *(psy)* black box
→ S-R-Modell
Schwarzer Markt m *(econ)* black market
Schwarzes Brett n **(Anschlagbrett** n**)** notice board
schwarzes Licht n *(phot)* black light
Ultra-violet lighting that causes phosphorescent paints to glow.
Schwarzfilm m *(film)* black leader, blacking, black spacing
Schwarzpegel m **(Austastpegel** m**)** *(TV)* black level
The minimal television voltage signal that establishes the blackness of the transmitted image.
Schwarzplatte f **(Konturenplatte** f, **Tiefenplatte** f**)** *(print)* black plate
The plate that prints black in multi-color printing.
Schwarzschildeffekt m *(phot)*
Schwarzschild effect
Schwärzung f *(phot)* density, blackening, optical transmission density, photographic transmission density
The degree of opacity of a photographic image.
Schwärzungsabstufung f *(phot)* density gradation
Schwärzungsbereich m *(phot)* density range

Schwärzungsdichte *f (phot)* density
→ Schwärzung
Schwärzungskurve *f* (**Dichtekurve** *f*) *(phot)* density curve
Schwärzungsmesser *m*
→ Densitometer
Schwärzungsstufe *f (phot)* density step, density value
Schwärzungsumfang *m*
→ Dichteumfang
schwarzweiß (schwarz-weiß) *adj* black-and-white (b & w, b and w, b/w, B & W, B and W, B/W)
Being reproduced in one color only, i.e. black on white paper, as distinguished from two or more colors.
Schwarzweißabbildung *f (phot/print)* black-and-white illustrations
Schwarzweißabzug *m (phot)* black-and-white print, black-and-white photo, monotone print, monotone, mono
Schwarzweißanzeige *f (print)* black-and-white advertisement, black-and-white ad, b & w ad
An advertisement printed only in black and white, as differentiated from one printed in two, three, or four colors.
Schwarzweißautotypie *f (print)* black-and-white halftone
Schwarzweißdruck *m* **1.** *(print)* (Verfahren) black-and-white printing, b & w printing, monochrome printing **2.** (Produkt) black-and-white print, b & w print
Schwarzweißempfänger *m*
→ Schwarzweißfernseher
Schwarzweißfernsehen *n* black-and-white television, black-and-white TV, b & w TV
Schwarzweißfernseher *m* black-and-white television set, black-and-white receiver, black-and-white set
Schwarzweißfilm *m (phot)* black-and-white film, (Material) black-and-white stock
Schwarzweißlinie *f* (**Schwarzweißstrich** *m*) *(print)* black-and-white line finish
A narrow black finish line, separated from the edge of a halftone plate by a white line of suitable width. The effect can be mechanically introduced with a lining beveler.
Schwarzweißmanier *f*
→ Schabmanier
Schwarzweißnegativfilm *m (phot)* black-and-white negative film, (Material) black-and-white negative stock
Schwarzweißphoto *n* (**Schwarzweißbild** *n*, **Schwarzweißphotographie** *f*) black-and-white photo, black-and-white picture, b & w photo, black-and-white photo print, b & w photo print, b/w photo
Schwarzweißphotographie *f* **1.** → Schwarzweißphoto **2.** black-and-white photography
Schwarzweißpositivfilm *m (phot)* black-and-white positive film, (Material) black-and-white positive stock
Schwarzweißraster *m* (**Schwarzweißmuster** *n*) *(TV)* chequerboard pattern
Schwarzweißreproduktion *f (phot/print)* black-and-white reproduction
Schwarzweißsprung *m (film/TV)* black-to-white transition, black-to-white step
Schwarzweißumkehrfilm *m (phot)* black-and-white reversal film, black-and-white reversible film, (Material) black-and-white reversal stock
Schwarzweißzeichnung *f* black-and-white drawing
Schwarzwert *m*
→ Schwarzpegel
Schwebung *f (TV)* beat
Schwebungsfrequenz *f (TV)* beat frequency
Schwebungsnull *f (TV)* zero-beat frequency
Schwedenschlüssel *m (survey res)* random number generator
Schweizerdegen *m (print)* compositor-pressman, *brit colloq* twicer
A compositor who is also educated and trained as a printer.
Schwellenangst *f (psy)* etwa fear of entering (a store), threshold anxiety
Schwellenpreis *m (econ)* line price *vgl.* Preisschwelle
Schwenk *m (film/TV)* pan, panning, panning shot, wipe, swivel shot, (mit dem Kran) caring, booming
A scene or sequence made by rotating, panning or gradually swinging the camera from left to right or right to left, as distinguished from a dolly shot, (→) Fahrtaufnahme, where the whole camera is moved on a wheeled platform to follow the action.

→ Horizontalschwenk, Panoramaschwenk, Reißschwenk, Vertikalschwenk, Diagonalschwenk
Schwenkarm m *(film/TV)* swivel arm,
panning handle, pan-and-tilt arm
schwenkbar *adj* swiveling, *brit*
swivelling, swivel-mounted, swinging
schwenken *v/t* *(film/TV)* (Kamera) to
pan, to swivel, to wipe, to arc, to
chinese, (senkrecht)
To rotate a camera in any direction in
order to keep an object in the picture or
to get a panoramic effect.
→ kippen
Schwenken n *(film/TV)* panning,
swiveling, *brit* swivelling
Schwenkgriff m
→ Schwenkarm
Schwenkkopf m *(film/TV)* panning
head, pan head
Schwenkkran m *(film/TV)* camera
boom, boom
A mount that enables a motion picture or
television camera to be raised above or
lowered to the action.
Schwenkstativ n *(film/TV)* camera
tripod
Schwerinkurve f *(res)* Schwerin curve
(Horace Schwerin)
Schwerin-Präferenz-Test m
(Schwerin-Test m**)** *(market res)*
Schwerin preference test, Schwerin
test, brand-preference change test,
brand-preference change study, gift
method (of investigating brand-
preference change), gift technique
(Schwerin Research Corporation)
A labory test used to pretest
advertisements or packages. The subjects
are invited to select a gift, then exposed
to advertising, normally television or
screen commercials, and thereafter
invited to select another gift. Their
choice of advertised product is
interpreted as an indication of a positive
advertising effect.
Schwerkraftgesetz n **im Einzelhandel**
(econ) law of retail gravitation
(William F. Reilly)
→ Gesetz der Agglomeration im
Einzelhandel
Schwindelzeitung f **(Phantomzeitung**
f**)** bogus paper
Schwingung f
→ Oszillation
Schwund m **(Fading** n**)** *(radio/TV)*
fading
Variation in the intensity of broadcast
signals, either audio or video.

Schwundausgleich m **(Schwund-
regelung** f**)** *(radio/TV)* fading control
Schwundgebiet n *(radio/TV)* fading
area
The area where fading, (→) Schwund, is
most noticeable for a given radio or
television station.
Scientific Management n
→ Operations Research
Scoringmodell n
→ Punktbewertungsverfahren
Screening n
→ Filterfrage, Filterinterview
Screening-Frage f
→ Filterfrage
Screening-Interview n
→ Filterinterview
Screening-Phase f
→ Filterphase
Scribble n
→ Rohzeichnung
Script n
→ Drehbuchmanuskript
Script-Girl n *(film/TV)* script girl,
continuity girl
An employee who keeps a detailed
written record of all the minutiae of the
actual shooting, set, costumes, action,
dialogue, and so forth.
Segment n *(stat/res)* segment
A section of a population which may be
characterized as homogeneous with
respect to one or more defined variables.
→ Marktsegment
Segmentation f **(Segmentierung** f**)**
1. *(stat)* segmentation
A term covering a variety of practices. It
means, as in common parlance, the
process of dividing up: in marketing
terms it refers to dividing the market
into distinct segments which can be
described as submarkets. There is a
variety of questionnaire and analysis
processes used to establish market
segments. The purpose of segmentation
analysis is to enable marketing activity
to be directed at specific groups of the
community. Markets can be segmented
according to behaviourial characteristics,
purchase or consumption characteristics,
or attitudinal characteristics. The term,
segmentation, is also used in the context
of products, as opposed to people, where
it is sometimes useful to group, say,
brands into those with common
characteristics. In the marketing context
it might be useful to think of groups of
brands as providing different sorts of
consumer satisfaction and therefore
appealing to different markets.
2. → Marktsegmentierung

Segmentationsanalyse *f* **(Segmentanalyse** *f*) *(res)* segmentation analysis, segment analysis, tree analysis
> The procedures designed to define "market segments" of the population that are relatively homogeneous with respect to the goals of the advertiser. Segments so defined may be appealed to differently, approached via different media and — if necessary, offered different products.

→ Baumanalyse

Segmentationsbaum *m (res)* segmentation tree
→ Baumanalyse

Segmentationsmethode *f* **(Segmentbildungsmethode** *f*) *(res)* segmentation method, segmentation technique

segmentiertes Marketing *n (econ)* segmented marketing, market segmentation
> The practice and strategy of dividing a market into subgroups with similar motivations and catering to the specific needs and wants of these market segments.

vgl. selektives Marketing

Segmentierung *f*
→ Segmentation

Segmentierungskriterium *n (res)* segmentation criterion

Segmentierungsmodell *n (res)* segmentation model

Segmentierungsvariable *f (res)* segmentation variable
> A variable used as a basis for segmentation (in marketing or in research). The most widely used bases for segmenting a market are: Demographics, geographics, personality, use of product, psychographics, preference, attitudes, values, and benefits.

Sehbeteiligung *f (TV)* share of audience, share
> Generally, the percentage of the aggregate television audience in some specified area at some specified time that is in the audience of a given network, station, or program. A share may be computed on a household basis or on an individual basis. The base for a share on a household basis is normally households using television a specified geographic area, over a specified time. Thus, a share on a household basis shows the percentage of those households using television that are estimated to be in the audience of a given network, station, or program, over a specified time.
> The base for a share on an individual basis is normally individuals using television in a specified geographic area, over a specified time. The base may include all such individuals, or some specified group of individual persons (such as those who have attained a specified age) that are using television. Thus, a share on an individual basis shows the percentage of these individuals using television that are estimated to be in the audience of a given network, station, or program, over a specified time.
> The shares of networks, stations, or programs in a given market may sum to more than 100 percent. One reason is that some households of individuals may be counted in the audience of two or more networks, stations, or programs, during a specified period of time. Or, these shares may sum to less than 100 percent because some households or individuals may be counted in the audiences of stations that are outside of the market or otherwise not reported.
> At times, shares may be computed on bases other than households using television or individuals using television. For example, one alternative method is to relate a particular station rating to the total of all station ratings in a given market, and call the ratio a share ("share (of total)").

→ Einschaltquote

Sehdauer *f* **(Verweilzeit** *f*) *(media res)* time spent viewing, viewing time
> A measure of viewer interest or involvement, expressed as the number of hours over a given period that a television set-owning household or any of its members spends in watching TV.

Seher *m*
→ Zuschauer

Seher *m/pl* **pro Sendung** *(media res)* broadcast audience, program audience, *brit* programme audience
> An estimate of the total or average number of individuals who have actually tuned in to a particular television program, as distinguished from an inherited audience which is defined as those persons who remain tuned in to a following program as a result of having actually tuned in to a particular preceding program.

Seher *m/pl* **pro Tag** *(media res)* viewers *pl* per day

Seherschaft *f*
→ Zuschauerschaft

Sehwahrscheinlichkeit f
→ Kontaktwahrscheinlichkeit
Seidenblende f *(phot)* silk scrim, silk, scrim, span, butterfly
   A gauze light diffuser.
Seidendruck m **(Seidenrasterdruck** m**)**
→ Siebdruck
Seidenpapier n tissue paper, tissue
   A semi-transparent paper.
Seite f **1.** (Zeitschrift/Zeitung) page **2.** (Schallplatte, Verkehrsmittel) side
Seitenabzug m **(Seitenfahne** f**)** *(print)* page proof, slip page
   A proof of type and plates in page form as they will finally appear, usually pulled after galley proofs have been corrected.
Seitenansicht f lateral view
Seitenantenne f *(electr.)* side antenna, brit side aerial
Seitenanzahl f **(Anzahl** f **der Seiten)** number of pages
Seitenband n *(radio)* side band, sideband
   The transmission frequency lying immediately above or below the carrier wave, (→) Trägerwelle.
Seitenbeachtung f *(media res)* page traffic, page traffic score
→ Lesevorgänge pro Seite
Seitenbeleuchtung f
→ Seitenlicht
Seitenfläche f
→ Rumpffläche
Seitenflächenposition f
→ Rumpfflächenposition
Seitenformat n **(Seitengröße** f**)** *(print)* page size, size of (the) page, (beschnitten) trim size
   The size of a full page in a periodical publication.
Seitenheftung f *(bookbinding)* side stitching, side sewing
   In binding a magazine or booklet, a method of stitching through the edges of the folded pages from front to back, so that the pages will not lie flat when opened.
Seitenhöhe f *(print)* depth of page, depth of space
   The vertical distance between the upper and lower edge of a full page.
Seitenkontakt m *(media res)* page exposure, (Lesevorgänge pro Seite) page traffic, page traffic score
→ Kontakt, Anzeigenseitenkontakt
Seitenlayout n *(print)* page design, page makeup, page layout
→ Layout

Seitenlicht n **(Seitenbeleuchtung** f, **seitliche Belichtung** f**)** *(phot/film/TV)* side light, side lighting, edge light, crosslighting, *colloq* kicker, (bei Portraits) Rembrandt lighting
   The technique of lighting a photographic subject, motion picture or television scene, etc., from one side. In portrait photography, a type of lighting giving a three-quarter view, in which the shadow side faces the camera.
Seitenmitte f *(print)* center of (the) page, brit centre of (the) page
Seitenmontage f *(print)* lithographic stripping, stripping of page, assembly of page negative, stripping of a flat
→ Montage
Seitennumerierung f *(print)* pagination, foliation
   The sequence, arrangement or assignment of numbers to pages of a publication.
Seitennummer f **(Nummer** f **der Seite)** *(print)* page number
Seitenpaar n
→ Doppelseite
Seitenplakat n
→ Rumpfflächenplakat
Seitenpreis m **(Preis** m **für eine ganzseitige Anzeige)** page rate, full-page rate, full-page advertisement rate, full-page adrate
   The advertising rate for a full-page advertisement in a magazine or paper.
Seitenrand m *(print)* page margin, margin (of a page)
   The space between the print and the edge of a page.
Seitenscheibenplakat n *(transit advtsg)* side-window poster, sidewindow display
→ Scheibenplakat
Seitenspiegel m *(print)* page plan, (gezeichnete Skizze) key drawing
   The arrangement of type proofs and prints of art used as a guide by the engraver in assembling all elements of a page.
Seitensteg m *(print)* side stick, side margin
→ Seitenrand
Seitenteil m **(Teil** m **einer Seite)** *(print advtsg)* fraction of a page, page fraction, fractional page space
   Any periodical advertising space occupying less than the whole area of a page.
seitenteilige Anzeige f fractional page advertisement, fractional page ad

Seitentitel *m* (**Seitenüberschrift** *f*)
→ laufender Kolumnentitel
Seitenumbruch *m* *(print)* page makeup, *brit* page make-up, page pasteup, *brit* page paste-up
→ Umbruch
Seitenumkehrung *f*
→ Seitenverkehrung
Seitenverhältnis *n* *(phot/print/TV)* aspect ratio
  The relationship between the width and height of a picture.
seitenverkehrt *adj* *(phot/print)* laterally reverse(d), reverse, flop
Seitenverkehrung *f* (**Seitenumkehrung** *f*) *(phot/print)* lateral reversal, reversal, flop
  The process, technique and result of turning a photographic image as to right and left position, achieved either with optical reversing devices, by stripping, or placement of the image in a transparency holder during photography.
→ Konterbild
Seitenzahl *f* 1. *(print)* (**Seitenziffer**) → Seitennummer 2. (Zahl der Seiten) number of pages
Sektorenblende *f* *(film)* rotary disc shutter, rotary disk shutter
Sektorenverschluß *m* *(phot)* segment shutter
Sekundäranalyse *f* (**sekundäre Analyse** *f*) *(res)* secondary analysis
→ Sekundärforschung; *vgl.* Primäranalyse
Sekundärbedarf *m* *(econ)* secondary demand
  In economics, the demand for a particular brand of product.
vgl. Primärbedarf
Sekundärbedürfnis *n* *(psy)* secondary need, acquired need
vgl. Primärbedürfnis
Sekundärdaten *n/pl* (**sekundäre Daten** *n/pl*) *(social res/stat)* secondary data *pl*
vgl. Primärdaten
Sekundärdatengewinnung *f* (**sekundäre Datengewinnung** *f*) *(social res)* secondary data collection
vgl. primäre Datengewinnung
Sekundärerhebung *f*
→ Sekundärdatengewinnung
Sekundärforschung *f* secondary research, desk research
vgl. Primärforschung
Sekundärgruppe *f* *(soc)* secondary group

  A group which an individual joins by conscious and deliberate choice, a special-interest group.
vgl. Primärgruppe
Sekundärinformationen *f/pl* secondary information
Sekundärkommunikation *f* secondary communication
vgl. Primärkommunikation
Sekundärleser *m*
→ Zweitleser, Folgeleser
Sekundärleserschaft *f*
→ Zweitleserschaft
Sekundärmaterial *n*
→ Sekundärdaten
Sekundärnachfrage *f*
→ Sekundärbedarf
sekundärstatistische Auswertung *f*
→ Sekundäranalyse
Sekundärstudie *f* (**Sekundäruntersuchung** *f*) *(res)* secondary investigation, secondary study, desk study
Sekundärwerbeträger *m* (**Nebenwerbemedium** *n*) fringe publication
vgl. Hauptwerbeträger
selbe Stelle — selbe Welle *f* *(radio/TV)* across the board
  A broadcast program aired seven days a week at the same time. Loosely applied to any program broadcast at the same time five or more days a week.
Selbstaktualisierung *f*
→ Selbstverwirklichung
Selbstauslöser *m* *(phot)* delayed-action device, delayed-action shutter, self-timer, automatic release, auto release
  An adjustment on a camera shutter by means of which the photographer may set the shutter and then take his place in a group or view so that he is included in the picture.
Selbstauslösung *f* *(phot)* delayed action, automatic release
Selbstauswahl *f*
→ Teilselbstbedienung
Selbstbedienung *f* (**SB**) *(retailing)* self-service
  The method used in retailing whereby the customer selects his own merchandise, removes it from the shelves or bulk containers, carries it to a check-out stand to complete the transaction and transports it to the point of use.
Selbstbedienungsgeschäft *n* (**Selbstbedienungsladen** *m*) *(retailing)* self-service store, self-service shop
→ Selbstbedienung

Selbstbedienungsgroßhandel m
(econ) **1.** (Funktion) cash-and-carry wholesaling **2.** (Institution) cash-and-carry wholesale trade, cash-and-carry trade
A type of wholesaling, (→) Großhandel, exhibiting the following features: customers call to pick up the merchandise, cash is required with the purchase, salespersons are not widely used to call on prospects.

Selbstbedienungsladen m
→ Selbstbedienungsgeschäft
Selbstbedienungswarenhaus n **(SB-Warenhaus** n) *(retailing)* self-service department store
→ Verbrauchermarkt
Selbstbeschränkung f **(Selbstbeschränkungsvorschrift** f) self-policing regulation
→ Wettbewerbsregeln
Selbstbeschränkungsabkommen n self-policing agreement, self-policing regulations pl
→ Wettbewerbsregeln
Selbstbild n **(Selbstimage** n)
→ Eigenimage
Selbsteinschätzung f **(Selbsteinstufung** f) *(res)* self-assessment, self-rating, self-ranking
Selbsteinschätzungsverfahren n **(Selbsteinstufungsverfahren** n) *(res)* self-rating technique, self-assessment technique, self-ranking technique
Selbstimage n
→ Eigenimage
Selbstklebeband n **(Tesafilm** m) self-adhesive tape, adhesive tape, Scotch tape
Selbstklebeetikett n self-adhesive label, adhesive label, pressure-adhesive label
Selbstklebefolie f self-adhesive film, adhesive film, self-adhesive foil, adhesive foil, self-adhesive acetate, adhesive acetate
Selbstklebepapier n self-adhesive paper, adhesive paper, pressure-adhesive paper
Selbstklebeumschlag m self-seal envelope, self-sealing envelope
Selbstkonzept n
→ Eigenimage
Selbstkosten pl **(Gestehungskosten** pl) *(econ)* prime cost(s) *(pl)*, first cost(s) *(pl)*
1. The direct or immediate cost of a commodity, specifically the cost or expenses of producing or obtaining a commodity exclusive of general expenses of management involved and of profit on capital.
2. The combined total of raw material or direct labor costs incurred in production.
Selbstkostenpreis m *(econ)* cost price; zum Selbstkostenpreis verkaufen: to sell at cost
A price which covers the seller's cost but does not make a profit.
Selbstleuchter m fluorescent substance
Selbstselektion f *(retailing)* self selection
→ Teilselbstbedienung
Selbstverwirklichung f *(psy)* self-actualization, self-realization, brit self-realisation
The process of developing one's capacities, accepting oneself, and integrating one's motives, i.e. becoming actualized in what one is potentially.
Selbstverwirklichungsbedürfnis n *(psy)* self-actualization need (Abraham H. Maslow)
The highest of the five levels in Maslow's hierarchy of needs, (→) Bedürfnishierarchie, after egoistic needs have been accommodated. Most people do not reach this level of self-fulfillment, to become whatever they are capable of becoming.
Selbstwahl f
→ Teilselbstbedienung
Selektion f selection
selektive Absatzpolitik f
→ selektiver Vertrieb
selektive Distribution f
→ selektiver Vertrieb
selektive Erinnerung f *(psy)* selective memory, selective retention, selective recall
The tendency of audience members who have been exposed to unsympathetic material to recall it less than they recall sympathetic material, and to forget it more rapidly.
selektive Kommunikation f selective communication
selektive Sensitivierung f selective sensitization
selektive Wahrnehmung f **(selektive Perzeption)** f *(psy)* selective perception, selective attention, selective exposure
The tendency of individuals to perceive or to expose themselves to mass communication material that is in accord with their existing attitudes or interests

selektive Werbung

and to avoid perceiving, or being exposed to, contrary attitudes.
selektive Werbung f selective advertising, selective demand advertising
Both advertising which strives to establish selective buying motives within the audience and a strategy for selecting media which is based on the common special interest of the product's users wherever they are located. Here the problem is not so much the cost, but just how to get the message to them.
→ gezielte Werbung
selektiver Verkauf m (econ) selective selling
The policy of selling to a limited number of customers in a market.
selektiver Vertrieb m (**selektive Absatzpolitik** f, **selektive Distribution** f) (econ) selective distribution, limited distribution
A distribution policy, (→) Vertriebspolitik, that uses only retailers who spend no less than a predetermined amount of money or who meet certain standards in their operations or consists in the wholesale distribution only of items that have a markup of no less than a predetermined rate and yet are competitively priced.
Selektivfrage f
→ Auswahlfrage
Selektivität f selectivity
Selenzelle f selenium cell
Self-Liquidator m (**Self-liqidating Offer** n)
→ SLO-Angebot
Selling Center n
→ Verkaufsgremium
seltener Leser m
→ gelegentlicher Leser
seltenster Wert m (**Minimumstelle** f) (stat) antimode
The variate value for which a frequency distribution, (→) Häufigkeitsverteilung, has a minimum. The expression is usually confined to the case where the minimum is not zero and is a true minimum.
Semantik f (res) semantics pl (construed as sg), auch significs pl (construed as sg)
That branch of science within linguistics that is concerned with the conveyance of meaning by the grammatical and lexical devices of a language.
semantische Forschung f semantic research

semantische Funktion f (res) semantic function
semantischer Raum m (res) semantic space
semantisches Differential n (**Polaritätenprofil** n) (social res) semantic differential, semantic differential scale (Charles E. Osgood)
A method of measuring attitudes, the meaning of words or concepts which normally employs bipolar scales separated by seven equal intervals. The scale helps to specify the connotative meaning which an individual has for any stimulus and to isolate statistically significant dimensions of connotation such as evaluation (good — bad), activity (active — passive), and potency (strong — weak).
semantisches Feld n (res) semantic field
semantisches Profil n (**Polaritätenprofil** n) (social res) semantic profile
Semidokumentation f
→ Dokudrama
Semiotik f (res) semiotics pl (construed as sg), auch semeiology
The theory of signs, i.e. linguistics, logic, mathematics, rhetoric, etc., subdivided into syntactics, semantics, pragmatics.
Sendeablaufplan m (**Sendeplan** m) (radio/TV) presentation schedule, transmission schedule, schedule
Sendeablaufprotokoll n (**Ablaufprotokoll** n) (radio/TV) presentation log, transmission log, station log, log
In broadcasting, an hourly chronological record of all programs and commercials aired by a station.
Sendeabwicklung f (radio/TV) broadcasting operations pl
Sendeanlage f (radio/TV) transmitting installation, transmitting station, transmitter
Sendeanstalt f (radio/TV) broadcasting corporation, broadcasting company, broadcasting organization, brit organisation
Sendeantenne f transmitting antenna, brit transmitting aerial
Sendeaufnahme f (radio/TV) taped broadcast, taped program, brit programme
Sendeauftrag m (radio/TV) broadcast order
Sendeaufzeichnung f (radio/TV) recorded broadcast, recorded program, brit programme, (zur zeitverschobenen Ausstrahlung) delayed

broadcast, *colloq* (Sendekonserve) canned broadcast, canned program, *brit* programme
Sendeausfall m *(radio/TV)* transmission breakdown, blackout, dead air
Sendeband n *(radio/TV)* transmission tape, (Frequenz) transmitting frequency range
Sendebeginn m *(radio/TV)* sign-on, (Ansage) station announcement; zu senden beginnen: *v/i* to sign on
  The time at which a station begins its broadcast day.
  vgl. Sendeschluß
Sendebereich m **(Sendegebiet** n, **Empfangsbereich** m, **Empfangsgebiet** n) *(radio/TV)* broadcasting area, signal area, service area, signal service area, signal service zone, service range, transmission area, coverage area, coverage, reception area
  The geographic area normally reached by any level of a broadcast signal.
Sendebetrieb m *(radio/TV)* broadcasting operations *pl*
Sendebild n *(TV)* outgoing picture
Sendedauer f *(radio/TV)* duration of transmission, transmission time
Sendeempfang m *(radio/TV)* broadcast reception, reception
Sendeform f **(Programmtypus** m**)** *(radio/TV)* format, type of broadcast
  The general character of the programs aired by a radio or television station. Distinction between the various formats is of minor importance under the German system of public-service broadcasting, (→) öffentlich-rechtlicher Rundfunk.
Sendefrequenz f *(radio/TV)* transmitting frequency, output frequency
Sendefrequenzbereich m *(radio/TV)* broadcast spectrum
  The segment of the total range of electromagnetic waves assigned to television and radio broadcasters.
Sendegebiet n
→ Sendebereich
Sendekanal m *(radio/TV)* broadcast channel, broadcasting channel, channel
  A group of wave lengths or operating frequencies assigned to radio and television stations.
Sendekonserve f *(radio/TV)* prerecorded broadcast, recorded broadcast, *colloq* canned broadcast, canned program, *brit* programme
Sendekopie f *(TV)* transmission copy, transmission print, transmission tape
Sendeleistung f **(Sendestärke** f**)** *(radio/TV)* effective radiated power (ERP), transmitting power, field strength, broadcast signal strength, signal strength
Sendeleiter m *(radio/TV)* production director, director of production, producer
Sendeleitung f *(radio/TV)* **1.** direction of production, production management **2.** (Übertragungsleitung) outgoing circuit, outgoing channel, distribution channel
Sendelizenz f *(radio/TV)* broadcasting license, *brit* licence
Sendemanuskript n
→ Drehbuch
Sendemodulation f *(radio/TV)* transmitted modulation
senden *v/t* **1.** (mit der Post) to send, to forward, to dispatch, *auch* to despatch, to mail, to ship, *brit* to post **2.** *(radio/TV)* to broadcast, to air, *(TV)* to telecast, *brit* to televise **3.** → übertragen
Sendenorm f
→ Fernsehnorm
Sendepause f *(radio/TV)* intermission, interval, break, station break
Sendeplan m
→ Sendeablaufplan
Sendeprotokoll n
→ Sendeablaufprotokoll, Sendungsprotokoll
Sender m **(Sendestation** f**) 1.** *(radio/TV)* broadcasting station, station, *brit* wireless station (Übertragungssender) transmitter, transmitting station, (Sendeverstärker) relay station, translator station, translator **2.** (Kommunikator) sender, communicator **3.** → Absender
Senderabstimmung f *(radio/TV)* station tuning, transmitter tuning, tuning
Senderaum m *(radio/TV)* broadcasting room, broadcasting studio
→ Sendesaal
Senderausfall m *(radio/TV)* station breakdown, station blackout, dead air
Senderbeteiligung f *(radio/TV)* network rating, station rating

Senderdia

Any rating calculated for a television or radio network. Because there are several different types of rating, (→) Einschaltquote, there are several different types of network rating. In general, however, this kind of rating shows the percentage of television or radio households, or the percentage of a group of individuals among those in a specified area, that is estimated to be in a network's audience over a specified time.
→ Sehbeteiligung
Senderdia n **(Senderkennungsdia** n**)** *(TV)* station identification slide, station ID slide, station identification, station ID
Senderechte n/pl *(radio/TV)* broadcasting rights pl, transmission rights pl
Senderegie f *(radio)* presentation suite, continuity suite
sendereigenes Programm n **(Eigenprogramm** n **eines Lokalsenders)** *(radio/TV)* station-produced program, sustaining program, sustaining show, sustainer
Sendereihe f *(radio/TV)* broadcast series, broadcast serial, serial broadcast, serial, series of broadcasts
Sendereinstellung f *(radio/TV)* station tuning, station selector
Senderkette f
→ Sendernetz
Senderleistung f
→ Sendeleistung
Sendernetz n **(Senderkette** f**)** *(radio/TV)* broadcasting network, network, broadcasting chain, chain, *colloq* net, web
Sendernetzprogramm n *(radio/TV)* network broadcast, network program, *brit* programme
Sendertreue f **(Senderbindung** f, **Senderloyalität** f**)** *(radio/TV)* channel loyalty, station loyalty
Senderverstärker m **(Übertragungssender** m**)** *(radio/TV)* relay station, common carrier, translator station, translator
  A radio or television station that rebroadcasts programs from another station on another channel, but has no local studio and does no originate programs or commercials locally.
Senderwahl f
→ Sendereinstellung
Senderweiche f *(radio/TV)* combining unit

Sendesaal m *(radio/TV)* broadcasting hall, concert hall, audience studio
Sendesatellit m *(radio/TV)* broadcast satellite, broadcasting satellite, communications satellite, *colloq* bird
Sendeschluß m *(radio/TV)* sign-off, closedown, (Absage) closing announcement; Sendeschluß machen: to sign off, to go off the air
  The time at which a station ends its broadcast day.
vgl. Sendebeginn
Sendesperre f *(radio/TV)* block-out, (für Werbung) blocked-out time
  Airtime that is not sold to advertisers.
Sendestärke f
→ Sendeleistung
Sendestation f
→ Sender
Sendestudio n *(radio/TV)* broadcasting studio, studio
Sendetechnik f radio and television engineering
Sendetermin m **(Sendezeitpunkt** m**)** *(radio/TV)* air date, airdate, air time, airtime
  The scheduled broadcast date for a television or radio program or commercial.
Sendetext m *(radio/TV)* broadcast script, script
  The witten text for a commercial, TV or radio program.
Sendeton m *(radio/TV)* program sound, *brit* programme sound
Sendetonband n *(radio/TV)* transmission tape
Sendeturm m radio tower
Sendeunterbrechung f (für Werbung) advertising break, commercial break, (Senderunterbrechung) station break, (Ausfall) dead air
  The time after, before, or within a program which is used for announcements.
Sendeverstärker m
→ Senderverstärker
Sendezeit f *(radio/TV)* broadcasting time, air time, airtime, transmission time, (für Werbung) commercial time, commercial occasion, *brit* commercial slot, (zugewiesene Sendezeit) allotted time
Sendezentrale f *(radio/TV)* **1.** (im Sender) master control room

2. (eines Sendernetzes) flagship station
3. (eines Kabelfernsehsystems) head end
Sendung f **1.** *(radio/TV)* broadcast, aircast, program, *brit* programme, show, transmission **2.** (Postaussendung) mailing **3.** (Warenaussendung) consignment, shipment
Sendungsprotokoll n *(radio/TV)* as produced script
  The script of a TV or radio commercial or program as it was actually broadcast or produced on fim.
senkrechte Halbseite f **(hochformatige Halbseite** f) *(print)* vertical half-page
  Half the entire width of the full height of a periodical page purchased for an advertisement.
vgl. waagerechte Halbseite
Senkrechtschwenk m **(Kippschwenk** m) *(film/TV)* tilt, tilting, (mit dem Kran) craning, booming, (nach oben) craning-up, booming-up, (nach unten) craning-down, booming down
  A camera movement along a vertical arc and from a fixed position.
vgl. Panoramaschwenk
Sensation f sensation
Sensationsblatt n **(Sensationszeitung** f) sensationalist paper, yellow paper
→ Boulevardzeitung
Sensationsjournalismus m sensationalist journalism, sensationalism, yellow journalism
  Journalism which emphasizes the obscene, the risqué, the gory, the sensational.
Sensationspresse f sensationalist press, yellow press
Sensationswerbung f stunt advertising
Sensibilisator m *(phot/print)* sensitizer
  In offset-lithography, a bichromated albumin solution used for making a plate sensitive to light; in the deep-etch lithographic process, a bichromated glue or gum used for coating the plate.
sensibilisieren
→ lichtempfindlich machen
Sensibilisierung f
→ Lichtempfindlichmachen
sensitiv
→ lichtempfindlich
Sensitivität f **(Empfindlichkeit** f) *(psy)* sensitivity

Sensitivitätsanalyse f *(psy)* sensitivity analysis
Sensitometer n *(phot)* sensitometer
Sensitometrie f *(phot)* sensitometry
Sensorium n (*meist pl* **Sensorien**) *(psy)* sensory receptor(s) *(pl)*
Separatabdruck m **(Separatdruck** m)
→ Sonderdruck
Sepiapapier n *(phot)* sepia paper
  A type of monotone film or photographic printing paper yielding brown tones instead of gray to black.
Sepiapause f
→ Braunpause
Sepiaphoto n sepia print, sepia
  A photographic print in brown, rather than black, tones, and made on sepia paper.
Sepiazeichnung f sepia drawing
Sepmag n **(separates Magnetband** n) *(film)* separated magnetic sound, sound on tape (S.O.T.)
  A separate tape on which the sound of a motion picture is recorded.
Sequentialanalyse f
→ Sequenzanalyse
Sequentialtest m **(sequentieller Test** m) *(res)* sequential test
  A test of significance, (→) Signifikanztest, for a statistical hypothesis which is carried out by using the methods of sequential analysis, (→) Sequenzanalyse.
sequentielles Marketing n sequential marketing
  The planning of the steps of a marketing campaign one at a time and in an orderly fashion on the basis of prior analysis.
Sequenz f sequence
Sequenzanalyse f **(Sequentialanalyse** f, **sequentielle Analyse** f) *(res)* sequential analysis
  A research procedure in which the total number of cases to be studied or observations to be made is not determined in advance, but is decided as the research proceeds through a process of periodic analysis of the data thus far gathered. At each stage the data are analyzed to determine if the hypotheses may be accepted or rejected or if more data are needed or possibly if more of a specific type of data are needed.
→ Sequenzstichprobenbildung
Sequenzstichprobe f **(sequentielle Stichprobe** f) *(stat)* sequential sample
Sequenzstichprobenbildung f **(Sequenzstichprobenverfahren** n, **Sequenzauswahl** f, **sequentielle Auswahl** f) *(stat)* sequential sampling

Serie

A method of obtaining a sample from a population by measuring one elementary unit at a time and cumulating the results until the probable sampling error is determined to be such that the standard error, (→) Standardfehler, is reduced to the level acceptable to decision-makers. In sequential sampling the members are drawn one by one (or in groups) in order, and the results of the drawing at any stage decide whether sampling is to continue. The sample size is thus not fixed in advance but depends on the actual results and varies from one sample to another.

Serie f *(radio/TV)* series, serial
A number of television or radio programs presented at regular intervals and united by title, cast, story theme, etc.

serielle Korrelation f
→ Reihenkorrelation

serieller Effekt m **(Reihenfolgeeffekt** m**)** serial effect

Serienanzeige f
→ Anzeigenserie

Serienkopie f
→ Verleihkopie

Seriennachlaß m
→ Wiederholungsrabatt, Malrabatt

Serienwerk n serial publication, serial
→ Fortsetzungsreihe, Schriftenreihe

Serife f **(Füßchen** n, **Serif** m**)** *(typ)* serif
The short cross strokes at the top and bottom of the characters in certain designs of type, especially those of the Roman race.

serifenlos adj
→ grotesk

serifenlose Schrift f
→ Groteskschrift

Serigraph m **(Serigraf** m**)**
→ Siebdruck

Serigraphie f **(Serigrafie** f**)**
→ Siebdruck

Service m
→ Kundendienst

Servicebereich m
→ Dienstleistungssektor

Service Fee f *(advtsg)* service fee
A fee paid by an advertiser to an advertising agency, either in the form of a retainer for general services or of a special compensation for unusual services.

Service-Fee-System n
→ amerikanisches Abrechnungsverfahren

Servicegrad m
→ Lieferbereitschaft

Serviceleistung f
→ Kundendienst

Service Merchandiser m
→ Regalgroßhändler

Service m **nach dem Kauf**
→ Kundendienst

setzen v/t *(typ)* to set, to set up, to typeset, to compose

Setzer(in) m(f) typesetter, compositor, (Taster) keyboard operator
→ Schriftsetzer

Setzergeselle m *(typ)* two-thirder
An advanced printing apprentice.

Setzerei f **(Setzersaal** m, **Setzsaal** m**)** *(typ)* composing room, case room, typesetting room, (Unternehmen) composition house

Setzerjunge m **(Setzerlehrling** m**)** *(print)* printer's devil, apprentice compositor, apprentice typesetter

Setzersaal m
→ Setzerei

Setzfehler m **(Satzfehler** m**)** *(typ)* typographical error, typo, printer's error
In the narrower sense, a mistake made in typing or in setting type. More in general, any type error or undesirable feature of a proof or the like that is deemed to be the fault of the printer and is therefore not charged to the publisher or author in correction.

Setzkasten m type case, case, letter case
→ Schriftkasten

Setzkosten pl **(Satzkosten** pl**)** cost(s) *(pl)* of typesetting, typesetting cost(s) *(pl)*, cost(s) *pl)* of composition, composition cost(s) *(pl)*

Setzlinie f *(typ)* setting rule, composing rule, type rule
One of a variety of lines, of various thicknesses, which the printer can insert in making up pages of type and engravings.

Setzmaschine f 1. typesetter, typesetting machine, composing machine
A machine used to produce single types and lines of type on one slug.
2. *(TV)* → Titelsetzmaschine

Setzregel f
→ Satzanweisung

Setzschiff n **(Satzschiff** n**)** *(print)* galley, composing galley
A printer's shallow tray in which type is placed for assembling or storage.

Setztisch m **(Satztisch** m**)** *(print)* composing table

Setzwinkel *m*
→ Winkelhaken
Sexappeal *m* (**Sex-Appeal** *m*) sex appeal
Sexkino *n* sex movie, sex cinema
Sexzeitschrift *f* sex magazine
Sheppardsche Korrektur *f* (**Sheppard-Korrektur** *f*) *(stat)* Sheppard's correction
Sheth-Modell *n*
→ Howard-Sheth-Modell
Shop-in-the-Shop-System *n* *(retailing)* shop-in-the-shop system
Shopping Center *n*
→ Einkaufszentrum
Shopping Goods *pl* (**Güter** *n/pl* **des gehobenen Bedarfs**) *(econ)* shopping goods *pl*
Those consumer's goods which the customer in the process of selection and purchase characteristically compares on such bases as suitability, quality, price and style. Examples of goods that most consumers probably buy as shopping goods are: millinery, furniture, dress goods, women's ready-to-wear and shoes, used automobiles, and major appliances. It should be emphasized that a given article may be bought by one customer as a shopping good and by another as a specialty or convenience good. The general classification depends upon the way in which the average or typical buyer purchases.
vgl. Convenience Goods, Specialty Goods
Sicherheit *f* (**Sicherheitsgrad** *m*, **Genauigkeitsgrad** *m*)
→ Signifikanzniveau
Sicherheitsband *n* (Frequenz) guard band
Sicherheitsbedürfnis *n* *(psy)* safety need, *auch* security need (Abraham H. Maslow)
In the hierarchy of needs, (→) Bedürfnishierarchie, needs for protection, physical safety, order, routine, familiarity, and certainty become the motivational force in human behavior after the physiological needs have been satisfied.
Sicherheitsbestand *m* *(econ)* safety stock(s) *(pl)*
An amount of a product carried in inventory in excess of normal requirements to reduce out-of-stock conditions caused by sales fluctuations, or by failures by suppliers to deliver as promised for whatever reason.
Sicherheitsfilm *m* *(phot)* safety film, safety stock, non-flam film

Sicherheitsgrad *n*
→ Signifikanzniveau
Sicherheitskopie *f (phot/film)* safety copy
Sicherheitsmotiv *n*
→ Sicherheitsbedürfnis
Sicherheitsspur *f (film)* guard band, guard track, safety track
Sicherheitswahrscheinlichkeit *f*
→ Signifikanzniveau
Sichtbarkeit *f* visibility
Sichtbarkeitstest *m (outdoor advtsg)* visibility test
Sichtbereich *m (outdoor advtsg)* field of visibility
Sichtpackung *f (packaging)* transparent box, transparent package, transparent pack
Sichtröhre *f (TV)* pattern tube
Sichtschirm *m*
→ Bildschirm
Sichtzeichen *n* visual signal, marker
Siebdruck *m (print)* 1. (Siebdruckverfahren) silk screen printing, screen printing, screen process printing, silk screen process, (Kunstdruck) serigraphy
A method of printing based on the stencil principle. Inks are squeezed through separate cloth screens one at a time that have the design to be printed imposed upon it, so that the ink of each color passes only through the area which is to be printed. The technique is used for the reproduction of posters, show cards, etc.
2. (Produkt) silk screen print, screen print; (Kunstdruck) serigraph
Siebdrucker *m (print)* silk screen printer, screen printer, (Kunstdrucker) serigrapher
Siebdruckfarbe *f (print)* screen printing ink, silk screen printing ink, silk screen color, *brit* colour
Siebdruckmaschine *f (print)* screen printer, screen printing machine
Siebdruckschablone *f (print)* silkscreen stencil, stencil, (Sieb) silk screen, screen
Siebseite *f (paper)* wire side
The under side of a sheet of paper as it comes off the papermaking machine.
vgl. Filzseite
Siegelmarke *f* paper seal
siehe Manuskript! *(typ)* (Satzanweisung) follow copy, folo copy, follow style, folo style, see copy

Sigma

Sigma n (σ, Σ) *(math/stat)* sigma
The shorthand method of expressing "the sum of..."

Signal n signal, natural sign
1. The physical embodiment of a message (an utterance, a transmission, an exhibition of sign-events).
2. An electrical impulse derived from and convertible to a visible picture and or audible sound.

Signalamplitude f signal amplitude

Signal-Detektionstheorie f theory of signal detectability, signal detectability theory, signal detection theory

Signallampe f *(radio/TV)* cue lamp, cue light, signaling lamp, brit signalling lamp, tally light, indicator lamp, warning light
A red warning light indicating that a camera is shooting a scene for transmission.

Signalmischer m signal mixer, signal combiner

Signalpegel m signal level

Signalstärke f signal strength

Signatur f **1.** → Bogensignatur
2. *(print)* nick
A notch in type which acts as a guide to the compositor.

Signet n emblem, logotype, logo
The signature or standard name plate of an advertiser.

signifikant *adj (stat)* significant

signifikanter Unterschied m *(stat)* significant difference

Signifikanz f **(statistische Sicherheit** f**)** *(stat)* significance
An effect is said to be significant if the value of the statistic used to test it lies outside acceptable limits, that is to say, if the hypothesis that the effect is not present is rejected.

Signifikanzniveau n **(statistische Signifikanz** f**)** *(stat)* level of significance, significance level
Many statistical tests of hypotheses depend on the use of the probability distributions of a statistic t chosen for the purpose of the particular test. When the hypothesis is true this distribution has a known form (at least approximately) and the probability $P(t-t_1)$ or $P(t-t_0)$ can be determined for assigned t_0 or t_1. The acceptability of the hypothesis is usually discussed, inter alia, in terms of the values of t observed; if they have a small probability, in the sense of falling outside the range t_0 to t_1 ($P(t-t_1)$ and $P(t-t_0)$ small, the hypothesis is rejected. The probabilities $P(t \geq t_1)$ and $P(t \leq t_0)$ are called levels of significance and are usually expressed as percentages.

Signifikanzprüfung f **(Signifikanztest** m**)** *(stat)* significance test
In hypothesis testing, (→) Hypothesentest, the attempt of obtaining an outcome that permits the rejection of a null hypothesis, (→) Nullhypothese. A significant value of a test statistic is one that exceeds the critical values. A significant difference between sample statistics is one that is large enough to reject the hypothesis that the corresponding population parameters are equal.

Signifikanzwahrscheinlichkeit f *(stat)* significance probability, p value
In reporting the results of a significance test, (→) Signifikanzprüfung, the probability of obtaining a difference as large or larger than the observed difference. Equivalently, it is the probability of obtaining a value of the test statistic that differs from the expected value by as much as or more than does the observed value, if the null hypothesis is true. If the obtained p value is less than the chosen level of significance, (→) Signifikanzniveau, the null hypothesis can be rejected.

Sikkativ n
→ Trockenmittel

Silberbad n *(phot)* silver bath
The acidified silver nitrate solution used for sensitizing plates in wet collodion photography.

Silberbild n *(phot)* silver image

Silberblende f *(phot/film/TV)* silvered reflector

Silberbromid n
→ Bromsilber

Silberdruck m *(print)* **1.** (Verfahren) silverprinting, saltprinting, brownprinting **2.** (Produkt) silverprint, saltprint, brownprint
A special type of photographic paper print whose emulsion is sensitized by silver salts, made by engravers to show the accurate cropping and assembly of art elements.

Silberfolie f silver foil

Silberhalogen n **(Silberhalogenid** n**)**
→ Silbersalz

Silberkorn n *(phot)* silver grain

Silbernitrat n
→ Silbersalz

Silberpapier n *(phot)* silver paper, tinfoil

Silbersalz n *(phot)* silver salt, silver, silver nitrate, silver halide

Silberschirm m *(film)* silver screen
Simulation f *(res)* simulation
The process of building a model to convey the preconception of how variables interrelate and to make predictions. It is a method for analyzing the behavior of a system by computing its time path for given initial conditions and given parameter values.
Simulationsexperiment n *(res)* simulation experiment
Any experiment employing simulation.
Simulationsmodell n *(res)* simulation model
Simulationstechnik f **(Simulationsverfahren** n) *(res)* simulation technique
Simultansendung f *(radio/TV)* simultaneous broadcast, simulcast
A broadcast on a television station and radio station at the same time, usually to permit video material to be accompanied by high fidelity, stereophonic audio.
Simultanbelichtung f **(Simultanaufnahme** f) *(phot/film/TV)* combination shot, double exposure, double print
A composite image created by two exposures of one film or blended images from two television cameras.
Simultanübertragung f
→ Simultansendung
Single-Linkage-Methode f **(Minimum-Distanz-Regel** f) *(stat)* single linkage technique, single linkage
vgl. Average-Linkage-Methode, Complete-Linkage-Methode
S-I-R-Modell n
→ S-O-R-Modell
sittenwidrige Werbung f etwa immoral advertising, unfair practice
Situationsanalyse f situational analysis (Lovell J. Carr)
In general, a way of viewing and analyzing problems as situation processes, and not in terms of single causes or of individual traits. In economics, the joint reference to analyses of a business firm's external environment and its internal situation.
Situationskomödie f *(radio/TV)* situation comedy, sitcom, *auch* sit com
A show whose comedy is based on a series of humorous situations.
situatives Marketing n situative marketing
→ Situationsanalyse
SK *abbr* Schlußklappe
Skala f *(res)* scale, *auch* scalometer

A series of numerical units or nonnumerical categories used to measure or classify data. In principle, the construction of a scale requires the selection of a set of items such that the acceptance or the rejection of one implies a different degree of favorability of unfavorability in attitude, (→) Einstellung.
Skalafrage f *(survey res)* scale question, *auch* scalometer question
A type of fixed-alternative question, (→) Auswahlfrage, that requires an evaluative choice as the response. The respondent may be presented with words such as "Never, Sometimes, Frequently, Always," or a purely numerical sequence used to mark a group of items in order of importance to the respondent.
→ Ratingskala
Skalenanalyse f *(stat)* scale analysis
Skalenbildung f
→ Skalierung
Skalendiskriminationstechnik f **(Diskriminationstechnik** f) *(stat)* scale discrimination technique (Allen L. Edwards/F.P. Kilpatrick)
Skalenniveau n
→ Skalierungsniveau
Skalenmodell n *(stat)* scale model
A model which differs only in scale from the real-world structure.
Skalenparameter m *(stat)* scale parameter
Skalenpunkt m *(stat)* scale point
Skalen-Reliabilität f
→ Skalenzuverlässigkeit
Skalenpunktwert m **(Skalenwert** m) *(stat)* scale score
Skalentest m *(stat)* scale test
Skalentyp m **(skalierbarer Typ** m) *(stat)* scale type
Skalenwert m *(stat)* scale value
Skalenziffer f **(Skalenzahl** f) *(stat)* scale number
Skalenzuverlässigkeit f **(Skalen-Reliabilität** f) *(stat)* scale reliability
→ Zuverlässigkeit
Skalierung f **(Skalieren** n, **Skalenbildung** f) *(stat)* scaling
The processes and techniques of ordering a number of related items, e.g. attitude statements or descriptive characteristics, to form a continuum in order to provide a means of quantitative measurement of qualitative variables.
Skalierungsmethode f **(Skalierungsverfahren** n, **Skalierungstechnik** f) *(stat)* scaling technique, scaling method

Skalogramm n *(social res)* scalogram, Guttman scale (Louis Guttman)
→ Guttmanskala
Skalogrammanalyse f *(social res)* scalogram analysis, Guttman scaling technique, Guttman scaling (Louis Guttman)
→ Guttmanskala
Skalometer n
→ Skala
Skalometerfrage f
→ Skalafrage
Skandalblatt n (**Skandalzeitung** f, **Skandalzeitschrift** f)
→ Sensationsblatt
Skandalpresse f
→ Sensationspresse
Skelettschrift f *(typ)* skeleton face type, skeleton type
Skimming-Politik f
→ Abschöpfungsstrategie
Skimming-Preis m
→ Abschöpfungspreis
Skin-Effekt m
→ Hauteffekt
Skizze f sketch, rough draft, rough, raw draft, outline, (eines Layouts) visualization, *brit* visualisation, visual
  A freehand drawing, quickly made, to show the visual concept and the general arrangement of an advertisement, an illustration, a scene, a setup, etc.
Skizzenmappe f sketchbook, sketch folder
Skizzenzeichner m sketcher
skizzieren v/t to sketch, to trace out, to outline, to make a sketch of, to make a rough draft of
sklavische Nachahmung f *(econ)* slavish imitation, servile imitation
Skonto m/n *(pl* **Skontos, Skonti; Barzahlungsrabatt** m) *(econ)* cash discount, *auch* prompt payment discount
  The amount allowed to be deducted from a bill if it is paid promptly within a specified period of time; in Germany a 2 percent cash discount is commonly given if payment is made within 10 days.
Skript n *(radio/film/TV)* script
  The complete sequential account of dialogue, actions, settings, etc. prepared by the author of a motion picture, a play or show.
Skylight-Filter m *(phot)* skylight filter
Slapstick m (**Radaukomödie** f, **Klamotte** f, **Slapstickkomödie** f) *(film/radio/TV)* slapstick, slapstick comedy
  A fast action comedy, employing knockabout humor, chases, and profuse properties and sound effects. The English term is widely integrated into German.
Slapstickfilm m (**Filmschwank** m) *(film/radio/TV)* slapstick picture, slapstick motion picture
Sleeper-Effekt m
→ Zeitzündereffekt (Spätzündereffekt), Wirkungsverzögerung, Carryover-Effekt
Slice-of-Life-Technik f (**Slice-of-Life-Werbung** f) slice-of-life advertising, slice-of-life method, slice-of-life technique, slice of life
  All advertising simulating a real-life situation as closely as possible and showing how an individual overcomes an obstacle to a goal by using the advertised product.
SLO-Angebot n (**SLO-Zugabe** f) *(econ)* self-liquidating premium, self-liquidator, self-liquidating offer (SLO), purchase-privilege premium
  A premium, (→) Zugabe, having a cost fully covered by the purchase price for which it is offered.
Slogan m slogan
  A sentence or phrase which through repeated usage is designed to become identified with the advertiser's product or service.
Slowmotion f *(film/TV)* slow motion
  The practice of speeding a film faster than normal through the camera, so that the action appears to be slowed down.
Slowmotion-Maschine f (**SMM**) *(film/TV)* slow motion machine
S/N-Verhältnis n signal-to-noise ratio, S/N ratio
→ Rauschabstand
Snob-Effekt m *(econ)* snob effect
  The extent to which demand for consumer goods is diminished because many others are using the same goods. This happens e.g. in the field of exclusive fashion in which the demand curve, (→) Nachfragekurve, is sloped positively until the design is copied and made available at popular prices, after which the curve becomes sharply negative as the patrons of such fashion dissociate themselves from the general public.
Snob-Appeal m snob appeal
Social-
→ Sozial-, Sozio-
Soffitenbeleuchtung f (**Soffitenleuchte** f, **Soffitenlampe** f) *(phot/film/TV)* festoon lamp, festoon light, strip light, tubular lamp

Sofortbefragung f *(survey res)* intercept interviewing
vgl. **Koinzidenzbefragung**
Sofortzugabe f *(promotion)* direct premium
→ Direktzugabe, Herstellerzugabe
Soften n
→ Weichzeichnen
Softlinse f *(phot)* soft lens, diffusing lens, diffuser, *auch* diffusor, *colloq* romanticizer
→ Diffusionslinse
Softscheibe f *(phot/film/TV)* diffuser, diffusion disk, *auch* diffusor, soft focus filter, *colloq* romanticizer, *brit* romanticiser, (Beleuchtung) net, scrim
  A device used to soften or diffuse harsh light or to blur the focus of a camera image.
Solarisation f **(Solarisierung** f) *(phot)* solarization, *brit* solarisation
  A reversal of the image in a negative or print caused by great overexposure.
Sollfrequenz f *(electr.)* nominal frequency
Sommerloch n **(Sommerflaute** f) *(econ/advtsg)* summer doldrums *pl*
Sommerschlußverkauf m *(retailing)* summer closing-out sale, summer sales(s) *pl*
→ Schlußverkauf
Sondage f
→ Befragung
Sonderabdruck m **(Sonderabzug** m)
→ Sonderdruck
Sonderanfertigung f *(econ)* custom-made product, custom product
  A result of creative selling in which at least part of a product or service is designed especially for a particular prospect.
Sonderangebot n *(econ)* bargain, bargain offer, bargain sale, special offer
  An offer providing unusual value, normally a reduction in price.
Sonderangebotsanzeige f bargain advertisement, bargain sales advertisement, bargain ad, bargain sales ad
  An advertisement making a bargain offer.
Sonderangebotsfläche f *(retailing)* (im Laden) bargain basement
Sonderangebotskaufen n *(retailing)* bargain buying, bargain sales buying, *colloq* cherrypicking

Sonderheft

  The practice of consumers to buy only or preponderantly bargain products or services.
Sonderangebotspackung f *(retailing)* price pack, price-off pack
  A special retail package announcing a temporary reduction from the standard retail price, used as a promotional inducement to purchasers.
Sonderangebotspolitik f **(Sonderangebotsstrategie** f) *(retailing)* bargain sales policy, bargain sales strategy
Sonderangebotstisch m *(retailing)* bargain counter, bargain sales counter
Sonderangebotsverkauf m *(retailing)* bargain sale(s) *(pl)*, bargain selling
Sonderangebotswerbung f *(retailing)* bargain sales advertising, bargain advertising
Sonderausgabe f **(Sonderheft** n) (Zeitschrift) special edition, special issue, (Themenheft) feature issue, (sehr umfangreich) directory issue, (Saisonausgabe) boom issue
Sonderauslage f *(POP advtsg)* special display
  Any retail merchandising display other than that ordinarily mounted for a product on a shelf.
Sonderausverkauf m
→ Ausverkauf
Sonderbeilage f (Zeitschrift/Zeitung) special supplement
Sonderbericht m **(Sondersendung** f, **Sonderprogramm** n) *(radio/TV)* special report, special feature, special
Sonderberichterstatter m special correspondent, (Reisekorrespondent) roving correspondent
Sonderbestellung f *(econ)* special order
Sonderdisplay n
→ Sonderauslage
Sonderdruck m **(Sonderabdruck** m) offprint, separate print
Sonderfarbe f *(print)* special color, *brit* colour
→ Schmuckfarbe
Sonderfläche f **(Sonderstelle** f) *(outdoor advtsg)* special-purpose site
Sonderformat n *(advtsg)* special shape
Sonderformatanzeige f special shape advertisement, special-shape ad
→ Flexformanzeige
Sonderheft n
→ Sonderausgabe

Sonderkorrespondent *m*
→ Sonderberichterstatter
Sondermeldung *f (radio/TV)* special announcement
Sondernachlaß *m*
→ Sonderrabatt
Sondernummer *f*
→ Sonderausgabe
Sonderpackung *f* special package, special pack, bonus package, bonus pack
 Any specially packaged product designed to provide purchasers with extra content, at the usual price.
Sonderplazierung *f (advtsg)* special position, special placement
 Insertion of an advertisement in what is regarded as a distinctive position in a publication, e.g. outside or inside covers, or facing matter. Such a selection frequently involves a higher charge being made to the advertiser and advance action on his part to secure it.
→ Vorzugsplazierung
Sonderpreis *m (econ)* special price, premium price *(advtsg)* special rate, off card rate, (für Sonderplazierung) premium rate
 Any price or rate other than the regular, advertised, standard, list, or retail price, or other than the card rate.
Sonderprogramm *n*
→ Sondersendung
Sonderrabatt *m (econ)* special discount, extra discount
Sonderseite *f* (Zeitung/Zeitschrift) special feature page, feature page, special page
Sondersendung *f* (**Sonderprogramm** *n*) *(radio/TV)* special broadcast, special program, *brit* programme, special
 A single radio or television program which temporarily replaces those programs which usually appear in the time period of its broadcast; often a spectacular.
Sonderstelle *f*
→ Sonderfläche
Sonderthemenheft *n*
→ Sonderausgabe
Sonderveranstaltung *f (retailing)* special event
 Any sales event programmed for special promotion purposes.
Sonderverkauf *m*
→ Sonderangebotsverkauf
Sonderverkaufsprämie *f* (für Einzelhändler) push money (P.M.,

PM), premium money, spiff money, spiff
 A cash reward offered by a manufacturer or owner to a retailer for selling that manufacturer's products.
Sonderzuschlag *m (econ/advtsg)* special surcharge
Sonnenblende *f (phot)* lens shade, lens hood, sunshield, sunshade, sun visor, (Aufheller) reflection screen
Sonntagsausgabe (Zeitung) Sunday edition, Sunday issue, (erste Versandausgabe) bullpup
Sonntagsbeilage *f* (**Sonntagssupplement** *n*) Sunday supplement, Sunday newspaper supplement
Sonntagsblatt *n*
→ Sonntagszeitung
Sonntagspresse *f* Sunday press, Sunday newspapers *pl,* Sunday papers *pl*
Sonntagszeitung *f* Sunday newspaper, Sunday paper
SOP *abbr* Streuplan-Optimierungs-Programm
SOR-Modell *n* (**S-O-R-Modell** *n*, **S-I-R-Modell** *n*, **Stimulus-Organismus-Reaktions-Modell** *n*) *(psy)* SOR model, S.O.R. model, S-O-R model, stimulus-organism-response model
vgl. S-R-Modell
Sorte *f* (**Warensorte** *f*) *(econ)* product item, item, product sort, merchandise sort
 One size and form of a product or service sold in an assorted variety. It is the smallest unit of merchandise assortment.
Sortiermethode *f* (**Kartensortiermethode** *f*) *(survey res)* card sorting technique, card sorting
 A research technique in which a respondent is presented a set of stimuli printed on cards differing along two or more dimensions and is asked to sort them into groups that belong together. It generally is left to the subject to discover what basis for classification is appropriate.
Sortiment *n* (**Warensortiment** *n*) *(econ/retailing)* merchandise assortment, assortment
 The ability to provide the products and services demanded by consumers at the right time and place, at an adequate level of profit, i.e. the ability to offer an effective merchandise assortment, is the very basis of any retailer's existence.

Sortimentsanalyse f *(retailing)* merchandise assortment analysis, assortment analysis
Sortimentsauslage f *(POP advtsg)* assortment display
Sortimentsbereinigung f *(retailing)* merchandise assortment adjustment, assortment adjustment, merchandise assortment cleaning, assortment cleaning
Sortimentsbreite f **(Breite** f **des Sortiments)** *(econ/retailing)* width of merchandise assortment, merchandise assortment width, width of assortment, assortment width
  The overall number of different kinds of products or product lines carried in the assortment. Product assortments of narrow width are those consisting of a relatively few product lines or products; assortments of broad width have a relatively large number of different products or product lines. Specialty stores, e.g. (→) Fachgeschäft, are characterized by narrow assortments; department stores, (→) Warenhaus, variety stores, (→) Gemischtwarenladen, and other general merchandise retailers are characterized by broad assortments.
  vgl. Sortimentstiefe
Sortimentsdimension(en) f(pl) *(econ/retailing)* dimension(s) *(pl)* of merchandise assortment
Sortimentsgroßhandel m general merchandise wholesaling, general merchandise wholesale trade
Sortimentsgroßhändler m general merchandise wholesaler, general-line wholesaler
  A merchant wholesaler who carries goods in a number of unrelated lines. Also a merchant wholesaler characterized by this attempting to carry a complete stock of merchandise within a given field.
Sortimentsgroßhandlung f general merchandise wholesaler
Sortimentskontrolle f *(econ/retailing)* merchandise assortment control, assortment control
Sortimentsoptimierung f *(econ/retailing)* merchandise assortment optimization, *brit* optimisation
Sortimentsplanung f *(retailing)* merchandise assortment planning process (MAPP), merchandise assortment planning, assortment planning

  The process of using consumer demand information to develop an effective merchandise assortment. A merchandise assortment is an effective one if it meets demands for the types and quantities of products desired by consumers, at the times and places consumers want them. Includes decisions with respect to (1) what types of merchandise to carry, (2) how much merchandise to carry, (3) when the merchandise should be available, and (4) where the merchandise should be available.
Sortimentspolitik f *(econ/retailing)* merchandise assortment policy
Sortimentsrabatt m *(econ/retailing)* etwa full product range discount
Sortimentstiefe f **(Tiefe** f **des Sortiments)** *(econ/retailing)* depth of merchandise assortment, merchandise assortment depth, depth of assortment, assortment depth
  The depth of a product assortment describes the degree of comprehensiveness and variation within a particular product line. A product assortment with a great deal of depth has many products in the line and a wide range of choice; an assortment that is shallow has relatively few products in the line and relatively little choice.
  vgl. Sortimentsbreite
Sortimentsverbund m *(retailing)* merchandise tie-in
Sortimentsverbundenheit f *(econ/retailing)* complementarity of merchandise assortment
Sortimentsversandhandel m *(retailing)* general merchandise mail-order trade
sozial auffälliges Produkt n **(soziale Produktauffälligkeit** f**)** *(econ)* socially conspicuous product, conspicuous product
  A product (or service) consumed primarily to raise one's prestige rather than to satisfy material needs.
soziale Distanz f *(social res)* social distance
  → soziale Distanzskala
soziale Distanzskala f *(social res)* social distance scale, Bogardus scale, Bogardus scale of social distance, Bogardus social distance scale, Bogardus-type scale (Emory S. Bogardus)
  In attitude research, (→) Einstellungsforschung, a measuring device for ascertaining the degree of sympathetic

soziale Erwünschtheit 478

understanding between persons and groups relative to one another.
soziale Erwünschtheit f (**soziale Desirabilität** f) *(survey res)* social desirability
The perception by respondents that the answer to a question will enhance or hurt their image in the eyes of the interviewer or the researcher.
soziale Gruppe f social group
soziale Interaktion f social interaction
The basic social process represented in communication and a mutual relationship between two or more individuals or groups. Interaction between persons is social behavior. Through language, symbols, and gestures people exchange meanings and have a reciprocal effect upon each other's behavior, expectations, and thought.
soziale Kategorie f
→ Sozialkategorie
soziale Klasse f
→ Sozialschicht
soziale Kontrolle f social control (Edward A. Ross)
soziale Norm f (**Sozialnorm** f) social norm
soziale Rolle f social role, role
soziale Schicht f
→ Sozialschicht
soziale Selbsteinstufung f (SSE) social class rating (Gerhard Kleining/ Harriet Moore)
Soziale Wahrnehmung f (**Soziale Perzeption** f) social perception
The orientation in psychology concerned with the effects of social and cultural factors on man's cognitive structuring of his physical and social environment.
sozialer Status m
→ Status
sozialer Wandel m social change
soziales Marketing n
→ Sozio-Marketing
Sozialforschung f social research
The application to any social situation of exact procedures for the purpose of solving a problem, or testing a hypothesis, or discovering new phenomena or new relations among phenomena.
Sozialindikator m social indicator
Sozialisation f socialization, *brit* socialisation
→ Konsumentensozialisation
Sozialmarketing n
→ Sozio-Marketing

Sozialprodukt n
→ Bruttosozialprodukt, Nettosozialprodukt
Sozialpsychologie f social psychology
Sozialschicht f social class, social stratum
A large category of people within a system of social stratification who have a similar socioeconomic status in relation to other segments of their community or society. A social class is not organized, but the individuals and families who compose it are relatively similar in educational, economic, and prestige status.
Sozialstatus m
→ Status
Sozialtechniken f/pl social skills pl, social techniques pl
Soziobiologie f sociobiology
Soziodemographie f social demography, sociodemography, demography
→ Demographie
soziodemographische Merkmale n/pl *(social res)* sociodemographic characteristics pl, sociodemographics pl, demographics pl, sociographics pl
→ demographische Merkmale
Soziogramm n *(social res)* sociogram
Sozioindikator m
→ Sozialindikator
Sozio-Marketing n (**Sozialmarketing** n, **soziales Marketing** n) social marketing, *auch* societal concept of marketing
A collective term used to describe all marketing activities involved in attempts to influence the acceptance of social ideas and to gain desired audience action to implement into socially useful programs what present knowledge permits. In a more limited understanding, the societal marketing concept is a management orientation which holds that the key task of the organization is to determine the needs and wants of target markets and to adapt the organization to delivering the desired satisfactions more effectively and efficiently than its competitors in a way that preserves or enhances the consumers' and society's well-being. The marketer will essentially have to become concerned with short- and long-run consumer interests, company interests, and society's interests, including creating a healthy environment and conserving resources. All of these concerns imply and require an expansion

of marketing's frame of reference, purpose, and skills.
Soziomatrix f *(social res)* sociomatrix
→ Soziometrie
Soziometrie f *(social res)* sociometry, sociometrics *sg*, sociometric analysis (Jacob L. Moreno)
The practice of sociometry consists of the administration of a questionnaire in which the subject chooses five other people in rank order of their attractiveness as associates, either generally or in relation to some specific activity. It was later extended to cover negative choices. The results are plotted on paper in diagrammatic form, hence the term sociogram. This technique, whilst simple, is only suitable for small groups.
sozioökonomischer Status m **(sozioökonomische Stellung** f**)** socioeconomic status (SES), socioeconomic position
In a system of social stratification, a combination of various social and economic indexes of rank that are used in research studies. The term is often used to deal with stratification in a society without the need for the assumption that there are distinct social classes. Social characteristics (family background, education, values, prestige of occupation, etc.) and economic status (income) are combined into one SES rating.
sozioökonomische Schicht f **(sozioökonomische Schichtzugehörigkeit** f**)** socioeconomic class, socioeconomic level
→ sozioökonomischer Status
Spaltbildkamera f *(phot)* one-shot camera
A portable color camera capable of making continuous tone three-color separation negatives with a single exposure through a single lens.
Spalte f **(Kolumne** f**)** *(print)* column
One of two or more sections of type composition separated by a rule or a blank space; e.g., newspaper column. It is the standard, vertical unit of editorial or advertising space on the page of a publication.
Spaltenbreite f *(print)* column width, width of column, column
The typical or standard width of column, (→) Spalte, used as a measure of size.
Spaltenhöhe f **(Spaltentiefe** f**)** *(print)* column depth, depth of column, column height, height of column, depth of space

The dimension of advertising space measured from top to bottom, usually in reference to a column.
Spaltenlinie f *(print)* column rule, column line, dividing line
A strip or rule used between columns.
Spaltenmaß n **(Kolumnenmaß** n**)** *(print)* column measure, measure
The width of a column or a line of type.
Spaltentiefe f
→ Spaltenhöhe
Spaltenüberschrift f *(print)* column heading, column head, top head
Spaltenzahl f *(print)* number of columns
Spannband n *(outdoor advtsg)* banner, wall banner, *(POP advtsg)* arch, banner, overwire hanger
Any eye-catching device made of paper, cloth, or plastic designed to be hung from its top. Usually rectangular or triangular, it may be taped to a window or wall, or strung overhead or between poles. Most often it carries an advertising message.
Spannplakat n
→ Spannband
Spannweite f **(Variationsbreite** f, **Extrembereich** m, **Schwankungsbereich** m, **Streuungsbreite** f**)** *(stat)* range
The difference between the largest and the smallest of a set of variate values.
Sparneigung f *(econ)* propensity to save
The percentage of disposable income that consumers may be expected to save.
vgl. Konsumneigung
Sparte f **1.** *(econ)* (Bereich) field, area, section, branch **2.** *(print)* (Zeitungsrubrik) section
Spartenorganisation f
→ produktorientierte Marketingorganisation
Spätausgabe f (Zeitung) evening edition, late evening edition, (Fernsehnachrichten) late-night news, late news, late-night edition
Spatienkeil m *(print)* spaceband
Spätnachmittagsprogramm n
→ Nachmittagsprogramm
Spätsendezeit f *(radio/TV)* late evening, late fringe, late off-peak, post peak time
spationieren v/t *(print)* to space, to space out
To provide an interval between any two elements of type.
→ ausschließen

Spationierung f *(print)* spacing
→ spationieren

Spatium n **(Ausschlußstück** n**, Ausschluß** m**)** *(print)* space

Spearmans Rangkorrelation f **(Spearmans Rangordnungs-korrelation** f*,* **Spearmansche Rangkorrelation** f*,* **Spearmansche Rangordnungskorrelation** f**)** *(stat)* Spearman's rank correlation, Spearman's rank-order correlation, Spearman rank correlation, Spearman rank-order correlation

Spearmans Rangkoeffizient m **(Spearmans Rangkorrelationskoeffizient** m**, Spearmanscher Rangkorrelationskoeffizient** m**, Spearmans rho** n**)** *(stat)* Spearman's rank correlation coefficient, Spearman's rank-order correlation coefficient, Spearman rank correlation coefficient, Spearman rank-order correlation coefficient, Spearman's rho(ρ), Spearman rho(ρ), rho(ρ)
A coefficient of rank correlation, (→) Rangkorrelation. If the two rankings are a_i, b_i, and defined $d_i = a_i - b_i$, $i = 1, 2, ...$ n, the coefficient is given by

$$\rho = 1 - \frac{6 \sum_{i=1}^{n} d_i^2}{n^3 - n}.$$

It is also the product-moment correlation between the rank numbers a and b.

Special-interest-Zeitschrift f
→ Spezialzeitschrift

Specialty Goods pl **(Spezialbedarfsgüter** n/pl*,* **Spezialbedarf** m**)** *(econ)* specialty goods pl
Those consumer goods with unique characteristics and/or brand identification for which a significant group of buyers are habitually willing to make a special purchasing effort. Examples of articles that are usually bought as specialty goods are: specific brands and types of fancy foods, hi-fi components, certain types of sporting equipment, photographic equipment, and men's suits. Price is not usually the primary factor in consumer choice of specialty goods although their prices are often higher than those of other articles serving the same basic want but without their special characteristics.
vgl. Convenience Goods, Shopping Goods

Speisekammertest m *(market res)* pantry check, pantry inventory, pantry poll, pantry audit
A consumer research survey of items actually found in respondent's homes.

Spektralanalyse f **(Fourieranalyse** f**)** *(stat)* spectral analysis
The analysis of time series, (→) Zeitreihe, by spectral methods measures the strength of various frequency components or periodic terms in the data, and when used to look at the relationship between two or more series it tries to establish how that relationship changes between different frequency components. The spectrum is a function that measures how the total variance of a stationary series is distributed between the different frequencies that may be present. It is closely related to the periodogram and indeed the latter is often used as a basis from which to estimate the spectrum (or spectral density function).

Spektralempfindlichkeit f *(phot)* spectral sensitivity

spektrale Sensibilisierung f *(phot)* spectral sensitization, brit sensitisation

Spektralfarbe f *(optics)* spectral color, brit colour

Spektralfarbenzug m
→ Farbdreieck

Spektrallinie f spectral line, spectrum line

Spektrogramm n spectrogram

Spektroskop n spectroscope

Spektrum n spectrum

Spendenmarketing n charity marketing

Spendenwerbemittel n **(Spendenwerbeanzeige** f**)** charity advertisement, charity ad

Spendenwerbung f charity advertising

Sperrdruck m
→ gesperrter Satz

sperren v/t *(print)* to space, to space out, to letterspace
To add space between letters, generally in headings, to fill a given space or for the sake of appearance.

Sperren n *(print)* spacing, letterspacing
Spacing between type characters to extend them over a wider type measure.

Sperrfilter m *(phot)* rejection filter

Sperrfrist f **(Sperrvermerk** m**)** embargo

In relation to news releases, a time or date before which a particular item of news must not be published.
Sperrgreifer *m* **(Justiergreifer** *m*) *(film/phot)* register pin
Sperrsatz *m*
→ gesperrter Satz
Sperrung *f*
→ Sperren
Spesen *pl (econ)* expenses *pl*
Spezialbedarf *m* **(Spezialbedarfsgüter** *n/pl*)
→ Specialty Goods
Spezialbefragung *f* **(Spezialumfrage** *f*, **Einthemenbefragung** *f*) *(survey res)* single-subject survey, specialized survey, (für einen einzigen Auftraggeber) single-client survey
vgl. Omnibusbefragung
Spezialberichterstatter *m*
→ Sonderberichterstatter
Spezialfarbe *f* **(Spezialdruckfarbe** *f*) *(print)* special ink
Spezialgeschäft *n (retailing)* specialty store, specialty shop
A retail store that makes its appeal on the basis of a restricted class of shopping goods.
→ Fachgeschäft
Spezialgroßhandel *m* 1. (Funktion) specialty wholesaling 2. (Institution) specialty wholesale trade, specialty wholesaling
Spezialgroßhändler *m* **(Spezialgroßhandlung** *f*) specialty wholesaler
Spezialgüter *n/pl*
→ specialty goods
Spezialhandel *m (econ)* specialty selling
Applied generally to the sale at the home or place of business of merchandise or services not available in stores, e.g. home improvements, insurance, encyclopedias, etc.
spezialisierte Organisation *f (advtsg)* specialized organization, specialized agency organization
A type of advertising agency that specializes in certain areas, e.g. food products, direct-mail advertising, industrial goods, etc. The advantage of a specialized agency is that the people really know a business, its marketing environment, regulatory considerations, etc. But when an agency becomes too specialized in one product category conflicts of interest arise.
vgl. Abteilungsorganisation, Gruppenorganisation.

Spezialisierung *f* specialization, *brit* specialisation
Spezialist *m* specialist
Spezialmittler *m* media broker
An independent agency, usually dealing exclusively with buying space or time in the media on behalf of a client; its work may or may not include media planning or other support services.
Spezialpreis *m*
→ Sonderpreis
Spezialstelle *f*
→ Sonderstelle
Spezialzeitschrift *f* **(Special-interest-Zeitschrift** *f*) special-interest magazine, special-interest publication, selective magazine
Special-interest magazines are a recent trend in consumer magazine, (→) Publikumszeitschrift, publishing which seeks to carve out distinct market segments. In general, a contrasting approach to the earlier magazine posture as serving a wide national market. They are a result of a growing realization that a magazine can serve a highly targeted audience that television cannot reach effectively.
Spezialzentrum *n (retailing)* special center, *brit* special centre
sphärische Aberration *f (phot)* spherical aberration
The inability of a photographic lens to convey marginal (not oblique) rays to a point at the same distance as the central rays, a defect manifesting itself by impairment of contrast, (→) Kontrast, and definition, (→) Auflösung, in the projected image.
Spiegel *m*
→ Satzspiegel
Spiegelbildimage *n* **(Spiegelimage** *n*)
→ Eigenimage
Spiegelblende *f (phot)* mirror shutter
Spiegelfassung *f* reflector mount
Spiegelfrequenz *f* image frequency, second frequency
Spiegellampe *f* **(Spiegelscheinwerfer** *m*) *(phot/film/TV)* mirror lamp, reflector lamp
Spiegellinse *f (phot)* mirror lens, reflecting lens
spiegeln *v/t (print)* (Klebeumbruch machen) to paste up, to make the paste-up
To produce artwork, particularly page layouts on which proofs of type and photostats have been pasted so that all may be reproduced together.

Spiegelreflexblende f *(phot)* reflex mirror shutter
Spiegelreflexkamera f *(phot)* mirror reflex camera, reflex camera
Spiegelscheinwerfer m
→ Spiegellampe
Spiegeltrick m **(Spiegeltrickverfahren** n, **Schüfftan-Verfahren** n) *(film/TV)* mirror shot, mirror shot technique
  A shot of an image in a reflecting surface.
Spielfilm m feature film, full-length film
Spielleiter m
1. *(film/TV)* → Regisseur
2. *(radio)* → Hörspielleiter
Spielplan m
→ Sendeplan
Spieltheorie f *(stat)* theory of games, game theory
  Generally, that branch of mathematics which deals with the theory of contests between two or more players under specified sets of rules.
Spieß m *(print)* work-up, pick
  A piece of the furniture used to fill in a form that has worked up to the level of the type under the pressure applied by the printing thus causing a blemish.
Spill-over-Effekt m **(sachliche Wirkungsübertragung** f) *(res)* spillover effect, spillover
Spinne f (Lautsprecher) spider
Spionspiegel m **(Einwegspiegel** m) *(social res)* one-way mirror, one way mirror
  A glass partition used to separate researchers from respondents in an adjacent room; by being only partially reflectorized, it serves to transmit light intact into the darker of the two rooms, while reflecting light as a mirror back into the brighter room.
Spiralbindung f
→ Spiralheftung
spiralgeheftet (spiralgebunden) adj spiral-bound
Spiralheftung f **(Spiralbindung** f) spiral binding
  A book bound with wires in spiral form inserted through holes punched along the binding side of the book.
Spiralentheorie f (der Werbung) spiral theory (of advertising)
  The theory about the way a product or service evolves with regard to its acceptance by prospective consumers, which holds that this is a continuous process, moving to a new beginning in the spiral as acceptance increases.

Spirituosenwerbung f
→ Alkoholwerbung
Spitzenhelligkeit f *(phot)* highlight brightness
Spitzenlicht n
→ Spitzlicht
Spitzenqualität f high quality, top quality
Spitzenunternehmen n *(econ)* blue-chip organization, blue-chip company
Spitzlicht n **(Spitzenlicht** n, **Glanzlicht** n) *(phot)* highlight
  The lightest and whitest part of a printed picture or part of a picture, represented in a halftone by the smallest dots or no dots at all.
Spitzlichtaufnahme f **(Spitzenlichtaufnahme** f, **Glanzlichtaufnahme** f) *(phot)* highlight exposure
Spitzlichtautotypie f **(Spitzenlichtautotypie** f, **Hochlichtautotypie** f) *(print)* highlight halftone, dropout halftone, dropout, blowout
  A halftone in which the fine screen of the white areas has been removed for greater contrast.
Spitzlichtblende f **(Spitzenlichtblende** f) *(phot)* highlight stop, detail stop
  The particular lens aperture used in halftone photography to join the highlights dots in the negative and to record highlight detail.
Spitzlichtnegativ n **(Hochlichtnegativ** n) *(phot)* highlight negative
  A halftone negative in which the dot formation in the highlights has been eliminated during exposure of the original.
Spitzlichtpunkt m **(Hochlichtpunkt** m) *(phot)* highlight dot
  The formation of small dots representing the highlights in a halftone negative and printing plate.
Split m **(Splitten** n)
→ gegabelte Befragung, Anzeigensplit
Split-Ballot m
→ gegabelte Befragung
Split-half-Verfahren n **(Split-half-Methode** f)
→ Halbierungsverfahren
Split-Run m **(Split-run-Verfahren** n)
→ Anzeigensplit
sponsern v/t to sponsor
Sponsor m sponsor
  An organization or individual financing sporting or other activities in order to gain coverage and prestige from its association with them.

Sponsorsendung f (gesponserte Sendung f)
→ Patronatssendung
Sponsorenschaft f sponsorship
spontan adj spontaneous, top-of-the-mind, top-of-mind
spontane Erinnerung f
→ ungestützte Erinnerung
Spontanhandlungsverfahren n **(Spontanverfahren** n) *(market res) etwa* spontaneous action technique, impulse action technique
Spontankauf m
→ Impulskauf
Sportplatzwerbung f
→ Bandenwerbung
Spot m
1. → Werbespot
2. → Spotscheinwerfer
Spotfotometer n **(Spotphotometer** n)
→ Spotmeter
Spotlight n
→ Spotscheinwerfer
Spotmeter n **(Spotphotometer** n, **Spotfotometer** n) spot photometer
Spotscheinwerfer m **(Spotlichtscheinwerfer** m, **Spotlicht** n) *(phot/film/TV)* spotlight, spot
  A light with a directed beam.
Spotvorsatz m *(phot/film/TV)* cone
Sprachaufnahme f voice recording, speech recording
Sprachband n *(film)* sound on tape (S.O.T.)
Sprachfrequenzbereich m voice frequency range, speech frequency range
Sprechblase f balloon, bubble, blurb
  The encirclement of printed words which are spoken or thought by a character, especially in cartoons or comic strips.
Sprecher(in) m(f) speaker
→ Ansager, Nachrichtensprecher
Sprechfunk m radiotelephony (RT)
Sprechkopf m sound head
Sprechprobe f *(radio/film/TV)* voice test, audition, run-through, read-through, (film/TV) dry rehearsal, dry run
  A rehearsal without cameras.
Springblende f *(phot)* automatic diaphragm, semi-automatic diaphragm
Spritzmanier f **(Spritztechnik** f) airbrushing, airbrush technique
  A method used in art studios to add shading to drawings by mechanical means. Air brush work requires the use of halftones for reproduction. An airbrush, (→) Luftpinsel, is a type of sprayer operating on compressed air capable of producing a very fine spray which gives subtle gradations of tone. Used principally in the retouching of photographs and for smooth backgrounds in posters, etc.
Spritzmaske f
→ Abdeckmaske
Spritzpistole f **(Luftpinsel** m) airbrush, air brush
→ Luftpinsel
Spritzretusche f airbrush retouching, air brush retouching, airbrushing
→ Spritzmanier
Spruchband n
→ Spannband
Sprung m *(film/TV)* (Sprungschnitt) jump cut
  A cut between shots executed in a manner adding an improper discontinuity to continuous action.
Sprungabtastung f *(TV)* interlaced scanning
  The sequential scanning of alternate lines on the television tube to create a complete picture in two passes; reduces flicker potential.
Sprungwand f *(TV)* camera trap
Sprungwerbung f **(Publikumswerbung** f) consumer advertising, consumer-directed advertising, national advertising
vgl. Fachwerbung (Werbung in Fachkreisen)
Spule f spool, reel
Spur f
→ Tonspur
S-R-Modell n **(Stimulus-Reaktions-Modell** n, **Black-Box-Modell** n) *(psy)* S-R model, stimulus-response model, blackbox model
S-R-Psychologie f **(S-R-Theorie** f)
→ Reiz-Reaktions-Psychologie
Staatsanzeiger m (Zeitung) official gazette, gazette
Staatsrundfunk m state-controlled broadcasting, state-operated broadcasting, government-controlled broadcasting, government-operated broadcasting
Stab m *(econ)* (im Gegensatz zur Linie) staff
  The group of specialists and technicians who perform advisory and research services for the line officials, (→) Linie, or the production segment of a formal

Stabantenne

organization, such as a large industrial corporation.
Stabantenne f *(electr.)* rod antenna, *brit* rod aerial, flagpole antenna, *brit* flagpole aerial
Stabdiagramm n **(Säulendiagramm** n, **Stäbchendiagramm** n) *(stat)* vertical bar chart, vertical bar diagram, vertical bar graph
 The pictorial representation of values of frequency mesurements, which exhibits each class in a distinct and disjoint form. Bar charts have no horizontal axes, they can be adapted to display measurements of attribute classes, as well as those of variate groups.
 vgl. Balkendiagramm
Stabilisator m *(phot)* emulsifier, emulsifying agent
stabilisieren (stabil halten, stützen) v/t *(econ)* (Preise) to peg
 To hold prices artificially at a given level below which they are not permitted to fall regardless of market forces. Usually involves government action, often in the form of a subsidy to affected producers.
Stabilisierungsbad n *(phot)* stabilization bath, *brit* stabilisation bath
Stabilisierungswerbung f
 → Erhaltungswerbung
Stabilität f
 → Preisstabilität
Stab-Linien-Organisation f **(Stab-Linien-System** n) *(econ)* line-and-staff organization, *brit* line-and-staff-organisation
 An organization based on both line and staff functions.
 vgl. Linienorganisation, Stabsorganisation
Stabsabteilung f *(econ)* staff department
Stabsorganisation f **(Stabssystem** n) *(econ)* staff organization, *brit* organisation
 vgl. Linienorganisation
Stadtauflage f *(Zeitung)* city zone circulation
 The portion of a newspaper's coverage area that includes the corporate city plus adjacent areas which have the characteristics of the city.
 vgl. Restauflage 2.
Stadtausgabe f *(Zeitung)* city edition, city zone edition
Städtewerbung f
 → Kommunalwerbung

Stadtgebietsausgabe f
 → Stadtteilzeitung
Stadtillustrierte f city magazine
Stadtpresseamt n city information office, city information department
Stadtverschönerungswettbewerb m city beautification contest
Staffage f decoration, staffage
Staffel f
 1. → Preisstaffel
 2. → Staffelei
Staffelei f easel
Staffelpreis m **(Staffeltarif** m) *(econ)* graduated price, graded price
Staffelrabatt m *(econ)* graded discount, graduated discount
 → Malrabatt, Mangenrabatt
Staffelwerbung f **(Staffelwerbeplan** m, **Stufenwerbeplan** m) even flighting schedule, even flighting, flighting, staggered scheduling
 The publication of several advertisements scheduled in two or more publications, arranged so that the dates of insertion are alternated or rotated.
 → Phasenwerbung; *vgl.* Klotzwerbung
Stagnation f *(econ)* stagnation
Stahldruck m
 → Stahlstich
Stahlstecher m *(print)* steel engraver, engraver on steel
Stahlstich m **(Stahldruck** m) *(print)*
 1. (Verfahren) steel engraving, steel-plate engraving, steel-die engraving
 Printing from a steel plate on which the image has been engraved below the surface (commonly used for engraved cards, formal announcements, etc.).
 2. (Produkt) steel engraving, steel-plate engraving
Stakkato-Schnitt m *(film/TV)* jump cut, series of jump cuts, (Vorgang) jumpcutting
 Cutting, (→) Schnitt, between shots that is executed in a manner adding an impression of discontinuity to continuous action.
Stammkino n
 → Familienkino
Stammkunde m *(econ/retailing)* patronizer, regular customer, steady customer
Stammkundschaft f **(Stammkunden** m/pl) *(econ/retailing)* patronizers pl, regular customers pl, steady customers pl, (Vorhandensein von

Stammkundschaft) patronage, consumer patronage
The habitual use by customers of particular sources of supply.
Stammleser m
→ regelmäßiger Leser
Stammleserschaft f **(Stammhörerschaft** f, **Stammzuschauerschaft** f) *(media res)* bedrock audience
→ regelmäßiger Leser
Stand m
→ Messestand
Standard m standard
Standardabweichung f **(mittlere quadratische Abweichung** f) *(stat)* standard deviation (SD), mean square deviation, root mean square deviation (RMS)
A measure of the variability or dispersion, (→) Streuung, in a set of scores that provides an indication of the average amount by which the scores deviate from the mean, (→) Mittelwert, of the distribution. It is the square root of the variance, (→) Varianz, so the symbols (σ for a population, s for a sample) and the general definitional formulae for the standard deviation are derived from those for the variance.
Standardausrüstung f standard equipment
Standardauszählung f *(res)* standard computation
Standardeinheit f **(z)**
→ Standardwert
Standarderhebung f
→ Basiserhebung
Standardfehler m **(mittlerer quadratischer Fehler** m, **mittlerer Fehler** m) *(stat)* standard error (SE), mean square error (MSE)
The standard deviation, (→) Standardabweichung, of a sampling distribution. Standard errors can be computed for a variety of sample statistics (e.g., sample means or proportions). For example, the standard error of a sample mean and a sample proportion, respectively, with their computational formulae, are

$$\sigma_{\bar{x}} = \frac{\sigma}{\sqrt{n}} \text{ and } \sigma_p = \sqrt{\frac{pq}{n}}$$

Standardgröße f **(Standardformat** n) standard size
→ Standardisierung
standardisierte Befragung f **(standardisiertes Interview** n) *(survey res)*

standardized interview, standardized survey
standardisierte Verteilung f *(stat)* standardized distribution
→ Standardnormalverteilung
standardisierter Fragebogen m *(survey res)* standardized questionnaire
standardisiertes Interview n
→ standardisierte Befragung
Standardisierung f **1.** *(econ)* (Normierung) standardization, *brit* standardisation
The determination of basic limits or grade ranges in the form of uniform specifications to which particular manufactured goods may conform and uniform classes into which the products of agriculture and the extractive industries may or must be sorted or assigned.
2. *(survey res)* standardization, *brit* standardisation
→ standardisierte Befragung
3. *(stat)* standardization, *brit* standardisation
→ z-Transformation, Standardnormalverteilung, Standardwert
Standardkopie f *(film)* standard print
→ Normalkopie
Standardmaß n
→ Standardwert
Standardnormalverteilung f **(standardisierte Normalverteilung** f) *(stat)* standard normal distribution, z distribution, *auch* unit normal distribution
The normal distribution, (→) Normalverteilung, with a mean, (→) Mittelwert, of zero and a standard deviation, (→) Standardabweichung, of 1.0.
Standardpreis m
→ Einheitspreis, Stückpreis
Standardpunktwert m
→ Standardwert
Standardschätzfehler m
→ Standardfehler
Standardsortiment n
→ Grundsortiment
Standardtest m *(res)* standard test
Standardwert m **(Standardpunktwert** m, **z-Wert** m, **z-Punktwert** m) *(stat)* standard score, standardized score, z score, z score statistic
The expression of the value of an observation using one standard deviation, (→) Standardabweichung, as the unit of measurement of its distance, i.e. positive or negative difference, from

Standarte

the mean, (→) Mittelwert, of the distribution of the variate.
Standarte f *(phot)* 1. (einer Filmkamera) lens mount, 2. (eines Photoapparats) lens carrier, lens standard
Standausstattung f **(Ausstattung** f **von Messe- oder Ausstellungsständen)** exhibition stand design, stand design
Standbau m **für Messen** exhibition stand construction
Standbild n **(Standphoto** n, **Standphotographie** f, **Standaufnahme** f) *(phot)* still picture, still photo, still photograph, (eines Films) film still, still frame, frozen picture
An ordinary photograph of a scene from a motion picture or television program taken during the filming or blown up from a frame from the film itself.
Standbildverlängerung f **(Standkopieren** n) *(film)* freeze frame, stop frame, hold frame, still copy, frozen picture, suspended animation
Both the technique of repeatedly reprinting the same single frame to give the effect that motion has stopped and the same frame of a television commercial film or motion picture repeated a number of times in sequence to give the effect of frozen or suspended motion.
Standbogen m **(Stellungsbogen** m) *(print)* pull for position, position pull, imposition sheet, register sheet
Standby-Spot m **(Standby-Werbespot** m) *(radio/TV)* standby preemptible spot, (jederzeit absetzbar) section III spot, (bedingt absetzbar) section II spot
A commercial substituted or held ready to be substituted for a scheduled one in case of emergency.
Ständer m stand, (Gestell) rack, (Säule) pillar, post, (Stütze) support
Standfoto n
→ Standbild
Standgestaltung f
→ Standausstattung
Standkopie f
→ Standbildverlängerung
Standkopieren n
→ Standbildverlängerung
Standmiete f exhibition stand rent, stand rent
Standmikrophon n **(Standmikrofon** n) static microphone
Standort m *(econ)* site location, site, placement position, location, position, (Einzelhandelsgeschäft) store location,

(Werbemittel) advertising location, advertising position, (Plakat, Anzeige) space position, (Anschlagstelle) poster site location, site location, placement position
The geographical place where a business firm, e.g. a manufacturer or a retailer, or an outdoor advertisement is located.
Standortagglomeration f
→ Einzelhandelsagglomeration (Agglomeration des Einzelhandels)
Standortanalyse f *(econ)* location analysis, site location analysis, (Einzelhandelsgeschäft) store site analysis, retail store site analysis
Standortbewertung f *(econ)* location evaluation, site location evaluation, site evaluation, (Einzelhandelsgeschäft) store site evaluation, retail store site evaluation, retail site evaluation, (Anschlagstelle) poster site evaluation, poster placement site evaluation
Standortentscheidung f *(econ)* location decision, site location decision, site selection decision, (Einzelhandelsgeschäft) store location decision, store site selection decision
Standortentscheidungsmodell n *(econ)* location decision model, site location decision model, site selection decision model, (Einzelhandelsgeschäft) store site selection model, store location decision model, store site decision selection model
Standortfaktor m *(econ)* location factor, site location factor, site factor
Standortforschung f *(econ)* location research, site location research, site research (Einzelhandel) store location research, store site location research, retail store location research, retail site location research
The systematic investigation designed to seek out best locations for business enterprises.
Standortgemeinschaft f **(Standortkooperation** f)
→ Agglomeration (des Einzelhandels)
Standortmedium n **(Positionsmedium** n) *(advtsg)* position medium
A collective term applied to outdoor, (→) Außenwerbung, and to transit advertising media, (→) Verkehrsmittelwerbung, POP advertising, (→) P.O.P.-Werbung, and nonstandardized signs.

Standortmerkmal n *(econ)* location characteristic, site location characteristic, site characteristic
Standortmodell n
→ Standortentscheidungsmodell
Standortplanung f *(econ)* location planning, site location planning, site planning
Standortpolitik f *(econ)* location choice policy, site choice policy, site location policy, site selection policy
Standortskizze f **(Anschlagstellenkarte** f**)** *(outdoor advtsg)* location card, spotted map, spotting map
  A map of a locale, such as a city, town, or market, marked to show the locations of a set of outdoor advertisements.
Standortstrategie f
→ Standortpolitik
Standortvergleich m *(econ)* site comparison, comparison of site, location site comparison, location comparison
Standortwahl f *(econ)* site selection, location choice
Standortzentrum n
→ Großhandelszentrum
Standphoto n **(Standfoto** n**)**
→ Standbild
Standtitel m *(film/TV)* static caption
vgl. Rolltitel
Stange f *(film/TV)* bar, rod, (Scheinwerfer) lighting pole, barrel
Stanniol n tin foil
Stanze f *(print)* punching machine, punch, stamp, die, (Kupferstich) matrix, *(film)* (Zeichen) changeover cue
→ Stanztrick
stanzen v/t *(print)* to punch, to die cut
Stanzform f *(print)* cutting die, cutting form, *brit* cutting forme
Stanzplakat n **(Ausstanzstück** n**, gestanztes Markensymbol** n**)** *(POP advtsg)* die cut
  A sheet of paper cut with a die to the shape desired.
Stanzpresse f **(Stanzmaschine** f**, Stanzautomat** m**, Stanztiegel** m**)** *(print)* cutting press, cutting machine, die cutting machine, stamping press, stamping machine
Stanztrick m **(Farbschablonentrick** m**, Schablonentrick** m**)** *(film/TV)* chroma key, blue screen
  A technical, electronic process in motion picture and television production for changing the background of a scene without disturbing the foreground.
Stanztrickkamera f *(film/TV)* chroma key
Stanzung f **(Stanzen** n**)** *(print)* punching, die cutting
Stapelartikel m *(pl)* **(Stapelgüter** n/pl **)** *(econ)* staple goods *pl,* staple items *pl,* staple products *pl,* staple
  The types of merchandise, such as grocery items, which customers expect to find in that particular store and which is in generally continuous demand. If out of stock, the store may lose the customer for a longer period than represented by that one sale.
Stapelfenster n **(Massenfenster** n**)** *(POP advtsg) etwa* jumble display window, classification dominance display window, wide-assortment display window, huge-assortment display window
  A type of retail store window display where merchandise is displayed in a more or less casual or apparently casual manner.
Stapelskala f **(Stapelskalometer** n**)** *(survey res)* Stapel scale, Stapel scalometer (Jan Stapel)
Stapeltisch m
→ Wühltisch
Starch-Formel f *(media res)* Starch formula (Daniel Starch)
Starch-Test m *(advtsg res)* reading and noting test, Starch rating test, Starch test, Starch procedure, Starch model
  A readership survey relating to selected advertisements in a given issue of a publication, to establish the number of persons who have noted an advertisement to the extent of recalling having seen it, and the name of the product advertised. Interviews are carried out with 100 to 200 men and 100 to 200 women on each issue studied of magazines of general interest. To qualify for an interview, respondents must state that they read the issue of the magazine under study prior to the interview. The interview technique involves the recognition method, (→) Wiedererkennungsverfahren. As the interviewer goes through the magazine with the respondent, the respondent tells whether and to what extent he or she read each advertisement a half-page or larger in that issue. The scores reported are:
  Noted: The percent of readers of the magazine who say they have previously

Starprodukt

seen the advertisement in the particular magazine.
Seen/associated: The percent of readers who say they have seen or read any part of the advertisement that clearly indicates the name of the product (or service) or advertiser.
Read most: The percent of readers who not only looked at the advertisement, but who say that they read more than half of the written material in the ad.

Starprodukt n *(econ)* star product, cash cow, bell cow, blue chip
A product that experiences a high growth rate and high relative market share. Stars are highly successful, profitable and the leaders in their market. They need a continual shot of cash to maintain their growth.

Starsystem n *(advtsg)* star system

Starrummel m **(Starreklame f)** *(advtsg)* star billing

Star-Werbesendung f
→ programmunterbrechende Werbesendung

Startauflage f (Erstauflage f) (Zeitung/Zeitschrift) first printing

Startauslösezeichen n *(radio/TV)* start pulse, starting mark, starting signal, start release signal

Startband n **(Startvorspann** m) *(film/TV)* start leader, head leader, leader, (nach den Richtlinien der amerikanischen Academy of Motion Picture Arts and Sciences mit einer Laufzeit von acht Stunden) Academy leader
A non-projected identification and audio and/or video timing countdown at the head of film or video tape material, for exact cueing purposes. Also, the head portion of film or tape "leading" it from the feed to the take-up reels through the projection or playback path.

Startimpuls m *(TV)* sync mark, synch mark, sync plop, synch plop

Startkreuz n *(TV)* sync cross, synch cross

Startmarkierung f (Startmarke f, Startzeichen n) *(film/TV)* start mark, cue
The editor's start point indication.

Startvorlaufzeit f (Startzählung f) *(tape/film/TV)* run-up time, roll-in time, pre-roll time, countdown, count down
The time-marked lead-in segment of a film or tape, cueing the technician so the production will start on time at the very beginning.

Startvorsprung m
→ Startband
Startzählung f
→ Startvorlaufzeit
Startzeichen n
→ Startmarkierung
Station f
→ Sender
stationärer Handel m *(econ)* stationary trade
vgl. ambulanter Handel
Stationsabsage f
→ Sendeschluß
Stationsansage f
→ Sendebeginn
Stationsdia n
→ Senderdia (Senderkennungsdia)
Stationskennung f (Stationskennzeichen n)
→ Kennung
stationseigene Sendung f
→ sendereigenes Programm
statische Aufladung f *(electr./phot)* static charge, (die durch Aufladung entstandenen Streifen auf einem Film) static marks pl
The dark streaks found on developed negatives, due to static discharge, (→) statische Entladung, when the film was drawn too quickly from the pack.
statische Entladung f *(electr./phot)* static discharge
Statist m
→ Komparse
Statistik f 1. statistics pl (construed as sg)
The body of methods for collecting, tabulating, presenting, and analyzing quantitative data. The data may consist of enumerations of measurements. Statistical techniques provide descriptive procedures for classifying and summarizing data so that a mass of quantitative facts may be converted into a comprehensible form. Statistics also provides inductive techniques for using principles of mathematical probability to obtain generalizations from sample data that may be applied to the larger population.
2. → statistische Tabelle
Statistiker m statistician
statistisch adj statistical
statistische Analyse f (statistische Auswertung f) statistical analysis
statistische Assoziation f **(Assoziation** f) statistical association, association
→ Assoziation

statistische Darstellung f (**statistische Deskription** f) statistical description
→ deskriptive Statistik
statistische Daten n/pl statistical data pl
statistische Datengewinnung f statistical data collection
statistische Entscheidungstheorie f statistical theory of decision-making, statistical decision-making theory, statistical decision theory
→ Entscheidungstheorie
statistische Funktion f statistical function
statistische Grundgesamtheit f
→ Grundgesamtheit
statistische Hypothese f
→ statistical hypothesis
statistische Hypothesenprüfung f (**statistischer Hypothesentest** m) statistical hypothesis test, statistical hypothesis testing
statistische Inferenz f (**statistisches Schließen** n, **statistische Schlußfolgerung** f, **statistische Induktion** f) statistical inference, statistical induction
→ Inferenzstatistik
statistische Interpretation f statistical interpretation, statistical data interpretation
statistische Karte f (**statistische Landkarte** f, **Kartogramm** n) statistical map, cartogram
statistische Marktdaten n/pl statistical market data pl
statistische Masse f
→ Grundgesamtheit
statistische Methode f (**statistisches Verfahren** n) statistical method, statistical technique
statistische Mortalität f statistical mortality, mortality, sample mortality
→ Mortalität
statistische Nachfrageanalyse f (econ) statistical analysis of demand, statistical demand analysis
statistische Norm f statistical norm
statistische Qualitätskontrolle f statistical quality control, quality control
→ Qualitätskontrolle
statistische Reihe f
→ Häufigkeitsverteilung
statistische Sicherheit f (**statistische Signifikanz** f)
→ Signifikanzniveau

statistische Tabelle f statistical table
→ Tabelle
statistische Theorie f (**Theorie** f **der Statistik**) statistical theory
statistische Wahrscheinlichkeit f statistical probability
→ Wahrscheinlichkeit
statistischer Fehler m statistical error
→ Standardfehler; Fehler 1. Art, Fehler 2. Art
statistischer Fehlschluß m (**statistischer Trugschluß** n) statistical fallacy
→ Fehlschluß, Fehler 1. und 2. Art
statistischer Schluß m
→ statistische Inferenz
statistischer Test m statistical test
statistisches Moment n statistical moment, moment
→ Moment
statistisches Verfahren n
→ statistische Methode
Stativ n (phot/film/TV) stand, support, (dreibeinig) tripod
A camera support.
Stativfahrwagen m (**Stativwagen** m) (film/TV) tripod dolly, dolly
Stativkamera f (film/phot/TV) stand camera
Stativkopf m (**Kreiselkopf** m) (film/phot/TV) tripod head, pam head, pan head, gyroscopic head
Stativspinne f (phot/film/TV) tripod base, spider
Stativverlängerung f (phot/film/TV) tripod extension
Status m (**sozialer Status** m, **Sozialstatus** m) status, social status
1. A defined position in the social structure of a group or society that is distinguished from and at the same time related to other positions through its designated rights and obligations. Because each status position in a social structure can be viewed in terms of its superiority or inferiority (advantages, disadvantages), people tend to equate status with rank and prestige or hierarchical positions.
2. A rank in a hierarchy.
3. A person's total standing in society, that is, the combination of his known statuses.
Statusangst f (**Angst** f **vor Statuswechsel**, **Statusunsicherheit** f) status anxiety
Statussymbol n status symbol
Any visible mark, object, such as a product, word, or activity that is intended to convey to others an individual's or

Stauchfalz

group's social status or status aspirations. Usually the term refers to social display to enhance one's prestige — to make it either equal or superior to the prestige of those persons one desires to impress.
Stauchfalz m (**Stauchfalzung** f) buckle folding
Steg m (print) stick, piece of furniture, (pl Stege) quotation furniture, furniture
A small piece of metal furniture used by compositors.
Stehbild n
→ Standbild, Standbildverlängerung
stehen lassen (typ) 1. stet
A proofreader's notation instructing the printer to ignore a change marked on a proof. A dotted line is placed under the change to which the notation applies.
2. keep standing, hold
An instruction to a typographer to keep type set up for future use.
Stehsatz m (print) live matter, pickup matter, pickup, holdover, standing matter, standing type, colloq pork
Composed type that has not been used and is kept standing for future use.
Steifleinen n (**Buckram** m) (binding) buckram
Steigetrichter m (**Plattenunterlage** f, **Schuh** m) (print) patent base, patent block, riser
Steilheit f
→ Gamma, Schwärzungsgrad
Stein m
→ Lithographiestein
Steindruck m
→ Lithogrphie
Steindrucker m
→ Lithograph
Steinzeichner m
→ Lithograph
Steinzeichnung f
→ Lithographie
Stelle f
→ Anschlagstelle, Position, Plazierung, Standort
Stellenangebot n (**Stellenangebotsanzeige** f) personnel wanted ad(vertisement), wanted ad, recruitment advertisement, recruitment ad, vacant position(s) ad(vertisement), (Rubriküberschrift in der Zeitung) vacancies pl, vacant positions pl, positions offered pl, positions pl, situations vacant pl, situations pl, personnel wanted

Stellengesuch n (**Stellengesuchanzeige** f) employment wanted ad(vertisement), situation wanted ad(vertisement), colloq want ad
Stellplakat n
→ Aufsteller
Stellprobe f (radio/film/TV) first rehearsal
Stellungsbogen m
→ Standbogen
Stempel m stamp, (Gummistempel) rubberstamp, rubber stamp, (Buchbinderstempel) tool, (Patrize) punch, die
Stempeldruck m rubberstamp printing, rubber-stamp printing, rubberstamping, rubber stamping
Sterbetafel f (**Absterbetafel** f) (stat) life table, mortality table
Stereo n 1. (print) (Stereotypplatte) electro, electrotype, stereo, stereo plate, stereotype
A duplicating printing plate cast from a matrix of impregnated paper pulp or plastic. Because stereotypes are used almost exclusively on rotary presses, they are generally in the form of one-half a cylinder, but any printing plate, flat or curved, cast from a paper matrix is properly called a stereotype. Stereos are made from mats, (→) Mater, mats are made from electros, (→) Galvano, electros are made from type and original engravings.
2. → Stereoaufnahme, Stereophonie
Stereoakustik f
→ Stereophonie
Stereoaufnahme f 1. (tape) stereo recording, stereophonic recording, (disk) stereo pickup, stereo transcription, stereophonic pickup, stereophonic transcription
2. (phot) stereograph, stereoscopic pair of pictures
Stereoaufzeichnung f
→ Stereoaufnahme 1.
Stereobetrachtungsgerät n (**Stereobetrachter** m) (phot) stereo viewer, stereoscopic viewer
Stereobild n
→ Stereoaufnahme 2.
Stereobox f stereo box, stereo loudspeaker box, stereophonic box, stereophonic loudspeaker box
Stereodia n (**Stereodiapositiv** n) (phot) stereo slide, stereographic slide, stereographical slide, stereoscopic slide

Stereoeffekt m stereo effect, *(sound)* stereophonic effect, *(phot)* stereoscopic effect, stereographical effect
Stereoempfang m *(radio)* stereo reception, stereophonic reception
Stereoempfänger m **(Stereogerät** n**)** *(radio/TV)* stereo receiver, stereo set, stereo tuner, stereophonic receiver, stereophonic set, stereophonic tuner
Stereofilm m
→ dreidimensionaler Film
Stereogerät n
→ Stereoempfänger
Stereokamera f *(phot)* stereo camera, stereoscopic camera
Stereolautsprecher m stereo loudspeaker, stereophonic loudspeaker
stereophon *adj* stereophonic, stereo, binaural
Pertaining to the use of two simultaneously recorded, parallel audio channels to create the auditory illusion of a sound stage.
stereophone Sendung f **(stereophone Rundfunksendung** f **)** *(radio/TV)* stereo broadcast, binaural broadcast, stereophonic broadcast
The broadcasting of two signals for reception on two separate sets in stereophonic sound. The two signals may be transmitted by a single station using multiplexing, or by two different stations — two FM, one AM and one FM, or a TV station plus either an AM or FM station.
Stereophonie f stereo sound, stereo, stereophony, stereophonic sound, binaural sound
Stereophotographie f **(Stereoskopie** f **)** stereo photography, stereographic photography, stereoscopic photography, stereoscopy
Stereoprogramm n *(radio/TV)* stereo program, *brit* programme, stereophonic program, *brit* programme
Stereosendebetrieb m *(radio/TV)* stereo transmitter operation, stereo operation, stereophonic transmitter operation, stereophonic operation
Stereosendung f
→ stereophone Sendung
Stereosignal n *(radio/TV)* stereo signal, stereophonic signal
Stereoskop n **(stereoskopisches Bild** n**)** *(phot/film)* stereoscope, stereograph
Stereoskopie f *(phot/film)* stereoscopy, stereography

Stereostudio n *(radio/TV)* stereo studio
Stereoton m **(Raumton** m**)** stereo sound, stereophonic sound, binaural sound
Stereotonbandgerät n stereo sound recorder, stereo tape recorder
stereotyp (stereotypiert) *adj (print)* stereotyped
→ Stereo
Stereotyp n
→ Stereotypie (Stereoplatte)
Stereotypdruck m **(Stereotypdruckverfahren** n**)** *(print)* stereotypography
Stereotypeur m *(print)* stereotyper, stereotypist, foundryman
Stereotypie f *(print)* 1. (Verfahren) stereotyping, stereotyping process, stereotyping technique, stereotypy, stereotype 2. (Stereotypplatte) →Stereo 1. 3. (Raum) stereotyping room, foundry
Stereotypiepapier n **(Stereotypiepappe** f**)**
→ Maternpappe
Stereotypieplatte f
→ Stereo, Galvano
stereotypieren *v/t (print)* to stereotype, to make a stereo, to make a stereotype, to make a stereotype plate, to make an electro, to make an electrotype
Stereotypplatte f
→ Stereo 1.
Stereoübertragung f *(radio/TV)* stereo transmission, stereophonic transmission, binaural transmission
Stereowiedergabe f **(stereophone Wiedergabe** f**)** stereo reproduction, stereophonic reproduction, binaural reproduction
Stereovorsatz m *(phot)* stereo attachment, beam-splitting attachment
Stern m **(Sternchen** n, **Sternchenzeichen** n, **Asteriskus** m**)** *(typ)* asterisk(*), (drei Sternchen) asterism (***)
stetige Daten n/pl
→ kontinuierliche Daten
stetige Häufigkeitsverteilung f **(stetige Verteilung** f**)**
→ kontinuierliche Häufigkeitsverteilung

stetige Grundgesamtheit f (stetige Population f, stetige statistische Masse f)
→ kontinuierliche Grundgesamtheit
stetige Skala f
→ kontinuierliche Skala
stetige Variable f
→ kontinuierliche Variable
stetige Verteilung f
→ kontinuierliche Häufigkeitsverteilung
stetige Zufallsgröße f
→ kontinuierliche Zufallsgröße
Steuerpult n
→ Kontrollpult
Steuerraum m (Steuerungsraum m)
→ Kontrollraum
Stich m
1. *(print)* → Kupferstich, Stahlstich
2. → Farbstich
Stichel m *(print)* engraver's tool, burin, graver
A cutting or shaping tool used by finishers or engravers.
Stichelarbeit f *(print)* tool engraving
Stichprobe f (Erhebungsauswahl f, Auswahl f) *(stat)* sample
A portion of a larger group of units, i.e. the population, (→) Grundgesamtheit, selected by some principle. If the selection is done so that the probability of selection is known, it is a probability sample, (→) Wahrscheinlichkeitsstichprobe. Inferences about the population can be made, then, according to the principles of statistical inference. If the sample is a nonprobability sample, (→) bewußte Auswahl, the kinds of inferences that can be made about the population are open to question, because there is no accepted theory of inferences about populations based on information from nonprobability samples.
Stichprobenanlage f
→ Auswahlplan
Stichprobenausfälle m/pl *(stat)* sampling loss
→ Ausfälle
Stichprobenauswahl f
→ Auswahl 4., Auswahlverfahren
Stichprobenbildung f *(stat)* sampling, sample selection
→ Auswahlverfahren
Stichprobeneinheit f
→ Erhebungseinheit (Auswahleinheit)
Stichprobenerhebung f (Teilerhebung f) *(stat)* sample survey, sampling survey, sample investigation, sampling investigation, sample study,

sampling study, (Mikrozensus) sample census, partial census
A survey which is carried out using a sampling method, i.e. one in which a portion only, and not the whole population, is surveyed.
Stichprobenfehler m
→ Auswahlfehler
Stichprobenfunktion f *(stat)* sample function
Stichprobenfusion f
→ Datenfusion
Stichprobengenauigkeit f *(stat)* sampling accuracy
→ Repräsentativität
Stichprobengröße f
→ Stichprobenumfang
Stichprobenmaßzahl f *(stat)* sample statistic
→ Maßzahl
Stichprobenmittel n (Stichprobenmittelwert m) *(stat)* sample mean
→ Mittelwert
Stichprobenplan m
→ Auswahlplan
Stichprobenpunkt m (Sample Point m) *(stat)* sample point, sampling point
→ Stichprobenraum
Stichprobenraum m *(stat)* sample space
A sample of n observations can be represented as a point or vector in an n-dimensional space. Such a representation is called a sample point, (→) Stichprobenpunkt. The set of all possible sample points constitutes the sample space. Generally the term is used to denote the set of all possible outcomes to a sample selection procedure, or to an experiment.
Stichprobenschätzung f *(stat)* sample estimate
Stichprobentechnik f
→ Auswahlverfahren
Stichprobentheorie f *(stat)* sampling theory, theory of sampling
Stichprobenumfang m (Stichprobengröße f) *(stat)* sample size
The number of units included in a sample. It generally refers to the number of elements in the sample. In multistage sampling, the sample size is the number of final stage units in the sample.
Stichprobenuntersuchung f
→ Stichprobenerhebung
Stichprobenvarianz f (Varianz f der Stichprobenverteilung) *(stat)* sampling variance

Stichprobenverfahren n
→ Auswahlverfahren
Stichprobenverteilung f *(stat)* sampling distribution
 The array of possible values for a specific sample design, of a sample statistic or estimator, each with its associated probability of occurrence, constitutes the sampling distribution of the statistic or estimator.
Stichprobenwert m *(stat)* sample score
Stichtagsbefragung f (**Stichtagserhebung** f, **Stichtagsermittlung** f, **Stichtagsuntersuchung** f) *(survey res)* instantaneous survey
 A survey whose interviews are conducted at a given instant, point or period of time.
Stichwort n catchword, catch word, *(radio/TV)* cue, word cue
Stichzeile f *(print)* catchline, catch line
Stichzeitraumbefragung f (**Stichzeitraumerhebung** f, **Stichzeitraumermittlung** f, **Stichzeitraumuntersuchung** f) *(survey res)* instantaneous survey
→ Stichtagsbefragung
Stil m style
 A characteristic or distinctive mode or method of expression, presentation, or conception in the field of some art.
Stimmprobe f
→ Sprechprobe
Stimmung f mood, (von Personengruppen) sentiment
→ Konsumentenstimmung
Stimmungsmusik f
→ Hintergrundmusik
Stimulation f *(psy)* stimulation
Stimulus m
→ Reiz
Stimulusgeneralisierung f
→ Reizgeneralisierung
Stimulusintensität f
→ Reizintensität
Stimulus-Organismus-Reaktions-Modell n
→ SOR-Modell
Stimulus-Reaktions-Modell n
→ Reiz-Reaktions-Modell (S-R-Modell)
Stimulusskala f *(stat)* stimulus scale
Stimulusskalierung f *(stat)* stimulus scaling, stimulus model of scaling
Stimulusvariable f *(stat)* stimulus variable

Stirnwand f *(transit advtsg)* (im Verkehrsmittel) bulkhead
Stirnwandaufkleber m (**Stirnwandplakat** n) *(transit advtsg)* bulkhead card
 An advertising message on a card that is normally posted on the end bulkheads of public transportation vehicles.
Stochastik f *(stat)* stochastics pl *(construed as sg)*
 The mathematical theory of variations in which at least one of the elements is a variate and of processes in which the system incorporates an element of randomness as opposed to a deterministic system.
stochastisch adj *(stat)* stochastic
stochastische Abhängigkeit f *(stat)* stochastic dependence
 The relationship between variates which are not independent as contrasted with mathematical dependence, which is a relationship between variables.
vgl. stochastische Unabhängigkeit
stochastische Beziehung f stochastische relationship
vgl. deterministische Beziehung
stochastische Gleichung f *(stat)* stochastic equation
stochastische Unabhängigkeit f *(stat)* stochastic independence
vgl. stochastische Abhängigkeit
stochastische Variable f (**Zufallsvariable** f) *(stat)* stochastic variable
stochastischer Fall m
→ Entscheidung unter Risiko
stochastischer Prozeß m (**Zufallsprozeß** m) *(stat)* stochastic process
stochastisches Experiment n *(res)* stochastic experiment (Johan Galtung)
vgl. deterministisches Experiment
stochastisches Modell n *(stat/res)* stochastic model
vgl. deterministisches Modell
Stock m
→ Druckstock
Stockholmer Wellenplan m Stockholm wave-length plan, Stockholm plan
Stoppbad n (**Stopbad** n)
→ Unterbrecherbad
Stopptrick m (**Stoptrick** m) *(film)* stop-camera effect, freeze-frame effect, freeze effect
→ Standbildverlängerung

Störabstand *m* (**S/N-Verhältnis** *n*)
signal-to-noise ratio, S/N ratio, signal-to-interference ratio
→ Rauschabstand
Store Erosion f
→ Ladenverschleiß *m*
stören *v/t* (Radioempfang) to interfere, to blanket (absichtlich) to jam
Store-Test *m*
→ Ladenbeobachtung, Ladentest
Störfaktor *m* (**Störvariable** f) disturbing variable
Störgeräusch *n* noise interference, noise, (beabsichtigt) jamming noise, jamming
Störkompensation f interference compensation
Störlicht *n* light interference
stornieren *v/t (econ)* to cancel
Stornierung f (**Storno** *n*) *(econ)* cancellation, cancelation
Stornierungsfrist f *(econ)* cancellation date, cancelation date
Störpegel *m* (**Geräuschpegel** *m*, **Rauschpegel** *m*) noise level
Störsender *m (radio)* jamming station, interfering transmission
Storyboard *n (TV)* storyboard, strip cartoon, photomatic
   A series of sketches, with accompanying copy, providing in parallel sequence the video and audio portions of a television program or commercial. A "layout" for television.
Storyboardtest *m (TV)* storyboard test
   An advertising test using a storyboard.
stoßweise Werbung f (**Stoßwerbung** f) burst advertising, impact scheduling, impacting
→ phasenweise Werbung
Strahlbreite f (**Strahlquerschnitt** *m*) *(TV)* beamwidth, beam width
Straßenbahn- und Omnibuswerbung f
→ Verkehrsmittelwerbung
Straßenhandel *m (econ)* street selling, street sales *pl*, street vending
Straßenverkauf *m* (**Straßenverkäufe** *m/pl*) (Zeitung) street sales *pl*, newsboy sales *pl*, boy sales *pl*
   The total or average number of newspapers sold by individuals on the street as distinguished from those sold by dealers with permanent shops or by a carrier boy or those being delivered to subscribers with a regular list of customers.

Straßenverkäufer *m (econ)* street vendor
Straßenverkaufszeitung f
→ Kaufzeitung
Strategie f strategy
strategische Marketingplanung f
→ strategisches Marketing
Strategischer Geschäftsbereich *m* (**SGB**) *(marketing)* strategic business unit (SBU)
   A combination of one or more products, brands, company divisions, or market segments that have something in common, such as the same distribution system, similar consumer benefits, or like technology.
strategisches Marketing *n* (**strategische Marketingplanung** f) strategic marketing, strategic marketing planning
   The process of establishing long-range corporate and marketing decisions anticipating future changes in a largely uncontrollable social and political environment.
Stratifikation f (**Stratifizierung** f)
→ Schichtung
stratifizieren
→ schichten
Stratifizierungseffekt *m*
→ Schichtungseffekt
Stratifizierungsfaktor *m* (**Stratifizierungsvariable** f)
→ Schichtungsfaktor
stratifizierte Auswahl f
→ geschichtete Auswahl
Strebeflächenplakat *n (transit advtsg)* bulkhead card
Strebung f
→ Sekundärbedürfnis
Streckenanschlag *m* (**Streckenplakat** *n*) *(transit advtsg)* railroad showing, railroad bulletin
   An outdoor bulletin or station poster conspicuously located to attract the attention of train passengers.
Streckengeschäft *n* (**Streckenhandel** *m*, **Streckengroßhandel** *m*) *(econ)* stockless retailing, nonstore retailing, nonstore wholesaling
vgl. Lagergeschäft
Streckenhandelsbetrieb *m* (**Streckenhändler** *m*) *(econ)* nonstore wholesaler, stockless dealer
Streckenwerbung f *(transit advtsg)* road sign advertising, railroad bulletin advertising, railroad advertising

Advertising using permanent and semi-permanent outdoor signs along the driving lanes of highways and the tracks of railroads.
streichen v/t **1.** (Textpassagen) to delete, to cross out, to strike out, to erase, to cancel **2.** *(print)* (Satz) to kill **2.** → beschichten
Streichsatz m *(print)* leftover matter, overmatter, overset matter, overset, overs *pl*
  Type set in excess of the amount alotted and therefore crowded out of the paper for lack of room.
Streichung f **(Streichen** n**)** (von Textpassagen) deletion, crossing out, cancelation, cancellation, cancel
Streifband n **(Kreuzband** n**)** wrapper, newspaper wrapper; per Streifband (Kreuzband): by book mail, *brit* by book-post
Streifbandzeitung f wrappered newspaper
Streifen m **1.** *(paper)* → Rippe **2.** *(phot)* (auf dem Negativ) streak **3.** *(film)* film strip, film **4.** *(video)* striation
Streifenanzeige f **(Leistenanzeige** f**)** strip advertisement, strip ad
Streifenbildanzeige f cartoon advertisement, cartoon ad, comic-strip advertisement, comic-strip ad
Streiflicht n *(film/phot)* rim light, glancing light
Stress m **1.** *(psy)* stress **2.** *(stat)* → Kruskals Stress
Stresswert m
→ Stress 2.
Streuagentur f
→ Mediaagentur
Streuanalyse f advertising analysis
Streuart f type of media planning
Streuauftrag m media buying order
Streubereich m *(media res)* coverage area, circulation area, circulation
Streubild n
→ Streudiagramm
Streudauer f advertising time, duration of advertising campaign
Streudiagramm n **(Streuungsdiagramm** n, **Streubild** n**)** *(stat)* scatter diagram, scattergram, scatterplot
  A diagram showing the joint variation of two variates. Each member is represented by a point whose coordinates are the values of the variates. A set of *n* observations thus provides *n* points on the diagram and the scatter or clustering of the points exhibits the relationship between the two variates.
Streudichte f advertising density, density of advertising
Streuen n
→ Streuung
Streufachmann m
→ Mediaplaner
streufähige Werbemittel n/pl above-the-line advertisements *pl*, above-the-line advertising, above the line
  Any advertisements for which a commission or fee is payable to a recognized advertising agency operating on behalf of its client(s) (Usually press, television, radio, cinema, and posters).
Streufeld n advertising zone, advertising area
Streugebiet n
→ Streubereich
Streukosten *pl* media buying cost(s) *(pl)*
Streulicht n *(phot)* diffused light, stray light, spill light, spill
  The unwanted or extraneous illumination from a single light source.
Streulichtfaktor m *(phot)* diffusion factor
Streulichtscheinwerfer m *(phot/film/ TV)* broadside, broad
  A large, 2000-watt, boxlike floodlight.
Streulichtschirm m **(Streuschirm** m**)** *(phot/film/TV)* diffusing light
Streumedium n
→ Werbeträger
Streumenge f number of advertisements
Streumittel n
→ Werbeträger
Streumittelanalyse f
→ Werbeträgeranalyse, Mediaanalyse
Streumittler m media broker
→ Spezialmittler
Streuperiode f
→ Werbeperiode
Streuplan m
→ Mediaplan
Streuplaner m
→ Mediaplaner
Streuplanung f
→ Mediaplanung
Streuprospekt m
→ Prospekt
Streupunktdiagramm n
→ Streudiagramm
Streuung f **1.** *(stat)* dispersion
  The degree of scatter shown by observations. It is usually measured as

Streuungsdiagramm

an average deviation about some central value or by an order statistic but may also be a mean of deviations of values among themselves.
→ Varianz
2. *(phot/opt)* diffusion, dispersion
→ Aberration, Diffusion
3. → Mediaplanung (Streuplanung), Mediaeinkauf, Mediaselektion
4. *(TV)* scattering
Streuungsdiagramm *n*
→ Streudiagram
Streuungsfachmann *m*
→ Mediaplaner
Streuungsmaß *n (stat)* measure of dispersion, statistic of dispersion
Streuungsparameter *m (stat)* dispersion parameter
Streuungszerlegung *f*
→ Varianzanalyse
Streuverluste *m/pl (media planning)* coverage waste, waste coverage
That portion of the circulation of a medium which cannot be considered to reach logical prospects for a product because they are unable to use it or unable to pay for it. Also, for instance, any advertising in a geographical area where the advertiser has no distribution for the advertised product.
Streuversand *m (Zeitschrift)* non-qualified distribution, non-controlled distribution
Streuweg *m* advertising delivery channel, audience delivery channel
Streuwertanalyse *f* media performance analysis
Streuwertfaktor *m (advtsg)* cost per conversion factor, conversion rate
Streuwinkel *m* **(Abtastwinkel** *m) (TV)* angle of scatter, angle of divergence, angle of spread, (Scheinwerfer) diffusion angle, angle of dispersion
Streuwirkung *f*
→ Werbewirkung
Streuzahl *f* advertising audience, audience
Streuzeit *f*
→ Streudauer
Streuzeitschrift *f* non-qualified distribution magazine, non-controlled distribution magazine
vgl. CC-Zeitschrift
Strich *m* **1.** *(print)* → Linie **2.** *(paper)*
→ Laufrichtung
Strichätzung *f* **(Strichklischee** *n)* *(print)* line cut, linecut, line block, line engraving, line etching, line photo-engraving, lineplate, line plate, zinc etching
An engraving made without a screen; it reproduces only solid lines or areas, without intermediate shades or tones.
Strichelmethode *f* **(Strichelverfahren** *n)* *(stat)* hand tallying, tallying, tallysheet method, tallysheet technique
→ manuelle Auszählung
stricheln
→ schraffieren
Strichelung *f*
→ Schraffur
Strichklischee *n*
→ Strichätzung
Strichlinie *f* **(gestrichelte Linie** *f*) broken line, dashed line
Strichliste *f (stat)* tally list
Strichlistenauszählung *f*
→ Strichelmethode
Strichpunktlinie *f* dot-dashed line
Strichraster *m* **(Linienraster** *m)* *(print)* line screen
Strichrasterbild *n (TV)* bar test pattern, bar pattern
Strichstärke *f* **(Stärke** *f* **des Drucks** *(print)* weight of type, weight
The relative darkness of the impression of a type face.
Strichvorlage *f (print)* line copy, line drawing, line artwork, line original
A photomechanical original in which the design or image is composed of lines or dots, and which can be reproduced in the form of line etchings.
→ Strichzeichnung
Strichzeichnung *f (print)* line drawing, line artwork
A brush or pen drawing consisting of solid lines or masses without tonal gradations.
strippen *v/t* → montieren **1.**
Strippen *n* **(Offsetmontage** *f)*
→ Montage **1.**
Strobe *m* **(Stroboskop** *n)*
→ Röhrenblitz
Strohpapier *n* strawpaper, straw paper
Strohpappe *f* strawboard
Struktur *f* structure
Strukturanalyse *f* **1.** structural analysis, structure analysis, analysis of structure **2.** *(media res)* audience structure analysis, analysis of audience structure
Strukturdaten *n/pl* structural data, structure data

Strukturerhebung f structural survey, structural data collection survey
strukturierte Beobachtung f *(res)* structured observation
strukturierte Frage f *(survey res)* structured question
strukturierter Fragebogen m *(survey res)* structured questionnaire, structured schedule
    Questionnaires, which specify the wording of the questions and the order in which they are asked. Unstructured questionnaires list the topics to be covered but leave the exact wording and order of questions to the interviewer's discretion.
    vgl. unstrukturierter Fragebogen
strukturiertes Interview n **(strukturierte Befragung f)** *(survey res)* structured interview
→ strukturierter Fragebogen
strukturiertes Tiefeninterview n *(survey res)* structured depth interview
Strukturmerkmal n structural characteristic
Strukturmodell n structural model
Strukturpolitik f structural policy
Strukturwandel m **(struktureller Wandel** m**)** structural change
Stückkosten pl *(econ)* unit cost(s) *(pl)*
Stückpreis m *(econ)* unit price
Student-Test m
→ t-Test
Student-Verteilung f
→ t-Verteilung
Studie f **(Untersuchung** f**)** *(res)* study, investigation
Studienleiter m research manager, research executive
Studio n studio
  1. *(phot)* A room in which a still photographer takes pictures.
  2. *(radio/film/TV)* A group of stages for motion picture or commercial production.
  3. *(advtsg)* A room in which an artist works.
  4. A group of artists and/or photographers organized to seek free-lance work through an agent.
  5. *(radio/TV)* An indoor origination point for television and radio programs.
→ Atelier
Studioausrüstung f studio equipment, studio facilities *pl*
Studiobeleuchtung f **(Studiolicht** n**)** *(phot/film/TV)* studio lighting, studio light(s) *(pl)*

Studiokamera f *(film/TV)* stand camera
Studio-Kino n film studio
Studioleiter m
→ Atelierleiter m
Studiolicht n
→ Studiobeleuchtung
Studiomeister m *(film/TV)* scene supervisor
Studioproduktion f studio production
Studioredakteur m **(Redakteur** m **im Studio)** *(TV)* anchorman, presenting editor
→ Moderator
Studioregisseur m *(radio/TV)* studio director
Studiosendung f **(Studioprogramm** n**)** *(radio/TV)* studio broadcast, studio program, *brit* studio programme
Studiotechnik f *(radio/TV)* studio engineering
Studiotest m
→ Labortest
Studiotonmeister m *(film)* floor mixer, production mixer
Stufenkeil m *(phot)* step wedge, stepped photometric absorption wedge
→ Graukeil
Stufenlinse f
→ Fresnel-Linse
Stufenmodell n **(der Werbewirkung)** step model (of advertising effect), stage model, phase model (of advertising effect)
Stufenplan m **(Stufenwerbeplan** m**)** *(advtsg)* cream plan
vgl. Zonenplan
Stufenrabatt m
→ Staffelrabatt, Funktionsrabatt
Stufenschalter m *(radio/TV)* step switch, sequence switch
Stufenwertzahlverfahren n **(der Standortpolitik)** *(econ)* zone score technique, zone scoring technique
stummer Verkäufer m *(promotion)* dummy salesman, silent salesman, counter display container, counter display, counter dispenser, dispenser
    Any point-of-purchase material embodying display and especially attention-getting contents used as a merchandising technique.
Stummfilm m 1. silent movie, silent film, silent picture

stümperhafte Anzeige

A picture with moving visual images recorded, projected, or broadcast without sound accompaniment.
2. (Stummfilmkino) silent pictures *pl*, silent movie
stümperhafte Anzeige *f* (**stümperhaft gemachte Werbung** *f*) buckeye
An unattractive, tasteless advertisement crude in design, overcrowded, using large, bold type.
stumpf *adj* → ohne Einzug
stumpffeine Linie *f (print)* blunt rule, blunt line
Stumpfklebelade *f* (**Stumpfklebepresse** *f*) *(film)* butt joiner
Stundenbericht *m*
→ Sendeablaufsprotokoll
stürzende Linien *f/pl (phot)* converging verticals *pl*
Stutzen *n* (einer Verteilung, einer Stichprobe) *(stat)* truncation (of a distribution, of a sample)
A truncated distribution is one formed from another distribution by cutting off (→) Abschneideverfahren, and ignoring the part lying to the right or left of a fixed variate value. A truncated sample is likewise obtained by ignoring all values greater than or less than a fixed value.
Stützmikrophon *n* (**Stützmikrofon** *n*) stand microphone
Stützplakat *n* (**Stützschild** *n*) backer card
A poster or other advertising card designed to fit on a pole or the back of a display bin.
Stützpreis *m (econ)* pegged price
A selling price which is held at a stable level, with the seller absorbing increased costs and possibly subsidized by government action. When undertaken on private initiative, it may enable the seller to win customers from rivals, or at least to maintain market share, especially during periods of inflation.
Styling *n* styling
Stylist(in) *m(f)* stylist
An artist who arranges materials such as food, hair, or apparel into attractive or suitable visual compositions.
subjektbezogene Marktforschung *f*
→ demoskopische Marktforschung
subjektive Schätzung *f (stat)* subjective estimate
Subkontraktor *m* (**Sub-Unternehmer** *m*) *(econ)* subcontractor
subliminale Wahrnehmung *f*
→ unterschwellige Wahrnehmung
subliminale Werbung *f*
→ unterschwellige Werbung

Submission *f*
→ Ausschreibung 2., 3.
Subskribent *m*
→ Abonnent
subskribieren
→ abonnieren
Subskription *f*
→ Abonnement
Subskriptionspreis *m* (**Vorbestellungspreis** *m*) *(advtsg)* advance rate, advance booking rate
Substitution *f (econ)* substitution
Substitutionalität *f (econ)* substitutionality
Substitutionselastizität *f (econ)* substitutionality, substitution elasticity
Substitutionsgüter *n/pl* (**Substitutionsprodukte** *n/pl*) *(econ)* substitutional goods
Goods or services related in use so that an increase in the price of one relative to a second results in an increase in the quantity demanded by the market of the second. The cross-elasticity value, (→) Kreuzpreiselastizität, if algebraically positive, is usually considered evidence that the two goods or services are substitutional, provided no change in the real income of the buyer has occurred.
Substitutionseffekt *m (econ)* substitution effect, substitutionality
→ Produktionsdifferenzierung
Substitutionskonkurrenz *f* (**Substitutionswettbewerb** *m*) *(econ)* substitutional competition
Substitutionsprozeß *m (econ)* substitution process
substitutive Güter *n/pl*
→ Substitutionsgüter
Subsystem *n* subsystem
subtraktive Farbmischung *f (phot/ print)* subtractive color mixing, *brit* subtractive colour mixing
vgl. additive Farbmischung
Suchanzeige *f* want advertisement, wanted ad
Sucher *m (film/phot)* viewfinder, finder
An optical device on a camera showing the operator the area within the field of view covered by the camera.
Sucherkasch *m* (**Sucherrahmen** *m*) *(film/phot)* viewfinder frame
Sucherlupe *f (film/phot)* viewing magnifier
Sucherobjektiv *n (film/phot)* viewfinder lens, viewing lens

Sucherokular *n (film/phot)* viewfinder eyepiece
→ Okular
Suffizienz *f (stat)* sufficiency
Suggestibilität *f* (**Empfänglichkeit** *f* **für Suggestion, Beeinflußbarkeit** *f*) *(psy)* suggestibility
Susceptibility to suggestion.
Suggestion *f* suggestion
A psychological process in which one person influences the attitude or behavior of another person indirectly, so that the person being influenced is uncritical and unaware of reasons for his acceptance of the communication.
suggestive Werbung *f* (**Suggestivwerbung** *f*) suggestive advertising
suggestiver Werbetext *m* (**suggestiver Anzeigentext** *m*) suggestive copy
Suggestivfrage *f* (**suggestive Frage** *f*) *(survey res)* suggestive question, leading question, loaded question
A question worded so that certain desired answers are more likely to be given by respondents. Loaded questions may be legitimately used to overcome a respondent's reluctance to report threatening behavior. The major illegitimate use of loaded questions is in surveys intended for lobbying or other persuasive purposes when the loading of an attitude question is in the direction of the views held by the question writer.
Suggestivverkauf *m* (**suggestives Verkaufen** *n*) *(econ)* suggestive selling, suggestion selling
Presenting selling arguments by suggestion, whereby the prospect may feel he has arrived at a conclusion (favorable to the selling agent) as a result of his own persuasions.
Suggestivwerbung *f*
→ suggestive Werbung
sukzessive Etatfestsetzung *f* build-up method (of advertising budget determination), build-up approach
A method of allocating the advertising budget to lines of offerings. It begins with requests for advertising budgets from those responsible for the lines. These are adjusted as necessary by the one in charge of promotion and then combined to produce a total.
Sulfatpapier *n* sulphate paper, sulfate paper
A strong paper made of sulphate wood pulp, not extensively bleached, used mainly for making bags, containerboard and the like.
Sulfatverfahren *n (papermaking)* sulfate process, sulphate process

Sulfatzellstoff *m* (**Holzzellstoff** *m*, **Papierbrei** *m*) *(papermaking)* sulphate pulp, sulfate pulp, sulphate wood pulp, sulfate wood pulp
A type of pulp prepared by digesting wood with a mixture of sulphate of soda, caustic soda, and sulphide of soda.
Sulfitpapier *n* sulfite paper, sulphite paper
A wood-pulp paper made from sulfite wood pulp and whitened through bleaching.
Sulfitverfahren *n (papermaking)* sulphite process, sulfite process
Sulfitzellstoff *m (papermaking)* sulphite pulp, sulfite pulp
A type of pulp made from wood chips cooked under a solution of bisulphite of lime.
summen *v/i* to buzz, to hum
Summenhäufigkeit *f* (**kumulative Häufigkeit** *f*) *(stat)* cumulative frequency
The sum of all the frequency values of a given variate below and inclusive of a given measure for ordinal or interval level variates.
Summenhäufigkeitsverteilung *f* (**kumulative Häufigkeitsverteilung** *f*) *(stat)* cumulative frequency distribution
Summenkurve *f* (**Summenhäufigkeitskurve** *f*, **Summenpolygon** *n*) *(stat)* cumulative frequency curve, cumulative frequency graph, cumulative frequency polygon, frequency polygon, summation curve
A frequency distribution polygon, which joins together plotted cumulative frequency values of a given variate.
Summenpolygon *n*
→ Ogive
Summensignal *n (radio/TV)* composite signal, mixed signal
Summenregler *m* (**Summensteller** *m*) group fader
Summierungsmethode *f* (**Summierungsverfahren** *n*)
→ Likertskala
Summenverteilung *f*
→ Summenhäufigkeitsverteilung
Super-8-Film *m (film)* super 8 film, super 8
An enlarged version of the older 8mm motion picture film.
Superette *f (retailing)* superette, bantam store, vest-pocket supermarket

superiore Güter

A retail store that is somewhat smaller than a supermarket, (→) Supermarkt, but otherwise possesses most of the same characteristics.

superiore Güter *n/pl (econ)* superior goods *pl*, superior products *pl*
Goods the demand for which decreases with rising price and vice versa.
vgl. inferiore Güter

Super-Ikonoskop *n (TV)* super-iconoscope, image iconoscope

Superlativwerbung *f* superlative advertising, advertising with superlatives

Supermarkt *m (retailing)* supermarket, (Hypermarkt) hypermarket, hypermarché, hypermarche
A large retailing business unit selling mainly food and grocery items on the basis of the low margin appeal, wide variety and assortments, self-service, and heavy emphasis on merchandise appeal. In its bid for patronage the supermarket makes heavy use of the visual appeal of the merchandise itself. Supermarket retailing involves (1) self-service and self-selection displays; (2) centralization of customer services, typically at the checkout counter; (3) large-scale physical facilities; (4) strong price appeal; and (5) a broad assortment of merchandise to enhance multiple item purchases. First developed by food stores during the depression, this method of retailing has spread to other types of retail and sporting goods fields.

Super-Orthicon *n (film)* superorthicon, image orthicon

Superposter *n* **(Superplakat** *n***)**
→ Großplakat, Mammutplakat

Super-16-Film *m (film)* super 16 film, super 16
An enlarged version of the 16mm motion picture film.

Super-Supermarkt *m (retailing)* super-supermarket, hypermarket, hypermarché, hypermarche
A very large retail store which makes heavy use of warehousing technology involving the use of palettized and collapsible wire racks for merchandise display.

Supplement *n* supplement, newspaper supplement, newspaper magazine, (Sonntagsbeilage) Sunday supplement, (nicht eigenproduziert) syndicated supplement
A special feature section, often in magazine format, distributed together with a newspaper.

supranationales Marketing *n* supranationales marketing

Surrogat *n* surrogate

surrogatfreies Papier *n*
→ Hadernpapier

Surrogatkonkurrenz *f* **(Surrogatwettbewerb** *m***)** *(econ)* surrogate competition

Symbiotik-Marketing *n* **(symbiotisches Marketing** *n***)** symbiosis marketing, symbiotic marketing
An arrangement whereby one firm sells and promotes a product made or controlled by another firm. It is a horizontal cooperative venture between two or more organizations involved in similar, sometimes noncompetitive, sometimes competitive business.

Symbol *n* symbol, conventional sign
An arbitrary sign that evokes a uniform social response. The meaning of a symbol is arbitrary in the sense that it is not inherent in the sound, object, event, etc., but is derived from the common learning and consensus of the people who use it in communications.

Symmetrie *f* symmetry

Synchro-Marketing *n* synchro marketing
The type of marketing that is designed to balance out seasonal or cyclical vacillations in demand.
vgl. Anreiz-Marketing, Entwicklungs-Marketing, Konversions-Marketing, Erhaltungsmarketing, Kontra-Marketing, Reduktions-Marketing, Revitalisierungs-Marketing

synchron *adj* synchronous

Synchronatelier *n* **(Synchronstudio** *n***)** *(film/TV)* dubbing studio
A studio that specializes in the introduction of sound in motion pictures which does not originate in the studio.

Synchronaufnahme *f (radio/TV)* direct recording
A recording made direct from a live performance or a real-life event while it happens.

Synchronbetrieb *m (radio/TV)* (Sender) common-wave operation

Synchronbild *n* synchronous picture

Synchronisation *f* **(Synchronisierung** *f***)** 1. (technisch) synchronization, *brit* synchronisation, synch, sync
→ Lippensynchronisierung

2. *(film/TV)* dubbing
   In motion pictures and broadcasting, the process of adding pictures or sound after the original recording has been made. Also, making duplicate recordings of original material.

Synchronisationssignal *n* sync signal, synch signal

Synchronisator *m (phot)* synchronizer, *brit* synchroniser, synchronizing unit, *brit* synchronising unit

Synchronisierbereich *m* hold range, locking range

synchronisieren *v/t* **1.** (technisch) to synchronize, *brit* to synchronise, to bring into step, to lock **2.** *(film/TV)* to dub

Synchronisieren *n*
→ Synchronisation

synchronisierte Kopie *f (film)* integrated print, final print, married print

Synchronisierung *f*
→ Synchronisation

Synchronität *f* synchronism

Synchronklappe *f (film)* clapper board, clapper, slate, clapstick, *brit* number board
   A special hinged slate device for the synchronization of picture and sound, inscribed with full production information and "clapped" on the camera before each double-system take.

Synchronkopf *m* synchronizing head, *brit* synchronising head

Synchronlauf *m (film/TV)* synchronous running

Synchronliste *f (film/TV)* dubbing cue sheet

Synchronmarke *f* **(Synchronzeichen** *n) (film)* synchronizing mark, *brit* synchronising mark, sync mark, synch mark, synchronizing cue, *brit* synchronising cue
   The film editor's start point indication.

Synchronregisseur *m (film/TV)* dubbing director

Synchronrolle *f (film/TV)* dubbing part

Synchronsatellit *n* synchronous satellite

Synchronschleife *f* dubbing loop, post-sync loop, post-synch loop

Synchronsignal *n* **(S-Signal** *n) (TV)* synchronization signal, *brit* synchronisation signal

Synchronsprecher *m (film/TV)* dubbing speaker, dubbing actor

Synchronstart *m* sync start, synch start

Synchronstimme *f (film/TV)* dubbing voice

Synchronstudio *n*
→ Synchronatelier

Synchronton *m* synchronous sound

Synchronumroller *m*
→ Synchronisator

Synchronwert *m* synchronizing level, *brit* synchronising level, sync level, synch level

Synchronzeichen *n*
→ Synchronmarke

Synektik *f* synectics *pl (construed as sg)*
   The art and science of developing creative strategy by the study of problem solutions by groups of individuals.

Synergie *f* synergy (Lester F. Ward)
   Both the unintended cooperative action (and the organizations and other cultural products resulting from such cooperative action) in which people engage as they pursue their own individual interests (in contrast to "true" cooperation wherein participants deliberately aim to help one another) and the combined effort, mutuality, and effect resulting from it.

Synergieeffekt *m* **(Synergiewirkung** *f)* synergistic effect

Synopsis *f* **(Synopse** *f)* synopsis

synthetisches Papier *n* synthetic paper

System *n* system
   An organization of interrelated and interdependent parts that form a unity. A system is a conceptual model used to facilitate investigation and analysis of complex phenomena. Systems are usually treated as though they are not part of larger systems, but in reality a system is usually an abstraction from a larger system, usually containing smaller systems.

System *n* **überlappender Gruppen**
→ Teamorganisation

Systemanalyse *f* systems analysis, *auch* systemic analysis
   A theoretical approach, in which emphasis is placed on analysis in terms of organization and interrelationships rather than on the study of separate units or entities. In contrast to earlier mechanical or organismic-type models, modern systems models emphasize the integration of the sociocultural system in terms of networks of information and communication. Thus systems analysis in

sociology is closely allied with cybernetics and information theory. Another important characteristic of systems analysis is that, by conceiving of systems as involved in a constant process of adaptation to their environment and internal reorganization, the attempt is made to build into the model conceptions of conflict, change, and process. In marketing, an approach which examines and analyzes the behavioral interrelationships among the various elements of the marketing structure, including the power structure and the communications network.

systematische Auswahl f **(systematisches Auswahlverfahren** n) *(stat)* systematic sampling, systematic selection
A sampling technique which consists of taking every kth sampling unit, (→) Auswahleinheit, after a random start. It differs from simple random sampling, (→) Zufallsauswahl, in that each combination of elements does not have an equal chance of being selected. There is also the possibility of introducing a recurring bias, (→) systematischer Fehler, of unpredictable significance if the element at the interval chosen is of a type more, or less, favorable to the hypothesis.

systematische Beobachtung f *(stat)* systematic observation

systematischer Fehler m **(Bias** m) *(stat)* bias, systematic error, constant error
The difference between the value reported and the true value. Sample bias results from the omission or the unequal selection of members of the population without appropriate weighting. Response bias for behavioral reports is the difference between what the respondent reports and the respondent's actual behavior.
vgl. Zufallsfehler

Systemeffekt m systems effect

Systemforschung f systems research
→ Systemanalyse

Systemgeschäft n **(Systemverkauf** m) *(econ)* systems contracting, systems selling
A form of selling which allows for little or no stock to be carried by the buyer. The purchase agreement is based on a catalog furnished by the supplier for the items agreed upon, usually a large group of repetitive materials. The supplier agrees to carry sufficient quantities of all items in the catalog and to respect the prices listed in it for a specified period of time. Requisitioners in the buyer firm's departments order directly, in approved quantities.

Systemtheorie f systems theory
An intellectual orientation stressing the development of principles or models of organization in such generally applicable terms that they can profitably be used as a basis for understanding all types of systems, from the simplest machine to the most complex, symbolically mediated, dynamic sociocultural formation.

Systemvergleich m (in der Werbung) *etwa* systems comparison
→ Fortschritts- und Systemvergleich

Systemverkauf m
→ Systemgeschäft

Systemzeitschrift f systems magazine, technology magazine

Szenario n **(Szenarium** n) *(econ)* scenario
A description or representation of a hypothetical sequence of events showing the alternative decisions at decision points and the possible consequences of each decision with their estimated probabilities.

Szenariotechnik f **(Szenarioverfahren** n) *(res)* scenario technique, scenario method

Szenarium n
→ Szenario

Szene f *(film/TV)* scene, shot

Szenenaufbau m *(film/TV)* box set, set

Szenenaufnahme f **(Szeneneinstellung** f) *(film/TV)* take, shot
→ Einstellung

Szenenausschnitt m *(film/TV)* bit, scene excerpt

Szenenausleuchtung f **(Szenenbeleuchtung** f) *(film/TV)* scenery illumination, set lighting, scene lighting
→ Ausleuchtung, Beleuchtung

Szenenbauplan m *(film/TV)* studio plan

Szenenbeleuchtung f
→ Szenenausleuchtung

Szenenbild n *(film/TV)* scenery, setting, set, decor

Szenenbildner(in) m(f)
→ Bühnenbildner

Szenenübergang m *(film/TV)* interscene transition, *brit* inter-scene transition
Any technique or means of moving from one scene to another in a motion picture or television broadcast. Can be done

musically, by fading out voices, by sound effects, and by other means.

Szenenwechsel *m (film/TV)* change of scenery, (mit der Kamera) intercut The abrupt transfer of camera from one scene to another.

Szondi-Test *m (psy)* Szondi test A projective technique, (→) projektive Technik, using pictures of mentally sick individuals, occasionally applied in motivation research, (→) Motivforschung.

T

T-Technik *f (stat)* t technique
t-Test *m* **(Student-Test** *m*, **Test** *m* **nach Student)** *(stat)* t test, Student test, Student's t test
 A statistical test used to determine the probability that a statistic, (→) Maßzahl, obtained from sample data is merely a reflection of a chance variation in the sample(s) rather than a measure of a true population parameter. The ratio of a statistic to its standard error, (→) Standardabweichung, is used to determine the level of significance, (→) Signifikanzniveau, of a statistic of a certain size obtained from a sample of a certain size. The t test is used instead of the critical ratio, (→) kritischer Quotient, when the size of the sample is small.

t-Verteilung *f* **(Student-Verteilung** *f*, **Verteilung** *f* **nach Student)** *(stat)* t distribution, Student distribution, Student's t distribution
 The distribution of the ratio of a sample mean to a sample variance in samples from a 'normal' population. The distribution is multiplied by a constant in order to make it a probability distribution. It is independent of the parent distribution and can be used to provide confidence intervals of the sample mean independently of the variance of the parent distribution. The sampling distribution of t does not exactly coincide with a normal frequency distribution curve, (→) Normalkurve, because, with a small sample, the probability of more extreme deviations is greater than with a large sample. As the size of the sample increases, the distribution of t approaches a normal curve. With very large samples the calculation of t for any statistic takes into account the size of the sample from which the statistic was obtained.

T-Wert *m (stat)* T score
tabellarisch *adj* tabular
tabellarisieren (tabellieren) *(v/t)* to tabulate
Tabelle *f* **(statistische Tabelle** *f*) table, statistical table
Tabellenkopf *m (stat)* boxhead, box head
Tabellensatz *m (print)* tabular matter

tabellieren
→ tabellarisieren
Tabellierung *f* **(Tabulation** *f*) *(stat)* tabulation
 The enumeration of the number of cases that fall in each category of class intervals of a variable. Tabulation is generally the first step in the analysis of data.
Tachistoskop *n (res)* tachistoscope, T-scope
 Any of various instruments for the presentation of visual stimuli, such as a picture, a word, or a group of symbols, or for successive presentation of a series of any such data, the duration of each single stimulus being extremely short.
tachistoskopische Methode *f* **(tachistoskopisches Verfahren** *n*, **Tachistoskopie** *f*) tachistoscope test technique, tachistoscope research technique, tachistoscope research, tachistoscopy, T-scope technique
Tachistoskoptest *m (res)* tachistoscope test, T-scope test
tachistoskopisches Verfahren *n*
→ tachistoskopische Methode
Tagblatt *n* **(Tageblatt** *n*)
→ Tageszeitung
Tagebuch *n (survey res)* diary
 A written record kept by respondents to report events, such as purchases of nondurable goods, media consumption, or illnesses, that are difficult to remember accurately at a later time. Diary keepers are requested to make entries immediately after the purchase or other event occurs.
Tagebuchmethode *f* **(Tagebuchtechnik** *f*) *(survey res)* diary method, diary technique, diary research, diary keeping method, diary keeping technique, diary keeping
 A survey technique in which an individual or a household provides a record, usually daily, of specified behavior, such as reading, listening, or viewing, or of product purchasing activities. In measuring the size of the audience for a broadcast medium, this method employs a notebook kept next to the set in which members of a family can record the stations and programs they attend. While there is always the

possibility of invalid entry, the advantages of this method are that all broadcast hours are covered, all members of the family are included, and additional information about the audience can be elicited. However, the method is not normally used in German broadcast media research. In readership research, a diary is kept by informants for recording, over a specified period of time, reading events in relation to all or a limited number of publications.

Tagebuchpanel n *(survey res)* diary panel
→ Tagebuch, Panel
Tagegeld n *(econ)* daily allowance, per diem allowance, perdiem
Tagesbericht n (eines Vertreters) daily report
A field report on sales and expenses made daily by a salesman.
→ Besuchsbericht
Tagesleuchtfarbe f daylight fluorescent ink, *(TM)* Day-Glo color, Day-Glo poster color, Day-Glo ink, Day-Glo
A luminously brilliant matte paint, available in a variety of colors, used mainly for display cards and outdoor advertisements.
Tageslicht n daylight
Tageslichtaufnahme f *(phot)* daylight shot
Tageslichtentwickler m **(Tageslichtentwicklungsgerät** n) *(phot)* daylight developer
Tageslichtfarbfilm m *(phot)* daylight color film, *brit* daylight colour film
Tageslichtfilm m *(phot)* daylight film
Tageslichtleuchte f **(Tageslichtlampe** f) *(film/phot)* daylight lamp
Tageslichtprojektor m
→ Arbeitsprojektor
Tagespresse f daily press, daily newspapers *pl*, daily papers *pl*, dailies *pl*
Tagesreichweite f *(radio)* (eines Senders) daytime service range, daytime range, diurnal service range, diurnal range
Tagessender m **(Tagesreichweitensender** m) *(radio)* daytime station, daytimer, limited-time station, part-time station
Tageszeitung f daily newspaper, daily paper, daily
Tageszeitungsanzeige f daily newspaper advertisement, daily paper advertisement, newspaper

advertisement, daily paper ad, newspaper ad
Tageszeitungsleseranalyse f *(media res)* daily newspaper audience analysis, newspaper audience analysis
täglich *adj* daily, *attr* every day *(radio/TV)* across the board
On the same station, at the same time, on every available day of the week, typically Monday through Friday.
Take m *(tape/film)* take
→ Einstellung
Talkshow f *(radio/TV)* talk show, *brit* chat show
Talmi m **(Plunder** m, **Talmiprodukt** n) *(econ) derog* borax, schlock merchandise
Any superficially impressive, but low-quality merchandise.
Tampon m *(print)* (zum Einschwärzen) ink ball, tampon
Tandem-Spot m *(TV)* double spot, piggyback commercial, piggyback, split commercial
Two broadcast commercials aired one after the other featuring two different products of the advertiser.
Tangierfell n **(Tangierfolie** f)
→ Rasterfolie
Tangiermanier f
→ Rasterdruck
Tangierraster m
→ Rasterfolie
Tanimoto-Koeffizient m **(Tanimoto-Ähnlichkeitskoeffizient** m) *(stat)* Tanimoto coefficient, Tanimoto proximity coefficient
Tante-Emma-Laden m *(retailing)* mom-and pop store, mom-and-pop shop
A very small neighborhood retailer, usually family-operated, and with restricted capital, especially in the food business.
Tarif m
→ Anzeigenpreis, Werbetarif
Tarifgemeinschaft f *(advtsg)* rate association
→ Kombinationstarif
Tarifkombination f *(advtsg)* rate combination, combined rate
→ Kombinationstarif
Tarifliste f
→ Anzeigenpreisliste, Werbepreisliste, Preisliste
Tarifstaffel f
→ Preisstaffel

Tarnwerbung
→ Schleichwerbung
Taschenbuch n paperback, paperback book, paper-bound book, pocketbook, pocket book, soft-cover book, softcover, papercover book
Taschenzeitschrift f pocket magazine, miniature magazine
Tastatur f keyboard
Taster m
→ Setzer
TAT abbr Thematischer Apperzeptions-Test
Tatsachenbericht n documentary report, documentary, (dramatisiert) docudrama
  A newspaper, magazine, motion picture, television, or radio presentation of actual events, especially as illustrations of a theme being discussed.
tatsächlich verbreitete Auflage f (**Vertriebsauflage** f)
→ verbreitete Auflage
tatsächlicher Empfänger m (**qualifizierter Empfänger** m) *(media res)* qualified recipient, proven buyer, proven reader-buyer
tatsächlicher Hörer m (**qualifizierter Hörer** m) *(media res)* qualified listener, proven listener
→ tatsächlicher Zuschauer
tatsächlicher Leser m (**qualifizierter Leser** m) *(media res)* qualified reader, proven reader, qualified issue reader
  A person who qualifies for examination on his reactions to a periodical advertisement by giving evidence in a survey interview of having read the issue in which an advertisement under investigation appeared.
tatsächlicher Zuschauer m (**tatsächlicher Seher** m, **qualifizierter Zuschauer** m, **qualifizierter Seher** m) *(media res)* qualified viewer, proven viewer
  A person who qualifies for examination on his reaction to a television commercial or program broadcast by giving some evidence of having watched the broadcast or commercial.
TAT-Test m
→ Thematischer Apperzeptions-Test
Tausch m *(econ)* barter, truck, (Umtausch) exchange
  A business transaction in which goods are exchanged without the use of money.
Tauschanzeige f
→ Gegengeschäftsanzeige

täuschende Reklame f
→ irreführende Werbung
Tauschexemplar n (Zeitung/Zeitschrift) exchange copy
Tauschgeschäft n
→ Gegengeschäft
Tauschhandel m *(econ)* barter trade, barter
→ Tausch
Täuschung f
→ Irreführung
Tausender-Auflagenpreis m *(media advtsg)* cost per thousand circulation, cost per thousand copies
  The total cost of an advertisement divided by the number of thousands in the circulation of the advertising medium.
Tausender-Kontaktpreis m (**Tausend-Kontakte-Preis** m) *(media advtsg)* cost per thousand exposures, (pro tausend Leser) cost per thousand readers, (pro tausend Hörer) cost per thousand listeners, (pro tausend Zuschauer) cost per thousand viewers, (pro tausend Haushalte) cost per thousand households, cost per thousand homes (pro tausend gewichtete Kontakte) cost per thousand weighted exposures
  The advertising cost incurred in reaching one thousand persons, homes, or other audience units, regardless of duplications.
Tausenderpreis m *(media advtsg)* cost per thousand (CPM, C.P.M., *brit* CPT, C.P.T.), cost per 1000
  The advertising cost of reaching one thousand units of a target audience with a particular media vehicle. CPM is calculated by dividing advertising unit cost by audience (in thousands). Generally, it is presented in terms of cost per thousand households, men, women, circulation, etc. This efficiency standard is used to compare ad units or media vehicles which vary in audience delivery and cost structure.
→ Tausender-Auflagenpreis, Tausender-Kontaktpreis, Tausend-Seitenpreis, Tausend-Leser-Preis
Tausend-Leser-Preis m *(media advtsg)* cost per thousand readers, cost per 1000 readers
  A figure obtained by dividing the advertising rate of a publication by the number of readers in thousands.

Tausend-Seiten-Preis m *(media advtsg)* cost per page per thousand circulation
   The cost per thousand copies of an issue of a periodical publication for placement of a full-page black and white advertisement in a publication.
Taxiwerbung f taxi-cab advertising
Taxonomie f *(res)* taxonomy
Teamorganisation n **(teamorientierte Marketingorganisation** f) team organization, *brit* organisation, team-oriented organization
   vgl. Matrixorganisation
Technik f **der Zufallsantwort (Random-Response-Methode** f) *(survey res)* random response technique, random response procedure, randomized response technique, *brit* randomised response technique, randomized response model, *brit* randomised response model
   A method that ensures respondent anonymity on questions dealing with socially undesirable or illegal behavior. The procedure involves asking two questions, one threatening and the other completely innocuous, both of which have the same possible answers, such as "yes" or "no." The respondent decides which question to answer on the basis of a probability mechanism, such as a box of red and blue beads with a window in which a single bead appears. Since the interviewer does not know what question is being answered, the response is completely anonymous, although some respondents may not believe this. By knowing the distribution of responses to the innocuous question (such as "Were you born in April?") and the probability mechanism, the researcher can estimate the response to the threatening question.
technische Einzelheiten f/pl **(technische Daten** n/pl) (bei Werbung) mechanical requirements pl, mechanical data pl
   The layout and makeup specifications of a periodical, to which prepared advertising printing material must conform.
technische Fachzeitschrift f technical journal, technical magazine, technical publication
technische Kosten pl
   → Herstellungskosten
technische Werbung f technical advertising

technische Zeitschrift f
   → technische Fachzeitschrift
Technologiefolgenabschätzung f **(technologische Vorhersage** f) technological forecasting
Technologiewirkungsanalyse f technology assessment
   The function of trying to determine the impacts of utilizing a particular technology in advance of its introduction.
Teilausverkauf m
   → Ausverkauf 2.
Teilbelegung f (Anzeigenwerbung) split-run advertising, split-run circulation, split run, (Anschlagwerbung) fractional showing, (Minimalbelegung bei Außenanschlägen) quarter showing, number 25 showing, quarter run, quarter service, spot coverage, 25 showing, (Halbbelegung) half showing, half run, half service, number 50 showing, 50 showing
   A schedule whereby the advertiser alternates with different copy in every other copy of the same issue of an advertising medium. The split-run makes it easy to compare coupon returns from two different advertisement under similar conditions.
Teilbelegungsanzeige f split-run advertisement, split-run ad
Teilbild n *(phot/film/TV)* partial image, partial picture, field
Teilerhebung f
   → Stichprobenerhebung
Teilgesamtheit f
   → Stichprobe
Teilkorrelation f
   → Partialkorrelation
Teilregression f
   → Partialregression
Teilkostenrechnung f *(econ)* direct costing
   An accounting method of producing a statement of costs which are directly attributable to a particular product, brand, or function. Especially significant at extreme ends of the product life cycle, e.g. during the growth and decline stages. It is a way of applying costs to products so that only the variable costs associated with a product are allocated to that product, while the fixed costs are charged off as expenses applied to the period in which they are incurred and not reflected in inventories. Under this method fixed costs affect net income more quickly than in the full costing

Teillieferung

method because none of the fixed costs linger in inventory valuations.
Teillieferung f *(econ)* **1.** *(Vorgang der teilweisen Lieferung)* part delivery, partial delivery, delivery in parts **2.** *(die teilweise gelieferte Ware)* part shipment, part consignment
Teilmarkt m
→ Marktsegment
Teilmarktstrategie f
→ Marktsegmentierung
Teilnahme f **1.** participation **2.** *(Btx)* user access
teilnehmende Beobachtung f *(survey res)* participation observation
Teilnehmer m **1.** participator **2.** *(Btx)* user
Teilselbstbedienung f **(Halbselbstbedienung** f, **Selbstauswahl** f) self-selection, semi-self service
  The method used in retailing by which the customer may choose the desired merchandise without direct assistance of store personnel.
Teilstichprobe f **(Unterstichprobe** f) *(stat)* subsample
  A sample, (→) Stichprobe, of a sample.
Teilstichprobenbildung f **(Unterstichprobenbildung** f) *(stat)* subsampling, subselection
teilstrukturiertes Interview n
→ halbstrukturiertes Interview
Tele n
→ Teleobjektiv
Tele-Banking n tele banking
Telebrief m **(Telefax** n, **Faxbrief** m) telecopied letter, telecopy
Telecine n
→ Bildabtaster
Telefax n
→ Telebrief, Fernkopierer
Telefonbefragung f **(telefonische Befragung** f) *(survey res)* **1.** *(Umfrage)* telephone survey, phone survey, telephone interviewing, phone interviewing
  Any survey conducted by telephone, rather than by mail or face-to-face interviewing.
2. → Telefoninterview
Telefonbuch n telephone directory, telephone book
Telefonbuchwerbung f telephone directory advertising, telephone book advertising
Telefongeschäft n
→ Telefonverkauf

508

Telefoninterview n **(telefonisches Interview** n) *(survey res)* telephone interview, phone interview (Telefonbefragung, telefonisches Koinzidenzinterview) telephone coincidental interview
  A telephone interview of television viewing or radio listening, conducted at the time the program is on the air.
→ Koinzidenzinterview
telefonische Befragung f
→ Telefonbefragung
telefonisches Interview n
→ Telefoninterview
Telefonmarketing n telephone marketing
Telefonverkauf m telephone selling
  Any selling operation in which the telephone is used to contact potential customers, and to solicit orders without any personal call upon customers' premises. It can be based on a cold canvass of the telephone directory, or prospective clients can be screened before calling. Another tactic is to use advertising that encourages consumers to initiate a call or to request information about placing an order.
Telefonwerbung f telephone advertising
telegen *adj* telegenic
Telegenität f telegenity
Telekommunikation f
→ Fernmeldetechnik (Fernmeldewesen)
Telematik f compunication (Simon Nora)
  Computer-assisted communication.
Tele-Mikrophon n **(Tele-Mikrofon** n)
→ Keule
Teleobjektiv n **(Tele** n, **Fernlinse** f) *(phot)* telephoto lens, tele lens, telephotographic lens, telescopic lens
  A camera lens used to photograph objects or action at a distance.
Teleprompter m **(Texttafel** f, **Souffliergerät** m) *(TV)* teleprompter, autocue, cue card, *colloq* idiot card
  A rolling script device used off-camera for performers who have difficulty in remembering lines. Lines are printed large enough to be read at a distance on a revolving sheet which keeps pace with the show's action, and which is not visible to viewers.
Teleshopping n *(econ)* teleshopping
Teletex m **(Teletext** m)
→ Ferntext
Television f
→ Fernsehen

Tendenz *f* tendency
Tendenzblatt *n* **(Tendenzzeitung** *f*)
→ Meinungsblatt
Terminabteilung *f* traffic department
In an advertising agency, the department that schedules the work of other departments and is responsible for its completion according to schedule. In broadcasting, the department responsible for the scheduling of all programs and announcements to be aired.
Terminanzeige *f* fixed date advertisement, fixed date ad
Terminauftrag *m* **(Anzeigenterminauftrag** *m*) *(advtsg)* wait order, hold order
An order to a medium to hold an advertisement for release at a date to be specified later.
Terminer *m* **(Terminüberwacher** *m*) (in einer Werbeagentur) accelerator, traffic manager, traffic controler
The head of a traffic department, (→) Terminabteilung.
Termingeschäft *n* *(econ)* futures business, forward business, futures transaction, forward transaction
Any transaction in a futures market, (→) Terminmarkt.
Terminkoordinator *m*
→ Terminer
Terminkoordinierung *f* **(Terminkoordination** *f,* **Terminplanung** *f*) **1.** (in einer Werbeagentur) traffic management, traffic control, (System der Terminkoordinierung) traffic system
→ Terminabteilung
2. *(econ)* traffic management
The planning, selection, and direction of all means and methods of transportation involved in the movement of goods in the marketing process.
Terminmarkt *m* *(econ)* futures market
That part of the market for a commodity in which contracts to buy or sell the commodity at some determinable future date are traded.
Terminplanung *f*
→ Terminkoordinierung, Zeiteinsatzplanung der Werbeeinsätze
Terminüberwacher *m*
→ Terminer
tertiärer Sektor *m*
→ Dienstleistungssektor
Tertil *n* *(stat)* tertile
Tesafilm *m*
→ Selbstklebefolie

Test *m* **(Versuch** *m*) test
A research instrument for the systematic measurement and comparison of subjects or objects in regard to a specified characteristic.
Test *m* **des Werbetextes** *(advtsg)* copy test
→ Copy-Test
Testaussendung *f* *(direct advtsg)* test mailing, sample mailing, trial mailing
A method of testing the applicability of a list and/or the efficacy of a mailing piece. By sending different mailings to different parts of a list to see which secures the best response, the particular mailing piece may be judged.
Testband *n* test tape, standard tape
Testbatterie *f* *(res)* battery of tests, test battery
Testbild *n* *(TV)* test pattern, test chart, test card, resolution chart
A card or chart used by television stations to adjust video equipment for proper transmission.
Testbildgeber *m* *(TV)* test pattern generator
Testeffekt *m*
→ Hawthorne-Effekt
testen *v/t* to test
Testen *n* *(res)* testing
Testfaktor *m* *(res)* test factor
Testfarbe *f* *(print/phot/film/TV)* test color, *brit* colour
Testfehler *m* **(Versuchsfehler** *m*) *(res)* test error
→ Fehler 1. Art, Fehler 2. Art
Testfilm *m* test film, test strip
Testfrage *f* *(survey res)* test question (Elisabeth Noelle)
vgl. Programmfrage
Testgeschäft *n*
→ Testladen
Testgruppe *f*
→ Versuchsgruppe
Testimonial *n* *(advtsg)* testimonial
An opinion given by the endorser of a product, directed toward inducing others to use the product.
→ Empfehlungsschreiben
Testimonialanzeige *f* testimonial advertisement, testimonial ad, testimonial
Testimonialsendung *f* **(Testimonial-Spot** *m,* **Testimonial-Werbesendung** *f*) *(radio/TV)* testimonial commercial, testimonial
Testimonialwerbung *f* testimonial advertising

Test-Item *m* (**Testaufgabe** *f,* **Einzelaufgabe** *f* **eines Tests**) *(res)* test item
Testkampagne *f* (**Werbetestkampagne** *f,* **Probekampagne** *f*) *(advtsg)* test campaign
An advertising tryout with limited circulation, to discover the effectiveness of copy before general release; usually a limited, short-term, advertising program designed to test selling offers, copy appeals or other factors such as media, size of ads, color, length of commercials, frequency, spending or pressure levels, etc. for efficiency and effectiveness in anticipation of a wider or national roll-out.

Testkauf *m (res)* test purchase, phantom purchase
→ Einkaufstest

Testkäufer *m (market res)* test shopper, comparison shopper, mystery shopper

Testkopie *f* (Kopierwerk) grading copy, first trial print, *(film)* rush print, rush

Testkriterium *n (res)* test criterion

Testladen *m* (**Testgeschäft** *n*) *(market res)* test store
A retail store used for tests of product movement rates, buying habits, selling practices, etc. in a store test, (→) Ladentest.

Testmarketing *n (market res)* test marketing
The execution in miniature of a complete program in one or several selected markets to test ideas, concepts, and techniques in product innovation, pricing, packaging, display, distribution, selling, sales promotion, advertising, publicity, etc. in real-life anticipation of a wider or national roll-out.

Testmarkt *m (market-res)* test market
A single market, usually one of several, in which marketing, advertising, and/or promotional ideas and strategies are tested for efficiency and effectiveness in anticipation of a wider or national roll-out.

Testmarkteffekt *m (market res)* test market effect

Testmarktkontrolle *f (market res)* test market control

Testmarkttest *m (market res)* test market test
→ Markttest

Testmarktverfahren *n* (**Testmarktmethode** *f*) *(market res)* test

marketing technique, test marketing method, test marketing
→ Testmarketing

Test-Retest-Anlage *f*
→ Wiederholungsanlage

Test-Retest-Methode *f*
→ Wiederholungstestmethode

Test-Retest-Reliabilität *f*
→ Wiederholungszuverlässigkeit

Testsendung *f (radio/TV)* (Programm) pilot program, *brit* programme, pilot, trial program, *brit* programme, (technisch) test transmission
→ Pilotsendung

Testsignal *n (radio/TV)* test signal

Testumfrage *f*
→ Probebefragung

Testverfahren *n (res)* test method, test technique

Testversand *m*
→ Probeaussendung

Testwert *m* (**Prüfwert** *m*) *(res)* test score

tetrachorische Korrelation *f (stat)* tetrachoric correlation

tetrachorischer Korrelationskoeffizient *m (stat)* tetrachoric correlation coefficient
A measure of correlation between two variables, each of which is expressed in a dichotomy, or two separate categories. The use of the tetrachoric correlation assumes that each variable is truly continuous, with a normal distribution that has been constricted into a dichotomy.

teuer *adj* expensive, high-priced

Texoprintverfahren *n (print)* Brightype conversion method

Text *m* **1.** *(print)* text, reading matter, text matter **2.** *(radio/TV)* (zum Ablesen) script, text script **3.** *(advtsg)* (Werbetext, Anzeigentext) copy, advertising copy, body copy

Text *m* **mit Sperrfrist** release copy
→ Sperrfrist

Textabbildung *f* text figure, text illustration

Textabteilung *f* (**Werbetextabteilung** *f*) copy department, copywriting department

Textanalyse *f* (**Werbetextanalyse** *f*) copy analysis

Textänderung *f*
→ Autorenänderung

textanschließend *adj/attr (advtsg)* following matter, following or next to reading matter, following reading

matter, following or next to reading, full position
  Alongside the editorial section of a periodical rather than surrounded by advertising

textanschließende Anzeige *f* full position advertisement, full position ad
  An advertisement position immediately adjacent to reading matter or editorial content.

Textanzeige *f* text-type advertisement, text-type ad, (reine Textanzeige) tell-all copy, all-copy ad(vertisement)
  An advertisement that gives all operational data and information necessary for making a decision to purchase and does not use any illustrations; used especially in business-paper advertising.

Textausschnitt *m* excerpt, *(tape)* cut
Textband *n* visual tape, written band
Textbandprojektor *m* visual tape projector, written-band projector
Textblock *m* (**Textabschnitt** *m*) *(advtsg)* copy block
  An area of running-text material in an advertisement.

texten *v/i (advtsg)* to copywrite, to write copy, to write advertising copy
Texten *n* (**Werbetexten** *n*) *(advtsg)* copywriting
Texter *m* (**Werbetexter** *m*) *(advtsg)* copywriter, copy writer
  An agency employee or a freelance professional who writes headlines and text for advertisements and promotional material, and usually creates advertising ideas and campaign themes.

Textkorrektur *f*
  → Autorenkorrektur
Textlänge *f* length of text, amount of copy
Textredakteur *m* copy editor
Textredaktion *f* copy editing
Textsatz *m*
  → Satz
Textschrift *f (typ)* straight matter, body type, text face, book face, text type
  Any type used for straight matter composition.

Texttafel *f*
  → Klapptafel
Textteil *m* (**einer Anzeige**) *(advtsg)* body matter, running body, body copy, running text
  The main copy block or blocks of an advertisement, as distinguished from headline, subheads, coupon copy, etc.

Textteilanzeige *f* full-position advertisement, full-position ad
  A preferred position advertisement, generally following and next to reading matter, (→) textanschließend, or top of column next to reading matter.

Textumfang *m (print)* amount of copy, copy size, amount of text
Textumrahmung *f (print)* (um eine Abbildung herum gesetzter Text) runaround copy, runaround matter, runaround
  A block of type, where a portion is set to less than full measure in order to leave space for an illustration, a large initial, etc.

Textverständlichkeit *f* reading ease, reading ease score
  → Lesbarkeit
Textwalze *f* (**Textrolle** *f*) *(film/TV)* crawl roll, title roll
  A drumlike device on which the titles and credits of a film are mounted so that their position can be continuously altered in printing on successive frames in order to create a creeping title, (→) Rollentitel.

Textzeile *f (print)* copy line, text line
Textvorlage *f* manuscript
  → Manuskript
Theaterkopie *f*
  → Verleihkopie
Theaterplakat *n* (**Theaterprogramm** *n*, **Theaterzettel** *m*) playbill
Theaterring *m* (**Lichtspieltheaterring** *m*) cinema circuit
Theke *f*
  → Ladentisch
Thekenaufsteller *m* (*POP advtsg*) (Aufstellerkarte) counter card, (stummer Verkäufer) counter dispenser, dispenser, (Auslage) counter display piece, counter display, (Auslagebehälter) counter display container
  A dispenser, a product, or an advertising message designed for display at the point of purchase on a retailer's counter.

Thema *n* 1. subject, topic, theme 2. *(advtsg)* (Leitmotiv eines Werbetextes) copy theme, advertising theme, copy platform, platform
  The overall rationale for an advertising campaign, implementing creative strategy and basic selling ideas.

Themamusik *f (film/TV)* theme music

Thematischer Apperzeptions-Test

Thematischer Apperzeptions-Test *m* (**TAT-Test** *m*, **TAT** *m*) *(res)* Thematic Apperception Test (TAT), TAT test (Henry A. Murray)
A projective technique, (→) projektive Technik, for the study of personality in which the subject is asked to respond to a series of ambiguous pictures by creating stories about each of them. An analysis of each of the stories is used to study the attitudes, values, and role conflicts the subject is experiencing or has experienced in actual social interaction, which he may not wish or be able to discuss directly. It is occasionally applied in motivation research, (→) Motivforschung.

Themenzentrum *n (retailing)* theme center

Themenheft *n* (**Sonderheft** *n*, **Sonderausgabe** *f* **zu einem Thema**) *(Zeitschrift)* feature issue
A special issue of a magazine focused on a special field of interest.

Theorem *n (res)* theorem
An established and accepted generalization based on empirical observations or derived by logical reasoning from postulates or other laws.

Theorem *n* **von Say**
→ Say'sches Theorem

theoretisches Konstrukt *n*
→ hypothetisches Konstrukt, Konstrukt

Theorie *f* theory
A set of interrelated principles and definitions that serves conceptually to organize selected aspects of the empirical world in a systematic way. A theory includes a basic set of assumptions and axioms as the foundation, and the body of the theory is composed of logically interrelated, empirically verifiable propositions.

Thermometerskala *f* (**Thermometerskalometer** *n*) *(survey res)* thermometer scale, thermometer scalometer

These *f* thesis

Thriller *m* thriller, suspense novel, suspense series, mystery show

Thurstone-Skala *f (res)* Thurstone scale, equal-appearing intervals scale, scale of mean gradations, mean gradations scale (Edward L. Thorndike/Louis L. Thurstone)
A type of attitude scale, (→) Einstellungsskala, consisting of a series of items (attitude statements) that the respondent rates, either as agree/disagree or by choosing the two or three he most agrees with. To construct it, the investigator gathers a large number of statements (usually several hundred) relating to the attitude, (→) Einstellung, being studied. These statements are given to from fifty to several hundred judges, who individually and independently classify the statements into eleven categories, from one extreme to the opposite. The middle (sixth) category is regarded as neutral. The classifications of the judges are compared. Those statements on which there is a great deal of disagreement among the judges are discarded. The investigator then selects a certain number of statements on which there is sufficient consensus among the judges and which provide an even representation of the categories. Each statement is given a scale value that is the value of the median category of the categories to which it was assigned by the judges. The respondent's scale score is the median or mean value of the statements with which he agrees.

Thurstone-Technik *f* (**Thurstone-Skalierungstechnik** *f*) *(res)*
Thurstone technique, method of equal-appearing intervals, Thurstone scaling, equal-appearing intervals scaling, mean gradations scaling (Edward L. Thorndike/Louis L. Thurstone)
A scaling procedure in which a respondent is presented with a number of stimuli that differ in magnitude along some dimension and is asked to sort them into a specified number of piles, usually from 7 to 11, in such a way that the differences between neighboring piles represent subjectively equal increments in stimulus magnitude.

Tiefätzung *f (print)* deep etching, intaglio etching, intaglio engraving, recess engraving, (Klischee) intaglio halftone
An image etched into a plate instead of appearing in relief, and usually made from a photographic positive. It is usually an additional etching of engravings to create proper molding depth or to sharpen the highlights of halftones. Also to add depth in type areas on combination line and halftone engravings.

Tiefdruck *m (print)* **1.** (Verfahren) intaglio printing, gravure, rotogravure, photogravure, copperplate printing, steel-plate engraving
Any of a variety of printing processes that employ plates in which the image is depressed below the plate surface. It is a printing method in which the image

areas of the printing plate have been etched below the plate surface to hold the ink from which the printing is done, as in gravure, rotogravure, color-gravure and steel-plate engraving.
2. *(Produkt)* intaglio print, intaglio, gravure, rotogravure, photogravure, copperplate print

Tiefdruckabzug *m (print)* intaglio proof
A proof, (→) Abzug, made from an intaglio plate, produced by depositing ink in the etched incisions or lines and wiping the surface of the plate clean before taking the impression on paper.

Tiefdruckautotypie *f* **(tiefgeätzte Autotypie** *f*) *(print)* intaglio halftone
A halftone plate etched in intaglio manner and made from a halftone positive.

Tiefdruckbeilage *f* (Zeitung) roto section, rotogravure supplement, rotogravure, roto
A newspaper supplement with a magazine-like format printed by a rotogravure process, (→) Tiefdruck 1.

Tiefdrucker *m (print)* gravure printer, rotogravure printer, photogravure printer

Tiefdruckpresse *f* **(Tiefdruckmaschine** *f*) *(print)* gravure press
A printing press, (→) Druckpresse, where the ink is transferred to the paper from depressions in the surface of the plate.

Tiefdruckplatte *f (print)* gravure plate
A printing plate used in gravure printing, in which the portions to be printed are etched out or depressed, rather than raised as in letterpress printing. The plate is covered by ink which is then scraped off, except for that remaining in the etched or depressed areas, which provides the printed impression.

Tiefdruckraster *m (print)* gravure screen

Tiefdruckrotationspresse *f* **(Tiefdruckrotationsmaschine** *f*) *(print)* rotogravure rotary, rotogravure machine, gravure rotary press, gravure rotary

Tiefdruckverfahren *n*
→ Tiefdruck 1.

Tiefdruckzylinder *m (print)* rotogravure cylinder, gravure cylinder
Tiefe *f* 1. *(print)* → Höhe 2. *(radio)* bass, bass note, low pitch 3. *(TV)* (des Bildes) dark-picture areas *pl*, dark areas *pl*

Tiefenabschwächung *f (radio)* bass boost, bass lift

Tiefeninterview *n* **(Tiefenbefragung** *f*) *(res)* depth interview, free interview
A type of research interview based on the use of open-end questions, (→) offene Frage, and stimulation of the respondent to talk freely and at length about the subject.

Tiefenplatte *f*
→ Schwarzplatte

Tiefenpsychologie *f* depth psychology

Tiefenschärfe *f* **(Schärfentiefe** *f*) *(phot)* depth of focus, depth of field
The depth between nearer and farther points of a scene that are in acceptably sharp focus. In theory, only one plane of the subject, that upon which the lens is focused, is sharply rendered in a photograph. In practice, objects before and behind this plane may also be rendered with adequate sharpness. The extent of this range of sharpness in the photograph is called depth of field. It is influenced by the lens aperture, (→) Blende, – a smaller aperture giving greater depth of field, by lens focal length, (→) Entfernungseinstellung, – shorter focal length lenses, for a given aperture, having greater depth of field, and by focusing distance – the depth of field being less, for given aperture and focal length, for close subjects than for distant ones.

Tiefenschärfebereich *m (phot)* zone of sharpness, field of focus
The range within which a camera may be moved toward or away from a subject, while the subject remains in acceptably sharp focus.

Tiefenschärfetabelle *f (phot)* depth of field chart, depth of focus chart

Tiefensperre *f (radio)* low-frequency rejection filter, bass cut

tiefgeätzt *adj (print)* deep-etched, intaglio
→ Tiefätzung

tiefgeätzte Autotypie *f*
→ Tiefdruckautotypie

Tiefpaß *m* **(Tiefpaßfilter** *m*) *(radio)* low-pass filter

tiefstehend (tiefgestellt) *adj (typ)* (Zahl/Buchstabe) inferior, subscript
Being set below the base line, (→) Schriftlinie, for normally set type.

Tiefton *m* low frequency, bass
Tieftonlautsprecher *m* bass loudspeaker, *colloq* woofer
Tiegel *m (print)* platen
An element in a printing press that presses the sheet to be printed against the printing surface.

Tiegeldruckpresse 514

Tiegeldruckpresse f **(Tiegeldruckmaschine** f) *(print)* platen press, platen machine
  A type of letterpress which makes impressions from a flat surface.
Tilde f *(typ)* swung dash, tilde
tilgen
  → auslassen
Tilgung f
  → Auslassung
Tilgungszeichen n
  → Deleaturzeichen
Tinte f ink
  → Druckerschwärze (Druckfarbe)
tintenfestes Papier n
  → geleimtes Papier
Tischgerät n table-top set, table set, table model
Tischkarte f **(Tischaufsteller** m, **Tischaufstellkarte** f) *(POP advtsg)* tent card
  A small, tent-folded card for table display.
Tischmikrofon n **(Tischmikrophon** n) table microphone, desk microphone
Titel m **1.** *(print)* title
  The name of a book or other written, typed, or typeset document.
2. (Motto) slogan, title, motto **3.** *(film/TV)* (Titelinsert) caption, title, credit title, credits *pl*
  The announcements or credits of a program produced on film, cards, or slides.
  → Zeitungstitel, Zeitschriftentitel
Titelaufnahme f *(phot)* **1.** (Bild) title photograph, title photo, caption **2.** (Tätigkeit) caption shooting, titling-bench work, titling
Titelband n *(film/TV)* title strip
  The footage preceding and following the actual story on which information is given about the title, who made the film, also, words which are superimposed on the film, as in silent pictures.
Titelbank f *(film/TV)* titling bench, rostrum
Titelbericht m **(Titelstory** f) cover story
Titelbild n (Zeitschrift) cover picture, cover photo, cover photograph
Titelblatt n
  → Titelseite
Titelbogen m *(print)* title sheet, prelims *pl,* preliminaries *pl,* front matter, *brit* oddments *pl*
Titelbox f *(advtsg)* ear, *meist pl* ears, (Titelboxplazierung) ear space
  Either one of the extreme upper corners of the front page of a newspaper, flanking the title; sold as preferred position advertising space.
Titelboxanzeige f ear
  → Titelbox
Titelei f
  → Titelbogen
Titelgerät n **(Titelmaschine** f) *(film/TV)* title printer, titler, titling bench, titling set, caption printer
Titelinsert n
  → Titel 3.
Titelkarte f *(media res)* masthead card, logo card
  A card containing the logotype of a newspaper or magazine to be presented to respondents in a readership survey as a recall aid, (→) Gedächtnisstütze. Masthead cards may be loose for card sorting methods or bound into a booklet.
Titelkartenheft n *(media res)* masthead card booklet, masthead booklet, masthead folder
  → Titelkarte
Titelkartenmethode f **(Titelkartenverfahren** n, **Kartenvorlage** f) *(media res)* masthead card technique, card sorting, card method
  → Titelkarte
Titelkarton m art board, fashion board
Titelkopfanzeige f
  → Titelboxanzeige
Titelkopfposition f
  → Titelbox
Titelkuller m
  → Titelbox
Titelmaschine f
  → Titelgerät
Titelmelodie f **(Titelsong** m) *(film/TV)* theme song
Titelmusik f *(film/TV)* title music
  The music serving as background for a motion picture or television title.
titeln (beiteln) v/t to title
Titelnegativ n title negative
Titelpositiv n title positive
Titelrolle f *(film/TV)* **1.** (Titelwalze) title roll, crawl roll **2.** (Hauptrolle) title role, title rôle, lead rôle, lead role, title part, lead part, name part
  → Textrolle
Titelsatz m *(print)* composition of (the) title, title composition, setting of (the) title

Titelschrift f 1. *(print)* titling face, title face **2.** *(film/TV)* caption lettering, title lettering
Titelseite f title page, front page, cover page, front cover, cover, first cover (C), outside front cover (OFC, O.F.C.)
Titelseiten-Wiedererkennung f *(media res)* cover recognition
→ Wiedererkennung
Titelständer m *(film/TV)* caption stand, titles easel
Titeluntergrund m *(film/TV)* title background, caption background
Titelvorspann m *(film/TV)* opening titles *pl*, opening credits *pl*, opening billboard, lead-in
→ Vorspann
Titelzeichner m *(film/TV)* caption artist, titling artist
Tochterband n (Tonbandkopie f) tape copy
Toleranz f (Toleranzbereich m, Toleranzintervall n)
→ Vertrauensbereich
Tolleisen n (Glockeisen n, Gaufriermaschine f, Kräuselmaschine f) goffer, gofer
Ton m 1. *(Schall)* sound, *(Klangfarbe)* tone, *(Tonqualität)* sound quality, tone quality, *(Tonhöhe)* pitch **2.** → Farbton, Tönung **3.** *(Ton aufdrehen)* up-and-over, *(Ton drosseln)* down-and-under
Tonabnehmer m (Tonabtaster m) sound pickup, pickup, sound head, head assembly, (Gerät) pickup
Tonabtaster m sound pickup, sound scanning, sound gate
Tonangel f *(film/TV/radio)* boom arm
Tonangler m *(film/TV/radio)* boom operator
Tonarchiv n *(radio/TV)* sound library, sound archives *pl*
Tonarm m pickup arm, pickup, *brit* pick-up arm
  The stylus, cartridge, arm, or head of a phonograph record player or audio tape player that converts signals from a disc or tape into electrical signals in an audio system.
Tonassistent m *(radio/TV)* sound man
  A technician responsible for sound engineering in the production of a program or commercial.
Tonatelier n
→ Tonstudio

Tonblende

Tonaufnahme f sound recording, audio recording, sound pickup
→ Tonbandaufnahme
Tonaufnahmeausrüstung f (Tonausrüstung f) recording channel
Tonaufnahmegerät n (Tonaufnahmemaschine f) sound recording equipment, sound recorder
Tonaufnahmepult n sound control desk, sound mixing desk
Tonaufnahmeraum m recording channel, recording room
Tonaufnahmestudio n sound recording studio, sound studio
Tonaufnahmetechnik f sound recording
Tonaufnahmewagen m
→ Aufnahmewagen
Tonaufzeichnung f
→ Tonaufnahme
Tonausblendung f *(radio/TV)* sound fade, sound fading
→ Tonblende, Blende
Tonausfall m *(radio/TV)* sound breakdown, loss of sound
Tonband n sound tape, audio tape, sound track, tape
  A ribbon of plastic bearing a layer of magnetizable particles and used to bear recorded audio signals.
Tonbandaufnahme f sound tape recording, audio tape recording, tape recording
Tonbandgerät n tape recorder, sound tape recorder, audio tape recorder, tape deck
Tonbandkassette f tape cassette, tape cartridge, cartridge
Tonbandlauf m tape travel
Tonbandmaschine f
→ Tonbandgerät
Tonbandtransport m tape transport
Tonbericht m sound report
Tonbezugsband n reference audio tape
Tonbezugspegel m reference audio level
Tonbildschau f sound-slide show, audiovisual show, sound-slide film
Ton-Bild-Versatz m *(film/TV)* (beabsichtigt) sound track advance, sound advance, sync advance, synch advance, (unbeabsichtigt) slippage of sound to picture
Tonblende f (Klangregler) sound fade, sound fader, (Frequenz) variable correction unit (VCU)

Tonblitz *m* sound flash, plop, blip, noisy join
Tonblubbern *n* bubbling, motorboating
Tondruck *m* (print) tinted flat color work, brit tinted flat colour work
Toneffekte *m/pl*
→ Geräuscheffekte
Toneinblendung *f* (radio/TV) fade-up
tonen *v/t* **1.** (phot) to tone **2.** (print) to tint, to scum
tönendes Dia *n* (tönendes Diapositiv *n*) (screen advtsg) sound slide
Tonfalle *f*
→ Tonsperre
Tonfarbe *f* **1.** → Tönung **2.** (music) timbre, color of tone, brit colour of tone
Tonfilm *m* sound motion picture, sound picture, sound film, *colloq* talk film, talkie
Tonfixierbad *n* (phot) tone fixing bath, fixing bath
Tonfolge *f* frequency run
Tonfolie *f* cellulose disc, acetate
→ Schallfolie
Tonfrequenz *f* audio frequency (AF), sound frequency, voice frequency
Tonfunk *m*
→ Hörfunk
Tongalgen *m*
→ Mikrofongalgen
Tongemisch *n* composite sound
Tongenerator *m* audio-frequency signal generator, audio oscillator
Tonhöhe *f* pitch, pitch of sound
Tonhöhenschwankung *f* pitch variation
Toninformation *f* audio information
Toningenieur *m* sound control engineer, sound engineer, audio engineer
Toninsert *n*
→ Tonschnitt
Tonkamera *f* (film) sound camera
Tonkanal *m* sound channel, audio channel
Tonklebestelle *f* sound join, sound splice
Tonkonserve *f* (Musikaufzeichnung *f*) canned music
Tonkopf *m* sound head, pickup head, pickup
Tonkopie *f* (film) sound print, sound copy
Tonkopieren *n* (film) sound copying, sound printing

Tonlampe *f* (**Tonprojektorlampe** *f*) sound exciter lamp
Tonlaufwerk *n* sound-film traction
Tonleitung *f* audio circuit, sound circuit
Tonmeister *m*
→ Toningenieur
Tonmischer *m* (film/radio/TV) sound mixer
Tonmischpult *n* (film/radio/TV) sound mixing desk, sound mixing console, mixing desk, mixing console, sound mixer
Tonmischung *f* (film/radio/TV) sound mixing, (film/TV) sound dubbing
Tonmotor *m* (radio/TV) capstan motor, capstan
  A rotating motor spindle used to transport recording tape at fixed speeds.
Ton-Negativ *n* (film) sound track negative, sound negative
Tonpapier *n*
→ Rastefolie
Tonpegel *m*
→ Geräuschpegel
Tonplatte *f* (**Untergrundplatte** *f*) (print) tint plate, ground-tint plate, tint block, background plate
  An unetched plate or flat-tone halftone used to print a light shade of ink for a background or other sizeable area.
Ton-Positiv *n* (film) sound positive, sound track positive
Tonprobe *f* sound level check
Tonprojektor *m* sound projector
Tonprojektorlampe *f*
→ Tonlampe
Tonqualität *f* sound quality, quality of sound, tone quality
Tonraum *m* (radio/TV) sound booth
Tonregie *f* (radio/TV) sound control, (Raum) sound control room, sound control studio
Tonregler *m* (radio/TV) sound control, sound fader
Tonreportage *f*
→ Hörfunkreportage
Tonrundfunk *m*
→ Hörfunk
Tonsäule *f* sound column, column loudspeaker
Tonschaltraum *m* sound switching area
Tonschleuse *f* sound gate
  A projector mechanism "reading" an optical soundtrack.

Tonschnitt m *(radio/film/TV)* sound editing
→ Schnitt
Tonschramme f sound scratch
Tonschwingung f sound vibration
Tonscript n sound script
Tonsender m sound transmitter
Tonsignal n sound signal, *colloq* beep
Tonspalt m headgap
Tonsperre f **(Tonfalle** f**)** sound trap
Tonspur f **(Tonstreifen** m**)** (am Tonfilm) sound track, voice track, music track, sound on film (S.O.F.)
   The audio portion of a motion picture print or videotape.
Tonstärke f **(Tonvolumen** n**, Volumen** n**)** sound volume, sound intensity, loudness, audio intensity
Tonstartmarke f sound start mark
Tonsteller m
→ Tonregler
Tonstörung f audio interference
Tonstudio n **(Tonatelier** n**)** sound studio, sound channel
Tontechnik f sound engineering, audio engineering
Tontechniker m *(radio/film/TV)* sound operator, sound mixer, sound-effects man, sound-effects operator, sound man, sound recordist, desk operator, program operations assistent, *brit* programme operations assistent (POA), *colloq* gaffoon
   The technician responsible for sound, sound effects, and sound mixing in the production of a motion picture, a broadcast program or commercial.
Tonträger m (Material) sound track support, base, (Funk) sound carrier, (Raum) recording channel, (Recht) phonogram
Tonüberblendung f *(radio/film/TV)* sound mixing, sound fading, crossfade
   The process and technique of allowing one audio source to rise out of another.
Tonübertragung f *(radio/TV)* sound transmission
Ton- und Bildübertragung f *(film/TV)* sound and vision transmission
Tonung f **(Tonalität** f**)** tone, tonality
   The skill with which an artist has reproduced the tonal gradations of his subject, or the effectiveness with which he has used tonal gradation to express an idea or feeling.

Tönung f *(print/phot)* (Schattierung) tint, hue, shade, tone, nuance
   The specific color or blend of colors of the spectrum composing any actual color.
Tonverzerrung f sound distortion
Tonvolumen n
→ Tonstärke
Tonwanne f line source unit, line source loudspeaker
Tonwert m *(phot/print)* tonal value, value
   The relative lightness of a hue, white having the highest value and black the lowest.
Tonwertumfang m *(print)* range of tonal values
Tonwertwiedergabe f *(print)* tonal value reproduction
Tonwiedergabe f sound reproduction
Tonwiedergabegerät n sound reproducer
Tonzuspielung f sound feed
Tor n **(Torblende** f**)**
→ Scheinwerfertor
Torschalter m gate circuit switch
Torschaltung f gate circuit, gate
Totalausverkauf m
→ Ausverkauf
Totalbelegung f **1.** *(outdoor advtsg)* → Netzanschlag **2.** *(transit advtsg)* total bus
   The contract arrangement in which an advertiser using transit advertising employs all the advertising space available on the vehicle.
Totale f **(Totalaufnahme** f**)** *(film/TV)* full shot (F.S.), long shot (L.S.)
   A shot showing an entire scene from some distance or a person or other object in full size from head to toe.
Totalerhebung f **(Vollerhebung** f, **Zensus** m, **Zählung** f**)** *(stat)* census, general census, complete census
   A complete survey of an entire population, (→) Grundgesamtheit.
   vgl. Teilerhebung
Totalimage n **(Gesamtimage** n**)** *(res)* multiple image
Tourenplanung f **(Tourenpolitik** f**)** *(econ)* (Außendienst) itinerary planning
Tourismus m
→ Fremdenverkehr
Tourismuswerbung f
→ Fremdenverkehrswerbung
Trade Mart m
→ Großhandelsdispositionszentrum
Trading-down n *(econ)* trading down

Trading-up

The strategy of selling at low prices to achieve high volume, which usually involves lower grade or deteriorated products. A German term is nonexistent.
vgl. Trading-up

Trading-up n *(econ)* trading up
The strategy of selling at high prices supported by a high level of service in order to secure exclusive custom and high profit ratios. An original German term does not exist.
vgl. Trading-down
Traffic-Abteilung f
→ Terminabteilung
Traffic-Manager m
→ Terminer
tragbare Fernsehkamera f hand-held TV camera, *Am colloq* creepie-peepie
Trägerfrequenz f (TF) carrier frequency
Trägerstelle f *(phot)* base side, emulsion side
→ Schichtseite
Trägerwelle f carrier wave (CW)
Tragetasche f **(Tragtasche** f, **Tüte** f) paper bag, (Plastik) plastic bag
An open-ended container for wrapping goods usually at the point of sale, made from paper or plastic, and sometimes including paperboard for added protection; often bearing distinctive printing indicating origin, and advertising goods or services.
Trägheit f
→ Fahnenziehen
Trailer m
→ Programmhinweis
Tranchenverkäufe m/pl (Zeitschrift) bulk sales *pl*, single copy sales *pl* in bulk
All single copies purchased in quantities of five or more which promote the business or professional interests of the purchaser, i.e. sales of copies of a single issue of a publication in quantities of five or more to one purchaser.
Transaktion f **(soziale Transaktion** f) transaction, social transaction
A unit of social or economic intercourse.
Transaktionsanalyse f **(transaktionale Analyse** f) *(psy)* transactional analysis (TA) (Eric Berne)
A form of group psychotherapy that focuses on how people interact and communicate with each other in social situations. Social interactions are viewed as coming from three separate components or roles of the individual's personality — the parent, child, and adult components — any of which may dominate at any particular time.

Cooperation or conflict among these components within the individual will contribute to his interactions with others. TA is especially concerned with describing how these components influence the individual in his social interactions and how they can lead to communication or misunderstanding in specific situations.
Transaktionsepisode f *(econ)* etwa transaction episode
Transaktionsprozeß m transactional process, transaction process
Transfer m transfer
Transfokator m
→ Vario-Objektiv
Transformation f transformation
Transistor m *(electr.)* transistor
Transit m transit
transparent
→ durchsichtig
Transparent n 1. (Durchscheinbild) backlighted transparency, transparency
2. → Spruchband
Transparentfolie f
→ Klarsichtfolie
Transparentpapier n transparent paper, glassine
A translucent paper permitting the passage of light.
→ Glanzfolie
Transparentschirm m transparent screen
Transversalaufzeichnung f transverse recording
Transversalkopf m transverse head
Travelling-Matte-Verfahren n
→ Wandermaskentrickverfahren
Traverse f (Stativ) cross arm
Treffgenauigkeit f **(Genauigkeit** f, **Akkuranz** f) *(stat)* accuracy
Lack of bias in a measurement. It is indexed by the mean of repeated measurements. The more accurate measurements are, the closer this mean is to the true value of the object being measured.
→ Genauigkeit; *vgl.* Wiederholungsgenauigkeit
Trend m *(stat)* trend
The steady change in a variable or set of related variables in a certain direction for a period of time. The term may be applied to an abstraction or to concrete objects. An essential feature of the concept of trend is that it is smooth over periods that are long in relation to the unit of time for which the series is recorded. In practice, trend is usually

represented by some smooth mathematical function such as polynomials in the time variable or logistic form, but graduation procedures by moving averages, (→) gleitender Durchschnitt, are also common.
Trendanalyse f *(stat)* trend analysis
Trendausschaltung f **(Trendeliminierung** f) *(stat)* trend elimination, elimination of trends
Trenderhebung f **(Wiederholungsbefragung** f) *(survey res)* tracking study, tracking investigation, tracking
Trendextrapolation f *(stat)* trend extrapolation
Trendforschung f *(survey res)* trend research, tracking research
Trendkorrektur f **(Trendanpassung** f) *(stat)* trend fitting
   The general process of representing the trend component of a time series, (→) Zeitreihe.
Trendprognose f *(econ)* trend forecast, trend prognosis, trend prediction
Trendstudie f **(Trenduntersuchung** f)
→ Trenderhebung
Trendvergleich m **(Vergleich** m **von Trends)** *(econ/stat)* trend comparison, comparison of trends
Trennlinie f **(Trennungslinie** f) *(print)* dividing rule, separatrix
Trennschärfe f (eines Tests) **(Güte** f, **Macht** f) *(hypothesis testing)* power (of a test)
   The ability of a test to reject a false hypothesis and to accept a correct one.
Trennschärfefunktion f **(Gütefunktion)** f (eines Tests) **(Testschärfefunktion** f) *(stat)* power function (of a test)
   When the alternatives to a null hypothesis form a class which may be specified by a parameter, the power of a test of the null hypothesis considered as a function of this parameter is called the power function.
Trennschärfekurve f *(stat)* power curve
→ OC-Kurve
Trennungslinie f
→ Trennlinie
Trennungszeichen n **(Divis** n) *(print)* hyphen
Tresen m **(Ladentresen** m)
→ Ladentheke
Tresenaufsteller m
→ Thekenaufsteller
Treuerabatt m *(econ)* patronage discount

A type of discount allowed on the basis of the amount of business done with one firm and intended to honor supplier loyalty.
Treuevergütung f *(econ)* patronage bonus
Trichterlautsprecher m horn loudspeaker, cone loudspeaker
Trick m **1.** *(film)* special effect(s) *(pl)*, animation, film animation
   The artificially produced audio and/or visual effects in motion pictures, television, and radio, apart from the live action.
2. → Werbetrick
Trickabteilung f *(film)* special effects department, special effects section, effects department, effects section, animation department
Trickaufnahme f *(film)* animation picture, rostrum shot
Trickbank f **(Tricktisch** m, **Trickpult** n) *(film)* animation board, animation stand, animation bench, rostrum bench, cartoon camera bench, animation desk, stop-frame rostrum, special effects desk, effects desk, vision mixer's desk
Trickblende f **(Trickblendeneffekt** m) *(film)* optical effect, optical, wipe
Trickeffekt m *(film)* special effect, stunt effect, (Zeichentrick) cartoon effect
Trickblendung f *(film)* animated intercut, *(electr.)* electronic inlay, superimposition
Trickfilm m *(film)* **1.** (Zeichentrickfilm) animated cartoon, animated film, rostrum film **2.** *(allg.)* special effects film, effects film, stunt film
Trickfilmherstellung f **(Zeichentrickfilmherstellung)** f) *(film)* cartoon animation, animation
   Any photographic technique utilizing still subject material to give illusion of actual motion.
Trickgraphik f **(Trickgrafik** f) *(film)* animated capiton
Trickkamera f **(Trickfilmkamera** f)
   A camera mounted vertically over a horizontal subject table for successive single-frame exposures; the movements of both camera and table are carefully coordinated.
Trickkameramann m **(Trickfilmkameramann** m) *(film)* animation cameraman, rostrum camera operator
Trickkopiermaschine f *(film)* optical effects printer, aerial-image printer

Trickmischer

Trickmischer m *(film)* 1. (Person) animation mixer 2. (Gerät) special effects mixer, special effects generator, animation mixer
Trickpult n
→ Trickbank
Trickstudio n *(film)* special effects studio, special effects room, effects studio, effects room, (Zeichentrick) animation studio, animation room
Tricktisch m
→ Trickbank
Tricktitel m **(Trickuntertitel** m) *(film)* animated caption, animated title
Tricküberblendung f *(film)* animation superimposition
→ Überblendung
Trickzeichner m *(film)* cartoonist, animator, cartoon-film artist, cartoon animator
Triffinischer Koeffizient m
→ Kreuzpreiselastizität
Tripackfilm m **(Tripack** m) *(phot)* tripack
Trockenkleben n *(film)* dry splicing
Trockenklebepresse f *(film)* dry film splicer
Trockenkopieren n
→ Xerographie
Trockenoffset m **(Trockenoffsetdruck** m, **Trockenoffsetverfahren** n) *(print)* dry offset printing, dry offset
  A printing process similar to conventional offset printing, (→) Offsetdruck, except that it employs a relief plate and does not require a water-dampening system. In dry offset, the areas to be inked are raised by etching around them, in contrast to the ordinary planographic form of offset printing.
Trockenoffsetmaschine f *(print)* dry offset machine, letterset press
Trockenplatte f *(phot)* dryplate, dry plate, gelatin dry plate
  A photographic glass plate sensitized with a film of gelatino-silver emulsion, the plate being exposed in a dry condition. The light-sensitive chemicals are carried in a layer of gelatin coated on the plate, a principle which has remained the basis of photography ever since.
Trockenplattenverfahren n **(trockenes Kollodiumverfahren** n) *(phot)* dry plate process
Trockenverfahren n **(Trockenkopierverfahren** n) *(print)* dry process

Trommelblende f *(film)* drum diaphragm, drum shutter, barrel shutter
Trotzreaktion f
→ Reaktanz
Trübung f *(phot)* milkiness, turbidity
  The appearance of developed and unfixed film, or film which has been incorrectly or insufficiently fixed.
Truca f *(TV)* optical printer
  An optical house printing machine producing a final optical negative.
Trucaaufnahme f *(TV)* process shot
Truppenkino n military movie theater, military cinema
Tülle f
→ Pförtner
Tusche f **(Zeichentusche** f, **chinesische Tusche** f) ink, India ink, Indian ink
→ Ausziehtusche
Tuschmanier n **(Tuschemanier** f, **(Tuschverfahren** n, **Tuscheverfahren** n) aquatinta, aquatint
Tüte f
→ Tragetasche
TV n
→ Fernsehen
TV-
→ Fernseh-
Typ m type
Type f
→ Letter
Typenart f *(print)* type face, typeface
→ Schriftart
Typendruck m *(print)* type printing
Typendrucker m *(print)* type printer
Trypendruckverfahren n
→ Typendruck
Typengießmaschine f *(print)* typecasting machine, typecaster
→ Schriftgießmaschine
Typensatz m
→ Satz
Typenträger m *(print)* font disc, *brit* fount disc
typische Auswahl f *(stat)* typical sampling
Typograph m **(Typograf** m) *(print)* typographer
Typographie f **(Typografie** f) typography
  The art of setting and arranging for printing or reproduction.
typographischer Punkt m typographical point
→ Punkt

Typologie *f (res)* typology
A classificatory scheme composed of two or more ideal types (or constructed types). The ideal types provide abstract categories in terms of which individual or group phenomena are analyzed. The differences between the ideal may be conceptualized as a gradual continuum or as discrete.
Typologie *f* **des Kaufverhaltens**
typology of buying behavior,
brit buying behaviour

Typologie *f* **des Konsumverhaltens**
(market res) typology of consumer behavior, *brit* behaviour
Typologisierung *(res)* typologization, *brit* typologisation
Typometer *n (print)* type gauge, type rule, line gauge, pica scale
typometrisches System *n*
→ Punktsystem
Typus *m*
→ Typ

U

U-Bahn-Plakat n (transit advtsg) subway poster, underground poster, brit tube card
U-Musik f
→ Unterhaltungsmusik
U-Test m
→ Mann-Whitney-Test
Ü-Wagen m
→ Übertragungswagen
überbelichten v/t (phot) to overexpose, colloq to cook, to burn
überbelichtet adj (phot) overexposed, too dense, (stark überlichtet) burned up, blocked up, colloq cooked
Überbelichtung f (phot) overexposure
  The photographic error of exposing light-sensitive material, such as a film, longer than required to light, resulting in a picture that is too light.
überblenden v/i (radio/film/TV) (Bild) to fade, to change over, to overlay, to inlay, to lap-fade, to crossfade, to dissolve, to superimpose, (Ton) to mix in, to fade, to blend in, to add
  The technique of combining two separate scenes into one.
Überblenden n
→ Überblendung
Überblender m (**Überblenderegler** m) (radio/film/TV) fader, (beim Projektor) changeover, brit change-over
Überblenderverschluß m (**Überblendungsblende** f) (film/TV) dissolving shutter
Überblendregler m
→ Überblender
Überblendung f (radio/film/TV) dissolve, fade, fading, lap dissolve, cross fade, fade-over, mix, mixing, (Einkopieren) superimposition, superimposure, short super-imp, overlay, inlay, (Durchblenden) superposition
  The technique of bringing one scene into full focus as a previous one fades or is wiped out. Also the imposition of the image from one camera over the image from another.
Überblendungszeichen n (**Überblendzeichen** n) (film/TV) changeover cue, brit change-over cue, changeover mark, changeover sign, cue dot
  The projectionist's changeover warning, usually consisting of several frames of a tiny white circle or triangle in advance of a film's beginning or end.
Überbrückungssendung f (radio/TV) bumper, cushion, pad
  Any extra tail program material.
Überdruck m (**Überdrucken** n) (print) (Produkt) surprint, overprint, (Verfahren, Vorgang) surprinting, overprinting
  The superimposition of additional printed matter over matter already printed, usually by means of a screen or different transparent color to prevent the underlying matter from being obscured. A combination plate made by superimposing a line negative on a halftone negative.
überdrucken v/t + v/i (print) to overprint, to surprint
Übereinanderblendung f (film/TV) overlap, superimposition, superimposure, short super-imp
  Both the process and the resulting composite image created by the superimposition of one camera image over another.
überentwickeln v/t (phot) to overdevelop
überentwickelt adj (phot) overdeveloped
Überentwicklung f (**Überentwickeln** n) (phot) overdevelopment, overdeveloping
Überflußgesellschaft f (**Gesellschaft** f **im Überfluß**) (econ) affluent society (John Kenneth Galbraith)
Übergang m 1. (radio/TV/film) transition, change, switch, bridge, segue, (Anschluß) changeover, brit change-over, junction, (Programm) continuity
  The transition from one scene to another by means of sound effects, music, or camera techniques, or the transition from one musical selection to another without interruption.

2. *(print)* break, (Seitenübergang) page break
The point at which a story turns from one column or one page to another.

Übergangsszene f *(radio/TV/film)* transition scene, transition

Übergangswahrscheinlichkeit f *(stat)* transition probability
In the theory of stochastic processes, the conditional probability, that a system in state E, will be in state E_k at some designated later time.

übergroße Welle f
→ D-Welle

Überhang m (**Überhänger** m) *(print)* kern, overhang
The part of the type face that extends beyond its main body so as to create a possible overlap with an adjacent letter.

überhängen (unterschneiden) v/i *(print)* to kern

Überhängen n *(print)* kerning

überhängend adj *(print)* kerned

überhängendes Bild n *(print)* kern
→ Überhang

Überkontakt m *(media res)* overexposure

Überlagerer m *(radio/TV)* beat frequency oscillator, beat oscillator

überlagern v/t (Radioempfang) to blanket

Überlagerung f (**Überlagern** n) *(radio/TV)* superimposition, superposition, (Frequenz) hetero-dyning, beating, (von Empfangssignalen) blanketing

Überlagerungsfrequenz f
→ Mischfrequenz

Überlänge f *(film/TV)* excessive length, overlength, (Schnitt) excessive duration, (Aufnahme) excessive footage

überlappen (sich überlappen) v/refl to overlap

Überlappung f overlapping, overlap
→ Duplizierung, Überschneidung

Überlappungsbereich m (**Überlappungsgebiet** n) *(radio/TV)* overlapping area, overlapping region, signal importation area

Überleitung f *(radio/TV)* transition, bridge, segue
→ Übergang

übermitteln (übertragen) v/t to relay, to transmit, to convey

Übermittlung f (**Übertragung** f) transmission, conveyance

Übermittlungsdauer f (**Übertragungsdauer** f) transmission time

Übernahme f *(econ)* takeover, brit take-over, *(radio/TV)* (einer Sendung) relay, rebroadcast

übernationale Marktforschung f
→ internationale Marktforschung

überörtliche Werbung f (**überregionale Werbung** f) nonlocal advertising, national advertising
The advertising of a manufacturer or wholesaler in contrast to the advertising of a retailer or local advertiser. Also, any advertising in media with nationwide circulation.

überprüfte Auflage f (Zeitung/Zeitschrift) audited circulation
→ Auflagenprüfung

überprüfte Erinnerung f *(media res)* proven recall
A respondent's recall of the content of advertising that is demonstrated by a repetition of the content.

überprüfte Markenerinnerung f (**überprüfte Marken-Werbeerinnerung** f) *(advtsg res)* proved name registration (PNR, P.N.R.), (Zahl der sich erinnernden Personen) proved name registration score, PNR score, P.N.R. score (Gallup & Robinson)
The proven recall, (→) überprüfte Erinnerung, display of the brand name.

überprüfte Werbeerinnerung f *(advtsg res)* ad-retention rate, at retention (W.R. Simmons & Associates)
A measurement that describes the communication value of a medium through the ability of its audience to correctly identify their exposure, (→) Kontakt, to its advertisements or commercials. In initial attempts to measure advertising recall, Simmons found that people often claim to have seen advertising messages which were not shown in the issue or the broadcast involved. To compensate for this readers or viewers were asked to pick out the advertisements (or commercials) they thought they were exposed to from a group which also included units that did not run. The difference between the correct and the incorrect identification is called the ad-retention rate.

Überquote f (**Überpräsentation** f) *(stat)* (in einer Stichprobe) oversample, overcoverage, (Vorgang) oversampling

Überredbarkeit f (**Beeinflußbarkeit** f) *(psy)* persuasibility, influenceability
The susceptibility to persuasive communication.

überreden (überzeugen) v/t to persuade
Überredung f **(Beeinflussung** f**)** persuasion
> The use of argumentative communication to secure the adoption by others of certain beliefs, connotations, attitudes, sentiments, lines of action, values, etc.

überregional adj national, nonlocal
überregionale Ausgabe f (einer Zeitung) country edition, nation-wide edition, national edition
überregionale Einschaltquote f **(nationale Einschaltquote** f**)** *(radio/TV)* national rating (program area basis), national rating (program station basis)
überregionale Presse f **(nationale Presse** f**)** national press, national newspapers pl and magazines pl
überregionale Werbung f **(nationale Werbung** f**)** national advertising, general advertising
überregionale Zeitung f **(nationale Zeitung** f**)** national newspaper, national paper
überregionaler Werbepreis m **(nationaler Werbetarif** m**)** national advertising rate, national rate
überregionaler Werbungtreibender m **(nationaler Werbungtreibender** m**)** national advertiser
überregionales Medium n **(überregionaler Werbeträger** m, **nationales Medium** n, **nationaler Werteträger** m**)** national medium
Überreichweite f *(radio/TV)* (eines Senders) transhorizon range, overshoot, (das Signal) distant signal, imported signal
> The situation that a broadcast media signal is received outside the normal reception area of a locality.

Übersatz m *(print)* overmatter, overset matter, overset
> Any type matter that has been set but not been used.

Überschichtung f
→ Schichtung
Überschlag m 1. *(print)* white line, (Vorschlag) sinkage 2. *(radio/TV)* flashover, brit flash-over, arc-over, sparkover, disruptive charge
überschneiden (sich überschneiden) 1. v/refl to overlap 2. v/t *(film)* to cut across, (sound) to cut
Überschneidung f *(media res)* overlapping, overlap

→ externe Überschneidung (Quantuplikation, Duplikation), interne Überschneidung (Kumulation)
Überschneidungskoeffizient m *(media res)* (externe Überschneidung) duplication coefficient, quantuplication coefficient, (interne Überschneidung) cumulation coefficient
Überschreitenswahrscheinlichkeit f
→ Irrtumswahrscheinlichkeit
Überschrift f 1. *(print/film/TV)* (Titel) heading, head, caption, title 2. *(print)* (Schlagzeile) headline, heading, head
> A short printed sentence or phrase summarizing or contents of the news or feature story which appears beneath it, or an attention-getting phrase or short sentence at a prominent place in an advertisement, in type size larger than the body or text copy.

3. *(print)* (über eine Spaltenbreite) crosshead, crossheading
→ Balkenüberschrift, Unterüberschrift, Zwischenüberschrift
Überschriftszeile f
→ Dachzeile
Überschußauflage f
→ Drucküberschuß
überschwemmter Markt m **(übersättigter Markt** m**)** *(econ)* glutted market
überschwingen v/t *(radio)* to overshoot, to ring
Überschwingung f **(Überschwingen** n**)** *(radio)* overshooting, ringing
Überschwingfaktor m *(radio)* overshoot ratio
Übersichtsskizze f
→ Skizze
überspielen v/t *(radio/TV)* to rerecord, brit to re-record, to transfer, to transscribe
> To make a new recording from existing recordings, as to mix several sound tracks into a single track or to equalize the sound levels of tracks recorded at different times.

Überspielung f *(radio/TV)* rerecording, transfer, transcription, (Leitung für eine Sendung) closed-circuit transmission
> The technique and process of mixing different audio effects, as music and voice, or leveling of volume from scene to scene.

übersprechen v/t *(film/TV)* to crosstalk
Übersprechen n *(film/TV)* crosstalk

übersteuern v/t *(radio/TV)* to overmodulate, to overload, to overdrive, (Mikrophon) to blast

Übersteuerung f **(Übersteuern** n) *(radio/TV)* overmodulation, overloading, overdriving, (Mikrophon) blasting
  The input of power or signal in an equipment beyond its capability to distribute or to reproduce.

überstrahlen v/t to irradiate, *(phot)* to flare

Überstrahlung f **(Überstrahlen** n)
1. irradiation, spill, dazzle, bloom
  The spreading of light in an emulsion due to reflection from the surfaces of the silver halide crystals.
  vgl. Ausstrahlung
2. *(TV)* irradiation, halation, halo effects, halo overshoot distortion, overthrow distortion
3. *(phot)* (Objektiv) lens flare, flare → Reflektionslichthof

Überstreuung f *(media planning)* saturation, supersaturation
  A media plan designed to achieve or inadvertently achieving excess impact, coverage, or both by means of large frequency and wide coverage over a relatively concentrated period of time.

übertragen v/t **1.** (kopieren) to copy, to transfer, to transcribe **2.** (senden) to broadcast, to transmit, to relay

Übertragung f **1.** (Kopie) copy, transfer, transcription **2.** *(radio/TV)* (einer Sendung) broadcast, transmission, relay, (Direktübertragung) remote pickup, nemo broadcast, nemo *brit* outside broadcast
  A broadcast originating from outside a studio usually picked up by a mobile unit. Also, the sending of television or radio signals.

Übertragungsdauer f **(Übertragungszeit** f) *(radio/TV)* duration of transmission, transmission time

Übertragungsdienst m **(Ü-Dienst** m) *(radio/TV)* outside broadcast operations *pl*, OB operations *pl*, remote pickup operations *pl*

Übertragungseffekt m *(res)* spillover effect, spillover

Übertragungsfehler m
1. (Kopieren) transcription error
2. (Sendung) transmission fault

Übertragungsfunktion f (von Kommunikationsmitteln) transfer function

Übertragungskabel n **(Leitungskabel** n) *(radio/TV)* feeder cable, program cable, *brit* programme cable, program line, *brit* programme line
  A coaxial cable or other type of cable that transmits signals from a cable-system trunk line to specific neighborhoods.

Übertragungskanal m *(radio/TV)* transmission channel, channel

Übertragungskette f *(radio/TV)* transmission chain, *(TV)* television chain

Übertragungsmedium n transmission medium

Übertragungssatellit m transmission satelllite

Übertragungssender m *(radio/TV)* relay station
  An individual station in a point-to-point pickup and retransmission system, amplifying the original signal.

Übertragungsstandort m *(radio/TV)* pickup point
  The outside location from which a remote broadcast originates.

Übertragungswagen m **(Ü-Wagen** m) *(radio/TV)* remote pickup mobile station, mobil unit, *brit* outside broadcast van, OB van
  A vehicle used to transmit program material, like sports news events, from locations outside of a broadcasting studio.

übertreibende Werbung f exaggerated advertising, *colloq* hyped-up advertising

überziehen *(radio/TV)* v/t (Sendezeit) to overrun

Überziehung f *(radio/TV)* (der Sendezeit) overrun

Ubiquität f *(econ)* (Markenartikel) ubiquity

Uhrenanlage f **(Uhrenwerbeanlage** f) *(outdoor advtsg/transit advtsg)* clock spectacular
  The elements of a clock spectacular are a large clock and an accompanying backlighted display. Sometimes a moving message may also be part of the display.

ultrafeine Welle f *(paper)* E flute

Ultrakurzwelle f (UKW) *(TV)* very high frequency (VHF)
  The relatively long-range television wave bands operating at from 54 to 216 mega-Hertz.

Ultraschall *m* ultrasound, ultrasonics
pl (construed as sg)
ultraviolettes Licht *n (phot)*
ultraviolet light
    That section beyond the violet end of the visible spectrum, the rays of which exert a high degree of photochemical action.
Ultraviolettfilter *m* (**UV-Filter** *m*)
(phot) ultraviolet filter, *brit* ultraviolet filter
umändern *v/t*
→ ändern
Umänderung *f*
→ Änderung
umbrechen *(print)* **1.** *v/t* + *v/i* to make up, (kleben) to paste up
→ Umbruch
2. *v/t* (eine Zeile) to overrun (a line)
Umbrechen *n*
→ Schirmwerbung
Umbruch *m (print)* makeup, *brit* make-up, making up, making-up, (Seitenumbruch) page makeup, page design, (Klebeumbruch) pasteup, pasting up, pasting-up
    Both the skill and art of assembling type and plates into complete pages, the art of arranging pictures and news matter in the most effective and artistic manner throughout the paper, and the result thereof, i. e. the arrangement of editorial and/or advertising elements on a page.
→ Klebeumbruch
Umbruchabzug *m (print)* (auch einzelnen Blättern) slip proof, slip page, (Abzug einer umbrochenen Seite) page proof, (auf Fahnen) makeup galley
    A proof of one or more made-up page(s).
Umbruchbildschirm *m (print)* makeup screen, *brit* make-up screen
Umbruch-Bildschirmgerät *n*
(**Umbruchgerät** *n*) *(print)* makeup display terminal, makeup terminal, *brit* make-up display terminal, make-up terminal
Umbruchredakteur *m (print)* makeup editor, *brit* make-up editor, makeup man, *brit* make-up man, maker-up
Umbruchskizze *f* (**Seitenspiegel** *m*) *(print)* key drawing, keyline, key, type mechanical
    An outline sketch of all typographic and visual elements of a printed page, an advertisement, brochure, mailer, etc., showing the size and position of each element.
Umbruchstadium *n (print)* makeup stage, makeup

Umbruchtisch *m (print)* makeup table, *brit* make-up table, making-up table
Umdruck *m* (**Umdruckverfahren** *m*) *(print)* transfer printing, transfer printing process, transfer
umdrucken *v/t (print)* to transfer
Umdrucker *m* (**Umdruckgerät** *n*) *(print)* transfer printer, duplicator
    A small-size machine for printing multiple paper copies of typing, drawings, etc. from a master or stencil.
Umdruckfarbe *f (print)* transfer ink
Umdruckpapier *n (print)* transfer paper
Umdruckverfahren *n*
→ Umdruck
Umfangsanalyse *f (media res)* analysis of advertising to editorial ratio, analysis of editorial to advertising ratio
Umfangsberechnung *f* (**Satzumfangsberechnung** *f*)
→ Satzberehnung
Umfeld *n* environment, (soziales Umfeld) social environment, (redaktionelles Umfeld) editorial environment, *(radio)* ambient field, outer field
    In the most general sense, all the external conditions, physical and sociocultural, which can influence an individual or a group.
Umfeldbild *n (TV)* cut-off area, cutoff, out-of-frame area
    That section of the transmitted television picture information that is hidden by the home receiver mask.
Umfeldhelligkeit *f (phot/film/TV* ambient brightness
    Any brightness that does not stem from the camera subject or its lighting.
Umfrage *f* (**Befragung** *f,* **demoskopische Befragung** *f*) *(survey res)* survey, *auch* inquiry, enquiry, interviewing, (soziale Übersichtsstudie) social survey
    A study that selects a sample from some larger population in order to ascertain the prevalence, incidence, and interrelations of selected social, social psychological, psychological, or market media variables. The survey is used primarily to determine the distribution of persons on some variable, and to determine interrelationships among variables.

Umfragegebiet n **(Erhebungsgebiet** n **einer Umfrage)** survey area
　The geographic area covered by a survey.
Umfragemethode f **(demoskopische Methode** f**)** survey method
Umfrageplan m **(Anlage** f **einer Umfrage)** survey design
Umfragetechnik f
→ Befragungsmethode
Umgebung f
→ Umfeld
Umgebungs-
→ Umfeld-
Umgebungsprüfungsmodell n
→ Permutationsverfahren
Umhängemikrofon n **(Umhängemikrophon** n**)** necklace microphone
Umkehr f *(phot/film)* (im Kopierwerk) reversal
Umkehrbad n *(phot/film)* reversing bath
Umkehrduplikat n *(phot/film)* reserval duplicate
Umkehremulsion f *(phot/film)* reserval emulsion
umkehren v/t *(phot/film)* to reverse
Umkehrentwicklung f *(phot/film)* reversal development, reversal processing, reversal process, reversal
Umkehrfarbfilm m *(phot/film)* reversal color film, *brit* reversal colour film, reversal-type color film, *brit* reversal-type colour film
Umkehrfilm m *(phot/film)* reversal film, reversal-type film
　Any film stock that can be made directly into positive transparencies without the use of negatives in the developing process.
Umkehrkopie f
→ Konterbild
Umkehrprozeß m **(Umkehrverfahren** n**)**
→ Umkehrentwicklung
umkopieren v/t (Bild) to print, (Ton) to record, *brit* to re-record
Umkopierung n **(Umkopieren** n**)** (Bild) printing, (Ton) rerecording, *brit* re-recording
Umlauf m **1.** (Rundschreiben) circular letter, circular **2.** *(print)* (umlaufender Artikel) carry-over article, carryover article, carryover, turn article, (umlaufende Kolumne) carry-over column, carryover column, carryover, (Umlaufenlassen) overrunning, (der umlaufende Teil eines Artikels) overrun, (umlaufende Überschrift) jump head
　A continuation of a story or article farther back in the publication.
Umlaufbahn f
→ (Satellit) orbit
Umlaufblende f
→ Sektorenblende
umlaufen v/t *(print)* (um ein Bild) to run around, (überlaufen) to run over
umlaufende Überschrift f
→ Umlauf 2.
umlaufender Artikel m
→ Umlauf 2.
umlaufen lassen v/t *(print)* to overun
Umlenkprisma n *(phot)* deviating prism, deviating wedge
Umlicht n **(diffuses Licht** n**)** *(phot/film/TV)* ambient light
　Any general lighting that is not directed at the camera object but contributes to the general illumination of the scene.
Umrahmung f
→ Rahmen
umranden
→ einrahmen
Umrandung f
→ Rahmen
Umrechnungsfaktor m *(stat)* conversion factor
Umrechnungstabelle f *(stat)* conversion table
umreißen
→ skizzieren
Umriß m outline
Umrißbild n **(Umrißskizze** f**)** outline picture, thumbnail sketch, thumbnail
　A rough layout sketch often rendered in a smaller size than the final advertisement.
Umroller m *(phot/film)* rewinder
　One of a pair of geared, hand-cranked devices used to spool off or rewind film reels.
Umrolltisch m *(film)* rewind bench
Umsatz m *(econ)* turnover
　1. In manufacturing, the cost of goods and/or services sold divided by the average inventory priced at cost.
　2. In retailing, total sales divided by the average inventory at selling prices.
vgl. Absatz
Umsatzabnahmerate f
→ Umsatzquote
Umsatzanalyse f *(econ)* analysis of turnover, turnover analysis
vgl. Absatzanalyse

umsatzbezogene Methode *f* (der Werbebudgetierung) sales ratio method (of avertising budget determination), function-of-sales method, (prozentual) percentage-of-sales method, (stückbezogen) unit rate method
  A method of setting an advertising budget under which a company takes past year's sales figures for a product and assigns a relatively arbitrary percentage of that amount to advertising for the upcoming year. A somewhat more advanced version of this approach is to forecast how large sales for the coming year are likely to be, and make the same determination.

Umsatzeffekt *m*
→ Umsatzwirkung

Umsatzerfolg *m* (der Werbung) (**Absatzerfolg** *m*) sales effect (of advertising)

Umsatzerfolgskontrolle *f (econ)* sales effectiveness control
  The control of the effectiveness of a communications medium or advertising campaign in selling a product or a service.

Umsatzerfolgsmessung *f (econ)* measurement of sales effectiveness

Umsatzkennziffer *f*
→ Absatzkennziffer

umsatzorientierte Methode *f* (der Werbebudgetierung)
→ umsatzbezogene Methode

Umsatzprognose *f*
→ Absatzprognose

Umsatzquote *f* (**Umsatzrate** *f*) *(econ)* turnover rate, sales ratio
  A portion of a sales forecast for a company as assigned to a territory, region, field representative, or branch. It is a part of the basic planning by means of which the company's goals are set. The sales quota is used primarily as a measurement and control device.

Umsatzreaktionsfunktion *f*
→ Reaktionsfunktion

Umsatzstatistik *f*
→ Absatzstatistik

Umsatzvolumen *n*
→ Absatzvolumen

Umsatzwirkung *f* (**Umsatzeffekt** *m*) *(econ)* sales effect

Umsatzziel *n*
→ Absatzziel

umschalten *v/t + v/i* to switch, to switch over

Umschalter *m* (**Umschaltknopf** *m*) *(radio/TV)* selector switch, changeover switch, *brit* change-over switch

Umschaltkennung *f (TV)* changeover identification, changeover ID, *brit* change-over identification
  An announcement of varying length within or between programs to identify the broadcasting station.

Umschaltpause *f (radio/TV)* (Sender) station break, switching period, (Programm) break in transmission, transmission break
  A period between two television or radio programs, used for network or station identification.

Umschaltung *f* (**Umschalten** *n*) *(radio/TV)* switching, switchover, changeover, *brit* change-over, commutation.

Umschlag *m* 1. (Schutzumschlag) cover, jacket, dust jacket, (Briefumschlag) envelope, (Schutzhülle) folder
  The outer faces of a book or magazine.
  2. *(econ)* (Warenumschlag) turnover, (im Lager) stockturn
  Both the rate of repetition in the purchase of a product by a consumer and, in retailing or wholesaling, the rate at which trading stock is sold and replaced.

Umschlagabbildung *f* (**Umschlagbild** *n*)
→ Titelbild

umschlagen 1. *v/t (print)* (Druckbogen) to work and turn, to print and turn
  To apply a printing method whereby the forms for both sides of the sheet are set side by side, to print first on one side of the sheet which ist then turned over left to right, using the same edge of paper as gripper, for printing on the other side, thus reducing total press time.
  2. *v/i (econ)* (Waren) to turn over

Umschlagfarbe *f* (Zeitschrift) cover color, *brit* cover colour

Umschlaggeschwindigkeit *f* (**Anschlaghäufigkeit** *f*) *(econ)* turnover rate, rate of stockturn
  The rate at which trading stock is sold and replaced.

Umschlaggestaltung *f* (Zeitschrift) cover design, (Buch) jacket design

Umschlagkarton *m* cover cardboard, cover paper, cover stock
  A special heavy paper or cardboard used for the cover of a pamphlet or magazine.

Umschlagklappe f (Buch) jacket flap, flap, (Rückenklappe) backflap
Umschlagpapier n
→ Umschlagkarton
Umschlagpappe f cover board
Umschlagpunkt m
→ Wendepunkt
Umschlagseite f cover page, cover (C), (Titelseite: U 1) outside front cover (OFC, O.F.C.), first cover (C), front cover, cover page, cover, (2. Umschlagseite: U 2) inside front cover (IBC, I.B.C.), (4. Umschlagseite: U 4) outside back cover (OBC, O.B.C.), fourth cover (4 C), back cover
Umschlagsgeschwindigkeit f **(Umschlagshäufigkeit** f)
→ Umschlaggeschwindigkeit
Umschlagtext m **(Waschzettel** m **auf dem Schutzumschlag)** flap blurb, jacket blurb, blurb
 A short piece of promotion copy printed on the jacket flap(s) of a book.
Umschlagtitel m cover title
umsonst
→ gratis, frei
umstellen v/t (print) to transpose, (Satzanweisung) transpose, tr, Tr
 Instructing the typographer to transpose type as indicated.
Umwälzverfahren n **(Wechselstreuung** f, **Wechselstreuplan** m, **Rotationsstreuung** f, **Rotationsstreuplan** m) (media planning) staggered advertising schedule. staggered schedule, rotary plan, rotation plan, wave posting, wave scheduling, pulsation
→ pulsierende Werbung
Umwelt f environment
 The surrounding conditions of any activity, such as marketing, the natural social, physical, geographical and psychological conditions.
Umweltbedingung f environmental condition
Umweltfaktor m environmental factor
Umweltforschung f environment research
Umweltschutz m environmental protection, protection of the environment
Umworbene m/pl
→ Zielgruppe, Zielperson
unabhängige Variable f **(unabhängige Veränderliche** f) (res) independent variable

A variable subjected to controlled change or manipulation in an experiment in order to observe associated changes in dependent variables.
vgl. abhängige Variable
Unabhängigkeit f independence
Unabhängigkeitsanalyse f
→ Independenzanalyse
Unabhängigkeitstest m **(Test** m **auf Unabhängigkeit)**
→ Chi-Quadrat-Test
Unähnlichkeit f **(Unähnlichkeitsmaß** n)
→ Ähnlichkeit, Proximitätsmaß
Unaided Recall m **(Unaided-Recall-Verfahren** n)
→ ungestützte Erinnerung
unangemeldeter Besuch m (econ/ survey res) (Vertreter, Interviewer) cold call
 Paying a visit to a prospect or a respondent without first making an appointment.
unangeschnittene Doppelseite f **(unbeschnittene Doppelseite** f) (print) two pages pl facing
 Two advertising pages opposite one another without printing in the gutter space between them.
unaufdringliche Maße n/pl **(unaufdringliche Meßinstrumente** n/pl) (social res) unobtrusive measures pl
→ unaufdringliche Messung
unaufdringliche Messung f **(unauffällige Messung** f) (social res) unobtrusive measurement, unobtrusive technique
 A research technique that can be used without the awareness of the subjects being studied. Unobtrusive measures include the study of records (such as birth, death, marriage, and sales records), the study of physical evidence (such as wear on library books, fingerprints on exhibits, the setting on automobile radio dials), unnoticed observers, and hidden cameras and tape recorders.
→ nichtreaktive Messung
unbedruckt adj (print) blank
unbedruckter Raum m (print) blank space
unbelichtet adj (phot) unexposed
unbeschnitten (nicht beschnitten) adj (print) non-bleed, untrimmed, uncut
vgl. beschnitten (angeschnitten)
Unbestimmtheitsmaß n **(Unbestimmtheitskoeffizient** m) (stat) coefficient of non-determination, coefficient of nondetermination (k^2)

unbunt

The proportion of variance, (→) Varianz, in a variable that is not explained, or accounted for, by its correlation with a second variable, i.e. the proportion of variance that is not predictable from variability in the second variable. It is equal to the square of the coefficient of alienation k (Alienationskoeffizient) or to $1 - r^2$ where r is the product-moment correlation coefficient, (→) Produktmomentkorrelation.
unbunt *adj (phot)* achromatic
Lacking chroma.
→ achromatisch
Unbuntbereich *m (phot)* achromatic focus, achromatic region
unbunte Farbe *f (phot)* achromatic color, *brit* achromatic colour
A color lacking chroma.
Und-Zeichen *n*
→ Et-Zeichen
undurchschossen
→ kompreß
undurchsichtig *adj (phot/print)* opaque, non-transparent
Not permitting the passage of light.
uneingeschränkte Zufallsauswahl *f (stat)* **1.** (Verfahren, Stichprobenbildung) unrestricted random sampling **2.** (Stichprobe) unrestricted random sample
A sample, (→) Stichprobe, which is drawn from a population, (→) Grundgesamtheit, by a random method without any restriction, i.e. all possible samples have the same chance of being selected.
Unendlichkeitseinstellung *f (phot)* infinity focusing, infinity adjustment, infinity focus
unentgeltlich vertriebene Auflage *f (Zeitschrift/Zeitung)* unpaid distribution, free copies *pl*
Unfolding-Technik *f*
→ Verfahren der transferierten Rangordnung
ungedruckt *adj* unprinted
ungefalzt (nicht gefalzt) *adj* unfolded
ungeleimt *adj (paper)* unsized
ungerade Seite *f* **(Seite** *f* **mit ungerader Seitenzahl)** *(print)* odd page, odd-numbered page
ungeschützt (urheberrechtlich ungeschütz)
→ gemeinfrei
ungestrichen *adj (paper)* uncoated
ungestützte Erinnerung *f* **(Erinnerung** *f* **ohne Gedächtnisstütze)** *(survey res)* unaided recall, pure recall

A research technique in which respondents must answer questions without any aids to memory.
vgl. gestützte Erinnerung
ungestützter Erinnerungstest *m (survey res)* unaided recall test, pure recall test
Ungewißheit *f*
→ Entscheidung unter Unsicherheit
ungezielte Streuung *f* **(von Werbemitteln) (Schrotflintenansatz** *m)* *(media planning)* non-selective advertising, shotgun approach
A way of trying to accomplish an advertising objective by spraying a large amount of activity over a broad area without aiming at a special target group, so that everyone can end up hitting no one.
univariate Analyse *f* **(univariate Datenanalyse** *f)* *(stat)* univariate analysis, univariate data analysis
The analysis of data consisting of measurements or observations of only one variable.
univariate Daten *n/pl* univariate data *pl*
→ univariate Analyse
univariate Grundgesamtheit *f (stat)* univariate population, univariate universe
→ univariate Analyse
univariate Verteilung *f* **(univariate Häufigkeitsverteilung** *f)* *(stat)* univariate distribution, univariate frequency distribution
→ univariate Analyse
univariates Verfahren *n* **(univariates Analyseverfahren** *n)* *(stat)* univariate technique, univariate analysis technique
→ univariate Analyse
Universalgenossenschaft *f*
→ Full-Service-Genossenschaft
Universalmesse *f (econ)* universal trade fair, universal fair, general trade fair, general fair
vgl. Fachmesse
Universum *n*
→ Grundgesamtheit
unlautere Werbung *f* unfair advertising, unfair practice in advertising
unlauterer Wettbewerb *m (econ)* unfair competition, unfair trade practice
Unlauterkeit *f (econ/advtsg)* unfairness, unfair practice

unliniiert adj (print) unruled
unmittelbare Marktforschung f (Karl Christian Behrens)
→ Primärforschung, Feldforschung
unregidiert adj unedited
unregelmäßig erscheinende Publikation f irregular publication
unrichtige Angabe f
→ irreführende Angabe
unsatiniert adj (paper) unglazed, uncalendered
unscharf adj (phot) out-of-focus, blurred, fuzzy
 The characteristic of a blurred, distorted image.
Unschärfe f (phot) lack of focus, lack of definition, blurring, fuzziness
Unschärfekreis m (phot) circle of confusion
Unsicherheit f
→ Entscheidung unter Unsicherheit
unstrukturierte Befragung f **(unstrukturiertes Interview** n) (survey res) unstructured interview
vgl. strukturierte Befragung
unten links bottom left, (Anzeigenposition links unten) bottom left position
unten rechts bottom right, (Anzeigenposition rechts unten) bottom right position
unter Text (unterhalb des Textes) (print) (Anzeigenposition) below text
unterbelichten v/t (phot) to underexpose
unterbelichtet adj (phot) underexposed
Unterbelichtung f (phot) underexposure, brit auch undertime
 Insufficient action of light on a sensitized photographic surface, resulting in thin or weak images and loss of detail.
Unterbrecherbad n **(Unterbrechungsbad** n) (phot) shortstop, short stop, stop bath
 A dilute acetic acid solution used as an intermediate bath between development, (→) Entwicklung, and fixing, (→) Fixieren, of photographic negatives and prints.
unterdrehen v/i (film) to shoot with low speed, to shoot for time lapse effect
unterentwickeln v/t (phot) to underdevelop
unterentwickelt adj (phot) underdeveleped

Unterentwicklung f (phot) underdevelopment
Unterführungszeichen n (print) ditto marks pl
Untergrund m (print) background, ground
Untergrundplatte f
→ Tonplatte
Unterhaltung f entertainment
Unterhaltungsfilm m entertainment film, feature film
Unterhaltungsmusik f (U-Musik f) light music, light entertainment music
Unterhaltungsprogramm n **(Unterhaltungssendung** f) (radio/TV) variety program, brit programme, variety show, light entertainment program, light entertainment show, show
Unterhaltungsquiz n (Quizsendung f) (radio/TV) game show, quiz game show
Unterhaltungssender m (Musiksender m) (radio) contemporary
Unterhaltungssendung f
→ Unterhaltungsprogramm
Unterkasten m (print) (Setzkasten) lower case, lowercase
vgl. Oberkasten
Unterkleber m (film) joiner tape, splicing patch
 A transparent tape for accurately joining edited film frames.
Unterkundengeschäft n (econ) subcontracting
Unterlänge f 1. (typ) descender, (Buchstabe mit Unterlänge) descending letter
 The longer lines extending below the body in some letters, as in lower case g or p.
 2. (film/TV) insufficient footage, (Schnitt) underlength, insufficient length
vgl. Oberlänge
untermalen v/t (film) to underscore, to score
Untermalung f (film) underscoring, underscore
Untermalungsmusik f
→ Hintergrundmusik
Unternehmensberater m (econ) management consultant
→ Managementberater
Unternehmensberatung f (econ) management consultancy
→ Managementberatung

Unternehmensforschung f operations research, management science
The approach to management that emphasizes the application of scientific methods for the improved understanding and practice of management.
Unternehmensgestalt f corporate design
Unternehmensidentität f corporate identity (CI, C.I.)
Unternehmensimage n **(Unternehemensbild** n)
The image or impression created in the public mind by the name or symbol of a company or organization.
Unternehmenskultur f corporate culture
Unternehmensphilosophie f *(econ)* corporate philosophy
Unternehmenspolitik f *(econ)* corporate policy
Unternehmensstrategie f *(econ)* corporate strategy
Unternehmenswerbung f **(Unternehmenskommunikation** f)
corporate advertising, corporate image advertising, corporate communication, institutional advertising
Advertising created primarily to build long-range goodwill or prestige for the advertiser, rather than stimulating immediate product purchase.
Unternehmensziel n *(econ)* corporate objective
Unternehmerrente f
→ Produzentenrente
Unterrichtsfernsehen n educational television, educational TV
Unterrichtsfilm m educational film, instructional film
Untersatz m *(promotion)* (für Getränke) drip mat, mat
Unterschlag m *(print)* footline
unterschneiden v/t 1. *(print)* to kern 2. *(radio/TV)* (Ton) to intercut, to overlay, to underlay
Unterschnitt m 1. *(print)* kern 2. *(radio/film/TV)* cut-in, (Ton) cut-in, overlay, underlay, (live) film insert, film inject
unterschwellig adj *(psy)* subliminal
unterschwellige Kommunikation f *(psy)* subliminal communication
A communication or message that is received by a person without his full or specific awareness. Frequently, it is apprehended as a part of a more central message and therefore it is not critically examined. In a sense, it is a hidden message. When responding to complex stimuli, a person's critical evaluations are focused on only a part of what he is experiencing. However, he also may be influenced by secondary messages that he may recall long after the experience and become "aware" of for the first time. If the secondary message is not specifically recalled but influences the person's behavior without his full awareness, or if it can be recalled but not in its original context, the message is called subliminal.
unterschwellige Konditionierung f *(psy)* subliminal conditioning
A type of conditioning by which the experimenter attempts to condition a nonverbal response to a stimulus whose intensity is lower than that capable of eliciting a discriminated verbal report. The conditioned response may be either a voluntary or an autonomic response, although the latter is more typical (for example, galvanic skin response, heart rate, pupillary contraction).
unterschwellige Wahrnehmung f *(psy)* subliminal perception
unterschwellige Webung f *(psy)* subliminal advertising
Any advertising presented below the threshold of perception, such as a split-second announcement on television.
→ unterschwellige Kommunikation
untersuchen v/t *(res)* to investigate, to study, to examine
Untersuchung f **(Studie** f) *(res)* investigation, study
Untersuchungsanlage f **(Untersuchungsanordnung** f)
→ experimentelle Anlage
Untersuchungsbericht m
→ Studienbericht, Bericht
Untertitel m subtitle, subheading, subhead
Unterüberschrift f **(Unterzeile** f)
subheading, subhead, deck head, step line, dropline, drop head, streamer line, (Spitzmarke) side heading
Both a secondary head or title for a newspaper article or the like and a display line within the body of a text, serving as a subtitle for the portion of the text that follows.
Untervertrag m *(econ)* subcontract
unverbindlich adj/adv recommended, on speculation, *short* on spec
Without any obligation of payment.
unverbindlicher Richtpreis m
→ empfohlener Preis (Preisempfehlung)
unveröffentlicht adj/adv unpublished

unveröffentlichtes Heft n (unveröffentlichte Ausgabe f) *(media res)* prepublished copy, prepublished issue, advance copy
→ Konfusionskontrolle
unverzerrte Auswahl f (unverzerrte Stichprobenbildung f, unverzerrtes Auswahlverfahren n, unverzerrtes Stichprobenverfahren n) *(stat)* unbiased sampling
unverzerrte Stichprobe f *(stat)* unbiased sample
unverzerrter Schätzwert m (unverzerrte Schätzung f)
→ erwartungstreue Schätzung
uraufführen v/t *(film)* to premiere, *brit* to première, to show for the first time
Uraufführung f *(film)* premiere, *brit* première, first performance, first run, first night, first showing
Uraufführungstheater n (Erstaufführungstheater n, Erstaufführungskino n) *(film)* first-run theater
Urheber m author, creator, designer
Urheberrecht n copyright
The legal protection granted an author or artist against the reproduction and sale of an original work without express consent. The period of grant in Germany is for the originator's lifetime plus 70 years.

Urheberrechtsgesetz n (UrhG) copyright law
Urheberrechtsgesetzgebung f copyright legislation
urheberrechtlich schützen v/t to copyright
Urnenmodel n *(stat)* urn model
Ursache f cause
Ursachenforschung f
→ Relationsforschung
Ursendung f (Erstsendung f) *(radio/ TV* first broadcast, *(TV)* first telecast (F.T.)
The date on which a program, commercial, or series of commercials is to be broadcast for the first time.
Urteilsindex m *(res)* reaction index
Usance f
→ Handelsbrauch
Utilität f (Utilitätsprinzip n)
→ Nutzen, Nutzenansatz
UV-Filter m
→ Ultraviolettfilter
Ü-Wagen m
→ Übertragungswagen
UWG *abbr* Gesetz gegen den unlauteren Wettbewerb

V

Vakuumaufnahmebrett *n*
(Vakuumaufnahmerahmen *m***)** *(phot)*
vacuum copyboard
  A board on process cameras, (→) Reprokamera, for holding originals in place during exposure, (→) Belichtung, by means of atmospheric pressure.
Vakuumlampe *f* **(Vakuumleuchte** *f***)** vacuum lamp, incandescent lamp
Vakuumpackung *f*
(Vakuumverpackung *f***)** vacuum package, vacuum pack
Vakuumrahmen *m*
→ Vakuumaufnahmebrett
Vakuumplatte *f* **(Vakuumsaugplatte** *f***)**
→ Ansaugplatte
Valenz *f*
→ Aufforderungscharakter
Validität *f* **(Gültigkeit** *f*,
Stichhaltigkeit *f***)** *(res)* validity
  In the broadest sense in research, the relevance to desired objectives of given methods, tools and procedures; more specifically, particularly as a convention in the behavioral sciences, the degree to which a scale, a test, or any other research tool measures what it purports to measure, i.e. the correspondence between what a measuring device is supposed to measure and what it really measures. The validity of a measuring device is usually determined by comparing the results obtained from that device with an independent and accepted measure of the same characteristic. The independent measure used for comparison may be a test the validity of which has been established, or an accepted objective criterion, e.g. income as a criterion of economic success.
validiert (gültig) *adj (res)* validated, valid
Validierung *f* **(Validitätsprüfung** *f***)** *(res)* validation, validity check
  The process of obtaining outside data to measure the validity, (→) Validität, of data. Validation may be at either an individual or a group level.
Variable *f* **(Veränderliche** *f***)** *(stat)* variable
  Any event or characteristic with values that can change from time to time or object to object. In research, specific types of variables include independent variables, (→) unabhängige Variable, and dependent variables, (→) abhängige Variable.
Variablensprache *f* **(Sprache** *f* **der Variablen)** *(social res)* language of variables
Varianz *f* **(Streuung** *f***)** *(stat)* variance
  A measure of the variability of scores defined as the mean for a sample or expected value for a population of the squared deviations from the mean. The variance of a population is expressed as $\sigma^2 = E(X - \mu)^2$, and the variance of a sample as $s^2 = \Sigma(X - \bar{X})^2/n$ where μ and $\bar{X}$ are the means of the population and sample, respectively, and n is the number of observations in the sample.
Varianzanalyse *f* **(Streuungszerlegung** *f***)** *(stat)* variance analysis, analysis of variance (ANOVA)
Varianzschätzung *f* *(stat)* variance estimate
Varianz-Verhältnis-Test *m*
→ F-Test
Variation *f* *(stat)* variation
Variationskoeffizient *m* *(stat)* coefficient of variation
Vario-Objektiv *n* **(Zoom-Objektiv** *n*, **(Zoom** *m***)** *(phot)* varifocal lens, variable focus lens, zoom lens, zoomar lens, zoom
  A camera lens, (→) Objektiv, capable of rapid changes of magnification, range and scene scale.
VDID *m abbr* Verband Deutscher Industrie-Designer e.V.
VDZ *m abbr* Verband Deutscher Zeitschriften-Verleger e.V.
Veblen-Effekt *m* *(econ)* Veblen effect, prestige effect
  The effect, observable for prestige products, that a price increase entails higher demand.
Vektor *m* *(math/stat)* vector
  A row or column of values, such as means, factor loadings, etc., or a line drawn from the origin of a set of axes to the point represented by these values.
Vektordiagramm *n*
(Vektorendiagramm *n***)** *(stat)* vector diagram

Vektormodell n (stat) vector model
Venn-Diagramm n (stat) Venn diagram
Veralterung f **(Obsoleszenz** f) (econ) obsolescence
→ Obsoleszenz
veranschaulichen v/t to visualize
Veranschaulichung f visualization
  A sketch made in the process of designing an advertisement which shows approximately how the finished display will look.
Verband m association, federation, society
Verband m **Deutscher Adreßbuchverleger e.V** Association of German Directory Publishers
Verband m **Deutscher Buch-, Zeitungs- und Zeitschriften-Grossisten e.V. (Presse-Grosso)** Association of German Book, Newspaper and Magazine Wholesalers
Verband m **Deutscher Industrie-Designer e.V. (VDID)** Association of German Industrial Designers
Verband m **Deutscher Zeitschriftenverleger e.V. (VDZ)** Association of German Magazine Publishers
Verbandsblatt n **(Verbandsfachzeitschrift** f, **Verbandszeitschrift** f) association journal, association magazine, association publication
Verbandsmarketing n association marketing
Verbandswerbung f association advertising
Verbandszeitschrift f
→ Optimierungsmodell
Verblitzung f (phot) electrostatic discharge, dendriform exposure of film
Verbrauch m
→ Konsum
Verbraucher m
→ Konsument
Verbraucheranalyse f (market res) consumer analysis
  The systematic research into consumer characteristics, attitudes, and behavior designed to establish psychological, sociological and demographic understandings as possible considering available time and resources.
Verbraucheranteil m (econ) consumer share
Verbraucheraufklärung f consumer education

Verbraucherwerbung

Verbraucherbefragung f
→ Konsumentenbefragung
Verbraucherbewegung f
→ Konsumerismus
Verbraucherforschung f
→ Konsumentenforschung
Verbrauchergenossenschaft f
→ Konsumgenossenschaft
Verbraucherinformation f
→ Konsumenteninformation
Verbraucherinteresse n **(Konsumenteninteresse** n) (econ) consumer interest
Verbrauchermarkt m **(Selbstbedienungswarenhaus** n, **SB-Warenhaus** n) (retailing) self-service department store, combination store
  A type of department store where customers help themselves to prepriced goods from shelves or other displays, and pay for their purchases at suitably located cash tills or in total upon departure.
Verbrauchernachfrage f
→ Konsumentennachfrage
Verbraucher-Ombudsmann m
→ Konsumenten-Ombudsmann
Verbraucherorganisation f consumer organization, brit organisation
Verbraucherpackung f consumer package, consumer pack
Verbraucherpanel n **(Konsumentenpanel** n) (market res) consumer panel survey, consumer panel test, consumer panel, consumer jury
  A method of pretesting products or advertisements by exposing them to potential purchasers or users.
Verbraucherpolitik f **(Verbraucherschutz** m) consumer protection
Verbraucherpreis m
→ Endverbraucherpreis
Verbraucherrabatt m
→ Konsumentenrabatt
Verbraucherrisiko n
→ Konsumentenrisiko
Verbraucherschutz m
→ Verbraucherpolitik
Verbrauchersouveränität f
→ Konsumentensouveränität
Verbraucherverband m consumer association, consumers' association
Verbraucherverhalten n
→ Konsumentenverhalten
Verbraucherwerbung f
→ Publikumswerbung

Verbraucherzeitschrift f
→ Kundenzeitschrift
Verbraucherzufriedenheit f
→ Konsumentenzufriedenheit
Verbrauchsdaten n/pl
→ Konsumdaten
Verbrauchselastizität f
→ Elastizität
Verbrauchsforschung f
(Konsumforschung f) consumption research, (Kaufverhaltensforschung) buyer behavior research, buying behavior research, *brit* behaviour
→ Konsumentenforschung
Verbrauchsfunktion f
→ Konsumfunktion
Verbrauchsgewohnheit f
→ Konsumgewohnheit
Verbrauchsgüter n/pl **(kurzlebige Konsumgüter** n/pl) *(econ)* nondurable consumer goods *pl*, nondurables *pl*
vgl. langlebige Konsumgüter
Verbrauchsgüterwerbung f
→ Konsumgüterwerbung
Verbrauchsverhalten n
→ Konsumverhalten
verbreitete Auflage f **(tatsächlich verbreitete Auflage** f, **Vertriebsauflage** f) (Zeitung/ Zeitschrift) total circulation
 The full number of copies of a publication distributed, including both copies sold to subscribers, (→) Abonnementsauflage, and single copy buyers, (→) Einzelverkauf, as well as complimentary copies, (→) Freistücke.
Verbreitung f 1. (Nachricht, Produkt) circulation, dissemination, spread, (Diffusion) diffusion, (Propagierung) propagation 2. (Zeitschrift, Zeitung) circulation, coverage, (Vertrieb) distribution
Verbreitungsanalyse f *(media res)* distribution analysis
 The analysis of the number of readers or subscribers a periodical has, usually broken down by geographic or sociodemographic characteristics.
Verbreitungsgebiet n 1. *(advtsg)* (Streugebiet) circulation area, coverage area, media market
 The geographic area as defined by the effective coverage pattern of media originating in the market.
2. *(radio/TV)* brodcasting area, service area, signal service area, coverage area, circulation area, signal area
 A geographic area within which a television or radio station actually obtains audiences. A circulation area is defined on a "do-receive" basis and should not be confused with a coverage area which is defined on a "can-receive" basis.
→ Empfangsbereich
Verbundaktion f *(advtsg)* tie-in campaign, tie-in
 Anything related and supplementary, as for instance one element in a promotion campaign and particularly a dealer's local advertisement, display, etc., repeating the theme or illustration of national advertising.
Verbundanzeige f **(Referenzanzeige** f) tie-in advertisement, tie-in ad, tie-in
 Any advertisement making reference to another advertisement in the same issue run by another advertiser, or to any other piece of promotion.
Verbundeffekt m
→ Ausstrahlungseffekt, Irradiation
Verbundmarke f *(econ)* tie-in brand, cross-ruff brand
 The result of a cooperative or promotional program involving couponing, product sampling, and premiums, and the like, in which two or more companies join to promote like brands. Companies engaging in this activity usuall deal directly with another and each continues to promote its own brands.
Verbundmarketing n tie-in marketing
 The development of a cooperative marketing effort between products, brands or marketers.
Verbundmarktforschung f
→ Gemeinschaftsmarktforschung
Verbundmessung f
→ konjunkte Analyse
Verbundpackung f **(Combipack** m) combipack, multiple-product package
Verbundwerbemittel n tie-in advertisement, tie-in ad, crossruff advertisement, crossruff ad
 A single advertisement intended to encourage the sale of more than one product, brand, or service. Also a small local advertisement placed by a dealer or agent near or in juxtaposition to a large advertisement placed by the national advertiser.
Verbundwerbesendung f
(Komplementärwerbesendung f)
(radio/TV) tie-in commercial, tie-in

A commercial announcement given by the local announcer after a break in a network program, or at the end of the network program.
Verbundwerbung *f* **(Komplementärwerbung** *f*, **Referenzwerbung** *f*) tie-in advertising, tie-in
→ Verbundanzeige, Verbundaktion, Verbundwerbemittel, Verbundwerbesendung
Verbundwirkung *f*
→ Ausstrahlungseffekt, Irradiation
Vercodung *f* **(Verkodung** *f*)
→ Kodierung, Verschlüsselung
Verdingung *f*
→ Ausschreibung
Verdrängungswerbung *f* **(Verdrängungswettbewerb** *m*) *(econ)* predatory competition
Setting prices so low that competitors will be driven out of business.
Verdrängungswettbewerb treiben *v/t (econ)* to make predatory competition
verdunkeln *v/i (film/phot)* to fade to black, to go to black
→ abblenden, Schwarzblende
Verdunkler *m (film/phot)* dimmer, dimming switch
An electrical device used for varying the intensity of lights.
→ Abblendregler
verdünnen *v/t* to dilute
Verdünner *m* diluting agent
Verdünnung *f* dilution
Vereinigung *f* **zur Förderung der Public Relations-Forschung e.V. (VFPRF)** Association for the Promotion of Public Relations Research
Vereinsblatt *n*
→ Verbandsblatt
Verfahren *n* **der ...**
→ Methode der ...
Verfalldatum *n* **(Frischestempel** *m*) *(econ)* (auf Lebensmittelpackungen)
→ Frischestempel
Verfasser *m* author
Verfasserkorrektur *f*
→ Autorenkorrektur
verfilmen *v/t* to filmize, to picturize, to cinematize
Verfilmung *f* **(Filmbearbeitung** *f*) film adaption, filmization, screen adaptation, motion picture adaptation, picturization, cinematization, cinemazation
Verfilmungsrechte *n/pl* screen rights *pl*, filmization rights *pl*

verfischen *v/t (print)* to pie, to pi (type)
To mix up or jumble type, thus making it unusable.
Verfolgerscheinwerfer *m* **(Verfolgerspot** *m*, *colloq* **Verfolger** *m*) *(film/TV)* follow spotlight, follow spot, follower
A moving spotlight to track a moving object.
Verfolgungsaufnahme *f (film/TV)* follow focus shot, follow shot
A camera move to track a moving object.
→ Fahraufnahme
verfügbare Kaufkraft *f*
→ Kaufkraft
verfügbares Eikommen *n* **(frei verfügbares Einkommen** *n*) *(econ)* disposable income, discretionary income, discretionary fund, (verfügbares Geld zum Einkaufen) open-to-buy amount (OTB amount)
1. The personal income remaining after the deduction of taxes on personal income and compulsory payment such as social security levies (disposable income).
2. That portion of personal income, in excess of the amount necessary to maintain a defined or historical standard of living, (→) Lebensstandard, which may be saved with no immediate impairment of living standards or may be as a result of consumer decision relatively free of prior commitment or pressure of need (discretionary income).
3. Discretionary income enlarged by the amount of new credit extensions, which also may be deemed spendable as a result of consumer decision relatively free of prior commitment or pressure of need.
Vergessen *n (psy)* forgetting, (Gedächtnisverfall) memory decay
Vergessenskurve *f (psy)* curve of forgetting, (des Gedächtnisverfalls) memory decay curve
Vergleich *m* comparison
vergleichen *v/t* to compare
vergleichende Werbung *f* **(vergleichende Reklame** *f*) comparison advertising, comparative advertising
Any advertising which directly compares the advertiser's product, brand, or service on one or more specific characteristics with at least one competing brand that is named or made clearly recognizable. German legislation and jurisdiction are very restrictive.

Vergleichsanalyse f (vergleichende Analyse f) *(res)* comparative analysis
Vergleichsgüter *n/pl (econ)* comparison goods *pl*
→ relevanter Produktmarkt
Vergleichsmethode f (der Werbebudgetierung) *(advtsg)* comparison method, comparison with total product group
→ konkurrenzorientierte Budgetierung
Vergnügungssteuer *f (econ)* admission tax, entertainment tax
vergrößern 1. *v/t (econ)* (Sortiment) to enlarge, to extend, to expand 2. *(phot/print)* to enlarge, to blow up, (im Maßstab) to scale up, (Brennweite) to increase (focus)
Vergrößerung *f* **(Vergrößern** *n***)** 1. *(econ)* (Sortiment) enlargement, extension, expansion 2. *(phot/print)* enlargement, blowup, blow-up
  Any reproduction that is larger than the original.
Vergrößerungsapparat *m* **(Vergrößerungsgerät** *n***)** *(phot)* enlarger
Vergrößerungskopie *f (phot)* enlargement, blowup, blow-up
Vergrößerungsmaßstab *m* **(Maßstab** *m***)** scale
  The proportion or yardstick by which a reproduction is enlarged.
Vergütung *f* 1. (Honorar) remuneration, payment 2. → Entspiegelung
vergütungsfähige Werbung *f* **(kommissionsfähige Werbung** *f***)** above-the-line advertising
Verhalten *n* **(Verhaltensweise** *f***)** behavior, *brit* behaviour
  In the most general sense, any change, movement, or response of an entity or system. In a more restricted sense, only that type of action that is related to environment, thus excluding intra organism activity, but including verbal statements and subjective experiences.
Verhaltensabsicht *f* **(Verhaltensintention** *f***)** behavioral intention (BI), *brit* behavioural intention
Verhaltensanalyse *f* **(Analyse** *f* **des Verhaltens)** behavioral analysis, *brit* behavioural analysis, behavior analysis, analysis of behavior, *brit* behaviour

Verhaltensbeobachtung *f* observation of behavior, *brit* behaviour, behavior observation, behavioral observation, *brit* behavioural observation
Verhaltensbiologie *f* biology of behavior, *brit* behaviour
Verhaltensdisposition *f* behavioral disposition, *brit* behavioural disposition
Verhaltenserwartung *f* behavioral expectation, *brit* behavioural expectation
Verhaltensforschung *f* **(Ethologie** *f***)** ethology
→ Verhaltenswissenschaften
Verhaltensfrage *f (survey res)* behavior question, *brit* behaviour question
  Questions that ask about behavior or facts, such as characteristics of people, things people have done, or things that have happened to them that are in principle verifiable by an external observer.
Verhaltensintention *f*
→ Verhaltensabsicht
Verhaltensmodell *n* behavioral model, *brit* behavioural model, behavior model, *brit* behaviour model
Verhaltensmuster *n* 1. A relatively uniform series of overt activities, i.e. the able regularity of conduct.
2. A type of conduct serving as a model.
Verhaltensregeln *f/pl* **(in der Werbung)** code of (advertising) practice, (advertising) standards *pl*, code of ethics (in advertising), ethical code (in advertising)
Verhaltenstheorie *f* **(Theorie** *f* **des Verhaltens)** behavior theory, *brit* behaviour theory
Verhaltenswissenschaft(en) *f(pl)* behavioral science(s) *(pl)*, *brit* behavioural science(s) *pl*
Verhältnis *n (stat)* ratio, proportion
  An expression of relative magnitude between two or more values in a series or between elements of the series and their total.
Verhältnis *n* **von Redaktion zu Anzeigen** editorial to advertising ratio, advertising to editorial ratio
Verhältnisschätzung *f (stat)* (Methode der Verhältnisschätzung) ratio estimation, ratio method, (Schätzresultat) ratio estimate,

(**Verhältnisschätzfunktion**) ratio estimator
An estimator (Schätzfunktion) which takes the form of a ratio between two random variables, as they are often used in sample surveys. The value obtained by using a ratio estimator is a ratio estimate.

Verhältnisskala f (**Proportionalskala** f, **Ratioskala** f, **Absolutskala** f) (stat) ratio scale
A scale, (→) Skala, for properties of objects and events that assumes same-size units throughout, in addition to a nonarbitrary zero point. It allows meaningful statements of proportion such as A is one-half the size of B. Ratio scales are more likely to involve physical than psychological measurements.

Verhältnisskalierung f
→ Verhältnisskala

Verhältniszahl f (**Verhältnisziffer** f) (stat) ratio
→ Verhältnis

Verifikation f (**Verifizierung** f) (res) verification
A process by which the truth or actuality of a hypothesis (→) Hypothese, or theory or doctrine or idea is demonstrated or disproved. Scientific verification consists in testing claims, by repetition of experiments or observations under similar or more refined conditions or with parallel control experiments for isolation of specific differential factors, or by attempting to reach similar findings with different instruments or methods.

verkabeln v/t to cable, to wire
Verkabelung f cabling, wiring
Verkabelungssystem n (cable TV) distribution system
Verkauf m (econ) 1. (Verkaufsakt) sale 2. (Verkaufen) selling, (jur auch) vending
The personal or impersonal process of assisting and/or persuading a prospective customer to buy a commodity or a service or to act favorably upon an idea that has commercial significance to the seller.
3. (Verkaufsabteilung) sales department
→ Absatz, Vertrieb

verkaufen v/t (econ) to sell, (jur auch) to vend
To encourage a sales transaction.

Verkäufer m (econ) salesman, saleswoman, seller, (Angestellter) salesclerk, salesperson, brit shop assistant

1. An employee of a wholesale or manufacturing distributor calling upon retailers or other potential customers soliciting orders. 2. A member of the retail staff in a store.

Verkäufermarkt m (econ) seller's market, sellers' market
A condition of the market in which vendors are able to prescribe the conditions of a transaction because demand exceeds supply.
vgl. Käufermarkt

Verkäuferstab m (**Verkäufer** m/pl) (econ) salesforce, sales staff, salespeople pl
The group of employees of a business organization responsible for personal development of sales and sales prospects.

Verkäufertest m (**Kontrollkauf** m, **Testkauf** m, **Testkaufaktion** f)
→ Kauftest

Verkaufsabteilung f
→ Verkauf 3.

Verkaufsagent m (econ) sales agent, selling agent
A person having the right to negotiate business with a third party on behalf of a principal, selling his goods or services according to laid down agreements. The essence of an agency is that the agent drops out of the contract once it has been signed by the principal parties.

Verkaufsaktion f (**Verkaufskampagne** f) (econ) sales campaign
The implementation of the selling strategy, e.g. mounting a specific selling operation for a product, a market segment, or a geographical area, in isolation from the normal sales activity.

Verkaufsanalyse f (**Absatzanalyse** f) (econ) sales analysis
→ Umsatzanalyse

Verkaufsanzeige f sales advertisement, sales ad, direct-action advertisement, promotional advertisement, promotional ad

Verkaufsappell m sales appeal

Verkaufsargument n sales argument, sales proposition, selling proposition, sales point, selling point

Verkaufsauflage f (**verkaufte Auflage** f) (Zeitung/Zeitschrift) number of copies sold, paid circulation, net paid circulation, total net paid circulation, total net paid, total paid, (einschließlich Sammelbezieher) total net paid including bulk, (ohne Sammelbezieher) total net paid excluding bulk; (durchschnittliche

Verkaufsauslage

Verkaufsauflage) average net paid circulation, average net paid
   The total average number of copies of a publication sold per issue through subscription, newsstand sales, but excluding free distribution.

Verkaufsauslage f *(POP advtsg)* sales display, merchandise display
→ Warenauflage

Verkaufsaußenorganisation f *(econ)* sales force, salesforce
→ Verkäuferstab

Verkaufsausschreibung f
→ Ausschreibung

Verkaufsautomat m *(retailing)* vending machine, automatic vending machine, vendor, automat, sales automat
   A purely automatic dispenser of merchandise upon insertion of a coin.

Verkaufsbehälter m *(POP advtsg)* counter display container, sales container, counter dispenser, dispenser
   A merchandise display containing a stock of items for immediate sale.

Verkaufsberater(in) m(f) *(econ)* sales consultant

Verkaufsbereich m
→ Absatzgebiet

Verkaufsbericht m
→ Vertreterbericht, Bericht, Besuchsbericht

Verkaufsbezirk m
→ Absatzbezirk

Verkaufsdatum n (Zeitschrift) on-sale date

Verkaufsdisplay n
→ Verkaufsauslage

Verkaufseinheit f sales unit, unit

Verkaufsfeldzug m
→ Verkaufsaktion

Verkaufsfiliale f *(retailing)* sales outlet, sales branch
   A selling or trading unit.

Verkaufsfläche f *(retailing)* selling space
   The area in a retail store where merchandise is actually offered for sale (the sales floor), in contrast to *nonselling space* which ist the area where merchandise is stored, received, price marked, repaired, etc.

Verkaufsflächenaufteilung f *(retailing)* selling space allocation
   There is no set ratio of selling to nonselling space. The figure varies according to the type of retailer, the size of the retail store, and the individual retailer's merchandise practices and preferences. Ideally, the retailer should allocate space for different kinds of merchandise in such a way as to allow for the optimum level of exposure for each type of merchandise is given just the amount of space that will realize maximum sales potential for the total merchinadise assortment.

Verkaufsförderer m sales promoter, merchandiser

Verkaufsförderung f sales promotion, merchandising, (beim Handel) trade promotion, (bei Konsumenten) consumer promotion
   1. In the most general sense, any sales activity that supplements or coordinates personal selling and advertising, but which cannot be strictly classified as either. 2. In a specific sense, those marketing activities, other than personal selling, advertising, and publicity, that stimulate consumer purchasing and dealer effectiveness, such as display, shows and exhibitions, demonstrations, and various non-recurrent selling efforts not in the ordinary routine. 3. In retailling, all methods of stimulating customer purchasing, including personal selling, advertising, and publicity.

Verkaufsförderungsabteilung f sales promotion department, merchandising department, promotion department
   1. The department of a manufacturing or wholesaling company responsible for the planning and implementation of all promotional activities. 2. A department of an advertising or public relations agency responsible for devising promotion plans for clients.

Verkaufsförderungsagentur f sales promotion agency
   An organization specializing in supplying sales promotion services to clients.

Verkaufsförderungsberater m (**Verkaufsförderungsfachmann** m)
→ Verkaufsförderer

Verkaufsförderungsleiter m (**Leiter** m **der Verkaufsförderung**) sales promotion manager, managing sales promoter, sales promotion executive, executive sales promoter

Verkaufsförderungsmaterial n sales promotion material, promotional material, sales aids *pl*, sales tools *pl*, *colloq* promotools *pl*, (Ausrüstung) promotional kit, promotional package
   Any of the various media and aids used in the promotional mix. Includes such activities and units as demonstrations,

contests, trade exhibits, free samples, catalogs, trading stamps.
Verkaufsförderungsmittel *n* sales promotion aid, promotion matter, promotional matter, *colloq* promotool
Verkaufsförderungs-Mix *n* sales promotion mix, promotional mix
  The combination of all means used to promote sales. It should be recognized that a great deal of substitutability exists among the various means.
Verkaufsforschung *f* sales research
  The study of field and office activities in an effort to discover means of improving sales force productivity.
  → Absatzforschung
Verkaufsgebiet *n*
  → Absatzgebiet, Vertriebsgebiet
Verkaufsgebietstest *m*
  → Gebietsverkaufstest
Verkaufsgespräch *n* personal sales transaction, personal selling
  The personal process of assisting and/or persuading a prospective customer to buy a commodity or a service, or to act favorably upon an idea that has commercial significance to the seller.
Verkaufsgondel *f (POP advtsg)* sales gondola, gondola
  An island of shelving in a retail store, usually open on two sides but may be open all around.
Verkaufsgremium *n* **(Selling Center** *n) (retailing)* selling center
  vgl. Einkaufsgremium
Verkaufshandbuch *n* **(Verkaufskatalog** *m,* **Verkaufsmappe** *f) (promotion)* sales manual, salesfolder, sales folder, sales portfolio
  A manual of information carried by a salesman for reference or display.
Verkaufshelfer *m*
  → Verkaufsförderer, Absatzhelfer
Verkaufshilfe *f (meist pl* **Verkaufshilfen)**
  → Händlerhilfen
Verkaufsinsel *f (POP advtsg)* island display, island
  A retail store display accessible on all sides.
Verkaufskampagne *f*
  → Verkaufsaktion
Verkaufskanal *m*
  → Absatzkanal, Vertriebskanal
Verkaufskatalog *m*
  → Verkaufshandbuch
Verkaufskontrolle *f*
  → Absatzkontrolle

Verkaufskooperation *f*
  → Absatzkooperation
Verkaufskosten *pl*
  → Abatzkosten
Verkaufskunst *f (econ)* salesmenship
  The art and skill of successfully persuading prospects or customers to buy products or services from which they can derive suitable benefits, thereby increasing their total satisfactions. It is the opposite of conmanship, and it includes the practice of informing and persuading persons or organizations of the value of a purchase and expressing that value in actual benefits unique to each prospect.
Verkaufsleistung *f* **(Verkaufseffizienz** *f) (econ)* sales effectiveness
Verkaufsleiter *m (econ)* sales manager, sales executive
  The executive who plans, directs, and controls the activities of salesmen.
Verkaufsleitung *f* **(Verkaufsmanagement** *n) (econ)* sales management
  The planning, direction, and control of the personal selling activities of a business unit, including recruiting, selecting, training, equipping, assigning, routing, supervising, paying, and motivating as these tasks apply to the personal sales force.
Verkaufsmesse *f (econ)* sales fair
  vgl. Mustermesse
Verkaufsmethode *f* **(Verkaufsform** *f)*
  → Bedienungsmethode
Verkaufsniederlassung *f (retailing)* sales outlet, outlet
  → Verkaufsfiliale
Verkaufsorganisation *f (econ)* sales organization, *brit* organisation, salesforce, (unternehmerische Funktion) sales management
  The structure and distribution of the sales personnel, head and branch offices or warehouses and possibly shops, where company-operated; sometimes also applied in the same way to the organization of the sales staff in a mail order operation.
Verkaufsort *m*
  → Kaufort
Verkaufspackung *f* consumer package, consumer pack, retail package, retail pack
Verkaufspersonal *n (econ)* salespeople *pl,* sales people *pl*
  → Verkäuferstab
Verkaufsplakat *n* commercial sign

Verkaufsplan

Verkaufsplan m
→ Absatzplan
Verkaufsplanung f
→ Absatzplanung
Verkaufspolitik f
→ Absatzpolitik
Verkaufspotential n
→ Absatzpotential
Verkaufsprämie f (**Verkäuferprämie** f) 1. salesman's premium
  A reward in excess of salary or commission provided to a salesperson in return for archieving a stated sales goal, or for extraordinary effort or for leadership in the amount sold.
2. sales incentive
  Promotional devices and gifts offered to trade buyers, potential customers, or to distribution channels, in order to promote sales or extra selling effort.
Verkaufspreis m (econ) selling price, auch sale price, (faktischer Preis nach Abzug des Händlerrabatts) code price, (Zeitschrift) cover price
→ Einzelhandelspreis, Endverbraucherpreis
Verkaufsprognose f
→ Absatzprognose
Verkaufsquote f (econ) sales quota, quota
  A projected volume of sales assigned to a marketing unit for use in the management of sales efforts. It applies to a specified period and may be expressed in monetary or in physical units. The quota may be used in checking the efficiency or stimulating the efforts of or in remunerating individual salesmen or other personnel engaged in sales work. A quota may be for a salesman, a territory, a department, a branch house, a wholesaler or retailer, or for a company as a whole. It may be different from the sales figure set up in the sales budget. Since it is a managerial device, it is not an immutable figure inexorably arrived at by the application of absolutely exact statistical formulas.
Verkaufsraum m (retailing) salesroom
Verkaufsschlager m (econ) seller, bestseller, sleeper
  A product or service that sells extraordinarily well.
Verkaufsschulung f
→ Verkaufstraining
Verkaufsständer m (POP advtsg) display container, dispenser, display rack, sales rack
Verkaufsstelle f
→ Kaufort, Verkaufsniederlassung

Verkaufsstrategie f (**Verkaufstechnik** f) (econ) sales strategy, selling strategy, sales technique, selling technique
Verkaufssystem n
→ Bedienungsform
Verkaufstätigkeit f (econ) selling, sales activity, (jur auch) vending
→ Verkauf 2.
Verkaufstechnik f
→ Verkaufsstrategie
Verkaufstest m
→ Ladentest
Verkaufstisch m
→ Auslagetisch
Verkaufstrainer m (econ) sales trainer
Verkaufstraining n (econ) sales training
Verkaufsverpackung f
→ Verkaufspackung
Verkaufsvertreter m (econ) sales representative
  A sales person usually associated with technical or professional selling.
Verkaufswagen m (retailing) mobile shop, merchandising bus
  A regular transit bus converted into a mobile showcase to display and sell products.
Verkaufswerbung f sales advertising, promotional advertising
→ Absatzwerbung
Verkaufswettbewerb m (promotion) sales contest
  A contest, (→) Wettbewerb, open to a business firm's sales personnel or to prospects, structured to reward superior performance or unusually large purchases.
Verkaufsziffer f
→ Absatzziffer
verkaufte Auflage f
→ Verkaufsauflage
Verkehrsfluß m
→ Verkehrsauffassung
Verkehrskreis m
→ beteiligte Verkehrskreise
Verkehrsmittelanschlag m (**Verkehrsmittelplakat** n) (transit advtsg) transit card, transit poster, car card, bus card, transportation poster
  An advertising sheet for display inside or outside a vehicle of public transportation.
Verkehrsmittelanschlagfläche f (transit advtsg) car panel, bus panel
Verkehrsmittelanschlag-Tarif m (Tarif m für Verkehrsmittel-

anschläge) *(transit advtsg)* car card rate, bus card rate, transit advertising rate
Verkehrsmittelbenutzer *m (transit advtsg)* car passenger, passenger, bus passenger
Verkehrsmittelplakat *n* **(Verkehrsmittelschild** *n)*
→ Verkehrsmittelanschlag
Verkehrsmittelwerbung *f* transit advertising, transportation advertising, transport advertising, car card advertising
    Any advertising associated with vehicles of public transportation, both inside and outside, and in their stations and shelters.
Verkehrswerbemittel *n*
→ Verkehrsmittelwerbung
Verkehrszählung *f (outdoor advtsg)* traffic count
→ Passantenzählung
Verkettung *f (stat)* chaining
verkleinern *v/t* 1. *(econ)* (Sortiment) to reduce, to dwindle down, to diminish 2. *(phot/print)* to reduce, (im Maßstab) to scale down, (Brennweite) to decrease (focus)
vgl. vergrößern
Verkleinerung *f* **(Verkleinern** *n)*
1. *(econ)* (Sortiment) reduction
2. *(phot/print)* reduction, (im Maßstab) scaling down
vgl. Vergrößerung
Verkleinerungskopie *f (phot)* reduction print, reduction
→ Verkleinerung 2.
Verkleinerungsmaschine *f (phot/ print)* reduction printer
Verkleinerungsmaßstab *m (phot/ print)* scale (of reduction)
Verlag *m* publishing company, publishing house, publisher
Verlagsanzeige *f*
→ Eigenanzeige
Verlagsbranche *f* **(Verlagsgewerbe** *n,* **Verlagswesen** *n)* publishing industry, publishing
Verlagsort *m*
→ Erscheinungsort
Verlagsstück *n* publisher's copy
Verlängerung *f (phot)* extension, prolongation
Verlängerungsfaktor *m* **(Belichtungsfaktor** *m) (phot)* extension factor, prolongation factor

Verläßlichkeit *f*
→ Zuverlässigkeit (Reliabilität)
Verlaufblende *f* **(Verlauffilter** *m)* *(phot)* graduated filter, gradual filter
verlaufende Autotypie *f (print)* vignetted halftone, vignette halftone, vignetted finish, outlined cut
    A halftone, (→) Autotypie, showing the background or a portion of the illustration gradually shaded off toward the edges; they blend gradually from full tones through succeeding lighter tones.
Verlaufschleier *m*
→ Verlaufblende
verlegen *v/t* + *v/i* to publish
Verleger *m* publisher
Verlegerfernsehen *n* newspaper publishers' television
Verlegerverband *m* publishers' association
Verlegerverband *m* **Deutscher Anzeigenblätter e.V. (VVDA)** Association of German Freesheet Publishers
Verleih *m*
→ Filmverleih
Verleiher *m*
→ Filmverleiher
Verleihfilm *m* distributor's film
Verleihfirma *f*
→ Filmverleih 2.
Verleihkopie *f* **(Theaterkopie** *f,* **Massenkopie** *f) (film)* distribution print, quantity print
    A multiple film print of a motion picture or a commercial prepared in order to permit its simultaneous use for projection in movietheaters or airing on a number of broadcasting networks or stations.
Verleihrechte *n/pl* **(Filmverleihrechte** *n/pl)* distribution rights *pl*
Verleihvertreter *m (film)* film salesman
Verlosung *f*
→ Lotterie
vermarkten *v/t (econ)* to market
Vermarktung *f (econ)* marketing
Vermittlungsvertreter *m (econ)* broker, merchandise broker
    An agent who does not have direct physical control of the goods in which he deals but represents either a buyer or seller in negotiating purchases or sales for his principal. His powers as to prices and terms of sale are usually limited by his principal.
Vernichtungswettbewerb *m*
→ Verdrängungswettbewerb

veröffentlichen v/t + v/i to publish, to publicize
Veröffentlichung f publication
verpacken v/t to pack, to package
Verpackung f packaging, packing
→ Packung
Verpackungsberater m packaging consultant
Verpackungsfachmann m
→ Packungsfachmann
Verpackungsforschung f packaging research
Verpackungsgestalter m (**Packungsgestalter** m, **Packungsdesigner** m) package designer
Verpackungsgestaltung f (**Packungsgestaltung** f, **Packungsdesign** n) package design
Verpackungsgutschein m
→ Packungsgutschein
Verpackungsmaterial n (**Packungsmaterial** n) packaging material, package material
Verpackungstest m
→ Packungstest
Verpackungswesen n packaging
Verpackungszugabe f
→ Packungszugabe
Versal m (meist pl **Versalien**) (typ) capital letter(s) (pl), cap(s) (pl), uppercase letter(s) (pl), uppercase (UC, uc), (Satzanweisung) all caps
  A capital letter, as opposed to a small letter.
Versalschrift f (typ) uppercase type, uppercase (UC, uc)
Versandauflage f (Zeitung/Zeitschrift) mail circulation
Versandhandel m (**Versandgeschäft** n) (retailing) 1. (Institution) mail-order trade, mail-order business 2. (Funktion) mail-order trading, mail-order retailing, mail-order selling
  In retailing, a method of generating sales through the mailing of catalogs, fliers, brochures, or sales letters and print or broadcast advertising, as opposed to distributors, wholesalers, retailers, or door-to-door salesmen. Customers buy direct by mail either in response to an advertisement or from a sales promotional catalogue. Deliveries are made through the mail, by carrier direct from warehouse or factory, or occasionally through a local agent.
Versandhaus n (**Versandhandelsunternehmen** n) (retailing) mail-order house, mail-order company, mail-order firm, mail-order business
  A retailing business that receives its orders primarily by mail or telephone and generally offers its goods and services for sale by means of a catalog or other printed material. Other types of retail stores often conduct a mail order business, usually through departments set up for that purpose, although this fact does not make them mail order houses. On the other hand, some firms that originally confined themselves to the mail order business now also operate chain store systems.
Versandhauskatalog m (**Versandkatalog** m) (retailing) mail-order catalog, brit catalogue
Versandhauswerbung f mail-order advertising
  Advertising designed to produce orders direct from prospects by mail; any type of medium may be used to deliver the advertising message.
Verschluß m (phot) shutter, camera shutter
  A mechanical device that revolves between the lens, (→) Objektiv, and the film in a camera, thus admitting light to the film which it covers for brief intervals. It can be opened and closed for a controlled length of time to permit exposure of the sensitive material. Most simple box cameras have rotary shutters permitting only instantaneous exposures (of about 1/25 of a second) and time setting, in which the shutter can be held open for a long period. Folding cameras often have more complex shutters, permitting a range of longer or shorter exposure times.
Verschlußauslösung f (phot) shutter setting, shutter scale
verschlüsseln (kodieren) v/t to code, to encode, (Anzeige chiffrieren) to key (an advertisement)
→ Verschlüsselung
verschlüsselte Anzeige f
→ Chiffre-Anzeige
Verschlüsselung f (**Verschlüsseln** n, **Kodierung** f, **Kodieren** n) (survey res) coding, encoding
  A research procedure in which the data collected by questionnaire or any other method are prepared for counting and tabulation by classification and codification. Categories or classes are devised so that observation will fall into one or another of a predetermined set of categories. The raw data are transferred into symbols, usually numerical, and can

then be transferred to punched cards or to tape and be rapidly processed.
Verschlüsselung f **(Chiffrieren** n**) (von Anzeigen) keying (of ads)**
A method of response control, (→) Anfragenkontrolltest, that consists in putting a code number or letter in a coupon or in the advertiser's address so the particular advertisement or medium producing an inquiry can be identified.
Verschlüsselungsplan m
→ Kodeplan
Verschlußgeschwindigkeit f **(Verschlußzeit** f**)** (phot) **shutter speed**
The time interval that a camera shutter, (→) Verschluß, exposes film.
Verschlußlamelle f (phot) **shutter blade, shutter leaf**
Verschlußzeit f
→ Verschlußgeschwindigkeit
Verschnitt m (paper) **offcut,** (film) **waste**
Verschwärzlichung f (phot) **blackening**
verschwommener Druck m **(verwischter Druck** m**) blurred print**
A print characterized by a loss of sharp detail and confused outlines.
Versicherungsmarketing n **insurance marketing**
Versicherungswerbung f **insurance advertising**
Versprecher m (radio/TV) **fluff, blooper**
In broadcasting, any minor mistake made on the air.
verstärken v/t **1.** (phot) (Licht) **to intensify 2.** (Kopierwerk) **to reinforce 3.** (electr.) **to amplify**
Verstärker m **1.** (phot) (Kopierwerk) **intensifier**
A chemical agent capable of intensifying photographic material.
2. (electr.) **amplifier (amp.)**
A device used for strengthening an electronic signal.
3. (communications) **reinforcer**
Verstärkerhypothese f **(Verstärkungshypothese** f**)**
(communications) reinforcement hypothesis (Paul F. Lazarsfeld/ Bernard Berelson/Hazel Gaudet)
Verstärkeranlage f (electr.) **amplifier equipment, amplifier**
Verstärkung 1. (phot) (Kopierwerk) **intensification**
The process of increasing the opacity of developed and fixed photographic

negatives by chemical treatment of the image.
2. (electr.) **amplification**
3. (communications) **reinforcement**
Verstärkungsbad n **(Verstärkerlösung** f**)** (phot) **intensifier**
Verstärkungswerbung f
→ Festigungswerbung, Erhaltungswerbung
versteckte Werbung f
→ Schleichwerbung, unterschwellige Werbung
verstecktes Angebot n (advtsg) **blind offer, buried offer, hidden offer, subordinated offer**
A special offer buried in the body copy of a print advertisement as a test of readership.
versteigern v/t (econ) **to auction**
Versteigerung f (econ) **auction**
The public sale of property to the highest bidder.
Versuch m **1.** (econ) (Prüfung) **trial, attempt, check 2.** (res) (experiment) **test, trial**
→ Experiment, Test
Versuchsanlage f **(Versuchsanordnung** f**)**
→ experimentelle Anlage
Versuchsfehler m
→ Fehler
Versuchsfilm m
→ Experimentalfilm
Versuchsgruppe f
→ Testgruppe
Versuchsleitereffekt m **(Experimenter-Effekt** m**)** (res) **experimenter effect, (verzerrender Effekt) experimenter bias**
Any unintentional effect an experimenter's behavior in an experiment may have on its outcome.
Versuchsperson f **(Testperson** f**)**
→ Testperson
Versuchsplan m **(Versuchsplanung** f**)**
→ experimentelle Anlage
Versuchsprogramm n **(Versuchssendung** f**)**
→ Testsendung (Pilotsendung)
Verteiler m **1.** (Versandliste) **mailing list**
A particular list of addresses used in direct mail advertising, in the distribution of publicity releases, or in any informative mailing.
2. → Umlauf
3. distributor, distribution frame, distribution board, manifold

Verteilerkontrolle f mailing list control
Verteilung f *(stat)* distribution, frequency distribution
→ Häufigkeitsverteilung
Verteilungsanalyse f
→ Distributionsanalyse
Verteilungsapparat m
→ Vertriebsapparat
verteilungsfreie Statistik f
→ parameterfreie Statistik
Verteilungsfunktion f *(stat)* distribution function
Verteilungskurve f *(stat)* distribution curve
→ Häufigkeitsverteilungskurve
Vertikalantenne f *(radio)* vertical antenne, *brit* vertical aerial
Vertikalauflösung f *(TV)* vertical definition
Vertikalauslage *(POP advtsg)* vertical case, vertical display
  Any display case that is higher than it is wide.
Vertikalaustastimpuls m *(TV)* field blanking pulse, vertical blanking pulse
vertikale Preisbindung f
→ Preisbindung der zweiten Hand
vertikale Preisempfehlung f
→ Preisempfehlung
vertikales Bildkippen n
→ Bildkippen
vertikales Marketing n vertical marketing, vertical marketing system
  The whole set of means organizations use to diminish the traditional autonomy of their suppliers, dealers, or customers such as vertical integration, franchises, cooperatives, or the leveraged application of scalar advantages.
Vertikalfrequenz f **(V-Frequenz** f**)** *(radio/TV)* field frequency, vertical frequency
Vertikalschwenk m
→ Kippschwenk
Vertragshändler m *(econ)* appointed dealer, franchised dealer
  An exclusive, selected or accredited dealer who is assured of freedom from competition and marketing support in return for quality of service and promotion of sales.
Vertragshändlersystem n *(econ)* appointed dealer system, franchised dealer system
Vertragsjahr n
→ Abschlußjahr

Vertrauensbereich m **(Konfidenzintervall** n**, Vertrauensintervall** n**, Mutungsbereich** m**, Fehlerspanne** f**)** *(stat)* confidence interval
  A range of numerical values that, with some specified probability, contains the true value of a population parameter, such as a mean, a standard deviation, a proportion, etc. The confidence interval is determined from data obtained from a sample taken from the population. The numerical values of the upper and lower boundaries of the confidence interval are referred to as confidence limits.
Vertrauenswerbung f goodwill advertising, patronage institutional advertising, institutional advertising
  Any advertising intended to build goodwill for the advertiser rather than to stimulate the immediate purchase of a product.
vertreiben (distribuieren) v/t *(econ)* to distribute
Vertreter m *(econ)* 1. (Repräsentant) representative, rep
  2. → Handelsvertreter
Vetreterbericht m **(Besuchsbericht** m**)** *(econ)* call report
  A summary, usually in writing, of a visit by a salesman to a customer.
Vertreterbezirk m **(Verkaufsbezirk** m**)** *(econ)* sales district, sales agent's district
  The geographical sales territory covered by one salesperson.
Vertreterorganisation f
→ Außendienstorganisation
Vertreterprovision f *(econ)* agent's commission, salesman's commission
→ Provision
Vertretervertrag m agency agreement, agent's agreement, representative's agreement
Vertreterwerbung f agent recruitment, sales agent's recruitment
Vertrieb m *(econ)* 1. (Absatz) sale, sales pl 2. distribution
  The function of dispensing the goods manufactured or warehoused to the locations where they will be consumed or received by customers. This involves the physical movement of goods to ultimate consumers and thus provides place utility.
Vertriebsabteilung f *(econ)*
1. (Absatzabteilung) sales department
2. distribution department, (Medienvertrieb) circulation department

Vertriebsauflage f
→ verbreitete Auflage
Vertriebsauslieferung f (Zeitung/ Zeitschrift) circulation delivery
Vertriebsbezirk m (Zeitung/ Zeitschrift) circulation district
Vertriebsbindung f
→ Abnehmerbindung, Absatzbindung
Vertriebsdichte f (Zeitung/Zeitschrift) circulation density
Vertriebserfolgsrechnung f
→ Absatzerfolgsrechnung
Vertriebserlös(e) m(pl) (Zeitung/ Zeitschrift) circulation revenue
Vertriebsetat m **(Vertriebsbudget** n) *(econ)* sales budget
  A tabulation of anticipated accounting figures covering sales revenue and direct selling costs, shown in predetermined divisions of time, products, territory or market segments. Used as a means of control by comparing actual with budgeted performance.
Vertriebsforschung f **(Distributionsanalyse** f) *(market res)* distribution research
Vertriebsgebiet n *(econ)*
1. → Absatzgebiet
2. (Zeitung/Zeitschrift) circulation area
Vertriebskanal m
→ Absatzkanal, Absatzweg(e)
Vertriebskennzahl f
→ Absatzkennzahl
Vertriebskontrolle f *(econ)*
1. → Absatzkontrolle 2. (Zeitung/ Zeitschrift) distribution control
Vertriebskooperation f
→ Absatzkooperation
Vertriebskosten pl *(econ)*
1. → Absatzkosten 2. distribution cost(s) pl
Vertriebskostenanalyse f **(Vertriebskostenrechnung** f) *(econ)* distribution cost analysis (DCA)
  That branch of marketing research and cost accounting that studies and evaluates, against profits or income, outgo for different methods of marketing and particularly the relative efficiency of personal selling and advertising.
Vertriebsleiter m *(econ)*
1. → Verkaufsleiter 2. (Zeitung/ Zeitschrift) distribution manager, circulation manager
Vertriebsmarketing n *(econ)* distribution marketing
Vertriebsmethode f *(econ)*
1. → Absatzmethode, Verkaufsmethode
2. (Zeitung/Zeitschrift) distribution method, circulation method
Vertriebsmodell n *(econ)* distribution model
Vertriebsorganisation f *(econ)*
1. → Absatzorganisation f, Verkaufsorganisation f
2. (Zeitung/Zeitschrift) distribution organization, *brit* organisation
Vertriebsplan m
→ Absatzplan
Vertriebsplanung f
→ Absatzplanung
Vertriebspolitik f **(Distributions-Mix** n, **Distributionspolitik** f) *(econ)* distribution policy, distribution mix
→ Distributions-Mix
Vertriebssystem n *(econ)* distribution system, circulation system
→ Absatzwegepolitik
Vertriebsverband m
→ Absatzkooperation
Vertriebsweg m
→ Absatzweg
Verursachungsziffer f
→ Beziehungszahl
vervielfältigen v/t to copy, to duplicate, to manifold, to reproduce, *colloq* to dittograph, *colloq* to ditto
  To duplicate or copy material which is typed, drawn, or written on special paper.
Vervielfältiger m
→ Vervielfältigungsapparat
Vervielfältigung f **1.** (Vorgang) reproduction, duplication, duplicating, copying, multiplication, manifolding
2. (Produkt) duplication, duplicate, copy, manifold, ditto
Vervielfältigungsapparat m **(Vervielfältigungsgerät** n) duplicator, copier, duplicating machine, manifolder, dittograph, multigraph, multilith, mimeograph, copy cat
  A small office machine used for printing multiple paper copies of typing, drawings, etc., from a master stencil.
Vervielfältigungspapier n duplicating paper
  Any type of paper suited for use with a duplicator, (→) Vervielfältigungsapparat.
Vervielfältigungsrecht n copyright
verwackeln v/t *(phot)* (Bild) to blur
verwackeltes Bild n *(phot)* blurred picture, double image

Verweigerung

A duplication of the outlines of a photograph as a result of movement of the camera or subject during exposure.
Verweigerung f (**Antwortverweigerung** f) *(survey res)* nonresponse, refusal
A missing observation, which results from the failure of a survey to obtain information from an elementary unit that is originally selected for the survey, because the respondent refused to participate in the interview.
→ Ausfälle
Verweigerungsrate f (**Verweigerungsquote** f) *(survey res)* nonresponse rate, *auch* refusal rate
→ Verweigerung
verweißlichen v/i *(phot)* to desaturate
Verweißlichung f *(phot)* desaturation
Verwender m (**Nutzer** m) *(econ)* user
Verwenderanteil m (**Nutzeranteil** m) *(econ)* share of users
Verzeichnung f (**Distorsion** f) *(phot)* (Abbildungsfehler) distortion
verzerrte Stichprobe f *(stat)* biased sample
A sample selected using a biased sampling method, i.e. a method which systematically discriminates in a nonquantifiable way against some part of the population. Consequently samples obtained using such a sampling procedure will be unrepresentative of the population.
verzerrter Schätzwert m *(stat)* biased estimate
Verzerrung f (**Bias** m)
1. → systematischer Fehler
2. (Nachrichtentechnik) distortion
Verzichtswerbung f
→ Reduktionsmarketing, Reduktionswerbung
Verzögerungseffekt m
→ Wirkungsverzögerung
Vexierbild n picture puzzle
VFPRF *abbr* Vereinigung zur Förderung der Public Relations Forschung e.V.
Video n
→ Videorecorder, Videotext
Videoaufnahme f (**Videobandaufnahme** f) video recording, videotape recording (VTR), video cassette recording (VCR)
Any television program or commercial recorded on a videotape, (→) Videoband.
→ Magnetbildbandaufzeichnung (MAZ)
Videoband n videotape

A magnetic tape on which both sound and picture are recorded simultaneously as opposed to audio tape which only records sound, and permits immediate playback and rapid editing.
Videobandkassette f
→ Videokassette
Videofilterkreuzschiene f video matrix
Videofrequenz f (**VF**) video frequency
Videogerät n (**Videorecorder** m) videotape recorder, video recorder, videoplayer, video cassette recorder (VCR)
A device used to play pre-recorded video programming or to record on-air broadcasts on video tape.
Videokabel n video cable
Videokamera f video camera
Videokassette f video cassette, video cartridge
A magnetic tape unit which can be used for video recordings, permanently housed within a case which includes takeup reels.
Videokopf m video head
Videomagnetband n
→ Videoband
Videomagnetbandaufnahme f
→ Videoaufnahme
Videomixer m video mixer
Videoplatte f
→ Bildplatte
Videoplattengerät n
→ Bildplattengerät
Videorecorder m (**Videorekorder** m)
→ Videogerät
Videosignal n *(TV)* video signal
Videospeichergerät n
→ Videogerät
Videospur f video track
→ Bildspur
Videoterminal m video display terminal (VDT), video terminal
Videotext m (**Videotex** m)
→ Fernsehtext
Vidikon n (**Vidicon** n) *(TV)* vidicon
A durable television camera pickup tube.
Vielleser m *(media res)* heavy reader
Vielseher m *(media res)* heavy viewer
viereckige Autotypie f *(print)* squared halftone
A halftone plate having four straight edges which can be mechanically cut or beveled in straight lines.
Vierergang m *(film)* four-frame motion

548

Vierfarbenätzung f *(print)* four-color block, *brit* four-colour block, four-color plate

Vierfarbendruck m **1.** (Verfahren) four-color process, *brit* four-colour process, four-color printing, *brit* four-colour printing **2.** (Produkt) four-color print, *brit* four-colour print
  A printing process that reproduces a full range of colors by overprinting red, yellow, blue, and black with four separate plates.

Vierfarbensatz m **(Vierfarbenätzung** f, **Farbklischeesatz** m **mit vier Farben)** *(print)* four-color process plate, *brit* four-colour process plate, four-color process printing plate, *brit* four-colour process printing plate

vierfarbig adj *(print)* four-color, *brit* four-colour, 4/C, 4/c
  Noting or pertaining to halftone printing in yellow, red, blue, and black in combination, to give a complete range of hues and tonal values to match the colors in the original.

vierfarbige Anzeige f **(Vierfarbenanzeige** f) four-color advertisement, *brit* four-colour advertisement, four-color ad, 4/C ad, 4/c ad

Vierfeldertafel f **(Vierfelderschema** n, **Vierfeldertabelle** f) *(stat)* fourfold table, two-by-two table, 2 × 2 table
  → Kontingenztabelle

vierte Umschlagseite f **(U 4** f) *(Zeitschrift)* outside back cover (OBC, O.B.C.), fourth cover (4 C), back cover

Vierteljahreszeitschrift f **(Vierteljahrespublikation** f) quarterly journal, quarterly publication, quarterly

vierteljährlich (vierteljährlich erscheinend) adj quarterly

Viertelseite f quarter page

viertelseitige Anzeige f quarter-page advertisement, quarter-page ad

vierzehntäglich (halbmonatlich) adj fortnightly, *auch* biweekly

vierzehntäglich erscheinende Zeitschrift f **(Halbmonatszeitschrift** f, **Zweiwochenzeitschrift** f) fortnightly magazine, fortnightly paper, fortnightly journal, fortnightly publication, fortnightly, *auch* (doppeldeutig) biweekly, bi-weekly
  A periodical publication issued every two weeks.

Vignette f *(phot)* **1.** vignette
  An illustration or photograph with an indefinite outer edge that blends into the surrounding blank area through shading.
  2. vignette, matte, mask
  A mask for a lens of a camera that gives a shot a vignette-like effect.

Vignettenautotypie f *(print)* vignette
  A halftone in which the edges fade out irregularly.

visualisieren v/t *(psy)* to visualize

Visualisierung f *(psy)* visualization
  The process of picturing in the mind a mental image of a situation as a whole on the basis of partial information, e.g. of how an ad will look before it is produced.

visuelle Kommunikation f visual communication

Vitrine f **(Auslagevitrine** f, **Schaukasten** m) *(POP advtsg)* display case, showcase, show case

VK abbr Verkauf

Vogelperspektive f *(phot)* bird's eye view, bird's eye perspective

Vollautotypie f
  → viereckige Autotypie

Vollbeleg m
  → Belegexemplar

Vollbelegung f *(advtsg)* (Zeitung) full run, every day (E.D.), every issue (E.I.), (Zeitschrift) full run, every issue (E.I.)
  The insertion of an advertisement in every edition of a daily newspaper during one day, or of all editions during one week; in transit advertising, one card in every vehicle of a fleet.

Vollerhebung f
  → Totalerhebung

voller Spaltensatz m **(in voller Spaltenbreite** f) *(print)* full measure
  A standard width of one column without any indentation.

Vollservice m
  → Full-Service

Vollsichtauslage f *(POP advtsg)* full display

Vollsichtregal n *(POP advtsg)* display rack, display shelf

vollständiges Belegexemplar n
  → Vollbeleg

Vollton m *(print)* solid tint

Volltonfläche f *(print)* solid plate, solid
  A plate having an even printing surface and bearing no etched or engraved design. Used for printing solid tints or uniform deposition of ink in any color.

Volltonklischee n **(Volltonautoypie** f, **Vollton** m) *(print)* fulltone
  A highlight halftone plate with the deepest shadows represented by solids.

Volumen n volume
vorabaufnehmen v/t to pre-record, (film) to prefilm
Vorabdruck m (print) advance copy, advance publication, preprint
  A reproduction of a periodical or any other piece of printed matter.
vorabdrucken v/t to preprint
Vorabdruckrecht n (print) first serial right(s) (pl)
Vorabexemplar n 1. → Vorabdruck 2. → unveröffentlichtes Heft
Vorankündigung f (**Voranzeige** f) advance notice, advance announcement
Voranschlag m
  → Kostenvoranschlag
Vorarbeiter m (print) (in der Setzerei) copycutter, brit copy-cutter
  An overseer in the composing room who divides copy into portions which are given to compositors to set in newspaper shops.
Vorausbesuch m (econ) (Vertreter) advance canvass
  A round of visits to retailers in a territory to obtain support for a promotional campaign.
Vorausdruck m
  → HiFi-Endlosfarbanzeige
Vorausexemplar n predate issue
  An edition of a publication that is released before the date it actually bears.
Vorauskorrektur f (print) (eines Manuskripts) copy editing, copy preparation
Voraussage f (**Vorhersage** f)
  → Prognose
Vorbildwerbung f
  → Leitbildwerbung
Vorblatt n (print) cover sheet
Vordergrund m (phot/film/TV) foreground
Vorderlicht n (**Frontallicht** n) (phot) front light, front lighting
  A technique of lighting a photographic subject or cinematic scene from the general direction of the camera or spectator.
Vorderseite f front page
Vordruck m
  → Vorabdruck
voreinstellen v/t (phot) to preset, to set up
vorfahren v/i (film/TV) (Kamera) to track in
Vorfahrt f (film/TV) track-in

Vorführband n (promotion) demonstration tape
Vorführdauer f (film/TV) running time, screen time
vorführen v/t (film) to show, to present, to project
Vorführer m
  → Filmvorführer
Vorführkabine f (film/TV) projection booth, projection room
Vorführkopie f (film) release print, viewing print
  A completed copy of a motion picture made available for distribution.
Vorführrabatt m (retailing) display discount, display allowance
  A merchandising allowance or discount granted to retailers in return for the opportunity to display off-shelf merchandise.
Vorführung f
  → Filmvorführung
Vorgabe f
  → Antwortgabe
vorgedruckt adj preprinted
vorgeschriebene Plazierung f
  → Plazierungsvorschrift
Vorhangblende f (phot) curtain shutter, curtain fading shutter, curtain wipe
Vorkorrektur f
  → Vorauskorrektur
Vorlage f
  → Druckvorlage, Reproduktionsvorlage
Vorlauf m (film) forward motion
Vorlaufband n tape leader, leader
Vorlaufzeit f leader duration, pre-roll time, (Leitung) line-up time, test period
Vormittagsprogramm n (radio/TV) morning program, brit morning programme
  → Frühstücksfernsehen
Vormontage f (film) (Schnitt) assembly
Vorpremiere f (film) advance showing, preview, Am auch prevue
  A special showing of a motion picture, a program or a commercial to a select audience before it is released.
Vorratsmarke f (**Vorratszeichen** n) (econ) blanket brand
Vorsatzblatt n (**Vorsatz** m) (print) endpaper, flyleaf, bookend
  A paper at either end of a book, lining the cover and forming a flyleaf.

Vorsatzlinse f (**Linsenvorsatz** m) (*phot*) attachment lens, lens attachment
→ Objektivvorsatz
Vorschaltzeit f (*radio/TV*) line-up time, test period
Vorschau f preview, (*film/TV*) trailer
  A promotional spot announcing a forthcoming television or radio program.
→ Programmvorschau
Vorspann m 1. introduction, introductory lines *pl*, headnote 2. (*film*) (Titel) opening credits *pl*, opening titles *pl*, opening credit lines *pl*, (Vorschau) preview, Am auch prevue, trailer, (zum Einfädeln) leader, film leader, head leader
  The lines at the beginning of a motion picture or television film that list the contributions of the production's various participants.
Vorspannband n leader tape, leader
Vorspannfilm m leader film, head leader
Vorspanntitel m
→ Vorspann 2.
Vorstellung f
→ Filmvorstellung
Vorstellungsbild n
→ Image
Vorstudie f (**Pilotstudie** f, **Voruntersuchung** f) (*survey res*) pretest, pilot study, pilot test
  A small field test, primarily of the questionnaire but also of other field procedures, before the main study is conducted. Pilot tests usually have small samples (ten to fifty cases) and are intended to alert the researcher to any respondent difficulties that were not anticipated in planning the study.
Vorverbraucherpanel n (*market res*) industrial user panel
Vorverkauf m (*econ*) advance sale

vorverpackte Ware f
→ Fertigware
Vorversuch m
→ Pretest
Vorwahl f
→ Teilselbstbedienung (Selbstauswahl)
Vorwärtsgang m (*film*) forward motion
Vorwärtsintegration f (**vertikale Diversifizierung** f) (*econ*) vertical diversification, vertical integration
  Both the merging of companies producing different things but contributing to the same ultimate product and the operation of a company at more than one level in channels of distribution, typically as both manufacturer and distributor.
Vorwort n preface, foreword
Vorzeichentest m (**Zeichentest** m) (*stat*) sign test
  A nonparametric test for the significance, (→) Signifikanztest, of the difference between two correlated sets of scores. Most commonly the test involves repeated measures where for each subject there is a pair of scores, one under each of two experimental conditions. The procedure involves finding the difference between the two scores, $X_1 - X_2$, for each subject, and noting whether the difference is positive, negative, or zero.
Vorzugsplatz m (**Vorzugsplazierung** f)
→ Plazierungsvorschlag
Vorzugspreis m
→ Sonderpreis
Vorzurichtung f (*print*) pre-makeready
VVDA m *abbr* Verlegerverband Deutscher Anzeigenblätter e.V.

W

W-Markt *m*
→ Wiederverkäufermarkt
Wabenlinse f *(phot)* (des Belichtungsmessers) multicellular lens
Wachsmatrize f *(print)* wax stencil, wax mold electrotype, wax
  A duplicate printing plate made from a wax mold of an original.
Wachspapier *n* wax paper, waxed paper
Wachstum *n (econ)* growth
Wachstumsfunktion f *(econ/stat)* growth function
  An expression giving the size of a population as a function of a time variable, and hence describing the course of its growth.
Wachstumsideologie f *(econ)* ideology of growth, growth ideology
Wachstumskurve f *(econ/stat)* growth curve
  Any curve, especially one that is theoretical or fitted to data, that shows the growth of some dependent variable. Growth curves generally are exponential in form.
Wachstumsmodell *n (econ/stat)* growth model
Wachtumsphase f **(im Produktlebenszyklus)** *(econ)* growth stage (in the product life cycle)
  The stage of a product's market-acceptance in which both sales and profits rise, often at a rapid rate. Competitors enter the market in large numbers if the profit outlook is particularly attractive. Sellers shift to a "buy-my-brand" rather than a "try-this-product" promotional strategy. The number of distribution outlets increases, economies of scale are introduced, and prices may come down a bit.
Wachstumspolitik f *(econ)* policy of growth, growth policy
Wachstumsstrategie f *(econ)* strategy of growth, growth strategy
Wahlspruch *m*
→ Slogan, Motto
wahrer Wert *m*
→ Erwartungswert
Wahrheit f **in der Werbung** truth in advertising
Wahrnehmung f *(psy)* perception
  The selection, organization, and interpretation by an individual of specific stimuli in a situation, according to prior learning, activities, interests, experiences, etc. Perception is a process and a pattern of response to stimuli. It is a function of the situational field, that is, of the total configuration of stimuli, as well as of previous social and cultural conditioning.
Wahrnehmungsabwehr f **(perzeptorische Abwehr** f) *(psy)* perceptual defense, *brit* defence
Wahrnehmungsgegenstand *m (psy)* percept
Wahrnehmungskarte f **(Wahrnehmungslandkarte** f) *(market res)* perceptual map, market map, connotative map, (Anfertigung von Wahrnehmungskarten) perceptual mapping, market mapping, connotative mapping
  A consumer research technique that rates consumer judgments of overall similarity or preference and finds literally a picture in which objects that are judged to be similar psychologically plot near each other in geometric space. However, in perceptual mapping the respondent is free to choose his own frame of reference rather than to respond to explicitly stated attributes.
Wahrnehmungspsychologie f perceptual psychology
Wahrnehmungsschwelle f
→ Reizschwelle
Wahrnehmungswirklichkeit f perceived reality
  Reality as it is perceived by relevant consumer groups. The term is increasingly used in court procedures and applies to the effects of advertising as they convey the image of a product to a consumer. Courts in Germany base decisions on wether a particular advertisement or campaign is misleading on what the audience perceives as real about the advertising, rather than by the literal meaning of the words in the message.
Wahrscheinlichkeit f *(stat)* probability
  The likelihood that out of a specified number of equally likely and mutually exclusive occurrences a given event or

relationship will occur. The concept thus refers to a proportion, i.e. the proportionate frequency with which a given outcome is expected out of the total frequency of all outcomes.

Wahrscheinlichkeit f **des Kaufs**
→ Kaufwahrscheinlichkeit

Wahrscheinlichkeitsauswahl f *(stat)*
1. (Verfahren) probability sampling
In the entire general process whereby inferences about a relatively large entity are drawn from parts of the entity, any type of sampling where there is a precise way of estimating the chances that particular parts, or combinations of parts, will be in a given grouping chosen for study.
2. (Stichprobe) probability sample
A sample drawn in such a way that each member of the population, (→) Grundgesamtheit, from which the sample is drawn, e.g. households or individuals, has a known probability of being included in the sample. In equal-probability samples, each member of the population has an equal probability of selection; in unequal-probability samples, certain types of members of the population are over- or undersampled — that is, are given a greater or lesser chance of falling into the sample than their proportion in the population would determine.

Wahrscheinlichkeitsdichte f *(stat)* probability density

Wahrscheinlichkeitsdichtefunktion f *(stat)* probability density function

Wahrscheinlichkeitsfunktion f *(stat)* probability function

Wahrscheinlichkeitsgrenze f *(meist pl* **Wahrscheinlichkeitsgrenzen**) *(stat)* probability limit(s) *(pl)*

Wahrscheinlichkeitsnetz n *(stat)* probability grid

Wahrscheinlichkeitspapier n probability paper

Wahrscheinlichkeitsrechnung f probability calculus

Wahrscheinlichkeitsstichprobe f *(stat)* probability sample
→ Wahrscheinlichkeitsauswahl

Wahrscheinlichkeitsstichprobenbildung f (**Wahrscheinlichkeitsauswahlverfahren** n, **Wahrscheinlichkeitsstichprobenverteilung** f) *(stat)* probability sampling
→ Wahrscheinlichkeitsauswahl

Wahrscheinlichkeitsverteilung f *(stat)* probability distribution

Wald-Wolfowitz-Test m (**Iterationstest** m, **Wald-Wolfowitzscher Iterationstest** m, **Wald-Wolfowitzscher Lauftest** m) *(stat)* Wald-Wolfowitz runs test, Wald-Wolfowitz test, runs test
A nonparametric test of significance, (→) Signifikanztest, usually used with independent samples to test for differences in central tendency. The data from the combined samples are arranged in order of magnitude, and the number of runs, (→) Iteration, is counted. For small samples the critical value for this statistic is obtained from a special table; for large samples there is an approximate z test, (→) z-Test.

Wald-Regel f
→ Minimax-Regel (Minimax-Kriterium)

Walze f *(print)* roller
→ Zylinder

Walzendruck m *(print)* cylinder printing
The type of printing with a printing press in which the paper is carried over and around a cylinder, which impress it on the type form.

Walzendruckmaschine f *(print)* cylinder printing machine

Walzenpapier n bowl paper

Walzentext m *(film/TV)* crawl, creeping title
→ Rolltitel

Wandbemalung f *(outdoor advtsg)* painted wall, wall painting
The use of outdoor advertisements in which the copy and art elements are manually painted on a building wall.

Wanderausstellung f *(econ)* traveling exhibition, *brit* travelling exhibition, traveling display
An exhibit of point-of-purchase material which is the property of the advertiser and is moved from one dealer or one location to another.

Wandermaske f *(film/TV)* traveling matte, traveling mat
A mask stretching over a number of motion picture or television frames, used to achieve certain optical effects.

Wandermaskentrick m (**Wandermaskenverfahren** n) *(film/TV)*
1. (Einzelaufnahme) traveling matte shot, traveling mat shot, matte shot, mat shot 2. (Verfahren) traveling matte, traveling mat
An optical effect in which one figure is superimposed over another and backgrounds in a manner which results in a convincingly integrated image.

Wanne

Wanne f *(radio/TV)* **1.** (Licht) lighting trough **2.** (Ton) line source loudspeaker, line source unit
Ware f *(oft pl* **Waren)** *(econ)* product(s) *(pl)*, merchandise, (Handelsware) commodity
Warenabsatz m
→ Absatz
Warenangebot n
→ Angebot, Sortiment
Warenaufsteller m **(Warenständer** m**)** *(POP advtsg)* floor stand, display stand
A standing mount used for the display of retail merchandise.
Warenauslage f *(POP advtsg)* product display, merchandise display, (im Geschäft) in-store display
The way merchandise is organized and arranged at each location in the store layout. Effective displays should attract customer attention and interest by enhancing the appeal of the merchandise on display. The ultimate objective of display is to raise the amount of customer purchases by increasing the level of the pass-buy-ratio. That is, the display should make merchandise so appealing that a higher proportion of shoppers who pass the display will decide to purchase the merchandise than would have done so in absence of the display. There are some general types of display approaches and strategies. Among the most important of these are 1. open displays, 2. theme displays, 3. lifestyle displays, 4. coordinated displays, 5. classification dominance displays, 6. vertical presentation displays, 7. use of flexible fixtures in display, and 8. use of videotapes in display.
Warenauslagefläche f *(retailing)* display space
Warenauslieferung f
→ Auslieferung
Warenausstattung f
→ Ausstattung
Warenausstellungswagen m **(Warenausstellungsbus** m**)** *(retailing)* merchandising bus
Warenauszeichnung f *(econ)* product labeling, labeling
The design of that part of products which conveys verbal information about the product or the seller. It may be affixed directly to the product itself, may be a part of the package, or may be a tag securely attached to the product.
Warenautomat m
→ Verkaufsautomat

Warenbehälter m *(retailing)* dump bin
A merchandiser built to contain merchandise as it is literally dumped into it from the shipping case. Only the one product is displayed in it.
Warenbestand m *(econ)* merchandise stock
Warenbörse f
→ Produktenbörse
Warengestaltung f
→ Produktgestaltung
Warengruppe f
→ Produktgruppe
Warenhaus n department store
A large retailing business unit which handles a wide variety of shopping and specialty goods, including women's ready-to-wear and accessories, men's and boy's wear, piece goods, small wares, and home furnishings, and which is organized into separate departments for purposes of promotion, service and control.
Warenköder m
→ Lockangebot (Lockvogelangebot)
Warenkorb m *(stat/econ)* commodity basket, market basket
→ Lebenshaltungskostenindex
Warenmarkierung f
→ Markierung
Warenmuster n **(Warenprobe** f**)** *(promotion)* sample, product sample, sample product, free sample, leave behind, (verkäuflich) salable sample, saleable sample
A representative item or portion used by salesmen to assist in convincing buyers of a product's quality.
Warenprozeßpolitik f
→ Marketinglogistik
Warenpyramide f *(POP advtsg)* floor pyramid
A merchandise display of several levels, approximately to eye height.
Warenrückvergütung f
→ Rückvergütung
Warensortiment n
→ Sortiment
Warenstapel m **(Stapelauslage** f**)** *(POP advtsg)* mass display, jumble display
A variety of products piled together in a bin, basket, or on a counter or table.
Warentest m **(vergleichender Warentest** m**)** *(econ)* product rating

Warentisch m (**Warenauslagetisch** m)
(POP advtsg) dump table, product
display table, display table
   A display table on which merchandise
   items are stacked or dumped.

Warenverpackung f
→ Verpackung

Warenzeichen n (econ) trademark,
trade-mark
   A brand or part of a brand that is given
   legal protection because it is capable of
   exclusive appropriation; because it is
   used in a manner sufficiently fanciful,
   distinctive, and abritrary, because it is
   affixed to the product when sold, or
   because it otherwise satisfies the requirements set up by law. Trademark is
   essentially a legal term and includes only
   those brands or parts of brands which
   the law designates as trademarks.

Warenzeichengesetz n (**WZG**) (econ)
trademark law
   The statute governing the registration of
   trademarks and the other identifying
   symbols on products and services.

Warenzeichenrecht n (econ)
trademark legislation

Warenzeichenregister n (**Warenzeichenrolle** f) (econ) principal
register
   The register in the German Federal
   Patent Office (Bundespatentamt) in
   which trademarks are registered. Entry
   in the register gives the registrant the
   exclusive right to use the mark in
   commerce. It also gives him the right to
   sue in German courts and to prevent
   importation of goods bearing an
   infringing mark. Marks must have been
   in lawful use in commerce for at least
   one year to be eligible.

Warenzeichenschutz m (econ)
trademark protection
→ Warenzeichen, Warenzeichenregister

Warmprägung f
→ Heißprägung

Warnhinweis m (**auf Werbemitteln**)
warning label (in advertisements)

Warnlicht n (film/radio/TV) cue light,
cue lamp, preview light, warning light
   A light used for signaling studio
   performers when the television camera
   or the microphone is on-the-air.

Warteschlange f (stat) queue, lineup,
line-up

Warteschlangenmodell n
(**Bedienungsmodell** n) (stat) queuing
model

Warteschlangenproblem n (stat)
queuing problem
   The problem of queues, or congestion,
   arises whenever there is a service to be
   offered and accepted rather than a
   product to be made. In general, the
   problem is concerned with the state of a
   system, e.g. the length of the queue (or
   queues) at a given time, the average
   waiting time, queue discipline and the
   mechanism for offering and taking the
   particular service. The analysis of
   queueing problems makes extensive use
   of the theory of stochastic processes,
   (→) Stochastik.

Warteschlangentheorie f (**Bedie-
nungstheorie** f) (stat) queuing theory

**Was-können-wir-uns-leisten-
Methode** f (der Werbebudgetierung)
→ finanzmittelbezogene Budgetierung

Waschzettel m (advtsg) blurb, (Buch)
flap blurb, jacket blurb
   A short piece of promotion copy.

Waschzetteltext m (advtsg) blurb
copy, canned copy

wasserabweisende Beschichtung f
water-repellent coating

Wasserfarbe f water color, brit water
colour, water ink
   A transparent water-base and water-
   soluble paint, especially one intended for
   use on paper.

Wasserzeichen n watermark, (auf
geripptem Papier) chain mark, chain
line
   A faint identifying design put into paper
   during manufacture, usually visible only
   when the paper is held against a light.

Wasserzeichenpapier n watermarked
paper

Wasserzeichenwalze f (**Egoutteur** m)
dandy roll, dandy roller, dandy
→ Egoutteur

WBZ abbr Werbender Buch- und
Zeitschriftenhandel

WDW abbr obsol Wirtschaftsverband
Deutscher Werbeagenturen

Wear-out-Effekt m
→ Werbeverschleiß

Wechselobjektiv n (phot)
interchangeable lens

Wechselsack m (**Dunkelsack** m)
(phot) changing bag
→ Dunkelsack

Wechselschalter m (radio/TV)
changeover switch, brit change-over
switch

wegretuschieren v/t (phot/print) to opaque, to block out, to stop out
   To eliminate areas from a photographic negative or print by retouching, masking or opaquing.
→ retuschieren
Wegretuschieren n (phot/print) blocking out, stopping out, opaquing
→ Retuschieren
Wegwerfpackung f
→ Einwegpackung
Wegwerfpreis m
→ Schleuderpreis
Wegwerfwerbung f (advtsg) ashcanning, junking
   In advertisement copy, the destruction of part of a competitive product, implying — often by means of illustration — that the knocked product is inferior and only fit to be thrown away. Acts of junking or mudslinging are derogatory to both product and industry, and offend against German unfair practice legislation.
weich adj (phot) (Bild) soft, blurred, (Negativ) weak, soft
   Pertaining to an image showing detail and gradation, but lacking proper contrast.
Weichbildscheibe f (phot) diffusion disk, diffusion disc
→ Softscheibe
Weichstrahler m (phot) diffuser, auch diffusor
Weichzeichner m (phot) soft-focus lens, soft-focus attachment, diffuser scrim
   A photographic lens giving soft or diffused images.
Weichzeichnung f (phot) soft focus, diffusion
Weißabgleich m (**Weißbalance** f) (film/TV) white balance
weißer Artikel m (**weiße Ware** f, **weißes Produkt** n)
→ anonyme Ware
weißer Kittel m (für Ärzte) (advtsg) (in Werbung) white coat (die das Tragen weißer Kittel in der Publikumswerbung untersagende gesetzliche Regel) white coat rule
   The restriction which prohibits advertisers from using spokesmen who purport or appear to be medical professionals (doctors, dentists, etc.) in advertisements, especially commercials.
weißer Rand m (outdoor advtsg) blanking area
   The white-paper area between the outside edges of an outdoor poster and the inside of the panel moulding.

weißes Papier n plain paper, white paper
weißes Produkt n
→ weißer Artikel
weißes Rauschen n (**Weißton** m) (sound) white noise
Weißfilm m white film, (Start) white leader, white spacing, blank film
Weißpegel m (**Weißwert** m) (TV) white level
Weißton m
→ weißes Rauschen
Weißwert m
→ Weißpegel
Weißzeile f (TV) white line
Weiteinstellung f (film/TV) extreme long shot (ELS), very long shot (VLS)
weiterkopiertes Einzelbild n (film/TV) stop frame, hold frame, freeze frame, frozen picture, still copy, suspended animation
   A single frame repeated serveral times to create an effect of suspended time and action.
→ Standbildverlängerung
Weiterverkauf m (econ) resale
→ Wiederverkauf
Weitester Empfängerkreis m (**WEK**) (Zeitschrift) etwa total number of (magazine) recipients
   The total number of individual and institutional recipients of a periodical publication who received at least one of 12 subsequent issues.
Weitester Hörerkreis m (**WHK**) (media res) total audience, total exposure, total listeners pl
→ Weitester Nutzerkreis
Weitester Leserkreis m (**WLK**) (media res) total audience, total audience impressions pl, total readers pl, total exposure, total effective exposure (TEE)
→ Weitester Nutzerkreis
Weitester Nutzerkreis m (**WNK**) (media res) total audience, total effective exposure (TEE)
   The total number of all readers, listeners, or viewers of an advertising medium with an exposure probability, (→) Nutzungswahrscheinlichkeit, higher than 0.
Weitwinkel m (phot) wide angle
Weitwinkelaufnahme f (phot) wide-angle shot, cover shot
Weitwinkelbereich m (phot) wide-angle range

Weitwinkelobjektiv *n* **(Weitwinkel** *m)*
(phot) wide-angle lens
A camera lens that covers a relatively larger area of a scene, with deeper perspective, than a normal lens at the same point.
WEK *abbr* Weitester Empfängerkreis
Welle *f* 1. *(radio)* wave
→ Wellenlänge
2. *(paper)* (Riffel) corrugation, flute
Wellenbahn *f (paper)* corrugated web
Wellenblende *f (film/TV)* wash dissolve, riffle dissolve
A move from one shot to the one following in which the new image appears as one or several wavy blurs that obscure the previous image.
Wellenlänge *f (radio)* wavelength, *brit* wave-length
Wellenlinie *f (print)* wavy rule, wavy line
Wellenplan *m (radio)* frequency allocation plan, frequency plan
Wellenschalter *m (radio)* waveband switch, band switch, wave changer
Wellenschwund *m (radio)* fading
→ Schwund
Wellpappe *f* corrugated board, corrugated cardboard, corrugated pasteboard, corrugated paper, cellular board
A container board composed of an inner corrugated thickness of paper glued to smooth outer faces.
Weltmarke *f (econ)* global brand, worldwide brand
A brand that is distributed and marketed worldwide, (→) Globalmarketing. The adoption of a policy of global brands is most useful when the company has a reputation of quality and technical excellence that can be carried into the international markets and where brands, (→) Markenartikel, are important to the consumer. A global brand policy has the following advantages: the ready-made base for the company's promotional effort provided by an already established brand; the preferences that exist in many countries for the foreign-made product; the desirability of better consumer recognition of the company's products; and the value of a reputation as an international firm with multinational resources and capabilities. Then the global brand leads to improved marketing communicatons, clearer identification of the company's products, and the possibility of better coordination of the company's worldwide advertising.

Welt-Urheberrechtsabkommen *n*
Universal Copyright Convention
Werbeabgabe *f*
→ Werbesteuer
Werbeabteilung *f* advertising department
Werbeabwehr *f* **(Abwehr** *f* **gegen Werbung)** advertising resistance
Werbeagent *m*
→ Werbefachmann
Werbeagentur *f* advertising agency, ad agency, agency
A professional organization that renders advertising services to clients, including such functions as planning, preparing, placing, and checking advertisements.
Werbeakademie *f* advertising academy
Werbeaktion *f* advertising campaign, promotional campaign
A coordinated advertising effort over a certain period of time in carefully selected media with a specific objective, such as by a bank to announce a new saving plan, or by a manufacturer to persuade the market of the superiority of his product's benefits so that his market share will rise.
Werbeaktivität(en) *f(pl)* advertising activity (activities *pl*)
Werbeakzidenzen *f/pl*
→ Akzidenzdruck (Akzidenzen)
Werbeanalyse *f* advertising analysis
Werbeanalytiker *m* advertising analyst
Werbeangebot *n*
1. → Sonderangebot
2. → Lockartikel
Werbeanhänger *m* advertising label
→ Anhänger
Werbeansage *f* **(Werbedurchsage** *f*) advertising announcement
→ Ansage
Werbeansatz *m* advertising approach
Werbeanschlag *m* advertising bill, advertising poster, advertising card
→ Anschlag
Werbeanstoß *m*
→ Werbekontakt
Werbeanstrengungen *f/pl* advertising efforts *pl*
Werbeanteil *m* **(Anteil** *m* **der Werbung)** advertising share, share of advertising (SOA)
Werbeantwort *f*
→ Rücklauf

Werbeantwortbrief m (**Werbeantwortumschlag** m) business reply envelope
→ Rückantwortbrief
Werbeantwortkarte f business reply card, advertising reply card
→ Rückantwortkarte
Werbeappell m advertising appeal, (eines Werbemittels) copy appeal
The means an advertiser uses to motivate a prospective.
Werbeargument n advertising point, advertising angle, copy angle, angle
Werbeart f (**Werbeform** f) type of advertising, kinds of advertising
Werbeartikel m advertising novelty, novelty, advertising specialty, specialty
A small, interesting, sometimes personally useful item with the name and the advertising message of the issuing company printed on it.
Werbeartikelhändler m (**Werbeartikelvertrieb** m) advertising novelty dealer, advertising novelty distributor, advertising specialty dealer, advertising specialty distributor
A wholesaler in the specialty advertising field handling various types of advertising novelties and providing assistance in planning advertising campaigns using such items.
Werbeassistent m advertising assistent
Werbeatelier n
→ Werbestudio
Werbeaufdruck m advertising imprint, imprint, (Händleraufdruck) dealer imprint
→ Eindruck
Werbeaufkleber m advertising label, poster stamp
→ Aufkleber
Werbeaufnahme f
→ Werbephoto
Werbeaufschrift f advertising label
Werbeauftrag m advertising order, advertisement order, (bei Werbung, die in Flächeneinheiten berechnet wird) space order, (bei Werbung, die in Zeiteinheiten berechnet wird) time order
Werbeaufwand m (**Werbeaufwendungen** f/pl) advertising expenditure, (Volumen) advertising weight, advertising volume, advertising support, support, (Höhe des Werbeaufwands) advertising level, level of advertising expenditure

The total amount of advertising in a specified period of time, as measured by the amount of money spent for it.
Werbeausbildung f (**werbliche Ausbildung** f) advertising education
Werbeausgaben f/pl advertising outlay(s) (pl), advertising expenses pl, advertising money
Werbeausgaben-Umsatz-Beziehung f (**Werbeausgaben-Absatz-Verhältnis** n) advertising-to-sales ratio, A/S ratio, conversion rate, cost per sale, cost per conversion, cost per order (cpo)
A measure of the effectiveness of advertising in terms of the sales value of the sales made divided by the cost of the advertising for the items sold.
Werbeaussage f
→ Werbebotschaft
Werbeaussendung f
→ Direktwerbeaussendung
Werbeauswirkung f
→ Werbewirkung
Werbebehauptung f advertising claim, copy claim
The benefit, or value, attributed to a product or service by an organization in its promotional activities.
Werbebeilage f
→ Beilage
Werbebeobachtung f advertising tracking, advertising observation
→ Trenderhebung
Werbeberater m advertising consultant, advertising counselor, brit counsellor
Werbeberatung f 1. (Beratungstätigkeit) advertising consultancy, advertising counsel
2. → Werbeberatungsbüro
Werbeberatungsbüro n advertising consultant, advertising counselor, brit counsellor
Werbeberichtigung f
1. → Berichtigungswerbung
2. → Werberevision
Werbeberuf m advertising profession
Werbeberührte m/pl (**Personen** f/pl **mit Werbekontakt**) exposed persons pl, exposed people pl
→ Kontakt
Werbeberührung f
→ Werbekontakt, Werbemittelkontakt, Kontakt
Werbebeschränkungen f/pl advertising restrictions pl
Both the legal and self-policing conditions imposed upon advertising by

governments, trade associations and media owners.

Werbebild *n* advertising picture

Werbeblock *m (radio/TV)* commercial pod, pod, commercial occasion, commercial break, clutter, clutter position, *brit* commercial slot
   In broadcasting, either a group of consecutive time periods reserved for advertising or the same time period from day to day. Under the German system of public-service broadcasting, (→) öffentlich-rechtlicher Rundfunk, commercials can only follow one another without intervening program time.

Werbebotschaft *f* **(Werbeaussage** *f***)** advertising message

Werbebranche *f* advertising industry, advertising trade, advertising profession

Werbebrief *m* advertising letter, sales letter, promotional letter
   A form of direct advertising consisting of a small sheet of paper printed on one or both sides for delivery by mail.

Werbebriefing *n* advertising briefing
   A more or less detailed statement of aim(s) in relation to the preparation of an advertisement, or series of advertisements, with the purpose of ensuring that copywriters are aware of their purpose and that their submissions may be evaluated by continuous reference to it.
   → Briefing

Werbebroschüre *f* advertising pamphlet, advertising folder, advertising booklet, advertising brochure
   → Broschüre

Werbebudget *n* **(Werbeetat** *m***)** advertising budget, (bewilligter Etat) advertising appropriation
   The amount of money set aside for spending on an advertising campaign or during a specified period of time, normally a fiscal year. Sometimes it represents the total sum available to cover all advertising expenditure including overheads.

Werbebudgetallokation *f* advertising budget allocation, advertising allocation, allocation of advertising expenditure, allocation
   The division of an advertising appropriation for specific purposes.

Werbebudgetierung *f* **(Bestimmung** *f* **des Werbeetats)** advertising budget determination, advertising budget appropriation, advertising budgeting, budgeting
   Advertisers use a variety of methods in determining advertising appropriations. However, there are three major methods for deciding how much a company is to spend on advertising in use by national advertisers: 1. the objective and task approach, (→) Ziel-Aufgaben-Methode, 2. budgeting by fixed guidelines, and 3. arbitrary budgeting, (→) intuitive Methode. There are three subcategories to the budgeting by fixed guidelines method of budget determination. The percentage-of-sales method, (→) umsatzbezogene Werbebudgetierung, is by far the most widely used, with some firms employing the unit-of-sale variation, (→) Verkaufseinheitsmethode. The third method uses advertising expenditures of competitors as the guide, (→) konkurrenzorientierte Budgetierung.

Werbebudgetplanung *f* advertising budget planning

Werbebüro *n* advertising office

Werbechancenanalyse *f* advertising opportunity analysis
   A stepwise procedure for integrating brand analysis, marketing objectives, marketing research, and judgment to produce an advertising strategy. The end result is a written strategy statement, a description of the opportunity for advertising that provides a road map for agency creatives and a benchmark for advertising evaluation.

Werbechef *m*
   → Werbeleiter

Werbedestinatare *m/pl*
   → Zielgruppe, Zielperson

Werbedia *n* **(Werbediapositiv** *n***)** advertising film slide, advertising slide
   → Dia(positiv), Diawerbung

Werbedosis *f* number of advertising exposures, advertising impressions *pl*

Werbedruck *m* advertising impact, advertisement impact, impact
   The degree to which or the force with which an advertising message, or campaign, affects the audience receiving it, measured by either the extent and degree of its awareness attainments, or the sales it produces.

Werbedrucksache *f* advertising matter

Werbedruckschrift *f*
   → Werbebroschüre

Werbedrucktest *m* **(Impakttest** *m***)** *(advtsg res)* advertising impact test, impact test

Werbedurchdringung

Werbedurchdringung f (Penetration f) advertising penetration, penetration
→ Penetration
Werbedurchführung f advertising execution, execution of advertising
Werbedurchsage f *(radio/TV)* advertising announcement, commercial announcement, spot announcement, announcement, spot
→ Durchsage, Ansage
Werbedynamik f dynamics pl *(construed as sg)* of advertising, advertising dynamics pl *(construed as sg)*
Werbeeffekt m
→ Werbewirkung
Werbeeffizienz f (Werbewirksamkeit f) advertising efficiency, efficiency of advertising
   The ability of advertising to reach (a) specified objective(s) with minimum cost.
Werbeeinblendung f *(radio/TV)* commercial cut-in, commercial break, (in eine Programmsendung) commercial integration, (eingeblendete Sendung) integrated commercial, blended commercial, cast commercial
   Any interruption in a broadcast program for a commercial, (→) Werbesendung.
Werbeeindruck m 1. (eingedruckte Werbung) advertising imprint, imprint
→ Eindruck
2. (allgemeiner Eindruck) commercial impression(s) *(pl)*, advertising impression(s) *(pl)*
Werbeeinfluß m advertising influence
Werbeeinkauf m
→ Mediaeinkauf
Werbeeinnahmen f/pl advertising receipts pl
Werbeeinsatz m
→ Werbeanstrengung, Werbeaufwand
Werbeelastizität f (der Nachfrage) *(econ)* advertising elasticity (of demand)
   The ratio of the percentage change of a company's sales to a percentage change in advertising expenditure.
Werbeelement n advertising element
Werbeentscheidung f advertising decision
Werbeerfolg m advertising effectiveness, (Einzelerfolg) advertising success
→ Werbewirkung, Werbewirksamkeit

Werbeerfolgsforschung f (Werbebewirkungsforschung f) *(advtsg res)* advertising effectiveness research
Werbeerfolgskontrolle f (Werbebewirkungskontrolle f) *(advtsg res)* advertising effectiveness control, effectiveness-of-advertising control
Werbeerfolgskriterium n criterion of advertising effectiveness
Werbeerfolgsmessung f *(advtsg res)* measurement of advertising effectiveness
Werbeerfolgsprognose f *(advtsg res)* advertising effectiveness forecast, forecast of advertising effectiveness, prognosis of advertising effectiveness, prediction of advertising effectiveness
Werbeergebnis n (greifbares Resultat n von Werbung) advertising result, *meist pl* advertising results
   Usually, the sales and profits outcome of advertising.
Werbeerinnerung f (Werbemittelerinnerung f) *(advtsg res)*
1. advertising recall, recall, (Texterinnerung) copy recall
   A person's ability to remember certain facts about his exposure, (→) Kontakt, to specific print or broadcast advertising, while being interviewed for research purposes.
→ Erinnerung
2. (an den Inhalt der Werbebotschaft) advertising playback, ad playback
3. (einen Tag nach Kontakt) day-after recall (DAR)
   An audience recall measured the day after an advertisement is exposed.
Werbeerinnerungstest m *(advtsg res)* advertising recall test, recall test, copy recall test
→ Werbeerinnerung
Werbeerlös m (Werbeertrag m) advertising revenue
Werbeerreichte m/pl
→ Werbeberührte
Werbeerträge m/pl
→ Werbeerlös
Werbeetat m
→ Werbebudget
Werbeetikett n advertising label, label
→ Etikett
Werbeevaluierung f advertising evaluation, (Werbemittelevaluierung) advertisement evaluation, ad evaluation, (Evaluierungsmethode) advertising evaluation technique, ad-evaluation technique

The process of and the techniques used in evaluating both the possible and actual results of an advertising campaign. The purpose of pretesting is much the same as that of laboratory or field tests of a new product, (→) Produktbewertung, before full production starts. Both types of research attempt to eliminate errors or weaknesses in design before a considerable sum of money is invested. Testing may apply to the advertisement or elements in it, such as the headline idea, basic theme, or illustrative treatment. It may apply to the proposition, such as a premium or special price, or to the use of a particular medium. The actual testing is usually carried out either by the advertising agency or by an independent research organization.

Werbeexemplar n **(Probeexemplar** n**)** (Zeitung/Zeitschrift) promotion copy
Werbefachhochschule f advertising college
Werbefachleute pl advertising experts pl, admen pl, adexperts pl
werbefachliche Ausbildung f
→ Werbeausbildung
werbefachlicher Beruf m
→ Werbeberuf
Werbefachmann m advertising expert, adexpert, advertising man, adman
    A specialist in preparing advertisements.
Werbefachschule f advertising trade school
Werbefachverband m advertising trade association, advertising association
Werbefachzeitschrift f advertising trade magazine, advertising trade journal, advertising magazine, advertising journal
Werbefachzeitung f advertising trade paper, advertising paper
Werbefaktor m advertising factor
Werbefaltprospekt m advertising folder
→ Faltprospekt, Prospekt
Werbefeldzug m **(Werbekampagne** f**)** advertising campaign
    An organized and coordinated course of advertising action, planned carefully to achieve predefined objectives.
Werbefernsehblock m
→ Werbeblock
Werbefernsehen n **(Fernsehwerbung** f**)** commercial television, commercial TV, television advertising, TV advertising

Werbefernsehkumulation f commercial clutter, clutter
→ Werbeblock
Werbefernsehzeit f commercial time, commercial time slot, commercial time segment, daypart, day part
Werbefernsehzuschauer m commercial television viewer, commercial viewer, (pl) commercial audience, commercial viewers pl
Werbefigur f trade character
    An animate being or animated object designed to identify and personify a product or an advertiser.
Werbefilm m advertising film, advertising picture, commercial picture, commercial film, commercial movie, publicity film, publicity picture
    A motion picture sponsored by an advertiser to promote a product through a selling message designed to create goodwill with selected groups of persons.
werbefinanziertes Fernsehen n sponsored television, sponsored TV
    A television broadcasting method where time periods are bought by companies, who provide their own producer, director, and artists for a show and during broadcasting advertise their company products. The method is not allowed in the German public-service broadcasting system,
    (→) öffentlich-rechtlicher Rundfunk.
werbefinanzierter Hörfunk m **(werbefinanziertes Radio** n**)** sponsored radio
→ werbefinanziertes Fernsehen
Werbefläche f advertising space, space
    The portion of a publication's pages, or outdoor or transit display areas, that may be purchased for advertising.
→ Anzeigenraum, Anschlagfläche.
Werbeflächenpächter m
→ Anschlagflächenpächter
Werbeflugblatt n advertising flyer, advertising flier, advertising handbill, advertising leaflet, advertising fly sheet, advertising bill
→ Flugblatt, Handzettel
Werbeform f
→ Werbeart
Werbeforschung f advertising research
    That branch of marketing research, (→) Marketingforschung, that studies the effectiveness of advertising, tests copy by different methods both before and after publication, conducts readership, recognition and recall studies, analyzes

Werbeforschungsbudget

coupon returns and other replies, and makes distribution cost analyses.
Werbeforschungsbudget n (**Werbeforschungsetat** m) advertising research budget
Werbeforschungsprojekt n advertising research project
Werbeforschungsstudie f (**Werbeforschungsuntersuchung** f) advertising research study, advertising research investigation
Werbefoto n
→ Werbephoto
Werbefotograf m
→ Werbephotograph
Werbefotografie f
→ Werbephotographie
werbefreie Zeit f (**werbefreie Sendezeit** f) (radio/TV) blocked-out time
Broadcasting time that is not sold to advertisers.
Werbefrequenz f
→ Werbehäufigkeit
Werbefunk m
→ Hörfunkwerbung
Werbefunkhörer m/pl **pro Tag** commercial radio listeners pl per day
Werbefunkhörer m/pl **pro Woche** commercial radio listeners pl per week
Werbefunkhöreranalyse f
→ Höreranalyse
Werbefunktion f advertising function
Werbefunkvertreter m (radio/TV) station representative, station rep
A person who solicits the purchase of commercial time from advertisers on behalf of a television or radio station.
Werbegabe f
→ Werbegeschenk
Werbegag m (**Reklamegag** m) advertising gimmick
→ Gag
Werbegedicht n advertising rhyme
Werbegemeinschaft f advertising cooperative
→ Gemeinschaftswerbung
Werbegemeinde m/pl
→ Zielgruppe
Werbegesamtausgaben f/pl total advertising expenditure
→ Werbeausgaben
Werbegeschenk n advertising gift, promotional gift, advertising specialty, specialty, advertising novelty, novelty, (einzelne Werbegabe) door opener

An inexpensive, possibly gimmicky gift, usually carrying an advertising message, a brand name or symbol.
Werbegesetz n advertising law
Werbegesetzgebung f advertising legislation
Werbegestalter m
→ Gestaltung
Werbegestaltung f advertising design
Werbegewinn m (**Werbeprofit** m) advertising profit, advertising payout
Werbegraphik f (**Werbegrafik** f) advertising art, creative art, commercial art
→ Gebrauchsgraphik
Werbegraphiker(in) (**Werbegrafiker(in)**) m(f) advertising artist, creative artist, commercial artist
→ Gebrauchsgraphiker
Werbegroßfläche f
→ Anschlaggroßfläche
Werbegrundsätze m/pl advertising policy
Werbehandzettel m
→ Werbeflugblatt
Werbehäufigkeit f (**Werbefrequenz** f) advertising frequency, frequency of advertising
Werbeheft n
→ Werbeexemplar
Werbehilfe f
→ Händlerhilfsmittel, Verkaufshilfe
Werbehinweis m
→ redaktioneller Hinweis
Werbehochschule f
→ Werbefachhochschule
Werbeidee f advertising idea
Werbeinserat n
→ Inserat, Anzeige
Werbeintensität f advertising intensity, intensity of advertising
Werbejargon m advertising slang, Madisonese
Werbejournal n
→ Werbefachzeitschrift
Werbekampagne f
→ Werbefeldzug
Werbekatalog m
→ Katalog
Werbekaufmann m
→ Werbefachmann
Werbeklub m advertising club
Werbekodex m (**Verhaltensregeln** f/pl **für die Werbepraxis**) code of advertising practice, advertising code,

code of advertising standards, advertising standards *pl*
   A code of ethical principles and rules governing the practice of advertising.
Werbekolonne *f*
→ Anschlagkolonne
Werbekommunikation *f* **(werbliche Kommunikation** *f*) advertising communication
Werbekonstante *f* advertising constant
Werbekontakt *m* advertising exposure, exposure to advertising
→ Kontakt, Werbemittelkontakt
Werbekontakter *m*
→ Kontakter
Werbekontrolle *f*
→ Werbeerfolgskontrolle
Werbekonzept *n* advertising concept
→ Konzept
Werbekonzeption *f* advertising conception
→ Konzeption
Werbekonzeptionstest *m*
→ Konzeptionstest
Werbekooperation *f*
→ Gemeinschaftswerbung
Werbekosten *pl* advertising cost(s) *(pl)*, cost(s) *pl* of advertising
→ Werbeaufwendungen; *vgl.* Werbungskosten
Werbekostenzuschuß *m* **(WKZ)** dealer promotion rebate, promotion rebate, promotion allowance, merchandising allowance
   An allowance made by a manufacturer or his agent to a wholesaler or retailer who agrees to promote the product purchased under allowance.
Werbekupon *m*
→ Kupon
Werbekurzfilm *m* advertising filmlet
→ Kurzfilm
Werbelehre *f* **(Werbekunde** *f*) advertising science
Werbeleistung *f* advertising performance
Werbeleistungsprüfung *f* **(Werbeleistungskontrolle** *f*) advertising performance audit
Werbeleiter(in) *m(f)* advertising manager, advertising executive
   An executive employee of an organization reponsible for the development, review and approval of advertising plans and, usually, executions of advertisements.
Werbeleitfaden *m* advertising guide

Werbeleitung *f* advertising management
→ Werbeleiter
Werbeleumund *m* advertising record
Werbelichtbild *n*
→ Werbedia
Werbemanagement *n*
→ Werbeleitung
Werbemanager(in) *m(f)*
→ Werbeleiter
Werbemann *m* **(Werber** *m*) advertising man, adman, ad man
→ Werbefachmann
Werbemannschaft *f*
→ Werbestab
Werbemappe *f* **(Angebotsmappe** *f*) advertising portfolio, advertising kit
Werbemarkt *m* advertising market
Werbemaßnahme *f* **(werbliche Maßnahme** *f*) advertising measure
Werbematerial *n* advertising material, advertising matter, advertising aids *pl*, promotion material, promotional material, leave behind
   An assortment of special materials sent to a dealer to help him tie in with the advertising theme of a product's manufacturer.
→ Händlerhilfen
Werbemedien *n/pl* **(Werbemedia** *n/pl*)
→ Werbeträger
Werbemethode *f* advertising method, advertising technique
Werbemittel *n* advertisement, ad, *auch* adv., advert
   An openly sponsored, multiply reproduced message, intended to persuade people to voluntarily produce a recommended behavior pattern, and presented by the purchased use of an advertising medium.
vgl. Werbeträger
Werbemittelanalyse *f* advertisement analysis, ad analysis, copy analysis
   Any research conducted to measure the effectiveness of a creative message.
Werbemittelbeachtung *f* advertisement noting, ad noting, noting
→ Starchtest
Werbemittelerinnerung *f* advertisement recall, ad recall, advertising recall, copy recall
→ Erinnerung
Werbemittelevaluierung *f* advertisement evaluation, ad

Werbemittelexperiment 564

evaluation, advertising evaluation, advertising copy evaluation, copy evaluation
→ Werbeevaluierung
Werbemittelexperiment *n* advertisement experiment, ad experiment, copy experiment
Werbemittelforschung *f* advertising copy research, copy research
   The analysis and evaluation of an advertisement, including the measurement of efficiency with which a particular idea can be communicated and of the degree of observation and audience it reaches.
Werbemittelfunktion *f* (der Werbung) copy function (of an advertisement) (Alfred Politz)
   The perception or readership (audience) of an advertisement.
   vgl. Werbeträgergestalter
Werbemittelgestalter *m*
→ Gestalter
Werbemittelgestaltung *f*
1. → Gestaltung
2. (Art der Gestaltung) advertisement format
   The general concept, form, makeup, or style of an advertisement.
Werbemittelgestaltungstest *m*
→ Gestaltungstest
Werbemittelkontakt *m* (**Werbekontakt** *m*) advertising exposure, advertisement exposure, exposure to an advertisement, exposure to advertising, ad exposure, (Starchtest) ad noting
→ Kontakt
Werbemittelkontaktchance *f*
→ Kontaktchance
Werbemittelkontaktmessung *f*
→ Kontaktmessung
Werbemittelleistung *f* (**Werbemittelqualität** *f*) copy performance, advertising performance
Werbemittel-Nachtest *m* (**Werbemittel-Posttest** *m*) advertisement post test, ad post test, copy posttest
→ Posttest
Werbemittel-Vorstudie *f* (**Werbemittel-Pretest** *m*) advertisement pretest, ad pretest, copy pretest
→ Pretest
Werbemittelreichweite *f*
→ Reichweite
Werbemittelstrategie *f* advertisement strategy, ad strategy, copy strategy

Werbemittelstreuung *f*
→ Streuung
Werbemitteltest *m* advertisement test, advertising test, copy test
   A preliminary trial of various types of copy appeals to measure their probable effectiveness in use.
Werbemittelumsätze *m/pl* advertising turnover
→ Werbeumsatz
Werbemittelwiedererkennung *f* advertisement recognition, ad recognition, advertising recognition, copy recognition
→ Wiedererkennung
Werbemittler *m* (**Werbungsmittler** *m*, **Werbemittlung** *f*) advertising broker, advertising contractor
   A broker of advertising space and/or time.
Werbemix *n* advertising mix
→ Kommunikations-Mix
Werbemobile *n*
→ Mobile
Werbemodell *n* advertising model
Werbemöglichkeit *f* advertising opportunity
→ Werbechance
Werbemonopol *n* advertising monopoly
Werbemusik *f* advertising music, music in advertising
werben *v/t* 1. (Werbung treiben) to advertise, *Am auch* to advertize
2. (Kunden, Abonnenten, Personal werben) to recruit, to solicit
3. (Haustürwerbung treiben) to canvass, *auch* to canvas
Werbenachlaß *m*
→ Werberabatt
werbende Führung *f* human relations *pl* (construed as sg)
→ Human Relations
Werbender Buch- und Zeitschriftenhandel *m* (WBZ) *etwa* subscription book and magazine trade
Werbenummer *f*
→ Werbeexemplar
Werbeobjekt *n* (**Werbegegenstand** *m*) advertising object
Werbeorganisation *f* advertising organization, *brit* organisation
Werbeoptimierung *f*
→ Optimierung
Werbeoptimierungsmodell *n*
→ Optimierungsmodell

Werbepackung f
→ Probepackung
Werbepause f advertising hiatus, hiatus, out period
A more or less extended, temporary cessation of advertising schedules between flights.
→ phasenweise Werbung
Werbeperiode f **(Werbephase** f**)** advertising period, advertising stage, advertising phase, flight
→ phasenweise Werbung
Werbephoto n **(Werbefoto** n**)** advertising photo, advertising photography
Werbephotograph m **(Werbefotograf** m**)** advertising photographer
Werbephotographie f **(Werbefotografie** f**)** 1. advertising photography 2. → Werbephoto
Werbeplakat n
→ Plakat
Werbeplakette f advertising button, advertising badge
→ Anstecknadel
Werbeplan m advertising plan, (Zeitplan) advertising schedule
The detailed program of planned advertisement insertions, showing detailed costs, timing, nature of media and the bookings to be reserved.
→ Mediaplan
Werbeplaner m advertising planner
Werbeplanung f advertising planning, campaign planning, (Zeitplanung) advertising scheduling, scheduling
Werbepolitik f advertising policy
Werbepraktikant(in) m(f) advertising intern
Werbepraktik(en) f(pl) **(Werbeusance** f**)** advertising practice
Werbepraktiker m advertising practitioner
Werbepraxis f advertising practice, practice in advertising
Werbeprämie f advertising premium, advertising bonus
→ Bonus, Prämie, Zugabe
Werbepräsentation f
→ Präsentation
Werbepreis m
→ Sonderangebotspreis
Werbepreisausschreiben n
→ Preisausschreiben
Werbepreisnachlaß m advertising discount, advertising allowance
→ Rabatt, Werbekostenzuschuß

Werbeprogramm n **(Grundkonzept** n **der Werbung)** advertising platform, copy platform, copy outline, advertising program, brit programme
The statement of the basic idea for an advertising campaign, and any instructions as to the order of significance of the various selling points and elements of any advertisement.
Werbeprospekt m
→ Prospekt
Werbeprovision f
→ Provision
Werbepsychologie f advertising psychology
Werbepublikation f advertising publication
Werbepublikum n advertising audience
Werber m 1. → Abo-Werber
2. → Propagandist
3. → Werbungtreibender
4. → Handelsvertreter
Werberabatt m advertising discount
→ Rabatt
Werberat m Am advertising review board, brit advertising standards authority
→ Deutscher Werberat
Werbereaktion f **(Reaktion** f **auf Werbung)** advertising response, response to advertising
→ Kaufreaktion
Werbereaktionsfunktion f advertising response function
A function describing the quantitative relationship between some input of advertising and some output or effect of presumed value for the advertiser.
Werberealisation f
→ Werbedurchführung
Werberecht n advertising law, advertising legislation, advertising regulations pl
werberechtliche Vorschriften f/pl advertising regulations pl
Werbereichweite f
→ Reichweite
Werbereim m advertising rhyme
Werberendite f advertising yield
Werberentabilität f advertising payout rate, payout rate of advertising, payout rate
The ratio
change in gross contribution − change in advertising expenditure = change in advertising expense.

Werberevision f advertising performance audit
Werberhythmus m advertising flight, flight schedule
→ phasenweise Werbung
Werberichtlinien f/pl
→ Verhaltensregeln
Werberundbrief m **(Werberundschreiben** n**)** advertising circular, circular letter
→ Werbebrief
Werbesaison f
→ Werbeperiode
Werbesatz m catchline, catch line, catch phrase
Werbeschaffender m
→ Werbeberuf
Werbeschild n
→ Schild
Werbeschlager m advertising hit
Werbeschreiben n
→ Werbebrief
Werbeschrift f
→ Werbebroschüre, Werbeprospekt
Werbeschulung f
→ Werbeausbildung
Werbeselbstkontrolle f self-policing of advertising
Werbesendezeit f **(Sendezeit** f **für Werbung)** commercial time, commercial occasion, availability, brit commercial slot, time slot
  The specific time period reserved for the broadcast of commercials.
Werbesendung f 1. *(radio/TV)* commercial, commercial broadcast, *(radio)* radio commercial, *(TV)* television commercial, TV commercial
  An advertising message of given length on television or radio.
2. → Werbeaussendung
Werbesendungskontakt m **(Kontakt** m **mit einer Werbesendung)** *(media res)* commercial exposure
  The number of sets actually tuned to a television or radio station at the time when a commercial is delivered.
Werbeslang m
→ Werbejargon
Werbesoziologie f advertising sociology, sociology of advertising
Werbespezialist m
→ Werbefachmann
Werbespot m **(Kurzwerbesendung** f**)** *(radio/TV)* spot announcement, spot, spot commercial, commercial spot
  By some miraculous way the term "Werbespot" or "Spot" (frequently pronounced "Shpot" has come to be more widespread in German as a term to describe a commercial broadcast than the original German word "Werbesendung".
Werbesprache f advertising language, language of advertising
→ Werbejargon
Werbespruch m advertising slogan, slogan
→ Slogan
Werbestatistik m advertising statistics *pl (construed as sg)*
Werbestempel m **(Freistempel** m**)** indicia, advertising indicia
  An envelope marking accepted by a postal service in lieu of stamps.
Werbesteuer f advertising tax, tax on advertising
Werbestil m advertising style, style of advertising
Werbestrategie f advertising strategy, (Werbemittelstrategie) copy strategy
  The overall plan behind an advertising campaign.
Werbestreifen m
→ Werbefilm
Werbestreuplanung f
→ Mediaplanung (Streuplanung)
Werbestreuung f
→ Streuung
Werbestudium n advertising studies *pl*
Werbesubjekt n advertising subject
→ Zielperson, Zielgruppe
Werbesymbol n advertising symbol
Werbetafel f
→ Anschlagtafel
Werbetaktik f advertising tactics *pl (construed as sg)*
Werbetätigkeit f **(Werbeaktivität** f**)** advertising activity
Werbeteam n **(Werbemannschaft** f, **Werbestab** m**)** advertising team, advertising group, advertising staff
Werbetechnik f
→ Werbemethode
Werbetechnikum n
→ Werbefachhochschule
Werbeterminologie f advertising terminology
Werbetest m advertising test, (Feldtest) advertising field test, advertiser's test
→ Test, Werbemitteltest
Werbetext m advertising copy, copy, advertising text, (Textteil eines Werbemittels) body copy

Broadly, all elements, both verbal and visual, which will be included in the finished advertisement. In a narrow sense, the verbal elements only, or the material to be set by a compositor.
Werbetextanalyse f advertising copy analysis, copy analysis, copy research
→ Werbemittelanalyse
Werbetexten n copywriting
Werbetexter m **(Texter** m) copywriter, copy writer, advertising copywriter, advertising copy writer
→ Texter
Werbetheorie f advertising theory, theory of advertising
Werbeträger m advertising medium, medium, advertising vehicle, vehicle
The medium that brings the advertising message to the attention of the consumer.
vgl. Werbemittel
Werbeträgeranalyse f
→ Mediaanalyse
Werbeträgerauswahl f
→ Mediaselektion
Werbeträgerbewertung f **(Werbeträgerevaluierung** f) advertising media evaluation, media evaluation
→ Mediaevaluierung
Werbeträgererinnerung f advertising media recall, media recall
→ Erinnerung; *vgl.* Werbemittelerinnerung (Werbeerinnerung)
Werbeträgerforschung f **(Mediaforschung** f) advertising media research, media research
→ Mediaforschung
Werbeträgerfunktion f (der Werbung) media function (of an advertisement) (Alfred Politz)
The exposure of an advertisement.
vgl. Werbemittelfunktion
Werbeträgergewichtung f
→ Mediagewichtung
Werbeträgerimage n
→ Medienimage
Werbeträgerkombination f
→ Mediakombination
Werbeträgerkontakt m *(media res)* media exposure
Exposure, (→) Kontakt, to an advertising medium, (→) Werbeträger.
Werbeträgerplanung f
→ Mediaplanung
Werbeträgerreichweite f
→ Mediareichweite
Werbeträgerstrategie f media strategy

The overall plan and method used to achieve the media objectives of an advertising plan; it is the idea behind the plan of action or final blueprint for bringing the advertising message to the consumers. The variables in media strategy are in selecting a media mix, (→) Media-Mix, from among the alternative offerings of magazines, newspapers, broadcast stations or networks, outdoor and car card representatives, and direct-mail services.
Werbeträgerverbreitung f
→ Verbreitung
Werbeträgervertrieb m
→ Medienvertrieb
Werbeträgerwiedererkennung f advertising media recognition, media recognition
→ Wiedererkennung
Werbetreibender m
→ Werbungtreibender
Werbeuhr f **(Reklameuhr** f) clock spectacular
→ Uhrenanlage (Uhrenwerbeanlage)
Werbeumsatz m **(Werbeumsätze** m/pl) advertising turnover, advertising sales pl
Werbeumwelt f advertising environment, environment of advertising
→ Umwelt
Werbe- und Verkaufshilfen f/pl
→ Verkaufshilfen, Händlerhilfen
Werbeunterlagen f/pl
→ Werbematerial
Werbeunterricht m
→ Werbeausbildung
Werbeusance f advertising practice
Werbevariable f advertising variable
Werbeveranstaltung f advertising event, advertising show, promotional event
Werbeverband m
→ Werbefachverband
Werbeverbot n advertising prohibition
Werbeverfahren n
→ Werbemethode
Werbeverkauf m
→ Sonderveranstaltung
Werbeversand m promotional mailing
Werbeverhalten n advertising behavior, *brit* behaviour
Werbevertrag m advertising contract, advertising agreement, (Agenturvertrag) agency agreement, (für Werbung, die in Flächeneinheiten

berechnet wird) space contract, (für Werbung, die in Zeiteinheiten berechnet wird) time contract
    A contractual agreement between an advertiser and a communications medium for advertising space or time; usually negotiated by an advertising agency.
Werbevolumen *n* advertising volume, advertising weight, adstock
    The total amount of advertising in a specified period of time, as measured by advertising expenditure.
Werbevorbereitung *f* preparation of advertising, campaign preparation, copy preparation
Werbevorspann *m* **(Vorspann** *m* **vor einem Werbefilm)** *(film/TV)* cowcatcher
Werbewagen *m*
→ mobile Großfläche
Werbewand *f* **(Werbefläche** *f* **)** billboard hoarding, hoarding
    A large, upright structure for poster advertising.
Werbeweg *m* advertising channel
Werbewert *m* advertising value
Werbewesen *n*
→ Werbung
Werbewiderstand *m* 1. advertising resistance, resistance to advertising 2. → Reaktanz
Werbewimpel *m* **(Werbefähnchen** *n*) advertising pennant, pennant, flag
Werbewirksamkeit *f* advertising effectiveness
Werbewirkung *f* advertising effect
Werbewirkungsanalyse *f* advertising effectiveness analysis, analysis of advertising effectiveness
Werbewirkungsforschung *f* advertising effectiveness research
Werbewirkungsfunktion *f* advertising response function
→ Werbereaktionsfunktion
Werbewirkungshypothese *f* advertising effectiveness hypothesis
Werbewirkungskontrolle *f*
→ Werbeerfolgskontrolle
Werbewirkungskriterium *n*
→ Werbeerfolgskriterium
Werbewirkungskurve *f* advertising response curve
→ Werbereaktionsfunktion
Werbewirkungsmessung *f*
→ Werbeerfolgsmessung
Werbewirkungsmodell *n* model of advertising effect

Werbewirkungsprüfung *f*
→ Werbeerfolgskontrolle
Werbewirtschaft *f* advertising industry, advertising trade, advertising
Werbewissenschaft *f* advertising science
Werbezeichner(in) *m(f)* advertising cartoonist
Werbezeichnung *f* advertising cartoon
Werbezeit *f* **(Werbesendezeit** *f,* **Sendezeit** *f* **für Werbung)** *(radio/TV)* commercial time
→ Werbesendezeit
Werbezeitschrift *f*
→ Werbefachzeitschrift
Werbezeitung *f*
→ Werbefachzeitung
Werbezettel *m*
→ Handzettel
Werbeziel *n* advertising objective, advertising goal, advertising end
    A specific communication task to be accomplished among a defined audience to a given degree in a given period of time.
Werbezone *f* **(Werbegebiet** *n,* **Streufeld** *n*) advertising zone
Werbezugabe *f* advertising premium, premium
→ Zugabe
Werbezweck *m* advertising purpose
Werbezyklus *m* advertising cycle
werblich *adj* advertising, advertisement, ad
werbliche Effizienz *f*
→ Werbeleistung
werbliche Kommunikation *f*
→ Werbekommunikation
werbliche Sozialisation *f* advertising socialization, *brit* socialisation
→ Konsumentensozialisation
Werbung *f* **(Reklame** *f,* **Werbewesen** *n*) advertising, *Am ungebr auch* advertizing
    Any paid form of non-personal presentation and promotion of ideas, goods, or services by an identified sponsor. It involves the use of such media as the following: magazine and newspaper space, motion pictures, outdoor (posters, signs, skywriting, etc.), direct mail, novelties (calendars, blotters, etc.), radio and television, cards (car, bus, etc.), catalogues, directories and references, programs and menus, circulars. Advertising is generally but not necessarily carried on through mass media. While the postal system is not

technically considered a "paid" medium, material distributed by mail is definitely a form of presentation that is paid for by the sponsor.
Werbung *f* **am Verkaufsort**
→ POP-Werbung
Werbung *f* **für Investitionsgüter**
→ Investitionsgüterwerbung
Werbung *f* **für Konsumgüter**
→ Konsumgüterwerbung
Werbung *f* **im Erzählstil** narrative advertising, narrative copy
An imaginative approach to the reader, listener, or viewer which presents a story about how the product or service played an important role in the life of someone with whom a member of the audience can identify. This type of copy generally consists of four parts: the predicament or problem being faced, the discovery of the solution (provided by the product or service), the happy ending, and the transition which ends with a direct suggestion to the audience.
Werbung *f* **in Fachkreisen (Fachwerbung** *f*) professional advertising
Any advertising a manufacturer of a product, a producer of a service, or other supplier addresses directly to persons or organizations who can specify it for use by those whom they advise.
vgl. Publikumswerbung
Werbung *f* **in streufähigen Werbemitteln** above-the-line advertising
All advertising in traditional, commission-paying media, such as the press, broadcast media, motion pictures, outdoor and transit media.
→ klassische Werbung; *vgl.* Werbung in nicht streufähigen Werbemitteln
Werbung *f* **in nichtstreufähigen Werbemitteln** below-the-line advertising
All advertising that does not take place in the traditional, commission-paying media, e.g. merchandising, point-of-purchase advertising, direct mail, trade shows and exhibitions, etc.
vgl. Werbung in streufähigen Werbemitteln
Werbungdurchführung *f*
→ Werbedurchführung
Werbungschaffender *m*
→ Werbeschaffender
Werbungskosten *pl Am* class B deductions *pl, brit* expenses *pl* against earnings
Werbungsmittler *m*
→ Werbemittler

Werbungsvertreter *m*
→ Abonnementswerber
Werbungtreibender *m* advertiser, (in Medien, deren Preise nach Flächeneinheiten berechnet werden) space buyer, (in Medien, deren Preise nach Zeiteinheiten berechnet werden) airtime buyer, time buyer, (Sponsor) sponsor
An organization, such as a business firm, or an individual who pays for advertising, i.e. the client of an advertising agency.
Werkaufnahme *f*
→ Standbild
Werkbruch *m*
→ Kreuzbruch
Werkdruck *m* bookwork, book printing
vgl. Akzidenzdruck
Werkschrift *f*
→ Brotschrift
Werkzeitschrift *f* **(Betriebszeitschrift** *f*, **Hauszeitschrift** *f*) company magazine, house journal, house magazine, house organ, internal house organ
A publication issued periodically by a business concern to further its own interests among its employees and its salesmen.
vgl. Kundenzeitschrift
Werkzeitung *f* company paper, company organ, house organ
→ Werkzeitschrift
Werkzeitungsredakteur *m* industrial editor
Wert *m* value
1. An abstract, generalized principle of behavior to which the members of a group feel a strong, emotionally toned positive commitment and which provides a standard for judging specific acts and goals. Values provide the generalized standards of behavior that are expressed in more specific, concrete form in social norms. They are essential organizing principles for the integration of individual and group goals.
2. The characteristic of a service or a product which induces people to sacrifice some portion of their purchasing power, past, present, or future, in order to obtain it.
3. The utility of a product measured in money terms.
Wertanalyse *f* value analysis, value engineering, value control
The process and technique of examining every constituent of a product to ensure

that its cost is no greater than is necessary to carry out its function. By investigating the performance of a material or a part in terms of its function and its unit price, this analysis attempts to develop the most effective specifications at the lowest ultimate product cost. It will consider the effects of various substitutes, different manufacturing methods, real labor cost, source factors, etc.

Wert-Erwartungs-Modell *n*
→ Fishbein-Modell

Wertedynamik *f* **(Wertewandel** *m***)** dynamics *pl (construed as sg)* of value change, change of values

Wertemarketing *n* value marketing
A concept of a marketing system which integrates marketing, design, and communications into a mix made specifically for a particular business situation. By methodical research and observation of the flow of goods and services in a market, factors not pertinent can be eliminated while packaging, product and corporate image activities, and trademark and environment design may be given the required emphasis.

wertentsprechender Preis *m (econ)* value-in-use price

Wertgutschein *m* **(Geschenkgutschein** *m***)** gift coupon, gift voucher, premium token
A special incentive to purchase, usually involving a money-off against the next purchase of a qualifying brand or providing an opportunity for a special purchase.

Wertmarke *f*
→ Sammelgutschein

Wertrabatt *m (econ)* cash discount
→ Skonto

Wertreklame *f*
→ Wertwerbung

Wertwerbung *f* **(Wertreklame** *f* **)**
→ Zugabewerbung

Wettbewerb *m* 1. *(econ)* (Konkurrenz) competition
→ Konkurrenz
2. *(promotion)* (Werbewettbewerb) contest
→ Schaufensterwettbewerb

Wettbewerber *m*
→ Konkurrent

Wettbewerbsanalyse *f*
→ Konkurrenzanalyse

Wettbewerbsbeschränkung *f (econ)* restraint of trade
→ Konkurrenzausschluß

Wettbewerbsgesetz *n*
→ Gesetz gegen den unlauteren Wettbewerb (UWG)

Wettbewerbs-Paritäts-Methode *f* (der Werbebudgetierung)
→ konkurrenzbezogene Methode

Wettbewerbspräsentation *f* speculative presentation, *colloq* pitch
A demonstration by an agency to a client, showing how the agency would handle the account if it is awarded the business.
→ Präsentation

Wettbewerbsrecht *n* unfair competion legislation

Wettbewerbsregeln *f/pl* self-policing rules *pl* against unfair competition

Wettbewerbsverbot *n*
→ Konkurrenzausschluß

Wettbewerbsverein *m*
→ Gebührenverein

Wettbewerbsvorteil *m (econ)* competitive advantage, competitive edge
Any benefit or value provided by a product or company, often unique to the organization concerned, that gives it superiority in the marketplace.

Wettbewerbswerbung *f*
→ Konkurrenzwerbung

wettbewerbswidrige Werbung *f* unfair practice (in advertising)

WHK *abbr* Weitester Hörerkreis

Wickelfalz *m* reverse accordion fold

Wickelfalzung *f* reverse accordion folding

Widerdruck *m (print)* perfecting, second printing, verso printing, backing up, back up
vgl. Schöndruck

widerdrucken *v/i (print)* to perfect, to back up

Widerdruckform *f* **(Widerdruckseite** *f* **)** *(print)* second form, second forme, wire side

Widerdruckmaschine *f (print)* perfecting machine, perfecting press, perfector press, perfector

Widersprüchlichkeit *f* **der Kommunikation** discrepancy, communication discrepancy

Wiederabdruck *m* reprint

Wiederaufführung *f* film rerun, rerun

Wiederaufführungshonorar *n* **(Wiederholungshonorar** *n***)** *(radio/film/TV)* residual, re-use fee, S.A.G. fee
A royalty paid to a performer or other person by a television or radio station or

advertiser for a broadcast of a program or commercial.

Wiederaufnahme f *(film)* retake
Wiedereinführung f
→ Produktvariation
Wiedererkennung f *(media res)* recognition, (eines bestimmten Hefts) issue recognition, (Werbemittelwiedererkennung) advertising recognition, (Werbeträgerwiedererkennung) advertising media recognition, media recognition
In psychology, the awareness of having experienced some event, situation, or object previously. In media and advertising research, the remembrance of prior exposure, (→) Kontakt, to an advertising medium or an advertisement provoked by repeated exposure.
Wiedererkennungsbefragung f **(Wiedererkennungsumfrage** f) *(media res)* recognition survey, recognition test
Wiedererkennungsmethode f **(Wiedererkennungsverfahren** n) *(media res)* recognition method, recognition technique, issue method, issue technique
A method for testing advertising copy or media exposure in which respondents are shown an advertisement or an advertising medium and asked whether they saw it, read the copy, noted the illustration, etc.
Wiedererkennungstest m *(media res)* recognition test
Wiedererkennungswert m *(media res)* recognition value, recognition score, (Quote) recognition rating
Wiedergabe f replay, reproduction, playback, *colloq* repro
Wiedergabegerät n recorder, playback machine, playback unit, reproduction unit
wiedergeben v/t to reproduce, to render
Wiederholung f repetition, reiteration
The reiteration of an advertisement, slogan, or theme to strengthen its impression.
Wiederholungsanzeige f repeat advertisement, rerun
→ Wiederholung
Wiederholungsbefragung f
→ Trenderhebung
Wiederholungsbesuch m *(econ/survey res)* (Vertreter/Interviewer) callback, call-back, return call
A second or third call made by a sales representative or an interviewer to a

prospective customer or respondent subsequent to a previous one, as to reach a previously unavailable prospect or respondent, or as one of a series of interviews.

Wiederholungsgenauigkeit f **(Präzision** f) *(res)* precision
In measurement, having small measurement error, as indexed by the standard deviation. The more precise a measuring instrument is, the smaller the standard deviation of the values obtained from repeated measurements of an object.
vgl. Treffgenauigkeit
Wiederholungsrabatt m
→ Malrabatt
Wiederholungssendung f *(radio/TV)* rebroadcast
A broadcast program repeated at a different time.
Wiederholungsverfahren n **(Wiederholungstestverfahren** n, **Test-Retest-Methode** f) *(res)* test-retest-method, test-retest design
Any procedure for measuring the reliability, (→) Reliabilität, of a test by correlating the test scores from the same group of people on two different occasions.
Wiederholungskauf m **(Wiederkauf** m) *(econ)* repeat purchase, (Vorgang) repeat purchasing (Kaufakt)
The ultimate goal of all marketing and advertising effort is to convert trial purchasers, (→) Erstkäufer, into repeat purchasers, (→) Wiederholungskäufer. Once an organization has effectively identified itself to a customer through its brand name, the satisfied customer will seek that company's products for repurchase. This is most vital in the case of products that are subject to frequent usage, usually of low unit value and bought regularly for habitual consumption. Convenience plays a large part in such purchasing and substitution will often occur if the preferred brand is not readily available.
Wiederkäufer m *(econ)* repeat buyer, repeat purchaser
→ Wiederholungskauf
Wiederkaufrate f **(Wiederkaufquote** f) *(econ)* repeat buying rate
→ Wiederholungskauf
wiederverfilmen *(film)* v/t to remake
Wiederverfilmung f *(film)* remake
A refilmed version of a previously filmed motion picture.

Wiederverkauf *m* (**Weiterverkauf** *m*)
(econ) resale
→ Handel
wiederverkaufen *(econ)* v/t to resell
Wiederverkäufer *m (econ)* reseller,
(Einzelhändler) retailer, (Großhändler) wholesaler
Wiederverkäufermarkt *m* (**W-Markt** *m*) *(econ)* reseller's market (Philip Kotler)
Wiederverkäuferrabatt *m*
→ Funktionsrabatt
Wiederverkaufsrate *f (econ)* resale rate
Wiederverkaufswert *m (econ)* resale value
Wiederverwendung *f (econ)* reuse, re-use
Wilcoxon-Test *m* (**Wilcoxon-Rangordnungs-Zeichentest** *m,* (**Wilcoxon-Test** *m* **für Paardifferenzen**) *(stat)*
Wilcoxon test, Wilcoxon signed ranks test, Wilcoxon T test, Wilcoxon's test, Wilcoxon matched pairs signed ranks test, signed ranks test
  A nonparametric test of significance, (→) Signifikanztest, for differences between paired observations, which takes into consideration not only the sign of the differences but also the magnitude of the differences. The absolute values of the differences are ranked, and then the ranks, (→) Rang, are assigned the sign of the corresponding differences. The test statistic is T, the sum of the ranks, (→) Rangsumme, with one sign, usually the ranks with the less frequent sign.
→ Mann-Whitney-Test
Wildanschlag *m* (**wilder Anschlag** *m*) *(outdoor advtsg)* **1.** (Vorgang) fly posting, sniping
  The posting of outdoor advertisements on sites for which a permission was not given or a rent not paid.
2. (einzelnes Plakat) fly poster
willkürliche Auswahl *f* (**Auswahl** *f* **aufs Geratewohl**) *(stat)* **1.** (Verfahren) accidental sampling, haphazard sampling, convenience sampling, street-corner sampling
  The most rudimentary form of nonprobability sampling in which subjects are selected indiscriminately until the desired sample size is reached. No attempt is made to control for biases and confounding errors. Street corner polls by mass media are typical of accidental sampling.

2. (unkontrollierte Zufallsstichprobe) accidental sample, haphazard sample, convenience sample
willkürliches Auswahlverfahren *n*
→ willkürliche Auswahl 1.
Windmaschine *f (film/TV)* blower, fan
Winkelhaken *m (print)* composing stick, compositor's stick, stick, setting stick, news stick
  In hand composition, (→) Handsatz, a compositor's device for holding hand-set individual type characters in sequence before they are transferred to a galley, (→) Setzschiff, for lock-up and proofing.
Winsorisation *f (stat)* Winsorization, *brit* Winsorisation
Winterschlußverkauf *m (retailing)* winter closing-out sale, winter sale(s) *(pl)*
→ Schlußverkauf;
vgl. Sommerschlußverkauf
Wirkdauer *f*
→ Streudauer
wirksame Reichweite *f (media res)* effective coverage, effective audience
Wirksamkeit *f* effectiveness
Wirksamkeitstest *m*
→ Werbewirksamkeitstest
Wirkung *f* effect
Wirkungsanalyse *f (advtsg res)* effectiveness analysis
Wirkungsbereich *m (outdoor advtsg)* effective circulation
  An estimate of the number of passers-by who might reasonably be considered capable of seeing an outdoor advertisement.
Wirkungsforschung *f* effectiveness research
Wirkungsfunktion *f* (**Wirkungskurve** *f*) *(res)* response function, response curve
→ Reaktionsfunktion
Wirkungsgewicht *n*
→ Kontaktgewicht
Wirkungshierarchiemodell *n*
→ Hierarchy-of-effects-Modell
Wirkungshypothese *f (res)* effect hypothesis
Wirkungskurve *f*
→ Wirkungsfunktion
Wirkungsmessung *f (res)* effect measurement, measurement of effect
Wirkungsmodell *n (res)* effect model
Wirkungspanel *n (media res)* impact panel
Wirkungstest *m (res)* impact test, effect test

A test of the degree to which an advertising message or campaign affects an audience in terms of awareness or behavioral response, such as sales.

Wirkungsverzögerung f *(res)* delayed response effect, carryover effect, delayed response, carryover, sleeper effect
  In the most general sense, any temporary or permanent change in an individual's behavior from prior exposure to one or more stimuli that may contaminate or otherwise modify his behavior. More specifically, in marketing the influence that is exerted on the sales of future periods by a marketing expenditure today. There is evidence enough to support a conclusion that an expenditure such as for a short advertising campaign may have a continuing effect indefinitely. Also, the propensity of a particular ad to be seen or recalled in periods following its deployment. This includes the building up of favorable attitudes and predispositions to buy in the mind of the consumer.

Wirtschaftlichkeit f *(econ)* profitability
Wirtschaftlichkeitsanalyse f *(econ)* profitability analysis
Wirtschaftlichkeitsvergleich m *(econ)* profitability comparison
Wirtschaftsadreßbuch n
  → Branchenadreßbuch, Handelsadreßbuch
Wirtschaftsblatt n
  → Wirtschaftszeitung
Wirtschaftsmagazin n **(Wirtschaftszeitschrift** f**)** business magazine, business journal
  A periodical publication dealing with management, manufacturing, sales or operation of industries or businesses, or some specific industry, occupation or profession, and being published to interest and assist persons actively engaged in the field it covers.
Wirtschaftspresse f business press
  A collective term for publications, advertising media, addressed to those in trade (merchandising trade papers), in production (industrial and vertical papers), in professions (professional), in executive of managerial positions (executive, horizontal) and, occasionally also in hotels, schools, hospitals, etc. (institutional).
Wirtschaftspublikation f business publication

Wirtschaftsredakteur m business editor, economics editor, economic editor
Wirtschaftsteil m (Zeitung) business section, business pages *pl*, commercial section, commercial pages *pl*
Wirtschaftsverband m **Deutscher Werbeagenturen e.V. (WDW)** Association of Medium-Sized German Advertising Agencies
Wirtschaftsverband m **inhabergeführter Werbeagenturen e.V. (WIW)** Association of Owner-Managed Advertising Agencies
Wirtschaftswerber m business advertiser
Wirtschaftswerbung f business advertising
  Any paid advertising for business purposes.
Wirtschaftswochenzeitschrift f business weekly, economic weekly, weekly business magazine
  → Wirtschaftspresse
Wirtschaftszeitschrift f
  → Wirtschaftsmagazin, Wirtschaftspresse
Wirtschaftszeitung f business newspaper, business paper
  → Wirtschaftspresse
Wischblende f *(film)* soft-edged wipe
wissenschaftliche Fachzeitschrift f scientific journal, science journal
Witzbild n
  → Karikatur
Witzseite f (Zeitung) comic section, funny page, funnies *pl*
WKZ *abbr* Werbekostenzuschuß
WLK *abbr* Weitester Leserkreis
WNK *abbr* Weitester Nutzerkreis
Wobbelbereich m *(radio)* frequency deviation range, sweep range, wobble range
Wobbelfrequenz f *(radio)* sweep frequency, wobble frequency
wobbeln *v/i (radio)* to sweep, to wobble, to wobbulate
Wobbeln n *(radio)* sweeping, wobbling, wobbulation
Wobbelsignal n *(radio)* sweep signal, wobble signal
Wobbelton m *(radio)* tone frequency run
Wobbler m **(Wobbelgenerator** m**)** *(radio)* wobbler, wobbulator, sweep-frequency generator

Wochenausgabe f (Zeitung/Zeitschrift) weekly edition
Wochenbericht m weekly report
Wochenblatt n
→ Wochenzeitschrift, Wochenzeitung
Wochenendausgabe f (Zeitung) weekend edition, Saturday edition, Sunday edition
Wochenendzeitung f weekend paper, Saturday paper, Sunday paper
Wochenmagazin n
→ Wochenzeitschrift
Wochenmarkt m *(econ)* weekly market
 A place where trading takes place once a week.
Wochenschau f *(film)* newsreel
Wochenschrift f
→ Wochenzeitung, Wochenzeitschrift
wöchentlich (wöchentlich erscheinend) *adj* weekly, *attr* every week (E.W.)
Wochenzeitschrift f (**wöchentlich erscheinende Zeitschrift** f) weekly magazine, weekly journal, weekly
Wochenzeitung f (**wöchentlich erscheinende Zeitung** f) weekly newspaper, weekly paper, weekly
Wohltätigkeitsanzeige f (**Spendenanzeige** f) charity advertisement, charity ad
Wohltätigkeitswerbung f (**Spendenwerbung** f) charity advertising
Wohnen- und Einrichten-Zeitschrift f (**Zeitschrift** f **für Wohnen und Einrichten**) home service magazine, home service book, shelter magazine, shelter publication, shelter book
 A magazine with editorial focus on the home, conveying such topics as home building, remodeling, decoration, and maintenance, and sometimes secondarily, family activities and problems.
Wölbung f (**Kurtosis** f, **Exzeß** m) (einer Verteilung) *(stat)* kurtosis, excess (of a distribution)
 The manner in which a frequency distribution, (→) Häufigkeitsverteilung, rises more or less sharply at the mode, (→) häufigster Wert, thus being more peaked (leptokurtic), more flat (platykurtic) or medium (mesokurtic).
Wolkenschreiber m
→ Himmelsschreiber
Wortassoziationstest m *(res)* word association test, association test
→ Assoziationstest
Wortergänzungstest m
→ Lückentest
Wortmarke f (**Wortzeichen** n)
→ Markenname
Wrattenfilter m *(phot)* Wratten filter
Wühlkiste f (**Wühlkorb** m) *(POP advtsg)* jumble basket, jumble display, dump table, dump bin, dumper
 A loosely arranged display of uniformly priced but heterogeneous objects offered for sale in a retail store.
Würfelsystem n
→ Matrixorganisation
Wurfsendung f direct-distribution advertising
Wz *abbr* Warenzeichen
WZG *abbr* Warenzeichengesetz

X

x-Achse *f*
→ Abszisse
x-Test *m (stat)* X test
Xenonlampe *f (phot)* xenon lamp
Xerographie *f* **(Trockenkopieren** *n*, **Trockenkopierverfahren** *n) (phot)*
xerography, xerographic process
 A photocopying process in which powdered ink is distributed electrostatically and made permanent by the application of heat.
xerographisch *adj (phot)* xerographic
Xerokopie *f (phot)* xerox copy
xerokopieren *v/t (phot)* to xerox
XL-Kamera *f*
→ Panographie

Y

y-Achse f
→ Ordinate
Y-Signal n *(radio)* luminance signal, y signal
→ Luminanz
Yagiantenne f *(TV)* yagi antenna, *brit* yagi aerial, *colloq* yagi
→ Luminanz
Yates-Korrektur f **(Yates'sche Korrektur** f, **Yates'sche Stetigkeitskorrektur** f, **Kontinuitätskorrektur** f) *(stat)* Yates' correction, Yates' correction for continuity, Yates' modified chi-square test
A relatively simple modification of a computed test statistic when the data are frequencies. It may be used when either the normal distribution, (→) Normalverteilung, or a χ^2 distribution (→) Chi-Quadrat-Verteilung, with one degree of freedom (→) Freiheitsgrad, is used to approximate the binomial distribution, (→) Binomialverteilung, (e.g., for a binomial test or test for independence), especially when one or more expected frequency value(s) is small. The correction consists in subtracting 0.5 from the absolute value of each difference between observed and expected frequencies.

Yule-Koeffizient m **(Yules Q** n) *(stat)* Yule coefficient, Yule's Q
A measure of association for categorical data classified on two dichotomous dimensions. Schematically, the data are arranged as follows: where a, b, c, and d are the cell frequencies. The coefficient of association is

$$Q = \frac{ad - bc}{ad + bc}$$

and ranges from -1 to +1, with 0 being no association and +/-1 being perfect association.

Z

z-Test *m stat)* z test
z-Transformation *f* **(Fishers z-Transformation** *f*) *(stat)* z transformation
   A log transformation of the sample values of a Pearson product moment correlation coefficient r, (→) Produkt-Moment-Korrelation. The z transformation is used for such purposes as testing the hypothesis that a sample is randomly selected from a population with a specified value of p other than zero, establishing a confidence interval for p, or testing the significance of the difference between two sample values of r.
z-Verteilung *f* **(Fishers z-Verteilung** *f*) *(stat)* z distribution
→ Standardnormalverteilung
z-Wert *m*
→ Standardwert
Zackenlinie *f* zig-zag line, zigzag line
Zackenrand *m* (Zeitung) serrated edge
Zackenschnitt *m* (Zeitung) serrated cut
Zackenschrift *f (film)* variable-area sound track
Zahlenzeichen *n (econ)* trademark number
   A trademark, (→) Warenzeichen, consisting of a combination of numbers.
Zahlteller *m (POP advtsg)* cash mat
ZAW *m abbr* Zentralausschuß der Werbewirtschaft e.V.
ZDF *n abbr* Zweites Deutsches Fernsehen
Zeichen *n* sign
Zeichenatelier *n*
→ Zeichenstudio
Zeichenbuchstabe *m* **(gezeichneter Buchstabe** *m*) drawn letter
Zeichenbüro *n* drawing office, drafting office
Zeichenergänzungstest *m (res)* sign-completion test
→ Ergänzungstest
Zeichenfeder *f*
→ Ausziehfeder
Zeichenfilm *m*
→ Zeichentrickfilm
Zeichenfolie *f* drawing acetate, drawing foil, drawing film

Zeichengerät *n* drawing instrument, (*pl* Zeichengeräte) drawing equipment, drawing set, drawing instruments *pl*
Zeichenkarton *m* bristol board, Bristol board, bristol, Bristol, drawing board, art board, illustration board
   A stiff, moderately heavy paper used for ink drawings.
Zeichenkohle *f* drawing charcoal, charcoal
→ Kohlestift
Zeichenpapier *n* bristol paper, Bristol paper, bristol, Bristol, drawing paper, plotting paper
   A paper with a smooth finish widely used for pen and ink drawings, available in a variety of weights and finishes.
Zeichenprisma *n* camera lucida
   A prism or series of lenses which transfer the image of a three-dimensional object onto a two-dimensional plane, enabling the image to be copied by hand in a larger or smaller size.
Zeichenrolle *f* **(Warenzeichenrolle** *f*) *(econ)* principal register, register of trademarks
→ Warenzeichenregister
Zeichenschutz *m*
→ Warenzeichenschutz
Zeichensetzgerät *n (typ)* character printer
   An instrument which prints one character at a time, such as a typewriter, as distinguished from a line printer which prints a whole line of type at one time.
Zeichenstift *m* drawing pencil, (bunt) crayon
Zeichenstudio *n* **(Zeichenatelier** *n*) drawing studio
Zeichentechnik *f* drawing technique
Zeichentest *m*
→ Vorzeichentest
Zeichentrick *m (film)* 1. (Verfahren) cartoon animation, animation 2. (Film/Aufnahme) animated cartoon, animated picture
   Movement added to static objects. Usually applied to cartoon drawings filmed for television, or to POP material

Zeichentrickfilm

or outdoor advertisements with moving parts.
Zeichentrickfilm m *(film)* animated cartoon
zeichnen v/t to draw
→ skizzieren, entwerfen
Zeichner m draftsman, drawer, *brit* draughtsman
Zeichnung f drawing
→ Skizze, Entwurf
Zeile f 1. *(print)* line, (Anzeigenzeile) Am agate line
A measure of the depth of space.
2. *(TV)* scanning line, line
The single horizontal path the electron beam traces across the television picture tube.
Zeilenablenkung f *(TV)* horizontal deflection, *brit* deflexion, horizontal sweep, line scanning
Zeilenabstand m 1. *(print)* interlinear space, line spacing 2. *(TV)* distance between lines
Zeilenabtastung f (**Zeilenaustastung** f) *(TV)* line scanning, line blanking
Zeilenanzahl f
→ Zeilenzahl
Zeilenberechnung f
→ Zeilenpreis
Zeilenbreite f *(print)* width of line, measure
→ Spaltenbreite
Zeilendauer f *(TV)* line duration, line period
Zeilendurchlauf m *(TV)* line traversal
Zeilendurchschuß m
→ Durchschuß
Zeilenende n (**Zeilenübergang** m) *(print)* line break, end of line, break
Zeilenfall m *(print)* quadding, line arrangement
Zeilenfangregler m *(TV)* horizontal hold
Zeilengießmaschine f (**Zeilengußmaschine** f) *(print)* line casting machine, line caster, linecaster, slug casting machine
Zeilenguß m *(print)* line casting, slug casting
Zeilenhonorar n line-by-line payment
Zeilenlänge f
→ Zeilenbreite
Zeilenmaß n (**Zeilenmesser** m) *(print)* line gauge, type gauge, gauge, type scale, type rule
Zeilenmillimeter m
→ Spaltenmillimeter

Zeilennorm f *(TV)* line standard
→ Fernsehnorm
Zeilenpreis m *(advtsg)* (bei Anzeigen) line rate, cost per line, (pro Millionenauflage) milline rate, (Höchstpreis pro Millionenauflage) maximil rate, (Niedrigstpreis pro Millionenauflage) minimil rate
Zeilenraster m *(TV)* line-scanning pattern
Zeilenrauschen n *(TV)* line noise, low-frequency noise
Zeilenreißen n *(TV)* line tearing
Zeilenrücklauf m *(TV)* line fly back, horizontal flyback
Zeilensatz m
→ Zeilenpreis
Zeilensetzmaschine f *(print)* line composing machine
Zeilensetz- und Gießmaschine f *(print)* line composing and casting machine
Zeilensprung m *(TV)* interlaced scanning, line interlace
The sequential scanning of alternate lines on the television tube to create a complete picture in two passes.
Zeilensprungverfahren n (**zeilensprungartige Abtastung** f) *(TV)* interlaced scanning, interlacing, line interlacing
Zeilensteuerung f *(TV)* line control
Zeilensystem n *(TV)* line system
Zeilentransformator m (**Leitungsübertrager** m) *(TV)* line transformer
Zeilenübergang m
→ Zeilenende
Zeilenumfang m (**Zeilenzahl** f) *(print)* lineage, linage
The total amount of advertising space in a paper or a magazine, named in the number of lines run.
zeilenweise adj *(print)* line-by-line, adv by the line
Zeilenzahl f *(print)* number of lines
Zeilenzwischenraum m
→ Zeilenabstand
Zeilenzähler m *(print)* line counter
Zeitablaufsmedien n/pl (**Ablaufsmedien** n/pl) time-bound media pl, transient media pl
Zeitansage f *(radio/TV)* time announcement, time check
Zeitaufnahme f *(phot)* time exposure, time shot
Zeitbelichtung f *(phot)* time exposure

Zeit-Belichtung f *(phot)* time exposure
Zeit-Blenden-Paarung f *(phot)* aperture-speed combination, stop-speed values *pl*
Zeitbudget n *(res)* time budget
→ Zeitbudgetforschung
Zeitbudgetforschung f *(res)* time-budget research
    A time budget is a log or diary of the sequence and duration an individual engages in over a specified period of time, most typically the 24-hour-day. Time-budget research involves the collection of numerous such protocols from members of a population to analyze main trends and subgroup differences in the allocation of time. Time-budget research is particularly widespread in analyses of media behavior and consumer research.
Zeitbudgetstudie f **(Zeitbudgetuntersuchung** f) *(res)* time-budget study, time-budget investigation
→ Zeitbudgetforschung
Zeitdehner m **(Zeitdehneraufnahme** f)
→ Zeitlupe
Zeitdehnerkamera f
→ Zeitlupenkamera
Zeitdehnung f
→ Zeitlupe
Zeitfehlerausgleich m *(film/TV)* 1. (Vorgang) time-base error correction (TBC) 2. (Vorrichtung) time-base error corrector (TBC), time-base corrector (TBC)
Zeitfilter m *(media res)* time period filter, time-related filter
    A filter question, (→) Filterfrage, screening in or out publications by reference to reading within a specific time period stated.
zeitliche Kontaktbereitschaft f
→ Leistungsbereitschaft
Zeitlupe f **(Zeitlupenverfahren** n, **Zeitdehnung** f) *(film/TV)* slow motion, slow-motion technique
    Any action shown slower than normal by shooting it on motion picture film at a rate faster than the standard rate of projection.
Zeitlupenaufnahme f *(film/TV)* slow-motion picture, slow-motion shot
Zeitlupeneffekt m *(film/TV)* slow-motion effect
Zeitlupenkamera f **(Zeitlupengerät** n) *(film/TV)* slow-motion camera, high-speed camera

Zeitlupentempo n *(film/TV)* slow motion
Zeitlupenverfahren n
→ Zeitlupe
Zeitmarke f time marker
Zeitnachlaß m **(Zeitrabatt** m)
→ Wiederholungsrabatt
Zeitplan m timetable, time schedule, schedule
Zeitrabatt m
→ Wiederholungsrabatt
Zeitraffer m **(Zeitrafferverfahren** n) 1. *(film/tape)* quick motion technique, fast motion, fast-motion technique
    A shot or sequence in which time appears compressed, and the rate of action accelerated; accomplished by recording film or tape at a slow rate, and using regular playback rates, or (less commonly) raising the playback rate above the regular rate at which the film or tape was recorded.
2. (beim Trickfilm) stop motion, stop-motion technique
    A photographic technique for animating inanimate objects.
3. *(phot)* time-lapse photography, time-lapse technique
    Single-frame photography at precise periodic intervals.
Zeitrafferaufnahme f *(film)* single-picture shot, single-picture taking, time-lapse shot, time-lapse shooting, stop motion
→ Zeitraffer
Zeitrafferaufnahmeverfahren n
→ Zeitraffer
Zeitrafferkamera f *(film)* quick-motion camera, fast-motion camera, stop-motion camera
Zeitraffertest m *(media res)* quick-motion test
Zeitraffung f
→ Zeitraffer
Zeitraum m **des Erscheinens**
→ Erscheinungsintervall
Zeitreihe f **(zeitliche Reihe** f) *(stat)* time series
    A set of observations on a random variable made at successive points in time, or indeed any ordered set of measurements of a random variable. A fairly simple model from a series (X_t) would be:
$$X_t = T_t + C_t + S_t + I_t$$
where T_t is the trend component at time t, C_t a cyclical (business cycle) component, S_t a seasonal component, and I_t an erratic or random component.

Zeitreihenanalyse

Seasonal adjustment, for example, would consist of estimating and then subtracting the term S_t.
Zeitreihenanalyse f (**Zeitreihenzerlegung** f) *(stat)* time series analysis
→ Zeitreihe
Zeitschrift f periodical, magazine, journal, *colloq Am* book
A periodical publication, usually bound, and generally published quarterly, bimonthly, monthly, or more frequently.
Zeitschrift f **für Wohnen und Einrichten**
→ Wohnen- und Einrichten-Zeitschrift
Zeitschriftenabfrage f (**Zeitschriften-Abfragemodus** m) *(media res)* question order, (jede Frage für alle Zeitschriften nacheinander) vertical question order, (alle Fragen zunächst für eine Zeitschrift, dann für die nächste) horizontal question order
Zeitschriftenabonnement n (**Zeitschriftenabo** n) magazine subscription, periodical subscription, subscription to a magazine, subscription to a periodical
→ Abonnement
Zeitschriftenabonnent m magazine subscriber, subscriber to a magazine
→ Abonnent
Zeitschriftenanzeige f (**Anzeige** f **in einer Zeitschrift**) magazine advertisement, magazine ad
→ Anzeige
Zeitschriftenart f type of magazine, type of periodical
Zeitschriftenartikel m magazine article, magazine story, contribution to a magazine
Zeitschriftenauflage f
→ Auflage
Zeitschriftenaufsatz m
→ Zeitschriftenartikel
Zeitschriftenausgabe f
→ Ausgabe
Zeitschriftenausschnitt m magazine clip, magazine clipping, magazine cutting
Zeitschriftenausschnittbüro n
→ Ausschnittbüro
Zeitschriftenbeilage f
→ Beilage
Zeitschriftendruck m magazine printing, printing of periodicals

580

Zeitschriftenformat n magazine size, periodical size
Zeitschriftengattung f magazine category, type of magazine
Zeitschriftengroßhandel m 1. (Funktion) magazine wholesaling, magazine wholesale 2. (Institution) magazine wholesale trade
Zeitschriftengroßhändler m magazine wholesaler
Zeitschriftengruppe f group of magazines, group of periodicals
Zeitschriftenhandel m 1. (Funktion) magazine selling, magazine trading 2. (Institution) magazine trade
Zeitschriftenhändler m magazine dealer
→ Zeitungshändler
Zeitschriftenhändler m magazine dealer
→ Zeitungshändler
Zeitschriftenherstellung f magazine production, periodical production, journal production
Zeitschrifteninserat n
→ Zeitschriftenanzeige
Zeitschriftenlayout n magazine makeup, makeup of a magazine
Zeitschriftenleser m magazine reader, reader of a magazine, periodical reader, reader of a periodical, journal reader, reader of a periodical
Zeitschriftenleserschaft f magazine audience, magazine readers pl
Zeitschriftenpapier n magazine paper, journal paper, periodical paper, (Hochglanzpapier) slick paper, glossy paper
Zeitschriftenraster m *(print)* magazine screen, periodical screen
Zeitschriftenredakteur m magazine editor
Zeitschriftenredaktion f editorial staff of a magazine, editorial department of a magazine
Zeitschriftenstand m (**Zeitschriftenständer** m) *(POP advtsg)* magazine rack, magazine stand
→ Kiosk
Zeitschriftentitel m (**Zeitschriftentitelzug** m) magazine title, magazine logo
→ Titel, Titelkopf
Zeitschriftentitelbild n
→ Titelbild
Zeitschriftenverlag m magazine publisher, periodical publisher,

journal publisher, magazine publishing company, magazine publishing house

Zeitschriftenverlagswesen *n* magazine publishing, periodical publishing, journal publishing

Zeitschriftenverleger *m* magazine publisher, periodical publisher, journal publisher, publisher of magazines, publisher of periodicals, publisher of journals

Zeitschriftenverlegerverband *m* **(Zeitschriftenverlegervereinigung** *f***)** magazine publishers' association, association of magazine publishers, association of periodical publishers, periodical publishers' association

Zeitschriftenvertreter *m* **(Zeitschriftenwerber** *m***)**
→ Abowerber

Zeitschriftenvertrieb *m* magazine distribution

Zeitschriftenwerbung *f* **(Werbung** *f* **in Zeitschriften)** magazine advertising, periodical advertising

Zeitschriftenwesen *n*
→ Zeitschriftenverlagswesen

Zeitstaffel *f*
→ Wiederholungsrabatt

Zeitüberschreitung *f* **(Zeitüberziehung** *f***)** *(radio/TV)* overrunning, overrun

Zeit-Umkehr-Probe *f (stat)* time-reversal test
vgl. Basis-Umkehr-Probe

Zeitung *f* newspaper, paper
A publication, usually a periodical, accepting advertising, issued in a manner that provides its public with comprehensive accounts of very recent events, and offered for sale.

Zeitung *f* **im Großfolioformat** blanket sheet

Zeitungsabonnement *n* newspaper subscription, subscription to a newspaper
→ Abonnement

Zeitungsabonnent *m* newspaper subscription, subscriber to a newspaper
→ Abonnent

Zeitungsagentur *f* **(Presseagentur** *f***)** newspaper agency, newspaper syndicate
→ Nachrichtenagentur

Zeitungsanzeige *f* newspaper advertisement, newspaper ad
→ Anzeige

Zeitungsanzeigenannahme *f*
→ Anzeigenannahme

Zeitungsarchiv *n* newspaper archives *pl*

Zeitungsart *f*
→ Zeitungstyp

Zeitungsartikel *m* newspaper article, newspaper story

Zeitungsauflage *f* newspaper circulation
→ Auflage

Zeitungsaufsatz *m*
→ Zeitungsartikel

Zeitungsausgabe *f* newspaper edition, newspaper issue

Zeitungsausschnitt *m* newspaper clip, newspaper clipping, newspaper cutting

Zeitungsausschnittbüro *n* **(Zeitungsausschnittdienst** *m***)**
→ Ausschnittbüro

Zeitungsauslieferung *f* **(Zeitungszustellung** *f***)** newspaper delivery

Zeitungsauslieferungswagen *m* **(Auslieferungswagen** *m* **)** newspaper delivery truck, delivery truck

Zeitungsausträger *m* **(Zeitungsjunge** *m* **)** newsboy, delivery man, carrier

Zeitungsautomat *m* newspaper slot machine, slot machine

Zeitungsbeilage *f*
1. → Beilage
2. → Supplement

Zeitungsbericht *m* newspaper report

Zeitungsberichterstatter *m*
→ Berichterstatter, Journalist

Zeitungsbesitzer *m* **(Zeitungseigentümer** *m***, Zeitungsinhaber** *m***, Eigentümer-Verleger** *m***)** newspaper proprietor, newspaper owner, (newspaper) publisher-owner

Zeitungsbote *m*
→ Zeitungsausträger

Zeitungsbranche *f* newspaper industry, newspaper publishing

Zeitungsdruck *m* newspaper printing

Zeitungsdrucker *m* newspaper printer

Zeitungsdruckpapier *n*
→ Zeitungspapier

Zeitungsente *f*
→ Ente

Zeitungsformat *n* newspaper size

Zeitungsgattung *f* newspaper category, type of newspaper

Zeitungsgroßhandel *m* 1. (Funktion) newspaper wholesaling, newspaper wholesale 2. (Institution) newspaper wholesale trade, newspaper wholesale business
Zeitungsgroßhändler *m* newspaper wholesaler, news agent
A distributor of papers or periodicals at wholesale.
Zeitungshandel *m* 1. (Funktion) newspaper selling, newspaper dealing 2. (Institution) newspaper trade
Zeitungshändler *m* **(Zeitungs- und Zeitschriftenhändler** *m*) newsdealer, newsagent, newsvendor
A merchant with fixed place of doing business who buys papers or periodicals to sell again at retail.
Zeitungsherstellung *f* newspaper production
Zeitungsinhaber *m*
→ Zeitungsbesitzer
Zeitungsinserat *n*
→ Zeitungsanzeige
Zeitungsjunge *m*
→ Zeitungsausträger
Zeitungskiosk *m*
→ Zeitungsstand, Kiosk
Zeitungskopf *m* (print) newspaper masthead, masthead, nameplate, name flag, logotype, logo
The name of a newspaper, usually at the top of the first page and frequently in a distinctive typographic style or arrangement.
Zeitungskorrespondent *m*
→ Korrespondent
Zeitungskunde *f*
→ Publizistik
Zeitungslesen *n* newspaper reading, paper reading
→ Lesen
Zeitungsleser *m* newspaper reader, paper reader
→ Leser
Zeitungsleserschaft *f* newspaper audience, paper audience, newspaper readers *pl*, paper readers *pl*
→ Leserschaft
Zeitungsnachricht *f*
→ Nachricht
Zeitungsnotiz *f* **(Pressenotiz** *f*)
→ Meldung
Zeitungspapier *n* **(Zeitungsdruckpapier** *n*) newsprint, newsstock
A coarse, unsized paper made from wood pulp, used primarily by newspapers.

Zeitungsraster *m* (print) newsprint screen, newspaper screen
Zeitungsredakteur *m* newspaper reporter, newspaper subeditor, newspaper editor
Zeitungsredaktion *f* editorial staff of a newspaper, editorial department of a newspaper, newsdesk, newsroom
Zeitungsreklame *f*
→ Zeitungswerbung
Zeitungssatz *m* (print) newspaper work, news work, newspaper composition
Zeitungsschreiber *m* **(Zeitungsmann** *m*)
→ Journalist
Zeitungssetzer *m* (print) newspaper compositor
Zeitungsspalte *f* (print) newspaper column
Zeitungsspaltenbreite *f* (print) newspaper column width
Zeitungsspaltenhöhe *f* **(Zeitungsspaltentiefe** *f*) (print) newspaper column depth, newspaper column height
Zeitungsstand *m* **(Zeitungskiosk** *m*) newsstand, brit news stall
→ Kiosk
Zeitungstitel *m* newspaper title
→ Zeitungskopf
Zeitungsträger *m*
→ Zeitungsausträger
Zeitungstyp *m* type of newspaper, newspaper type
Zeitungstypographie *f* newspaper typography
→ Typographie
Zeitungstypologie *f* newspaper typology
Zeitungsverkauf *m* newspaper selling, (einzelner Verkaufsakt) newspaper sale
Zeitungsverkäufer *m*
→ Zeitungshändler
Zeitungsverlag *m* newspaper publisher, newspaper publishing company, newspaper publishing house
Zeitungsverlagswesen *n* newspaper publishing
Zeitungsverleger *m* newspaper publisher
Zeitungsvertrieb *m* newspaper distribution
Zeitungswerbung *f* **(Werbung** *f* **in Zeitungen)** newspaper advertising

Zeitungswesen n 1. → Zeitungsverlagswesen 2. → Journalismus
Zeitungswissenschaft f journalism, science of journalism
→ Publizistik, Kommunikationswissenschaft
Zeitunterschreitung f **(Zeitunterziehung** f) *(radio/TV)* underrunning, underrun
Zeitverschluß m *(phot)* time shutter
zeitversetzte Sendung f *(radio/TV)* delayed broadcast
zeitversetztes Senden n *(radio/TV)* delayed broadcasting
Zeitzündereffekt m **(Spätzündereffekt** m)
→ Wirkungsverzögerung
Zellengewichtung f
→ Kontaktgewichtung, Redressement
Zellstoff m *(papermaking)* cellulose
  A fibrous substance used to make paper obtained from cotton, linen, hemp, and wood.
Zellstoffbrei m
→ Papierbrei
Zellstoffpapier n *(papermaking)* pulp paper
  Paper made from pulp, (→) Pulpe.
Zensus m
→ Totalerhebung (Vollerhebung)
Zentralausschuß m **der Werbewirtschaft e.V. (ZAW)** etwa German Advertising Federation
Zentrale f **zur Bekämpfung unlauteren Wettbewerbs e.V.** etwa German Better Business Bureau
Zentralverschluß m *(phot)* diaphragm shutter, between-the-lens shutter
Zentralwert m
→ Median
zentrieren v/t *(print)* to center, brit to centre
  To place in the center of a sheet, a column, or line.
Zentrieren n centering, brit centring
→ zentrieren
zentriertes Interview n *(survey res)* focused interview, focused group interview brit focussed
  An interview that concentrates the investigation on selected aspects of a specific event or situation experienced by the respondent. Focused interviews are usually held with a number of respondents who have had a common experience — for example, having read the same propaganda leaflet, seen the same movie, or having been involved in the same event. „The distinguishing characteristic of the focussed interview is that the interwiewees have been exposed to concrete situations, the „objective" character of which is known to, and has been previously analyzed by the interviewer. The interviewees have seen a film, heard a radio program, read a pamphlet, magazine or advertisement; participated in a psychological experiment. In other words, the interview focusses on an experience of the respondent — exposure to a given stimulus situation, a situation which the interviewer has subjected to a „content analysis" which in turn has formed the basis of an interview guide... The focussed interview...aims to particularize the effective stimuli in the objective situation, and to characterize the subject's response to it." (Robert K. Merton)
Zentroidverfahren n *(stat)* centroid technique
Zerfallsverfahren n
→ Deformationsverfahren
Zerreißprobe f **(Reißprobe** f, **Zerreißtest** m, **Reißtest** m) *(paper)* pop test
Zerstreuungskreis m *(phot)* circle of divergence, circle of confusion
  The diameter of the circle created by a lens photographing a true point; the smaller the circle of confusion, the sharper the print.
Zerstreuungslinse f *(phot)* diverging lens, divergent lens, concave lens, negative lens
Zettelkleber m
→ Plakatkleber
Zeug n **(Defekten** m/pl) *(print)* broken types pl
→ Defekten
Zeugkiste f **(Defektenkasten** m) *(print)* hellbox, hell
Zickzackanzeige f zig-zag spread, zigzag spread
  A magazine (or, less common, a newspaper) flexform advertisement spreading in a zig-zag shape over a full or double page.
Zickzackfalz m
→ Leporellofalz
Zickzackfalzung f
→ Leporellofalzung
Ziel-Aufgaben-Methode f (der Werbebudgetierung) objective-and-task method (of advertising budget determination), plunge method, task method, target sum method
  A budgeting method by which an organization uses advertising to further the smooth functioning of the marketing

Zielgruppe system by allocating specific amounts to achieve specific objectives.
Zielgruppe f target group, (Gesamtheit) target population
  In the widest sense, a group which is the object of special action, such as a marketing or advertising campaign.
Zielgruppenaffinität f affinity
  → Affinität
Zielgruppenanalyse f target group analysis
Zielgruppenauswahl f target group selection
Zielgruppenbeschreibung f target group description
Zielgruppenbestimmung f target group determination
Zielgruppendemographie f
  → demographische Martsegmentierung
Zielgruppenforschung f target group research
Zielgruppengewicht n (media planning) target group weight
Zielgruppengewichtung f (media planning) target group weighting
Zielgruppenkommunikation f target group communication
Zielgruppenpsychographie f
  → psychographische Marktsegmentierung
Zielgruppenzeitschrift f demographic magazine, demographic edition, horizontal publication
  A periodical intended for a specific demographic group or to individuals of similar functions, interests, or responsibilities.
Zielmarkt m target market, target consumers pl
  A market toward which a marketing and/or selling effort is directed.
Ziel-Mittel-Beziehung f means-end relation
zielorientierte Budgetierung f
  → Ziel-Aufgaben-Methode
Zielperson f target person, (Konsument) target consumer
Zierleiste f (Zierrand m) (print) ornamental border
Zierlinie f (print) ornamental rule, ornamental line
Ziffernanzeige f
  → Chiffre-Anzeige
Ziffergebühr f
  → Chiffre-Gebühr

Zimmerantenne f (electr.) room antenna, brit room aerial, indoor antenna, brit indoor aerial
Zinkätzung f (Zinkätzungsverfahren n) 1. (print) zinc etching, zincography, zinc engraving 2. → Zinkklischee
Zinkdruck m (print) zinc-plate printing, zincography
Zinkklischee n (Zinkätzung f, Zinko n) (print) zinc etching, zinc engraving, zinc plate, zincograph, zinco
  A halftone on a zinc plate, with a coarser screen than that of a copper halftone.
Zinklithographie f (Zinklithografie f) (print) 1. (Verfahren) zinc-plate lithography 2. (Produkt) zinc-plate lithograph
Zinko n
  → Zinkklischee
Zinkweiß n (Zinkoxyd n) zinc white, zinc oxyde, Chinese white
Zischen n (Zischlaute m/pl) (radio) sibilance
zitierende Werbung f
  → allegatorische Werbung
Zone f (marketing) zone
  → Werbezone
Zonenplan m (Gebietsplan m, Zonenwerbeplan m) (marketing) zone plan
  → Testmarkt
Zoom m (Gummilinse f)
  → Vario-Objektiv
zoomen (phot) v/t to zoom
Zoomen n (phot) zooming
Zoomaufnahme f (phot) zoom shot
  → optische Fahrt
Zoom-Objektiv n
  → Vario-Objektiv
Zubringer m (Zubringerkabel n, Zubringerleitung f) feeder, feeder cable, feeder line
Zufall m stat 1. (systematischer Zufall) chance, random event
  A process or event in which occurrences are determined strictly by chance, so that the probability of occurrence is the same as the probability of the event in the population.
  2. (unkontrollierter Zufall) accident, haphazard event
zufälliges Ereignis n
  → Zufall
Zufallsantworttechnik f
  → Technik der Zufallsantwort
Zufallsauswahl f (Wahrscheinlichkeitsauswahl f) (stat)

1. (Zufallsauswahlverfahren) random sampling, probability sampling, random selection
   Drawing a sample in such a way that each element in the population has an equal probability of being included in the sample. The probability that a given element will or will not be included in the sample is not influenced by whether any other particular element or elements were or were not selected. A random sample may be defined also as one selected so that all possible samples like that are equally likely to be chosen. A random sample is considered to be representative of the population from which it is selected regardless of sample size.

2. (Zufallsstichprobe) random sample, probability sample
   Strictly speaking, a random sample is one type of probability sample, in which the sample is drawn by means of a strict random procedure, such as a table of random numbers. In practice, the term "random sampling" is frequently used loosely to mean any kind probability sample. The term "nonrandom sample" is most often used to mean any sort of nonprobability sample — such as a quota sample, a convenience sample, or a haphazard sample.

Zufallsereignis n
→ Zufall

Zufallsexperiment n *(stat)* random experiment

Zufallsfehler m **(Auswahlfehler** m**, Stichprobenfehler** m**)** *(stat)* random error, chance error, accidental error
   An error of measurement or observation that cannot be attributed to any specific cause. Random errors vary in directions and magnitude from observation to observation with respect to both magnitude and sign, and thus, tend to average to zero over the long run. Random errors generally are considered to be normally distributed, (→) Normalverteilung.
   vgl. systematischer Fehler

Zufallskunde m
→ Laufkunde m

Zufallskundschaft f
→ Laufkundschaft

Zufallsprozeß m **(zufälliger Prozeß** m**)** *(stat)* random process, stochastic process

Zufallsreihe f **(Zufallsfolge** f**)** *(stat)* random series
   A series the numbers of which may be regarded as drawn at random from a fixed distribution.

Zufallsschwankung f *(stat)* random fluctuation

Zufallstart m *(stat)* random start
   In selecting a systematic sample at intervals of n from an ordered population, it is sometimes desirable to select the first sample unit by a random drawing from the first n units of that population. The sample is then said to have a random start.

Zufallsstichprobe f **(Zufallsauswahl** f**, Wahrscheinlichkeitsprobe** f**)** *(stat)* random sample, probability sample
→ Zufallsauswahl

Zufallsstichprobenbildung f **(Zufallsstichprobenverfahren** n**)**
→ Zufallsauswahl 1.

Zufallsvariable f **(Zufallsgröße** f**)** *(stat)* variate, random variable, stochastic variable
   A variable whose different values occur with probabilities that are, at least theoretically, specifiable.

Zufallsweg m *(stat)* random walk, random route
→ Random-Route

Zufallszahl f *(stat)* random number
   One of an array of numbers constructed in such a way that each of the digits 0 through 9 has an equal chance of being in any position and that successive digits are independent.

Zufallszahlengenerator m **(Schwedenschlüssel** m**)** *(stat)* random digit generator, random number generator

Zufallszahlentafel f **(Zufallszahlentabelle** f**)** *(stat)* random number table

zuführen v/t *(print)* to feed

Zuführer m
→ Anleger

Zuführung f *(print)* feed, feeding

Zugabe f **(Werbezugabe** f**)** advertising premium, premium
   An offer of merchandise, either free, at a reduced cost, or at nominal cost, as an immediate inducement to purchase a product.

Zugabeangebot n **(Warenangebot** n **mit Zugabe)** *(econ)* premium offer
   A special offer of merchandise at a reduced price in consideration of purchasing a particular product, as evidenced by the sending in of a qualifying number of labels or coupons; frequently conducted as a self-liquidating operation.

Zugabeartikel m *(econ)* premium product

Zugabenserie f
→ Sammelzugabe
Zugabentest m **(Zugabetest** m) *(econ)* premium test
Zugabeverordnung f **(ZugabeVO** f)
(econ) premium regulations *pl*
Zugabewerbung f premium advertising
Zugangskennung f *(Btx)* password
Zugartikel m *(econ)* puller
Zugfilm m *(film)* leader film, leader
A blank segment of film at the beginning of a reel.
Zugkraft f **(der Werbung)** pulling power, pull, drawing power, draw, attraction
The effectiveness of advertising in persuading the public to buy a product, make inquiries, send in coupons, or take some other positive action.
Zugnummer f audience puller, puller
Zugpferd n *(econ)* drawing card
Zugstrategie f
→ Pull-Strategie
ZugVO f *abbr* Zugabeverordnung
Zuhausehören n *(media res)* in-home listening, at-home listening
Zuhausehörer m *(media res)* in-home listener, at-home listener
Zuhausehörerschaft f **(Zuhausehörer** m/pl) *(media res)* in-home audience, at-home audience, in-home listeners *pl*, at-home listeners *pl*
Zuhauselesen n *(media res)* in-home reading, at-home reading
Zuhauseleser m *(media res)* in-home reader, at-home reader
Zuhauseleserschaft f **(Zuhauseleser** m/pl) *(media res)* in-home audience, at-home audience, in-home readers, *pl*, at-home readers *pl*
Zuhausesehen n **(Zuhause-Fernsehen** n) *(media res)* in-home viewing, at-home viewing
Zuhauseseher m **(Zuhausezuschauer** m, **Zuhausefernsehzuschauer** m) *(media res)* in-home viewer, at-home viewer
Zuhauseseherschaft f **(Zuhausezuschauerschaft** f, **Zuhausezuschauer** m/pl, **Zuhauseseher** m/pl) *(media res)* in-home audience, at-home audience, in-home viewers *pl*, at-home viewers *pl*
Zuhörer m
→ Hörer

Zuhörerschaft f
→ Hörerschaft
zukreisen v/t *film/TV* (Blende) to iris out, to circle out
To end a scene by closing an iris, so that the scene appears within a shrinking circle.
Zukunftsforschung f
→ Futurologie
zulängliche Stichprobe f **(adäquate Stichprobe** f) adequate sample
→ adäquate Stichprobe
Zuordnungsskala f
→ Ratingskala
Zuordnungstest m
→ Szonditest
Zurichtebogen m **(Zurichtungsbogen** m) *(print)* overlay, makeready sheet
In letterpress makeready, a piece of paper placed in the packing to make part of the form print more heavily in that place; in offset-lithography, the transparent or translucent covering on the copy on which directions or work to be overprinted are placed, in the preparation of artwork.
zurichten v/t *(print)* (die Form) to make (the form) ready
Zurichtung f *(print)* makeready
The adjustment or building up of the press form, in letterpress printing, so that the light and heavy areas print with the correct or desired impression.
zusammendrucken v/t *(print)* to gang up
Zusammendrucken n *(print)* ganging up, ganging, gang printing
Arranging a group of type pages, engravings, or other printing units arranged together for printing with a single impression.
zusammenfallen v/i *(print)* (Satz) to pie, to pi
To jumble, get mixed or disarranged and therefore impossible to use.
zusammengesetztes Bildsignal n *(TV)* composite video signal, composite video waveform
Zusammensetzung f **(der Leserschaft...)**
→ Leserschaftszusammensetzung, Hörerschaftszusammensetzung
Zusammentragen n *(print)* assembly, assembling, (von gefalzten Bogen) gathering
The process of assembling the signatures or sheets of a book or booklet, often confused with collating.

(von einzelnen Blättern) collation, collating
  Gathering the different printed forms of a periodical, a catalog, or a booklet in proper sequence preparatory to binding.
Zusatzfarbe f
→ Schmuckfarbe
Zusatzlicht n **(Zusatzbelichtung** f, **Zusatzbeleuchtung** f) *(phot)* fill-in light, fill light, booster light, balancing light
→ Ausgleichsbeleuchtung
Zusatznutzen m **(Erbauungsnutzen** m, **Geltungsnutzen** m) (Wilhelm Vershofen) *(econ) etwa* additional utility, prestige utility
vgl. Grundnutzen
Zusatzqualität f
→ Integralqualität
Zuschauer m **(Fernsehzuschauer** m) television viewer, viewer, *auch* televiewer, (*pl* die Zuschauer) audience
Zuschaueranteil m *(media res)* share-of-audience, audience share
→ Sehbeteiligung, Einschaltquote
Zuschauerbeteiligunsprogramm n **Zuschauerbeteiligungssendung** f) *(TV)* audience participation program, *brit* programme, audience-participation show
  A broadcast which depends, in part on the participation of the program audience for its entertainment or educational value.
Zuschauerdaten n/pl *(media res)* audience data *pl*, viewer data *pl*
Zuschauerfluß m **(Zuschauerfluktuation** f) audience flow, audience turnover
  A measure of television tuning activity in homes; specifically, a measurement of audience generation, mobility, and/or loss with respect to sources and inheritors. It is hence, a measurement of the frequency with which a program's audience changes over a period of time; more specifically, the ratio of the net unduplicated cumulative audience over several time periods to the average audience per one time period.
Zuschauerforschung f **(Zuschauerschaftsforschung** f) *(TV)* audience research, TV audience research, broadcast audience research, *auch* viewer research
Zuschauergewohnheiten f/pl **(Sehgewohnheiten** f/pl) viewing habits *pl*

Zuschauermessung f **(Zuschauerschaftsmessung** f) *(media res)* audience measurement, television audience measurement, television audience measurement, TV audience measurement, broadcast audience measurement
Zuschauerschaftspanel n *(media res)* panel of television viewers, panel of viewers, viewer panel, television audience panel, audience panel
Zuschauerschaftsstudie f **(Zuschauerschaftsuntersuchung** f) *(media res)* audience study, audience investigation, TV audience study, television audience study, TV audience investigation, television audience investigation, viewer study, viewer investigation
Zuschauerschaftsstruktur f **(Zuschauerstruktur** f) *(media res)* audience structure, television audience structure, TV audience structure, audience characteristics *pl*, audience composition, audience comp, audience setup, *brit* set-up, audience profile, viewer structure, viewer characteristics *pl*, viewer profile
  The characteristics of television audience by standard demographic groupings, such as age, income, family size, etc. These are generally presented in the form of percentage distributions which can be compared with similar data for the population as a whole.
Zuschauerverhalten n viewer behavior, *brit* viewer behaviour
Zuschuß m
→ Papierzuschuß
Zuschußbogen m
→ Papierzuschuß
Zusendung f **unbestellter Waren**
→ negative Option
Zuspielband n insert tape, (Mischband) mixing tape
zuspielen v/t to play in, to feed, to insert, to inject
Zuspielen n *(radio/TV)* remote contribution inject, remote contribution insert
Zuständigkeit f **(eines Werbeträgers)** **(Z-Wert** m) *(media res) etwa* media competence
Zustelldienst m *(econ)* delivery service, home delivery service
Zusteller m *(econ)* delivery man

Zustellpreis m *(econ)* delivery price
→ Lieferpreis
Zustelltermin m *(econ)* delivery date, date of delivery
→ Liefertermin
Zuverlässigkeit f **(Reliabilität** f) *(stat)* reliability
   In the technical sense, as used in psychology and survey research, the degree to which multiple measures of the same attitude or behavior agree. These multiple measures may be over time or at the same point in time. If repeated in the same questionnaire, the same item should not be asked in exactly, or nearly exactly, the same way, since this irritates the respondent and distorts the estimate of reliability.
Zuwendung f **(Zuwendungsindex** m) *(media res)* affinity, affinity index
zuziehen v/t *(film/TV)* (Blende) to fade out, to fade down, to zoom out
→ ausblenden, abblenden
Zweibadverfahren n *(phot)* two-bath process
vgl. Einbadverfahren
Zweibandtaster m *(TV)* Sepmag telecine
→ Sepmag
Zweibandabtastung f *(TV)* Sepmag telecine system, double-headed system
Zweibandkopierung f *(TV)* double-track printing
Zweibandprojektor m *(TV)* Sepmag projector
Zweibandverfahren n
→ Zweibandabtastung
zweidimensionale Morphologie f *(marketing)* two-dimensional morphology
Zweidrittelseite f *(print)* two-thirds page
Zweiereinstellung f *(film/TV)* two-shot
   Two persons in frame.
Zweierpackung f **(Zweierpack** n) *(packaging)* twin pack
   A promotion event calling for two product units to be sold as one, at a discounted price; usually implemented by packaging which physically unites the two units and flags the savings offered.
Zweifachbelegung f **(Doppelbelegung** f) *(transit advtsg)* double-carding
   An arrangement in transit advertising whereby two messages of one advertiser are specified for each vehicle.

Zweifarbenätzung f *(print)* two-color process etching, *brit* two-colour process etching
Zweifarbendruck m *(print)* 1. (Verfahren) two-color printing, *brit* two-colour printing, two-color process, *brit* two-colour process
   A method of reproduction in which two plates, line or halftone, are printed in two practically complementary colors to give a full-color effect.
2. (Produkt) two-color print, *brit* two-colour print
zweifarbig *adj (phot/print)* two-color, *brit* two-colour
Zweiflügelblende f *(phot)* two-blade shutter, two-wing shutter
Zweiggeschäft n **(Zweigniederlassung** f) *(retailing)* branch store, branch shop, (einer Handelskette) chain store
   One of a system of two or more stores of similar type which are centrally owned and managed.
→ Filiale
Zweigstelle f
→ Filialbetrieb
Zwei-Hemisphären-Theorie f *(brain res)* two-hemisphere theory
Zweijahresschrift f **(Zweijahrespublikation** f) biennial publication, biennial journal
zweijährlich (alle zwei Jahre erscheinend) *adj* biennial
Zweikilowatt m **(Zweikilowattscheinwerfer** m, **Zwei-KW** m) *(film/TV)* broad light, broad
   A 2000 watt, boxlike motion picture or television floodlight.
Zweikomponentenentwicklung f *(phot)* two-component development
zweimal gefalteter Bogen m *(print)* quarternion
zweimal täglich *adj* twice daily
zweimal wöchentlich *adj* twice weekly, biweekly, bi-weekly
   Issued twice a week.
zweimal wöchentlich erscheinende Zeitung f biweekly newspaper, bi-weekly newspaper, biweekly paper
zweimonatlich (Zweimonats-) *adj* semi-monthly, bimonthly, bi-monthly
Zweimonatsschrift f semi-monthly publication, semi-monthly magazine, bimonthly publication, bimonthly magazine, semimonthly, bimonthly
→ Vierzehntagezeitschrift

Zweipack m **(Zweischichtfilm** m)
(phot) bipack
→ Bipack
Zweipackverfahren n *(phot)* bipack procedure
Zweireihenkorrelation f
→ biserielle Korrelation
Zweiraumkassette f *(phot)* double-chamber magazine
Zweischichtenpappe f **(zweischichtige Pappe** f) two-ply board
Zweiseitenbandempfänger m *(radio)* double-sideband receiver
zweiseitige Kommunikation f interactive communication
zweiseitiger Test m **(Zwei-Segment-Test** m) *(stat)* two-tailed test, double-tailed test, two-sided test
   A statistical test used to test a hypothesis when the direction of the difference between samples or relationship between variables is not predicted in the hypothesis. That is, the null hypothesis merely states that there will not be a significant difference between the samples, or relationship between the variables, and the alternative hypothesis does not specify which sample will be further in a given direction (score higher, be more favorable, etc.) if there is a difference, or if there is a relationship between the variables whether it will be positive or negative. The term two-tailed refers to the fact that there is a region of rejection of the null hypothesis at both ends (or tails) of the sampling distribution.
vgl. einseitiger Test
zweispaltig *adj (print)* double-column
Zweispur f *(tape)* dual track, double track, twin track
Zweispuraufnahme f *(tape)* dual-track recording, double-track recording, twintrack recording
Zweispurgerät n **(Zweispuraufnahmegerät** n, **Zweispurmaschine** f) dual-track tape recorder, twin-track tape recorder
Zweistreifenverfahren n
→ Zweibandabtastung
Zwei-Stufenfluß m **(der Kommunikation)** two-step flow (of communication) (Paul F. Lazarsfeld)
   The flow of information, advertising influence, etc., from a communications medium to a relatively small group of interested and informed opinion leaders, (→) Meinungsführer, and in turn from this group to a larger group of less interested and less informed persons.

Zweitbelichtung f *(phot)* double exposure, re-exposure
→ Doppelbelichtung
Zweitbesuch m
→ Nachfaßbesuch
Zweitdruck m
→ Nachdruck
zweite Umschlagseite f **(U 2 f)** (Zeitschrift) inside front cover (IFC, I.F.C.)
Zweitempfänger m **(Zweitgerät** n) *(radio/TV)* secondary receiver, second home set
Zweitentwicklung f *(phot)* secondary development
Zweites Deutsches Fensehen n **(ZDF)** Second German Television Channel
Zweitfarbe f
→ Schmuckfarbe
Zweitfilm m
→ Duplikat
Zweitkorrektur f *(print)* revised proof
→ Maschinenkorrektur
Zweitleser m **(Sekundärleser** m, **Folgeleser** m) *(media res)* secondary reader, pass-along reader, pass-on reader, non-buyer reader
   A person who reads a magazine or newspaper which he or another member of his household did not purchase. Readers who purchase a magazine consist of both primary and pass-along readers.
vgl. Erstleser
Zweitmarke f
→ Billigmarke
Zweitnutzen m
→ Zusatznutzen
Zwei-Weg-Kommunikation f two-way communication, interactive communication
→ Zwei-Stufen-Fluß
zweiwöchentlich
→ zweimal wöchentlich
Zweizeilenfall m *(print)* two-deck headline
Zweizeilenkorrelation f
→ biserielle Korrelation
zweizeilig *adj (print)* double-spaced
Zwei-Zyklen-Fluß m **(der Kommunikation)** two-cycle flow (of communication) (Verling C. Troldahl)
Zwiebelfisch m *(typ)* pie, pi, printer's pie, printer's pi, wrong font (WF), *brit* wrong fount
   A mixed-up or jumbled type, therefore not usable.

Zwischenduplikat n *(film)* intermediate duplicate, intermediate dupe
Zwischenfrequenz f **(ZF)** intermediate frequency
Zwischenkopie f *(film)* intermediate copy
Zwischenlinie f *(TV)* interline
Zwischenmodulation f *(radio/TV)* intermodulation
Zwischennegativ n
→ Internegativ
Zwischenpositiv n
→ Interpositiv
Zwischenraum m *(print)* space, spacing
The interval between letters, words, and lines in printed copy.
Zwischenring m *(phot)* adapter ring, intermediate ring
Zwischenschlag m *(print)* blank line, white line, white space
The blank area of a piece of printing not covered with type matter or illustration.
Zwischenschnitt m *(film)* cut-away, insert, continuity shot

Zwischensprung m *(TV)* interlace
The sequential scanning of alternate lines on a television tube to create a complete picture in two passes.
Zwischentitel m **(Zwischenüberschrift** f**)** **1.** *(print)* caption, subheading, subheadline, subhead, subcaption
A second or subordinate headline in an advertisement or a news or magazine story.
2. *(TV)* title link, time link, cut-in, information caption, caption
Zwischenverkäufer m
→ Wiederverkäufer
Zwischenzeile f **1.** → Zwischentitel
2. → Zwischensprung
Zwischenzeilenverfahren n
→ Zeilensprungverfahren
Zwischenzeilenflimmern n *(TV)* interline flicker, wave flicker
zyklische Werbung f
→ prozyklische Werbung
Zylinder m
→ Druckzylinder
Zylinderflachformpresse f
→ Schnellpresse
Zylinderlinse f *(phot)* cylinder lens
Zylinderpresse f *(print)* cylinder press
→ Walzenpresse